166644
VC GP-MA

Jerome
KAGAN
Harvard University

Julius
SEGAL

E I G H T H
E D I T I O N

PSYCHOLOGY
An Introduction

THE HARCOURT PRESS

HARCOURT BRACE COLLEGE PUBLISHERS

FORT WORTH   PHILADELPHIA   NEW YORK   ORLANDO   AUSTIN   SAN ANTONIO
TORONTO   MONTREAL   LONDON   SYDNEY   TOKYO

Publisher: Ted Buchholz
Acquisitions Editor: Christina Oldham
Senior Developmental Editor: Meera Dash
Production Manager: Cynthia Young
Picture Editor: Cindy Robinson
Cover Design: Burl Sloan

Requests for permission to make copies of any part of the work should be mailed to:
Permissions Department, Harcourt Brace & Company, 6277 Sea Harbor Drive, Orlando,
Florida 32887-6777

Address editorial correspondence to:
301 Commerce St., Suite 3700
Fort Worth, TX 76102

Address orders to:
6277 Sea Harbor Dr.
Orlando, FL 32887
1-800-782-4479 (outside Florida)
1-800-433-0001 (inside Florida)

Acknowledgments begin on page C–1 and constitute a continuation of this page.

ISBN: 0-15-501476-5

Library of Congress Card Number 94-35276

Printed in the United States of America
0 1 2 3 4 5   069   11 12 13 14 15

TO THE INSTRUCTOR

The eighth edition of *Psychology: An Introduction* contains significant revisions of a textbook that began its life nearly three decades ago. So swift has been the pace of psychological research during those years that this revision is in essence a different book. Perhaps the most eloquent evidence of this knowledge explosion will be found in the current index, where a very high proportion of the topics listed—all essential to an understanding of what psychology is all about in the mid-1990s—were not even a part of any psychologist's vocabulary when the first edition appeared.

We have always aimed to serve instructors and students eager for a book that, as one journal review of an earlier edition put it, "combines brevity, clarity, rigor, and relevance." And although the book retains that basic approach—striving for brevity and equal attention to scientific rigor and students' need for clarity and relevance—individual chapters have been reorganized and substantially rewritten.

To keep the book brief, we have continued to seek extreme economy in writing style and to concentrate more than ever on the main thrust and meaning of psychology. To keep the book rigorous and relevant, we have constantly asked ourselves: Of all the knowledge that now exists, what elements are *most* important to students—both those preparing for advanced courses and those who will have no further exposure to psychology?

If we can help students grasp the significance of key psychological principles and disabuse them of the false and often harmful beliefs about human behavior that are popular among those who have never taken a psychology course, we will feel gratified.

Changes in the Eighth Edition

We have made substantial changes in the structure of the book, most notably moving from 17 to 14 chapters. The first half of the book deals primarily with universal human—and sometimes animal—qualities, including the physiology and chemistry of the brain, sensation, perception, learning, memory, language, and the nature of emotions, motives, and drives.

The second half of the book deals with the differences among people, which are a function of both heredity and experience. Some of the most important sources of variation among individuals are intelligence, personality, response to stress, capacities to cope with difficulties, abnormal symptoms, developmental trajectories, and styles of social interaction.

Sensation and perception are now combined into a single chapter. The way the senses operate to inform us about the world continues to be one of psychology's major interests. Of equal importance, however, is the related process of perception—the way the mind organizes and interprets the evidence that is received from the senses. New scientific discoveries are revealing the error of separating the reactions of the sensory receptors from the perceptual processes. This chapter helps the student to appreciate the close relation between the patterns of light and sound that encroach on us and the meaning each of us puts on that information.

The related topics of emotions, drives, and motives are also discussed in a single chapter so that the student can more easily understand the relations among all three processes. The drives of hunger, thirst, and sex create strong emotional states, and many human motives derive their urgency from the emotional feelings that accompany them.

Intelligence and personality are combined in a chapter because each represents a significant cause of differences among people. Further, psychologists recognize that motivation and anxiety can influence the quality of mental performance. This chapter also demonstrates how both intelligence and personality can be influenced, often subtly, by a combination of heredity and experience.

A number of new topics, suggested both by scientists and instructors as being of importance as well as of practical value to students, have been added. Prominent among them are expanded discussions of various forms of memory, aggression and violence, the role of women in the workplace, and aspects of physical health that are related to stress and coping.

We have increased our emphasis on the changes in psychological processes from infancy through old age so that the student can appreciate how experience and maturation, acting together, alter the basic mental and emotional features of humans. The ability to remember the past, for example, is fragile during the first year of life and again during the last decade of the average life span. Although children and adults are capable of fear and anxiety, the sources of anxiety change in a dramatic way with development. The adoption of this life span perspective will enrich the student's understanding of psychological processes.

We have also put a spotlight on the use of psychology by the media. We hope that the exploration of such issues will compel students to take a critical look at the many arenas in which psychology is discussed.

Our increased emphasis on the life span and the media reflect our individual strengths as authors. In addition, the study guide, prepared by Julius Segal and Robert McCall, is incorporated into the textbook (see the "To the Student" section). And finally, we have added a margin glossary with pronunciation guide. Adding this element, assisted by Barbara Hermann of Gainesville College, enabled us to revisit every single term and definition in the book. We trust that students will benefit greatly from this process.

Pedagogical Features

Some special features warrant additional mention.

First, the book contains three types of boxes: Psychology in Action, Life Span Perspective, and Psychology and the Media. Each type of box provides the student with a valuable perspective on a particular psychological issue covered in the chapter.

The Psychology in Action boxes explore practical applications of psychological research and show the relevance of psychology to the student's everyday world. We have kept the most popular ones from the seventh edition and brought in new ones as well.

The new Life Span Perspective boxes survey how a particular phenomenon is manifested over the course of a life and expand the student's appreciation of the dynamics of human development. For example, the one in Chapter 14 (Social Psychology) queries, "How Much Can People Change" at different ages.

The new Psychology and the Media boxes enrich the student's insights into themes and controversies that appear in newspapers, magazines, and books. Chapter 9 (Stress, Coping, and Health) excerpts an article from the *Washington Post* on Alice Isen's work and poses questions for the student about testing the hypothesis and using humor. Each of these boxes ends with questions addressed to the student.

We have retained and updated the Test Yourself questions at the end of each section. Improved placement in the margin will facilitate the use of this feature, enabling students to use it without interrupting the flow. These questions foster progressive critical thinking and application of the material. Answers appear at the end of the chapter after the extensive Chapter Summary.

After the *Preface* in a section addressed to the student, we have included a set of instructions on "How To Study This Book," detailing the SQ3R method and contents of the Study Guide.

In addition, we have devised a Test of Essential Psychological Information (TEPI), which can be used as Pretest/Posttest tool. It can be applied to assess the level of psychological sophistication of the students as they begin the course and the changes that the course has helped bring about. The thirty True-False items of this test reflect key elements of psychological content in the introductory course.

The Ancillary Package

A Test Bank, completely revised for the eighth edition by Carolyn Meyer of Lake Sumter Community College, is available in printed and software versions. The test bank includes more than 100 multiple-choice and essay items per chapter. Each item is classified as "recall" or "application," assigned one of three levels of difficulty, and keyed to the learning objective and page number in the textbook. Items that come from boxes are so identified. The computerized test bank is available in IBM®, Microsoft Windows™, and Macintosh® formats. EXAMaster™ software allows instructors to create tests using fewer keystrokes, guided step-by-step by easy-to-follow screen prompts. EXAMaster™ has three test creation options: EasyTest™, which compiles tests from a single screen based on the instructor's choices; FullTest™, which includes a larger range of options and editing of items; and RequesTest™, a test compilation service for the instructor who has no computer. EXAMaster™ comes with EXAMRecord™, a customized gradebook software program.

An Instructor's Manual, prepared by Thomas Gerry of Columbia Greene Community College, is expanded to three times its previous size. Each chapter has objectives, lecture outlines, teaching suggestions, and many other useful elements. An extensive video and videodisc instructor's guide and course planning suggestions also appear in the manual.

Overhead Teaching Transparencies, full-color transparency acetates, illustrate key psychological concepts. They contain information to supplement (not duplicate) material in the textbook.

Personal Discovery Software is an interactive software program designed to assist students in applying psychological knowledge and principles to practical uses in their everyday lives. Students gain experience with psychological models, theories, and ideas and learn to use them.

Psychlearn, an interactive software program for students, contains five experiments for IBM and Apple computers: Schedules of Reinforcement, Short-term Memory, Reaction Time, Self-consciousness Scale, and Social Dilemma. This full-color program comes with a guide containing instructional information and discussion questions for each lesson.

Brainstack, an interactive software program for Macintosh users, provides students with a self-guided tour of the cerebral cortex, giving valuable information about brain-behavior relationships. Major topics include the motor and sensory cortex, visual and auditory cortex, memory, thinking, pattern recognition, facial identity, and the language system.

The Psychology Experimenter, an interactive program for IBM users, performs psychological experiments and records and analyzes data. It also enables users to duplicate four classic memory and perception experiments and to modify experiments of their own design.

Supershrink II: Jennifer is an interactive microcomputer simulation program for use on an IBM system. Users take the role of a counselor at a helpline clinic and conduct an interview with the client, Jennifer. This program is especially helpful to introductory psychology students learning concepts in psychopathology, personality, and assessment.

The Psychology Video Library houses various video programs, from which instructors can choose, based on the Harcourt Brace video policy. The series programs include the introductory psychology telecourses, *Discovery Psychology* and *The Coast Telecourse,* the *Discovering Psychology* teaching modules, *The Brain, The Mind, Infinite Voyage,* and selected videos from *Films for the Humanities and Sciences.* Instructors also have access to developmental psychology videos. See your Harcourt Brace representative for details.

Harcourt Brace Quarterly Videos come from the "CBS Nightly News," "CBS This Morning," "48 Hours," and "Street Stories with Ed Bradley." Every three months, excerpts from these programs are selected to keep students engaged in thinking about the many applications of psychology. Each Quarterly is accompanied by instructor's notes.

Harcourt Brace Psychology videodiscs include *Dynamic Concepts in Psychology, Discovering Psychology* Teaching Modules, *Infinite Voyage,* and *Fires of the Mind.* These videodiscs provide a variety of animated sequences, film and video footage, demonstrations, and still images (from the textbook as well as other sources). The fully integrated package includes *LectureMaker,* software available in IBM®, Microsoft Windows™, and Macintosh® formats, for creation of custom lectures, and complete documentation. Adhesive bar code labels facilitate access to images during lectures.

Acknowledgments

We are especially grateful to Paul Sirovatka and Elizabeth Stark for their assistance in the preparation of various chapters of this edition. Joanne Gholl provided assistance in the preparation of the References.

We are indebted to Barbara Hermann for her work on the margin glossary, Bob McCall for his help with the Study Guide, Tom Gerry for his creation of the Instructor's Manual, and Carolyn Meyer for her work on the Test Bank. We also thank the following reviewers of the eighth edition:

Betty Andrews, Jefferson Community College

Linda Campbell, William Rainey Harper College

Parnell Cephus, Jefferson State Junior College

Tom Gerry, Columbia Greene Community College

John Greaves, Jefferson State Junior College

Barbara Hermann, Gainesville College

Charles Jeffreys, Seattle Central Community College

Sammy LaClair, McHenry County College

Vance Rhoades, Brewton-Parker College

Jerome Kagan

Julius Segal

TO THE STUDENT

There are many possible ways to use the eighth edition of *Psychology: An Introduction* to learn the material effectively. Your instructor may suggest a method geared to the classroom approach to the course. Or you may want to experiment and discover your own method, based on your individual study habits. The following suggestions are merely some general guidelines for taking full advantage of the possibilities.

Studying Each Chapter

The textbook and built-in *Study Guide* are designed to assist in applying the SQ3R system of studying. This system, which has proved highly effective, is used by many proficient students—either after learning about the system or because they have discovered on their own the value of combining some or all of the system's five steps. The SQ3R system includes the following steps: survey, question, read, recite, and review.

1. Survey

Before starting to read a chapter, you should have a general notion of what it contains and the key points it makes. This survey need not take long. Note the title (for Chapter 1, *The Science and Practice of Psychology*), which is in itself a very brief description of what is to come. Then look at the outline that precedes each chapter. The primary section headings list the main points covered in each chapter. (In Chapter 1, the first two are *The Scope of Psychology* and *The Varieties of Psychology and Psychologists*.)

This may be enough of a survey. Or you may want to take a little more time and thumb through the chapter, noting how much space is devoted to each of the main sections, some of the secondary headings found under each, and the illustrations (which help illuminate some of the points). The whole purpose of the survey is to provide a framework that will help you organize the chapter's facts and ideas as you encounter them.

Make a similar survey at the start of each major section of the chapter, starting with the primary heading. Thumb through the section and examine the words printed in italics and boldface for emphasis and the points that are made in the illustrations. Note especially the secondary headings, marking subsections of the discussion. In other words, take a few moments to get a general idea of what this particular section of the book is going to tell you.

2. Question

This step applies to the secondary headings in the book. Each time you come to a new subsection and before you start reading it, turn its heading into a question that will pique your curiosity and orient you toward finding the answer. For the secondary heading *The Mission of Psychology* you might ask yourself: "What is this science trying to accomplish, and why?" Or you can put the question in any other way that makes you wonder why the book is going to discuss the matter and eager to learn more about it.

3. Read

How much to read in one chunk is largely a matter of individual preference. Some students find it best to study the entire chapter as a whole, a technique they find helpful in understanding the pattern of the materials and the way the individual topics and facts relate to one another. Some study one major section at a time (five to ten pages), others only a subsection (less than a single page). You may want to experiment with what works best for you—and vary the size of the chunk for various parts of the book. Some parts are more or less familiar and can be taken in fairly easily. In others new ideas may tend to crowd together and get confusing if taken in too large a dose.

Whatever you decide, read with the idea that you will make an active search for the answer to the question you have asked for each secondary heading, and that you want to comprehend and remember it. As the author of the SQ3R system has pointed out, "Reading textbooks is work"—and readers must know what they are looking for, find it, and then organize their thoughts about it.

4. Recite

You can recite what you have read by talking, either aloud or in your mind. But a much better way is to jot down notes summarizing what you have read. The notes should be brief—just a single word or a very few at most—and in your own language. They should be written *after* you have finished reading. (Many students make the mistake of taking notes as they go along, without really comprehending their meaning.)

The best method is to stop at the end of each subsection, look away from the book, and try to recite the answer to the question you asked and any other important information you have learned. Then jot down a brief note that summarizes the subsection.

A possible alternative to taking notes is to go back and underline the key words and key points in the subsection. This works for some students but is generally less helpful, in part because it does not force you to put the point into your own words. Moreover it may lead to reading just for the sake of finding important sentences and marking them without any real attention to the meaning. You can, of course, use both techniques—first make notes, then underline the words in the book that relate to your notes, as well as details that you want to remember.

5. Review

When you get to the end of a major section of the chapter, look over the notes you have jotted down on the subsections and find how the various points are organized and related to one another. Or, if you have used under-lines instead of notes, go back through the section and examine the points you have marked. Then, since this step is closely related to the previous one, cover up your notes or look away from the book and recite the points. If you have trouble recalling any of them, or what any of them means, take another look at your notes or the book and try again. In addition, respond to the Test Yourself questions and check your answers with those provided at the end of the chapter.

Turn also to the summary at the end of the chapter, where the most important points are presented briefly. For convenience in applying the SQ3R system, the summary is divided into the major sections of the chapter, with each identified by the same heading used in the chapter. Read the sum-mary for the section you have been studying and make sure you are aware of all the ideas it contains, understand them, and can explain them. If you can-not do so, go back to the chapter and do some more reading of what you have missed. Your review will probably take no more than five minutes in all—but it will be of tremendous value in making sure you have grasped all the points made in the section and fixing them in your memory.

When you have completed the chapter and your review of the final major section, make another review of the chapter as a whole. The *Study Guide* at the end of each chapter will assist you in this review.

The list of *Learning objectives* that begins the *Study Guide* should be part of your final review of what you have learned after completing the chapter. The objectives called "For an understanding of the science" include the most important facts and principles—valuable in their own right and almost always covered in your classroom tests. If you have a thorough understanding of these facts and principles, you have genuinely mastered the subject matter. The objectives called "For application to life situations" are a guide to how you can use your knowledge to understand your own and other people's behavior and perhaps achieve greater self-fulfillment in your day-to-day life.

The *Programmed unit* that follows the learning objectives is the core of the *Study Guide*. It is a step-by-step, easily mastered summary of the most important points in the chapter. You will note that the programmed unit is divided into brief "frames," each containing blank spaces for you to fill in as you go along. The correct word or words to fill in are printed in the margin. When you study the unit, keep the answers covered with a ruler or a long strip of paper, and move it down the page each time you fill in a blank. This process serves two purposes. First, it enables you to combine the reading and reciting steps of SQ3R. Second, by learning if your answer was right, you get immedi-ate feedback on your performance and can act at once to correct any mistakes.

The *Review of important terms* allows you to verify your mastery of new words and topics. Go through this list and make sure that you know and can explain each term.

The *Practice test* is useful in your review of what you have learned, after you have finished studying the entire chapter. Taking the test offers further feedback on your performance, and checking your answers enables you to catch and correct any mistakes.

The *Exercises* at the end of each chapter are suggestions for simple demonstrations you can perform to apply or illustrate some of the scientific findings presented in the chapter.

Diagnostic Test: Measuring How Much You Will Learn

As you study this book, you will be learning many facts about psychology, a sizable proportion of which may be surprising to you. Indeed, some of them may run contrary to the beliefs you now have about various aspects of human behavior.

To measure the extent to which this book enlarges your understanding of the field of psychology, we have developed the following Test of Essential Psychological Information (TEPI). The items will test your knowledge of various facets of human personality and behavior, and allow you to gauge how much new information you have accumulated from this book and course.

Listed are thirty statements about various aspects of behavior and mental functioning that reflect the typical content of introductory courses in psychology. Facts about each of these statements is contained in this book. Read each statement carefully, and record your judgment of it by circling **True** or **False.**

To compare your present knowledge about the field of psychology with what you learn from this course, you may opt to take this test again at the end of the semester. A scoring guide and the correct answers are provided at the end of the test.

1. A ten-year-old has more synapses—that is, nerve connections in the brain—than does a one-year-old.
2. Acupuncture is effective in dulling subsequent pain in a patient because it may stimulate the brain's endorphins.
3. The tongue can detect six different pure tastes.
4. The sense organs that allow us equilibrium, or sense of equilibrium, or balance, are located in the thyroid gland.
5. Your memory for a telephone number would remain in your mind for about only 30 seconds if you didn't repeat it to yourself.
6. Eyewitness testimony at a trial is generally accurate and reliable.
7. If you were to work with chimpanzees for a long time, they could be made to be as sophisticated with their word skills as are children.
8. Intelligence test scores are the best predictor of future mental health.
9. When a person feels frightened, the right side of the brain is likely to be more active than the left.
10. Our brains are sometimes more active when we are sleeping than when we are awake.
11. Lifetime behavior patterns are pretty much set by age five.
12. Certain images in our dreams—such as fire or guns—have the same meaning for everybody.
13. If you're being attacked on the street, you're most likely to get help if there is one rather than six bystanders.
14. Firstborns are more motivated to achieve in school than are later borns.

15. Sexual preferences are formed mainly as a result of experiences with one's parents in the first two years.
16. A person's environment can alter personality patterns that are partly genetic in origin.
17. Most children who are raised permissively become poor parents.
18. Scores on all components of intelligence tend to decrease as people grow older.
19. Psychological symptoms of depression are always caused by a psychological problem.
20. First impressions have a strong influence on interpersonal relationships.
21. Lie detectors generally reveal who is telling a lie.
22. You can overcome a phobia without understanding how it began.
23. The environment begins its influence the moment a person is born.
24. If two siblings grow up in the same home with the same parents, they usually share major personality traits.
25. ESP is not accepted as a valid scientific phenomenon.
26. Most creative individuals are psychologically abnormal.
27. Most two year olds can understand the difference in meaning between right and wrong.
28. The suicide rate in the United States is highest among men over 85 years old.
29. Some young children develop better in daycare than they do at home.
30. Most of the time divorce leads to long-standing psychological problems in children.

Scoring:

Not knowledgable = 18 or below
Barely knowledgable = 19–21
Basically knowledgable = 22–24
Knowledgable = 25–27
Very knowledgable = 28–30

Answers:

1. False		16. True	
2. True		17. False	
3. False		18. False	
4. False		19. False	
5. True		20. True	
6. False		21. False	
7. False		22. True	
8. False		23. True	
9. True		24. False	
10. True		25. False	
11. False		26. False	
12. False		27. True	
13. True		28. True	
14. True		29. True	
15. False		30. False	

BRIEF CONTENTS

CONTENTS

C H A P T E R   3

Sensation and Perception   96

C H A P T E R   6

Language and Thought   252

CHAPTER 9

Stress, Coping, and Health 426

C H A P T E R 10

Abnormal Behavior 478

C H A P T E R 1 1

Psychotherapy and Other Treatment Approaches 526

C H A P T E R 1 2

Infancy and Childhood 572

CHAPTER 13

Adolescence, Adulthood, and Old Age 622

C H A P T E R 1 4

Social Psychology: How We Relate to Each Other 668

A P P E N D I X

Statistical Methods 715

To Julius Segal

a wise and compassionate friend

C H A P T E R   1

The Science and Practice of Psychology

Psychology can perhaps best be described as a modern attempt to deal with a subject that has interested and puzzled humanity since the dawn of time: what human beings do, think, and feel—and the reasons for their behavior. Thus, more than any subject you are likely to study, psychology is about a topic that should be of intense interest to you. It is about yourself. The field embodies an effort to answer the kinds of questions you have often asked about your makeup and behavior.

The questions addressed by psychology are endlessly fascinating: Were you born the way you are or did your personality evolve over time? Are you the master of your fate or a helpless pawn of your environment? Can you change if you want to? What accounts for the differences within the human species? Why are some people so quick to learn, others so slow? Why do some people crumble in the face of everyday stress, while others can overcome even seemingly devastating crises? Why are some people generally cheerful, others generally glum; some aggressive, others passive; some withdrawn, others friendly? Why do some people appear to be perfectly sane and rational, while others behave in ways that are regarded as strange and abnormal?

Those questions are dealt with every day in popular books, magazines, television talk shows, and conversations with friends. But psychology offers scientific rather than "armchair" answers. Psychology's insights are based on the careful efforts of both scientists and clinical practitioners to gather a solid body of information about the nature of human functioning—namely, about what human beings do, think, and feel and the reasons for their behavior.

Psychologists do not pretend to have all the answers, of course. Human behavior is so complex that it may forever defy full scientific analysis. But psychologists do have some of the answers and clues to many others, and they are constantly making new discoveries. This much seems certain: When you finish studying this book, you will know more about the human experience than anybody in the world did a century ago, when the first psychology laboratory was opened, and the science of psychology was begun.

The Scope of Psychology

Because psychology is a relatively new science, however, and because so many unfounded opinions of human behavior persist, there is still considerable confusion over what the field is actually all about. An introductory textbook must begin, therefore, with a description of the varied domain of psychology, and how it is related to the subject matter of other sciences.

Defining Psychology's Boundaries

Psychology

The systematic study of behavior and mental processes—including thought and emotion—and the factors that influence them.

A definition of **psychology**, although brief, covers an enormous realm. It is *the systematic study of behavior and mental processes—including thought and emotion—and the factors that influence them*. In those few words are covered a range of subject matter whose boundaries are enormously wide.

To begin with, the word *behavior* means a host of things. Our physical actions begin each morning when we wake, yawn, stretch, dress, and eat breakfast, and they do not end until we go back to bed and fall asleep—after a long day in which we walk, talk, study, work, play, and sometimes laugh or cry.

Inside ourselves is another world of activity: the *mental and emotional processes* of thought and feeling. We develop ideas, we learn, we remember,

Psychologists search for the characteristics that people have in common—but also those that make each of us unique.

and we forget. We feel hunger and thirst—and such emotions as anger, fear, joy, and sadness. We have stirrings of desire for accomplishment and success, friendship, and sometimes revenge. We worry over problems and seek ways to cope with them. Thus the subject matter of psychology includes not only the observable behaviors that we exhibit, but also the hidden processes constantly going on within us—our thoughts, emotions, motives, and conflicts.

The *factors that influence behavior and mental processes* are also many and varied. The most important is the human brain, an organ that is immensely complex—made up of billions of nerve cells, of scores of different kinds performing different functions, that are intricately connected and interconnected and constantly exchanging messages coded into electrical and chemical activity. The brain would be useless without the help it gets from other parts of the body. It would not know anything about the environment without the specialized nerve cells of the sense organs, sensitive to light, sound, smell, taste, and pressure. It would not even know hunger or thirst without signals provided by the bloodstream and some of the visceral organs. It would not produce emotions without the aid of various chemicals in the brain.

Psychology must study all these relationships between the brain and the rest of the body. It must investigate heredity—and the extent to which our conduct is governed by tendencies handed down to us from the countless generations of forebears from whom we are descended. At the same time it must examine the influence of environment, including the ways we learn from our experiences, remember them, and apply them. In particular it must look at the ways the actions of other people affect our own behavior—which turns out to be much more significant and far-reaching than we might suspect.

Our definition of psychology includes the words *systematic study* because psychology uses the rigorous and disciplined methods of science. It does not rely on some mysterious explanation for human behavior, as our earliest ancestors did. It is not content to describe behavior as a philosopher of the past, however brilliant, may have imagined it to be. Psychology is skeptical and demands proof, based on controlled experiments and on observations made with the greatest possible precision and objectivity—which means freedom from personal prejudices or preconceived notions. Consider the fact that many Europeans in the fifteenth century believed that illness and depression could be caused by people believed to be witches. Because no carefully controlled experiment was done to test the truth of that idea, it survived even as late as the seventeenth century—for example, in the famous Salem witch trials.

Without the scientific approach, it is difficult to reach valid conclusions about human behavior. The nonscientist is almost bound to commit numerous mistakes of observation and interpretation and to make judgments based on faulty or insufficient evidence. All of us tend to generalize from our own feelings and experiences—but as this book will make clear, what we see in ourselves is not necessarily characteristic of people in general. Or we generalize from the actions and opinions of the people we know, which again are not necessarily universal.

The Mission of Psychology

The field of psychology has a dual mission: most importantly *to understand behavior and mental processes* and (2) *to predict their course*. Indeed, understanding and predicting are goals of all sciences. Chemists, for example, have sought from earliest times to understand why wood burns and gold does not—and to predict what will happen when a chemical substance is subjected to flame or combined with another chemical in a test tube. Psychologists seek, among other things, to understand why individuals behave as they do in a family or in a social situation—and to predict what will happen if certain environmental changes are made. For example: Would children be less anxious if divorce were impossible?

Some scientists seek not only to understand and predict events but to control them as well. Chemists want to be able to control the substances they deal with so that they can develop useful new purposes for chemicals such as the various synthetics now used in clothing and automobiles. To a certain extent, some psychologists also look for ways to "control" human behavior. This is especially true of those who devote their careers to helping people overcome mental and emotional problems. They want to modify the behavior of their clients by trying to relieve their problems—perhaps an unreasonable fear of going out in public, an inability to establish satisfactory sexual relationships, or alcohol addiction.

But dealing with humans is far different from mixing chemicals in a test tube. The possibility of controlling human behavior raises thorny questions of social policy. Therefore psychologists have mixed feelings about whether control of behavior should be considered a third goal of the science. Some psychologists have argued that human behavior is always under some kind of control—the control of parents over their children, the control of school systems, the business world, and the nation's laws—and that it would be better to have the control exercised in a scientific fashion by scientists dedicated to improving the human condition (Skinner, 1971). Most psychologists, however, shun the responsibility—and the dangers of abuse—inherent in efforts to manipulate human behavior.

Related Fields

Psychology is one member of a family of sciences often called the **behavioral** and **social sciences.** It is generally recognized that understanding human

Behavioral science
The scientific study of behavior from the perspectives of psychology, sociology, anthropology, and biology.

behavior requires that we study not only the individual but also other facets of human functioning—from the activity of individual brain cells to the social and cultural setting in which humans function. Thus the subject matter of these sciences range from the neurochemical bases of memory and motivation to the dynamics of global commerce and international conflict (Gerstein et al., 1988). Such a broad perspective is necessary because humans continually think about what is happening to them and in the world around them. Thus, for example, the quality of sleep of an African-American in Chicago can be affected by a TV news story about what is happening to blacks in South Africa.

Scientists who work as members of the behavioral and social science family come from fields as seemingly different as **genetics** (the study of hereditary mechanisms) and **physiology** (the study of the biological functions and activities of living organisms) on the one hand. On the other hand, social science includes *anthropology* (the study of cultures and races), *economics, linguistics* (the study of language), *education, sociology* (the study of social institutions, groups, and relationships), and *political science* (the study of political and governmental institutions and processes).

Although psychologists represent a distinct field, the areas of study they undertake are so varied that they often maintain close connection with many of their "siblings" in the behavioral and social science family. For example, psychologists exploring the role that heredity plays in intelligence might work in concert with geneticists, and those studying how schools affect children might collaborate with education specialists. In doing so, psychologists seek not only to draw from work in other disciplines but to contribute to them as well. But what is common to all psychologists is an interest in the study of behavior, and of mental and emotional processes.

Social science
The study of human behavior in its social and cultural settings.

Genetics
The study of hereditary contributions to physical and psychological traits.

Physiology
The study of the biological functions and activities of living organisms.

The Varieties of Psychology and Psychologists

In the last half century, the number of psychologists in the United States has grown dramatically. The percentage of all doctoral degrees awarded in the United States to psychologists has risen from 4 percent in 1945 to over 9 percent in 1987 (Coyle & Thurgood, 1989). More than 100,000 individuals are engaged in some form of psychological endeavor, and more than 60,000 are members of the field's professional organization, the American Psychological Association (APA) (Stapp, Tucker, & VandenBos, 1985). The expanding ratio of women in the field is discussed in the Psychology in Action box on "Closing the Gender Gap in Psychology."

The number of books, magazine articles, and TV shows built around psychological themes has also grown. Oddly enough, the popularity of psychology is something of a handicap to the student embarking on an introductory course—who may find the field to be somewhat different in scope and content than expected.

Basic and Applied Psychology

Some psychologists, as pictured in Figure 1.1, are concerned with **basic science**—that is, knowledge for the sake of knowledge. Their chief activities are teaching and research. Their major areas of interest are shown in Figure 1.2.

Basic science
The search for fundamental knowledge without specific attention to its practical implications.

Closing the Gender Gap in Psychology

Although their contributions have often been overlooked or ignored, women have been involved in psychology since its early years. When a professional psychological organization was formed in 1892, women quickly began joining; they contributed to the new journals and presented papers at the annual meetings. Mary Calkins, Christine Ladd-Franklin, and Margaret Washburn are three of the best known turn-of-the century female psychologists. In 1894 Washburn was the first woman to earn a doctorate in psychology, from Cornell University. Both Calkins and Ladd-Franklin completed the requirements for their doctorates, but they were not awarded the degree because their universities, Harvard and Johns Hopkins, would not grant doctorates to women.

Margaret Washburn (1871–1939)

These female pioneers all faced major obstacles in their attempts to pursue psychology. Society was opposed to the notion of a working wife or mother, so most women were forced to abandon their professional pursuits once they married. Even those who decided to forgo marriage faced more limited career options than did their male colleagues. Yet, these early female psychologists were not relegated to "women's work," as were women in other scientific fields. Their academic interests covered the realm of psychology.

During this century, psychology has attracted more women than any other science and has proved to be a popular undergraduate major among women. As far back as 1950, more women earned their bachelor's degrees in psychology than in any other field. Over the past few decades, as more and more women have pursued doctorates, the number of women earning Ph.D.'s in psychology has also risen. In 1950 women earned 15 percent of the doctorates awarded in psychology; by 1984 women received 50 percent of those in the field.

Despite the greater opportunities for women in psychology, women today face many obstacles similar to those of a century ago. Since society still expects women to carry most of the burden of child care, choices between career and family are often as difficult to resolve now as they were then. Discrimination still exists, although it is more subtle than it was

at the turn of the century. Universities no longer exclude women from their graduate programs, yet women with Ph.D.'s in psychology are underrepresented in tenured faculty positions. Female psychologists also earn lower incomes than their male colleagues. A 1983 study from the National Science Foundation found that male psychologists earned $57,000 more a year than women with equal experience and training.

Nevertheless, opportunities for women in psychology have greatly improved over the past 100 years (Scarborough & Furumoto, 1987). As of 1985, women comprised 34 percent of the membership of the American Psychological Association. By the early 1990s, far more women than men will earn doctorates in the field. And despite subtle forms of discrimination, many female psychologists are rising to the ranks of their profession. For example, two of the APA's recent presidents, Janet T. Spence and Bonnie R. Strickland, are women (Howard et al., 1986; Furumoto & Scarborough, 1986).

Experimental psychologists are interested in the ways we perceive the world, and in such basic processes as learning, memory, and motivation. *Comparative psychologists* focus their efforts on comparing the behavior of different species—and relating animal behavior patterns to those found in humans. *Physiological psychologists* seek information about the structure and function-

FIGURE 1.1 Basic and applied psychologists at work Pictured here are psychologists working in the two diverse fields of psychology—basic research (top) and applied (bottom).

ing of the brain, and they examine chemical substances that influence our nervous systems and emotions. They, as well as many other psychologists, are interested in animal organisms as well as people; because the study of the brain requires direct access to it through surgical techniques, animals are frequently used as subjects in the hope that what is learned about their brains and behavior will be applicable to humans. *Developmental psychologists* study how individuals grow and change throughout their existence. *Personality and social psychologists* study the enduring characteristics of people and the social conditions that influence human behavior. Some basic psychologists, of course, deal directly with the many forms that behavior takes, and they cannot therefore be pigeonholed easily into one subspecialty. The percentages of psychologists working in these areas of basic science are shown in Figure 1.2.

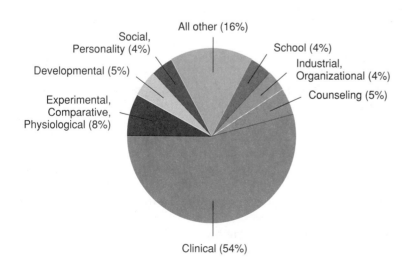

FIGURE 1.2 The varieties of psychologists Shown here are the major groupings of both basic and applied psychologists.

Applied science

Using knowledge to help society carry on its everyday tasks, tackle its problems, and improve the quality of life.

Clinical psychologists

Psychologists who diagnose and treat psychological disorders in individual and group settings.

Psychotherapy

A technique using the discussion of problems as a way to modify attitudes, emotional responses, and behavior.

Psychoanalysis

A type of psychotherapy developed by Freud, in which the patient gains insight into unconscious conflicts through free association, study of dreams, slips of the tongue, and transference.

Counseling psychologists

Psychologists who help with milder problems of social and emotional adjustment like career guidance and marital problems.

Other psychologists, also pictured in Figure 1.1, are concerned not so much with basic science as with **applied science,** or using knowledge to help society carry on its everyday tasks, tackle its problems, and improve the quality of life. *School psychologists* test and evaluate pupils, analyze learning problems, and counsel both teachers and parents. *Industrial and organizational psychologists* help select and train workers and improve working conditions, employee morale, and staff cooperation. The percentages of psychologists working in these applied areas are indicated in Figure 1.2.

Psychology includes a number of additional subfields grouped together in Figure 1.2 as "All other." Within them, for example, are *educational psychologists* concerned with the impact of educational processes and techniques—including teaching methods, curriculum, and textbooks—on students. Included also are a number of additional subfields of applied psychology. *Environmental psychologists* are especially interested in researching and solving ecological problems like smog, water pollution, crowding, and noise—and with helping our industrial society maintain an environment that preserves the balance of nature and enables human beings and other organisms to continue to thrive. *Community psychologists,* sometimes called specialists in *community mental health,* are concerned with the social environment and the way schools and other institutions might better serve individual human needs. *Forensic psychologists* work on behavioral issues important in the legal, judicial, and correctional systems. And, as one more example, *health psychologists* study and apply ways to improve health by altering behavior.

The line between basic science and its applications is by no means rigid. Indeed many of the findings from basic research have found important uses—for example, in the education of young children who have learning difficulties and in the treatment of various forms of abnormal behavior (Silver & Segal, 1984).

The Practice of Clinical and Counseling Psychology

Most applied psychologists, the largest group of all psychologists in the United States, are in the fields of *clinical* or *counseling* psychology. They use the findings of science to help individuals solve the various problems in society that trouble people from time to time—everything from deciding on a suitable line of work, to dealing with marital or sexual maladjustments, to overcoming crippling depression and anxieties. As indicated in Figure 1.2, of all professionally trained psychologists in the nation, nearly 60 percent are in this particular arena of psychology (Pion, 1990).

Clinical psychology is the diagnosis and treatment of psychological disorders—all of the traits and behaviors that are thought of as abnormal, described in Chapter 10. Clinical psychologists sometimes work with individuals, sometimes with groups. They use the technique called **psychotherapy**—treatment through discussing problems, trying to get at the root of them, and modifying attitudes, emotional responses, and behavior.

Psychotherapy as we know it today began with Sigmund Freud, an Austrian physician and neurologist who asked his troubled patients to lie on a couch (see Figure 1.3) and talk about themselves, their experiences, and what was troubling them, simply letting their thoughts roam in any direction. By analyzing this flow of ideas, as described in Chapter 13, Freud tried to dis-

FIGURE 1.3 The birth-place of psychoanalysis It was in this room, on this couch, that psychoanalysis began. The photograph was made in the office of Sigmund Freud about 1895.

cover the origin of the problems and eventually to lead his patients to under-stand and overcome them.

Psychotherapy was originally the sole province of specialists who, like Freud, were physicians with advanced training in **psychoanalysis,** as Freud's method is called. The first psychologists who entered the field also used Freud's technique, and many of today's clinical psychologists continue to be influenced to some degree by Freudian theory. But others have developed different methods of approaching the special problems of the individuals they are trying to help. There are now far more clinical psychologists than psy-choanalysts in the United States, using a wide array of psychotherapy tech-niques, as described in Chapter 11. (Unlike psychiatrists, who have an M.D. degree, clinical psychologists do not assess the physiological roots of psycho-logical problems, nor do they prescribe drugs or use other medical therapies also described in Chapter 13.)

In general, **counseling psychology** involves helping those with milder problems of social and emotional adjustment. Some counselors provide assis-tance to people who need guidance on such temporary problems as difficul-ties in school or choice of a vocation. In their search for the best solution, counselors often administer tests that have been developed by psychology for everything from general intelligence to aptitude for specific tasks. One of psy-chology's most important findings, as you will see in Chapter 8, is that peo-ple are usually very good at doing some things but only mediocre to poor at others—and one secret of success, in both school and work, is to take advan-tage of individual strengths. Psychological counselors attempt to discover and encourage these strengths.

Some counselors specialize in helping married couples overcome diffi-culties in their relationships—often caused not so much by deep-seated emo-tional problems as by poor communication or stressful circumstances. Like clinical psychologists, these marriage counselors sometimes work with indi-vidual couples, sometimes with groups.

TEST YOURSELF

c) During the past 100 years, how has psychology com-pared to other sciences in the matter of attracting women to the field?

d) Two psychologists are interested in the subject of risk-taking behavior. The first is studying the range of physiological changes people undergo when they are faced with a risky task, while the second is helping the government select personnel for dangerous missions. Which psycholo-gist's work is *basic* and which is *applied?*

e) A mother of an adolescent girl is concerned that her daughter is constantly depressed and speaks of suicide. If she seeks psy-chological help, which field of psychology is that per-son likely to be in?

The Methods Psychologists Use

In every science, the methods of study depend on the subject matter. Because behavior takes such a wide variety of forms, psychologists have had to use various approaches. No single method can be applied. Therefore psychologists have had to adopt a number of different ways of studying their subject matter—and they are constantly seeking new ways. The most prominent methods of study in use are described in the following pages.

Observation: Learning by Watching

In many cases, psychologists do what astronomers do—that is, they observe events, such as the actual behavior of people in various kinds of social situations. In a sense all humans continually use the technique of observation. Everybody observes the behavior of other people and draws some conclusions from their actions. If we note that a woman student rarely speaks up in class and blushes easily in social situations, we conclude that she is shy, and we treat her accordingly. (We may try to put her at ease, or, if we feel so inclined, we may enjoy embarrassing her and making her squirm.) Psychologists make their observations in a more disciplined fashion. They try to describe behavior objectively and exactly, and they are loath to jump to conclusions about the motives behind it. For example, a psychologist, studying the reactions of students to the stress of an exam, might record that the "students continuously shifted position"—not that they were "nervous."

In studying behavior through observation, psychologists try to remain apart from what is going on in order to avoid influencing events in any way. They practice **naturalistic observation,** trying to be as inconspicuous and anonymous as possible, lest their presence affect the behavior they are studying. Sometimes they even arrange to be unseen, as illustrated in Figure 1.4.

Naturalistic observation

A scientific method in which the investigator, by being as inconspicuous and anonymous as possible, does not affect the behavior of the subjects under observation.

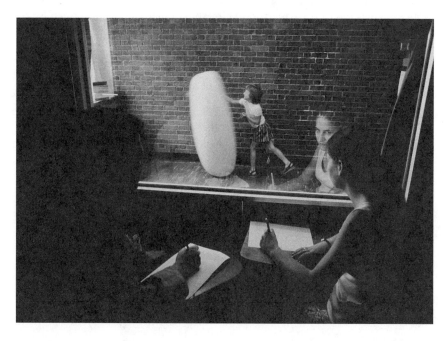

FIGURE 1.4 Invisible observers study child behavior Unseen behind a one-way mirror, investigators use the method of naturalistic observation to study a child at play. To the observers outside the room, the wall panel looks like a sheet of clear glass. To the child inside, it looks like a mirror.

Some of our most valuable knowledge about the behavior of infants and the way they develop has come from observers who used this method. The famous Masters and Johnson findings on sexual response were obtained in part in this manner, and in part through indirect observations—that is, through the use of videotapes, film, or a remote microphone (Masters, Johnson, & Kolodny, 1985). Naturalistic observations have also been used to study the behavior of animals—for example, the social behavior of primates as they operate day-to-day in their natural surroundings (Goodall, 1986).

At other times, psychologists engage in **participant observation.** They take an active part in a social situation—sometimes deliberately playacting to see how other people behave toward someone who seems unusually withdrawn or hostile. Or they may interact in a group to study their own as well as other people's reactions.

Participant observation

A scientific method in which the investigator takes an active part in a social situation in order to study how other people behave.

Interviews and Case Histories: Asking and Digging Back

Another way to discover how people behave and feel is to ask them—and therefore psychologists often use **interviews,** questioning subjects in depth about their life experiences. A special application of the interview method is the **case history,** in which many years of a person's life are reconstructed to show how various behavior patterns have developed. Often, interviews and the construction of case histories are used in concert. Such an approach has been taken, for example, to provide insights into the various effects on parents and children of family breakup (Wallerstein & Blakeslee, 1989).

Interview

A scientific method in which the investigator questions subjects in depth about their life experiences.

Case history

An application of the interview method in which the investigator describes a person's background to show how behavior patterns have developed.

Questionnaires and Opinion Surveys

Closely related to the interview is the **questionnaire,** which can be especially useful in gathering information quickly from large numbers of people. A questionnaire is a set of written questions that can be answered easily, usually with a check mark. Most studies of personality, for example, require the use of questionnaires, which ask people to indicate how sad, happy, fearful, or shy they are. To produce accurate results, a questionnaire must be worded with extreme care. The creation of a reliable questionnaire is a fine art, for the slightest change in the way the questions are worded may completely distort the results.

Questionnaire

A set of written questions that can be answered and scored quickly; used to gather information from large numbers of people.

Questionnaires and interviews are sometimes challenged on the grounds that people do not respond truthfully. But experienced investigators have ways of spotting people who are lying or exaggerating. Interviews and questionnaires cannot always reveal the complete truth. When carefully planned and administered, however, they can be extremely useful.

Questionnaires and interviews find a special use in the study of public opinion, in which psychologists are also active. Scientific methods of choosing a sample of people to poll, and analyzing the results, have made it possible to show how all the people in the United States are divided on any controversial issue, within a few percentage points of possible error, by questioning a mere 1,500 or so.

Public opinion surveys are a valuable contribution to the democratic process because they provide an accurate picture of how citizens actually feel about such issues as taxation, defense expenditures, foreign policy, abortion, and laws regulating sexual conduct and the use of drugs. Before such infor-

Public opinion survey

A sampling of attitudes providing a picture of how citizens feel about such issues as taxation, abortion, sexual conduct, and drugs.

mation was available, there was no accurate way to gauge public opinion—and often small but vociferous minorities were able to convince politicians that they represented the majority view by waging intense publicity campaigns. Now many congressional and other political leaders base their votes on the will of the majority (which is often unorganized and silent) as expressed in polls.

Some well-known, though less important, uses of public opinion surveys include predictions of election results and the Nielsen ratings, which measure the popularity of television shows. Business firms use surveys to measure public response to new products and to sales and advertising campaigns.

Tests: Assessing Traits and Behaviors

Among the oldest tools of psychology are the tests that have been developed for many human characteristics, abilities, and achievements. You have probably taken a number of such tests—for example, the Scholastic Assessment Test (SAT), which is a form of intelligence test, or examinations that showed your elementary and high school teachers how your progress in reading or mathematics compared with the national average. When applying for a job, you may be asked to take tests that psychologists have devised for measuring ability at specific tasks, ranging from clerical work to being an astronaut. If you have occasion to visit a clinical psychologist, you may be tested for various personality traits.

The construction of scientific tests—which actually measure what they are supposed to measure and do so accurately and consistently—is much more difficult than is commonly supposed. Many of the so-called psychological tests in newspapers and magazines, which claim to tell you how happy, self-fulfilled, or neurotic you are, or how good you are likely to be as a husband, wife, or parent, have no value at all. They are simply casual games dreamed up by self-styled "experts," and any score you may make on them, good or bad, is not to be taken seriously. Even psychology's best tests have weaknesses despite all the scientific knowledge and effort that have gone into creating them. But they also have their uses, and the search goes on constantly for new and better versions.

Physiological Measures: Activities of Brain and Body

Measurement
The assignment of an orderly system of numbers to behaviors or traits.

Psychologists are also interested in the **measurement** of any physiological characteristics that have a bearing on behavior. They have found, for example, that certain abnormal states such as severe depression may be triggered by disturbances in the chemistry of the brain. They have also shown that the feelings of hunger are not necessarily caused by activity of the stomach, as popularly believed, but by measurable changes in the composition of the bloodstream. They have also shown that the body may respond at times with changes in hormones that are related to anxiety, although the individual reports feeling no emotion.

As described in the next chapter, new techniques now allow researchers to study the brain directly—its structure, blood flow, chemistry, and electrical activity—while the individual is engaged in a variety of activities or while experiencing unusual states of consciousness such as those produced by sleep, drugs, or hallucinations. Researchers have measured the activity of the glands that influence emotions, and the way the arousal of emotions produces changes in the heart rate, blood pressure, and breathing. They have measured muscle tension and brain wave activity in states of stress and relaxation. In identifying some of the chemicals, produced in nerve endings, that transmit nervous impulses, they have found how irregularities in these chemicals play a part in mood and behavior.

Often it turns out to be important to use physiological measures in conjunction with other methods since they may reveal information otherwise unavailable. For example, individuals suffering certain brain injuries have reported being unable to recognize familiar persons in photographs. However, when electrodes are placed on their palms to measure the **galvanic skin response (GSR)**—that is, the electrical changes associated with sweating—it is clear that the photographs of familiar persons do indeed arouse a response (Tranel & Damasio, 1985). This means that at some deep, unconscious level, recognition is taking place.

Galvanic skin response (GSR)
Electrical changes in the skin associated with the activity of the sweat glands.

Measuring the Differences Among Us

Psychology's methods have been particularly helpful in adding to our knowledge of **individual differences** among people. Every person is indeed unique, and physical and psychological traits, from height and muscular strength to intelligence and emotional sensitivity, vary over a wide range.

Individual differences
Variations between members of the same species.

In studying individual differences, the science relies heavily on mathematical techniques known as **statistics**, which are described in the Appendix of this book. Many human traits, from height and weight to intelligence, fall into a similar pattern. Regarding height, for example, the measurements for adult American men range all the way from around 3 feet to around 8 feet. But most cluster around the average, which is now about 5 feet 9 inches, and the number found at each point in the range goes down steadily with each inch up or down from the average. Note the graph in Figure 1.5, which shows how IQs as measured by intelligence tests range from below 40 to above 160—but with the majority falling close to the average of 100, and only a very few at the extreme low or high levels.

Statistics
A branch of mathematics that analyzes and summarizes data and then draws conclusions from that data.

The pattern shown in Figure 1.5 is so typical of the results generally found in all tests and measurements that it is known as the **normal curve of distribution.** The message of the curve is that in many measurable traits, physical and psychological, most people are average or close to it, some are a fair distance above or below, and a few are very far above or below. Those who are about average have a lot of company. Those who are far removed from the average—in intelligence the geniuses and the mentally retarded, in height the seven-footers and the four-footers—are rare.

Normal curve of distribution
A bell-shaped curve illustrating that for many events in nature most cases cluster around the average and decline near either extreme.

The curve of normal distribution helps explain a great deal about behavior, including the general similarities displayed by most people and the wide deviations shown by a few others. The curve applies to performance in school. (Most students have to do an average amount of struggling; some can make A's without turning a hair; some cannot handle the work at all.) It applies to musical talent, athletic skill, and interest or lack of interest in sex—as well as to the intensity of emotional arousal and the strength of motives for achievement, power, and friendship. These and many other individual differ-

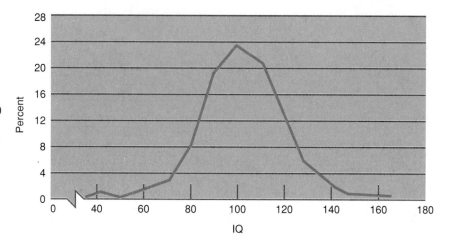

FIGURE 1.5 Individual differences in IQ The graph was obtained by testing the IQs of a large number of people in the United States. Note how many people scored right around the average of 100. (A total of 46.5 percent showed IQs between 90 and 109.) Note also how the number falls off rapidly from the midpoint to the lower and upper extremes. Fewer than 1 percent of all people showed IQs under 60 and only 1.33 percent were at 140 or over (Terman & Merrill, 1937).

ences are the reason you cannot generalize about humanity as a whole from your own traits—especially on a matter in which you happen to fall at an unusually low or high point on the curve.

Correlation: To What Extent Is "A" Related to "B"?

Consider a question that has interested psychologists almost from the beginning of the science: Do children resemble their parents in intelligence? This question has many implications for study of the part played by heredity and environment—which, as you will see a little later, is one of the basic issues in psychology. How would you try to go about answering it?

A person untrained in the methods of science might jump to conclusions based on personal experience: "No, obviously not. My neighbors the Smiths are both smart people—they went to college and have good jobs—but their two kids are having a terrible time in school." Or, "Certainly. My neighbors the Joneses are geniuses and their two daughters are the smartest kids in their school."

A more sophisticated approach would be to look at a much larger sample of children and parents than provided by just the Smiths or the Joneses—and give both generations intelligence tests rather than to rely on personal impressions of how smart they seemed to be. This would be a good start toward a scientific answer. But the results would be difficult to interpret, because the tests would show contradictions. One mother and father, both with IQs of 120, turn out to have an only child whose IQ is also 120—but another couple with the same IQ has an only child with an IQ of 90. One mother at 95 and father at 85 have an only child with an IQ of 90—but a similar couple has a child whose IQ is 125. Even in the same family the tests would sometimes show three children with IQs as far apart as 85, 115, and 135. Without some method of analyzing and interpreting the test results, any scientific answer to the question would still be elusive.

In this type of situation, psychologists apply a statistical tool called **correlation.** This is a mathematical method used to examine two different measurements (such as the IQs of parents and the IQs of their children)—and to determine what relationship, if any, actually exists between the two. The

Correlation

A statistical method examining the relationship between two measures.

method, which is explained in the appendix, computes a **coefficient of correlation** ranging from 0.00 (no relationship at all) to 1.00 (a one-to-one or absolutely perfect relationship). In the case of parents and children, the coefficient of correlation between IQs has generally been found to be about 0.50—indicating a fairly high, though by no means perfect, relationship.

You will find many correlations mentioned throughout this book, but a word of caution is in order. Correlations reveal the existence and extent of relationships, but they do not necessarily indicate cause and effect. Unless they are carefully interpreted, correlations can be misleading. There is a high correlation between the number of permanent teeth in children and their ability to answer increasingly difficult questions on intelligence tests. But this does not mean that having more teeth causes increased mental ability. The correlation is high because increasing age accounts for both the new teeth and the mental development. Usually when two traits are correlated it is because a third process is the cause of both of them.

Coefficient of correlation
A statistic that describes the degree of a relationship between two factors.

The Conclusive Method:
Conducting an Experiment

In an **experiment,** the psychologist makes a careful and controlled study of cause and effect, setting up one set of conditions and determining what kind of behavior takes place under those conditions. Then the conditions are changed and the effect of the changes, if any, is measured. It is possible, of course, to learn a great deal about the world without doing experiments, as, for example, in the case of astronomy. But the most powerful tool of all sciences, including psychology, is the experiment.

Experiment
A scientific method in which the experimenter makes a careful and controlled study of cause and effect.

Independent and Dependent Variables

Every psychological experiment is, in effect, an attempt to discover whether behavior changes when conditions change. The change in conditions is set up and controlled by the experimenter. Note the example illustrated in Figure 1.6, in which the change in conditions is the fact that the experimenter has trained parents to read picture books to their children. The technique being used is designed to stimulate verbal interaction with the children and, therefore, their language development (Whitehurst et al., 1988). Since the change is manipulated by the experimenter rather than being dependent on anything the subjects—in this case, the parents—do or do not do, it is called the **independent variable.**

Independent variable
The factor that is manipulated by the experimenter.

The behavior that occurs in response to the independent variable—in Figure 1.6, the child's capacity to use language—is called the **dependent variable.** In all experiments, the experimenter arranges to change the independent variable, then measures the dependent variable as exhibited by a group of subjects.

What if it turned out—as it actually did—that the result for the children in the reading experiment was a better-than-average capacity to use language? This might seem to suggest at first blush that parents who are specially trained in reading picture books to their young children are likely to advance their language development.

Dependent variable
A change in behavior that results from the manipulation of the independent variable.

FIGURE 1.6 Does parent training help children's language development? In this experiment the researcher provided a group of parents with special training in how to read picture books to their children in ways intended to speed up language development. For a month, the parents made sure to do such things as ask questions as they read, encourage the child to name objects pictured on the page, repeat words, and correct the child's errors. The parent training comprised the *independent variable,* and the resulting language development of the children comprised the *dependent variable.* To find out whether the program had any effect, refer to Figure 1.7.

But does it? As you have already doubtless decided, such a conclusion is unwarranted. It is impossible to figure out, from such a finding alone, what if anything would be demonstrated if the experiment went no further. There are obvious questions to be asked: What would have happened if the subjects had *not* been read to in a special way? What level of expressive language skills would they then have shown?

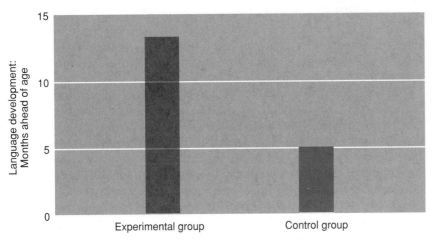

FIGURE 1.7 Does parent training help children's language development? Yes, it does. In the experiment shown in Figure 1.6, the use of a *control group* along with an *experimental group* permitted the researchers to conclude that parent training did indeed have a significant effect on the children's level of language development. The bar chart shows that the difference between the two groups of children is about 6 months—in favor of the experimental group (after Whitehurst et al., 1988).

The Need for Experimental and Control Groups

The problem is solved by using a second group for comparison's sake, and measuring *their* use of language as well. As shown in Figure 1.7, the researchers study not only (1) an **experimental group** of children whose parents were specially trained to read to them, but (2) a **control group** whose parents read to them in the customary way. Only by determining the difference in results between the experimental and the control groups is it possible to get a clear indication of the effect of the experimentally introduced independent variable. In this instance, as demonstrated in Figure 1.7, the evidence is clear: The use of the parent training program (the independent variable) had a marked beneficial effect on the children's use of language (the dependent variable).

If an experiment is to be meaningful, the experimental and control subjects must be chosen with great care. In the case of the reading experiment just described, the children studied had to be matched in terms of such factors as age, sex, number of children in the family, education level of the parents, and frequency of reading to the child. Moreover, the experimenter had to make certain by pretesting the children that they were all starting out from the same level—that is, that the status of language development of both groups was roughly comparable to begin with.

Experimental group

A group of subjects whose behavior is observed while the experimenter manipulates the independent variable.

Control group

A group whose behaviors are used for comparison with those of an experimental group.

Single-Blind and Double-Blind Experiments

How would you conduct an experiment on the effects of marijuana on driving ability? Psychologists would probably begin by dividing their subjects into an experimental group that was under the influence of the drug and a control group that was not. But a further precaution would be necessary—for the subjects' performance might be affected by their knowledge that they had taken the drug and their expectations of how it might affect them. To avoid this possibility, it would be important to keep the subjects from knowing whether they had received the drug. This could be done by giving half the subjects an injection of the drug's active ingredient, THC, and the other half an injection of a salt solution that would have no effect, without telling them which was which. This method, in which subjects are not told whether they belong to the experimental group or the control group, is called the **single-blind technique.**

There is the further danger that the experimenter's own ratings of the subjects' performance might be affected by knowing which of them had taken the drug and which had not. To make the experiment foolproof, the drug or salt solution would have to be injected by a third party, so that even the experimenter would have no way of knowing which subjects had received which kind of injection. This method, in which neither the subject nor the experimenter knows who is in the experimental group and who is in the control group, is called the **double-blind technique.** It is particularly valuable in studying the effects of drugs, including the tranquilizers and antidepressants used to treat mental disturbances. It is also used in any other experiment in which knowledge of the conditions might affect the judgment of the experimenter as well as the performance of the subjects.

The double-blind experiment is psychology's most powerful tool. Its power is enhanced by the fact that the experiment can undergo **replication**— that is, it can be repeated by another experimenter at another time and in another place, ruling out the possibility that the results were accidental or influenced by extraneous variables, among them the first experimenter's personality or preconceived notions of what would happen.

Psychology's Rich History and Promising Future

The psychological experiment—and psychology itself—has come a long way since the science began. At the start, the idea of taking a scientific approach to the study of behavior required a radical shift in human thinking and the invention of new techniques of study.

The year that the science was founded is usually put at 1879, when Wilhelm Wundt opened the first psychological laboratory at Germany's University of Leipzig. Wundt had studied to be a physician, then, instead of practicing medicine, taught as a professor of physiology. But he soon lost interest because he, like other early European psychologists, was much more concerned with human consciousness than with the workings of the body. He and his colleagues would have individuals sit for hours in the laboratory listening to sounds and looking at colors—at the same time asking them to report what they perceived. In this way he hoped he would discover the relation between stimulation and mental phenomena.

Wundt was the most popular professor at his university, and no classroom was big enough to hold all the students who wanted to hear his lectures. A few years later, similar acclaim came to Sir Francis Galton, one of the first British psychologists. Galton, who was interested in individual differences in mental abilities and personality, invented numerous devices to test hearing, sense of smell, color vision, and ability to judge weights, all of which he believed comprised an index of intelligence. At one time he set up his equipment as a feature at an International Health Exhibition in London—and peo-

TEST YOURSELF

f) Later in this book, in Chapter 10, you will be learning that there is a correlation between serious feelings of depression and certain biochemical changes in the brain. From that fact alone, can you tell for sure which is cause and which is effect?

g) If you were to do an experiment on the effects of praise on mathematics performance, would the praise be the independent or dependent variable?

Single-blind technique

A method in which subjects do not know whether they are in the experimental group or the control group.

Double-blind technique

A method in which neither the subject nor the experimenter knows who is in the experimental group and who is in the control group.

Replication

The repetition of an experiment by another experimenter at another time and in another place.

ple flocked in to be his subjects, gladly paying an entrance fee for the privilege. Even in those early years, when psychology was just taking a few tentative steps into the vast realm of human behavior, it captured the public's imagination.

The Era of Introspection

Like Wundt, most of the pioneers concentrated on an attempt to discover the nature, origins, and significance of conscious experiences. Their chief method of investigation was **introspection,** or looking inward. They tried to analyze the processes that went on inside their minds, asked their subjects to do the same, and recorded their findings, as objectively as possible, for comparison with other observers.

The most prominent of the early American psychologists was William James, who came to the science from an unusual background. Like Wundt, he studied medicine but never practiced. Indeed he had a difficult time finding his true vocation. At one time he wanted to be an artist, then a chemist, and once he joined a zoological expedition to Brazil. In his late twenties he suffered a mental breakdown and went through a prolonged depression in which he seriously thought of committing suicide. But he recovered—largely, he believed, through what he called "an achievement of the will"—and went on to become a Harvard professor and prolific writer on psychology and philosophy.

James had no doubt about the mission of the new science. A textbook he wrote began with the words: "Psychology is the study of mental life" (James, 1890). The distinguishing feature of this mental life, he felt, was that human beings constantly seek certain end results and must constantly choose among various methods of achieving them.

The Rise of Behaviorism

Was William James's introspective approach really scientific or just another form of mere speculation about the human condition? Soon a new breed of psychologists began to question the usefulness of introspection as a source of information, and their questions raised nagging doubts as the years went by. In 1913 another American, John Watson, revolutionized psychology by breaking completely with the use of introspection and founding the movement called **behaviorism.**

Watson declared that "mental life" is something that cannot be seen or measured and thus cannot be studied scientifically. Instead of trying to examine any such vague thing as "mental life" or consciousness, he argued, psychologists should concentrate on actions that are plainly visible. In other words, he wanted the science to study what people *do*, not what they think or feel.

Watson did not believe in anything like "free will," or the ability to control our own destiny. Instead he believed that everything we do is predetermined by our past experiences. He considered all human behavior to be a series of actions in which a **stimulus**—that is, an event in the environment—produces a **response**—that is, an observable muscular movement or some physiological reaction, such as increased heart rate or glandular secretion, which can also be observed and measured with the proper instruments. (For

John B. Watson (1878–1958)

Introspection
Looking inward to examine the processes within the mind.

Behaviorism
The psychological study of overt behavior rather than "mental life" or consciousness.

Stimulus
An event in the environment that produces a response.

Response
A behavioral or physiological reaction that can be observed and measured.

example, shining a bright light into the eye is a stimulus that causes an immediate response in which the pupil of the eye contracts.) Watson believed that through the establishment of **conditioned reflexes,** a type of learning discussed in Chapter 4, almost any kind of stimulus can be made to produce almost any kind of response. He once said that he could take any dozen babies at birth and, by conditioning them in various ways, turn them into anything he wished—doctor, lawyer, beggar, or thief.

Watson conceded that human beings had thoughts, but he believed that these were simply a form of talking to themselves, by making tiny movements of the vocal cords. He also conceded that people have what they call feelings, but he believed that these were only some form of conditioned response to a stimulus in the environment.

For almost five decades behaviorism was the dominant force in psychology. Watson was succeeded as leader of the movement by B. F. Skinner, who was chiefly interested in the learning process and revised and expanded Watson's ideas. Skinner made many important contributions to our knowledge of how patterns of rewards and punishments help shape the organism's behavior—often in the most complex ways. To Skinner, people are not totally responsible for their conduct, nor are they deserving of blame for their failures or of credit for their achievements. They are the creatures of past experience. Their behavior depends on what they have learned and especially on which of their actions have been rewarded. According to Skinner, a "social engineer" aware of all the principles of learning could mold people into any form desired, whether for good or for evil.

The behaviorists, in their efforts to avoid introspective speculation and confine their investigations to forms of behavior that could be seen and measured, often chose to experiment with animals. Skinner built his principles of learning on the behavior of rats and pigeons. Other behaviorists have worked with various animals to explore motives, aggression, cooperation, conflicts, and even abnormal behavior. The thrust of the science was to find universal laws that applied to all organisms, rather than just to some unique mental quality, spiritual superiority, or "achievement of the will" possessed by human beings. As is evident throughout this textbook, the behaviorist view is still evident among many psychologists—for example, among those who study conditioned fear in rats and mice in the hope that what is learned will help explain the origins of fear and anxiety in humans.

The behaviorists, with their search for simple and observable knowledge, pushed psychology into a more disciplined channel—and to the realization that a science must be based on controlled experiments and measurements of behavior. On the other hand, behaviorism was always controversial. Many psychologists rejected the idea that we are all pieces of machinery that automatically perform in a certain way whenever a certain button is pushed. In particular, they disagreed with Skinner's belief that we have no real freedom of choice or responsibility for our own actions. We do seem, as William James pointed out, to make choices. We have complicated thoughts, feelings, emotions, and attitudes that are difficult to explain through a simple push-button theory.

Gestalt psychology

A psychological movement holding that all psychological phenomena must be studied as a whole and in the context in which they occur.

Gestalt Psychology

One movement of considerable historic importance in the opposition to behaviorism was **Gestalt psychology,** which originated in Germany at about the same time Watson's ideas were becoming influential in the United States. The movement took its name from a German word that has no exact English equivalent. **Gestalt** is roughly translated as "pattern" or "configuration," but it means something more than that. The Gestalt school believed that in studying any psychological phenomenon, from a perceptual process to the human personality, it is essential to look at events considered *as a whole*.

Gestalt psychologists also stressed the importance of the entire situation, or context, in which the "whole" is found. A demonstration is shown in Figure 1.8. Note how your interpretation of the highlighted characters is dictated by the rest of what you see in each row of characters. Though the Gestalt movement is no longer active, many of its ideas survive in today's emerging view of mental activity and human behavior in general as a pattern and a unity.

Gestalt

(guess-TAHLT) A "pattern" or "configuration."

The Cognitive Approach and Its Influence

In a sense the opposite directions taken by the behaviorists and the introspectionists were like the efforts of a gunner who first aims too far to the left, next too far to the right—and then, with the target bracketed, scores a direct hit. Both schools of thought were wide of the mark, yet both were essential to the growth of psychology into its present form. Many aspects of "mental life" have now been drawn back into the field of study, and psychologists in recent years have been busy exploring the human use of language, thinking, and memory, as well as human emotions, motives, and social relationships. Yet at the same time, thanks to the influence of Watson and Skinner, the study has become more disciplined and systematic, relying on observations of actual behavior rather than mere introspection.

A major trend today is called **cognitive psychology**—"cognitive" referring to the ways in which we learn about our environment, store the knowledge in memory, think about it, and use it to act intelligently in new situations. These various forms of mental activity are often referred to as **information processing,** a term borrowed from computer science. They begin with what in a computer would be called the inputs—the raw data about the environment that we gather through our sense organs as they respond to light and sound waves, the mechanical forces of pressure and heat, and the chemical forces that cause sensations of taste and smell. Our brain tries to make sense out of this jumble of stimuli, comparing it to previous information and interpreting its significance (through the process of perception, as described in Chapter 4). The information, thus transformed into meaningful patterns, is then stored in memory, where it is associated with other information to which it bears some relationship. We call on the information whenever we need it—as a computer would tap its memory bank—to help us think, understand, and solve problems.

The cognitive psychologists reject the behaviorist proposal that people are mere passive creatures of the environment, responding in reflex fashion to incoming stimuli. Instead they view the human organism as "an active seeker of knowledge and processor of information," from which each individual actively builds "mental representations of the world" (Klatzky, 1980). These **mental models of reality** are a core idea in cognitive psychology.

To put this another way, the cognitive psychologists think of the human mind as a mental executive that organizes stimuli into perceptual patterns

Cognitive psychology

A movement studying the ways in which we learn about our environment, store that knowledge in our memory, process that knowledge, and use it to act intelligently in new situations.

Information processing

A term that cognitive psychologists use to describe the mental processes entailed in perception, learning, and thinking.

Mental models of reality

A key idea in cognitive psychology defined as patterns of knowledge about the world that the mind builds through its information processing.

A B C D E
11 12 13 14 15

FIGURE 1.8 How the context, or surrounding, influences the Gestalt The highlighted item in each row is, of course, exactly the same— but what you see in each case is quite different. The reason is explained in the text.

(for example, perceiving a girl or a boy rather than a collection of arms, legs, and body), makes comparisons, and processes the information it receives into new forms and categories. It discovers meanings and uses its stored knowledge to find new principles that aid in constructive thinking, making judgments, and deciding on appropriate behavior. These ideas have influenced most of today's psychologists in one way or another, in all the branches of the science from the study of the senses to psychotherapy.

The Humanistic Trend

Humanistic psychology
A movement emphasizing the uniqueness of the individual.

Psychology has of course taken other directions, as would be expected in a science embracing such a wide field of inquiry. One of today's prominent movements is **humanistic psychology,** which stems in part from the Gestalt school. Like the Gestalt psychologists, the humanists prefer to view the human personality as a pattern. To try to study human behavior by breaking it down into fragments, such as individual responses to stimuli, is regarded as futile and a display of "disrespect" for the unique quality of the human spirit (Matson, 1971).

The humanistic psychologist takes the view that human beings are totally different from dogs or monkeys. They are distinguished by the fact that they have values and goals and seek to grow, to express, and fulfill themselves, and to find peace and happiness. Their thoughts and aspirations, which Watson considered inappropriate for study, appear to the humanistic psychologist to be the important aspects of behavior.

The humanistic psychologists are more oriented toward philosophy, literature, and religion than toward the investigative methods of the sciences. Many humanistic psychologists have been associated with efforts to expand consciousness and achieve unity of mind and body through encounter groups, sensitivity training, and other kinds of mental and physical "reaching out."

Sigmund Freud and Psychoanalysis

Hysterical conversion
A disorder in which psychological conflict and stress are converted into physical symptoms such as the loss of functioning of some part of the body.

Sigmund Freud, as mentioned earlier, was not a psychologist but a physician, yet he had a profound influence on many aspects of psychology. Beginning his career in the 1880s in Vienna, he turned his attention to psychological processes as a result of his experience with patients who were suffering from physical impairments—including paralysis of the arms or legs or blindness—without any apparent physical cause. He described such cases as **hysterical conversion,** believing that the patient converted emotional conflicts into physical symptoms. The theories he developed—over a lifetime of treating many kinds of abnormal behavior and analyzing his own personality—are the basis of psychoanalysis, announced to the world at the turn of the century.

In his youth Freud himself suffered from feelings of anxiety and deep depression, and he retained some neurotic symptoms all his life. He was a compulsive smoker of as many as 20 cigars a day, was nervous about traveling, and was given to what were probably hypochondriacal complaints about poor digestion, constipation, and heart palpitation. However, he managed to overcome his early inclinations toward depression and lived a rich professional, family, and social life—an indication that in his case the physician had managed to heal himself, at least in large part.

One of Freud's great insights was the discovery of how the human personality is influenced by **unconscious processes,** especially motives of which the person is unaware. At first his ideas were bitterly attacked; many people were repelled by his notion that human beings, far from being completely rational, are largely at the mercy of irrational unconscious thoughts. Many were shocked by his emphasis on the role of sexual motives (which were prominent among those motives that the society of that period preferred to deny). Over the years, however, the furor died out. There remains considerable question about the value of psychoanalytic methods in treating emotionally disturbed patients, but even those who criticize psychoanalysis as a form of psychotherapy are influenced by Freud's basic notions about personality and its formation. His theories will be discussed in detail in Chapter 10, and the methods of psychoanalysis will be discussed in Chapter 11.

Psychology's rich history includes many influential people, only some of which we have room to discuss in this book. Table 1.1 lists several contributors.

Unconscious processes
The thought and motives of which a person is usually unaware.

TABLE 1.1   Some Influential People in Psychology's History

Name	Main Contributions
Wilhelm Wundt (1832–1920)	One of the founders of **psychology** who established the first psychological laboratory at Germany's University of Leipzig; one of the first to study the process of attention in a systematic manner.
William James (1842–1910)	The author of *Principles of Psychology,* a book dealing with all of the important issues in psychology and still being read by students and scholars today; became a professor at Harvard University.
Sigmund Freud (1856–1939)	The founder of **psychoanalysis.**
Edward B. Titchener 1867–1927	One of the founders of **experimental psychology;** spent much of his life as a professor at Cornell University.
John B. Watson (1878–1958)	The first **behaviorist** who popularized Pavlov's discoveries of conditioning.
Max Wertheimer (1880–1943)	One of the founders of **Gestalt psychology;** emigrated from Europe during World War II and was a professor at the New School for Social Research.
E. C. Tolman (1886–1959)	An influential figure in theories of learning and cognition; spent most of his career at the University of California at Berkeley.
Jean Piaget (1896–1980)	One of the major theorists of **cognitive development;** spent his career at the University of Geneva.
Lois B. Murphy (1902–)	A key figure in theories of **developmental psychology;** originally taught at the City University of New York, then moved to the Menninger Foundation in Topeka, Kansas.
Magda Arnold (1903–)	An important contributor to theories of **emotion;** spent most of her career at Loyola University in Chicago.
Donald O. Hebb (1904–1985)	Author of *The Organization of Behavior,* which was very important in stimulating the field of **physiological psychology;** taught at McGill University.
B. F. Skinner (1904–1990)	One of the most famous **behaviorists;** spent most of his career at Harvard University.
Eleanor J. Gibson (1910–)	One of the most influential theorists in **perceptual development;** spent most of her career at Cornell University.

New Perspectives in Psychobiology

Psychobiology
The study of how various facets of behavior are associated with bodily processes.

Among psychologists today are a growing number who focus on **psychobiology,** the study of how various facets of behavior are associated with processes in the body. You will be reading of their work throughout the book—for example, in studies of the psychological functions of various areas of the brain (Chapter 2), the influence of brain chemistry on emotions and drives (Chapter 7), the bodily changes associated with stress (Chapter 9), the use of drugs to alleviate anxiety and depression (Chapter 11), the role of inherited genes in shaping human development (Chapter 12), and how hormonal changes can affect the adjustment of adolescents (Chapter 13).

In one sense, all behavior is rooted in some manner in the activity of the brain and nervous system, and, as will be discussed later in this book, new techniques allow us now to actually visualize what electrical and chemical changes the brain undergoes when we perceive an object, think, remember, or experience a hallucination. Indeed advances in brain research have led some scientists to conclude that everything we experience and do will one day be explained by the operations of the brain. Even psychologists have wondered if "psychology is in danger of losing its status as an independent body of knowledge" (Peele, 1981).

Most scientists and biologists as well as most psychologists think not. For one thing, the workings of the brain are so complex as to defy complete understanding and will always remain something of a mystery. More important, no matter how complete our understanding of the brain, its structures and circuits do not work independently as if in a vacuum. The brain works instead as an instrument through which behavior is altered by experience. Roger Sperry, when he received the Nobel Prize for his research on the brain (Chapter 2), emphasized this point. We cannot depend on the brain to tell us everything about the operation of the conscious mind (Sperry, 1988). Thus, psychologists will always need to know something about the prior history and psychological state of the person being studied.

Three Key Issues in Psychology Today

Subsequent chapters of this book will be concerned with specific facts that psychologists have discovered about human behavior—from the role of brain cells to social interactions. Before beginning this kind of detailed discussion, however, it is useful to examine some of the major issues to which modern psychology is addressing itself. By and large, these issues go to the very core of human experience. Since they cut so deep, they are difficult to study or resolve. On none of them are all the facts in, and on many of them there is widespread disagreement. But these are the big issues to which psychology, in the broadest sense, is now dedicated.

Heredity and Environment: Their Joint Influence

A major issue of continuing concern to psychology is the nature of the relation between inborn biological factors and life experiences as they affect human personality and behavior.

The relative importance of inherited biological characteristics and experiences has long been a subject of considerable debate. William James, for example, believed that much of our behavior is regulated to a great extent by powerful human instincts present at birth—including pugnacity, rivalry, sociability, shyness, curiosity, acquisitiveness, and love. Watson, on the other hand, believed the newborn child can be turned into almost any kind of adult through conditioned reflexes established by the environment. The debate is often called the **nature-nurture controversy.** It still continues—though it has been modified greatly by findings in **behavior genetics,** the study of the role of inherited traits in shaping behavior.

Today we know that it is not possible to treat biological nature and life experiences as separate, independent forces (Plomin & McClearn, 1993). In order to become a great basketball star, for example, a child would typically have to inherit a combination of height, speed, and endurance. But without exposure to the sport and opportunity to practice, even the best-endowed child would never become skilled at this activity. Thus it is not possible, when looking at a basketball hero, to say exactly how much of his ability is due to what he inherited and how much to his environmental opportunities. As you will see in many other examples throughout this book—whether it is in the development of language, the display of intelligence, or the onset of abnormal behavior—the two forces operate in tandem to give each of us our unique identity.

Continuity and Change

No one would argue with the fact that you are quite different today from the human being you were at birth, or the person you will be in the closing years of your life. But how different? Is human development marked by continuity—that is, a series of gradual and cumulative changes, with the echoes of each stage of life embedded in the later ones? Or are there significant discontinuities—that is, changes so dramatic that some characteristics vanish and new ones emerge?

It is possible to find examples of both stability and change in behavior, and human development appears to be a mix of both themes. Psychologists who study memory claim that once a memory is formed, it can never be entirely lost, and studies of mentally ill individuals often suggest that early trauma, such as abuse in childhood, can leave profound effects in adult life. But on the other hand, the brain undergoes marked changes over time, with some circuits phasing out and new ones added—dramatically changing our repertoire of behaviors. And new experiences—a different job, marriage, a sudden trauma—can dramatically shift the course of development for good or ill. Psychology must study both continuity and change. It must strive to understand to what extent we become just different versions of our earlier selves, and to what degree we can become "a different person," difficult to recognize from our earlier identity.

Context: How Setting Affects Who We Are

For many decades, psychology was chiefly interested in the individual. The science was content to separate the individual person from others—much like a zoologist cutting one elephant out of the herd for measurement and labeling—and to study this person's behavior. Any characteristic was assumed to represent a consistent pattern of behavior—as stable as height or weight. A

Behavior genetics
The study of the role of heredity in behavioral characteristics.

Context
The particular situation in which a behavior occurs.

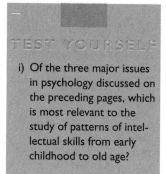

TEST YOURSELF

i) Of the three major issues in psychology discussed on the preceding pages, which is most relevant to the study of patterns of intellectual skills from early childhood to old age?

person found to be helpful and generous would be helpful and generous in general under most circumstances. An aggressive person would always tend to be aggressive, an anxious person always anxiety prone, an achievement-oriented person always focused on achievement.

It is now clear, however, that our behavior is not as consistent as was once believed. Our actions depend on the **context**—that is, on the particular situation in which the behavior occurs. We may be generous at home but selfish at work, aggressive with a spouse but submissive with friends, anxious in an unfamiliar place but calm and relaxed in familiar surroundings. A major issue in psychology, therefore, is to understand more fully how our behavior depends on where we are—and particularly on the people around us.

The manner in which the situation and the people in it can influence behavior is the primary concern of the specialists in social psychology, which is the subject of Chapter 14. But all branches of psychology have been greatly influenced by the rise of this important issue. More and more it appears that we cannot always fully understand individuals by studying them in isolation.

Psychology's Ethical Standards

In studying the effects of special tutoring on disadvantaged children, a psychologist may probe for details of each child's family life and then, in an experiment, provide an enriched teaching program to half the children while denying it to the others. In analyzing the dynamics of family communication, a psychologist may contrive a situation to generate family conflict and then record the interactions among husband, wife, and child. In studying the effects of sleep deprivation on the brain, a team of psychologists may deprive monkeys of sleep to the point of total collapse. As these three examples suggest—and you can think of many more—there are occasions when the work of psychologists raises moral dilemmas.

The American Psychological Association has devoted considerable effort to develop a code of ethics for guiding its members in resolving ethical dilemmas they might encounter in the course of their work. In pursuing their goals of studying behavior and the factors that influence behavior, psychologists must "make every effort to protect the welfare of those who seek their services and of the research participants that may be the subjects of study" (American Psychological Association, 1981). The APA is prepared to expel any member who clearly violates the ethical guidelines, a few of which are discussed here.

Safeguarding a Subject's Confidentiality and Rights

In gathering information from others, psychologists are required to ensure **confidentiality.** Whether the information is gained during testing, in a counseling or therapy session, or as part of an attitude survey, or an experiment on learning with college students doesn't matter. Whatever the context, to violate the confidentiality of the information provided by the psychologist's clients or subjects would be a breach of ethical principles.

An even broader principle requires that psychologists protect the **rights of subjects** participating in psychological research. No matter how sincere the psychologist's research aims, this principle is intended to ensure that psychologists must consider both the benefits to society and the dignity and welfare of the research subjects themselves. A specific requirement obliges psychologists to try to avoid concealing the aims of an experiment or deceiving subjects, if at all possible, in the course of conducting a study.

Of course, some methods of studying behavior are clearly unacceptable. For example, no psychologist would consider urging a brain operation just for the sake of studying its effects. But in other cases, the line is more difficult to draw. When are psychologists justified in deceiving their subjects—for example, by telling them they are administering electric shocks to another person, when in fact the other person is a confederate who is only pretending to be shocked? There are, of course, many borderline cases that psychologists can decide only by carefully weighing the possible harm to their subjects against the value to humanity of the knowledge they may discover. In any case, psychologists are required to obtain the consent of potential participants in research studies, and to explain the nature and purposes of the research in advance—or, if necessary, afterward.

Care in the Use of Animals for Research

Throughout this book, you will be reading about research with animals that is intended to shed light on various aspects of human behavior—on the operations of the brain, the basic elements of learning and memory, the nature of emotions and drives, the effects of stress on health, the influences of genes and environment on development, and much more. About 7 percent of psychological studies use animals as subjects (Miller, 1985a). During the past few years, there has been a great deal of discussion concerning the use of animals in behavioral research. Indeed various animal rights organizations have

Psychological research often requires animal subjects—but they must be treated humanely.

charged the field of psychology with outright abuse and even torture of monkeys, rats, and other animals.

Such charges have proved groundless (Coile & Miller, 1984) and, moreover, the contributions made through animal research are impressive—among them understanding and alleviating the effects of stress and pain; discovery and testing of drugs to help the mentally ill; new knowledge about the mechanisms of alcohol and drug addiction; and insights into communication abilities (National Institute of Mental Health, 1991). Such advances are possible because psychologists can vary the environments and experiences of animals in ways that would be out of the question for human subjects. Nevertheless, the APA requires that its members take special care in the use of animals in psychological research, avoiding needless harm and exploitation. Living conditions for animals used in research are carefully prescribed by veterinarians and other experts on the species being studied (National Institute of Mental Health, 1992). Indeed, researchers who maintain nonhuman primates in captivity are required to house the animals in a manner that takes into account their psychological as well as physical well-being—for example, by monitoring signs of distress and evaluating coping responses (Novak and Suomi, 1988). Psychologists must proceed with a sure sense of ethical behavior and the humane treatment of all forms of life.

TEST YOURSELF

j) One psychologist is studying the effects of long-term sleep deprivation, and another is studying the relative effectiveness of two forms of psychotherapy. Which one is more likely to use animals as subjects for the research?

SUMMARY REVIEW

The Scope of Psychology

1. Psychology is *the systematic study of behavior and the factors that influence behavior.*
2. The goals of psychology are to *understand behavior and mental processes* and to *predict behavior.*
3. Psychology is one member of a family of sciences known as the **behavioral and social sciences.**

The Varieties of Psychology and Psychologists

4. Many psychologists are concerned only with **basic science,** or knowledge for the sake of knowledge. Others are chiefly interested in **applied science,** or the use of psychological findings to help society carry on its everyday tasks, tackle its problems, and improve the quality of life.
5. Among psychologists concerned with basic science are:
   a) *Experimental psychologists,* who study such basic processes as learning, memory, and motivation.
   b) *Comparative psychologists,* who concentrate on relating animal behavior patterns to those found in humans.
   c) *Physiological psychologists,* who study the role of brain and body functions in behavior.
   d) *Developmental psychologists,* who study how individuals grow and change throughout their existence.
   e) *Personality* and *social psychologists,* who study how people differ in their enduring inner characteristics and traits, and how they influence and are influenced by others.
   f) *Educational psychologists,* who are concerned with the impact of educational processes and techniques on students.

6. Examples of psychologists interested in applied science are:
   a) *School psychologists,* who test and evaluate pupils, analyze learning problems, and counsel both teachers and parents.
   b) *Industrial and organizational psychologists,* who help select and train workers, and improve working conditions, employee morale, and staff cooperation.
   c) *Environmental psychologists,* who deal with ecological problems like pollution and overcrowding.
   d) *Community psychologists,* who deal with the social environment and how it could better serve human needs.
   e) *Forensic psychologists,* who work on behavioral issues important in the legal, judicial, and correctional systems.
   f) *Health psychologists,* who focus on ways to improve health by altering behavior.
7. **Clinical psychologists** help diagnose deep-seated psychological problems and treat such problems through **psychotherapy.**
8. **Counseling psychologists** help those with milder problems of social and emotional adjustment—such as school difficulties, choice of vocation, or marriage conflicts.

The Methods Psychologists Use

9. The methods used by psychology to study behavior include **naturalistic observation, participant observation, public opinion surveys, interviews** and **case histories, questionnaires, tests** and **measurements,** and **physiological measures.**
10. The results of tests and measurements are analyzed through mathematical techniques called *statistics.*
11. Psychological statistics have greatly enhanced our knowledge of **individual differences** by showing that almost all physical traits (like height) and psychological characteristics (like intelligence) follow the **normal curve of distribution**—with most measurements clustering around the average and only a few falling at the lowest or highest extremes.
12. **Correlation** is a statistical tool used to determine what relationship, if any, exists between two different measurements—such as the IQs of parents and their children.

The Conclusive Method: Conducting an Experiment

13. The *experimental method,* which is the science's most powerful tool, is an attempt to discover cause and effect through a rigidly controlled examination of whether behavior changes when conditions change.
14. The experimenter controls the **independent variable,** which is set up independently of anything the subject does or does not do, and then studies the **dependent variable,** which is a change in the subject's behavior resulting from a change in the independent variable.
15. Experiments often use both an **experimental group,** whose behavior is studied under new conditions, and a **control group** that is not placed under the new conditions.

16. In a **single-blind** experiment, the subjects do not know whether they belong to the experimental group or the control group. In a **double-blind** experiment, neither the subjects nor the experimenter knows.

Psychology's Rich History and Promising Future

17. Psychology was founded in 1879 when the first laboratory was opened by Wilhelm Wundt at a German university. The early psychologists, including the American William James, were chiefly interested in human consciousness, which they studied through **introspection,** looking inward at mental processes.

18. The school of **behaviorism,** a rebellion against introspective studies, was founded by John Watson, who declared that mental processes cannot be seen or measured and therefore cannot be studied scientifically. Watson believed that psychologists should study what people do, not what they think.

19. Watson held that human behavior is a series of actions in which a **stimulus**—that is, an event in the environment—produces a **response**—that is, an observable muscular movement or some physiological reaction, such as secretion, that can also be observed and measured with the proper instruments. He believed that through establishment of **conditioned reflexes,** a type of learning, almost any kind of stimulus could be made to produce almost any kind of response.

20. B. F. Skinner, who succeeded Watson as leader of the behaviorist school, agreed that human beings are creatures of their environment whose behavior depends on the kinds of learning to which they have been subjected—and who are therefore not to blame for their failures or deserving of credit for their achievements.

21. **Gestalt psychology,** which takes its name from a German word meaning "pattern" or "configuration," maintained that events must be considered as a whole in studying any psychological phenomenon—from a perceptual process to personality—because "the whole is greater than the sum of its parts." The Gestalt school also stressed the entire situation, or context, in which the "whole" is found.

22. Many of the Gestalt ideas survive in today's trend toward **cognitive psychology,** which is interested in all the ways we learn about our environment, store knowledge in memory, and use it to think and act intelligently in new situations. These various forms of mental activity are often called **information processing.**

23. A core idea in cognitive psychology is that we build **mental models of reality** from information about the world provided by our sense organs, which we can then examine for meanings and guidance in behavior.

24. Today's **humanistic psychology** also stems in part from the Gestalt school. The humanists believe we are unique organisms because we have values and goals and seek to grow and to express and fulfill ourselves, and to find peace and happiness.

25. The opposite of humanistic psychology is Sigmund Freud's **psychoanalysis,** which is based on the idea that behavior is often influenced by **unconscious processes,** especially motives of which we are unaware.

26. A growing number of psychologists today focus on **psychology,** the study of how various facets of behavior are associated with processes in the body.

Three Key Issues in Psychology Today

26. There is a continuing debate, often called the **nature-nurture** controversy, over the relative importance of heredity and environment in establishing behavior.
27. The nature-nurture controversy has been modified greatly by modern findings in **behavior genetics,** the study of the role of inherited traits in shaping behavior.
28. Human development is a mix of both continuities (a series of gradual and cumulative changes) and discontinuities (dramatic changes that cause some characteristics to vanish and new ones to appear).
29. Human behavior is not as consistent as was once believed; often a person's actions depend on the context in which the behavior occurs.

Psychology's Ethical Standards

30. A code of ethics developed by the American Psychological Association requires its members to protect the **confidentiality** and **rights of subjects.**
31. The American Psychological Association also requires that its members take special care in the use of animals in psychological research, avoiding needless harm and exploitation.

TEST YOURSELF ANSWERS

a) The researcher is a psychologist since his or her project involves the study of behavior (aggression) and mental processes (anger)—and possible factors (childhood experiences) that influence them.

b) The second researcher is most likely in the field of anthropology—which is the study of cultures and races.

c) Psychology has attracted more women than has any other science.

d) The work of the first psychologist is basic since it involves primarily the search for knowledge for the sake of knowledge. The work of the second is applied since it involves the use of knowledge to help society carry out its everyday tasks.

e) The psychologist is likely to be in clinical psychology—which is devoted to the diagnosis and treatment of psychological disorders.

f) As in the case of all correlations, you cannot tell. In this case, the depression may have caused the brain changes, or the brain changes may have caused the depression.

g) The praise would be the independent variable since it would be introduced by you as the experimenter and would not be dependent on anything the individuals you are studying do or do not do. The behavior that occurs in response to the praise—that is, the math performance—constitutes the dependent variable.

h) You would be more likely to focus on the latter since psychobiology is devoted to the study of how various facets of behavior are associated with processes taking place in the body.

i) The issue of continuity and change is most relevant since the study described deals with the degree to which a human characteristic—in this case, intellectual ability—remains the same or alters over time.

j) The first psychologist is more likely to use animals as subjects.

Study Guide

Chapter 1   The Science and Practice of Psychology

LEARNING OBJECTIVES

After studying this chapter, you should be able to:

For an Understanding of the Science

1. Define psychology as the systematic study of behavior and mental processes—including thought and emotion—and the factors that influence them; recognize that the goals of psychology are to understand and to predict behavior.

2. Distinguish between the activities of psychologists who are concerned mainly with basic science, or knowledge for the sake of knowledge, and those concerned with applied science, or the use of psychological knowledge to improve the quality of life.

3. Describe the variety of methods psychology uses to study behavior, including naturalistic observation, participant observation, interviews and case histories, questionnaires, tests and measurements, and experiments.

4. Understand the importance of statistics as a tool for analyzing and interpreting tests and measurements and the results of observations and experiments; describe the normal curve of distribution and correlation.

5. Discuss the characteristics of psychological experiments, including independent and dependent variables, experimental and control groups, and single-blind and double-blind techniques.

6. Describe the history of psychological thought, including introspection, behaviorism, Gestalt psychology, cognitive psychology, humanistic psychology, and the psychoanalytic school.

7. Debate the issues of nature-nurture, continuity-change, and individual-context.

For Application to Life Situations

8. Describe how the subject matter of psychology applies to almost every aspect of your daily life, and recognize how often you practice introspection ("Why did I do that?" "Why am I angry?"), cognitive psychology ("Which of these two cars is the best value?"), and psychoanalysis ("I wonder what unconscious motives make Harold act so angrily?").

9. Argue that understanding human nature—all the ways in which we resemble each other and differ from each other in our physical actions, dreams, aspirations, loves, hates, worries, and joys—was not possible until modern science began to learn how the brain, sense organs, and glands operate and the role played by heredity and biology.

10. Identify the different types of applied psychologists and their specialties in the event that you or someone you know needs specialized help.

11. Discuss the ethical issues of conducting observations and experiments as well as delivering psychological services.

PROGRAMMED UNIT
THE SCOPE OF PSYCHOLOGY

1. Psychology is defined to be *the systematic study of behavior and mental processes—including thought and emotion—and the factors that influence them.* The term "systematic study," meaning the use of rigorous and highly disciplined methods of science rather than relying on judgments based on insufficient evidence or unwarranted generalities, distinguishes _____ from the views of behavior proposed in philosophy and literature.

psychology

2. Psychology studies our physical activities—everything we do from the time we wake up in the morning until we go back to bed and fall asleep. All these forms of activities are the _____ that the science of psychology studies.

behavior

3. Psychologists also study the activities that take place inside of us—the ways we learn, remember, forget, feel hungry, become angry or joyful. Such _____ _____, which include _____ and _____, are also embraced by the study of psychology.

mental processes
thought, emotion

4. In addition, psychology studies the things and events that influence behavior and mental processes, including the human brain, sense organs, chemicals in the bloodstream, heredity, the actions of other people, and so forth. These _____ that influence behavior and mental processes are a third category of items studied by psychologists.

factors

5. Psychology, then, is the _____ _____ of _____ and _____ _____—including _____ and _____— and _____ that influence them.

systematic study
behavior, mental processes,
thought, emotion, factors

6. The missions of psychology are (1) *to understand behavior and mental processes* and (2) *to predict their course.* For example, psychologists try to _____ why individuals behave as they do in a classroom or in social situations to _____ how they would behave in school or in a social environment.

understand
predict

7. The missions of psychology, similar to the goals of all sciences, are to _____ behavior and mental processes and to _____ their course.

understand, predict

8. Psychology is one member of a family of sciences often referred to as the *behavioral and social sciences.* Subject matter ranging from the neurochemical basis of memory and mental illness to the dynamics of global commerce and international conflict constitute the domain of the _____ and _____ _____.

behavioral
social sciences

9. Scientists who study genetics, physiology, anthropology, economics, linguistics, education, sociology, and political science are all members of the _____ and _____ _____, and those who study behavior and mental processes in particular are part of the field of _____.

behavioral, social sciences
psychology

THE VARIETIES OF PSYCHOLOGY
AND PSYCHOLOGISTS

basic science

10. Some psychologists are concerned with *basic science*—that is, knowledge for the sake of knowledge. Psychologists who are interested in the way forms of energy affect the sense organs, how chemical substances influence the nervous system and emotions, how individuals grow and change throughout their lives, and how characteristics of individuals are influenced by the behavior of others are all students of _____ _____.

applied science

11. In contrast, other psychologists are concerned with *applied science*. They use knowledge to help society carry on its everyday tasks, tackle its problems, and improve the quality of life. School psychologists, industrial and organizational psychologists, educational psychologists, environmental psychologists, community psychologists, forensic psychologists, health psychologists, and clinical and counseling psychologists are all interested in _____ _____.

basic science, applied science

12. Studies that are motivated by the simple desire to learn about behavior often produce principles that are then used in subsequent work to improve learning in school, performance on the job, or happiness in life. This is an example of principles discovered by _____ _____ that are incorporated in _____ _____.

clinical, counseling

13. Most applied psychologists, indeed the largest group of all psychologists in the United States, are in the fields of *clinical* and *counseling* psychology. Psychologists who use the findings of science to help people solve various problems in their lives are _____ and _____ psychologists.

clinical

14. Clinical psychology consists of the diagnosis and treatment of psychological disorders—all of the traits and behaviors that are thought of as abnormal. Individuals with severe problems of behavior should consult a _____ psychologist.

psychotherapy

15. Clinical psychologists use the technique of *psychotherapy* to help their clients. Discussing problems, trying to get at the root of them, and modifying attitudes, emotional responses, and behavior are part of _____.

psychoanalysis

16. Psychotherapy began with Sigmund Freud, an Austrian physician and neurologist, whose method was called *psychoanalysis*. The analysis of a client's flow of ideas in an attempt to discover the origin of problems and helping the client to understand and overcome them is fundamental to _____.

counseling

17. Counseling psychology involves helping those individuals with milder problems of social and emotional adjustment. Psychologists who specialize in resolving marital problems or the difficulties people have adjusting to the social and academic demands of school, for example, are _____ psychologists.

clinical
counseling

18. Psychologists who help individuals overcome problem behavior are of two general kinds: those who deal with serious problems and abnormal behavior are _____ psychologists while those who deal with milder problems of social and emotional adjustment are _____ psychologists.

psychotherapy

psychoanalysis

19. Clinical psychologists, for example, treat their patients with _____, which may take many forms, one of which originated with Sigmund Freud and is called _____.

THE METHODS PSYCHOLOGISTS USE

20. One method of studying behavior in a _____ manner is to make careful *observations* of it.

    systematic

21. One type of _____ is the practice of *naturalistic observation* in which the behavior is monitored in its typical context by an inconspicuous observer.

    observation

22. Watching nursery school children play from behind a one-way window constitutes _____ _____. Psychologists also engage in *participant observation,* which means that they take an active part in the social situation.

    naturalistic observation

23. A psychologist might enter a nursery school playroom and reprimand a misbehaving child to observe the effects of that scolding on the behavior of other children; this action would constitute _____ _____.

    participant observation

24. When an observer does nothing to alter or interfere with the behavior under study, the observation is _____; when an observer actively attempts to influence the behavior under study, it is _____ observation.

    naturalistic
    participant

25. Another approach to making behavioral _____ is to use the *interview* method (questioning subjects), a special application of which is the *case history* (reconstructing the entire story of a person's life).

    observations

26. Questioning subjects in depth about their life experience or attitudes about a given topic, for example, constitutes an _____, while reconstructing a description of a person's life over many years to show how various behavior patterns have developed constitutes a _____ _____.

    interview

    case history

27. Instead of asking questions in person, as in the _____ method, written questions can be administered to large numbers of people in a form known as a *questionnaire.*

    interview

28. *Public opinion surveys* gather information about people's attitudes and opinions by using both telephone _____ and written _____.

    interviews, questionnaires

29. Among the oldest tools of psychology are the *tests* it has developed. Many human characteristics, abilities, and achievements are systematically assessed by a variety of psychological _____.

    tests

30. Psychologists also make *physiological* measures that may have a bearing on behavior. Disturbances in the chemistry of the brain, for example, may produce severe depression, and electrical changes on the skin are associated with various states of anxiety. So, in addition to assessments of mental and personal behavior, psychologists also take _____ measures.

    physiological

31. An important finding made through the use of tests and measurements is that there are wide-ranging *individual differences* in all kinds of physical and psychological traits. Each person is indeed unique, because a set of measurements of behavior, mental processes, and physiological characteristics always contains _____ _____ that distinguish one person from another.

    individual differences

32. These _____ _____ and the other _____ made by psychologists are often described and analyzed with *statistics.*

    individual differences, measurements

33. The average grade in your class is one example of a simple _____.

    statistic

34. Most characteristics measured in a large group of individuals form a *normal curve of distribution* when the frequency of particular scores are plotted as

a function of score value. Typically, scores near the average have many frequencies while scores both higher and lower than the average have progressively fewer frequencies. A graph of individual differences for most physical and psychological characteristics takes the form of the

normal curve of distribution

_____ _____ _____ _____.

35. The fact that the IQs of most people center around the value 100, while those who are genius and mentally retarded are relatively infrequent conforms to the _____ _____ _____ _____.

normal curve of distribution

36. This distribution describes _____ _____ in IQ and is a major tool of the methods of _____.

individual differences
statistics

37. Sometimes individual differences on one _____ are associated with _____ _____ on another measurement. When this happens, psychologists say that a *correlation* exists.

measurement
individual differences

38. Tall men, for example, tend to be heavier while small men tend to be lighter in weight, indicating that there is a relationship or _____ between height and weight.

correlation

39. A numerical index of the degree of _____ is called the *coefficient of correlation*. For example, tall men are not necessarily smarter than shorter men, so no _____ exists between height and intelligence and the numerical index, called the _____ _____ _____, would be near zero.

correlation

correlation
coefficient of correlation

40. Psychologists often study individual differences by using _____ and _____, describing such observations by using _____, including the _____ _____ of _____, and searching for a relationship or _____ between individual differences on one measurement and _____ _____ on another. The degree of relationship is expressed numerically with the _____ _____ _____.

tests, measurements
statistics, normal curve
distribution, correlation
individual differences
coefficient
of correlation

THE CONCLUSIVE METHOD: CONDUCTING AN EXPERIMENT

41. Psychology's most powerful tool is the method of study known as the *experiment*. When a psychologist sets up one set of conditions and determines what kind of behavior takes place, then changes the conditions and measures any change in behavior, the psychologist is using a powerful method called the _____.

experiment

42. Both the possible behavior change and the change in conditions are called *variables*. The systematic manipulation and observation of whether change in one _____ leads to change in another _____ constitutes an _____.

variable, variable
experiment

43. In an experiment, the researcher sets up and manipulates a change in the conditions; this change is called the *independent variable*. The fact that such changes are under the researcher's control and not influenced by anything the subject does is the reason this change is called the _____ _____.

independent variable

independent variable

44. In contrast, behavior that occurs in response to the _____ _____ is called the *dependent variable*.

independent, dependent

45. In all experiments, the experimenter arranges to change the _____ variable, then measures the _____ variable on the subjects.

46. The subject displays the _____ variable, while the experimenter manipulates the _____ variable. Stated another way, the purpose of an _____ is to observe the influence of the _____ variable on the _____ variable.

dependent
independent
experiment, independent
dependent

47. If a psychologist is interested in the influence of a highly structured curriculum versus a free-play preschool experience on the ability of children to learn certain principles of their physical world (e.g., gravity, force), then in the psychologist's experiment, learning would be the _____ variable and type of preschool curriculum would be the _____ variable.

dependent
independent

48. Sometimes experiments consist of two groups, an *experimental group* and a *control group*. Typically, special treatment is given to the subjects in the _____ group but not to the subjects in the _____ group.

experimental, control

49. A scientist wants to know whether parents who read extensively to their children improve the language ability of those children. Some parents are asked to read additional amounts to their children while others are not. Those who read additionally in response to the experimenter's request constitute the _____ group, while those given no special instructions to read to their children comprise the _____ group.

experimental
control

50. The presence or absence of additional reading experience constitutes the _____ variable in the above _____, while children's language ability constitutes the _____ variable.

independent, experiment
dependent

51. In many experiments, subjects might be affected by knowing which group they are in. For example, in an experiment in which the independent variable is taking marijuana and any change in the subjects' driving ability is the _____ variable, the subjects' driving performance might be influenced by their knowledge that they had taken the drug and their expectations of how it would affect them.

dependent

52. Therefore, the experimenter might give half the subjects an injection of the drug's active ingredient and the other half of the subjects an injection of a salt solution that would have no effect, without telling them which was which. When subjects do not know whether they belong to the experimental or to the _____ group, the experimenter is said to be using the *single-blind technique*.

control

53. Keeping the subjects from knowing whether they belong to the control or to the experimental group is called the _____-_____ technique.

single-blind

54. There is also the danger that the experimenters' own assessment of driving performance might be influenced by knowing which subjects had taken the drug and which had not. To guard against this possibility as well, the two kinds of injection could be administered by a third party, a method called the *double-blind technique* in which the experimenter as well as the subjects do not know who belongs to the _____ group and who belongs to the _____ group.

experimental
control

55. When neither the experimenter nor the subjects know which subjects are in which group, the experimenter is using the _____-_____ technique.

double-blind

56. Even with careful control and observation, and even if the _____-_____ or _____-_____ techniques are used, the validity of the results of an experiment is improved if the experiment can undergo *replication*.

single-blind, double-blind

57. That is, if another experimenter at another time and in another place repeats the original experiment and obtains the same result, then the possibility that the original results were accidental or influenced by other factors is minimized by this process of _____.

replication

PSYCHOLOGY'S RICH HISTORY AND PROMISING FUTURE

58. Most of the early psychologists concentrated on an attempt to discover the nature, origins, and significance of conscious experiences through *introspection,* or looking inward and trying to analyze the processes that went on inside their minds. They made a start toward the systematic study of behavior by recording what they found through _____ as objectively as possible, for comparison with other observers.

introspection

59. *Wilhelm Wundt,* a German who founded the first psychological laboratory in 1879, and *William James,* the most prominent American psychologist around the turn of the century, were among the pioneers who tried to analyze their conscious experiences through _____.

introspection
Wundt

60. The first psychology laboratory was established in Germany by _____, while the most prominent American psychologist of this early period was _____.

James

61. In contrast to psychologists who were interested in studying mental life, such as _____ and _____, American *John Watson* revolutionized psychology by breaking completely with those who emphasized the method of _____ and founding the movement called *behaviorism.*

Wundt, James

introspection
Watson

62. The school of behaviorism was founded by _____, who held that psychologists should concentrate on actions that are plainly visible, not on a "mental life" that cannot be seen or measured.

behaviorism

63. Watson and his followers in the school of _____ believed that all human behavior is simply a series of actions in which a *stimulus*—that is, an event in the environment—produces a *response*—that is, an observable muscular movement or a physiological reaction, such as increased heart rate or glandular secretion, that can be measured.

stimulus
response

64. Watson held that almost any kind of environmental _____ can be made to produce in an organism any kind of _____ through the establishment of a *conditioned reflex,* a type of learning.

conditioned reflex

65. The type of learning stressed by the behaviorists was the _____ _____.

stimulus

66. Since Watson was convinced that all behavior is a response to a _____, he believed he could take any dozen babies at birth and turn them into anything he wished by establishing many _____ _____.

conditioned reflexes

67. Watson was later followed by *B. F. Skinner,* who became the leader of the _____ school. Skinner believed that a "social engineer" versed in all the principles of learning could mold people in any form desired, whether for good or for evil.

behaviorist

68. The great contribution of the leaders of the behaviorist school, both _____ and _____, was to pull psychology back from the danger of becoming a mere branch of philosophical speculation and to pro-

Watson, Skinner

mote a more objective study based on controlled experiments and measurements of behavior.

69. In opposition to the belief that behavior is simply a series of stimuli and responses, as the _____ school would suggest, *Gestalt* psychology emphasized that events must be considered as a whole.
behaviorist

70. The insistence that the whole is more than simply the sum of its parts and that behavior is influenced by the entire context in which it occurs, not simply a single stimulus, characterized the view of _____ psychologists.
Gestalt

71. Today's trend is toward *cognitive psychology,* which studies the "mental life" that interested _____ and _____ but in the more systematic and disciplined ways suggested by the behaviorists _____ and _____.
Wundt, James
Watson
Skinner

72. A core idea in the school of thought known as _____ psychology, is that we learn about our environment, store the knowledge in memory, think about it, and use it to act intelligently in new situations. These various forms of mental activity are often referred to as *information processing.*
cognitive

73. When we think about, understand, and solve problems, we engage in _____ _____, and one of the results of this activity is the creation of *mental models of reality.*
information processing

74. Representations that aid constructive thinking, making judgments, and deciding on appropriate behavior are called _____ _____ of reality, which are created through learning and _____ _____.
mental models
information processing

75. Another of today's prominent movements is *humanistic psychology,* which views human beings as quite different from other organisms. A focus on human values, goals, expression, growth, fulfillment, and the search for peace and happiness characterizes _____ psychology.
humanistic

76. A growing number of today's psychologists specialize in *psychobiology,* the study of how various facets of behavior are associated with processes taking place in the body. Bodily changes associated with stress, the use of drugs to alleviate anxiety and depression, and the role of genes in shaping human development are some topics that characterize the study of _____.
psychobiology

THREE KEY ISSUES IN PSYCHOLOGY TODAY

77. Several issues have dominated the study of human behavior over the years. One question, which asks whether heredity or environment controls human behavior, is known as the *nature-nurture* controversy. The debate over whether human behavior is controlled by heredity or environment is called the _____-_____ controversy.
nature-nurture

78. Among psychology's historic figures, William James believed that our behavior is regulated to a considerable extent by powerful human instincts present at birth. Thus, James took the _____ side of the controversy.
nature

79. John Watson, on the other hand, believed that our behavior depends on conditioned reflexes established by various kinds of stimuli provided by the environment, thus taking the _____ side of the controversy.
nurture

80. A relatively new field of study, *behavior genetics,* is concerned with the role of inherited traits in shaping behaviors. Therefore, the field of _____ _____ studies directly the issue of _____-_____.
behavior genetics
nature-nurture

change

81. A second issue debated for decades is that of *continuity versus change*. Obviously, you are not the same person today that you were at birth, which indicates that human beings are capable of substantial _____.

continuity

82. But you also may have an interest in music, an assertive personality, and vivid memories of being abused by your parents that span decades of your life and have a continuing influence on your behavior, which would indicate that there is some _____.

individual

83. A third issue concerns whether behavior is more influenced by the *individual* or the *context*. Years ago, personality traits were thought to exist within the individual and that an aggressive person would always tend to be aggressive and an anxious person would always be prone to anxiety. In short, the characteristics were thought to reside within the _____.

context

84. On the other hand, it is clear that a person's actions depend on the particular situation, and that a person may be generous at home but selfish at work or aggressive with a spouse but submissive with friends. Obviously, a person's behavior is partly dependent on the _____.

ethical guidelines

85. As with any profession, psychologists have the opportunity to use other people for their own benefit, to deceive them, and to practice unfairly. For this reason, the American Psychological Association, the principal society representing the profession of psychology, has developed *ethical guidelines* to help its members resolve ethical dilemmas they might encounter in the course of their work. Principles governing how psychologists should treat the subjects of their research and the clients they serve are summarized in the _____ _____.

right
confidentiality

86. Specifically, psychologists are pledged to safeguard the *confidentiality* of their subjects or clients and to protect the *rights* of subjects, both human and animals, who participate in their research. For example, clean and healthful living environments is a _____ of animal subjects, and privacy or _____ is a right of human subjects.

REVIEW OF IMPORTANT TERMS

applied science (10)

basic science (7)

behavior genetics (27)

behavioral and social sciences (6)

behaviorism (21)

case history (13)

clinical psychology (10)

cognitive psychology (23)

conditioned reflexes (22)

confidentiality (28)

context (28)

control group (18)

correlation (16)

counseling psychologist (10)

dependent variable (17)

double-blind technique (20)

experiment (17)

experimental group (18)

galvanic skin response (GSR) (15)

genetics (7)

Gestalt psychology (22)

humanistic psychology (24)

hysterical conversion (24)

independent variable (17)

individual differences (15)

information processing (23)

interviews (13)

introspection (21)

measurements (14)

mental models of reality (23)

naturalistic observation (12)

nature-nurture controversy (27)

normal curve of distribution (15)

participant observation (13)

psychoanalysis (10)

psychobiology (26)

psychological statistics (15)

psychotherapy (10)

public opinion survey (13)

questionnaire (13)

replication (20)

response (21)

rights of subjects (28)

single-blind technique (20)

stimulus (21)

unconscious processes (25)

PRACTICE TEST

_____ 1. Psychology can best be defined as the

    a. analysis of human behavior.

    b. the systematic study of personality and interpersonal problems.

    c. the systematic study of behavior and mental processes—including thought and emotion—and the factors that influence them.

    d. the application of scientific experimentation to the study of human behavior.

_____ 2. The missions of psychology are to

    a. understand and experiment with behavior.

    b. conduct controlled experiments and use the scientific method.

    c. control and manipulate human behavior.

    d. understand and predict behavior.

_____ 3. Psychologists who are basic scientists are mostly interested in

    a. knowledge for the sake of knowledge.

    b. understanding and controlling behavior.

    c. applying the scientific method.

    d. learning about human behavior.

_____ 4. The largest number of applied psychologists are engaged in

    a. clinical psychology and counseling.

    b. school psychology.

    c. research psychology.

    d. community psychology.

_____ 5. The difference between counseling and clinical psychology is that clinical psychology

    a.   works with more severe disorders.

    b.   works with individuals, not groups.

    c.   does not do psychotherapy.

    d.   uses psychoanalysis as the main treatment.

_____ 6. In contrast to a laboratory experiment, naturalistic observation requires psychologists to

    a.   control the situation.

    b.   make correct interpretations about why the observed behavior occurred.

    c.   be intimately acquainted with the causes of the behavior.

    d.   minimize their influence on the situation.

_____ 7. Questionnaires

    a.   are not always answered truthfully.

    b.   depend greatly for results on the precise wording of the questions.

    c.   take less time to administer than interviews.

    d.   all the above.

_____ 8. The degree of relationship between two variables on the same or related individuals is expressed by

    a.   the normal curve of distribution.

    b.   individual differences.

    c.   the relationship index.

    d.   the coefficient of correlation.

_____ 9. An experiment seeks to determine the influence of

    a.   the independent variable on the dependent variable.

    b.   the dependent variable on the independent variable.

    c.   the experimental group on the control group.

    d.   single-blind versus double-blind techniques.

_____ 10. A major difference between an experiment and naturalistic observation is that one

    a.   is objective and the other is not.

    b.   studies variables and the other does not.

    c.   is pure and the other is applied science.

    d.   manipulates variables and conditions in the situation and the other does not.

_____ 11. In a single-blind experiment

   a. the experimenter does not know which subjects are in the experimental and control groups.

   b. subjects do not know whether they are in the experimental or the control group.

   c. both the experimenter and the subjects are unaware of who is in which group.

   d. the experimenter does not know the dependent variable.

_____ 12. Which of the following is most closely associated with Watson?

   a. mental life

   b. first psychology laboratory

   c. stimulus and response

   d. human goals

_____ 13. Which statement is *not* likely to be associated with B. F. Skinner?

   a. People are creatures of their environments.

   b. People are not responsible for their conduct.

   c. Most accomplishments are achievements of the will.

   d. Psychologists should study observable stimuli and responses.

_____ 14. The school of psychology most likely to be associated with the statement that "the whole is greater than the sum of its parts" is

   a. humanistic psychology.

   b. Gestalt psychology.

   c. holistic psychology.

   d. psychoanalysis.

_____ 15. An important notion in cognitive psychology is

   a. unconscious processes.

   b. information processing.

   c. self-fulfillment.

   d. the nature-nurture issue.

_____ 16. Psychologists who study how heredity influences behavior are called

   a. behavior geneticists.

   b. behavior environmentalists.

   c. nature-nurture psychologists.

   d. Gestalt psychologists.

_____ 17. Which of the following is most closely associated with Sigmund Freud?

   a. conditioned reflexes

   b. hysterical conversion

   c. the study of mental life

   d. mental models of reality

_____18. Which of the following is *not* a prominent approach today?

    a.   cognitive psychology

    b.   introspection

    c.   psychobiology

    d.   humanistic psychology

_____19. The fact that some people are aggressive with their husband or wife but very compliant with their boss illustrates a part of the

    a.   continuity vs. change issue.

    b.   individual vs. context issue.

    c.   nature vs. nurture issue.

    d.   all of the above.

_____20. Which historical figure is likely to be most sympathetic with the nurture rather than the nature position?

    a.   Watson

    b.   Galton

    c.   James

    d.   Freud

ANSWERS TO PRACTICE TEST

1. c	6. d	11. b	16. a
2. d	7. d	12. c	17. b
3. a	8. d	13. c	18. b
4. a	9. a	14. b	19. b
5. a	10. d	15. b	20. a

EXERCISES

I.   Interview two people you know well and attempt to construct a case history for each person. Begin by asking what they think are their major characteristics—intelligent, outgoing, athletic, and so on. For each characteristic, such as athletic, ask their first recollections of such behaviors. Why do they think they have developed that characteristic, and what factors or events in their past were influential in contributing to it? Concentrate on asking why they did the things they did, what they felt might have happened to them if they did or did not do certain things, and how they felt about themselves and other people. Then try to piece together a cohesive explanation for how the particular characteristic developed in each person. Provide different interpretations of this development from the perspective of behaviorism, Gestalt, cognitive, and humanistic perspectives as well as from the standpoint of the nature-nurture, change-continuity, and individual-context issues.

II.   The experimental method is the primary approach psychologists use to determine the causes of certain behaviors. Subjects are frequently sampled and then divided into an experimental and a control group. The experimental group is treated in a special way while the control group is not. The difference in behavior between the experimental and control groups presumably indicates the causal effect of the independent variable. But research is not usually that simple, and very often the difference in behavior between experimental and control groups can be explained by something other than the independent variable.

Below are descriptions of a few hypothetical experiments and conclusions. Write a short discussion of each, pointing out the inadequacies of the experiment for drawing the stated conclusions. Try to suggest factors other than the one mentioned that might have produced the results. There may be more than one way to view each situation.

1. Newborn babies in one nursery were played recorded human heartbeats while newborn babies in another nursery were not played any particular sounds. Babies cried less when they heard the heartbeat sounds than when they heard no particular sounds. The researcher concluded that the heartbeats reminded the infants of being in the womb and that playing recorded heartbeats, rather than other sounds and methods, was a particularly good way to calm infants.

2. To test the effects of marijuana on driving performance, some subjects were asked to smoke one marijuana cigarette while other subjects were asked to smoke one tobacco cigarette before taking a test of driving ability. The marijuana group did more poorly on the test, and the researcher concluded that marijuana impairs driving performance.

3. Children who watch a great deal of violent television programming are themselves more aggressive and violent in their play with other children than are children who do not watch so much violent programming. Therefore, watching violent television programming leads to aggressive social behavior.

4. A popular columnist asked parents to write to tell her whether they would have children again if they could relive their married lives. Ten thousand people responded, and three out of four said they would not have children again if they had to do it all over again. The columnist concluded that most American parents regret having children.

C H A P T E R   2

Brain, Body, and Behavior

- It perches on top of your spine, beneath your skull—three pounds of grayish-pink, soft, strangely wrinkled tissue the size of a grapefruit.
- In weight it makes up less than 2 percent of the human body, yet it works so hard that it consumes about 20 percent of the oxygen that the body uses when at rest.
- Nature has devised ways to protect it. Encased in the skull's thick bone, it is surrounded by a fluid that helps cushion it from injury in case of sudden impact. And when the body is deprived of food, it is the first to get its share of whatever nutrients are coursing through the blood.

Those facts help portray the human brain, pictured in Figure 2.1, and described as "the most marvelous structure in the universe" (Miller, 1990). All the human capacities you will read about in this book—gathering information, learning and remembering, acting intelligently, moving about, developing skills, feeling emotions, coping with stress, relating to others—are managed within the brain. Think of all the things you did in the last 24 hours. Whatever you did—sleep, dream, wake up, shower, get dressed, drive your car, play tennis, study, get angry, make love—you accomplished through the capacities of your brain.

The energy to operate the brain comes from the activity of billions of nerve cells that are in constant communication with each other and with their counterparts throughout the body. The result is a network of brain-and-body systems that is surely one of the great miracles of nature. Knowledge of how these systems work—and exactly what they accomplish—is essential to an understanding of the entire field of psychology.

FIGURE 2.1 The human brain The brain perches on top of your spine, beneath your skull—three pounds of grayish-pink, soft, strangely wrinkled tissue the size of a grapefruit. How this small mass of matter accomplishes all its tasks is the subject of this chapter.

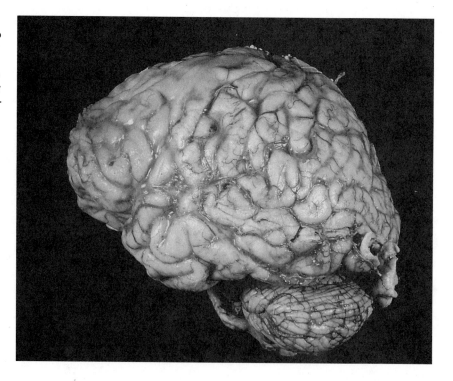

How the Brain Governs Human Behavior

To appreciate the remarkable powers of the brain, it is important to understand how lower organisms manage to function. A one-celled animal such as a paramecium does not have any nervous system at all. Its entire single-celled "body" is sensitive to heat and light and capable of initiating its own movements. Larger and more complicated animals, however, must have some kind of nervous system, composed of specialized nerves in the shape of fibers that reach from one part of the body to another and are capable of conveying messages back and forth.

The key to the brain's mastery is precisely such a web of powerful connections within itself and with other parts of the body. The brain carries out its many functions through a constant exchange of messages, speeding through its untold billions of pathways. Indeed, without them the brain would be helpless to direct and manage our behavior.

The Brain's Communication System

The brain contains a staggeringly large number of separate **neurons,** or nerve cells. Estimated to be more than 100 billion in number (Shatz, 1992), they are woven into an intricate tapestry of connections and interconnections. Each of these fiberlike cells may receive messages from thousands of other neurons, process these messages in various ways, then pass its own messages along to thousands more. The total number of possible connections is so great that it defies the imagination. One estimate places it at an unthinkable 50 trillion (Rosenzweig & Lieman, 1982). Little wonder that the brain has been described as "the most complex structure in the known universe" (Fischbach, 1992).

The primary job of most brain cells is transmitting messages—for example, to the nerves that serve the hand and permit it to move. Others, however, perform different tasks. The brain, for example, has some cells, called **glia** (from the Greek word for "glue") which help keep the neurons in place and provide them with nourishment. Some glia operate very much like sense organs—serving as the brain's "eyes" and "ears" to observe changes in the bloodstream and thus detect when the body needs food or water. Others are sensitive to changes in the body's internal temperature; they are responsive to the body's thermal sensors and initiate panting to cool the body, or shivering to heat it. The brain also has neurons that operate like miniature glands, producing complicated chemicals called **hormones** (from the Greek word meaning "activators" or "exciters"). These hormones are released into the bloodstream and travel through the body, stimulating many kinds of physical activity.

It is hard to imagine the resulting extraordinary hubbub of activity taking place in your nervous system. Right now, for example, messages rich in information are being "flashed" back and forth to every part of your body. The messages take the form of nervous impulses, produced by the neurons, that resemble tiny electrical charges, each barely strong enough to move the needle of the most sensitive recording device. The neurons start sending their messages long before birth and continue humming with activity throughout life. If every neuron in the brain fired off its impulse at the same instant, the entire amount of electricity produced would be just about

Neuron

The nerve cell; the basic unit of the nervous system.

Glia

A type of brain cell that helps keep the neurons in place and provides them with nourishment.

Hormones

Chemicals produced by the endocrine glands and secreted directly into the bloodstream.

Dendrites

The "receiving" parts of the neuron.

Cell body

The part of the neuron that performs the process of metabolism and converts food supplied by the bloodstream into energy.

Nucleus

The core of a neuron; contains the genes.

Receptor sites

Spots on the cell body of neurons that can be stimulated by the axon of another neuron.

Axon

A fiber of the neuron that carries the nervous impulse to the end branches.

End branches

The part of the neuron that acts as a "sender" of messages to other neurons or to muscles and glands.

Myelin sheath

A whitish coating of fatty protective tissue that covers many neurons.

Nodes

Constrictions on the axon of a neuron that speed up the transmission of the nervous impulse.

enough to power a small transistor radio. Yet these tiny impulses somehow account for all the accomplishments of the brain and are viewed as the key to arriving at an understanding of the physical roots of behavior (Hoyenga & Hoyenga, 1988).

Although neurons show many variations, they all resemble the drawing in Figure 2.2 in a general way. The **dendrites** are the "receivers." When they are properly stimulated, they set off the nervous impulse, which travels the fiberlike length of the neuron to the other end. In between is the **cell body,** which has a **nucleus,** or core, containing the genes that caused the cell to grow into a neuron in the first place. The cell body performs the process of metabolism, converting food supplied by the bloodstream into energy. Moreover, the surface of the cell body is dotted with numerous **receptor sites** that are also capable of responding to stimulation, like the dendrites, and setting off nervous impulses, which travel down fiberlike **axon** to the **end branches,** which are the neuron's "senders."

The axon's **myelin sheath,** found in many but not all neurons, is a whitish coating of fatty protective tissue that increases the speed at which the nervous impulse travels. Transmission is further improved by the **nodes,**

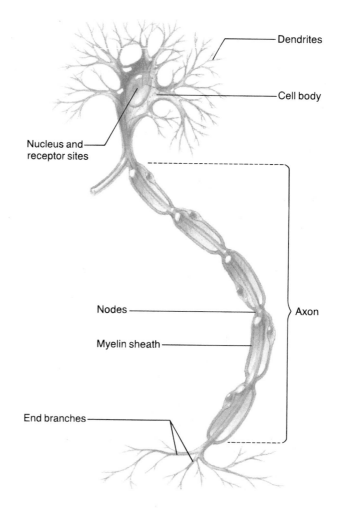

FIGURE 2.2   A more or less typical neuron A typical *neuron* is a fiber-shaped cell with *dendrites* at one end, an axon at the other end, and a *cell body* somewhere in between. The functions of the various structures are explained in the text.

which are constrictions of the sheath acting as little booster stations that help nudge the impulse along to the end branches, the "senders" that deliver the neuron's message.

Some neurons have their end branches in glands or muscles, which their impulses stimulate into action. Most neurons, however, particularly in the brain, have end branches that connect with other neurons. Their job is communication—passing messages along to other neurons.

How Neurons Send Their Messages

The nervous impulse—the tiny charge of electricity that passes down the length of the neuron fiber—can best be compared to the glowing band of fire that travels along a lighted fuse. The neuron ordinarily operates on what is called the **all or none principle.** That is to say, if it fires at all, it fires as hard as it can. The nervous impulse can only travel the length of the neuron that produces it—from dendrites or receptor sites to the end branches of the axon. There it stops. It can go no farther. It can, however, influence other neurons by delivering its message.

The key to transmission of the message is the **synapse,** the connecting point where an end branch–sender of one neuron is separated by only a microscopic distance—a millionth of an inch—from a dendrite–receiver of another neuron. At the synapse, where the two neurons almost touch, the first can influence the second in various ways. Sometimes the electrical charge arriving at the synapse is enough in itself to produce an effect. Usually, however, the action is chemical. The senders of the axon contain small amounts of chemical substances called **neurotransmitters.** When the neuron fires, a burst of these substances is released at the synapse. The chemicals flow across the tiny gap between the two neurons and act on the second neuron.

Figure 2.3 is a photograph of parts of the neuron that play an especially important role in the transmission of messages—the little swellings called **synaptic knobs** at the very tips of the branches of the axon. It is these knobs that actually form synapses with other neurons at their dendrites or cell body receptor sites. An enlarged drawing of a synapse is shown in Figure 2.4.

In the first neuron the neurotransmitter is produced in the cell body and delivered down the length of the fiber to the **synaptic vesicles,** where it is stored until called upon. When the neuron fires, the nervous impulse reaching the synaptic knob causes the vesicles to release their transmitter chemicals. These neurotransmitters flow across the **synaptic cleft** and act on the receptors of the second neuron. Some of the neurotransmitters act as stimulants, urging the second neuron to fire off its own nervous impulse. Others, however, do the opposite, instructing the second neuron to refrain from action. They act to inhibit any activity in the second neuron.

Whether the neuron fires or not depends on the whole pattern of messages it receives. Ordinarily it will not fire in response to a single message arriving at one of its many dendrites or on its cell body. Instead, the firing process requires multiple stimulation—a whole group of messages arriving at once or in quick succession from the other neurons with which it has synaptic contact. Moreover, the messages that represent signals to fire must outweigh the messages that inhibit it from firing.

Although the electrochemical messages travel in complex ways, the process is highly organized. Nerve cells are arranged in ways that permit those

All or none principle
The principle that a neuron, if it fires at all, fires as hard as it can.

Synapse
The connecting point and space between the end branches of an axon of one neuron and the dendrites of another neuron.

Neurotransmitters
Chemicals released at the synapse.

Synaptic knobs
Swellings at the tips of the end branches.

Synaptic vesicles
Tiny sacs in the synaptic knob that contain neurotransmitters.

Synaptic cleft
Tiny spaces between the end branches of the axon of one neuron and the dendrites of another.

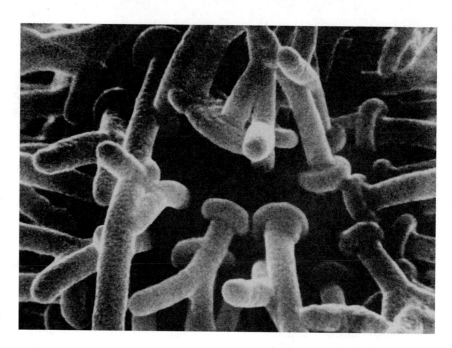

FIGURE 2.3 The synaptic knobs This photograph, taken at magnification of about 2,000 times life size, was the first ever made of the *synaptic knobs*. It shows some of the structures in a snail (Lewis, Zeevi, & Everhart, 1969).

engaged in similar tasks to work together. The chemical receptors on the neurons are also quite specific; they will recognize only certain kinds of neurotransmitters. Neurons that send or receive the same neurotransmitters form special pathways or circuits, and these are often grouped together in particular parts of the brain to perform as a team the specific tasks described in the remainder of this chapter. Small wonder that the human nervous system is capable of so many accomplishments. By comparison with the brain, the nation's telephone network is a simple child's toy.

FIGURE 2.4 Where neuron meets neuron: The synapse The axon of the first neuron ends in a synaptic knob, separated from the second neuron by only a tiny gap called the *synaptic cleft*. What happens at the cleft is described in the text.

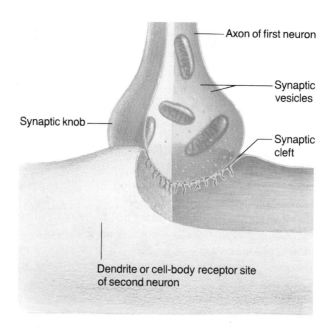

Axon of first neuron

Synaptic vesicles

Synaptic cleft

Synaptic knob

Dendrite or cell-body receptor site of second neuron

The Links of the Nervous System

The neurons of the brain can affect our behavior only because there are links between them and other parts of the body. These links are forged by the rest of the nervous system, composed of neurons of various kinds that connect with the brain. The neuron fibers of the nervous system—the axons identified in Figure 2.2—extend throughout the body. The axons that lie outside the brain and the **spinal cord** comprise the **peripheral nervous system** (PNS), a network that extends to the fingertips and feet. All the neurons of the peripheral nervous system eventually connect to the **central nervous system** (CNS)—made up of the spinal cord, which is in part a sort of master cable to the brain, and the brain itself.

Neurons differ not only in length but in kind. They can be grouped into three classes based on their function: (1) **Afferent neurons** originate in the sense organs and body, and they carry messages from our eyes, ears, and other sense organs toward the central nervous system. (2) **Efferent neurons** carry messages from the central nervous system in an outward direction—ordering muscles to contract and directing the activity of the body's organs and glands. (3) **Connecting neurons,** which are the most numerous, are communications neurons that carry messages between other neurons. Every moment of our lives, day and night, afferent neurons carry information to the brain, and efferent neurons dispatch the brain's decisions and directions. As the center of this ceaseless activity of the nervous system, the brain performs all the essential and wondrous functions that will be discussed later.

The Cerebral Cortex—and How It Makes Us Human

If the top of a person's head were transparent and you looked down from above, you would see the brain as shown in Figure 2.5: a mass of gray tissue so rich in blood vessels that it takes on a pinkish cast. It resembles a walnut,

Spinal cord
The thick cable of neurons connecting the neurons in the spinal column to the brain.

Peripheral nervous system (PNS)
The network of nerves outside of the brain, including the neurons that make up those nerves.

Central nervous system (CNS)
The brain and the spinal cord.

Afferent neurons
Neurons that carry messages from the senses to the central nervous system.

Efferent neurons
Neurons that carry messages from the central nervous system to the muscles and glands.

Connecting neurons
Neurons that carry messages between neurons; sometimes called association neurons.

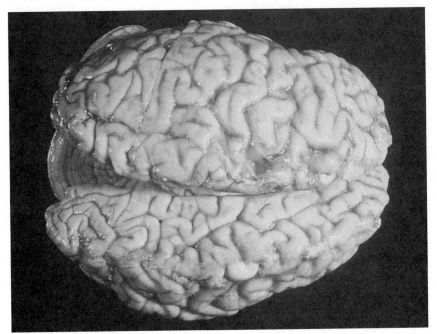

FIGURE 2.5 A topside view of the brain The photograph shows the human brain as seen from above, displaying the elaborate folds and creases. Note especially the vertical line, resembling a narrow ditch, running down the middle from the top of the photo (which is the front of the brain) to the bottom. This is a deep fissure that divides this top part of the brain into two separate halves, or hemispheres.

TEST YOURSELF

a) A doctor is examining a football team's quarterback, injured when he was tackled while trying to throw a pass. The patient reports that he feels no sensation in his hand—even when the doctor pushes hard on the skin with an instrument—but he can pick up a ball and throw it a good distance. Which neurons—afferent or efferent—are likely to have been affected by the injury?

b) On March 30, 1981, James Brady, press secretary to President Ronald Reagan, was shot above the left eye by would-be assassin John Hinckley. The bullet went through Brady's brain and lodged in the right hemisphere. Why is it unlikely that he will ever be able to fully recover his lost capacities to function—for example, to walk, speak, or express himself as normally as he did before?

but it is soft and pulsing with life. This is the part of the brain that is chiefly responsible for remembering, thinking, and planning—the activities that make humans more intelligent than other animals. It is called the **cerebral cortex,** and nature has made it larger in proportion to body size in human beings than in most other species. As can be seen in Figure 2.6, it is really too large to fit comfortably into the human head. But it has been ingeniously compressed to fit into the skull by the intricate foldings and refoldings apparent in Figure 2.5. What you see in the photograph is in fact only about a third of the cerebral cortex. All the rest is hidden in the creases.

The cortex is actually the surface, about one-eighth of an inch (3 mm) thick, of the human brain's largest single structure, the **cerebrum,** which lies on top of all the other parts of the brain. As is apparent in Figure 2.5, the cerebrum is split down the middle into a left half, or **left hemisphere,** and a right half, or **right hemisphere.**

Although the two hemispheres look like mirror images, they differ slightly in form and are often engaged in different activities—almost as if we have two brains doing our thinking. This arrangement has provoked a number of fascinating questions that will be discussed later.

Beneath the cerebrum, and totally hidden by its bulk when the brain is viewed from above, lie a number of other structures with their own special roles to play in our behavior. We share with other forms of animal life a number of these structures—those, for example, that generate our emotions and maintain our basic life functions. But it is the cerebrum and its cortex, comprising 80 percent of the human brain, that make us special. Without them, we humans are "almost a vegetable, speechless, sightless, senseless" (Hubel & Wiesel, 1979).

Because of the brain's vast and complex responsibilities, injury to it—for example, in an automobile accident or from a gunshot wound—can critically affect vital psychological and physical functions. And generally, damage to the brain is lasting. In contrast to other organs—for example, the liver—the brain is without the power to regenerate. Once neurons suffer damage, they are typically gone for good—and with them whatever behavioral functions they made possible. Nevertheless, scientists continue to study the brain's **plasticity**—its power to reorganize and shift functions. Their work is discussed in a Psychology in Action box entitled "The Brain's Repair."

FIGURE 2.6 The surprising size of the brain's cerebral cortex If it were laid flat, its many folds "ironed out," the cortex would measure about 1.5 square feet (.14 square meters) in area (Ornstein & Thompson, 1984).

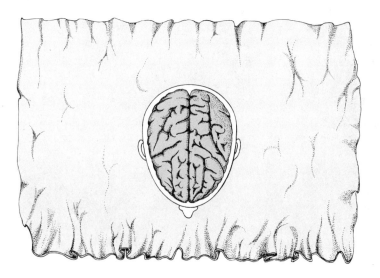

The Brain's Repair

We have all read of cases in which surgeons have reattached severed fingers and toes—which then regained their function. Although similar feats have not been possible in the damaged brain and its connecting nerve fibers, there is evidence that the brain and its functions can undergo renewal—and that they can sometimes be helped to do so.

Following harm to some areas of the brain, adjoining areas may eventually appropriate a number of lost functions. The healthy, neighboring neurons may make up for the loss by forging new connections that substitute for those that have been erased. As we grow older, for example, the dendrites of certain neurons increase in length—allowing them to receive messages despite the age-related destruction of neighboring neurons (Selkoe, 1992). And there is evidence that areas of the brain's cortex can shift their functions when neural pathways connected to them are damaged (Barnes, 1990). Recent findings, based on studies of mice, suggest that certain brain cells will divide into nerve tissue, including neurons, when exposed to a stimulating protein (epidermal growth factor, or EGF), in the test tube (Reynolds & Weiss, 1992).

Related studies show that it may be possible to graft healthy tissue to replace diseased or injured portions of the brain (Wyatt & Freed, 1983). It seems clear that the brain is usually less likely to reject newly grafted tissue than are body organs (Wyatt & Freed, 1985).

What are the prospects for restoring behavioral functions and health through such research? Right now they are strictly experimental, and considerable research is still necessary before new technologies can be widely applied. Yet the possibilities are there, including the transplantation of tissue from the adrenal gland—just above the kidney—to portions of the brain affected in the neurological disorder known as Parkinson's disease (Wyatt & Freed, 1985); the grafting of entire eyes to restore lost vision (Bjorkland & Steveni, 1984; Freed, de Medinaceli, & Wyatt, 1985), and the restoration of tissue that produces the right brain chemicals to treat Alzheimer's disease. Perhaps we are truly on the threshold of translating research on the operations of the brain into enormous help for millions of incapacitated people (Kiester, 1986).

The Brain's Functions: 1. Experiencing the World

You are driving down the street, and a child darts into the path of your car. In a twinkling, the muscles of your right leg tense and your foot hits the brake, bringing your car safely to a stop. Or you are in bed sound asleep. Suddenly there are shouts of "Fire!" You awake with a start, jump out of bed, and dash out of the house to safety.

Though we tend to take our behavior in such situations for granted, it is actually remarkable. Such acts require the teamwork of millions of neurons, receiving and sending messages with blinding speed. Our capacities to get information from the world, process that information, and respond to it all depend on the intricate functioning of the brain, both the cerebral cortex and the related structures lying below it, as well as the brain's links to the peripheral nervous system.

Sensing and Interpreting the Environment

Most of the information picked up by our sense organs is eventually transmitted, by way of the brain's many pathways, to the cerebral cortex. As shown in Figure 2.7, the cortex has specialized areas that receive the sensory messages for vision and hearing. It also contains a long strip, known as the **somatosensory cortex,** that receives messages for touch from the feet (at the

Cerebral cortex
The part of the brain responsible for remembering, thinking, and planning.

Cerebrum
The large brain mass that is covered by the cerebral cortex.

Left hemisphere
The part of the cerebrum that receives sensory messages from and controls the movements of the right side of the body.

Right hemisphere
The part of the cerebrum that receives sensory messages from and controls the left side of the body.

Plasticity
The power of the brain to reorganize and shift functions.

Somatosensory cortex
The specialized area of the cerebral cortex responsible for analyzing and interpreting messages from the sense organs.

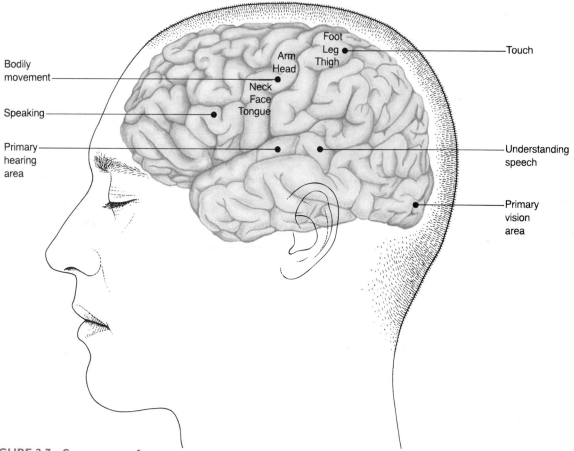

Bodily
movement

Speaking

Primary
hearing
area

Neck
Face
Tongue

Arm
Head

Foot
Leg
Thigh

Touch

Understanding
speech

Primary
vision
area

FIGURE 2.7 Some areas of the cerebral cortex with special functions On this drawing of the cerebral cortex as it would be seen from the left side of the body, the labeled portions represent areas that are known to perform some of the special jobs described in the text (Geschwind, 1979, p. 186).

top) to the head (at the bottom). In these specialized areas, the messages are analyzed and interpreted. The brain decides which messages are important and what they mean. The sounds of speech—which are of particular importance because language plays such a large role in human behavior—have an area of their own especially concerned with understanding the meaning of words and sentences.

The importance of the cerebral cortex in registering and processing sensory information becomes dramatically clear in cases of harm to any of these portions of the brain. Depending on the location and extent of injury to the back part of the cortex responsible for vision, for example, an individual might suffer varying degrees of blindness, even though the eye and its own muscles and nerves remain perfectly intact. Moreover, depending on the specific area of damage to the cerebral cortex, patients may be unable to recognize a familiar person's identity from their face but retain the capacity to recognize them from their walk. Thus different parts of the brain and different neural systems are evidently responsible for the learning of different types and levels of knowledge about the same entity (Damasio, 1990).

If the area for understanding speech is injured, an individual might no longer be able to interpret what is being said, even though all parts of the ear are perfectly healthy and the sounds of the words spoken are clearly heard. In such cases, the afflicted persons literally cannot get the words "through their heads."

Processing and Transmitting Sensory Information

Sensory information from the outside world is also processed and organized in the lower parts of the brain just a few milliseconds before it ever reaches the cortex. Serving as a relay station for sensory messages from the body to the cortex is the **thalamus,** shown in Figure 2.8. (The thalamus also acts as a relay station for some of the messages traveling in the opposite direction, especially some of the messages going out from the cortex calling for body movements described in the next section.)

Sensory information is processed as well in a network of nerve cells near the base of the brain called the **reticular activating system** (RAS). The network gets its name from the fact that it appears under a microscope as a criss-crossed (or reticulated) pattern of nerve fibers. As shown in Figure 2.8, it

Thalamus
The brain's relay station for sensory messages to and from the body and cortex.

Reticular activating system (RAS)
A network of nerves in the brain stem that serves as a way station for messages from the sense organs.

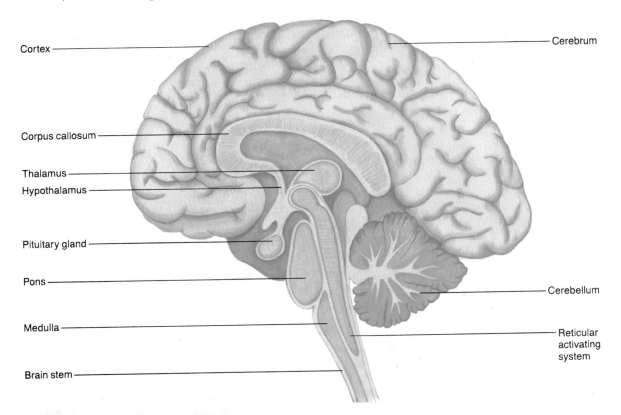

- Cortex
- Corpus callosum
- Thalamus
- Hypothalamus
- Pituitary gland
- Pons
- Medulla
- Brain stem
- Cerebrum
- Cerebellum
- Reticular activating system

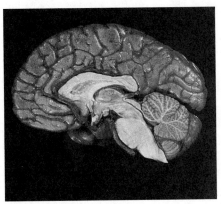

FIGURE 2.8   A sectional view of the brain Individual parts of the human brain are shown here as they would be seen if the brain were divided down the middle from front to back. The function of the various structures are described in the text (London, P. *Beginning Psychology.* The Dorsey Press 1978). The inset shows an actual photograph of the brain taken from the same perspective (courtesy the Warder Collection).

extends downward to the bottom part, or stem, of the brain, where the brain and spinal cord join together.

Nerve pathways carrying messages from the sense organs to the cerebrum have side branches in the reticular activating system. These side branches stimulate the system to send its own nerve impulses upward to the cerebrum, arousing it to a state of alertness and activity. Animals whose reticular activating system is destroyed remain permanently unconscious for lack of such arousal. If the reticular activating system is electrically stimulated, sleeping animals will awaken immediately (Rosenzweig & Lieman, 1982).

The reticular activating system also helps us to focus selectively on those sensory signals that are the most important. For example, when you are reading a newspaper, it blocks unimportant messages—the sounds in your room or flashes of lightning outside—and prepares the cortex to receive the ones that matter.

Generating Body Movements

Sometimes the reactions of the nervous system are immediate—as when you quickly move your hand away from a hot stove. Such responses do not require commands from the brain but are instead the results of connections in the spinal cord. But most of the movements you make—from the gross muscular adjustments of the arms and legs when lifting things or running, to the tiny adjustments of finger muscles when threading a needle or playing the guitar—are initiated in the cortex (Evarts, 1979).

The actual sequence of events in the brain that results in voluntary movements is complex and not yet completely understood, but we do know that many parts of the brain are engaged in the process. A specialized strip on the cortex, shown in Figure 2.7, controls body movements from feet to head. Known as the **motor cortex,** it initiates body movements in response to orders from other parts of the brain. In the case of the simple act of picking up a glass, for example, you must first have an intention of performing the act before actually executing the action (Libet, 1985).

Motor cortex
The specialized strip on the cerebral cortex that controls body movements.

Without the brain's cerebellum, such feats would be impossible.

The cortex also has an area for speaking that moves the vocal cords and muscles associated with them in a way that produces meaningful sounds. When a stroke or other injury damages this area of the cortex, the result is often a loss of the incomparable human gift of speech—the ability to formulate and utter precisely words that convey ideas. It is this portion of the brain that also manufactures the sounds that give voice to feelings—a shriek of delight when you see your home team score a winning touchdown, a groan of despair when you hear about the death of a friend, or a sigh of contentment when you feel the embrace of a loved one.

Managing the Miracles of Coordination and Balance

As shown in Figure 2.8, there lies below the cerebrum and attached to the back of the brain stem a bulging structure that looks like a tree in full bloom. Called the **cerebellum,** it is essential for many aspects of movement. The cerebellum, which has been called a "magnificently patterned, orderly and fantastically complex piece of machinery" (Hubel, 1979), has many connections with parts of the cerebral cortex that initiate muscular activity.

One of the special roles of the cerebellum is to coordinate all the various finely regulated muscular movements of which we are capable, such as typing or playing the piano. If the cerebellum is damaged, movements become jerky, and great effort and concentration are required to perform even what was once such an automatic activity as walking. Victims of damage to the cerebellum also have difficulty speaking, which requires well-coordinated movements of the muscles of the vocal cords, windpipe, and mouth.

The cerebellum also controls body balance and is the part of the brain that keeps us right side up. It plays an important role in allowing us to do things that require great equilibrium. An example is shooting a pistol at a target. Studies of champion marksmen in the Russian army showed that, although many parts of their body moved, the pistol remained virtually immobile (Evarts, 1979). With millions of neurons sending their trillions of messages to and fro—from the eyes, the cerebral cortex, the arms and fingers—somehow the brain, thanks largely to the cerebellum, is able to integrate all these messages into an act of exquisite balance and precision. Like the cerebrum, the cerebellum is divided into two lobes, or hemispheres. The left and right lobes are connected by the **pons,** which gets its name from the Latin word for bridge. The neurons of the pons serve as a bridge or cable that transmits messages between the two hemispheres of the cerebellum.

Cerebellum
The brain structure controling balance and movement.

Pons
The brain structure connecting the two hemispheres of the cerebellum.

The Brain's Functions: 2. Managing Thought and Memory

The brain areas responsible for monitoring sensations and controlling movements make up only about a quarter of the cerebral cortex. The rest of it, all the unshaded parts in Figure 2.7 (p. 58), helps us reason, relate past experiences to present ones, and plan for the future—in other words, all the intellectual processes that raise us far above the level of other organisms.

These unspecified areas, known as the **association cortex,** also contribute to our ability to be aware of ourselves and our relationship to the world, our ability to contemplate what has been and what might yet be. No other species has so much of its cortex devoted to association areas, a clue to their importance in uniquely human capabilities.

Association cortex
An area of the cortex contributing to self-awareness and the ability to think about the past and imagine the future.

The Miracles of Thinking and Planning

Frontal lobes
The front portions of the brain that play a key role in problem solving and planning.

The association areas in the front portion of the brain—called the **frontal lobes**—seem to play a key role in such human capacities as solving problems, planning, and relating the past with the present. Though we take our consciousness for granted, it is a strange and wonderful thing, allowing us to examine our own lives, understand those of others, and create the ideas, arts, and technologies that are hallmarks of human society.

Evidence of the importance of the frontal lobes in higher mental processes comes, in part, from observations of individuals in whom the area is injured or damaged. Such persons may be able to remember facts and to make high scores on intelligence tests, but they cannot plan ahead and initiate an activity. Such a person, for example, might easily remember his child's birthday but be incapable of the steps necessary to plan the child's party. Individuals with damaged frontal lobes also lose their normal social inhibitions and begin saying and doing inappropriate things—as if propelled by momentary impulses rather than "thinking through" a particular situation. For example, after losing that area of the frontal cortex responsible for processing information on emotional state, one man turned dramatically from a model citizen to an impulsive and irresponsible human being (Damasio, Tranel, & Damasio, 1990).

Further evidence comes from studies of early development. Very young children are typically impulsive in their behavior; they are not very good at thinking things through and purposefully planning ahead. Significantly enough, at this point in development the frontal lobe is not yet fully developed, and its connections with other important centers of the brain are not yet established (Diamond, 1991).

How Memories Are Stored and Retrieved

In recent years, researchers have made especially notable progress in understanding the role of the brain in memory (as well as in emotions, as will be described later in this chapter). For a number of years, it was thought that memory could be tracked to a single location in the brain. Now, however, it appears clear that multiple areas are involved. For example, the memory for the name of a person and a schematic representation of that person are each stored in separate parts of the brain—which explains why, with age, we might forget the names of people but still be able to call up images of their faces (Hart & Gordon, 1992).

A variety of studies show that memory is managed primarily in the association areas of the cortex, especially in the frontal lobe (Goldman-Rakic, 1992). Here resides the capacity to store newly gained information and to link it to relevant information stored long ago (Baddeley, 1986). For example, patients suffering from damage to the frontal lobe display an inability to use the knowledge they gain to guide how they behave from moment to moment.

Hippocampus
The part of the brain that transforms information from short-term memory to long-term memory.

The complex task of storing and retrieving information seems to require the cooperation of other parts of the brain as well, however—most notably the **hippocampus** (Passingham, 1985; Murray & Mishkin, 1985). The hippocampus lies beneath the cortex close to the area involved in processing speech shown in Figure 2.7, but it is difficult to illustrate clearly. It appears to

A stimulated childhood environment may speed the rate at which the young brain grows.

be essential in transforming new information into long-lasting memories (Mishkin & Appenzeller, 1987). In animals and birds, when the hippocampus is destroyed, old memories do not vanish, but newer ones cannot be retrieved (Squire, 1992).

Studies have shown that adults suffering from amnesia, or a severe breakdown of memory, display patterns of forgetting—for example, of objects they have just seen—very much like those shown by monkeys with damage to the portion of the brain that includes the hippocampus (Squire, Zola-Morgan, & Chen, 1988). From studies of both animals and humans, it appears that the hippocampus is essential for **semantic memory;** this includes memory for people's names, and for words, facts, and ideas. However, the hippocampus is not essential for **procedural memory,** which includes the ability to remember motor skills and habits such as tying shoelaces or playing golf or tennis (Squire, 1992). A primary role of the hippocampus is to consolidate new memories and relate separate events, especially to relate an event to the place where it occurred (McDonald & White, 1993). The frontal cortex is more essential for the retrieval of prior facts, names, and rules from long-range storage in the association cortex in order to help solve a problem at hand.

Semantic memory
Conscious recall of facts, information, and ideas.

Procedural memory
Memory for motor skills and behavioral habits.

The Growing Brain and the Developing Intellect

The highly developed abilities of human beings depend in large measure on the cerebrum and its cortex. Even before birth, in the darkness of the womb, they grow so rapidly that they almost seem to explode, as Figure 2.9 shows. Growth continues at a furious pace after birth—so much so that the baby's brain triples in weight in the first six months of life. By the age of two, the brain reaches three-quarters of its ultimate weight (finally achieved in the late teens to early twenties), and it is precisely during these opening years that the child makes remarkable strides in motor skills, speech, and the human capacity to remember and reflect. All the various stages of children's intellectual

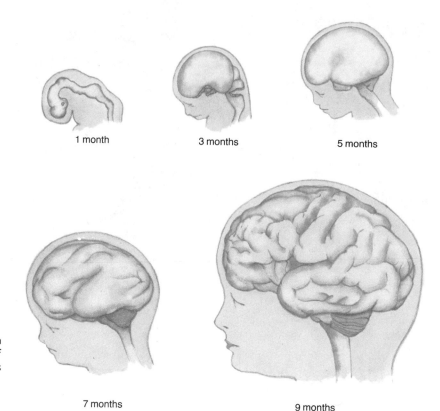

FIGURE 2.9 The brain's explosive growth before birth During each minute in the womb, the brain of the infant-to-be gains tens of thousands of new brain cells. The folds on the brain's surface begin to appear at about the middle of pregnancy—as the cortex grows rapidly to fill the top of the tiny fetal skull of the brain (Cowan, 1979).

1 month

3 months

5 months

7 months

9 months

development described later in the book are dependent on the progressive growth and maturation of the cerebral cortex (Tanner, 1978).

Although the number of neurons remains relatively constant, the number of synapses peaks early in the first two years of life (Rakic et al., 1986). Indeed, as the child learns more information and learns new skills, the number of synapses actually decreases. Experience appears to prune the cortex into a more efficient form—much like a sculptor, given an unformed piece of marble, chips away and prunes the material to develop the final product containing less substance than the original. For a further discussion of the role of the brain's development over time, see the Life Span Perspective box, "As the Brain Matures."

Left Brain, Right Brain

As was noted in Figure 2.8 (p. 59), the topmost part of the brain—the cerebrum and the cerebral cortex—is divided into two halves, or hemispheres. Each half seems to have somewhat different responsibilities for memory, reasoning, and language.

Most of the nerve fibers connecting the brain with all the various parts of the body through the spinal cord cross from one side to the other. This means that the left hemisphere ordinarily receives sensory messages from and controls movement in the right side of the body. The right hemisphere deals with the left side of the body. If like most people you write with your right hand, it is your left hemisphere that directs the movements. The left hemi-

LIFE SPAN PERSPECTIVE

As the Brain Matures

Various aspects of the brain are altered over the life course. Moreover, those changes are often reflected in behavior and well-being. Three examples follow:

- One notable change takes place in the levels of the neurotransmitter dopamine in the brain (Rosenzweig & Leiman, 1982). Concentrations of dopamine rise during childhood, with a major increase taking place during adolescence. As will be described in Chapter 10, a significant increase in dopamine may be associated with schizophrenia—a serious mental disorder that often surfaces during late adolescence and early adulthood. Some scientists have suggested that the timing of the disorder may be more readily understood in the light of developmental changes in the brain's chemistry: A large increase in dopamine in the brain of a young individual genetically predisposed to schizophrenia might well produce the bizarre symptoms characteristic of this disorder.

  At a much later period in the life span, changes in the brain—again involving dopamine—lead to the development of a neurological disorder. Parkinson's disease, appearing in late adulthood and old age, causes tremors to occur and body movements—even walking—to become uncoordinated. The disorder appears to be caused by damage to an area of the brain where neurons normally secrete dopamine (Wyatt & Freed, 1985). When patients are given replacement therapy with a chemical that normally leads to the production of dopamine, their symptoms are relieved.

- A second developmental change in the brain is revealed in sleep. As will be described in Chapter 7, a major component of sleep is the period known as **REM** (*rapid eye movement*) sleep, marked by dreaming. This is a period of intense physiological activity, which is prominent even during prenatal life and consumes about half of the newborn's sleep. In later infancy and early childhood, the proportion of sleep time spent in REM diminishes dramatically, falling to less than 20 percent in adulthood. It is believed that the REM period is essential "exercise" for the rapidly developing nervous system of the fetus and infant (Hobson, 1989).

- A third change takes place in the weight of the brain itself. Almost all the brain's neurons are present at birth. The number increases afterward only by a small amount, and only in certain areas (Greenough, 1982). Yet the brain quadruples in weight from birth to adulthood, with the most rapid growth taking place in the first five years of life. Some of the added weight comes from the growth of supporting tissue. But perhaps more important is the growth of new offshoots from nerve cells—much as a young tree develops new branches. By sprouting new branches, neurons increase their interconnections with other neurons, thus providing new pathways for messages in the brain. ∎

Rapid eye movement (REM)
Small movements of the eyes that occur during dreaming.

Corpus callosum
The structure of the brain that connects the right and left hemispheres of the cerebrum and enables those hemispheres to interact.

TEST YOURSELF

e) When an aging grandfather complains that his memory constantly fails him, what structure in his brain is likely to be undergoing change?

f) If you were to meet an elderly man with severe hand tremors and coordination difficulties, what brain disorder might come to mind—and what neurotransmitter might be diminished in that man's brain?

g) For whom is the right hemisphere of the brain often likely to be more active than the left—a stand-up comic or an architect?

FIGURE 2.10   A normal subject tackles a spatial task. What do his brain waves show? This subject has been fitted with a skull cap that holds electrodes against various parts of his scalp. The electrodes are hooked up to an electroencephalograph (EEG) that records the electrical activity beneath them.

sphere also has greater control of the use of language—speaking and understanding the speech of others. Thus in most people the left hemisphere is the dominant one—and the one most used and relied on.

The two hemispheres cooperate very closely. They have numerous interconnections, especially through a structure known as the **corpus callosum** (shown in Figure 2.8), which resembles a thick telephone cable between the two hemispheres. Thus each half of the cerebrum and cerebral cortex communicates with the other half.

What would happen if the corpus callosum were cut or missing and the two halves of the brain could not communicate? We know the answer because surgeons sometimes cut the connecting link as a last resort to relieve patients of crippling epileptic seizures. This "split-brain" operation produces some strange results. Patients may show little change in their intelligence, personality, or general behavior, yet careful testing reveals that in some ways they act as if they have two independently functioning brains.

Experiments with individuals who have undergone split-brain surgery show that the two hemispheres, when separated, perform different functions. Although the hemispheres look symmetrical overall, certain areas are slightly larger on the left side, while others are slightly larger on the right. These physical differences have been seen even in unborn fetuses, an indication that they are innate rather than acquired through experience and learning (Galaburda, 1984).

A number of psychologists have concluded that the left hemisphere is more skilled at dealing with symbolic information—like words and numbers, considered one by one in a logical sequence. This is the kind of mental work we call "reasoning," in which we arrive at logical conclusions in a step-by-step fashion. The left hemisphere is also particularly adept at language, in which sounds are put together in logical order into words, and words are arranged into sentences. By contrast, the right hemisphere appears to be more skilled at considering whole patterns—seeing the forest, not the trees. For example, it excels at the perception of visual information such as paintings or spatial locations, the melodies in a song or symphony, and the tone of a person's voice.

However, our knowledge about the division of labor between the two hemispheres in normal people remains incomplete. There is evidence that the two hemispheres are both active in most things we do, although for specific tasks one may be more active than the other. For example, as shown in Figure 2.10, when a normal person was trying to master the delicate feat of judging space and movement to get a steel ball through a labyrinth (a spatial task), measurements of his brain's electrical activity indicated that his right hemisphere sphere was doing most of the work. When he switched to writing a letter (a language task), there was more activity in the left hemisphere (Ornstein, 1978).

The Brain's Functions: 3. Overseeing Emotions and Survival

The remarkable feats of the brain described thus far—allowing us to make sense of our environment, move about in the world, and think as humans— are impressive in their own right. But even with them, our lives would be flat and barren were it not for the deeply moving experiences we call emotions. True, the emotions of fear and anger are often upsetting and sometimes destructive. However, they also help us cope with the world and meet its crises, motivating us to action. And there are other emotions that greatly enrich our lives, such as love and joy. These feelings, too, are produced by our brain, working in concert with our body.

The brain not only regulates our emotions; it also ensures our personal physical survival by keeping our body in healthy working order. It oversees the fundamental functions of breathing, pumping blood, and maintaining adequate blood pressure. It also tells us when we need food or drink, and it keeps body chemistry in balance. The brain seems to watch out for our survival as a species, too; it is deeply involved in our sexual development and behavior. Our lives are finally at an end only when the brain ceases its last flicker of activity.

The Wellsprings of Passions and Feelings

Of special importance in our emotional life is a network of brain structures and pathways near the brain's center known as the **limbic system.** Making up about one-fifth of our brain, it is illustrated in Figure 2.11.

The limbic system consists of many components, one of which, the hippocampus, plays a role in memory, as has already been described. In effect, it receives information and "decides" if the information is familiar or unfamiliar. If it is unfamiliar—and therefore potentially significant or threatening—another structure, the **amygdala,** comes into play. The amygdala sends axons to other parts of the brain and body. The activity of these parts leads to the experience of intense emotions such as anger and fear. Through its connections with other portions of the brain, the amygdala can also trigger actions that are appropriate to an emotional state.

Limbic system
The set of interconnected pathways in the brain involved with smell, eating, and emotion.

Amygdala (ah-MIG-da-la)
The part of the limbic system that plays a role in intense emotions like anger and fear.

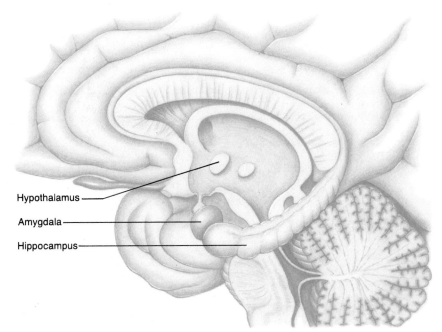

Hypothalamus

Amygdala

Hippocampus

FIGURE 2.11   The brain's limbic system The word *limbic* means "bordering," and the *limbic system* is so named because its parts form a border, or loop, around the deepest core of the cerebrum. Because it is in close contact with both the frontal lobes of the cortex and the brain stem, the limbic system is strategically located for its role in vital brain functions. Those functions and some of the key parts of the system are described in the text.

In one experiment, researchers showed that the startle response of rats to a sudden, very loud noise is greater when the rats have been conditioned to fear a shock in advance of the noise. That is, the state of fear leads to a larger startle response. But when the amygdala is surgically removed, the exaggerated startle response produced by the fear vanishes—demonstrating that it is the amygdala that mediates the fear experience (Hitchcock & Davis, 1991). As portrayed in Figure 2.12, it is the right amygdala, rather than the left, that is especially activated when fear is present. (As will be described later, the right hemisphere of the brain is especially responsible for regulating negative emotions.)

The limbic system has connections to another key player in our emotional lives and our physical survival: the **hypothalamus,** the brain's most direct link to the body glands that are active in fear, anger, and other emotions. The hypothalamus is attached to the master gland, the **pituitary** (see Figure 2.8, p. 59), which is actually its partial master. Working in concert with other portions of the limbic system and the cortex, the hypothalamus delivers messages that help produce the "stirred-up" bodily processes that accompany emotion. A discussion of the possible tie between the hypothalamus and homosexuality is contained in the Psychology and the Media box, "Zone of Brain Linked to Men's Sexual Orientation."

In lower mammals, the limbic system appears to contain the programming that directs the instinctive patterns in which they feed, mate, fight, and escape from danger. There is evidence that when animals learn to anticipate that a stressful experience—such as a shock—is coming, the limbic system becomes active (Herrmann, Hurwitz, & Levine, 1984). Laboratory experiments have shown that surgery or electrical stimulation of various parts of the limbic system can cause animals to behave in ways that appear unusually docile or unusually aggressive, as illustrated in Figure 2.13. Damage to one part of the limbic system will reduce the fear and avoidance that many animals display when faced with a novel stimulus, while damage to another part will erase inhibitions on attack behavior and make many animals vicious.

Hypothalamus

The portion of the brain that serves as a mediator between the brain and the body; helps control metabolism, sleep, hunger, thirst, body temperature, sexual behavior, and emotions.

Pituitary gland

The master endocrine gland that secretes hormones controling growth and sexual development at puberty and regulating other endocrine glands.

FIGURE 2.12 The amygdala and painful emotion
When squirrel monkeys were placed in a room where they had experienced earlier shock, there was a more marked increase in delta waves—slow brain waves that typically emerge during emotional upheaval—in the right amygdala than in the left (adapted from Lloyd & Kling, 1991).

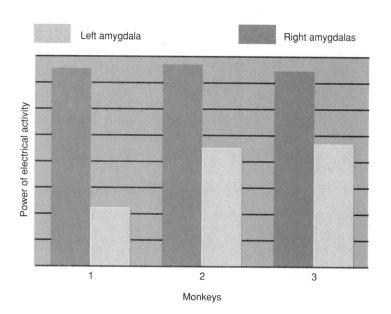

Staying Alive and Physiologically in Tune

The body's well-being depends on keeping its many functions on a reasonably even keel despite the many events and environmental changes it continually encounters. For example, the body must keep internal temperature stable in all seasons and levels of exertion, and it must maintain a proper supply of oxygen, water, and various other substances that cells need to function well. The state of dynamic equilibrium achieved when these processes are working right and all physiological systems are well-balanced is called **homeostasis.**

The air we breathe, the water we drink, and the food we eat are the raw materials required to keep our cells properly supplied and working correctly. We need a central management system to order these supplies, make sure they arrive on time, distribute them where they are needed, and see that they are processed properly. The brain provides that management.

For example, the hypothalamus, besides being a center for emotional behavior, helps to maintain homeostasis by signaling when the body needs more food or water and by regulating states of wakefulness and sleep. It also acts like a highly accurate thermostat, keeping body temperature close to 98.6°F by reacting to messages from temperature sensors in the skin and from its own temperature-sensing cells.

Our continuing survival depends as well on the **medulla,** shown in Figure 2.8 (p. 59), a structure in the brain stem that is responsible for coordinating vital bodily processes such as breathing, heart rate, blood pressure, and digestion. Infants who die suddenly without any apparent cause (victims of so-called sudden-infant-death syndrome) often have a medulla that is not fully developed and, therefore, does not react quickly to loss of oxygen when there is a breathing problem that might otherwise have proved insignificant (Valdes-Dapena, 1980).

The Autonomic Nervous System: The Brain's Busy Deputy

In controlling bodily processes, the brain has an effective assistant in the form of the **autonomic nervous system** (**ANS**). The word autonomic means independent or self-sufficient—and in many ways the autonomic nervous system operates on its own, as its name suggests, without much if any conscious

Homeostasis
A state of equilibrium or balance in any physiological system.

Medulla
The structure in the brain stem that helps regulate breathing, heart rate, blood pressure, and digestion.

Autonomic nervous system (ANS)
The nerve network connecting the central nervous system with glands and smooth muscles.

The spontaneous smiling and joyful posture shown here are influenced by circuits in the brain that are excited by desired events.

Zone of Brain Linked to Men's Sexual Orientation

The brains of homosexual men are structurally different from those of heterosexual men in a region thought to influence male sexual behavior, a scientist says he has found.

The discovery, if confirmed, would be the first detection of a distinct pattern in the brain that could help explain sexual preference among men.

"The main result of this research is to show that it is possible to study sexual orientation at the biological level," said Dr. Simon LeVay, a neurobiologist at the Salk Institute in La Jolla, Calif. "It's not just the province of the psychologists and the psychoanalysts anymore."

In the new work, Dr. LeVay reports that in homosexual men, one segment of the hypothalamus, an important structure in the forebrain, is only a quarter to a half the size of the same region in heterosexual men. Dr. LeVay's study appears in today's issue of the journal *Science,* which relies on evaluations of independent researchers before publication.

"It's quite a striking observation, and as far as I know it's unprecedented," said Dr. Thomas R. Insel, a behavioral neuroscientist at the National Institute of Mental Health in Rockville, Md. "Simon LeVay is a top-notch, world-class neuroanatomist, and this is a very provocative paper."

But other researchers warned that the findings are highly preliminary, and that they involve only a small number of brain tissue samples. They said the results by no means prove homosexuality is caused by a particular variation in the brain, or anywhere else in the body for that matter.

Studies With Lab Animals

Dr. LeVay proposes that the hypothalamic segment could be responsible for inspiring males to seek females, and that its absence in men would be one possible element predisposing them toward homosexuality.

In studies of male rats and monkeys, researchers have found that injury to this portion of the brain causes males to lose interest in females while continuing to express sexual vigor by such activities as masturbation.

But Dr. LeVay and many other researchers emphasize that the results remain to be confirmed in follow-up studies. And even if definitively proved, they said the brain discrepancy is likely to be only a small part of the story of how male sexuality unfolds.

"How Did It Get There?"

Dr. LeVay also said it was not yet known if the difference arises during the development of the brain, or whether a man's homosexual preferences could somehow influence the contours of certain neural pathways later in life. If that were the case, he said, his finding would be a mere consequence of homosexuality, rather than one of its possible causes.

"It's axiomatic that sexual orientation is going to be represented in the brain somewhere," said Dr. John Money, a professor emeritus at Johns Hopkins School of Medicine in Baltimore who has long studied the origins of sexual behavior. "The really interesting questions are when did it happen and how did it get there?"

Dr. LeVay believes the variation in hypothalamic size probably arises dur-

---

control. Even if we try, we cannot ordinarily command our stomach muscles to make the movements that help digest food. We cannot order the muscles of the blood vessels to channel a strong flow of blood to the stomach to aid digestion—or to redirect the flow of blood toward the muscles of the arms or legs when we have to do physical work. We cannot make our hearts pump faster or slower. But the ANS can do all these things and does so constantly, even when we are asleep or in a deep coma caused by an anesthetic or a brain injury.

Endocrine glands (ductless glands)
Glands that discharge hormones directly into the bloodstream, resulting in a variety of physiological changes.

In addition, the ANS exercises considerable independent influence on important bodily structures called **endocrine glands,** or glands of internal secretion (also called **ductless glands**), which are also resistant to conscious control. Unlike the sweat glands that deliver perspiration to the skin, or the salivary glands that deliver fluids to the mouth, the endocrine glands discharge their products directly into the bloodstream. These substances, as

ing the growth of the fetus. But whether that alteration is caused by genetic programming that is hardwired into the baby's DNA, he said, or by fluctuations during pregnancy of critical hormones known to affect fetal brain development, remains a mystery.

Other caveats of the new report abound. The gay men whose brain samples were examined all died of AIDS, a disease that infiltrates the central nervous system. But Dr. LeVay said that factor was unlikely to account for the discrepancy observed in the hypothalamus because six of the men presumed to have been heterosexual also died of AIDS, contracted as a result of intravenous drug use. Nevertheless, these men had hypothalamic structures several times the size of those in gay men, he said.

But Dr. LeVay also said he did not know for certain that the men he assumed to have been heterosexual actually were.

"For most men who die, there's nothing mentioned about their sex lives in their medical charts," he said. "You just obtain tissue and say the likelihood is they're heterosexual just because of the numbers."

Dr. LeVay, who is a homosexual himself, said the gay men he has discussed his work with are in general pleased by the idea that sexual orientation may be at least partly inborn.

"They say their sexual personality is something very deeply ingrained in them," he said, "so they're not surprised to be told there are structural differences in the brain."

In the new research, Dr. LeVay examined thin slices of autopsied brain tissue from 19 homosexual men, 16 presumed heterosexual men and six women also thought to have been heterosexual. The average age at the time of death for all three groups was about 40, and thus the brains had not yet undergone the profound changes known to be associated with age. He focused on a particular segment of the hypothalamus known as the third interstitial nucleus of the anterior hypothalamus, which previous studies had shown to differ significantly between men and women. Measuring the volume of cells in the region, he found that in the heterosexual men it averaged about the size of a large grain of sand, but that in the women and the gay men it was almost indetectable. Although the region is tiny, the discrepancy between heterosexual and homosexuals is significant.

"Most of us who look at the influence of the brain on behavior work at the molecular level," said Dr. Insel. "But this is a rather gross anatomical difference, and that's a dramatic finding."

Source: From "Zone of Brain Linked to Men's Sexual Orientation" by Natalie Angier, 1991, *The New York Times,* August 30.

Issues to Consider

1. Is it possible that the scientist's own sexual orientation might have influenced the conclusions from his study?
2. Is a cause-effect relationship certain from the findings?
3. What additional studies do you think are needed to clarify the relationship between the brain's structure and homosexuality?

mentioned earlier, are called hormones. They influence many bodily activities, including those associated with emotional behavior. As illustrated in Figure 2.14, the endocrine glands include the pituitary, parathyroid, thyroid, and adrenal glands and the pancreas, ovaries, and testes.

The autonomic nervous system exerts its impact on important body processes through a number of centers called **ganglia,** as shown in Figure 2.15. These are like small brains scattered throughout the body. They consist of masses of nerve cells packed together and connected with one another—as in the brain itself but on a much smaller scale. Some of these neurons, as indicated in Figure 2.15, have long fibers over which they send commands to the glands, the heart muscles, and the muscles of the body's organs and blood vessels. Others are connected to the brain and the spinal cord—which means that the ANS, though independent in many ways, does take some orders from above. In the case of being wakened by shouts of "Fire!" your ears send

Ganglia

Masses of nerve cells and synapses that form complex and multiple connections.

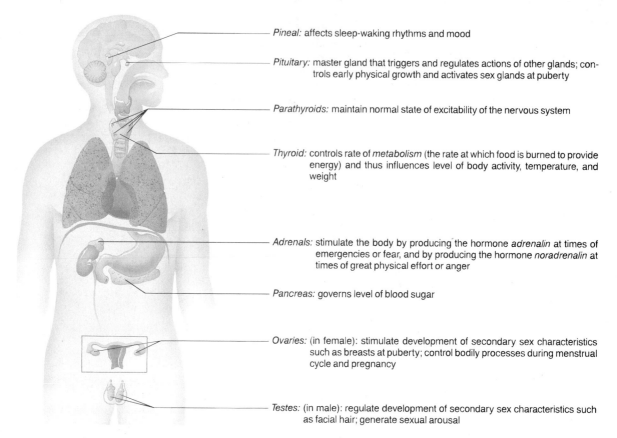

Pineal: affects sleep-waking rhythms and mood

Pituitary: master gland that triggers and regulates actions of other glands; controls early physical growth and activates sex glands at puberty

Parathyroids: maintain normal state of excitability of the nervous system

Thyroid: controls rate of *metabolism* (the rate at which food is burned to provide energy) and thus influences level of body activity, temperature, and weight

Adrenals: stimulate the body by producing the hormone *adrenalin* at times of emergencies or fear, and by producing the hormone *noradrenalin* at times of great physical effort or anger

Pancreas: governs level of blood sugar

Ovaries: (in female): stimulate development of secondary sex characteristics such as breasts at puberty; control bodily processes during menstrual cycle and pregnancy

Testes: (in male): regulate development of secondary sex characteristics such as facial hair; generate sexual arousal

FIGURE 2.14   The human endocrine glands The *endocrine glands* receive messages from the brain and ANS that make them spring into action or sometimes slow down. The glands influence the excitability of the brain and the rest of the nervous system, helping create emotional experiences.

Parasympathetic division
A part of the nervous system made up of scattered ganglia near the glands or the muscles of organs; helps maintain heartbeat and digestion.

a message to your brain, which then sends an emergency command to the ANS, which in turn springs into action through its various connections with the glands and muscles.

As shown in Figure 2.15, there are two divisions of the ANS, differing in structure and function: the parasympathetic and the sympathetic.

The Parasympathetic Division: Running the Ordinary Business of Living The **parasympathetic division** connects with the stem of the brain and the lower part of the spinal cord. It is made up of a number of widely scattered ganglia, most of which lie near the glands or muscles of organs to which it delivers its messages. Because it is so loosely constructed, it tends to act in piecemeal fashion, delivering its orders to one or several parts of the body but not necessarily to all at once.

In general, the parasympathetic division seems to play its most important role during those frequent periods when no danger threatens and the body can relax and go about the ordinary business of living. It tends to slow down the work of the heart and lungs. It aids digestion by stimulating the salivary glands, producing wavelike motions of the muscles of the stomach and intestines, and encouraging the stomach to produce digestive acid and the liver to produce the digestive fluid called bile. It also brings about elimination

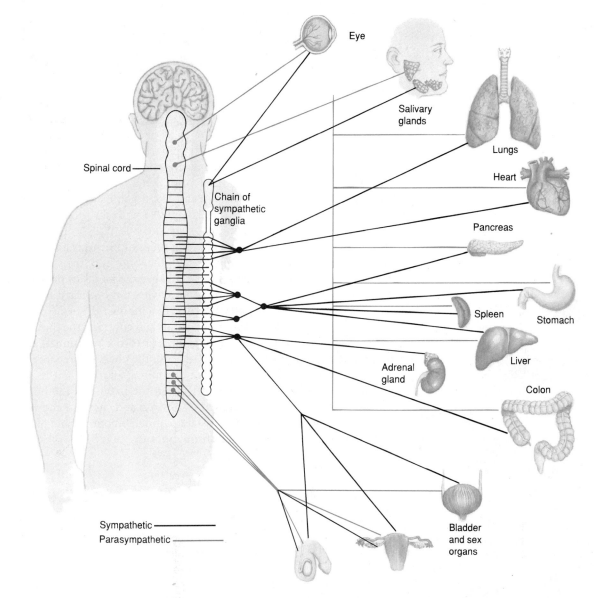

FIGURE 2.15 **Autonomic nervous system** The long chain of ganglia of the *sympathetic division* extends down the side of the spinal cord, to which it makes many connections. (There is a similar chain on the other side of the body.) The *parasympathetic division* has small ganglia near the glands and smooth muscles that both divisions help control, though in different ways (after Crosby, Humphrey, & Lauer, 1962).

of the body's waste products from the intestines and bladder. At times, however, the parasympathetic division abandons these usual tasks and helps mobilize the body for emergency action. When it does this—operating in ways that are not yet understood—it seems to assist and supplement the work of the other part of the autonomic system, the sympathetic division.

The Sympathetic Division: Meeting Emergencies The **sympathetic division** is shown in Figure 2.15 as a long chain of ganglia extending down the sides of the spinal cord. There is a similar chain, not shown, on the other

Sympathetic division
A long chain of ganglia that extends down the sides of the spinal cord and activates glands and smooth muscles for "fight" or "flight."

side of the cord. All the many ganglia of the sympathetic division are elaborately interconnected. Note that many of the nerve fibers going out from the chains of ganglia meet again in additional ganglia in other parts of the body, where they again form complicated interconnections with nerve cells that finally carry commands to the glands and smooth muscles. For this reason the sympathetic division, unlike the parasympathetic, tends to function as a unit.

When the sympathetic division springs into action, as it does when we experience fear or anger, it does many things all at once. Most notably, it commands the adrenal glands to spill their powerful stimulants into the bloodstream. By acting on the adrenal glands, liver, and pancreas, it increases the level of blood sugar, thus raising the rate of metabolism and providing additional energy. It causes the spleen, a gland-like organ in which red corpuscles are stored, to release more of these corpuscles into the bloodstream, thus enabling the blood to carry more oxygen to the body's tissues. It changes the size of the blood vessels—enlarging those of the heart and muscles of body movement and constricting those of the muscles of the stomach and intestines. It makes us breathe harder. It enlarges the pupils of the eyes, which are controlled by muscles, and slows the activity of the salivary glands. ("Wide eyes" and a dry mouth are characteristic of a number of strong emotions such as fear.) It also activates the sweat glands and contracts the muscles at the base of the hairs of the body, causing the hair to rise on animals and producing gooseflesh in human beings. In general, the changes prepare the body for emergency action—such as fighting or running away.

Clearly there is a very close marriage between the brain and the body, linked together as they are through numerous physical and chemical connections. The implications of this link for our state of mind, emotions, and physical and mental well-being are discussed throughout this book.

The Brain's Hemispheres and the Regulation of Emotion

As described on pages 64–66, psychologists have concentrated in the past on studying the differing roles of the two brain hemispheres in cognition. More recent studies, however, point to differences between the two sides of the brain in the regulation of emotional behavior as well. In general, the frontal area of the right hemisphere appears to be more active in regulating negative emotions such as sadness and fear, while the corresponding area of the left hemisphere appears to be more active in regulating positive emotions such as happiness (Davidson & Tomarken, 1989).

The pattern appears to hold both for infants and adults. For example, it has been found that infants of 10 months who cried when separated from their mothers were more likely in earlier testing to have displayed relatively high activity in the right frontal area (Davidson & Fox, 1989). And in studies of adults, it has been found that those who respond with intensely negative feelings to emotion-arousing films were similarly more likely to display high activation of the right frontal area (Tomarken, Davidson, & Henriques, 1990; Tomarken et al., 1992).

One laboratory experiment demonstrating the roles of brain hemispheres in emotion is summarized in Figure 2.16. It shows that stimuli with an unhappy connotation get a faster response from the right hemisphere, while the opposite is true for stimuli with a happy connotation (Reuter-

TEST YOURSELF

h) What evidence can you cite to suggest a biological basis for male homosexuality?

i) "His hormones are raging." That description is sometimes applied to an adolescent who begins to take an intense interest in sex. What gland is in charge of this development?

j) A friend tells you that she spent a relaxing period last evening finishing a crossword puzzle—but that later on in the evening, while getting ready for bed, she had a period of intense panic when she kept hearing strange sounds in the basement. In which of those two periods was the sympathetic division of your friend's autonomic nervous system more likely to have been active?

k) Which of the two hemispheres of your brain is typically the more active when you are feeling happy?

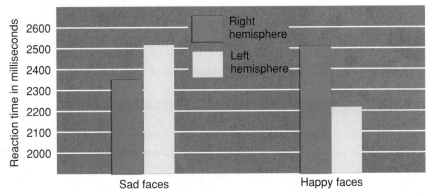

FIGURE 2.16 **Right for sad, left for happy** When subjects were presented with pictures of sad faces to their left visual field, which connects with the right brain hemisphere, the reaction time was faster than when the same pictures were presented to the right visual field, which connects with the left hemisphere. The opposite was true for happy faces (Reuter-Lorenz & Davidson, 1981).

Lorenz & Davidson, 1981). A more recent study suggests that differences in the activation level of the two hemispheres is related to the function of the body's **immune system**—which produces antibodies, or so-called "killer cells," to help fight infection and disease. This is the body's intricate defense network of organs and tissues that produces protective cells such as lymphocytes (white blood cells). Researchers showed that adult women having a relatively high activation of the right frontal area had lower levels of natural killer cell activity. Those women who had a greater left frontal activation showed a much more vigorous immune response than did those with greater right frontal activation (Kang et al., 1991). The finding is of special interest, given the evidence that an upbeat, optimistic mood is associated with good health (Seligman, 1990).

Immune system

An intricate network of organs and tissue producing antibodies and special cells to fight infection and disease.

Neuroscience: New Investigations of the Brain-Behavior Link

Recent advances in various aspects of brain research have led to the establishment of the field of **neuroscience**, a fusion of several scientific disciplines—biochemistry, physiology, anatomy, pharmacology, and psychology—all geared to acquiring a fuller understanding of how the brain operates (Pachuna & Martin, 1991). The role of psychology in this family of sciences has grown considerably in recent years, focusing on studies of the behavioral functions of the brain (Davis et al., 1988).

Neuroscience

The branch of science that fuses biochemistry, physiology, anatomy, pharmacology, and psychology in order to explain how the brain operates.

Studies of brain and behavior are described throughout this book. They include explorations of the complex functions of attention, reasoning, language, learning, motivation, emotion, and the various abnormal conditions that continue to afflict humankind. To end this chapter, however, it is important to consider the major challenge addressed by investigators in the field: to explain the mechanisms that link the operations of the brain with various facets of human behavior.

Brain Imaging: How Scientists "See" the Brain in Action

Analyses of the relationship between brain activity and behavior have been enriched in recent years by new techniques for actually viewing the intact brain in operation. Those who studied the brain in the past had to depend on inferences about it rather than on the organ itself. In contrast, a number of modern techniques have made it possible for researchers to study the brain in action—its electrical activity, structure, blood flow, or chemistry. Each of these approaches produces either a display of the brain's activity or an actual image of the brain.

The best known technique, introduced more than a half century ago, is the standard **EEG (electroencephalogram)**, which consists of amplified tracings of the brain's continuous "waves" of electrical activity recorded through electrodes placed on the scalp. Although valuable, the EEG has been able to provide information only about overall electrical activity of the brain. Now, however, new methods employing computer technology make possible the translation of the brain's electrical activity into specific "maps" at various intervals. These are used, for example, to monitor the brain's responses to various medications.

Even more revealing are new **brain-imaging** techniques that produce overall views, or scans, of the brain itself. The **CAT (computerized axial tomography) scan,** for example, provides a look at a particular "slice" of the brain by means of thousands of X-ray images collected from various angles around the skull. The pictures are processed by a computer, revealing a clear image of a specific area of the brain and any damage to it. Even more sensitive is the **MRI (magnetic resonance imaging) scan,** which produces three-dimensional images of the brain by safely exposing the skull to magnetic fields; this technique has now been refined as the so-called fast MRI, which uses special hardware to speed the imaging process, and advanced computer programs to convert still brain images into movies (McCarthy, 1993). Recent years have witnessed, too, the development of the **PET (positron emission tomography) scan,** which requires very small injections of a radioactive substance later traced by sensitive detectors. As depicted in Figure 2.17, use of

**FIGURE 2.17 The Brain in
Action** These PET scans reveal
how various portions of the
brain are activated while a subject is performing a series of verbal tasks. They reveal that blood
flow in the brain shifts to different areas of the brain according
to the type of task being performed (Fischbach, 1992).

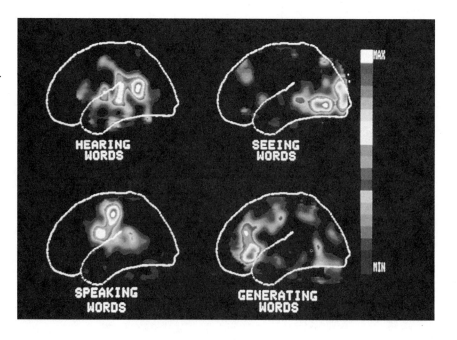

this technique has provided remarkable insights into the functioning of various portions of the brain while the individual is engaged in a specific activity. The radioactive substance is often most pronounced in those areas of the brain that are most actively involved.

These and other brain-imaging techniques will be referred to in connection with various studies described throughout this book. By revealing in sharp detail both brain structures and functions, these techniques offer great promise for clarifying the links between brain and behavior. They will allow researchers to pierce even further the mystery of how the brain works to help us accomplish three basic tasks: to take in and respond to what is going on in the outside world; to engage in remarkable intellectual operations such as thought and memory; and to express emotion and maintain our very survival.

Transforming Electricity and Chemistry into Meanings and Feelings

One of the great mysteries in psychology is how the electrical and chemical activity in the brain can produce thought and emotion. We know from neuroscience studies that the nervous impulses, those tiny electrical charges discussed early in this chapter, represent the basic activity that goes on inside the nervous system. Each neuron ordinarily produces only one kind of impulse, its own little unvarying "beep." Yet somehow these monotonous beeps—by the rate at which they are produced, the patterns they form, and the way they are routed through the brain—manage to account for the miracles of human cognition and consciousness. They tell us what our eyes see and our ears hear. They enable us to learn and to think. They direct our glands and internal organs to function in harmony. They direct our muscles to perform such intricate and delicate feats as driving an automobile or playing a violin.

Different neurons, in transmitting their nervous impulses, release different kinds of neurotransmitter chemicals at the synapse. These chemicals must be properly balanced if the whole enterprise is to function properly. Anything that affects the amount and effectiveness of these chemicals in the brain cells is likely to profoundly influence our thoughts, feelings, and activities.

A growing number of brain chemicals are generally recognized as neurotransmitters. Some investigators suggest the existence of as many as 300, and many others are likely to be identified (Kandel & Schwartz, 1985). They are necessary for normal brain functioning and behavior, and, when the balance is disturbed, serious psychological problems may arise.

Three of the best known neurotransmitters are **acetylcholine,** which is involved in motor activity as well as the memory problems of patients with Alzheimer's disease; **norepinephrine,** involved in arousal as well as states of depression; and **dopamine,** involved in goal-related motor behaviors as well as Parkinson's disease.

In addition to the neurotransmitters, there are other essential chemicals known as **peptides.** Some of these chemicals act like neurotransmitters. But most are more like hormones, because they are usually released into the bloodstream and affect both parts of the nervous system and distant organs outside it. Scientists first discovered some of these substances in locations far from the brain, such as in the intestines.

Brain peptides can be as powerful in their effects as synthetically manufactured drugs prescribed by doctors. Some seem to affect parts of the brain

Acetylcholine (uh-see-til-KOH-leen)
The neurotransmitter involved in motor activity and the memory problems of Alzheimer's patients.

Norepinephrine (nor-ep-pee-NEFF-rin)
The neurotransmitter involved in arousal and depression.

Dopamine
The neurotransmitter involved in goal-related motor behaviors and Parkinson's disease.

Peptides
Hormone-like chemicals affecting the nervous system and distant organs.

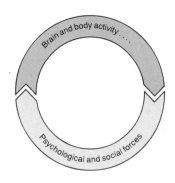

FIGURE 2.18 Biological and behavioral forces: A two-way affair Just as the functioning of the brain and body can affect behavior, the reverse is true as well—as explained in the text.

Corticotropin-release factor (CRF)

A peptide secreted by the hypothalamus.

Cortisol

The hormone secreted by the adrenal gland during emotional upset.

Endorphins

Peptides or brain chemicals affecting pain and mood.

Testosterone

The male sex hormone.

associated with pain and with emotion and mood (Bloom, Lazerson, & Hofstadter, 1985). Others have profound influences on behavior—including, for example, drinking, muscular movement, and memory (Iversen, 1982). One important peptide, called **corticotropin-release factor,** (**CRF**), is secreted by the hypothalamus. Through stimulation of the pituitary, it leads to the production of **cortisol** by the adrenal gland in response to emotionally stressful events and pain. More than 100 peptides have already been identified, with new ones continuously emerging (National Institute of Mental Health, 1988; Snyder, 1984).

One group of brain peptides has been named **endorphins**—from the Greek word meaning "the morphine within"—because it is similar in structure and effect to the powerful painkiller morphine (Thompson, 1985). The endorphins may help explain the mystery of acupuncture (sticking fine needles into various parts of the body), an ancient technique widely used by Chinese physicians to reduce pain and treat physical ailments. Applying needles in this way seems to increase production of the brain's own brand of morphine—as if a natural pain barrier is set up when the needle is inserted (Facklam & Facklam, 1982). There are hints that substances derived from endorphins can help in treating schizophrenia (Snyder, 1982), but the therapeutic uses of these chemicals are just beginning to be explored.

Our understanding of brain peptides, and of endorphins in particular, is accelerating by leaps and bounds. However, because much of this knowledge is quite new (the first endorphins were discovered only in 1975), our picture of how many brain peptides there are and what they can do is still sketchy. It is clear, however, that they play an important part in our feelings and behavior.

The Interplay of Biological and Psychological Forces

As this chapter has shown, biological factors—for example, hormone levels, neurotransmitter activity, or brain injury—can affect behavior. It is important to recognize also, however, that behavioral factors—our environment, our social interactions—can affect our biological state. As indicated in Figure 2.18, the relationship between biological and psychological forces is reciprocal.

Consider this example, drawn from animal research. It is known that the sexual activity of male monkeys reflects the level of **testosterone,** the male sex hormone. Studies have shown, however, that levels of testosterone vary as a function of the social situation in which an animal finds himself. If a male is placed in contact with female monkeys in an environment that excludes other males, his testosterone level will increase—and these increased levels are accompanied by increased sexual activity. On the other hand, when the male is placed in a setting in which he is dominated by other males, his testosterone levels will decrease—leading, in turn, to lower levels of sexual activity. While hormones affect behavior, hormonal activity appears to be regulated by the social milieu (Moberg, 1987).

A similar reciprocal relationship between biological and psychological factors is evident in many studies of humans as well. As will be described later in this book, for example, it is known that biological factors—genetic inheritance, brain malfunctions—play a role in the development of serious forms of mental illness. But it is equally true that these vulnerabilities are triggered when individuals encounter experiences that give rise to psychological turmoil and stress (National Institute of Mental Health, 1989a).

Studies of these sorts serve as an important reminder of the danger of trying to reduce all behavior to its biological correlates. Seymour Kety, a leading investigator of the biological foundations of behavior, acknowledges that remarkable progress has been made in understanding the structures of the brain, the relationships among its parts, and the effects of brain chemistry on behavior. But he maintains that biology is not able with its tools alone to unravel the mysteries of human personality and experience (Kety, 1982). Nobel Prize–winning brain scientist John Eccles has observed: "I go all the way with my fellow scientists in understanding the brain physically. But it doesn't explain me, or human choice, delight, courage, or compassion. I think we must go beyond. . . . There is something apart from all the electricity and chemistry we can measure" (Facklam & Facklam, 1982). As Roger Sperry has put it, "the events of inner experience" are important to study in their own right as causal factors in human behavior (Sperry, 1988).

Psychologists work to understand human behavior at many different levels—from analyzing the most minute workings of brain cells to the broad interactions of people with one another in groups, from observing behavior in animals to plumbing the breadth and depth of human feelings. All of these approaches are needed to answer the central question: How and why do we behave as we do? Understanding how the brain works is an essential part of the picture, but it is only one part. The remaining chapters will show how other aspects of psychology also help to answer the same question.

SUMMARY REVIEW

How the Brain Governs Human Behavior

1. The *brain* governs all our psychological and physical functions through its connections with other parts of the body.

2. The brain contains more than 100 billion **neurons,** or nerve cells; each neuron receives, processes, and transmits messages to thousands of others throughout the body.

3. In addition to transmitting messages, some neurons act as sense organs sensitive to changes in body temperature and blood chemistry (thus detecting when the body needs more food or water), while others act as glands that secrete chemicals into the bloodstream (thus stimulating many kinds of bodily activity).

4. Each neuron in the nervous system is a fiberlike cell with receivers called **dendrites** at one end and senders called **end branches** at the other. Stimulation of the neuron at its dendrites—or at **receptor sites** on its cell body—sets off a nervous impulse that travels the length of the fiber, or **axon,** to the **end branches,** where the impulse activates other neurons, muscles, or glands.

5. A neuron ordinarily fires on the **all or none principle,** meaning that if it fires at all, it fires as hard as it can. Most neurons have a maximum firing rate of several hundred times a second.

6. The key to the transmission of nervous messages is the **synapse,** a junction point where a sender of one neuron is separated by only a microscopic distance from a receiver of another neuron.

7. The sending neuron can stimulate the receiving neuron electrically at times, but it usually releases chemical **neurotransmitters** that flow across the tiny gap of the synapse and act on the receiving neuron.

8. The neurons of the brain affect behavior through the rest of the nervous system, which is made up of various kinds of neurons connected with the brain. The **peripheral nervous system** is made up of the outlying neurons throughout the body. The **central nervous system** is made up of the brain and spinal cord.

9. **Afferent neurons** carry impulses from the sense organs to the brain. **Efferent neurons** carry messages from the brain to the glands and muscles. **Connecting neurons** are the intermediaries between other neurons.

10. The topmost and largest part of the brain is the **cerebrum,** covered by the **cerebral cortex.**

11. The cerebrum and its cortex are split down the middle into a **left hemisphere** and a **right hemisphere.**

12. The cerebral cortex, larger in human beings in relation to body size than in any other species, is the part of the brain responsible for remembering, thinking, and planning.

The Brain's Functions: I. Experiencing the World

13. The specialized areas of the cerebral cortex responsible for analyzing and interpreting messages from the sense organs are referred to as the **somatosensory cortex.**

14. The **thalamus** is a relay and processing center for messages from the sense organs and for motor commands from the cerebral cortex to the peripheral nervous system.

15. The **reticular activating system** helps keep the top part of the brain in a state of arousal and activity.

16. The specialized strip on the cerebral cortex that controls body movements and speech is called the **motor cortex.**

17. The **cerebellum** controls body balance and the coordination of complicated muscular movements.

The Brain's Functions: 2. Managing Thought and Memory

18. The **association cortex,** which makes up the unspecified areas of the cerebral cortex, is concerned with consciousness—the awareness of self and the ability to think about the past and imagine the future.

19. The association areas in the front portion of the brain—called the **frontal lobes**—seem to play a key role in such human capacities as solving problems, planning, and relating the past with the present.

20. The **hippocampus** appears to be essential in the transformation of new information into long-lasting memories.

21. The rapid development of the cerebral cortex in early life is related to the growth of the child's intellectual abilities.
22. The **right hemisphere** of the brain deals with the left side of the body. The **left hemisphere** controls the right side of the body and the use of language; in most people it is the dominant hemisphere.
23. The two hemispheres are in constant communication through the **corpus callosum,** a thick cable of interconnecting neurons.
24. Experiments with patients whose corpus callosum has been cut—split-brain patients—indicate that the left hemisphere specializes in individual items of information, logic, and reasoning, while the right hemisphere specializes in information about form, space, music, and entire patterns, and is the intuitive half of the brain.

The Brain's Functions: 3. Overseeing Emotions and Survival

25. The **limbic system,** a network of brain structures and pathways, helps regulate emotional behavior.
26. One of these structures, the **amygdala,** comes into play in the experience of such intense emotions as anger and fear, and through its connections with various portions of the cortex, triggers the actions taken in response.
27. A prominent part of the limbic system is the **hypothalamus**—the brain's most direct link to the body glands that are active in emotions. The master gland, the **pituitary,** is attached to the hypothalamus.
28. The hypothalamus also plays a role in maintaining the body's **homeostasis,** the state of stability in such matters as internal temperature and chemical balance.
29. The **medulla** is responsible for a number of essential bodily processes including breathing, heart rate, and digestion.
30. The **autonomic nervous system** exercises a more or less independent control over the glands, the heart muscles, and the muscles of the body's organs and blood vessels. It helps regulate breathing, heart rate, blood pressure, and digestion. In times of emergency it works in conjunction with the endocrine glands to mobilize the body's resources for drastic action.
31. The **endocrine glands,** or ductless glands, influence behavior by secreting hormones (or activators) into the bloodstream. The most important endocrine glands are:
    a) The *pineal,* which affects sleep-waking rhythms and mood.
    b) The *pituitary,* which is the master gland, producing hormones that control growth, cause sexual development at puberty, and regulate other glands.
    c) The *parathyroids,* which maintain a normal state of excitability of the nervous system.
    d) The *thyroid,* which regulates metabolism and affects levels of body activity, temperature, and weight.

e) The *adrenals,* which secrete the powerful stimulants adrenalin (active in states of emergency or fear) and noradrenalin (active during physical effort or anger).

f) The *pancreas,* which governs blood sugar level.

g) The female *ovaries* and male *testes,* which regulate sexual characteristics and behavior.

32. The autonomic nervous system is composed of two parts: (1) the **parasympathetic division,** which is most active under ordinary circumstances; and (2) the **sympathetic division,** which is active in emergencies.

33. There may be differences between the two sides of the brain in the regulation of emotion; the right hemisphere appears to be more active in regulating negative emotions, while the left hemisphere appears to be more active in regulating positive emotions.

Neuroscience: New Investigations of the Brain-Behavior Link

34. Advances in brain research have led to the establishment of the field of **neuroscience**—which combines elements of several scientific fields, including psychology and its study of the behavioral functions of the brain.

35. Those who studied the brain in the past had to depend on inferences about it rather than on the organ itself. Today, in contrast, techniques are available that make it possible for researchers to study the brain in action—its electrical activity, structure, blood flow, and chemistry.

36. In addition to the standard **EEG (electroencephalogram),** which provides tracings of the brain's continuous "waves" of electrical activity, new brain-imaging techniques include the **CAT (computerized axial tomography) scan** and the **PET (positron emission tomography) scan;** these permit insights into the functioning of the brain while the individual is engaged in a specific activity.

37. Anything that alters the amount and effectiveness of neurotransmitters in the brain is likely to profoundly influence thoughts, feelings, and activities.

38. Among the best-known neurotransmitters are **acetylcholine** (which seems to be involved in the memory problems of patients with Alzheimer's disease), **norepinephrine** (involved with other neurotransmitters, in major depression), and **dopamine** (involved in schizophrenia and Parkinson's disease).

39. **Peptides** are chemicals that act like neurotransmitters but are more like hormones, since they are released into the bloodstream and affect both parts of the nervous system and the distant organs outside it. One group of brain peptides, called **endorphins,** is similar in structure and effect to the powerful painkiller morphine.

40. Just as biological factors can affect human behavior, so, too, can behavioral factors—our environment, our social interactions—affect our biological state.

a) The afferent neurons were likely affected. They carry messages from the sense organs—including the skin—to the brain. In contrast, the efferent neurons carry messages from the brain outward, thus directing the activities of the body—for example, the muscular activity involved in throwing a football.

b) Jim Brady's brain was badly damaged, and damage to the brain is lasting because its neurons cannot regenerate and thus rekindle the powers that have been destroyed.

c) The soldier is likely to have problems seeing. As shown in Figure 2.7 on page 58, the back part of the cortex is responsible for vision.

d) The cerebellum coordinates the kind of finely regulated finger movements a violinist uses, and the kind of body balance and equilibrium a ballerina requires.

e) Grandfather's hippocampus is probably involved. It is a key structure of the brain in storing and retrieving information.

f) The brain disorder that would come to mind is Parkinson's disease, and the neurotransmitter diminished in the brain would be dopamine.

g) The right hemisphere of the brain is more heavily involved than the left when dealing with visual and spatial information; therefore it is more active in the work of the architect.

h) The evidence is that one portion of the hypothalamus appears to be considerably smaller than normal in the brains of homosexual men.

i) The pituitary gland (see Figure 2.14, page 72) sparks the body's sex hormones to begin to flow more actively at puberty.

j) The second experience undoubtedly caused the sympathetic division to spring into action—for it does so whenever we feel intense emotions such as fear or anger.

k) The left hemisphere is likely to be more active when you're feeling happy.

l) She would be most likely to use the PET scan. The EEG gives only a picture of the overall activity of the brain—but the PET scan allows us to actually see which portions of the brain are involved as a person engages in specific activities.

m) The researcher would be more likely to study the role of brain chemistry. Neuroscience focuses on the relationship between the brain—including its chemical activity—and behavior.

Study Guide

Chapter 2   Brain, Body, and Behavior

LEARNING OBJECTIVES

After studying this chapter, you should be able to:

1. Understand that there are more than 100 billion neurons in the human brain—and especially in the cerebrum and cerebral cortex—that govern all our behavior.

For an Understanding of the Science

2. Recognize the fact that the brain has at least 100 different types of neurons—specialized to perform tasks like transmitting messages, serving as miniature sense organs to detect changes in the body's chemical balance and temperature, and directing the secretion of hormones that influence many bodily and psychological activities.

3. Describe the structure of a typical neuron; the functions of the dendrites, axons, and neurotransmitters; and know the all or none principle of how neurons produce messages.

4. Understand how the brain and spinal cord, which make up the central nervous system, exchange messages with a peripheral nervous system that extends throughout the body, and the different roles of the network's afferent, efferent, and connecting neurons.

5. Describe the brain structures that perform the important function of sensing what is going on in the world and taking action; these structures include the cerebral cortex and its specialized areas (for receiving and interpreting messages from the sense organs and for sending signals that control bodily movements) and the cerebellum (which coordinates muscular movements).

6. Recognize that the cerebral cortex is also largely responsible for the important function of enabling us to remember (and thus to learn), think, and plan for the future.

7. Understand how the cerebrum and its cortex are divided into two hemispheres that cooperate through an interconnecting cable called the corpus callosum, with the left hemisphere largely responsible for language and logical thinking and the right hemisphere for spatial relationships, considering things as a whole, and intuition.

8. Describe how the brain performs other important functions by controlling bodily processes, which it keeps in a state of homeostasis, and regulating our emotions.

9. Understand the part played in physical well-being by the brain's hypothalamus and medulla, and the part played in emotion by the brain's limbic system, the autonomic nervous system, and the various endocrine glands.

For Application to Life Situations

10. Understand that the human brain—especially its cerebrum and cerebral cortex, which are proportionately much larger and more highly developed than in any other species—accounts for our remarkable ability at information processing and gives us each our special identity as a human being.

11. Describe how the hormones and other chemicals directed by the brain play an important part in moods, emotions, and resistance to pain, and that our increasing knowledge of brain chemistry may someday explain and perhaps point to cures for such mental disturbances as schizophrenia and Alzheimer's disease.

12. Understand that although fear and anger can be upsetting and destructive, our emotions help us cope with the world and meet its crises, and that without the capacity for emotions such as joy and love our lives would be flat and barren.

PROGRAMMED UNIT
HOW THE BRAIN GOVERNS HUMAN BEHAVIOR

1. The *brain,* which contains more than 100 billion individual nerve cells or *neurons,* is a miracle organ that accounts for all human capabilities—from information processing and feeling emotion to coping with stress and relating to other people. Everything we do from waking in the morning to closing our eyes at night—and even when we are sound asleep—is accomplished by the remarkable powers of the human _____.

   brain

2. The brain's nerve cells or _____ are all intricately connected with each other and with other nerve cells throughout the body.

   neurons

3. The primary job of most of the brain's cells or _____ is transmitting messages. Some cells in the brain, called *glia,* serve to keep the neurons in place and to provide them with nourishment, while other cells operate much like miniature glands, producing complex chemicals called *hormones,* from the Greek word meaning "activators" or "exciters."

   neurons

4. The chemicals produced and directed by the brain, which travel through the bloodstream and influence many physical and psychological activities, are known as _____. The nutritional and structural support cells in the brain are called _____.

   hormones
   glia

5. At one end of the nervous system's basic cellular unit, known as the _____, are the *dendrites,* which are branching structures that receive messages from other neurons.

   neuron

6. When a single neuron is stimulated, the message is often received by the _____, but impulses can also be received along the cell body at numerous *receptor sites.*

   dendrites

7. A neuron can thus be stimulated at the _____ as well as at other _____ _____. Once initiated, the nervous impulse travels down the fiber-like *axon* to the *end branches.*

   dendrites, receptor sites

8. The sending end of a neuron consists of the _____ and the _____ _____. Between them lies the *cell body* containing a *nucleus.*

   axon, end branches

9. Receptor sites are located along the _____ _____, while the cell's genetic material is contained in the _____. The entire neuron may be covered with a protective *myelin sheath.*

   cell
   body
   nucleus

10. A whitish coating of fatty protective tissue that increases the speed at which the nervous impulse travels along the neuron is the _____ _____.

    myelin sheath

11. The *synapse* is the point at which two _____ almost touch.

    neurons

12. Impulses are transmitted from one neuron to another across the _____. The impulse is assisted in jumping this gap by chemical substances called *neurotransmitters.*

    synapse

13. When a neuron fires, the sending structures of the neuron release _____ at the _____, which aid the transmission of the impulse from one neuron to the next.

    neurotransmitters
    synapse

14. The actual synapse with another neuron occurs at the *synaptic knobs,* the neurotransmitters are stored in the *synaptic vesicles,* and they flow across the *synaptic cleft* to act on the receptors of the second neuron. So the neu-

vesicles
knobs, cleft

rotransmitter is released by the synaptic _____, travels to the synaptic _____, and bridges the synaptic _____ to stimulate the
receptors of another neuron.

neuron
dendrites, receptor
sites, cell
body
nucleus
axon, end branches

15. To summarize, the main cell of the nervous system, the _____,
receives impulses at the _____ or at the _____
_____ located along the _____ _____. The impulse
travels down the cell body, past the cell's genetic material contained in
the _____, toward the sending end or _____ which contains
the _____ _____.

myelin sheath

16. The speed of the impulse along the cell body is increased if the neuron is
wrapped with a _____ _____.

synapse, neurotransmitters
vesicles
knobs
cleft

17. The neural impulse is sent to another neuron at the _____. Chemicals, called _____, are stored in the synaptic _____. They are
transferred to the synaptic _____ and injected into the synaptic
_____ to facilitate the transmission of the impulse to the next
neuron.

receptor sites

18. Whether a neuron fires or not depends on a whole pattern of messages
it receives. A single neuron may be stimulated simultaneously at different
_____ _____, some of which cause the neuron to fire while
others inhibit its firing. The result depends on the total collection of such
impulses. But ordinarily, once a neuron fires, it follows the *all or none*
principle.

all or none

19. That is, if a neuron fires at all, it fires as hard as it can, or essentially
_____ _____ _____.

neurons

20. The brain, with its 100-plus billion intricately interconnected _____,
is one part of the *central nervous system*. The other part is the *spinal cord,* a
sort of master cable carrying messages to and from the brain down the
length of the spine.

spinal cord
central nervous

21. The brain and the _____ _____ make up the _____
_____ system, which has many elaborate interconnections with the
outlying nerve cells of the body from head to fingertips and toes. Those
outlying nerve cells are the *peripheral nervous system,* which is a network
extending throughout the body.

brain, spinal cord
peripheral

22. The central nervous system, consisting of the _____ and the
_____ _____, gets messages from and controls movements in
all parts of the body, because it connects with the wide-reaching network
of the _____ nervous system.

peripheral nervous
system

23. All the neurons we possess, in the brain, spinal cord, and the _____
_____ _____, fall into three classes. One class is *afferent* neurons, which carry messages from the eyes, ears, and other sense organs to
the brain.

afferent

24. In addition to the neurons that carry messages toward the brain, known as
_____ neurons, we also have *efferent* neurons that carry messages
away from the brain and spinal cord to the body's muscles, organs, and
glands.

efferent

25. The brain's messages are directed outward toward the rest of the body
through _____ neurons.

afferent

26. The third class of neurons, besides the _____ neurons that carry

messages toward the brain and the _____ neurons that carry messages away from the brain, is the *connecting neurons,* which, as their name indicates, carry messages between other neurons.

efferent

27. Nerve cells that carry messages between other nerve cells are _____ neurons.

connecting

28. If you could look down through the top of the skull, you would see the important part of the _____ called the *cerebral cortex.* It is larger in proportion to body size in human beings than in most other species, and it is chiefly responsible for the ability to remember, think, and plan—all skills that make human beings more intelligent than lower animals.

brain

29. Human skill at all kinds of information processing is governed by the _____ _____, which is the surface—like the thick wrinkled skin of a prune—of the brain's largest single structure, the *cerebrum.*

cerebral cortex

30. The largest single structure of the brain, overlaid by the cerebral cortex, is the _____.

cerebrum

31. The cerebrum and its covering, the _____ _____, are split down the middle into a *left hemisphere* and a *right hemisphere.*

cerebral cortex

32. The two halves of the _____ are the left and right _____.

cerebrum, hemispheres

THE BRAIN'S FUNCTIONS: 1. EXPERIENCING THE WORLD

33. Most of the information picked up by the sense organs is eventually transmitted to the cerebral cortex, especially to a long strip known as the *somatosensory cortex.* Messages for touch from the feet to the head are received by the _____ _____.

somatosensory cortex

34. Information from the outside world is also processed and organized in the lower parts of the brain before it reaches the cortex, for example by the *thalamus.* A relay station for censoring messages from the body to the cortex is the _____.

thalamus

35. Sensory information is also processed in the network of nerve cells near the base of the brain called the *reticular activating system.* Nerve pathways carrying messages from the sense organs to the cerebrum have side branches to an area near the base of the brain, which under a microscope appears to be a criss-crossed pattern of nerve fibers, known as the

_____ _____ _____.

reticular activating system

36. Once the brain is stimulated by the _____ _____ _____, the motor cortex of the brain may instruct the muscles of the body to act.

reticular activating system

37. Initiating and controlling bodily movements is accomplished by the _____ _____, but the *cerebellum* plays an important part in coordinating finely regulated muscular movements such as typing and playing a musical instrument.

motor cortex

38. People have great difficulty performing such coordinated muscle movements as walking or talking if they suffer damage to the brain structure called the _____.

cerebellum

39. Like the cerebrum, the cerebellum is divided into two lobes or _____, which are connected by the *pons.*

hemispheres

40. The bridge or cable that transmits messages between the two hemispheres of the _____ is the _____.

cerebellum, pons

cortex

41. The brain's function of sensing the world and taking action, as has just been explained, is performed largely by the specialized areas of the cerebral _____. These specialized areas make up about a quarter of the cortex, and the remaining three-quarters is called the *association cortex,* which is responsible for all our intellectual processes.

association
cortex

42. The ability to remember, think, plan for the future, and process information in ways that raise human beings far beyond the level of other organisms is performed by unspecified areas that make up the _____ _____.

association cortex

frontal lobes

43. The front portion of the _____ _____ includes the *frontal lobes.* The areas apparently involved in solving problems, planning, and relating the past with the present are the _____ _____.

frontal
lobes, association cortex

44. A brain-damaged person who can remember her child's birthday but cannot plan the child's birthday party may have a disability in the _____ _____ of the _____ _____.

hippocampus

45. The brain relies on another of its structures, called the *hippocampus,* to establish long-term memories. A brain structure involved in forming long-term memories that may be damaged in some people who have amnesia is the _____.

hippocampus
explicit, semantic memory
implicit, procedural
memories
hemispheres

46. The hippocampus, however, seems to be essential for *semantic memory* but not for *procedural memory.* A person with damage to the _____ might have difficulty remembering names, words, facts, ideas, and other kinds of _____ but not tying shoes, playing golf, or other kinds of _____.

47. As explained earlier, the cerebrum and its cortex are divided down the middle into left and right _____. The left half, dominant in most people, controls language and the right side of the body. The right half controls the left side of the body and seems to specialize in interpreting form and space.

right
left

48. The left hemisphere controls language and the _____ side of the body, while the right hemisphere controls the _____ side of the body and the processing of form and space.

49. Although the two hemispheres have different emphases, most functions we perform use both sides of the brain, which are coordinated very closely through numerous interconnections, especially through a cable called the *corpus callosum* that connects the left and right _____ of the cerebrum.

hemispheres

corpus callosum

50. The master cable between the two halves of the cerebrum and its cortex is the _____ _____.

THE BRAIN'S FUNCTIONS: 3. OVERSEEING EMOTIONS AND SURVIVAL

51. Of special importance in emotional life is the *limbic system,* which makes up about one-fifth of the brain. Anger and fear as well as sexual behavior are controlled by the _____ _____.

limbic system

52. One part of the limbic system is the *hippocampus,* which, as mentioned

above, is involved in long-term memory. If the _____ decides a new stimulus is threatening, then the *amygdala* may come into play.

hippocampus

53. The part of the _____ _____ involved in intense emotions such as anger and fear is the _____.

limbic system
amygdala

54. Another part of the limbic system is the *hypothalamus*. The brain's most direct link to the body's *glands* is the _____.

hypothalamus

55. The organs that secrete substances that help produce the "stirred-up" bodily processes that accompany fear, anger, and other emotions are the _____. The body's master gland is the *pituitary*, which is attached to the hypothalamus.

glands

56. There is a direct link from the limbic system to the body's master gland, the _____.

pituitary

57. The hypothalamus, besides the role it plays in emotion in cooperation with other parts of the _____ system and the _____, also contributes to physical well-being by keeping the body in a state of *homeostasis*, or stability, in such matters as internal temperature and chemical balance.

limbic, glands

58. The hypothalamus signals when the body needs food, water, or sleep, thus contributing to the state of bodily stability or balance called _____.

homeostasis

59. In addition to signaling when the body has a need for food, water, or sleep, the _____ also acts like a thermostat that controls bodily temperature.

hypothalamus

60. Our physical well-being demands not only a state of stability or _____ in temperature and chemical balance, but also the steady performance of vital bodily processes such as breathing, heart rate, and digestion. These bodily processes are coordinated and kept working smoothly by another brain structure called the *medulla*.

homeostasis

61. Coordinating vital processes such as breathing and heartbeat is the responsibility of the _____.

medulla

62. In controlling bodily process and maintaining a state of _____, the brain has a valuable assistant in the *autonomic nervous system,* or ANS for short. The word "autonomic" means independent or self-sufficient, and the _____ _____ _____ operates largely on its own, without much conscious control.

homeostasis

autonomic nervous system

63. The ANS can command the heart to beat faster or slower and the blood vessels to channel a strong flow of blood to the stomach to aid digestion or toward the arms and legs when physical work is to be done. The largely self-sufficient system, called the _____ _____ system, exercises considerable power over the body's *endocrine glands,* or glands of internal secretion, which also operate without much direct conscious control.

autonomic nervous

64. The ANS influences the _____ glands, whose secretions (or hormones) are discharged into the bloodstream, travel to all parts of the body, and affect many bodily activities, including those associated with emotional behavior.

endocrine

65. The ANS, or _____ _____ _____, exerts its impact on important bodily processes through a number of neural centers called *ganglia*. The "small brains" composed of masses of connected nerve cells packed together and distributed throughout the body are called _____.

autonomic nervous system

ganglia

ANS

66. The autonomic nervous system, known for short as the _____, has two divisions: the *sympathetic division* and the *parasympathetic division*. Both are connected to the endocrine glands and other organs.

67. The sympathetic division acts in various ways to prepare the body for emergency action—such as fighting or running away. The other part of the ANS, the _____ division, seems to play its most important role when no danger threatens and the body can relax and go about the ordinary business of living.

parasympathetic

68. Meeting emergency situations—by taking such steps as ordering the glands to pour powerful stimulants into the bloodstream and enlarging the blood vessels that carry oxygen to the heart and muscles of body movement—is the function of the _____ _____ of the ANS.

sympathetic division

69. When no danger threatens and the body can relax, the autonomic nervous system's _____ _____ slows down the heart and encourages digestion by ordering the stomach to make wavelike motions and produce digestive acid.

parasympathetic division

70. In emergency situations, the _____ division is active. In contrast, when the body goes about the typical business of living, the _____ division is active.

sympathetic parasympathetic

NEUROSCIENCE: NEW INVESTIGATIONS OF THE BRAIN-BEHAVIOR LINK

71. The relation between brain and behavior is part of a new field called *neuroscience*. A science consisting of the fusion of elements of several disciplines, including biochemistry, physiology, anatomy, pharmacology, and psychology, all geared to acquiring a fuller understanding of how the brain governs behavior, is called _____.

neuroscience

72. Neuroscientists study the activity of the cortex and cerebrum with the help of the *electroencephalogram* (*EEG*) and newer *brain-imaging* techniques. A method introduced more than a half century ago, which consists of amplified tracings of the brain's continuous "waves" of electrical activity recorded through electrodes placed on the scalp, is the _____.

electroencephalogram

73. While information about the overall electrical activity of the brain can be provided by the _____, or _____ for short, overall views or scans of the brain itself are produced by the newer _____-_____ techniques, including the *computerized axial tomography* scan (*CAT*) and the *magnetic resonance imaging* scan (*MRI*).

electroencephalogram, EEG brain-imaging

74. X-ray images collected from various angles around the skull, a technique called the _____ _____ _____ scan, provides a particular look at a "slice of the brain," while a three-dimensional picture of the brain can be obtained by the _____ _____ _____ scan.

computerized axial tomography magnetic resonance imaging

75. A third _____-_____ technique is the *positron emission tomography* (*PET*) scan. Injections of small amounts of a radioactive substance are traced with the _____ _____ _____ scan.

brain-imaging positron emission tomography

76. The new study of _____ also examines the roles of many chemicals on brain functioning.

neuroscience

77. For example, recall that impulses are transmitted from one neuron to another with the help of chemical neurotransmitters, three of which

are acetylcholine, norepinephrine, and dopamine. In addition to these _____, other essential chemicals known as *peptides* act like neuro-transmitters, but most are like hormones because they are usually released into the bloodstream and affect both parts of the nervous system and different organs outside of it.

neurotransmitters

78. One of these _____ is *corticotropin-release factor*. Secreted by the hypothalamus, _____-_____ _____ leads to the production of cortisol in response to emotionally stressful events and pain.

peptides
corticotropin-release factor

79. Another group of these brain _____ has been named *endorphins*, from the Greek word meaning "the morphine within." Chemicals similar in structure and effect to the powerful painkiller morphine are called _____. These may help explain the mystery of acupuncture as well as the ability of the body to resist the pain in marathon running.

peptides

endorphins

80. The new set of different scientific disciplines, collectively called _____, studies the relations between brain functioning, its physiological and chemical makeup, including _____ and _____, and its effects on behavior.

neuroscience

neurotransmitters, peptides

REVIEW OF IMPORTANT TERMS

acetylcholine (77)

afferent neuron (55)

all or none principle (53)

amygdala (67)

association cortex (61)

autonomic nervous system (ANS) (69)

axon (52)

brain imaging (76)

CAT (computerized axial tomography) scan (76)

cell body (52)

central nervous system (CNS) (55)

cerebellum (61)

cerebral cortex (56)

cerebrum (56)

connecting neuron (55)

corpus callosum (66)

corticotropin-release factor (CRF) (78)

cortisol (78)

dendrite (52)

dopamine (77)

EEG (electroencephalogram) (76)

efferent neuron (55)

end branches (52)

endocrine gland (ductless gland) (70)

endorphins (78)

frontal lobes (62)

ganglia (71)

glia (51)

hippocampus (62)

homeostasis (69)

hormone (51)

hypothalamus (68)

immune system (75)

left hemisphere (56)

limbic system (67)

medulla (69)

motor cortex (60)

MRI (magnetic resonance imaging) scan (76)

myelin sheath (52)

neurons (51)

neuroscience (75)

neurotransmitter (53)

nodes (52)

norepinephrine (77)

nucleus (52)

parasympathetic division (72)

peptides (77)

peripheral nervous system (PNS) (55)

PET (positron emission tomography) scan (76)

pituitary (68)

plasticity (56)

pons (61)

procedural memory (63)

rapid eye movement (REM) (65)

receptor site (52)

reticular activating system (RAS) (59)

right hemisphere (56)

semantic memory (63)

somatosensory cortex (57)

spinal cord (55)

sympathetic division (73)

synapse (53)

synaptic cleft (53)

synaptic knobs (53)

synaptic vesicles (53)

testosterone (78)

thalamus (59)

PRACTICE TEST

_____ 1. Within a neuron, the nervous impulse travels from
   a.   axon to dendrites.
   b.   cell body to dendrites.
   c.   dendrites to end branches.
   d.   nucleus to cell body.

_____ 2. The principal function of the myelin sheath is to
   a.   make the neuron more sensitive.
   b.   increase the strength of the nervous impulse.
   c.   protect the dendrites.
   d.   increase the speed of the nervous impulse.

_____ 3. The all or none principle is that
   a.   a neuron stimulates all the other neurons in the ganglion if it stimulates any one of them.
   b.   a neuron will not fire unless all its receptor sites are stimulated.
   c.   all neurotransmitters are secreted at the synapse.
   d.   if a neuron fires at all, it fires as hard as it can.

_____ 4. The part of the brain that does most of our remembering, thinking, and planning is the
   a.   medulla.
   b.   cerebellum.
   c.   limbic system.
   d.   cerebral cortex.

_____ 5. The spinal cord is part of the
   a. peripheral nervous system.
   b. central nervous system.
   c. reticular activating system.
   d. parasympathetic system.

_____ 6. When a sense organ sends a message to the brain that results in a bodily movement, the sequence of neurons involved is
   a. connecting, afferent, efferent.
   b. efferent, connecting, afferent.
   c. afferent, connecting, efferent.
   d. afferent, efferent, connecting.

_____ 7. The major relay station for sensory messages passed from the body to the cortex is the
   a. thalamus.
   b. hypothalamus.
   c. reticular activating system.
   d. corpus callosum.

_____ 8. A sleeping animal can be awakened immediately by electrical stimulation applied to the
   a. hypothalamus.
   b. reticular activating system.
   c. limbic system.
   d. cerebellum.

_____ 9. The brain structure that coordinates the finely regulated muscular movements of a musician or typist is the
   a. sympathetic nervous system.
   b. limbic system.
   c. cerebellum.
   d. medulla.

_____ 10. An adult whose hippocampus has been damaged might have trouble
   a. remembering childhood events.
   b. remembering a new telephone number.
   c. speaking clearly.
   d. walking a straight line.

_____ 11. As the child develops into an adult,
   a. the number of neurons increases dramatically.
   b. the number of neurotransmitters and peptides increases.
   c. experiences have less effect on the brain.
   d. the number of synapses decreases.

_____ 12. The two hemispheres of the cerebrum communicate through the

    a.   corpus callosum.

    b.   hippocampus.

    c.   pons.

    d.   cerebellum.

_____ 13. The left hemisphere is more skilled at

    a.   interpreting speech and language.

    b.   seeing the forest, not the trees.

    c.   analyzing the melodies in a song.

    d.   judging the symmetry in a photograph.

_____ 14. The part of the brain chiefly responsible for emotion is the

    a.   limbic system.

    b.   reticular activating system.

    c.   thalamus.

    d.   hippocampus.

_____ 15. The master gland is the

    a.   thyroid.

    b.   adrenal.

    c.   parathyroid.

    d.   pituitary.

_____ 16. Homeostasis refers to

    a.   chemical balance within the body.

    b.   a stable relationship between the brain and the endocrine system.

    c.   an equal dominance of right and left hemispheres.

    d.   the ability to keep physical balance and to know up from down.

_____ 17. Coordination of vital bodily processes, such as breathing, heart rate, and digestion, takes place in the

    a.   synapse.

    b.   medulla.

    c.   somatosensory cortex.

    d.   frontal lobes.

_____ 18. The part of the nervous system that plays its most important role during periods of quiet when there is no threat or need for unusual action is the

    a.   sympathetic division.

    b.   ganglia.

    c.   parasympathetic division.

    d.   autonomic nervous system.

_____ 19. The parasympathetic and sympathetic divisions are part of the

    a. limbic system.

    b. central nervous system.

    c. peripheral nervous system.

    d. autonomic nervous system.

_____ 20. Acetylcholine, norepinephrine, and dopamine are all

    a. peptides.

    b. hormones.

    c. endorphins.

    d. neurotransmitters.

ANSWERS TO PRACTICE TEST

1. c	6. c	11. d	16. a
2. d	7. a	12. a	17. b
3. d	8. b	13. a	18. c
4. d	9. c	14. a	19. d
5. b	10. b	15. c	20. d

EXERCISES

I. Trace the path of a nervous impulse from its initiation at a single neuron through its transmission to another neuron. Specify the parts of the neuron and their functions, consider the role of chemicals in the process, and indicate what factors influence the speed or course of the impulse. Also, describe what changes occur in the development of the neuron during infancy and childhood.

II. Consider a man who is asleep on a couch, breathing regularly. He is awakened by an automobile horn, sits up, and looks around. When he stands, he has some trouble coordinating himself. He recognizes what the sound was, sits down, and works a crossword puzzle. Suddenly there is a noise in the rear of the house, sounding like a burglar. Alarmed, he rushes to the back room, but he finds nothing and soon relaxes again on the couch.

    Discuss the actions of this man in terms of what you know about the nervous system. Be specific about which structures may have played a part in each action and in what way.

C H A P T E R   3

Sensation and Perception

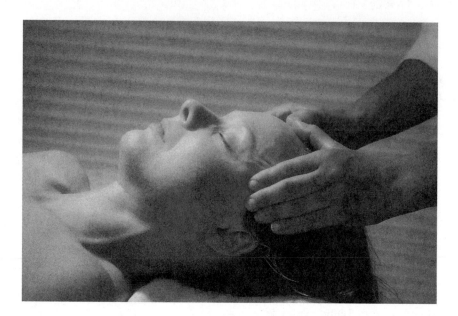

Massage of the skin excites receptors for touch and transmits the information to the brain.

All about us in our daily lives lies a wealth of information vital to our well-being. With total effortlessness, we experience constant interaction between the information coming to us from the environment and our responses to it. It is a process that we take completely for granted. The information-gathering structures of the nervous system are, in their own way, as remarkable as the brain itself.

Sensation

The process by which sense organs gather information about the environment.

Our senses are our windows on the world, and in studying **sensation,** we are exploring *the process by which the sense organs gather information about the environment.* Thus this chapter addresses one of psychology's basic questions: How do we become aware of all that is happening in the world outside ourselves? The manner in which the sense organs send their information to the brain—and the way the sensory areas of the cortex manage to understand the messages and translate them into our conscious sensations—is another of the marvels of the nervous system.

Perception

The process that permits us to become aware of our environment by selecting, organizing, and interpreting evidence from our senses.

Somehow we humans manage automatically to make sense of the ever-shifting stimulation the world provides to our sense organs. As illustrated in Figure 3.1, most of the time our central nervous system allows us to extract the precise information that is important to us without any conscious effort on our part. We know almost instantaneously what it all means. The key to this remarkable accomplishment is **perception,** which can be defined as *the process through which we become aware of our environment by selecting, organizing, and interpreting evidence from our senses.*

How Our Senses Function: Some General Principles

Stimulus

Any form of energy activating a sense organ.

Our sense organs vary, of course, in the sensations they produce, but they all work on a few basic principles. They have to be activated by a **stimulus**—any form of meaningful energy activating a sense organ. Take the case of vision, for example. The visual stimulus you are experiencing at this very moment is the light waves reflected off your book. But sense organs must also have a **receptor,** a nervous structure capable of responding to that particular kind of stimulus. When you read, the receptors are the light-sensitive cells in your eyes. You cannot see the book in a totally blackened room because there are no light waves, nor through your ears or fingertips because they have no receptors for light.

When receptor cells for vision are activated by a stimulus, they set off bursts of nervous impulses routed to the sensory areas for vision of the cerebral cortex. There they are translated into our conscious sensation of vision. The very same process—with different stimuli and different receptors—apply to all the other senses.

Our Thresholds for Sensory Experience

One principle that holds for all the senses is that they are activated only by a stimulus that is at or above their **absolute threshold,** the minimum amount of stimulus energy to which a receptor can respond at least 50 percent of the time. Any weaker stimulus has no effect and therefore goes unnoticed. When a physician tests your hearing by noting from how far away you can follow the ticking of a watch, the physician is making a rough estimate of your absolute threshold of hearing.

Receptor

A specialized nerve ending of one of the senses that is capable of responding to a stimulus.

Absolute threshold

The minimum amount of stimulus energy to which a receptor will respond at least 50 percent of the time.

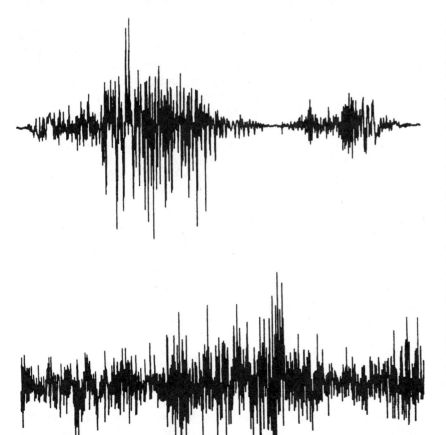

FIGURE 3.1   Making Out a Word in a Din of Conversation Both of the sound waves shown here depict the actual sound pressure generated by a human male voice saying the word "science." The top figure resulted when the voice spoke the word in the stillness of a soundproof chamber and the bottom figure resulted when the voice was masked by noise that simulated a roomful of people talking—for example, at a loud cocktail party. Neither the human eye nor any computer can detect the top wave form embedded in the bottom one; in other words, they cannot extract the sound waves made by saying "science" from the jumble of additional waves made by the noise. But miraculously, a normal listener has no trouble at all hearing and understanding the word through the accompanying noise (Gerstein et al., 1988).

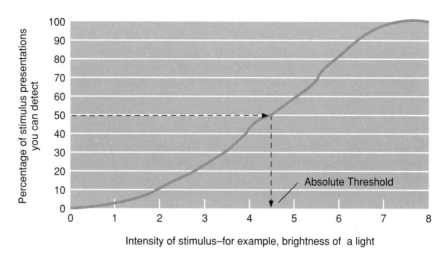

FIGURE 3.2 Estimating the Absolute Threshold As this figure indicates, the absolute threshold is actually not absolutely fixed. At times you may be able to detect a stimulus of a given intensity, at other times you may not. Your absolute threshold is the intensity required for you to make out the stimulus—in this case, a light—half the time.

Difference threshold

The smallest increase in intensity of a stimulus that permits the detection that it is different.

Sensory adaptation

The tendency of sensory receptors to adjust to a stimulus and stop responding after a time.

Wavelength

A characteristic of light waves that determines hue.

Intensity

The amount of energy in a visual stimulus that affects the sensation of brightness.

Brightness

A dimension of visual sensation dependent on intensity.

In scientific studies of the relationship between physical stimuli and sensations, more precise measurements are used. These show that stimuli of borderline intensity are sometimes detected and sometimes missed. As portrayed in Figure 3.2, the absolute threshold is defined as the energy level at which a subject can detect a stimulus 50 percent of the time. However, the absolute threshold will vary some, depending on the conditions under which the stimulus is presented. For example, background noise may affect whether a sound is detected, and motivation may affect the ability to make out a flashing light.

The senses also have a threshold for the ability to discriminate between two stimuli that are similar in strength but not identical. For example, suppose you see a flash of light, followed immediately by a different flash. How much more intense would the second light have to be before you could notice a difference? The answer is 1.6 percent. This is the **difference threshold** for light, also known as the *just noticeable difference,* or j.n.d. For sound the difference threshold is about 10 percent, with slight differences for high- and low-pitched sounds.

The rule that the difference threshold is a fixed percentage of the original stimulus is called *Weber's law,* in honor of the physiologist who discovered it more than a century ago. The law holds primarily over a large part of the range of stimulation. In practical terms, it means this: The more intense the sensory stimulation to which the human organism is being subjected, the greater the increase in intensity required to produce a recognizable difference. In a room where there is no sound except the soft buzz of a mosquito, you can hear a pin drop. On a noisy city street you can hear the loud honk of an automobile horn but may be completely unaware of a friend shouting to you from down the block.

The Sensory Adaptation Process

When you undress, you sometimes notice marks on your skin caused by a wristwatch, belt, or elastic band in your clothing. Surely those areas of skin have been subjected all day to a considerable amount of pressure. Why did you not feel it?

The answer lies in the principle of **sensory adaptation,** which means that after a time your senses adjust to a stimulus—they get used to it, so to speak—and the sensation produced by the stimulus tends to disappear. If you hold saltwater or a bitter fluid in your mouth, the taste goes away. The strong smell that greets you in a fish market also seems to disappear. Your eyes may strike you as an exception, because your vision never goes blank no matter how long you stare at an object, but this is only because the eyes are never really still. The muscles controlling the eyeballs constantly produce spontaneous, pendulum-like motions at the rate of as many as 100 a minute, which means that light rays never keep stimulating the same receptor cells for very long. By attaching a miniature slide projector to the eyeball, casting a continuing image on the same receptor cells despite any movements, it has been found that the image quickly fades from sight (Pritchard, 1961).

All the senses demonstrate adaptation in one way or another—though a new stimulus will immediately produce a new response. In practical terms, the principle of adaptation means that our sensory equipment is built to inform us of changes in the environment—exactly the kind of information that is most valuable.

The Power of Vision

The most remarkable thing about our eyes is the vast number of conscious sensations they produce. You can concentrate your vision on a single black word on the white page of this book—or look out the window and see an entire landscape full objects in what seems to be an infinite variety of shadings and hues. You can see a whole range of brightness from pure white through various grays to jet black, plus all the colors of the rainbow, in hues that run from vivid blue to muddy red. According to one estimate, our eyes are capable of distinguishing among 350,000 just noticeable differences in color and brightness—which means that the sense of vision has a tremendous scope.

Light Waves: The Visual Stimulus

The stimulus for vision is light waves, which are pulsations of electromagnetic energy. Light has three qualities that determine the sensations it produces:

1. **Wavelength,** the distance between the peaks of the waves, determines the hue, the scientific term for the color we see. White light is a mixture of all the hues.

2. **Intensity,** the amount of energy in the light wave, determines the sensation of **brightness,** although not entirely. The same intensity of light ordinarily produces greater brightness at the yellow and green wavelengths.

3. **Complexity,** the degree to which the predominant wavelength is somewhat mixed with other wavelengths, determines the sensation called **saturation.** The purer the wavelength, the greater the saturation and the more vivid the hue. When other wavelengths are mixed in, we see a hue that we often describe as duller or muddier. A pure or saturated red is strikingly colorful. If other wavelengths are added to reduce the saturation, what we see is "less red."

Complexity
A characteristic of a sound wave that determines the timbre we hear.

Saturation
The amount of pure hue present in a color as compared to amount of other light wavelengths mixed in.

Iris

The circular arrangement of smooth muscles that contract and expand to make the pupil smaller in bright light and larger in dim light.

Pupil

The opening in the iris that admits light waves into the eyeball.

Lens

The transparent structure of the eye that changes shape to focus images on the retina.

FIGURE 3.3   The structure of the eye Light waves first strike the *cornea,* a transparent bulge in the outer layer of the eyeball. The cornea serves as a sort of preliminary lens, gathering light waves from a much wider field of vision than would be possible if the eyeball merely had a perfectly flat window at the front. The light waves then pass through the *pupil,* which is an opening in the *iris,* a circular arrangement of smooth muscles that contract and expand to make the pupil smaller in bright light and larger in dim light. (When you look at your eyes in a mirror, the pupil is the dark, almost black circle at the center. The iris is the larger circle around it containing the pigments that determine eye color.) Behind the pupil lies the transparent *lens,* the shape of which is controlled by the *ciliary muscles.* The lens focuses the light rays on the *retina,* which contains the light-sensitive receptors of the eye. The receptors are most tightly packed in the *fovea,* where visual acuity is the greatest. Messages from the receptors are transmitted to the brain by way of the *optic nerve,* which exits from the back of the eyeball, a little off center. Attached to the eyeball are muscles that enable us to look up, down, and sideways. The space inside the eyeball is filled with a transparent substance, as is the space between the cornea and the iris (Bloom & Fawcett, 1968).

Light-wave energy can travel over long distances—as when light from a star reaches us across the vast expanses of empty space. The light waves travel at 186,000 miles (300,000 kilometers) a second, the fastest speed known and presumably the fastest possible. This is such a great velocity that a light wave, if you could manage to reflect it around the world, would make the long journey and get back to you in less than one-seventh of a second.

Light waves are closely related to many other forms of pulsating energy that range in wavelength from small cosmic rays to household electricity, with its wavelengths of 100 million meters. In this broad range of wavelengths of electromagnetic energy, light occupies only a very small niche. The band of waves we can see ranges from about 380 billionths of a meter to about 780 billionths. The shortest waves, which are seen as violet, are just a little bit longer than the invisible ultraviolet rays that cause sunburn. The longest, which are seen as red, are just a little bit shorter than the invisible infrared waves produced by a heating lamp.

The Structures of the Eye and How They Work

If you have ever taken photographs—especially with a camera that must be properly set and focused before the shutter is snapped—you should feel right at home with the diagram of the eyeball in Figure 3.3. The **iris** serves the same purpose as the diaphragm in a camera. When the smooth muscles of the iris open to maximum size, as they do under dim conditions, the **pupil,** which is the opening in the iris, admits about 17 times as much light as when it is contracted to its smallest size. The **lens** of the eye serves the same purpose as the lens of a camera but in a way that would not be possible with even the most carefully designed piece of glass. The lens of a camera has to be moved forward and backward to focus on nearby or faraway objects. The lens

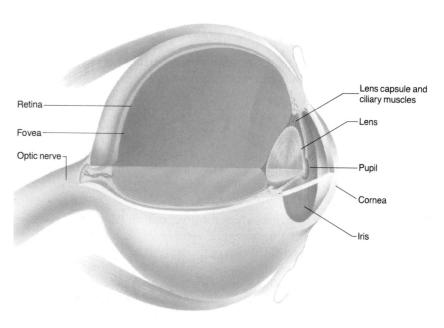

Retina

Fovea

Optic nerve

Lens capsule and ciliary muscles

Lens

Pupil

Cornea

Iris

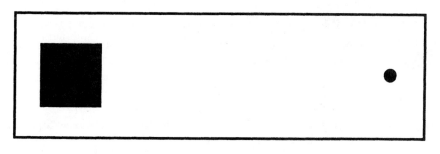

FIGURE 3.4 A demonstration of the blind spot Hold this book at arm's length, close your right eye, and look at the circle on the right. Now move the book slowly closer. When the image of the square at the left falls on the blind spot of your left eye, it will disappear. To demonstrate the blind spot of the right eye, repeat with the left eye closed and your gaze concentrated on the circle at the left.

of the eye remains stationary but changes shape. The action of the **ciliary muscles** makes the lens thinner to bring faraway objects into focus and enables it to thicken to focus on nearby objects. Sharp images created by the lens are cast on the **retina,** the eye's equivalent of film.

The receptor cells in the retina trigger nervous impulses that leave the eyeball by way of the **optic nerve.** At the point where this cable of neurons exits, there is a small gap in the retina known as the **blind spot,** containing no receptors. We are never aware of this gap in our visual field in ordinary life, but you can discover it for yourself by examining Figure 3.4. The optic nerve terminates in the thalamus, which serves as a relay station in the brain for visual stimuli. Here neurons in the thalamus send the visual information on to the portion of the cerebral cortex responsible for vision. The entire visual pathway is portrayed in Figure 3.5.

Ciliary muscles

The muscles in the eye that control the shape of the lens.

Retina

A patch of tissue at the back of the eyeball; contains nerve endings called rods and cones that are the receptors for vision.

Optic nerve

The visual input pathway from the eye to the brain.

Blind spot

The gap in the retina that contains no receptors.

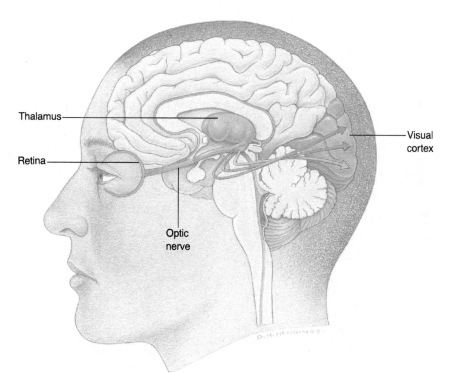

FIGURE 3.5 The pathway for vision Light travels via the retina of the eye to the optic nerve, and from there to the thalamus—where it is relayed to the visual cortex.

Thalamus

Retina

Optic nerve

Visual cortex

The Visual Receptors—in Good Light and Bad

Although a good camera has a sharper lens and a diaphragm with a much wider range than the iris, no photographic film can begin to compare with the efficiency of the retina. The receptors are sensitive to low intensities of light that would not register at all in a camera and can also function under high intensities that would burn the film.

Each retina, if flattened out, would be an irregular ellipse with a total area of just about three-fourths of a square inch (slightly under five square centimeters). Packed into this small area are about 127 million receptors of the kind shown in Figure 3.6. The great majority of the receptors are long and narrow, a fact that has given them the name **rods.** The rest, numbering about 7 million, are somewhat thicker and tapered; these are called **cones.** Both rods and cones respond to different intensities of light. The rods function chiefly under conditions of low illumination and send information to the brain about movement and about whites, grays, and blacks but not about color. Our eyes are so sensitive that on a clear, black night they can spot a candle flame more than 30 miles away. The cones function in strong illumination and provide sensations not only of movement and brightness from white to black but also of hue or color.

The cones are most numerous toward the middle of the retina. The area called the **fovea,** near the very center of the retina, contains only cones, packed together more tightly than anywhere else. This is where our vision is sharpest. When we read or do anything else that requires a very sharp image, we keep the object in the center of our field of vision so that its light waves fall on the fovea.

The manner in which light waves stimulate the receptors of the retina was discovered many years ago when physiologists managed to extract a substance called **rhodopsin** from the rods. Rhodopsin is a pigment that absorbs light, which bleaches it at a rate depending on intensity and wavelength.

Rods

The receptors for light intensity.

Cones

The receptors for colors.

Fovea

The most sensitive part of the retina, containing only cones.

Rhodopsin

(row-DOP-sin)   A light-sensitive substance associated with the rods of the retina.

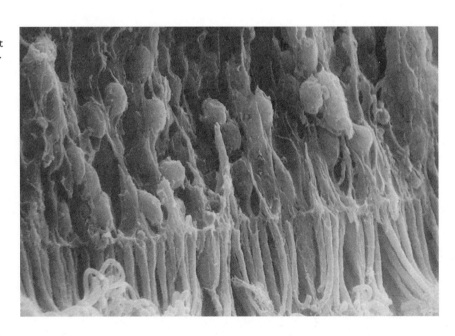

FIGURE 3.6   The retina's receptor cells The shapes that give the names to the eye's light-sensitive rods and cones can be seen clearly in this photograph of the retina, magnified about 45,000 times.

Thus light waves striking the retina produce chemical changes in the rhodopsin, and these changes act to stimulate the neurons next in the pathway that carries messages from receptors to brain (Wald, 1951).

The cones contain certain pigments that operate in much the same way, except that there are three different types. The first is most sensitive to blue wavelengths, the second to green, and the third to waves in the green-yellow portion of the spectrum. However, all three types are broadly tuned, and their pigments respond to some degree to many wavelengths.

One of the most valuable aspects of our visual equipment is its ability to function under an extremely wide range of illumination. Note what happens when you walk through bright afternoon sunlight into a movie theater where there is hardly any light at all. At first the theater seems pitch-black, and you can hardly find your way down the aisle to an empty seat. But after a while your eyes undergo what is called **dark adaptation**—and you can clearly see the aisle, the seats, and the faces of the people around you.

Dark adaptation depends mostly on the rods, whose rhodopsin builds up to high levels when it goes unbleached for a time by strong light. (The production of rhodopsin, in turn, requires vitamin A—which is why people who suffer from night blindness, or inability to adapt, are advised to eat carrots.) Full adaptation to dark takes about 30 minutes, by which time the eyes are about 100,000 times more sensitive to light than they were in the bright sunlight. Note that you do not see colors in a dimly lighted place such as a theater—nothing but shades of gray. This is because the color-sensitive cones cannot function at low intensities of light. Only the rods respond.

Dark adaptation
The ability of the eyes to adapt from a brighter to darker illumination.

The Capacity for Color Vision

Color does not actually exist in the objects themselves. Instead it is a psychological phenomenon—an aspect of sensory experience that is created when the brain processes the wavelengths contained in light.

The three types of cones, each responding in its own way to different wavelengths, permit us to distinguish the hues of the rainbow. But the ability also depends on the coding that takes place in the complex pathway of neurons that leads from the eye to the sensory areas of the cerebral cortex, through a number of switching points including a major relay station in the thalamus.

The pathway begins with neurons in the retina that make contact with the receptor cells—sometimes with just one, sometimes with a number of them—and are stimulated to a greater or lesser degree by the chemical activity of the receptors. The nervous impulses in these neurons, in turn, stimulate the neurons of the optic nerve, which send their impulses to the thalamus. There appear to be four kinds of cells responsible for color vision in the thalamus, each behaving in a different way in response to the messages it receives.

One type of nerve cell fires a rapid burst of impulses in response to messages indicating a blue stimulus but is turned off by a yellow stimulus. Another does just the opposite—it shows a high rate of activity in response to yellow and is turned off by blue. The third type is activated by red and slowed by green, the fourth type activated by green and slowed by red. There are also two other types of neurons that appear to be responsible for black-and-

Opponent-process theory
A pattern theory maintaining that our visual sensation of color results from three types of cones and nerve cells.

Color blindness
A deficiency in color discrimination.

white sensations and brightness. One is turned on by white or bright stimuli and turned off by black or dark stimuli. The other works in the opposite fashion, on for dark and off for bright (De Valois & Jacobs, 1968).

This explanation of vision is known as the **opponent-process theory.** A visual stimulus sets up a pattern of chemical response in the rods and the three kinds of cones in the retina. This pattern in turn stimulates the neurons of the visual system into their pattern of nervous activity, with the six opponent-process cells for blue-yellow, red-green, and bright-dark all behaving in different ways. It is this pattern of nervous impulses, arriving at the visual centers of the brain, that determines what we see.

Color Blindness

Some people—about 2 percent of all of us—are deficient in the capacity to detect colors; most are male (Gouras, 1985; Hubel, 1988). A small proportion of them never experience the sensation of hue at all; these people are totally **color blind** and see the world only in shades of gray, like a black-and-white photograph. The rest are color blind to some extent. The most common difficulty is distinguishing reds and greens. Less common is reduced sensitivity to blues and yellows.

Most people who are color blind do not know it. One reason is that light waves reaching the eye are seldom a fully saturated single wavelength. Both blue and yellow paints, as has been mentioned, reflect some green. Most red objects reflect some yellow waves, and most green objects some blue rays. (Traffic lights are deliberately designed this way to help people with red-green difficulties.) Color-blind people learn to use subtle differences in saturation—as well as brightness and other clues—to recognize and name hues they never see as the normal person experiences them. Their deficiencies can be readily detected, however, with tests that are useful in steering people away from jobs in which color blindness would be a handicap (or, as in the case of flying an airplane, a hazard).

TEST YOURSELF

e) If the ciliary muscles of a person's eye were suddenly to turn totally rigid, what would likely be the resulting defect in vision?

f) In a discussion of vision, someone tells you that if forced to choose, she would rather do without cones than rods. What might that indicate to you concerning the individual's feelings about color?

Hearing: From Sound Waves to Sounds

Our sense of hearing is just as versatile as vision. We can distinguish tones ranging from the lowest notes of the tuba to the highest notes of a shrill whistle, changing in loudness from the merest hint of a whisper to the most deafening clap of thunder, taking such diverse and varied forms as the tick of a watch, the human voice, and the blended richness of a hundred instruments in a symphony orchestra. Our world contains many kinds of sound stimuli—and our ears, like our eyes, have a remarkable capacity to sense all the stimuli and tell them apart.

How Is Sound Made?

The stimulus for hearing is sound waves, traveling unseen through the atmosphere. The waves are little ripples of contraction and expansion of the air, typically produced by the vibration of a piano string or the human vocal cords or by two objects banging together. They have three qualities that determine the sensations they produce:

1. **Frequency,** or the number of sound waves per second, determines the sensation of **pitch.** The lowest sounding note on a piano measures about 27 hertz, or Hz, the scientific term for the number of cycles of contraction and expansion per second. The highest is around 4,200 Hz. Our full range of hearing extends from about 20 to 20,000 Hz.

2. **Amplitude,** or the strength of the wave, determines the degree of loudness we hear, although not entirely. Our sense of hearing is most sensitive to the frequencies between about 400 and 3,000 Hz, which is about the range of the human voice. Frequencies higher or lower than that do not sound as loud even when they have exactly the same amplitude. A wave of 1,000 Hz sounds louder than 10,000 Hz, which in turn sounds louder than 100 Hz, because we are least sensitive of all to low notes. The way waves vary in amplitude and frequency is illustrated in Figure 3.7.

3. Complexity determines the sensation of **timbre,** which is the quality that distinguishes a middle C on the piano from the same note on a clarinet or violin. Complexity results from the fact that virtually all sources of sound produce not just a single frequency but others as well. For example, while the middle C piano string is vibrating at 256 Hz, sections of the string also vibrate at higher frequencies though with lower amplitude. Each half vibrates at 512 Hz, twice the basic fre-

Frequency
The number of sound waves per second; determines the tone or pitch.

Pitch
The property of being high or low in tone.

Amplitude
The characteristic of a sound wave that determines the loudness of what we hear.

Timbre
The quality of sound that contributes to the complexity of the sound wave.

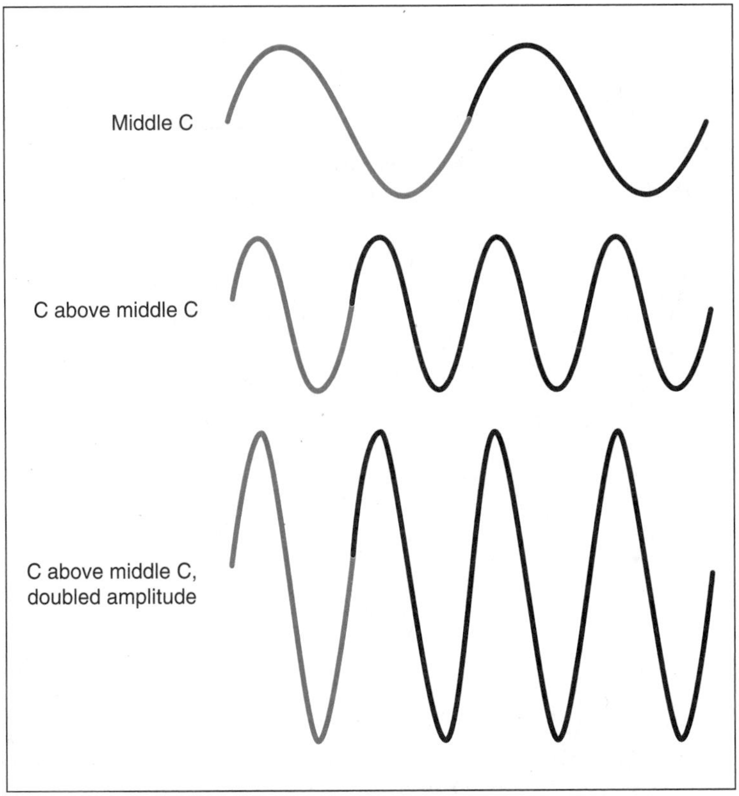

FIGURE 3.7   Sound waves: Frequency and amplitude
The wave at the top, for the pure tone of middle C, has a frequency of 256 Hz. The wave in the middle, for the C above middle C, has twice as many cycles of contraction and expansion per second, or 512 Hz. Sounding this same note with twice the force produces the wave at the bottom, which continues at a frequency of 512 Hz but has double the amplitude, as indicated by the height of the wave. The colored portions of the wave show a single cycle of contraction and expansion.

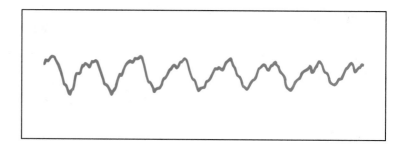

FIGURE 3.8 A pattern of complexity and timbre
Unlike the "pure" waves shown in Figure 3.7, the waves that usually reach our ears take this complex form. The note shown here comes from a violin. It maintains a basic frequency that produces our sensation of pitch, but each cycle of contraction and expansion is modified by overtones that change the pattern of the wave and result in our sensation of the violin's own special timbre.

Outer ear

The visible portion of the ear that collects sound waves and directs them to the hearing receptors.

Eardrum

The membrane between the outer ear and the middle ear.

Middle ear

An air-filled cavity containing three small bones that conduct vibrations.

quency, each third at 768 Hz, and so on. These additional vibrations are called overtones. All the various frequencies combine into a complex sound wave with the shape illustrated in Figure 3.8, which produces the sensation of a middle C with the timbre characteristic of its source.

The Ear and Its Hearing Receptors

What we call the ear—the flap of tissue at the side of the head—is in fact the least important part of our hearing equipment. The working parts, including the receptors, lie hidden inside the skull.

The structure of the ear is shown in Figure 3.9. The **outer ear,** or visible portion, merely collects the sound waves. The waves create vibrations of the **eardrum** that are passed along through the **middle ear,** an air-filled cavity containing three small bones that conduct vibrations. The last of these bones,

FIGURE 3.9 A diagram of the hearing apparatus Sound waves enter the *outer ear,* pass through the *auditory canal,* and set up vibrations of the *eardrum.* The three bones of the *middle ear* transmit the vibrations to the *cochlea* through its *oval window.* The *auditory nerve* carries messages from the hearing receptors inside the cochlea to the brain. The *Eustachian tube,* traveling from middle ear to throat, keeps the air pressure inside the middle ear at the same level as outside. (When the tube is temporarily clogged, as sometimes happens when you have a cold or ride in an airplane or elevator, you can feel a difference in pressure against the eardrum.) The *semicircular canals* play no part in hearing but are responsible for our sense of equilibrium, as discussed later.

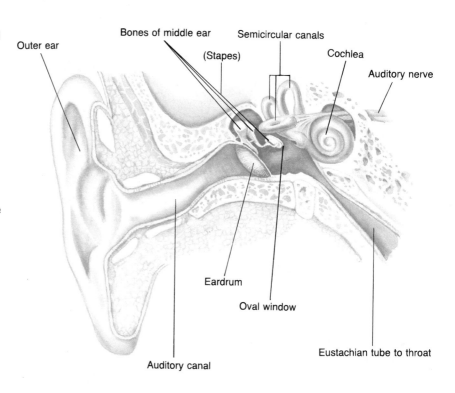

Outer ear

Bones of middle ear

(Stapes)

Semicircular canals

Cochlea

Auditory nerve

Eardrum

Oval window

Eustachian tube to throat

Auditory canal

called the **stapes,** is mounted like a piston on the **cochlea**—a bony structure about the size of a pea and shaped like a snail's shell. It is the cochlea, receiving the vibrations transmitted by the stapes, which contains the receptor for hearing of the **inner ear.**

The cochlea is filled with fluid. Stretched across it, dividing it more or less in half, is a piece of tissue called the **basilar membrane.** When the vibrations of sound reach the cochlea, they set up motions of the fluid inside, thus bending the basilar membrane. Lying on the membrane is the **organ of Corti,** a collection of hair cells that are the receptors for hearing.

How the Hearing Receptors Work

With over a million essential working parts, our auditory receptor organ, the cochlea, has been described as "the most complex mechanical apparatus in the human body" (Hudspeth, 1985). Sound waves cause the entire basilar membrane to respond to wave-like, up-and-down motions that travel along its length and breadth, in turn activating the hearing receptors resting on the membrane. The unique feature of these receptor cells is a bundle of protruding hairs. When the floor beneath the receptors moves, the hairs move and bend like tiny dancers. This stimulates the neurons of the **auditory nerve,** to which the receptors connect, to produce the nervous impulses that are routed toward the sensory areas of the cerebral cortex. The potential behavioral impact of sounds in the environment is the subject of a Psychology and the Media box titled "Loud Noises."

Stapes
One of the bones of the middle ear.

Cochlea
(COCK-lee-ah) The bony structure that receives the vibrations transmitted by the stapes.

Inner ear
The part of the ear that contains the cochlea, vestibule, and semicircular canals.

Basilar membrane
The piece of tissue that divides the cochlea.

Organ of Corti
(KOR-tie) A collection of hair cells that are the receptors for hearing located on basilar membrane.

Auditory nerve
The pathway from the ear to the brain.

PSYCHOLOGY AND THE MEDIA

Loud Noises

Arlene Bronzaft, a psychologist, discovered that exposing children to chronic noise "amplifies aggression and tends to dampen healthful behavior." in a study of pupils in grades 2–6, at PS 98, a grade school in Manhattan, she showed that children assigned classrooms in the half of the building facing the elevated train tracks were eleven months behind in reading by their sixth year, compared to those on the quieter side of the building. After the N.Y. City Transit Authority installed noise abatement equipment on the tracks, a follow-up study showed no difference in the two groups. Parents don't stop to worry about which side of a building their child is going to be sitting on, and yet an eleven-month retardation in the course of only four years of school is disastrous. A child would have to struggle hard to catch up. And we wonder why kids can't read, we wonder why the drop-out rate is so high in New York. Jackhammers, riveting, and other construction noises are part of what we associate with life in big cities, but by hanging steel-mesh blankets over the construction site to absorb sound it is possible to erect a building quietly. As civilization swells, even sanctuaries in the country could become too clattery to endure, and we may go to extremes to find peace and quiet: a silent park in the Antarctic, an underground dacha.

Source: Excerpted from "Loud Noises," in *A Natural History of the Senses,* by Diane Ackerman, New York: Random House, 1990, pp. 187–188.

Issues to Consider

1. Do you think loud noise adversely affects adults as well as children?
2. Can you think of an experiment to test the effects on behavior of loud noises in the environment?
3. What steps do you believe the government might take to protect citizens from loud noise?

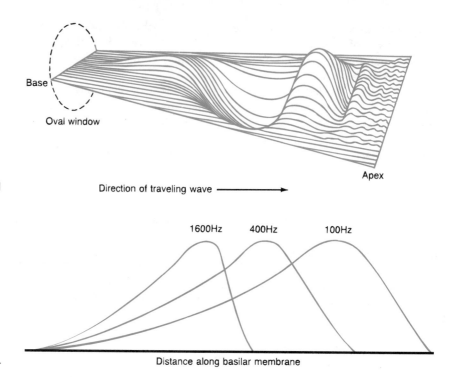

FIGURE 3.10 Waves of sound along the basilar membrane The *basilar membrane,* shown in the top part of the figure, is narrowest and stiffest along its base, where vibrations caused by the sound waves first enter the *cochlea* at its *oval window.* The membrane then becomes progressively wider and more flexible toward its other end, or *apex.* As the lower part of the figure shows, the narrower portions of the membrane—and the receptor cells at those points—move most vigorously in response to high-frequency sound waves. The wider portions and their receptors show a greater response to low frequencies. Loudness is represented on the basilar membrane by the size and expansiveness of the waves.

Exactly how the basilar membrane operates is described in Figure 3.10. The code of nervous impulses in which hearing messages eventually reach the cerebral cortex seems to depend in part on which receptors, at which locations along the membrane, are stimulated. The code in which hearing messages reach the cerebral cortex—and are translated into our sensations of pitch, loudness, and timbre—appears to depend also on the number of receptors stimulated, the rate at which each sets off nervous impulses, and especially the entire pattern of the impulses (Uttal, 1973). In fact, for the very low frequencies—those below about 400 Hz—the code does not seem to depend at all on the exact location of the receptor, because these frequencies make the basilar membrane move as a unit, to an equal degree throughout its length and breadth.

Where Sounds Come From

If you hear an automobile pass by, unseen, you can tell at once in which direction it is moving. Something about the sound waves and the manner in which they stimulate your hearing receptors tells you where they come from and in what direction they are moving. The ability to determine location seems to depend on the fact that slightly different sound waves reach the two ears. A sound wave from the left arrives at the left ear a tiny fraction of a second before it strikes the right ear, and in a slightly earlier phase of its cycle of contraction and expansion. By the time the sound wave reaches the right ear it has slightly less amplitude because it has traveled farther. And because high frequencies are more likely than low ones to be absorbed by any object that gets in the path of sound waves, the pattern of overtones has been altered by contact with the head, thus slightly changing the timbre.

The structure of the outer ear also seems to play a part, because its intricate shape bounces sound waves around much as the walls and furniture in a room affect the music from a stereo set. The two outer ears, receiving waves from different directions, reflect them toward the eardrum in different ways. Thus in a number of ways the receptors in the two ears are stimulated somewhat differently and produce slightly different patterns of nervous impulses, which the brain can usually decode into an instant judgment about the location of the sound. We are probably not so skillful at locating sounds as are animals with movable outer ears—like dogs and horses that prick their ears when curious about a noise—but we manage well enough.

Taste, Smell, Touch—and the Two Forgotten Senses

It is popularly assumed that we are endowed with five senses: vision and hearing, already discussed, and taste, smell, and touch—to be discussed in this section.

It is true that these five senses are our sole sources of inputs from the outside world. Yet we have two other senses—bodily movement and equilibrium—that we seldom even consider but that bring us essential information about our own bodies. Without these two forgotten senses, we would find it difficult to walk or even keep from falling down and impossible to play tennis or operate a typewriter. All the seven senses are important to the information processing we do.

Taste and Its Many Inputs

Though we can recognize a great variety of foods, and either relish or reject them, taste is probably the least efficient of our senses. The flavor of food actually depends only in small part on our taste receptors. Much of the sensation is produced by other factors—warmth, cold, the consistency of the food, the mild pain caused by certain spices, and above all smell. The next time your nose is stuffed up by a cold, notice that your meals seem almost tasteless.

The taste receptors are more or less out in the open. If you examine your tongue in a mirror, you will notice that it is covered with little bumps, some tiny, others a bit larger. Inside each of the bumps, a few of which are also found at the back of the mouth and in the throat, are the **taste buds,** the receptors for the sense of taste. Each bump contains about 245 taste buds, and each taste bud contains about 20 receptors sensitive to chemical stimulation by food molecules. Food dissolved in saliva spreads over the tongue, enters small pores in the surface of the bumps, and sets off reactions in the receptors. These reactions trigger activity in adjacent neurons, which fire off nervous impulses toward the brain.

The taste receptors appear to respond to many kinds of chemical stimulation, but they seem to respond most vigorously to four basic taste qualities: sweet, salty, sour, and bitter. As shown in Figure 3.11, the receptors for each are concentrated in various areas of the tongue.

Taste buds
The receptors for the sense of taste.

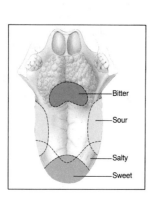

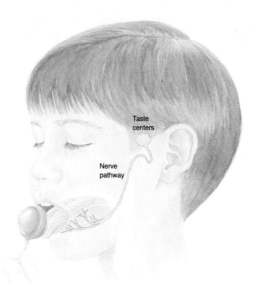

FIGURE 3.11   **How the taste sense works**   Taste sensations originate at specific points on the tongue, and the stimuli are relayed via neural connections through the thalamus to areas of the cerebral cortex where various tastes are "recognized."

Smell and Its Powers

The receptors for the sense of smell, as shown in Figure 3.12, lie at the very top of the nasal passages leading from the nostrils to the throat. As we breathe normally, the flow of air from nostrils to throat takes a direct path, as the figure indicates, but a certain amount rises gently to the top of the nasal passage, where it encounters the **olfactory epithelium,** which contains the receptor cells for smell. Sensitivity to odors seems to depend on the total number of receptors. Animals that have more receptors have keener senses of smell. Humans, who are at the lower end of the scale of smell sensitivity, have about 10 million olfactory receptors; in contrast, dogs, who have great sensitivity to smell, have about 200 million such receptors.

In a way still not well understood, the receptors are stimulated to respond by the molecules of chemical substances suspended in the air. The olfactory receptors apparently respond to the shape of the molecule—like locks activated by one particular key. Recently, researchers have identified a key protein, found in animals and undoubtedly in humans as well, that actually carries odor molecules along the path that begins at the tip of the nose into the brain. The protein, called "odor binding protein," probably acts to concentrate odorants so that even tiny amounts can be smelled (Pevsner et al., 1988). Many lower animals rely on the sense of smell to track down their prey

Olfactory epithelium

The part of the nasal passage that contains receptor cells for smell.

or to detect the approach of an enemy—and even as a means of communicating with one another. They "speak" through **pheromones,** volatile chemical secretions whose odor has a powerful effect on others of the same species. Frightened rats, for example, produce a pheromone that serves as a warning signal to other rats (Valenta & Rigby, 1968). Dogs secrete a pheromone in their urine that tells other dogs to stay away from their territory.

Comparable studies in humans have been less compelling, but there is evidence, nevertheless, that the sense of smell can influence human functioning. One study of dormitory residents at a women's college produced provocative results. When the college term began, the subjects reported wide differences in the dates when their menstrual periods began. Six months later, however, those who were spending a lot of time together as roommates or close friends reported that the dates were considerably closer together, as if there was a growing tendency for their menstrual cycles to coincide (McClintock, 1971). Perhaps pheromones secreted during the cycle had a mutual effect on the timing—a possibility that is reinforced by later experiments on the role of pheromones in synchronizing the estrous cycles of groups of rats (McClintock, 1984). The power of smell to influence sexual activity is discussed in the Psychology in Action box titled "The Scent of Sex."

The Taste-Smell Connection

A considerable factor in the experience of flavors of food and drink is the odor involved (Murphy & Cain, 1980). The fact that smell operates as a partner with taste is obvious when we have a head cold. The food we eat seems to be without flavor—despite the fact that it is our nasal passages that are clogged, interfering with the work of the smell receptors, while the tongue and its taste receptors are undisturbed. As shown in Figure 3.13, some of the most easily identified tastes become difficult to recognize when we are without the sense of smell.

Pheromones
Body secretions whose odor affects the behavior of members of the same species.

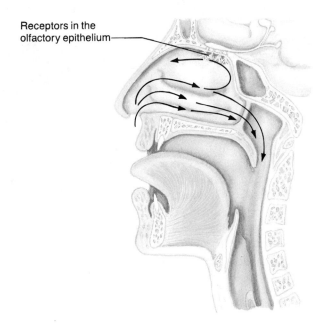

Receptors in the olfactory epithelium

FIGURE 3.12 The nose and its smell receptors This cross section of the human head shows the position of the receptors for the sense of smell. The arrow indicates how some of the air we breathe rises to touch the receptors. An odor, an assortment of molecules floating in air, goes in the nose and makes its way to the very top of the nasal passages, where it meets a collection of nerve cells making up the *olfactory epithelium* and having direct connections to the brain. The odor is converted into electrical signals matching the molecules being smelled, and these signals are transmitted to the brain.

Men's colognes are often marketed with the message that certain scents influence sexual attraction and behavior.

One way to demonstrate the smell-taste connection is to pinch your nostrils before approaching a food or drink you are about to taste. Then place some of the substance in your mouth, move it around, and try to grasp its flavor. The difficulty you find in doing so is likely to disappear once you let go of your nostrils and begin allowing air to enter normally.

In one survey, about three-fourths of the respondents reported at least occasional problems with the sense of smell, and many of them—often older persons—reported difficulties quite often (Gilbert & Wysocki, 1987). It is likely that such difficulties in the elderly help account for their frequent complaint that foods have lost their flavor.

The Scent of Sex

Many female animals, including dogs and cats, secrete pheromones that signal when they are sexually receptive. In female rhesus monkeys, for example, certain chemical substances termed *copulins* affect vaginal odor—and indicate to the male that mating is welcome. And a female moth can emit a pheromone sufficiently strong and compelling to attract males from miles away. Males, too, exude a pheromone that signals sex. One such substance is called *androstenol*. The boar produces androstenol in its testes, and when it secretes it in its saliva, the odor causes the sow to turn immobile—and thus amenable to the boar's sexual advances.

Because androstenol is also secreted in humans from underarm glands, and because humans are able to discriminate among various underarm odors, it has been thought to be a factor in human sexual attraction as well. A few studies have shown intriguing results. In one, women in photographs were rated as more appealing sexually by both men and women wearing surgical masks saturated with androstenol than by those wearing masks without it (Kirk-Smith et al., 1978). And when a seat in the waiting room of a dentist's office had been sprayed with the substance, more women than men chose to sit in it (Kirk-Smith & Booth, 1980). Evidently women can detect musk-like odors, which are characteristic of the sex pheromones secreted by male animals, more readily than men can. Moreover, their sensitivity to these odors is greatest during the time in their menstrual cycle when the amount of the hormone estrogen in their bodies is at its peak (Vierling & Rock, 1967).

Thus there are some indications that there may also be human pheromones that influence sexual behavior, though without our conscious awareness. Perfume and men's cologne manufacturers have, in fact, assumed that we are strongly attracted to another person through some mysterious language that only the nose understands.

Overall, the evidence leads to this conclusion: while it is possible that scents can affect human sexual responses, there is no reason to deduce that our sex life is regulated by them to the degree found in lower animals and insects (Rogel, 1978). For one thing, human responses to odors are variable. Like monkeys, for example, human females also manufacture copulins—but the male's reaction to vaginal scents is far from uniform (Labows, 1980). Moreover, for humans, visual stimulation can be equally exciting, as can psychological factors such as early memories and prior associations. In effect, "human sexual choice, contrary to the claims of some perfume manufacturers, is apt to be more a matter of higher mental processes than of primitive responses to sexual odors" (Coren & Ward, 1989).

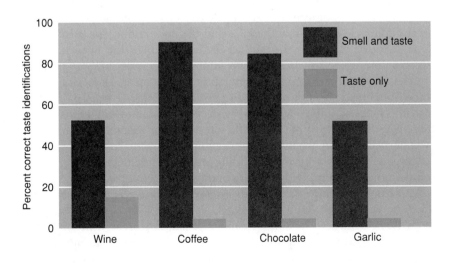

FIGURE 3.13   The role of smell in taste Note the sharp decline in the capacity to identify some common foods when the sense of smell is absent (from Mozel et al. 1969).

These wine tasters provide a good example of how much the sense of smell contributes to the sense of taste.

The Subtle Nature of Touch: Our Skin Senses

The receptors for the skin senses are nerve endings scattered throughout the body, just under the surface. They are sensitive to four basic types of stimulation—pressure, pain, cold, and warmth. As with the other senses, the sensation they produce appears to depend on the pattern of nervous impulses set off by a number of broad-tuned nerve endings. Indeed, manipulation of the pattern can fool us into experiencing a sensation that is totally at odds with the actual stimulation. This has been demonstrated with the device illustrated in Figure 3.14. When cool water is passed through both coils, the device feels cool to the touch. When warm water is passed through both coils, it feels warm. But when one coil is warm and the other is cool, the device produces a sensation of heat—so great that anyone who grasps it immediately pulls away. Somehow the pattern of nervous impulses set up by this kind of stimulation completely fools the sense of touch.

There are variations in skin sensitivity to pain throughout the body. The nerve endings in the back of the knee and the neck region, for example, are more sensitive than those in the ball of the thumb or the tip of the nose (Coren, Porac, & Ward, 1984). Nerve endings for pain are also found in our muscles and internal organs. Indeed, some of the most excruciating pains come from muscle cramps or from distention of the intestines by gas. Yet the receptors in most of the internal organs do not respond to stimuli that would cause pain if applied to the skin. The intestines, for example, can be cut or even burned without arousing any sensation of pain.

Pain sensations pose many baffling questions. Athletes in the heat of competition may suffer blows severe enough to produce deep bruises—yet feel no pain until later. People with intense and long-term pain can sometimes be relieved through hypnosis (Goleman, 1977). Chinese surgeons often use no anesthetic, just the technique of acupuncture in which little needles are stuck in various spots of the patient's skin, shown in Figure 3.15, often far removed from the part of the body undergoing the operation. Elec-

FIGURE 3.14 When you touch this harmless coil, watch out! This device can fool the skin senses in startling fashion. The coils are completely separate and can be connected to different sources of water. The surprising result described in the text is obtained by running cool water through one coil and pleasantly warm water through the other.

trical stimulation applied to the spinal cord or brain—or for that matter even a placebo, which is a mere sugar pill with no medical effect—may make severe pain disappear. Why?

The answer is not known. One theory is that many of these phenomena occur because the brain is induced in one way or another to increase its output of the morphine-like painkillers it can produce (Iversen, 1979). Another theory is based on indications that there seem to be two different pathways carrying pain messages through the spinal cord and into the brain. One is made up of "fast" fibers that signal sharp, localized pains like a pinprick. The other consists of "slow" fibers that signal duller, more generalized pains like those produced by many illnesses (Liebeskind & Paul, 1977). Some investigators believe that these two kinds of fibers interact at a **gate-control mechanism** in the spinal cord, either opening it to let pain messages through or shutting it to cut off the sensations (Melzack, 1973). Such a gate might be activated by nervous impulses set up through acupuncture or electrical stimulation. In the case of hypnosis or placebos, the brain might send signals to the control mechanism.

Though we can only theorize about the way pain operates, we do know that it serves a purpose. Without the warning provided by pain, we might hold a hand in a flame until the tissues were destroyed, or cut off a finger while peeling an apple. Even the pain of headache, though we cannot attribute it to any specific cause, is probably a warning that we have been under too much physical or psychological strain. By forcing us to slow down

"Fast" fibers
Fibers that signal a sharp and localized pain.

"Slow" fibers
Fibers that signal a duller and more generalized pain.

Gate-control mechanism
A theoretical process of the spinal cord that either lets messages through or shuts them off.

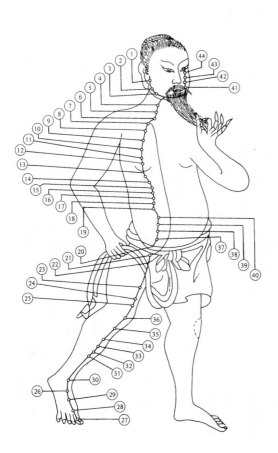

FIGURE 3.15   An acupuncture chart The numbers shown here indicate the spots at which needles can be inserted into the skin of a patient seeking relief from pain.

or even take a day off, the headache takes us away from a situation that, if continued, might cause some serious damage to the tissues of our bodies or to our mental stability.

Bodily Movement and Equilibrium

Even in a pitch-black room, you know exactly how to move your hand to point up, down, or to either side, and to touch the top of your head or your left knee. This may not seem like much of an accomplishment—but it would be completely impossible without the generally ignored and unappreciated sense of **bodily movement,** which keeps us constantly informed of the position and motion of our muscles and bones.

The receptors for the sense of bodily movement are nerve endings found in three parts of the body. The first are in the muscles, and they are stimulated when the muscles stretch. The second are in the tendons that connect the muscles to the bones and are stimulated when the muscles contract and put pressure on the tendons. The third, and apparently most important, are in the linings of the joints between the bones and are stimulated by movements of the joints. Without the information provided by these three receptors, we would have trouble performing any of the bodily movements we now take for granted. Even to walk, we would have to concentrate on using our eyes to guide our legs and feet into the right position for each step.

The other forgotten sense is **equilibrium,** which keeps our bodies in balance and oriented to the force of gravity. Thanks to this sense, our bodies stay erect—and, if we should start to fall, we catch our balance through reflex action, without even thinking about it.

The receptors for the sense of equilibrium are hairlike cells found in fluid-filled passages that are part of the inner ear, as illustrated in Figure 3.16. The three **semicircular canals** lie at such angles to one another that any movement of the head moves the thick fluid in at least two of them, stimu-

Bodily movement
The body sense that keeps us informed about the position and motion of our muscles and bones.

Equilibrium
The body sense that keeps us in balance and oriented to the force of gravity.

Semicircular canals
Three fluid-filled canals in the inner ear that contain receptors for the sense of equilibrium.

This performance totally depends on the human sense of equilibrium.

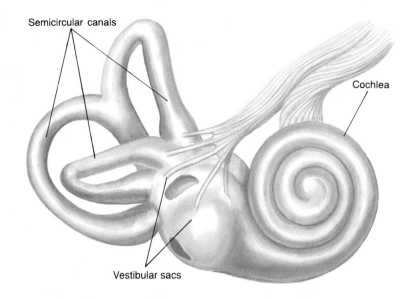

Semicircular canals

Cochlea

Vestibular sacs

FIGURE 3.16 The sense organs for equilibrium The receptors for the sense of equilibrium lie in these passages of the inner ear.

lating the receptors they contain. In the **vestibular sacs,** the receptors are matted together and tiny pieces of stone-like crystal are embedded in the mattings. The crystals are heavy enough to be pulled downward by the force of gravity, putting pressure on the receptors. Thus the receptors in the vestibular sacs keep us aware of being upright even when we are not moving.

Among them, the receptors for the sense of equilibrium constantly monitor the position of the head and any change in position. Besides keeping us right side up and in balance, they provide information essential to our sense of vision. By stepping toward a mirror, you can observe that your head bobs around when you walk—as it also does in many other circumstances. Unless the muscles controlling movement of the eyeballs made constant adjustments to hold your gaze steady, your field of vision would jiggle and blur. These adjustments are made by reflex action in response to messages from the sense of equilibrium. No matter how much you bob or shake your head, the world you see remains firmly in place.

Some people experience motion sickness when the various pathways of the sense of equilibrium become overloaded. Medicines such as dramamine act to prevent motion sickness by inhibiting some of the nervous activity.

Vestibular sacs
The sacs containing receptors for the sense of equilibrium.

TEST YOURSELF

h) If the taste buds on the tip of your tongue were to be destroyed, what would a lollipop taste like?

i) If someone told you that your pet dog is extremely sensitive to pheromones, what might that tell you about the dog's pattern of sexual behavior?

Perception and Survival

Despite our ability to sense changes in light or loudness, it is our perceptual processes that permit us to make sense of the constantly shifting stimuli in the outside world. Consider, for example, the familiar act of crossing the street. To do so, we must perceive the shapes of objects accurately, and detect their movement and speed. How long would you last in big-city traffic if you had to keep asking yourself: "That patch of blue light waves out there—is it an automobile or something else? Is it moving? How fast and in what direction? Is it dangerous or can I ignore it?" Or, consider the act of calling out for help. If you were in trouble and pleading for a friend to come to your side, it would be absolutely essential that the listener be able to make out that the voice is yours—no matter how loud or soft, whether high-pitched or low, whether on the phone or in the next room.

How long do you suppose it would take you to read this page if you had to work at deciphering every visual stimulus that reaches your eyes? That is to say, if you had to figure out each time that a vertical line with a little horizontal dash across it is a *t,* a vertical line with a curve an *h,* a partial circle with a horizontal line across it an *e*—and that a combination of *t, h,* and *e* means *the?*

But you do not have to stop and think. You perceive a *the*—or a moving automobile, or a familiar voice—without even trying. In fact, in most cases you cannot help perceiving what you do, even if you make a deliberate effort, because perception is a process over which we have little conscious control.

The Built-in "Wiring" of Feature Detectors

Part of our skill to perceive the world depends on the structure of the nervous system—the way it is "wired" to extract information from the environment. The nerve pathways from the sense organs to the brain, and the sensory areas of the brain, contain a great number of specialized cells that automatically detect important features of the environment. In the visual system these cells, called **feature detectors,** are especially sensitive to patterns and to movement. In hearing, the feature detectors are especially sensitive to pitch and changes in pitch. Thus the cells are ideally suited to respond immediately to stimuli that represent such important information as the direction of a line, the shapes and motion of objects, and the flow of conversation.

Much of our knowledge of feature detectors comes from the research of David Hubel and Torsten Wiesel, who shared a 1981 Nobel Prize for their work. Hubel and Wiesel measured the nervous impulses in individual cells of the visual cortex of cats and monkeys, while the animals looked at a screen on which various kinds of stimuli were flashed. They found that some of the brain cells responded vigorously to a vertical bar on the screen but did not respond at all to a horizontal bar, as shown in Figure 3.17. Other cells acted in the opposite fashion, responding to a horizontal bar but not to a vertical one. Others responded most vigorously to angles, and still others to movement (Hubel & Wiesel, 1965).

Similarly it has been found that the sensory areas of the brains of animals—and presumably of humans as well—contain feature detectors specialized to respond to various characteristics of sound waves. Some are activated most strongly by low-pitched sounds, others by high-pitched sounds, and still others only by a change in pitch (Whitfield & Evans, 1965).

The concept of feature detectors has been extended to apply to the perception of speech. Feature detectors for speech have been thought of as specialized neurons capable of detecting specific elements of the speech signal—as if, as a result of continued exposure to speech, the brain is able to store auditory templates, or molds, containing representations of recognizable speech patterns (Coren & Ward, 1989). Such a view of feature detectors raises a broad issue: whether we come into the world neurologically predisposed to perceive the world in particular ways, or whether we learn how to perceive a person from experiences in the environment.

Feature detectors
The cells that are sensitive to the orientation of lines and the movement of stimuli.

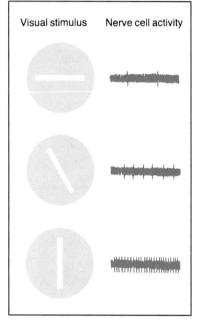

Visual stimulus   Nerve cell activity

FIGURE 3.17   How a feature-detector cell works
The spikes in the graph lines are recordings of the nervous impulses in one of the feature-detector cells of a cat's brain. In response to a horizontal bar, the cell displays only its normal amount of spontaneous activity. To an oblique bar, there is also a small response. To a vertical bar—the kind of feature to which this cell is specifically sensitive—there is a sharp burst of activity (Hubel, 1963).

The Skill of Perception: Inborn or Learned?

There has been a continuing controversy over the relative contribution of the central nervous system we are born with versus experience in explaining our perceptions. One view claims that there are inborn structures in the brain that allow us to perceive size and color. A contrasting view is that our perceptions are the result of accumulated psychological interpretations of the sensations we experience over time. Neither of these extreme views is likely to be correct.

On the one hand, there is evidence for inborn wiring. In the case of feature detectors, Hubel and Wiesel studied both newborn and very young monkeys kept from any visual stimulation since birth—and found feature detector cells in full operation. These cells were activated by the very first stimulation of the eye's receptors, responding in much the same way as the cells of older animals with visual experience (Wiesel & Hubel, 1974). There is indirect evidence that the human nervous system is wired in the same way (McCullough, 1965). It appears that the pathways of the sensory system not only receive the inputs provided by the sense organs but begin the information processing by making an initial selection and interpretation of these inputs. It has been said that they "condense the information present in the world down to certain features that are essential to the organism" (Levine & Shefner, 1981). Even young infants, although they have had very little experience, can perceive depth and shape.

On the other hand, we know that in complicated situations, especially when the stimuli are ambiguous, we must rely on past experience. When you are driving at dusk, for example, and try to make out an object on the road, you are going to be influenced by what you have previously learned. The most appropriate way to view perception, therefore, is as a skill derived from basic, inborn physiological mechanisms—but shaped and modified by learning experiences.

Our Special Skill: Recognizing Change, Movement, and Contrast

Our inborn skills are particularly adept at spotting any *change* in stimulation, which is often the most useful information of all. In general, change in stimulation is the most potent way to attract the attention of a baby. This makes sense, since the elements of change—for example, of temperature, or brightness—usually contain the most useful information in the environment. Throughout our lives, our nervous system finds it impossible to ignore change. If a radio is playing softly in the background while you are reading, you may pay no attention to it—but you cannot help noticing if the sound stops. You are instantly aware of a change if the light in the room becomes brighter or dimmer. And you can recognize even extremely subtle variations in the appearance of a face, such as a narrowing of the mouth or eyes (Haig, 1984).

Movement, which is a form of change, is such a compelling stimulus that even very young babies try hard to follow any moving object with their eyes. Indeed the newborn infant arrives with an automatic tendency to select and pay attention to movement. When you look at a pasture full of horses, you are most aware of those that are running. An advertising sign that uses items in motion demands your attention far more than a sign that remains stationary.

Movement
A stimulus that is a compelling form of change.

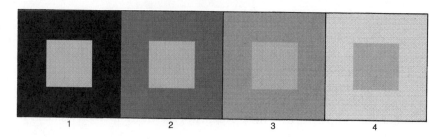

FIGURE 3.18 The same but different: a study in contrasts The central squares in each of the four larger squares are actually the same gray. The amount of light and the wavelength reaching your eye is the same from each one. But the perceived levels of brightness of these small squares are not equal. The grays printed on dark backgrounds appear lighter than those printed on light backgrounds, as explained in the text (adapted from Coren & Ward, 1989).

Contrast

A sharp difference in the intensity of light reflected by two objects in the field of vision.

Simultaneous brightness contrast

The differences in the amount of light reflected from adjacent objects.

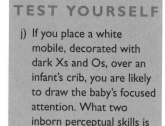

TEST YOURSELF

j) If you place a white mobile, decorated with dark Xs and Os, over an infant's crib, you are likely to draw the baby's focused attention. What two inborn perceptual skills is the infant demonstrating?

Selection

The ability to pay attention to only some of the stimuli that bombard our sense organs.

The reason movement leaps immediately to awareness probably also depends on inborn characteristics of the nervous system. It appears that the wiring of the visual system contains separate cells for motion (Sekuler & Levinson, 1977). This is a characteristic of great potential value in survival, for there are many situations in which it is more important to detect and respond quickly to the movement of an object than to know what the object may be. To our ancestors, for example, the sudden approach of a wild animal meant danger regardless of whether the animal happened to be a lion or a bear.

Another compelling stimulus is **contrast**—any sharp difference in the intensity of light reflected by two objects in the field of vision. Even babies are attracted by contrast (Salapatek & Kessen, 1966). Newborns also recognize and react to black-and-white contrast as well as to changes in loudness and pitch. Their early interest in the human face occurs because they notice the high degree of contrast between a light face and dark eyes or hairline, or between a dark face and the whites of the eyes and teeth. Our perception of the relative brightness of an object often depends on differences in the amount of light reflected from adjacent objects (Shapley, 1986). This perceptual effect, called **simultaneous brightness contrast,** is demonstrated in Figure 3.18.

Besides change, movement, and contrast, two other stimulus characteristics have an effect on perception. One is *size,* with large objects more compelling than small ones. When you look at the front page of a newspaper, you notice the biggest headlines first. The second is *intensity.* When you drive at night along a business street where all the signs are of equal size, the brightest one is the most compelling. When you stand on a crowded subway, you may ignore the pressure of the people pressed against you—but you quickly notice if someone accidentally pokes an elbow in your ribs.

Selection and Attention

Of the three functions of perception—selection, organization, and interpretation—**selection** heads the list. This is because we cannot possibly cope with all the varied and changing stimulation that bombards our sense organs. To avoid confusion, we have to select and pay attention to only a small part of it. What we select depends on many factors, ranging from automatic and involuntary to conscious and deliberate.

What's Behind the Selection Process?

What we select from the environment depends not only on choices dictated by the inborn tendencies of our nervous system but also on choices colored

Advertisers assume that we will pay more attention to large signs—and we usually do.

by experience. As an example of the latter, consider the kinds of choices that might be made by a man working as a forest ranger as he stands on a high observation tower looking out over a wide expanse of hills, valleys, open spaces, trees, and streams. Scanning the scene, he thinks he spots a plume of smoke. He raises his binoculars and focuses his eyes on this single aspect of the landscape. Only now, after selecting this small spot on which to concentrate, can he try to find some organization in the stimuli reaching his eyes (do they really represent a plume of smoke or something else?) and make an interpretation (if it is smoke is it coming from a cabin or is it the start of a forest fire?). Between the two extremes are many gradations that are difficult to classify. The in-between choices seem to depend partly on inborn tendencies and partly on learning and experience; often it is hard to say whether we make them consciously or unconsciously.

Because so many factors can influence selection, people looking at the same event in the environment may perceive it in different ways. We are likely to pay attention to events that interest us for one reason or another. When people look at words flashed only briefly for their inspection, they are better at recognizing terms related to their own special interests than unrelated terms. Subjects interested in religion are quick to perceive words like *sacred*. Subjects interested in economics are quick to perceive *income* (Postman, Bruner, & McGinnies, 1948).

You can observe for yourself how mood affects selection. When you are feeling out of sorts, you are likely to pay attention to anything in the environment that is potentially irritating—a noise in the next room, a watchband that feels too tight, another person's frown. When you are feeling on top of the world you may be especially aware that the sun is shining, everybody seems to be friendly to you, and there are a great many attractive people walking around. As the old saying goes, a pessimist sees a glass that is half empty, an optimist a glass that is half full.

Trying to Attend to Simultaneous Inputs

As we all have noticed at one time or another, it is difficult to pay attention to more than one event in the environment at a time, and selecting one stimulus usually means losing perception of the other possible inputs. A frequent example occurs in driving an automobile. As you drive along a highway where the traffic is light, you are listening to the radio—to a football game or a news broadcast that is about to give a weather report. But now you come to a busy intersection. The traffic lights are changing. You have to slow down, veer into another lane, watch out for a car that has moved into your path. When all this activity ends, you find to your surprise that the score in the football game has changed or that the news is over and you have missed the weather report. While your attention was directed elsewhere the radio was on just as loud as before, but your perceptual processes missed it entirely.

Laboratory experiments have shown that it is especially difficult to process two different inputs, especially if they arrive in the same sensory channel. In studying two sounds heard at the same time, experimenters have used earphones that deliver one spoken message to the right ear and a completely different one to the left ear. Subjects can pay attention to and understand either one of the two messages, but not both at once. The same applies to visual stimuli—for example, trying to take in what is happening in two films shown simultaneously, one showing a boxing match and the other a football game (Neisser & Becklen, 1975).

It is somewhat easier to pay attention to two things at once when two different senses are being stimulated. You may have noticed, for example, that you can continue to read with fairly good comprehension while listening to a radio or a telephone conversation. Apparently the mental processes required for perception can operate more efficiently with two different kinds of sensory information than with two messages in the same sensory channel. It is as if the brain has more than one area for paying attention (Wickens, 1984).

Selection and Exploration

What selection does, in the last analysis, is to help us perceive what is likely to be important to us, ignore all the many other inputs provided by our sense organs, and concentrate on using the rest of our information-processing talents to the best possible advantage. When we notice something unusual out of the corner of the eye—usually because of movement or contrast—we move the eyes to bring the image to the center of the retina where our vision is sharpest. Then we make a series of scanning movements, as illustrated in Figure 3.19. These scanning movements occur even when we think we are staring fixedly at a stimulus like the photograph in that figure, which means that the eyes send the brain information about first one part of the photo, then another, and then still others. Somehow the brain manages to piece together this rapid succession of fragmentary bits of information into a perception of the photograph as a whole. The way this is done resembles the creation of a mosaic from tiny bits of tile—but how it is done is only dimly understood.

TEST YOURSELF

k) The fact that a baseball player is able to follow the flight of a pitched ball—despite all the crowd noise, the chatter of the catcher, and the movement of the players on the field—reflects what aspect of human perception?

l) A mother says: "When I'm lying in bed and anxious about my baby, I notice every sound she makes. But when I'm relaxed, the baby's sounds blend in with everything else—the outside traffic, the murmur of a conversation downstairs, the TV in the next room. What general rule about the selection process in perception is this mother describing?

m) Suppose that one day you tried to listen to a lecture and a pocket radio at the same time, and that the next day you tried to listen to a lecture while looking out the window to see whether your taxi was arriving. Which would be easier to do—the first or the second—and why?

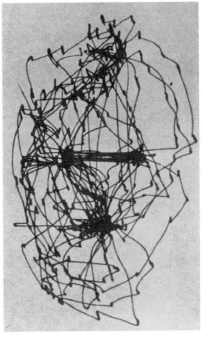

FIGURE 3.19 The scanning process The pattern of lines was made by bouncing a light beam off the white of one man's eye, thus recording his eye movements as he looked for a few minutes at the photograph of a girl. Note how many movements took place and how they provided information about all the important elements of the photo (Yarbus, 1967).

Organizing Our Perceptions

When we select a stimulus in the environment for further exploration, often the first thing we want to know is *What is it?* To answer this question, we have to see or hear the stimulus as something that hangs together as a unit of some kind, separate and distinguishable from all the other stimuli the environment provides. We must see light waves organized into some whole object—an animal, an automobile, a face, something. Or we must hear a string of sound waves organized into the meaningful pattern of human speech, or a rap at the door, or an approaching car.

In vision we organize stimuli into an object largely by the perceptual principle of **figure and ground.** As you read this page, for example, your eyes are stimulated by the white space and many little black lines, curves, squiggles, and dots. Your perceptual process organizes these stimuli into black figures—letters, words, and punctuation marks—seen against a white ground. This is also the way you perceive a chair, a face, or the moon in the sky. The figure hangs together, into an organized shape. The ground is a neutral and formless setting for the figure. What separates the two and sets the figure off from the ground is a clearly perceived dividing line called a contour. The separation depends in part on our inborn skill at perceiving contrast, probably because of the way feature detectors operate. An interesting example of how we organize visual stimuli into figure and ground is shown in Figure 3.20. In the drawing you may perceive some strange shapes against a white ground. Or you may perceive white shapes forming the word TIE against a black ground. But you cannot perceive both at once.

Figure and ground

In perception, the tendency to see an object as a figure set off from a neutral ground.

FIGURE 3.20 The principle of figure and ground When you look at the drawing, you probably perceive some shapes that look like little pieces of a jigsaw puzzle. But you can also perceive some thing quite different, as explained in the text.

Some Rules of Organization

Although the same stimuli can sometimes be grouped into different patterns, there are a number of rules of organization that generally apply. The most important are the following:

Closure

The ability to fill in the gaps in figure perception.

- **Closure** refers to the fact that we do not need a complete and uninterrupted contour to perceive a figure. If part of the contour is missing, our perceptual processes fill in the gaps. This rule of perception is illustrated in Figure 3.21. The rule of closure also operates for sounds. A tape recording of a spoken message can be doctored so that many of the sounds are missing—consonants, vowels, syllables, or entire words. Yet if you hear the tape, you will have no trouble perceiving the message.

Continuity

The tendency to perceive continuous lines and patterns.

- **Continuity,** which is closely related to closure, is the tendency to perceive continuous lines and patterns. An example is shown in Figure 3.22. The two lines at the left, seen separated in space, have their own continuity, but when they are put together as at the right, a different kind of continuity makes us perceive them quite differently. In looking at any kind of complex visual stimulus, we are likely to perceive the organization dictated by the most compelling kind of continuity.

Similarity

The way the factor of likeness affects perceptual organization.

Proximity

The way the factor of nearness affects perceptual organization.

- **Similarity** *and* **proximity** are illustrated in Figure 3.23. The checkerboard lettered A, with blocks all the same color and equal distances apart, has no real pattern inside it. If you keep looking at it and shift your eyes from one point to another, your tendency to find organization is likely to make you perceive some patterns—vertical rows, horizontal rows, or groups of squares arranged in pairs, squares, or

FIGURE 3.21 Some examples of closure Though the figures are incomplete in one way or another, we perceive them at once for what they are.

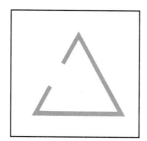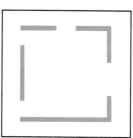

FIGURE 3.22 An example of continuity At the left we clearly perceive two continuous lines that are combinations of straight and curved segments. When the two lines are put together as at the right, however, we find it difficult to perceive the original pattern. Instead we perceive a continuous wavy line running through another continuous line of straight horizontal and vertical segments.

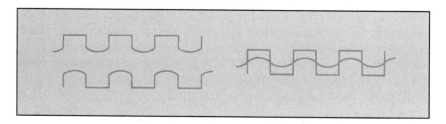

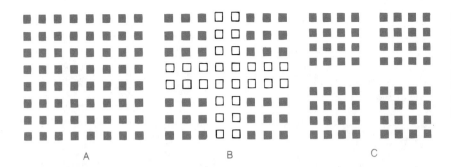

FIGURE 3.23 **The effects of similarity and proximity** Drawing A has a simple pattern. But note what happens to your perception when some of the colored squares are changed to white, as in B, or moved apart, as in C.

A   B   C

rectangles—but these patterns are not compelling and are likely to keep shifting. In B, however, removing the color from some of the blocks makes a white cross fairly leap off the page. This demonstrates the rule of similarity, which is that we tend to group stimuli that are alike.

In variation C of the checkerboard, some of the colored blocks have been moved closer together, and now a pattern of four squares can be clearly perceived. This demonstrates the rule of proximity, which is that we tend to group together stimuli that are close together in space. The rule also applies to sounds. When we hear a series of sounds that are all alike, the pattern we hear depends on the timing. When we hear click-click . . . click-click . . . click-click (with the dots indicating a pause), the rule of proximity dictates that we organize the sounds into pairs. When we hear click-click-click . . . click-click-click, we perceive patterns of three. Even different sounds presented this way—click-buzz-ring . . . click-buzz-ring—are perceived in groups of three.

Finding Stability and Consistency

In trying to answer the question *What is it?* we have to overcome some serious handicaps. Though the objects visible in the world may have a definite and unchanging shape, the light rays they reflect to our eyes take many different patterns, depending on the angle from which we view them. A dinner plate, for example, casts its true circular image only when we look straight down at it or hold it vertically in front of our eyes. From any other angle it casts different images—all sorts of ovals and ellipses. A door is a rectangle only when seen at right angles to the eyes. From other angles, as when it swings open or shut, it forms various images that are trapezoids.

This variation seldom bothers us. Regardless of the shape of the image cast on our eyes, we know immediately that we are looking at a round plate or a rectangular door. Thanks to what is called **perceptual constancy,** we perceive a stable and consistent world. The form of perceptual constancy demonstrated by the plate and the door is called **shape constancy.** Some other forms are the following:

- **Size Constancy** refers to the tendency to recognize the actual size of an object regardless of whether the image it casts on the eye is large, as when seen close up, or small, as when seen from a distance. Figure 3.24 demonstrates how the actual size of the image creates a distorted view of the world on the film in a camera. We ourselves, viewing the same scene from the same place as the camera lens, would perceive every-

Perceptual constancy
The perception of a stable and consistent world.

Shape constancy
The tendency to perceive objects as retaining their shape regardless of the nature of the sensory information that reaches the eye.

Size constancy
The tendency to perceive objects in their correct size regardless of the size of the actual image cast on the eyes.

FIGURE 3.24 What the world would look like without size constancy? This is how two people on a beach look to a camera held at close range. If you were holding the camera, your eyes would see much the same kinds of images—hands of different sizes, exaggerated torsos, undersized heads. But you would not be aware of the distortion.

FIGURE 3.25 Salad plate or dinner plate? For a clear demonstration of size constancy, put a dinner plate on the table. Then move a salad plate up and down until its image exactly blots out the dinner plate. Without changing the height at which you hold the salad plate, move it to one side. The images cast on your eyes by the two plates are exactly the same size—but what do you perceive?

thing in proper perspective. You can experience a perhaps even more convincing demonstration of size constancy by trying the experiment illustrated in Figure 3.25. If you follow the instructions, the images cast on your eyes by the small salad plate and the large dinner plate will be exactly the same size. Yet you will find that what you perceive—and in fact cannot help perceiving—is a small plate fairly close to you and a larger plate farther away.

- **Brightness Constancy** can best be explained by the example of how you might perceive a black shoe lying on a sidewalk in bright sunlight and the same shoe lying on a snowbank in deep shade on a cloudy winter day. In either case the shoe looks black, its background white. But if you made some measurements with a photographer's light meter, you would discover something strange. The shoe in sunlight would register just as bright on the meter as the snow in the shade—perhaps even brighter. Regardless of the actual intensity of the light waves reaching your eyes, brightness constancy provides consistent impressions of blacks, whites, and grays and the contrasts between them. Part of the explanation seems to be the ratio of light intensity, which is about the same between sunlit shoe and sidewalk as between cloudy-day shoe and shaded snow (Hochberg, 1978).

The Perception of Distance and Depth

Another important question, as we explore the world, is: *Where is it?* In order to avoid bumping into walls and other people, we must not only perceive objects but also know how far away they are. Before we step off a bus we must know how deep a drop there is to the pavement. Fortunately, we perceive distance and depth without thinking.

The ability seems to depend partly on inborn wiring, as has been demonstrated with the apparatus shown in Figure 3.26. This device, known as a

FIGURE 3.26 A baby avoids a fall on the visual cliff At left a baby fearlessly crawls toward its mother on the glass covering the shallow-looking side of the *visual cliff*. But at right the baby stops—seeming afraid to cross the glass that covers the apparently deep side (Gibson & Walk, 1960).

"visual cliff," is a piece of heavy glass suspended above the floor. Across the middle of the glass is a board covered with checkered cloth. On one side of the board the same kind of cloth is attached to the bottom of the glass, making this look like the solid, or shallow, side of the cliff. On the other side the cloth is laid on the floor, and to all appearances there is a drop on that side.

As the figure shows, a nine-month-old baby crawls without hesitation over the shallow-looking side but hesitates to crawl on the deep side. Lower animals show this tendency before any kind of learning presumably has had time to take place. Baby lambs and goats tested as soon as they are able to walk avoid the deep side. This ability seems to be the secret of how even very young animals—particularly mountain goats born into an environment full of sharp and dangerous drops—manage to avoid falls. Other factors that aid the perception of depth and distance are difficult to classify as either inborn or learned. It seems that they are a combination of the two (Hochberg, 1978).

One influential factor is **binocular vision,** which refers to the fact that the two eyes receive different images because of the distance between them, which is about 64 millimeters or 2½ inches. Like the two lenses of a three-dimensional camera, the eyes view objects in the visual field from slightly different angles. The images they receive are put together by the brain into a three-dimensional pattern that greatly assists the perception of depth and distance.

Other factors that aid in distance and depth perception include **interposition,** which, as shown in Figure 3.27, has to do with the fact that nearby objects block off part of our view of more distant objects; **linear perspective**—a distance cue that pertains to the phenomenon that parallel lines, like highway lanes, seem to draw closer together as they recede into the distance; and **relative size,** referring to the perception that larger objects are close and smaller ones are more distant.

When Illusions Mask Reality

The process of perception, aided by the inborn characteristics of the nervous system, is the source of our first quick impressions of what is going on around

Brightness constancy

The tendency to perceive objects to be of consistent brightness regardless of the amount of light they actually reflect under different conditions of illumination.

Binocular vision

The condition in which each eye receives slightly different images of any object.

Interposition

The condition in which nearby objects block off part of the view of more distant objects.

Linear perspective

A cue to distance perception in which parallel lines seem to draw closer together as they recede into the distance.

Relative size

The perception that larger objects are close and smaller objects more distant.

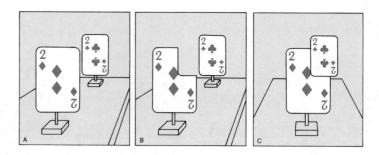

FIGURE 3.27 Fooling the eye with interposition The drawings illustrate an experiment that shows how your perception of distance can be thrown off by manipulating the clue of interposition. Two ordinary playing cards are arranged as shown in *A* and are the only objects visible in an otherwise dark room. You perceive clearly that the two of clubs is farther away. Now a corner is clipped from the two of diamonds, as shown in *B,* and the stand holding this card is moved to the right. If you now look at the cards through one eye and see them as shown in *C,* you perceive a small two of clubs close by and a larger two of diamonds farther away (Krech & Crutchfield, 1969. Reprinted by permission).

us. Usually, it is accurate. The process is not perfect, however. Our first impressions are not always in accord with the facts. For example, you may have had the experience, when riding along a highway, of being sure you saw a dead dog at the side of the road—only to discover, as you got closer, that it was just a piece of rumpled cloth. Your perceptual process, in its effort to make sense out of the visual stimulation reaching your eyes, signaled "dog" when in fact there was no dog at all. Students of perception have shown that you can be fooled in many ways. Some of these are called optical illusions, a few of which are illustrated in Figure 3.28.

Perceptual illusions occur in senses other than vision as well. The ancient Greek philosopher-scientist Aristotle called attention to an illusion of touch, illustrated in Figure 3.29. Perceptual illusions also take place during what are

FIGURE 3.28 How do you perceive these drawings? Is line *a* or line *b* longer in no. 1? In no. 2? In no. 3? Which of the two inner circles in no. 4 is larger? In no. 5, are the horizontal lines straight or curved? After you have made your judgments, you can discover with a ruler that all the lines *a* and *b* are the same size, and so are the two circles in no. 4. The lines in no. 5 are parallel.

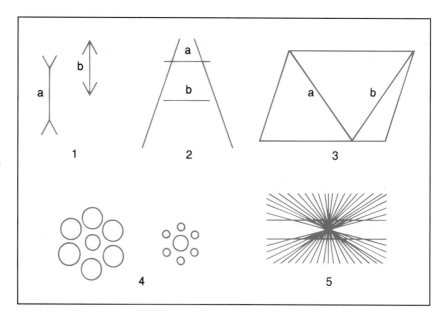

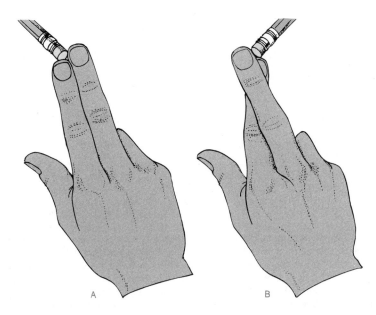

FIGURE 3.29 **One pencil or two?** Hold your fingers as pictured in figure A and touch the point between them with a pencil. You will perceive one pencil. But if you simply cross your fingers as shown in figure B and now touch the pencil, you will perceive two distinct pencils. (If you keep your eyes closed, thus denying yourself the vision of reality, the effect may be stronger.) The best explanation of the illusion is that when the pencil is stimulating the inside of the two fingers as in figure A, the touch information is being sent to adjacent or overlapping areas of the brain cortex responsible for touch sensations. But when the pencil is stimulating the outside of the two fingers as in figure B, the information is sent to two separate areas of that part of the cortex (adapted from Coren, Porac, & Ward, 1984).

called **altered states of consciousness** (ASC)—for example, during dreams, under hypnosis, or under the influence of alcohol and mind-altering drugs, states that are described in various later chapters of this book.

Most of the time, however, our perceptions give us an accurate view of what is going on in the world. Our first impressions, arrived at quickly and automatically, are usually correct and useful.

How We Interpret What We Perceive

Selection answers the question Which one of all the many objects and events in the environment is worthy of attention and exploration? Organization helps answer other questions: What is it, and where is it? But one important question remains: What does it mean? Finding the answer requires the third element of perception, which is **interpretation.**

Of all the elements, interpretation is the most clearly dependent on learning rather than on inborn characteristics of the nervous system. We compare the information provided by the senses with old information acquired in the past. Note for example the symbols in Figure 3.30. You probably have never seen anything exactly like them before—but you perceive at once that all of them are the letter *E*. You have stored in memory what students of perception call a **prototype** or **schema**—a sort of generalized picture of what the letter *E* looks like. You can identify the new symbols because they

Altered states of consciousness (ASC)

States of consciousness such as those produced by dreams, sleep, hypnosis, alcohol, or mind-altering drugs that differ from normal waking experiences.

Interpretation

The meaning we attach to stimuli affecting the sense organs.

Prototype or schema

A generalized picture or model on which a concept or perception is based.

FIGURE 3.30   You know what these are—but how do you know? These symbols are unlike any *E*'s you have seen before, yet you recognize them at a glance. For the explanation, see the discussion of *prototypes* in the text.

FIGURE 3.31   A little perceptual magic: now it's a man, now it's a rat Cover both rows of drawings, then ask a friend to watch while you uncover the faces in the top row one at a time, beginning at the left. The friend will almost surely perceive the final drawing as the face of a man. Then try the bottom row in similar fashion on another friend. This friend will almost surely perceive the final drawing as a rat. The psychologists who devised this experiment found that 85 to 95 percent of their subjects perceived the final drawing as a man if they saw the other human heads first, as a rat if they saw the animals first—though of course the final drawings are exactly alike (Bugelski & Alampay, 1961).

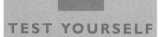

TEST YOURSELF

n) You are driving along the highway in a patchy fog, and up ahead you see one headlight, one double set of tires, and part of a large windshield. "That's a truck," you tell yourself. What rule of perception allows you to make this assumption?

o) If you were to watch a basketball game from a seat 50 rows up in the stands, the images of the players on the retina of your eye would be quite different in size from the images cast by the players if you were in a front row seat. Nevertheless, you would be able to keep the *actual* size of the players in perspective. What aspect of perception does this fact demonstrate?

p) You probably have never actually seen the strange figure on page 133, Figure 3.33. But still, you undoubtedly perceived it right away as a facial profile. How did you accomplish this feat?

resemble this prototype. Similarly, you have prototypes that help you recognize the human face, a tree, the animal called a dog, and all the other objects and events you have become familiar with.

Experience has led us to expect certain events to happen in our world in certain familiar ways. We have a mental set toward the environment. What we perceive and how we interpret it depends to a considerable extent on our set—in other words, on our **perceptual expectations.** Laboratory experiments have shown that manipulating people's expectations can greatly affect their perceptions. Would you believe, for example, that two people could look at exactly the same drawing—yet that one would see a man and the other would see a rat? To convince yourself, try the demonstration illustrated in Figure 3.31.

The drawing, of course, was specially designed. The final figure was deliberately made ambiguous, so that it looks both like a man's face and a rat. You can just as easily perceive one as the other. But many of the sights we encounter in real life are also ambiguous—and the way we perceive them is also likely to depend on what we expect to see.

In a similar way, interpretation also depends on the situation in which we encounter a stimulus—that is, the **context** in which it is found. For a demonstration, note Figure 3.32. There you see exactly the same unusual symbol in the middle of each of the two words. If you saw it set apart by itself, you would hardly know what it was supposed to be. You might even guess that it was a set of goal posts. In the context of the words, you immediately perceive the first of the identical symbols as an *H* and the second as an *A*.

To show how our internal state can affect interpretation, an experimenter once asked subjects to describe pictures they were told they would see dimly on a screen. Actually there were no real pictures, only blurs and smudges. But hungry subjects, who had gone 16 hours without eating before the experiment, thought they saw all kinds of foods and food-related objects (McClel-

Perceptual expectations
The mental sets that influence interpretation.

Context
The situation in which we encounter a stimulus.

FIGURE 3.32 Same symbol, different context, different interpretation

FIGURE 3.33

land & Atkinson, 1948). It appears that we begin our information processing by perceiving not only what we expect to see and what the situation indicates we are likely to see but also what we want to see.

Thus it is clear that our inborn perceptual skills, so important in helping us survive, are enriched and given meaning by the experiences we encounter throughout our lives (Rock, 1984).

SUMMARY REVIEW

How Our Senses Operate: Some General Principles

1. The *senses* are the information-gathering structures of the nervous system.
2. The two requirements for sensation are (a) a **stimulus,** a form of meaningful energy activating a sense organ, and (b) a **receptor,** a nervous structure capable of responding to that particular stimulus.
3. To activate a sensory receptor, a stimulus must be above the **absolute threshold,** or minimum intensity required to make the receptor respond.
4. To be distinguished as different, two stimuli must vary by at least the amount of the **difference threshold,** also called **just noticeable difference,** or j.n.d. for short. According to *Weber's law,* for each sense the difference threshold is a fixed percentage of the original stimulus (10 percent for sound, 1.6 percent for light).
5. All the senses display **sensory adaptation**—meaning that the sensation produced by a constant stimulus disappears after a time, though a new stimulus creates an immediate new response. Thus our senses are best equipped to provide information about change in the environment.
6. The information that a sense organ receives travels to the brain as millions of tiny impulses. These impulses are deciphered by the brain, enabling us to experience sensation.

The Power of Vision

7. The stimulus for *vision* is *light waves,* a pulsating form of electromagnetic energy. Light waves occupy a small portion of the range of electromagnetic radiation, which extends from cosmic rays (the shortest) to household electricity (the longest). Violet waves are a little longer than

the invisible ultraviolet waves that cause sunburn. Red waves are slightly shorter than the invisible infrared waves produced by a heating lamp.

8. Light waves vary in **wavelength, intensity,** and **complexity.** Wavelength determines *hue,* the term for the sensation produced by a colored object. Intensity determines **brightness** (though not entirely). Complexity determines **saturation,** or the sensation of a vivid or dull hue. White light is a mixture of all the wavelengths, as can be demonstrated by passing it through a prism and obtaining a spectrum of the hues.

9. Light waves enter the eyeball through the **pupil,** which is the opening in the **iris.** They then pass through a transparent **lens,** which can change shape by the action of the **ciliary muscles** to focus the waves sharply on the **retina** at the back of the eyeball. The retina contains the receptors for vision—nerve structures called **rods** and **cones.**

10. The rods function chiefly under low illumination and send information to the brain about movements and about whites, grays, and blacks but not color. The rods contain **rhodopsin,** a pigment bleached by light.

11. The cones function in strong illumination and send information to the brain about not only movement and brightness but also color. There are three kinds of cones, containing pigments that are broadly tuned but most sensitive to either blue, green, or green-yellow.

12. **Dark adaptation,** which makes the eyes about 100,000 times more sensitive under low illumination than in strong light, depends mostly on the rods. At low intensities only the rods function. Because the cones do not respond, color vision is absent.

13. The modern explanation of color vision is **opponent-process theory,** which holds that nervous impulses set off by the rods and three types of cones enter a pathway to the brain containing six different types of neurons. These neurons respond differently to different color stimuli, (or brightness) and black (or darkness). The total pattern of nervous impulses—activated by the response of the rods and cones to a stimulus, then carried to the visual area of the brain by the six types of neurons—accounts for our visual sensations.

14. The ability to distinguish colors varies among individuals. About 2 percent of all people are **color blind.** Some see the world in only black and white; others learn to recognize subtle distinctions, and never know they are color blind.

Hearing: From Sound Waves to Sounds

15. The stimulus for *hearing* is *sound waves,* which are ripples of contraction and expansion of the air. Sound waves vary in **frequency, amplitude,** and **complexity.** The frequency determines our sensation of **pitch.** Amplitude determines *loudness* (though not entirely). Complexity determines **timbre.**

16. Sound waves are collected by the **outer ear,** the visible portion of the ear. The waves create vibrations of the **eardrum,** which are then passed along by the three bones (including the **stapes**) of the **middle ear** to the **cochlea** of the **inner ear.** In the cochlea, the vibrations set up complicated wavelike motions of the **basilar membrane.** These motions activate the hairlike receptors for hearing in the **organ of Corti,** lying on the basilar membrane. The bending of the hairlike receptors stimulates the neurons on the **auditory nerve** to produce the nervous impulses that are routed toward the sensory areas of the cerebral cortex.

17. The basilar membrane is narrowest and stiffest at the end where sound enters the cochlea, and the receptors at this end respond most vigorously to high-frequency waves. The membrane becomes progressively wider and more flexible toward the other end, which is most sensitive to low frequencies.
18. Our ability to know which direction a sound comes from depends on the fact that the hearing receptors in the two ears receive a slightly different pattern of stimulation and send slightly different patterns of nervous impulses to the brain.

Taste, Smell, Touch—and the Two Forgotten Senses

19. The receptors for *taste* lie mostly in the **taste buds** of the tongue. They are broadly tuned to respond to chemical stimulation—but there are four types especially sensitive to either sweet, salty, sour, or bitter.
20. The **olfactory epithelium** contains the receptors for smell; they lie at the top of the nasal passages leading from the nostrils to the throat, and they are sensitive to gases and to molecules of chemicals suspended in the air.
21. Humans have been found to respond to the scent of volatile chemical substances called **pheromones.** The sense of smell has also been found to influence sexual activity in humans as well as animals.
22. The senses of taste and smell are closely intertwined; if the ability to smell is not present, food can become practically tasteless.
23. The receptors for the *skin senses* are nerve endings lying just beneath the surface. They account for our sensations of pressure, pain, cold, and warmth.
24. The sense of **bodily movement** keeps us informed of the position of our muscles and bones and is essential to such complex movements as walking. The receptors are nerve endings in the muscles, tendons, and joints.
25. The sense of **equilibrium** keeps us in balance and oriented to the force of gravity. The receptors are hairlike nerve cells in the inner ear's three **semicircular canals** and **vestibular sacs.**

Perception and Survival

26. Our skill at perception depends in part on the inborn structure of the nervous system and specialized nerve cells called **feature detectors,** found in the pathways from the sense organs to the brain and in the brain itself. In vision, some feature detectors respond sharply to patterns (such as a vertical or a horizontal line, or an angle) and others to movement. In hearing, some feature detectors are strongly activated by either low-pitched sounds, high-pitched sounds, or changes in pitch.
27. Our inborn perceptual skills are particularly adept at spotting any **change, movement,** or **contrast** among the stimuli reaching our senses.
28. In addition, we are proficient in the perception of stimuli of substantial *size* and **intensity.**

Selection and Attention

29. **Selection** is a key element in perception because we can perceive only a few of all the many stimuli that constantly bombard our senses.

30. Selection depends on the inborn structure of the nervous system and on such learned factors as interests, motivation, emotional states, and personality.

31. When we select and pay attention to one event, we usually lose perception of other stimuli. It is especially difficult to process two different inputs if they arrive in the same sensory channel—for example, to pay attention to two conversations at the same time.

32. Selection helps us explore the environment, perceive what is likely to be most important, ignore the rest, and concentrate on using the rest of our information-processing talents to the best possible advantage.

Organizing Our Perceptions

33. *Organization* is a key element because, in order to answer the question *What is it?*, we have to see or hear a stimulus that hangs together in some kind of unit—a human face or a meaningful pattern of human speech.

34. An important factor in organization is **figure and ground,** which is the tendency to perceive an object as a meaningful unit set off from a neutral background by a dividing line called a *contour.*

35. Organization generally follows the rules of:
    a) **closure,** which refers to the fact that we do not need a complete and uninterrupted contour to perceive a figure.
    b) **continuity,** which is the tendency to perceive continuous lines and patterns.
    c) **similarity,** which is the ability to group stimuli that are alike.
    d) **proximity,** which dictates that we tend to group together stimuli that are close in space.

36. **Perceptual constancy** is the tendency to perceive a stable and consistent world even though the stimuli that reach our eyes are inconsistent and potentially confusing. Perceptual constancy includes **shape constancy, size constancy,** and **brightness constancy.**

37. In perceiving distance and depth, we rely on clues provided by movements of the *eye muscles,* **binocular vision, interposition,** and **linear perspective.**

38. Our perceptions of the world are usually—but not always—in accord with the facts. Among the exceptions are perceptual illusions and distortions during **altered states of consciousness** (like those produced by hypnosis or drugs).

39. **Interpretation** is a key element because it answers the question *What does it mean?* Interpretation is ordinarily made by comparing new information provided by the senses with old information acquired in the past.

40. We interpret and identify a new stimulus by matching it against generalized models that we have stored in the memory of familiar events and objects—like the letter E or the human face. Such a model is called a **prototype** or **schema.**

41. Our interpretations are influenced by **perceptual expectations,** or mental sets acquired because we have learned to expect certain events to occur in certain familiar ways. They are also influenced by the **context** in which the new stimulus is found and to some extent even by mood, physical condition, and wishes.

a) Your acquaintance is describing the ability called perception—that is, the ability to select, organize, and interpret evidence from our senses. Without it, the person you called would be left only with a confusing jumble of sound impulses generated by the sound waves you created in saying "hi."

b) It is called the absolute threshold—that is, the point at which there is a minimum amount of stimulus energy (in this case, the odor of food) to which sensory receptors (in this case, receptors for smell) can respond.

c) Your friend is trying to tell you that it was impossible to discriminate between the loudness of the sound before and after you raised the volume. To your friend's ears, the change was not enough to pass the difference threshold, or j.n.d.— which stands for just noticeable difference.

d) You have just left the state of sensory adaptation—meaning that after a while, your ears adjusted to the constant hum of traffic sufficiently for the sensation of the sound to disappear.

e) The resulting defect would be an inability to focus clearly. The ciliary muscles allow the lens of the eye to become thinner in order to bring distant objects into focus and to thicken to do the same for nearby objects.

f) The statement would indicate that the person puts a higher priority on the sensation of color than on whites, grays, and blacks. Rods are responsible for the former, cones for the latter.

g) The hardening of the bones would make them incapable of conducting the vibrations of sound on their way from the eardrum to the inner ear's receptors for hearing.

h) The lollipop would be essentially tasteless since it is sweet, and as can be seen from Figure 3.11 on page 112, the taste buds responsible for the sensation of sweetness are located primarily toward the tip of the tongue.

i) Your dog is likely to be relatively well tuned in to sexually receptive dogs—who secrete pheromones, a volatile chemical substance, in order to attract mates.

j) The infant is demonstrating the inborn skills of being able to spot movement (the rotation of the mobile) and contrast (the contrast between the dark decorations against a white background).

k) It reflects selection—the ability to perceive only a limited number of the stimuli that keep showering our senses and competing for attention.

l) She is describing the general rule that the selection process depends, among other things, on our emotional state.

m) The second would be easier to do since it is somewhat simpler to pay attention when two different senses (in this case, hearing and vision) are being stimulated simultaneously than when a single sense (in this case, hearing alone) is receiving two stimuli.

n) It is one of the rules of organization, called the rule of closure. The rule is based on the fact that we do not need to have a complete and uninterrupted contour of a figure (the truck) in order to perceive it. You are able instinctively to fill in the gaps—in this case, the other headlight, the cab and body of the truck, the tires, and all the rest of the truck's characteristics missing in the fog.

o) It demonstrates the aspect of perception referred to as size constancy—that is, the capacity to recognize the actual size of an object regardless of the size of the image it creates as a result of your distance from it.

p) You did so by having stored in your memory a prototype—that is, a generalized model—of what a human profile looks like, and then fitting the figure to the prototype.

Study Guide

Chapter 3   Sensation and Perception

LEARNING OBJECTIVES

After studying this chapter, you should be able to:

For an Understanding of the Science

1. Describe the operation of the senses and how it depends on stimuli and receptors capable of responding to different stimuli.

2. Understand the principles of absolute threshold, difference threshold, and sensory adaptation.

3. Discuss the seven senses of vision, hearing, taste, smell, touch, bodily movement, and equilibrium, and list the stimuli and receptors responsible for each.

4. Describe the visual sensations of hue, brightness, and saturation and their corresponding physical characteristics of wavelength, intensity, and complexity; the structure of the eye and the process by which it translates light waves into the sensation of vision; and the opponent-process theory of color vision.

5. Describe the auditory sensations of pitch, loudness, and timbre and the corresponding characteristics of the sound wave—namely, frequency, amplitude, and complexity; and the structure of the ear and the process by which it translates sound waves into the sensation of hearing.

6. Understand that perception is the process through which we become aware of our environment by selecting, organizing, and interpreting the evidence from our senses almost instantaneously and without any conscious effort.

7. Discuss how the selection of stimuli is influenced by a built-in tendency of the nervous system and its feature detectors to pay special attention to change, movement, contrast, size, and intensity.

8. Describe how the way we organize stimuli is influenced by the perceptual rules of figure and ground, contour, closure, continuity, similarity, and proximity.

9. Understand how our ability to perceive a stable and consistent world depends in part on shape, size, and brightness constancies.

10. Explain how perception of distance and depth is helped by clues provided by movements of the eye muscles, binocular vision, interposition, linear perspective, and relative size of objects.

11. Understand how we answer the question *What does it mean?* through the element of perception called interpretation, which depends in large part on learning of prototypes or schemas, perceptual expectations, contexts, and internal states.

For Application to Life Situations

12. Explain how we can respond only to those features of the environment to which our sense organs are sensitive—for example, that we can detect light waves but not the very similar waves of radio, X rays, and household

electricity, and understand the limitations and advantages of the human senses.

13. Describe the process of translating light waves into visual sensations beginning in the retina, and the relation of this processing to visual sensitivity, acuity, and color vision.

14. Understand that the way we perceive the world is influenced by our perceptual expectations, the context in which a stimulus occurs, and our interests, physical condition, and even mood of the moment.

15. Cite examples illustrating that the process of perception does not always operate perfectly and that we are subject to a number of perceptual illusions.

16. Understand that it is difficult to pay attention to more than one stimulus at a time, and discuss the implications of this fact for distractions when driving or studying.

PROGRAMMED UNIT

1. *Sensation* is the process by which the sense organs gather information about the environment. The eyes, ears, nose, tongue, and other sense organs provide us with information about the environment and are the crucial detection instruments for the process of _____.

    sensation

2. *Perception* is the process through which we become aware of our environment by selecting, organizing, and interpreting the evidence from our senses. Adding meaning to sensory information is the task of _____.

    perception

3. Taking in information about the environment is the province of _____; interpreting that information is the role of _____.

    sensation
    perception

HOW OUR SENSES FUNCTION: SOME GENERAL PRINCIPLES

4. A sense organ contains *receptors,* special organs that are sensitive to a particular form of energy called a *stimulus.* Light is the _____ that energizes special _____ in the eye.

    stimulus
    receptors

5. For all the senses, there is an *absolute threshold,* the minimum amount of stimulus energy to which the receptors can respond. If a clock ticks close to your ear, you hear it. If the clock is moved farther and farther away, eventually you can no longer hear it because the energy of its _____ has become so weak that the ear's _____ do not respond.

    stimulus
    receptors

6. The minimum amount of stimulus energy to which a receptor can respond is called its _____ _____.

    absolute threshold

7. The senses also have a *difference threshold,* a threshold that involves the ability to discriminate between two stimuli that are similar but not exactly alike. If one light is flashed and then a second light is, the second must be 1.6 percent brighter (or dimmer) for the eyes to notice a difference. A second sound must be 10 percent "louder" (or "softer") than the first. So 1.6 percent is the _____ _____ for light.

    difference threshold

8. For sound, the difference threshold is _____ percent.

    10

9. The rule that the difference threshold is a fixed percentage of the original

difference threshold

stimulus is *Weber's law.* It was Weber who discovered that 10 percent is the _____ _____ for sound.

10. The difference threshold is also called the *just noticeable difference,* or *j.n.d.* for short. The rule that the j.n.d. or difference threshold is a fixed percentage of the original stimulus is _____ law.

Weber's

just noticeable difference

11. A 1.6 percent increase in light level will produce a _____ _____ _____ in illumination.

12. In practical terms, Weber's law means that the more intense the stimulation that a sense organ is receiving, the greater the increase in intensity required to produce a detectable difference. On a noisy city street you may notice the loud honk of an automobile horn but never be aware that a friend is shouting to you from down the block. This is because the horn, but not the voice, has enough energy, over and beyond the stimulation you already hear, to produce a _____ _____ _____ or to reach your _____ _____.

just noticeable difference
difference threshold

13. If you enter a fish market, you will smell fish at first, but eventually the fishy smell seems to go away. This is because of *sensory adaptation,* which means that our senses adjust, or _____, to a stimulus after a time, and the conscious sensation produced by the stimulus tends to disappear.

adapt

14. The tendency of our conscious sensations to fade away after steady and continued stimulation is called _____ _____.

sensory adaptation

15. Of course, if a new stimulus occurs, we will respond to it. Therefore, our senses are designed to inform us of changes in stimulation, because we tend not to respond to continuous stimulation according to the principle of _____ _____.

sensory adaptation

THE POWER OF VISION

16. The energy or _____ for the sense of vision is *light waves,* which consists of pulsations of electromagnetic energy that have three qualities that determine our visual sensations: *wavelength, intensity,* and *complexity.*

stimulus

17. The first quality is the distance between the pulsations or waves, which is called _____. It determines our sensation of *hue,* or color.

wavelength

18. The physical characteristic of _____ produces our sensation of _____, which is the scientific name for the sensation of color.

wavelength
hue

19. Light waves also have a second quality, the amount of energy, which is called _____, and determines the sensation of *brightness.* A 100-watt light bulb looks brighter than a 50-watt bulb because the light waves have greater _____.

intensity

intensity

20. A very short light wave with low intensity looks different from a very long wave with high intensity with respect to color or _____ and intensity or _____.

hue
brightness

21. Besides color, which is determined by _____, and brightness, which is determined by _____, light waves also have *complexity,* which consists of the number of other wavelengths that are mixed together.

wavelength
intensity

22. The relative purity of the light wave, called its _____, determines the sensation of *saturation.* A source of light that is very pure is seen as a vivid hue. If other wavelengths are mixed in, it is seen as a duller or muddier color, which we say has less _____.

complexity

saturation

23. Three physical qualities of light energy produce three different visual sensations. The amount of energy or its _____ produces the sensation of _____. Color or _____ is determined by the _____ of the light, and the purity or _____ of the light creates our sense of _____.

intensity
brightness, hue
wavelength, complexity
saturation

24. Figure 3.3 (page 102) is a diagram of the human eye. Light passes through the *pupil,* the opening you see in your mirror as a small black circle surrounded by the colored *iris,* which is muscle tissue. Like the diaphragm of a camera, the muscles of the _____ contract to minimize the size of the _____ to admit less light in strong illumination.

iris
pupil

25. After light passes through the opening or _____ formed by the colored _____, it then goes through the transparent *lens.* The lens, also as in a camera, focuses the light waves sharply on the back of the eyeball.

pupil
iris

26. Light waves are focused by the _____, the shape of which is controlled by the *ciliary muscles.*

lens

27. While the iris controls the size of the _____ and thus the amount of light that enters the eye, the shape of the lens, which focuses the waves, is controlled by the _____ _____.

pupil

ciliary muscles

28. The receptors for vision are light-sensitive nerve cells packed tightly together in the *retina* at the back of the eyeball. The ciliary muscles adjust the _____ to focus the image on the light-sensitive _____.

lens, retina

29. The visual receptors, located at the back of the eyeball in the _____, are of two kinds: *rods,* which are sensitive to movement, blacks, grays, and whites but not to color; and *cones,* which are sensitive to color as well as to brightness and movement.

retina

30. The visual receptors sensitive only to movement and brightness from black to white are the _____.

rods

31. The visual receptors sensitive to hue, and therefore responsible for color vision, are the _____.

cones

32. The cones are most numerous toward the middle of the _____, especially in an area at the very center, called the *fovea,* which contains only _____ packed together more tightly than anywhere else. In contrast, the periphery of the retina contains mostly _____.

retina

cones
rods

33. It is in the center part of the _____, called the _____, that we see color and where our vision is sharpest.

retina, fovea

34. When we read or do anything else that requires a very sharp image, we keep the object in the center of the field of vision so that its light waves fall on the _____.

fovea

35. The impulses from the rods and cones leave the eyeball by way of the *optic nerve.* The connection between the nerves from the eyes' receptors and the brain is the _____ _____.

optic nerve

36. The place on the retina where the optic nerve is connected has no receptors and so constitutes a *blind spot.* It is difficult to see an image that falls on the _____ _____ of the _____.

blind spot, retina

37. The rods and cones, located in the light-sensitive _____, contain pigments that absorb light, which bleaches the pigments at a rate that depends on the intensity and wavelengths of the light, and these chemical

retina

rhodopsin

changes cause the neurons to fire. One such pigment found in the rods is *rhodopsin*. When light strikes the rods, it bleaches _____, which causes the neurons to fire.

38. The visual system operates under a wide range of illumination. One feature that helps you see in dim light is *dark adaptation*. The fact that you see better in a movie theater after several minutes illustrates the process of _____ _____.

dark adaptation

39. After spending time in the dark, the rod's light-sensitive pigment, _____, builds up, producing extra sensitivity—almost 100,000 times more sensitive after 30 minutes of _____ _____.

rhodopsin
dark adaptation

40. The modern explanation of the way the sense of vision operates is the *opponent-process theory*, which is a pattern theory based in part on the differences in sensitivity among the rods and the three types of _____.

cones

41. We see the great variety of images and colors that we do because of patterns of firing from the receptors according to the _____-_____ theory of vision.

opponent-process

42. A few people, about 2 percent, are *color blind*—that is, they have difficulty seeing some colors. Often, this is caused by a deficiency in one or another of the three types of color receptors, called _____.

cones

43. The inability to detect the difference between reds and greens is more common than between blues and yellows among _____ _____ individuals.

color blind

HEARING: FROM SOUND WAVES TO SOUNDS

44. The physical stimulus for the sense of hearing is *sound waves*, which are invisible little ripples of contraction and expansion of the air. Compressions and expansions of the air, called _____ _____, vary in a number of ways that affect our sensations. One is *frequency*, or the number of waves per second.

sound waves

45. The number of sound waves per second, called _____, determines the *pitch* of the sound we hear, from the lowest boom of a foghorn to the highest tweet of a piccolo.

frequency

46. The sensation of _____ is governed by the physical sound wave's _____.

pitch
frequency

47. The sensation of *loudness* is determined by the sound wave's *amplitude*, or strength. If you touch the piano key for middle C gently, then strike it hard, the second sound wave has greater _____ than the first, even though both have the same _____.

amplitude
frequency

48. Psychologically, the second tone has greater _____, even though both have the same sensation of _____.

loudness
pitch

49. Overtones, which make sound waves vary in their physical *complexity*, are caused by the fact that virtually all sources of sounds produce not a single frequency, like middle C, but other frequencies as well. When a piano string vibrates at middle C, parts of the string also vibrate with reduced amplitude at other frequencies. These additional vibrations produce _____, which reflect the _____ of the sound wave.

overtones, complexity

50. The pattern of basic frequency plus overtones constitutes the sound wave's physical _____, which produces the psychological sensation of *timbre*.

complexity

51. Middle C could be played with the same amplitude on a piano and the clarinet, but the two tones will sound different because they have different _____, even though they have the same main _____ and _____.

timbre, pitch loudness

52. Since human vocal cords also vibrate in different ways and produce different patterns of overtones, their sound waves also vary in _____ and in the sensation of _____ they create.

complexity timbre

53. To summarize the relation between characteristics of a sound wave and the sensations they produce, the wave's frequency determines our sensation of _____, its amplitude determines _____, and its complexity determines _____.

pitch, loudness timbre

54. Our sensation of pitch depends on the sound wave's _____, loudness on its _____, and timbre on its _____.

frequency, amplitude, complexity

55. You may have noted a resemblance between the ways in which the physical qualities of light and sound waves affect vision and hearing. Just as the frequency of sound waves determines _____, the wavelength of light determines _____.

pitch hue

56. Just as the amplitude of sound waves determines _____, the intensity of light determines _____.

loudness brightness

57. And just as the complexity of sound determines _____, the complexity of light waves determines _____.

timbre saturation

58. Figure 3.9 (page 108) is a diagram of the parts of the human ear. Sound waves gathered by the *outer ear,* or visible portion, cause vibrations to travel to the *eardrum.* Sound waves, collected by the _____ _____, vibrate the _____, which moves three small bones in the *middle ear.*

outer ear eardrum

59. The three bones of the _____ _____ amplify the sound, and the last bone, called the *stapes,* is mounted like a piston on the *cochlea.*

middle ear

60. After amplification, the sound vibration is conducted via the last bone of the middle ear, the _____, to the _____ of the *inner ear.*

stapes, cochlea

61. A bony structure the size of a pea and shaped like a snail's shell is the _____, which contains the receptors for hearing in the _____ _____.

cochlea inner ear

62. The cochlea is divided roughly in half by the *basilar membrane,* stretched across it from one end to the other. The hearing receptors lie atop this _____ membrane, which makes wavelike motions as the fluid inside the cochlea responds to the vibrations.

basilar

63. It is the wavelike motions of the _____ _____ inside the _____ that jiggle the hearing receptors, called the *organ of Corti.*

basilar membrane, cochlea

64. The hair cells, or _____ of _____, located atop the _____ _____, dance in sympathetic vibration with the sound wave and send nervous impulses along the *auditory nerve* to the brain that produce our sense of hearing.

organ, Corti, basilar membrane

65. The specialized cells, called the _____ of _____ atop the

organ, Corti

basilar membrane, cochlea, inner ear, auditory nerve	_____ _____ in the _____ of the _____ _____ send their impulses to the brain along the _____ _____.
taste buds	66. Our sense of taste is typically associated with the *taste bud* receptors that line the tongue and back of our mouths. But the flavor of food is influenced by its temperature, smell, and other factors in addition to its sweet, sour, salty, and bitter characteristics detected by the _____ _____.
olfactory epithelium	67. The receptors for smell are in the *olfactory epithelium,* located at the top of the nasal passage. Sensitivity to odors appears to depend in part on the number of receptors contained in the _____ _____.
pheromones	68. Animals often give off odors, called *pheromones,* that signal danger, territory, or sexual receptivity. While less obvious, humans may also produce sexual _____.
bodily movement **equilibrium**	69. Often forgotten are the senses of *bodily movement* and *equilibrium.* Receptors in the muscles, tendons, and joints provide information about our _____ _____, while receptors in the *vestibular sacs* of the *semicircular canals* of the inner ear help to keep our bodies in balance or _____.
vestibular sacs, semicircular canals, equilibrium	70. Tiny pieces of stone-like crystal whose movement can be detected by receptors in the _____ _____ of the _____ _____ help us stay balanced or in a state of _____ with respect to the force of gravity.
overloaded	71. Some people experience motion sickness in an airplane or car when the sense of *equilibrium* becomes _____.

PERCEPTION AND SURVIVAL

perception **sensations**	72. The process by which we become aware of our environment by selecting, organizing, and interpreting sensory information is called _____, and our ability to add meaning to _____ is greatly assisted by the presence of specialized cells called *feature detectors.*
feature detectors	73. Cells that respond immediately to stimuli representing such important information as the shapes of objects, motion, and the changes in sound that make up the flow of conversation are called _____ _____.
change, feature detectors	74. Our inborn skills are particularly adept at spotting any *change* in stimulation, which is often the most useful information of all. Our ability to perceive _____ sometimes depends on special cells called _____ _____ and other inborn characteristics of the nervous system.
change	75. One form of _____ in stimulation is *movement.* To our ancestors, the sudden approach of a wild animal meant danger regardless of whether the animal was a lion or a bear—an example of the survival value of rapid detection of _____.
movement	
change, movement **feature detectors** **contrast, size** **intensity**	76. Besides _____ and _____, other compelling stimulus attributes are *contrast, size,* and *intensity.* Apparently inborn characteristics of the nervous system, including _____ _____, make us sit up and take notice of a _____ in brightness, the _____ of objects in our field of vision, or the _____ of stimuli that are bright or loud.

77. In summary, much of our knowledge of the environment comes through _____, which is partly determined by the inborn structure of the nervous system, including _____ _____ that are sensitive to _____, _____, _____, _____, and _____.

perception
feature detectors
change, movement
contrast, size, intensity

SELECTION AND ATTENTION

78. Of the three functions of perception—selection, organization, and interpretation—*selection* heads the list. This is because perception must start with the _____ of stimuli to attend to.

selection

79. Although much selection of stimulation depends on the inborn structure of the nervous system, learned dispositions, such as *interests, motives,* and *moods* also influence our _____ process.

selection

80. When subjects are asked to identify words flashed very briefly on a screen, business people are quick to recognize words like "income" and ministers are quick to recognize "sacred." This is an example of the way our _____ influence perception.

interests

81. Under the same condition, ambitious people are especially quick to perceive words like "strive" and "perfect," an example of how perception is influenced by _____.

motives

82. You have probably noticed that when you are feeling on top of the world you are aware that the sun is shining and everybody seems to be smiling. But when you are out of sorts you are quick to notice anything that is potentially irritating, like noise outside the window or a watchband that feels too tight. This is an example of how perception is influenced by one's _____ of the moment.

mood

83. Selection is difficult if two different stimuli arrive in the same *sensory channel*. Using earphones that deliver one spoken message to the right ear and a different message to the left ear, experimenters have found that subjects can pay attention to and understand the message, from only one _____ _____ but not both ears at the same time. They must _____ one message only.

sensory channel
select

ORGANIZING OUR PERCEPTIONS

84. After we make a _____ of one of the many stimuli in the environment for further exploration, we strive to find an *organization* that forms the stimulus into some kind of meaningful unit.

selection

85. Light waves that hang together as some kind of object, like a face or an automobile, or sound waves that form a pattern of meaningful speech or a rap at the door are examples of how we _____ sensations into meaningful units.

organize

86. In vision, determining what an objective is through _____ is dictated largely by the perceptual principle of *figure and ground*. As you read this page, your eyes are stimulated by the white space and many little black lines, curves, squiggles, and dots. You perceive all this as black _____—letters and words—seen against a white _____. What separates the figure from the background is a clearly perceived dividing line called the *contour*.

organization

figures, ground

figure, ground
contours

organize

closure

continuity

closure, continuity

similarity

proximity

organization, closure
continuity, similarity
proximity

perceptual constancy

perceptual, shape
size constancy

brightness constancy

distance, depth

perception

87. Perceiving a chair as a unit standing out from the rest of the room or a face as a unit clearly distinguishable from the wall behind it, are examples of a _____ seen against a _____ separated by dividing lines called _____.

88. Even with the aid of figure and ground, a number of rules help to _____ our perceptions. One rule is that of *closure,* which refers to the fact that we do not need a complete and uninterrupted contour to perceive a figure.

89. We will perceive an object as a circle even if portions of the curved figure are missing because of the principle of _____. Another principle is *continuity,* which is the tendency to perceive continuous lines and patterns.

90. We are more likely to see a line as wavy rather than as a series of scallops because of our tendency toward _____.

91. In addition to the principles of _____ and _____, we organize stimuli according to their *similarity* and *proximity.*

92. Instead of seeing three red and five green blocks as a set of eight, we are more likely to see two sets of different colored blocks because of the _____ of colors.

93. Pauses after commas and periods when we read a sentence help the listener to group the words between these punctuation marks by the principle of _____.

94. Therefore, the rules of perceptual _____ include _____, _____, _____, and _____. But alone they are not sufficient, for we also perceive a stable and consistent world because of our tendency toward *perceptual constancy.*

95. For example, when we look at a dish, we perceive it as round no matter what angle we look at it from. The dish does not seem to change its shape regardless of the image it casts on our retinas because of the tendency toward _____ _____.

96. We perceive the shape of a dish as constant, due to what is called *shape constancy. Size constancy* also exists and refers to the tendency to recognize the actual size of an object regardless of whether it is near or far. Two examples of _____ constancies are _____ and _____ _____.

97. Also, because of *brightness constancy,* we perceive the brightness of objects to be the same even when the actual level of illumination changes dramatically. A black shoe on a sidewalk in bright sunlight is perceived as black just as the same shoe is perceived as black when lying on a brown carpet in a dimly lit room. This is an example of _____ _____.

98. Not only must we organize perceptions to determine what stimuli are, but we need to know where objects are located. Just to walk around without bumping into chairs and other people, we must be able to perceive *distance* and *depth,* for example. Two skills that help us locate objects are _____ and _____ perception.

99. Two factors that aid distance and depth _____ are *binocular vision* (the fact that the two eyes, set 2½ inches apart, receive slightly different images) and *interposition* (the fact that nearby objects block off our view of more distant objects).

100. The fact that the two eyes receive slightly different images, a clue to distance and depth perception, is known as _____ vision.

binocular

101. If we see a boy blocking off part of our view of a tree, we know that the boy is closer than the tree. If the tree obscures part of the boy, we know the tree is closer. This is the clue of _____.

interposition

102. Artists provide additional clues to the perception of _____ and _____ by the use of *linear perspective* and *relative size*.

distance, depth

103. In a photograph, two railroad tracks seem to draw closer together as they recede into the distance, which illustrates how _____ _____ contributes to the perception of distance and depth. Similarly, larger objects are usually perceived as closer than smaller ones because of the principle of _____ _____.

linear perspective

relative size

104. Four clues to perceiving distance and depth are the fact we have two eyes (i.e., _____ _____), near objects occlude more distant objects (i.e., _____), parallel lines converge in the distance (i.e., _____ _____), and nearer objects usually appear larger (i.e., _____ _____).

binocular vision
interposition
linear perspective
relative size

105. In attaching meaning to our sensations, we pick some stimuli and not others to attend to by the process of _____, we determine what and where an object is by the process of _____, and we attach further meaning through the process of *interpretation*.

selection
organization

106. The perceptual process of finding meaning, called _____, is clearly more dependent on learning than on inborn characteristics of the nervous system. For example, how do you know that the object you have selected for attention and oganized into a pattern of head, furry body, and wagging tail is a dog and not a cat? You perceive this immediately because you have stored in memory what is called a *prototype* or *schema*—a sort of generalized picture of what a dog and a cat look like.

interpretation

107. Since the new stimulus resembles the _____ or _____ you have learned, you can quickly make an _____ of what the stimulus means.

prototype, schema
interpretation

108. In quickly deciding what a stimulus means, we are often influenced by *perceptual expectations*. The mental set we have, which is the result of learning to expect certain things to happen in our environment, constitutes a _____ _____.

perceptual expectation

109. In addition, interpretation depends on the *context* in which a stimulus is located. From a distance, a soccer ball and a basketball might be indistinguishable, but we would interpret the ball to be a basketball if it were located near a basketball goal rather than a soccer goal, thus making the interpretation on the basis of _____.

context

110. *Internal states* can also influence our interpretations of objects. Alcohol can contribute to the perception of movement, and hunger can cause us to interpret certain ambiguous stimuli as food. Both alcohol and hunger show how our _____ _____ can influence our _____ of stimuli.

internal state
interpretation

REVIEW OF IMPORTANT TERMS

absolute threshold (99)

altered states of consciousness (ASC) (131)

amplitude (107)

auditory nerve (109)

basilar membrane (109)

binocular vision (129)

blind spot (103)

bodily movement (118)

brightness (101)

brightness constancy (129)

ciliary muscles (103)

closure (126)

cochlea (109)

color blindness (106)

complexity (101)

cones (104)

context (133)

continuity (126)

contrast (122)

dark adaptation (105)

difference threshold (100)

eardrum (108)

equilibrium (118)

"fast" fibers (117)

feature detectors (120)

figure and ground (125)

fovea (104)

frequency (107)

gate-control mechanism (117)

inner ear (109)

intensity (101)

interposition (129)

interpretation (131)

iris (102)

lens (102)

linear perspective (129)

middle ear (108)

movement (121)

olfactory epithelium (112)

opponent-process theory (106)

optic nerve (103)

organ of Corti (109)

outer ear (108)

perception (98)

perceptual constancy (127)

perceptual expectation (133)

pheromone (113)

pitch (107)

prototype (131)

proximity (126)

pupil (102)

receptor (99)

relative size (129)

retina (103)

rhodopsin (104)

rods (104)

saturation (101)

schema (131)

selection (122)

sensation (98)

semicircular canals (118)

sensory adaptation (101)

shape constancy (127)

similarity (126)

simultaneous brightness contrast (122)

size constancy (127)

"slow" fibers (117)

stapes (109)

stimulus (98)

taste buds (111)

timbre (107)

vestibular sacs (119)

wavelength (101)

PRACTICE TEST

_____ 1. Weber's law states that

    a.   the absolute threshold is the same for all stimuli.

    b.   repeated exposure to a stimulus makes the sensation for that stimulus progressively weaker.

    c.   the just noticeable difference is always the same fraction of the absolute threshold.

    d.   The difference threshold is a fixed percentage of the original stimulus over a wide range of stimuli within a given sense.

_____ 2. Which of the following is _incorrect?_

    a.   Intensity is to brightness as amplitude is to loudness.

    b.   Complexity is to saturation as overtones is to pitch.

    c.   Wavelength is to hue as frequency is to pitch.

    d.   All of the above are correct.

_____ 3. When you first enter a fish market, the smell is strong and perhaps unpleasant. If you stay for a long time, the odor seems to go away. This demonstrates

    a.   the difference threshold.

    b.   just noticeable difference.

    c.   sensory adaptation.

    d.   broad-tuned receptors.

_____ 4. The pattern theory of sensation

    a.   applies primarily to vision and hearing but not to taste, smell, or touch.

    b.   explains why we are able to sense highly specific stimuli even though individual receptors are broadly tuned to fire when stimulated by a wide range of stimuli.

    c.   explains why we tend to look at something we hear.

    d.   none of the above.

_____ 5. When many other different wavelengths are added to a green, the light appears

    a.   to have more timbre.

    b.   more complex.

    c.   less intensely green.

    d.   more saturated.

_____ 6. The eye's ciliary muscles control

    a.   the direction the eyeball is oriented.

    b.   the size of the pupil.

    c.   the sense of bodily movement.

    d.   the shape of the lens of the eye.

_____ 7. Relative to rods, cones are
   a. more numerous.
   b. more sensitive to dim light.
   c. concentrated in the center of the retina.
   d. filled with rhodopsin, which when stimulated by light, produces impulses corresponding to the three basic color types.

_____ 8. The sensation of the pitch of a sound is most closely associated with what sensation of light?
   a. wavelength
   b. hue
   c. intensity
   d. complexity

_____ 9. The correct sequence in which sound is transmitted to the brain is
   a. cochlea, bones of the middle ear, the basilar membrane.
   b. stapes, organ of Corti, eardrum.
   c. eardrum, stapes, cochlea, basilar membrane, organ of Corti.
   d. outer ear, eardrum, middle ear, cochlea, stapes

_____ 10. A nerve cell that responds to a vertical line but not a horizontal line is an example of a
   a. feature detector.
   b. linear perspective system.
   c. pattern analyzer.
   d. selection and organization process.

_____ 11. Cells in the nerve pathways from eye to brain are especially sensitive to
   a. pattern and movement.
   b. color.
   c. brightness and saturation.
   d. distant objects.

_____ 12. The fact that a nearer object may obscure a more distant object from view is called
   a. the simultaneous brightness contrast.
   b. figure and ground.
   c. proximity.
   d. interposition.

_____ 13. If you are trying to follow two football games on different TV sets, you will do best if you
   a. turn off the sound on one set, watch that game, and listen to the other game.
   b. use single earphones that send the sound from one set to the right ear and from the other set to the left ear.

c. close your eyes and listen to the two games.

d. turn off the sound on both sets and watch both games.

_____ 14. When you listen to a person speaking in a foreign language with which you are familiar, you may miss some words but you understand the meaning because of

a. similarity.

b. closure.

c. perceptual constancy.

d. continuity.

_____ 15. As you walk toward your breakfast table, the dishes cast oval images on your eyes, yet you always perceive the dishes as circular. This is an example of perceptual

a. closure.

b. constancy.

c. illusion.

d. interpretation.

_____ 16. Three-dimensional movies, but not other films, utilize the perceptual clue of

a. binocular vision.

b. perspective.

c. movements of the eye muscles.

d. interposition.

_____ 17. Railroad tracks that seem to draw closer together as they recede into the distance are an example of

a. linear perspective.

b. relative size.

c. binocular vision.

d. feature detection.

_____ 18. The element of perception most clearly dependent on learning rather than on inborn traits is

a. organization.

b. selection.

c. interpretation.

d. feature detection.

_____ 19. A generalized picture or model of an object or event—learned in the past and stored in memory—is a(n)

a. perceptual expectation.

b. prototype or schema.

c. shape constancy.

d. opponent process.

_____20. Our interpretation of a stimulus may be affected by

    a.   our body chemistry.

    b.   our mood or physical condition at the moment.

    c.   our personality.

    d.   all of the above.

ANSWERS TO PRACTICE TEST

1. d	6. d	11. a	16. a
2. b	7. c	12. d	17. a
3. c	8. b	13. a	18. c
4. b	9. c	14. b	19. b
5. c	10. a	15. b	20. d

EXERCISES

I. Perceptual expectations can influence how we perceive an object. Follow the directions in the caption for Figure 3.31 on page 132 of your text to illustrate this fact.

II. Figures 3.34 and 3.35 are diagrams of the eye and ear with several parts located but not labeled. Write in the correct name for each part indicated.

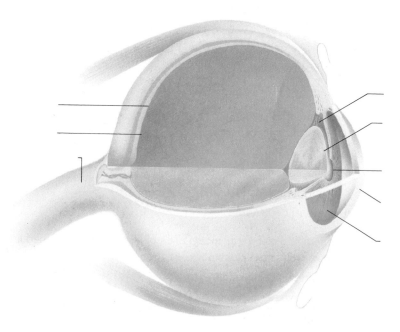

FIGURE 3.34

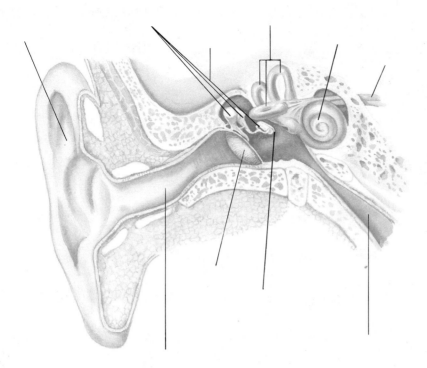

FIGURE 3.35

Then, without looking at the diagrams, write a paragraph, one for vision and one for audition, that describes the path a stimulus takes from receptor to brain, mentioning as many parts of the sensory system as you can and telling the function each part plays.

Explain for both vision and audition how variations in the stimulus—wavelength, intensity, complexity for vision and frequency, amplitude, complexity for audition—are translated into different patterns of nervous impulses that the brain can then interpret as different sensations.

CHAPTER 4

C H A P T E R   O U T L I N E

Classical Conditioning

Pavlov and the salivating dogs

Conditioned terror: The baby who feared Santa Claus

Conditioning feelings of illness

Conditioning and the immune system

The essentials of classical conditioning

The Power of Conditioning: Influential Factors

The effects of timing and frequency

The predictability of reinforcement

The power of expectation: Drug reactions without drugs

The extinction and recovery of conditioned responses

Stimulus generalization and discrimination

The role of built-in predispositions in learning

Operant Conditioning

B. F. Skinner's magic box

Some basics of operant conditioning

Behavior shaping

How superstitions take shape

Some features of reinforcement

Partial reinforcement schedules

Behavior modification and token economies

PSYCHOLOGY IN ACTION
Learning through biofeedback

Escape and Avoidance, Punishment, and Learned Helplessness

Escape and avoidance in everyday life

How punishment affects behavior

Punishment with animals—and with people

Learning to feel helpless

Helplessness and failure: Antidotes

Cognitive Learning: A Contemporary View Rooted in the Past

The case of the ingenious chimps

Learning in the absence of reinforcement

Can there be learning without a response?

Cognitive maps, expectancies, and knowledge

LIFE SPAN PERSPECTIVE
Learning and age

Observational learning

Summary Review

"Test Yourself" Answers

Study Guide

Learning: Basic Principles

The behavior and mental activity of each of us depend to a large extent on the process of learning—a subject which, from the very beginning has been a central concern to psychology. Indeed, virtually everything discussed in the introductory psychology course at least in part involves learning—for example, the process of perception with which we view the world (Chapter 3), the events that trigger our emotions (Chapter 1), our motivations (Chapter 7), and our relations with the society in which we find ourselves (Chapter 14).

Instincts
A built-in pattern of behavior.

True enough, some of the creatures that inhabit our earth manage to go about their lives without learning much new. Most of what they need to know to subsist is already present in the wiring of the nervous system with which they are born—and they require, if anything, only a minimal degree of experience to deal with life. Guided solely by their **instincts,** or *built-in patterns of behavior,* they can find food, build shelters, mate, and survive.

Human beings, however, are quite different. To be sure, there are certain basic behaviors—sucking is one example—that appear at the very start of life without any apparent learning. But we have no inborn blueprints in the nervous system to put us on "automatic pilot" and steer us through life. We have to learn how to find food, keep warm, build shelters. We must learn to form social arrangements that provide the safety of numbers and enrich our lives by providing through joint effort what no individual could manage alone.

Over the years, psychology has taken two notably different approaches to the study of learning. In the period when most psychologists preferred to study observable actions and ignore mental life and human consciousness, learning was generally regarded as a process that produced clear-cut and readily apparent changes in behavior. Many psychologists concentrated on lower animals and the way their behavior could be altered by experience. The science searched for laws that applied not just to humans but to all forms of animal life.

Even during this period, however, there were some psychologists who believed learning could not be fully understood without considering the subtle workings of the human brain. The rise of the cognitive school has popularized this view of learning as the acquisition of knowledge—one of the steps in "the human being's active interaction with information about the world" (Klatzky, 1980). It is such learning that allows us to accomplish the learning necessary, for example, to play the piano, to write a novel, or to develop computer programs.

Learning
Any relatively permanent change in behavior produced by experience.

Both these approaches have been fruitful, and although many learning theorists today believe that all human learning is cognitive in nature, each will be described in turn in this chapter. Together, they represent what is today a generally accepted definition of **learning:** *Any relatively permanent change in behavior (or behavior potential) produced by experience* (Tarpy & Mayer, 1978). The words "behavior potential" refer to the knowledge we acquire and remember—like the nursery rhyme "Old Mother Hubbard"—without necessarily displaying any change in the way we act. The definition also covers the universal laws of learning that psychologists have established by observing the actual behavior of humans and lower animals.

Classical Conditioning

Many of us seem to have seemingly inexplicable preferences for certain things, especially certain kinds of people. We may be instantly attracted to men who have mustaches or men who are bald, or to small women or women who are tall and broad shouldered. We may feel unexplained warmth toward a certain tone of voice or the way a person walks, gestures, or dresses. We know that these matters have nothing to do with what the person is really like, yet we find ourselves irresistibly drawn.

Similarly, many of us are troubled by unreasonable fears. You may, for example, suffer from a strange reluctance to be in any kind of small, enclosed place. It frightens you to step into an elevator or a closet. You breathe faster; you feel a sinking sensation in your stomach; your hands tremble. You know that this fear, which is called **claustrophobia,** makes no sense. But you cannot help it. You are frightened without knowing why.

These unreasonable preferences and fears are learned responses—though often we do not know how we have learned them. In many cases they seem to be the result of **classical conditioning,** which can best be explained by discussing the work of Ivan Pavlov, a Russian scientist who performed one of the most famous experiments in the history of psychology.

Pavlov and the Salivating Dogs

Pavlov conducted his experiment in the early years of this century in Saint Petersburg, Russia. His subjects were dogs, and his experimental apparatus was the simple but effective device illustrated in Figure 4.1. His concern was focused on the type of behavior called a **reflex,** an automatic action exhibited by all organisms that possess a nervous system. One such reflex is the knee jerk. When you have your legs crossed, with one foot dangling in the air, a sharp tap just below the kneecap makes the foot jump. Another reflex makes your pupils smaller whenever a bright light strikes your eyes. The bodily changes associated with emotions are also reflex responses. For example, when a baby hears a sudden loud noise, this stimulus automatically triggers the nervous system into producing the changes in heartbeat and limb movement that are characteristic of fear.

All reflex responses take place without conscious effort, because our nervous system is wired in such a way that the stimulus automatically produces the response. The reflexes are built in, not learned. The question that interested Pavlov was this: Can reflexes be modified by learning?

Pavlov set about answering the question by investigating the salivary reflex, which results in secretions by the salivary glands of the mouth when

Claustrophobia

An abnormal fear of being in any kind of small, enclosed space like a closet or elevator.

Classical conditioning

A type of learning process through which a reflex becomes associated with a previously neutral stimulus.

Reflex

An automatic action exhibited by an organism.

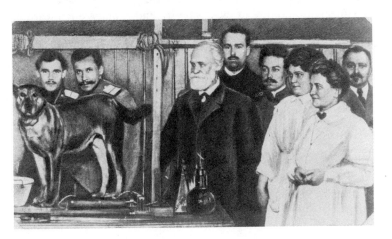

Pavlov is shown (center) in his laboratory with his assistants, his apparatus, and one of his dogs.

FIGURE 4.1 *Pavlov's dog*
A tube attached to the dog's salivary gland collects any saliva secreted by the gland, and the number of drops from the tube is recorded on a revolving drum outside the chamber. The experimenter can watch the dog through a one-way mirror and deliver food to the dog's feed pan by remote control. Thus there is nothing in the chamber to distract the dog's attention except the food, when it is delivered, and any other stimulus that the experimenter wishes to present, such as the sound of a metronome. For the discoveries Pavlov made with this apparatus, see the text (Yerkes & Morgulis, 1909).

food is presented. He strapped a dog into the harness shown in Figure 4.1 and then introduced a sound, such as the beat of a metronome. The dog made a few restless movements, but there was no flow of saliva. This was what Pavlov had expected. The stimulus for reflex action of the salivary glands is the presence of food in the mouth—not the sound of a metronome. When food was delivered and the dog took it into its mouth, saliva of course flowed in quantity.

Now Pavlov set about trying to connect the neutral stimulus of the sound with the reflex action of the salivary glands. While the metronome was clicking, he delivered food to the dog, setting off the salivary reflex. After a time he did the same thing again—sounded the metronome and delivered food. When he had done this many times, he tried something new. He sounded the metronome but did not deliver any food. Saliva flowed anyway (Pavlov, 1927). The dog had learned—through the form of learning now called classical conditioning—to exhibit the salivary reflex in response to a totally new kind of stimulus.

In the more than 60 years since Pavlov, psychologists have studied classical conditioning with a wide variety of techniques and with various species of animals—mostly domesticated rats, pigeons, and rabbits. Such learning has been shown to be possible even in the primitive sea snail (Carew, Hawkins, & Kandel, 1983). An example of one technique—for conditioning the rabbit to blink—is described in Figure 4.2. Because rabbits do not ordinarily blink their eyes, the researcher can be fairly certain that the response occurs as a result of conditioning (Gormezano, Kehoe, & Marshall, 1983).

Conditioned Terror: The Baby Who Feared Santa Claus

What salivating dogs and blinking rabbits tell us about more complicated forms of human behavior was demonstrated in another famous experiment— this one performed by John Watson, the founder of behaviorism. Watson's subject was an 11-month-old boy named Albert. His experiment was an

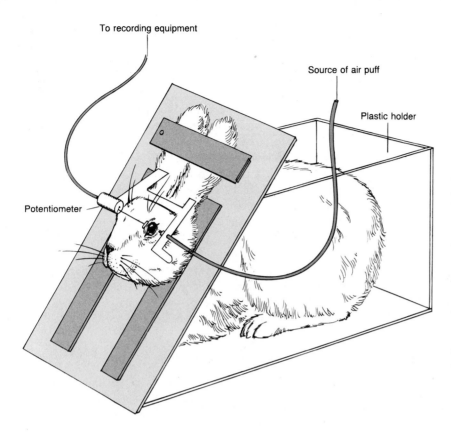

FIGURE 4.2 **Learning to blink the eye** The rabbit is placed in a plastic holder, with the head protruding from it. One end of a fine string is attached to the upper lid of one eye. The other end is attached to a small potentiometer—a device through which eyelid movements can be translated into electrical impulses and then recorded. The stimulus for the eye-blink reflex is a puff of air to the surface of the eye. In various conditioning experiments, rabbits have learned through classical conditioning to blink in response to totally new stimuli—including lights, tones, and even vibration of the animal's abdomen with a hand massager (after Domjan & Burkhard, 1986).

attempt to establish whether the reflex response of fear produced in infants by a loud noise could be conditioned to take place in response to other and previously neutral stimuli.

At the start Albert had no fear of a white rat. But every time he touched the animal, a loud noise was sounded. After a number of pairings of animal and sound, Albert began to cry when he saw the rat. He also showed strong signs of fear toward some other furry objects, including a dog and a fur coat, and a suspicious attitude toward a bearded mask of Santa Claus (Watson & Rayner, 1920). If the fear persisted, Albert may have come to be afraid of sidewalk Santa Clauses at Christmas—without ever knowing why.

The Albert experiment casts considerable light on the unexplained fears we often display as adults. A number of them are conditioned responses, learned in childhood through some long-forgotten pairing of stimuli— through an experience that may not even have impressed us much at the time. Similarly, the experiment helps explain many of our unreasonable preferences. A liking for people of a certain type may go back to a childhood experience in which a person with that kind of face or body build or mannerisms elicited reflex responses of warmth and pleasure.

Conditioning Feelings of Illness

In one experiment, rats were put into a coma with a heavy dose of insulin, producing the drastic reaction known as insulin shock. The drug was administered with a hypodermic needle while a bright light was shining. The concurrent association of needle, light, and coma resulted in a spectacular kind of conditioning. The same kind of light was turned on, the same needle was used to inject a harmless shot of salt water—and the animals went into a coma characteristic of insulin shock (Sawrey, Conger, & Turrell, 1956). More recent research demonstrates that, by pairing the injection of insulin (which reduces blood sugar level) with normally irrelevant stimuli such as a strange odor, noise, and light, it is possible to condition a decrease in blood sugar level in humans (Fehm-Wolfsdorf et al., 1993).

Such experiments indicate the ways in which classical conditioning can produce some of the strange physical symptoms that may bother us as adults. An asthma sufferer may have been conditioned—not in the laboratory but by some real-life experience—to have an attack when walking into a particular room or seeing a particular person or even looking at a certain kind of picture on a television screen. Events that occur in our lives, unimportant in themselves but associated with past experiences, may make us have headaches or become sick to our stomachs. We may suddenly and inexplicably show all the symptoms of having a cold, or we may experience heart palpitations, high blood pressure, dizziness, or cramps.

Conditioning and the Immune System

More recent studies show that our immune system, which produces antibodies to help us fight infection and disease, can be influenced by conditioning. Rats were conditioned to associate a novel taste with unpleasant physical reactions to a drug that suppresses the immune system. Later, when the animals were exposed only to the novel taste but not to the drug, the production of immune system antibodies was suppressed (Ader, Cohen, & Bovbjerg, 1982). This research demonstrates that each of us is potentially vulnerable to changes in our resistance to disease as a result of classically conditioned responses occurring without our awareness.

The conditioning process plays a role in the development of some of life's more pleasant physical responses as well. Think, for example, of the reaction of your stomach glands to the mention of a restaurant in which you have enjoyed a series of memorable dinners. Or think of the sexual response you might feel to the odor of a particular perfume or shaving lotion that you associate with an attractive friend.

The power of such conditioning was demonstrated in a study of male rat pups that suckled females whose nipples and vaginal odors were altered with a distinct lemon scent. The rats were then weaned and never exposed again either to females or to the lemon scent until they were sexually mature. At that point they were paired with sexually receptive females. The vaginal areas of some females were treated with lemon scent, but others were not. As shown in Figure 4.3, the contrast in sexual response was dramatic. The male rats placed with the lemon-scented females became more excited and ejaculated readily, while the other rats were considerably slower to respond (Fillion & Blass, 1986).

In a more recent study, five-day-old rats were exposed to an orange scent, followed by an injection of morphine. When they were 10 days old, they showed a marked preference for the scent of orange, a preference that was reversible by the injection of an opiate-blocker drug. Thus it would

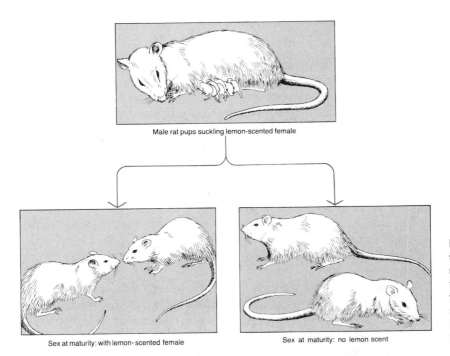

Male rat pups suckling lemon-scented female

Sex at maturity: with lemon-scented female

Sex at maturity: no lemon scent

FIGURE 4.3 Early conditioning of later sexual response As explained in the text, male rat pups that suckled females treated with a lemon scent became sexually aroused by the smell after they reached puberty (Fillion & Blass, 1986).

appear that exposure to the orange scent in previously conditioned rats caused a release of opiate-like chemicals in the brain. This conclusion is reinforced by the data shown in Figure 4.4; the conditioned rats, when exposed later to orange scent, had a higher threshold for pain. Such studies portray what powerful effects early conditioning can have on later behavior.

The Essentials of Classical Conditioning

With these facts in mind about the potentially far-reaching effects of classical conditioning, let us now return to Pavlov's experiment and discuss this type of learning in more detail. To understand the process we must first consider

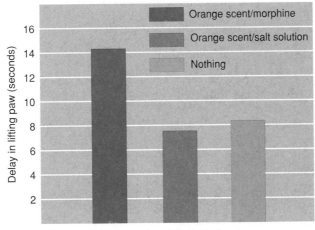

Rat pups placed on heated surface

FIGURE 4.4 When the smell of orange can act as a pain-killer Three groups of 10-day-old rat pups were placed on a heated surface while being exposed to the scent of orange, and the delay in their lifting their paws to escape the heat was measured. Note that the rats who had been conditioned five days earlier to associate orange scent with morphine took more than twice as long to lift their paws than did those rats who were treated with a simple salt solution rather than morphine, or those who were altogether untreated.

Unconditioned stimulus

Any stimulus that naturally and automatically, without prior exposure, produces a response.

Conditioned stimulus

A previously neutral stimulus that, when paired with an unconditioned stimulus, acquires the ability to set off or elicit a response.

Unconditioned response

A response that is built into the wiring of the nervous system and takes place automatically, without prior learning.

Conditioned response

Any response resulting from a change in the nervous system produced by the pairing of the conditioned stimulus with an unconditioned stimulus.

Reinforcement

The process of assisting learning by the pairing of a response with something the organism finds rewarding.

Forward pairing

The sequence in which the conditioned stimulus is presented just before the unconditioned stimulus.

its five essential elements, using the terms that Pavlov himself used to describe them.

1. The food used in the experiment was the **unconditioned stimulus**—the stimulus that naturally and automatically, without prior exposure, produces the salivary response.
2. The sound of the metronome was the **conditioned stimulus**—neutral at the start but eventually producing a similar response.
3. The reflex action of the salivary glands when food was placed in the dog's mouth was the **unconditioned response**—the response that is built into the wiring of the nervous system and takes place automatically, without prior learning.
4. The response of the salivary glands to the sound of the metronome was the **conditioned response**—resulting from some kind of change in the dog's nervous system produced by pairing the conditioned stimulus with the unconditioned stimulus and therefore with the salivary response.
5. The presentation of the food (the unconditioned stimulus) in the context of the sound (the conditioned stimulus) was the **reinforcement**—the key to conditioning. (In more everyday terms, reinforcement would take place if you were to present your dog with a bone every time it brought you the newspaper from the front lawn.)

These elements, illustrated in Figure 4.5, are common to all cases of classical conditioning. In Watson's Albert experiment, the unconditioned stimulus was the loud noise; the conditioned stimulus was the rat; the unconditioned response was the automatic display of fear following the noise; the conditioned response was the learned display of fear; and the reinforcement was the pairing of the loud noise with the rat.

The Power of Conditioning: Influential Factors

The power of conditioning can be affected by a variety of factors—among them, for example, the timing and frequency of the process, the consistency with which it unfolds, and even the biological predisposition of the learner. These factors—and others—are discussed in the following section.

The Effects of Timing and Frequency

It appears in general that the conditioning process is most effective when the conditioned stimulus (the metronome in Pavlov's experiment) is presented just before the unconditioned stimulus (the food)—a sequence called **forward pairing.** Less effective is **simultaneous pairing,** the presentation of both at exactly the same time. Least effective of all is **backward pairing,** the presentation of the conditioned stimulus after the unconditioned stimulus. The three types of pairing are shown in Figure 4.6.

The number of pairings of the conditioned and unconditioned stimulus necessary to produce a conditioned response also varies depending on the

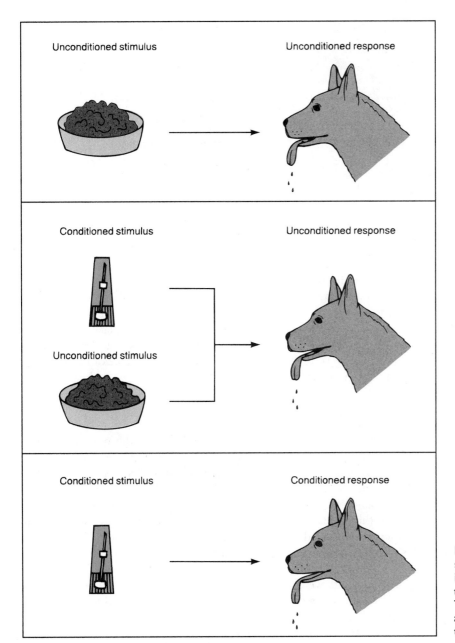

Unconditioned stimulus   Unconditioned response

Conditioned stimulus   Unconditioned response

Unconditioned stimulus

Conditioned stimulus   Conditioned response

FIGURE 4.5   The basic steps in classical conditioning Sketched here in brief are the steps in Pavlov's experiment. The same steps are followed in all instances of classical conditioning—as described in the text.

behavior being conditioned. Fear reactions in animals are readily conditioned in the laboratory. After only several presentations of a neutral conditioned stimulus with a painful conditioned stimulus such as electric shock, the conditioned stimulus will produce bodily reactions symptomatic of fear—crouching, trembling, urination, defecation—indicating that the animal has learned that the conditioned stimulus signals that a shock is coming.

Recent studies have identified the brain mechanisms that appear to be involved in conditioned fear responses. Normally, when a rat is exposed to a sudden loud sound, it displays a startle reaction. But it is possible to produce

Simultaneous pairing

The sequence in which the conditioned stimulus and the unconditioned stimulus are presented at the same time.

Backward pairing

The sequence in which the conditioned stimulus is presented after the unconditioned stimulus.

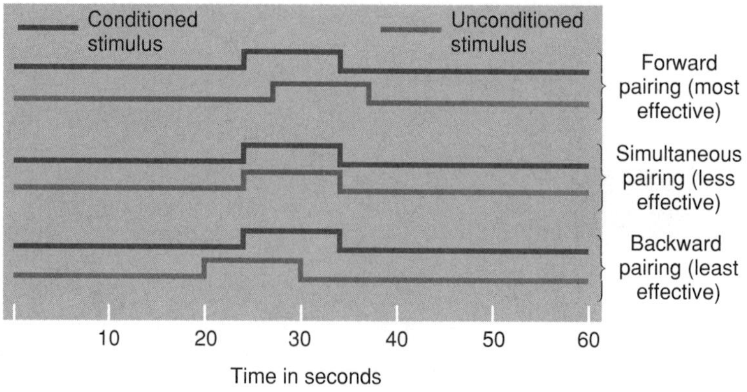

FIGURE 4.6 The difference timing makes The timing of the presentation of conditioned and unconditioned stimuli determines the effectiveness of the conditioning process—as described in the text.

Potentiated startle

An enhanced or increased startle to a loud noise or bright light produced by a conditional structure.

a **potential startle**—that is, an enhanced or increased startle—by first conditioning the rat to expect a shock each time a light is flashed, and then presenting the conditioned light stimulus just prior to the loud sound. It has been shown that a circuit from the central area of the amygdala (described on page 67) to the brain stem mediates the potentiated startle (Hitchcock & Davis, 1991). This is further evidence of the important role of the amygdala in the expression of fear responses.

The Predictability of Reinforcement

For most reactions, however, the critical factor is not the number of times that the conditioned stimulus is paired with an unconditioned stimulus but rather the reliability with which the conditioned stimulus predicts the unconditioned stimulus (Rescorla & Holland, 1982). In one experiment, dogs were first trained to jump back and forth over a barrier in a so-called shuttle box so that they could escape an electric shock. After the dogs had learned to jump, they were divided into two groups. For one group, tones and electric shocks were presented haphazardly—so that a tone just as often came before a shock as after it. For the second group, the tone was usually followed by a shock. All the dogs were then presented only with tones—that is, with no shock. If learning an association between hearing a tone and feeling a shock only required that tones and shocks occur together, then the first group should have learned to jump as quickly as the second group—for both groups had experienced the same number of tones and shocks. But if learning to jump is easier when the tone *predicts* when the shock will occur, then the second group should have learned more quickly. The results showed that the dogs in the second group had the greater tendency to jump when they heard the tones.

This study suggests that we are more likely to develop a conditioned response—for example, a distaste for a particular food—if encounters with it are consistently followed by unpleasant experiences. If exposure to the food and unpleasant experiences occur together only in an unsystematic rather than a predictable fashion, it is less likely that the conditioned response will develop.

The Power of Expectation: Drug Reactions Without Drugs

In the view of many psychologists today, conditioning can be best explained by the development of **expectancies.** In other words, what animals and humans learn in conditioning is the *expectation* that a particular conditioned stimulus will be followed by an unconditioned stimulus (Leahey & Harris, 1989). In humans, for example, it is possible to condition the "sweaty palms" measured by the galvanic skin response (GSR) if subjects are simply told that they will receive a shock every time they hear a tone. It is not necessary for the experimenter to deliver the shock; the expectation of the outcome is sufficient to produce the response.

It is now believed that Pavlov's dogs learned to salivate to the sound of the metronome because they learned to expect the sound to be followed by the food. And indeed Pavlov himself concluded that all organisms respond not only to stimuli but also in anticipation of the stimuli. In one series of experiments, Pavlov paired the sound of a bell with the injection of a drug, apomorphine. It turned out that the anticipation of the drug on hearing the bell produced symptoms—including salivation, agitation, and vomiting. After a period of time, the bell sound wasn't essential. Simply opening the container of hypodermic needles was sufficient to produce the symptoms (Siegel, 1983).

A dramatic example of this phenomenon has been observed among former drug addicts, who begin to show the symptoms of withdrawal and a return to drug-taking when they are simply exposed to drug paraphernalia, other individuals who use drugs, or the neighborhood where they secured their drugs. It is for this reason that those who work with the rehabilitation of drug addicts suggest that they move to a new setting where encounters with the cues of drug-taking are less likely to take place—that is, where the environment does not elicit expectations of a "high." Evidently the critical element in classical conditioning is that the organism—animal or human—is learning that a connection exists between the conditioned stimulus and some event, or the expectation of that event, in the environment.

The Extinction and Recovery of Conditioned Responses

Once Pavlov had established the conditioned salivary response, he wanted to find out how long and under what circumstances it would persist. When he merely kept sounding the metronome without ever again presenting food—in other words, when he removed the reinforcement—he found that in a very short time the flow of saliva in response to the sound began to decrease, and soon it stopped altogether, as shown in Figure 4.7. In Pavlov's terminology, this disappearance of the conditioned response is called **extinction.** (In the same way, your dog would stop bringing you the newspaper if you always withheld the accompanying presentation of a bone.) When Pavlov occasionally followed the sound with food—thus providing reinforcement not every time but sometimes—he found that he could make the conditioned response continue indefinitely.

Pavlov also tried another approach. He withheld reinforcement and let the conditioned response undergo extinction, then gave the dog a rest away from the experimental apparatus, and later tried again to see if there would be

Expectancies
The anticipation that one event will lead to another.

Extinction
The disappearance of a conditioned response that results from the withdrawal of reinforcement.

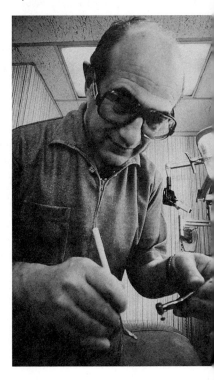

The dentist often becomes the object of conditioned fear.

FIGURE 4.7 The conditioned reflex: going, going, gone The graph shows what happened to Pavlov's dog when the conditioned stimulus of sound was no longer accompanied by the unconditioned stimulus of food. The conditioned salivary response, very strong at first, gradually grew weaker. By the seventh time the metronome was sounded, the conditioned response had disappeared. Extinction of the response was complete.

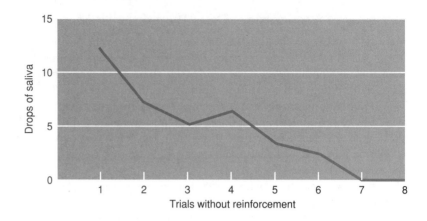

Spontaneous recovery

The tendency of a conditioned response that has undergone extinction to reappear after a period of rest.

Stimulus generalization

The tendency of an organism to respond to any stimulus that is similar to the original stimulus.

Stimulus discrimination

The ability to discriminate between similar stimuli.

any response to the metronome. Under these circumstances, the conditioned response that had seemed to be extinguished reappeared. Pavlov called this **spontaneous recovery**—a phenomenon that may account for real-life situations in which unreasonable fears or preferences, learned originally through conditioning, suddenly crop up again after seeming to have vanished.

Stimulus Generalization and Discrimination

In Pavlov's experiments, there was nothing magic about the sound produced by the metronome. He later used many other kinds of stimuli—and found that he could just as easily condition the salivary response to the sound of a bell or to the flash of a light. He also discovered that a dog conditioned to the sound of a bell would salivate just as readily to the sound of a different bell or even a buzzer. This phenomenon is called **stimulus generalization**—meaning that once an organism has learned to respond to a particular stimulus, it tends to display that behavior toward similar stimuli as well. Stimulus generalization explains why little Albert feared not only rats but also a bearded mask. It also explains why we find certain stimuli so appealing. For example, we tend to perceive people with childlike facial features—round face, large forehead, round eyes—as being like children in their warmth, submissiveness, and naïveté (Berry & McArthur, 1986). Like Albert, we generalize our emotional reactions from one stimulus to another.

After Pavlov had established the principle of stimulus generalization, he went on to demonstrate its opposite, **stimulus discrimination.** Here, by continuing to reinforce salivation to the bell by presenting food and omitting food when he sounded a different bell or a buzzer, Pavlov soon taught the dog to salivate only to the sound of the original bell, not to the other sounds. The dog had learned to discriminate between the stimulus of the bell and the other stimuli.

Pavlov also discovered that by taking advantage of the stimulus discrimination effect he could condition dogs to behave in abnormal ways. First, he projected a circle and an ellipse on a screen and conditioned dogs to discriminate between the two. Then he gradually changed the shape of the ellipse so that it looked more and more like a circle. Even when the difference in appearance was very slight, the dogs still made the discrimination successfully.

But when the difference became too small for the dogs to recognize, and discrimination was impossible, the dogs acted strangely disturbed. They became restless, destructive, or apathetic and developed muscle tremors and tics.

Pavlov's experiments suggest that abnormal human behavior may also result from problems and difficulties that occur through classical conditioning. This possibility will be explored later in this chapter in connection with the phenomenon known as **learned helplessness,** which can have profound effects on human behavior.

The Role of Built-in Predispositions in Learning

The power of conditioning depends on the degree to which the organism is prepared by its biological nature to learn to associate a particular pairing of stimuli. Thus one cannot use just any conditioned stimulus to condition any response.

For example, it is easy to condition an animal to avoid water with a distinctive taste when the drinking of that water is followed by illness. But when the act of drinking plain water is paired with a noise, the animal does not learn to avoid the water when it hears the noise even though the drinking is followed by illness (Holder, Bermudez-Rattoni, & Garcia, 1988). This means that it is difficult to form a conditioned association between an auditory stimulus and an illness, but easy to associate a distinctive taste stimulus with subsequent illness.

Important, too, is the environmental context in which conditioned responses are being learned. In one study, rabbits were conditioned to blink their eyes in response to a tone by learning to associate that tone with a puff of air to the eye. But when they were shifted to a different setting, the number of conditioned responses decreased. The ability to recognize the shift in context, the investigators demonstrated, depends on the functioning of the brain's hippocampus. For those rabbits in whom the hippocampus was surgically removed, changing the context did not decrease the number of conditioned responses (Penick & Solomon, 1991).

Each species is predisposed by heredity to learn to react to some stimuli but not to others. For example, experiments show that in contrast to rats, birds relate sickness not to taste but to visual cues. In humans, too, the pairing of conditioned stimulus with the response is stronger in some combinations than others. Studies of situations under which people learn food aversions, for example, show that they usually learn them as a result of illness—and not when eating the food is associated with accidents such as breaking a limb or getting cut. Moreover, the illness is much more likely to result in conditioned aversion to the actual foods involved rather than to related factors such as where the food was eaten (Garb & Stunkard, 1974; Logue, Ophir, & Strauss, 1981).

Learned helplessness
The condition found in both humans and animals in which organisms give up because their own efforts to succeed in a task seem to make no difference.

Operant Conditioning

Classical conditioning changes reflex behavior that, in the absence of any learning, would occur only in response to specific stimuli—like salivation to the presence of food. But reflexes are not the only form of behavior. For example, if a rat is placed in a cage, it exhibits many types of behavior that seem to be spontaneous and self-generated, not mere predetermined responses to any kind of stimulus. The rat may sniff at the cage, stand up to get a better look at things, scratch itself, wash itself, and touch various parts of the cage. Similarly, babies in their cribs display many spontaneous actions. They move their arms and legs, try to turn over or grasp a blanket or the bars of the crib, turn their heads and eyes to look at various objects, and make sounds with their vocal cords.

Such actions are not reflexes set off by some outside stimulus. The actions are initiated by the rat or the baby—put in motion by the organism itself. So instead of having something in the environment produce a response, we have here just the opposite. The rat or the baby is acting on the environment. It might be said that the organism is "operating" on the world around it—and often bringing about some kind of change in the environment. Hence this type of activity is called **operant behavior.**

Like inborn reflexes, operant behavior can also be modified through learning. One way is through a form of learning that, since it resembles classical conditioning in a number of respects, is called **operant conditioning.**

Operant behavior

Behavior that is not elicited by a specific stimulus but that does produce a change in the environment.

Operant conditioning

The process by which an operant behavior becomes attached to a specific conditioned stimulus.

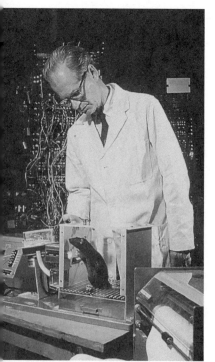

FIGURE 4.8 **Learning in the Skinner box** With this simple but ingenious invention, a box in which pressure on the bar automatically releases a pellet of food or a drop of water, Skinner demonstrated many of the rules of operant behavior.

B. F. Skinner's Magic Box

A classic demonstration of operant conditioning was performed by B. F. Skinner with the special kind of cage shown in Figure 4.8. When Skinner first placed a rat in the cage, it engaged in many kinds of spontaneous operant behavior. Eventually, besides doing other things, it pressed the bar. A pellet of food automatically dropped into the feeding cup beneath the bar. Still no learning took place. In human terms, we might say that the animal did not "notice" any connection between the food and the bar, and it simply ate the food and continued its random movements as before. Eventually it pressed the bar again, causing another pellet to drop. After several times, the animal "noticed" what had happened and formed an association between the act of pressing the bar and the appearance of food. The rat now began pressing the bar as fast as it could eat one pellet and get back to the bar to release another (Skinner, 1938).

To put this another way, the rat operated on the cage (the "Skinner box") in various ways. One particular kind of operant behavior, pressing the bar, had a rewarding result—it produced food. Therefore the rat repeated that behavior. Using the same language that is applied to classical conditioning, we say that the presentation of the food was a reinforcement of the bar-pressing behavior. The rule in operant conditioning is that operant behavior that is reinforced tends to be repeated—while operant behavior that is not reinforced tends to be abandoned.

Some Basics of Operant Conditioning

The Skinner box prompted a host of new studies of learning. It was found that operant conditioning followed many of the laws laid down by Pavlov for classical conditioning. Conditioned operant behavior, like the conditioned reflex response, was subject to *extinction*. That is, if the rat was no longer rewarded with food for pressing the bar, it eventually stopped pressing. *Spon-*

taneous recovery also occurred: After a rest away from the Skinner box, the rat started pressing again.

Experiments with pigeons, which are especially good subjects in their own version of the Skinner box, clearly showed stimulus generalization. A pigeon that had learned to obtain food by pecking at a white button would also peck at a red or green button. But if only the operant behavior toward the white button was reinforced, the pigeon displayed *stimulus discrimination*. In that case the pigeon learned to peck only at the white button and to ignore the red and green ones.

Behavior Shaping

Psychologists interested in operant conditioning have developed a method of teaching animals many complicated and unusual forms of behavior, a process called **shaping**. Figure 4.9 illustrates one way this process can be used. A pigeon is led step by step, through reinforcement by food as it gets closer and closer to performing the desired activity, to exhibit a form of behavior that it might never have hit upon spontaneously. Pigeons shaped in this manner have become excellent quality control inspectors in manufacturing plants—watching drug capsules roll by on a conveyer belt and signaling when a defective one appears (Verhave, 1966). Shaping is also the technique used to train animals to perform unusual and spectacular tricks.

Shaping
A step-by-step process used to teach complex behaviors; also called successive approximations.

FIGURE 4.9 Shaping a pigeon's behavior How can a pigeon be taught to peck at that little black dot in the middle of the white circle on the wall of its cage? When first placed in the box, the bird merely looks about at random (*A*). When it faces the white circle (*B*), it receives the reinforcing stimulus of food in the tray below (*C*). Step by step, the pigeon is first rewarded for looking at the circle (*D*), then not until it approaches the circle (*E*), then not until it pecks at the circle (*F*). The next step, not illustrated here, is to withhold the reward until the pigeon pecks at the dot.

A   B   C

D   E   F

How Superstitions Take Shape

Do you have a "lucky" sweater that you always wear to exams because it helps you get good grades? Do you win more tennis matches if you wear the same pair of socks and carefully pull on the right one before the left one?

If so, you are probably exhibiting the effects of **autoshaping**—a process discovered when investigators showed that, in the course of operant conditioning, certain behaviors take shape automatically (Brown & Jenkins, 1968). The researchers presented hungry pigeons in a Skinner box with a stimulus—a colored light on a response key that they could peck at—at various intervals. No matter whether the pigeons pecked at the response key or not, food appeared for a four-second interval every seven seconds. Even though the delivery of the food was totally independent of the pigeon's behavior—that is, the pigeon could neither expedite nor delay the appearance of the feeder—after only 10 pairings of the light and food, the pigeons began to peck at the light on the response key. The pigeons behaved as if they "believed" the operant behavior of pecking was producing the food even though it clearly was not. Their behavior appeared to be based on superstitions.

Skinner himself had observed this process when he retooled one of his boxes so that it delivered food from time to time without any rhyme or reason, and regardless of what the pigeon in the box did or did not do. As a result, the birds developed some strange and unusual habits. A bird that happened to be flapping its wings when the food appeared might continue to flap incessantly, as if it "believed" that this produced food. Some pigeons learned to crane their necks, or to peck at a blank wall, or to keep moving in circles. Thus, as in classical conditioning, the behavior displayed by the pigeons indicated that they had developed an expectation—in this case that such acts as pecking would produce food.

For humans as well, it is possible to develop an expectation when the reinforcement does not follow the response in a predictable fashion. Many human superstitions, not only our own individual quirks but those common to many people, probably originated in such a manner. One widely held superstition may have been started by a boy who walked under a ladder and promptly fell into a mud puddle. Another may have been started by a girl who found a clover with an extra leaf, then promptly found a penny. Like the pigeons pecking or flapping, a behavior was shaped automatically through operant conditioning.

Some Features of Reinforcement

The term reinforcement, as you have probably noticed, keeps cropping up in these discussions of operant conditioning. It lies at the very core of the process. With animals, it is easy to provide reinforcement. Food and water constitute an obvious kind of reward, and experimenters in operant conditioning call them **primary reinforcers.** But humans seldom do any learning in order to receive food or water. Instead they usually seem to learn for less tangible rewards, such as praise or acceptance. Indeed even animal trainers often use the reward of affection rather than food. Such rewards are called **secondary reinforcers,** and it has been assumed that they have gained their value through a conditioning process that linked them originally with primary reinforcers. A simple example of secondary reinforcement is illustrated in Figure 4.10.

Autoshaping

A process that sometimes occurs in operant conditioning in which certain behaviors take shape automatically.

Primary reinforcer

A reward like food and water that motivates animals to respond.

Secondary reinforcer

A reward like money or prizes that has value because it is linked to primary reinforcers.

FIGURE 4.10 The chimp and the poker chip Why is the chimpanzee dropping the chip into the slot? The reason is that the chip was used as a secondary reinforcer in a learning experiment—and now, when placed in a vending machine, it produces a primary reinforcement by making food drop into the tray.

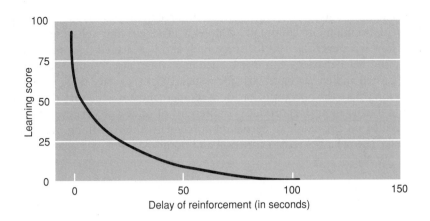

FIGURE 4.11 Oops . . . the reinforcement came too late The steep drop in the curve shows how rapidly learning fell in an experiment in which reinforcement—food presented when rats pressed the bar in a Skinner box—was delayed for intervals ranging from a few seconds to about two minutes. Note that there was no learning at all when the reinforcement was delayed for slightly more than 100 seconds (Perin, 1943).

The exact properties of an event that constitutes reinforcement are not easy to define, but one element is that the event carries an element of surprise. That is, learning is facilitated by an experience that violates the animal's expectations (Staddon & Ettinger, 1989). For example, if two different tastes—one novel and the other ordinary—both lead to feeling ill, conditioning would be much more likely to occur in the case of the novel one. Effective reinforcements—whether in classical conditioning or operant conditioning—are attention-getting. In classical conditioning, too, a loud noise or metronome is attention-getting. Thus a reinforcement, which increases the probability of a particular response, is usually like a punctuation mark— an event that is a surprise to the animal or person.

As for the timing of reinforcements, it has been found in most animal experiments that immediate reinforcement produces the most rapid learning. Any delay reduces the amount of learning, and too long a delay produces no learning at all, as is shown in Figure 4.11. The same thing holds true for young children. It is difficult to teach a four-year-old to stay out of the street, for example, if the child is not rewarded at once for doing so, or punished for not doing so (Wickelgren, 1977).

Nevertheless, there are specific instances in which animals and humans will learn an association even when the delay between the conditioned stimulus and reinforcement is relatively long. For example, in the experiments in which rats learned to avoid a particular taste when it was followed by bodily discomfort, the delay between the taste and the discomfort could be several hours without impeding the learning process. And we humans can think about an event for a long time and, therefore, learn associations despite considerable intervening delays.

Experimenters have also studied the effects of **constant reinforcement** (reward for each performance) as compared with **partial reinforcement** (reward on some occasions but not on others). They found that although learning generally takes place more rapidly with constant reinforcement, the behavior is more persistent (that is, more resistant to extinction) with partial reinforcement (Robbins, 1971). This finding has many applications to real-life situations. For example, parents who want their children to acquire a lasting tendency to work hard in school and get good grades will probably accomplish more with partial than with constant reinforcement. The trick is not to offer reinforcement for every good grade, but rather to bestow praise and affection (and possibly material rewards as well) a little more sparingly.

Constant reinforcement
A reward delivered for each correct behavior or performance.

Partial reinforcement
A reward delivered for some but not all correct behaviors or performances.

The long-lasting effects of partial reinforcement may also create problems in bringing up children. Suppose a little girl starts having temper tantrums whenever she asks for something and it is denied. Her parents try to ignore her behavior—but every once in a while, just to quiet her down, they give in and let her have what she wants. What they have done is set up a situation where the operant behavior of temper tantrums (the very thing they would like to eliminate) produces the reward of candy, or whatever it is the girl wants, on a schedule of partial reinforcement (the very thing most likely to make the behavior resist extinction and occur over and over again).

Partial Reinforcement Schedules

Psychologists differentiate between two basic types of partial reinforcement schedules, as indicated in Figure 4.12. In the first, called **ratio schedules,** the reinforcement is delivered only after the subject responds correctly a certain number of times. (In the case of Skinner's rats, the animal would receive a pellet of food only after pressing the bar, say, three, or four, or five times.) In the second, called **interval schedules,** the reinforcement is delivered only after a certain period has passed. (For example, the rat would receive a pellet, say, every minute, or every two or three minutes.)

For both types of schedules, another differentiation can be made. If either the ratio or interval is the same each time, the schedule is termed **fixed.** On the other hand, if the ratio or interval changes to some degree each time, the schedule is termed **variable.**

Although Figure 4.12 provides examples of reinforcement schedules in both animal and human learning, it seems clear that they apply more to animals than to ourselves. The reason for this is that in the case of humans, learning is often less a reflection of the actual appearance of reinforcements set up by an investigator in the laboratory than of what we *believe* is happening (Leahey & Harris, 1989). As will be shown later in this chapter, human learning is dominated less by objective schedules of reinforcement than by subjective beliefs about what is going on in the environment.

Ratio schedule

Reinforcement delivered only after the subject responds correctly a certain number of times.

Interval schedule

Reinforcement delivered only after a certain period of time has passed.

Fixed schedule

A schedule based on a set number of responses or set amount of time.

Variable schedule

A schedule based on a varying but average number of responses or amount of time.

FIGURE 4.12   Schedules of partial reinforcement Reinforcers for learning may be delivered in four major ways as discussed in the text.

TYPE OF REINFORCEMENT SCHEDULE	WHEN REINFORCERS ARE GIVEN	EXAMPLE
Ratio		
Fixed	After a fixed number of responses	Getting paid after every ten office files you finish
Variable	After a variable number of tries around some average	Making a sale after anywhere from one to twenty tries—but on the average, after five
Interval		
Fixed	For first response after a fixed interval of time has passed	Getting paid every week as soon as you turn in a file
Variable	For first response after a variable amount of time has passed	Making a sale after anywhere from one to seven days—but on the average, after three

Behavior Modification and Token Economies

Parents who want their children to stop throwing temper tantrums and animal trainers who want their dolphins to jump through hoops have something in common: both are trying to mold behavior. All of us are constantly trying to influence behavior—our own actions as well as those of the people around us (Stolz, Wienckowski, & Brown, 1975). We try to lose weight, quit smoking, get higher grades, perform better on the job, or overcome a block in writing (Boice, 1982). We try to influence other people to give us a good grade or a raise, to show us more appreciation and respect, or to stop doing things that annoy us. In so doing we often practice what psychologists call **behavior modification,** a technique based largely on operant conditioning and the use of secondary reinforcement.

As psychologists use the term, behavior modification means any deliberate program designed to influence and change behavior through learning. The assumption is that behavior is controlled to a considerable degree by its consequences. If a certain type of behavior "works"—that is, if it results in reinforcement through some reward or praise or even just a feeling of self-esteem—it is likely to be learned and repeated. If it does not produce satisfactory results, it will be abandoned. In this fashion, it has been possible, for example, to raise the level of children's social skills (Yule, 1985), and to teach brain-damaged patients to reduce their socially inappropriate actions (McGlynn, 1990).

Experiments in behavior modification have produced some dramatic results. One of the first attempts was made with a three-year-old girl in a nursery school who was too shy and withdrawn to take part in any of the group activities. Instead she tried to hide by staying on the floor, either motionless or crawling. How could she be led to get up, start moving around, and join the other children? The secret turned out to be very simple. As long as she was on the floor, her teachers ignored her. As soon as she got up on her feet, they flattered her with attention. Given this reinforcement, she quickly became an active member of the group (Harris et al., 1965). The same kind of behavior modification—ignoring undesirable actions and rewarding desirable ones—has since been successful in many other situations. One special kind of behavior modification, in which the reinforcement is a sort of make-believe cash payment for desirable behavior, is called a **token economy.** It is used in mental hospitals, where it was originated as an attempt to improve the general atmosphere and the daily lives of patients. For dressing properly, eating in an acceptable manner, and working at useful jobs, patients are rewarded with tokens that they can use like money to "buy" such privileges as movies, rental of radios or television sets, cigarettes, candy, and opportunities for privacy. These token economies have produced some remarkable changes in behavior, as can be seen in Figure 4.13.

Token economies have also been used successfully in schools, particularly to help retarded or emotionally disturbed children and those with learning problems (O'Leary and Drabman, 1971). Token economies and behavior modification in general are not infallible, but they have been found to be clearly effective in many situations. Another attempt to apply the principles of conditioning—in this case in the fields of medicine and health psychology—is discussed in the Psychology in Action box called "Learning Through Biofeedback."

Behavior modification
The technique of helping someone change behavior by manipulating the rewards and punishments given.

Token economy
A form of behavior modification in which tokens are earned for appropriate behavior and can then be exchanged for privileges or goods.

TEST YOURSELF

d) By continuing to play regularly, Marcia gets better and better at tennis. What kind of learning is Marcia undergoing?

e) What do psychologists call the kind of learning an elephant undergoes in order to do stunts in the circus?

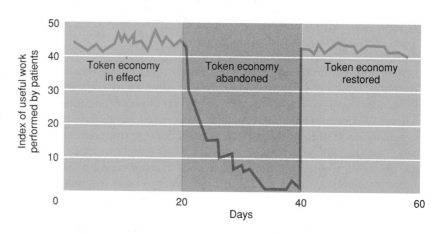

FIGURE 4.13 **Behavior modification revolutionizes a hospital** Under a token economy, patients worked actively at useful jobs and helped run the hospital (line in blue area at left). From the 20th to 40th days of the experiment, the token economy was abandoned and the patients quickly went back to their old passive ways (line in center area). As soon as the token economy was put back in effect, they again pitched in as shown by the line at the right (Ayllon and Azrin, 1968).

Biofeedback

A method in which control is achieved over bodily and brain functions.

Escape and Avoidance, Punishment, and Learned Helplessness

Operant conditioning can be established with two very different kinds of reinforcement. The first, called **positive reinforcement,** has already been described. It relies on the use of such desirable rewards as food, praise, and

P S Y C H O L O G Y   I N   A C T I O N

Learning Through Biofeedback

The word **biofeedback** did not appear in dictionaries published less than two decades ago, but it is now widely used. Attempts have been made to apply biofeedback to all the various bodily activities over which we ordinarily have no conscious control, including heart rate, blood pressure, and the movements of the stomach muscles. Perhaps one reason we cannot control these activities is that we are not usually aware of them. We do not know how fast our heart is beating, whether our blood pressure is high or low, or whether our alimentary canal is busy digesting food. Nor are we aware of many other bodily events—for example, tenseness in our forehead and neck muscles (which

appears to be the cause of tension headaches), spasms of the blood vessels in our head (migraine headaches), or the patterns of our brain waves (which may be related to epilepsy and also, in another form, to feelings of relaxation, peace of mind, and happiness).

Biofeedback procedures attempt to give us control over these activities by providing a moment-to-moment reading of what is going on in the body. With headache patients, for example, electrodes are attached to the muscles of the forehead and neck and connected to a device that clicks rapidly when the muscles are tense, more slowly when they begin to relax. Given this knowledge of what is going on, patients may learn to control the activity of their muscles. Similarly, through devices that monitor and report the

volume of blood in the forehead, migraine sufferers may learn to direct the flow of blood away from the vessels in the head that cause the problem (Tarler-Benlolo, 1978).

Even in the treatment of headaches, where biofeedback has had its greatest successes, the results have varied from patient to patient and have not always been satisfactory. One reason may be that people show wide individual differences in the ability to learn to control their bodily activities, just as they differ in other skills. Although the technique has not yet proved nearly so spectacular as the publicity often suggests (N. E. Miller, 1985b), biofeedback is being studied further by psychologists and researchers in numerous hospitals and medical schools.

valuable tokens. The other kind, called **negative reinforcement,** is the termination of something painful or otherwise unpleasant—for example, the cessation of a form of punishment.

When negative reinforcement is used in the laboratory, animals usually learn very quickly. This has been demonstrated by placing dogs in a device called a shuttle box that has two compartments separated by a barrier. The barrier is high enough to discourage the animal but low enough to jump over when there is a real incentive. One of the compartments has a metal floor through which an electric shock can be administered; the other does not.

As shown in Figure 4.14, when a dog is placed in the wired compartment and the electricity turned on, the animal quickly learns to jump across the hurdle to the other side to escape the shock. This behavior is called **operant escape.** But if some kind of warning is given, such as a light turned on or off a few seconds before the shock is administered, the animal will quickly learn to jump the hurdle when the light changes and thus avoid the shock entirely. This behavior is called **operant avoidance.**

Escape and Avoidance in Everyday Life

A great deal of everyday human behavior seems to represent some form of operant escape and avoidance, learned through negative reinforcement. For

Positive reinforcement
The process of encouraging desired behaviors through the use of rewards.

Negative reinforcement
The termination of something painful or unpleasant by the removal or cessation of the unpleasant stimulus.

Operant escape
Behavior in which the organism seeks to escape something unpleasant.

Operant avoidance
Behavior in which the organism attempts to avoid an unpleasant event before it occurs.

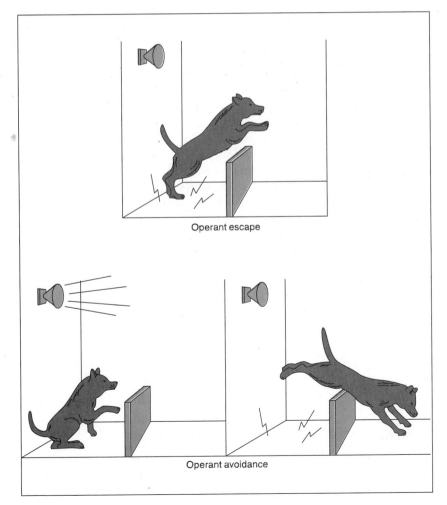

Operant escape

Operant avoidance

FIGURE 4.14 Learning from negative reinforcement The dog, placed in a shuttle box, is learning to respond to a shock as described in the text.

example, a young boy finds the presence of a stranger in his home distasteful—and he wants to escape. He may run and hide his head in his mother's lap to shut out the sight of the stranger. Having learned the reinforcing consequences of this escape behavior, he may generalize this response to other situations. He may become an adult who avoids social functions that, he anticipates, will generate anxiety, or he may avoid volunteering for challenging responsibilities in his job.

You may also know people who try to avoid anxiety by deliberately insulating themselves from situations that might upset them—for example, social events, travel, or difficult jobs. The price they pay for this form of operant avoidance is often a limited lifestyle with few adventures or satisfactions.

Many defenses against events that arouse unpleasant anxiety appear to be forms of operant escape and avoidance. You may have noticed that many people who are made anxious by criticism become overapologetic. This may be a form of conditioned avoidance behavior that in some way served as a successful escape from anxiety in the past—perhaps with a mother who stopped criticizing and showed affection when her child apologized.

How Punishment Affects Behavior

Operant behavior can also be conditioned through the use of punishment. Here the goal is not to reinforce a response, and therefore make it likely to occur again in the future, but to eliminate a response by following it with an unpleasant experience. Most people and indeed society as a whole seem to believe in the effectiveness of punishment as a form of behavior modification. Toddlers are punished by a slap on the hand if they grab at a fragile lamp or by a slap on the bottom if they whine too much. Older children are punished if they are "sassy," get into fights, or refuse to do their homework.

Researchers studying marriage have found that it is not uncommon for one or both partners to use punishment in an attempt to change the other's behavior. Note this case: A husband was annoyed because whenever his wife was in a bad mood, she had the habit of swearing at the children if they misbehaved. In an effort to change her behavior, he yelled at her, or stormed out of the house for the evening, or stopped sharing in household chores when she swore at the child. The wife, in turn, was annoyed because the husband always left the den in a mess—with newspapers, magazines, and books scattered over the floor and on top of the television set. In an effort to change his behavior, she threw out his magazines, stopped talking to him, and rejected his sexual approaches whenever he left his den in a mess (Patterson, Hops, & Weiss, 1975). Both were saying, in effect, "Yes, I'm punishing you by being as unpleasant as I can—and I'll do it until you change your ways."

The question is: Does punishment really work? In the case of the couple just described, it did not. They wound up taking their problems to a marriage counselor. But the question cannot always be answered with a simple yes or no. It is surrounded by many complications, all bearing on our attempts to get along in society and with our fellow human beings.

Punishment with Animals—and with People

In general, punishment often results in rapid and long-lasting learning by animals (Solomon, 1964). As might be expected from what was said earlier about delayed reinforcement, the punishment is most effective if administered as soon as possible after the behavior that the experimenter wants to eliminate (Campbell & Church, 1969).

The punishment is most effective of all when combined with reward—that is, when the "wrong" behavior is punished and the "right" behavior is rewarded. This has been shown by placing a rat in a simple T-shaped maze. The animal starts at the bottom of the T and has the choice, when it reaches the top, of turning either right or left. The rat will learn the "correct" turn very quickly if rewarded with food when it turns right and punished with shock when it turns left. A real-life demonstration of the same principle is provided by the housebreaking of a young puppy, which, as countless dog owners have discovered, is best accomplished by punishing the animal immediately by slapping it with a rolled-up newspaper when it wets the rug and showing it that the same act is praiseworthy when performed outdoors.

In at least some cases, punishment also helps babies and small children to learn. Its use is sometimes unavoidable. A slap on the hand when a child reaches toward a forbidden object may be the only way to prevent damage, as when the object is a fragile lamp, or even serious injury, if the object happens to be a sharp knife.

With older children and adults, however, the effectiveness of punishment is much less clear. One reason is that it is impossible to say how any given individual feels about any particular kind of supposedly punishing treatment. If that statement strikes you as peculiar, consider this situation: A mother and father make it a regular practice, when their children misbehave, to raise a great fuss. They yell at the children, call them to task, bawl them out, threaten them with everything from being sent to bed without supper to a thorough spanking. They believe that this punishment will make the children mend their ways. The children, however, may view the situation in an entirely different light. Let us say that their parents ordinarily ignore them, displaying very few signs of interest or affection. Thus, to the children, the intended punishment is actually a form of attention, which they desperately crave. It constitutes a positive reinforcement that they are likely to seek again and again. In these cases even a spanking may be regarded as a positive reinforcement.

Psychologists are well aware that punishment often achieves exactly the opposite of its intended effect (Feshbach, 1983). It can create a vicious circle within a family: The child misbehaves, the parent punishes, and the punishment leads to further misbehavior (N. E. Miller, 1975). Punishment may also have far-reaching side effects. Studies of children who received drastic verbal or physical punishment have shown that they tend to acquire a dislike for the people who punish them, such as their parents or teachers. These children often become aggressive and punishing toward other children—and as adults frequently are cruel to their own offspring.

Learning to Feel Helpless

Most of the time, when we expect unpleasant experiences, we do whatever we can to avoid them. A student manages to avoid taking a difficult course, or a person allergic to ragweed gets away from it in the fall of the year. But there are some conditions in which such coping responses do not occur, and instead we become apathetic and appear to be helpless.

This was first demonstrated in an experiment in which a dog was strapped into the kind of harness used by Pavlov. The dog then received a series of 64 electrical shocks, each lasting five seconds, delivered at random intervals. There was no way the dog could avoid the shocks or escape from them before the five seconds were up. The next day the dog was placed in a shuttle box. From time to time the light inside the box was dimmed, and a few seconds later a shock was administered through the floor of the compartment in which the dog had been placed. The animal could avoid the shock altogether by jumping over the hurdle into the other compartment when the warning light was dimmed, or it could escape the shock by jumping after the electricity was turned on. If the dog did not jump into the other compartment, the shock continued—this time for a full 50 seconds.

The results of the experiment, shown in Figure 4.15, were dramatic. A number of dogs were used in the experiment. All had 10 trials in the shuttle box during which they could learn to avoid or escape the shock. But the amount of learning that took place was small. Most of the animals simply accepted the shock for the full 50 seconds, making no attempt to leap over the hurdle. They behaved in totally different fashion from a control group of dogs that had not previously received inescapable shocks. These "normal" dogs learned very quickly to leap the hurdle in time to avoid the shock or to escape in a hurry once the shock had begun.

How are we to account for the failure of the experimental dogs to learn—for their acceptance of a severe and long-lasting shock? The experimenters attribute it to what they have called *learned helplessness*. That is, while the dogs were in the Pavlov harness they learned that nothing they could do would have any effect on whether they received a shock or for how long. In human terms, they had no hope that they could do anything about the shock, even when moved to the shuttle box, and they therefore had no incentive to try to escape (Maier, Seligman, & Solomon, 1969).

Humans as well as animals can be led to acquire learned helplessness through simple laboratory procedures. In one experiment, for example, college volunteers were subjected to an earsplitting noise. They were told that they could stop the noise by learning how to manipulate some control devices—but actually these devices had no effect. Later, when placed in another situation where it would have been easy to move a control lever and

FIGURE 4.15 Results of an experiment in learned helplessness The rapid rise in the solid line shows how quickly "normal" dogs learned how to cope with an electric shock delivered in a shuttle box, as explained in the text. The dashed line shows the very different behavior of animals that had acquired *learned helplessness*—and therefore seemed incapable of learning how to do anything about the shock.

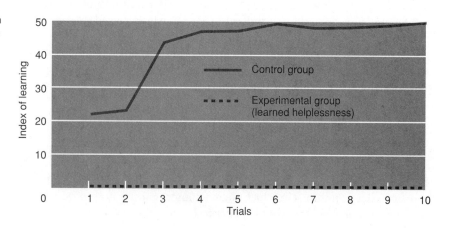

turn off the noise, the subjects made no effort and simply put up with the noise until the experimenter called a halt (Hiroto, 1974).

Children who are continually yelled at or spanked no matter what they have done may very well acquire learned helplessness. They may decide that they have no control over when, how, or why they are punished. They may give up trying to learn what their parents are trying to teach them, in which case the attempts to punish them into learning the difference between good behavior and bad become self-defeating. Some scientists believe that children growing up in a deprived, ghetto environment and who see no way to escape are vulnerable to adopting a helpless mental attitude.

Helplessness and Failure: Antidotes

The original experiment on learned helplessness, performed with dogs in the late 1960s, opened up a new line of psychological investigation. Punishment, it has been found, is not the only possible cause of learned helplessness. An even more common cause is failure—at any of the tasks we face throughout life, in the classroom, or in the outside world.

Although everyone experiences failure, not everybody suffers drastic consequences. One of the contributions of studies of learned helplessness has been to offer some clues as to when, how, and why this unhappy result is likely to occur—and what might be done about it.

Suppose you are in love—but the object of your affections rejects you. It makes a great deal of difference whether you blame yourself, blame her or him, or blame women or men in general. Blaming yourself usually results in a loss of self-esteem and is associated with lack of confidence in the future (Garber & Hollon, 1977). Sometimes it produces significant depression (Rizley, 1978). The particular way in which you blame yourself is also important. If you merely blame your behavior in that one particular relationship, your feelings of helplessness will probably be less severe. But if you blame yourself in

The inevitable failure experienced in life can produce learned helplessness under certain conditions.

general—your own worth and character, so to speak—you are much more likely to be in trouble (Peterson & Seligman, 1984). Thus it is better to think, "Well, I just did the wrong thing that time," than to decide, "That's the way I am and it seems I'm just plain unattractive to women (or men)."

If you blame the other party or the other sex in general—thereby attributing your failure to outside factors—you preserve your self-esteem. But this does not necessarily exempt you from the symptoms of helplessness. Again it appears that if you make a sweeping condemnation—of all women (or all men)—your helplessness is likely to generalize and handicap you in other situations. If you blame one particular person—"She (or he) is overly competitive and rejecting"—there is less likelihood that the incident will affect other relationships (Abramson, Seligman, & Teasdale, 1978).

Any form of learned helplessness can cause serious problems. One group of investigators has cited the example of an accountant who gets fired from his job. If his symptoms do not generalize to other situations, he may continue to be a good husband and father and to function well in social situations. But the symptoms may cripple him nonetheless. He may be unable to prepare his own income tax return or try for a new job in accounting. If the helplessness becomes generalized, his entire life may be affected. He may become sexually impotent, neglect his children, and avoid any social contacts (Abramson, Seligman, & Teasdale, 1978).

Though most of us suffer at times from learned helplessness—when failure makes us question our own abilities and we believe ourselves to be incompetent, lazy, unattractive, and generally good for nothing—our pessimistic attitudes fortunately do not usually last very long. We have trouble with math but overcome it by working a little harder—or make up for our lack of mathematical ability by doing well in another subject. Though one person of the opposite sex rejects us, we soon find someone else who likes us a great deal. After being fired, we find another job at which we are more efficient—and we end up feeling much better about ourselves and the world.

When we do this, we provide our own very effective therapy—for we are doing exactly what a therapist would try to do if our problems were so severe that we had to seek help. The best treatment for learned helplessness, it has been found, is to give people some evidence that they do have the ability to succeed (Teasdale, 1978). Sometimes they have set their goals impossibly high and have to be taught to be more realistic. Sometimes they have to work at developing their skills at performing their jobs or conducting their social relationships. But mostly therapists seek to provide situations in which people who suffer from learned helplessness can and do succeed, thereby discovering that they are more competent at more things than they thought they were. This new confidence generalizes to other situations (Bandura, Jeffery, & Gajdos, 1975), and they begin to feel a growing faith in their ability to control their own futures.

Cognitive Learning: A Contemporary View Rooted in the Past

For a period, the laws of classical and operant conditioning dominated psychology's view of learning. The behaviorist school thought of all human behavior as conditioned more or less by events in the environment. The prevailing belief was that there is little difference between humans going about

TEST YOURSELF

f) If a psychologist suggests using positive reinforcement to help a child overcome thumb-sucking, what approach is being recommended—punishment or reward?

g) "I've learned to recognize muscle tension and how to reverse it," says Mary. What technique is she likely to be using?

their daily lives and a rat negotiating its way through a simple T maze. The rat's behavior could be accurately predicted if we knew in which arm of the T it has previously been rewarded with food and in which arm it has been punished by a shock. The view was that we could also predict people's behavior fairly well if we simply knew which of their actions had been rewarded in the past and which had been punished, and in what way and to what extent (Miller & Dollard, 1941).

Even during the heyday of this view, however, there were dissenters since some experimental results, even with rats, did not fit easily into the laws of conditioning. It was felt that even in apparently simple, stimulus-response learning, it was essential to account for the perceptions and thoughts that take place between the stimulus and the response. Embedded in this outlook was the modern view which, as earlier portions of this chapter have made clear, is that when animals as well as humans learn to relate a conditioned and unconditioned stimulus, what they are actually learning is an expectation. Pavlov's dogs learned to salivate to the sound of the metronome because they expected the sound to be followed by food. In operant conditioning, rats in a Skinner box learn to press the bar because they anticipate the action to be followed by food.

Thus there was ingrained in the history of learning research all along what is now generally accepted as the contemporary view of learning: That the organism, human or animal, far from being a passive product of experience, is always actively interacting with the environment.

The Case of the Ingenious Chimps

One of the first influential experiments along cognitive lines was reported by the German psychologist Wolfgang Köhler as far back as the 1920s. Köhler worked with chimpanzees, creating situations in which they had to demonstrate considerable ingenuity to get at a banana placed tantalizingly out of reach. Sometimes the food was just a little farther than arm's length away from a chimp behind a barrier. Sometimes it was suspended overhead, too high to reach by jumping. So near and yet so far.

Could the chimpanzees learn to get the food? As it turned out, they managed in a number of clever ways. The animals behind the barrier found they could use sticks, available within arm's reach, to rake in the banana. The animals who saw the food overhead hit upon several strategies, two of which are illustrated in Figure 4.16. To Köhler, this kind of learning went far beyond any stimulus-response connections established by conditioning. He held that the animals had learned through **insight**—or what today would be called cognition. That is, they evaluated the situation, called on their past knowledge about sticks and boxes, and processed all this information in terms of cause and effect.

Insight
The sudden realization that allows the solution of a previously unsolved problem; the "aha" principle.

Learning in the Absence of Reinforcement

Another influential experiment, reported in 1930 and performed with rats in a maze, produced results that cast doubt on the theory that reinforcement is essential to learning (Tolman & Honzik, 1930). The rats were divided into three groups. Group 1 always found food at the end of the maze—a clear-cut and immediate reinforcement. The Group 2 rats were simply placed in the maze and permitted to move around in any way they chose, never finding any

FIGURE 4.16 **You can't keep a good chimp down** Faced with the problem of reaching a banana suspended high overhead, the chimpanzee at left has managed by balancing a long stick beneath it and quickly climbing up. The chimpanzee at right has hit upon the "insight" of piling three boxes on top of each other as a makeshift step stool (Köhler, 1925).

food. Group 3 was treated the same way as Group 2 for the first 10 days, receiving no reinforcement. Then, after the tenth day, food was placed at the end of the maze, as it had been all along with Group 1.

How the three groups performed, as measured by how direct a route they took without entering blind alleys, is illustrated in Figure 4.17. Note that the rats in Group 1 learned rapidly, as the laws of operant conditioning would have predicted, improving every day right from the beginning. As might also have been predicted, the rats in Group 2, which were never reinforced, did not display much learning. But note the strange behavior of Group 3. For the first 10 days this group also showed little learning. Then, on the eleventh day, when a reward was provided at the end of the maze, the rats immediately began running the course like veterans. Even in just wan-

FIGURE 4.17 **A funny thing happened on the way through the maze** The graph shows the surprising behavior of three groups of rats placed in a maze under different conditions of reinforcement. For the meaning of the lines, which chart the rats' progress in learning the way through the maze, see the text (Tolman and Honzik, 1930).

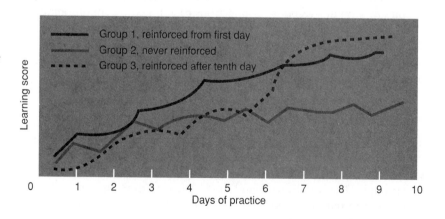

dering about the maze for 10 days, without any reinforcement, they apparently had learned a great deal about the correct path. As soon as a reward was provided, they began to demonstrate this knowledge.

The experiment seemed to show that even lower animals can learn without the immediate reinforcement considered essential to classical and operant conditioning—and in fact without any reinforcement at all. In cognitive terminology, the rats moving around the maze without any reward had acquired knowledge about the pathway, which they could call on when it was useful in helping them get to food as rapidly as possible.

Such experiments along with others suggest that reinforcement, as described earlier, is an event that attracts and focuses attention (Rescorla & Holland, 1982). Think, for example, of the sudden taste of food when an animal is hungry or an unexpected frown from a teacher when a student has given a wrong answer. Both are events that alert the organism, leading it to concentrate on the behavior just performed. The effectiveness of a reinforcing event is thus related to its capacity to evoke attention to the behavior just displayed.

Can There Be Learning Without a Response?

Just as the maze experiment demonstrated that learning is possible without reinforcement, other experiments have shown that learning can take place without a response. In one of the most famous studies, the subject was a dog in a Pavlov-type harness. The unconditioned stimulus was an electric shock to the paw, the unconditioned response the pulling away of the paw, and the conditioned stimulus a high tone sounded just before the shock was delivered. The animal, of course, was quickly conditioned to pull its paw away at the sound of this tone—and it also showed stimulus discrimination by ignoring a low tone that was never followed by shock. So far just a routine example of classical conditioning and stimulus discrimination.

But now the experimenter did the same thing with another dog—except that this dog's leg was paralyzed with a drug, so that it would not be pulled away. When the high tone was sounded and the shock delivered, the animal could not respond. Yet when the process was repeated later, after the drug had worn off, the dog pulled its paw away immediately at the sound of the high tone while ignoring the low tone. It had learned to avoid the shock and to discriminate between the two tones—even though the establishment of a stimulus-response connection was impossible during the conditioning trials (Solomon & Turner, 1962). The learning involved an association between the tone and the expectation of being shocked.

Cognitive Maps, Expectancies, and Knowledge

The various experiments just described—Köhler's chimpanzees and their "insight," the rats that acquired learning without any reinforcement, and the paralyzed dog that learned to avoid a shock—led many psychologists to seek a new definition of learning. Granted, humans as well as lower animals often establish a simple stimulus-response connection through classical and operant conditioning, with reinforcement a part of the process. But in cases where some other kind of learning occurs, in ways not accounted for by the laws of conditioning, just what is it that the organism learns—and how does the learning take place?

Cognitive map
A person's knowledge of the spatial features of the environment.

Edward Tolman, who collaborated on the experiment with the three groups of rats in the maze, suggested the term **cognitive map** (Tolman, 1948). From many studies of behavior in mazes, Tolman concluded that even animals learn not just responses that propel them to a reward but a knowledge of the spatial features of the environment—of where things are and "what leads to what." Reinforcement does not produce the learning but instead leads animals to use what they have learned. If a reward is provided in one part of the cognitive map, they will somehow manage to go there. If there is punishment, they will avoid that spot.

Subsequent experimenters, working with types of learning that did not pose the spatial problems found in mazes, enlarged Tolman's terminology into the idea of acquiring *expectancies* (Bolles, 1972). As pointed out earlier, even in studying classical and operant conditioning, investigators concluded that what was important was the subject's anticipation, or belief, about what would take place.

Knowledge
The results of complex mental processing, according to cognitive psychologists.

Today's cognitive psychologists have expanded these suggestions into the all-embracing term **knowledge.** What is learned, according to the cognitive school, is all sorts of knowledge—the "maps" of pathways acquired by Tolman's rats, the expectancies about food acquired by Pavlov's dogs, and a human's knowledge that Main Street is one block north of Broadway, an aspirin can be expected to relieve a headache, $2 \times 4 = 8$, the past tense of *swim* is *swam,* and the earth is round. Indeed we now know that different parts of the brain are involved in different types of learning. For example, the learning of a classically conditioned response, an operant response, an association between two words, and a motor habit all involve different neurological circuits and different principles of learning.

The cognitive psychologists regard "the human organism as an active seeker of knowledge and processor of information"—with learning being the step in which we acquire information that we then modify, manipulate, store, and use in various ways (Klatzky, 1980). They view learning as one element in a closely related series of processes—notably perception, memory, and language and cognition—that are discussed in other chapters of this book. Psychologists are also aware that learning capacities differ at various points in our lives, as discussed in the Life Span Perspective box titled "Learning and Age."

The behavior of children is often modeled from observations of the adults around them.

LIFE SPAN PERSPECTIVE

Learning and Age

Although it is true that humans are born with all the neurons they will ever have, the overall mass of the brain in infancy totals only about one-fourth that of the adult brain. The brain grows bigger over time because its neurons grow in size, and the number of axons and dendrites as well as the scope of their connections increases (Shatz, 1992). Because the brain changes with growth, we should expect that the ease of learning new ideas and skills or achieving insights should also change dramatically over the life span.

During the first year of life, before the child has acquired any language, learning consists of the acquisition of new perceptual skills and new habits. If the new skill is one for which the infant is biologically prepared, then learning takes place quickly. An example is the skill of reaching for objects. Infants can learn rapidly to reach for a rattle when its sounds are close by, and to ignore it when the sounds are from a distance. However, if the task is not one for which the infant is innately prepared—for example, turning the head to the right upon hearing a particular sound—the learning rate can be prolonged. Thus the ease of learning is clearly a function of the nature of the task.

After two or three years of age, the child is using symbols and, therefore, can relate new experiences to a very large and complex set of ideas. From three to seven years of age, there is an obvious improvement in the speed of learning a new habit or set of rules. If the task is to reach for the one object of three that is different from the other two (for example, a cup but not the two adjoining glasses), the older child will learn this new rule very quickly compared with a two-year-old.

From adolescence to about 30 years of age, many researchers believe, the brain is optimal for learning new ideas and manipulating complex concepts. It is noteworthy, for example, that many mathematicians and physicists make their most important discoveries in their twenties. Many of the Nobel laureates in physics made their important discoveries before they were 30 years old.

The learning of middle and old age involves mainly the integration of past experiences, or what many would call wisdom. A 60-year-old cannot learn new ideas as quickly as the younger person. For example, if the task is to learn a series of 100 digits, with the individual attempting to learn 10 new digits each day, the 30-year-old can master the assignment much more quickly than the older person. But, as will be seen in Chapter 13, the older person has accumulated a richer set of experiences, permitting greater insights into complex events in the world. Freud's most important ideas came after he had reached midlife, and George Bernard Shaw wrote some of his best plays in his "later years." ■

Observational Learning

One way of acquiring knowledge is **learning through observation** (or, as some psychologists prefer, **learning through modeling** or **learning by imitation**). All three terms refer to the process through which we learn by observing the behavior of others.

It has been known for some time that even lower animals learn by observation and imitation. In one of the early experiments, a cat was taught in a Skinner box to obtain food by pressing the bar when a light went on. Another cat, which had been watching, was then placed in the box. This second cat began very quickly to press the bar when the light went on. Through observation, it had learned much faster than the first cat (John et al., 1968). Subsequent experiments have demonstrated many kinds of observational learning by many animals, from mice to dolphins.

With humans, one of the most dramatic examples of observational learning was recorded on film by Albert Bandura. In this experiment, children watched a movie showing an adult striking a large doll with a hammer. When

Learning through observation

A process in which learning occurs by observing the behavior of others; includes learning through modeling and imitation.

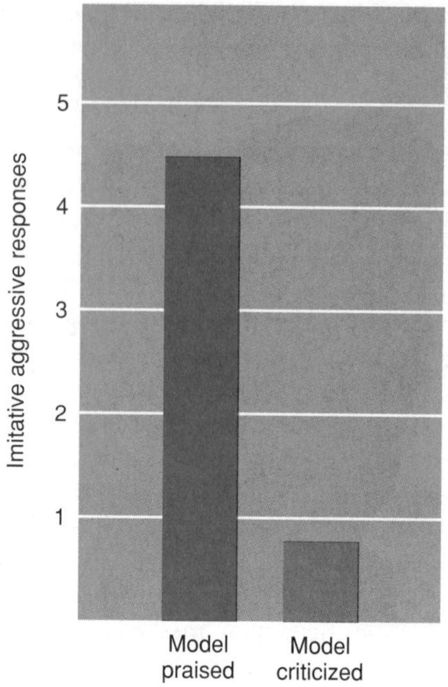

FIGURE 4.18 Imitation Through Observation Children were much more likely to imitate aggressive behavior when they observed such behavior being praised rather than criticized. (Adapted from Rosekrans & Hartup, 1967).

the children then had an opportunity to play with the doll themselves, they showed remarkably similar behavior. In a similar study involving real-life figures, children watched an adult beating and poking a large doll. Another adult, observing the action, either praised the aggressive behavior or criticized it. As illustrated in Figure 4.18, the children were most likely to imitate the aggressive behavior when they not only observed it but heard it admired.

Cognitive theorists do not think of observational learning as an automatic and unthinking imitation of what we have seen. Rather they believe that we begin in early childhood, and continue throughout our lives, to observe what goes on around us and to store the information that the observation provides. We observe what other people seem to value, how they go about getting what they value, their behavior in general, and the results of their behavior. At the same time, we make judgments. We may or may not decide to value what they value. We may imitate their behavior, adopt some but not all of it, or reject it entirely. As Bandura has stated, learning by observation is "actively judgmental and constructive rather than a mechanical copying" (Bandura, 1974).

Closely akin to observational learning, of course, is the kind of learning you are doing at this moment—and that people do in many ways in many situations. This is learning by receiving instruction from someone else, as when reading a textbook (or a recipe) or listening to a teacher in the classroom (or to a tennis pro telling you how to improve your serve). The cognitive psychologists would say that in our information processing we have the benefit not only of the knowledge stored in our own memories but, through language, of all the knowledge possessed by our fellow human beings and indeed the wisdom of the ages as recorded in our libraries and computer data bases.

TEST YOURSELF

h) Johnny uses "bad words" every time he gets angry at school—just as his father does at home. What kind of learning is Johnny demonstrating?

SUMMARY REVIEW

Classical Conditioning

1. Learning is *any relatively permanent change in behavior (or behavior potential) produced by experience.*

2. One of the simplest and most universal forms of learning concerns the **reflex,** which is an inborn and built-in response to a stimulus.

3. Through learning, a reflex response can become attached to a stimulus that did not originally cause the response. This process was demonstrated when Pavlov taught a dog to respond to a sound with the salivary reflex, which originally was caused only by the presence of food in the mouth. This type of learning is called **classical conditioning.**

4. In classical conditioning, the stimulus that naturally sets off the reflex (in Pavlov's experiment, the food) is called the **unconditioned stimulus.** The previous neutral stimulus to which the reflex becomes attached (the sound) is called the **conditioned stimulus.**

5. The original reflex response (in Pavlov's experiment, salivation) is called the **unconditioned response.** The response to the conditioned stimulus is the **conditioned response.**

The Power of Conditioning: Influential Factors

6. The pairing of the unconditioned stimulus and the conditioned stimulus is called **reinforcement.** Conditioning turns out to be most effective through the use of **forward pairing** (the conditioned stimulus precedes the unconditioned stimulus by a short interval). Less effective is **simultaneous pairing** (presentation of both at the very same time), and the least effective of all is **backward pairing** (presentation of the conditioned stimulus after the unconditioned stimulus).

7. In the view of many psychologists today, conditioning can be explained best by the development of **expectancies**—that is, what animals and humans learn is the expectation that a particular conditioned stimulus will be followed by an unconditioned stimulus.

8. When reinforcement is no longer provided (in Pavlov's experiment, when food no longer accompanies the sound), the conditioned response tends to disappear—a process called **extinction.** After a rest period, however, the conditioned response may reappear—a process called **spontaneous recovery.**

9. When a response has been conditioned to one stimulus, it is also likely to be aroused by similar stimuli—a process called **stimulus generalization.** Through further conditioning, however, the organism can learn to respond to one particular conditioned stimulus but not to other stimuli that closely resemble it—a process known as **stimulus discrimination.**

10. Classical conditioning by past events accounts for many of the unreasonable fears and preferences displayed by human adults—also for such strange physical symptoms as unexplained headaches or nausea.

11. The power of conditioning depends on the strength of the organism's native tendency to respond to the actual pairing of stimuli used. Evidently various species are prepared by nature to make stronger associations between particular stimuli and responses than to others.

Operant Conditioning

12. Another type of learning, demonstrated by Skinner, concerns operant behavior—the random or exploratory activities in which organisms engage, not in reflex response to a stimulus but as a self-generated way of "operating" on the world around them.

13. Skinner showed that a rat in a cage containing a bar would eventually press the bar as part of its operant behavior—and would learn to keep pressing if rewarded with food. This form of learning is called **operant conditioning.**

14. In operant conditioning, the *reinforcement* is the reward (in Skinner's experiment, the food). The rule is that operant behavior that is reinforced by a reward tends to be repeated, while operant behavior that is not reinforced tends to take place only at random intervals or is abandoned.

15. Like classical conditioning, operant conditioning also displays *extinction, spontaneous recovery, stimulus generalization,* and *stimulus discrimination.*

16. Through operant conditioning, animals can be taught to perform complex tasks by rewarding them for the successful completion of each step that leads to the desired behavior. This process is called **shaping.**

17. Rewards that the organism finds basically satisfying, such as food and water, are **primary reinforcers.** The less tangible rewards for which human beings often learn, such as praise or acceptance, are **secondary reinforcers.**

18. Operant learning usually takes place fastest with **constant reinforcement** or reward for each performance. But learning is usually more resistant to extinction with **partial reinforcement,** or rewards on some occasions and not on others.

19. The two basic types of partial reinforcement schedules are:
    a) **ratio schedules,** in which the reinforcement is delivered only after the subject responds a certain number of times
    b) **interval schedules,** in which reinforcement is delivered only after a certain period has passed. If either ratio or interval is the same each time, the schedule is termed **fixed.** On the other hand, if the ratio or interval changes to some degree each time, the schedule is termed **variable.**

20. The use of rewards to influence human activities—for example, praising a withdrawn nursery school child to encourage sociable behavior—is called **behavior modification.**

21. A special form of behavior modification, widely used in mental hospitals, provides reinforcement in the form of tokens that can be spent like money for goods and privileges. This method is called a **token economy.**

22. **Biofeedback** is an operant conditioning technique that attempts to relieve physical ailments through devices that provide the subject with moment-to-moment readings of such bodily activities as muscle tension and blood flow.

Escape and Avoidance, Punishment, and Learned Helplessness

23. Operant conditioning can be established through either **positive reinforcement,** in the form of desirable rewards, or **negative reinforce-**

ment, which is the termination of something painful or otherwise unpleasant, like an electric shock.

24. Experiments with negative reinforcement have shown that animals are very quick to learn **operant escape,** or how to get away from the shock, and **operant avoidance,** or how to prevent the shock by taking some kind of action before it occurs. Many human defenses against events that arouse unpleasant anxiety appear to be forms of operant escape or avoidance.

25. In *punishment,* the goal is not to reinforce a response, and therefore make it more likely to occur in the future, but to eliminate a response. Although punishment often produces rapid learning in animals, it is of questionable value in influencing human behavior.

26. One result of punishment, in both animals and human beings, may be **learned helplessness**—a tendency to believe that events cannot be controlled and to give up trying to learn.

27. Learned helplessness can be caused not only by punishment but also by failure. The effects depend partly on whether victims blame themselves or outside factors.

28. Learned helplessness may apply only to one kind of activity or situation, or it may become generalized and affect the victim's entire approach to life.

29. Therapists try to treat learned helplessness, which can result in seriously abnormal behavior, by persuading victims that they have more ability to succeed than they realize.

Cognitive Learning: A Contemporary View Rooted in the Past

30. Ingrained in the history of learning research is what is now regarded as the contemporary view of learning: That the human organism is far from being a passive product of experience. Instead learning is a process— with the human organism actively interacting with the environment.

31. Among the experiments that helped lead to the cognitive view are
a) Köhler's findings that chimpanzees learn through **insight,** or what is known today as cognition
b) the discovery that rats in a maze may display a special type of learning—which takes place without reinforcement and lies dormant until there is reason to use it
c) the temporarily paralyzed dog that learned how to escape from a shock even though it could not make a response during the learning trials.

32. Various psychologists have suggested that what is learned is not just a simple stimulus-response connection but a **cognitive map** (of a maze, for example) or an expectancy (for example, that food will follow the sound of a metronome). The cognitive view now includes both theories in the all-embracing idea that what we learn is knowledge of many kinds.

33. One form of acquiring knowledge is **learning through observation** (also called **learning through modeling** or **learning by imitation**). Closely akin to observational learning is the familiar process of learning through instruction—for instance, by listening to a teacher or reading a book.

Study Guide

Chapter 4   Learning: Basic Principles

LEARNING OBJECTIVES

After studying this chapter, you should be able to:

For an Understanding of the Science

1. Understand the process of classical conditioning and the meaning of unconditioned stimulus, unconditioned response, conditioned stimulus, and conditioned response.

2. Distinguish between classical conditioning and operant conditioning.

3. Define and illustrate the principles of reinforcement, extinction, spontaneous recovery, stimulus generalization, and stimulus discrimination, and know how they apply to both classical and operant conditioning.

4. Understand positive and negative reinforcement, operant escape and avoidance, and the pros and cons of using punishment as a form of negative reinforcement with human beings.

5. Explain the cognitive view of learning, its emphasis on the acquisition of knowledge including expectancies and learning through observation, and its argument that conditioning cannot explain all forms of learning.

For Application to Life Situations

6. Describe how classical conditioning in childhood may account for unreasonable fears and preferences as well as some of the strange physical symptoms that may bother us as adults.

7. Give examples of how operant conditioning is used in behavior modification.

8. Discuss the implications of studies on learned helplessness: how we can acquire it through punishment or failure, how it may cripple us, and how it can be combated through therapy or self-therapy that demonstrates that we are more competent at more things than we realize.

9. Explain the implications of cognitive theory that we learn from other people by observing what they seem to value and how they go about getting it and the consequences of their behavior. Explain how we decide whether to imitate certain behaviors, adopt some but not all of them, or reject them entirely.

PROGRAMMED UNIT
CLASSICAL CONDITIONING

1. *Learning* is any relatively permanent change in behavior (or behavior potential) produced by *experience*. When we touch a hot stove, the experience teaches us to avoid contact with the stove in the future—a lasting change in our behavior produced by _____. **learning**

2. Learning is any lasting change in behavior (or behavior potential) produced by _____. But learning from experience can even be applied to behaviors that originally are not learned but are inborn. For example, a *reflex* is an inborn response to a specific stimulus. **experience**

3. Whenever a bright light strikes your eyes, it makes your pupils smaller. This type of automatic response, which is inborn, is called a _____. **reflex**

4. Another type of inborn behavior is an *instinct*, which is an inborn pattern of behavior. The nest-building behavior of birds constitutes an _____. **instinct**

5. An inborn, automatic, single action is a _____, while an inborn pattern of behavior is an _____. **reflex instinct**

6. Although reflexes and instincts are inborn and not _____, *Ivan Pavlov*, a Russian scientist, was interested in whether a reflex could for example, through learning, be made to occur in response to a stimulus that originally did not evoke it. **learned**

7. The process of learning to associate a reflex with a new stimulus—the type of learning of interest to the Russian scientist _____—is called *classical conditioning*. **Pavlov**

8. Pavlov taught a dog to respond to a sound with a salivary reflex, which was originally caused only by putting food in the dog's mouth. This type of learning is called classical _____. **conditioning**

9. In the process of learning to associate a reflex with a new stimulus, called _____ _____, the stimulus that naturally sets off the reflex is called the *unconditioned stimulus*. **classical conditioning**

10. In Pavlov's experiment, food was the natural stimulus for the reflex of salivation. In classical conditioning terms, food was the _____ _____. **unconditioned stimulus**

11. The unconditioned stimulus naturally produces a _____, and in classical conditioning terminology, this unlearned reflex to a stimulus is called the *unconditioned response*. **reflex**

12. In Pavlov's experiment, salivation was the _____ _____. **unconditioned response**

13. The *unlearned* stimulus and response in classical _____ are called the _____ _____ and the _____ _____, respectively. **conditioning, unconditioned stimulus, unconditioned response**

14. The learning in classical conditioning involves "teaching" a new stimulus, called the *conditioned stimulus,* which does not usually produce a response, to elicit salivation. The sound of a metronome was the _____ _____ in Pavlov's experiment.

conditioned stimulus

15. The metronome, or _____ _____, was sounded just before the food, or _____ _____, was given to the dog.

conditioned stimulus
unconditioned stimulus

16. Eventually, after several pairings of the _____ and _____ stimuli, the metronome alone produced the salivation, a behavior that is then called the *conditioned response,* because it is learned.

conditioned, unconditioned

17. When salivation occurs as an unlearned reflex to the stimulus of food, it is called the _____ response; when it occurs as a learned response to the metronome stimulus, it is called the _____ response.

unconditioned
conditioned

18. In the form of learning called _____ _____, a previously neutral stimulus, the _____ _____, is associated with another stimulus, the _____ _____, which reflexively produces the _____ _____. When the conditioned stimulus produces this same response through learning, the behavior is then called the _____ _____.

classical conditioning
conditioned stimulus
unconditioned stimulus
unconditioned response
conditioned response

19. The pairing of the conditioned stimulus with the unconditioned stimulus is called *reinforcement.* In Pavlov's experiment, following the metronome with food was a _____.

reinforcement

20. In general, reinforcement occurs in classical conditioning when a _____ stimulus is paired with an _____ stimulus, and such _____ eventually lead to learning that the two stimuli will occur together.

conditioned
unconditioned, reinforcements

THE POWER OF CONDITIONING: INFLUENTIAL FACTORS

21. Simple learning, such as _____ _____, is influenced by several factors. One is the sequence in which the conditioned and unconditioned stimuli are presented. The traditional sequence described above is to first present the _____ stimulus followed by the _____ stimulus, a sequence called *forward pairing.*

classical conditioning

conditioned
unconditioned

22. Learning occurs most rapidly under conditions of _____ _____. Less effective is *simultaneous pairing,* and least effective is *backward pairing.*

forward pairing

23. If the conditioned stimulus precedes the unconditioned stimulus, it is called _____ _____; if the unconditioned precedes the conditioned stimulus, it is _____ _____; and if they are presented together, it is _____ _____.

forward pairing
backward pairing
simultaneous pairing

24. The difference in effectiveness of these pairings to produce learning or _____ demonstrates that the crucial experience is not simply the pairing of conditioned and unconditioned stimuli but that the conditioned *predicts* the unconditioned stimulus.

conditioning

25. The organism learns that the conditioned stimulus _____ the unconditioned stimulus—that is, it learns an *expectation*—and this _____ is most easily acquired under conditions of _____ _____.

predicts
expectation
forward pairing

26. Indeed, learning can occur even if the organism is immobilized with drugs and prevented from responding to the unconditioned response, because what is learned is not the response but the _____ that the _____ stimulus will be followed by the _____ stimulus.

expectation
conditioned, unconditioned

27. As might be expected, if reinforcement is no longer given—that is, if the conditioned stimulus is no longer followed by the _____ stimulus—the learned _____ weakens and eventually the conditioned response no longer occurs following the conditioned stimulus, a phenomenon called *extinction*.

unconditioned
expectation

28. In Pavlov's experiment, if the sound is no longer followed by food, the dog will eventually cease to salivate to the sound. When that happens, the conditioned response has undergone _____.

extinction

29. In short, when Pavlov discontinued _____, then the conditioned response underwent _____. After a rest period, however, a conditioned response may reappear—a process called *spontaneous recovery*.

reinforcement
extinction

30. If after a period of rest, an extinguished conditioned response reappears following the next presentation of the conditioned stimulus, this phenomenon is called _____ recovery.

spontaneous

31. Once learning has occurred to a particular conditioned stimulus, the conditioned response may occur to other stimuli similar to the original conditioned stimulus in a process called *stimulus generalization*. If a dog learns to salivate to the sound of a metronome, the dog may also salivate to the sound of a bell by the process of _____ _____.

stimulus
generalization

32. But if a deliberate attempt is made to follow the metronome, but not the bell, with the unconditioned stimulus (i.e., food powder), then the dog will learn to salivate only to the metronome and not to the bell, a process called *stimulus discrimination*. The opposite process to stimulus _____ is stimulus _____.

generalization
discrimination

33. Albert initially learned to fear a rat, but he also was apprehensive about Santa Claus's beard, evidence of _____ _____. If Albert had then been given experience with Santa's beard without its being paired with the unconditioned stimulus—that is, without _____—eventually the apprehension to the beard, but not the rat, would undergo _____ and the result would be that Albert learned _____ _____.

stimulus generalization
reinforcement
extinction
stimulus
discrimination

OPERANT CONDITIONING

34. In addition to changes in reflex behavior, which is the subject of _____ conditioning, another important form of behavior in the study of learning is called *operant behavior*. The seemingly random activity initiated by the organism as a way of "operating" on the environment is called _____ _____.

classical

operant behavior

35. When a rat is placed in a strange cage, it may explore, sniff, and climb about. This seemingly random activity, initiated by the rat as a way of exploring and perhaps changing the environment, is a form of _____ behavior.

operant

36. Through learning, such behavior can become associated with a specific stimulus, also called a *reinforcement,* which increases or decreases the likelihood that the organism repeats the _____ behavior, a learning process called *operant conditioning*.

operant

37. The learning process by which the occurrence of operant behavior is increased or decreased by following that behavior with a _____ is called _____ _____.

reinforcement
operant conditioning

38. If a rat learns to press a bar to produce food, psychologists say _____

operant

conditioning has occurred. Through such conditioning, animals can be taught to perform complex tasks by the process of *shaping*, which consists of rewarding them for the successful completion of each step leading to a desired behavior.

39. In teaching a pigeon to peck a black dot inside a white circle, the pigeon might first be rewarded with food for merely facing the circle. Later, when this is learned, the bird might be rewarded only for approaching the circle and then only for touching it with its beak. Finally, the pigeon must actually peck the black dot to receive the reward. This process of rewarding the pigeon for successive approximations until the desired behavior is learned is called _____.

shaping

reinforcements

40. Sometimes rewards and punishments, which psychologists call _____, accidentally teach an unintended lesson in a process called *autoshaping*.

41. When a reward occurs, it tends to encourage the organism to repeat whatever _____ behavior was occurring at the time, whether it actually produced the reinforcement or not. Animals and people can learn "superstitious" behavior and beliefs by this process of _____.

operant

autoshaping

42. Any stimulus that will increase or decrease the likelihood that a particular behavior will be repeated is a _____. Some stimuli that are basically rewarding, such as food and water, are called *primary reinforcers*.

reinforcement

43. In addition to rewards that are inherently satisfying, or _____ reinforcers, there are less tangible rewards that human beings often learn to desire, such as praise and acceptance. These are called *secondary reinforcers*, and they may acquire their reward value through association with primary reinforcers.

primary

44. Six-year-old John is learning to read faster because his mother rewards his successes with praise, which is a _____ reinforcer. John's dog is learning to retrieve the morning paper more regularly because he is rewarded with a biscuit, which is a _____ reinforcer. In either case, when rewards are offered for each and every performance of the desired behavior, the process is called *constant reinforcement*.

secondary

primary

45. Learning generally takes place more rapidly when reinforcement follows each time the organism displays the desired response, which is _____ reinforcement. But learning is usually more resistant to extinction if it is acquired with *partial reinforcement*, the delivery of a reinforcement on some occasions but not on others.

constant

46. Because one does not catch a fish every time a line is cast into the water, fishing behavior is usually encouraged by _____ _____.

partial reinforcement

constant
extinction
partial

47. Behaviors are learned more rapidly when reinforcement is _____, but such behaviors persist longer in the face of _____ when reinforcement is _____. There are two types of partial reinforcement schedules. The first is called a *ratio schedule*, in which the reinforcement is delivered only after the subject responds a certain number of times. The second is called an *interval schedule*, in which the reinforcement is delivered only after a certain period of time.

ratio
interval

48. If a rat receives food only after pressing a bar three times, the reinforcement schedule would be a _____ schedule; if the rat receives food every two minutes, the reinforcement would be an _____ schedule.

For both types of schedules, if the ratio or interval is always the same, the schedule is said to be *fixed;* if it changes over time, the schedule is said to be *variable.*

49. Intermittent reinforcement, called _____ reinforcement, can be given after a specific number of correct responses, called a _____ schedule, or after so much time, called an _____ schedule, and the ratio or interval can be constant, or _____, or changing, called _____.

partial
ratio
interval
fixed, variable

50. Most employees are paid every two weeks or every month, which constitutes a _____ _____ schedule. But fishing or shooting baskets in basketball is typically rewarded on a _____ _____ schedule.

fixed interval
variable ratio

51. Any deliberate attempt to use reinforcement and other learning principles to change behavior is called *behavior modification.* A shy young girl was deliberately ignored by her teachers when she played alone but given their attention when she joined the play of other children. This systematic attempt to help the child overcome shyness by using reinforcements and other techniques of learning is an example of _____ _____.

behavior
modification

52. Deliberately "teaching" people to change their behavior is known as _____ _____, a special form of which is called a *token economy.* This method, widely used in mental hospitals, provides reinforcement for positive behavior in the form of tokens that patients can spend like money for goods and privileges.

behavior modification

53. Mark, who is in an institution for the mentally retarded, receives tokens every time he laces his shoes. Later he can buy toys with the tokens. Mark is being rewarded by the method known as a _____ _____ system, and, because the tokens become associated with good things, they act as _____ reinforcements.

token economy

secondary

ESCAPE AND AVOIDANCE, PUNISHMENT, AND LEARNED HELPLESSNESS

54. Operant conditioning, a process in which a particular _____ behavior is increased or decreased in frequency by _____, may involve *positive* or *negative reinforcement.*

operant
reinforcement

55. Providing desirable rewards, such as food, praise, and valuable tokens, to encourage a behavior constitutes _____ _____, while terminating something painful, unpleasant, or undesirable to promote a behavior constitutes _____ _____.

positive reinforcement

negative reinforcement

56. Teaching a rat to press a bar to receive food is an example of _____ reinforcement, while teaching a dog to jump to the other side of a shuttle box to escape or avoid being shocked with electricity is an example of _____ reinforcement. In fact, animals are very quick to learn *operant escape,* or how to get away from something painful or otherwise unpleasant, like an electric shock.

positive

negative

57. If one-half of the floor of a compartment delivers an electric shock to the feet of an animal, the animal will quickly learn to run to the other side, which is a demonstration of _____ _____.

operant escape

escape	58. In addition to learning to get away from or to _____ something painful or unpleasant, animals also learn *operant avoidance,* or how to prevent something painful like an electric shock by taking some kind of action before it occurs.
	59. An animal, warned by a signal that a shock will soon be administered, can run to the side of the compartment that is safe. In doing so, the animal is
operant avoidance	demonstrating _____ _____.
	60. Once negative reinforcement has begun, most animals will learn operant
escape	_____. If a signal warns that negative reinforcement is coming, they
avoidance	will learn operant _____. Operant behavior can also be conditioned through the use of *punishment,* the goal of which is to discourage or eliminate rather than encourage or increase a response.
	61. A mother who slaps her toddler on the hand for reaching for an electric socket is attempting to eliminate the child's response through the use of
punishment	_____, which can produce rapid learning in animals but is of less consistent value when applied to humans.
	62. Sometimes procedures that eliminate responses through the use of
punishment	_____ can lead in both animals and human beings to *learned helplessness,* or a tendency to believe that events cannot be controlled and to give up trying to learn or act.
punishment	63. Frequent experiences with failure or _____ can lead to the tendency to believe that events cannot be controlled and to give up trying, which is
learned helplessness	called _____ _____.

COGNITIVE LEARNING: A CONTEMPORARY VIEW ROOTED IN THE PAST

classical, operant	64. Historically, some psychologists once thought that essentially all human learning was acquired through _____ and _____ conditioning. But not all learned behavior can be explained by these principles, as illustrated by the example of *insight,* or what today would be called cognition.
	65. For example, in one early experiment, chimpanzees faced with food placed at a distance and given some sticks, "figured out" how to use the sticks to
insight	rake in the food. This cognition is called _____.
operant, reinforced	66. The chimps had never before raked in food with sticks, so such behavior did not constitute _____ behavior that was _____ by food as
operant	in _____ conditioning.
unconditioned	67. Similarly, such behavior was not reflexively produced by an _____
classical	stimulus and then associated with the presence of sticks as in _____ conditioning.
insight	68. Instead, the chimpanzees appeared to learn by cognitive means, in this case by _____. In other situations, animals and people can also learn
reinforcement	without receiving positive or negative _____ or without actually making a response, as in *learning through observation.*
	69. A child who watches a movie of another child hitting a large doll and who later hits the same doll in a play session, illustrates learning through
observation	_____, which is also called learning through *modeling* or learning by *imitation.*

70. Evidence that some children learn aggressive behavior by watching violence on television supports the view that learning takes place through _____, _____, or _____.

observation, modeling, imitation

71. Recall that what was learned during conditioning was not a response but an _____ of what stimulus _____ another stimulus. Similarly when we study a map of a city, we may not learn a particular route of left and right turns to a specific destination, but rather we may acquire a *cognitive map* that allows us to go many different routes and even improvise a new route if we suddenly get lost.

expectation, predicts

72. According to cognitive psychologists, what is learned in all these situations is *knowledge*. The expectancies of conditioning, the sudden solving of a problem by _____, learning by _____, and the acquisition of _____ _____ are all examples of the acquisition of _____, not simple stimulus-response connections.

insight, observation cognitive maps knowledge

REVIEW OF IMPORTANT TERMS

autoshaping (170)

backward pairing (163)

behavior modification (173)

biofeedback (174)

classical conditioning (157)

claustrophobia (157)

cognitive map (184)

conditioned response (162)

conditioned stimulus (162)

constant reinforcement (171)

expectancy (165)

extinction (165)

fixed schedule (172)

forward pairing (162)

insight (181)

instincts (156)

interval schedule (172)

knowledge (184)

learned helplessness (167)

learning (156)

learning through observation (or modeling or imitation) (185)

negative reinforcement (175)

operant avoidance (175)

operant behavior (168)

operant conditioning (168)

operant escape (175)

partial reinforcement (171)

positive reinforcement (175)

potential startle (164)

primary reinforcer (170)

ratio schedule (172)

reflex (157)

reinforcement (162)

secondary reinforcer (170)

shaping (169)

simultaneous pairing (163)

spontaneous recovery (166)

stimulus discrimination (166)

stimulus generalization (166)

token economy (173)

unconditioned response (162)

unconditioned stimulus (162)

variable schedule (172)

PRACTICE TEST

_____ 1. Which statement is *not* true about learning?
  a. A reflex response can become attached to a stimulus that did not originally cause that response.
  b. Learning can occur without observable behavioral activity.
  c. Learning differs from an instinct because of the role of experience.
  d. Reflexes and instincts are inborn and are not modified by learning.

_____ 2. Some prejudices and fears are caused by
  a. classical conditioning.
  b. stimulus generalization.
  c. operant conditioning.
  d. all the above.

_____ 3. In Pavlov's experiment the conditioned response is
  a. the food.
  b. salivation to the metronome.
  c. the metronome.
  d. salivation to the food.

_____ 4. In the "Albert experiment" the unconditioned stimulus is
  a. fear of the sight of the rat.
  b. the rat.
  c. the loud noise.
  d. Santa's beard.

_____ 5. A type of learning not initially dependent on a specific stimulus to produce a specific response is called
  a. operant conditioning.
  b. reflex learning.
  c. discrimination learning.
  d. classical conditioning.

_____ 6. Albert showed fear or suspicion toward a dog, a fur coat, and a bearded mask of Santa Claus because of
  a. operant conditioning.
  b. stimulus generalization.
  c. stimulus discrimination.
  d. spontaneous recovery.

_____ 7. Human beings prone to asthma attacks because of an allergy to dust or pollen could suffer an attack when exposed to a harmless substance because of
  a. operant conditioning.
  b. stimulus discrimination.

    c.   classical conditioning.

    d.   spontaneous recovery.

_____ 8. Insight and cognitive maps are concepts most closely associated with

    a.   behavior modification.

    b.   Pavlov.

    c.   cognitive psychology's view of learning.

    d.   John Watson.

_____ 9. A concept primarily related to operant but not to classical conditioning is

    a.   reinforcement.

    b.   shaping.

    c.   spontaneous recovery.

    d.   stimulus generalization.

_____ 10. Pavlov discovered that he could make dogs restless, destructive, apathetic, and neurotic by

    a.   reinforcing these behaviors.

    b.   giving the dogs an impossible discrimination problem.

    c.   having them solve an impossible stimulus generalization problem.

    d.   all the above.

_____ 11. When toddlers are brought into a strange room one at a time, they walk around it, explore the furniture, and play with the objects that are in the room. This type of activity is called

    a.   operant behavior.

    b.   spontaneous recovery.

    c.   operant conditioning.

    d.   behavior modification.

_____ 12. Some people believe that certain objects are good-luck pieces and help them perform better. Such superstitions may be the result of

    a.   a program of behavior modification.

    b.   insight.

    c.   autoshaping.

    d.   token economy systems.

_____ 13. Learning is likely to occur most rapidly and be most persistent if

    a.   partial reinforcement is used.

    b.   constant reinforcement is used.

    c.   partial reinforcement is used first, followed by constant reinforcement.

    d.   constant reinforcement is used first, followed by partial reinforcement.

_____ 14. The schedule of reinforcement that operates in fishing or shooting baskets is most likely a

    a.   variable ratio schedule.

    b.   variable interval schedule.

    c.   fixed ratio schedule.

    d.   fixed interval schedule.

_____ 15. Poker chips that can be used to buy privileges and are given for desired behavior constitute

    a.   secondary reinforcers.

    b.   primary reinforcers.

    c.   constant but not partial reinforcers.

    d.   negative reinforcers.

_____ 16. A parent who deliberately ignores a child's temper tantrum is attempting to discourage tantrums by

    a.   negative reinforcement.

    b.   extinction.

    c.   operant avoidance.

    d.   learned helplessness.

_____ 17. The assumption that behavior is controlled to a considerable degree by its consequences underlies

    a.   behavior modification.

    b.   autoshaping.

    c.   biofeedback.

    d.   all the above.

_____ 18. In the study in which a light is illuminated just before an electric shock is turned on, the animal learns

    a.   operant escape and then operant avoidance.

    b.   operant avoidance and then operant escape.

    c.   only operant escape.

    d.   only operant avoidance.

_____ 19. Punishment is most effective when combined with

    a.   reward for the correct behavior.

    b.   secondary reinforcement.

    c.   extinction.

    d.   partial reinforcement.

_____ 20. Learned helplessness in children may be caused by

    a.   frequent and inconsistent punishment.

    b.   frequent failure.

    c.   continually being pressured to perform better than their true capabilities.

    d.   all the above.

ANSWERS TO PRACTICE TEST

1. d	6. b	11. a	16. b
2. d	7. c	12. c	17. d
3. b	8. c	13. d	18. a
4. c	9. b	14. a	19. a
5. a	10. b	15. a	20. d

EXERCISES

I. Father Flanagan's Boys Town operates a residential treatment facility for adolescent boys and girls who have had difficulty getting along with their parents, other youth, teachers, and society in general. A youth who comes to Boys Town lives with eight or nine other youths and a married couple called family-teachers. Family-teachers provide a home-like setting in which there are rules, responsibilities, and privileges, and they teach the youth appropriate social behavior.

Because these young people have had so much difficulty in the past, the rules, responsibilities, and privileges are spelled out very clearly. The youths are motivated to learn appropriate behavior by an elaborate point system. Each boy or girl must earn 10,000 points by 9 P.M. each day to have a set of privileges granted for the next day. The privileges may include TV time, snacks, listening to the radio or tapes, participating in recreational activities, and so forth. Points can be earned for positive behaviors, such as studying, doing assigned chores, negotiating politely, taking criticism without becoming angry, spontaneously doing something nice or helpful for someone else, and listening to instructions. Points can be also be deducted (that is, a youth may be "fined") for swearing, leaving personal belongings in common rooms (for example, the kitchen or living room), failing to carry out a request, and so forth. Each youth has a card on which the points earned and points deducted are recorded throughout the day.

This point system helps the family-teacher motivate the youth to behave in socially acceptable ways. For example, here's what a typical interaction might be like.

"John," says a family-teacher, "you just finished an hour of hard studying. You have earned 2,000 points. Good job!"

"Thanks," John replies. "May I go to the gym now?"

"I'm sorry, John, you did not earn your 10,000-point minimum yesterday, so you are not permitted to go to the gym today. But you are well on your way to earning that privilege for tomorrow."

"That's a crock," John screams. "You know I earned my points yesterday. You're lying."

"John, I can see that you are angry, but when you disagreed with me you yelled and accused me of lying. I am going to fine you 1,000 points for that. You can earn back some of the points you lost by disagreeing politely. Say calmly, 'I think you are wrong. I am pretty sure I earned my points yesterday. Could we check them?' "

"That's silly," jeers John.

"It may sound silly to you, but that's how we disagree here. And you will find when you leave here that other people will respect you and you are more likely to get your way if you disagree with them in this way. Why don't we try it?"

"Well . . . you're wrong," John insists but in a softer voice. "I know I earned my points yesterday."

"That's a big improvement. Thank you, and I'll give you 200 points back for softening your voice. But I think you can do better."

"Okay. I think you're wrong. I am certain I made my points. Could we check it?"

"That was terrific! Give yourself 500 more points. You requested, instead of demanded, and in a nice tone of voice. Super. Now let's go check it out."

Given the above information, describe the Boys Town family-teaching program and the example using the terminology you have learned in this chapter. Go to the list of important terms in this chapter and try to use as many of them as possible in describing the Boys Town family-teaching program and the example. You may make up additional examples of this sort to illustrate terms not covered by the example above.

II.   **A.** Suppose you are a psychologist who attempts to help people with their problems through the use of behavior modification. Think about the following situations:

(1) You are a school psychologist and a teacher reports to you that Sally is a very shy first-grade girl who rarely plays with other children. Most of the time she plays alone in the corner or tries to do special favors for the teacher. What would you suggest the teacher do to help this child become more social and become less of a pest for the teacher?

(2) You are in charge of a ward in a hospital for mentally retarded children. Many of these youngsters have not learned to dress themselves, eat properly, wash themselves, brush their teeth, or refrain from hitting other children. How would you design a token economy system to help these children? Describe not only what you would do using proper learning terminology, but say why it should work.

(3) You are a child psychologist and some parents come to you because their three-year-old son throws a temper tantrum whenever he does not get his own way. He yells and screams, throws himself on the floor, kicks, and pounds. How would you explain to the parents how such behavior might have developed in the first place, and what would you suggest be done about it?

In all these situations, of course, there may be some circumstances that you do not know. And it is understood that you probably have had no actual experience with such cases. Moreover, although actual psychologists would apply some of the principles you have studied in this chapter, they might treat some of the people differently from others, depending on their individual characteristics. Thus you cannot offer universally "correct" answers to these questions. However, bring your responses to these situations to class and compare them with your student colleagues. Discuss the possible merits and liabilities of various approaches and the limitations and responsibilities involved in their use.

B. There is considerable debate about the ethics of using such behavioral principles in schools, hospitals, and at home. Some people claim this constitutes manipulating individuals against their will, and that no one has the right to exert such control over others in our society. In contrast, those who favor the use of behavioral principles argue that children who disrupt classrooms and patients who need help are already coerced and manipulated by schools, hospitals, policy, and other members of society in one way or another whether behavioral principles are used or not. They claim behavior modification is singled out—and receives more blame than does sending a child to the principal's office or committing an individual to a mental hospital—simply because behavior modification is more likely to be effective. Write a discussion presenting details and examples of both these opposing arguments, and then state your personal position and justify it.

Memory: How We Remember and Why We Forget

At every stage of life, memory is an important element of human behavior.

"I'm sorry, I seem to have forgotten your name."

"I meant to send you a birthday card, but I just forgot."

"I knew the answer, but I couldn't remember it."

Most of us have had occasion to make statements such as these. We sometimes have trouble remembering a phone number, a tune, or what time we said we would meet a friend for lunch. Little wonder that human memory is often blamed, apologized for, and agonized over.

Yet, no matter how imperfect our memories, and no matter how frustrated we feel at times when we forget, there is an enormous amount of knowledge stored somewhere—and somehow—within the nervous system. It is not rare for adults to know the meanings of many thousands of English words and perhaps some foreign words as well, plus rules of mathematics, and many basic facts about geography, science, and history. Not to mention such practical matters as how to drive a car, read a map, operate a calculator, make a phone call, and shop for food and clothing. The marvel is not how much we forget but how much we remember.

Psychologists and other scientists devote considerable effort to studying just how human memory works. How is it that items as fleeting a childhood conversation, the smell of a spring rain, or a baseball player's batting average can be kept "in the head" even for a short time, let alone for many years? One thing seems clear, as this chapter will explain. Human memory, rather than being a single capacity as once thought, is made up of different kinds of memory (Mitchell, 1989). Verbal memory—for example, remembering what this chapter contains—is quite different from memory for events, or the memory that allows us to remember how to ride a bicycle, or the memory for previously experienced faces, sounds, and smells.

The various types of memory systems probably involve different brain mechanisms (Squire, 1987), and to a degree, some of them are amenable to improvement through various techniques. These techniques will be described later in the chapter—but first it is important to understand the nature of the remarkable human capacities to remember.

The Range and Content of Human Memory

To cognitive psychologists, with their emphasis on knowledge as a key part of the human experience, learning and memory are, of course, closely related. Learning refers to the ways we acquire the many forms of knowledge we possess and utilize. Memory has two distinct meanings. First, it is the "storehouse" in which we keep all our knowledge—carefully sorted and saved so that we can find it quickly when we need it; second, it is the process by which we are able to retrieve the information we have accumulated.

We do not always succeed, as we all know, in our efforts to remember. Sometimes we let a piece of information slip through our hands, so to speak, and we say we have forgotten—perhaps permanently, perhaps just for the time being. How well we remember information depends in large part on how well we have learned it in the first place, and how carefully we have stored it away. Consider these three examples, all of them dealing with memory of verbal material:

- You are driving to the beach and hear on the radio that the temperature is 87 degrees. But at that moment you have to swerve to avoid an oncoming car. When the crisis is over, you try to remember what the temperature is, but you find that you have completely forgotten. It seems as if the information never registered at all in your memory.
- You are in a phone booth and look up a friend's phone number. You start repeating the number as you turn from the book and drop a coin into the phone. You have successfully remembered the number. But you get a busy signal—and by the time you fish the coin out of the return slot, drop it back into the phone, and wait for the tone, you find you have forgotten the number.
- You are not very good at remembering names, but at a party you meet a man whose name is Ronald Marston. You remark on the coincidence: his first name is the same as your brother's, and his last name is the same as your best friend's. Two years later, you meet the man again. You have absolutely no trouble saying, "Hi, you're Ronald Marston, aren't you?"

As these examples suggest, memories may persist over a time span that varies over an extremely wide range: a mere fraction of a second (like the weather report heard while driving); less than a minute (like the telephone number you forget right after looking it up); or a lifetime (like the name that has a special meaning for you). This section deals with the temporal aspects of memory—that is, the range of time over which we remember information like words, numbers, and sentences. For convenience, psychologists divide the range into three stages of memory, illustrated in Figure 5.1. It will be helpful to refer to the figure as you read the description of the three stages in the following pages.

Sensory Memory: Gone in an Instant

Every event that impinges on our sense organs seems to remain available at least for a brief instant, but sometimes no longer. These very brief memories, of which we are typically unaware, are called **sensory memory.** They contain

Sensory memory
The memory system that includes very brief memories composed of lingering traces of information sent to the brain by the sense organs.

FIGURE 5.1 **The three stages of memory** This diagram offers a quick summary of how the three stages of memory operate. The sights, sounds, and other stimuli in the environment register briefly in *sensory memory*. Some are promptly lost but others are transferred to *short-term memory*. There again some are lost but others are rehearsed and "kept in mind" long enough to be transferred to *long-term memory*—a more or less permanent storehouse from which they can later be retrieved (Shiffrin & Atkinson, 1969).

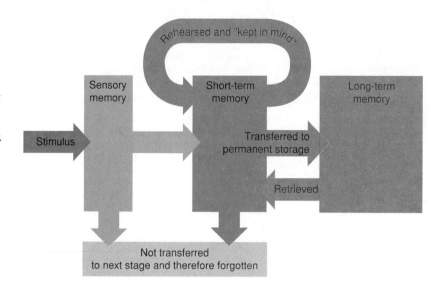

just the lingering traces of a great deal of information sent to the brain by the sense organs.

The nature of sensory memory was demonstrated many years ago in the experiment shown in Figure 5.2. Twelve letters and numbers were shown briefly to subjects, who were then asked how many of the letters and numbers they could remember. Without any kind of help, they remembered an average of four. But if a signal was given asking them to try to remember the letters and numbers on one particular line, they could usually recall at least three and often four of the symbols on this line. This was true no matter which of the three lines was signaled, suggesting that the subjects retained a brief impression of almost the entire pattern of the dozen letters or numbers (Sperling, 1960).

FIGURE 5.2 **The fleeting nature of sensory memory** Arrangements of twelve letters and numbers, such as those given here, were shown briefly to subjects. Through a method described in the text, the amount of information they held in sensory memory was then analyzed. As the bars show, the amount was quite high at the start but declined very quickly. (The base line for the bars is four because that was the average number of items remembered after the sensory memory had faded completely.)

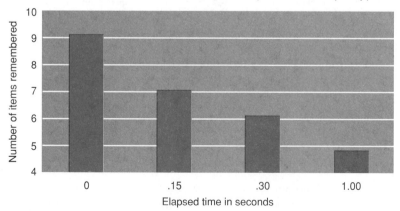

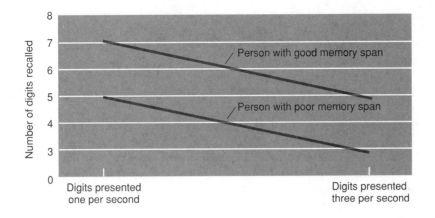

FIGURE 5.3 The brief lifespan of short-term memory Even individuals with a relatively good memory span have a limited capacity to recall digits immediately after they are presented—and however good or poor the memory span, the capacity gets weaker when the digits are presented more rapidly (after Lyon, 1977).

While the experiment showed that we can see and recall a good bit, it also showed—as indicated in Figure 5.3—that the information in sensory memory deteriorates very rapidly. There is probably a sensory memory process for each of the senses—so that, for example, we are able to remember for an instant the sight of lightning after it has flashed across the sky, the scent of flowers in a garden we have just walked by, or the sound of a car horn after it has passed. But these traces begin to vanish very quickly—usually within a half second if it is something we have seen, and within two to ten seconds if it is something we have heard (Cowan, 1984). To retain the traces longer, they must be transferred to the second of the three stages of memory.

Short-Term Memory: How Information Is Retained

The second of the three temporal stages is **short-term memory,** into which some but not all of the information from sensory memory is transferred. Unless some processing takes place within short-term memory, however, information held there deteriorates and seems to be forgotten completely within about 30 seconds (Shiffrin & Atkinson, 1969). So much information is lost in this way that one psychologist has described short-term memory as a "leaky bucket" (Miller, 1964). However, this is not entirely a disadvantage. For example, a bank teller remembers only briefly that he is cashing a customer's paycheck for $150.89. By the time the next customer steps up to the window, the figure $150.89 has already vanished from his memory. This is just as well—for he would be totally confused by the end of the day if he recalled every transaction starting with the first one of the morning.

It appears that much of the forgetting we do from short-term memory is intentional (Bjork, 1972). We have no need to remember the information. We do not want to remember it—and it would only get in our way, for the capacity of the short-term memory is quite small in terms of amount of information as well as time span, as portrayed in Figure 5.3. On the average, in the adult, it holds seven unrelated items—exactly the number of digits in a phone number—although for some people the limit is only five and for others it is as many as nine. When short-term memory is near capacity with its five to nine items, new information can be added only by dropping some of the old (or by grouping some of the items, as will be described later). We often throw out the old items deliberately. We do so by manipulating the processes that go on in short-term memory (Sperling, 1967).

Short-term memory
The memory system that holds information up to 30 seconds and then the information is either forgotten or transferred to long-term memory.

Scanning

A process in which some items are selected as worthy of attention.

Encoding

A process that transforms information in a way that is easy and simple to handle.

Schema

The mental representations of the information to be remembered.

Rehearsal system

A technique in which information is deliberately repeated to keep it in mind and to prevent it from slipping out of short-term memory.

Primacy effect

The preferential recall of items encountered in the first part of a series of stimuli.

Recency effect

The recall of items encountered at the end of a series.

Long-term memory

A memory system in which information is held more or less permanently.

Transfer process

The effect of prior learning on new learning.

First, although we remain unaware of it, there must be some kind of internal **scanning** of the information that is being held briefly in sensory memory. From the constant flow of sights, sounds, and other messages from the sense organs, some particular items must be selected as worthy of attention.

To help with the processing, the information held in short-term memory is usually transferred in a way that makes it as simple and easy to handle as possible. This process is called **encoding,** for it resembles the manner in which a computer can take complicated facts—for example, the information on your tax return—and codify them for easy processing. The encoding can take the form of a **schema,** or mental representation of the information to be remembered; the verbal meaning of the information; or its physical characteristics. For example, suppose you happen upon two dogs engaged in a fight. You can encode the event as the visual scene of the fight, verbally as "a dogfight," or as the sounds of snarling and barking. Or, of course, you can use all three forms of encoding. Some psychologists believe that verbal encoding allows information to be remembered with the greatest accuracy over a long period.

If information selected for attention and encoded is to be held for any length of time, some sort of **rehearsal system** must be set up. That is, the information must be deliberately repeated to be kept in mind and prevented from slipping out of the "leaky bucket." Through rehearsal, information can be kept in short-term memory as long as desired—though the amount of information that can be kept alive is quite small. From a list of learned items, what we are most likely to remember is governed by the **primacy effect** and the **recency effect**—meaning that we tend to remember the earlier and later portions. For instance, if you are introduced to seven or eight people at a party, you will probably remember the first two and the last two persons better than the middle ones.

Finally, if the information is to be remembered more or less permanently, it must be passed along and stored in **long-term memory.** The process seems to take place somewhat as follows. The new information, held in short-term memory and kept alive through rehearsal, is associated with any relevant pieces of information that already exist in long-term memory. Comparisons are made and relationships sought. Further encoding and recoding take place. When this so-called **transfer process** is successful, the new information is more or less permanently fitted into long-term memory, like a new item dropped into an appropriate file.

Long-Term Memory: Holding On to Information Indefinitely

How long is long-term? As we have all surely discovered to our sorrow at times, it is not always as long as we would wish. Nevertheless, it is longer than we might assume. A recent experiment, illustrated in Figure 5.4, showed that forgetting in long-term memory can be gradual, and continue for many years (Squire, 1989). Indeed many long-term memories persist for a lifetime. An elderly person may hear a tune and remember the lyrics learned decades earlier. As for how much information we can store in long-term memory, there is really no way of knowing. Certainly the capacity is very large.

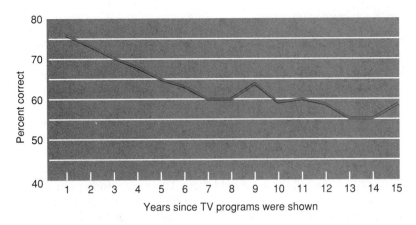

FIGURE 5.4   The surprising staying power of long-term memory From four alternative titles of television programs, three of which were fabricated, subjects were asked to identify the actual titles of a number of one-season television programs that had been shown nationally within the past 15 years. As indicated in the bar chart, the percentage of correct answers dropped steadily with the passing years—but even after a dozen years, the chances of remembering a long-abandoned television program was still better than 50–50 (Squire, 1989).

Most people have the meanings of tens of thousands of words stored in memory. Some have vocabularies that run into the hundreds of thousands. With the help of these words we accumulate all kinds of facts about the world. It has been estimated that the items of information and relationships held in memory must number in the tens of millions, and all of these pieces of information are somehow represented in the brain. It may even be that the memory storehouse has an unlimited capacity—though this is a matter of debate.

This much seems clear: Long-term retention depends to some degree on the nature of the material learned earlier. In a study especially relevant to students of psychology, nearly 400 former students in a psychology course taught over a period of 12 years were given memory tests to assess their retention of the material. As expected, the longer the elapsed time, the poorer was the retention—although overall, even after 10 years, the students did fairly well (Conway, Cohen, & Stanhope, 1991). As shown in Figure 5.5, however, there were some differences in retention depending on the particular topics.

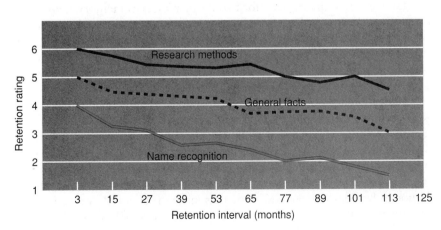

FIGURE 5.5   Remembering a psychology course 10 years later Over a 10-year period, students in a cognitive psychology course were best able to retain material dealing with research methods, and less so material dealing with general facts. They did most poorly when tested on the recognition of names of psychologists in the field (Conway, Cohen, & Stanhope, 1991).

The Retrieval Process

We cannot possibly be conscious at any given moment of all the millions of items of information we hold in long-term memory. Most of the information just lies there, unused. Then there comes a time when a situation calls for us to use a particular piece of information. Let us say that you are reading one evening by the light of a single lamp. Suddenly the light goes out—and you are left in the dark. The situation calls for action, and for the use of the knowledge you have stored in long-term memory about lamps, electricity, and alternative sources of light.

An order has arrived at memory's storage house, calling for the immediate delivery of some of the items held there. You need information, and to be able to use it you must engage in the process called retrieval. That is, you must find the right items, pull them out, and deliver them to short-term memory, where you can actively think about them.

Look back at Figure 5.1 (p. 208) and note the two arrows showing the interaction between short-term and long-term memory. One arrow indicates the process in which new information is transferred from short-term memory into more or less permanent storage. The other arrow indicates the retrieval process, in which information that has been stored in long-term memory is called back into short-term memory, or in other words back into consciousness, where you can think about it and use it.

The human retrieval process operates in wondrous ways, more directly and efficiently than most computers. We do not have to rummage through all the items stored away to find what we need. Instead we are capable of what has been called direct-access retrieval (Wickelgren, 1981). Our storehouse is organized in such a way that we can ordinarily go directly to the right "place," put our hands on the items we need, and deliver them promptly to short-term memory. The way we accomplish this highly efficient organization is discussed later in the chapter.

The Substance of Memory

Until now, this section has dealt with the time span of our memories. Equally important, however, is the content of those memories. What kinds of information are actually stored for later retrieval?

Humans have the capacity for two distinct kinds of memory. The first is **semantic memory,** or the retrieval of facts or bits of knowledge that are without any context. For example, in remembering that London is in England, you probably have no idea when or where you learned that fact. The second is **episodic memory,** or the retrieval of personal experiences (Tulving, 1989)—for example, remembering your first day of college.

The difference between the two is dramatically exemplified in the case of K. C., whose extensive brain injuries as a result of a motorcycle accident left him in a severe state of amnesia. As described by memory researcher Endel Tulving, his case is unique in that he is unable to remember *any* personal happenings in his life—meaning that he has no episodic memory. He cannot recollect having experienced any situation, or having participated in any event. Although he does not *remember* any personally experienced events, he does *know* many things about the world. He has knowledge of history, geography,

Skating is an example of a behavior that may depend on memory traces established many decades earlier.

TEST YOURSELF

a) What's wrong with this statement? "I can usually keep a landscape in my sensory memory for years."

b) A friend tells you that whenever she tries to memorize a telephone number, she experiences the primacy effect. What is happening?

c) "I seem to be having trouble with my semantic memory." If a friend were to say that to you, what kinds of things would he be having trouble remembering—names and dates, or the events surrounding his courtship and marriage?

politics, music, and various other fields of endeavor. But he knows about his own life from the point of view of an observer rather than as a participant. For example, as shown in Figure 5.6, he has retained his knowledge of how to play chess—but he cannot remember having played chess ever before, with anyone. A similar pattern has been found among others with amnesia suffered as a result of brain disorders or injuries. Among these individuals, there is often little correlation between remembering facts, or semantic memory, and remembering the sources of the facts, or episodic memory (Shimamura & Squire, 1987).

Episodic and semantic memory systems appear to be supported by different types of brain activity. Episodic memory seems to depend to a greater extent on the functioning of the brain's frontal lobes than does semantic memory. A discussion of the capacities for memory among older people is found in the box on Life Span Perspective titled "Remembering and Forgetting in Adulthood and Old Age."

FIGURE 5.6   The difference between remembering and knowing Patient K. C., despite massive brain injuries, remembers how to play chess—but he has totally forgotten all of his past experiences as a chess player (Tulving, 1989).

Semantic memory
The retrieval of words, ideas, or facts without any context.

Episodic memory
The memory or retrieval of personal experiences or events together with the context.

LIFE SPAN PERSPECTIVE

Remembering and Forgetting in Adulthood and Old Age

Does the ability to retain routine information decline with age? In one experiment, both young and older adults kept a diary of occasions in which they could not readily come up with a familiar word that was "on the tip of the tongue." The older adults reported many more such episodes (Burke & Harrold, 1988). Older adults also have more trouble than younger adults in recalling the names of people to whom they have been introduced (Crook & West, 1990)—as demonstrated in Figure 5.7.

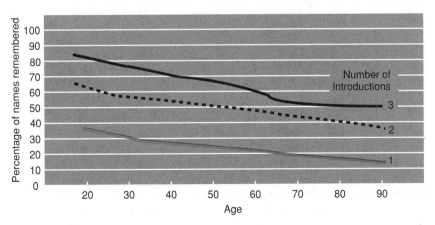

FIGURE 5.7   "I'm sorry, what was your name again?" More than 1,000 people were tested on their ability to recall the names of individuals "introduced" via videotape. As shown here, no matter at what age, memory for the names improved after repeated introductions—but the older the learner, the fewer the names remembered (adapted from Crook & West, 1990).

Such data, however, do not provide a full picture of the memory capacities of older people. To begin with, not all aspects of memory appear to be equally affected with the passing years. Aging seems to affect the capacity to retrieve previously stored information rather than the storage capacity itself. In other words, while old people often have problems *recalling* items that they had learned, they do no worse than younger people in *recognizing* those items.

Equally significant is the ability of older persons to apply the information they have learned over the years in the solution of problems. Researchers asked young, middle-aged, and older adults to think aloud about how they would solve several difficult life problems faced by fictitious individuals of varying ages. The researchers were trying to measure "wisdom," which they defined as uncommon insight into human development and exceptional judgment about difficult life problems, based on remembering experiences of the past. There was little difference between the age groups, with older adults contributing an equal share of wise responses (Smith & Baltes, 1990).

Such data demonstrate that human memory is far more than simply a matter of remembering isolated facts—and, equally important, that some of the popular generalizations about the intellectual capacities of older people are untrue and unfair.   ■

Why We Forget

Memory cannot be discussed without also discussing forgetting. They are opposite sides of the same coin. We learn something—that is, we store some piece of information in our memory. Sometimes this information persists and we can call on it whenever we need it. We say that we remember. Sometimes the information seems to disappear or elude us—and we say we have forgotten. Why do we remember some things and forget others?

How Remembering and Forgetting Are Measured

Attempts to investigate the twin processes of remembering and forgetting face many obstacles. There is no way psychologists can examine the nervous system to see what kinds of changes have been laid down in it by learning and how well these changes persist. They can only devise tests to determine how much is remembered and how much is forgotten. Unfortunately, these tests can never make a direct measure of memory. All they can measure is how well people *perform* on the tests—and their performance is not an entirely accurate indication of how much they remember. Memory may be adversely affected by poor motivation, anxiety, distractions, and many other factors. The tests of remembering and forgetting must always be viewed with reservations. But psychologists, in their effort to do the best they can and recognizing that one measure alone may be a misleading index of an individual's capacity to remember, have adopted three methods for measuring what is remembered—recall, recognition, and relearning.

Recall

A way of demonstrating what has been learned by reciting information that has been stored in memory.

Recall   If you want to show that you have learned the Gettysburg Address, you can recite it—a process demonstrating that you can **recall** it, or bring it out intact from wherever it is stored in your memory. In school, a common use of recall is in the essay type of examination. When teachers ask, "What is classical conditioning?" they are asking you to recall what you have learned.

Recognition   Often we cannot recall what we have learned, at least not completely, but we can prove that we remember something about it by being able to demonstrate our **recognition** of it. For example, you may not be able to recall the Gettysburg Address, but if someone asks you what speech begins with the words "Fourscore and seven years ago," you might immediately recognize the speech, thus demonstrating that you certainly remember something about it. As shown in Figure 5.8, even patients suffering from amnesia, or severe breakdown of memory, can do well in recognizing words they have learned but fail at recalling them (Graf, Squire, & Mandler, 1984).

In multiple-choice examinations you are asked to choose the right answer from among several possible answers and thus prove that you recognize it. Because recognition is easier than recall, many students would rather take a multiple-choice test than an essay examination. But the capacity to recognize material learned earlier is diminished with the passage of time.

Tests of the sort just described measure **semantic memory,** so-called because it involves a clear-cut, intentional recall of information. There is, however, a specific type of recognition called **procedural memory,** which involves the retention of information without an awareness of remembering. An individual who reads a list of 40 familiar words will later be able to recognize most of them. But suppose the individual is shown only fragments of some of these words along with fragments of words not seen earlier. For example, the person might see on a screen the following fragment of the word "wagon": _a_on. If the word had been on the earlier list, the subject would be more likely to guess that the word is "wagon" than if it had not been on the list. Seeing the word earlier evidently readied the individual for the word-completion task, demonstrating the ability to retain implicit knowledge without awareness (Schacter, 1987; Roediger, 1990).

Relearning   The most sensitive method of measuring memory—is seldom used the method of **relearning**—because it is so cumbersome. All of us once learned the Gettysburg Address, or, if not that, then some other well-known piece of writing (anything from a nursery rhyme to Hamlet's soliloquy). We may not be able to recite these pieces now; so we would fail on the recall test.

Recognition
A way of demonstrating what has been learned by selecting the correct information when cued in some form.

Semantic memory
The conscious, intentional recall of information.

Procedural memory
The retrieval of information without an awareness of remembering it.

Relearning
A method of measuring memory in which someone is asked to relearn something.

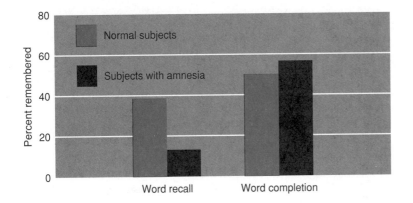

FIGURE 5.8   The difference the test makes   When amnesia sufferers were compared with normal subjects on various tests of memory, they did only about a third as well when the task was to recall words learned earlier. But they did just as well when the task was to complete the words after recognizing a few of the letters (after Graf, Squire, & Mandler, 1984).

We might recognize them if we saw or heard them again. This would prove that we remember something but would not be a very precise measure of how much. If we set about relearning them, however, the length of time this would take would serve as a highly accurate measure.

Theories of Forgetting

Relearning was the measurement used in one of psychology's earliest and most famous studies of forgetting, conducted by a nineteenth-century German named Hermann Ebbinghaus. For his experiments, Ebbinghaus invented the nonsense syllable. He learned lists of such syllables and then measured how long it took him to relearn the lists to perfection after various intervals. He came up with the **curve of forgetting,** shown in Figure 5.9. The curve does not always apply, because we learn some things so thoroughly that we never forget them. However, it tells a great deal about the forgetting of such varied kinds of learning as motor skills, poems that have been memorized, and college courses taken. Its message is this: *When we learn something new, often we quickly forget much of it, but we remember at least some of it for a long time.*

As to why we forget, the answer is not yet fully known. But there are a number of factors worth considering. All the factors may be important at least in part, for forgetting may be such a complex process that it takes place in different ways under different circumstances.

Theory 1: Fading of the Memory Trace

Every time we store a new piece of information in long-term memory, the brain—indeed we ourselves—are somehow changed. We can do something—recall a new fact or engage in a new kind of behavior—that we could not do before. Obviously something has happened inside. But what?

FIGURE 5.9 **Ebbinghaus's famous curve of forgetting** Ebbinghaus memorized lists of 13 nonsense syllables similar to those shown here, then measured how much he could remember after various intervals. After 20 minutes, he remembered only 58 percent and after about an hour only 44 percent. After the initial sharp dip, however, the curve flattened out. After one day he remembered about 34 percent and after two days about 28 percent. Although the graph line does not extend that far, he recalled 21 percent after a month (Ebbinghaus, 1913).

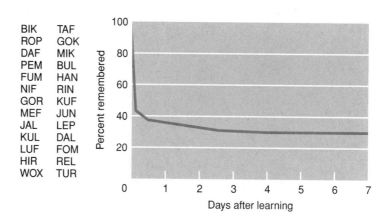

By continually rehearsing their required lip and finger movements, these flute players are less likely to forget them with the passage of time.

Psychologists do not know for sure. They must confine themselves to saying that a **memory trace** has been established—representing some kind of change in the nervous system, typically in the highest part, or cortex, of the brain. When we learn something, nervous impulses are routed over a particular pathway, passing through a number of synapses in a particular pattern. The various kinds of nervous activity that take place along this pathway presumably have a lasting effect that makes it possible to reactivate the pattern on future occasions—thus enabling us to remember what we have learned. The possibility of enhancing the process through chemical means is discussed in a box on Psychology and the Media titled "Drug Is Found to Improve Memory in Tests on Rats."

One of the oldest ideas about forgetting assumes that the memory trace, whatever its physical nature, is subject to decay—that it begins to fade as time goes on and sometimes disappears entirely. This view regards the memory trace as resembling a path worn into a plot of grass. It can be kept functioning through use, as a pathway can be kept clear by continuing to walk over it. But without use the memory trace may vanish, as a pathway becomes overgrown when abandoned.

Many of today's memory theorists continue to believe that the memory trace has some physical quality that changes with the passage of time, often reducing the likelihood that it can be retraced or reactivated. This view is supported by findings that show changes in brain synapses with learning (Rakic et al., 1986). The trace is thought to have two qualities. The first is its **strength**—how likely it is to "pop into mind." This quality, the strength of the memory trace, is at its peak immediately after learning and declines with the passage of time. The second quality is **resistance to extinction**—how well the trace can manage to survive and become immune to fading or decay (Wickelgren, 1977).

Establishing a resistance to extinction takes a certain amount of time. It requires what memory theorists call **consolidation,** a period during which

Memory trace

A theory maintaining that learning represents some kind of change in the nervous system, typically in the cortex.

Strength

A quality of a memory trace referring to how likely it is to "pop into mind."

Resistance to extinction

A quality of a memory trace referring to how well the trace can survive and be immune to fading or decay.

Consolidation

The time during which a memory trace becomes more resistant to extinction.

Drug Is Found to Improve Memory in Tests on Rats

Scientists say they have found a drug that greatly enhances memory in laboratory animals.

The experiments are important because drugs to improve memory have been sought for many years without much success, and because the drug is the first in a new class that stimulates the operation of neurons in the brain rather than dampening them, as other psychiatric drugs do.

The drug, the culmination of several decades of work on human memory, enables neurons to form more efficient connections, which are more or less permanent. These links allow the neurons to be reactivated easily, and the reactivation constitutes memory.

A report on the research will appear on Tuesday in The Proceedings of the National Academy of Sciences. The authors of the report were Dr. Gary Lynch of the University of California at Irvine, Dr. Ursula Staubli of New York University and Dr. Gary Rogers of the University of California at Santa Barbara. In the study, rats were given the drug just before they were given tasks to learn. A second group of rats did not get the drug.

There were three memory tasks. In one, the animals were trained to distinguish between two smells. If they went toward the source of one, they received a reward, and if they searched out the other, there was no reward.

Dr. Staubli said: "After 5 or 10 exposures to the odors, the rats will remember which is the good one and which is the bad one for months. It is a long-term memory task. We gave the drug to some of the rats before they went into the task, and they were able to learn it faster. It took half the amount of training for them to acquire a stable memory."

A second test was carried out in a circular maze with eight passageways with hiding places at the ends. The rats first learned where the eight hiding places were and that chocolate chips or sugar-coated cereal would be hidden there. Soon they visited each of the eight hiding places to get the treats, making no detours.

Then, the experimenters put the rats in the maze and allowed them to uncover only four treats before they were taken back to their home cage for a timeout. After four hours, if they were put back in the maze, they remembered well which four hiding places they had checked and so went immediately to the next four.

But after eight hours, the memory was gone, and they began to search randomly again. If the drug was given just before the rats were set in the maze, however, even after eight hours the rats remembered almost perfectly where the undiscovered treats lay.

The rats that received the drug performed only slightly better than those that did not on the third test. That test involved having the rats swim to a hidden platform remembered from previous swims.

Breakthrough for Scientists

"This represents the first time ever that scientists have been able to go into the machinery of the brain and try to turn it up," said Dr. Lynch, the senior author of the paper. Other psychiatric drugs, like antidepressives and antipsychotics, work by dampening the activity of the neurons because the illness has made them overactive.

Dr. Daniel Alkon, a neuroscientist at the National Institutes of Health who is an expert on the molecular systems of memory, said the paper "seems to demonstrate that the drug can enhance memory in animals." . . .

Researchers do not yet know whether the effect seen in rats will hold true in humans, and whether the types of memory enhanced by the drug will be those that are important to humans.

Source: From "Drug Is Found to Improve Memory in Tests on Rats" by Philip J. Hilts, 1994, *New York Times,* January 15.

Issues to Consider

1. What precautions would you have to take if you were to conduct a similar study on humans?
2. Do you believe that studies such as this one demonstrate the importance of animal research in understanding human behavior?

---

the trace undergoes a process that might be compared with the hardening or "setting" of a newly laid sidewalk. The consolidation process takes place most rapidly in the first minutes after learning—but it continues, though at a gradually slowing rate, over time—especially if the person rehearses the information.

Theory 2: Failure of Retrieval

Some memory traces, once established as part of long-term memory, may persist for as long as we live. But the information may be unavailable for recall. We cannot retrieve it, and we say we have forgotten it—although the memory trace still exists. Thus forgetting may not be due to the loss of a memory trace but rather a failure in retrieval (Kintsch, 1977).

Temporary forgetting caused by failure in retrieval is an everyday experience. There undoubtedly have been many occasions when you found yourself unable to remember some item of information, then later on recalled it perfectly, especially if something happened to "jog your memory." There is evidence suggesting that this difference may depend on the kind of material involved. In one study, for example, researchers compared what adult subjects could remember after having been exposed in turn to both words and pictures viewed on a screen. When the subjects were asked simply to recall what they had seen, they did better in the case of the pictures; however, when they were tested by means of a word completion test (for example, having to remember "lemon" when shown only the letters "l-e-m"), then recall was much better for words than for pictures (Rajaram & Roediger, 1993).

It has been found that important similarity between conditions at the time of retrieval and at the time of learning and encoding may serve as a cue that stimulates the memory. The principle has been stated thus: "When the conditions of encoding and recall are most similar, then recall will be best" (Klatzky, 1980). Some kinds of information are more easily retrieved in the same physical setting in which the learning took place (for example, the same classroom)—or even through visualizing the setting (Smith, 1979). This suggests that we might find it helpful, when trying to remember a name, to try to recall the physical circumstances in which we met or last saw that person.

Theory 3: Interference

Another possible explanation for failure of retrieval is that the ability to remember any given piece of information is interfered with by other information stored in memory. Our memory for what we learn today is often adversely affected by what we have learned in the past and also by what we will learn in the future. The various pieces of information compete for attention and survival—and not all of them can prevail. There are two major types of interference: proactive and retroactive.

Proactive Interference　When old information causes us to forget new information, the process is called **proactive interference.** The phenomenon of proactive interference can be demonstrated through simple laboratory procedures, such as asking subjects to try to learn and remember several lists of words. The results of one such experiment are illustrated in Figure 5.10. Note the steady decline in the subjects' ability to remember new materials caused by more and more proactive interference from prior learning.

The reason for proactive interference is a matter of debate. But it is known to be greatest when we try to learn new information that is similar to old information already stored in memory—as was the case with the word lists used in the experiment shown in Figure 5.10. Proactive interference is considered less troublesome when the new information is substantially dif-

Proactive interference
A process in which old information causes us to forget new information.

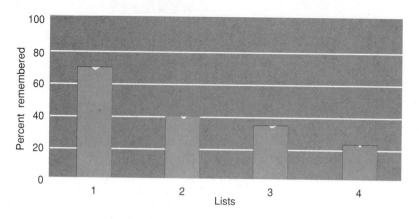

FIGURE 5.10   How the old interferes with the new   In one of the classic experiments on *proactive interference,* subjects learned a list of paired adjectives. Two days after learning, they were tested for their recall of list 1 and asked to learn list 2. After a similar interval they were tested on list 2 and learned list 3. Two days later they were tested on list 3 and learned list 4. Finally, after another two-day interval, they were tested on list 4 and the experiment ended. The steady decline in the height of the bars shows how learning list 1 interfered with memory for list 2, how learning lists 1 and 2 interfered with memory for list 3, and so on (Underwood, 1957).

ferent from the old, as is illustrated in Figure 5.11. In this experiment, one group of subjects watched four videotaped broadcasts of news items that all fell into the same general category, for example national political developments. Another group watched similar news items on the first three tapes. But the fourth tape abruptly switched the subject—for example, from national politics to foreign affairs. As the figure shows, both groups remembered less and less over the first three trials. On the final tape, the first group

FIGURE 5.11   Changing the subject as an antidote to proactive interference   The bars show the results of an experiment in which subjects watched a series of four videotapes of old news broadcasts. After each tape they were tested on how much of it they remembered. For both groups, the recall scores began a steady decline as listening to tape 1 interfered with their ability to remember tape 2 and listening to tapes 1 and 2 interfered with their memory for tape 3. But note the discrepancy between the two groups on tape 4. Group 1 subjects continued to show a decline, but group 2 suddenly displayed a sharp improvement (Gunter, Berry, & Clifford, 1981). For the reason, see the text.

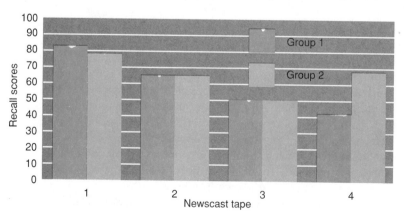

continued to display a decline caused by proactive interference—but the second group, with proactive interference reduced because of the change to a different topic, did much better. The same phenomenon is apparent when we try to remember a number of songs we have heard in the past. We have the least difficulty remembering those that are least similar to others (Halpern, 1984).

In everyday life, you experience proactive interference when you have been studying the same course material—for example, this chapter on memory—for several hours. Your ability to remember what you have read in the third hour becomes poorer. The reason is not just fatigue. If you were to turn to entirely new material—for example, history—it is likely you would remember more from your third hour of study.

Retroactive Interference   In proactive interference, old information gets in the way of remembering new information. The opposite situation—when new information causes us to forget old information—is called **retroactive interference.** Again, the similarity between old and new materials plays an important role in recall. When subjects learn a new list of words with the same meaning as the words in a previously learned list (synonyms), they experience more retroactive interference than when the new list contains very different materials, such as nonsense syllables. Moreover, it has been shown that information that violates our expectations will be recalled and recognized better than information consistent with our expectations (Pezdek, et al., 1989).

Retroactive interference
A process in which new information causes us to forget old information.

Perhaps the most interesting—and consoling—fact about retroactive interference is that it has a greater effect on unimportant materials that are not worth remembering anyway (like lists of words learned in a laboratory) than on important and meaningful materials. Retroactive interference often makes us forget the specific details of what we have learned, especially if the details are not essential, but it is not nearly so likely to make us forget the basic theme and meaning of what we have learned (Christiaansen, 1980). Thus you will probably forget some of the things you learn in this course because of retroactive interference from information you will learn in future courses and from your life experiences. You may not remember the exact meaning of such terms as classical conditioning and reinforcement, but you will probably always remember the general principles of learning and of how memory operates. Moreover, there is evidence that while you may have difficulty recalling old information because new information interferes, your capacities for *recognition* of the old material will be less affected (Graf & Schacter, 1987).

Theory 4: Motivated Forgetting

The fact that we seem to forget some things deliberately was mentioned earlier in connection with the processes that take place in short-term memory. Many theorists believe that at times we also forget information stored in long-term memory because we want to forget it, whether consciously or not. It may be emotionally uncomfortable to remember the name of a person we dislike, or the painful emotional problems we had at a certain stage of life.

Motivated forgetting is often referred to as *repression* by psychoanalysts, who believe that it often plays a part in dealing with anxiety. They find that

Motivated forgetting (repression)
An attempt to forget emotionally uncomfortable information.

TEST YOURSELF

d) A student is preparing for exams in German, French, and history. According to the principle of retroactive interference, in what order should he study the three subjects to do best on each exam?

e) You meet someone who has the same name as someone who treated you cruelly five years ago. Within a few minutes, you have trouble remembering the name of your new acquaintance. What kind of forgetting has taken place?

people can be motivated not only to forget upsetting events, but to distort their recollections to make them more bearable (Erdelyi, 1985). Indeed most of us are troubled by persistent memories of embarrassing and painful events that we would gladly forget if only we could.

The Encoding and Transfer Process

The factors that help explain why we forget offer some valuable hints on how we can avoid the handicap and embarrassment of forgetting. The motivation factor suggests that we are more likely to remember when we want to remember. The other factors indicate that we will be most efficient at remembering if we can manage to store information in such a way that the memory traces will not fade away with the passage of time and that the information can be retrieved when we want it—remaining more or less intact despite interference from previous and future learning.

All these matters depend on how we encode and transfer information to long-term memory. Thus the key to remembering lies in two related questions: What is the nature of the encoding process that creates our store of knowledge and how can we do the processing more effectively—and learn and remember to greater advantage?

Chunking—Or Putting Many Little Items into One Neat Package

One of the important elements in encoding can best be explained by taking another look at short-term memory, with its capacity to store about seven unrelated items. Note what happens if you look briefly at this string of letters:

tvfBIYmcasATNbcnASA

You will probably find it impossible to remember all 19 letters, or anywhere near that number. But note what happens with just a slight change:

tvFBIymcaSATnbcNASA

The 19 letters are now turned into a mere six units—each containing familiar combinations of initials—and fall well within the limits of short-term memory. You would have no trouble remembering them after a few seconds of study (after Bower, 1970).

This process, in which a number of individual units of information are combined into one—wrapped together securely, so to speak, in a single neat package—is called **chunking** (G. A. Miller, 1956). Chunking greatly increases the scope of short-term memory, which can hold about seven big packages of information just about as well as it can handle seven small individual items. We encode many forms of information into chunks—letters into words (as illustrated in Figure 5.12), words into phrases (*frying pan, chicken chow mein*), phrases into sentences (*Mary had a little lamb*), individual digits into memorable dates (1492, 1776), and so on.

Obviously chunking requires some interaction between short-term and long-term memory. We would not readily form the chunks TV and FBI, for example, unless we were already familiar with these combinations of letters. And obviously much of the information in long-term memory has been

Chunking

A technique to improve the scope of short-term memory in which a number of individual units of information are combined into one.

FIGURE 5.12 A classroom demonstration of chunking
The instructor first shows the blackboard as in the upper photo. How many of the 49 letters can the class possibly remember after studying the board for a minute or two? Not many, because each line in the column contains seven letters—and seven is about the capacity of short-term memory. But then she shows the board in the lower photo. The task becomes much easier, for each line of letters has been rearranged into a familiar word that constitutes a single chunk, and there are now just seven chunks to deal with instead of 49 individual letters.

encoded and stored there in chunks. For example, as we come to understand a body of knowledge such as American history, we chunk it into periods: the Revolution, the Civil War, World War I, World War II, the Vietnam War, and so on. This makes it easier to remember the many specific facts associated with each period.

The Associative Network

Most researchers now believe that memory can best be described and explained as a complicated network in which thousands upon thousands of words and ideas are all connected and interconnected by long and far-reaching strands of association (Anderson & Bower, 1973). As new information is encoded into the network, new linkages are formed to old information already contained there. Some of these links or associations are direct, others more roundabout. Some are strong, some weak. Some are long-lasting, resistant to forgetting, and easy to retrieve. Others are weaker and less likely to be recalled.

This view of memory, called the **associative network theory,** accounts for the extraordinary human ability to retrieve information. Leading to every fact or chunk of information in the network are countless linkages. Through one link or another we can usually find a quick and direct route to what we need—and, once we have it, we can then also pull out any or all the other chunks with which it is connected.

Associative network theory
A theory that accounts for the extraordinary human ability to retrieve information.

We encode new information into long-term memory by noting how it relates to what we have already stored—and thus we add it to the network along with all the appropriate associations to existing information. A new fact or chunk of facts is woven into the network, attached by many far-reaching new strands through which, if they are solid and strong enough, we can reach and retrieve it when we need it.

What We Encode, Remember, and Retrieve

In the encoding process we add something new to the associate network. But just what is it that we add? Is it an exact copy of something we have done, seen, or heard—like a movie or a tape recording? Or is it something else?

In some cases what we encode is clearly a faithful copy. An experimenter once asked college students to recite the words to *The Star Spangled Banner,* Hamlet's soliloquy, and other familiar passages of verse and prose. Whatever they remembered at all, it turned out, was almost a word-by-word reproduction (Rubin, 1977). But this kind of verbatim encoding and retrieval is rare. In most cases we seem to engage in what is called constructive processing. We encode and retrieve not an exact copy of the information we receive—as from a printed page or a lecture or a conversation—but whatever meanings and associations we have found. We remember not "what was out there" but what we ourselves "did during encoding"—that is, the way we processed the information and related it to the knowledge already held in long-term memory (Craik & Tulving, 1975).

In most cases, therefore, we remember what we consider important—the theme or underlying meaning—and forget or distort many of the details, such as the exact wording. One study has suggested this analogy: When we read or hear something, we make mental notes—like the brief reminders you might jot down in your notebook while listening to a lecture. It is these notes, not the actual words we read or heard, that we store in some appropriate "pigeonhole in memory" until we need them. While stored in the pigeonhole, the various factors that cause forgetting may cause some of the notes to become smudged. Some of them may even get lost. Thus, when we try to retrieve the information, we find that it is incomplete—only a sketchy reminder of what we actually read or heard. All we can do is "fetch the notes from their pigeonhole and from this fragmentary information reconstruct what . . . was in the original message"—or rather what we now have come to believe was in it (Clark & Clark, 1977). The same process applies to our memory for other items such as melodies heard, scenes observed, or people encountered.

With the brief and sometimes smudged or incomplete mental notes, we do the best we can. We try to make sense out of them. We fill in the missing details—sometimes accurately and sometimes not. Sometimes, new and contradictory information gets in the way, and leads us to believe erroneously in the accuracy of our memories (Loftus, 1993). Thus a great deal of what we think we remember never really happened—or, if it did, it was different in many respects from the way we remember it. Memory, as one scholar has said, is often "unreliable, given to invention, and even dangerous" (Bower, 1978). These omissions and distortions pose serious problems at times—especially in legal trials where precise details may be crucial to the outcome.

The memory for a new telephone number will be lost after about 30 seconds unless the person rehearses it several times.

Emotional States and Retrieval

Experiments have been performed in search of factors that might affect the memory trace for better or worse. One such factor is the emotional content of a memory.

Like most people, you undoubtedly have graphic recollections of events in your life that carried great emotional impact. Many individuals possess a mental photograph of their wedding day, for example. Others can tell you precisely what they were doing and their surroundings at the moment when they heard that a loved one had died. If we have a strong emotional reaction—for example, as many did to the assassination of President Kennedy, the attempted shooting of President Reagan, or the explosion of the space shuttle Challenger—it is likely that we will remember many details about the event (Pillemer, 1984). Indeed many people are able to remember their experience of emotional events in such photographic detail—exactly where they were, who they were with, who said what—that the phenomenon has been given the name **flashbulb memory** (Brown & Kulik, 1982).

Such vivid recollections may exist because memory is closely tied to the limbic system, the brain's seat of emotions (Mishkin, 1986). Indeed there is evidence that emotional, as contrasted with informational, elements of memory may be stored in their own, distinct regions of the brain (Mishkin & Appenzeller (b), 1987). There is evidence, too, that neurotransmitters released during emotional arousal enhance learning and memory (McGaugh, 1983).

Whatever the mechanism, all of us manage to preserve clear mental pictures of special episodes in our experience. Among a sample of college students, prominent flashbulb memories include such events as a car accident, high school graduation, an important romantic encounter, or the moment of opening the letter reporting SAT scores (Rubin, 1985). The impact of any event is always unique to the individual, and details of events that are of considerable personal consequence are more likely to be recalled (Rubin & Kozin, 1984).

Also affecting memory is our present emotional state. There is evidence that the capacity to recall accurately is, in part, a function of our mood when we are trying to remember (Eich & Metcalfe, 1989). As shown in Figure 5.13, when we are depressed, recall is less sharp than when we are not (Ellis et al., 1985).

Flashbulb memory
A photographically detailed memory of an emotionally charged event or experience.

TEST YOURSELF

f) "I'm going to try to 'chunk' this list of words so I can remember them better," says a classmate in your French course. What is your classmate going to do?

g) "I can still recall every detail of my scary first-grade classroom 60 years ago," says a grandmother. What does her ability imply about the relationship between emotional states and memory?

Linkages in Learning

The associative network of long-term memory is so large and complex, and its linkages so intricately connected and interconnected, that tugging at one strand can produce far-reaching and sometimes unpredictable results. Suppose, for example, that you are asked to retrieve everything you remember about the word *angel*. You might begin by pulling out information from paintings you have seen of winged figures in white robes, with halos and playing harps. From there you might move on to describe the churches you have seen, the prayers you have learned, and the principles underlying the world's major religions. You might go on to talk about morality, then about a priest or rabbi who played a significant part in your life.

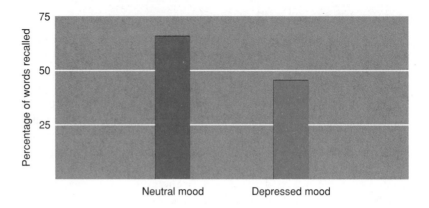

FIGURE 5.13 How mood affects memory In one study, college students were asked to study a list of sentences. A depressed mood was induced in some of them by having them read a series of depressing statements, while the others remained in a neutral state. The results showed a significantly poorer capacity by the depressed-mood subjects to recall certain key words in the sentences (after Ellis et al., 1985).

Your progression of associations may lead almost anywhere—and if you are asked to do the same thing tomorrow, the pathway may take an entirely different route. Of course, the associations vary from person to person. To another individual, the word angel may immediately suggest the California baseball team and lead to a discussion of Yankee Stadium, Babe Ruth, candy bars, and eventually some unsuccessful personal experiences with dieting.

As these examples of retrieval indicate, every item of information in long-term memory is associated with many other items, which in turn lead to innumerable other associations. How likely you are to remember and retrieve any new information depends on how well you manage to add it to this network—that is, how many strong associations you form to linkages that already exist. Effective encoding sometimes takes place without much effort. You do not have to make any deliberate attempt, for example, to remember important events in your life or the names and faces of people who have played significant parts in it. But often—and especially in school or when trying to master a new skill, like chess or repairing electronic equipment—you have to work hard to form the associations.

Thus memory is closely related to learning. How well we remember generally depends on how well we learn in the first place—that is, on how many links or associations we establish between new information and information already stored in the network. This kind of encoding depends in turn on how thoroughly we analyze and understand the new information and how many relationships we can find between the new and the old. The richer and more elaborate our analysis, the more likely we are to form a long-lasting memory that will resist being forgotten and will be easy to retrieve (Kintsch, 1977).

The Role of Meaning and Organization

In studying a page like this one, it is futile just to read and reread the words without making any attempt to understand them. The words may eventually begin to seem familiar, like old friends—but mere familiarity, without careful attention and analysis, is no guarantee of successful encoding. We sometimes learn and remember surprisingly little about familiar objects and events. What counts in learning is something quite different:

> The critical thing for most of the material you learn in school is to understand it, which means encoding it in a way that makes it distinctive from

unrelated material and related to all the things it ought to be related to in order for you to use it. . . . The time you spend thinking about material you are reading and relating it to previously stored material is about the most useful thing you can do in learning any new subject matter (Wickelgren, 1977).

To put this another way, the key to successful encoding is to figure out the meaning of new information and organize it into some unified and logical pattern that can be readily associated with other information. Because meaning is so important, some things are just naturally easier to learn and encode into memory than others. If the materials themselves make sense—that is, if they are intrinsically meaningful—we have a good head start on our processing. Thus it is much easier to remember lists of actual three-letter words (such as SIT, HAT, BIN, COW) than lists of three-letter nonsense syllables. In fact it is easier to remember lists of nonsense syllables that resemble real words than syllables that are truly nonsensical. An experiment performed many years ago showed that subjects are about 50 percent better at remembering syllables like DOZ, SOF, LIF, and RUF, all of which remind most people of actual words, than totally unfamiliar syllables like ZOJ, JYQ, GIW, and VAF (McGeoch, 1930). Similarly, we are more likely to encode and remember passages of poetry than prose since poetry has not only meaning but a kind of internal logic and organization provided by the cadence and rhymes.

Successful encoding may take a variety of forms, depending on the material being learned. If you were to be a teacher of science, for example, there is evidence that you would be helping your students understand scientific concepts if you were to present analogies relevant to those concepts with the brute facts. For example, if the concept were a pulsar, students would be better able to make accurate inferences about the nature of a pulsar if they understood that it is analogous to a beacon from a rotating lighthouse (Donnelly & McDaniel, 1993).

The increased emotion and motivation that occur when students study together sometimes results in better registration of the information.

Using Rules to Learn and Remember

Both meaning and organization help account for the fact that we usually remember longer if we learn by **rule** (that is, if we try to understand the underlying principles or logic) than if we learn by **rote** (trying to memorize materials simply by repeating them mechanically without any regard to what they mean).

Some things, of course, have to be learned by rote. There is no other way to learn the multiplication tables or the sequence of letters in the alphabet. And, as these examples suggest, some information learned by rote is never forgotten. But most college courses would be almost impossible to encode into lasting memory by rote—and fortunately most courses readily lend themselves to learning by rule. They have patterns of meaning and organization, built around underlying principles, and are presented by instructors and in textbooks in ways designed to help you find, understand, and analyze those patterns. They can be studied and encoded effectively through logical approaches like the SQ3R system that is described in the Preface to this book.

Learning often depends more on the kind of cognitive processing and encoding we do than on the amount of time we spend (Craik & Tulving, 1975). Thus even a small amount of time spent finding meaning, organiza-

Rule

A memory technique in which one tries to understand the underlying principles or logic of the stored information.

Rote

A technique to memorize material by repeating it mechanically without regard to its logic or structure.

tion, and relationships is generally more effective than a great deal of time devoted merely to rehearsing what is on a page more or less verbatim.

Nevertheless, time is ordinarily an important factor. Most of the time, effective encoding requires deliberate effort—we have to work at it—and a certain amount of time. You can safely assume that the more time you spend the more you are likely to remember—provided, of course, that you use the time effectively. There are no shortcuts in learning. For example, nothing is gained through "speed reading," which is the popular name for techniques that are supposed to enable you to read a printed page much faster while still comprehending everything the words mean. In fact, studies have shown that the faster you read the less you are likely to understand and remember (Graf, 1973).

There are certain advantages, of course, in saving time through the rapid scanning of materials that you do not need to remember, or when you are glancing through a long and complicated article or book in which there are only a few specific pieces of information that you want to seek out and concentrate on. But in general any increase in reading speed, beyond your normal rate, saves time only at the expense of remembering. The kind of encoding that results in long-lasting memory, like the weaving of a strong and farflung net, simply cannot be rushed.

Law of overlearning

A principle stating that after you have learned something, further study tends to increase the time that the information is remembered.

Even after new information has been encoded into memory, it usually pays to spend some more time studying it—possibly because practice and repetition somehow increase the strength and retrievability of the memory traces in the network. This fact is expressed in the **law of overlearning,** which states: After you have learned something, further study tends to increase the length of time you will remember it. The law of overlearning seems to explain why we never forget such childhood jingles as "Twinkle, twinkle little star," or the stories of Cinderella and Goldilocks and the Three Bears. Long after we knew these things by heart, we continued to recite or listen to them over and over again. We not only learned but overlearned them.

The law of overlearning also explains why cramming is not a satisfactory way to learn the contents of a college course. By cramming, students may learn enough to get a passing grade on an examination, but they are soon likely to forget almost everything they learned. A little overlearning, on the other hand, is like time spent thinking about new materials and trying to understand them and relate them to previous information. It is a good investment in the ability to remember for a long time.

Building a Storehouse for Learning

Another practical implication of psychology's studies of encoding is this: The more we already know, the easier it is to learn and remember something new. As we go through school and college, we acquire a bigger vocabulary, more mathematical symbols and rules, more knowledge of the general principles of science, human behavior, and the workings of our society. All this previously stored information helps us understand the new information, relate it to past knowledge, and encode it solidly into our memory network.

The fact that learning builds on learning has never been expressed more eloquently than by William James, even though James lived and wrote many years before the discovery of most of what is now known about encoding and memory.

The more other facts a fact is associated with in the mind, the better possession of it our memory retains. Each of its associates becomes a hook to which it hangs, a means to fish it up by when sunk beneath the surface. Together, they form a network of attachments by which it is woven into the entire tissue of our thought. The "secret of a good memory" is thus the secret of forming diverse and multiple associations with every fact we care to retain (James, 1890).

Of course, the possession of a great deal of information increases the possibility of proactive and retroactive interference. But any tendency to forgetting that this may create is more than offset by the increased chances of finding more associations between new and old and thus weaving the new information more solidly into the network.

Learning How to Learn and Remember

All of us get better and better at encoding and remembering new information as time goes on. Our classroom work and our life experiences provide us with something that is perhaps even more valuable than facts and general principles. We learn how to learn.

One need not be a great scholar. Even the monkey shown in Figure 5.14 learned to learn. Asked to perform a long series of learning tasks that were

TEST YOURSELF

h) If a student in a biology course had to memorize the parts of the body, would she do better if she simply listed all the parts alphabetically and then began to memorize them, or instead tried to learn them according to where in the body they are found?

FIGURE 5.14   What is this monkey learning? All the monkey seems to be learning is that it will find food under one of the two objects in front of it but not under the other. When the photo was taken, the food was always under a funnel and never under a cylinder, regardless of which was on the left or right. At other times, the food was under a circle but not a rectangle, a cube, but not a sphere, a black object but not a white object, and so on. At first the monkey had trouble learning where to find the food. But after the experiment had gone on long enough—with several hundred pairs of objects—the monkey mastered the problem on the very first trial. Whether or not it found the food under the first object it examined, it went almost unerringly to the correct object the next time the pair was presented (Harlow, 1949).

Learning set

A successful strategy for approaching the learning of new information.

similar in general but different in detail, the monkey showed remarkable improvement. It developed what is called a **learning set**—a successful strategy for approaching the learning task. In an experiment with humans, using a similar but more difficult series of problems, the results were much the same. It was also found, as might be expected, that college students were quicker to develop effective learning sets or strategies than fifth-graders. In turn the fifth-graders were quicker than preschool children (Levinson & Reese, 1967).

How Categories Help

Categories

Mental representation of the features that are shared by dissimilar events.

One useful strategy that all of us adopt, in one way or another, helps us deal with materials that do not at first glance seem to hang together of their own accord. We often manage to organize and encode this type of information by breaking it down into **categories**—a method best explained by the example shown in Figure 5.15(a). Note that the 18 words on the list, presented at random, do not seem to have much in common. They do not fall into any kind of obvious pattern—and you might think that, if you wanted to encode them into memory, you would have to learn them by rote. This is the way the experimenter's control group went about trying to memorize them—painfully and, as will be seen in a moment, without much lasting success.

Another group of subjects, however, got some help. To these subjects, the words on the list were presented in the manner shown in Figure 5.15(b). The subjects were helped to see that all the words fell into the general category of minerals, that this category could be broken down into the subcategories of metals and stones, and that these subcategories could again be divided into three different kinds of metals (rare, common, and alloys) and two different kinds of stones (precious stones and stones used in masonry).

FIGURE 5.15 An experiment on categories as an aid to encoding The control group saw the list of 18 words presented at random. The experimental group saw them as arranged in the diagram. For how well the two groups learned and remembered, see the text and Figure 5.16.

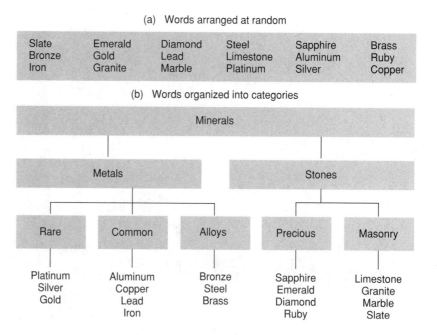

(a) Words arranged at random

Slate	Emerald	Diamond	Steel	Sapphire	Brass
Bronze	Gold	Lead	Limestone	Aluminum	Ruby
Iron	Granite	Marble	Platinum	Silver	Copper

(b) Words organized into categories

Minerals

Metals — Stones

Rare — Common — Alloys — Precious — Masonry

Platinum / Silver / Gold — Aluminum / Copper / Lead / Iron — Bronze / Steel / Brass — Sapphire / Emerald / Diamond / Ruby — Limestone / Granite / Marble / Slate

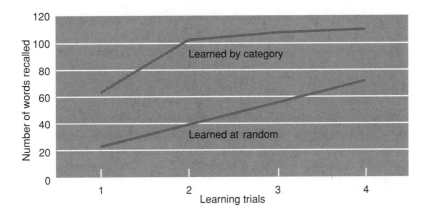

FIGURE 5.16 **Did the categories make a difference? Yes, indeed.** The top line shows how rapidly the experimental subjects were able to learn as a result of seeing the words in Figure 5.15 arranged in categories. Subjects who tried to memorize the words by rote (bottom line) did not do nearly so well.

The control group and the experimental group were both asked to try to learn several such lists, containing 112 words in all, within four trials. The difference in the amounts learned by the two groups was striking. As Figure 5.16 shows, the subjects who had been helped to organize the words into categories proved far superior. They remembered all 112 words perfectly on the third and fourth trials—a level never even approached by the subjects who tried to learn the words by rote (Bower et al., 1969).

Clustering—Packaging Information for Long-Term Memory

Organizing materials into categories bears considerable resemblance to the chunking process that enables us to hold seven large packages of information in short-term memory as readily as seven small individual items. In both cases a number of small units of information are lumped together into a single unit. When the process refers to short-term memory, it is called *chunking;* when it relates to long-term memory, it is called **clustering,** a method of organizing information into categories, by meaning, or logic, or in other ways. Information stored in some form of cluster tends to hang together in a solid unit that becomes a strong part of the associative network.

Clustering also aids retrieval. Within each tightly bound and cohesive cluster there are a number of individual items of information. In the search of memory that goes on during retrieval, we have a much better chance of finding one of many items than any single item. And when we manage to find this one item, we can pull the whole cluster of information out with it.

An example might occur on an essay examination where you are asked to define the term *stimulus generalization*. At first the meaning of the term eludes you. You seem to have forgotten it. But then, as you continue to search through your memory network, the word *stimulus* leads you to the term *conditioned stimulus*—and thus to the whole package of information that falls into the category of classical conditioning. Out pour all the facts you have clustered there, including the meaning of *stimulus generalization*.

One interesting way we encode clusters into long-term memory is demonstrated by how much we remember of the things we read, such as stories. If the story moves in a straight line, with one event leading logically to the next, we can usually remember a good deal of it. If the story jumps

Clustering

A long-term memory aid that organizes materials into meaningful groups or categories.

around, switching from one point of view to another, we are less likely to remember it (Black, Turner, & Bower, 1979).

We seem particularly adept at clustering together materials that have a cause-and-effect relationship that binds them into a logical entity. An indication comes from an experiment in which two groups of college students studied slightly different versions of the same story. Version 1 contained pairs of sentences like these:

> He lowered the flames and walked over to the refrigerator, seeing a bowl he had left on the table. Suddenly it fell off the edge and broke.

> While he was sitting on a huge log he found an old pocket knife. He felt sad as they took a few more pictures and headed back.

In version 2 the sentence pairs were changed to read like this:

> He lowered the flames and walked over to the refrigerator, bumping a bowl he had left on the table. Suddenly it fell off the edge and broke.

> While he was sitting on a huge log he lost an old pocket knife. He felt sad as they took a few more pictures and headed back.

Note that the changes, though small, create a cause-and-effect relationship in the version 2 sentence pairs that does not occur in version 1. *Bumping a bowl* (version 2) is a logical reason for the bowl to fall off the table; *seeing a bowl* (version 1) is not. Someone who *lost an old pocket knife* is likely to have felt sad, while someone who *found an old pocket knife* is not. As is illustrated in Figure 5.17, establishing the cause-and-effect relationship produced a significantly better memory for the version 2 sentences (Black & Bern, 1981).

Similarly, it has been demonstrated that one good way to remember a list of unrelated items is to make up a story about them that ties them all together. Let us say, for example, that you are going to a supermarket to buy

FIGURE 5.17 If one event causes another, you are likely to remember both The bars show the results of the experiment, described in detail in the text, with two versions of the same story. Note how much more was remembered by subjects who read version 2 (the cause-and-effect version) than subjects who read version 1—when tested for either "free recall" (how well they remembered without prompting) or "cued recall" (how well they could remember the second of two sentences after the first was read to them).

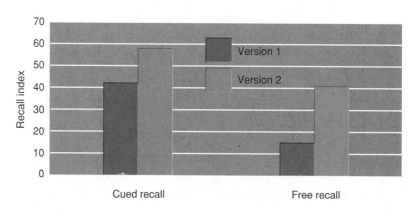

the following 10 items, listed in the order you would find them along the route you take through the aisles:

1. coffee	6. light bulbs
2. hamburger	7. matches
3. charcoal	8. facial tissues
4. milk	9. broom
5. paper cups	10. dog food

One way you can be almost sure of remembering everything in proper order is to make up a story like the one presented in Figure 5.18. Such stories have been found remarkably helpful. The experiment in Figure 5.19, for example, found an extremely large difference in recall of word lists between subjects who wove the words into stories and subjects who did not.

FIGURE 5.18 Remembering a shopping list The ten supermarket items listed in the text can be easily recalled in order by making up this story: I was sitting in my kitchen one evening drinking a cup of *coffee* when my neighbor came in with her child to invite me to a Saturday cookout. She said we would grill *hamburgers* over *charcoal*. I asked her to sit down and join me for coffee, and I poured the child some *milk* in a *paper cup*. While we were talking the *light bulb* burned out, and my neighbor lit some *matches* to help me replace the bulb. In the darkness the child spilled some milk, and we wiped it up with *facial tissues*. I heard my dog at the door and went to let it in. There was another dog that wanted to enter, but I chased it away with a *broom* and fed my pet its *dog food* while my neighbor and I finished our coffee (after Bower, 1978).

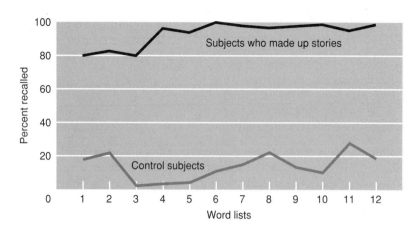

FIGURE 5.19 How well do made-up stories work? *Extremely* well. The graph lines show the results of an experiment in which one group of students made up stories to help them remember a dozen lists of words, while a control group was merely asked to try to memorize the lists. When tested later, the subjects who made up stories remembered their lists almost perfectly. The other subjects had forgotten most of their words (Bower & Clark, 1969).

Preserving Visual Information

Imagery

A mental picture of an event.

Mnemonic (knee-MON-ick) **device**

A memory technique based on the ability to encode information in ways that make it easier to remember.

Mnemonic

The Greek word for memory.

TEST YOURSELF

i) How does clustering help memory?

j) If a law student formed a mental picture of a law case in order to remember the details of the case better, what technique would she be using?

Made-up stories are particularly helpful if you try to form a mental picture or image of the events, like the drawings in Figure 5.18. Studies have shown that there are many situations in which the use of **imagery** helps to encode, remember, and retrieve information (Bower, 1972). One reason seems to be that we have an extraordinary ability to remember visual information. This was demonstrated in a famous experiment in which subjects looked at a set of over 600 colored pictures—then were tested on how many they could recognize when the pictures were shown again, now paired with another picture they had not seen before. In all, the subjects spotted 97 percent of the original pictures—a far better performance than could ever be attained with the same large number of words (Shephard, 1967).

The ability to encode visual information and imagery is the basis of techniques known as **mnemonic devices,** discussed in a Psychology in Action box, "Developing Your Own Strategies for Remembering."

One interesting sidelight is that lower animals encode considerable amounts of information into memory without the help of language—which makes possible the search for meaning and organization that characterizes so much of human encoding. Studies show that even a monkey, an animal far lower in intellectual development than its cousin the chimpanzee, can perform much like a human being on a test of memory for pictures (Sands & Wright, 1982). Encoding visual characteristics seems to be a more fundamental skill than the human encoding of verbal information—but we do not know whether the two are different in kind or merely in degree.

Developing Your Own Strategies for Remembering

In ancient Greece, orators used to develop devices to help them remember the points they wanted to make in their long speeches. We now call such devices **mnemonic**—after the Greek word for memory. The method of the ancient orators was based on the spatial arrangement of a temple with which they were thoroughly familiar—that is, the order in which they walked past the doorways, rooms, statues, and other objects within the temple walls. For each location, they created a mental image associating the spot with a topic in their speech. For example, if they wanted to start by discussing medicine, they might visualize a famous physician of the day pushing through the temple entrance. To try this method yourself, you can base it on the layout of your home, its rooms, and its prominent pieces of furniture.

A somewhat more complicated mnemonic system, for remembering things like shopping lists or chores to be done during the day, has been used in a number of psychological experiments and found extremely helpful. You begin by memorizing this jingle:

> One is a bun; two is a shoe;
> Three is a tree; four is a door;
> Five is a hive; six is sticks;
> Seven is heaven; eight is a gate;
> Nine is wine; ten is a hen.

To use this device to help remember the supermarket shopping list mentioned earlier, the trick is to form a mental image connecting the items on the list (coffee, hamburger, and so on) with the words in the jingle that rhyme with the numbers (bun-one, shoe-two, and so on). Similar systems, more elaborate in that they can provide memory hooks for as many as 100 items, are the secret behind the seemingly incredible feats performed by the "memory experts" who quickly learn long lists of objects or people's names. For remem-

bering things that do not hang together through any organization or logic, mnemonic devices are unquestionably useful. One reason is that they take advantage of the well-established value of imagery. Another is that they provide a ready-made framework into which the new information can be clustered. Some simple little mnemonic devices with which you are probably familiar include the jingle that begins "Thirty days hath September" (for remembering how many days there are in each month), the sentence "Every good boy does fine" (for remembering the notes in music), and "I left port" (for remembering the difference between the port, or left side, of a ship and the starboard, or right side). Note that the value of all mnemonic aids is limited to materials that would otherwise have to be encoded and stored by rote. For most of the knowledge we acquire, there is no substitute for the kind of information processing that seeks meanings, organization, relationships, and rules.

SUMMARY REVIEW

The Range and Content of Human Memory

1. Memories may last from a fraction of a second to a lifetime. The range is divided into three stages of memory:
   a) **sensory**
   b) **short-term**
   c) **long-term**
2. **Sensory memory** is made up of the lingering traces of information sent to the brain by the senses. The information is forgotten within a second unless transferred to short-term memory.
3. **Short-term memory** has a capacity of about seven unrelated items of information, which are forgotten within about 30 seconds unless further processing takes place.

4. The information processing in short-term memory includes:
   a) **scanning** of the information in sensory memory and selection of some items as worthy of attention
   b) **encoding** of information (to make it simple and easy to handle)
   c) **rehearsal** (to keep information in mind for more than 30 seconds)
   d) further encoding that results in **transfer** of the information to long-term memory.
5. Encoding can take the form of a **schema,** or mental picture, that represents the information to be remembered, the verbal meaning of the information, or its physical characteristics.
6. Through rehearsal, information can be kept in short-term memory as long as desired—although the amount of information that can be kept alive is quite small. From a list of learned items, we are most likely to remember the earlier and later portions rather than the middle items. This is called the **primacy effect** and the **recency effect** in short-term memory.
7. **Long-term memory** is a more or less permanent storehouse of information.
8. **Retrieval** is the process that recalls information held in long-term memory back to short-term memory, where we can actively think about it and use it.
9. Exactly what happens inside the nervous system when we store information in long-term memory is not known. Psychologists say that a **memory trace** has been established, but they can only speculate as to what this trace is, how it is formed, and why it sometimes seems to persist forever and sometimes seems to vanish.
10. Formation of the memory trace seems to depend at least in part on:
    a) the brain's **neurotransmitters**
    b) the strengthening of existing synapses rather than the addition of new ones.
11. Neurotransmitters are the chemicals that pass along messages from one neuron to another. It appears that neurotransmitters increase the efficiency of the synapse. The neurotransmitter that has received attention in recent years is **acetylcholine,** which appears to be decreased in patients suffering from **Alzheimer's disease,** a disorder of the brain whose victims suffer progressive deterioration of the memory and other intellectual functions.

Why We Forget

12. How well we remember and how much we forget can be measured only by how well we perform on tests of memory. Three methods used by psychologists to test performance are:
    a) **recall**
    b) **recognition**
    c) **relearning.**
13. Tests of performance show that we often quickly forget much of what we have just learned, but remember at least some of it for a long time. The fact that we forget rapidly at first but more slowly later on is shown by the **curve of forgetting.**
14. There are four theories of why we forget, all of which may be true at least in part and at certain times:

a) *fading of the* **memory trace**
b) *failure of* **retrieval**
c) *interference from other information stored in memory*
d) **motivated forgetting,** or forgetting because we want to forget.

15. The trace is thought to have two qualities: *strength,* or how likely it is to "pop into the mind;" and *resistance to extinction,* meaning how well the trace can manage to survive.

16. Establishing a resistance to extinction requires **consolidation,** a period during which the trace undergoes a process of hardening, or setting.

17. Some kinds of information are more easily retrieved in the same physical setting in which the learning took place.

18. When old information causes us to forget new information, the process is called **proactive interference.** The opposite, when new information causes us to forget old information, is called **retroactive interference.**

The Encoding and Transfer Process

19. The manner in which we encode and transfer information to long-term memory determines how well we will be able to remember and retrieve it.

20. In the process called **chunking,** we combine a number of individual units of information into one neat package—such as when we combine four individual digits (1, 4, 9, 2) into a single memorable date, 1492.

21. Chunking increases the scope of short-term memory, which can hold around seven big packages of information about as well as it can handle seven small items. In the interaction between short-term and long-term memory, information is often transferred to storage in chunks.

22. The prevailing view is the **associative network theory,** which describes memory as a complex network in which countless items of information are connected and interconnected by long and far-reaching strands of association.

23. The theory holds that we encode new information into long-term memory by noting how it relates to what we have already stored—and thus add it to the network with all the appropriate associations of existing information.

24. Sometimes we encode and can retrieve a faithful copy of the information—as when we recite a familiar poem word for word. More frequently we engage in constructive processing—encoding and retrieving the theme or underlying meaning and trying to fill in the details, sometimes accurately and sometimes not. It has been said that memory is often "unreliable, given to invention, and even dangerous."

25. The brain's complex responsibilities in memory are revealed when considering our capacities for two distinct kinds of memory: **semantic memory,** or the retrieval of facts; and **episodic memory,** or the retrieval of actual experiences. The first appears to depend on the functioning of the brain's frontal lobes, while the second does not.

Linkages in Learning

26. How well we remember generally depends on how well we have learned in the first place—that is, on how thoroughly we understand new information and how many associations we find between new and old.

27. Finding meaning and organization is useful in forming associations. It is generally more effective to learn by **rule** (trying to understand the underlying principles) than by **rote** (simply trying to memorize materials by repeating them mechanically without any regard to what they mean).

28. The **law of overlearning** states: After you have learned something, continuing to work at learning it tends to increase the length of time you will remember it.

Learning How to Learn and Remember

29. **Clustering** is the encoding and storing into long-term memory of information organized into packages composed of a number of small units (like chunking in short-term memory). Clusters of information can be formed by categories, meaning, logic, or in other ways.

30. Made-up stories are a method of clustering items of information that would not otherwise hang together. Made-up stories are particularly helpful if you try to form a mental picture or image of the event.

31. **Imagery** is helpful because we have an extraordinary ability to remember visual information—a fact that has led some psychologists to believe we have two separate ways of encoding and storing information—one for physical attributes and the other for knowledge that can be put into words.

32. **Mnemonic devices** are tricks, like the "Thirty days hath September" jingle, that help provide a memory framework for materials that otherwise would have to be learned by rote. Many mnemonic devices rely on imagery for their effectiveness.

TEST YOURSELF ANSWERS

a) Sensory memories are very brief, containing only fast-disappearing traces of information received by the brain from the sense organs.

b) Your friend is finding that she tends to remember the initial numbers best.

c) Your friend would be having trouble remembering impersonal facts—for example, names and dates—rather than personal experiences.

d) He should study either of the two languages, then history, then the second language. Old information learned gets in the way of new information—especially when the items to be learned are similar. So breaking up the language studies with history makes sense.

e) Motivated forgetting has occurred.

f) Your classmate is going to combine a number of words into individual, discrete packages.

g) Her abilities indicate that highly emotional experiences tend to stay in memory for long periods.

h) She would do better by taking the second approach. It helps to organize information into some uniform pattern that makes sense—and that can readily be associated with other information.

i) Clustering organizes the information into smaller units for long-term memory.

j) She would be using a technique known as imagery.

Study Guide

Chapter 5   Memory: How We Remember and Why We Forget

LEARNING OBJECTIVES

After studying this chapter, you should be able to:

1. Describe sensory, short-term, and long-term memory and the processes that transfer information from one system to another.

2. Understand that learning and remembering cannot be measured directly but only through performance, and that psychologists measure memory as best they can through recall, recognition, and relearning.

3. Draw the curve of forgetting and recognize that we remember at least some of what we learn for a long time.

4. Discuss four theories of why we forget—fading of the memory trace, failure in retrieval, proactive and retroactive interference, and motivated forgetting—and why all of them may be correct at times.

5. Describe the associative network theory of memory.

6. Improve memory by spending time processing the information during learning—that is, to understand the information and to discover meaning and organization that make it hold together and become firmly associated with what you already know.

7. Discuss why such processing is aided by learning by rule rather than by rote, clustering, and allowing a period of time for consolidation, and why speed reading is not ordinarily a good study method.

8. Understand how to use made-up stories, imagery, and mnemonic devices to help remember materials that would otherwise resist attempts to find meaning and organization.

For an Understanding of the Science

For Application to Life Situations

PROGRAMMED UNIT
THE RANGE AND CONTENT OF HUMAN MEMORY

1. The range of memory is divided into three stages. The first, *sensory memory,* is made up of the lingering traces of information sent to the brain by the senses. The image of a car license plate that remains in mind for less than a second illustrates the operation of _____ _____.

   sensory memory

2. Some, but not all, of the information that arrives in _____ _____ is transferred to the second system, *short-term memory.*

   sensory memory

3. Information stored in _____-_____ memory is retained somewhat longer than in sensory memory, perhaps up to 30 seconds. A telephone number remembered long enough to dial is held in _____-_____ _____.

   short-term

   short-term memory

sensory
memory

short-term memory

4. When you walk through a crowd, many images pass before you and are immediately forgotten. They have entered and left your _____ _____. However, you may observe a street sign and remember the name long enough to check a map, in which case the name probably was held in _____-_____ _____.

5. Short-term memory has been described as a "leaky bucket," because much information is quickly lost unless attempts are made to process and retain the material. Processing activities begin with *scanning* of the information briefly held in _____ memory.

sensory

6. The transfer of material from sensory to short-term memory is aided by this _____ process.

scanning

scanning

7. The information in sensory memory must undergo _____ to determine which items should be selected for further attention and then perhaps *encoding*, which is transforming information in some way that makes it easier to handle.

encode

8. If you see two dogs fighting, you may _____ the event as a "dogfight." The verbal code "dogfight" is a *schema*.

encoding, schema

9. A mental representation of the information to be remembered created by the process of _____ is called a _____.

scanning, encoding

10. In addition to the processes of _____ and _____, some sort of *rehearsal system* can keep information active in short-term memory for longer periods of time.

rehearsal system

11. When you silently repeat a phone number until you have finished dialing it, you are using a _____ _____ to keep information active in short-term memory.

short-
term
rehearsal system

12. Only a small amount of information can be maintained in _____-_____ memory, even when it is maintained there by using a _____ _____, and the particular items that are remembered will be influenced by the *primacy* and *recency effects*.

primacy effect
recency effect

13. If you meet 10 people at a party, you are most likely to remember the names of the first person or two because of the _____ _____ and the last person or two because of the _____ _____.

sensory, short-
term

14. The third kind of memory, along with _____ and _____-_____ memory, is *long-term memory*. This is a relatively permanent storehouse of information.

long-
term memory

15. Your own name and birth date are stored unforgettably in _____-_____ _____.

long-term

16. Material is passed from short-term to _____-_____ memory by some kind of *transfer process*, which includes additional encoding and relating the new information to information that already exists in long-term memory.

transfer process

17. Recognizing that a phone number corresponds to the numerical code for your birth date is part of the _____ _____ that helps establish long-term memories.

retrieval processes

18. Material is also transferred in the reverse direction by *retrieval processes*. The recall of information from long-term to short-term memory is accomplished by _____ _____.

19. One factor in this recall process is *direct-access retrieval,* which means that we are able to go into long-term memory and locate information placed there by a _____ process, and then recall the material immediately.

transfer

20. The content of a memory is of two kinds, *semantic* and *episodic.* The memory of facts is typically encoded into memory in the form of words and language and is called _____ _____. Memory for episodes in your experience is called _____ _____.

semantic memory
episodic memory

21. Remembering your first day at college or a car accident is _____, whereas remembering that London is in England or that 3 is the square root of 9 is _____.

episodic

semantic

WHY WE FORGET

22. Unfortunately, tests of learning and memory only measure how well an individual *performs* on the tests, and performance may not be an entirely accurate indication of how much is actually remembered. How well you score on a history quiz is not only influenced by learning and memory but also by anxiety, distractions, and other factors. So a test score should be regarded as a measure of how well you _____ on the test.

perform

23. There are three principal ways to measure learning and memory through tests of _____. The first is to ask people to *recall* information they have learned.

performance

24. In an essay test, learning and memory performance are measured by the method of _____. Another approach is to measure *recognition*—for example, with a multiple-choice exam in which you must select the right answer from several alternatives.

recall

25. If you did not study much for a history test, you might be able to pick out the correct answer in a multiple-choice question, but you are likely to have a harder time writing an essay in which you must produce the facts yourself, because recall tends to be more difficult than _____. Thus a poorly prepared student might prefer to be tested by the method of _____ rather than _____.

recognition

recognition, recall

26. Multiple-choice examinations tend to measure *semantic memory,* the clear-cut intentional retrieval of information. The practice tests in this study guide assess _____ _____.

semantic memory

27. In contrast, some information is retained without an awareness of remembering, which is called *procedural memory.* Sometimes you experience a person or place that seems familiar but you know you have never met the person or been there before—you have an _____ _____ of something that is similar to the new person or place but you cannot identify that item.

procedural memory

28. A third method of measuring learning and memory _____ is *relearning.*

performance

29. If it takes you less time to learn something the second time you study it than the first, this difference reflects how much you remembered from the first time and is a measure of _____.

relearning

30. Hermann Ebbinghaus used this very sensitive method of _____ to draw a *curve of forgetting.* He discovered that when we learn something

relearning

new, we quickly forget much of what we have learned, but we remember at least some of it for a long time.

31. In graph form, Ebbinghaus's results showed a rapid drop in memory performance followed by a leveling off, which is the typical shape of a _____ of _____.

curve
forgetting

32. Why do we forget? One possible answer is that forgetting is caused by *fading of the memory trace*. According to this idea, a path through a field that disappears with time unless it is continually used resembles the _____ of the _____ _____.

fading, memory trace

33. The memory trace has two qualities. First is its *strength*. How likely the memory is to "pop into mind" is a reflection of its _____.

strength

34. The second quality of the _____ _____ is *resistance to extinction,* meaning the ability of a memory to survive and become immune to fading or decay.

memory trace

35. Resistance to _____ of a memory trace requires what memory theorists call *consolidation*. This is a period of time during which the memory "sets." The hardening of newly poured concrete is analogous to the _____ of a memory trace.

extinction

consolidation

36. During the process of firming up a memory, called _____, the qualities of a memory _____, namely its _____ and _____ to _____, are improved.

consolidation
trace, strength, resistance
extinction

37. A second explanation of forgetting suggests that it is essentially a *failure in retrieval* more than a failure to maintain the _____ _____.

memory trace

38. The memory trace, once established, may be permanent, but it is not always available because of a _____ in _____ of the information stored in memory.

failure, retrieval

39. Sometimes being located in the same place or even visualizing the place where original learning took place helps to facilitate _____.

retrieval

40. A third possible explanation of _____ is that our ability to remember any given piece of information may suffer from *interference* from other information stored in memory.

forgetting

41. There are two general kinds of _____. *Proactive interference* occurs when old information causes us to forget new information. For example, learning a list of fruits is made more difficult by having previously learned a list of vegetables, which illustrates _____ interference.

interference

proactive

42. The second kind, *retroactive interference,* occurs when new information causes us to forget old information. When individuals learn a new list of words that are synonyms (that is, they mean the same thing as words in a previously learned list), it is more difficult to remember the original words because of _____ interference.

retroactive

43. Suppose a student first learns Spanish and then French. If remembering French is made more difficult by having previously learned Spanish, _____ _____ has occurred. If the memory for Spanish is disturbed by the subsequent learning of French, then _____ _____ has occurred.

proactive interference
retroactive
interference

44. A fourth possible cause of _____ is *motivated forgetting,* or the fact that we may deliberately forget information we do not want to remember.

forgetting

45. Gamblers are notoriously prone to remember the times they won and forget the times they lost. Their distorted recollection of how well they have done over the years illustrates _____ _____.

motivated forgetting

46. The four theories that help explain forgetting suggest that forgetting may consist in part of a _____ of the _____ _____, a failure to recall or _____ information, a disturbance caused by the _____ of other material, and selective or _____ _____.

fading, memory trace
retrieve
interference, motivated
forgetting

THE ENCODING AND TRANSFER PROCESS

47. Recall that information from short-term memory is _____ to long-term memory with the help of some _____ process. One such process is *chunking,* in which we combine a number of individual units of information into one package for storage in long-term memory. For example, the seven letters UCPIRTE can be remembered much better if they are rearranged into the word PICTURE and stored as a single unit, a process called _____.

transferred
encoding

chunking

48. Organizing otherwise disconnected information into more meaningful but fewer units, called _____, is consistent with the *associative network theory,* which describes memory as a complex network in which countless items of information are interconnected by long and far-reaching strands of association. Linkages are formed between the new information being encoded and old information already in memory. The linkages depend on the similarities and differences in such material along many dimensions according to the _____ _____ _____.

chunking

associative network theory

49. For example, after being introduced to a person, you may remember his or her name because it is the same as that of your best friend in high school, because of the way the individual looks, the color of his or her clothes, a particularly interesting conversation between the two of you, or several other linkages with existing memories, which illustrate the _____ _____ _____.

associative
network theory

50. A special linkage that occurs for emotional events that you remember in graphic detail is termed a *flashbulb memory.* Remembering standing at the alter on your wedding or what you were doing at the moment a loved one or famous person died are examples of _____ _____.

flashbulb memories

LINKAGES IN LEARNING

51. How well we remember often depends on how well we have learned or _____ information into our associative network in the first place. Encoding is easier if we can find *meaning* and *organization* in the material.

encoded

52. Syllables that are real words are much easier to learn than nonsense syllables, and disjointed material that can be put into a coherent sequence is easier to remember than material that cannot. These examples illustrate the importance of _____ and _____ during initial _____ in helping us remember material.

meaning, organization,
encoding

53. Finding _____ and _____ in information helps us learn material by *rule* rather than by *rote.*

meaning, organization

rote
rule

54. Simply learning nonsense syllables by "gut memory" and repetition is to learn them by _____, while trying to attribute some meaning or logic to the nonsense syllables is to learn them by _____.

rule, rote

55. The *law of overlearning* states that after you have learned something, either by _____ or _____, continuing to work at learning the material tends to increase the length of time you will remember it.

law
overlearning

56. Certain nursery rhymes and the alphabet, which are frequently repeated during childhood, may be remembered forever because of the _____ of _____.

LEARNING HOW TO LEARN AND REMEMBER

learning set

57. As individuals continue to learn the same general kind of material, they develop a *learning set*. In a sense, learning how to learn certain material, or acquiring a _____ _____, helps encoding.

learning set

58. Freshmen in college are often overwhelmed by the amount of material they are expected to learn, but after a few years they are able to handle the same amount or even more material quite efficiently because they have developed a _____ _____ for it.

categories

59. Another aid to encoding is to use *categories*. Sometimes information cannot be organized into a single unit, but the elements of the information can be broken down into a few _____.

categories

60. If you are required to learn a list of words, it may be helpful to group these words into _____ first.

short-term

61. Earlier, we learned that chunking consists of organizing material in _____-_____ memory. When carried on in long-term memory, the same process is called *clustering*.

clustering, long-term

62. Information can be organized by categories, meaning, logic, and other ways in this _____ process, and the result is better _____-_____ memory and retrieval.

clustering

63. We seem particularly adept at _____ materials together if they have a *logical* relationship. Cause-and-effect sequences and narrative stories are often easy to encode and remember because they contain _____ relationships among elements of the material.

logical

64. Not all material is easily organized, so sometimes we must impose meaning on it by creating a *made-up story* about the material. If you want to remember the words "coffee," "idea," and "light," you might say to yourself, "After a cup of coffee, I had an idea that turned on like a light bulb in my head" to cluster the items, you have created a _____-_____ _____ about them.

made-up
story

65. *Imagery* is also helpful when encoding memory and retrieval. If you can create a mental picture of events, memory might be improved by the process of _____.

imagery

66. Another way to impart meaning to material is to create a *mnemonic device*. A jingle like "30 days hath September" helps us remember information through the use of a _____ _____.

mnemonic device

REVIEW OF IMPORTANT TERMS

acetylcholine (236)

Alzheimer's disease (236)

associative network theory (223)

categories (230)

chunking (222)

clustering (231)

consolidation (217)

curve of forgetting (216)

encoding (210)

episodic memory (213)

flashbulb memories (225)

imagery (234)

law of overlearning (228)

learning set (230)

long-term memory (210)

memory trace (217)

mnemonic (234)

mnemonic device (234)

motivated forgetting (repression) (221)

neurotransmitter (236)

primacy effect (210)

proactive interference (219)

procedural memory (215)

recall (214)

recency effect (210)

recognition (215)

rehearsal system (210)

relearning (215)

resistance to extinction (217)

retroactive interference (221)

rote (227)

rule (227)

scanning (210)

schema (210)

semantic memory (213)

sensory memory (207)

short-term memory (209)

strength (217)

transfer process (210)

PRACTICE TEST

_____ 1. The memory system described as a "leaky bucket" because it typically retains material for less than 30 seconds is

    a.   sensory memory.

    b.   short-term memory.

    c.   long-term memory.

    d.   transfer memory.

_____ 2. Short-term memory is capable of holding approximately how
many items of unrelated information:

    a.   one

    b.   two to four

    c.   five to nine

    d.   ten to twelve

_____ 3. The process through which we associate information in short-term memory with information in long-term memory is called

    a.   scanning.

    b.   transfer.

    c.   rehearsal.

    d.   chunking.

_____ 4. The very brief mental image of the color of a fast-moving car constitutes

    a.   short-term memory.

    b.   sensory memory.

    c.   semantic memory.

    d.   procedural memory.

_____ 5. The analogy of memory as a path worn into a plot of grass is used by those who think of forgetting as

    a.   the fading of the memory trace.

    b.   a failure in retrieval.

    c.   a lack of consolidation.

    d.   failure to achieve overlearning.

_____ 6. The most sensitive test of memory is

    a.   relearning.

    b.   recall.

    c.   a multiple-choice test.

    d.   an essay examination.

_____ 7. If you have "crammed" for an examination, you would probably prefer a test requiring

    a.   recall.

    b.   recognition.

    c.   relearning.

    d.   procedural memory.

_____ 8. The typical curve of forgetting indicates that we

    a.   continue to forget substantial amounts of material long after original learning.

    b.   forget nearly everything within a very short time after learning.

    c.   do not forget much immediately after learning but forget rapidly thereafter.

    d.   forget most rapidly immediately after learning but retain something for remarkably long periods of time.

_____ 9. A period of time following learning during which a memory becomes more firmly established is called

    a.   consolidation.

    b.   overlearning.

c. transfer period.

d. constructive processing.

_____ 10. In contrast to those younger, older people

    a. have generally poorer memories for most things.

    b. have better recall of explicit rather than implicit material.

    c. have more problems recalling material but recognize items equally well.

    d. have more "wisdom," that is better insight into and judgment concerning solving difficult life problems.

_____ 11. You cannot recall the name of a city you once visited in Mexico or anything about it. Then the name strikes you—and suddenly you also remember the name of your hotel, the street, and your favorite shop. This illustrates

    a. procedural memory.

    b. "tip of the tongue" phenomenon.

    c. motivated recall.

    d. clustering.

_____ 12. Learning French after having learned Spanish may make French harder to remember because of

    a. retroactive interference.

    b. proactive interference.

    c. motivated forgetting.

    d. overlearning.

_____ 13. Flashbulb and episodic memory are similar because they both are likely to involve

    a. a memory for an event in a person's experience.

    b. associations with extreme emotions or significant life events.

    c. both semantic and procedural memories.

    d. all of the above.

_____ 14. When we fail to remember an unpleasant experience, we may be displaying

    a. retroactive interference.

    b. motivated forgetting.

    c. a failure in retrieval.

    d. constructive processing.

_____ 15. The two qualities of strength and resistance to extinction are represented in which of the following?

    a. Learning

    b. Consolidation

    c. Memory trace

    d. Interference

_____ 16. Memory for particular events is called

    a.   semantic.

    b.   sensory.

    c.   semantic.

    d.   episodic.

_____ 17. Chunking occurs in short-term memory. What is the similar process called when it occurs in long-term memory?

    a.   clustering

    b.   categorization

    c.   making up a story

    d.   rule learning

_____ 18. People who learn and remember well and efficiently often have

    a.   a rich associative network.

    b.   more knowledge and information in general.

    c.   many learning sets.

    d.   all of the above.

_____ 19. Studies of speed reading indicate that

    a.   increases in reading speed beyond normal rates result in declines in remembering the material.

    b.   speed and comprehension can both be increased markedly over normal rates with sufficient practice.

    c.   very rapid readers are more efficient information processors.

    d.   slow readers spend too much time on the important points.

_____ 20. People who must frequently learn different examples of the same general type of material may become very efficient at such learning because of

    a.   a learning set.

    b.   the law of overlearning.

    c.   procedural memory.

    d.   improved relearning potential.

ANSWERS TO PRACTICE TEST

1. b	6. a	11. d	16. d
2. c	7. b	12. b	17. a
3. b	8. d	13. d	18. d
4. b	9. a	14. b	19. a
5. a	10. c	15. c	20. a

EXERCISES

I.   Figure 5.20 contains a list of 10 nonsense syllables and a list of 10 words. Ask a friend to learn the list of nonsense syllables in the following manner: Study the

Memory Lists	
TAC	WEEDS
MIH	SKY
BOK	BOWL
SIW	CARPET
PUR	TRAY
FEX	COLUMN
DOS	PLUG
WOL	ASHES
CUK	SCREEN
JAD	PAPER

FIGURE 5.20

list for 30 seconds; then write down as many of the nonsense syllables as possible within a one-minute time limit. After resting 15 seconds, study the list again for 30 seconds and then write it down again. Repeat this procedure until all the words have been recalled correctly in two consecutive trials—or until 10 trials have been attempted. Keep track of how many syllables are recalled at the end of each trial, plot the scores on the graph provided in Figure 5.21 and connect the points with a solid line.

Now spend five minutes talking to your subject about the weather, a sporting event, or any other matter unrelated to nonsense syllables. Then ask the subject to write down the syllables again. Plot on the graph the number of syllables recalled on this retest. Also ask whether the subject used any special kind of strategy in trying to remember the list.

With another subject, follow the same procedure, but with the list of words rather than the nonsense syllables. Plot the results on the same graph, but connect the points with a dashed line.

Now consider the following questions:

1. Are the curves for the syllables and words the same? If there are any differences, can you speculate why they occurred? What do the curves tell you about the learning process?

FIGURE 5.21

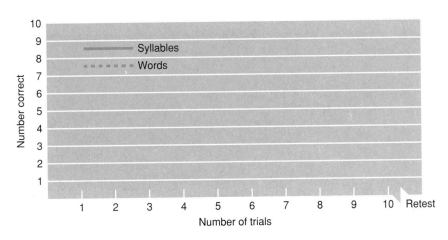

Number Lists

Numbers in Set	Sets
4	8-3-2-9
5	6-8-5-1-4
6	8-8-2-7-4-6
7	2-9-6-3-2-9-8
8	5-4-0-5-2-4-1-6
9	8-0-4-1-2-7-0-6-3
10	7-3-1-2-5-7-4-3-0-5

FIGURE 5.22

2. Which task—learning and remembering the syllables or the words—seemed easier? Explain why. Which list was remembered better on the retest following the five-minute break? Why? Did the two subjects apply any techniques that gave the list more meaning, such as, making up stories, mnemonic devices, clustering, and so forth? Did such techniques seem to help?

II. It has been suggested that short-term memory can hold approximately seven plus or minus two items at a time, or between five and nine items simultaneously. This exercise represents an informal test of this idea. Ask a small group of volunteers to listen to you read the first set of numbers given in Figure 5.22. Say the numbers in a monotone, approximately one per second. When you have finished reading a number set, have your subjects write down as many of the numbers in the order presented as possible. Then proceed to the next set until all sets have been presented. After testing, check how many numbers in each set your subjects recalled correctly.

If several students are doing this exercise, the instructor may wish to determine how many subjects can perfectly recall each set of numbers. It is unlikely that everyone will be able to recall perfectly a 10-number set. The average should be approximately seven.

Now try the same approach with the numbers given in Figure 5.23. Notice that the numbers are grouped into sets of two numbers. That is, they have been chunked. When reading the numbers to your subjects, read the members of a pair rather rapidly, pausing longer—but only for a second—between pairs. For example, say "seven five . . . one four . . . six zero" for the first set. Tabulate the number of individuals who can correctly recall each number set in the same manner as above.

Numbers in Set	Groups in Set	Sets
6	3	75-14-60
8	4	72-85-46-97
10	5	94-72-69-48-03
12	6	30-41-80-49-25-73
14	7	14-20-39-05-42-68-92

FIGURE 5.23

Are people able to recall more digits when they are chunked into pairs than when they are not so grouped? What are the implications of this result for remembering telephone numbers and area codes, for example?

III. Describe an ideal method of studying textbook material for a course such as this one. Use as many of the concepts of learning, memory, and retrieval described in this chapter as seem appropriate. After each point in your study method, identify the relevant concept and provide a rationale and evidence as to why this step should help.

C H A P T E R 6

Language and Thought

Language communicates thoughts and feelings.

How do we humans acquire and use language?

That question has puzzled scientists, philosophers, and educators for centuries. Interest in the subject is understandable. Somehow, we are able to produce and understand a limitless number of sentences never spoken or heard before. Indeed, we can identify every familiar spoken word we hear in less than a third of a second, drawing on more than 100,000 word forms stored in a "mental dictionary." For those who know more than one language, the miracle is even more awesome. Moreover, as we process the sounds we hear, we are able almost instantaneously to assemble them into meaningful sentences that reflect the message intended by the speaker (Gerstein et al., 1988).

The everyday miracle of language is made possible in part because the human brain is especially constructed to acquire and speak language. Granted, as will be discussed later, that some animals are able to understand certain symbols, no other species can communicate with others of its kind in a way that approximates human language—no matter how well developed its vocal apparatus or how intricate its social organization. In contrast, all human beings have the capacity for human language, no matter how primitive or isolated the society. To put it another way, the use of complex and infinitely varied language seems to be a behavior dictated by our biological inheritance. In evolutionary terms, language is a "uniquely human activity" that gives us a tremendous advantage over all other animals (Miller, 1981). Just as fish are born to swim and moles to burrow, we seem born to speak.

The two topics covered in this chapter—language and thought—are significantly related. It is true enough, of course, that thinking does not necessarily require language. Animals obviously do some kind of thinking, and so do human babies before they have learned to speak. An artist working on a painting thinks in terms of mental images—a mind's-eye picture of what the details and final results should look like. Musicians compose and orchestrate by manipulating "sounds" that they hear only inside themselves. Mathematicians manipulate their own symbols and formulas. But most of us generally think in words, and language greatly enlarges the scope of our thinking. Indeed much of the thinking we do would be impossible without the use of words and the ideas they represent. Together, the ability to generate complex thoughts and to communicate them in language represents one of the supreme attainments of the human species.

The Function and Structure of Language

The origin of human language is lost in the mists of antiquity. But we can assume that its first purpose was to exchange messages of vital concern to survival—to enable people to establish **communication** with one another about food supplies and how to obtain them, about danger and how to avoid it. In our own everyday lives, one way we use our knowledge is to communicate with others—and thus engage in the cooperative activities essential to carry on the basic tasks of human society. Language has the power to convey messages understood by all of us, enabling us to work, play, and live together. We use language to tell each other how we feel, what we need, what we desire. We use it to amuse ourselves in conversation, to form friendships, and to help one another grow and transport food, build houses and office skyscrapers,

Communication

The exchange of information and feelings between two or more people.

and manufacture and distribute clothing. With language, we can express everything from a child's simple request for a glass of milk, to a lover's declaration of passion, to the most complex scientific theories.

Moreover, through reading we not only gather knowledge and information but a greater sense of identification with our society and culture. Language helps us acquire information by providing labels for the objects and events in the environment. It allows us to reason—to make inferences and deductions. And it helps establish and maintain social relationships with others. It helps us encode information into memory by providing many of the linkages in the associative network of memory. It helps us think and solve problems.

Other species lower on the evolutionary scale—from bees to chimpanzees—also manage to communicate in one way or another. But only humans have developed a method of exchanging so many messages of so many varied and complex meanings.

The Basic Sounds of Language

In effect, language is an agreement among those of us who speak the same language that certain sounds, put together according to rules that all of us know and use, convey meaningful messages intended by the speaker and understood by the listener. The sounds that constitute language depend on the capacity of the human brain and vocal cords to produce them—and the number is limited. This may seem hard to believe, in view of the apparent complexity and variety of all of the sentences that can be heard in various countries and cultures of the world—but it is true. No language contains more than 85 basic sounds, and some contain as few as 15. English has about 40, or a few more depending on regional dialects.

The basic sounds, called **phonemes,** might be described as the building blocks of language. In English, the phonemes include such sounds as the short *a* in *pat,* the long *a* in *pate,* the consonant *p* as in either *pat* or *pate,* the *ch* in *chip,* the *th* in *the,* and the *sh* in *shop.* Thus the word *pat* contains three phonemes. By changing any of the three, you can produce many different words. Changing the first phoneme will give you *bat, cat, chat,* and so on. Changing the second creates *pate, pet, pit, pout,* and others. A new sound at the end creates *pack, pad, pal, pan,* and more. If you play around with the word *pat* in this way, changing just one of the three phonemes at a time, you will find that you can produce more than 30 different words. As shown in Figure 6.1, infants only one week old can already discriminate even between phonemes that sound very much alike.

Phonemes
The basic sounds that form the building blocks of language.

Units That Convey Meaning: The Morphemes

By themselves, the phonemes usually have no meaning. (Although some meaningful units, like the first person pronoun *I,* are made up of a single phoneme.) But they can be put together, in combinations of two or more, to form units that do have meaning. For example, we can start with the phoneme *t,* add the phoneme pronounced as *ee,* then add the phoneme *ch,* and arrive at the combination *teach.* The result is called a **morpheme**—a combination of phonemes that possesses meaning in and of itself. Like *teach,*

Morpheme
The combination of phonemes that possesses some meaning in and of itself.

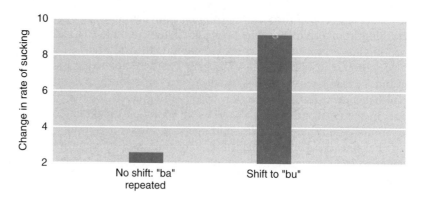

FIGURE 6.1 **The early capacity to distinguish between spoken sounds** The rate at which infants engaged in sucking was measured while they heard a phoneme ("ba") repeated. As the infants became bored with hearing the same phoneme, their rate of sucking decreased. At this point, a slightly different phoneme was introduced. If the infants were to discriminate the new sound, they would become more aroused and, as a consequence, increase their sucking rate. That is precisely what happened. The results showed a significant increase in sucking rate when there was a slight shift in the sound of the phoneme (from "ba" to "bu"), indicating that the infants did indeed differentiate one sound from another (Bertonici, et al., 1988).

many morphemes are words. Others are prefixes or suffixes, which can in turn be combined with other morphemes to form words. For example, we can combine the three morphemes *un* (a prefix), *teach* (a word in itself), and *able* (a suffix) to form the word *unteachable*. Or we can start with the same morpheme *teach*, add *er* (meaning *one who*) and *s* (to denote the plural), and form the word *teachers*. The plural *s* is one of the most commonly used morphemes, as is *ed* to indicate the past tense of a verb (walk*ed*, talk*ed*).

Some very long words represent a single morpheme—for example, *hippopotamus*. But most long words are combinations of morphemes and therefore of meanings. Note the following:

piti ful

dis join ted

in sur mount able

The building blocks of language, though simple, make possible a tremendous variety of expression. The 40 English phonemes (which are written using only the 26 letters of the alphabet) are combined in various ways to produce more than 100,000 morphemes. These are in turn combined with one another to produce the 600,000 or more words found in the largest dictionaries.

The Rules of Grammar: Building Sentences from Words

Semantics

The meaning of morphemes and words in language.

Language is not possible with words alone. True, we must understand and agree on what is called **semantics,** or the meaning of the words in our language. But, in addition, we must establish the grammatical rules of our language in order to string the words together into meaningful sentences. Thus every language has two essential elements: (1) a **vocabulary** of meaningful morphemes and words, and (2) a set of rules, called **grammar,** for combining the words into an almost infinite number of sentences that can be constructed to express an almost infinite variety of semantic meanings. In this book alone there are thousands of sentences that you have never before encountered, yet whose meaning you understand immediately.

Vocabularies differ from one language to another, of course, and often greatly. The English word *house* is *maison* in French and *casa* in Spanish, and in Chinese it is pronounced something like *ook*. The rules of grammar, however, though they vary in detail, share some basic similarities in all languages—including the dead languages of the past as well as those spoken today. Presumably this is because people everywhere have the same abilities and limitations in the use of language (Clark & Clark, 1977).

How the Rules of Syntax Prevent Chaos

Among the most important rules of grammar are those called **syntax,** which relate to sentence structure. The rules of syntax regulate the manner in which nouns, verbs, adjectives, and adverbs are placed in proper order to form phrases—and the way the phrases are combined to form sentences that convey a meaning readily understood by anyone who speaks the language. Without these rules, language would be a jumble. For example, even very young children know the meaning of the individual names and words. *Bill, quickly, who, the, down, was, street, saw, walking, John, a, sweater, his, in, yellow, friend.* But when presented in that order, the words do not convey any message. Rearranged according to the rules of syntax, they become the meaningful sentence:

> John, who was walking quickly down the street, saw his friend Bill in a yellow sweater.

If that is the message you want to convey about John and Bill, you have to arrange the words in that order. Any change in the arrangement might convey an entirely different meaning, as for example:

> John, who was in a yellow sweater, quickly saw his friend Bill walking down the street.

> Bill saw his friend John, who was walking quickly down the street in a yellow sweater.

You will find that you can use the 16 words to express several other meaningful sentences, simply by altering the syntax.

The rules of syntax vary somewhat from language to language. Thus in English we place adjectives before nouns (*red house*), while the French place them after the nouns (*maison rouge*). Some languages permit the speaker to say "Ice the man slipped on" to emphasize it was ice that caused the person to fall. But the pattern has a logic: "what belongs together mentally is placed close together syntactically" (Vennemann, 1975). We may not be aware of all the rules either as children or as adults, but we follow them even if we cannot explain what they are. In combination with the agreed-on meanings of morphemes and words, rules are the magic key to human communication (Chomsky, 1965). They probably form the only kind of system that could meet the needs of our civilization.

Vocabulary

An essential element of language that includes meaningful morphemes and words.

Grammar

An essential element of language that includes a set of rules for combining words into meaningful sentences.

Syntax

The rules of grammar that relate to sentence structure.

The Effect of Social Context on Meaning: Pragmatics

In addition to semantics and syntax, there is a third, related aspect of language that affects the nature of our communications. Known among language scholars as **pragmatics,** it is the social purposes of language. That is to say, the actual meaning of what we say may depend largely on the situation in which we say it.

Consider the following question: "How much money do you need?" Without knowing the context in which it was asked, the question sounds like it might have been addressed by a kindly person to an individual in need. In fact, however, it is a question asked by tennis star John McEnroe of fellow professional Ivan Lendl during a stormy meeting in which Lendl expressed concern over a possible decrease in tournament fees (Vescey, 1989). Far from a kindly inquiry, the communication was actually belligerent in the social setting in which it was uttered.

Together, the three aspects of language discussed in this section—semantics, syntax, and pragmatics—give our utterances a structure and a range of functions that set human communications far apart from that of other species.

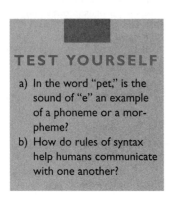

TEST YOURSELF

a) In the word "pet," is the sound of "e" an example of a phoneme or a morpheme?

b) How do rules of syntax help humans communicate with one another?

Generating Messages— and Comprehending Them

The signs shown at the right are commonly used in public places and on highways in various parts of the world. Each of them conveys a single, simple message: "No smoking here," "Curvy road ahead," and "Deer may be crossing the road."

Suppose that your language, which is your own communications system, worked the same way. For each idea that you wanted to express—everything from "Let's eat" to "Psychology is the systematic study of behavior"—you would need a separate sign of some kind, in the form of a spoken or written word. How many signs or spoken words—each conveying only one simple message—would you need to convey everything that you now say in the course of an ordinary day? How long would it take just to tell a classmate that you would like to go along to a movie but have a history examination tomorrow and must study, and besides you have to do some laundry and return a book to the library—so all in all, though you appreciate the invitation and would like a rain check, you feel you must say no?

The number of signs you would need, each conveying its own message, is almost beyond imagination. Most of the thoughts you express in the course of an ordinary day take the form of sentences you have never used or heard before—sentences you make up on the spot. Your listeners, in most cases, have never before heard the same combination of words. Our system, combining the simple building blocks of a small number of phonemes according to the established rules of grammar, enables us to exchange an unlimited number and variety of messages. It would be difficult indeed to imagine any other system that could possibly enable us to live in the complex societies we have developed.

However, producing language—speaking or writing new sentences created spontaneously—requires thinking and planning. Understanding language also demands the most complex kind of mental activity. Especially in the case of the spoken word, communication requires as well close cooperation between speaker and listener. The speaker, having a purpose in mind, must carefully choose words and produce sentences that will "get the message across." The listener then must interpret the meaning and intention of the combination of sounds reaching the ear.

Suppose, for example, you are in a room with a friend who is sitting near a window. You want the window opened wider. How, exactly, shall you phrase the suggestion? From all the possible words and syntactic arrangements available, you decide to say, "It's hot in here." Now your friend has to do some processing—for the words "It's hot in here" can be interpreted in a number of different ways. Your friend has to decide: Were you merely stating a fact? Do you mean that you want the window opened wider—or shut? Are you perhaps suggesting that both of you move to a different room? The possibilities have to be considered and accepted or rejected. Your friend will probably get the message, but not without working at it. For both speaker and listener, the use of language demands the full use of all of our varied cognitive abilities (Gerstein et al., 1988).

The Challenge for the Speaker

One way to get some idea of the difficulty of producing language is to make a tape recording of some of your own utterances, especially when you are trying to explain something fairly complicated. Hearing the tape afterward, you will probably be shocked at how tongue-tied you sound, for the spoken word is not nearly so smooth and fluent as is generally believed. As we talk, we often have to stop and think. Our speech is full of long pauses, *and-uhs* and *ers*. We make mistakes or fail to express ourselves clearly and have to amend our utterances with phrases like *I mean* or *that is to say*. Sometimes we stop in the middle of a sentence, leave it unfinished and start all over. We make "slips of the tongue" and end up saying something quite different from what we intended, often when we are preoccupied or distracted (Reason, 1984).

When we produce sentences, we must first think of the meaning we want to convey—perhaps a message that will be several sentences long. Then we have to plan each sentence and each part of a sentence. We have to find the right words to flesh out the sentence and then put the words in their proper places. Finally we have to command all the muscles we use in speech to carry out the program we have planned—even as we are mentally racing ahead to what we want to say next (Clark & Clark, 1977).

The Difficulties of the Listener

When you listen to someone speak, and try to interpret the meaning and intent, you have to engage in what is probably an even more difficult form of information processing. The only raw data you have are the sound waves produced by the speaker's voice and transmitted through the air to your ears. Ordinarily these waves meet with considerable competition from other sounds elsewhere in the vicinity. Other people are carrying on conversations in the same room. Footsteps thud against the floor. A telephone rings. A door slams. You may think you hear every word and every syllable uttered by the speaker—but in fact you do not. Many of the sounds are blotted out.

Even if you heard all the words, your ears could not immediately identify them. Many English words sound pretty much alike—for example *writer* and *rider, wave* and *waif.* Moreover, most of us are very careless about the way we pronounce words. We say not *I'm going to* but *I'm gonna,* not *Won't you* but *Woncha?,* not *Give me* but *Gimme.* Regional accents further confuse matters. Bostonians say not *Harvard* but *Havad.* Many Southerners say not *whether* but *whethah.*

Two psychologists once made high-fidelity tape recordings of some everyday conversations, then cut up the tapes so that they could play back separate portions—anything from a single word to longer phrases. Listeners to these excerpts had a hard time recognizing what they heard. When they listened to a single word, they failed to identify it more than half the time. Even when they heard a phrase three words long, they missed it nearly 30 percent of the time (Pollack & Pickett, 1964). What this shows is that making sense out of the sound waves that strike our ears is as difficult as trying to read a page on which paint has been splattered, making it impossible to recognize many of the words.

In listening we carry out many mental processes all at the same time. We simultaneously try to recognize sounds, identify words, look for syntactic patterns, and search for semantic meaning. When sounds and words are in themselves vague or unintelligible—as so often happens in everyday speech—the processing for syntax and semantics creates order out of chaos (Clark & Clark, 1977). All this takes place so smoothly that we are not even aware of the mental work we do when listening or the handicaps we overcome.

The Challenge to Schoolchildren with a "Different" Language

Many children growing up in homes where two languages are spoken learn rapidly to use both. During the second year of life, such children are already able to understand that a certain word in English has the same meaning as another word in the second language. One mother, for example, kept a diary describing her child, who was learning both English and Estonian. By the age of two, the child knew enough to use English when speaking to people outside the home, and Estonian while speaking to relatives inside (Vihman, 1985).

The United States, as a melting pot for people from all over the world and with many different language backgrounds, has always faced an important educational challenge. Today the challenge centers mostly on the Spanish-speaking population. We have more than 14 million citizens of Hispanic origin—including many children who have grown up in homes where only Spanish is spoken. These children—like their predecessors from homes where only Italian or German or Polish or Yiddish was spoken—often face serious difficulties in acquiring knowledge in English-speaking schools.

How can these children receive the American ideal of equal educational opportunity? One possible way—urged by many Spanish-speaking parents—is to have them taught in Spanish by Spanish-speaking teachers. It has been suggested that this should be done throughout the early grades of elementary school. Later, English would be introduced and taught as a second language (as many English-speaking American children are now taught Spanish or French). Even after the children began to learn English, they would con-

Exposure to two languages during childhood need not interfere with school success and, in some cases, may help it.

tinue to devote as much time to Spanish and Latin-American history and culture as to U.S. history and English literature.

The suggestion has considerable appeal. It would preserve a cultural heritage—that is, fluency in the language of origin and familiarity with the traditions and customs of the Spanish-speaking world. Especially for children in the early grades, it would avoid the dislocations and handicaps of attending schools that use an unfamiliar language—and possibly the loss of self-esteem caused by failure.

But to function fully and efficiently as members of our English-speaking society, all children must eventually become adept at English. And psychological findings raise some serious questions about delaying the process. Studies of children who spoke a dialect of Spanish and a little English, but who were expected to use English in their classrooms, show that they often had difficulty in making the switch—and that many became discouraged and left school (W. S. Hall, 1986). There is no evidence that growing up in a two-language home poses a problem for most children. In fact, economically disadvantaged children who learn both Spanish and English have a slight advantage in intellectual skills (Diaz, 1985). Moreover, as will be shown in the next section, the ability to pronounce unused phonemes decreases with age (Werker, 1989). Most people who acquire a new language after childhood never manage to speak it without an accent (Oyama, 1973), and learning a new language at all becomes more difficult.

It would seem that Spanish-speaking schools represent a trade-off, with certain advantages but also some dangers that would not be apparent without psychology's studies of language. The same findings apply to children from homes where American Indian languages are spoken, and also to black

TEST YOURSELF

c) With your skills of sensation intact, you can see the
person who is talking to
you, and you can hear
clearly every word spoken.
Is that enough for you to
understand what that per-
son is telling you?

children whose parents speak what is sometimes called "black English" as opposed to "standard English." Children initially taught the standard form of two languages may get off to a slow start, but they become attuned to the flexibility of language and do well over time (W. S. Hall, 1986).

How We Learn Language

Given all the mental processing necessary to understand and speak language, it seems miraculous that children learn to use it at all. Yet they do—and quickly.

Most infants begin to understand words late in the first year—many more, it is believed, than they are able to produce. Because parental reports of children's early word comprehension may not be accurate, one investigator devised a more objective technique. He showed infants pairs of slides containing, for example, a kitten and a tree, and then asked the tiny subjects: "Show me the kitty. Where is the kitty?" The investigator reasoned that if the infant responded by fixing her gaze on the slide containing the kitty, it would mean that she understood the word. The results showed that infants do, indeed, comprehend words early—with a steady increase from 8 to 20 months (Reznick, 1990).

By the end of their second year, many children are already speaking such sentences as "Baby drink milk." By the age of five, they understand the meaning of about 2,000 words (M. E. Smith, 1926). By about the age of six, they have learned virtually all the basic rules of grammar. They can string words together according to the rules to create meaningful new sentences of their own. And they understand the meaning of sentences they have never heard before. By the time they are 10, children are able to produce a veritable torrent of language—about 20,000 to 30,000 words each day (Wagner, 1985).

Along the way, too, children learn to make remarkably subtle interpretations of the language they hear. Until about the third year, children use language literally—that is, they use it to describe events in the real world. Moreover, they assume that other people who speak intend their words to have a literal meaning. For example, when the grandfather of one young child died, the youngster heard his mother say, "They're flying the body home tomorrow." His response was immediate: "What happened to Grandpa's head?" he asked. But by the fourth birthday, children begin to understand the nonliteral meanings of words and phrases, and by age six, some are expert even at appreciating irony. For example, when the child hears his father say "Boy, is this nice morning" as rain clouds gather, he has no problem understanding the intended meaning. To reach such sophisticated uses of language, however, requires a phenomenal amount of learning in a short time.

From Babbling to Language

Everything about the use of language must be learned except how to create the sounds, which is an inborn ability common to all normal children. Early in life, all babies begin to produce many sounds that resemble the phonemes of language—presumably because of movements of the muscles of the mouth, throat, and vocal cords associated with breathing, swallowing, and hiccupping. This "**babbling**" occurs spontaneously. It is not an attempt to

Babbling
The early sounds produced spontaneously by babies that resemble the phonemes of language.

imitate sounds that have been heard—as was demonstrated by observations of a deaf baby whose parents were deaf and mute. This baby never heard a sound yet did the same kind of babbling as any other child (Lenneberg, 1967).

It appears that children of all nationalities make the same sounds in their earliest babbling. For example, there are no differences among the babbling sounds of infants born to families that speak English, Russian, or Chinese (Atkinson, MacWhinney, & Stoel, 1970). American infants have been observed to utter sounds that are not used by English-speaking adults but only by people who speak French or German (G. A. Miller, 1951). Soon, however, babies begin to concentrate on the sounds appropriate to their own language, which they hear from their parents and others around them. The other sounds, not used in English, fade away through disuse. As shown in Figure 6.2, infants have a remarkable capacity to discriminate between syllables in a strange language, but adults have great difficulty with the same sounds, far removed from the ones they have been used to hearing and using (Werker, 1989). Thus, over the course of development, adults lose the ability they had as babies to discriminate certain phonemes.

As a result, those of us who try to learn foreign languages after we have grown up find the task quite difficult. Many of us who try to pick up French or German, for example, are never able to hear some of the phonemes properly, even though we may have done so quite naturally when we were babies.

How Human Interaction Affects Language Skills

As for how children learn all the many other things required for the use of language, psychologists have some clues and some theories—but as yet they have found no single and totally satisfactory explanation. Mere exposure without interaction—for example, exposure to television—does not appear to be enough (Snow et al., 1976; W. S. Hall, 1986). More important, are the everyday social interactions between adult and child. For example, while

Talking directly to the infant and responding to the baby's babbling contributes in an important way to the child's language development.

FIGURE 6.2 Infants can, but adults cannot Infants from six to eight months old were tested on their ability to discriminate two Hindi syllables not used in English and rare in the world's languages—one made with the tip of the tongue touching the front teeth, another made with the tongue curled under the palate. These infants from English-speaking families did nearly as well as Hindi-speaking adults. But English-speaking adults found the task extremely difficult (after Werker et al., 1981).

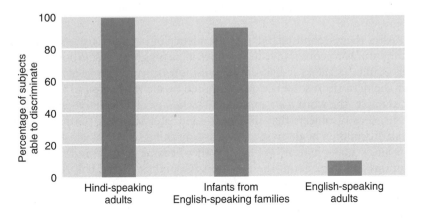

playing together, the more time a mother spends pointing out objects to her child, gesturing and talking about them, the greater the child's vocabulary is likely to be at 18 months (Smith, Adamson, & Bakeman, 1988).

In the interaction between child and mother or some other intimate caretaker, the two communicate from the very beginning. In speaking to their babies, mothers and other caretakers use a special tone of voice, rhythm, and style—called "motherese"—that seems to help stimulate linguistic development since it is especially well suited to the young infant's perceptual and attentional capacities (Fernald, 1983). When mothers of infants a few days old are asked to speak in this fashion without their children present, they actually speak quite differently (Fernald & Simon, 1984). The reciprocal interaction between caretaker and infant is evident beyond the opening months of life. It appears that mothers of toddlers follow their children's leads in using words that connote internal feeling states. For example, as toddlers begin to show a growing understanding of what it means to feel empathy and compassion toward others, their mothers begin to use words like "good" or "bad" more frequently (Lamb, 1991).

Partly as a result of such early interactions, and also, as a result of the child's own developing cognitive capacities, the child quickly acquires an understanding of the structure of language and a mastery of the processes of producing and understanding it (Gleitman, Newport, & Gleitman, 1984). Some of the steps are described in the Life Span Perspective box titled "Growth of Language in Babies and Toddlers."

LIFE SPAN PERSPECTIVE

Growth of Language in Babies and Toddlers

The first accomplishment of children is to speak a few meaningful single words that name objects: *baby, mama, milk*. A few months later, they begin to string two words together by adding a verb: *baby walk, see mama*. The average length of their utterances increases at a steady rate. Some children learn more quickly than others—but all normal children show consistent progress.

After their second birthday, the tendency of babies to use speech rather than gestures to communicate becomes increasingly strong (Shore, O'Connell, & Bates, 1984). Children's acquisition of words proceeds in concert with their efforts to solve the puzzles posed by the world around them. Thus, for example, the word *gone* appears only when a child begins to grapple with the mystery of objects that disappear—and later reappear (Gopnik, 1984). Similarly, children begin to speak words connoting success at a task ("there"), or failure ("no—oh, dear") only when they become aware of right and wrong solutions and think about these matters (Gopnik & Meltzoff, 1984).

In general, during the first two years, maturation of the brain is a major determinant of language development. There is no evidence of an infant under eight months old who could speak and understand words. Once the brain's growth permits language, environmental experiences begin to assume a greater role. It has been shown, for example, that the tendency of children in the second year of life to point to and to name objects such as a dog, cat, or pup is an outgrowth of interactions in the previous year with mothers who usually labeled objects in the environment as they interacted with their children (Goldfield, 1990). In another study of three- and four-year-old children from low-income families, it was found that children who are relatively good at narrating events in their experience were growing up in homes where their mothers interacted with them frequently and provided a great deal of information to their children in everyday conversation (Snow & Dickinson, 1990). ■

The Discovery of Grammar

Even at an early age, children acquire some of the rules of grammar practiced by the adults around them. At about the age of two, for example, children are likely to say such things as *gooses swimmed*. Even though the statement is not put correctly, it shows that they have learned something about the rules. They have discovered that ordinarily a noun can be made plural by adding an *s* and a verb can be turned into the past tense by adding an *ed*. We can hardly blame them for the fact that our language is not always consistent and decrees that the plural of goose is geese and the past tense of *swim* is *swam*.

Children learn the rules of grammar in a remarkably consistent pattern. Whether they are fast learners or slow, and regardless of the size or nature of their vocabularies, they seem to acquire their knowledge in a predictable order. In English, one of the first such morphemes is usually *ing*, added to a verb to denote an action going on at the moment. Somewhat later comes the addition of an -*s* to words to make them plural. And still later the use of an -'*s* to indicate possession. Most children learn to use some of the articles (*the, a, an*) before they add an *ed* to a verb to convey the past tense (R. Brown, 1973). In other languages the order may be different, but in general, the order of learning morphemes is determined by the distinctiveness of their sounds and the regularity with which they are used. The English sounds *ing* and '*s*, for example, satisfy both criteria, and, therefore, tend to be learned early (Slobin, 1985).

With minor variations, the first two-word utterances of children are similar regardless of whether they are learning to speak English, Russian, or Samoan (Slobin, 1971). Children usually put nouns before verbs ("mommy eat," not "eat mommy"), and verbs before objects ("throw ball," not "ball throw"). They seem to go about learning the rules in much the same way (Slobin, 1973)—with the ultimate aim of using them to make sense.

Theories to Explain Language Learning

At one time some psychologists believed that the manner in which language is learned could be explained fully in terms of operant conditioning. They thought that some of the sounds babies make in their early babbling are reinforced by their parents' smiles, fondling or other forms of approval. These sounds tended to be repeated. The same process of reinforcement was believed to account for the manner in which babies start to string sounds together into meaningful sentences (Skinner, 1957).

Later, some psychologists who became impressed by the importance of learning through observation proposed a different theory. They suggested that language is learned not through operant conditioning but through imitation of the way parents combine phonemes into meaningful morphemes, then string morphemes together into meaningful words and sentences.

Both these theories may account for some language learning, but neither offers a complete explanation. It is difficult to see how operant conditioning can lead children to acquire rules that will enable them to create new sentences of their own—especially since scientists have found that children may receive positive reinforcement in the form of approval for grammatically incorrect utterances that are factually right (*Mama isn't boy; he a girl*), and disapproval when their grammar is correct but the facts are wrong (*Walt Disney comes on Tuesday*). It is also difficult to see how imitation can result in completely new and original sentences—and in fact there is evidence that children who do very little imitating learn language just as well as children who do a lot of it (de Villiers and de Villiers, 1978).

Innate mechanism

The inborn wiring of the brain that allows humans to learn and use language, according to Noam Chomsky.

A totally different theory has been proposed by linguist Noam Chomsky. Chomsky suggests that the human brain is wired in such a way that we are born with some kind of **innate mechanism** for learning and using language (Chomsky, 1965). This innate mechanism enables us as children to do some rapid information processing on the language we hear from our elders. We quickly develop our own notions of how adults string sounds together to convey meaning. Later we modify and expand these notions as we get more experienced at communicating with others—and soon we are using the rules of grammar in such a sophisticated fashion that we can understand or express almost anything. The Chomsky theory holds that, in a sense, we cannot help learning language and using it the way we do. This is simply the way our brains operate—a behavior for which we are prepared by our biological inheritance. Just as fish are born to swim and moles to burrow, we are born to speak and understand language.

Do Apes Use Language?

Many attempts have been made in recent years to explore the question of whether any other animals, especially chimpanzees and other apes, may possibly share the human talent for language. One problem is that even the apes seem unable to use their vocal cords to make the sounds of human speech. Therefore experimenters have tried substitutes—for example, the sign language used by deaf people, which was the basis of an early study made by Beatrice and Allen Gardner with the chimpanzee named Washoe shown in Figure 6.3.

After about four years of training, Washoe had learned a vocabulary of more than 130 signs, including *you, please, cat, enough,* and *time.* Moreover, she could string the signs together into statements like *hurry gimme toothbrush* (Gardner & Gardner, 1972). She even made up a word of her own

FIGURE 6.3   A chimpanzee "talks" At the age of 2½, the chimpanzee named Washoe makes the sign language signal for "hat."

using the signs available to her—*water-bird* to describe a duck—almost as if she learned sign language in much the same way that a human child learns the spoken word.

Another approach was taken by David Premack with a chimpanzee named Sarah, who was taught to communicate by using symbols made of plastic cut into various shapes. The pieces each represented a word, and the words could be arranged in order on a magnetized board. Sarah learned the meanings of numerous words and sentences like *Mary give apple Sarah*. Once she understood the meaning of the words *take, dish,* and *red,* she obeyed a command expressed in a sentence she had never seen before: *Sarah take red dish* (Premack, 1976). Later, a four-year-old chimp named Kanzi demonstrated even more developed linguistic capacities (Savage-Rumbaugh et al., 1985). For example, in a limited way, Kanzi appeared capable of using symbols to identify ideas, and to request items such as food and drink that were out of his sight.

It is believed by most psychologists that there is a qualitative difference between the human capacity for communication and that of apes (Premack, 1985). That is the conclusion of Herbert Terrace, who conducted a long-term study of a chimpanzee playfully named Nim Chimpsky. Terrace began with high hopes of showing that Nim could acquire human facility with language. After five years, however, he reached the reluctant conclusion that most of Nim's communication was little more than a "subtle imitation" of his teachers, learned for the sake of obtaining rewards. There seemed to be no indication of any knowledge about syntax or of the human child's growing ability to produce longer and more complex messages.

TEST YOURSELF

d) Language development in the early years depends on two factors. The first is the growth of the brain. What is the second?

e) Jon says the communication between chimps is just as effective as that between humans. Mary says it is not. Who is right?

The Doubly Useful Words Called Concepts

One feature of our language deserves special attention because it makes possible our great flexibility in the use of words for both communication and information processing in general. This is the fact that only a few of the words we use are the names of specific, one-of-a-kind objects—for example, the planets Mars and Venus. Most words, on the contrary, represent whole groups of objects, events, actions, and ideas. Even a simple word like *water* means not only the colorless fluid in the glass we hold in our hands but also any somewhat similar substances anywhere, including the salty contents of the oceans and the raindrops that fall from the sky. The word *justice* represents many different abstract ideas held by people around the world at various times in history and embodied in various legal codes and practices.

Such words are called **symbolic concepts**—which can be defined roughly as mental representations of similarities between objects or events that we know are also different from one another. For example, to know the concept *water* is to know that the substances in drinking glasses, oceans, and raindrops, though they take different forms, are in fact similar in some basic way. Many kinds of similarities can contribute to the formation of concepts. Some concepts grow out of the physical attributes of objects as they appear to our senses—for example, similarities in the appearance of roses and tulips (*flowers*), the sound of a singing voice and a brass band (*music*), and the feel of a piece of paper and a windowpane (*smooth*). Some are based on similarities in relationships between physical attributes: *bigger* applies to such diverse pairs of objects as fly-to-gnat, adult-to-child, and Texas-to-Delaware, and *louder* applies to shout versus whisper or thunderclap versus shout. Other concepts take note of similarities in function. Dwelling, for example,

Symbolic concepts

The mental representations of the similarities between different objects and events.

These 3-year-olds in a Head Start program are learning letters of the alphabet while learning concepts for shapes.

embraces a one-family house, a high-rise apartment, a tepee, and an igloo. An abstract concept like *justice* lumps together events that share the idea that a person is treated fairly by an authority whether the person is a criminal and the authority is a judge, the person is a minority member and the authority is a state, or the person is a football player and the authority is a referee.

Whether or not two words or ideas are viewed as belonging to the same concept depends on the individual's knowledge and on the ability to detect an aspect of similarity (Murphy & Medin, 1985). Thus for a child, *robin* and *Paris* do not belong to a concept, but for many adults they are linked to the concept of spring.

Concepts Without Words: Perceptual Concepts

Though words that express concepts make up a large part of our vocabulary, concepts can be formed without any language. These are called **perceptual** *or* **schematic concepts,** an illustration of which is provided in Figure 6.4. Many experiments have shown that animals, which have no language, can acquire perceptual concepts of triangles and other qualities. Dogs obviously have some concept of *tree,* and will behave toward a tree they have never seen before just as they behave toward more familiar trees. Pigeons display a similar skill. For example, they can detect a tree in pictures of scenes containing a wide variety of trees (Herrnstein & de Villiers, 1980).

Many of our concepts are, of course, both symbolic and perceptual in nature. Thus, for example, our concept of a bird involves language—words such as *feathers, beak,* and *song*—along with perceptual representations of birds, including, for example, their shape and texture.

Perceptual (schematic) concepts

Concepts based on physical similarities instead of language.

How Language Enriches Our Concepts— and the Other Way Around

If language is not essential for acquiring concepts, however, it is certainly a great help. Much of our communication and thinking depends on words that represent complex concepts embedded within other concepts, in a way that would be impossible without language. Note, for example, the term *human being.* What the term means to us goes far beyond any physical attributes (two legs, erect posture, and so on) or functions (being students, working at jobs). We have a far richer concept of human being as the highest (which is itself a concept) of mammals (another concept)—a mammal being a particular kind of organism (still another concept) that produces (another) its young (another) inside (another) the body (another) of the mother (another), which nurses (another) the baby (another) after (another) birth (still another).

Language helps us find meanings, relationships, and similarities and thus build concepts on top of concepts. Without language, it would be difficult to find much resemblance between a two-legged human being walking on the land and a whale swimming in the ocean. Our concept word *mammal,* however, includes both of them.

Just as our language enriches our symbolic concepts, so do our perceptual concepts enrich our language. Concept words make it possible to use the 26 letters and 40-odd phonemes of the English language to express an

FIGURE 6.4 **It all adds up to a coffee mug** The perceptual concept of a coffee mug can entail representations of its shape and texture, as well as the smell and taste of the coffee, and even the direction one's hand takes to bring the mug from the table to the lips. All such representations, stored in various parts of the brain, are reconstructed instantaneously and "add up" to a coffee mug (adapted from Damasio & Damasio).

The emotion in our voices and faces enriches the sentences that people exchange with each other.

unlimited number of messages. Suppose we lacked the concept *people* and had to talk about each individual by a different and distinct name. Or we had no concept *dwelling* and had to use a different word for each place where someone lives—and the same for every item of furniture and food.

Concepts and Inferences

The use of both symbolic and perceptual concepts lends a tremendous variety and versatility to the kind of information processing we call thinking. When we encounter a new object or experience, we do not ordinarily have to deal with it as a unique event of which we have no prior knowledge and must learn about from scratch. Instead we can fit it into some already existing concept (Bruner, Goodnow, & Austin, 1956). A dog of a species we have never seen before is instantly recognizable as a dog. A strange new sculpture by a modern artist is immediately recognizable as a piece of art. Concepts "give our world stability. They capture the notion that many objects or events are alike in some important respect, and hence can be thought about and responded to in ways we have already mastered" (Smith & Medin, 1981).

One important way concepts help us think can be demonstrated by this example: Someone says to you, "There is a bird in Brazil called a cariama. Does it have wings?" Almost immediately, you answer, "Yes." You do not know this from your own experience, but have reached your answer through the useful form of thinking called **inference**—or drawing logical conclusions from facts already known. You have been told that a cariama fits into the concept bird. Your concept of bird includes the fact, previously learned and stored in memory, that birds have wings. Therefore it is reasonable to infer, even though you have never seen a cariama, that it too has wings.

The process of inference enables you to think about many matters without having any direct knowledge of the situation (Collins & Quillian, 1972). At the end of a long day's drive, you feel confident that you will find a motel room if you push on another 50 miles toward Atlanta. You can make this

Inference

A form of thinking in which a person comes up with an idea from a set of known facts.

inference because, even though you have never been there before, you know Atlanta is a big city and your concept of cities includes the presence of motels on their outskirts.

Our inferences are sometimes wrong. Suppose, for example, that the question about the Brazilian bird was, "Does a cariama fly?" Again you would probably answer yes, because your concept of birds includes flight. But there are a few birds that do not fly, and the cariama may just happen to be one of them.

Most of our inferences, however, are correct and valuable. Just as the rules of grammar enable us to generate sentences we have never spoken before and to understand sentences we have never heard before, so does the process of inference enable us to think about all kinds of matters we have never actually encountered. We can generalize about the new and unfamiliar from what we have observed about similar objects or events. Most of what we know—or think we know—is based on inference rather than on direct observation.

Concepts, Learning, and Memory

While reading these pages on concepts, you may have been reminded of the topic discussed in the previous chapter on memory—that is, the way categories help us organize information and encode it into long-term memory. Concepts are one of the ways language helps us learn and remember. They make possible all kinds of chunking and clustering that help us process information in short-term memory and encode it efficiently into a network of long-term memory.

As we acquire more information, we change our symbolic and perceptual concepts in many ways—refining or enlarging them and forming new ones. Out of our simplest concepts, like faces, food, and furniture, we build increasingly complex concepts that serve as high-level clusters of related information and ideas. Thanks to these new "and ever more complex combinations of simpler ideas," we can remember and "think about complex subject matter just about as easily and efficiently as we could previously think about simpler subject matter" (Wickelgren, 1981).

Language accounts to a great extent for the fact that learning builds on learning—or, in William James's words, that new items of information "cluster and cling like grapes to a stem." It does so both by helping us acquire concepts and giving us specific words that help us remember and think about specific details. It is difficult to imagine, for example, how a surgeon could be trained without all the words that medical science has developed over the years to describe the human body—some representing the general principles of how the body is put together and functions, others identifying specific anatomical structures. Effective surgery would probably be impossible without an "effective language" (Bross, 1973).

The relation between language and learning and memory is a two-way street. As one study stated, "Learning new words enables children to conquer new areas of knowledge, and these new areas enable them to learn new words, and so on" (Clark & Clark, 1977). This is one reason, unfortunately, that children from poorly educated families often have a difficult time in school, thus continuing a vicious circle that leads one generation after another to have trouble getting along in society. Children whose parents have very little formal education and use a limited vocabulary start school with a severe handicap. There are hundreds of words and concepts that they have never heard of but that are already familiar to children whose parents are better educated. They simply do not have the same kind of "effective language" that makes it easy to find similarities and relationships between the new information presented in school and their prior knowledge.

A Lingering Puzzle: What Exactly Is a Concept?

Though concepts play such a large and useful part in our learning and thinking, and have been studied extensively by psychologists and linguists, they continue to be something of a puzzle. The exact nature of concepts is not clear and there are a number of conflicting points of view.

One view, suggested by Eleanor Rosch, is that from our observations of events in the world we form a notion of a typical bird (or vegetable or fruit or anything else). Based on both symbolic and perceptual concepts, for most Americans, the typical bird seems to be a robin—which is rather small, has two short legs and two wings, flies, sits in trees, and sings. Then we lump other living creatures into our prototype of bird, or reject them, depending on how much family resemblance they bear to our typical bird, the robin. We know immediately that thrushes and song sparrows, which are very similar to robins, fit into our concept of birds. We need a little more time to decide that a chicken is a bird, because it is a good deal larger than a robin and does not fly or sit in trees (Rosch & Mervis, 1975).

Sometimes, Rosch has pointed out, the boundary lines for family resemblances are extremely "fuzzy." Therefore we may have trouble deciding whether a bat fits the concept of bird or animal and whether a tomato is a vegetable or a fruit (Rosch, 1973). The same "fuzziness" in the way we form concepts makes it difficult to classify an 18-year-old female as a girl or a woman, and rheumatism as a disease or something else. Our concepts and categories—and indeed our thinking in general—are not always as neat as we would like them to be. But perhaps this simply reflects the fact that our world does not readily match the concepts we invent and is not, therefore, easy to describe in cut-and-dried terms.

Sometimes we rely on factors other than family resemblances to establish what is typical—including the degree to which the item represents an ideal, or how often we encounter it (Barsalou, 1985). The typical food to be eaten while on a diet, for example, is not determined by its physical features but by notions about the ideal diet food in that category or the frequency with which it occurs.

It appears that we are more apt to notice similar features in things that are in many ways dissimilar when our information is symbolic—that is, verbal—rather than visual. In one experiment, when subjects were asked to read pairs of sentences about Eskimos and Americans, they judged the two groups to be more similar than when they were asked to look at pictures of the two types of people (Gati & Tversky, 1984). Because a concept contains a "bundle" of features, the specific ones we pick out and use will change with the situation—as is illustrated in Figure 6.5.

FIGURE 6.5 "Hot"—what does the concept mean? As illustrated here, the concept "hot" contains features that vary from one context to another. For example, it can mean overheated, "cool," or on a winning streak.

Does Language Shape Our View of the World—or Vice Versa?

One of the interesting questions about language and thinking is this: Is it possible that language restricts our information-processing abilities? Does it perhaps serve as a pair of faulty eyeglasses through which we get only a limited and sometimes distorted view of the world?

A prominent language theorist, Benjamin Whorf, suggested that people who use different languages have very different ways of looking at the world and different concepts about the similarities and relationships that it displays. In studying many languages, Whorf found one group of American Indians who lump together with a single word things that fly—insects, airplanes, and even airplane pilots. He found other languages that do not have any devices for distinguishing the past, present, and future tenses of verbs (Whorf, 1956). In Whorf's view, such differences are bound to affect the way people who speak these languages conceive the world, organize it, and think about it.

This is an intriguing theory—and it seems to receive a certain amount of support from some of the matters discussed in the last few pages. The trained surgeon, with an "effective language" of anatomy, looks at and thinks about the human body differently from the rest of us. Children who start school with impoverished vocabularies probably conceive of the world in more limited fashion than their more fortunate classmates. It would appear that information processing can be influenced not only by the use of different languages but also by differences in the vocabularies of people who speak the same language.

There is a great deal of evidence, however, that language is usually tailored to human thinking, rather than vice versa. Among all the many languages of the world, there are more basic similarities than differences. Certainly on the matter of the physical objects and everyday events found in the world, people everywhere seem to perceive them, find names for them, organize them into concepts and categories, and think about them in ways that are often very similar.

Some colors, for example, seem particularly striking—doubtless because of the way the sense organs of the eye and the process of perception operate. And, though languages differ in the number of colors for which they have names, the names usually refer to the colors that "hit the eye," like red and yellow, not to all the many other hues and shades found in nature (Kay, 1975). Similarly, most languages have terms for shapes that human perception seems to find compelling, such as squares and circles. Most languages also have terms for basic emotions like fear and anger, for dimensions of objects like height and length, and for distance and direction (Clark & Clark, 1977).

Rosch has suggested that our concepts about the physical world are based on what is actually "out there" in nature. That is to say, they are molded by and reflect the physical realities of the environment. Objects just naturally fall into groups like birds and animals, vegetables and fruits—and our language acknowledges this fact (Rosch, 1977). Our brains are wired to notice certain attributes of the objects and events we encounter—and family resemblances in these attributes form the basis of our concepts.

How New Thinking Yields New Language

Another indication that language is tailored to human thinking is the fact that language changes when people's thinking changes. Note, for example, all the new words that football has created while developing to its present highly technical level. There were no such terms in the English language, even a few years ago, as *cornerback, noseguard,* and *safety blitz.* All grew out of the need to find new terms for new concepts developed by inventive coaches.

Designing circuitry on a computer demands a specialized vocabulary.

When we need a new word, we coin it—or borrow it from another language. (Many everyday "English" words are borrowed—*goulash* from Hungarian, *whiskey* from Gaelic, *sabotage* from French.) And as additions to the language become more and more widely used, we often shorten them to make them more convenient (Zipf, 1949). Thus the original term *moving picture* has been condensed to *movie, gasoline* to *gas, telephone* to *phone.* Specialists in certain areas of knowledge, such as surgeons, coin or borrow their own vocabulary and often engage in their own form of shortening terms for simplicity and convenience.

All in all, though thinking may in some ways be molded and limited by language, as Whorf has pointed out, the human brain seems remarkably capable of adapting this useful tool to its own advantage. One study stated: "Apparently when people lack a word for a useful concept, they soon find one. . . . What this suggests is that language differences reflect the culture and not the reverse" (Clark & Clark, 1977). The moral for all of us is that we have in language a tool of virtually infinite possibilities—limited, for all practical purposes, only by how well we learn to handle it.

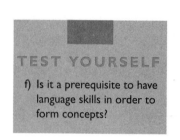

TEST YOURSELF

f) Is it a prerequisite to have language skills in order to form concepts?

Thinking and Problem Solving

Sometime when you are engaged in thinking—about anything at all, from your plans for the next meal to your ideas about religion and politics—stop yourself and examine what kind of process has been going on. Most likely you will find you have been talking to yourself—thinking through the use of language, and especially words that represent concepts.

Thinking is one of those terms that everybody understands but nobody quite knows how to define. It is probably best described as the "mental manipulation of information." In the learning and memory stages of information processing, we build a store of knowledge about the objects and events we have encountered—a sort of mental representation of the world and the way it operates. In the thinking stage, we process this inner representation in various ways to add to our understanding of the world and solve the problems it presents. Our thinking is often entirely independent of physical objects and actual events. We can think about objects that are not present at the moment (like an architect planning a house that does not yet exist), about events that occurred in the past (a childhood birthday party), or about abstract concepts that have no physical reality at all (religion and politics).

We think about many things in different ways. As we observe the world around us, we seek to find some kind of order in its objects and events. We look for meanings and relationships that enable us to form concepts and categories. As we accumulate more knowledge, these concepts change and become more and more refined and elaborate. The mind, it has been said, is constantly working on its knowledge (Bowerman, 1974)—trying to understand and absorb the new and revising the old in light of the new.

Thinking
The mental manipulation of information.

Some Tools of Thinking: Rules and Premises

Among the important pieces of information we process during our thinking are the rules that govern the relationships and interactions among the objects and events in the environment—in other words, the facts we have learned about the way the world operates. We have learned from experience that water, if heated enough, will boil and turn to steam. We have also discovered that an egg placed in boiling water will start to turn hard, and if left long enough will become hard-boiled. In thinking about cooking, these are some of the rules we manipulate.

Some of the rules we use come from our own observations—that is, from the kind of pragmatic, everyday experience that helps us reason and solve problems (Cheng, 1985). Others represent the pooled observations of many people—the kinds of information found in our libraries. When we think about the sky and the solar system, we utilize astronomy's rule that the moon revolves around the earth and the earth and other planets revolve around the sun. When we think about the distance around a circular lake that we know to be a half mile wide, we use the mathematician's rule that the circumference equals the diameter (here .5 mile) times π (3.1416).

We also base much of our thinking on what are called **premises,** or basic beliefs that we accept even though they cannot be proved. The line between a premise and a rule is often hazy and difficult to draw, for many generally accepted beliefs may not really be true. It is universally believed, for example, that no object can be in two places at the same time—even though modern physics teaches that the tiniest particles of matter, called "photons" can indeed accomplish this fact. In other areas of science, too, such ideas as the theory of evolution and many advanced mathematical theories are still only premises, though they are in accord with the best observations currently possible and have at least a certain claim to validity.

Many premises are the result of individual experience. They are not necessarily based on objective observation, and they vary greatly from one person to another. Some of us, from what we have observed, believe that most people are honest—and much of our thinking about other people is based on this firmly held premise. Others hold just as firmly to the premise that most people are dishonest. Some think and act on the premise that it is wise to keep one's nose to the grindstone, others on the premise that all work and no play makes Jack a dull boy.

Premises
The basic beliefs that are accepted and used in thinking even though they cannot be proved.

Logical and Illogical Ways of Thinking

When you express an opinion and explain why you have reached it, a friend may say, "That's logical. I agree." Or, on the contrary, "Your logic is wrong. I disagree." Logical thinking means drawing conclusions that follow inescapably from the rules we have learned and the premises we have adopted. Suppose, for example, you are a contestant on a quiz show and are asked this question: *Does a whale nurse its young?* If you had learned the rule that all mammals nurse their young, and if you knew that a whale is a mammal, it would follow logically that, yes, a whale must nurse its young.

Illogical thinking, in contrast, means drawing conclusions that are not justified by such evidence as rules, facts, and premises. For example, a young woman may decide to become a schoolteacher as a result of this line of thought: "My mother says she was extremely happy when she was teaching. Therefore I will be happy teaching." Her thinking is illogical because she may have very different interests and talents from her mother's and the teaching profession may have changed in the meantime. A man with a stomachache takes a pill that was once prescribed for a friend, thinking, "The pill helped him, and therefore it will help me." But his stomachache may have an entirely different cause, and may be worsened by the medicine.

When we accuse people of being illogical, we are often incorrect. Their logic is perfectly sound, granted their premises, and it is the premises that we disagree with. Was it illogical for Christopher Columbus's critics to believe he would fall off the earth if he kept sailing west? No, for they based their reasoning on the premise that the earth was flat—and, if so, Columbus's ships would indeed fall off like plates pushed to the edge of a table. Their logic was right but their premise was wrong, because the earth is not flat. There is evidence that many people do not apply the same logical rules of reasoning in every situation; instead, much depends on the subject matter at hand. Thus, for example, a person might reason correctly about the economy, but not about crime. An individual's prior knowledge and beliefs vary from one issue to another—and thus the content at hand typically affects the line of reasoning (Gigerenzer & Hug, 1992).

Many arguments and misunderstandings among diplomats and nations as well as between friends and family are caused not so much by fallacies in logical thinking as by starting from different premises. One economist, using flawless logic, may conclude that taxes should be raised. An equally brilliant economist, using equally flawless logic, may conclude that taxes should be lowered. One person decides, after much reasonable thought, that capital punishment is wrong. Another person, after equal consideration, decides it is essential. Which of the opinions on the economy and on capital punishment is right and which is wrong? We cannot really say, because we have no way of establishing the validity of the premises on which they are based.

We cannot be sure that a premise is wrong unless it clearly violates the truth, and this is seldom the case. We know for a fact, as the navigators of Columbus's time did not know, that the earth is spherical rather than flat. If a man claims to be Napoleon, we know he is unquestionably wrong and we doubt his sanity. But mostly we hold our premises more or less on faith. We can agree or disagree with another person's premises but cannot usually prove them right or wrong. Thus people whose thought processes are totally logical can reach entirely different conclusions.

Using Algorithms and Heuristics

Problem solving

The form of thinking directed toward the solution of a problem.

Algorithm

(AL-go-rith-m) A problem-solving technique that produces a correct solution by following a series of steps.

Much human thinking is directed at **problem solving,** the attempt to cope with the innumerable problems faced by all human beings. Some practical suggestions on this subject are provided in the Psychology in Action box titled "Taking Steps to Solve a Problem."

The most effective overall strategy, when it is available, is to use what is called an **algorithm.** The word originally was used to describe mathematical formulas and procedures—which of course guarantee a correct solution to any problem that deals with numbers, provided we understand the problem and know the proper algorithm to apply. The term has now been broadened to include any specific technique that can be followed step by step and will produce a correct solution without fail. An example would be the problem of calling a friend who is not listed in the phone book. You know the number begins 445-57—but have forgotten the last two digits. You can use an algo-

Taking Steps to Solve a Problem

As a student, you must solve not only the theoretical problems in your math courses but also many everyday problems. You have a certain number of dollars available for tuition, books, clothes, housing, food, and entertainment. How can you best allot the dollars to these expenses? A person starting a long automobile trip must ask: What highways will provide the best route? How can the trip best be broken up into how many days on the road? A mechanic looking at a stalled automobile must ask: What is wrong? How can I fix it?

Many studies have been made of problem solving—the traps to avoid and the most effective ways to go about it. One finding is that the process requires four distinct steps. These steps should be undertaken whether you understand them or not, and knowing about them is one way to improve your skill (Wessels, 1982).

1. *Define the problem.* Clarify in your own mind the nature of the problem you are addressing and the solution or goal that you seek.
2. *Devise a strategy.* Come up with a plan of attack that shows reasonable promise of reaching the goal.
3. *Carry out the strategy.* This is best done by calling on any rules and other knowledge that may be useful and by avoiding distractions and focusing attention on the task.
4. *Evaluate progress toward the goal.* It is essential to stop from time to time to see if you are getting closer to the solution and should continue with your strategy or switch to a different approach.

Although these steps may at first blush strike you as obvious, it is surprising how often we impulsively bypass them—and thus become embroiled in activities that deplete our energies and delay the resolution of a problem.

---

rithm by trying every possible number from 445-5700 through 445-5799. The method may keep you busy for a long time—especially if the correct number turns out to be 445-5799—but it cannot fail.

For most of the problems we face, no algorithm is available and we have to rely instead on what are called **heuristics.** These are rules of thumb—approaches that have worked for us in the past, in somewhat similar situations, and may work again, though there is no guarantee. A driver who comes to a fork in an unfamiliar country road, while trying to get to a town known to be somewhere toward the west, chooses the path that seems from the position of the sun to head more westerly—though it may later curve and turn south. A chess player, who cannot possibly predict all the possible moves in the game, follows the rule of thumb of trying to control the center of the board—which does not guarantee winning but usually helps.

Heuristics
(hu-RIS-tiks) A problem-solving technique that has worked in similar situations in the past but does not guarantee success in all kinds of situations.

Trap 1 in Problem Solving: Failure to Analyze the Problem

One of the most common dangers we face in our efforts to solve problems is the failure to analyze the situation thoroughly—to jump to an incorrect view of the nature of the problem and the possible solution. This trap is beautifully illustrated by the experiment shown in Figure 6.6, which you should try for yourself before going on to the next paragraph.

The problem presented in the figure is fairly simple—yet few people manage to solve it. The answer is that you must turn over cards 1 and 3. If

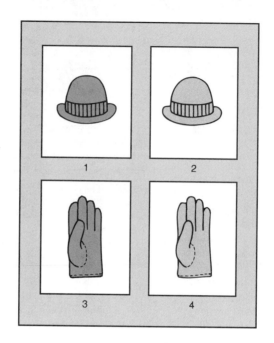

FIGURE 6.6 Can you solve this problem? The four cards, which have symbols on both sides, lie on a table so that you can see them as shown here. You are told that each card has on one side a hat, which may be either blue or gray, and on the other side a glove, which also may be either blue or gray. You are asked to prove or disprove this statement: *Every card that has a blue hat on one side has a gray glove on the other side.* How many cards—and which ones—would you have to turn over to find out whether the statement is true or false? For the answer, see the text (after Wason, 1971).

card 1 has a blue glove on the back, or if card 3 has a blue hat on the back, then the statement you are asked to prove or disprove is false. But if card 1 has a gray glove on the back, and card 3 has a gray hat on the back, then the statement is true.

Most people insist that the cards to turn over are 1 and 4. But in fact card 4 has no bearing on the problem. Regardless of whether the hat on the back is blue or gray, this card cannot prove or disprove the statement. The reason people tend to fall into the error of picking this card seems to be that they take too much for granted in reading the problem. From the statement given in the experiment, *Every card that has a blue hat on one side has a gray glove on the other side,* they assume that it is also true that every card that has a gray glove on one side must have a blue hat on the other side. But this has never been stated and is not part of the problem. The psychologist who devised the experiment made many similar studies and found that most people have this tendency to jump to unwarranted assumptions about the nature of the problem (Wason, 1971). The tendency is most pronounced when the task at hand is unfamiliar, but less so when it relates to our own interests.

Trap 2: Thinking What You Are Prepared to Think

Closely allied to the error of failing to analyze the problem and making unwarranted assumptions is the fact that we sometimes tend to let our personal biases get in the way. We try hard—and sometimes against all the weight of evidence and logic—to find the answer we would like to find (Metcalfe, 1986). The ways this tendency can affect problem solving has been demonstrated by the experiment shown in Figure 6.7. Try it yourself before going on to the next paragraph.

Not every subject solved the problem, of course. But the interesting development was the difference between those who succeeded and those

FIGURE 6.7 The problem of the dishonest coin salesman Here is a problem posed to students taking an introductory psychology course:
A stranger approached a museum curator and offered him an ancient bronze coin. The coin had an authentic appearance and was marked with the date 544 B.C. The curator had happily made acquisitions from suspicious sources before, but this time he promptly called the police and had the stranger arrested. Why?
On a scale of 1 to 10, how sure are you that you know the correct answer? Now decide on an answer. After you have done so, see the text and Figure 6.8 for the correct answer—plus the results of the experiment and what they tell us about a trap in problem solving.

who failed in their degree of confidence that they were onto the correct solution. On the average, those who felt more certain about the answer were less likely to be right, as Figure 6.8 shows. We all have a tendency to reach conclusions based on our instincts of the moment and on what we would prefer to be the case. Seeing a problem the way we would like does not always lead to the best solution.

Trap 3: Functional Fixedness

Another tendency we all share is to get into a rut in our view of the world and the way it operates. In particular, we tend to think of an object as functioning only in a single way—and therefore to ignore its other possible uses. This pitfall, called **functional fixedness,** is best demonstrated in the famous old

Functional fixedness
The tendency to think of an object in terms of its usual functions rather than other possible functions.

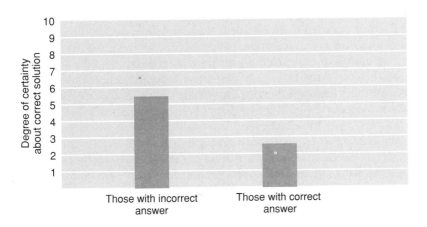

FIGURE 6.8 Dead certain? Dead wrong. The correct answer to the problem is that the coin could not have been authentic because it would have been impossible for someone who had actually lived in 544 B.C. to know that eventually the calendar would change to mark a date that itself was still 544 years in the future. The date is a giveaway. Note that those students who got it wrong were more likely to say that they were certain they had the right answer (after Metcalfe, 1986).

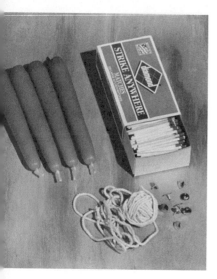

FIGURE 6.9 **Problem: how to mount the candle on a door so it won't drip on the floor** These were the objects used in an experiment described in the text. Subjects were asked to figure out a way to turn them into an improvised candle stand. Try it yourself before looking at Figure 6.10 for an illustration of how it can be done.

FIGURE 6.10 **The candle stand solution** The problem posed in Figure 6.9 can be solved only by finding an unusual way of using the box that held the matches. Just use the thumbtacks to fasten it to the door—and, lo, you have a candle stand to catch the drippings.

experiment illustrated in Figure 6.9. Examine the figure and see if you can solve the problem before you read on to the next paragraph. The problem is especially difficult when you have only a photograph and cannot actually manipulate the objects—but, with effort and luck, you may find the answer.

The problem can be solved, as you will see when you turn to Figure 6.10, only by forgetting about the way a box is ordinarily used. You have to empty the box of all the matches, tack it to the door, and turn it into your candle stand. Though this seems simple enough once you know it, fewer than half the subjects thought of it when the experiment was first performed (Duncker, 1945).

Functional fixedness reduces our efficiency at solving many everyday problems. A nail file is for filing nails—and we may completely overlook the possibility of using it to tighten a screw and thus repair a broken lamp. A goldfish bowl is for holding fish—and the first person who converted one into a terrarium for growing house plants had to break some powerful old associations.

Functional fixedness is one form of a more general phenomenon called **persistence of set.** Over the years we develop a mental set toward problems—that is, our own habitual way of approaching them. We tend to follow the same approach even in situations where other methods would be more appropriate. One almost sure way to improve our ability to solve new problems is to work at greater flexibility by trying at the very start to think of several possible ways to define the problem and the goal, as well as a number of different strategies that might work.

Trap 4: Relying Solely on Information Readily Available

The fourth common pitfall is best explained by indulging in a bit of fantasy. Suppose your life depends on a modern-day version of one of those old mythical tests—like slaying a dragon—devised by a king seeking a worthy heir to his throne. The test is this: The king pulls a book from his library shelves. He turns at random to a page and circles the first word he finds that either begins with an *r* (like *road*) or has *r* as its third letter (like *carpenter*). You have to guess which. If you are right, the kingdom is yours. If you are wrong, off with your head.

How would you go about deciding? Most people, it has been found, start by trying to figure the odds. They see how many words they can recall that begin with an *r*, then how many they can recall with *r* as the third letter. They find it much easier to think of words starting with *r*, decide the chances are heavily weighted in that direction—and make the wrong guess. As it happens, there are more words in which *r* is the third letter rather than the first. But we pay much more attention to the first letter than any other when encoding words into memory, and therefore words like *road* and *rock* are more readily available than words like *cork* and *farm* (Tversky & Kahneman, 1973).

Much of our real-life thinking and problem solving also depend on the availability of information we have stored in memory. Recent events are likely to have an especially strong influence on our thinking—sometimes unduly. A good example comes from the world of sports, where we are often influenced by what we know about the recent performance of athletes. Both basketball

Boats use flags as symbols to communicate with one another.

players and fans believe that a player's chances of making a shot are greater if he has just made one than if he has just missed. But the actual records of players on two professional teams show that this belief in a player's "hot hand" or "streak shooting" is not supported by the facts (Gilovich, Vallone, & Tversky, 1985). We are also more influenced by an event that has a personal impact than by something we read in a newspaper. (A homeowner is more likely to buy additional fire insurance after watching a neighbor's house burn down than after watching televised fires in other parts of the city.)

Our reliance on the most readily available information often serves a useful purpose, because by and large our memory operates to make the most important information the easiest to recall. But there are times when relying on the readily available prevents us from solving a problem or causes an error (Tversky & Kahneman, 1973). Note this common occurrence: If we associate with people who lean strongly toward a certain lifestyle and opinions, we may accept their judgment as the representative wisdom of all humanity—and be influenced accordingly in important decisions about career, purchases, marriage, and morals. In actual fact, their behavior and beliefs may be just a minority phenomenon that is not typical of most people—and not at all suitable for us.

As in the case of functional fixedness, the availability pitfall can be avoided by being flexible in approaching the problem. Somewhere in your memory storehouse you have many kinds of information that might help. The first information that comes to mind, as you start searching your memory may or may not help. You may do better to stop and think: What other information do I have that bears on the problem? How can I think about the problem in a way that will help me find this other information? Thinking, as has been said, is the manipulation of information—and, in problem solving, the more we manipulate the information the better.

Persistence of set

The tendency in problem-solving to develop a mental set that leads to solving problems in a habitual way.

TEST YOURSELF

g) If you were lost in the forest in the late afternoon, and you looked at the position of the sun in the sky in order to head east toward safety, what kind of problem-solving rule would you be using?

h) Your friend is trying to open a bottle of soda but cannot locate an opener. So he gives up the idea of a drink—despite the fact that he is standing at the sink and could use the side of the sink to open the bottle. Your friend's behavior is an example of what pitfall in problem solving?

SUMMARY REVIEW

The Function and Structure of Language

1. Language is a uniquely human activity made possible by the structure and dynamics of the human brain.
2. The basic function of language is **communication.** It enables us to exchange an unlimited number and variety of messages and pass knowledge along from one generation to the next.
3. Language also helps us acquire information (by providing labels for the objects and events in the environment), to encode information into memory, and to think and solve problems.
4. The building blocks of language are the basic sounds called **phonemes.** English has about 40 phonemes, and no language has more than 85.
5. Phonemes are combined into meaningful sounds called **morphemes,** which may be words, prefixes, or suffixes. English has more than 100,000 morphemes, which are combined in turn to produce more than 600,000 words.
6. **Semantics** is the meaning of a language's morphemes and words.
7. Every language has two essential elements:
   a) a **vocabulary** (or set of morphemes and words with meanings dictated by semantics)
   b) a **grammar** (or set of rules for putting morphemes and words together).
8. An important part of grammar is the rules of **syntax,** which govern sentence structure.
9. **Pragmatics** refers to the social purposes of language, and acknowledges that the actual meaning of what we say may depend largely on the situation in which we say it.

Generating Messages—and Comprehending Them

10. When we produce sentences, we must:
    a) think of the meaning we wish to convey
    b) plan each sentence and part of a sentence
    c) find the right words to flesh out our thoughts
    d) put the words in their proper order.
11. In listening, we carry out many mental processes all at the same time. We simultaneously try to recognize sounds, identify words, look for syntactic patterns, and search for semantic meaning.
12. When we listen to speech, the individual sounds and words are often vague or unintelligible but our information processing makes order out of chaos—so smoothly that we are not even aware of the mental work we do or the handicaps we overcome.

How We Learn Language

13. Children display a remarkable ability to learn language. At the age of two most children speak three-word sentences; at five they understand the meaning of about 2,000 words; at six they have acquired virtually all the basic rules of grammar; and at 10 they are able to produce a veritable torrent of language—about 20,000 to 30,000 words each day.

14. Everything about the use of language must be learned except the inborn ability to create sounds. In early infancy, the use of sounds that resemble the phonemes of language are called **babbling.**

15. In learning language, the crucial factor appears to be communication and interaction between child and mother, or some other intimate care-taker.

16. In general, during the first two years of development, maturation of the brain is a major determinant of language development. During the later years, environmental experiences assume a greater role.

17. Learning the rules of grammar appears to proceed in much the same fashion for babies the world over, regardless of what language they are learning to speak.

18. Some theorists have suggested that language is learned through operant conditioning, others that it is acquired through observation, learning, and imitation. In contrast, Noam Chomsky has proposed the theory that the human brain is wired in such a way that we have an **innate mechanism** for learning and using language.

19. At one time it was thought that apes are capable of using sign language in much the same way human beings use words. More recent evidence, however, suggests that their abilities are very limited.

The Doubly Useful Words Called Concepts

20. Only a few words are names of specific, one-of-a-kind objects. Most are **symbolic concepts,** which can be defined roughly as mental representations of similarities between objects or events that are also different from one another.

21. Some concepts are based on similarities between physical attributes. Some are based on similarities in relationships between physical attributes (*bigger, louder*), and some on similarities in function (*dwelling, furniture*). Concepts like justice and religion lump together abstract ideas that are in some way similar.

22. Young babies and animals can acquire some concepts without language—but language enables us to build concepts on top of concepts and adds tremendous variety and versatility to our thinking and communication.

23. Our knowledge of concepts enables us to make useful **inferences** by drawing logical conclusions about new and unfamiliar objects and events from what we already know.

24. Many concepts represent categories, or groupings that help us organize information and encode it into long-term memory.

25. A number of theories have been proposed to explain the exact nature and formation of concepts. Eleanor Rosch has suggested that from our observations of the world we form a notion of a typical object—for example, a robin that seems to be a typical bird—then lump other creatures into our concept of bird, or reject them, depending on how much family resemblance they show to a robin.

26. Benjamin Whorf has suggested that people who use different languages have different ways of looking at the world, organizing it, and thinking about it. There is considerable evidence, however, that we tailor our language to our thinking, adding new words whenever we need them.

Thinking and Problem Solving

27. **Thinking,** defined as *the mental manipulation of information*, can be accomplished without language—but language is chiefly responsible for the fact that our thinking is independent of physical objects and events and can range widely in space and time.

28. Among the important pieces of information we use in our thinking are the rules we have learned that govern the relationships and interactions among objects and events.

29. We also base our thinking on **premises,** which are basic beliefs that we accept even though they cannot be proved.

30. The most effective strategy in problem solving is an **algorithm**—a mathematical formula or other procedure that will guarantee a correct solution if followed step by step.

31. When an algorithm is not available, we use **heuristics** or rules of thumb that have worked in similar situations and may work again.

32. Traps in problem solving include:
    a) failure to analyze the problem
    b) thinking what you are prepared to think
    c) functional fixedness
    d) relying on the most readily available information.

33. The pitfalls can often be avoided by greater flexibility in analyzing a problem, thinking of several possible ways to define the problem and the goal, seeking a number of different strategies that might work, and searching memory for additional information that may help (instead of concentrating solely on the most readily available information).

TEST YOURSELF ANSWERS

a) It is a phoneme—one of the many basic sounds that are the building blocks of language.

b) They regulate the way words are placed in proper order to form phrases—and the way these phrases are combined to form sentences. Without rules of syntax, language would be incomprehensible.

c) It would not be enough. To understand speech, you must carry out the varied perceptual and cognitive tasks—for example, recognition, understanding, interpretation—involved in information processing.

d) The second is the child's environment—specifically, exposure to language in interactions with mother and other adults.

e) Mary is likely to be right. While there are some points of similarity between chimp communication and human language, there is little evidence that chimps can learn syntax, for example, or produce complex messages.

f) It is not. Language is the basis for our symbolic concepts—words that connote our mental representations of distinct classes of objects or events. But we are also capable of developing concepts without words—called perceptual concepts—through a sensory awareness of the attributes of a class of objects.

g) You would be using a heuristic—that is, a rule of thumb or an approach that has worked for you in the past in similar situations.

h) It is an example of functional fixedness—the tendency we have to get into a rut in our view of the world and of how things operate.

Study Guide

Chapter 6 Language and Thought

LEARNING OBJECTIVES

After studying this chapter, you should be able to:

1. Recognize that the human ability to use language probably depends on the special structure and dynamics of the human brain and is a uniquely human behavior that requires active communication and interaction with another speaker.

For an Understanding of the Science

2. Discuss that the building blocks of the English language are its approximately 40 basic sounds called phonemes and that these are combined into more than 100,000 meaningful units called morphemes, which are words or can be combined with one another to form words.

3. Recognize that every language must have a vocabulary of meaningful sounds and words (its semantics) and a set of rules for combining words into sentences (its grammar), an important part of which are the rules of syntax that govern sentence structure.

4. Understand the complex mental processes required for the use of language, the special problems of the speaker and listener, and the active processing needed for speech comprehension.

5. Discuss that children from different language environments seem to babble and learn the rules of grammar in roughly similar ways, and describe the pros and cons of the theories of language acquisition based on operant conditioning, learning through observation, or Chomsky's "innate mechanism."

6. Describe how language and thinking are related and how human thinking both affects and is affected by language. Recognize the special importance of concepts in acquiring new information, storing it in memory, and using it effectively.

7. Discuss the types of thinking called inference and problem solving.

8. Describe how language serves as a tool of virtually infinite possibilities, limited only by how well we learn to handle it. Recognize how language helps learning build on learning—how acquiring a large effective or working language enables us to acquire more easily new concepts and knowledge, which, in turn, enables us to learn new words and concepts more easily.

For Application to Life Situations

9. Understand the steps in problem solving and the common traps people fall into when trying to solve problems.

PROGRAMMED UNIT
THE FUNCTION AND STRUCTURE OF LANGUAGE

1. *Language* is a communication system that enables human beings to exchange an almost infinite variety of messages. Although other animals

language

language

communication

can communicate with one another, human beings alone can convey an almost endless number of messages through _____.

2. *Communication* is the basic function of _____.

3. We intend to influence people with language—to inform, warn, order, and question them, for example. These purposes all serve the _____ function of language. The building blocks of the English language are about 40 basic sounds called *phonemes*.

phonemes

4. In our language "ah" and "th" are basic sounds and are among the _____ of English.

phonemes

5. These _____ are combined into meaningful sounds—words, prefixes, and suffixes—called *morphemes*.

morphemes

6. *Hat, pre,* and *ed* are called _____.

phonemes
morphemes

7. English has about 40 elementary meaningless _____ and more than 100,000 meaningful basic _____.

communication

8. Every language must have two essential elements for _____ to take place. The first is a *vocabulary*—the meaningful morphemes and words of our language.

vocabulary

9. The morphemes and words of English constitute its _____, but we also must agree on the meaning of those morphemes, called *semantics*.

semantics

10. Every speaker of a language must understand and agree on the meaning or _____ of words.

language

11. The second essential element of a _____ is its *grammar*—the set of rules for combining words together into an almost infinite number of sentences.

grammar

12. Among the most important rules of _____ are those called *syntax*, which relate to sentence structure.

syntax

13. The rules governing the manner in which nouns, verbs, adjectives, and adverbs are placed in proper order to form phrases and the way the phrases are combined into sentences that convey a meaning readily understood by anyone who speaks the language composes the _____ of a language.

syntax

14. In English, an adjective is placed before a noun (for example, "red house"); in French, the adjective is placed after the noun ("maison rouge"), which illustrates a difference between the languages in _____.

semantics
syntax

15. In addition to meaning or _____ and sentence structure or _____, a third aspect of language is *pragmatics*, which is the social purpose of language.

pragmatics

16. The sentence, "How much money do you need," means one thing if a parent is asking a child who is about to go to the store and another thing when tennis star John McEnroe challenged Ivan Lendl's concern that fees for playing in tournament were decreasing. The contribution that such social contexts make to meaning in language is called _____.

HOW WE LEARN LANGUAGE

babbling

17. Before babies can talk, they utter meaningless sounds that we call *babbling*. Infants from many different language environments all make more or less the same sounds while _____.

18. Technically speaking, babbling consists of a great many elementary sounds or _____. Infants of all nationalities make the same sounds in their earliest _____, but eventually sounds that do not belong to the language the infant hears no longer occur in the infant's _____.

phonemes
babbling
babbling

19. Although psychologists do not know exactly how children learn a _____, a crucial factor appears to be *verbal interaction* between the child and a language-speaking caretaker.

language

20. Instead of simply listening to language—for example, as heard on television—the child must be in active _____ _____ with someone who speaks the language. One of the things they learn in this manner are the *rules of grammar.*

verbal interaction

21. Using the articles (in English, *the, a, an*), making different verb tenses (*go, going, went*), and forming plurals (*dog, dogs*) occur in very similar developmental sequences in different languages, illustrating the universality of how children learn the _____ of _____.

rules, grammar

22. Various theories have been offered to explain how children learn _____. Some have suggested that it is learned by *operant conditioning.*

language

23. The idea that parents, for example, reward their children's language with praise and understanding is at the heart of the _____ _____ theory.

operant conditioning

24. Others have proposed that children learn language by *imitation*. Presumably, children hear language spoken and then repeat it by _____.

imitation

25. Noam Chomsky suggested that neither _____ _____ nor _____ were the major factors. Rather, he proposed that children have an *innate mechanism* for language learning.

operant conditioning
imitation

26. Chomsky suggested that all children possess a strong tendency to speak, which he called an _____ _____.

innate mechanism

27. Attempts to teach language to apes using one or another symbol system have shown that they have some ability but it is limited, presumably indicating that the human's _____ _____ for language is better than that of the apes.

innate mechanism

THE DOUBLY USEFUL WORDS CALLED CONCEPTS

28. Only a few words in any language are names of specific, one-of-a-kind objects; otherwise most words represent whole groups of objects, events, actions, and ideas, which are called *symbolic concepts*. Mental representations of *similarities* between objects or events that we know are also different are _____ _____.

symbolic concepts

29. Whether physical attributes, functions, or more abstract ideas, individual examples of a single _____ _____ all possess certain _____.

symbolic concept
similarities

30. In humans, concepts are primarily represented by words and phrases, which is why they are called _____ concepts. But concepts can be formed without language, even among lower animals, in which case they are called *perceptual* or *schematic concepts.*

symbolic

31. Dogs have a concept of a tree, although they have no language, which illustrates a _____ or _____ _____.

perceptual, schematic concept

32. Concepts help us think, and one kind of thinking involves making *inferences,* that is, drawing logical conclusions from facts already known. When you decide you can find a motel if you drive closer to Denver because you know Denver is a big city and it has been your experience that all big cities have motels on their outskirts, you have made an _____.

inference

33. If someone tells you that there is a bird in Brazil called a cariama, you immediately know that it has wings even though you have never seen such a bird. You conclude this by making an _____ on the basis of knowing the _____ of bird.

inference
concept

34. Many concepts represent *categories* or groupings that help us organize information by chunking and clustering material. Many categories are _____ and many concept words describe _____.

concepts, categories

35. Since learning builds on _____, it is helpful to have a broad "effective language." Children from advantaged circumstances often enter school with knowledge of many different concepts and words, and it is this _____ _____ that makes it easier for them to find similarities in relationships between the new information presented in school and their prior knowledge.

learning

effective
language

36. Language not only helps us learn new concepts, but it may limit our thinking as well. Some small cultures in remote Brazil only have three words for quantities—the equivalent of "one," "two," and "many." These people are much less able to solve simple problems involving the difference between four and six objects, for example, which illustrates that _____ may limit _____.

language
thinking

37. But does language lead or follow concepts and thinking. Perhaps the Brazilian group, which lives in the very remote jungle, has never needed to distinguish three, four, five, six, or more objects, whereas some Eskimo groups do need to distinguish 20 or 30 kinds of snow and have separate words for them. Both _____, including _____, and _____ depend on our needs and experience and probably reflect this common basis.

language, concepts, thinking

THINKING AND PROBLEM SOLVING

38. *Thinking* is the mental manipulation of information. Among the important pieces of information we manipulate during our _____ are the *rules* that govern relationships and interactions among the objects and events in the environment.

thinking

39. The facts we have learned about the way the world operates constitute some of the _____ we use during thinking. We also base much of our thinking on *premises,* which are beliefs that we accept even though they cannot be proved.

rules

40. *Logical thinking* means to draw conclusions that follow inescapably from the _____ we have learned and the _____ we have adopted.

rules, premises

41. If you know the rules that all mammals nurse their young and that a whale is a mammal, then the conclusion that whales nurse their young is an example of _____ _____.

logical thinking

42. When a conclusion is false, it may be because of illogical thinking or because of the use of an incorrect _____ or _____. Critics who argued that Christopher Columbus would fall off the earth if he sailed west were wrong because they thought the world was flat, a faulty _____, but their thinking was _____.

rule, premise

premise, logical

43. Much of human thinking is an attempt at *problem solving*. Determining how long it will take you to drive 100 miles or how to balance the national budget both require _____ _____.

problem solving

44. The most effective strategy for _____ _____ is to use a mathematical formula or other procedure that will guarantee the solution if followed step-by-step. Such a procedure is called an *algorithm*.

problem solving

45. Most of the time, however, no certain, step-by-step _____ is available, and we must rely on *heuristics*, rules of thumb that have worked previously in similar situations and may work again.

algorithm

46. Determining how long it will take you to drive 100 miles at exactly 50 miles per hour is solved by using an _____, but trying to find the way between two towns 100 miles apart without a map would probably require _____.

algorithm

heuristics

47. One of several common traps in faulty problem solving is a *failure to analyze the problem* thoroughly. It is crucial to know exactly what the task is, what facts are available, and what limitations constrain the solution, otherwise the problem will be difficult to solve because of a _____ _____ _____ _____ _____.

failure to analyze the problem

48. In addition to a _____ to _____ the _____, another reason we can have difficulty solving a problem is that we may let our personal *biases* get in the way.

failure, analyze, problem

49. The fact that people often seem to find flaws in even the most logical reasoning if they disagree with the conclusion is an example of letting our _____ interfere with our logical thinking. Another problem-solving trap, called *functional fixedness*, is the tendency to think of objects as functioning only in a certain way and to ignore their other possible uses.

biases

50. People who cannot think of a variety of creative uses for a brick or paper clip have the problem of _____ _____.

functional fixedness

51. Functional _____ is one form of a more general phenomenon called *persistence of set*, habitual ways of approaching problems or situations.

fixedness

52. The "this is the way we have always done it" approach to problem solving works well in many situations but can be an obstacle to solving problems that appear, but are not really, similar to our previous experience. When that happens, we call the error a _____ of _____.

persistence, set

53. A fourth trap of _____ _____ consists of *relying solely on readily available information*. Often we attempt a solution based on information that we have recently acquired or believe strongly, even though that information may be no more relevant to the problem than other information available to us.

problem solving

54. The tendency to drive more carefully after seeing an accident or to buy more insurance after a neighbor's house burns illustrate our tendency of _____ solely on the _____ _____ _____.

relying, readily available information

REVIEW OF IMPORTANT TERMS

algorithm **(278)**

babbling **(262)**

communication **(254)**

functional fixedness **(281)**

grammar **(257)**

heuristics **(279)**

inference **(271)**

innate mechanism **(266)**

morpheme **(255)**

perceptual (schematic) concept **(269)**

persistence of set **(282)**

phoneme **(255)**

pragmatics **(258)**

premises **(277)**

problem solving **(278)**

semantics **(256)**

symbolic concepts **(268)**

syntax **(257)**

thinking **(276)**

vocabulary **(257)**

PRACTICE TEST

_____ 1. The difference between the communication systems of humans and of lower animals is that human beings

    a.   use sounds and gestures.

    b.   use symbols.

    c.   communicate meaning.

    d.   can communicate a vastly greater variety of thoughts.

_____ 2. A phoneme is

    a.   a basic sound.

    b.   the smallest meaningful unit of language.

    c.   a syllable.

    d.   all the above.

_____ 3. The English language has how many phonemes?

    a.   85

    b.   40

    c.   35

    d.   25

_____ 4. A morpheme may be

    a.   a word

    b.   a combination of phonemes.

    c.   a prefix.

    d.   all the above.

_____ 5. Semantics is most closely associated with

    a.   grammar.

    b.   meaning.

    c.   syntax.

    d.   word order.

_____ 6. Syntax

    a.   does not contribute to the meaning of a sentence.

    b.   is not usually learned by children before age six.

    c.   is more concerned with word order than with word meaning.

    d.   reflects meaning rather than grammar.

_____ 7. Which is *not* true about the language learning of children?

    a.   They typically speak in two- or three-word sentences by age two.

    b.   They do not learn all of the basic rules of grammar until age 12.

    c.   They understand the meaning of about 2,000 words by age five.

    d.   They can string words together according to grammatical rules to create meaningful new sentences by age six.

_____ 8. The early babbling of infants

    a.   begins at birth.

    b.   is a learned characteristic.

    c.   seldom occurs in deaf babies who cannot hear sounds.

    d.   contains more or less the same sounds in infants from all language environments.

_____ 9. Which is *not* true about language learning

    a.   Children exposed mostly to Spanish in their home and a little English had difficulty in school switching from Spanish to English.

    b.   Children exposed to two languages have no particular language problems.

    c.   Poor children who learn two languages have slightly better intellectual skills than poor children exposed to only one language.

    d.   People who learn a second language after childhood can often speak it without an accent.

_____ 10. Perhaps the most crucial experience in acquiring a first language is

    a.   active language interaction with another speaking person.

    b.   sheer exposure to a language.

    c.   a parent who speaks slowly, in simple sentences, and repeats key words.

    d.   none of these, the "innate mechanism" is sufficient.

_____ 11. Language is probably learned

    a.   by operant conditioning.

    b.   by imitation.

    c.   as a result of an "innate mechanism" for learning and using language.

    d.   all the above.

_____ 12. Attempts to teach apes language have demonstrated that

    a. It is impossible to teach an ape the language skills of even a three-year-old child.

    b. apes are as capable of understanding symbols, communicating with them, and engaging in various kinds of information processing as many primary schoolchildren.

    c. apes can use language to produce long and complex messages.

    d. apes are able to create new sentences they have never experienced before by combining words or symbols they already know into a new sequence.

_____ 13. Concepts

    a. require language.

    b. cannot be learned by lower animals.

    c. are based on similarities among objects, events, and relationships.

    d. are first learned when babies begin to talk.

_____ 14. Drawing logical conclusions from facts already known is a thought process called

    a. semantics.

    b. imitation.

    c. inference.

    d. none of these.

_____ 15. The notion of "effective language" is most closely associated with

    a. the principle that learning builds on learning.

    b. skills in public speaking.

    c. proper syntax.

    d. schematic concepts.

_____ 16. The idea that the nature of language influences how people conceive the world, organize it, and think about it is primarily associated with

    a. Whorf.

    b. Aristotle.

    c. Rosch.

    d. Chomsky.

_____ 17. A false conclusion may derive from

    a. incorrect facts.

    b. faulty premises.

    c. illogical thinking.

    d. all the above.

_____18. One noted economist argues that taxes must be lowered; another says taxes must be raised. They probably disagree on

    a. rules.

    b. premises.

    c. logic.

    d. semantics.

_____19. A rule is to a premise as

    a. an algorithm is to a heuristic.

    b. illogical is to logical thinking.

    c. an assumption is to a conclusion.

    d. schematic is to symbolic concepts.

_____20. Functional fixedness is a

    a. motor impairment.

    b. special form of persistence of set.

    c. type of personal bias.

    d. lack of mechanical ability.

ANSWERS TO PRACTICE TEST

1. d	6. c	11. d	16. a
2. a	7. b	12. d	17. d
3. b	8. d	13. c	18. b
4. d	9. d	14. c	19. a
5. b	10. a	15. a	20. b

EXERCISES

I. Concepts are based on similarities in physical attributes, functions, relationships, and abstract ideas. The concept of "bird" involves wings and feathers, for example. But concepts and their examples also have implied meanings in addition to the more obvious physical or functional similarities that define them. These implied meanings have such qualities as goodness or badness, strength or weakness, activity or passivity, and so on. Even clear examples of the same concept may have very different implied meanings. The eagle may imply strength but the hummingbird weakness, the hawk may be active while the dove is regarded as passive.

One method of assessing the implied meanings of concepts is the semantic differential developed by C. E. Osgood. The semantic differential consists of pairs of opposite ends of a line containing seven equally spaced marks along it. A person rates the concept being assessed by placing a mark on the line according to how weak or strong, small or large, etc. the rater feels the concept represents.

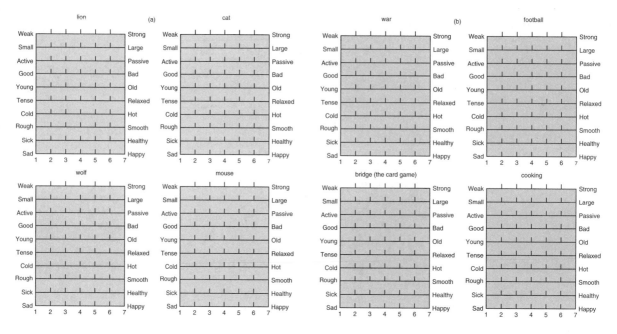

FIGURE 6.11

Specifically, select several of your friends to rate the following concepts:

lion	war
cat	football
wolf	bridge (the card game)
mouse	cooking

Figure 6.11 contains eight examples of the semantic differential assessment form. You may wish to duplicate them for as many subjects as you expect to use. At the top of each form is the word to be evaluated. Have your subjects place a check along each line at a point that describes their relative feelings about the concept named at the top. When they are finished rating each concept, you can draw a line from point to point within each form to construct a profile of what the concept implies to each subject. Further, you may have several ratings of each concept, either from the several subjects you test or from your classmates. You can then construct a profile for each concept. To do this, use as scores the numbers 1 through 7 along the bottom of the form. Assign a score to each check made by a subject, and average the scores across subjects for each concept. Then plot a group profile for each concept. You may wish to determine a group profile separately for male and female subjects. Consider these questions:

1. Examine the ratings for each concept within the two sets of four concepts. How are they similar and how are they different? For example, among the animals, which represent examples of the same concept, how is the lion related to the cat and to the wolf? How is the cat related to the mouse? Explain the similarities and differences. Do the same for the other four words.

2. Did people show more or less agreement about their ratings for some words than for others? Why?

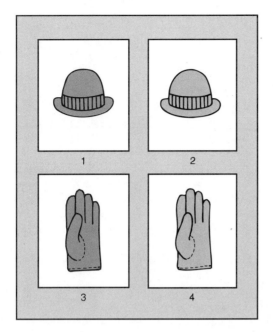

FIGURE 6.12 Place the four cards, which have symbols on both sides, on a table so that you can see them as shown here. Each card has on one side a hat, which may be either blue or gray, and on the other side a glove, which also may be either blue or gray. Prove or disprove this statement: *Every card that has a blue hat on one side has a gray glove on the other side.* How many cards—and which ones—would you have to turn over to find out whether the statement is true or false?

3. Do male and female raters differ in the way they perceive the meanings of certain concepts?

4. Relate your results to the issue of defining a concept and to the idea of meaning.

II. Figures 6.12 and 6.13 present two problems to solve. Have several friends attempt to solve these problems. After they give their first answer, ask them to explain their reasoning. If they are wrong, tell them they are wrong and have them try again and explain their next answer. From their wrong answers, try to determine what error or common trap they fall into attempting to solve the problem. The answers are in the text (pp. 280–281).

FIGURE 6.13 Turn to page 281 and look at Figure 6.7. A stranger approached a museum curator and offered him an ancient bronze coin. The coin had an authentic appearance and was marked with the date 544 B.C. The curator had happily made acquisitions from suspicious sources before, but this time he promptly called the police and had the stranger arrested. Why?

On a scale of 1 to 10 how sure are you that you know the correct answer?

CHAPTER 7

Emotions, Drives, and Motives

The gaining of a desired goal after prolonged effort usually releases a lot of emotion.

- In 1993, when Israeli Prime Minister Yitzhak Rabin and PLO Chairman Yasser Arafat signed a peace pact between their peoples, the jubilation of most Israelis and Palestinians was offset by angry protests on both sides.
- During the 1994 Winter Olympic games, Ukranian figure skater Oksana Baiul sobbed uncontrollably after finishing her performance and realizing that she had probably won a gold medal.
- In London a few years ago, as she watched her son being beaten, the mother of a professional boxer jumped into the ring and began flailing away at the winning boxer with her shoe.

These examples illustrate the striking ways in which *emotions* influence behavior. Occasionally we hear about more extreme episodes: People in the grip of rage who commit murders, or people in panic who fight to escape from a burning building.

In more ordinary situations as well, emotions affect our behavior. For example, even mild excitement or eagerness often helps us learn faster or accomplish a task more efficiently. At the same time, emotions involving fear and anxiety can make us forget everything we studied when we sit down to take an important examination or strike us dumb when we get up and try to make a speech.

Fundamentally important in the regulation of our existence, emotions defy easy definition. There is far from perfect agreement as whether or not a particular state of feeling should be considered an emotion (Shields, 1984).

What is an emotion? What actually happens when we become angry or sad, happy or ashamed? Why do some people lose control of their emotions and begin to behave in strange and irrational ways?

In addition to emotions, a second group of related psychological states, called **drives**—for example, hunger, thirst, sleep—have a pronounced effect on behavior. A state of hunger can make us jumpy, jittery, and unable to concentrate. Indeed, the urge to find food or water, when the body lacks either of them, can be just as strong as the tendency to run away in fear or strike back in anger. In one famous case of a party of pioneers stranded by an 1846 blizzard in the Donner Pass, the urge overrode all moral and esthetic scruples and turned some of them into cannibals. And the need for sleep can cause a sleep-deprived prisoner of war to turn from defiance to submission.

This chapter also addresses the related topic of **motives.** Unlike emotions and drives, which have an inherited and universal biological component, human motives are rooted in psychologically potent ideas that direct behavior toward goals such as power over others, friendship, and achievement. Although these goals are not essential to life, the desire to attain more power or to master a skill can be so intense that people will devote a great deal of planning and effort to its satisfaction. While it is true that motives are universal and, therefore, part of the human heritage, they are maintained to a far greater degree than emotions and drives by cognitive factors. Striving for a goal with symbolic value is a hallmark of being human.

Drives

Physiological states (like hunger, thirst, and sleep) that have a pronounced effect on behavior.

Motives

The psychologically potent ideas that direct behavior toward goals such as power over others, friendship, and achievement.

Biological Underpinnings of Emotion

Although there is some disagreement on the best definition of an emotion, most psychologists would agree that an **emotion** is comprised of (1) a precipitating event that is (2) accompanied by changes in physiology that are (3) evaluated cognitively, and (4) may lead to a change in feeling. The qualifier "may lead to a change in feeling" is important. Although some physiological changes produced by an event are consciously felt—and are interpreted by the person as fear, sadness, or joy—similar changes can occur without being consciously felt. In the second case, although behavior may change, the person is not aware of being in an emotional state. For example, a person rejected by a friend may become preoccupied and forgetful without actually feeling consciously angry or sad. These two types of emotional states are quite different.

Because the most salient feature of an emotion is a change in the body's physiology, the first part of this chapter addresses these biological underpinnings of emotional states. There is, however, disagreement on how many basic emotions there are. One psychologist has suggested that there are ten basic emotions, listed in Figure 7.1.

As the above definition makes clear, the most important characteristic that differentiates emotions from other psychological states—for example, perception or thought—is that they are accompanied by widespread and pronounced bodily changes that can alter blood circulation, heart rate, stomach activity, muscle tension, and concentrations of neurotransmitters and hormones.

You can assume, for example, that you are in an emotional state when you blush or become pale, or when your muscles grow taut, or when your mouth turns so dry that you can hardly speak. You also know that you are in

Emotion

The changes in physiology that are evaluated cognitively and may lead to a change in conscious feeling.

The ten basic emotions	
anger	guilt
contempt	interest-excitement
disgust	joy
distress	shame
fear	surprise

Four important complex emotions
anxiety
(fear plus anger, distress, guilt, interest, or shame)
depression
(distress plus anger, contempt, fear, guilt, or shame)
hostility
(a combination of anger, contempt, and disgust)
love
(interest plus joy)

FIGURE 7.1 One psychological view of the range of emotions The fundamental human emotions, according to one investigator, are those listed at the top of the table. Other emotions that we frequently experience, notably those at the bottom, are combinations of some of the fundamental feelings (after Izard, 1977).

an emotional state, even if you are able to conceal all outward signs, when you feel that you are shaking inwardly or are "hot under the collar," or when your pulse is racing or your stomach is "full of butterflies." There are also quieter emotions that occur when the body seems to be especially relaxed. These are the calm and contented feelings experienced when you enjoy a beautiful piece of music or a satisfying meal. In these cases, too, the body is changed in a specific manner.

The bodily changes associated with emotion do not, however, exist in a vacuum. Rather, as the definition of emotion makes clear, they are linked to two other factors: an event in the environment and the thoughts, ideas, or images triggered by that event. All of the emotions we experience—whether sadness, anxiety, or joy—contain the same three factors: a particular event (or the memory of an event); changes in the body and brain; and thoughts generated by the event (Shields, 1984)

Pinpointing Bodily Changes in Emotion

"I could hardly breathe."

"I had butterflies in my stomach."

"My face was beet red."

Such statements about bodily changes are often heard from people who have been emotionally aroused, and they raise the question whether particular emotions are linked to changes in particular areas of the body.

One team of researchers attempted to answer this question by asking subjects to reminisce about specific emotions they underwent and to indicate on detailed diagrams of the body where, especially, they sensed each one (Nieuwenhuise, Offenberg, & Frijda, 1987). In general, the subjects were able to identify the "location" of specific emotions. For example, most people said that they felt disgust especially in the stomach and throat; fear in the abdomen, legs, genitals, and stomach; contempt and shame in the face; surprise in the lower back; joy in the arms and legs; and anger virtually everywhere, but mainly in the arms and legs.

The tendency to associate specific emotions with parts of the body may be the result of the actual physiological responses related to particular feeling states. For example, disgust is likely to be ascribed to the stomach and throat because of sensations of nausea and gastric upset. Shame may be located in the face as a result of the tendency to blush. Such associations originate in the different physiological changes that accompany specific emotional experiences.

The Body's Often Hidden Changes

The fact that emotion is accompanied by changes in different parts of the body is most apparent in the behavior of lower animals, such as the cat pictured in Figure 7.2. It is often less obvious among humans, for most of us have learned to hide many outward signs of emotion. But the changes can be measured with laboratory equipment. When we experience a strong emotion, such as fear, our heartbeat may increase from the normal rate of around 72 beats per minute to as high as 180. Blood pressure may rise sharply, and blood is often diverted from the stomach to the muscles of movement and to the surface of the body, resulting in flushed cheeks and a sensation of warmth. The composition of the blood changes. The number of red corpuscles, which carry oxygen, increases markedly. Secretion of hormones by the endocrine glands produces changes in the level of blood sugar, the acidity of the blood, and the amount of adrenaline and noradrenaline (powerful stimulants secreted by the adrenal glands and autonomic system) in the bloodstream.

The normal movements of the stomach and intestines, associated with the digestion and absorption of food, usually stop during anger. Some emotional states may lead to nausea or diarrhea, a higher metabolic rate to create additional energy, and gasping or panting. The salivary glands may stop working, causing a feeling of dryness in the mouth often associated with fear and anger. The sweat glands, on the other hand, may become overactive, as shown by the dripping forehead that may accompany embarrassment or the "cold sweat" that sometimes accompanies fear. The tiny muscles at the base of the hairs may contract and raise goose flesh. Finally the pupils of the eyes may enlarge, causing the wide-eyed look that is characteristic of fear, rage, excitement, and pain. Of course, all of these reactions do not necessarily take place in every episode of strong fear or anger (Campos, et al., 1983), but they tend to form a pattern.

The Role of the Autonomic Nervous System and Glands

Some bodily changes that accompany emotion are regulated by the autonomic nervous system and the endocrine glands, over which—as described in Chapter 2—we ordinarily have no conscious control. It is when the sympathetic division of the autonomic nervous system is activated that we experience such physiological changes as a rise in heart rate and blood pressure, muscle tension, dilation of the pupils, and inhibition of stomach and intestine activity.

It is not surprising, therefore, that we do not seem to have much control over our emotions. They often seem to boil up of their own accord, and we feel them even if we manage to hide all outward signs. Even in situations in which we are determined to remain calm, we often find ourselves unaccountably angry, frightened, or overcome with joy.

FIGURE 7.2   An open display of emotion in the cat An angry cat shows many outward bodily signs of emotion. The animal crouches and growls. Its hair stands on end, its ears are laid back, and its eyes are wide and staring (Young, 1961).

Cortisol

A hormone secreted by the adrenal gland.

Although a pattern of bodily changes characterizes each of the major emotions, certain changes are linked to several different emotions. For instance, the adrenal glands produce the hormone **cortisol** when anger and fear are experienced. Our pupils dilate when we experience fear, but also in response to milder emotions such as interest or the excitement of a tennis match (Rose, 1980). Thus psychologists have found it difficult to match a particular bodily state with a particular emotional experience. Moreover, on separate occasions, the same person reporting feelings of joy may show a different pattern of bodily change. And a group of people who report feeling exactly the same emotion (joy or distress) may show different patterns. Thus it is difficult to determine through physiological measurement alone what particular emotion a person is experiencing. Nevertheless, a variety of physiological measures are used in conducting lie detector tests, discussed in the Psychology in Action box entitled, "How Truthful Are Lie Detectors?"

The Facial Muscles and Emotion

A number of bodily changes that accompany emotion do not involve the autonomic nervous system, glands, or visceral organs. These changes represent activity of the muscles of movement over which we ordinarily do have conscious control.

You probably have been aware of some of them—for example, muscular tension (as when the teeth are clenched in anger) or trembling (which occurs when two sets of muscles work against each other). When emotionally excited, many people have a tendency to blink their eyes or make nervous movements, such as brushing back their hair or drumming their fingers. Emotions are often expressed vocally in laughter, snarls, moans, and screams—or revealed by changes in the speed, pitch, and loudness of speech, as shown in Figure 7.3. Emotions are also revealed in facial expressions, like smiles, grimaces, and frowns. In fact, even just thinking about experiences that are happy, sad, or infuriating can produce strikingly different patterns of activity in the muscles of the face. Though the changes are often too small to be seen, they can be detected by measuring the electrical activity of the muscles (Schwartz, 1982).

The psychologists who maintain that facial expressions are a key factor in emotional experience hold that every basic emotion is accompanied by a char-

FIGURE 7.3 Examples of speech patterns that reflect emotion Speech patterns often vary sharply depending on the emotion experienced. The patterns are so consistent that some emotional states can be identified with surprising accuracy just from the sound of a person's voice (Scherer, 1986). From the opening "hello" of a telephone conversation, for example, we can often tell whether the person on the other end is happy or sad.

Emotion	Patterns of speech		
	Tempo	Pitch	Volume
Happiness	Fast	High	Loud
Sadness	Slow	Low	Soft
Contempt	Slow	Low	Loud

How Truthful Are Lie Detectors?

It has been estimated that at least a million Americans a year are asked to take a lie detector test. Some are defendants, plaintiffs, or witnesses in legal cases. Others are job applicants or workers in chain stores, banks, supermarkets, or other companies that try to spot dishonesty. Still others are executives in industrial firms or government agencies that require periodic loyalty checks.

The lie detector device is essentially a version of the polygraph machine, which produces a continuous record of bodily processes—breathing, blood pressure, sweating—that often change under a given emotional state.

Many people believe the polygraph is an infallible scientific instrument and place absolute confidence in its results.

The test is certainly based on a sound principle—namely, that people are likely to become physiologically "stirred up" when they feel so threatened by a question that they answer it untruthfully. But psychology has found that a perfectly innocent person may react emotionally to a critical question—and thus appear to be lying when actually telling the truth. And career criminals who are veteran liars can feel no anxiety or guilt about anything—and can therefore tell outrageous untruths without showing the slightest emotional ripple. This can lead to some seriously mistaken conclusions (Kleinmuntz & Szucko, 1984).

To complicate matters, scoring test results may be influenced by the purely subjective impressions of the examiners. Their interpretation of the tracings of physical reactions to test questions may be colored by personal biases about the subject's age, sex, social class, or race. All in all, the great weight of psychological evidence is that lie detector tests have no real claim to being "scientific" or infallible (Lykken, 1981), and we should never reach a final conclusion about whether a person is lying based solely on their results (Ekman, 1985). Based on these findings, the American Psychological Association has developed a policy statement arguing against the use of lie detection programs.

Lie detector testing has become a thriving American industry, and it is likely that a significant number of legal and administrative decisions are unfairly influenced by the results. This is a good example of psychology misapplied—how the science can be warped when its findings are used without sufficient safeguards and caution.

---

acteristic facial pattern that occurs automatically because of the manner in which our bodies and brains are programmed by heredity (Izard, 1977). The various patterns, they believe, are the product of evolution. Especially for animals that do not have a spoken language, it is an advantage to be able to avert aggression through a facial expression, signalling friendliness or submission. Facial expressions of fear can alert other members of the group to the presence of danger. Thus the process of natural selection has favored the survival of individuals who carry genes for specific facial expressions (Andrew, 1965).

This view is based, in part, on a study that used photographs of individuals exhibiting certain emotions. The photos were shown to people in a number of very different societies, who were asked to identify the emotions being displayed on the photo. As shown in Figure 7.4, there was remarkable agreement on the specific emotion on the face, not only among subjects in the United States, but in a variety of countries and cultures around the world (Ekman, 1971). The various facial expressions are sufficiently unique that even pigeons can be trained to differentiate among them (Bhatt et al., 1988).

The study summarized in Figure 7.4 indicates that the facial expressions that accompany some emotions seem to be universal and unlearned, as if they were genetically programmed—set by nature rather than nurture. More recently, similar agreement across cultures has been found in judgments of the facial expression of contempt (Ekman & Friesen, 1986). Furthermore,

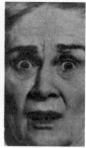

FIGURE 7.4 Strong agreement across cultures These photos of faces showing different emotions were shown to subjects in the various countries identified. Note the high percentages of subjects who linked the photos with the emotions (Ekman, 1973).

	Happiness	Sadness	Disgust	Surprise	Anger	Fear
United States	97%	84%	92%	95%	67%	85%
Brazil	95%	59%	97%	87%	90%	67%
Chile	95%	88%	92%	93%	94%	68%
Argentina	98%	78%	92%	95%	90%	54%
Japan	100%	62%	90%	100%	90%	66%

most adults agree on the emotion they believe is reflected by the different facial expressions of young babies (Izard & Dougherty, 1982), as shown in Figure 7.5. "Reading" the facial expressions of older persons is more difficult for all of us, although women appear generally to be better at the task than men. Still, research has shown that certain emotions—for example, amusement or peacefulness—are easier to read than others such as happiness, sadness, anger, or disgust (Wagner, 1990).

Can We Hide Our Emotions?

The difficulty of concealing the facial movements that accompany some emotional experiences was demonstrated by a team of investigators who attached electrodes to the facial muscles of individuals during an interview, and, by measuring the electrical activity of these muscles, detected the intensity of reaction to emotionally toned material (Cacioppo et al., 1988). Because certain facial muscles are difficult to control voluntarily, they some-

FIGURE 7.5 Emotions of infants: written all over their faces Notice the similarity of these facial expressions to those of the happy and sad adults pictured in the first two photos of Figure 7.4.

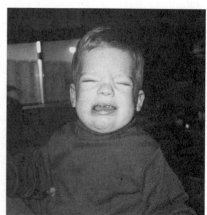

times provide clues to an emotion the individual is fighting to hide. When we are worried or under stress, for example, we might try to act as if nothing is wrong—but there is a fair chance that we cannot keep at least one clue from revealing our actual state of tension: The inner part of the eyebrows tend to rise (Ekman, 1985).

Habituated
The state of becoming accustomed to a stimulus.

There are times, of course, when the face does not reveal an individual's internal emotional state. In one experiment, 72 women experienced intense pain when they immersed their hands and arms in extremely cold water. Initially, they showed the expected facial changes that accompany pain: cheeks raised, eyelids tight, eyes closed in a blink, and upper lips raised and the corners pulled back. But even though the subjects experienced increasing pain as the experiment went on, their facial displays of "pain" became much less apparent as they became **habituated,** or accustomed, to their uncomfortable situation (Craig & Patrick, 1985). But by and large, the face can be more revealing than spoken words. And sometimes words aren't needed at all—as when we say to a friend, "I could tell something was wrong by just looking at you."

The judgments we make of people by "just looking" at them can often be uncannily reliable, even if time permits only a swift first impression. Psychologists have examined, for example, the impact that a person's nonverbal, unconscious "body language" has on the emotional attitudes of others toward them. When a group of female college students were asked to form an impression of a teacher on the basis of three 10-second silent videotape segments of that teacher in a classroom, their impressions were found to correlate strongly with end-of-semester evaluations of that teacher by actual students (Ambady & Rosenthal, 1993). Empathy, too, plays a role in our ability to judge the emotional states of others. In one study, subjects were asked to identify the emotions being expressed by a couple videotaped in conversation. Their ability to recognize when the conversing couple was angry was linked to a high level of cardiovascular arousal—a physiologic state shared by the couple at that point in their conversation (Levenson & Ruef, 1992).

Mechanisms of Emotion

One of the earliest and most challenging questions to confront the fledgling field of psychology involved the origins of emotion. What causes changes to take place in the body, welling up without conscious control and often despite our determination to suppress them? The common sense answer to the question of the origins of emotion—that we cry because we are sad, strike out because we are angry, tremble and run because we are afraid—begs the question. Are emotions a product of brain activity? Or of "heart"? Even today, this issue remains an intriguing question in scientific psychology.

The James-Lange and Cannon-Bard Theories

Nearly a century ago, William James, one of psychology's founding fathers, offered a radical proposal that turned the conventional wisdom upside down. James proposed that emotion occurs when specific stimuli in the environment set off physiological changes in the body. These changes, he said, stimulate sensory nerves leading to the brain, and it is the brain's reaction to these sensory messages that we perceive as emotion. In other words, we do not cry because we are sad. On the contrary, we feel sad because we are crying. Similarly, we do not tremble because we are afraid, but feel afraid because we are trembling (James, 1890).

Much more recent research suggests that even bodily sensations stemming from posture may have an effect on emotional response. In an experiment in which college students were asked to complete a series of simple cognitive and motor tasks, some students were seated in a normal, "upright" position, while others were provided seating that required them to "slump." When the experimenter told them how they had performed, posture was shown to have a striking effect: Those who were slumped over when they heard their rating felt significantly less proud than those who were sitting upright (Stepper and Strack, 1993).

Startling as James's idea initially was to most of his contemporaries, it complemented the thinking of the Danish scientist, Carl Lange. He, too, reasoned that physiological changes in the body come first and that the perceived conscious emotion is the result of feedback from those changes. In the absence of any plausible opposition, the **James-Lange theory** of emotion, which is illustrated in Figure 7.6, held sway for many years. The principal weakness of the theory was the difficulty involved in matching any particular kind of bodily state—and its physiologic feedback—with any particular emotion.

Not until half a century passed did psychologists refine the classic James-Lange theory, by linking it to the role of the facial muscles. The new thinking held that feelings of emotion are influenced by feedback from bodily sensations—but not so much from the visceral organs as from the muscles of the face, which they believed were programmed by nature to respond in definite ways to certain events in the environment (Tomkins, 1962).

Building on this proposal, researchers recently have suggested that muscle movements that accompany changes in facial expressions modify the pattern of face-to-brain bloodflow, thus affecting the release of neurotransmitters by the brain—and these, in turn, affect our mood (Zajonc,

James-Lange theory
A physiologically based theory of emotion suggesting that stimuli in the environment set off the physiological changes in an individual and that these are followed by the perceived conscious emotion resulting from the perception of feedback of those changes.

FIGURE 7.6 The James-Lange theory As shown here, the James-Lange theory maintains that the psychological experience we call emotion follows the experience of bodily responses to a stimulus. If the shadowy figure at the left is perceived as a menacing intruder, the body responds—and the experience of fear ensues.

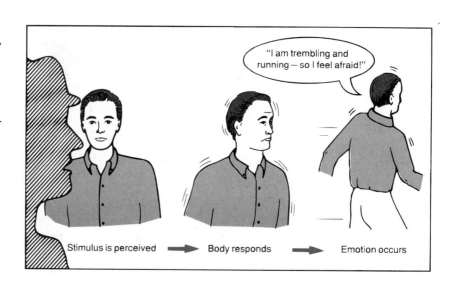

"I am trembling and running—so I feel afraid!"

Stimulus is perceived → Body responds → Emotion occurs

1989). For example, when a group of students were asked to adopt either a "worried" (negative) or "smiling" (positive) facial expression while recollecting events in their past life, subjects who had assumed a "worried" expression tended to rate themselves as less self-assured at the time of a given event than did those who were smiling (Stepper & Strack, 1993). And although individuals normally cannot control many of the bodily changes that accompany emotions, recent research suggests that the activation of specific facial muscles in smiling can generate some of the changes in regional brain activity known to occur during spontaneous enjoyment (Ekman & Davidson, 1993). Thus it may be that emotions do not necessarily "happen to" an individual but may be produced voluntarily.

The increasing specificity of these ideas, however, does not solve the formidable difficulty of matching the feedback from specific facial expressions to the experience of specific emotions. Proponents of the facial feedback theory believe that the matching exists (Izard & Dougherty, 1982), but other psychologists remain skeptical (McCaul, Holmes, & Solomon, 1982).

As psychologists grappled with the concept of emotions as the result of bodily feedback, two American scientists emphasized the fact that brain activity changes with emotion. According to the **Cannon-Bard theory,** certain events in the environment trigger hypothalamic activity. As shown in Figure 7.7, neurochemical events in the hypothalamus lead to arousal of the autonomic nervous system to produce the various physiological changes associated with emotion and alert the cerebral cortex, which translates the message into conscious feelings of emotion. This theory minimizes the importance of feedback of bodily sensations; it considers the physiological changes to be a

Cannon-Bard theory

A neurologically based theory of emotion suggesting that stimuli in the environment set off patterns in the hypothalamus and that these patterns cause bodily changes in emotion and conscious awareness of the feelings of emotion simultaneously.

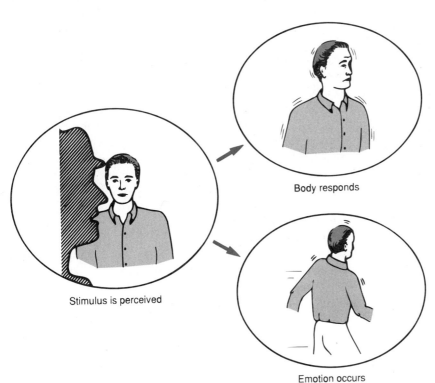

Stimulus is perceived

Body responds

Emotion occurs

FIGURE 7.7 The Cannon-Bard theory In contrast to the *James-Lange theory* (see Figure 7.6), the *Cannon-Bard theory* holds that the psychological experience of emotion and the body's response to a stimulus occur simultaneously—as explained in the text.

Cognitive theory

A contemporary theory of emotion suggesting that the mind plays a commanding role in emotion and leads the individual to appraise and interpret events that occur in the environment.

sort of side effect—useful in preparing the body to take appropriate action but not essential to the conscious experience of emotion.

The James-Lange and Cannon-Bard theories seem to contradict each other. But as psychologists use more sophisticated methods to probe the relationship of brain and behavior, it is likely that each idea will prove to have some correct components.

Today's Cognitive Perspective of Yesterday's Theories

The contemporary **cognitive theory** of emotion holds that the cortex plays the commanding role by appraising events that occur in the environment and feedback from the body simultaneously. At any given moment, the information received by the cortex from both sources may be neutral in terms of emotional impact; in this case we make a cognitive decision that we are not in an emotional state. Or, on the other hand, the sensory information may lead the cognitive process to decide we are in a state of joy, anger, or fear. We experience a change in our internal sensations, which we then try to appraise and interpret, given our context (Schachter & Singer, 1962). For example, a student sitting alone in the library at night becomes aware of unusual bodily sensations and interprets them as feelings of loneliness. A student who has the same pattern of sensations the night before a difficult examination may interpret them as anxiety. Another who has put in an unusually hard day's work may decide that he is fatigued.

As indicated earlier, some physiological states are detected consciously, some are not. Imagine, for instance, two mothers, each of whom is dealing daily with the troubled behavior of a preschool child, and experiencing similar physiologic changes. One mother, detecting her physiology, recognizes that her emotional state is one of worry. The other mother may fail to detect the subtle changes in her physiology, and is unable, in turn, to recognize the depth of her anguish.

Our cognitive appraisal of the environment is often immediate and automatic (Arnold, 1960)—something like the rapid first impression that occurs in perception. If we find a snake in our path, for example, everything seems to happen at once. Our hearts jump. We feel afraid. We leap back. All this seems to occur without any conscious decision making. At other times our appraisal is more complex and deliberate (Lazarus & Averill, 1972). An example is the "slow burn" we sometimes experience when we hear a remark and have no immediate reaction. But when we think about it and decide it was insulting, we become angry.

The cognitive view accepts parts of the Cannon-Bard theory and that part of the James-Lange theory claiming that bodily sensations are an essential aspect of emotion. The mind and body work together during emotional experiences. In sum, the cognitive view maintains that bodily states alone are not enough to account for the different emotions we experience. When we become aware of bodily changes, what determines our emotion is our cognitive evaluation of the changes and the environmental situation in which those changes occur.

Individual Differences in Emotions

Some differences in emotional behavior appear to be inborn, as discussed more fully in Chapter 12. Studies of infants have shown, for instance, that some are more inclined to smile than others, while some have a pronounced tendency to cry at the slightest provocation.

There is considerable evidence that one inborn difference affecting emotions is the sensitivity of the autonomic nervous system (ANS), which controls many of the bodily changes associated with emotion. Some people seem to react to weaker stimulation of the ANS than others—and to react more rapidly and with greater intensity. Patterns of ANS activity also vary. In the same kind of emotional situation, one person may show a rapid heartbeat, while another may show only a small change in heart rate but a pronounced increase in skin temperature (Lacey & Lacey, 1958). Differences of this kind can be observed in children (Tennes & Mason, 1982). When feeling challenged, two-year-olds who are chronically anxious, timid, and shy have been found to have a heart rate that is unusually high and stable. In similar circumstances, two-year-olds who are far less fearful usually have a heart rate to challenge that is low and more variable (Kagan, 1989a).

Certainly any abnormality of the glands or nervous system can have significant effects on emotional experience. In humans, for example, malfunctioning of the pancreas as a result of an undiagnosed cancer can produce symptoms that mimic severe psychological depression (Goodwin & Jamison, 1990). And in animals, an interruption of the flow of information from the visual areas of the cortex to the brain's limbic system disrupts emotional reactions, causing them to treat once-feared stimuli—for example, a threatening gesture—in a casual manner (National Institute of Mental Health, 1988).

We all know people who seem to "overreact" to even minor events in their lives, and others who don't seem to be fazed by even major upheavals. One individual who loses his wallet may be in a stew for days, while another who learns that she needs serious surgery may go on with her normal routine with little feeling. Such differences between people are apparent at the very start of life and tend to remain as a major dimension of personality. Some people seem to crave variety and novelty in their lives. They have been described as "sensation-seekers," and they tend to pursue an existence that is more complex than do most individuals (Zuckerman, 1991). Still other people respond to life events with more intense reactions no matter whether the events evoke positive or negative emotions (Larsen, Diener, & Emmons, 1986).

Unfortunately, most unpleasant emotional experiences stay with us for longer periods than do pleasant ones. Students were asked to try to remember the last time they had something happen to them, either good or bad, that affected them emotionally. They remembered negative episodes and their emotional fallout more clearly and reported them more than twice as often as positive experiences (Scherer & Tannenbaum, 1986). Perhaps it has proved adaptive for animals and humans to remember those events that harm them more clearly than those that give pleasure. Avoiding a mountaintop where you almost fell off and experienced extreme fear is more important than remembering the mountaintop on which you saw a lovely sunset and felt serenity.

TEST YOURSELF

e) People clearly differ in the way they experience and express emotions. Are people born with such differences, or are they learned in the course of life?

Drives and Their Impact on Behavior: Hunger and Thirst

As pointed out at the start of this chapter, emotions are not the only states that involve changes in the body and behavior. We turn now to another group of states, called drives, which do so as well.

No clear dividing line exists between emotions and drive states like hunger and thirst. As in the case of emotions, the hunger drive, for example, consists of three components: an event in the environment (in this case, the deprivation of food), bodily changes (for example, changes in the body's stores of fat), and a cognitive component (thoughts about food and the search for it). Both emotions and drives produce strong bodily sensations, and both trigger behavior—sometimes of the most explosive kind. For instance, just as an insult produces the bodily reactions and brooding behavior that we call anger, deprivation of food produces the physiological responses and cranky behavior of hunger.

Yet there is a difference, and even in ordinary conversation we do not refer to hunger—or thirst, or the drive for sleep—as an emotion. A drive involves the process of **homeostasis,** or the maintenance of bodily stability; an emotion does not. It is one of the brain's functions, as was explained in Chapter 2, to preserve homeostasis by making sure the body has a constant supply of the substances the cells require to perform efficiently. When the body lacks any of these substances, a **drive state** is created, which can be defined as a pattern of brain and bodily activity resulting from physiological imbalances that threaten homeostasis. Two major drives are **hunger** (caused by the lack of food), and **thirst** (caused by the lack of water, which makes up two-thirds of our bodies).

The pattern of brain and bodily activity that constitutes a drive makes us seek whatever our bodies need to maintain homeostasis. By so doing—for example, by finding food or water—we restore the physiological balance, change the pattern of brain activity, and thus satisfy the drive.

The Body's Hunger Signals: Not Just an "Empty Stomach"

All infants respond to an important fact of life: Taking in nutrients is vital to survival and well-being. Because food is critical for all living creatures, our bodies must have the means to signal to us that it is time to eat.

But how do we actually know that we are hungry?

Common sense tells us that we have hunger pangs in the stomach, which feels empty and overactive and sometimes actually growls for food. This explanation is partially true. There are nerve fibers that carry messages from the stomach (Ball, 1974), the mouth, throat, and intestines, to the brain. Moreover, the sustained distension of the stomach will indeed make us feel satiated and affect eating behavior (Stellar, McHugh, & Moran, 1985).

But the role of the stomach is not so simple. Animals stop eating when their stomachs are far from full—when they have eaten a substance that is especially nutritious. If the stomach is filled with an equal amount of nonnutritious bulk, the animal will continue eating. This indicates that the stom-

Homeostasis

A state of equilibrium or balance in any physiological system.

Drive state

A pattern of brain and bodily activity resulting from physiological imbalances that threaten homeostasis.

Hunger (drive)

A major drive caused by the lack of food.

Thirst (drive)

A major drive caused by the lack of water.

ach's walls contain receptors that are sensitive to nutrients that are dissolved in the stomach acids. Evidently these receptors relay the message to the brain that nutritious material is on its way into the system (Deutsch, Puerto, & Wang, 1978). The message is probably facilitated through the action of an intestinal hormone (Stellar, McHugh, & Moran, 1985). Whatever the mechanism of communication, more is involved in hunger than the state of the stomach—and its messages to the brain.

The Body's Set Point and How It Works

The drive to eat involves a number of interrelated physiological mechanisms governed by the body's **set point**—an innate physiological mechanism that keeps an individual's body weight at a genetically "programmed" level. In effect, the set point is a homeostatic mechanism that leads us to return to our "natural" body weight after we have tried to go above it (by overeating) or below it (by dieting).

A popular view has been that the maintenance of the set point is facilitated by hunger messages originating in the liver, which plays the role of manager of the body's food metabolism. The evidence seemed clear enough: After we eat, there is an overly generous supply of glucose in the blood, and the extra glucose is converted to **glycogen,** or "animal starch," in the liver. While the liver is actively manufacturing glycogen, we are not hungry. But when we have not eaten for a time, the liver begins to pour glucose into the blood from its store of glycogen, and this change in glucose level in the blood leads to hunger and to eating (Le Magnen, 1984).

However, a new view suggests that blood sugar is less important as a primary regulator of eating behavior than the amount of fat stored within the body. The body contains a large number of cells, in diverse locations, that are designed for the storage of fatty compounds. In evolutionary terms, survival of the species presumably depended on the ability of these **fat cells** to store up energy that would tide the body over the prolonged periods of starvation that humans in the past experienced frequently (and still do in many places). Under ordinary circumstances, the hunger drive keeps these cells filled to an appropriate level with fatty molecules. But when the body lacks other sources of food and energy, the fat cells are emptied and their contents used as fuel for energy. This raises the level of fatty compounds in the bloodstream, and that change, like the change in glucose in blood, serves as one of the triggers for the hunger drive.

The current view is that the amount of fat in the body is represented in some way in the brain—and the brain directs eating behavior to maintain the individual's optimal fat level. In effect, each person's brain tries to maintain a certain level of fat within that person's body. One proof for this view is that when an animal is starved and loses weight, it will, when it is allowed to eat as much as it wants, overeat until it has gained back the fat that was lost and, therefore, approach its usual fat level. The same process works in reverse when an animal is overfed (Bloom & Lazerson, 1988). One is reminded of the workings of a thermostat that manages, by turning a furnace on and off, to keep a building within a temperature range of one or two degrees.

Set point
An innate physiological mechanism that keeps an individual's body weight at a genetically "programmed" level.

Glycogen
The "animal starch" in the liver that is converted from glucose in the blood after eating.

Fat cells
The cells that are scattered throughout the body and designed for the storage of fatty compounds.

The Psychology of Hunger

Incentive objects

The stimuli that arouse a drive or motive.

Insulin

A hormone secreted by the pancreas that metabolizes blood sugar to provide the body with energy.

The hunger drive is also affected by outside stimuli called **incentive objects.** These may include, for example, the smell of food from a restaurant kitchen or the sight of pastries in a bakery window—or our eating habits and the social relationships we have built around eating. We tend to feel hungry around our usual dinner time regardless of our physiological condition, and we usually eat more when we are with family or friends than when we are alone.

Although the physiological mechanisms involved in hunger are the same in all of us, there are wide variations in the ways we seek to satisfy the hunger drive. Some snack continuously, while others generally eat only one meal each day. Individuals whose eating is initiated more readily by the presence of food in their environment rather than by internal physiological needs are referred to as "externals." Such individuals, when exposed to smell and sight of inviting food, undergo an increase in the hormone **insulin** in the blood (Rodin, 1985). Since insulin acts to reduce blood glucose and may well be the primary medium for signaling "I am hungry" to the brain (Bloom & Lazerson, 1988), this finding serves as another demonstration of how external factors can affect internal physiology.

Clearly, hunger appears to be the result of an intricate system of bodily and psychological states—among them the action of intestinal hormones, the level of glucose in the blood, the activity of the brain, the stores of fat in the body, and the presence of cues for eating in the environment and the nature of our reactions to them. Here, once again, we encounter one of the major issues in psychology described in Chapter 1: the interaction of biological and psychological forces in shaping behavior.

Displays like this can play a role in the experience of hunger.

What Makes Some People Fat?

It is estimated that somewhere between a quarter and a third of all adult Americans are at least 20 percent over their ideal weight—some by as much as 20 or 50 or even 100 pounds (Kolata, 1985). The reason is a mystery that many psychologists have spent years trying to unravel—in part because obesity can lead to severe psychological problems as well as to physical disorders such as high blood pressure, diabetes, and heart disease (Grinker, 1982). In addition to its deleterious impact on physical health, research has shown that the adverse social and economic consequences of obesity, especially in women, often are greater than those of other chronic physical conditions (Gortmaker, et al., 1993). In this longitudinal study, women who were overweight (above the ninety-fifth percentile in weight for age and sex) were found to complete fewer years of school, earn significantly less per year, and have higher rates of household poverty. Overweight men were 11 percent less likely to be married than their slimmer counterparts.

In some cases, obesity seems to stem from metabolic disturbances. Instead of turning food into energy at the normal rate, the body stores an excessive amount in fat. In most cases, however, obesity is simply the result of eating too much and exercising too little (Stunkard, 1985).

But why do people eat too much? Sometimes the reason seems to be **emotional stress.** Clinical psychologists have found that many overweight patients overeat to relieve anxieties over competition, failure, rejection, or sexual performance. A study of both lower-class urban residents and Ameri-

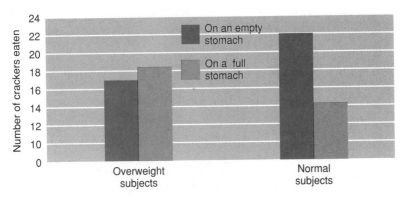

FIGURE 7.8 One clue to overeating An experimenter worked with two groups of subjects, one group of normal weight and the other anywhere from 14 to 75 percent overweight. When the subjects arrived at the laboratory, having skipped the previous meal, half from each group were fed sandwiches, the other half nothing. They then took part in what they thought was an evaluation of the taste of five different kinds of cracker presented to them in separate bowls. They were told that they could eat as few or as many of the crackers as they wished in making their judgments. As the graph shows, the amount eaten by the subjects of normal weight was considerably lower if they had just eaten sandwiches. The overweight subjects, however, actually ate somewhat more on a full stomach than on an empty stomach. For a possible explanation of these results, see the text (Schachter, 1971).

can Indians showed that individuals who undergo a great deal of stress and have an opportunity to eat will do so—and that the process, maintained over time, will lead to obesity (Pine, 1985).

The eating patterns of many fat people are unusual in several respects. For one thing, fat adults tend to eat whenever they have the opportunity, even if they have already had a meal and should not be hungry. This was demonstrated in striking fashion in the experiment illustrated in Figure 7.8. Overweight people tend to eat more and eat faster (Schachter, 1971). They are particularly likely to eat a lot when the food tastes unusually good—and more likely than people of normal weight to be turned off by food that tastes bad (Nisbett, 1968).

It is possible that overweight people have a form of brain abnormality affecting the hypothalamus. Or it may be that the bloodstream of overweight people carries some kind of chemical, produced by a quirk in the manner in which their alimentary canals and livers process food, that overstimulates the hypothalamus and thus creates more frequent and more intense feelings of hunger (N. E. Miller, 1975). Whatever the source of obesity, the condition is best dealt with through programs of management of eating behavior (Stunkard, 1985).

Yet for some obese people, even rigorous adherence to good nutrition practice will not yield great dividends. For these individuals, the problem may be in the cells that store fatty compounds. It has been found that at least some overweight people have an unusually large number of these cells in their bodies (Björntorp, 1972). These cells may be voracious consumers of fatty compounds carried by the bloodstream.

Thus overweight people, because of their excessive number of fat cells, may be constantly hungry for reasons they cannot control by an act of will

Emotional stress

The wear and tear on the body created by the physical changes that result from emotional states.

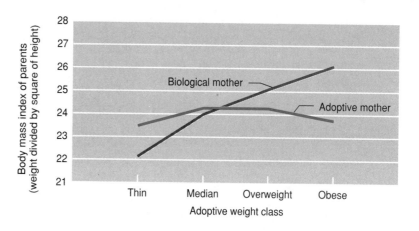

FIGURE 7.9 Fat parents, fat children Adults who had been adopted as children turned out to be thin, plump, or fat according to the size of their biological mothers rather than the size of the mothers who reared them. The pattern applies equally in the case of fathers as well (Stunkard, Foch, and Hrubec, 1986).

power. Their hunger may become particularly intense if they try to diet. It has been suggested that many fat people, because of the social pressure against obesity, are actually underweight rather than overweight in terms of the requirements of their own bodies (Nisbett, 1972).

Why do some people have more fat cells than others? The answer seems to lie partly in heredity. Identical twins, who have inherited the same genes, are twice as likely to be in the same weight range as are fraternal twins (Stunkard, Foch, & Hrubec, 1986). Additional evidence for a strong hereditary factor comes from studies of adoptive children, as illustrated in Figure 7.9.

One approach to solving the obesity problem may be to urge mothers not to push babies to overeat during the early period when the number of fat cells is being established. But this approach comes too late for overweight people beyond the age of childhood, who continue to have their difficulties despite everything that has been learned thus far about the hunger drive.

The Nature of Thirst

The thirst drive resembles the hunger drive in many respects. The common sense observation—that we get thirsty when our mouths are dry—again turns out to be partially true. The drive does depend in part on messages carried to the brain from the mouth—as well as from the throat, which seems to signal how much water has passed through, and from the stomach, which signals whether it is empty or full (Blass & Hall, 1976). But this is not the full explanation.

As with hunger, the hypothalamus plays an important role. A lack of water causes the cells of the body to become dehydrated, and certain nerve cells in the hypothalamus appear to be sensitive to this change (Rolls & Rolls, 1982). Moreover, when water is lost, the body immediately activates mechanisms to conserve it. A lack of water reduces the volume of blood flowing through the body, causing sensory receptors in the heart and blood vessels to send signals to the brain (Epstein, Kissileff, & Stellar, 1973). The reduced volume of blood also causes the kidneys to produce a chemical that stimulates the hypothalamus (Epstein, Fitzsimons, & Simons, 1969). Water loss results in the release of a hormone that helps prevent further loss through urination (Rolls & Rolls, 1982). Thus the thirst drive is triggered by various signs of imbalance in the body's water supply.

TEST YOURSELF

f) A friend whose pattern of eating varies periodically says that it's all a function of the body's set point. What is your friend trying to say?

g) Your roommate pleads with you not to expose him to any incentive objects in the refrigerator. What is being asked of you?

h) "All day, my brain has been getting signals of imbalances in my body's water supply." How would you make that statement in simpler terms?

The Sleep Drive: How We Spend a Third of Our Lives

All humans sleep. Between the darkness out of which we are born and the darkness in which we end, there is a tide of darkness that ebbs and flows each day of our lives to which we irresistibly submit. A third of life is spent in sleep—that most usual yet profoundly mysterious realm of our existence. By the time you are 70, it is likely that you will have slept a total of over 20 years.

There seems to be something special about a period of rest every 24 hours, the solar day caused by one revolution of our tilted planet in its yearly spin around the sun. It is almost impossible to find a living creature whose activity does not subside for at least one period each day. Lobsters become immobile. Butterflies fold their wings at night, attach themselves firmly to a blade of grass and refuse to budge until a civilized hour in the morning. At night some fish lie on their sides at the bottom of their aquarium. Others float on the surface of the sea. Frogs, lizards, and turtles grow still for long periods. Birds and mammals sleep. Every creature seems to reflect in its alternation between activity and rest the biological necessity for sleep.

Why do we sleep? Why do we and the animal world plunge into these periods of stillness? Why does the **sleep drive** play such an important part in the rhythm of our daily lives? And what causes us to experience dreams? Scientists have not yet fully answered these questions, but they have made considerable headway in tracking some of the unseen forces that govern the sleep-wake rhythm.

Sleep drive
A major drive aroused by the physiological requirements for sleep.

A Night's Journey: The Stages of Sleep

Sleep may feel like a blanket of darkness, punctuated by a remembered dream, a time when the mind is totally "out of it." Nothing could be less true. Studies have shown clearly that sleep is by no means a state of suspended animation in which the body and brain are shut down for a time. Instead it is a kind of activity in its own right. The brain continues to be highly active—though in a different way. All night a person drifts through different levels, or stages, of consciousness and inward activity. Using the EEG machine, which traces the pattern of the brain's electrical changes, as well as other physiological measures of body temperature, pulse, and respiration, researchers like the one pictured in Figure 7.10 have charted the stages of the average person's journey into sleep.

Imagine you are watching your own descent into sleep, standing over the shoulder of the sleep researcher pictured in Figure 7.10. You are about to see a journey you make each night, yet one of which you are scarcely aware. As graph paper slowly moves under the pens of the EEG, a small pinched scrawl emerges. From the shapes of these waves the researcher can see when you closed your eyes. There, on one line, the rise and fall of breathing has become even. On another line is the metronome flick of the pulse, also steady and even. Body temperature is gradually going down. The brain waves are showing a very definite, even frequency of about 9 to 13 waves per second, known as the **alpha rhythm.** Seeing this, the researcher knows that you are in a state of relaxation. You are awake but serene, and soon you will pass into sleep.

Alpha rhythm
A state in which brain waves show a dominant frequency of about 9 to 13 waves per second, usually when the person is relaxed, with eyes closed.

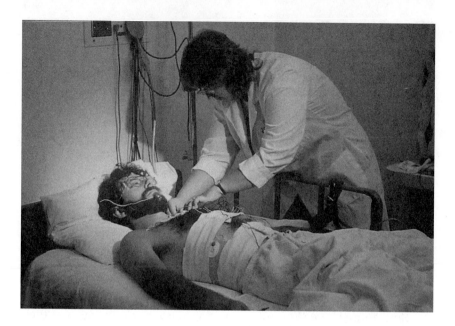

FIGURE 7.10 **Sleeping for science** Volunteers and patients by the hundreds of thousands have slept in sleep laboratories while researchers have recorded the changes taking place in the brain and body. Here a subject is readied for a night of sleep.

Myoclonic jerk

A sudden spasm in the body caused by a tiny burst of brain activity.

Sleep stages (I, II, III, and IV)

The changes in the brain waves indicating light sleep to deep sleep.

A sudden spasm of your body may now awaken you for a fraction of a second. This is a sign of neural changes. it is known as the **myoclonic jerk,** resulting from a tiny burst of activity in the brain, and children often describe it as a feeling of "falling off the bed." This phenomenon is normal in human sleep. It is finished in a fraction of a second and the descent continues. Even if your eyes were partly open, you would be blind now. If an object were held before your eyes for a moment and you were awakened, you would not remember having seen it.

Your journey includes **sleep stages (I, II, III, IV).** From the threshold of sleep, you sink into *Stage I*. The pens trace waves that are small and pinched, showing that the voltage from the sleeping brain is small and rapidly changing. Your muscles relax and pulse slows, but you might not feel asleep. If awakened, you might insist that you were wide awake.

If not disturbed, you will sink in a few minutes into *Stage II* of sleep, in which the pens trace out quick bursts of brain activity, brain waves that are rapidly growing larger. The lines recording eye movements show shallow waves as your eyes slowly roll from side to side. If you were awakened now, you might say that you had been awake all along—but you might be much less certain of that. At this point you have been asleep for about 10 minutes. You might recall vague thoughts as mundane as shopping lists, yet intermixed with strange images.

You are now descending into deeper sleep and are growing progressively harder to awaken. Within about 30 minutes you are probably immersed in *Stage III*. Now the pens trace brain waves that resemble a profile of buttes and mountains. As these brain waves show, the voltages are now much higher, and the changes are occurring more slowly. You may move. You may mutter. But your muscles are relaxed. Your breathing is even. Your temperature and blood pressure are still falling slightly, and it would take a loud noise to awaken you.

Stage III soon merges into *Stage IV*. It is the bottom of the lagoon, also called **delta sleep,** for the large but slow brain waves that are known as delta waves. These have the profile of mountain ranges, and they signify the silent darkness of the ultimate depths. Stage IV seems to be a relatively dreamless oblivion. Sounds that might have awakened you 10 minutes ago may not penetrate consciousness now. If someone shakes you, rings a bell, or calls your name, you will reluctantly rise to the surface. Most likely you would remember nothing and would say your mind was blank. This is the sleep of the weary, and probably the state that most people like to consider sleep. Yet, it is only a fraction of the total night of sleep. You do not remain in the lower depths. After about 20 minutes you start drifting upward into lighter sleep.

About 70 to 90 minutes after falling asleep, you approach the surface. You may turn over in bed, or even thrash around for a moment. However, instead of breaking through into wakefulness, or simply floating on the threshold of consciousness, something odd has happened. You are so removed from the world that it would take a loud sound to awaken you. The EEG script, irregular and small, is a low voltage rapidly changing brain wave that resembles waking. You are entering **REM sleep,** or **rapid-eye-movement sleep**—so named because, among other changes in the body, the eyes begin darting rapidly under closed eyelids. During REM, your body physiology reflects a state of great excitement. Your heart beats irregularly. Your blood pressure fluctuates as it might during a period of intense waking emotion. Your genitals may indicate arousal—an erection if you are a male and vaginal lubrication and congestion if you are a female—even though the dream content may be bland. Despite the storm of internal activity, your body is as relaxed as a piece of cloth. Because the brain's activity is similar to the waking state but the muscles are almost totally relaxed, the period is also referred to as **paradoxical sleep.**

As shown in Figure 7.11, during the night you repeat the entire cycle four or five times, as if slowly sinking and rising on a recurrent tide—and if you have a bed partner who falls asleep when you do, chances are that you both enter and leave each stage of sleep at about the same time (Hobson, 1989). Toward morning, you no longer sink to the bottom in delta sleep, and your REM periods are longer. Sleep is lighter. Your body temperature begins to rise. Your blood chemistry is changing. Soon you will awaken. You may remember a dream fragment, a moment of awakening, or nothing at all. Yet your mind was active throughout that time, and you were dreaming for a total of several hours. Altogether about a quarter of the night is spent in this period, marked by dreaming, which is such a unique aspect of sleep that its possible functions will be described and in more detail shortly.

Delta sleep
The deep sleep of Stage IV, indicated by large but slow delta brain waves.

REM (rapid-eye-movement) sleep
A type of sleep in which the brain waves resemble a waking state and the eyes begin to dart rapidly under closed eyelids.

Paradoxical sleep
A type of sleep in which brain waves resemble a waking state but the muscles of the body are in an almost totally relaxed state.

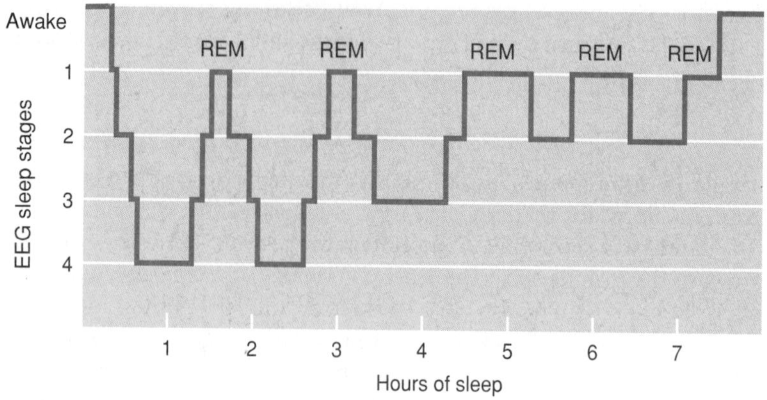

FIGURE 7.11 The cycles of a night of sleep During a normal night, the sleeper moves through the various stages of sleep in cycles described in the text.

The Need for Sleep

The amount of sleep an individual needs varies considerably from one period of life to another. At birth, an infant sleeps as many as 18 hours a day. By age 4, the amount is reduced, on the average, to 9 to 10 hours, and by adolescence to 7½ hours—after which it declines gradually to about 6½ in old age (Hauri, 1982).

At any age, however, sleep would seem to be one of the most essential needs of higher mammals. Merely lying in bed and resting is no substitute for real sleep (Mendelson et al., 1984). In fact, any lack of sleep below your natural requirements, whether from insomnia or other causes, is likely to make you feel tired, irritable, and generally below par. Despite the profound importance of sleep, millions of Americans do not get enough of it, a deficit that often has severe repercussions, as discussed in the Psychology and the Media box entitled "The Great American Sleep Debt."

Although some people have been known to go without sleep entirely for a number of days without suffering any apparent damage (Webb & Cartwright, 1978), the older we get the more our performance and well-being suffer. A person can survive starvation for over three weeks, but three weeks' loss of sleep can produce symptoms that resemble mental illness. Prolonged sleep deprivation can lead not only to a loss of mental efficiency, but also to disturbances of perception and hallucinations—effects quickly overcome once the individual is allowed to sleep (Horne, 1988).

Even when only the normal cycles of sleep and waking are disrupted, we pay a price. This can be seen whenever there is a significant shift in schedules—for example, when we travel across time zones, and jet lag makes us feel as if our normally routine functioning is terribly out of kilter. Investigators have found that shift work has the same effect, creating inefficiency, irritability, fatigue, physical symptoms, depression, and a reduction of mental acuity (Akerstedt, Torsvall, & Gillberg, 1982).

The sleep drive appears to be triggered by imbalances in brain chemistry, and possibly body chemistry as well, that build up when we are awake and active. When we sleep, we correct the chemical imbalances and wake up ready to function again at full efficiency. Moreover, a sleep-producing chemical substance, called acetylcholine, has been found in the brains of animals and in human urine. When even very tiny amounts of this chemical are injected into the brains of other animals, it causes about a 50 percent increase in very deep, dream-free sleep (Maugh, 1982). If the chemical factor could be produced synthetically, it might solve the problems of people who experience sleep disorders. At present, however, investigators have to process more than 4 tons of urine to obtain about a millionth of an ounce of the chemical.

Why We Dream: The Functions of REM

As described earlier, the period known as REM sleep is different from the rest of the night, and it can easily be observed in the sleep laboratory. When it occurs—roughly every 90 minutes—your eyes move as if you were watching a TV show or movie, and the chances are 85 percent that you are experiencing a vivid or at least describable dream.

The dreams that occur during REM sleep can be so vivid that the content of dreams has been used by psychologists and psychiatrists since Freud to help understand some of the hidden emotional aspects of a person's life. But the REM period is also a unique physiological state, common to all mammals. Because REM sleep periods are of longer duration in the young, psychologists reason that its functions must be "strictly and deeply biological" (Hobson, 1989) and perhaps spur neural growth in young organisms. Supporting this hypothesis is the fact that the rate of protein synthesis in the brain is at its highest during REM sleep (Hobson, 1989). By restoring brain proteins essential for learning and memory, REM may work to keep brain tissues in good working order.

Both people and animals have more than their normal amount of REM sleep when, in their waking lives, they are involved in novel situations that require learning or new challenges. Moreover, a higher proportion of REM sleep occurs among individuals experiencing significant psychological problems (Hartmann, 1984).

Yet another function of REM sleep may be, to borrow a term from computer technology, "file maintenance" for the brain's memory banks. REM sleep may afford an opportunity for the brain to arrange memories in a hierarchy of psychological and emotional importance—and to discard items that are no longer needed (Crick and Mitchison, 1983).

TEST YOURSELF

i) If someone is extremely difficult to awaken, what stage of sleep is that person most likely to be experiencing?

j) What physiological features of REM sleep account for its also being called paradoxical sleep?

Pain and Temperature: Safeguarding the Body

"If I could get rid of this toothache, I'd never complain about another thing in my life." Such words of anguish are often spoken by individuals engulfed in pain. Try to remember the last episode of a severe headache, burn, cut, or bump you had to endure. You probably felt you would be glad to try anything to be relieved of the pain. It should not surprise us that we pay billions of dollars each year for "pain killers" and submit to operations meant to bring relief from pain.

In Chapter 3, you read about both pain and changes of temperature as sensations, and learned about the central nervous system mechanisms through which we become aware of them. Here we will consider these topics briefly once again—but this time as events that threaten our safety and well-

The Great American Sleep Debt

Americans are sleepy people. That is the conclusion of the National Commission on Sleep Disorders Research, which issued its final report last week. The commission, which was established by Congress to research sleep and its impact on society, estimated that 40 million Americans have sleep disorders and millions more suffer from a simple lack of sleep that can have grave repercussions.

The resulting sleepiness, according to commission chairman William Dement, chairman of the Stanford University Sleep Disorders Center, "makes them extremely vulnerable to inappropriate and often catastrophic sleep episodes and undermines their intellectual and emotional capacity."

Those episodes include serious traffic accidents caused by drowsy drivers, industrial accidents and lost productivity from employees who fall asleep on the job. The commission estimated that in 1990 sleep problems cost at least $16 billion in lost productivity, medical costs and sick leave. This does not include costs of catastrophic disasters in which sleep deprivation played a role. The commission report said that the study of sleep has been neglected and what is available is fragmented and uncoordinated. It called for leadership in sleep research, including the establishment of a center for sleep disorders and research at the National Institutes of Health.

Commission officials said sleep disorders are commonly overlooked by physicians and their patients. They identified 17 specific disorders such as sleep apnea (repeated cessation of breathing during sleep causing numerous wakenings each night and leading to cardiovascular complications), narcolepsy (uncontrollable sleep episodes) and chronic insomnia. They estimated 95 percent of cases go undiagnosed.

"A river of seriously ill sleep-disordered patients [is] flowing past the unseeing eyes of physicians, [and therefore] the lives and health of literally millions of Americans are in jeopardy," said Dement.

But just as important, Dement and other commission members said, is "the American sleep debt," the chronic scrimping on sleep that affects uncounted millions. The resulting fatigue can erode performance, interpersonal relations, child rearing, learning, psychological well-being and behavior, they argued.

"The sleep debt, we believe, is every bit as important as the national debt," said commission member James K. Walsh, a special commission adviser and sleep specialist at Deaconess Hospital in St. Louis. Walsh is president of the American Sleep Disorders Association. "Whether it is caused by sleep disorders or sleep deprivation or daily rhythm factors, sleepiness is extremely prevalent . . . , and the consequences in the workplace and on the roads . . . are very costly."

"Using any yardstick," he said, "whether it be pain and suffering, profit and loss or life and death, our country is paying a steep price."

The commission said that 56 percent of night workers report falling asleep on the job at least once a week, and more than 50 percent of these report

---

being. Safeguarding the body from noxious stimuli such as pain or extreme heat can be considered to constitute a physiologically based drive. For when we succeed in doing so, we alter a physiological imbalance that threatens homeostasis and both our physical and psychological survival.

Internal Responses to Pain

Pain drive

A major drive that leads us to avoid events that would damage our bodies.

The **pain drive** leads us to avoid events that would damage our bodies. It accounts for such learned behavior as keeping our hands away from flames, being careful with sharp objects, and taking medicine to relieve a headache. Studies show the validity of what many of us have subjectively perceived. Careful measurements of subjective pain demonstrate that, in sufficient doses, aspirin does indeed reduce pain (Forster et al., 1988), and so does alcohol when it is in an amount equivalent to two cocktails (Woodrow & Eltherington, 1988).

errors by themselves or coworkers that are caused by lack of sleep. Sleep researcher Mary Carskadon, from Brown University and a member of the commission, said that the brain has an inherent daily rhythm of sleepiness, for most people during two periods, the main one between 2 a.m. and 6 a.m. and another during the midafternoon. Studies have shown that night-shift workers, even those who have slept well during the day, often notice these drowsy periods.

Walsh said his studies have found that someone working at night is roughly as sleepy as a day worker who had four hours of sleep the night before.

The researchers said the sleep deficits have gradually developed in this century, in large part as a response to the flexibility in lifestyle that followed the introduction of electric lights. Carskadon, who specializes in sleep problems of children and adolescents, noted that in 1910, children ages 10 to 12 averaged 10½ hours of sleep a night. In 1990, the average was closer to nine hours. In 1910, teens between 13 and 17 slept about 9½ hours a night. In 1990, it was a bit over eight hours in 13-year-olds and 7½ hours in 17-year-olds.

"We do not fully know all the consequences of this chronic sleep insufficiency, but we do know about 25 percent of teens report falling asleep in school at least once a week and more than 10 percent say they're late for school at least once a week because they've overslept," she said.

"Sleepiness," she said, "is not caused by a warm room, a dull lecture, a big meal, a long drive. These situations simply unmask or uncover the brain's sleepiness that is already present."

Carskadon said surveys show that fewer than half of American adults get eight hours of sleep each day and a quarter get less than seven hours. The exact amount needed varies, of course, from individual to individual, and there is a debate about the exact needs of the population as a whole. Carskadon believes that nearly all adults require at least seven hours of sleep "to avoid accumulating a sleep debt," and most adults require at least eight hours. Among the most dramatic examples of problems caused by lack of sleep cited by the commission members were:

- The 1989 Exxon Valdez oil spill in Alaska, in which transportation officials found that the third mate who was piloting the ship had fallen asleep.
- The 1979 Three Mile Island nuclear plant accident, in which fatigued workers at 4 a.m. did not respond to a mechanical failure.

Source: From "The Great American Sleep Debt" by Sandy Rovner, 1993, *Washington Post,* January 12.

Issues to Consider

1. What modern technological innovations in addition to electric lights may disrupt the brain's inherent daily rhythms for sleepiness? Can you list behaviors that interfere with natural sleep rhythms?
2. Assuming you have normal sleep patterns, at what time of day might you be least well-prepared to take a difficult exam, according to this article?

In addition, however, our nervous system provides protection against intolerable pain by producing its own painkillers. As described in Chapter 2, researchers have demonstrated the existence in both animal and human brains of a group of peptides called **endorphins,** whose effect is similar to the painkiller morphine. Although the perception of pain is essential to warn us of threats to the body, unrelenting pain would eventually disable us. Endorphins regulate the degree of pain we experience (Bloom & Lazerson, 1988).

Sensitivity to pain varies widely from person to person. There are people who claim never to feel any significant pain, and at the other extreme are those who feel excruciating pain even from slight bumps or abrasions—perhaps because their production of endorphins is poor. Or, perhaps, individuals who are exquisitely sensitive to pain are by nature sensitive to discomfort. Some people, for example, who are naturally anxious and focus on their symptoms report more aches and pains than those who are not (Ahles, Cassens, & Stalling, 1987). The perception of pain can vary not only from

Endorphins
The peptides or brain chemicals that affect the part of the brain associated with pain and mood.

one person to another, but within the same individual from one time to another. It has been shown that when we are with friends, we are likely to cope more effectively with pain than when we are with strangers (Spanos et al., 1984)—still another example of the powerful role that social contact plays in shaping behavior.

Psychological Dimensions of Pain

The study just described demonstrates that the behaviors associated with the pain drive do not depend on physiological factors alone. Such psychological factors as suggestibility and attentiveness are at play as well.

Even mere suggestion can alter pain perception. When placebos—non-active sugar or salt pills or injections—are given to experimental subjects as a painkiller, some people actually experience pain relief. Just the expectation of relief appears to cause the release of endorphins. Some current evidence points to the existence of pain-relief systems within the body that are separate from the endorphin system. Hypnosis works through another pain-relief pathway, integrated at the highest levels of the nervous system and involving cognitive and memory factors. Perhaps this pain-relief pathway is put to use by people, such as long-distance runners or football players, whose intense concentration on their goals enables them to ignore or subdue pain. Ballet dancers, too, can execute triumphant performances on bloody feet.

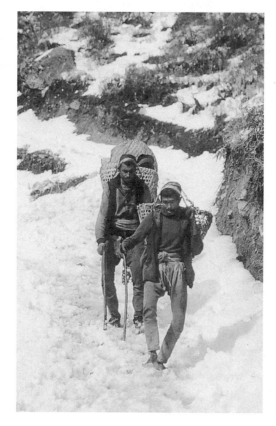

These Nepalese Sherpas define pain in a different way than do people in the Western world.

If we can manage somehow not to pay attention to pain, we are better able to endure it. The role of distraction was demonstrated in a study in which college students were exposed to painful pressure on their skin. One group, however, was preoccupied by the task of tracing letters. Their perception of the pain was considerably less pronounced than those who specifically paid attention to the painful stimuli (Dubreuil, Endler, and Spanos, 1987–88).

Cultural factors are at play as well. Although the thresholds for sensing pain are likely to be the same across various cultures, the degree of pain perceived by an individual depends to a surprising degree on social and cultural background. An example of how culturally defined learning defines human perception of pain can be seen in the contrasting perceptions of childbirth from one society to another. In some societies, women pursue their daily tasks until just before a baby is to be delivered and return to their normal routines within a few hours. In other societies, women have learned to anticipate significant and disabling pain. The Lamaze method of training for "natural childbirth" is based on the premise that women in most Western cultures have been conditioned to expect and fear the pain of giving birth. "The fear produces changes in their muscle tone and breathing patterns that hamper the process and make it more painful. The Lamaze methods teach breathing control and provide exercises to strengthen pelvic muscles. They also explain the entire process of birth, so women know what to expect. Thus, learning, which takes place in the higher cortical regions, can modify the experience of pain" (Bloom and Lazerson, 1988).

How Temperature Is Regulated

The **temperature drive** is common to all warm-blooded animals. In humans its goal is to maintain the body's inner temperature at about 98.6° Fahrenheit (37° centigrade). It appears to be controlled by neurons in the hypothalamus that are sensitive to temperature changes in the body.

When stimulated by increased warmth, these cells send off messages that cause perspiration (which cools the body through evaporation) and that also cause more blood to move toward the surface of the body, where it loses heat more quickly. Even when we feel the heat of emotional upset, we may begin to sweat to "cool off." When we are ill and "run a fever," it may be that the body is "putting the heat on" the invading bacterial organisms, which are vulnerable to the increased temperature and are destroyed. Another reason may be that the higher body temperature helps stir into action certain antibody-producing cells—thus causing the white blood cells to move faster to the area of infection and overwhelm the body's invaders (Bloom & Lazerson, 1988).

When the temperature-sensitive cells of the hypothalamus detect a drop in body temperature, they cause the sympathetic nervous system to route blood away from the skin and toward inner muscles and vital organs so that the body will not lose heat. At the same time, this mechanism causes an erection of fur or feathers in animals in order to trap a layer of warm air next to the skin—a phenomenon experienced by humans as "goose bumps." The "shivers" (caused by a constriction of blood vessels of the skin) also help generate heat, as does a rise in the body's basal metabolism rate—that is, the rate at which the body burns up oxygen.

Temperature drive

A major drive that attempts to keep the body's internal temperature at about 98.6° Fahrenheit or 37° centigrade.

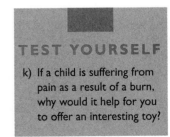

TEST YOURSELF

k) If a child is suffering from pain as a result of a burn, why would it help for you to offer an interesting toy?

Sex: An Emotion, Drive, and Motive

The subject of sexual behavior provides a transition from consideration of drives to a discussion of motives, for motives are directed at psychological goals rather than at attaining goals that affect the body directly, like food, water, and sleep. Sexual behavior in humans is, of course, a drive state controlled by the brain—but it is also a powerful motive.

Hormones, the Brain, and Sex

If this were a book about animals, sex could be discussed in much simpler terms. Among nonhuman mammals, sex is almost as direct a drive as hunger, though less frequently triggered. Usually the female sex drive is quiescent, and over long stretches of time the female is not sexually attractive to the male of her species. At regularly recurring periods, however, the ovaries release hormones that activate a sex control mechanism centered in the hypothalamus of the brain. During these periods, which vary in frequency and length from species to species, the female seeks sexual contacts and engages in the kind of courtship and copulation characteristic of the species. The female's readiness is apparent from such clues as odors, vocal signals (the sex "calls" of cats), or changes in the color and size of the genitals. These cues in turn prompt the male to initiate sexual behavior.

Estrogen

The chief female sex hormone.

Androgens

The male sex hormones.

The hormones that determine animal sexual behavior are present in humans as well. **Estrogen** and **androgen**—the female and male sex hormones—circulate in us as they do, for example, in mice. And, as in mice, they influence the activity of certain nerve cells in the hypothalamus and other parts of the brain's limbic system. These, in turn, influence the production of additional hormones. But that is where the basic similarity between humans and animals ends. The specifics of human sexual behavior are quite different from those of mice (Bloom & Lazerson, 1988).

Menopause

The period when the ovaries cease to function and menstruation ends.

Sexual responsiveness, especially in human females, does not seem to be strongly tied to hormones. To begin with, the desire for sex among women is not significantly keyed to monthly fluctuations in hormone levels (Harvey, 1987). While the female animal without ovaries is totally unreceptive to sex and typically fights off the male's overtures, a woman without ovaries—and, therefore, without a supply of estrogen—is still motivated for sexual activity. After the female **menopause,** when the ovaries no longer function and menstruation ends, sexual interest and activity not only do not wane but may increase. The disappearance of a totally human, psychological concern—about becoming pregnant—may be the reason.

Although it is true that human males without any male hormone are less active sexually, such effects are hardly universal. Again there is a marked contrast between lower animal species and humans. In rats, for example, castration leads to a progressive reduction and, eventually, an end to sexual activity. In human males with cancer of the testicles who must undergo chemical treatment that prevents the formation of male sex hormones, the effect is far less clear. Although some of these men no longer pursue sex, others maintain their usual sex life (P. A. Walker, 1978). Moreover, recent studies of men with underactive testicles (and, therefore, low sexual desire) show that, while doses of testosterone may help enhance the motivation for sex, they play little or no role in the sexual act itself (J. Davidson et al., 1988).

Clearly, the extent to which hormones determine sexual behavior is less pronounced for humans than for animals. Nor does human sexual behavior depend on some "sex center" in the brain that operates like an on-off switch. Thus, biology alone cannot explain all of human sexual behavior. For example, it is often the emotional fallout of marital conflict—not hormonal changes—that is the occasion for reduced sexual desire among couples.

The Power of Psychological Influences

Sexual expression is influenced not only by basic biological urges but by a whole array of desires and preferences that we begin to learn in childhood and may continue to revise throughout our lives. For a discussion of how sexual behavior varies over the years, see the Life Span Perspective box, "The Sexual Motive from Infancy to Old Age."

LIFE SPAN PERSPECTIVE

The Sexual Motive from Infancy to Old Age

Like many other human behaviors, sexual behavior evolves across the life span. Changes reflect not only biological capacities for sex at various stages of life, but also the different psychological and social meanings attached to the motive for sex during distinct periods.

- Ultrasound photographs of male fetuses, revealing erections in the womb (Calderone, 1983), suggest that the basic physiological activities symptomatic of sexual arousal are in place at the very start of life. Researchers have observed masturbatory actions and orgasm-like behavior in baby boys not yet a year old (Kinsey, Pomeroy, & Martin, 1948), and in infant girls (Kinsey et al., 1953). Although it is not clear how prevalent or purposeful masturbation is among children, it does seem that the motive for sex exists in rudimentary form well prior to maturity; still, while many infants and children exhibit sexual behavior, they do not do so in the kind of goal-directed way found later on in their development (Offir, 1982). Observations and interviews with children suggest that a motivated interest in sex—playing "doctor," asking questions about body parts and the "facts of life"—must await the child's cognitive maturation.
- Adolescence brings the first serious attempts to build relationships with the opposite sex. Sexuality emerges as a prominent concern, not only because of the physical changes of puberty but also because adolescents must establish their sexual identities as they cope with all the other difficulties of becoming adults. The challenges of these years intensified beginning in the 1960s, many believe, when much of society adopted more permissive attitudes toward sex. By the 1980s, about half of white

females and three-fourths of black females were having intercourse before age 18 (Furstenberg, Brooks-Gunn, and Chase-Lansdale, 1989). The figures for teenage boys—traditionally higher—have not changed as much, but today fewer male adolescents have sexual experiences exclusively with prostitutes or "bad" girls, and more with friends or classmates.

- During young adulthood, there is less peer pressure to engage in sex and fewer demands from parents to set limits—new freedoms that allow opportunities for sexual experiences dictated from within rather than without. Yet external factors still influence sexual behavior. Despite more liberal attitudes, young American adults appear to exercise growing care in the selection of partners (Ehrenreich, Hess, & Jacobs, 1986). Indiscriminate, casually initiated sexual encounters—both among heterosexual as well as homosexual couples—have decreased mainly in response to the threat of AIDS. At the same time, however, sex outside of marriage has become more common. This recent trend is especially apparent among women, whom some studies indicate are as likely as their mates to engage in extramarital relationships (Seagraves, 1989; Wyatt, Peters, & Guthrie, 1988).

- Through the adult years, many persons remain happily active sexually with their mates of many years. A complex interplay of physical and psychological factors can—and often does—enrich a sexual relationship in adulthood. For others, motivation for sex with one's mate may diminish at this time, and sexual dysfunctions may appear that often are regarded as symptomatic of marital tensions and the accompanying feelings of anger (Clifford and Kolodny, 1983). Seeking to understand the factors at work makes the topic endlessly puzzling to individuals and societies—and challenging to scientists.

- Sexuality in old age continues to reflect an interplay of physiological changes and social attitudes. Biologically, the sexual response changes. Older men take longer to become sexually excited and erections tend to be less frequent and less firm. As a result of a sharp drop in estrogen, some women experience a decrease in vaginal lubrication, making sexual intercourse painful (Sarrel, 1990). Other earlier signs of sexual excitement—nipple erection and clitoris enlargement—may abate. And, for both sexes, the orgasm is marked by fewer contractions. Social attitudes, too, exert an effect. In a youth-oriented culture, older persons are not expected by society to be sexual and may be looked upon as strange if their sexual motives are still strong at this time of life (Crooks & Baur, 1990). Despite the problems, the zest for sex—and the pleasure of the experience—are not universally extinguished with age. Studies following subjects over long periods reveal that earlier patterns of sexual interest and ability often are maintained. Given reasonably good health, sexual activity can play a vibrant role throughout the "declining" years (Adams & Turner, 1985). ■

Sexual excitement can arise without physical contact. Some people find that even fantasizing about a sexual encounter can bring about not only sexual arousal but orgasm (Bloom & Lazerson, 1988), and a disinterest in sex can be reversed simply by thoughts of novel sexual experiences. In one study,

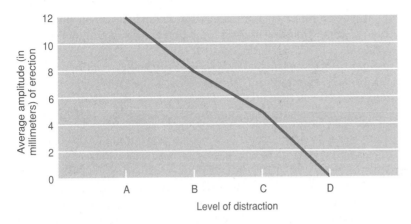

FIGURE 7.12 The effect of distractions on sexual arousal A group of men listened through earphones to an erotic audiotape—first without any distraction (*A*), and then simultaneously with each of three tapes containing increasingly distracting material. The distracting tapes required the subjects to write down a series of numbers (*B*); add successive pairs of digits and write down the results (*C*); and classify pairs of digits according to a complex scheme (*D*). Note that as the level of distraction rose, penile erection faltered (adapted from Geer and Fuhr, 1976).

a group of both women and men saw a sexually explicit film on four consecutive days. At the end of the fourth day, they became bored, and some even reported a negative effect. Half the subjects then saw a film with the same actors performing different sex acts, and half with different actors performing the same acts. All of the subjects reported being aroused again by the novelty (Kelley & Musialowski, 1986).

Conversely, the excitement phase of the sexual cycle is often aborted by purely psychological factors—especially by anxiety, or by distracting stimuli such as a knock on the door or a ringing telephone (Geer & Fuhr, 1976). From the study of college-aged men portrayed in Figure 7.12, it would seem that the more distracting the outside stimulus, the greater the impact on arousal.

Even in animals, sexual functioning can be strongly influenced by the environment. As one example, research on monkeys has shown that levels of the male sexual hormone testosterone vary as a function of the social situation in which an animal finds himself. If a male is placed in contact with female monkeys in an environment that includes other subordinate males, his testosterone level will increase—and these increased levels are accompanied by increased sexual activity. On the other hand, when the male is placed in a setting in which he is dominated by the other males, his testosterone level will decrease—leading, in turn, to lower levels of sexual activity (Moberg, 1987). While hormones affect behavior, hormonal activity in turn is regulated by the social milieu.

Social and Cultural Influences

- In the United States, thin women are regarded as sexually attractive—but in parts of Africa, lanky American fashion models would be viewed as revolting. There, women spend a period before their marriage in a "fattening hut" where they are placed on diets intended to increase their bulk—and thus enhance their sexual seductiveness (Gregersen, 1983).

- Petting, or foreplay, as a prelude to intercourse is virtually universal in the Western world, but among some Polynesians, petting follows rather than precedes sexual union.
- To most Americans, sexual intercourse with a close relative—parent, sister, brother—is repugnant. Not so to the Kubeo tribe of South America, who *demand* that a boy have intercourse with his mother to highlight officially the start of his sex life (Gregersen, 1983).

Those are just a few examples of how sexual behavior in humans is shaped by the values and standards of the society in which individuals live—a potent reminder of the role of social context in human behavior. To social historians, this would hardly seem surprising. Over the centuries, every shade of sexual attitude has been enthusiastically adopted in one setting but condemned in others. Homosexual acts were punishable by death among the ancient Hebrews but taken for granted by the Greeks. The early Christians held that abstinence was the only way to deal with the sex urge—at about the same time the Romans were staging their orgies. In the early years of this century, mention of sex, in either print or conversation, was virtually taboo. Today there is almost complete freedom to discuss or write about sex, and movies often present sex as a major theme.

Evidence of how society's attitudes have revolutionized sexual behavior in America is not hard to find. Fifty years ago, for example, marriage was seen by most Americans as the main avenue to sexual activity, while today premarital and even extramarital sex are more widely accepted (Crooks and Baur, 1990). Most people are no longer mortified when someone in public life, male or female, acknowledges homosexual behavior—and the gay liberation movement is prominent in many cities and colleges.

Whether in a remote African village or a teeming American city, social and cultural forces clearly shape the drive and motive for sex. An evolutionary perspective is useful in linking the various influences, as well as in clarifying certain gender-based differences in sexual attitudes and emotions. In a study addressing that point, U.S. college students, both men and women, were asked to visualize their partner engaging in sexual relations with another person and, separately, forming a strong emotional relationship with another person. The students' responses to each scenario were recorded, using several physiologic measures—skin conductance, pulse rate, and muscle activity. While both sexes were distressed over both types of infidelity, men were more upset by the notion of sexual infidelity of a mate than by emotional infidelity, as depicted in Figure 7.13. Women felt just the opposite (Buss et al., 1992). The researchers ascribed the differences to evolutionary-based sex roles: Women are more threatened by the loss of a mate's investment in the task of rearing offspring, while men are more threatened by the risk of investing their resources in genetically unrelated offspring.

Sexual Orientation

Sexual orientation

The attraction felt toward persons of a given sex.

Heterosexual

A strong sexual attraction to members of the opposite sex.

The direction taken by the motive for sex defines our **sexual orientation**—the attraction felt toward persons of a given sex. The majority of men and women are **heterosexual,** feeling strong sexual attraction to members of the opposite sex. Those who are **homosexual** are drawn to members of their own sex. Those who are open to both homosexual and heterosexual experiences are termed **bisexual.**

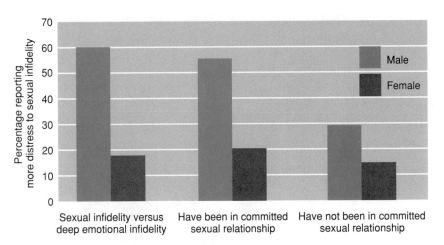

FIGURE 7.13 Sex differences in jealousy Men said they would be more distressed by a sexual infidelity in a mate than by emotional infidelity, and men who actually had experienced a committed sexual relationship were most likely to be distressed over the thought of a mate's sexual infidelity. In contrast, women were more distressed by a partner's emotional infidelity than by his sexual infidelity, a response that held true whether or not the women had experienced a committed sexual relationship.

It is estimated that from 2 to 4 percent of the male population and 0.5 to 1 percent of the female population are purely homosexual in their orientation (Katchadourian and Lunde, 1980; Ellis & Ames, 1987). In addition, it is fairly common for people to report having engaged on occasion in homosexual fantasies, and many adults describe themselves as having had one or several homosexual experiences. These typically take place during the adolescent years, and most often among boys (Dreyer, 1982).

What causes an individual to develop a homosexual orientation? This question, which has long attracted the interest of researchers in psychology and other behavioral sciences, is now being addressed as well by neuroscientists. No definitive answers have been found.

Some psychologists have examined the idea that many homosexuals grew up with a weak and unavailable father and a strong, authoritarian mother. But studies of the backgrounds of hundreds of homosexuals do not reveal this pattern in an obvious way. Researchers have also explored a variety of other environmental factors—among them, for example, the sexual adventures of childhood, sibling and peer relationships, and experiences in dating. But the patterns of homosexuals and heterosexuals do not reveal significant contrasts (Bell, Weinberg, & Hammersmith, 1981). Nor does homosexuality appear to result from conditioned learning—that is, from early homosexual episodes that provide pleasurable, reinforcing rewards. Indeed, the best predictor of homosexuality in adulthood is the existence of homosexual feelings prior to any homosexual activity (Bloom & Lazerson, 1988).

This fact suggests the possibility of a biological basis for homosexuality. The brain's exposure to an abnormal level of sex hormones during a critical period of prenatal development may predispose a person to adult homosexuality. For example, animal studies have revealed that stress during pregnancy can affect levels of male hormonal concentrations in the brain of the fetus, leading to the "feminization of offspring" (Moyer, Herrenkohl, & Jacobowitz, 1978; Jacobowitz, 1989). And when human homosexual males are injected with estrogen, many show a biochemical response of the brain's pituitary gland typical of women—a response not found among heterosexual males (Gladue, Geen, & Hellman, 1984). Despite such findings, the actual levels of sex hormones within any given individual do not correlate with that individual's sexual orientation.

Homosexual

A strong sexual attraction to members of the same sex.

Bisexual

A sexual attraction to both sexes.

The origins of homosexuality are still not clear.

The possibility of an innate biological basis for some homosexuality appears to be buttressed by research reports of specific anatomical differences in the brains of homosexual and heterosexual men. Reported differences have included the finding of an enlarged suprachiasmatic nucleus in homosexual men (Swaab & Hofman, 1990); another investigator reported that post-mortem analyses revealed a part of the anterior hypothalamus in homosexual men was anatomically more similar to the brain structure typically found in women, as opposed to heterosexual men (LeVay, 1991). Because the hypothalamus is known to govern sexual behavior, this finding may be more than simply a correlation, but, as noted in Chapter 2, more research is needed to tell us if the difference is a cause or an effect of homosexuality.

The preliminary evidence for some biological underpinnings of homosexuality is receiving new support from recent genetics studies that have examined rates of homosexuality among identical and fraternal twins, non-twin biological siblings, and adoptive siblings, in samples of men (Bailey & Pillard, 1991) and women (Bailey et al., 1993). As shown in Figure 7.14, findings suggest a substantial—but not exclusive—genetic contribution to sexual orientation. Subsequent to these reports, investigators at the National Cancer Institute described a preliminary genetic linkage analysis, in which the DNA of 33 out of 40 pairs of brothers both declaring themselves to be exclusively homosexual pointed to the possible role of a maternally transmitted gene in influencing homosexual behavior (Hamer et al., 1993). Although the researchers issued a number of caveats about the finding and called for replication studies, the study generated considerable media attention.

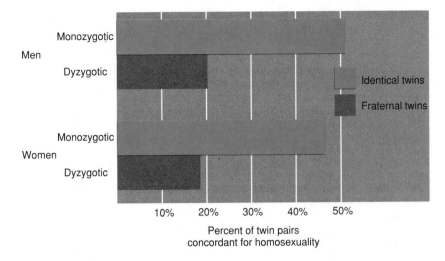

FIGURE 7.14 Is sexual orientation an inherited trait? Over the years, reports of the rate of concordance, or agreement, in sexual orientation among identical twins has ranged from 100 percent to 10 percent. These recent, well-publicized studies which found significantly higher concordance for homosexual orientation among identical, or monozygotic, twins than among nonidentical, or dyzygotic, twins is consistent with what would be expected of a heritable trait. But, among both men and women, more than half of identical twins—who share genes, as well as prenatal and, presumably, family environments—are *discordant* for the "trait" in question. Thus even if the existence of a specific "homosexual gene" were proven, more sophisticated models for the interaction of biological, psychological, and social-environmental factors will be required to answer the question.
Source: The data for women are from Bailey et al., 1993; those for men are from Bailey and Pillard, 1991.

These neuroscientists, like other researchers, emphasize that homosexuals are far from uniform not only in their biological makeup but also in their early development, family histories, and personality characteristics. As is the case for so many human traits, sexual orientation undoubtedly arises from a complex interaction of biological, psychological, and social factors (Money, 1987), and for now the conditions that lead to homosexuality are impossible to define.

The recognition of diversity among homosexuals has been partly responsible for reducing the stigma associated with being gay or lesbian. Although far from erased, negative attitudes have waned in recent years as a more accepting attitude toward sexual orientation has emerged in our society. Today it is generally acknowledged that we do not choose our sexual preferences, nor can we readily alter them. Homosexuality is no longer considered a sexual disorder, as evidenced by the fact that, two decades ago, the American Psychiatric Association deleted homosexuality from its official catalog of mental disorders.

TEST YOURSELF

m) One friend argues that homosexuality arises from purely biological factors, another that it arises from purely psychological and social factors. Who is right?

Motives for Achievement, Power, and Hostility

"I want so much to win at tennis, I can taste it."
"If I work hard at it, I'm sure I can graduate with honors."
"If she would only lose that client—then *I* would make partner!"

Because a hallmark of being human is an ability and propensity to strive for symbolic goals, such feelings are familiar to most people. For some, the self-imposed pressure to achieve a psychologically valued goal can be as relentless as a biologically based drive, although biology certainly does not press one to make the dean's list, amass a fortune, or see a competitor suffer an embarrassing loss. Rather than physiological drive, the impetus is the cognitive appraisal of the desirability of a given goal. The motives that compel our behavior have diverse roots and can lead in unexpected directions, with both positive and negative outcomes. Without motives, however, our lives would be humdrum, indeed.

The Achievement Motive

Achievement motive
The urge to attain optimal levels of performance on valued tasks.

All of us are typically motivated to use our talents to master certain goals. Beginning in childhood, we want to improve our ability and performance at those tasks valued by society—whether it be farming, hunting, or learning to read. This urge to attain optimal levels of performance on valued tasks is called the **achievement motive.**

Very few people, of course, have a uniformly high standard of achievement in all their undertakings. For some people, the achievement motive is directed mostly at athletic prowess, for others at intellectual mastery, musical skills, or making money. People with a strong achievement motive tend to work hard at the things they tackle and to make the most of their talents. They engage in "competition with a standard of excellence" (D. C. McClelland, 1985).

The impetus to strive for a realization of certain talents can be so strong that individuals often manage to overcome serious obstacles. Some people devote themselves single-mindedly to achieving their "personal best" despite poverty and lack of education, or even threats of bodily harm and psychological pain. An example of the latter can be found in a study of six of the world's highest ranking stunt performers—five men and one woman who regularly performed dangerous feats for television and the movies. Contrary to popular expectation, they were motivated not by the thrill of courting danger, but rather by the desire to achieve mastery over the specific challenge they faced (Piet, 1987).

The Origins of Achievement Motivation

Why do some of us develop a stronger desire for achievement than others? There are many reasons, including our experiences in home and school, what we read and what we see on television, and the people we come to admire (and therefore try to imitate) or dislike. Our estimate of our own abilities, which may be accurate or distorted, also plays a part. We tend to be motivated to persist with tasks in which we are talented, and to withdraw when we feel we cannot gain a goal because we do not have sufficient skill (Reeve, Cole, & Olson, 1986). In some instances, even if a required skill or aptitude is present, the way we define ourselves—or allow society to "define" us—also helps determine our level of achievement motivation. One recent study found that intelligent women whose quantitative SAT scores in mathematics would make pursuit of a career in science an eminently reasonable goal nonetheless tended to shy away from that choice simply because they had a low expectancy of success or a high level of anxiety about their mathematical ability (Chipman, Krantz, and Silver, 1992).

The way our parents treated us as children may be a crucial factor. In one early study, a group of children was divided into those who scored high and those who scored low for achievement motive. Their mothers were then asked at what ages they had demanded that the children start to show signs of independence—that is, go to bed by themselves, entertain themselves, stay in the house alone, make their own friends, do well in school without help, and later earn their own spending money and choose their own clothes. Questions were asked about 20 such forms of independent behavior. The children who turned out to be high in achievement motive were urged to be independent at much earlier ages than others (Winterbottom, 1953). A number of studies have since reinforced the conclusion that encouraging independence in early childhood seems to strengthen the achievement motive—and that parents who make few demands for mature behavior seem to discourage it (Mussen et al., 1990).

Parents who cultivate high achievement motivation in their children leave little doubt in the child's mind about the value of achievement, rewarding their children when they perform well and admonishing them when they do not. They talk about achieving individuals as the kinds of people they admire, holding them up as models. Moreover, the parents make their own aspirations obvious. And they stimulate in their young not only self-reliance, but curiosity, and exploration (Segal & Segal, 1985). There is evidence, too, that parents who endure financial hardships and are dissatisfied with their own life accomplishments increase the desire of their children to achieve a better outcome in life (Flanagan, 1989).

The nature of achievement motivation, like that of many other characteristics discussed in this text, is often a function of social context—serving once again as a reminder of one of the basic psychological issues introduced in Chapter 1. As one example, the relatively poor performance in mathematics of American high school children as compared with Asian children, has been explained in part by cultural contrasts in achievement motivation. Compared with children in China and Japan, for instance, more American children grow up in families that value "happiness" to a greater degree than they value achievement in academic skills. American parents are also more likely to ascribe achievement to the child's native ability rather than to hard work and self-application, and, as shown in Figure 7.15, they are more satisfied with their children's level of school achievement (Stevenson & Lee, 1990).

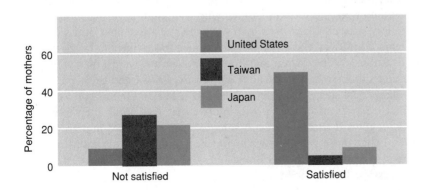

FIGURE 7.15 How parents influence children's achievement motivation The bars show the degree of satisfaction expressed by mothers over the schoolwork of their first-grade children. Note the contrast between Oriental and American mothers (Stevenson and Lee, 1990).

But research across diverse racial and ethnic groups shows that the influence of parents and family values on academic achievement are modified strongly by the influence that a student's peers exert on motive to achieve. In a study examining academic achievement among white, African American, Asian American, and Hispanic students, the value that peers attached to academic success could either augment or undermine achievement motivation. For Hispanic and white students, parents were the most potent sources of influence, but the low value attached to school success by a Hispanic student's ethnically similar peers diluted the parental influence. The high value attached to achievement by Asian American students and peers augmented a motive to achieve instilled by family values (Steinberg, Dornbusch, & Brown, 1992).

The Motive for Power—and "Power-Hungry" People

Power motive

The desire to be in a position of control over others and to influence them.

The desire to be in a position of control over others and to influence them—to be the boss, to give orders, to command respect and obedience—is called the **power motive.** At first glance, it may seem like the achievement motive. But the achievement motive is directed toward performing well at whatever one decides to pursue. The power motive, on the other hand, has less to do with excellent performance than with being "top dog." Studies of American presidents have shown that those who had a strong power motive (as judged from their speeches) tended to take strong and decisive actions and had a great impact on our society—but were not necessarily good presidents who made important and constructive contributions (Winter & Stewart, 1978).

As measured on relevant tests, college students who have a strong power motive tend to be officers in campus organizations, serve on student-faculty committees, and work for the school newspaper and radio station. They like to have nameplates, credit cards, and possessions associated with prestige, such as tape recorders, television sets, and framed pictures. They are quick to take up new fashion trends (Winter, 1973).

Though people with a strong power motive often become leaders of their group, they do not always necessarily serve the group's best interests. Evidence demonstrates that they provide the members with less information and fewer options than do leaders with a weaker urge for power. They also show less concern for moral issues raised by the group's activities and decisions (Fodor & Smith, 1982).

In men, the power motive often seems to interfere with establishing satisfactory relationships with the opposite sex. A study of college students who were going together found that men who were high in power motive tended to be less satisfied than other men with their relationships, and so did their partners. Moreover, these couples were much more likely to break up (Stewart & Rubin, 1976). When men high in power motive do marry, they seem to prefer submissive wives (Winter & Stewart, 1978), and their marriages are less likely to be successful (McClelland et al., 1972). One reason for this may be that frustrations of their power motive may lead some men to assaultive behavior toward their spouses. A study of men embroiled in marital conflict showed that those who physically attacked their wives displayed not only a more intense need for power but also less adequate verbal abilities to express their desires (Dutton & Strachan, 1987).

In a complex society such as ours, the power motive doubtless serves a useful purpose. Somebody has to run the government, the corporations, and all the other organizations that are essential to the functioning of an industrial nation. Moreover, though people who aspire to positions of power may pay a price in their personal relationships, they seem to find many satisfactions. Among the U.S. presidents of this century, it appears that those highest in power motive were the ones who enjoyed the job the most (Barber, 1972). But the power motive probably also directs the behavior of dictators, gang leaders, and the builders of fraudulent financial empires.

The Hostility Motive

The universal emotion of anger is associated with the **hostility motive,** defined by psychologists as a desire to know that harm, physical or psychological, has come to a person or group who is perceived as frustrating or threatening. This motive can last long after the acute emotion of anger has passed, and it need not lead to any aggressive behavior. Many people have strong hostility toward others and will live with it all of their lives. Younger brothers may hold hostility to their successful older siblings, poor neighbors may hold hostility to their more successful neighbors, and one religious group may hold hostile motivation to another living in the same neighborhood or city.

Scientists believe that those who hold intense hostile motives for long periods of time are characterized by so-called Type A personality, and put themselves at risk for heart disease, as discussed in Chapter 9. But hostility occasionally can lead to achievement motivation. James Watson, who won the Nobel Prize with Francis Crick for discovering the nature of the gene, wrote in his book, *The Double Helix,* that some scientists want to demonstrate to other scientists that the former are much smarter. In order to gratify their hostility toward others, they will persist in scientific research in order to make an important discovery.

Hostility motive
The desire to know that physical or psychological harm has come to a person or group who is perceived as frustrating or threatening.

TEST YOURSELF

n) If a person has a high achievement motive in undertaking one task, can you be sure it will be high in undertaking other tasks as well?
o) What motive would be weak in a person described as a "follower" rather than a "leader?"
p) Is it true that the power motive always leads to trouble?
q) What risk may be incurred by a person who is motivated by hostility?

Motives for Affiliation, Certainty, and Meeting Standards

The motives that have just been discussed—sex, achievement, power, and hostility—are those that have received the most attention from psychologists. Other motives, however, also influence us, sometimes strongly.

Needing Others: Motives for Affiliation and Dependency

All young children seek close attachments with parents and, later, all seek friendly relationships with others. The strength of this tendency, however, varies widely. Some people maintain close ties with their parents all their lives and are extremely sociable in general. They are "joiners" who always like to be in a group and prefer to work in jobs where they cooperate with and have the help of others. Other people prefer to spend their time alone and to be on their own in their work. Some even appear to be loners who care very little for human companionship.

Affiliation motive
The desire to be around other people and have close relationships with them.

The desire to be around other people and have close relations with them is called the **affiliation motive.** It is particularly noticeable in people who are experiencing unpleasant emotions, for there seems to be considerable truth in the adage that "misery loves company." This fact was demonstrated by an experiment in which university women were asked to visit a psychology laboratory. When they arrived, they found a frightening piece of apparatus awaiting them and were told it was designed to deliver severe electrical shocks. After having been made anxious about the nature of the experiment, they were told that they had their choice of waiting their turn alone or in company. Fully 63 percent preferred company, with most of the rest saying they did not care one way or the other. In a control group of women who had not been made anxious about the experiment, the number who preferred company while waiting was only 33 percent (Schachter, 1959).

In jobs that call for a group effort, it has been found that people high in affiliation motive would rather be with their friends even when they could work with strangers who were more competent and could offer more help. They are more pleased by signs that their group is getting along well than by its accomplishments. There is some evidence that students with a strong affiliation motive make better grades in classes where everyone is friendly and the instructor takes a personal interest in the students. For those with a low need for affiliation, grades appear to deteriorate under comparable conditions (McKeachie et al., 1966).

Dependency motive
The desire to rely on others.

Closely allied to the desire for affiliation is the **dependency motive,** which also exists in all humans. The dependency motive probably stems from our experiences as babies, when we are completely dependent on our parents. This tendency to rely on others—at least at times and for certain things—never leaves us. We continue to have a strong urge to depend on others to organize our lives, set up our schedules, help us with our work, comfort us, and give us support and pleasure. Like affiliation, the dependency motive is especially prominent in troubling situations. Hospital patients, for instance, often have mixed feelings. Despite their illness and worry, they may seek opportunities to be dependent on their physicians and nurses.

Behavior that stems from the dependency motive has been found to be more common among American women than men. But this is because our society, until recently, has considered dependency to be more appropriate for women. The motive itself is probably equally strong in men—but they are less likely to display it because society has frowned on dependent behavior by males. Often the motive is gratified by men in subtle ways—perhaps by taking their problems to a professor or a boss (though usually under the guise of being logical rather than emotional).

The Motive for Certainty

Motive for certainty
A desire to feel at home in one's world, to know where one stands, and to avoid the discomfort of unfamiliar and surprising events.

Even very young children display a strong **motive for certainty**—that is, a desire to feel at home in their world, to know where they stand, to avoid the discomfort of unfamiliar and surprising events. They clearly enjoy the certainty represented by their own bed, their own toys, the presence of familiar people and objects in their environment. As they grow a little older, they like to have rules set for their conduct; they like the certainty of knowing what they are permitted, and not permitted, to do. The prospect of uncertainty—being taken care of by a strange baby-sitter, going to school for the first time—is likely to upset them.

Adults, too, tend to be motivated toward the known and away from the unknown—to avoid inconsistency and novelty that they cannot handle well. Although some individuals such as explorers and astronauts seem to thrive on novelty, most people operate with a strong desire for certainty most of the time. We like to feel that we know how our relatives and friends will act toward us, what is likely to happen tomorrow in the classroom or on the job, and where and how we will be living next year.

In some people, the motive for certainty is so strong that they seem to avoid any kind of change, even when the price of inaction is very high—for example, people who persist in marriages they have long since decided are hopeless. Apparently they would rather stay with the known, no matter how unpleasant, than face the unknown. For most of us, however, the desire for certainty is not overpowering and simply operates to keep our lives on an even keel.

Playing by the Rules: The Motive to Meet Standards

All of us, as we grow up, begin to set rules for our own behavior. Through learning what society values and through identification with our parents and other adults, we acquire inner standards of many kinds. We also acquire a strong **motive to live up to our standards.** Most people want to be attractive, responsible, friendly, skillful, generous, honest, and fair. Some, because of a different early environment, have standards that motivate them to be domineering, tough, rebellious, or even asocial.

Our standards form what is called our **ego ideal**—our notion of how we would always think and act, if we were perfect. Many of us acquire such high standards that we cannot possibly live up to all of them at all times. In fact, the motive to live up to inner standards often requires us to suppress other powerful motives. Our standards may tell us that we should not take food from another person even if we are hungry, that we should be kind even to people toward whom we feel hostile, that we should play fair no matter how much we want to win. As a result, we often feel shame and guilt over our thoughts if not our actual conduct. In popular terms, our conscience hurts. When we fail to meet our standards, the pangs of conscience can be painful indeed.

Motive to live up to our standards
The desire to live up to the inner standards we have acquired from our parents, other adults, and society in general.

Ego ideal
Our notion of how we would always think and act, if we were perfect.

TEST YOURSELF

r) What motive would be lacking in a "loner"?
s) "When my 5-year-old sleeps over at a friend's house," says one father, "I suddenly realize how strong his motive for certainty is." What might this father be referring to?

How Motives Affect Behavior

One reason we are not very good at detecting the motives of other people is that motives may not necessarily result in any actual behavior. For one thing, action may be thwarted by the circumstances of our lives over which we have no control. The key idea here is opportunity—for we cannot fulfill any of our motives unless we have the right situation. The achievement motive is often the victim of lack of opportunity. For example, a young woman wants very badly to have a professional career, but for lack of money she cannot get the necessary education. A young man wants very badly to work in advertising, but cannot find any advertising firm that will hire him.

Lack of opportunity may also thwart the affiliation motive. For example, young people eager for the companionship of the opposite sex may live in a community where young men greatly outnumber young women, or vice versa. And for older people, the lack of opportunity is caused by the fact that women live much longer than men. Among Americans who are 45 or older, there are almost 8 million more women than men (U.S. Bureau of the Census, 1989c).

Motive Hierarchies

Hierarchy of motives
An individual's pattern of motives, from the strongest to the weakest.

All of us seem to have motives for achievement, power (or avoidance of power), affiliation, dependency, certainty, living up to standards, and (as we shall see in the next chapter) self-actualization. But there are great differences among people in the strengths of each motive. Each of us has built up a highly individual **hierarchy of motives** in which some motives have a high priority, while others are much less urgent—often depending on the intensity of the emotion associated with them. The position each motive occupies in our hierarchy determines how hard, if at all, we try to satisfy it (Atkinson, 1974). Some of us have such a strong affiliation motive that we are willing to ignore a weaker desire for achievement to avoid making our friends jealous. On the other hand, some of us are so intent on achievement or power that we are willing to sacrifice the friendships dictated by a weaker affiliation motive.

Gauging Our Odds of Success

Another factor that affects our decision to act or not to act on our motives is our estimate of how good our chances are to gain what we want. We are not likely to try very hard unless we feel we have a reasonable expectation of success. The college woman invited to try out for the campus play will probably turn down the suggestion if she believes that she has absolutely no chance—even though she wants to get a part. A male student may be highly motivated to call up a woman he has met in one of his classes. But if he feels shy and awkward around women and considers himself unattractive and uninteresting, he will probably take no action.

In gauging our chances of success, we try to make a realistic appraisal of the situation. We may decide not to try out for a campus play because we have never had any acting experience. We may abandon any thought of a career in accounting because we always have trouble in math courses. But often we are influenced not so much by the facts as by our self-image—our own perception of ourselves and our abilities. Some people have an exaggerated opinion of their talents and are inclined to try anything (a tendency that may bring them one disappointment after another). On the other hand, people who have acquired learned helplessness tend to be pessimistic about their chances, whatever the situation. In some instances, even if a required skill or aptitude is present, expectations may be a decisive factor. It has been found, for example, that intelligent women whose quantitative SAT scores in mathematics would make pursuit of a career in science an eminently reasonable goal nonetheless tended to shy away from that choice simply because they had a low expectancy of success or high level of anxiety about their mathematical ability (Chipman, Krantz, & Silver, 1992). Some individuals may be capable of far more success—at fulfilling their motives for achievement, affiliation, and other goals—than they themselves believe.

SUMMARY REVIEW

Biological Underpinnings of Emotion

1. **Emotions** are always accompanied by bodily changes.
2. The changes our body undergoes when we experience emotion are linked to two other factors: a specific event in the environment and thoughts triggered by the event.
3. Many of the bodily changes in emotion are controlled by the autonomic nervous system and the endocrine glands. These changes include:
   (a) heart rate (b) blood pressure (c) blood circulation (d) the composition of the blood (e) activity of the digestive organs (f) metabolic rate (g) breathing (h) salivation (i) sweating (j) goose flesh (k) pupil size
4. Other bodily changes in emotion are controlled by the muscles of movement. These changes include:
   (a) muscular tension (b) trembling (c) eye blinking and other nervous movements (d) vocal expressions of emotion (e) facial expressions
5. One theory holds that every basic emotion represents in part a characteristic pattern of facial expression programmed by heredity, and it is often difficult, therefore, to hide our emotions from others.

Mechanisms of Emotion

6. According to the **James-Lange theory,** emotions occur when a stimulus in the environment sets off physiological changes. Feedback from these changes, sent to the brain from the body's sensory nerves, is then perceived as emotion. We do not tremble because we are afraid, but rather we feel afraid because we are trembling.
7. According to the **Cannon-Bard theory,** emotions occur when a stimulus in the environment sets off patterns of nervous activity in the hypothalamus. These patterns were considered to have two simultaneous effects:
   (a) they are sent to the autonomic nervous system, where they trigger the bodily changes of emotion
   (b) they are sent to the cerebral cortex, where they cause perception of emotion
8. Today's cognitive psychologists regard emotions as composed of many complex factors. These include:
   (a) information about events in the environment that are delivered to the cerebral cortex by the sense organs
   (b) the brain's ability to store information, which helps appraise and interpret new events
   (c) patterns of nervous activity in the hypothalamus and the rest of the brain's limbic system, which trigger the autonomic nervous system into producing bodily changes
   (d) feedback from the bodily changes
9. The cognitive view agrees with James-Lange theory that feedback of physiological changes is important—and with Cannon-Bard theory that activity of the hypothalamus plays a part. But it holds that neither theory is the full explanation. What really determines emotions is the cognitive activity resulting from the stimulus that has produced the bodily

changes and the entire environmental situation in which it occurs. This cognitive activity shows wide individual differences because of prior experience and learning.

10. Some individual differences in the experience of emotion are the result of learning, others the result of inborn factors—including:
    (a) sensitivity of the autonomic nervous system
    (b) the size and activity of the endocrine glands

11. The degrees of emotional reaction to a given experience are often apparent at the very start of life and tend to remain as a major dimension of personality.

Drives and Their Impact on Behavior: Hunger and Thirst

12. A **drive** is a pattern of brain activity resulting from physiological imbalances that threaten **homeostasis**—the maintenance of bodily stability.

13. The **hunger drive** depends on the activity of the hypothalamus, a key brain region discussed in Chapter 2, as well as on **incentive objects** in the environment (the sight or smell of food) and by eating habits and social relationships built around eating.

14. The drive to eat involves a number of interrelated physiological mechanisms governed by the body's **set point**—an innate physiological mechanism that keeps an individual's body weight at a genetically "programmed" level.

15. Although the hunger drive operates to keep most people at a normal weight, it is estimated that between a quarter and a third of American adults are at least 20 percent overweight. Possible explanations of obesity include:
    (a) metabolic disturbances
    (b) overeating to relieve anxiety
    (c) overeating simply as a matter of habit
    (d) an unknown chemical in the bloodstream, caused by abnormalities in the way the alimentary canal and liver process food
    (e) an excess of the bodily cells that store fatty compounds

16. The **thirst drive** depends on:
    (a) nerve cells in the hypothalamus that are sensitive to dehydration
    (b) signals sent to the brain from the heart and blood vessels when the volume of blood is lowered by lack of water
    (c) stimulation of the hypothalamus by a chemical produced by the kidneys

The Sleep Drive: How We Spend a Third of Our Lives

17. The **sleep drive** plays an important role in the rhythm of daily life. Rather than a state of suspended animation, sleep is a brain and body activity in its own right, marked by different stages during a normal night of sleep. These include the **alpha rhythm;** the **sleep stages** (I, II, III, and IV) marked by increasingly deep levels of sleep; and **REM,** or **rapid-eye-movement, sleep,** marked by vivid dreaming.

18. The function of sleep is not only to allow the brain and body to recoup from the wear and tear of daily activity, but also to conserve limited supplies of energy and to restore chemical imbalances in brain chemistry incurred during waking life.

19. REM sleep is also known as **paradoxical sleep,** which occurs for about a quarter of the night. During this period the brain's activity is very similar to the waking state but the bodily muscles are almost totally relaxed.

Pain and Temperature: Safeguarding the Body

20. The **pain drive** leads us to avoid events that would damage our bodies. However, sensitivity to pain varies from person to person over a considerable range.
21. The perception of pain depends to a degree on attention mechanisms as well as on social and cultural factors.
22. The goal of the **temperature drive** is to maintain the body's inner temperature at about 98.6° Fahrenheit, and it appears to be controlled by cells in the hypothalamus that are sensitive to temperature changes in the body.

Sex: An Emotion, Drive, and Motive

23. Sex is among the major human **motives**—that is, the *desires humans have to reach goals that have value to them.*
24. The hormones that determine sexual behavior are **estrogen** in the female, and **androgen** in the male.
25. Sexual expression in humans is influenced not only by basic biological urges but by desires and preferences first learned in childhood, and by the social and cultural environment.
26. The direction taken by the motive for sex defines **sexual orientation**— that is, the attraction felt toward persons of a given sex.
27. The majority of men and women, described as **heterosexual,** feel strong sexual attraction to members of the opposite sex. Those described as **homosexual** are drawn to those of their own sex. Those who seek both homosexual and heterosexual experiences are termed **bisexual.**
28. Although there are evidences of sexuality in early childhood, a motivated interest in sex must await the child's physical and cognitive maturation.
29. Sexuality is a prominent concern during the adolescent years not only because of the physical changes of puberty but also because adolescents must establish their sexual identities.
30. Despite more liberal attitudes toward sex, a major shift in sexual behavior has taken place among young American adults—that is, a growing care in the selection of partners.
31. Despite the biological and environmental changes of old age, the zest for sex—and the pleasure of the experience—continue among many elderly persons.

Motives for Achievement, Power, and Hostility

32. The **achievement motive** is the urge to attain optimal levels of performance on valued tasks.
33. Among the factors that determine the strength of achievement motivation are experiences at home and school, whom we choose as role models, and the estimates we make of our own abilities.

34. The desire to be in a position of control and to influence others is called the **power motive.**

35. Individuals who hold intense hostile motives—that is, the desire to know that harm has come to a person or group perceived to be frustrating or threatening—for long periods of time may put themselves at risk for heart disease.

Motives for Affiliation, Certainty, and Meeting Standards

36. Motives for **affiliation, dependency, certainty,** and **living up to inner standards** can also shape our behavior.

How Motives Affect Behavior

37. Often a motive cannot be fulfilled because of lack of opportunity. In particular, we may never have the opportunity to gratify all our desires for achievement.

38. All of us seem to possess all the human motives but to a widely varying degree. An individual pattern of motives, from strongest to weakest, is a **hierarchy of motives.**

39. Key factors that help determine whether we will try to fulfill a motive include:
    (a) the strength of the motive (determined by the motive hierarchy)
    (b) the way we perceive our chances of success

TEST YOURSELF ANSWERS

a) You would be experiencing no emotion. In order for an emotion to occur, bodily changes must be present—linked to an event (in this case, the perception of the shadowy figure), and to thoughts triggered by the event (in this case, the question of the figure's identity). Since no physical changes occurred, there was no emotion.

b) The theory is the James-Lange theory of emotion—which holds that it is the feedback of physiological changes sent to the brain that is perceived as emotion.

c) The Cannon-Bard theory emphasizes the role of the hypothalamus in arousing the autonomic nervous system, which triggers the various physiological changes associated with emotion.

d) You would be representing the cognitive view of emotions.

e) Such individual differences—like others discussed throughout the book—are the result of both innate patterns and learning.

f) Your friend is saying that the drive to eat is regulated by an inborn physiological mechanism—the so-called set point—that keeps our body weight at a predetermined level. It leads us to return to our natural body weight after we have gone above or below it.

g) You are being asked not to stock the refrigerator with too many tempting food items, which—like other incentive objects such as the smell of food, or even talk of food—are among the outside stimuli that can affect the hunger drive.

h) You might say "I've felt thirsty all day." The thirst drive is triggered by such imbalances.

i) The person is likely to be in Stage IV sleep—the deepest stage of the sleep cycle.

j) It is termed "paradoxical" because the brain's activity is similar to the waking state, but the muscles are almost totally relaxed.

k) The toy might cause the child to pay less attention to the pain. Distraction reduces the perception of pain.

l) You might use any two of the following facts: (1) Unlike sex in lower animals, human sex is not altogether tied to glandular cycles. (2) In humans, just thinking about sex can lead to arousal. (3) For both men and women, psychological factors can act as a powerful "turn off." (4) Sexual practices differ widely from one human society to another.

m) Neither is right. Homosexuality appears to develop from a complex interaction of all three factors.

n) You cannot be sure. For a variety of psychological reasons—for example, ability, interest, self-concept—some individuals tend to be motivated to persist with some tasks but not with others.

o) The power motive would be weak.

p) It is not true. For example, some people with a highly developed power motive might end up as creative and dynamic leaders of social movements or government agencies—while others, of course, might end up as tyrannical spouses, gang leaders, or dictators. The presence of a motive does not tell us how it will be expressed.

q) Holding the hostility motive for a prolonged period may lead to heart disease and related health problems.

r) The affiliation motive would be lacking.

s) He is undoubtedly referring to evidence that, in sleeping away from home, his son shows discomfort in being in an unfamiliar environment—preferring the certainty of being in the presence of familiar things and people.

Study Guide

Chapter 7   Emotions, Drives, and Motives

LEARNING OBJECTIVES

After studying this chapter, you should be able to:

1. Understand how the experience of an emotion involves a particular event (or the memory of an event), changes in the body and brain, and thoughts generated by the event.

   For an Understanding of the Science

2. Describe the bodily changes that take place in emotion—in the glands, organs, and muscles controlled by the autonomic nervous system as well as in the facial and other muscles that are ordinarily under conscious control.

3. Trace the development of theories of emotion from the James-Lange theory (based on feedback from bodily changes), through the Cannon-Bard theory (based on patterns of activity in the hypothalamus), to the cognitive theory (based primarily on mental processes in the cortex).

4. Discuss the cognitive theory of emotion as a complex mental process entailing the interpretation of information from the environment, patterns of brain activity that trigger the autonomic nervous system, and feedback of sensations from the bodily changes produced by the autonomic nervous system.

5. Understand how individual differences in the arousal and display of emotion depend both on learning and on inborn differences in the autonomic nervous system, and possibly the glands.

6. Know that a drive is a pattern of brain activity resulting from a physiologic balance that threatens homeostasis.

7. Know the physiological conditions that result in the hunger drive, and how the hunger drive can be affected by outside stimuli, or incentive objects.

8. Know the physiological conditions that result in the thirst drive.

9. Describe the various stages of sleep—how they differ both physiologically and in terms of the depth of sleep.

10. Recall the theories that explain the functions of sleep and dreams.

11. Understand how the pain and temperature drives operate to protect the body.

12. Discuss the role of biological, psychological, and social influences on human sexual behavior.

13. Understand the differences between males and females and differences in sexual orientation.

14. Describe prominent characteristics of sexual behavior at various stages along the life span—including infancy and childhood, adolescence, the adult years, and old age.

15. Understand that motives are desires to reach goals that have value for the individual. Realize that some psychologists believe motives arise from the biological demands of drives, while others believe that motives are cognitive processes established largely by learning.

16. Discuss the motives for achievement, power, affiliation, dependency, certainty, living up to inner standards, and hostility.

17. Understand that our motives exist in a hierarchy, from strong and easily aroused to weak and seldom aroused—and that the strength of the motive at any given time depends on the presence of motive targets, or the people to whom our various motives are directed.

For Application to Life Situations

18. Realize the implications of the cognitive theory of emotions—especially its emphasis on the situations in which we find ourselves and our interpretation of the situation.

19. Understand that while we can sometimes learn to hide some of the outward signs of emotion, our emotions typically involve bodily changes over which we exert little conscious control.

20. Realize that people differ in the intensity of their emotions, and that such differences tend to appear at the very start of life.

21. Understand the implications of the findings on the relationship among the body's fat cells, the intensity of the hunger drive, and obesity.

22. Realize how the sleep drive plays an important part in our lives, why we pay a price when the normal cycles of sleep and waking are disrupted.

23. Understand that humans display a wide range of sexual attitudes and behavior, which are influenced by a mix of biological, psychological, and social factors.

24. Realize that the motive for sex plays an important role throughout the life span.

25. Understand that people with a strong achievement motive tend to surpass others of equal ability in many situations, including college performance. Understand the implications of studies indicating that the achievement motive is encouraged by parents who urge independence and self-sufficiency early in life.

26. Describe the factors that determine whether and how hard we try to satisfy our motives. Know that one important factor—expectation of success—can independently increase or diminish the likelihood that we will satisfy a given motive.

PROGRAMMED UNIT
BIOLOGICAL UNDERPINNINGS OF EMOTION

1. An *emotion* occurs when an event is accompanied by thoughts associated with the event and by bodily changes. When John thinks about the unfairness of his boss, his heart beats faster and his mouth turns dry—which suggests that John is experiencing an _____.　　**emotion**

2. Many of the bodily changes accompanying _____ are regulated by the *autonomic nervous system* and are not ordinarily under conscious control.　　**emotion**

3. John tries as hard as he can not to blush when he is embarrassed. But he always does anyway because, like the rest of us, he cannot consciously _____ the bodily changes associated with emotion.　　**control**

4. Without any command from the brain, our emotions are accompanied by changes in such functions as heart rate, blood pressure, muscle tension, and stomach activity—all of them controlled by the _____ nervous system.　　**autonomic**

5. The _____ changes accompanying emotion are also controlled by the *endocrine glands,* which secrete powerful hormones into the bloodstream.　　**bodily**

6. Many of the physical changes we feel in emotion are controlled by both the autonomic _____ _____ and the _____ glands. Eye blinking, finger drumming, and various facial expressions are all examples of bodily changes in emotion consciously controlled by the muscles of movement.　　**nervous system, endocrine**

7. The emotions of anger or fear lead to production of the hormone _____ by the adrenal glands.　　**cortisol**

8. The facial expressions that accompany emotions are examples of bodily changes that are ordinarily under _____ control. Some psychologists maintain that every basic emotion represents in part a characteristic pattern of facial expression programed by heredity.　　**conscious**

9. Facial expressions typical of certain emotions seem to be universal and unlearned, lending support to the theory that such characteristic expressions are programmed by _____.　　**heredity**

habituated

10. Facial displays of pain may become less apparent as one becomes accustomed, or _____, to an uncomfortable situation.

MECHANISMS OF EMOTION

emotion

11. The *James-Lange* theory held that the bodily changes accompanying _____ send feedback messages to the brain, and that these messages produce emotional feelings.

James-Lange

12. If feedback from bodily changes is the key to emotion—which is what the _____-_____ theory held—then it follows that we do not tremble because we feel afraid, but instead feel afraid because we are trembling.

emotion
feedback

13. The James-Lange theory of _____ emphasized the importance of bodily changes, especially the _____ of such changes to the brain.

bodily

14. Unlike the James-Lange theory, which held that emotion is caused by the feedback of _____ changes to the brain, the *Cannon-Bard* theory held that emotion originates in patterns of brain activity.

brain

15. The Cannon-Bard theory stressed the role of _____ activity in emotion—specifically the activity of the hypothalamus, which arouses the autonomic nervous system to produce the bodily changes associated with emotion, and also sends messages to the cerebral cortex that result in our feelings of emotion.

Cannon-Bard
hypothalamus

16. According to the _____-_____ theory, emotions result from patterns of nervous activity in the brain structure called the _____. *Cognitive theory* emphasizes the role of mental processes in such feelings as joy, anger, and fear rather than the role of bodily changes and the brain.

mental

17. Cognitive theory emphasizes the role of _____ processes in emotion.

cognitive

18. Feedback of bodily changes and the role of the hypothalamus, although important, cannot fully explain emotion, according to the _____ theory.

differences

19. Both the stimuli that arouse emotions and the behavior that results from emotion are subject to wide individual _____ that are partly the result of learning.

inborn

20. Some individual differences in emotion may reflect _____ differences rather than different learning experiences.

emotional

21. Any abnormality of the glands or nervous system can have significant effects on _____ experience.

sensitivity

22. The fact that some people seem to "overreact" to minor events, while others are unmoved even by major upheavals, appears to suggest differences from person to person in the _____ of the autonomic nervous system.

differences

23. The fact that such contrasting reactions are apparent at the very start of life suggests the importance of inborn _____.

DRIVES AND THEIR IMPACT ON BEHAVIOR: HUNGER AND THIRST

emotions

24. A group of psychological conditions called *drives* depends on bodily activities—which is true also in the case of _____. Psychologists define a

drive as a pattern of brain activity resulting from physiological imbalances that threaten the body's homeostasis—or the maintenance of the body's stability.

25. The *hunger drive* is aroused when lack of food threatens the body's
    _____.   **homeostasis**

26. Drives center on the process of homeostasis, or the maintenance of the
    body's _____.   **stability**

27. The drive to eat is governed in part by the body's _____, an innate   **set point**
    physiological mechanism that keeps an individual's body weight at a geneti-
    cally "programmed" level.

28. As the liver manages the body's metabolism of food, it helps maintain the
    set point by converting extra glucose into _____ for long-term stor-   **glycogen**
    age of energy.

29. Another view holds that rather than blood sugar (glucose) or glycogen as
    the primary trigger for the hunger drive, it is the level of fatty compounds
    in the bloodstream, which is regulated when _____ recognize that   **fat cells**
    the body needs fat for fuel and empty their contents into the bloodstream.

30. The hunger drive, in addition to being aroused by activity in the part of the
    brain called the _____, is affected by outside stimuli—called *incentive*   **hypothalamus**
    objects—such as the sight or smell of food.

31. Pastries seen in a restaurant window that arouse the hunger drive can be
    classified as _____ objects.   **incentive**

32. When exposed to incentive objects, some people experience an increase
    in the hormone _____ in the blood; by reducing blood sugar, this   **insulin**
    _____ may be the primary mechanism for alerting the brain to   **hormone**
    hunger.

33. Some obesity may result from _____ _____ as people   **emotional stress**
    overeat to relieve anxieties over competition, failure, rejection, or sexual
    performance.

34. The *thirst drive* is triggered by various signs of imbalance in the body's water
    supply. Just as eating is a response to the _____ drive, drinking is a   **hunger**
    response to the thirst drive.

35. Like all drives, the thirst drive centers on the process of _____, or   **homeostasis**
    the maintenance of bodily stability.

36. Like the _____ drive, the thirst drive depends in part on the activity   **hunger**
    of nerve cells in the hypothalamus—in this case, nerve cells that are sensi-
    tive to dehydration.

37. Both the hunger and thirst drives depend on activity of the part of the
    brain called the _____. The thirst drive depends as well on signals   **hypothalamus**
    sent to the brain from the heart and blood vessels when the volume of
    blood is lowered by lack of water.

38. When the volume of blood is lowered by lack of water, the heart and
    blood vessels send signals to the brain that trigger the _____ drive.   **thirst**

THE SLEEP DRIVE: HOW WE SPEND A THIRD OF OUR LIVES

39. Although sleep may feel like a blanket of darkness, the brain continues to
    be active during sleep—which proceeds through different levels, or stages.

drive

imbalances

alpha

myoclonic jerk

brain

stages

Stage, delta

REM

paradoxical

dream

sleep, paradoxical

The fact that all humans sleep, and that sleep helps maintain the body's homeostasis indicates the importance of the sleep _____.

40. The sleep drive appears to be triggered by _____ in brain and body chemistry.

41. During the brief phase of serene relaxation that immediately precedes sleep, the pulse is steady, body temperature is dropping gradually, and brain waves show an even frequency called the _____ rhythm.

42. Just before entering the first stage of sleep, neural changes may generate a fleeting sensation of "falling;" this normal phenomenon is called the _____ _____.

43. During sleep, the _____ continues to be very active, as the sleeper proceeds through a series of levels, or _____. The deepest of these is *Stage IV*, or *delta sleep*.

44. A sleeper who is extremely difficult to awaken is probably engaged in the deep sleep of _____ IV, also known as _____ sleep. The need for sleep appears to be triggered by imbalances in brain and body chemistry that build up when we are awake and active.

45. The period of sleep marked by dreaming is known as *rapid-eye-movement sleep*, or REM. Because the brain's activity during this period is similar to the waking state, but the muscles are almost totally relaxed, this period is also known as _____ sleep.

46. A person who is in the midst of REM sleep is probably having a _____. This period is regarded as essential in restoring the brain's ability to function.

47. The brain's ability to function appears to be restored as a result of REM _____, also known as _____ sleep because the brain appears active—yet the muscles are relaxed.

PAIN AND TEMPERATURE: SAFEGUARDING THE BODY

homeostasis

pain

endorphins

hypothalamus

temperature drive

hypothalamus

48. The *pain drive* leads us to avoid events that would damage our bodies. As such, like other drives, it helps maintain the body's stability, or _____.

49. We are led by the _____ drive to avoid events that threaten to damage our bodies. In part, this occurs through the brain's production of its own morphine-like painkillers called *endorphins*.

50. Painkilling chemicals produced by the brain, called _____ constitute one of the body's responses to pain.

51. The brain's _____ plays an important role in the *temperature drive*, the goal of which is to maintain the body's inner temperature at 98.6° Fahrenheit.

52. The _____ _____ has as its goal the maintenance of the body's inner temperature at 98.6° Fahrenheit. An important role in this is played by the brain's _____.

SEX: AN EMOTION, DRIVE, AND MOTIVE

motive

53. A *motive* is a desire to reach a goal that has value for the individual. Sexual behavior is a drive state, but also is a powerful _____.

54. In contrast to the fulfillment of the drive for food and water, satisfaction of the motive for sex is not absolutely vital for survival. A person might die of hunger or thirst, but not of deprivation of _____.   **sex**

55. Among nonhuman mammals, sex is almost as direct a drive as hunger and is triggered by the release of the sex _____, *androgen* in males, and *estrogen* in females.   **hormones**

56. In humans, especially in females, sexual responsiveness does not seem to be tied to hormones; instead, sexual activity is influenced by an array of _____, social, and cultural factors.   **psychological**

57. The female and male sex hormones—_____ and _____—are present in humans, and influence activity of the brain's hypothalamus; but hormonal activity is not required for sexual behavior, nor is it a sole, sufficient impetus for such behavior.   **estrogen, androgen**

58. When monthly fluctuations in a woman's hormone levels end with cessation of menstruation, at the _____, sexual activity may actually increase.   **menopause**

59. In humans, sexual activity is colored by _____ as well as social and cultural factors. The direction taken by the motive for sex defines our *sexual orientation*—that is, the attraction we feel toward persons of a given sex.   **psychological**

60. Sally feels strongly attracted to members of her own sex—which defines her sexual _____. The majority of men and women, described as *heterosexual*, feel strong attraction to members of the opposite sex.   **orientation**

61. Those people who feel strong attraction to members of the opposite sex are described as _____. In contrast, people drawn to those of their own sex are described as *homosexual*.   **heterosexual**

62. The sexual orientation of Sally (described in Item 60) is _____. Those who seek both homosexual and heterosexual experiences are termed *bisexual*.   **homosexual**

63. Mark, who seeks sexual contact with both men and women, can be described as _____.   **bisexual**

64. Sexual orientation, like sexual activity in general, is determined by an _____ of biological, psychological, and social factors.   **interaction**

65. Like later patterns of sexual behavior, sexual behavior in childhood is an outgrowth of both _____ and psychological factors. Sexuality is a prominent concern during the adolescent years.   **biological**

66. Sexuality plays a significant role during the _____ years, partly because of the physical changes of puberty.   **adolescent**

67. The physical changes of _____ help usher in a heightened awareness of sexuality.   **puberty**

68. Although the zest for sex is not universally extinguished with age, biologically, the sexual _____ changes in some respects.   **response**

MOTIVES FOR ACHIEVEMENT, POWER, AND HOSTILITY

69. A desire to reach a goal that has value for the individual is a _____. Among the most important motives influencing our behavior is the *achievement motive*, or the desire to perform well and succeed.   **motive**

achievement

school

abilities

power

achievement

hostility

motive

desire

aggression

70. People who tend to try harder than others and to attain more success in many kinds of situations are likely to have a strong _____ motive—the result of many factors, including experiences in home and school and our estimate of our own abilities.

71. The strength of the achievement motive depends on many factors, among them experiences in home and _____.

72. The strength of the achievement motive depends also on our estimate of our own _____.

73. People with a strong desire to be in a position of control have a strong *power motive*. John, who always wants to be top dog and to boss others, has a strong _____ motive.

74. His brother, Alexander, who constantly strives to be successful at virtually everything he undertakes, has a strong _____ motive.

75. Humans also have a desire to see others display signs of worry, fears of discomfort, and actual pain—which is the *hostility motive*. Thus mental and physical cruelty are examples of the _____ motive.

76. The argumentative and sarcastic person is also displaying the hostility _____, which frequently gives rise to behavior called *aggression*.

77. The hostility motive is the _____ to harm others.

78. A good deal of human history seems to revolve around the hostility motive and the behavior to which it gives rise, called _____.

MOTIVES FOR AFFILIATION, CERTAINTY, AND MEETING STANDARDS

power

affiliation

affiliation

dependency

motives

certainty

value

standards

ideal

79. Unlike the desire to be in control of others, or _____ motive, the *affiliation motive* is the desire simply to be around other people.

80. Judy, who constantly yearns for the company of others, has a strong _____ motive.

81. The desire to be close to other people is the _____ motive. Closely allied to it is the *dependency motive*—which is the desire to rely on others to fill our needs, as our parents did for us.

82. Our urges to have other people organize our lives, help us with our work, and comfort us in our troubles are examples of the _____ motive.

83. In addition to the desires for achievement, power, affiliation, and dependency—all of them strong human _____—there are other desires that influence all of us. One is the desire to feel at home in the world, to know where we stand, and to avoid the discomfort of unfamiliar and surprising events, called the *motive for certainty*.

84. The desire to know how our friends will behave toward us and what will happen at school tomorrow is an example of the motive for _____.

85. Still another powerful motive—or the desire to reach a goal of personal _____—is the *motive to live up to standards*, which is the desire to behave in accordance with our own ideas of what is right or wrong.

86. Mary, who is motivated by the belief that she should play fair no matter how hard she wants to win, displays the motive to live up to her _____.

87. Our notion of how we would always think or act if we were perfect is called our ego _____.

HOW MOTIVES AFFECT BEHAVIOR

88. All of us seem to have desires to reach a variety of goals of value to us. But there are great differences in the strengths of these desires, or _____, and an individual's pattern of desires from strongest to weakest is called a *motive hierarchy.*

motives

89. If an individual has a very strong urge for success, the achievement motive occupies a very high place in that person's motive _____.

hierarchy

90. Our pattern of desires from strongest to weakest is our _____ _____. The strength of a motive at any given moment depends on the presence of *motive targets,* or the people to whom the various motives are directed.

motive hierarchy

91. One key factor that influences whether or not a _____ will affect behavior is *expectation of success.*

motive

92. A man who wants to be a doctor but thinks he could never get through medical school will probably never try to satisfy the motive because he has a low _____ of success.

expectation

93. People who believe they have no chance of satisfying their motives may refrain from acting on them because they have a low expectation of _____.

success

REVIEW OF IMPORTANT TERMS

achievement motive **(334)**

affiliation motive **(338)**

alpha rhythm **(317)**

androgens **(326)**

bisexual **(331)**

Cannon-Bard theory **(309)**

cognitive theory **(310)**

cortisol **(304)**

delta sleep **(319)**

dependency motive **(338)**

drives **(301)**

drive state **(312)**

ego ideal **(339)**

emotion **(301)**

emotional stress **(315)**

endorphins **(323)**

estrogen **(326)**

fat cells **(313)**

glycogen **(313)**

habituated **(307)**

heterosexual **(330)**

hierarchy of motives **(340)**

homeostasis **(312)**

homosexual **(331)**

hostility motive **(337)**

hunger drive **(312)**

incentive objects **(314)**

insulin **(314)**

James-Lange theory **(308)**

menopause **(326)**

motives **(301)**

motive for certainty **(338)**

motive to live up to our standards **(339)**

myoclonic jerk **(318)**

pain drive **(322)**

paradoxical sleep **(319)**

power motive **(336)**

REM (rapid-eye-movement) sleep **(319)**

set point **(313)**

sexual orientation **(330)**

sleep drive **(317)**

sleep stages (I, II, III, and IV) **(318)**

temperature drive **(325)**

thirst drive **(312)**

PRACTICE TEST

_____ 1. All of the emotions that we experience contain
   a. a particular event or memory.
   b. changes in the body or brain.
   c. thoughts generated by the event.
   d. all of the above.

_____ 2. Most of the changes in the body that take place during times of high emotion are controlled by the
   a. thyroid gland.
   b. right hemisphere of the brain.
   c. autonomic nervous system.
   d. cerebral cortex.

_____ 3. Research has shown that facial expressions of some emotions
   a. are very similar in different cultures.
   b. are easier to interpret in women.
   c. need to be learned.
   d. are uncommon among animals other than humans.

_____ 4. Walking in the forest, you are suddenly confronted by a huge bear. You begin to tremble and say to yourself, "I've never been so scared in my whole life." According to the James-Lange theory, you are afraid because you
   a. have a conditioned fear of bears.
   b. are uncertain what the bear will do next.
   c. are trembling.
   d. have generalized your fear of other animals to bears.

_____ 5. The Cannon-Bard theory of emotion stresses the importance of
   a. physiological changes.
   b. the hypothalamus.
   c. the individual's perception of the situation.
   d. all the above.

_____ 6. Two students drink several cups of coffee at lunch, and the caffeine in the coffee arouses both. One student, who has just failed a test, interprets the effect as unusual anger. The other student, who has done well on the test, feels unusually happy. What theory of emotion best explains the difference?
   a. Stimulus variability
   b. Cannon-Bard
   c. Cognitive
   d. James-Lange

_____ 7. Lie detector test results can be influenced unduly by
   a. time of day test is given

b. subjective impressions of examiner

c. age of subject

d. sex of subject

_____ 8. Homeostasis is most closely associated with

a. drives.

b. emotions.

c. motives.

d. arousal.

_____ 9. The center for the thirst drive is the

a. hypothalamus.

b. stomach.

c. mouth.

d. right hemisphere of the brain.

_____ 10. A sudden spasm experienced while drifting off to sleep is known
as the

a. alpha rhythm.

b. myoclonic jerk.

c. sleep reflex.

d. waking reflex.

_____ 11. REM sleep is associated with the experience of

a. insomnia.

b. dreaming.

c. Stage IV sleep.

d. ordinary sleep.

_____ 12. Endorphins that can kill pain are produced by the

a. blood.

b. adrenal glands.

c. brain.

d. digestive tract.

_____ 13. The direction taken by the motive for sex defines our

a. sexual orientation.

b. sexual attitudes.

c. lack of inhibition.

d. sexual energy.

_____ 14. Changes in sexuality in older adults are partly the result of

a. biological changes.

b. bereavement.

c. retirement.

d. inhibitions.

_____ 15. The desire to be in a position of control is the
   a. achievement motive.
   b. affiliation motive.
   c. power motive.
   d. motive for certainty.

_____ 16. Behavior stemming from the hostility motive is called
   a. aggression.
   b. anger.
   c. conflict.
   d. frustration.

_____ 17. The desire to be close to other people is the
   a. dependency motive.
   b. affiliation motive.
   c. power motive.
   d. motive for certainty.

_____ 18. The child's preference for familiar things in the environment is related most directly to the motive for
   a. certainty.
   b. achievement.
   c. affiliation.
   d. dependency.

_____ 19. The ego ideal is a key factor in the motive for
   a. dependency.
   b. living up to standards.
   c. affiliation.
   d. power.

_____ 20. The notion of a motive hierarchy refers to the fact that
   a. motives can be served by a large number of behaviors.
   b. some motives are more broadly defined than others.
   c. our various motives range from strong to weak.
   d. all motives interact with one another.

ANSWERS TO PRACTICE TEST

1. d	6. c	11. b	16. a
2. c	7. b	12. c	17. b
3. a	8. a	13. a	18. a
4. c	9. a	14. a	19. b
5. b	10. b	15. c	20. c

EXERCISES

I. Figure 7.4 (p. 306) shows photographs of six faces expressing various emotions. Cover the rest of the page and show these photographs to at least a dozen individuals who are as different in age and background as possible, asking them to try to identify the emotions being displayed. Give each individual a list of emotions from which to choose, and ask them to record the judgments made. You may want to create a table, to expedite recording and tallying. Make the list twice as long as the actual emotions:

1. anger	7. love
2. disgust	8. contempt
3. fear	9. shame
4. joy	10. guilt
5. sadness	11. interest-excitement
6. anxiety	12. surprise

When you have completed collecting the responses, tally the number of individuals who identified each emotion correctly. Then consider these questions:

1. Did most of your subjects agree about the emotions expressed?
2. Which facial expressions, if any, were especially difficult for them to identify correctly?
3. Which ones were the easiest?
4. Are you convinced, as one theory maintains, that facial expressions of emotions are universal?

II. Review the definitions of the following motives on pages 334–339.

1. the achievement motive
2. the power motive
3. the hostility motive
4. the affiliation motive
5. the dependency motive
6. the motive for certainty
7. the motive to meet standards

Keeping the definitions for each in mind, place the motives in rank order (from 1 to 7) in terms of how strongly you believe they apply to you. Do the same for a close friend, and have the friend do the same sets of rankings. Then compare the results. How easy was it to assign the rankings? How similar are the rankings made by you and your friend—both for yourselves and each other? The results may demonstrate that our motives are often mixed and difficult to evaluate—but that at least one or two of them seem to stand out as especially strong or especially weak.

C H A P T E R   8

Intelligence and Personality

From the beginnings of psychology in the nineteenth century, scientists have been interested in discovering what is common to all human beings. Until now, this book has dealt primarily with such universal human—and, sometimes, animal—qualities. Among them are the chemistry of the brain; capacities of sensation and perception; the processes of conditioning, memory, language, and thought; and the arousal of emotions and drives. Although there are, of course, wide variations among people in these characteristics, all human beings possess these psychological features.

Individual differences

Differences among individuals of the same species.

Another of psychology's interests, however, is the study of **individual differences.** No two human beings, not even identical twins, are exactly alike, and psychologists want to know the reasons for this variation. What is it that causes one person to be verbally fluent and another hesitant, one friendly and another withdrawn, one timid and another bold? This chapter considers differences in two major domains of human functioning that have been studied extensively: intelligence and personality. The first domain is concerned with variation in a number of cognitive processes, the second with differences in patterns of motives and emotions. Both are influenced by a combination of heredity and experience which, as the chapter will show, cannot readily be teased apart.

The Nature of Intelligence

Intelligence

The capacity to understand the world and the resourcefulness to cope with its challenges.

Try asking several of your friends what they mean when they use the word *intelligence*. You are likely to end up with several different definitions. Perhaps the most practical definition of intelligence was proposed by David Wechsler, who constructed a number of today's most widely used intelligence tests. He defined **intelligence** as *the capacity to understand the world and the resourcefulness to cope with its challenges.* That is to say, you are intelligent if you know what is going on around you, can learn from experience, and therefore act in ways that are successful in your particular circumstances. Your behavior is intelligent if it has meaning and direction and is rational and worthwhile (Wechsler, 1975).

Clearly, what is rational and worthwhile will vary with where and when we live. What Wechsler's definition seems to say is that a person who was considered highly intelligent in Egypt in 500 B.C., for example, might not be considered so in the United States in the 1990s. A problem plaguing all investigators is that intelligence can mean different things to different people—and has done so from time to time and place to place throughout human history. The ancient Greeks considered a person intelligent if he had a talent for oratory. Until the twentieth century, the Chinese emphasized mastery of the written word, which is a different skill. Some tribes in Africa attribute intelligence to a person with hunting ability; many South Pacific islanders believe a person who can navigate a canoe is highly intelligent.

The subject of intelligence raises five major questions:

1. Is intelligence best viewed as a single ability or a combination of different abilities?
2. Can a person be highly skilled in some areas of mental ability but well below average in others?

Cultures differ in the skills that have to be learned in order to adapt to the society.

3. What is actually measured by intelligence tests? If, for example, one of today's intelligence tests shows that a person has an IQ of 110 (or 90 or 100 or 120), how much does that tell us about that person's chances for doing well in school—and, more important, for leading a happy and successful life?
4. How is intelligence related to creativity?
5. Assuming that some people are more intelligent than others, what roles do heredity and environment play in such differences?

A great deal of psychological research has been devoted to these questions, and many are still topics of considerable debate.

Intelligence as a Single General Ability

One influential theory of intelligence was suggested years ago by Charles Spearman, who applied sophisticated statistical analysis to the scores on tests of many kinds of abilities, from reading comprehension to visualization of spatial relationships. Spearman concluded that the score on any test depends in part on an *s* factor, meaning a specific kind of skill for a particular task. But people with a high level of *s* factor on one task also tend to make high scores at other tasks—a fact that Spearman believed could only be explained by a pervasive, general mental ability that he called the *g* factor, or **general intelligence factor** (Spearman, 1927).

Psychologist L. L. Thurstone rejected the idea of general intelligence and set out to disprove it. He, too, gave dozens of different tests to schoolchildren, measuring their ability at a wide range of tasks. But despite his original aim, he too wound up convinced that a *g* factor affects many different skills.

s factor
A specific kind of skill for a particular task.

g factor (general intelligence factor)
A pervasive, general mental ability.

Primary mental abilities

The seven basic abilities that make up intelligence, according to psychologist L. L. Thurstone.

Thurstone proposed the theory that intelligence is composed of a general factor plus seven specific skills that he called **primary mental abilities:**

1. *Verbal comprehension*—indicated by size of vocabulary, ability to read, and skill at understanding analogies and the meaning of proverbs. (Example: *How are cotton and wool alike?*)
2. *Word fluency*—the ability to think of words quickly, as when making rhymes or solving word puzzles. (Example: *In the next ten seconds, think of as many words as you can that have to do with a car.*)
3. *Number*—the ability to solve arithmetic problems and to manipulate numbers. (Example: *If seven shirts cost $126.00, how much does one shirt cost?*)
4. *Space*—the ability to visualize spatial relationships, as in recognizing a design after it has been placed in a new context. (Example: *Using the four blocks illustrated here, make the design shown below.*)

5. *Associative memory*—the ability to memorize quickly, as in learning a list of paired words. (Example: *Memorize these pairs of words—dog-pencil, leaf-ocean, cup-pipe—so that if you hear one word of a pair, you can remember the other.*)
6. *Perceptual speed*—the ability to grasp visual details quickly and to observe similarities and differences between patterns and pictures. (Example: *What is missing in this picture?*)

7. *General reasoning*—skill at the kind of logical thinking that was described in Chapter 6. (Example: See Figures 6.9 and 6.10, page 282.)

As the next section will show, studies of intelligence during the past two decades have tended to support Thurstone's view. The examples given above for primary mental abilities 1, 4, and 6 are from contemporary tests of intelligence developed by Wechsler, which will be described later in this chapter. The results of such tests reveal that individuals appear to differ dramatically in their patterns of specific abilities (Kail & Pellegrino, 1985).

Intelligence as Many Specific Skills

Today's intelligence tests usually measure performance on most of the seven primary abilities proposed by Thurstone. But people who are skillful at any one of them do not always do well on others. The correlations among them are so low that a few psychologists continue to question the existence of the *g*, or general, intelligence factor (Gardner, 1983).

J. P. Guilford, of the University of Southern California, extended the work of Thurstone and concluded that intelligence is made up of no less than

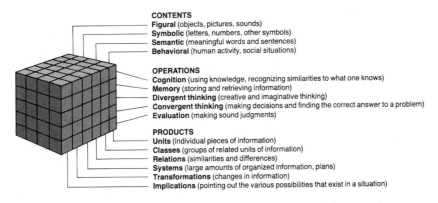

CONTENTS
Figural (objects, pictures, sounds)
Symbolic (letters, numbers, other symbols)
Semantic (meaningful words and sentences)
Behavioral (human activity, social situations)

OPERATIONS
Cognition (using knowledge, recognizing similarities to what one knows)
Memory (storing and retrieving information)
Divergent thinking (creative and imaginative thinking)
Convergent thinking (making decisions and finding the correct answer to a problem)
Evaluation (making sound judgments)

PRODUCTS
Units (individual pieces of information)
Classes (groups of related units of information)
Relations (similarities and differences)
Systems (large amounts of organized information, plans)
Transformations (changes in information)
Implications (pointing out the various possibilities that exist in a situation)

FIGURE 8.1   Guilford's 120-factor theory of intelligence The separate kinds of ability suggested by Guilford are represented by the small individual blocks contained in the cube. The theory maintains that each factor is the ability to perform one of five different types of mental *operations* on one of four different kinds of material, or *contents*, with the aim of coming up with one of six different kinds of end results, or *products*. Thus the total number of abilities that make up intelligence (or blocks in the cube) is 5 × 4 × 6, or 120. Followers of the theory measure the mental operation called "divergent thinking" by asking a question such as "How many uses can you think of for a brick?"— and noting how many different answers the individual can come up with and how imaginative the answers are. One test of the mental operation called "evaluation" is to present the four words *cat, cow, mule,* and *mare* and ask whether these are best categorized as: (a) farm animals, (b) four-legged animals, or (c) domestic animals. The answer will be found at the bottom of page 425.

120 different kinds of abilities. The 120-factor theory, illustrated in Figure 8.1, maintains that an individual may display a very high level of ability on some tasks, average ability on others, and low ability on others. Guilford and his associates devised tests for many of the 120 factors—and found very little relation between subjects' scores on one test and scores on many of the others (Guilford, 1967).

Guilford found that people differ widely in their abilities to deal with different kinds of materials (or *contents,* as they are termed in Figure 8.1). For example, some people are very good at handling words (**semantic contents**). These people might be outstanding as writers and philosophers. Others excel at working with numbers (**symbolic contents**). These people might be most productive as mathematicians or accountants. Others do best with perceptual images or schemata (**figural contents**). These people seem best suited to becoming commercial artists or master mechanics.

Howard Gardner, a recent theorist, also believes that individuals display a set of seven fundamental, but separate, intelligences. He calls them (1) linguistic ability, (2) skills in logic and mathematics, (3) the ability to use spatial concepts, (4) musical ability, (5) skills of motor movement and coordination, (6) interpersonal skills, and (7) the ability to understand one's self (Gardner, 1983). Another view, advanced by Robert J. Sternberg, proposes a three-part theory of intelligence claiming that intelligence involves (1) the ability to adapt to the particular environment in which one is required to function; (2) the capacity to deal with new situations; and (3) the possession of practical knowledge and the ability to apply it in the various contexts—work, travel, social relationships—in which people find themselves (Sternberg, 1985a).

Semantic contents

The meanings of words and sentences.

Symbolic contents

The meanings of symbols, like mathematics.

Figural contents

Meanings based on perceptual images or schemata.

Intelligence Tests

Despite the work of Thurstone, Guilford, Gardner, and Sternberg, the measurement of intellectual ability has been restricted for most of this century to a particular kind of test called an **intelligence test.** Thus when psychologists and educators talk about intelligence, they are most often referring to the score on this form of test. Few people grow to adulthood without taking one or more intelligence tests.

A Brief History

Intelligence tests began as a psychologist's solution to a problem faced by Paris schools at the beginning of the century, with the beginning of compulsory education. Many classrooms were crowded, and slow students were holding up the progress of the faster ones. One solution, it seemed, was to identify the children who lacked the mental capacity required by the standard curriculum and put them in a separate school of their own. But how could they be recognized?

A French psychologist named Alfred Binet realized that the task of identifying the poorer students could not safely be left to the teachers. There was a danger that teachers would show favoritism toward children who had pleasant personalities and would be too harsh on those who were troublemakers. There was also the question of whether teachers could recognize children who appeared quiet but in fact could have done the work if they had tried (Cronbach, 1949).

To avoid these pitfalls, Binet developed a test designed to measure potential ability at school tasks—and to produce the same scores regardless of the personalities or prejudices of those who gave or took the test. First published in 1905, Binet's test has been revised as recently as 1985 and is still used widely today. In fact, all modern intelligence tests bear a considerable resemblance to Binet's original test.

Measuring the Intelligence Quotient

In the United States, one of the best-known current versions of the original test is the **Stanford-Binet Intelligence Scale.** With simple physical equipment such as a paper doll and various toys, it can be given successfully even to children who are too young to have developed a wide range of language skills. Older children and adults are asked questions that measure such things as vocabulary, memory span for sentences and numbers, and reasoning ability. Some of the test items used at various age levels are shown in Figure 8.2.

The average **intelligence quotient** (**IQ**) derived from the Stanford-Binet and comparable tests, is 100. The ability to pass items above one's age level results in an IQ of more than 100. The inability to pass all the items appropriate for one's age level results in an IQ of less than 100. In actual practice, the IQ of an individual taking the Stanford-Binet or other intelligence tests is now determined from tables that translate the individual's raw score on the test and chronological age into an IQ number. The way IQs are distributed in the population, according to the Stanford-Binet test, is shown in Figure 8.3. Keep in mind that the classifications used are arbitrary and should not be considered as rigid labels.

Alfred Binet (1857–1911)

Intelligence test
A form of measuring the various factors that make up intelligence.

Stanford-Binet Intelligence Scale
A well-known intelligence test.

Intelligence quotient (IQ)
A numerical value assigned to an individual as a result of an intelligence test.

Two years old	On a large paper doll, points out the hair, mouth, feet, ear, nose, hands, and eyes. When shown a tower built of four blocks, builds one like it.
Four years old	Fills in the missing word when asked, "Brother is a boy; sister is a _____" and "In daytime it is light; at night it is _____."
Nine years old	Answers correctly when examiner says, "In an old graveyard in Spain they have discovered a small skull which they believe to be that of Christopher Columbus when he was about ten years old. What is foolish about that?" Answers correctly when asked, "Tell me the name of a color that rhymes with head." "Tell me a number that rhymes with tree."
Adult	Can describe the difference between laziness and idleness, poverty and misery, character and reputation. Answers correctly when asked, "Which direction would you have to face so your right hand would be toward the north?"

FIGURE 8.2 Some Stanford-Binet test items As shown by these examples, the questions asked very young children do not demand fluency in language. The questions increase in difficulty, particularly in matters of language and reasoning, at higher age levels.

Individual and Group Intelligence Tests: Some Examples

The Stanford-Binet is only one of many tests now used. Even more widely used are three tests devised by David Wechsler—the *Wechsler Adult Intelligence Scale* (or WAIS for short), another for children aged 7 to 16, and still another for children 4 to 6½. The distinguishing feature of the Wechsler tests is that they contain two separate categories of items, verbal and performance. The verbal items measure vocabulary, information, general comprehension, memory span, arithmetic reasoning, and ability to detect similarities between concepts—related to Thurstone's factors 1, 3, and 5. The performance items measure ability at completing pictures, arranging pictures, working puzzles, substituting unfamiliar symbols for digits, and making designs with blocks as shown in Figure 8.4. These are more closely related to Thurstone's factors four and six.

FIGURE 8.3 Ranges of IQ and how many people are found at each level
Administering the Stanford-Binet test to thousands of people has shown that one person in a hundred comes out with an IQ over 139 and can be classified as "very superior." (In popular terminology, this person is a "genius.") Three in a hundred come out with IQs below 70 and are classified as "mentally retarded." Almost half of all people have IQs in the "average" range of 90 to 109.

IQ	Classification	Percentage of People
Over 139	Very superior	1
120–139	Superior	11
110–119	High average	18
90–109	Average	46
80–89	Low average	15
70–79	Borderline	6
Below 70	Mentally retarded	3

FIGURE 8.4   A perfor-mance item on a Wechsler test With colored blocks of various patterns, the subject is asked to copy a design as one of the performance items on a Wechsler Intelligence Scale. The examiner notes how long the task takes as well as how accu-rately it is performed.

Individual tests

A test given to one person at a time by a trained examiner.

Group tests

Tests given to many people at the same time typically taking the form of printed questions with quick-scoring answer forms.

Aptitude tests

A form of testing that measures a person's ability to learn new skills or perform unfamiliar tasks.

A subject's IQ can be calculated for the test as a whole or for the verbal and performance items separately. This feature is often an advantage in test-ing people who lack skill in the use of the English language, for they may score much higher on the performance items than on the verbal items.

Both the Stanford-Binet and the Wechsler are **individual tests,** given to one person at a time by a trained examiner. The advantage of individual tests is that the examiner can readily detect if the results are being influenced by such factors as poor vision, ill health, or lack of motivation. Their disadvan-tage, of course, is that they cannot conveniently be used to test large numbers of people, such as all the pupils in a big school.

Available for large-scale testing of many people at the same time are a num-ber of **group tests**—typically taking the form of printed questions that are answered by making penciled notations. Among the widely used group tests are the Scholastic Assessment Tests, or SAT, taken each year by about a million high school juniors and seniors and used by many colleges and universities as one method of judging applicants. The SAT has two parts, one for verbal abil-ity and the other for mathematics, with the possible score on each part ranging from 200 to 800. In recent years the average scores have been around 431 on the verbal scale and 475 on the mathematical. Since the students taking the test are a selected group who have already proved their ability to do well in school, the 431 and 475 averages represent an IQ of over 100.

Because a number of colleges and universities have a cutoff point for SAT scores and will rarely admit a student who falls below that level, the SAT ter-rifies many high school seniors. Actually, however, the SAT affects college admissions less often than is generally supposed. It has been established that high school grades do just as well as SAT scores in predicting success in col-lege (Trusheim & Crouse, 1982).

Differentiating Aptitude from Achievement

Intelligence tests have also been called **aptitude tests** because they measure a person's ability to learn a new skill or perform an unfamiliar task. Aptitude tests are, in theory, different from **achievement tests,** which measure how much learning or skill a person has actually acquired. Intelligence tests attempt to determine how well the individual will be able to perform academic work in the future. Academic achievement tests, on the other hand, show how much the individual has accomplished in the past. For example, the Iowa and Stanford achievement tests, widely used in elementary and high schools, test how much pupils have learned about reading and arithmetic—and how they compare with other pupils around the nation. A final exam in college is, in essence, an achievement test, the purpose of which is to measure how much a student has learned about a course.

Although it is difficult to test aptitude without taking into account academic achievement, intelligence tests try to minimize differential education and experience. But because this is impossible, there is always a certain amount of bias in intelligence tests. In a nation containing as many diverse social and ethnic groups as the United States, not all people are exposed to the same kinds of basic knowledge. The tests favor those who have acquired the knowledge and language skills typical of the middle- and upper-middle classes and fostered by a school system largely staffed by middle-class teachers.

Moreover, cultural attitudes and values can influence such factors as the individual's motivation, competitiveness, attitude toward the task of taking tests, rapport with the person administering the test, and even the sense of comfort in the testing environment—all of which can affect the outcome (Anastasi, 1988). Thus there appears to be little question that IQ test results are affected by past experience, although psychologists differ in their assessments of how much bias actually exists in such tests.

Achievement tests

A form of testing that measures how much learning or skill a person has acquired.

TEST YOURSELF

a) How did Spearman explain the fact that a person who gets a high score on a test of reading comprehension also usually gets a high score on other tasks such as spatial visualization and memory?

b) What is the essential difference in intent between tests of intelligence and tests of achievement?

What IQ Tests Do and Do Not Tell Us

Our society values intelligence and is highly competitive. Given these two societal characteristics, the significance that we tend to attach to IQ test scores is perhaps not surprising. Yet while IQ tests have many legitimate uses and an impressive record of predicting accurately an individual's potential for accomplishment in many realms, intelligence test scores are not infallible predictors of achievement. Effective use of an individual's tested intelligence can and often does open the way to gaining opportunities and earning rewards; still, many factors intervene between raw intelligence scores and the productive use of intelligence.

IQ and Accomplishment in School

Wechsler pointed out that the word *intelligence* represents a value judgment. We call people intelligent when they have qualities that we ourselves—or our society as a whole, or the special part of society in which we live—consider resourceful and worthwhile. In general, American culture admires fluency in language and talent for mathematics and science. The most intelligent people, according to the consensus, are those who can analyze facts, reason about them logically, and express their conclusions in convincing words. These are the very qualities that are associated with doing well in our schools—and, as it turns out, our intelligence tests measure academic ability better than anything else.

Standard intelligence tests cannot hope to measure, with pinpoint accuracy, an individual's disembodied "capacity to understand the world," as Wechsler put it. Nonetheless the IQ, as determined by any of the standard group or individual tests, is a good indication of how well a person will do in school. Many studies of the relation between IQ and grades in school—from elementary school to the university level—have found correlations ranging from .40 to .80 (Wing & Wallach, 1971; Ceci, 1991).

Although an IQ score is a good predictor of school grades, it is also true that the extent and quality of an individual's school experience correlates with IQ. That is because schooling has a direct impact on the accumulation of knowledge and the development of cognitive skills that underlie performance on most IQ tests. In taking an IQ test, a person has the opportunity to apply the fund of information gained in the classroom and to use test-taking skills honed through academic experience—for example, the ability to categorize and manipulate information, to sit still and focus on questions posed, and to monitor and time one's own response to questions—all of which can affect the test outcome (Ceci, 1991).

Scores on intelligence tests also depend on many personality characteristics—for example, cooperativeness, attention, persistence, and ability to sit still (Scarr, 1981). Motivation is especially important—and therefore it is not surprising that middle-class children, who are strongly encouraged to take pride in the mastery of reading, writing, spelling, and arithmetic, make higher scores on the average than lower-class children, who are less motivated toward academic success.

The relationship between IQ and school achievement stems from Binet's basic aim in designing the original test items, which were used to predict how well an individual pupil could be expected to perform in the classroom. It would perhaps be more fitting to say that his test and its modern counterparts measure an individual's AQ, or academic quotient, rather than IQ, or intelligence quotient. The fact that the tests are called measures of intelligence, rather than something more modest, is one reason they have come under attack in recent years by psychologists as well as by outside critics and the legal system.

IQ, Occupational Status, and Success on the Job

Though the IQ is a good predictor of success in school, there is some question as to how well it predicts anything else. What about jobs, for example? Does a high IQ mean you are destined for a high-level occupation, a low IQ for a low-level job?

One massive body of evidence bearing on these questions comes from a study of the thousands of men who took the Army's group intelligence test during World War II (Harrell & Harrell, 1945). The results indicate that there is a relation between IQ and occupation—but often less than one might expect. The average IQ of such professionals as accountants and engineers was around 120, and the average for truck drivers and miners was below 100. But there was a wide range of IQs in every occupation.

One explanation for these findings undoubtedly is the amount of education the men in the study had received. Of two people with equal IQs, the one able to go to college may become an accountant or engineer. The other, unable for some reason to go to college or even complete high school, may have to settle for a job of lower prestige. In fact, other studies have shown that education is the chief factor in determining occupational status (Duncan, Featherman, & Duncan, 1972).

In general, college graduates have better paying, more challenging jobs than high school graduates, who in turn have better jobs than those who have not completed high school. The relation between IQ and job status, such as it is, seems to depend chiefly on the fact that people with higher IQs generally manage to acquire more education than others, barring such circumstances as illness or financial problems. Performance and advancement in one's job and career, however, frequently depends not so much on IQ level as on what has been described as "practical intelligence"—which involves the style used in thinking about issues, getting along with people, and grappling with problems effectively. Individuals with high practical intelligence can manage to reconcile and integrate a number of goals simultaneously—an ability that often comes from down-to-earth, on-the-job experience rather than academic knowledge (Sternberg, 1985).

Does IQ Foretell Attainment in Life?

One of the most important questions about IQ is the extent to which it relates not just to classroom grades or choice of occupation but to successful living. This is a difficult question to answer, for success in life is an elusive concept. It can hardly be defined in terms of income, for many people do not have the motivation or opportunity to make a great deal of money. Other types of success—efficiency and pleasure in one's job, good human relations, happiness in general—are hard to measure.

One study that has led many psychologists to consider a high IQ to be a great asset in achieving success of any kind was made with a group of 1,500 California schoolchildren who qualified as mentally gifted, with IQs of 140 or more, putting them in the top 1 percent of the population. The study was begun in 1921 by Lewis M. Terman and continued by him and his associates as the children grew into adulthood and middle age.

As children, Terman's subjects were superior in many respects other than IQ. They were above average in height (by about an inch), weight, and appearance. They were well-adjusted and showed superiority in social activity and leadership. In later life, despite some exceptions, the group was generally successful. A large proportion went to college, achieved above-average and often brilliant records, and went on to make important contributions in fields ranging from medicine and law to literature and from business administration to government service. They also seemed to display a high level of physical and mental health, a death rate lower than average, and a lower divorce rate.

Still, a number of investigators, after studying not just the mentally gifted but all people, have reported finding little relation between IQ and success outside the classroom. Grades in school, closely correlated with IQ, have been found to be unrelated to actual efficiency at such diverse jobs as bank teller, factory worker, or air traffic controller (Berg, 1970)—or even scientific research (Taylor, Smith, & Ghiselin, 1963)—as long as the IQ scores are average or higher.

Some scholars have concluded that IQ bears on success only to the extent that an IQ in the lower ranges may make it impossible for a person to complete high school, perform successfully in college, or qualify for certain demanding jobs. For people in or above the 110–120 range, differences in IQ do not seem to have much effect on actual achievement in later life (Wallach, 1976), including income (Jencks, 1972). The issue of real-life success in relation to IQ is discussed in a Psychology in Action box titled "Why Some Smart People Fail."

IQ and Creativity

Creativity
The capacity to regularly solve problems or fashion new products in one or more domains of activity.

Although we can all point to individuals who would be universally regarded as creative, the exact nature of *creativity* has proved elusive. As in the case of "intelligence," people tend to refer to the term casually—in contexts as different as schools, industry, advertising, and the arts—as if there were a common understanding of its meaning. Nevertheless, the definition of **creativity** as *the capacity to regularly solve problems or fashion new products in one or more domains of activity* (Gardner, 1988) is one on which most would agree.

Overall, the correlation between intelligence and creativity is weak for people with IQ scores over 100 or 110 (Barron & Harrington, 1981). A reasonably high level of intellectual ability appears necessary for creativity—more so in some fields than in others. Among painters and sculptors, for example, there seems to be very little if any correlation between IQ and creative ability (Barron, 1968). Among creative writers, the relationship between creativity levels and intelligence test scores is modest. Most fields seem to require what has been called a "threshold" IQ, higher in the sciences than in literature or

PSYCHOLOGY IN ACTION

Why Some Smart People Fail

Almost all of us know seemingly intelligent people who consistently fail at what they do. As psychologist Robert J. Sternberg has pointed out, many people come into the world with remarkable intellectual gifts, but because of other factors that get in their way, they find that all their native abilities are of little consequence. Here is a list of 20 such factors (Sternberg, 1986):

1. Lack of motivation
2. Lack of impulse control—for example, "shooting from the hip" with the first solution to a problem instead of giving thought to other possibilities
3. Lack of perseverance
4. Using the wrong abilities—that is, not capitalizing on strengths
5. Inability to translate thought into action
6. Unwillingness to apply oneself to produce a tangible product
7. Inability to complete tasks and to follow through
8. Failure to take the initiative—usually out of an unwillingness to make a commitment
9. Fear of failure
10. Procrastination
11. Blaming others—or oneself—for no reason
12. Excessive self-pity
13. Excessive dependency
14. Wallowing in personal difficulties
15. Distractibility and lack of concentration
16. Spreading oneself too thin or too thick
17. Inability to delay gratification
18. Inability or unwillingness to see the forest for the trees
19. Not applying the right abilities in the right situation
20. Too little self-confidence—or too much

Undoubtedly we can think of other factors to add to this list. In any case, few would argue with Sternberg's view that what really matters is not just intelligence but also how it is managed. Our goal, he maintains, should be to realize fully whatever abilities each of us has.

For creativity to flourish, children must be motivated from within.

music. But above that minimum requirement creativity depends less on intelligence than on other factors (Crockenburg, 1972; Wallach, 1985).

A clue to the other factors comes from studies showing that creative people tend to have a number of traits in common that are not shared by most other people. Many were lone wolves in childhood. They either were spurned and rejected by other children or sought solitude themselves. If being different from other children caused them anxiety, they eventually overcame it. They grew up with little need to conform to the people and the ways of life of those around them. Creative people *want* to be different and original. Willing to examine even the most foolish-seeming ideas, they are not worried about success or failure. Many can be aggressive; indeed hostility and a striving for power can be a strong driving force for creativity.

A frequent characteristic of those whose lives are marked by creative pursuits is the quality of their motivation. Creative individuals tend to display **intrinsic motivation**—that is, *the incentive to pursue an activity because it is inherently compelling, enjoyable, and satisfying.* They are less influenced by **extrinsic motivation**—*the desire for tangible rewards offered by others* (Amabile, 1989). Later in life, creative individuals tend not only to stand out from others in the quality of their output but in the style with which they approach their work. They emerge as more independent, self-confident, and unconventional. They also display a greater sense of alertness, ambition, and commitment to work (Gardner, 1988)—characteristics that are not wedded to IQ.

Intrinsic motivation

The incentive to pursue an activity because that activity is inherently compelling, enjoyable, and satisfying.

Extrinsic motivation

The desire for tangible rewards offered by others.

The Social Implications of IQ Testing

The history of intelligence testing has taken a curious twist. Until the 1960s it was "generally considered to be one of psychology's major success stories" (Tyler, 1976). In recent years, it has become a controversial aspect of the science—passionately criticized by many "concerned citizens and parents, teacher organizations . . . psychologists . . . and consumer advocate groups"

(Glaser & Bond, 1981), though also stoutly defended by many (Snyderman & Rothman, 1987).

The basic issue is as much a matter of social policy as of scientific validity. Critics question not only the accuracy of the tests and the way they are administered and scored but also the social consequences—on the ground that testing perpetuates advantages now enjoyed by middle-class and upper-class Americans and is unfair and harmful to the lower classes and to minorities, notably African-Americans and Hispanics (Carroll & Horn, 1981). They point out that the lower average scores made by minority groups bar a disproportionate number of them from jobs and promotions in industry and civil service, and also cut off many educational opportunities.

Most psychologists view intelligence tests, if properly used, as only one of a number of items of information helpful in guiding individuals toward suitable and rewarding goals, and all would agree that such tests should never be used in any way that might impede the progress of any group or individual (Snyderman & Rothman, 1987).

TEST YOURSELF

c) Which do traditional IQ tests predict better—the grades a child will get in school, or the success a child will attain in life?

d) Mark insists that, to be creative, you have to be extremely intelligent. Leon disagrees. Who is right?

e) If, in her work, Connie is driven mainly by a yearning for praise and higher pay, is she likely to be creative?

IQ and the Issue of Heredity Versus Environment

Like many other human qualities, intelligence is influenced by heredity as well as environment. Most psychologists agree that the two forces work in tandem—that a child's inherited predispositions work in conjunction with environmental factors to shape the development of intelligence (Rose & Wallace, 1985). But there is disagreement on the relative contribution of each (Plomin, 1989).

Some researchers maintain that heredity is more important than environment (Eysenck, 1981), while others believe the reverse (Kamin, 1981). This "either-or" position has created confusion for parents and educators (Weinberg, 1989). On no other issue has the nature-nurture controversy been waged more heatedly. One reason is that the evidence on both sides can be interpreted in so many different ways (Walker & Emory, 1985).

Family Resemblances in IQ: A Product of Genes or Environment?

Many studies have indicated that the more closely related two people are—that is, the greater their similarity in genetic background—the more similar their IQs are likely to be (DeFries, Plomin, & LaBuda, 1987). A number of such studies are summarized in Figure 8.5. Note the bar that shows the relationships found between parents and children: The correlations range up and down from a midpoint of about .50. The correlations between brothers and sisters reared together with their parents have also been found to cluster around .50. Children of the same parents, even when separated and brought up in different homes, still display a fairly high correlation, with the figures clustering around .35. Identical twins, who have inherited the same genes, show very high correlations when brought up together, and impressively high correlations even when reared apart from each other.

Much of the case for the nature side of the debate rests on those data—and especially on correlations between identical twins reared in different

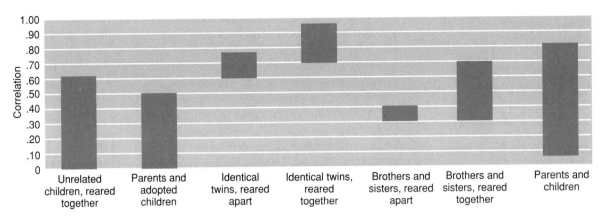

FIGURE 8.5 Family resemblances in IQ The bars show the range of correlations—and the midpoint within the range— found in various studies of comparisons in IQ between blood relatives and also between people who lived in the same home even though they were not related. The correlation between unrelated people who grew up in different homes would of course be zero. For a discussion of the correlations shown here—and how they have been interpreted—see the text (Erlenmeyer-Kimling and Jarvik, 1963; Jencks et al., 1972; Walker and Emory, 1985).

homes. If people with exactly the same genes show a correlation of somewhere between .62 and .77 even when they grow up in different environments, the influence of heredity on IQ would appear to be strong indeed.

The correlations, however, do not convince those on the nurture side of the debate. The figures on identical twins who grew up in different homes, for example, have been challenged on a number of grounds—including the small number of subjects (such twins are difficult to find), the kinds of intelligence tests that were used, and possible bias in the way the tests were administered and scored. Leon Kamin of Princeton University, who has carefully examined the studies, also concluded that the environments in which the twins grew up were probably more similar than the term "reared apart" would imply. This tendency toward similarity in environment might be just as responsible as the identical genes for the high correlations in IQ (Kamin, 1981).

The pro-nurture side also points to correlations, ranging up to .50, between foster parents and the adopted children to whom they were genetically unrelated. Note also in Figure 8.5 the bar for unrelated children who were brought up together, usually through adoption into the same home. One study found a zero correlation for such children—the figure that would be expected for unrelated people chosen at random—but other findings have ranged as high as around .60. These values indicate the influence of environment on IQ (Walker & Emory, 1985).

One widely accepted suggestion to emerge from the various studies is that the inherited genes set a top and bottom limit on an individual's possible IQ score—and the environment then determines where within this range the score will actually fall. Some believe that the range is around 20 to 25 points (Scarr-Salapatek, 1971)—in other words, that a more or less average person may wind up with an IQ of 85 if brought up in a deprived environment but 105 to 110 if brought up under ideal conditions.

The Interaction Between Heredity and Environment

There is some evidence that not all of the components of intelligence as measured by IQ tests are equally influenced by heredity. Among identical twins, for example, there is a greater similarity in verbal than in nonverbal skills (Segal, 1985), suggesting that the former are more heavily influenced by genetic factors. One idea, of which Sandra Scarr is the chief proponent, holds that many genetic traits influence the environmental experiences that a child will encounter. Scarr suggests that these influences take three different forms. First, parents who are themselves intelligent, and therefore likely to pass along to their offspring the genes associated with a high IQ, are also likely to provide a favorable environment. Second, children who have inherited favorable genes, for not only intelligence but appearance and personality, are more likely to evoke favorable responses from their environment. And third, as children grow older, they take an active part in creating their own environments—and in choosing what aspects of the environment they will respond to and learn from; thus, their inherited tendencies are related to their environmental encounters that, in turn, enhance the original tendencies (Scarr, 1981).

Some psychologists challenge Scarr's view of the importance of genetic factors. For example, Diana Baumrind, a child psychologist at the University of California, contends that the role of genes is not fixed and that the IQ level any individual can reach depends on how facilitating the environment is. Citing research suggesting that genetic inheritance has a much greater degree of "plasticity" than was once believed, Baumrind argues that the functional intelligence of some children who have very low IQ scores can be greatly improved by a suitably enriching environment (Baumrind, 1993). Jacquelyn Jackson, an African-American psychologist who studies African-American children also notes the growing consensus among behavioral geneticists that the interaction of genes and environment is the critical determinant of differences in intelligence and personality traits. Her position is buttressed by the success of several studies designed to improve the IQ of children deemed to be at risk by virtue of a mother's low IQ and disadvantaged living conditions (Jackson, 1993).

How Environment and Other Factors Can Alter IQ

It is clear that numerous influences can—and do—account for shifts in IQ over the life span. Poor nutrition may play a role, for it can stunt the development of a child's nervous system. In a study conducted in South Africa, undernourished children were found to have IQs that averaged 20 points lower than children who had received an adequate diet (Stock & Smythe, 1963). Even deficiencies in certain dietary components such as iron can have a depressing effect on both IQ and school achievement (Pollitt et al., 1989).

The psychological environment is also important in the relation of IQ to social class. Middle-class mothers spend more time than lower-class mothers talking to their young children, playing with them, and encouraging them to learn and to solve problems on their own. A high correlation of .76 has been found between children's IQ and parents' scores on a scale that measures how much encouragement and help they offer in using language and increasing vocabulary, how much motivation and reward they provide for intellectual accomplishment, and the opportunities for learning they provide in the home, including personal help, books, and other forms of stimulation (R. M. Wolf, 1963).

An insight into the explanation for shifts in IQ was gained through a study nearly four decades ago in which the progress of 140 girls and boys was carefully followed over a 10-year period, from the time they were 2 years old until they were 12 (Sontag, Baker, & Nelson, 1958). Intelligence tests given every year revealed that for half of the children there were changes upward or downward that in some cases reached striking proportions. Individual records from this study note that one child's IQ rose from about 110 to 160, and another's dropped from 140 to 110. The study found some personality differences between the children who showed increases and those who showed declines. The children whose IQ went up were more independent, competitive, and likely to take the lead in conversation. They showed strong motivation to master intellectual problems, worked harder in school, and persisted at even the most difficult tasks.

Thus the IQ is by no means a constant, unchanging trait like a person's fingerprints, and a score made on any given day is by no means an unerring guide to the future. This rarely recognized fact constitutes a warning to parents and teachers not to give up on a child who has a low score on an intelligence test or to expect too much from a child who has made a high score. "Although genetic endowment will always influence the acquisition of intellectual skills, the environments and opportunities we create for children do make an important difference" (Weinberg, 1989).

Race and Intelligence—and the Nature-Nurture Issue

One of the notable—and sometimes bitter—aspects of the nature-nurture debate is the vast amount of attention given in recent decades to the question of possible racial differences in intelligence. Many dozens of scholarly articles have argued the question pro and con. Countless news stories have reported the newest scraps of evidence and the latest shifts in opinion.

All this attention centers on the consistent findings that—on the average—blacks score 10 to 15 points lower on IQ tests than whites (Reynolds & Gutkin, 1981). The issue is the explanation for the disparity. Although a few psychologists and biologists have in the past expressed the view that there is probably an innate, genetically determined difference between the races (A. R. Jensen, 1969; Eysenck, 1981), available data do not support such a conclusion (Mackenzie, 1984). Indeed the evidence for the importance of the role of environmental factors is strong and compelling (Elliot, 1988; Montie & Fagan, 1988).

It appears that the progress of many nonwhite children is retarded as the result of their unstimulating home environment or failure and criticism in the early years of school. Children from low-income homes, in particular, may become so discouraged that they never take full advantage of their abilities, displaying a good deal less intelligence than they actually have. Their environments can lead them to make low scores on intelligence tests, which in turn leads them and their teachers to have lower expectations. The low expectations produce an apathy toward displaying the skills measured by the tests.

One study showed that black and interracial children adopted by white families with above-average incomes and education score 15 points higher on IQ tests than disadvantaged black children who continue to live with their biological parents (Scarr & Weinberg, 1976). The earlier the adoption, the better, suggesting that environment is important during the earliest months of life. It is noteworthy that no differences have been found between black and white infants in intellectual skills (Bayley, 1965; Montie & Fagan, 1988). But at three years of age, certain significant differences emerge—for example, in the mental manipulation (or visualization) of spatial relationships. These differences can be accounted for by differences in the availability of early learning experiences (Montie & Fagan, 1988).

It is important to keep in mind that both blacks and whites show a wide and overlapping range of individual differences in IQ, and scores are not affected by the average for the race or ethnic group to which a child belongs. There is no way of deciding on the origins of black-white differences in IQ scores until we are able to build a society in which blacks and whites are exposed to similarly favorable—and nondiscriminatory—environments (Kamin, 1981). That day hardly seems at hand. Recent data show that in 1987, black and Hispanic children were almost three times more likely to be living in poverty than were white children (U. S. House Select Committee on Children, Youth, and Families, 1989).

TEST YOURSELF

f) Is it possible to say that either heredity or environment is altogether responsible for a person's level of intelligence?

Personality and Its Meaning

So far, this chapter has dealt with differences among people in intelligence. But people differ from each other also in the strength of their motives, the quality of their moods, and their behavior toward others. These are called *personality* differences. How would you describe your own personality? What factors in your life do you think helped shape your personality? Is it essentially the same as it was, say, ten years ago?

If you have trouble answering such questions, don't be discouraged. The human personality is one of the most baffling of psychological phenomena, discussed and argued about at least since the ancient Greeks. What we casually refer to as personality is such a complex phenomenon that the English language has at least 18,000 words to describe the myriad traits that comprise it. The characteristics that define personality are based on the intricate processes covered in this book: the patterns of emotions, the intensities of drives, and the hierarchies of motives described in the previous chapter; the characteristics of temperament with which you were born; the surges of anxiety and stress that you experience and the diverse efforts you make to cope with them; and your beliefs about the people and the world about you. Small wonder that the concept of personality is so difficult to understand and describe.

Psychologists attempt to create a comprehensive theory of personality—in other words, a set of general principles that will explain why people are alike in some ways and very different in others. Some psychologists have developed theories that stipulate which personality traits are important, the patterns of relations among these traits, the manner in which these patterns become established in individuals, and (at least by implication) how they can be changed. Some of the main theories developed over the years have been accompanied by their own techniques of treating people suffering from personality disturbances, as will be seen in Chapter 10. First, however, we must define personality and explain what personality theories try to accomplish.

Personality

The total pattern of characteristic ways of thinking, feeling, and behaving that constitutes the individual's distinctive method of relating to the environment.

What Does "Personality" Mean?

Personality can best be defined as the *total pattern of characteristic ways of thinking, feeling, and behaving that constitute the individual's distinctive method of relating to the environment*. There are four key words in the definition: (1) *characteristic*, (2) *distinctive*, (3) *relating*, (4) *pattern*.

To be considered a part of personality, a way of thinking, feeling, or behaving must have some continuity over time and circumstance. It must be *characteristic* of the individual. We do not call a man bad tempered if he "blows up" only once in 10 years. We say that a bad temper is part of his personality only if he shows it often and in many different circumstances.

The way of thinking, feeling, or behaving must also be *distinctive*—that is, it must distinguish the individual from other individuals. This eliminates such common American traits as eating with a knife and fork, placing adjectives before rather than after nouns, and carrying a driver's license—all of which are more or less the same for every American and do not distinguish one person from another.

Though these first two elements are essential, they are not the whole story. For example, a woman might always wear a ring that is a family heirloom and the only one of its kind in the world. Wearing the ring is therefore both characteristic and distinctive. But this would hardly be considered part of her personality (unless perhaps she attached some deep significance to the ring, regarding it as a symbol of self-esteem and social acceptance). To be a part of personality, a trait must play a part in how a person goes about *relating* to the world, especially to other people. It is because of this element of relating that personality traits are often thought of as positive or negative. A positive trait, such as friendliness, helps the individual relate to people and events in a constructive manner. A negative characteristic, such as fear of social contacts, may produce loneliness.

Of the multitude of possible personality traits, all of us possess some but not others. It is the particular *pattern* of characteristics we possess and display—the sum total and organization—that is the core of the definition of personality.

The exchange of different ideas often helps to clarify each person's concepts.

Traits That Stand Out: The Personality Hierarchy

The various traits that make up a person's personality—the characteristic and distinctive ways of relating to the environment—exist in a hierarchy from salient and strong to less salient and weak. Salient qualities are easily and frequently aroused; less salient ones are less likely to be provoked. In a social situation, for example, an individual can be talkative or quiet, friendly or reserved, boastful or modest, bossy or acquiescent, more at ease with men or more at ease with women. One person may characteristically withdraw into the background, and we say that such a person is shy. Another may characteristically display warmth and try to put the others at their ease, and we say that such a person is outgoing. Another may be talkative, boastful, and domineering, and we say that such a person is aggressive or "pushy." In each of the three individuals, certain responses are strong in the personality hierarchy and easily aroused.

Each person's hierarchy of qualities is stable over time and consistent in similar situations. The shy person is usually quiet with many different strangers; the domineering person is consistently boastful and pushy with friends. But these qualities are often limited to particular situations and may not be seen when the circumstances change in a major way. For example, a young woman who is typically shy with older people may be sociable and relaxed only with a few friends her own age.

Personality Theory's Four Components

Many general theories of personality have been proposed over the years. They differ in many respects, but they all have four elements in common (Maddi, 1972):

Core of personality

The tendencies and traits common to all human beings.

1. Every theory is based on some fundamental viewpoint toward the basic quality of human nature. It assumes that there is a **core of personality** composed of tendencies and traits common to all of us. Different theories take different views of this common core, but all of them acknowledge that it exists and is a force in shaping personality. In general, for example, most theories of personality assume that all human beings possess the kinds of motives described in the previous chapter—for power over others, for friendships and loving relationships, and for hostility in the face of frustration.

Development

Orderly changes in competence, mood, and behavior throughout the life span.

2. Every theory maintains that the tendencies and traits that make up the common core of personality are channeled in various different directions in different individuals by the process of **development**—all the experiences we encounter, from our childhood relationships with our parents throughout the rest of our lives. Thus various theories agree that personality is the product of both nature (the common core that is part of our heritage) and nurture (the effect of individual experiences). As an example, while affiliation with others is a basic motive that cuts across cultures, the Japanese show a stronger desire to maintain close ties with family members than do Europeans or Americans—the result of values bred by the culture and early experience.

Peripheral traits

All of the distinctive ways in which people relate to the environment.

3. Every theory is concerned with what are called **peripheral traits**—that is, all the distinctive ways in which people relate to the environment. The peripheral traits are viewed as the inevitable result of the way indi-

vidual development has acted on the common core of personality. Consider, for example, a peripheral trait such as stubbornness. In a large urban area, a person who is stubborn will probably not have many friends. But in a small, remote village of 500 persons, a stubborn person will have many relatives and friends to whom he can relate.

4. Finally, every theory is concerned with the task of identifying and defining the inner processes, or dynamics, by which the peripheral traits are laid down and maintained. As we shall soon see, for example, the processes of conditioning and identification with significant figures are among those playing an important role in establishing personality traits.

TEST YOURSELF

g) José once saw Harry hand a homeless man a bag of fruit and concluded that "Harry has a generous personality." Why might that conclusion be premature?

The Psychoanalytic View: Sigmund Freud and His Break-away Disciples

The most famous of all views of personality is Sigmund Freud's psychoanalytic theory. Freud's writings about personality development and the treatment of psychological disorders have been widely read and debated. His views have had a profound influence on many psychologists and on society in general, especially in the United States.

A key idea in Freud's theory of personality is that all humans—children as well as adults—possess a basic energy, called **libido,** directed at maximizing pleasure. Many of the acts that bring pleasure, however, cause conflict as well—for example, revenge to relieve anger, promiscuous sexual behavior, or retaining dependent ties with parents beyond childhood. As a result, some of the motives that arise from the libido are repressed—causing the kinds of adjustment problems and abnormal symptoms discussed in Chapter 10. One of Freud's most imaginative ideas, detailed later in this section, was that the kind of symptoms a person develops depends on the stage of early development when repression occurs.

Libido

A basic energy source in all humans that is directed at maximizing pleasure.

The Unconscious

Freud believed that anxiety is the central problem in mental disturbance—so painful an emotion that we will go to almost any length to eliminate from conscious awareness a motive or thought that threatens to cause anxiety.

The **unconscious mind,** composed in part of repressed motives and thoughts, was another of Freud's most influential concepts. He was the first to suggest the now widely held theory that the human mind and personality are like an iceberg, with only a small part visible and the rest submerged and concealed.

One idea that has influenced many psychologists is that human activities are often a response to **unconscious motives**—that is, wishes and desires that we are not aware of but that influence our behavior nonetheless. The idea of unconscious motives raises some thorny psychological problems, among them the question of how a desire that is unconscious can operate to produce relevant behavior. This idea explains some aspects of human behavior that would otherwise be baffling.

One example of an unconscious motive is the phenomenon known as **posthypnotic suggestion.** While subjects are under hypnosis, they may be

Unconscious mind

The part of the mind composed mainly of repressed motives and thoughts.

Unconscious motives

The wishes and desires that we are not directly aware of but do influence our behavior.

Posthypnotic suggestion

A suggestion urging a person under hypnosis to undertake some kind of activity after the hypnotic trance ends.

told that after they awaken from the trance they will raise a window the first time the hypnotist coughs—even though they will not remember having received this instruction. Later the hypnotist coughs, and, sure enough, the subjects do open a window. If asked why, they say that the room was getting stuffy or that they felt faint. They have no idea that the reason was to comply with the hypnotist's demand.

Other examples are all around us. A mother may seem to believe sincerely that she has generous, affectionate, and even self-sacrificing motives toward her daughter. Yet an unprejudiced observer might say that the mother's real motives are to dominate the daughter, keep her from marrying, and hold on to her. A man may earnestly deny that he has any hostile motives. Yet we may see that he performs subtle acts of aggression against his wife, his children, and his business associates. The idea that the roots of our everyday behavior lie submerged in the unconscious unfortunately gives rise to a good deal of naive psychology.

All of the details of Freud's theory are difficult to summarize, for he revised and enlarged on them throughout a prolific career that spanned four decades. Moreover, Freud's followers have continued to refine his ideas, especially his later ones. This discussion is confined to the basic principles (especially those that have had the greatest influence on psychologists) as they are now viewed by psychoanalytic theorists who regard themselves as true Freudians.

Three Forces: Id, Ego, and Superego

Freud conceived of the human personality and mind as composed of three major parts that he called the id, ego, and superego.

1. The **id,** or most basic and primitive of the three parts, springs from what Freud held to be two inborn drives that all humans possess. One of these drives is the *libido,* consisting of sexual urges and such related desires as to be kept well-fed, warm, and comfortable. The other is a drive toward aggression—to attack anyone or anything that interferes with gratification.

   The drives arouse the id to a state of excitement and tension. In seeking to relieve the tension, the id operates on what Freud called the **pleasure principle.** To satisfy the libido, the id seeks possession of everything desired and loved. To satisfy the drive for aggression, it wants to destroy everything that gets in the way. As we grow up, we learn to control the demands of the id, after a fashion. But it remains active and powerful throughout life.

   Freud believed that human sexual development takes place in a series of stages in which the sexual energy of the libido focuses on different parts of the body. During the **oral stage,** from birth to about 18 months, desires and gratifications concern the mouth, tongue, and such activities as sucking and eating. This is followed by the **anal stage,** from about age 1½ to 3, in which the desires and gratifications are concerned with the act of emptying the lower bowel or refraining from the act. Next comes the **phallic stage,** in which the libido is principally focused on the external sex organ, male or female. At puberty the child enters the **genital stage,** which represents the adult and final step in sexual development, characterized by love for another person.

Id
A basic and primitive part of the mind, which springs from inborn drives toward aggression and sexual desires.

Pleasure principle
The demand of the unconscious id for immediate and total gratification.

Oral stage
The stage in which the energy from the libido focuses on the desires and gratifications concerned with the mouth, tongue, and such activities as sucking and eating.

Anal stage
The stage in which the energy from the libido focuses on the desires and gratifications concerned with the act of emptying or refraining from emptying the lower bowel.

Phallic stage
The stage in which the energy from the libido focuses on the desires and gratifications concerned with the external genital organs.

Genital stage
The stage in which the libido focuses on the desires and gratifications concerned with the love of another person.

Freud believed that either excessive or insufficient gratification of a motive would result in a fixation—meaning that the original focus of that motive would persist to an abnormal degree into adult life. Thus a fixation during the infant's oral stage might be displayed in adult life as an extreme dependence on others or an excessive concern with eating or smoking. And a fixation during the anal stage might cause either a passion for order and cleanliness or the hoarding of money.

2. The conscious part of the mind that develops as we grow is called the **ego.** This is the "real" us as we think of ourselves, including our knowledge, skills, beliefs, and conscious motives. The ego operates on the **reality principle.** The ego does our logical thinking and tries to help us get along in the world. Freud believed that our intellectual and social skills develop because we must learn, beginning in childhood, how to deal with the demands of the id. To the extent that these demands can be satisfied in some reasonable way, the ego permits satisfaction. But when the id's demands threaten to get us rejected by society, the ego represses them or tries to provide substitutes that are socially acceptable. Freud held that artistic creativity, for example, represents a channeling of the libido away from open sexual expression and into the production of paintings and literature.

3. The ego, in its struggle to meet the irrational demands of the id in some rational way, has a strong but troublesome ally in the **superego,** the third part of the mind conceived by Freud. In addition to our desires and our ability to gratify them, we also possess a conscience, a sense of right and wrong. But Freud's concept of the superego is much stronger and more dynamic than the word "conscience" implies. Much like the id, the superego is mostly unconscious, exerting a far greater influence over our behavior than we realize.

Ego
The conscious part of the mind that includes our knowledge, skills, beliefs, and conscious motives.

Reality principle
The principle on which the conscious ego operates as it tries to mediate and balance the demands of the unconscious id and the realities of the environment.

Superego
The largely unconscious part of the mind that threatens punishment for transgressions.

The superego is largely acquired as a result of the **Oedipus complex,** an important element in Freudian thinking. The theory holds that all children between the ages of about 2½ and 6 are embroiled in a conflict of mingled affection and resentment toward their parents. The young boy's libido drives him to want the total love of his mother and to take the place of his father with her. But fearing retaliation from his father and frustrated by his inability to obtain his mother or to replace her in his father's affections, he becomes overwhelmed with strong feelings of mingled love, rage, and fear toward both parents.

Oedipus complex
The conflict of mingled love and hate toward the same-sex parent experienced by boys between the ages of about 2½ to 6.

This period of turmoil takes its name from the Greek legend in which Oedipus unwittingly killed his father and married his own mother and then, when he discovered what he had done, blinded himself as penance. Girls, according to Freudian theory, go through similar torments, except that their love becomes directed mostly toward their father.

The Oedipus complex is resolved through the process of identification with the parents. That is, we resolve our feelings of mingled love and hate for our parents by becoming like them, by convincing ourselves that we share their strength and authority and the affection they have for each other. In this process, we adopt what we believe to be the standards of our parents. What we conceive to be their moral judgments, become our superego, which helps us restrain the demands of the id.

But the demands of the superego are as insatiable as the demands of the id. The superego's standards of right and wrong and its rules for punishment are far more rigid, relentless, and vengeful than anything in our conscious minds. Formed at a time when we are too young to distinguish between a bad wish and a bad deed, the superego may sternly disapprove of the merest thought of some transgression—which explains why some people who have never actually committed a bad deed still have strong feelings of guilt throughout life.

The Internal Battle

The three parts of the mind are often in conflict, and Freud regarded conflict as the core of human personality. One result of the conflict is anxiety, which is produced in the ego whenever the demands of the id threaten to create danger or when the superego threatens to impose disapproval. Anxiety arouses the ego to fight the impulses or thoughts that have created it. In one way or another—by using repression and the other defense mechanisms, by turning the mind's attention elsewhere, by gratifying some other impulse of the id—the ego defends itself against the threat posed by the id or the superego and gets rid of the anxiety.

To the extent that our behavior is controlled by the ego, it is realistic and socially acceptable. To the extent that it is governed by the passions of the id and the unrelenting disapproval of the superego, it tends to be maladjusted and neurotic.

If the ego is not strong enough to check the id's drives, a person is likely to be selfish, impulsive, and antisocial. But if the ego checks the id too severely, other problems may arise. Too much repression of the libidinal force can make a person incapable of enjoying a normal sex life or giving a normal amount of affection. Too much repression of aggression can seriously handicap a person in competition. If the ego is not strong enough to check the superego, the result may be vague and unwarranted feelings of guilt and unworthiness, even an unconscious need for self-punishment. Thus it is the conflict among ego, id, and superego, according to Freud, that often results in abnormal behavior.

TEST YOURSELF

h) "For the life of me, I can't figure out why I got so angry at my friend." If Freud were to hear you say those words, what would he probably conclude about the nature of your motives for having gotten angry?

i) Does the term *libido* refer only to sexual urges?

After Freud: Voices of Dissent

Freud was an important innovator who made many contributions to understanding the human personality. He was the first to recognize the role of the unconscious and the importance of anxiety and defenses against it. He also dispelled the myth, widely accepted before his time, that children did not have sexual urges or hostile impulses. He was a pioneer in recognizing the effect of childhood experiences on personality development and in highlighting the conflict between our private impulses and the need to adapt to society.

Freud's theory, however, has had many critics, especially today, and the unwavering belief in his ideas has declined in recent years. To begin with, it has proven impossible to demonstrate the existence of an id, an ego, or a superego. Moreover, there is no validation of the existence of the libido, nor in Freud's belief that the stage at which fixation occurs determines adult symptoms.

Many critics believe that Freud overemphasized the role of sexual motivation and conflict by generalizing from the experiences of patients who had grown up in Europe during the repressive Victorian age. Western Society has performed an experiment to test Freud's emphasis on sexuality. Although we have witnessed in recent decades considerable relaxation of social restraints on sexual behavior (and presumably much less repression of sexual wishes), there has not been an accompanying decrease in the incidence of neurotic symptoms. This fact suggests that sexual conflict is not the major cause of mental health problems.

But even in Freud's lifetime, some of his disciples broke from him and established competing schools of psychoanalytic thought.

Jung Versus Freud: Temperament Versus Sexuality

Carl Jung believed that Freud did not give enough emphasis to the importance of culture and inherited temperaments. Anticipating modern research, Jung viewed differences in temperament as related to the ability of the brain to deal with new experiences and stress.

Jung invented the terms **introvert** and **extrovert.** Introverts prefer to live with their thoughts and avoid socializing. Extroverts, Jung proposed, are interested in other people and in the events around them. The human personality requires a combination of both introversion and extroversion, but in each person one of these traits tends to develop at the expense of the other. Some people are very concerned with their own thoughts and feelings; others are very preoccupied with people and external events.

Introvert

Individuals who prefer to live with their own thoughts and avoid socialization.

Extrovert

Individuals who are interested in other people and the events around them.

Jung believed that Freud overestimated the importance of sexuality. He felt that the human libido was far richer and more complex—an all-encompassing life force that included a person's view of life, death, virtue, and religion. Jung placed more emphasis than Freud on intellectual and, especially, spiritual qualities of the human personality, and less on sex and aggression. Whereas Freud was relatively skeptical about human nature, Jung perceived heroism in humanity as well as idealism and romanticism. In doing so, he gave early voice to the humanistic views of personality to be described in the next section.

Jung proposed that humans possess a **collective unconscious**—a set of inherited mental structures that represent past events in human history. In a sense, modern neuroscience supports this idea. As we saw in Chapter 3, the human brain allows all humans to perceive and experience the world in ways that are universal. For example, all one-year-old infants are fearful of strangers; all six-year-olds believe that when a large and a small object are paired side-by-side, the larger one is masculine and the smaller one feminine. The collective unconscious contains traces of humanity's fears, superstitions, beliefs in magic, and search for a god. Because of the collective unconscious, every person embodies a great deal of human experience. Jung believed that each of us, of whatever sex, possesses elements of both woman and man, mother and father, hero, prophet, sage, and magician.

Collective unconscious

A set of inherited mental structures that represent past events in human history.

Freud viewed psychological symptoms—anxiety, depression—as the outcome of internal conflict within the individual. Jung anticipated contemporary views by being more sensitive to the role that society and the individual's life environment play in the development of such mental problems. This emphasis on the impact of social factors on personality was carried considerably further by other psychoanalytic theorists who followed Freud.

Adler and Horney: The Influence of Social Forces

Another early disciple who rejected Freud's focus on sexuality was Alfred Adler, whose theory of **individual psychology** emphasized instead the innate tendency of people to be cooperative and psychologically tuned-in to the lives of others. Adler believed that individuals encounter problems in life because they develop inappropriate goals and patterns of living that block the realization of their social interest. While the theory remains unproven, psychologists have attempted to differentiate among various groups of individuals—for example, felons as contrasted to church volunteers—in terms of their degree of concern for the social welfare of others (Crandall, 1980).

Adler also proposed that we are born with a tendency to strive for superiority—not necessarily in terms of influence or success in competition with others, but rather of self-perfection and self-realization. He viewed the motives for power and aggression as distortions of the more basic urge for personal fulfillment. Adler observed that many people appear to be engaged in constant efforts to overcome feelings of inferiority, based not only on physical flaws but psychological and social ones as well. Such efforts often begin early, based, for example, on the young child's perceptions of the capacities of an older sibling. One of Adler's most insightful observations was the importance of birth order in shaping personality—a subject of modern research described in a Life Span Perspective box titled "Sibling Order and Human Development."

Karen Horney (1885–1952)

Individual psychology

A theory that emphasizes the innate tendency of people to be cooperative and psychologically tuned-in to the lives of others.

LIFE SPAN PERSPECTIVE

Sibling Order and Personality Development

Were you the firstborn in your family—or did you come along later? This may seem like an odd question to ask in a discussion of personality, but it is more relevant than it may appear.

Firstborn children are more likely than others to have a strong motive for achievement. For example, students who are firstborns get higher grades than later-borns. They are also more competitive and have higher educational aspirations (Falbo, 1981). Their high achievement motive has led many firstborns to become outstandingly successful. They are more likely to become national merit scholars, get Ph.D.'s, and be listed in Who's Who (Sutton-Smith, 1982). Any list of prominent people—eminent scholars, even presidents of the United States—contains a high proportion of firstborns. The well-known people whose photos are shown in Figure 8.6 all were firstborn children.

One possible explanation is that parents treat firstborn children differently from later children. They devote more time to the firstborn, are more protective, take a greater part in the child's activities, interfere more, and expect more (Hilton, 1967; Scarr & Grajek, 1982). The firstborn child is criticized more often, and expected to conform to adult standards (Baskett,

FIGURE 8.6 Besides success, what do these people have in common? All these people, whose careers would indicate a high level of achievement motive, share another attribute—all were firstborn children. Clockwise from top left, they are: Wayne Gretzky, Hillary Rodham Clinton, Martin Luther King, Jr., Eleanor Roosevelt, Spike Lee, Candice Bergen.

1984). Later children receive less attention and guidance from their parents and are more influenced by their relations with other children, including their siblings.

Among other possible explanations is that firstborns may be driven to do better than the newcomers to the family because they feel anxious over being

Intelligence, drive, boldness, and energy characterize self actualizers.

cast aside—in Adler's words, "dethroned"—by their siblings' arrival. The motive to excel is thus driven by the wish to retain parental approval (Adler, 1928). More likely, the tendency toward achievement by firstborns may be the result of the fact that they are more apt to do better in school at earlier ages and go on to college (Sutton-Smith, 1982). On the average, firstborn children score higher on standard intelligence tests—again probably because they enjoy special benefits in their family relationships. They are the ones who benefit most from enriching, one-to-one contacts with their parents. From studies of large populations of children, one investigator finds that the more children there are in families—especially without wide gaps between them—the lower their average intelligence level is likely to be (Zajonc, 1986).

In addition to achievement and intelligence patterns, psychologists have sought to identify other characteristics among firstborns as well. Firstborn children, again perhaps because of their early close interactions with their parents, have been found to be more trusting of authority than later-born children (Suedfeld, 1969). Because of this characteristic and the related tendency to conform, firstborns are more reluctant than later-borns to generate or accept beliefs that depart from those of the majority. Among scientists, for example, firstborns are more likely to support the status quo, while later-borns are more likely to come up with ideas that threaten "the establishment." Thus Copernicus, who insisted that the earth revolved around the sun rather than the other way around was a later-born, as was Charles Darwin, who argued against the Biblical message of creation and suggested that taught that humans evolved from animals. The overall chances that a firstborn will support a scientific revolution is only half of that of later-borns. A similar preponderance of later-borns is found among social reformers—whether the issue is civil rights or the emancipation of women (Sulloway, 1990).

Another pattern: Just as the youngest child in the family seems to fear and shun power, firstborns often rate high in the motive to attain power. There seems to be some truth in an observation made by Adler, who once described the firstborn child as a "power-hungry conservative" (Adler, 1928).

There are of course many exceptions to all these generalities. Each human being is unique—and the product of many more factors than simply the order in which birth happened to occur.   ■

Another student of Freud who broke with him was Karen Horney, whose view of the human personality, like Adler's, was essentially optimistic. She also believed humans to be capable of growth and self-realization. The capacity is sometimes blocked, however, by a pattern of responses to life's **basic anxiety**—the feeling of being isolated and helpless in a potentially hostile world (Horney, 1945). Horney's views on the importance of the child's early experiences of love and security are reflected in much of the research on early attachment described in Chapter 12, and she was among the first psychoanalytic theorists to shift the view of women in society away from the male perspective that dominated earlier theories (Feshbach & Weiner, 1986). For example, she took exception to Freud's notion that penis envy is a state shared by women as a result of their biological nature, and she contended that Freud, her teacher, did not appreciate how society's view of women produces problems of self-confidence and self-fulfillment. Horney was, in the view of one of her biographers, "the first, and perhaps the best, critic of Freud's ideas about women" (Quinn, 1987).

In departing from Freud's theories of personality, both Adler and Horney turned their view away from the internal struggles of the individual, and focused attention instead on the importance of the ways we relate to others in society—a modern emphasis of psychology discussed in the final chapter of this book.

Basic anxiety
The feeling of being isolated and helpless in a potentially hostile world.

Some Later Trends in Psychoanalysis

In recent years, psychoanalysts have added to and in some ways revised Freud's theories—as he himself did constantly throughout his lifetime. These **neopsychoanalysts,** or new psychoanalysts, have tended to move away from Freud's emphasis on the id and its biologically determined instincts and toward greater concern with the ego and its attempts to deal with reality. One group, led by Heinz Hartmann, has concentrated on such ego processes as perception, attention, memory, and thinking. They regard the ego as an important force in itself rather than a mere mediator between the id and the superego (Hartmann, 1951).

Another group of neopsychoanalysts have turned their attention to cultural and social influences on personality, which were largely neglected by Freud. One prominent member of this group was Erich Fromm, who suggested that personality problems are caused by conflicts between the basic human needs and the demands of society. The core of personality, according to Fromm, is the desire to fulfill oneself as a human being—that is, to achieve a kind of unity with nature in the special way that is dictated by the human ability to think. Lower animals have no need to seek such unity, for they are simply a part of nature. They are not aware of any separation between themselves and their environment, including their fellow animals. But people must

Neopsychoanalysts
The recent psychoanalysts who emphasize a concern with the ego and its attempts to deal with reality.

1. Relatedness	This need stems from the fact that human beings have lost the union with nature that other animals possess. It must be satisfied by human relationships based on productive love (which implies mutual care, responsibility, respect, and understanding).
2. Transcendence	The need to rise above one's animal nature and to become creative.
3. Rootedness	The need for a feeling of belonging, best satisfied by feelings of affiliation with all humanity.
4. Identity	The need to have a sense of personal identity, to be unique. It can be satisfied through creativity or through identification with another person or group.
5. A frame of orientation	The need for a stable and consistent way of perceiving the world and understanding its events.

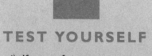

TEST YOURSELF

j) If you refer to someone as an introvert or extrovert, whose personality theory are you drawing from?

k) Why do you think Karen Horney's view of personality would have been widely endorsed by today's feminist leaders?

seek the unity through their own efforts; they must fulfill what Fromm regarded as the five basic and unique human needs (listed in Figure 8.7).

It would be possible, Fromm believed, to create a society in which these needs could be harmoniously fulfilled. But no such society has ever existed. Therefore all of us tend to experience frustrations and personality problems. It is society, Fromm said, that is "sick"—and it will remain so until people can relate to one another "lovingly" and "in bonds of brotherliness and solidarity," can transcend nature "by creating rather than by destroying," and can gain a sense of self-hood through their own individual powers "rather than by conformity" (Fromm, 1955).

Positive Growth: Humanistic Theories of Personality

Much closer to the theories of Adler, Horney, and Fromm than to Freud's are the humanistic theories of personality. These theories assume a core of personality almost opposite to the Freudian assumption. Freud believed that the core was conflict, springing in large part from the ruthless and pleasure-seeking demands of the id. Humanistic theories, on the contrary, hold that human nature is basically good and that the core of personality is the desire to perfect our skills and find peace and happiness.

Carl Rogers: The Power of Self-Image

Phenomenological self

The self-image that represents the way we perceive ourselves as functioning human beings.

Among the prominent humanistic theorists was Carl Rogers, who stressed the critical role of the self-image all of us carry around. This self-image, or **phenomenological self,** represents the way we perceive ourselves as functioning human beings. It consists of our judgments about our abilities, accomplishments, attractiveness, and relationships with other people. In part it is based on our own observations of our behavior and the reactions of other people. But it is also highly subjective, depending on our feelings about ourselves and the way we evaluate ourselves. Thus the phenomenological self does not necessarily correspond to reality. Many people who are considered successful and are highly respected by others perceive themselves as unworthy failures.

We must grow up in a family and social environment that treats us with what Rogers called **unconditional positive regard.** That is, we must be valued and trusted. Our opinions and behavior must be respected. We must be accepted and loved for what we are, even when we do things of which others may disapprove. Unfortunately, few people grow up in such a completely favorable atmosphere. Most are treated with what Rogers called **conditional positive regard.** Their families and later society at large respond warmly to only some of their thoughts and actions, disapprovingly to others. The "forbidden" thoughts and actions are likely to become a source of maladjustment.

All of us, said Rogers, try to perceive our experiences and to behave in a way that is consistent with our images of ourselves. When we are confronted with new experiences or new feelings that seem inconsistent with the image, we can take one of two courses: We can recognize the new experiences or feelings, interpret them clearly, and somehow integrate them into our image of self—which is a healthy reaction, or we can deny the experiences or feelings or interpret them in distorted fashion.

Rogers believed that the second course of action is likely to cause trouble. He concluded that maladjusted people tend to regard as a threat any experience that is not consistent with their self-image. Their phenomenological self, as they conceive of it, does not match their true feelings and the actual nature of their experiences. They must set up more and more defenses against the truth, and more and more tension results. Well-adjusted people, on the other hand, are those whose self-image is consistent with what they really think, feel, do, and experience—and who are willing to accept themselves as they are. Instead of being rigid, their phenomenological self is flexible and changes as new experiences occur.

Maslow and the Quest for Self-Actualization

The humanistic psychologists believe that the most powerful motivating force in human beings is the aspiration toward benevolent and spiritual goals. The humanists' view of human personality is expressed in the **theory of self-actualization,** which holds that people will always pursue the highest and most idealistic aims unless their development is warped by a malevolent social environment.

The theory was formulated by Abraham Maslow, who believed that humans are innately inclined to seek beauty, goodness, truth, and the fullest possible development of their own unique potentialities for perfection and creativity. For Maslow, self-actualization meant an all-encompassing self-fulfillment. Self-actualizing people have satisfied their search for such aesthetic pleasures as order, symmetry, and beauty. They accept themselves and others and the realities of existence, and they rejoice in the experience of living. Self-actualizers are spontaneous and creative and have a keen sense of humor. They have made the most of their abilities and have become all they are capable of becoming (Maslow, 1970). All this represents the goal toward which all humans by their very nature are motivated—though deprivation and social pressures may prevent some of them from ever reaching this ideal level of development.

Unconditional positive regard
The total acceptance of individuals for who and what they are even if one disagrees with their actions.

Conditional positive regard
The approval of some but not all aspects of an individual's behavior.

Theory of self-actualization
A humanistic view of human personality holding that people will always pursue the highest and most idealistic aims unless their development is warped by a malevolent social environment.

Maslow's theory does not in general lend itself to experimental proof or disproof. It must be taken largely on faith. To many psychologists, the theory has the intuitive ring of truth. To others, it seems too optimistic.

The Behavioral View of Personality

Behavioral theories

A set of theories that regard personality as largely composed of learned habitual ways of responding to the situations that arise in one's life.

Humanistic theories hold that the core of personality is the urge to grow in a constructive way. Freud's psychoanalytic theory holds that the core is conflict. Another prominent group of theories take still another view. These are the **behavioral theories,** which reject Freud's notion of the primitive drives of the id and do not necessarily take any stand at all on the question, so vital to the humanistic approach, of whether human nature is basically good or evil. Instead, behavioral theories regard personality as largely composed of habits—that is, of habitual ways of responding to the situations that arise in each of our lives. Beginning at birth, our experiences mold us in accordance with the principles of learning that were discussed in Chapter 4. Depending on what responses we have learned to display to events in the environment, we may either cope successfully or become helpless and troubled by anxiety or depression.

Personality as Learned Behavior

Cue

The stimulus for a response, according to Dollard and Miller.

Response

The behavior that follows the cue, according to Dollard and Miller.

Drive

An urge or need, according to Dollard and Miller.

Reinforcement

The event that strengthens a habit just displayed.

One of the earliest behavioral theories of personality was developed in the 1940s by John Dollard and Neal Miller, who attempted to use learning theory to explain some of the murkier psychoanalytic concepts of Sigmund Freud. Dollard and Miller proposed that to understand an individual's behavior—whether normal or not—it was necessary to focus on four factors: **cue** (stimulus), **response, drive,** and **reinforcement** (Dollard & Miller, 1950). Consider a concrete case: Suppose a friend always becomes hostile and sarcastic whenever you beat her at tennis. The cue for her is your sharp game, and her response is aggression. The drive could be an urge for power, and the reinforcement for her behavior the look of pain on your face. Or the drive could be a need for attention, and the reinforcement could be the comfort of a consoling arm around her shoulder. The central point for Dollard and Miller was that what we call personality is learned in the same way as any other conditioned behavior.

Unlike Dollard and Miller, B. F. Skinner, who was among the best known advocates of the behavioral approach to personality, rejected the existence of internal processes such as drives altogether (Skinner, 1953). Skinner maintained that we can understand personality only by applying the operant-conditioning laws described in Chapter 4. Rejecting the belief that humans possess a free will, Skinner's theory argues that we learn to be a particular kind of person just the way we learn anything else in life—through positive or negative reinforcement. External circumstances, not some inner motivation, ultimately define personality. In effect, we could predict a human's behavior if only we knew the full story of which of this person's actions had been rewarded by society and which had been punished.

Although Skinner's behavioristic view has been attacked because it regards humans as too passive, the view does open up the possibilities for change. Once it is known what reinforcers maintain a certain pattern of behavior, logic dictates that withdrawing them can cause extinction of that behavior. And by the same token, new reinforcers can be used to shape alternate ways of behaving. Such processes are the basis of many forms of treatment known as **behavior therapy,** described in Chapter 11.

The Theory of Social Learning

When behavioral theories of personality based on learning were formulated, most of psychology's knowledge of learning was confined to classical and operant conditioning. Thus the theories originally stressed the way unreasonable fears can be acquired through classical conditioning and the role of reinforcement in molding operant behavior. Considered especially important were the rewards and punishments provided first by the family and later by society in general.

Most learning theorists today take a more cognitive view of the manner in which experience creates habitual forms of behavior. They agree that rewards and punishments influence learning, but they believe that people learn by means other than direct reinforcement. And factors inside the person—such as inner standards—are also important.

One prominent social-learning theorist is Albert Bandura, whose concept of **reciprocal interaction** regards humans as highly active processors of information who are constantly interacting with the environment (Bandura, 1977). The environment affects us, but the opposite is true as well. For example, in the case described earlier, losing at tennis may cause your friend to behave in a hostile manner—and eventually lead you to respond in kind, causing friction in the friendship. But your friend would create a far different environment if she were "a good sport" and lost graciously. What this implies is that we are not just passive responders—we can choose how we want to affect the world around us. We have a "uniquely human capacity" for self-direction (Bandura, 1974).

According to Bandura and other learning theorists, we adopt many of our responses to the environment through a process called **observational learning.** Often without even being aware of it, we take on important behavior patterns that define personality by modeling the actions of others.

Describing Personality

Since antiquity, efforts have been made to "type" people's personalities. The ancient Greeks believed that fluids inside the body determined whether people were happy or depressed, hot-tempered or lethargic. These beliefs were not necessarily primitive; indeed, as discussed in the Psychology and the Media box, the search for a direct biological marker of personality continues today.

In the absence of physical descriptors of personality, the theories of Freud and those who followed him dictated the personality traits that were most important—traits described by terms like anxious, obsessive-compulsive, paranoid, repressed, or fixated. But, as psychoanalytic theory lost its popularity and psychologists abandoned their faith in the personality traits that Freud emphasized, it became necessary to seek new ideas. No strong theory, however, was available to replace psychoanalytic concepts. As a result, a different strategy was chosen. Psychologists decided to be less theoretical and to let

Behavior therapy

A form of therapy that applies the principle of learning theory and conditioning to help relieve the person of troubled symptoms and problems.

TEST YOURSELF

l) If you were to say that "I seem to be having trouble with my phenomenological self," what view of personality would you be basing your statement on, and what would you believe to be the problem?

m) How much emphasis did Skinner place on conditioning as a basis of personality?

n) When a parent says "monkey see, monkey do," about a child, what type of learning is being described, and what school of personality is being called upon to explain the child's behavior?

Reciprocal interaction

A concept suggesting that humans are highly active processors of information who are constantly interacting with the environment.

Observational learning

The process of taking on behavioral patterns that define our personality by imitating and modeling the actions of others.

Spit Testing May Be Hard to Swallow in the Workplace

Psychologist Collects Samples, Seeing Testosterone Levels As a Clue to Personality

The Romans believed that human saliva has mystical properties. Indeed, legend had it that any man could slay a serpent by spitting into its throat.

Now *that's* the kind of guy James M. Dabbs Jr. would like to meet.

Dr. Dabbs, a psychology professor at Georgia State University here, is making his career in spit. He has collected some 2,500 saliva samples—from murderers, ministers, lawyers, farmers, the rich and the poor, men and women—and then measured testosterone levels in the specimens.

He is interested in exactly how abnormally high levels of the hormone affect human behavior. Physiologically, the male sex hormone is associated with bigger muscles, deeper voices and baldness. Its effects on how people act—on competitiveness, criminality and such—are matters of rather more controversy.

Bloodless Procedure

The reason for a spit test is that it is easily administered, much simpler than a blood test requiring needles, and could even be done on you by your boss in the office, much as polygraphs and personality tests, for better or worse, are used in the workplace. "I'm on the cutting edge of spit," Dr. Dabbs says.

Dr. Dabbs's research, unsavory as it might seem, appeals to the National Science Foundation, which provides about $50,000 a year for his work. It's the envy of two dozen other researchers in the same field, if only for the volume of Dr. Dabbs's holdings—the contents of 2,500 little plastic cups to which volunteers were asked to contribute by students of his who knock on doors and stop people on the street asking them to spit.

When Dr. Dabbs first began studying saliva in the early 1980s, he would keep little vials of it in his refrigerator at home. But storing the stuff with the family groceries struck his wife as vile indeed. The samples soon were rusticated to a freezer outside his university office.

Donors weren't at all hard to come by. Nearly 700 inmates at the Lee Arrendale Correctional Facility in Alto, Ga., were happy to part with some sputum. Several offered to work as lab assistants. In animal tests, a group of chimpanzees proved to be particularly accommodating. ("It was monkey see, monkey do," says Dr. Dabbs. "We would spit in a cup, then they would spit in a cup.")

The process for collecting and treating samples is pretty straightforward. First, volunteers are asked to chew gum to encourage salivation, the glandular secretion of the thin, viscous fluid that aids in swallowing and digestion.

The fluid, tested for testosterone levels in a lab, shows pronounced differences in men and women, in ministers and prison inmates.

In women, relatively small amounts of testosterone are produced by the ovaries and adrenal glands. In men, the

---

the evidence decide which traits were most important. They devised many questionnaires that asked people to describe their behaviors and their moods and analyzed the results of these studies to ascertain which personality traits were most important. Personality questionnaires that are used today are derivatives of those developed earlier in the century.

Some psychologists selected from a dictionary all the words that described differences in human beings. After eliminating synonyms, they came up with a core set of adjectives. They then asked large numbers of adults to describe themselves with these adjectives and, following an analysis of these data, decided that there was a small number of basic personality traits. Today, these traits are suggested to be the "Big Five," or five most important personality traits (Goldberg, 1981; Digman and Inouye, 1986). Summarized in Figure 8.8, they include the complementary traits of (1) extroversion vs introversion that Jung made famous, (2) a calm vs highstrung profile, (3) a preference for new experiences versus liking what is familiar, a cooperative, trusting manner vs. a stubborn, more difficult per-

hormone is produced by the testes. The average woman has a testosterone level of about one to two nanograms per deciliter of saliva, while most men fall in the eight to 10 nanogram range. (A nanogram is a billionth of a gram, while a deciliter equals about half a cup.) According to Dr. Dabbs, a violent female prisoner typically shows a slightly elevated testosterone reading—about a three or four—while a violent man usually exhibits a substantial increase over the average (a 17 or more). Ministers typically fall in the five to six range.

So, who has got all the testosterone? Dr. Dabbs's researchers have found high levels of the hormone in, among others, attorneys, prisoners, cold-call salespeople and the unemployed. On the low end of the scale are ministers, farmers and most white-collar managers.

Cause and Effect

Dr. Dabbs, who got his doctorate from Yale in 1962, has written about 20 scholarly papers on testosterone and is highly regarded in the field, doesn't make wild claims that testosterone causes certain men to commit crimes. The causation of behavior is very hard to pin on a hormone found in all men. Dr. Dabbs merely looks at correlations. And meanings aren't always clear. The hardest-charging executives often exhibit only average or low levels of testosterone, Dr. Dabbs remarks. But Dr. Dabbs and his associates have observed an apparent link between elevated testosterone and acts of violence. And despite that, some people seem to be proud of a high testosterone score. Atlanta attorney Mary Thompson heard about Dr. Dabbs's work and invited him to her law practice to measure the staff. Ms. Thompson—who says she is capable of "yelling, pounding and jumping up and down at breakfast"—suspected she was high in testosterone, and she was right. But she isn't jumping to conclusions: "I don't know what it really proves," she says.

Those sentiments are shared by some scientists. "We're like detectives," says Brian Gladue, a senior scientist at the American Psychological Association. "We don't want to make a conviction," says Dr. Gladue, "until all the evidence is on the table. Correlations are clues—but they're not the case . . . You can make a case for any type of behavior and men, and you can make the case that men have a lot of testosterone."

Issues to Consider

Can you think of reasons that might encourage psychologists to continue to search for biological "markers" of personality, such as hormonal levels? If found, would such a marker be likely to be more or less objective than the results of personality tests?

What social and ethical risks might be associated with establishing biological tests as the basis for assessing personality?

Source: Excerpted from "Spit Testing in the Workplace May be Hard to Swallow," by Anita Sharpe, *Wall Street Journal,* November 29, 1993.

sonality, and, finally, a conscientious, well-organized profile versus a less reliable, careless style.

Despite the widely acknowledged conceptual value of the "Big Five," this scheme is not without its critics. Among the principal shortcomings is that the five dimensions constitute a "psychology of the stranger," (McAdams, 1992). That is, information about each of the five traits would enable one to make a quick appraisal of personality features that typically are relevant to interpersonal interactions in Western cultures. But these dimensions do not seem to be universal, nor do they give a comprehensive perspective on the many elements of personality. It is important, too, psychologists caution, not to be lulled into thinking that the availability of terms, however accurate, to describe personality implies an understanding of the actual structure of personality (Briggs, 1992).

The list of the "Big Five" personality traits is probably not a final, unified theory of personality. Psychologists disagree over the number of qualities that will make up the important dimensions or categories of human personality.

Dimension	Definition of Extremes	
Extroversion/ introversion	Outgoing	Withdrawn
	Fun-loving	Serious
	Affectionate	Aloof
	Spontaneous	Inhibited
Emotional stability	Calm	Fearful
	Secure	Uncertain
	Strong self-concept	Weak
	High-strung	Easygoing
Openness to experience	Imaginative	Down-to-earth
	Likes variety	Likes *status quo*
	Independent	A follower
	Inquisitive	Disinterested
Agreeableness	Kind	Mean
	Trusting	On guard
	Cooperative	Unamenable
	Courteous	Thoughtless
Conscientiousness	Careful	Careless
	Organized	Chaotic
	Rigorous	Haphazard
	Self-disciplined	Without resolve

FIGURE 8.8 Dimensions of personality: the "Big Five" As described in the text, this portrayal of five principal factors of personality reflects a continuing effort to define the essential dimensions along which individuals differ—and to do so in as meaningful and economical a way as possible (adapted from McRae & Costa, 1986).

Some argue that five is much too small a number; others believe that the number might be even smaller (McAdams, 1990). One notable effort to depict the human personality was undertaken by Hans Eysenck, a British psychologist who proposed that many variations in human behavior can be explained by two key dimensions (Eysenck, 1981). One of them—extroversion-introversion—is among the "Big Five" summarized in Figure 8.8, and echoes the typology proposed by Jung. The second is stability-instability. As shown in Figure 8.9, these two dimensions are defined by Eysenck by a variety of specific personality traits.

However logical and neat they seem, all trait theories are beset by a nagging question: How consistent are our personality characteristics over time and across different life situations?

The Consistency of Personality

Conclusions about the consistency of personality depend, of course, on the source of evidence. Those who subscribe to psychoanalytic theory and rely on behavioral observations and people's reports of their moods in a therapeutic context believe there is considerable consistency. By contrast, psychologists who use questionnaires as the primary source of information find less consistency.

The evidence that some personality traits remain consistent over long periods of time is derived from a number of studies (Moss & Susman, 1980). In studies spanning age five to early adulthood, for example, investigators have observed that aggressive behavior is moderately consistent over time (Olweus, 1981). In one long-range study, the investigator assessed 100 men

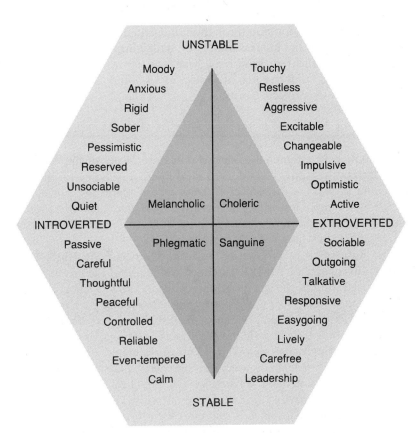

UNSTABLE

Moody   Touchy
Anxious   Restless
Rigid   Aggressive
Sober   Excitable
Pessimistic   Changeable
Reserved   Impulsive
Unsociable   Optimistic
Quiet   Active

Melancholic | Choleric

INTROVERTED   EXTROVERTED

Phlegmatic | Sanguine

Passive   Sociable
Careful   Outgoing
Thoughtful   Talkative
Peaceful   Responsive
Controlled   Easygoing
Reliable   Lively
Even-tempered   Carefree
Calm   Leadership

STABLE

FIGURE 8.9 **Eysenck's two personality dimensions** Shown here are various traits that make up the two major personality dimensions proposed by Eysenck. Note that the four combinations that emerge bear a startling resemblance to the basic personality types described by the early Greeks.

men and women over a span of 25 years and found that they retained to a remarkable degree, their level of dependability, emotional control, and aesthetic interest. But, as noted earlier, many people behave differently at home, at work, or on a date.

The Challenge of Personality Measurement

If psychologists had a test that measured all of personality accurately and reliably, it would be one of their most valuable tools. Clinical psychologists could quickly analyze their clients' strengths and weaknesses, pinpoint sources of stress and anxiety, and determine the most effective way of helping in the struggle to cope. Guidance counselors would have a surefire guide to jobs and careers, for personality is a major factor in determining whether a person will be happy and successful as a salesperson, teacher, police officer, or accountant. Research psychologists would have an invaluable aid in studying the conditions that foster or inhibit the flowering of personality.

Psychologists have spent a great deal of time, effort, and ingenuity on the creation of personality tests. Their goal, unfortunately, has been elusive. They have devised several hundred tests that are useful in many ways, but have yet to find the perfect set of tests. Perhaps they never will. Personality is such a complex matter—the product of a tangled weaving together of experiences beginning at birth, continuing throughout life, and unique for each individual—that the difficulties in measuring it are staggering.

All the personality tests now in use have some virtues but also many limitations. The tests fall into three major classes: (1) objective tests, (2) situational tests, and (3) projective tests.

Objective Tests

Objective tests

A group of personality tests whose results are not affected by the opinions or prejudices of the examiner.

Many people have attempted to devise a measure of personality that meets the standard of objectivity considered ideal in any psychological test. They have come up with some **objective tests** whose scores are not seriously affected by the opinions or prejudices of the examiner. Since these tests are administered according to a standard procedure, the results should be the same regardless of who gives or scores them.

Minnesota Multiphasic Personality Inventory (MMPI)

A widely used objective personality test that helps diagnose patterns of emotional disorders and assesses personality traits.

The most widely used objective test is the **Minnesota Multiphasic Personality Inventory,** or **MMPI.** Intended originally to identify individuals with mental disorders, the inventory was revised in 1989 to reflect changes in the American culture in the half century since it was first developed (Hathaway et al., 1989). Since its appearance, the test has come to be used around the world not only to help diagnose patterns of emotional disorders but also to assess personality traits—in job applicants, for example.

California Personality Inventory (CPI)

An objective personality test that measures such dimensions as dominance, sociability, self-acceptance, self-control, and responsibility.

The MMPI is made up of nearly 600 statements like those shown in Figure 8.10. For each statement, subjects are asked to check whether or not it is true of their own behavior or to mark "cannot say." The method of scoring compares the individual subject's responses with those made in the past by large numbers of other people—especially with the scores made by people known to have such personality traits as tendencies to pessimism and depression, anxiety over health, emotional excitability, delinquency, or tendencies toward mental illness. The recent revision of the MMPI also permits assess-

FIGURE 8.10 Some items from a personality test The *Minnesota Multiphasic Personality Inventory* is made up of statements like these, which subjects are asked to mark true, false, or cannot say of their own behavior. (Source: *Minnesota Multiphasic Personality Inventory.* Copyright 1943, renewed 1989 by the University of Minnesota. Published by the University of Minnesota Press, Minneapolis. All rights reserved.)

T	F	Cannot say	
☐	☐	☐	I have certainly had more than my share of things to worry about.
☐	☐	☐	I think that I feel more intensely than other people do.
☐	☐	☐	I have never done anything dangerous for the thrill of it.
☐	☐	☐	I think nearly everyone would tell a lie to keep out of trouble.
☐	☐	☐	I am happy most of the time.
☐	☐	☐	I tend to be on my guard with people who are somewhat more friendly than I had expected.
☐	☐	☐	My mother or father often made me obey even when I thought that it was unreasonable.
☐	☐	☐	I feel uneasy indoors.
☐	☐	☐	I refuse to play some games because I am not good at them.
☐	☐	☐	I find it hard to keep my mind on a task or job.

ment of characteristics of more general interest such as tendencies toward anger, cynicism, low self-esteem, and difficulties functioning on a job.

The MMPI has served as the basis for the development of other widely used objective tests of personality. One example is the **California Personality Inventory, or CPI.** This test contains nearly 500 items, yielding scores that measure such dimensions of personality as dominance, sociability, self-acceptance, self-control, and responsibility. Various combinations of scores on the scales of the CPI have been found to be typical of persons who succeed in school and various fields of work (Anastasi, 1982).

Situational Tests

In a **situational test,** the examiner observes the behavior of the subject in a situation deliberately created to bring out certain aspects of personality. For example, in a situational stress test, subjects might be asked to carry out some difficult mechanical task with the assistance of "helpers" who are in fact stooges and who behave in an uncooperative and insulting fashion (U.S. Office of Strategic Services, 1948). Or subjects might be put through what is called a stress interview, in which the people asking the questions are deliberately hostile (MacKinnon, 1967a).

Situational tests have been widely applied in efforts to identify personality characteristics as they might emerge in everyday life. Young children, for example, have been placed in group situations of free play with other, unfamiliar children in order to identify which ones tend to be shy and which ones do not (Kagan et al., 1988). Such tests have also been used to select people with personality traits that are appropriate for particular jobs—for example, as police officers or spies. One weakness of these tests is that it is difficult to know whether the situation actually seems real to the subjects and whether their motivation and behavior are the same as in real life. Moreover, two different examiners watching a subject's behavior may reach different conclusions about it. Thus situational tests, though they may give valuable clues to personality traits, must be used and interpreted with caution.

Projective Tests

The term *projection* was mentioned previously as a defense mechanism in which people attribute to others some of their own anxiety-causing motives. **Projective tests** of personality assume that a similar mental process can be observed and measured, even in people who are not using it as a defense mechanism, by providing conditions that encourage it. In the **Thematic Apperception Test (TAT),** these conditions are created by asking the subject to make up stories about pictures like the one in Figure 8.11, which you should examine before reading on.

The picture in Figure 8.11 is deliberately ambiguous. It could mean almost anything. Thus, in responding to it, you are likely to project some of your own personality traits. The story you make up may reveal something about your own motives, feelings, anxieties, and attitudes. Sometimes the amount of self-revelation is dramatic, as in this story made up by one subject:

> The older woman represents evil and she is trying to persuade the younger one to leave her husband and run off and lead a life of fun and gaiety. The

Situational test

A type of personality test in which the examiner can observe the behavior of the subject in a deliberately created situation.

Projective tests

A type of personality testing in which subjects are expected to project aspects of their own personalities into responses to ambiguous pictures or inkblots.

Thematic Apperception Test (TAT)

A projective personality test in which the subject is asked to make up stories about a series of pictures.

FIGURE 8.11   A projective test What story does this picture tell? What led to the situation? What is happening? How will events turn out? These are the questions asked in the *Thematic Apperception Test* (TAT), which uses drawings similar to this one. Try making up your own story before reading the discussion of the TAT in the text. (© Murray, 1971. Reprinted by permission of the Harvard University Press.)

younger one is afraid to do it—afraid of what others will think, afraid she will regret the action. But the older one knows that she wants to leave and so she insists over and over again. I am not sure how it ends. Perhaps the younger woman turns and walks away and ignores the older woman.

Rorschach Test

A projective personality test in which the subject is asked to explain what is perceived in an inkblot.

Word association test

A less formal projective personality test in which the subject is asked to respond with a word as quickly as possible immediately after the examiner calls out a word.

Draw-a-person test

A less formal projective personality test in which a subject is asked to draw a picture of a person on a blank piece of paper.

Sentence completion test

A less formal projective personality test in which the subject is asked to complete a series of incomplete sentences.

The **Rorschach Test** uses inkblots like the one shown in Figure 8.12. When subjects are asked what they see in the blots, they ordinarily mention 20 to 40 things of which they are reminded. Their responses are scored for various characteristics that seem to reveal personality. For example, a tendency to respond to the blot as a whole may indicate that the subject thinks in terms of abstractions and generalities, while a tendency to pick out minor details that most people ignore may indicate an overconcern for detail.

A number of other less formal projective techniques have been developed (Anastasi, 1982). In a **word association test,** the examiner calls out a word, such as "mother" or "bad" or "money" and the subject is asked to respond as quickly as possible with the first word that comes to mind. The examiner notes the nature of the associations that the test words suggest and also the speed with which the subject responds. Any unusual delay in responding is taken to indicate that the test word arouses some kind of conflict. In a **draw-a-person test,** the subject is simply asked to draw a picture of a person on a blank sheet of paper. The sex of the drawing, its size, the facial expression, and other characteristics may contain personality clues. In a **sentence completion test,** the examiner gives the subject a series of partially completed sentences such as the following:

I sometimes feel. . . .

When by myself. . . .

When I was young. . . .

The subject is asked to complete the sentences with the first thoughts that come to mind. The responses, like the TAT stories, may suggest motives and conflicts.

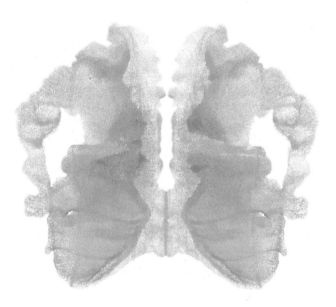

FIGURE 8.12   Another projective test: what do you see? This is an inkblot like those used in the *Rorschach Test.* Subjects are asked to examine it and report everything they see in it (Klopfer and Davidson, 1962).

Testing the Scientific Way

Clearly, many questions remain unanswered about the origins and elements of intelligence as well as about personality. Yet practicing psychologists must deal with each of these topics, even in the absence of definitive answers. Thus it is all the more important that when testing either for intelligence or personality, certain criteria are met. These include objectivity, reliability, validity, and standardization.

Requirement 1: Objectivity

A satisfactory test should be **objective**—that is, it should provide results that are not affected by the personal opinions or prejudices of the person who gives and grades it. The first intelligence test was an attempt to obtain a more objective measure of a child's ability to profit from classes in school than could be provided by the opinion of the teacher.

Insofar as is possible, psychological tests are designed so that any qualified person can present them to the subject in the same manner and under the same testing conditions. A uniform method is provided for scoring the results. Thus the person taking the test should get the same score regardless of who administers and scores it.

Objectivity
A criterion for good testing that should provide results that are not affected by the personal opinions or prejudices of the examiner.

Requirement 2: Reliability

To show why a test must also be **reliable,** an analogy can be drawn between a test and an oven thermometer. If the thermometer is reliable—that is, if it gives the same reading every time for the same amount of heat—the cook can count on roasts and pies to come out of the oven in perfect shape. If the thermometer is unreliable, it may read 300 degrees on one occasion and 400 degrees on the next, even though the actual temperature is exactly the same. In this case the food is likely to be somewhat disappointing.

Just as a good thermometer must produce consistent temperature readings, a good test must produce consistent scores. One way of determining the reliability of a test is to compare the same person's score on all the odd-numbered items with the score on all the even-numbered items; these two scores should be similar. Or two versions of the test can be constructed and given to the same person on two different occasions. Again, the scores should be similar.

Reliability
A criterion for good testing that should provide results that are consistent when the test is repeated.

Requirement 3: Validity

The most important requirement of all is **validity.** That is, a test must actually measure what it is intended to measure. There are a number of ways to determine this. Common sense is one of them; the items in the test must bear a meaningful relationship to the characteristic being measured. But common sense is not always enough. A better way is to observe the behavior of people who have taken the test and determine whether they behave as their test scores predicted. Thus the validity of intelligence tests, as measures of academic ability, has been shown by the high correlations between IQ and school grades. A test of aptitude for dentistry could be proved valid or invalid by following the careers of people who took it—or, to save time, by determining the test scores of dentists who are already practicing and whose abilities and performance are already known.

Validity
A criterion for good testing that suggests that a test measures what it is intended to measure.

Standardization

A criterion for good testing in which the test score of an individual can be compared with the scores of a large and representative sample of the population.

Percentile

A statistical term used to describe the position of an individual score within the total group of scores.

TEST YOURSELF

o) If a clinical psychologist were to ask you to make up a story about each of a series of drawings, what kind of personality test would he be giving you?

p) Can a test be perfectly reliable and still not be valid?

The final requirement of scientific testing can best be explained by imagining this situation: A psychologist has drawn up a 100-question test that can be given and scored objectively. It has proved reliable, and it seems to be a reasonable and valid measure of aptitude for working with computers. Another psychologist decides to use the test and gives it to a college student, who answers 60 of the items correctly. What does this score of 60 tell the psychologist? By itself, not very much. The psychologist cannot know, after giving the test to a single person, whether a score of 60 indicates exceptional aptitude, very low aptitude, or something in between.

As this example indicates, the results of a test are generally not very useful unless they can be compared with the scores of other people. Thus most tests, before they are considered ready for use, are themselves tested by administering them to a large and representative sample of the population. Records are kept of how many people score at all the possible levels from highest to lowest. This process, called **standardization,** makes it possible to determine whether the score made by an individual is average, low, or high. The individual's ranking can even be pinpointed precisely. We can say that the score falls (let us say) on the 71st **percentile**—that is, the individual has done better than 71 percent of all people, while 29 percent of all people make the same or a higher score.

All the accepted intelligence tests have been standardized on large samples of the population. They meet the requirements of objectivity and reliability and have proved valid for predicting academic success. Many other kinds of tests, devised for special purposes, have also been constructed with the greatest possible regard for scientific accuracy.

SUMMARY REVIEW

The Nature of Intelligence

1. **Intelligence** is the capacity to understand the world and the resourcefulness to cope with its challenges.
2. One theory is that intelligence is composed of a pervasive mental ability called the g **factor,** for general intelligence, plus a number of s **factors,** or specific kinds of skill at a particular task.
3. Thurstone suggested that the specific skills are for verbal comprehension, word fluency, number, space, associative memory, perceptual speed, and general reasoning—which he called the seven **primary mental abilities.**
4. Several theories stress the importance of specific rather than general abilities. Guilford theorized that intelligence is made up of no less than 120 kinds of ability and that a person may rank high in some of them but low in others. Gardner proposed the existence of seven fundamental but separate "intelligences." Sternberg suggested a three-part theory of intelligence that includes the planning and executing of mental activity and the capacity to deal with novelty and to adapt to the environment.

Intelligence Tests

5. **Intelligence tests** provide a measure of **intelligence quotient** (**IQ**). The intelligence quotient gets its name from the fact that it was originally determined by comparing a child's *mental age* (as shown by the ability to pass test items that can be passed by the average child of various ages) with *chronological age* (or actual age).

6. The average IQ is 100, and almost half of all people score between 90 and 109.

7. An **individual test** is given by a trained examiner to one person at a time. Two widely used individual intelligence tests are the **Stanford-Binet Intelligence Scale** and the Wechsler Adult Intelligence Scale.

8. A **group test** of intelligence can be given to many people at the same time. One well-known example is the Scholastic Assessment Tests (SAT).

9. Intelligence tests are also called **aptitude tests**, because they measure ability to learn a new skill or perform an unfamiliar task. In theory, aptitude tests are different from **achievement tests**, which measure how much skill or learning a person has actually acquired. However, it is usually impossible to measure ability without any regard for past achievement.

10. Intelligence tests are biased to some extent in favor of children who have acquired the knowledge, language skills, and motivation typical of the middle- and upper-middle classes. Such children achieve higher average scores than children from lower-class homes, and city children score higher than rural children. Blacks and members of other ethnic cultures make lower average scores.

11. Scores on intelligence tests also depend on motivation, adjustment, and other personality factors.

What IQ Tests Do and Do Not Tell Us

12. Although the tests cannot hope to measure sheer, disembodied skill at information processing, they are good predictors of success in school. Studies have found correlations of .40 to .80 between IQ and grades in classes from the elementary through the college level. Correlations within subject areas may be affected by emphasis assigned by families or schools to that particular area.

13. Psychologists disagree about the extent to which IQ is related to occupation and success in general. Any correlation may depend on the fact that a certain minimum IQ is required to complete high school and college and to perform successfully in some of the more demanding occupations.

14. **Creativity** has been defined as the capacity to regularly solve problems or fashion new products in one or more domains of activity.

15. Although *gifted* individuals may be capable of extraordinary achievement, they may not necessarily be creative.

16. Overall, the correlation between intelligence and creativity is weak. Most fields seem to require a "threshold" IQ, but above that minimum requirement creativity depends less on intelligence than on other factors—for example, a disdain for conformity and success, and a willingness to examine even the most preposterous ideas.

17. Creative individuals tend to display **intrinsic motivation**—that is, the incentive to pursue an activity because it is inherently compelling, enjoyable, and satisfying. They are less influenced by **extrinsic motivation**—the desire for tangible rewards offered by others.
18. It has proved difficult to devise tests that predict creative potential, in large part because it is difficult to capture the creative process in any standard, objective fashion.

IQ and the Issue of Heredity Versus Environment

19. Psychologists agree that intelligence is clearly influenced by both heredity and environment. But controversy exists over which factor is more important.
20. One suggestion is that inherited genes probably set a top and bottom limit on an individual's potential IQ score and that environment then determines where within this range the score will actually fall. The possible difference in IQ score that is due to growing up in a deprived environment vs. an ideal one has been estimated at around 20 to 25 points—and perhaps even greater for individuals born with the possibility of superior intelligence.
21. Scarr has suggested that many genetic traits play a part and that their interaction with the environment takes three forms:
    a) parents likely to pass along favorable genes are also likely to provide a favorable environment
    b) children with favorable genes for intelligence, appearance, and personality are likely to evoke more favorable responses from the people around them
    c) as children get older, they play an active part in creating their own environments.
22. Even when brought up in what seems to be an unchanging environment (same home, parents, and social class), children sometimes show changes in IQ over the years ranging as high as 50 points up or down. The shifts may be related to motivation and other personality factors, health, and emotional adjustment.

Personality and Its Meaning

23. **Personality** is the total pattern of characteristic ways of thinking, feeling, and behaving that constitute the individual's distinctive method of relating to the environment. The various traits that make up the personality exist in a hierarchy from strong to weak.
24. Personality theories are concerned with four aspects of human behavior. They assume
    a) that there is some **core of personality** common to all human beings
    b) that these common tendencies and characteristics of human beings are channeled in various directions by the process of **development**
    c) that the core of personality as modified by development makes each person a unique individual displaying a unique pattern of the **peripheral traits** that are generally known as personality

d) that identifying and defining inner human qualities help to explain the peripheral traits.

The Psychoanalytic View: Sigmund Freud and His Break-away Disciples

25. Freud's psychoanalytic theory assumes that the core of personality is conflict—springing from a basic, pleasure-seeking energy called the **libido.**

26. Psychoanalytic theory holds that the human mind has three parts or forces:
    a) the unconscious **id**
    b) the largely conscious **ego**
    c) the largely unconscious **superego**

27. The primitive id contains the person's instinctive drives toward sensuality and aggression. The drives arouse the id to a state of excitement and tension. In seeking to relieve the tension, the id operates on what Freud called the **pleasure principle.**

28. In regard to the libido, Freud believed that human sexual development takes place in four stages:
    a) **oral**
    b) **anal**
    c) **phallic**
    d) **genital**

29. The ego is the conscious part of the mind that operates on the **reality principle**—and does our logical thinking and tries to help us get along in the world.

30. The superego is acquired largely as a result of the **Oedipus complex,** a conflict of mingled love and hate toward the parents that all children are assumed to undergo between the ages of 2½ and 6. Children resolve the conflict by identifying with their parents and adopting what they consider to be their parents' moral judgments, which form the superego.

31. The central problem in mental disturbances, according to psychoanalytic theory, is anxiety—produced in the ego when the demands of the id threaten to create danger or when the superego threatens to impose disapproval or punishment.

32. The following are among the successors of Freud who have proposed variations in his theory:
    a) Carl Jung, who introduced the concepts of **introvert** and **extrovert** and of a **collective unconscious.**
    b) Alfred Adler, who rejected Freud's focus on sexuality and developed the theory of **individual psychology**—placing greater emphasis on the innate tendency of people to be cooperative and to strive for self-perfection.
    c) Karen Horney, who believed human beings are capable of self-realization if they are not blocked by **basic anxiety**—the feeling of being isolated and helpless in a potentially hostile world.
    d) Heinz Hartmann, who emphasized the role of such ego processes as perception, attention, memory and thinking in dealing with reality.
    e) Erich Fromm, who stressed the importance of social and cultural influences on personality.

Positive Growth: Humanistic Theories of Personality

33. Humanistic theories hold that human nature is basically good and that the core of personality is the desire to perfect our skills and find peace and happiness.

34. Rogers's humanistic theory stresses the self-image, or **phenomenological self,** which represents the way we see ourselves, our abilities, and our relationships with other people. Maladjustments occur when people fail to integrate all of their experiences, desires, and feelings into the phenomenological self, which is therefore at odds with reality.

35. Humanistic theorist Abraham Maslow formulated the **theory of self-actualization.** It maintains that people will always pursue the highest and most idealistic aims unless their development is warped by a malevolent social environment.

The Behavioral View of Personality

36. **Behavioral theories** regard personality as largely composed of habits—that is to say, of habitual ways of responding to situations that arise in one's life.

37. Dollard and Miller's behavioral theory of personality proposed that in order to understand an individual's behavior, it is necessary to focus on four factors:
    a) **cue** (*stimulus*)
    b) **response**
    c) **drive**
    d) **reinforcement**

38. The *behavioral theory* of B. F. Skinner rejects the existence of internal processes and maintains that personality can be understood only by applying the laws of operant conditioning.

39. *Social learning theories* hold that the core of personality is the habitual ways we have learned to respond to events in the environment. The theories originally stressed classical and operant conditioning and reinforcement through rewards or punishments. Many of today's social learning theorists take a more cognitive view and emphasize inner standards, self-reinforcement, and self-punishment.

40. A prominent social learning theorist is Albert Bandura, whose concept of **reciprocal interaction** regards human beings as highly active processors of information who are constantly interacting with the environment.

Describing Personality

41. Personality questionnaires constitute an attempt to describe personality through individuals' own assessments of themselves.

42. The "Big Five" important personality traits include extroversion versus introversion; calm versus high-strung; seeking new experience versus familiar ones; cooperative-trusting versus stubborn; and conscientious and well-organized versus unreliable and careless.

43. Personality traits tend to remain consistent over long periods of time.

The Challenge of Personality Measurement

44. *Personality tests* attempt to measure all the many traits that make up personality and to distinguish between normal and maladjusted patterns.

45. There are three types of personality tests:

a) **Objective tests,** such as the **Minnesota Multiphasic Personality Inventory (MPPI)** and the **California Personality Inventory (CPI).**

b) **Situational tests,** in which the examiner observes the behavior of the subject in a situation deliberately created to reveal some aspect of the subject's personality.

c) **Projective tests,** such as the **Thematic Apperception Test (TAT)** and the **Rorschach Test,** in which subjects supposedly insert or project aspects of their own personality into the kinds of objects they see in inkblots. Other more informal types of projective techniques include **word association, draw-a-person,** and **sentence completion tests.**

Testing the Scientific Way

46. To qualify as scientifically sound a test should be:

a) **Objective**—meaning that the subject will receive the same score regardless of who administers and scores the test.

b) **Reliable**—yielding similar scores when the same person is tested on different occasions.

c) **Valid**—actually measuring what it is supposed to measure.

d) **Standardized**—pretested on a large and representative sample so that an individual's score can be interpreted by comparison with the scores of other people.

TEST YOURSELF ANSWERS

a) Spearman believed that our specific skills are related to an overall mental ability he termed general intelligence, or the g factor.

b) The intent of intelligence tests is to measure aptitude, or the ability to learn, while the intent of achievement tests is to measure how much learning has actually already been acquired. But it is extremely difficult to build an IQ test without tapping, to some degree, prior learning.

c) IQ predicts grades better because they are typically designed to get at the very qualities—for example, reasoning, verbal ability, number skills—that figure heavily in school success. Success in the world outside the classroom, however, depends on a variety of factors not measured in IQ tests.

d) Leon is right. Granted that creativity in most pursuits requires some "threshold" level of intelligence, the overall correlation between creativity and IQ is not very high.

e) Not likely. Creative people are not typically influenced by such extrinsic motivation—that is, the desire for tangible awards offered by others. Instead, they are "turned on" by intrinsic motivation—that is, the desire to pursue an activity because it is inherently compelling and fulfilling.

f) It is not possible, since both factors constantly interact. Heredity may very well set the range within which an individual's IQ is likely to fall—but environmental factors help determine where within that range the individual's IQ level will actually fall.

g) José based his conclusion on only one episode. To be considered a part of personality, a particular behavior must be characteristic of the individual. Harry's generous behavior would have to have some continuity at different times and in different circumstances.

h) Freud would probably conclude that your motives in this case were unconscious. He believed that we are often unaware of our true wishes and desires—but that our behavior is, nonetheless, influenced by them.

i) That is how the term is popularly used, but Freud meant it to stand for a basic energy force—embracing sexual urges, but also such related desires as to be kept warm, well-fed, and content.

j) You are drawing from Carl Jung, who invented the term, and felt that the balance between the two is an important element in the human personality.

k) Horney took issue with Freud's view of the importance of women's biological nature, contending that Freud did not sufficiently emphasize how society's view of women can produce problems with self-confidence and barriers to self-fulfillment.

l) You would be basing your statement on the humanistic view of personality as expressed by Carl Rogers, and you would be convinced that you were having a problem with your self-image—the way you feel about and evaluate yourself.

m) Skinner was convinced that learning through positive and negative reinforcement is the entire basis of human personality.

n) The parent is describing observational learning and is calling upon a cognitive view of personality.

o) He would be giving you a projective test of personality.

p) Yes, it can. For example, a test intended to measure mechanical aptitude may produce consistent scores, meaning that it is reliable enough. But it may not really be measuring mechanical aptitude at all, meaning that it is not valid.

Study Guide

Chapter 8   Intelligence and Personality

LEARNING OBJECTIVES

After studying this chapter, you should be able to:

For an Understanding of the Science

1. Think critically about the virtues and limitations of Wechsler's definition of intelligence as "the capacity to understand the world and the resourcefulness to cope with its challenges," including understanding that different societies and various groups within our own society may have different standards of what constitutes resourcefulness and intelligent behavior.

2. Understand the key difference between Thurstone's theory of a "general factor" in intelligence and the Guilford theory that intelligence represents 120 different abilities.

3. Appreciate how intelligence testing began and the concept of intelligence quotient, which refers to a subject's intelligence test score in relation to his or her age.

4. Distinguish between individual and group tests and between aptitude and achievement tests.

5. Understand why the IQ is very good at predicting success in school but realize that its relation to occupational success and happiness is controversial.

6. Distinguish between intelligence and creativity, and understand the components of the creative process.

7. Discuss the debate over the relative contributions of heredity and environment to IQ.

8. Understand why the definition of personality includes the words *characteristic, distinctive, relating,* and *pattern,* and describe how personality traits are organized into a hierarchy.

9. Recognize that all personality theories deal with four aspects of human behavior: (a) a core of personality common to all human beings; (b) the manner in which development channels these core tendencies in different directions; (c) the peripheral characteristics, or distinctive ways of thinking, feeling, and behaving that each individual displays, and (d) the inner human qualities that help explain peripheral traits.

10. Discuss the different views of personality held by psychoanalysts, social learning theorists, humanistic psychologists, and behavioral psychologists.

11. Explain the meaning of such psychoanalytic terms as *id, ego, superego,* and *Oedipus complex,* and describe how Freud's original theories have been revised by Jung, Adler, Horney, and Fromm.

12. Understand the humanistic theory of personality and its emphasis on *unconditional positive regard* and the *phenomenological self.*

13. Describe the behavioral approach to personality—its early emphasis on classical and operant conditioning, and today's increased emphasis on social learning, inner standards, self-reinforcement, and self-punishment.

14. Understand how trait and type theories attempt to describe rather than explain behavior—as comprehensively and meaningfully as possible.

15. Describe the various types of tests—including *objective, situational,* and *projective*—used in efforts to measure personality characteristics. Understand their potential value and present weaknesses.

For Application to Life Situations

16. Understand how the Guilford theory applies to the college experience—that is, the value of using these years to discover your own special abilities and weaknesses and preparing for an occupation tailored to your talents.

17. Recall that we must be wary of judging ourselves and others too quickly on the basis of IQ score—particularly because intelligence tests are biased against people from certain environments and because IQs often show considerable spontaneous change.

18. List the characteristics often found in creative persons—and appreciate the difficulty in devising tests to identify such persons.

19. Appreciate that knowledgeable scholars disagree as to whether the core of personality is conflict (Freud), a basic urge toward self-fulfillment and harmony (the humanistic theorists), or the tendency to learn and change with experience (the behaviorist approach). Evaluate skeptically any claims of a simple new explanation for a complex phenomenon that has puzzled scientists for many years.

20. Envision the enormous number of possible personality traits and understand the ways they can be organized into hierarchies. Recognize how difficult it is to describe one's own or someone else's personality—especially since personality traits may be displayed in some situations and not others.

21. Recognize that our traits usually interact with the situations in which we find ourselves—but that there is typically a kernel of consistency that comes through across various life situations.

22. Understand that personality tests have their limitations, and that those who purport to be able to "read" all of the important dimensions of personality from a single test are claiming more than psychological research supports.

23. Cite and discuss the four requirements of a scientific test: that it be *objective, reliable, valid,* and *standardized;* and recognize that many so-called tests published in newspapers and magazines do not meet these requirements.

PROGRAMMED UNIT
THE NATURE OF INTELLIGENCE

1. *Intelligence* is a complex quality that has been defined as the capacity to understand the world and the resourcefulness to cope with its challenges. Being able to know what is going on, learn from experience, and behave in a rational and worthwhile way are all part of _____.

intelligence

2. A society's view of intelligence depends on which skill it particularly admires. In our own society people are considered intelligent if they can analyze facts, reason logically, and express their conclusions in fluent language. These same people, in a society that places higher value on the ability to run fast and hit a moving target with a spear, would not necessarily be regarded as having much _____.

intelligence

intelligence

3. Spearman's theory is that _____ is made up of a *g factor,* for general intelligence, and a number of specific skills, or *s factors.* His theory was based on tests of many people for many kinds of abilities from reading comprehension to the visualization of spatial relationships.

4. His finding that people who scored well on one test also tended to do well on others convinced him of the existence of a *g* factor, for

general intelligence

_____ _____.

5. He also found that people's scores varied somewhat for different kinds of abilities, which suggested the existence of specific skills, or _____

s

factors

_____.

6. Thurstone enlarged on Spearman's work by suggesting that there are seven specific skills that he called *primary mental abilities.* Thurstone's theory emphasizes an all-around mental ability, or _____

g

factor

_____, plus the primary mental abilities.

7. Thurstone found seven specific skills—verbal comprehension, word fluency, number, space, associative memory, perceptual speed, and general reasoning—that he called _____ _____ _____.

primary mental abilities

8. The theory that intelligence is made up of a *g* factor plus seven primary mental abilities was proposed by _____.

Thurstone

9. An entirely different theory comes from Guilford, who devised finely differentiated tests for many specific skills. Guilford has found little correlation between his subjects' scores on one test and their scores on many others, convincing him that intelligence is made up of many separate and different specific skills. He therefore rejects the idea of the _____ or _____ factor proposed by Spearman and Thurstone.

g
general

10. Guilford believes that intelligence is composed of no less than 120 different kinds of ability—and that the same individual may score high on some, average or low on others. He therefore rejects the notion of a *g* factor and believes there are many _____ skills.

specific

11. The number of specific skills suggested by Guilford is _____.

120

12. Guilford found that people differ widely in their ability to deal with various kinds of materials, or _____, such as words, numbers, or specific objects.

contents

13. Highly verbal or literate people tend to be good with words, or _____ contents.

semantic

14. A mathematician would likely be skilled in handling _____ contents, or numbers.

symbolic

15. Pleasure in working with specific objects or pictures, termed _____ contents, might lead one into the arts or crafts.

figural

INTELLIGENCE TESTS

16. The first *intelligence test* was created in France by Alfred Binet, who devised a wide range of items increasing step by step in difficulty. Binet found how many items the average child could pass at the age of 6, 7, 8, and so on—and the ability to make this average score on the tests was considered an indication of average _____.

intelligence

17. The usefulness of Binet's original _____ test is reflected in the fact that a revision of it is still widely used in the United States today, in the form of the _____ Intelligence Scale.

intelligence

Stanford-Binet

18. A formula that relates one's raw score on an _____ to one's age yields an individual's intelligence _____.

intelligence test
quotient

19. An intelligence test that is given to one person at a time by a trained examiner is an _____ test; tests that are administered to testing many people at once are _____ tests.

individual
group

20. All _____ tests fall into the general class of *aptitude tests,* meaning that they are intended to measure how well the individual will be able to perform in the future at a new skill or an unfamiliar task.

intelligence

21. Tests that estimate your ability to learn or perform in the future are called _____ tests.

aptitude

22. Tests like college exams, which measure how much learning or skill you have already acquired, are *achievement tests.* Achievement tests measure

	primarily what you have learned in the past, not how much ability or _____ you have for learning in the future.
aptitude	
achievement	23. Tests that show how much skill you have already acquired are called _____ tests.
aptitude **achievement**	24. An intelligence test is an _____ test. A college exam is an _____ test.
	25. Unfortunately aptitude tests must depend to some extent on the individual's existing knowledge. Thus intelligence tests reflect past learning of language, mathematics, and other skills. But they try to rely only on knowledge that all individuals of that age would normally have acquired—and measure ability to use that knowledge in a novel way. Thus the IQ is, insofar as possible, an index of aptitude for future learning, not of _____ in the past.
achievement	

WHAT IQ TESTS DO AND DO NOT TELL US

academic	26. Because intelligence tests tap qualities associated with doing well in school, they tend to measure _____ ability better than anything else.
experience	27. In addition to reflecting classroom skills and academic _____, IQ tests depend on personality characteristics such as *motivation*.
Intelligence **Academic**	28. It can be argued that tests such as the Stanford-Binet _____ Test do not measure one's intelligence quotient as much as they measure an _____ Quotient, or AQ.
practical	29. Performance in one's career frequently depends less on the person's IQ score than on his or her "_____ intelligence."
intelligence	30. *Creativity* has been defined as the capacity to regularly solve problems or fashion new products in one or more domains of activity. Since it is displayed by only a few people with IQs over 140, clearly a high level of _____ is no guarantee of creativity. Other factors, especially personality, seem more important.
creativity, personality	31. The capacity to regularly solve problems or fashion new products is an indication of _____, which seems related more to _____ than to intelligence. One characteristic that seems important is the quality of *motivation*.
intrinsic	32. Creative individuals tend to pursue an activity because it is inherently compelling, enjoyable, and satisfying; they are driven by _____ motivation.
intrinsic	33. Creative individuals tend to pursue activities that are inherently compelling, enjoyable, and satisfying—meaning that they display _____ motivation. They are less influenced by *extrinsic motivation,* or the desire for tangible rewards offered by others.
intrinsic, extrinsic **rewards**	34. Creative people are more influenced by _____ than _____ motivation, meaning that they pursue activities because they really like them rather than out of a desire for tangible _____. The process of creativity usually requires a high degree of persistence.

IQ AND THE ISSUE OF HEREDITY
VERSUS ENVIRONMENT

35. Like most human traits, the IQ is influenced by the pattern of genes we have inherited, which influences the way our nervous system and brain operate. In describing how the nature-nurture question applies to intelligence, almost all psychologists agree that IQ is affected by _____.

nature (or heredity)

36. But IQ is also influenced by our interaction with, and learning from, the world around us, or our _____.

environment

37. Psychologists disagree, often heatedly, on the relative contributions of _____ and _____ to IQ.

heredity, environment

38. One argument for the influence of heredity is that IQ tends to "run in families." It has been established that the more closely related two people are—that is, the more similarity in the patterns of _____ they have inherited—the more similar their IQs are likely to be.

genes

39. Correlations in IQ between parents and children cluster around .50, between brother and sisters in the same home also around .50. For identical twins, who have inherited exactly the same pattern of _____, studies have shown correlations of .70 to more than .90.

genes

40. The correlations in IQ between parents and children, and between brothers and sisters in the same home, cluster around _____.

.50

41. For identical twins, studies have shown correlations of _____ to more than _____.

.70
.90

42. Even for identical twins separated and brought up in different homes, correlations have been found to run between .62 and .77. The fact that people with the same genes show such high correlations even when brought up in different environments is a strong argument for the influence of _____.

heredity (or nature)

43. However, children not related by heredity who were brought up in the same home also have IQs that are correlated to some extent, which is a strong argument for the influence of _____.

environment (or nurture)

44. Many psychologists have concluded that heredity probably sets a top and bottom limit on the IQ of any individual, and the environment then determines where within this range the IQ will actually fall. Thus the possible range of IQ is set by _____, the exact figure within this range by _____.

nature (or heredity)
nurture (or environment)

45. Some believe the possible range set by heredity is around 20 to 25 points. This would mean that a girl born with more or less average genes might wind up with an IQ as low as 85 (the low end of her range) if brought up in a very unfavorable environment—but in an ideal environment she might reach the high end of her range, or as high as _____ to _____.

105, 110

46. A puzzling fact about IQ is that it sometimes changes up or down by as much as 50 points even when the child remains in the same environment. There are indications that the changes are related to motivation and other personality factors, physical health, and emotional adjustment. Thus in assessing a pupil's chances of succeeding in school, teachers should probably consider the child's entire personality as well as the present score on an _____ test.

intelligence

environment

intelligence

differences

47. Children from low-income homes may become so discouraged by an unstimulating _____ or by failure and criticism in their early schooling, that they fail to take advantage of their abilities, and display less _____ than they have.

48. Both blacks and whites show a wide and overlapping range of individual _____ in IQ.

PERSONALITY AND ITS MEANING

personality

behaving

49. *Personality* is defined in part as a person's ways of thinking, feeling, and behaving. Such traits as thinking logically or illogically, feeling cheerful or sad, and behaving in a friendly or unfriendly manner are all elements of the human _____.

50. Psychologists define personality in part as a person's ways of thinking, feeling, and _____. To be considered a personality trait, however, these must be *characteristic* of the individual.

characteristic

thinking

51. We do not describe a man as bad-tempered if he "blows up" once in 10 years. But if he displays a bad temper often and under many circumstances, it is a personality trait because it is _____ of him.

52. Personality traits—which characterize a person's ways of _____, feeling, and behaving—are also *distinctive*. This means that they distinguish the individual from other individuals.

distinctive

characteristic

53. John carries a driver's license. Because many people do the same thing, John's behavior is not _____ and, therefore, not a personality trait.

54. Personality traits, in addition to being _____ and distinctive, constitute the individual's way of *relating to the environment*.

relating

55. Mary wears a ring. Although doing so may be characteristic and distinctive, it is not a personality trait because it plays no significant part in _____ to her environment.

environment

56. Mary is also friendly and outgoing. This constitutes a personality trait because it does play a significant part in relating to her _____.

personality

57. A person's way of thinking, feeling, and behaving make up an individual's _____—which is not just a single trait, but the individual's total *pattern* of traits.

pattern

58. Mark has a bad temper. This does not define his personality because it is just a single trait rather than a total _____ of traits.

distinctive

59. Although there are many theories of personality—defined as the total pattern of characteristic and _____ ways of relating to the environment—all theories assume that there is some kind of *core of personality* composed of tendencies and characteristics common to all of us.

core

60. A theory that assumes human nature is basically good views goodness as the _____ of personality.

personality

61. All personality theories assume that there is some kind of core of _____ and also that *development* channels the core characteristics in different directions in different people.

development

62. Personality theories have to do with the way the core tendencies are channeled by experience—in other words, with the _____ of personality.

63. Personality theories, in addition to being concerned with _____ characteristics and their development, are also concerned with the *peripheral traits of personality,* or the way we think, feel, and behave at any given moment.

core

64. The personality characteristics we display at any given moment, resulting from the way our core of personality has been modified by development, are our _____ traits.

peripheral

THE PSYCHOANALYTIC VIEW: SIGMUND FREUD AND HIS BREAK-AWAY DISCIPLES

65. Sigmund Freud, in his *psychoanalytic theory,* proposed that the tendencies or characteristics common to human nature known as the core of _____ are the result of conflict.

personality

66. Psychoanalytic personality theory, developed by _____, emphasizes the role of anxiety in human behavior and as the central problem in mental disturbance.

Freud

67. Freud believed that the core of human personality is _____, and that the central problem in mental disturbance is _____.

conflict
anxiety

68. Freud, who originated _____ personality theory, proposed the concept of the *unconscious,* composed partly of repressed motives and thoughts.

psychoanalytic

69. Mark, who is not aware of hostile motives but reveals them in ways observable to others, displays the workings of the _____ mind.

unconscious

70. Wishes and desires that we are not aware of but that influence our behavior in any event, were termed unconscious _____ by Freud.

motives

71. An example of an _____ motive can be seen when a person who has been hypnotized acts upon an instruction given during the course of a *hypnotic* trance.

unconscious

72. When he acts on a _____ suggestion, a subject is unaware of having received an instruction during the trance.

posthypnotic

73. According to psychoanalytic theory the unconscious is composed partly of _____ motives and thoughts. The main element of the unconscious is the *id,* which is one of the mind's three parts, or forces, and contains the person's powerful inborn drives.

repressed

74. Freud believed that the core of the unconscious, or the _____, contains our instinctive drive to obtain pleasure, which he termed *libido,* as well as our drive toward aggression.

id

75. According to psychoanalytic theory, the inborn drive that seeks comfort and pleasure, including sexual pleasure, is known as the _____.

libido

76. In acting to relieve the tension created by its quest for material and sexual pleasure, the id acts on the _____ principle.

pleasure

77. Freud believed that during four successive _____ of human _____ development, which he termed *oral, anal, phallic,* and *genital,* the libido focuses on discrete parts of the body.

stages
sexual

78. For the infant, the gratification that comes from sucking and eating comprise the _____ stage of development.

oral

anal

phallic

genital stage

id

ego

reality

psychoanalytic

superego

id

Oedipus

conflict
id
ego, superego
personality

Jung

collective

temperamental

79. For the toddler, gratification during the _____ stage is derived from learning to control the bowel.

80. A fascination with the external sex organ is the defining feature of the _____ stage for both males and females.

81. At puberty, with the ability to love another person, the adolescent enters the fourth and final _____ of sexual development.

82. A second part of the human mind or personality proposed by Freud is the *ego* which, unlike the _____, is largely conscious and is the person's contact with reality.

83. According to psychoanalytic theory, the conscious part of the mind—the "real" us as we would like to think of ourselves—is called the _____.

84. As our conscious link with reality, Freud said, the ego acts on the _____ principle.

85. In addition to the id and the ego, a third part of the mind proposed by Freud in his _____ theory is the *superego*—a largely unconscious but stern and powerful judge of behavior that threatens punishment even for thoughts of transgression.

86. In attempting to resolve our *Oedipus complex,* or mixed feelings of affection and resentment toward our parents, we adopt what we believe to be our parents' standards as the core of our _____.

87. Freud believed that the three parts of the mind are often in conflict—as the ego wages a constant struggle to satisfy the sexual and aggressive drives of the _____ without incurring the punishments of the superego.

88. The psychoanalytic theory of personality holds that the superego, a largely unconscious judge of our behavior, stems from how we resolved our _____ complex.

89. Psychoanalytic theory holds that the core of human personality is a three-way _____ among the three parts of the mind.

90. Freud believed that the three parts of the mind are the _____, _____, and _____.

91. Freud's psychoanalytic theory of _____, emphasizing the conflict between our private impulses and the need to adapt to society, had its critics. One Freudian who broke away was Carl Jung, who believed that Freud did not give enough emphasis to the importance of culture and inherited temperaments or to the spiritual qualities of the human personality.

92. In emphasizing the spiritual qualities of the human personality, Carl _____ proposed that humans possess a *collective unconscious*—an inheritance from all the events that have occurred in human history.

93. Carl Jung believed that humans possess a _____ unconscious. Another disciple who rejected Freud's focus on sexuality was Alfred Adler, whose theory of *individual psychology* placed great emphasis on the tendency of people to be cooperative and psychologically tuned in to the lives of others.

94. In Jung's view, a key _____ difference among people was the distinction between those whom he termed *introverts,* people who are more reflective at the expense of frequent socializing, and *extroverts,* who are primarily interested in other people and events around them.

95. While all of us are part _____ and part _____, in each of us one style tends to develop at the expense of the other.

introvert, extrovert

96. The theory of individual psychology was developed by Alfred _____, who believed that individuals encounter problems in life because they develop inappropriate goals that block the realization of their social interest. He also believed that individuals struggle constantly to overcome feelings of inferiority.

Adler

97. The constant struggle to overcome feelings of inferiority is a feature of the theory of _____ psychology proposed by _____. Another student of Freud who broke with him was Karen Horney, who felt that life's *basic anxiety* is the feeling of being isolated and helpless in a potentially hostile world.

individual, Adler

98. Our responses to feelings of isolation are important in the development of personality, according to the view of Karen _____.

Horney

99. Feelings of isolation, in the view of Horney, comprise life's basic _____. Horney was among the first psychoanalytic theorists to shift the view of women in society away from the male perspective.

anxiety

100. Horney introduced to psychoanalytic theory a view of women different from the traditional _____.

male

101. Three disciples of Freud who broke with him were Carl _____, Alfred _____, and Karen _____. In recent years, new psychoanalysts, called *neopsychoanalysts,* have added to and revised Freud's theories.

Jung
Adler, Horney

102. Psychoanalysts who in recent years have added to and revised Freud's theories are called _____. One of these, Erich Fromm, emphasized the role of cultural and social influences on personality.

neopsychoanalysts

103. Social and cultural influences on personality figured strongly in the view of Erich _____.

Fromm

POSITIVE GROWTH: HUMANISTIC THEORIES OF PERSONALITY

104. In contrast to Freud, who believed that the core of personality is _____ over urges to sexuality and aggression, *humanistic theories* hold that human nature is basically good and that the core of personality is the desire to grow in positive ways—to perfect our skills and find peace and happiness.

conflict

105. Carl Rogers was among the prominent advocates of humanistic personality theory, which holds that the core of personality is the desire to grow in _____ ways.

positive

106. Carl Rogers, a leading proponent of _____ personality theory, stressed the importance of the self-image, or *phenomenological self.*

humanistic

107. The phenomenological self, or self-_____, is the way we see ourselves, our abilities, and our relationships with other people.

image

108. Rogers stressed the importance of the way we see ourselves, our abilities, and our relationships with other people or what he calls the _____ self.

phenomenological

unconditional	109. If those around us when we are growing up value and trust us, and respect our opinions and behavior, we benefit from what Rogers termed _____ positive regard.
conditional	110. When we are reared in an environment of _____ positive regard, only some thoughts and actions receive approval; those which do not are likely to become a source of maladjustment.
humanistic	111. According to _____ psychologists, the most powerful motivating force for human beings is to achieve and realize benevolent and spiritual goals for the self.
self-actualization	112. For humanistic psychologist Abraham Maslow, what he perceived as an innate tendency of people to pursue beauty, goodness, and truth, and to fulfill one's own potential, prompted his theory of _____.

THE BEHAVIORAL VIEW OF PERSONALITY

core	113. In contrast to the humanistic theories, which hold that the _____ of personality is to grow in positive ways, *behavioral theories* take no stand on whether human nature is basically good or evil. They hold instead that personality is simply the habitual ways we have learned to respond to events in the environment.
behavioral theories	114. Stressing the importance of an individual's response to his environment, one of the earliest _____ focused on four factors—*cue (or stimulus), response, drive,* and *reinforcement*—that serve to condition an individual's behavior.
cue, response drive reinforcement	115. When a friend becomes angry whenever you play tennis with her, your excellence at the game may be a _____ for her angry _____. The _____ for your friend may be an urge to power, and the _____ could be your embarrassment when she wins.
B. F. Skinner	116. The notion that external circumstances, not inner motivation, define personality was held by _____.
behavioristic	117. Skinner's _____ view has been attacked on the grounds that it regards humans as too passive.
therapy	118. By demonstrating how certain stimuli can be used to elicit specific behaviors, behaviorism provided a foundation for clinical behavior _____.
reinforcement behavior	119. Today's social learning theories, in addition to emphasizing _____ through rewards and punishments, take a cognitive view of the manner in which experience creates habitual forms of _____.
cognitive	120. Modern social learning theories, in taking a _____ view of personality, hold that personality factors such as inner standards are important in creating habitual forms of behavior.
learning	121. Social _____ theorist Albert Bandura introduced the term *reciprocal interaction* as a means of saying that the environment affects us, but the opposite is true as well.
interaction	122. Our style of reciprocal _____ helps to establish the nature of the environment in which we interact.
behavior	123. By observing others, we take on _____ patterns that contribute to defining our personality.

124. According to the social learning theorists, we adopt many of our responses to the environment by _____ learning.

observational

125. According to contemporary social learning theories, inner _____ and other factors inside the personality are as important as outside reinforcement in creating habitual forms of behavior.

standards

126. Theories maintaining that personality is largely composed of learned responses to the environment are _____ _____ theories.

behavioral learning

DESCRIBING PERSONALITY

127. Theories maintaining that _____ is largely composed of learned responses to the environment are behavioral in their point of view. In contrast to such theories—as well as psychoanalytic and humanistic theories—are those which focus on how we differ rather than why. These are known as *type* and *trait theories*.

personality

128. Proponents of _____ and _____ theories of personality are intent on describing personality rather than explaining it. One effort to identify key adjectives that describe personality types reduced the core list to five descriptors.

type, trait

129. Psychologist Hans Eysenck proposed that many variations in human behavior can be explained by two dimensions: extroversion versus _____, and stability versus _____.

introversion instability

130. An important question in considering trait theories is whether personality characteristics remain _____ across time and different life situations.

consistent

THE CHALLENGE OF PERSONALITY MEASUREMENT

131. Because personality is such a complex matter, its measurement is difficult. An important assumption in testing personality is that there are basic constants that make up the total pattern of characteristic ways of thinking, feeling, and behaving—or _____.

personality

132. An important assumption in personality _____ is that personality is comprised of basic constants. *Objective tests,* which make up one type of personality test, produce scores least likely to be affected by the views of the examiner.

testing

133. One widely-used _____ test is the *Minnesota Multiphasic Personality Inventory,* or *MMPI,* which compares an individual's responses on 600 items to the responses of large numbers of other people, including people with clearly defined personality traits.

objective

134. The widely-used _____ served as the basis for another objective test, the *California Personality Inventory,* or _____.

MMPI CPI

135. Personality tests least likely to be influenced by the examiner are called _____ tests. In *situational tests,* the examiner observes the subject in a situation deliberately created to bring out certain aspects of personality.

objective

136. A test in which a job applicant for police officer is asked to respond to a typical police call would be a _____ test. *Projective tests* are based on the assumption that people tend to attribute to others—that is, to project—some of their own anxiety-causing motives.

situational

projective

137. The *Thematic Apperception Test* (*TAT*) in which a person is asked to make up stories about pictures, invites the attribution to others of anxiety-causing motives. It is, therefore, in the category of _____ tests. A well-known test in the same category is the *Rorschach Test,* in which people are asked to tell what they see in inkblots.

TAT

picture, sentence

138. In contrast to the _____, wherein a subject is asked to make up a story about a prepared picture, other projective tests ask a subject to draw a _____ or complete a _____; from the subject's input, the examiner infers personality clues.

Rorschach

139. A projective test using inkblots is the _____ Test.

word

140. Yet another projective technique consists of an examiner calling out a word, and the subject responding with a _____ association that comes to mind.

TESTING THE SCIENTIFIC WAY

141. Constructing useful tests is actually a science in itself. A first requirement is that a test provide results that are not affected by the personal opinions or prejudices of the person administering it; that is, the test must be

objective

_____.

reliability

142. A test that produces consistent scores is said to have _____, but the most important requirement of a test is that it should have *validity,* that is, it should actually measure what it is intended to measure.

143. One morning, Nancy used a thermometer to find out whether she had a fever. Because the thermometer gave her a different reading each time she used it, she decided correctly that it was not _____.

reliable

144. A test that purports to gauge creativity but instead gauges verbal fluency, cannot be said to have _____ since it does not measure what it is intended to measure.

validity

145. An intelligence test predicts grades in school rather well but it does not predict adult income very accurately. Therefore the IQ test has _____ as a measure of school performance but not income.

validity

tests

146. A fourth requirement of _____ is *standardization.* That is, the test is given to a large group of people so that one can determine how good relative to the group an individual's score is.

standardization

147. Gathering the test information on the group is known as _____.

objectively
reliability, validity
standardization

148. The four requirements of a test are that it is administered and scored _____, that it possesses high _____ and _____, and that adequate _____ has been conducted.

percentile

149. Standardization enables an individual's ranking on a test to be pinpointed precisely by means of a percentile; at the 71st _____, one has done better than 71 percent of others who have taken the same test, while 29 percent of people have made the same or a higher score.

REVIEW OF IMPORTANT TERMS

achievement test (367)

anal stage (380)

aptitude test (366)

basic anxiety (387)

behavior therapy (391)

behavioral theories (390)

California Personality Inventory (CPI) **(396)**

collective unconscious **(383)**

conditional positive regard **(389)**

core of personality **(378)**

creativity **(370)**

cue **(390)**

development **(378)**

draw-a-person test **(398)**

drive **(390)**

ego **(381)**

extrinsic motivation **(371)**

extrovert **(383)**

figural contents **(363)**

g factor **(361)**

general intelligence factor **(361)**

genital stage **(380)**

group tests **(366)**

id **(380)**

individual differences **(360)**

individual psychology **(384)**

individual test **(366)**

intelligence **(360)**

intelligence test **(364)**

intelligence quotient **(364)**

intrinsic motivation **(371)**

introvert **(383)**

libido **(379)**

Minnesota Multiphasic Personality Inventory (MMPI) **(396)**

neopsychoanalysts **(387)**

objective tests **(396)**

objectivity **(399)**

observational learning **(391)**

Oedipus complex **(381)**

oral stage **(380)**

percentile **(400)**

peripheral traits **(378)**

personality **(376)**

phallic stage **(380)**

phenomenological-self **(388)**

pleasure principle **(380)**

posthypnotic suggestion **(379)**

primary mental abilities **(362)**

projective tests **(397)**

reality principle **(381)**

reciprocal interaction **(391)**

reinforcement **(390)**

reliability **(399)**

response **(390)**

Rorschach test **(398)**

s factor **(361)**

semantic contents **(363)**

sentence completion test **(398)**

situational test **(397)**

social learning theories **(391)**

standardization **(400)**

Stanford-Binet Intelligence Scale **(364)**

superego **(381)**

symbolic contents **(363)**

Thematic Apperception Test (TAT) **(397)**

theory of self-actualization **(389)**

unconditional positive regard **(389)**

unconscious mind **(379)**

unconscious motives **(379)**

validity **(399)**

word association test **(398)**

PRACTICE TEST

_____ 1. Wechsler's definition of intelligence emphasizes the ability to

    a.   do well in school.

    b.   communicate.

    c.   understand and cope with the world.

    d.   think logically.

_____ 2. Mary gets good grades in all her classes but does better at mathematics than at reading comprehension. Her performance is in line with

    a. Spearman's g factor plus s factors.

    b. Guilford's theory of intelligence.

    c. Piaget's stage of formal operations.

    d. The environmental viewpoint.

_____ 3. The number of primary mental abilities suggested by Thurstone is

    a. 6.   c. 8.

    b. 7.   d. 9.

_____ 4. The first intelligence test was created by

    a. Binet.

    b. Spearman.

    c. Thurstone.

    d. Wechsler.

_____ 5. The WAIS is mainly a(n)

    a. achievement test.

    b. aptitude test.

    c. group test.

    d. personality test.

_____ 6. The correlation between the IQs of parents and their children reared in their home is around

    a. .30.   c. .50.

    b. .40.   d. .60.

_____ 7. Of those below, the highest correlations in IQ are found between

    a. parents and children in the same home.

    b. brothers and sisters, reared together.

    c. adopted children, reared together.

    d. identical twins, reared in different homes.

_____ 8. Intelligent or gifted people may fail due to

    a. lack of motivation.

    b. fear of failure.

    c. excessive dependency.

    d. any of the above.

_____ 9. Heredity combines with environment in contributing to intelligence in which way?

    a. Intelligent parents provide better environments for their children.

    b. Genetically bright children provoke encouragement from other people.

c. Genes dispose a child to seek environments that promote intellectual growth.

d. All of these.

_____ 10. To be considered part of our personality, a way of thinking or behaving must be

a. innate.

b. distinctive.

c. unchanging.

d. observable.

_____ 11. Every personality theory maintains that the core tendencies and traits are channeled in various directions by the process of

a. development.

b. differentiation.

c. maturation.

d. fixation.

_____ 12. According to Freud, the main element of the unconscious is

a. the id.

b. the ego.

c. the superego.

d. none of the above.

_____ 13. Which of the following best describes the structure of the human personality as Freud saw it?

a. The superego is caught between the id and the ego.

b. The id is caught between the superego and the ego.

c. The ego is caught between the id and the superego.

_____ 14. The term "inferiority complex" was first used by

a. Adler.

b. Freud.

c. Jung.

d. Hartmann.

_____ 15. The high achievement often characteristic of first-born children is not explained by

a. fear of being "dethroned" by siblings.

b. higher parental expectations.

c. greater early freedom from parents' interference.

d. likelihood of attaining a higher education.

_____ 16. Humanistic theories of personality are most closely associated with the name of

a. Fromm.

b. Bandura.

c. Jung.

d. Rogers.

_____ 17. A prominent social-learning theorist associated with the concept of reciprocal interaction is

    a. Skinner.

    b. Fromm.

    c. Freud.

    d. Bandura.

_____ 18. Theories of personality that seek to describe rather than explain behavior are called

    a. situational and projective theories.

    b. type and trait theories.

    c. humanistic theories.

    d. psychoanalytic theories.

_____ 19. Personality tests that require paper-and-pencil responses to specific items are called

    a. projective tests.

    b. situational tests.

    c. objective tests.

    d. behavior tests.

_____ 20. If a test measures what it is supposed to measure, it has

    a. objectivity.

    b. reliability.

    c. validity.

    d. standardization.

ANSWERS TO PRACTICE TEST

1. c	6. c	11. a	16. d
2. a	7. d	12. a	17. d
3. a	8. d	13. c	18. b
4. a	9. d	14. a	19. c
5. b	10. b	15. c	20. c

EXERCISES

I. On page 360 of your text, this chapter begins with the suggestion that you ask a half dozen or so of your friends what they mean when they describe someone as "intelligent." Extend the number to 15 or 20 friends and acquaintances, and keep a record of the various definitions given. When you have collected a few dozen, try to group them into a smaller number of categories (5–10). How do these compare with the components of intelligence described on page 362? Do you believe most of the people you interviewed see intelligence as a single general ability or as many specific skills? What is your own view of the most appropriate and meaningful definition of intelligence?

II. A central point in Carl Rogers' humanistic personality theory, as explained in the text, is that well-adjusted people have a self-image that closely corresponds to reality. Poorly adjusted people, on the other hand, have a self-image that does not match their true feelings and the actual nature of their experiences.

Psychologists have found that normal people are reasonably satisfied with their perception of themselves. In other words, their self-image is not very different from what might be called their ideal image, or the way they would like to be. People with personality problems, however, are dissatisfied with their perception of themselves. Their self-image is often very different from their ideal image.

By using the items listed in Figure 8.13 on page 424, you can perform an informal experiment* that will give you at least a rough idea of how well your own self-image matches your ideal image. Copy and cut the items into the rectangles indicated by the lines. Shuffle them or mix them up in a hat and spread them out on a desk or a table in the random order in which they fall. Now look at all 16 carefully and try to decide which item describes you best, which is least true of you, and where the others rank somewhere in between. Arrange them in a line from your left, starting with the statement that describes you best, to your right, ending with the one that describes you least. When you have finished, use Figure 8.14 on page 425 to write down the order of the items as you have arranged them, from 1 at the extreme left to 16 at the extreme right. Do this under "Rank on list 1."

Next reshuffle the items, place them in front of you again, and this time arrange them in the order that best describes not what you are but what you would like to be. Put the statement that you wish were most true of you at the extreme left, and the one you wish were least true of you at the extreme right. When you have completed this pattern of what you would like to be, again use Figure 8.14 to write down the order of the items as you have arranged them, this time under "Rank on list 2."

For a rough measure of how your self-image differs from your ideal image, note the difference in rank of each item from list 1 to list 2, disregarding whether it ranked higher on list 1 or list 2. For example, if item A was sixth on list 1 and eighth on list 2, the difference is two. If item A was eighth on list 1 and sixth on list 2, the difference is also two. Total the differences. The smaller the total, the greater is the correspondence between what you think you are and what you would like to be. The average person usually shows a total difference of between 50 and 60. A difference as low as 35 shows an extremely high correspondence between self-image and ideal image. A score of more than 75 indicates an unusually low correspondence. However, if you score 75 or even much higher, do not leap to the conclusion that you are suffering from a personality problem. On a short and informal test such as this, many factors can influence the result. The exercise is designed only to cast some light on the Rogers theory, not to diagnose personality.

By doing a little further arithmetic, you can get a more accurate measure. For each card, square the number found in the column showing difference in rank and enter it in the next column called "Difference squared." Then total the numbers you have just placed in this column. Divide the total by 680, and subtract the answer from 1.

---

*This exercise is based on J. M. Butler and G. V. Haigh. Changes in the relationship between self-concepts and ideal concepts consequent upon client-centered counseling. In C. R. Rogers and R. F. Dymond, eds. *Psychotherapy and personality change: coordinated studies in the client centered approach.* Chicago: University of Chicago Press, 1954, pp. 55–76.

I usually manage to stay even tempered. A	I consider myself a leader. I
I spend too much time daydreaming. B	I am a shy person. J
I am a very likable person. C	I am physically attractive. K
I have to admit that I am rather selfish. D	I often feel blue and discouraged. L
I can work as hard as anybody when I want to. E	I am more intelligent than most people. M
I have a hard time standing up for myself. F	I worry about what other people think of me. N
Nothing frightens me. G	I have a good sense of humor. O
I often feel tense around other people. H	I wouldn't be above cheating. P

FIGURE 8.13

What you have just done is compute a coefficient of correlation, which is a statistical measure of the relationship between the two factors, by one of the methods described in the textbook's Appendix A (one indication that psychological statistics are not so difficult as students often assume). In the study on which this exercise is based, the correlation between self-image and ideal image for subjects who had never sought psychotherapy was .58. For subjects who were seeking treatment for personality problems, the correlation was 0, but it rose to .34 after they received psychotherapy. However, the original study and this informal exercise differ in important ways, and the results are not completely

Card	Rank on List 1	Rank on List 2	Difference In Rank	Difference Squared
A				
B				
C				
D				
E				
F				
G				
H				
I				
J				
K				
L				
M				
N				
O				
P				

Total of differences _____

Total of squared differences _____

$$\text{Correlation coefficient} = 1 - \frac{(\text{Total of squared differences})}{680} = \underline{\hspace{2cm}}$$

FIGURE 8.14

comparable. Moreover, it must again be pointed out that the experiment is not intended as a diagnosis of personality, and a zero or even a minus correlation is not to be considered alarming.

Although all three of the answers to the question posed in Figure 8.1 are correct, the best answer is (c) domestic animals. This makes the finest and neatest distinction between the four animals and other kinds of animals. "Farm animals" is not the best answer because a cat is often found elsewhere, "Four-legged animals" is not the best answer because almost all animals have four legs.

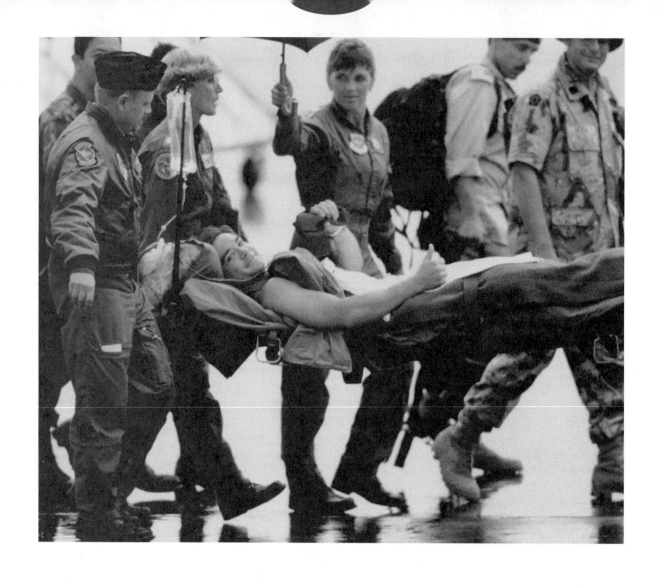

CHAPTER 9

Stress, Coping, and Health

Sooner or later, all of us encounter times when either the minor irritations or major problems of living pile up and seem almost unbearable. The result may be distressing physical symptoms: a racing heart, shortness of breath, trembling hands, queasy stomach, headaches, and even lingering physical ailments. Or, we may suffer troublesome psychological reactions—an inability to concentrate, anxiety, or a case of "the blues." Whether our symptoms are physical or psychological, we are experiencing typical reactions to the strains and pressures of life—what we often refer to as stress.

The word *stress* has firmly entered our daily consciousness and even our slang. People talk casually, for instance, about being "stressed out." And, as a solution, many attend "stress management workshops." Although most people have no trouble saying when they feel under stress, little agreement exists about its definition—either among laypersons or professionals (Elliot & Eisdorfer, 1982; Rutter, 1983b).

Most psychologists view **stress** as *a physical and psychological response to a harmful or potentially harmful circumstance*—that is, to anything that threatens to damage the organism. Such a stress reaction can be caused by a disease-carrying virus, air or noise pollution, the physical danger of an earthquake, or the psychological danger posed by the loss of a job or the death of a loved one. Note that the term *stress* applies not to these circumstances, but to the person's physiological and psychological reactions to them. In everyday language, of course, many people apply the term to the circumstances themselves. But these are best called **stressors**—*the events or conditions that put a strain on the organism and pose a challenge to adjust.*

Some people are convinced that stress is more severe today than ever before, while others question whether contemporary life is more difficult than in the past, when the concept of stress was less well known to the general public (Averill, 1989). In either case, stress clearly plays a significant role in both physical and mental health. Psychologists have carefully studied the responses we make to stressful events, and in doing so, they have identified ways to handle stress that can help us maintain our well-being—both of body and mind.

Sources of Stress: Life's Varied Stressors

- After six years of happy marriage, your husband dies a slow death from a ravaging cancer. A few years later, you are married again—to a kind, devoted man. But after three contented years, he is killed while crossing the street.
- You are an engineering student facing three exams, but instead of studying, you have to spend precious time hunting for a summer job or else you won't be able to pay your debts. Meanwhile, you are struggling with a conflict. Your girlfriend wants to get married now, but you think you should wait until you finish school.
- You are driving along the freeway, on your way to a job interview you have anticipated for months. Suddenly, you get a flat tire. You try desperately to flag down a passing motorist, but by the time someone stops to pick you up, you are already late and still miles from a phone.

Those three vignettes are taken from real life. They are not unusual. Stress can be caused by a sudden, overwhelming event, the daily grind of work, or an accumulation of a series of relatively small incidents on a day in

Stress

A physical and psychological response to a harmful or potentially harmful circumstance.

Stressors

The events or conditions that put a strain on the organism and pose a challenge to adjustment.

Intense stress, if prolonged, can affect our health.

which everything seems to go wrong. What we so often refer to as "the stresses of life" range from everyday irritations to devastating catastrophes—a lost wallet and bereavement, being stuck in an elevator and being taken hostage, failing to make a deadline and losing a job.

Certainly most of us would agree that some experiences are more devastating than others. Missing an appointment, for example, is hardly as devastating as finding out that you have incurable cancer. Yet we experience stress from both the major crises and the seemingly minor problems of life. Moreover, although most of us think of stress as the result of outside events, the occasion for stress can arise also from *within* the individual—for example, as a result of internal conflicts of motives. Life's varied sources of stress are not restricted to any particular period of life. Instead, they are our constant companions—as detailed in the Life Span Perspective box, "Stress From Infancy to Old Age."

LIFE SPAN PERSPECTIVE

Stress from Infancy to Old Age

From the moment of birth, humans confront the reality of a world replete with stressors—experiences that are, for the newborn unsettling, disturbing, or noxious (Lipsitt, 1990). During the first three months, pain, hunger, and cold are primary sources of stress—manifested by irritability and difficulties in feeding and sleeping. From 4 to 12 months, unpredictable events that are hard for the infant to assimilate—the presence of an unfamiliar adult, a mother's departure—become typical stressors, leading to such behaviors as withdrawal and crying. During the second year, parental restriction, punishment, prolonged separation, and even the presence of an unfamiliar child can evoke stress—as evidenced, for example, by clinging behavior or apathy. Later, as toddlers and schoolchildren, most youngsters eventually encounter a variety of stressors—the loss of a loved one, illnesses, separations, family conflicts, failures, or just the everyday griefs and disappointments that life inevitably brings (Garmezy & Rutter, 1985).

As will be evident in Chapter 13, the adolescent years are especially filled with stressful experiences. Over an average of just four years, the child is transformed in physical characteristics into an adult (Petersen, 1987; Mussen et al., 1990). These changes usher in the turbulence of heightened sexuality, a striving for autonomy, and a search for personal identity. For teenagers, a host of conflicts are to be found in the disparity between the values of the adolescent peer culture and familial values. All the while, society demands evidences of the transition to adulthood—for example, the achievement of independence from parents, responsible sexual behavior, the completion of required academic goals, and preparation for an occupation.

For college students, too, stress is often a major factor. Today's students feel pressured by the high cost of education, an uncertain job outlook, and stiff competition from their peers for everything from seats at a varsity basketball game to slots in a graduate program. As a result, serious stress-related illnesses such as depression, migraine headache, and eating and sleeping disorders appear—a pattern referred to by one investigator as "student shock" (Gottschalk, 1983).

The popular generalization that life gets easier with age hardly holds for most people. The challenges of young adulthood—establishing a career, finding a mate, becoming a parent—produce significant stress. Later on, in midlife, crises of career change, marital discord, and financial worries induce stress reactions. And the closing years, bringing the specter of physical and psychological decline, usher in an entirely new set of stressors that challenge the coping capacities of many elderly persons.

Moreover, certain stressors found in contemporary society appear to affect all of us, irrespective of age. An example is the ever-present threat of violence. Each day, newspaper headlines and TV newscasts assault us with reports of violent acts threatening the well-being and lives of people at all stages of life. Countless children, for example, are frightened by stories of abductions and molestations. Many teenagers are affected by the aura of violence on the streets and even in the schools. In many communities, elderly retirees live in fear of muggings, break-ins, and carjackings.

In sum, stress clearly appears to be our companion along the entire life span. At every point, however, we humans show a remarkable range of responses to the problems and crises that beset us. ■

Life Crises

A crippling accident, divorce, bankruptcy—at one time or another, each of us is likely to be faced with a seemingly overwhelming personal crisis. Indeed, it is probably fair to say that no life is without its episodes of trauma and loss—that eventually, we must all confront the kind of stressors that test our limits.

One investigator, reviewing various studies, has identified three kinds of events that have been found to be especially stressful (Rutter, 1983b): (1) events that signal the loss of an important relationship—for example, divorce; (2) events that cannot be controlled and therefore produce a feeling of helplessness—for example, a tragic accident; and (3) events that pose a long-term threat because they have lasting consequences—for example, a lingering illness or the loss of a job, or caring for years for a desperately ill and dying spouse (Kielcolt-Glazer et al., 1987). Such circumstances often produce the kind of physical and psychological stress responses that can significantly affect a person's health (Dohrenwend et al., 1982).

When personal crises pile up, the stress reactions are likely to be compounded. In a study of alcoholics who had completed a treatment program, chronic stress led to relapse—although less severe stress did not (Brown, et al., 1990). The same pattern holds for children. Among youngsters, a single hospital experience is not apt to be associated with psychological problems, but two such experiences are more likely to be so. The same is true among children who experience the crisis of parental divorce two or three times (Garmezy & Rutter, 1985).

Transitions as Stressors

The kinds of crises just described—for example, bereavement or divorce—constitute major life transitions, and because they are unhappy events, we can understand that they are especially likely to produce stress. But transitional milestones that are positive can be the occasion for stress as well. For example, stress can result from such basically joyous occasions as going off to college, getting married, or gaining a new family member. The following account by a young man, just graduated from law school, is not unusual: "I'm drowning in stress," he says. "I'm about to start a new job in a law firm, my girlfriend and I have decided to get married, and we've got our eye on the house we want to buy." Exposure to a number of such seemingly positive events within a short period of time can be stressful, and, at least in some individuals, can lead to illness (Maddi, Barone, and Puccetti, 1987).

The underlying element in such experiences is change. Today most people expect change to occur in their lives. We shift schools, jobs, or places of residence, experiencing abrupt alterations of environment when we do so. The result can be considerable stress—as has been demonstrated in studies of animals as well as humans. In one experiment, for example, individual monkeys were moved from one social group to another so that they constantly had to fight for social position within the group. Unlike other monkeys, who were allowed a stable social life, these animals on-the-move developed severe damage to their arteries (Bloom and Lazerson, 1988).

Catastrophes—Natural and Otherwise

Powerful earthquakes, severe hurricanes, and other natural disasters can also usher in stress for those in the environment. After the Mount Saint Helens volcanic eruption and ashfall in 1980, researchers studied the people living in the nearby town of Othello, Washington. As shown in Figure 9.1, emergency room visits rose by about a third as compared with the same period a year earlier. Moreover, mortality rates rose by about a fifth, and problems presented at the mental health clinic doubled (Adams & Adams, 1984).

FIGURE 9.1 Health implications of a major catastrophe Shown here is the rise in emergency room visits after the eruption of Mount Saint Helens volcano near Othello, Washington—as described in the text (after Adams and Adams, 1984).

The effects of exposure to catastrophic events can be revealed in more subtle ways as well. In a study spanning a three-week period following the 1989 earthquake in San Francisco, 40 percent of those living in the area reported experiencing nightmares about an earthquake. In a comparison group in Tucson, Arizona, the percentage of residents experiencing such nightmares following the earthquake was only about a tenth as large (Wood et al., 1992). Similar stress effects were undoubtedly also produced by the Los Angeles earthquake of 1993.

Stress often follows when people are exposed to a harmful substance which, they soon become aware, may cause their health to suffer at some time in the future. In effect, their exposure sets off what seems to them like a time bomb. This happened, for example, to a group of firemen who fought a large warehouse fire in New Jersey in 1985. Inside the warehouse was illegally stored polyvinyl chloride, the fumes from which are toxic and can have long-term harmful effects. Unaware of the presence of the polyvinyl chloride, the firemen did not at first put on masks to protect themselves—and only later learned of the risk that they had endured.

A single traumatic experience can produce a strong and persistent fear.

Researchers studied these firemen, comparing them with others who had not fought the fire a month or two after the event and again 22 months later. In contrast to the control subjects, those who had fought the dangerous fire were sadder, more anxious, and had more physical complaints. They were also significantly more angry and subject to confused thinking even as long as two years after the fire (Markowitz, 1989). As will be shown later, uncertainty and doubt can be potent sources of stress, and these elements undoubtedly contributed to the symptoms suffered by the exposed firemen.

Comparable reactions may also follow catastrophes brought about when technology fails us. When an accident damaged the nuclear power plant located at Three Mile Island, it exposed those nearby to potentially devastating radiation. Although some residents of the area moved away, others stayed on. People who continued to live there after the accident found themselves in a situation of chronic emotional tension. As long as 17 months after the incident, they showed more physiological signs of stress and reported more depression and anxiety than did control subjects (Schaeffer & Baum, 1984; Kiecolt-Glaser & Glaser, 1991).

Everyday Hassles

"It's not the large things that send a man to the madhouse . . . No, it's the continuing series of small tragedies that send a man to the madhouse . . . not the death of his love but a shoelace that snaps with no time left . . ." That view, expressed in a poem by Charles Bukowski, is reflected in the work of a number of psychologists, who have concluded that **daily hassles,** or seemingly minor irritations, can lead to as much stress as major life events. These are the "little things" that go wrong in life—the burnt toast, the washing machine that breaks down, the traffic tie-up that makes us late for work, the friend who forgets a lunch engagement.

Granted that, taken individually, such episodes usually do no more than turn a sweet day sour (Clark & Watson, 1988). But hassles that pile up have been shown to constitute a potent stressor (Lazarus & Folkman, 1984; Wein-

Daily hassles
The seemingly minor irritations that can lead to as much stress as major life events.

How much stress do you think this family is under?

berger, et al., 1987). The greater the number of daily hassles we encounter, the greater the number of psychological symptoms we are likely to experience (Zika & Chamberlain, 1987). Moreover, the occurrence of such physical problems as flu, backaches, and headaches have been tied to the stress posed by daily hassles (DeLongis, Folkman, & Lazarus, 1988).

Conflict as a Source of Stress

Should I stay in my room and study for tomorrow's test, or go out to a movie with friends?

Should I get married to that special person in my life, or continue living a life free of obligations?

Should I let my boss know what I really think of him, or keep quiet and not risk losing my job?

Such choices create **conflict**—which psychologists define as *the simultaneous arousal of two or more incompatible motives, resulting in unpleasant emotions such as anxiety or anger*. The phrase "unpleasant emotions" is an essential part of the definition. A person whose motives are in genuine conflict experiences anxiety, uncertainty, and the feeling of being torn and distressed. This is why conflict is a significant source of stress—and, in extreme cases, a threat to mental health. The types of conflicts faced in life are varied.

Life is full of such conflicts over pairs of goals that cannot be attained, all falling in general into four classes:

1. **Approach-approach conflict:** Takes place between two motives that both make us want to approach desirable goals. However, we cannot reach both goals, for attaining one of them means giving up the other. We cannot simultaneously satisfy the motive to watch the late movie on television and the motive to get a good night's sleep. We cannot simultaneously roam around the world and settle down in a career. Thus we are often torn between alternatives—each of which would be thoroughly pleasant except for our regret over losing the other.

2. **Avoidance-avoidance conflict:** Occurs between two motives that make us want to avoid two alternatives that are both unpleasant. For example, you are too keyed up over tomorrow's examination to get to sleep. You would like to avoid the unpleasantness of tossing and turning in bed, and you could do so by taking a sleeping pill. But you would also like to avoid the grogginess you will suffer tomorrow if you do take the sleeping pill.

3. **Approach-avoidance conflict:** Occurs when fulfilling a motive will have both pleasant and unpleasant consequences. As in the example given earlier, the thought of getting married often creates an approach-avoidance conflict. Being married has many attractions—but it also means added responsibilities and loss of freedom.

4. **Double approach-avoidance conflict:** The most complex and unfortunately the most common type of all, takes place when we are torn between two goals that will both have pleasant and unpleasant consequences. A college woman from a small community wants to become a certified public accountant. But she knows that the best opportunities in this field exist in large cities, and she is worried about the crowded and impersonal aspects of big-city life. Now she falls in love with a

Conflict

The simultaneous arousal of two or more incompatible motives, resulting in unpleasant emotions such as anxiety or anger.

Approach-approach conflict

A type of conflict in which a person must select one of two positive alternatives.

Avoidance-avoidance conflict

A type of conflict in which a person must select one of two negative alternatives.

Approach-avoidance conflict

A type of conflict in which a person must select an alternative that has both positive and negative consequences.

Double approach-avoidance conflict

A type of conflict in which a person must select from two alternatives, both of which have positive and negative consequences.

classmate who plans to go into business with his father, who runs a small-town automobile agency. She wants very much to marry this man and she likes the idea of living with him in a small community. But she knows that this community will give her very little opportunity for her chosen career as an accountant. Which way shall she turn?

Often there is no fully satisfactory solution to the conflicts we face in everyday life. But understanding their stressful nature can help us cope—and arrive at sensible resolutions.

Uncertainty and Doubt as Sources of Stress

Whenever the future is shrouded in uncertainty and doubt, stress is likely to arise. For example, because hostages never know whether they will ever be released, the experience of captivity becomes especially stressful. On a more mundane level, you may experience stress when you come to class to take an important exam, sit in the doctor's office waiting to learn what your X-rays tests show, or drive on the highway and suddenly see the flashing light of a police car looming behind you. Even astronauts, trained for years to face their complex tasks, show evidence of physiological stress as they sit at their controls, knowing that in a few seconds they will blast off into the void of space.

One experiment showed that uncertainty may affect even rats. Pairs of rats were placed in a device, shown in Figure 9.2, where they could not move, and they were then given series of electric shocks to their tails. The shocks came at

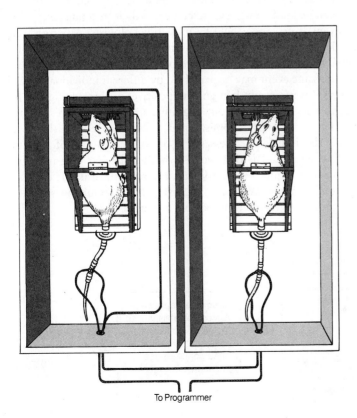

FIGURE 9.2 The effects of not knowing what lies ahead The stressor—shocks to the tail—was the same for both rats, but the experience produced different results for each, as described in the text.

To Programmer

the same time and were of equal strength. However, one rat in each pair received a warning tone before each shock, while the other heard meaningless, random beeps. The rats who never knew when the shocks would come engaged in erratic eating and drinking behavior and developed severe stomach ulcers as a consequence of their stress. Those who could predict when the shocks would arrive displayed far fewer signs of stress (Weiss, 1970).

In general, the more knowledge people have as they prepare to face a stress-provoking experience, the better they feel. But the result appears to depend to some degree on how apprehensive they are to begin with. For those who are usually very worried, information about what lies in store may actually increase the impact of the stressor. In one study, a group of women, about to have their hands immersed in painfully cold water, received detailed information about what to expect. The information helped reduce the stress of those who were not overly concerned about the experience—but it compounded the stress of the women who approached the experiment with extreme foreboding (McCaul, 1980).

Stress as an Individual Experience

"Grief is a matter of relativity; the sorrow should be estimated by its proportion to the sorrower; a gash is as painful to one as an amputation is to another." Those are the words of poet Percy Bysshe Shelley, writing early in the nineteenth century. His view has now been documented by psychologists, who have demonstrated the uniqueness of individual reactions to stressful events.

Some early investigators studying animals assumed that the effects of stressors can be studied without reference to their meaning to the individual. But this view is no longer held by most psychologists. A person's **cognitive appraisal,** or subjective interpretation, of a potentially stressful episode strongly influences that individual's response (Lazarus & Folkman, 1984). As a result, the same event may be perceived by different individuals in widely different ways—as irrelevant, benign, and positive, or threatening and harmful.

As shown in Figure 9.3, our cognitive appraisal of a stressful stimulus is of two kinds: primary appraisal and secondary appraisal. In **primary appraisal,** the individual assesses the personal meaning of the stressor at hand. How significant is this event—whether the loss of a neighbor, a job shift, or a surprise quiz—to me? In **secondary appraisal,** the question is one of coping alternatives. What can I realistically do about this situation? What are my options? Am I going to be able to handle this?

Cognitive appraisal

A person's subjective interpretation of a potentially stressful episode.

Primary appraisal

A type of cognitive appraisal in which the individual assesses the personal meaning of the stressor.

Secondary appraisal

A type of cognitive appraisal in which the individual deals with coping alternatives.

FIGURE 9.3   The stress experience A given event may or may not produce stress, depending on the individual's interpretation of it (after Taylor, 1986).

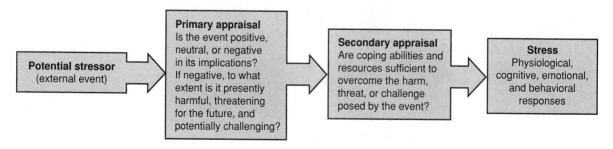

Because of the range of appraisals that humans make to stressful events, one person may experience severe stress over an occurrence that leaves another person relatively calm. For one person, a given stressor produces chronic feelings of anxiety; for another, it leads to little if any tension. You doubtless know men and women who carry on in normal fashion and even appear relatively calm and cheerful despite serious physical handicaps or tragic disappointments. You probably know others who are reduced to panic or temper tantrums if the breakfast bacon is too crisp.

Even apparently traumatic stressors such as being the victim of a crime do not yield the same responses from everyone. "The degree of violation experienced by an individual victim finally depends on the meaning of the crime in that person's life. What seems a minor incident to one target may be a personal catastrophe for another." It is the victim's subjective interpretation of the crime that determines how traumatic that event actually turns out to be (Bard & Sangrey, 1986).

Stress and Physical Health

Although all of us do not respond to life's stressors in the same way (Manuck, et al., 1991), in general, our body reacts in a fairly uniform pattern. A number of physiological changes take place, involving the brain and various organ systems, as portrayed in Figure 9.4. These changes mobilize our physical resources for "fight or flight." That is, they enable us to fight for our survival harder and longer than would otherwise be possible or to run away from danger faster and farther.

The fact that our physiology is altered under stress constitutes a rather mixed blessing, for some of the changes produce wear and tear on the body and symptoms of illness. In the case of a purely physical stress, such as sudden injury, our body will take steps to limit the damage—for instance rushing antibodies to the site of the injury. This could mean the difference between life and death. The fight-or-flight response may be equally valuable in situations where we must make split-second decisions and take quick action. We may, for instance, need to deal with a sudden fire in the kitchen, avoid an oncoming car in our lane of traffic, or rescue a drowning friend.

Yet many stresses of modern life are complex, ongoing, and seemingly inescapable. How can the fight-or-flight response help us deal with an overbearing boss, a seriously ill relative, a difficult chemistry class that we cannot drop? Such situations cannot be fought in the same way that our distant ancestors fought off a saber-toothed tiger. And we cannot really run from them. It is this dilemma that so frequently gets us into difficulties. To appreciate why this is so, it is necessary to understand in more detail how the body responds to stress.

Stress and the General Adaptation Syndrome

Much of what we know about the physiological effects of stress goes back to experiments performed on animals by Hans Selye in the 1950s and 1960s. The reactions he analyzed seem to be much the same as those produced in humans by any form of external or internal pressure, including prolonged emotional tension. Selye exposed animals to a variety of physical stressors—

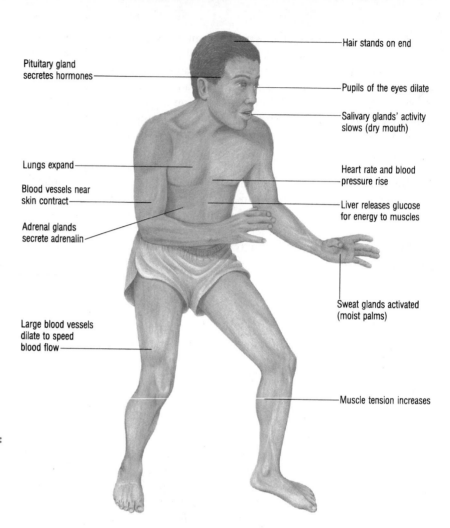

Pituitary gland
secretes hormones

Lungs expand

Blood vessels near
skin contract

Adrenal glands
secrete adrenalin

Large blood vessels
dilate to speed
blood flow

Hair stands on end

Pupils of the eyes dilate

Salivary glands' activity
slows (dry mouth)

Heart rate and blood
pressure rise

Liver releases glucose
for energy to muscles

Sweat glands activated
(moist palms)

Muscle tension increases

FIGURE 9.4 Fight or flight: The body's responses to a stressful event Faced with an emergency, a variety of physical reactions takes place in the body.

General adaptation syndrome (GAS)

The sequence of events, according to Selye, involved in prolonged stress including the alarm phase, the resistance phase, and the exhaustion phase.

such as extreme cold, fatigue, or doses of poison not quite strong enough to kill. He expected to find a different physiological response to each physical stress. Surprisingly, the animals responded in basically the same way no matter what he did to produce stress. Selye coined the phrase **general adaptation syndrome** to describe what he observed.

Selye distinguished three phases in the general adaptation syndrome: the alarm stage, the resistance stage, and the exhaustion stage. During the alarm stage, the body mobilizes its resources to meet the threat. Selye found that when an animal was injected with poison, its body automatically tried to defend itself. Most notably, its endocrine glands immediately sprang into action. The adrenal glands in particular showed striking changes. They became enlarged and produced more adrenalin. They also discharged their stored-up supply of the hormones known as steroids, which make many contributions to the body's well-being. Because of this high level of activity of the adrenal glands, numerous physical changes occurred in the animals. For example, tissue was broken down into sugar to provide energy. The amount of salt normally found in the bloodstream was sharply reduced.

FIGURE 9.5   The three phases of the general adaptation syndrome Illustrated here are the three stages of Selye's general adaptation syndrome. In the alarm phase (phase A), when the body first reacts to stress, resistance is lowered. As the stress continues, the body enters the resistance stage (phase B). Resistance is above normal, and the body appears to be doing well. In the exhaustion stage (phase C), resistance plummets (after Taylor, 1986).

Selye named the second phase of the general adaptation syndrome the resistance stage. At this point, as Figure 9.5 shows, the body seems to be doing better. Selye's animals, for example, seemed to adapt after a few days of continued exposure to stress-producing conditions. The adrenal glands returned to normal size and began to renew their supply of steroids. The salt level in the blood rose to normal or even higher. Apparently the animals had adjusted to the situation and were perfectly normal.

Yet Selye discovered that during this period, the animals were not so normal as they seemed. If a second source of stress was introduced during this stage, the animals quickly died. In attempting to adapt to the original stress, apparently they had used their defenses to the maximum and were helpless against a new form of pressure.

Even if only the original stress continued, the animals' recovery was temporary. After several weeks of continued resistance to stress, they entered the third stage, the exhaustion stage. Their adrenal glands again became enlarged and lost their store of steroids. The level of salt in the blood fell drastically. The kidneys, as a result of receiving an excess of hormones, underwent some complicated and damaging changes. Eventually the animals died, as if from exhaustion. They had been killed, so to speak, by an excess of the hormones they had produced in their own defense (Selye, 1956).

Psychosomatic Illness: How Stress Can Make Us Sick

Like Selye's animals, humans can mobilize the body's resources in order to react quickly and effectively to an immediate stressor. Yet if stress is long-lasting, our bodies can be severely damaged by the very mechanisms that would save it in the short run. Since stress—especially psychologically induced stress—is often prolonged and not easily remedied, it can lead to physiological damage and disease. For example, cortisol—a hormone released in the body when we experience stress—works to our benefit in the short run, but it is harmful if secreted at high levels over long periods.

Stress caused by frustration, conflict, or prolonged emotional upset can be as drastic as the kind Selye produced by injecting poison. The physical results often take the form of **psychosomatic illnesses,** a form of bodily ailments that stem at least in part from mental and emotional causes. Recent evidence shows, for example, that over the course of four decades, individuals who live under tension are twice as likely to develop hypertension, or high blood pressure, as are those whose lives are relatively free of stress (Markovitz

Psychosomatic illnesses
A form of bodily ailments that stem, at least in part, from mental and emotional causes.

Some jobs create chronic stress because of the requirement for continued vigilance and anxiety over mistakes that have serious consequences.

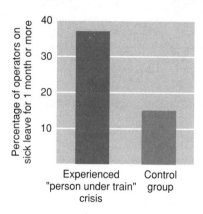

FIGURE 9.6   Out sick after a traumatic crisis "Person under train!" That shocking message has been heard on occasion by subway train operators. Those operators who experienced such an unfortunate event—that is, having a person hurt or killed after falling under the moving train—were far more likely to lose time due to illness during the following year (Theorell, et al., 1992).

et al., 1993). Other diseases that frequently seem to be psychosomatic include ulcers, bronchial asthma, and headache (Taylor, 1986).

As many people have discovered, the illness-producing stresses can be related to the work environment. It has been found, for instance, that air traffic controllers, especially in high-traffic airports, have a greater incidence than other workers of stomach ulcers and hypertension (Rose, Jenkins, & Hurst, 1978). And a recent study of subway train drivers showed that major, work-related crises can erode health and well-being, as described in Figure 9.6.

The onset of health problems following stress need not be immediate. For example, during the first three months, there was no difference between the two groups of subway drivers identified in Figure 9.6. The same pattern was shown in a study of men enrolled in a Navy submarine school. The subjects completed a survey of life experience covering the past year, dating each experience and rating its desirability and impact. Analysis of this information in relation to the subjects' medical records revealed a strong positive correlation between stressful life events and subsequent illnesses occurring as long as six months to a year later (Antonini, 1985).

Some researchers believe that, at least in humans, different types of stressors may affect the body differently and produce varying physiological responses (Taylor, 1990). For example, there are some indications that stressful events that evoke feelings of loss and depression are linked to a vulnerability to cancer (Jensen, 1987). In any case, it would seem that under ordinary conditions our bodies are able to resist such external causes of illness as viruses and bacteria. When our usual defenses are weakened by stress, we are likely to get sick.

Stress and Survival

Can stress actually kill, as it killed Selye's animals? Some evidence comes from a study of the backgrounds of middle-aged men who died suddenly of heart attacks. The results showed that four out of five had been feeling overwhelmed and depressed for periods ranging from a week to several months. Moreover, just before the fatal attack, at least half of them had been in a situation likely to produce sudden and intense emotional arousal—in some cases an unusually heavy workload or other bustle of activity, in other circumstances a high level of anxiety or anger (Greene, Goldstein, & Moss, 1972).

Additional evidence comes from a study of children who experienced life-threatening asthma attacks. The researchers found significant differences between the children who died from the attacks and those who survived. The children who died were more likely to be unusually sensitive to separation or loss. Often, they had experienced a recent loss through death, divorce, or abandonment. In addition, the children who succumbed were more likely to have a history of family turmoil, and to have expressed hopelessness or despair within a month before the fatal attack (Miller & Strunk, 1989). For both groups—the asthmatic children and the men who suffered heart attacks—it seems likely that stress was at least a contributing factor in their deaths.

Are Some Stressors Worse Than Others?

Everybody undergoes stressful experience—yet not everybody comes down with a psychosomatic illness. Why? One reason seems to be that no two people have the same experiences, and even if they do, as discussed earlier, two people may not view the same stressful experience in the same way. After studying the life experiences and medical records of large numbers of people, one group of investigators developed the Life Stress Scale shown in Figure 9.7, which assigns a numeric value to the amount of stress that adjusting to various new events seems to create. Note that these events include not only misfortunes but pleasurable happenings—such as getting married, achieving something outstanding, and even going on vacation or celebrating Christmas. Indeed getting married, assigned a figure of 50, was found fully half as stressful as the death of a husband or wife, which tops the list with 100.

The likelihood of psychosomatic illness, the investigators concluded, was determined by the total number of stress units that occurred within a single 12-month period. When the number exceeded 200, more than half the people in the study developed health problems. And when the total exceeded 300, nearly 80 percent of the subjects became ill.

Experience	Stress Units	Experience	Stress Units
Death of spouse	100	Change to new kind of work	36
Divorce	73	Change in work responsibilities	29
Separation	65	Trouble with in-laws	29
Jail term	63	An outstanding achievement	28
Death of close family member	63	Wife starts job or stops	26
Getting married	50	Begin or end school	26
Being fired	47	Trouble with boss	23
Reconciliation in marriage	45	Change in work conditions	20
Retirement	45	Move to new residence	20
Getting pregnant	40	Changing schools	20
Sex problems	39	Changing social activities	18
New member in family	39	Vacation	13
Change in finances	38	Christmas holidays	12
Death of close friend	37	Minor law violation	11

FIGURE 9.7   A scale of stress produced by various events These are some of the figures in the Life Stress Scale, discussed in the text (Holmes & Rahe, 1967).

Some critics regard the Life Stress Scale and others like it as arbitrary (Rabkin & Struening, 1976). For one thing, many psychologists believe that, when all other things are equal, happy events seldom lead to physical symptoms (Taylor, 1986). In addition, stress scales ignore individual differences both in the way we appraise the stressors we encounter and in the coping skills and outside emotional support we have available (Holahan & Moos, 1986).

The physical effects of stress may depend also on our level of physical fitness. One investigation showed that an abundance of stress is clearly associated with poor health for people who are not very fit to begin with, but less clearly for those who are in good shape (Roth & Holmes, 1985). As an example, both physical and emotional stress appear to produce abnormal—and potentially dangerous—heart activity in patients with coronary artery disease but not in healthy individuals (Rozanski et al., 1988).

Stress and the Body's Immunity to Disease

Immune system
A body's intricate network of cellular organs and tissues that protects cells against diseases.

We do not stay healthy by chance. One factor that keeps us healthy from day to day is a well-functioning **immune system,** *the body's intricate defense network of cellular organs and tissues that protect cells against diseases.* The immune response springs into action against any intruder that threatens the organism—from bacteria, viruses, and new growths (such as tumors) to ragweed pollen and bee venom.

Psychoneuroimmunology
A new field of research that focuses on the interaction of psychological and physiological processes influencing the body's capacity to fend off disease.

The immune response is extraordinarily complex, and researchers have only begun to penetrate its secrets. One important area of their work is called **psychoneuroimmunology,** a new field of research activity that focuses on the interaction of psychological and physiological processes that influence the body's capacity to fend off disease. Work in this field has reinforced the view that the net effect of stress is suppression of immunity—and thus increased vulnerability to illness.

Studies of animals subjected to stress consistently demonstrate a weakening of the immune system (Coe, 1993). One of the main consequences of the fight-or-flight response is the release of certain hormones—epinephrine, norepinephrine, and cortisol. These hormones, it turns out, act to suppress the body's lymphocytes, or white blood cells, reducing the capacity of the body to fight infection and disease (Marx, 1985).

There is growing evidence that the same pattern takes place in humans. Many of the stressors identified earlier in this chapter appear to be correlated with a weakened immunity. For example, following the death of a spouse from cancer, bereaved survivors showed a lowered immunity level—lower even than when their spouses were critically ill and dying. Separation and divorce also appear to have the same effect—as does the stress of a poor marriage. Moreover, a similar pattern emerges in studies of individuals exposed to chronic environmental stress. Residents of Three Mile Island, the site of a damaged nuclear power plant described earlier, developed lower immunity than those who lived 80 miles away (Kiecolt-Glaser & Glaser, 1991).

Milder forms of stress may also reduce immune response. A study of medical students, portrayed in Figure 9.8, showed that the activity of white blood cells that help fend off viral infections such as flu was significantly decreased at final examination time as compared to one month earlier. There was even greater suppression of these protective cells among students who were experiencing especially stressful life events and who were also especially

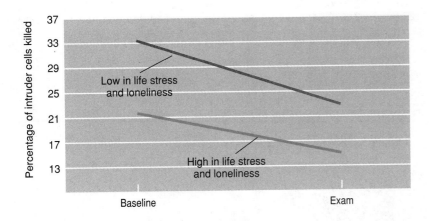

FIGURE 9.8 The body's immune response to stress Immune system protection (measured by the percentage of intruder cells killed) declined for students as they approached examination time. Protection was especially weak among students high on a scale of stressful life changes as well as on a scale of loneliness (adapted from Kiecolt-Glaser, et al., 1984).

lonely. The results suggest that there may be some truth to the popular belief that we are more likely to suffer a bout of flu or the common cold in the wake of a stressful period (Kiecolt-Glaser et al., 1984).

Moreover, the drugs prescribed by doctors to protect against illness may be less helpful when we feel under heavy stress. In one study, a group of medical students was given inoculations against hepatitis during examination time. For those students who had difficulties coping and were overwhelmed by anxiety, the inoculations were less effective in raising immunity against the disease (Glaser et al., 1992).

Not all bereaved spouses experience reduced immunity, of course, nor do all students taking examinations. There is evidence that individuals differ substantially in the responses of their immune system to stress. Such differences appear to depend, at least in part, on the nature of the individual's sympathetic nervous system. Healthy volunteers were subjected to a 20-minute period of acute stress by having to perform demanding cognitive tasks—for example, math problems—under time pressure and in a distracting environment. There was a suppression of immune function only in those individuals whose sympathetic nervous system is highly activated—as evidenced, for example, by heightened cardiovascular activity—when under stress (Manuck et al., 1991).

Type A Personality and Stress-Related Illness

How an individual fares under stress can also depend on the overall psychological makeup, or personality, of the individual. In assessing the chances of suffering a heart attack, some investigators have found that the greatest risk is among people whose behavior they have termed Type A, people who are typically hard-driving and successful, including numerous corporation executives (National Institutes of Health, 1981). These people have an extremely high achievement motive and believe they can overcome any obstacle if only they try hard enough. They are ambitious, impatient, and competitive and have a sense of urgency about getting tasks done on time. They usually work to the limit of their endurance and sometimes beyond it (Wright, 1988; Taylor, 1990). The probability of suffering a heart attack, some investigators find, is considerably less among so-called Type B people—who are more easygoing and place less value on success (Friedman & Rosenman, 1981).

Positions of responsibility can produce stress if the people in the job believe they cannot control risk or are temperamentally prone to anxiety.

When thwarted, Type A individuals typically react with feelings of hostility and anger. A number of researchers believe anger is the Type A behavior likely to be a special culprit in the development of coronary heart disease (Taylor, 1990). The emotion may be especially hurtful if held in, whether consciously or unconsciously (Wright, 1988). For example, unresolved hostility typical of Type A individuals appears to reduce the chances of recovering after a heart attack (Case et al., 1985).

It is possible that generally hostile individuals operate with a nervous system different from other people. When they get angry and their adrenalin begins to flow, their parasympathetic nervous system does not do its usual job of slowing down the work of the heart and lungs. Instead it remains aroused—and the heart rate and blood pressure show atypical increases (Suarez & Williams, 1989). At the same time, their interactions with people take on an aggressive edge (Williams, 1989).

Not everyone agrees that anger or hostility is the major ingredient in Type A behavior. Some investigators, for example, have found that people who harbor a cynical mistrust of other people's motives are the ones who are at risk for heart disease. Such people are likely to express a low opinion of human nature. Even though psychologists do not yet agree on exactly how Type A personality is related to heart disease, it has been found that working with people to reduce their Type A behavior appears to lower the risk of coronary heart problems (Taylor, 1990). In any case, it seems clear that anger carries with it potentially powerful ramifications for our well-being. Some suggestions for handling this emotion are found in the Psychology in Action Box entitled "Using Anger Constructively."

The Power Motive, Anger, and Hypertension

In a remarkable study spanning two decades, a group of men in their early thirties were assessed for their motivation and for their tendency either to gratify or inhibit certain motives. Twenty years later, their patterns of blood

Using Anger Constructively

Although anger is a universal emotion, some of us get angry more easily and more often than others. We now know that excessive anger may harm our bodies as well as our relationships. How can we learn to deal with anger? Here are some points to consider (Institute for Mental Health Initiatives, 1988):

- Don't fear that anger will drive others away. Friendships and romantic relationships cannot endure if either party is afraid to honestly express at least some angry feelings. By a wide margin, people report that such honest expression of anger is helpful rather than harmful. Even those who are the targets of another person's anger frequently say that they come to realize their own shortcomings because of the angry reactions of others. Anger is not pleasant. But it need hardly spell the end of an otherwise healthy relationship.
- Avoid expressing unnecessary and corrosive anger. The anger we waste on trivia is most likely to act upon the victims we least

intend—ourselves. On the other hand, it is not always wise to suppress legitimate anger. Some people overcompensate for the anger they feel by becoming overly ingratiating—at great personal cost. Suppressed anger can fester and end up misdirected at a friend or coworker.

- Keep in mind that there is a vast difference between our thoughts and our actions. All people have a "dark side." In the privacy of our own minds, we can be infantile, petty, vicious, murderous, perversely spiteful, cruelly sadistic, and worse. Although they seem so alien, the dark impulses are hardly abnormal; instead they are an inescapable part of being human. We are allowed to think anything without feeling guilty. Fantasies never hurt anyone.
- The main purpose of expressing anger should be to improve an upsetting situation, not to gain revenge. Anger can be used constructively to improve the quality of a relationship. It should not be manipulated to prove that one is right or used as a weapon to cause another person to feel bad or guilty.

- Accept the angry feelings of others. Friends and intimates are quick to pick up signals that we are unprepared to accept their angry feelings. The result is often confusion and misunderstanding on both sides. If we can recognize that the anger of others often stems from a deep sense of caring and if we can accept anger without self-pity or resentment, our relationships will be significantly enriched.
- Try to convert anger-energy into constructive action. Too often anger becomes the habitual springboard for feeling soured on life and resentful toward others. The result is apt to be unhappiness and scarred relationships. Yet we can use anger as an opportunity for growth. That is what the prophets of old did when they transformed their wrath and indignation into working for social change. And that is what the great civil rights leaders did when they redirected their outrage into the service of a noble human cause. We too can convert anger into constructive action—by effecting change in ourselves, in others, or in social institutions.

pressure were measured. The early tests of motivation were surprisingly accurate in predicting which of the men would have high blood pressure in later life. By far the greatest number of cases occurred among men who, in their thirties, had a strong power motive which they tried to inhibit (McClelland, 1979). Presumably "bottling up" the strong motivation for power produced frequent anger and chronic stress (McClelland, 1989).

This study is one of a number showing that many people with high blood pressure tend to conceal strong feelings of anger and resentment (Weiner, 1982). It has been suggested that this may be one reason why high blood pressure is twice as prevalent among blacks—many of whom have resented their status in society but have kept their anger in check—as among whites (Krantz et al., 1981). In one study, for example, black students were shown

TEST YOURSELF

e) A doctor hears the following account from a patient who, although unhurt, had been involved in a terrifying auto accident. "For a while I seemed to be doing O.K. But then, after a few days, I began to feel so exhausted, I had trouble getting through the day." What term did Selye apply to this pattern?

f) If someone were to describe your stomachache as "just psychosomatic," would that mean that the problem was purely a product of your imagination?

g) A scientist is interested in finding out why people who experience stress tend to be more vulnerable to colds and other illnesses. In what new field of investigation is that scientist working?

h) What useful purpose can anger serve?

Anxiety
An unpleasant feeling accompanied by a premonition that something undesirable is about to happen.

several scenes from a film. Racist scenes raised the students' blood pressure more than scenes that were anger-provoking but not racist in content—and emotionally neutral scenes did not raise blood pressure at all. Those students who tended to hold their anger in check had higher blood pressure after viewing the anger-provoking scenes than those who were more open about their anger (Armstead et al., 1989).

Stress and Mental Health

"The thought of hunting for a job makes me anxious all the time."

"I'm so upset about my neighbor's divorce that I just can't keep my mind on my work."

"When I lost my dog, I just felt like staying in bed forever."

Those statements begin to suggest the range of psychological experiences that accompany the body's responses to stress. When stressful events can be overcome, they may lead to positive feelings of mastery and self-esteem. But when they are perceived as overwhelming, they introduce painful feelings of anxiety and a draining of intellectual resources. Often, too, they lead to feelings of depression—of hopelessness and despair. Because stress influences the way we feel, think, and behave, it can powerfully affect the quality of our lives from day-to-day—the way we function at work or school, how we relate to others, and the degree to which life itself seems worth living.

Stress and Anxiety

One prominent response to stress, particularly to prolonged or repeated stress, is **anxiety,** *an unpleasant feeling accompanied by a premonition that something undesirable is about to happen.* It is closely related to the emotion of fear, but while fear is the result of a specific stimulus such as a menacing intruder in the home, the source of anxiety is not always easy to pinpoint, making it particularly difficult to handle.

Although all the causes of anxiety are difficult to define, there are five types of stressful situations that are likely to lead to anxiety:

1. We have conflicting motives of the kind discussed earlier, on page 434. (For example, we want to dedicate our lives to helping others, yet at the same time we want the solitude to write great novels.)
2. We experience a conflict between our behavior and an inner standard. (For example, we do something we believe to be wrong.)
3. We encounter some unusual event that we cannot immediately understand and adjust to. (For example, we arrive on a new campus, not knowing what kind of behavior is expected.)
4. We are faced with events whose outcome is unpredictable. (For example, we don't know what score we will make on an important test.)
5. We confront the loss of a beloved person. (For example, a close friend or parent becomes desperately ill.)

In all these cases, the emotion of anxiety is clearly related to a motive. In situations 1 and 2, it is produced by a conflict between motives or between a motive and an inner standard. In situations 3 and 4 it is produced by frustration of the motive for certainty. And in situation 5, it is produced by frustration of the affiliation motive.

Meeting new people is stressful for those who worry about how they will be evaluated.

Anxiety and Cognitive Performance

Anxiety evoked by stress can put a considerable strain on our cognitive resources. One reason is that when we are under stress, we devote energy to understanding what the stressful event is, as well as trying to determine whether it is likely to continue. As a result, we have less time and energy to devote to careful, reflective thought—which leads to poor performance on tasks. Another reason is that a stressful situation requires us to stay alert for signs of danger. Like the cowboy hero in the Old West movie, we must always be vigilant—which reduces our ability to concentrate (Taylor, 1986).

Of particular interest to college students is the influence of anxiety on the ability to learn and on grades. Although it appears that people high in anxiety do not do more poorly when the learning tasks are simple, their performance does suffer when the learning tasks are difficult (O'Neil, Spielberger, & Hansen, 1969). Presumably their high anxiety impairs the intense focusing required for the learning of complicated materials. They seem distracted, as if their anxiety forces them to concentrate on the way they feel rather than on the tasks at hand (Holyrod et al., 1978). People high in anxiety seem to do particularly badly at complex reasoning when they are put under pressure, such as being told they have a short time to answer test questions (Leon & Revelle, 1985).

Post-Traumatic Stress Disorder: Scars That Linger

In the studies just described, the levels of anxiety felt by subjects typically arose from the kind of stressful experiences that all of us can recognize. Some people, however, are unlucky enough to endure traumatic stressors that lie far outside the range of usual human experience. They include victims not only of disasters such as floods and fires, but also of shocking experiences that human beings themselves devise—among them war, captivity, torture, rape, and other crimes.

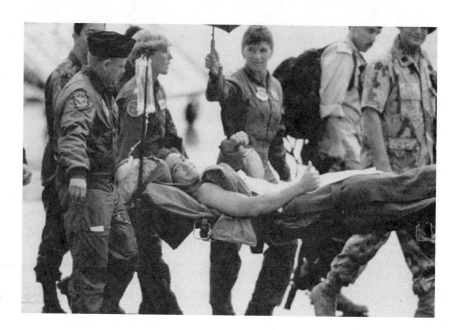

Uncertainty over possible harm can create chronic stress.

Post-traumatic stress disorder

A type of anxiety disorder in which a person reacts to a traumatic situation or experience that is far outside the usual range of human experience.

Survivors of such overwhelming events are sometimes left with special anxiety problems called **post-traumatic stress disorder** (**PTSD**). Some survivors act as if they have been numbed by the shock of their ordeal. Their interest in life is diminished, and they feel alienated from the people around them (Walker, 1981). Others develop a tendency to remain constantly on the alert—as if disaster is sure to strike again at any moment. They tend also to startle easily. People who have lived through auto crashes may panic at the sound of cars in the night. Those who have endured a mugging or rape may respond with a start whenever they hear strange sounds, and some former POWs and hostages report similar reactions whenever they hear approaching footsteps. As demonstrated in Figure 9.9, even words that evoke memories of an earlier trauma can be emotionally disturbing (McNally et al., 1990).

Survivors of psychological trauma are also likely to keep reliving their experience. They suffer from nightmares in which the shattering episode is reenacted in all its terrifying detail, and by day they find themselves suddenly overwhelmed by harrowing memories whenever they are exposed to situations that even remotely resemble the original event.

Some people get over a traumatic experience soon enough, but others are troubled by symptoms for many years. One team of investigators studied 27 women who had been raped, some as long ago as 16 years earlier. The victims continued to suffer from episodes of depression, tension, and fatigue. They experienced not only sexual problems but difficulties in developing close personal relationships. Two of the women eventually became so disturbed that they had to be hospitalized, and four reported that they subsequently returned to long-abandoned patterns of alcohol and drug abuse (Ellis, Atkeson, & Calhoun, 1981). A number of elderly concentration camp survivors broke down completely decades after their ordeal was over when they had to be hospitalized for medical reasons. The experience was sufficiently similar to imprisonment to reopen fully the old psychological wounds (Edelstein, 1982). Recent studies suggest that this lingering pattern may have a biological basis. The experience of terrorizing, traumatic events may alter the chemistry of the brain, rendering victims more vulnerable over time (Mason et al., 1990).

Although PTSD is not a universal consequence of trauma (Helzer, Robins, & McEvoy, 1987), there is some evidence that traumatic episodes inflicted by others leave worse scars than those occurring by accident or as a result of a natural catastrophe (American Psychiatric Association, 1980). Crime victims, hostages, and combat veterans are examples of those likely to suffer especially from their ordeals. Among Vietnam War veterans, 15 percent have showed signs of the disorder, and their suicide rate is considerably higher than that for the population at large (Roberts, 1988).

Stress and Depression

The physical and psychological effects of stress are sometimes difficult to separate. This is especially true in the case of **depression,** a common emotional disturbance that can range from low to high degrees of severity and that affects 1 in 12 Americans (National Institute of Mental Health, 1991).

As will be detailed in the next chapter, a tendency to become depressed, especially in its more extreme forms, appears to be at least partly the result of heredity. Apparently some people are born with a type of brain chemistry that is prone to low levels of the neurotransmitter noradrenalin, shown to be associated with depression (Goodwin & Jamison, 1990)—just as other people are born with weak stomachs or weak hearts that are vulnerable to damage by stress. At any rate, depression is an emotional disturbance in which the physical and psychological aspects of stress appear closely intermingled.

Even though a biological vulnerability may be present, depression is frequently precipitated by a stressful experience—bereavement, unemployment,

Depression
A common emotional disturbance that can range from low to high degrees of severity.

FIGURE 9.9   When words bring back painful memories Fifteen Vietnam combat veterans suffering from posttraumatic stress disorder (PTSD) were asked to name the color in which each of a series of randomly presented words were printed. The speed with which they responded was compared with that of 15 Vietnam veterans without PTSD. The PTSD group took significantly longer to name the colors of those words (PTSD words) associated with their Vietnam experience. Apparently, these words—for example, "bodybags" and "firefight"—activated memories of their trauma, which interfered with the cognitive task at hand. Note that the three other categories of words used in the experiment produced no significant difference in response time between the two groups of veterans (McNally et al., 1990).

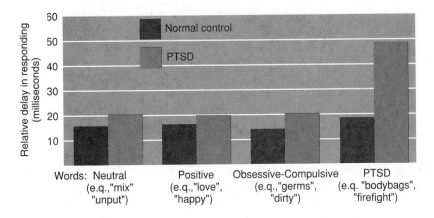

family breakup—especially one that is associated with a sense of loss. There is some evidence that life events that produce disturbed interpersonal relationships lead to depression (Rutter, 1983). Often such events destroy an individual's sense of identity and feelings of worthiness (Dohrenwend et al., 1987). Depression can also be one of the consequences of chronic pressure to work, without adequate emotional rewards. That is one of the reasons given for the fact that one in eight medical school students suffers bouts of depression (Zeldow, 1987).

Even among individuals suffering from depression clearly related to **endogenous causes**—that is, causes that are biological rather than only environmental—stressful events apparently play a role. A study of 68 depressed patients showed that the degree to which earlier life events were perceived as stressful—including events revolving around marital difficulties, child rearing, and health—was related to the severity of the depression. Moreover, those individuals without major stressors besetting them were more likely to recover from their symptoms (Reno & Halaris, 1990). Stresses that are chronic—marital and social problems, poor family relationships, continuing employment and financial crises—appear especially to lead to severe and recurrent depressive symptoms (Hammen et al., 1992).

For some people, echoes of stressful events appear to produce depression years later—that is, when those events are sharply reawakened by similar experiences. Thus, for example, the death of a parent in childhood, or the divorce of parents may serve to sensitize the youngster and increase vulnerability to later losses (Rutter, 1983b). And long-term studies have traced the existence of depression in some individuals for as long as a half century after the economic depression and job disruptions of the 1930s (Gerstein et al., 1988).

The Ways We Cope

The stressors we encounter in our lives can produce a wide range of responses—from depression and self-pity to optimism and heroism. Some people may throw up their hands, while others may try to fight off the stressor. Those who fail to overcome their difficulties, as is sometimes inevitable, may find a way of reconciling themselves to the situation—or, on the other hand, they may develop physical ailments, or crippling psychological symptoms. Indeed, to a considerable extent, all abnormal behavior is the result of unsuccessful coping. Some sort of maladjustment occurs between the individual and the environment—especially the social environment: family, friends, fellow workers, bosses, teachers. The individual experiences stress and wants to relieve it—but does not know how (Lazarus, 1978).

Many psychologists today focus on the factors that allow individuals to remain resilient rather than on those factors causing a person to break down (Segal, 1986). Even in the face of major stressors—whether bereavement, severe illness, or being held hostage by terrorists—people show a surprising ability to cope. Some held captive as prisoners of war or hostages, for example, have used their time in prison to teach themselves new languages, learn new skills, write poetry or books, or plan for the years ahead. Under severe stress, many people in everyday life also more than rise to the occasion—thus helping to protect their physical and mental health (Lazarus & Folkman, 1984).

Endogenous causes
Causes of depression that are biological rather than only environmental.

TEST YOURSELF

i) "Luckily, my post-traumatic stress disorder just lasted for a couple hours after the earthquake." What is wrong with that statement?

j) What psychological impact do stressful events involving loss—for example, bereavement or divorce—seem to have?

Coping Assertively

Some psychologists refer to constructive attempts to deal with stress as **assertive coping.** Often such responses take the form of direct attempts to change the stressful situation. Whether the stressor is as mundane as a flat tire that will make us late for an appointment, as challenging as school difficulties, or as harrowing as captivity by cruel enemies, we can usually do something to prevail over our predicament. A motorist frustrated by a flat tire can get busy changing it or find a phone to seek help. A student who wants to be an engineer but is weak in certain areas of mathematics can find a tutor to help master them. Even prisoners of war and civilians seized as hostages—brutally stripped of every physical and psychological means of defending themselves—have found ways to change dire situations.

Americans taken prisoner during the Vietnam War coped assertively for years with the stress of isolation and loneliness. Some adopted a program of physical exercise. Others passed the time by inventing new games, or by memorizing stories. A few kept busy by keeping a careful census of the insects in their cells. Without toothbrushes to preserve their teeth, they kept busy by making picks of bamboo sticks and wire, and dental floss out of threads of their clothing or blankets. Similarly bold coping techniques were used by the 52 American hostages held for 14 months in Iran. As one of them, Ambassador Bruce Laingen, said after his release: "We're like tea bags. We don't know our own strength until we get into hot water."

Assertive coping

Constructive and direct attempts to change stressful situations.

Three Varieties of Coping

We do not need to suffer extreme deprivation in order to cope assertively. We can find constructive ways of dealing with the stresses of everyday life. For example, let's say that we are experiencing frustration, and one of our motives has been blocked. We feel bad about the situation and may even suffer anger so intense that it amounts to rage and sets the stomach churning. Yet, if we can keep our wits about us, perhaps we can somehow manage to overcome the obstacle. We can face up to the difficulty and try to find some way through or around it. We can regard the situation as an exercise in problem solving and get busy seeking the answer, which may take one of the following three forms:

1. Changing the Environment Even a hungry animal, barred from getting food by a closed door, often tries to outwit its environment by gnawing through the barrier. Adolescents growing up in an impoverished and harsh environment work hard to build a life of greater security and comfort. Parents anxious over the threat of a child molester in the community arrange to post monitors at all public playgrounds.

Coping assertively with the environment consists of making a meaningful attempt to change the situation in a constructive way that has a reasonable chance of success. Even though the attempt may fail, the effort itself seems to combat the damaging effects of stress.

2. Changing Behavior In many cases, the stress we suffer comes not so much from the environment as from our own behavior. Failure in college can result from inattention in class or insufficient study. Social unpopularity may reflect a grumpy, timid, or overly aggressive approach to other people. (The way our own actions largely determine other people's behavior toward us is one of the concerns of Chapter 14.)

Thus at times the only effective way to reduce stress is to change our own behavior. For example, people with financial problems often can escape only by setting up a strict budget and resisting their urge to spend (Ilfeld, 1980). The couple who enters marriage counseling will probably find that both partners have to make adjustments in the ways they act toward each other. Indeed people who seek counseling or therapy of any kind are in effect asking for help in changing their behavior and attitudes.

3. Managing the Internal Wear and Tear   Sometimes a stressful situation persists no matter how hard we try to change the environment or our own behavior. During severe economic recessions many people continue to suffer the strains of unemployment and lack of money no matter how far they travel in search of a job. Efforts to cope with the situation by changing their own behavior—such as training themselves for a new line of work—may fail. A person may also be helpless to do anything about such sources of stress as the illness of a family member, the breakup of a love affair, or immovable social, sexual, or racial discrimination.

In situations of genuine helplessness—not learned helplessness—there is just no escape from the source of stress. The only form assertive coping can take is an effort to control the effects. We must somehow keep the physical and emotional wear and tear within bounds, so that they do not destroy us physically or psychologically. There is no magic formula for this kind of coping, but many people have succeeded at it—even those enduring major personal tragedies, or the hundreds of thousands of people who somehow kept their sanity and spirit in the horror of concentration camp captivity. One element in their resilience appears to be the conviction that they had not altogether lost control of their lives.

Staying in Control: A Vital Facet of Coping

The capacity to exert control is important in reducing the amount of stress we experience in a potentially damaging situation. Researchers studied executives of a midwestern utility company, all of whom had experienced various stressful situations, including transfer to a new job in a new city. A comparison was made of the personality traits of those who became ill and those who did not. The executives who escaped illness turned out to have much more of what the researchers termed "hardiness." They tended to have a sense of being responsible for their own destiny. They made vigorous attempts to face and solve their problems, in contrast to the more passive approach of those who became ill (Maddi & Kobasa, 1984).

To be sure, some situations allow us more latitude for control than do others. One study analyzed how the stressors of routine military flight affected pilots and crews. Preflight measurements of cortisol, a stress hormone, were found to be the same for both groups. However, postflight levels were higher in crew members whose activities only indirectly affected the safety of the flight (radio operators, navigators) than they were in pilots—those with their hands literally on the controls of the aircraft (Leedy & Wilson, 1985).

Similarly, among individuals who suffer a chronic disease or disability, those who believe they can manage either the course of their illness or its day-to-day symptoms appear to adapt better psychologically to their condition. There is some evidence, too, that the progress of the disease itself is influenced. For example, a number of studies suggest that cancer, once it has developed, is more apt to spread rapidly in those who readily resign themselves to their fate and "give in" than in those who maintain a fighting attitude (Taylor, 1990).

What happens to people who find themselves chronically in situations where they cannot control what happens to them? Heart disease appears to be more common among those in low-level jobs, particularly jobs that are demanding but where the worker has little opportunity for mastery—for example, jobs on an assembly line (Karasek et al., 1988). A similar finding comes from another study, in which researchers examined the effect of job stress on men across a range of occupations—both white- and blue-collar. Those who had both a highly demanding job and little opportunity for making decisions were more likely to suffer from high blood pressure as well as from undesirable structural changes in the heart (Schnall et al., 1990).

The Importance of Social Support

Another influential element in coping appears to be the quality of our relationships with others. A number of studies have underscored the common wisdom that a **social support network**—including devoted family, friends, colleagues, or fellow members of organizations—appears to offer one of the most effective avenues through which people can escape the damaging consequences of stress (Taylor, 1990; Greenblatt, Becerra, & Serafetinides, 1982).

The importance of social support has been demonstrated in laboratory studies of animals subjected to stress. They show, for example, that merely the presence of a familiar member of the same species lessens the impact of stress (House, Landis, & Umberson, 1988). When the social group is unsta-

Social support network
The network of family, friends, colleagues, or fellow members of organizations that aid a person in escaping the damaging consequences of stress.

Talking with others who share your problems can be therapeutic.

ble—that is, when its composition is changed regularly—the result is a reduction in the capacity of the stressed animal's immune system to function effectively. That is especially true if the animal is by nature a "loner" who finds it difficult to affiliate with others (Coe, 1993).

The availability of social support appears to "inoculate" against depression among people facing difficult life events (Holahan & Moos, 1991)—even such major stressors as family breakup, illness, and job loss. Moreover, sick people who have social supports available to them recover more quickly from physical illness (House, Landis, & Umberson, 1988).

Post-traumatic stress symptoms are also much less likely to take hold in the presence of strong social support. This was true, for example, even for some who survived the incredibly hideous conditions of Nazi concentration camps during World War II (Schmolling, 1984). And combat veterans of the Vietnam War who returned home to supportive family and friends were relatively free from post-traumatic stress problems that so heavily afflicted their comrades (Martin, 1982).

Children also manage to weather stress better if they enjoy social support. In a study of elementary school students, researchers found that youngsters had fewer behavior problems after such uncontrollable stressful events as the death of a parent, parental divorce, or a move to a new home if they received high levels of social support from their family and other children (Dubow & Tisak, 1989).

Members of a social network can provide support in a variety of ways—for example, companionship and assistance with daily tasks and hassles (Rook, 1987); reassurance and emotional strength (Schaefer, Coyne, & Lazarus, 1981); practical advice guidance; and, perhaps, most critical, the sense that one is important, valued, and cared about (Sarason & Sarason, 1985).

Just the simple act of confiding one's thoughts and feelings can have a potent stress-reducing effect. That conclusion has emerged from a variety of studies, among them one involving more than 2,000 people who had suffered trauma of various sorts—including physical abuse, rape, or the death of a loved one. Survivors were healthier if they managed to talk to someone about the event. Those who hadn't discussed their experiences developed more frequent illnesses of various types—from headaches to respiratory disease (Pennebaker, 1989). In another study, students who were asked to reveal, in writing, details of their most traumatic experiences—physical and sexual abuse, abandonment, humiliation—showed more effective immune activity than those who were not asked to do so (Pennebaker, Kielcolt-Glaser, & Glaser, 1988).

The Benefits of Optimism

"Each patient carries his own doctor inside him," said famed physician and humanitarian Albert Schweitzer. There is now reason to believe that attitudes under stress may indeed affect the ways in which the body responds. For example, people with a negative, pessimistic approach to life, particularly those who tend to become depressed or anxious, appear more likely than others to develop coronary artery disease, asthma, headache, ulcers, and arthritis.

We don't yet know why this happens. It may be, of course, that people with a negative attitude act in ways that harm their health, such as smoking or overeating (Taylor, 1990). But it is likely, too, that a pessimistic view of the

Pessimist	Optimist
Internal: "I can't do these math problems. I'm just naturally stupid."	*External:* "These problems were rigged."
Stable: "Math has always been a difficult subject and always will be."	*Unstable:* "With a different teacher, things would be a lot better."
Global: "Doing poorly in math is going to undermine everything I do."	*Specific:* "One test score doesn't make a career."

FIGURE 9.10   Contrasting attributions for stressful events In interpreting stressful events, some individuals show a pessimistic perspective, while others are decidedly more upbeat. This style of reacting makes a difference in the resistance to stress when crises occur (Peterson & Seligman, 1984).

future and the accompanying feelings of depression act to impair the body's immune system through biochemical changes in the nervous system (Rodin, 1980). One source of evidence is a study of a group of Harvard graduates who were evaluated over a period of 40 years. Initially, there were no significant health differences between those identified as optimists and pessimists; all were in good health at age 25 when the study began. But the health of the pessimists started to deteriorate at age 45 and continued to do so through age 60 (Seligman, 1988), reflecting a weakened immunity to disease.

Optimists and pessimists make sharply contrasting interpretations of the events in their lives. As Figure 9.10 shows, some people are quick to conclude that the crises they face are entirely of their own doing, that their reaction will last, and that it will undermine everything they do. These are essentially pessimists. Others, who are optimists, view the crises they face as arising from external circumstances, as transient, and as unrelated to the rest of their lives. The sources of such contrasting attitudes are undoubtedly varied, including temperamental and environmental influences. It has been found, for example, that members of fundamentalist religious groups have more optimistic attitudes than those of moderate or liberal groups. The differences may well be accounted for by the relatively hopeful attitude toward life that fundamentalism engenders, along with the greater optimism reflected in the actual content of religious services (Sethi & Seligman, 1993).

Whatever its sources, there is evidence that an upbeat, positive view of life can significantly enhance well-being and perhaps even longevity. The evidence comes from a study of the causal explanations of events on the ball field given by members of the Baseball Hall of Fame. Explanations of the outcome of games were gathered from the sports pages of the *New York Times* and the *Philadelphia Inquirer.* Interviewed by reporters after the game, some players displayed an optimistic, explanatory style—for example, "We lost because our top hitter had a sore finger, but he'll be OK in a day or two," or "We picked off the runner because my catcher and I have perfected our signals." Other players gave neutral or pessimistic explanations of events on the ball field— for example, "My aim is still good but I don't have the stuff I used to." It turns out that those who interpreted the game results optimistically lived considerably longer than the others (Seligman, 1986).

There is growing evidence that thoughts, expectations, and hopes affect the body's stress reactions more than the actual stressful experience itself. Even laughter may be beneficial. One researcher showed college students funny movies and discovered that this activity temporarily raised their immunity levels (D. C. McClelland, 1989). The role of humor in fighting stress is further discussed in the Psychology and the Media box entitled "Stress? Laugh It Off."

Stress? Laugh It Off

Humor is one of the best on-the-spot stress busters around. It's virtually impossible to belly laugh and feel bad at the same time. If you're caught in a situation you can't escape or change (a traffic jam, for example), then humor may be the healthiest form of temporary stress release possible.

Even when you can change the situation, humor helps. Research by Alice M. Isen, a psychologist at Cornell University, in Ithaca, N.Y., shows that people who had just watched a short comedy film were better able to find creative solutions to puzzling problems than people who had either just watched a film about math or had just exercised. In other studies, Isen found that shortly after watching or experiencing comedy, people were able to think more clearly and were better able to "see" the consequences of a given decision.

The physiological effects of a good laugh work against stress. After a slight rise in heart rate and blood pressure during the laugh itself, there's an immediate recoil: muscles relax and blood pressure sinks below pre-laugh levels and the brain may release endorphins, the same stress reducers that are triggered by exercise. A hearty ha-ha-ha also provides a muscle massage for facial muscles, the diaphragm and the abdomen. Studies show it even temporarily boosts levels of immunoglobulin A, a virus-fighter found in saliva. While our cave-dwelling ancestors were stressed by actual life-threatening situations like bumping into a woolly mammoth, times have changed. "Nowadays, stress is usually not caused by the situation itself, but by how we perceive that situation," says Allen Elkin, program director of Manhattan's Stress Management and Counseling Centers. Getting a new perspective is what comedy is all about. Several philosophers and writers have pointed out that comedy and tragedy are different ways of looking at the same stressful event. Comedy works by stepping back from

a situation and playing up its absurdities. The same kind of disinterested observation makes the tale of your disastrous vacation seem funny—after you get safely home. For stress busting, the trick is to find ways to laugh at the situation while it is happening. Even if you don't consider yourself much of a comedian, here are a few simple techniques you can use:

- **The Bart Simpson Maneuver.** How would your favorite cartoon character or comedian react to the situation? "Imagining what would happen can give you a chuckle, making the situation less annoying. You can pretend you're the star of a TV comedy, and this frustrating episode is tonight's plot," says Steve Allen Jr., an assistant professor of family medicine at SUNY Health Science Center, Syracuse (yes, he is the son of comedian Steve Allen).
- **Ballooning.** In your mind, consciously exaggerate the situation:

There is much still to be learned about the extent to which our outlook serves as a healing force. No doctor can prescribe hopeful optimism. Yet, as illustrated in Figure 9.11, this seems to aid the recovery of people with serious illnesses, occasionally to the point of enabling them to defy all medical predictions (Cousins, 1989).

Exercise as a Means of Coping

It seems to be commonly assumed that exercise makes us feel better. Millions of us engage in regular exercise routines such as walking, jogging, running, and biking, or we participate in classes that feature exercise regimens—and many of us do so, at least in part, because we feel a greater sense of well-being as a result.

Are such subjective experiences corroborated through research? In general, the answer is yes. People of all ages—from early childhood through mature adulthood—who stay fit through exercise show less evidence of stress when faced with difficult stressors than those who do not (Stephens, 1988;

Blow it completely out of proportion and into absurdity—into a comedy routine. In that long, long checkout line, don't say, "This waiting is killing me; I hate this." Say: "I'll never get to the front of this checkout line. The woman ahead of me is covered in cobwebs. The guy in front of her grew a beard standing in line. The cashier must be part snail. The continental drift moves faster." This maneuver helps take the edge off the situation, redirects your tension and helps you see things as not so impossible after all. Your running commentary, however, is probably best kept to yourself. If people stare at you because you seem to be laughing for no reason, pretend you're reading the scandal sheets. You don't have to be a master of one-liners to be funny. There are gentler forms of humor that can defuse anxiety in a group without making anyone feel like the butt of the joke.

- **Pick a Target.** Making fun of your own foibles can save face in an embarrassing situation—you'll have people laughing with you, rather than at you. Inanimate sources of frustration, like computers and copying machines, are also safe objects of humor.
- **Laying It on the Line.** Sometimes just telling the truth or pointing out the obvious can get a laugh. People are accustomed to exaggeration and truth-bending (too many TV commercials, perhaps), so plain speaking can come as a refreshing shock. For example, after delivering a series of lengthy explanations during a question-and-answer period, some people have been known to put everyone in stitches by simply replying to the next question with "Gee, I don't know." "This kind of humor is a way of fighting stress by accepting our shortcomings," says Joel Goodman, director of the Humor Project in Saratoga

Springs, N.Y.
- **Clip a Cartoon.** Keep a file of jokes and cartoons that make *you* laugh. Paste a few up where you're likely to need them—at work, on the refrigerator, wherever.

Issues to Consider

1. Can you think of an experiment that might test the hypothesis put forth in this article?
2. This chapter began with a discussion of the various types of stressors we are likely to face in life. For which of them do you think the use of humor would be most appropriate, and for which most inappropriate?

Source: From "Stress? Laugh It Off" by Stephen Lally, 1991, *Washington Post,* August 28.

J.D. Brown, 1991). There is some evidence, too, that sustained exercise can be an effective way to improve mood—as illustrated in Figure 9.12.

It is not clear, however, what mechanisms are involved in producing such results. Among the possibilities are that exercise produces deeper, more relax-

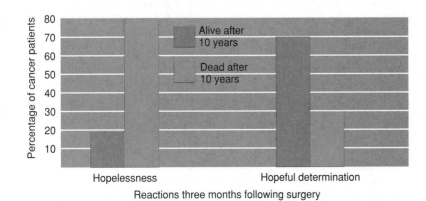

FIGURE 9.11 Attitude and longevity after cancer surgery After breast cancer surgery, women who felt their cause was hopeless had a much lower survival rate than those who harbored a sense of optimistic determination (Pettingale, et al., 1985).

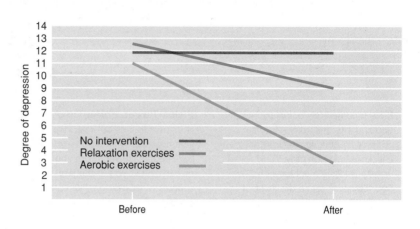

FIGURE 9.12 **Exercise and depression** A group of mildly depressed women engaged in one of two self-help programs, while a third group engaged in neither. As shown here, those that practiced aerobic exercise clearly enjoyed the greatest improvement (after McCann and Holmes, 1984).

Defense mechanisms
The unconscious psychological processes that people develop to relieve anxiety.

ing sleep (U. S. Department of Health and Human Services, 1981), or that it enhances the individual's sense of worth and self-concept (Hogan, 1989), or even that it raises the level of mood-altering endorphins produced by the brain. Perhaps all of these—and more—are involved. Even without knowing why exercise reduces stress reactions, the pursuit of regular physical activity would appear to be a wise approach for helping us handle the variety of stressors that inevitably come our way.

Defense Mechanisms: Problematic Coping Through Self-Deception

Unfortunately, not everyone handles stress in a positive fashion, using techniques of assertive coping. Many individuals use less successful ways to deal with the painful psychological consequences of stressful events. Prominent among them are devices called **defense mechanisms,** first described by Sigmund Freud. Freud regarded these mechanisms as unconscious psychological processes that people develop to relieve anxiety. Unlike assertive coping, defense mechanisms are not deliberate efforts to change the environment or one's own behavior or to deal realistically with stress and anxiety. All defense mechanisms are based to some degree on self-deception and distortion of reality. Yet everybody adopts some of them at one time or another.

By and large, defense mechanisms are not as effective as assertive coping in dealing with stress. They may serve as stopgaps in an emergency. They may even be practiced over long periods, as a sort of life strategy, with some success and without serious damage. But when carried to extremes, they carry a serious risk. They lie in a sort of gray area between successful coping and downright failure to cope—or, in other words, between normal and abnormal behavior.

Rationalization

One defense mechanism has been recognized ever since Aesop started the phrase "sour grapes" with his fable about the fox. (The fox, unable to reach an inviting cluster of grapes, consoled itself by deciding they would have been

Exercise will not make problems disappear, but it can help us manage the wear and tear of stress.

sour anyway.) Freud's name for this defense mechanism is **rationalization**—an attempt to deal with stressful situations by claiming that the stressor was of minimal importance and may have even had beneficial effects.

People often resort to rationalization to explain away their frustrations. A man, rejected by a woman, convinces himself that she was not nearly so attractive or interesting as he had supposed. A woman, turned down when applying for employment, convinces herself that the job was not really worth having. People also use rationalization to reduce the stress and anxiety caused by conflicts between motives and inner standards. As an example, a student cheats on an examination and rationalizes by claiming that everybody cheats.

Repression

As discussed earlier, people sometimes feel stress because of internal conflict over their motives. To deal with the anxiety this causes them, they may try to banish the offending motive from their conscious thoughts—to the point where they seem to be totally unaware of their original desires. This defense mechanism is called **repression.** People who at one time suffered severe stress and anxiety over sexual motives may repress these motives so thoroughly that they no longer seem to be aware of any sexual feelings or desires at all. Other people seem oblivious to the fact that they have any desires for dependency or hostility. Some cases of amnesia, or loss of memory, appear to be exaggerated forms of repression.

Sublimation

A motive that causes conflict and anxiety may also be transformed unconsciously into a different but related motive that is more acceptable to society and to oneself. This defense mechanism is known as **sublimation,** a process that enables a "shameful" motive to find expression in a more noble form. Freud believed that works of art are often the result of sublimation—that the

Rationalization

A defense mechanism in which a person attempts to deal with stressful situations by claiming that the stressor was of minimal importance and may have even had beneficial effects.

Repression

A defense mechanism in which a person tries to banish the offending motive from the conscious thoughts to the point of being totally unaware of the original desires.

Sublimation

A defense mechanism in which a person unconsciously transforms conflict and anxiety into a different but related motive that is more acceptable to society and to oneself.

Shakespeares and Michelangelos of the world may very well have channeled forbidden sexual urges into artistic creativity. Similarly, Freud believed that people may sublimate their urges toward cruelty into a socially approved desire to become surgeons, prosecuting attorneys, or even teachers with the authority to discipline the young.

Identification

Identification

A defense mechanism in which a person takes on the virtues of an admired person.

Another mechanism for relieving stress and anxiety is to take on the virtues of some admired person or group that seems free of such anxiety. This process is called **identification.** An example would be a man, anxious about his own lack of courage, who identifies with a brave movie hero or a group of mountain climbers so that he can believe he too possesses their daring. A woman anxious about her lack of social acceptance may identify with a popular roommate.

In a more complex form, identification may be established with a figure of authority who is resented and feared. Thus a young man may defend himself against the anxiety aroused by hostile feelings toward his boss by identifying with the boss. He may imitate the boss's mannerisms and express the same opinions, thus persuading himself that he possesses the same power. This type of identification may also be made with a group. Young people, anxious about their feelings of envy and hostility toward an exclusive clique, may identify with the group and adopt its standards.

Reaction Formation

Reaction formation

A defense mechanism in which a person pretends to possess motives that are the opposite of the motives that are causing conflict and anxiety.

People who display a trait to excess—that is, in an exaggerated form that hardly seems called for by the circumstances—may be using the defense mechanism called **reaction formation.** They are pretending to possess motives that are the exact opposite of the motives that are actually causing them conflict and anxiety. For example, a woman appears to be the soul of politeness. She is constantly holding doors for other people, always smiling, agreeable, and apologetic for her mistakes. This exaggerated politeness and concern for others may simply be a defense mechanism she has adopted to conceal the fact that she has very hostile motives that make her anxious. A man who dresses in a flamboyant manner and is constantly flirting and telling risqué stories may be concealing his anxiety and sexual inhibitions.

Projection

Projection

A defense mechanism in which a person attributes to others the motives or thoughts that have caused personal conflict.

The woman who claims that everybody is dishonest and the man who is convinced of the immorality of the younger generation may have reached their conclusions through honest examination of the evidence. On the other hand, they may be exhibiting another defense mechanism called **projection,** in which people attribute to others—that is, project onto them—their own motives or thoughts that cause them conflict. The woman who complains too much about dishonesty may be concealing her own strong tendencies toward dishonesty. The man who talks too much about the immorality of young people may be concealing his own promiscuity.

Projection often plays a part in disagreements between the sexes. A woman may complain that her mate is distant and remote, although a disinterested observer may clearly see that it is she who is actually withdrawn and inaccessible. A man who is torn by sexual conflicts and urges toward infidelity may falsely accuse his partner of being unfaithful. A marriage counselor who hears accusations by one partner of unacceptable behavior or improper motives always looks for the possibility that the complaints represent projection rather than truth. Projection is one of the most powerful and dangerous of the defense mechanisms. It works very effectively to reduce anxiety, but it does so at the risk of a completely distorted view of the truth about oneself and others.

Other Defense Mechanisms

The six defense mechanisms just discussed are the most common and easily recognizable. There are numerous others, however, that are called into play as means for coping with intolerable stress (Horowitz, 1988). Among them, for example, are the following:

- **Denial**—The attempt to dispel anxiety by refusing altogether to accept reality. (How many heavy drinkers, for example, successfully block out the fact that their habit can cause serious problems?) We humans are remarkably ingenious at finding new ways to delude ourselves. In one way or another, we persuade ourselves that we did not really want the goals we cannot achieve, that our motives are completely admirable, that we are living up to our own and society's standards, that our disappointments are somehow bearable, and that a threatening situation is really no threat at all.

- **Displacement**—The attempt to escape the discomfort of unwanted ideas or feelings by transferring them onto another person, situation, or object. Thus a person angry at her boss may suddenly pick a quarrel with a friend; in that way the friend rather than the boss becomes the

Denial
A defense mechanism in which a person attempts to dispel anxiety by refusing altogether to accept reality.

Displacement
A defense mechanism in which a person tries to escape the discomfort of unwanted ideas or feelings by transferring them onto another person.

Some adolescents who feel that they cannot deal with a problem at home run away to avoid the source of stress. By doing so, however, they expose themselves to new anxieties.

object of the anger. A person worried about the possibility that his mind is failing may transform this into worry about his body; he might then develop an exaggerated fear of having cancer.

Acting out

A defense mechanism in which a person takes action impulsively without weighing the consequences in order to avoid the stress of having to spend the time weighing conflicting courses of action.

- **Acting out**—Taking action impulsively without weighing its consequences, thus avoiding the stress of having to spend time weighing conflicting courses of action. An unhappy teenager, for example, may suddenly run away from home instead of considering such alternative steps as a confrontation with his parents or giving in to their demands.

Regression

A defense mechanism in which a person retreats toward behaviors that usually characterize a lower level of maturity.

- **Regression**—A retreat toward behaviors that usually characterize a lower level of maturity. Displays of regression as a reaction to frustration and stress are common. Frustrated adults may regress to such childish behavior as throwing temper tantrums. Many parents have described how their children, faced with frustration, begin to behave in a manner more appropriate to younger levels of development. The arrival of a new and competing sibling can be the occasion for a child already in the first grade to begin bed-wetting for example, or thumb-sucking. People who are victims of extreme emotional disturbance sometimes display striking degrees of regression, as illustrated in Figure 9.13.

When Defenses Falter

Because conflict and stress are so common, all of us use defense mechanisms from time to time—either those that have been mentioned or others of our own invention. Though these defense mechanisms are usually irrational, they often serve a useful purpose. They may help us through crises that would otherwise overwhelm and disable us. If nothing else, they may gain us time in which we can gather the strength, maturity, and knowledge needed to cope more realistically and constructively with our anxiety and stress. This is

FIGURE 9.13 A case of regression The girl at the left, a 17-year-old psychiatric patient, found the old photograph of herself in the center, taken when she was 5. She then cut her hair and made every attempt to look as she had at 5, as at the right (Masserman, 1961).

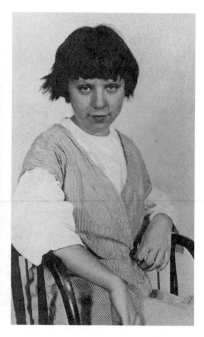

often true, for example, of cancer patients who practice denial until they are emotionally ready to face up to their bleak prognosis (Breznitz, 1983).

In extreme cases, of course, the use of defense mechanisms slips over into the realm of the abnormal. When efforts to cope by employing defense mechanisms no longer work, and when such problematic devices as acting out or regression get out of hand, the human personality falls apart. The result is one or another of the various psychological disorders to be described in detail in the next chapter.

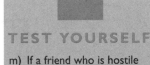

TEST YOURSELF

m) If a friend who is hostile accuses you of being angry, what defense mechanism is being displayed?

SUMMARY REVIEW

Sources of Stress: Life's Varied Stressors

1. Most psychologists view **stress** as a physical and psychological response to a harmful or potentially harmful circumstance.

2. The circumstances that produce stress are best referred to as **stressors**—the events or conditions that put a strain on the organism and pose a challenge to adjust.

3. Throughout the life span, humans confront the reality of a world filled with stressors—from the hunger of the newborn to the physical and psychological decline of the aged.

4. Among the circumstances that constitute stressors are life crises such as bereavement and divorce, transitions such as getting married or starting a new job, catastrophes such as earthquakes and fires, and daily hassles— that is, an accumulation of seemingly minor irritations.

5. Three kinds of life crises are especially damaging psychologically
   a) the loss of an important relationship
   b) uncontrollable events
   c) events that pose long-term threats.

6. Stress can also arise from within the individual. Involved are frustration—which is the blocking of motive satisfaction by some kind of obstacle; and **conflict**—the simultaneous arousal of two or more incompatible motives, resulting in unpleasant emotions such as anxiety or anger.

7. Four types of conflict are
   a) **approach-approach** (seeking two desirable goals)
   b) **avoidance-avoidance** (seeking to prevent two undesirable alternatives)
   c) **approach-avoidance** (choosing a goal that will have both pleasant and unpleasant aspects)
   d) **double approach-avoidance** (having to choose between two goals that both have some desirable and some undesirable aspects).

8. Any situation clouded with uncertainty has a built-in potential for creating stress.

9. A person's **cognitive appraisal,** or subjective interpretation, of a potentially stressful episode strongly influences that individual's response.

10. In **primary appraisal,** the individual assesses the personal meaning of the stressor at hand. In **secondary appraisal,** the individual assesses the options available for coping.

Stress and Physical Health

11. The damaging potential of stress was demonstrated by Hans Selye in experiments with animals subjected to small doses of poison. Selye found that the body automatically tries to defend itself in ways that include striking changes in activity of the endocrine glands, especially the adrenals. After a time the body seems to adapt and the glands return to normal. If the stressful conditions continue, however, the recovery proves to be only temporary and the animal dies—killed by an excess of hormones the body produced in its own defense. This sequence of events is called the **general adaptation syndrome.**

12. The bodily changes described by Selye also seem to occur in human beings, often as part of the stress caused by frustration, conflict, or any prolonged emotional upset. They often take the form of **psychosomatic illnesses,** bodily ailments that stem at least in part from mental and emotional causes.

13. The reasons why some people get sick and some do not can be attributed to differences in
    a) interpretations of any given stressful event
    b) coping skills
    c) outside emotional support
    d) level of physical fitness.

14. The **immune system** is the body's intricate defense network of cellular organs and tissues that protect cells against diseases. Studies of the impact of stress on the human immune system suggest that the net effect is a depression of immunity, and, therefore, a vulnerability to becoming ill.

15. **Psychoneuroimmunology,** a new field of research activity, focuses on the interaction of psychological and physical processes that influence the body's capacity to fend off disease.

16. How an individual fares under stress often reflects the overall psychological makeup, or personality, of the individual.

Stress and Mental Health

17. One prominent response to stress is **anxiety**—which can be defined as a vague, unpleasant feeling accompanied by a premonition that something undesirable is about to happen.

18. People high in anxiety do better than others at simple learning tasks but more poorly at difficult learning tasks. In college, anxiety does not seem to affect the grades of students of either highest or lowest learning ability. Among students of average ability, those with high anxiety make significantly lower grades than those with low anxiety.

19. Survivors of extremely traumatic events are sometimes left with special anxiety problems, called **post-traumatic stress disorder** (**PTSD**), marked by symptoms of stress that can linger for years.

20. The psychological effects of stress include **depression,** a common emotional disturbance often triggered by experiences that leave an individual with a sense of loss.

The Ways We Cope

21. **Assertive coping** is an effective defense against stress. It may take three forms:
    a) changing the environment and relieving the stressful situation
    b) changing one's own behavior
    c) keeping the emotional and physical wear and tear within bounds.
22. Successful coping often entails the ability to maintain a sense of control over the environment, the availability of a social support network, and an attitude of hopeful optimism.

Defense Mechanisms: Problematic Coping Through Self-Deception

23. Among questionable forms of coping are the **defense mechanisms** described by Freud. These are unconscious psychological processes, mental or symbolic, developed to relieve anxiety. They include:
    a) **rationalization**   d) **identification**
    b) **repression**   e) **reaction formation**
    c) **sublimation**   f) **projection.**
24. Other questionable reactions to anxiety and stress include:
    a) **denial**   c) **acting out**
    b) **displacement**   d) **regression.**

TEST YOURSELF ANSWERS

a) The experience is correctly referred to as a stressor—that is, an event that puts a strain on an individual and poses a challenge to adjust. It is the physical or psychological reaction to the house-robbing that is correctly referred to as stress.
b) There is no such age, for stress is a factor to reckon with throughout the life span.
c) They are trying to avoid uncertainty and doubt.
d) Your friend is overlooking the importance of cognitive appraisal—in other words, the subjective interpretation of a potentially stressful episode.
e) The term Selye applied to this pattern is the general adaptation syndrome.
f) Psychosomatic complaints are not imaginary. They concern actual bodily ailments that stem in part from mental and emotional causes.
g) The scientist is working in the field of psychoneuroimmunology—which is devoted to the study of the interaction of psychological and physiological processes that influence the body's capacity to fend off disease.
h) Anger can be a springboard for constructive action.
i) That statement is wrong because post-traumatic stress disorder is made up of a set of symptoms that tend to last for a long time—even for many years.
j) Such events typically produce depression.
k) It might be helpful by providing the child with some sense of control over the stressful experience.
l) All three are appropriately termed a social support network.
m) Your friend is displaying projection.

Study Guide

Chapter 9   Stress, Coping, and Health

LEARNING OBJECTIVES

After studying this chapter, you should be able to:

For an Understanding of the Science

1. Understand the distinction between the terms "stress" and "stressor."

2. Describe the various sources of human stress.

3. Describe Selye's general adaptation syndrome, which explains what takes place in the body during periods of prolonged stress, and the relationship between stress and psychosomatic illness.

4. Comprehend the impact of stress on the body's immune system.

5. Be familiar with the two prominent psychological experiences that accompany stress: anxiety and depression.

6. Realize the impact that anxiety can have on human behavior and performance.

7. Understand the three forms of assertive coping: (a) changing the situation, (b) changing behavior, and (c) managing internal wear and tear.

For Application to Life Situations

8. Grasp that the defense mechanisms people use are unconscious attempts to reduce anxiety; define the defense mechanisms known as rationalization, repression, sublimation, identification, reaction formation, and projection.

9. Understand that the stress response is an individual matter, colored by the individual's cognitive appraisal, or subjective interpretation, of a potentially stressful episode.

10. Know what is meant by frustration and conflict—and how these can give rise to stress.

11. Know how stress can cause bodily illness. Recall Selye's prescription for leading a healthy and fulfilling life: to live to the hilt in savoring excitement and emotionality but not to go beyond your own individual ability to tolerate stress.

12. Remember that stressful events include not only misfortunes but pleasurable happenings—such as getting married, having a baby, or getting a new job.

13. Remember that high levels of anxiety, unless overcome, can affect the ability to learn.

14. Keep in mind that a sense of inner control, the availability of social supports, and an optimistic outlook are important keys to coping.

PROGRAMMED UNIT

SOURCES OF STRESS: LIFE'S VARIED STRESSORS

1. Most psychologists view *stress* as a physical and psychological response to a harmful or potentially harmful circumstance—in other words to anything that threatens to damage the organism. Thus events such as an earthquake

or the loss of a loved one can produce the physical and psychological response we call _____.

stress

response

2. Stress is the _____ we make to anything that threatens to damage the organism. These events and conditions that put a strain on the organism and pose a challenge to adjust are known as *stressors.*

3. John faces both a critical final exam and a broken romance. Such events, which put a strain on him and pose a challenge to adjust, are known as

_____.

stressors

4. An event or condition that can produce stress is known as a _____. These can range from everyday irritations to devastating catastrophes. Personal crises such as a crippling accident, divorce, or financial ruin are usually referred to as life crises.

stressor

5. Stressors involving personal upheavals such as a crippling illness or the breakup of a marriage are referred to as _____ _____. These constitute major life transitions, or changes, which can also produce stress even if they are basically joyous—for example, marriage or beginning college.

life crises

6. Marriage as well as divorce can be a source of stress since each is a major _____, or change. Another major source of stress is comprised of events such as earthquakes, fires, hurricanes, floods—or catastrophes.

transition

7. Both a job change and a damaging flood put a strain on the individual's capacity to adjust, and, therefore, are _____. Floods, like fires or tornadoes, represent a type of _____ that can be described as a _____. Another source of stress is referred to as *daily hassles,* or seemingly minor irritations.

stressors

stressor

catastrophe

8. When compared to a life crisis or major catastrophe, a flat tire seems like a minor irritation. Yet such irritations, or daily _____ can be a source of stress. So can *conflict,* which psychologists define as the simultaneous arousal of two or more incompatible motives, resulting in unpleasant emotions.

hassles

9. When two or more incompatible motives are aroused at the same time, the result is called _____.

conflict

10. When we are torn between studying and going to a movie, we are in conflict because of the simultaneous arousal of incompatible _____.

motives

11. The simultaneous arousal of incompatible motives results in unpleasant

_____.

emotions

12. Unpleasant emotions are the likely result of _____, one type of which occurs between a motive and an inner standard.

conflict

13. When a student is tempted to cheat on an examination to get a good grade but feels inwardly that cheating is wrong, the student is experiencing a conflict between a motive and an inner _____. Another type of conflict occurs because of the arousal of two motives aimed at different and incompatible goals.

standard

14. When we are torn between studying and going to the movies, we are in conflict because our motives are aimed at two different and _____ goals.

incompatible

15. When the aroused motives are directed toward two desirable goals, both of which the person wants to approach and attain, it is called an *approach-approach conflict.* As in all cases of conflict, the result is likely to be unpleasant _____.

emotions

approach

approach-approach

desirable

avoidance-avoidance

unpleasant

approach-avoidance, double

cognitive, stressor

appraisal

stress
cognitive appraisal

primary

cognitive, secondary

stressor

16. A conflict between motives directed toward two desirable goals is an _____-approach conflict.

17. A student who wants to stay up and watch a late-night movie—and at the same time wants to get a good night's sleep—faces an _____-_____ conflict.

18. Fred is a college sophomore who must now declare a major area of study. He always dreamed of being a lawyer, but he also wants to enter the field of electronics. Fred faces an approach-approach conflict, or a conflict between motives directed toward two _____ goals. A conflict may also occur between motives to avoid two unpleasant alternatives; this is called an *avoidance-avoidance conflict.*

19. Jane, too keyed up to sleep, wants to avoid the unpleasantness of tossing and turning in bed—but she also wants to avoid the grogginess she will feel tomorrow if she decides to take a sleeping pill. Jane faces an _____-_____ conflict.

20. Mary hates to go to the dentist and would like nothing better than to cancel her appointment. But she has lost a filling and knows that her tooth will soon start to hurt. She faces an avoidance-avoidance conflict, or a conflict between motives to avoid two _____ alternatives. In contrast, an *approach-avoidance conflict* occurs when fulfilling a motive will have both pleasant and unpleasant consequences.

21. Because having a baby creates both pleasant and stressful circumstances, it can turn out to pose an _____-_____ conflict. A _____ *approach-avoidance conflict* takes place when we are torn between two goals, each of which has both pleasant and unpleasant consequences.

22. The experience of stress depends on the subjective interpretation, or _____ appraisal, we make of a stressful event, or _____.

23. One person faces an illness with little stress, another with a great deal. The difference lies in the cognitive _____ of the condition. Such subjective interpretations of stressors are of two kinds. In the first, or *primary appraisal,* the individual assesses the personal meaning of the stressor at hand.

24. The physical or psychological response we make to a harmful or potentially harmful circumstance is known as _____. The response depends on our _____ _____ of the event or circumstance.

25. The assessment of the personal meaning of the stressor at hand is known as _____ appraisal. In *secondary appraisal,* we assess the coping alternatives available.

26. Mary, who is facing surgery, wonders what she can do to handle the situation. In surveying her coping alternatives, she is engaging in one of the two forms of _____ appraisal referred to as _____ appraisal.

STRESS AND PHYSICAL HEALTH

27. In experiments with animals subjected to small doses of poison, Selye found that the body automatically tries to defend itself from stress through activity of the endocrine glands, especially the adrenals. In these experiments, the introduction of poison was the threatening event, or what psychologists call the _____.

28. Selye, in describing what he called the *general adaptation syndrome,* found that after the body is subjected for a time to stressful conditions, it seems to adapt and return to normal. But if the stressful conditions continue, the recovery process proves to be only temporary and the animal dies—killed by an excess of hormones produced in its own defense by the body's endocrine glands, primarily the _____.

29. To describe the sequence of events that takes place during prolonged stress, Selye coined the term _____ _____ _____.

30. A pattern of bodily changes by which the body attempts to adapt to stress was described by _____.

31. Stress in human beings caused by frustration and conflict can be just as drastic as the kind Selye produced by injecting _____ into animals. The physical results often take the form of *psychosomatic illness,* meaning bodily ailments that stem at least in part from mental and emotional causes.

32. In human beings, the workings of the general adaptation syndrome often produce bodily ailments called _____ _____.

33. Jim, who gets an attack of severe indigestion every time he is forced to work under intense pressure, is a victim of _____ _____.

34. The likelihood of psychosomatic illness is determined in part by the amount of _____ a person experiences—but also by individual differences in physical as well as psychological reactions to outside pressures.

35. Mark developed asthmatic attacks when his parents were divorced, but his twin brother apparently suffered no ill effects. This can be explained in part by individual _____ in response to stressful experiences.

36. Selye, who coined the phrase "general _____ syndrome," believed that the secret of a healthy and fulfilling life is to live to the full extent of our capabilities—but within the limits of our own ability to tolerate stress. In some cases, an overload of stress affects the *immune system*—the body's intricate defense network of organs and tissues that produce protective cells such as white blood cells.

37. Stress can affect the body's _____ system, which produces the body's protective cells. A new field of research, called *psychoneuroimmunology,* focuses on the interaction of psychological and physical processes that influence the body's capacity to fend off disease.

38. A psychologist who studies the interaction of psychological and physical processes that influence the body's capacity to fend off disease is working in a field called _____.

STRESS AND MENTAL HEALTH

39. Along with the body's stress responses, often producing _____ illness, go a number of painful psychological effects. Prominent among them is *anxiety,* which is an unpleasant feeling accompanied by a premonition that something undesirable is about to happen.

40. Stress can produce painful _____ effects as well as physical symptoms.

41. Among the painful psychological effects of stress is _____, an

adrenals

general adaptation syndrome

Selye

poison

psychosomatic illness

psychosomatic illness

stress

differences
adaptation

immune

psychoneuroimmunology

psychosomatic

psychological

anxiety

unpleasant feeling accompanied by a premonition that something undesirable is about to happen. The feeling is closely related to fear.

anxiety

fear

cognitive

stress
disorder

PTSD

post-traumatic

depression
physical

stress

depression

noradrenalin

low
reduced

endogenous

42. "I go around with the sense that something bad is going to happen any minute now." A person who says that is experiencing _____.

43. The feeling of _____ is closely related to anxiety, which can affect cognitive performance.

44. High anxiety can keep a student from achieving his usual grades—showing that anxiety can affect _____ performance. Some people who endure extremely traumatic stressors such as natural disasters, rape, accidents, or war combat are left with special anxiety problems called *post-traumatic stress disorder, or PTSD.*

45. Survivors of deadly fires or of concentration camps are among those left with special anxiety stress problems called post-traumatic _____ _____.

46. This condition is also known as _____.

47. PTSD is a short term for _____-_____ stress disorder. Another psychological outcome of stress is an emotional disturbance known as *depression,* which can have physical causes as well.

48. Along with anxiety, stress can result in feelings of _____, a common emotional disturbance arising from both psychological and _____ causes.

49. Depression seems to be associated with low levels or reduced efficiency of the brain's supply of the neurotransmitter called noradrenalin—which demonstrates how the physical and psychological effects of _____ are sometimes intermingled.

50. A common emotional disturbance in which the physical and psychological effects of stress are difficult to separate is _____.

51. Depression appears to be related to the activity of the brain's supply of the neurotransmitter called _____.

52. In depression the brain's supply of noradrenalin is _____, or its efficiency is _____.

53. When depression is caused by internal, or biological, factors rather than only environmental ones, it is referred to as _____ depression.

THE WAYS WE COPE

stressors

cope

psychosomatic
depression

assertive

assertive
coping

54. Some people try to deal with the causes of stress, or the _____ they face, which means they are trying to *cope.*

55. A person who tries to deal with the causes of stress is attempting to _____. Psychologists apply the term *assertive coping* to constructive attempts to deal with anxiety and stress. Failure to cope may result in physical ailments, called _____ illness, or psychological problems such as the common disturbance called _____.

56. A student who tries to overcome his anxiety over a failing grade by studying harder is engaging in _____ coping.

57. Constructive attempts to deal with anxiety and stress are called _____ _____, one form of which is to change the environment and thus relieve the stressful situation.

58. A motorist suffering anxiety over a flat tire that has delayed a trip can cope assertively by changing the tire or seeking help, thus attempting to _____ the environment.

change

59. In many cases, the stress we suffer comes not so much from the environment as from our own behavior—and changing that behavior is another form of assertive _____.

coping

60. At times the only effective way to reduce _____ is to change our own behavior.

stress

61. People who seek counseling or therapy are asking for help in coping by changing their _____.

behavior

62. Assertive coping, in addition to changing the _____ or our own _____, can take the form of managing the internal wear and tear produced by stress.

environment
behavior

63. A person may be helpless to do anything about some sources of stress such as the illness of a family member. In such cases, the only form assertive coping can take is to keep the internal _____ and _____ within bounds. The capacity to exert control is important in reducing the amount of stress we feel in a potentially damaging situation.

wear, tear

64. Individuals facing difficult stressors are likely to suffer less stress if they feel they have the capacity to exert _____ over the situation. Another influential element in coping appears to be the quality of our relationship with others—that is, our *social support network,* made up of family, friends, colleagues, or fellow members of organizations.

control

65. The harmful effects of stress can be reduced by the availability of good relationships with family, friends, colleagues, or fellow organization members—that is, by a _____ support _____.

social, network

DEFENSE MECHANISMS: PROBLEMATIC COPING THROUGH SELF-DECEPTION

66. Some questionable forms of coping with stress lie in the gray area between successful coping and downright failure to cope, which can lead to both _____ and _____ symptoms.

physical, psychological

67. Prominent among questionable forms of coping with _____ are *defense mechanisms,* which are unconscious psychological processes based to some degree on self-deception and distortion of reality.

stress

68. Defense mechanisms, first described by Freud, are _____ processes.

unconscious

69. Forms of coping described as unconscious psychological processes that are based to some degree on self-deception and distortion are called _____ _____.

defense mechanisms

70. *Rationalization,* one of the defense mechanisms first described by _____, is an attempt to deal with stressful situations by claiming that they never occurred.

Freud

71. Aesop's fable about the fox, unable to reach the grapes, that consoled itself by deciding they would have been sour anyway is a good example of _____.

rationalization

72. A college student who, after failing to make the team, convinces himself that he did not want to waste his time on athletics anyway is probably using the _____ _____ called rationalization.

defense mechanisms

unconscious	73. People suffering anxiety over their motives may use the defense mechanism known as *repression*—or simply banishing the motives from their thoughts. Like rationalization, repression is an _____ psychological process.
repression	74. John frequently behaves in ways other people consider hostile, yet seems totally unaware of any hostile motives. He is probably using the defense mechanism known as _____.
repression	75. Unlike _____, by which people banish anxiety-provoking motives from their awareness, *sublimation* allows people to transform such motives into different but related ones that are more acceptable to themselves and to society.
sublimation	76. A composer who channels forbidden sexual impulses into musical creativity is employing the defense mechanism known as _____.
defense mechanisms, deception distortion	77. Rationalization, repression, and sublimation are among our _____ _____, all of them based to some degree on self-_____ and _____ of reality.
identification	78. An individual who takes on the virtues of some admired person or group is displaying the defense mechanism known as _____.
reaction	79. When people pretend to possess motives that are the exact opposite of the motives actually causing them anxiety, they are practicing the defense mechanism called _____ formation.
psychological, process	80. *Projection* is a defense mechanism by which people foist off (or project) onto others their own anxiety-provoking motives or thoughts. Like other such mechanisms, it is an unconscious _____ _____.
projection	81. A person who hides tendencies to dishonesty by claiming that everyone else is dishonest is practicing _____.
coping	82. One of the most common reactions to anxiety and stress is *aggression*, which is often produced by frustration. Like defense mechanisms, it is a questionable form of _____.
denial	83. If your friend tries to dispel anxiety by refusing altogether to accept reality, you would be correct in seeing this as an example of _____, a defense mechanism.
displacement	84. In the defense mechanism known as _____, the individual escapes the discomfort of unwanted ideas or feelings by transferring them onto another person, situation, or object.
acting	85. The defense mechanism called _____ out involves taking action impulsively, thus avoiding the conflict involved in weighing conflicting courses of action.
regression	86. A retreat toward behaviors that typically characterize a lower level of maturity is typical of those practicing the defense mechanism known as _____.

REVIEW OF IMPORTANT TERMS

acting out (462)

anxiety (446)

approach-approach conflict (434)

approach-avoidance conflict (434)

avoidance-avoidance conflict (434)

assertive coping (451)

cognitive appraisal (436)

conflict (434)

daily hassles (433)

defense mechanism (458)

denial (461)

depression (449)

displacement (461)

double approach-avoidance conflict (434)

endogenous causes (450)

general adaptation syndrome (GAS) (438)

identification (460)

immune system (442)

post-traumatic stress disorder (PTSD) (448)

primary appraisal (436)

projection (460)

psychoneuroimmunology (442)

psychosomatic illness (439)

rationalization (459)

reaction formation (460)

regression (462)

repression (459)

secondary appraisal (436)

social support network (453)

stress (428)

stressors (428)

sublimation (459)

PRACTICE TEST

_____ 1. Stress is defined as

    a. a response to threats to the organism.

    b. psychological discomfort.

    c. an emotional response to conflict.

    d. the frustration of a psychological goal.

_____ 2. An individual's subjective interpretation of a potentially stressful episode is referred to as the individual's

    a. stressor.

    b. stress response.

    c. projection.

    d. cognitive appraisal.

_____ 3. The sources of stress are referred to as

    a. primary appraisals.

    b. cognitive responses.

    c. stressors.

    d. cognitive stimuli.

_____ 4. Life's seemingly minor irritations are known as

    a. minor stresses.

    b. daily hassles.

    c. stressful transitions.

    d. minor trauma.

_____ 5. Stress is known to exist
   a.   especially in adolescence
   b.   when we grow into adulthood
   c.   primarily in the later years
   d.   from infancy to adulthood

_____ 6. To be classified as a conflict, the simultaneous arousal of two or more incompatible motives must result in
   a.   approach-avoidance.
   b.   unpleasant emotions.
   c.   violation of an inner standard.
   d.   aggression.

_____ 7. The person who first demonstrated and named the general adaptation syndrome was
   a.   Selye.
   b.   James.
   c.   Cannon.
   d.   Freud.

_____ 8. In the general adaptation syndrome, the animal eventually dies from
   a.   lack of oxygen.
   b.   starvation.
   c.   an excess of white blood cells.
   d.   an excess of its own hormones.

_____ 9. Psychosomatic illnesses
   a.   result in psychotic behavior.
   b.   have mental and emotional causes.
   c.   cause a decrease in motivation and drive.
   d.   have only imaginary symptoms.

_____ 10. Selye suggests that the way to stay healthy is to
   a.   determine our optimum pace of living.
   b.   avoid all stress.
   c.   change our general anxiety into specific anxiety.
   d.   increase the effectiveness of our defense mechanisms.

_____ 11. Anxiety is most closely related to the emotion of
   a.   anger.
   b.   fear.
   c.   grief.
   d.   joy.

_____ 12. Extremely stressful experiences such as military combat or captivity can result in

    a.   cognitive disorder.

    b.   poor appraisal.

    c.   post-traumatic stress disorder.

    d.   psychosomatic stress.

_____ 13. A common emotional illness that can be caused by stress is

    a.   depression.

    b.   psychosomatic.

    c.   post-traumatic stress disorder.

    d.   cognitive disorder.

_____ 14. Assertive coping is a

    a.   strategy to overcome depression.

    b.   new structure for interpersonal interaction.

    c.   constructive effort to deal with stress.

    d.   defense mechanism.

_____ 15. Defense mechanisms are not

    a.   mental processes.

    b.   conscious.

    c.   attempts to relieve anxiety.

    d.   a form of self-deception.

_____ 16. Defense mechanisms were first described by

    a.   Selye.

    b.   Maslow.

    c.   Freud.

    d.   Aristotle.

_____ 17. When we try to be like some admired person who seems to be free of the anxiety that troubles us, we are using the defense mechanism called

    a.   reaction formation.

    b.   sublimation.

    c.   rationalization.

    d.   identification.

_____ 18. Mark, who feels anxious about his excessive hostility, is the soul of politeness and courtesy. His behavior is an example of the defense mechanism called

    a.   identification.

    b.   sublimation.

    c.   repression.

    d.   reaction formation.

_____ 19. When we falsely accuse other people of the motives that are making us feel guilty, we are using the defense mechanism called

   a. identification.

   b. projection.

   c. reaction formation.

   d. sublimation.

_____ 20. Retreating to activities characteristic of a lower level of maturity is called

   a. regression.

   b. depression.

   c. reaction formation.

   d. withdrawal.

ANSWERS TO PRACTICE TEST

1. a	6. b	11. b	16. c
2. d	7. a	12. c	17. d
3. c	8. d	13. a	18. d
4. b	9. b	14. c	19. b
5. d	10. a	15. b	20. a

EXERCISE

I. On pages 458 to 462 of the text you will find a description of defense mechanisms and other questionable forms of coping that we all use to some degree when faced with anxiety and stress. Six of them are listed below:

   a. Rationalization

   b. Reaction formation

   c. Projection

   d. Acting out

   e. Displacement

   f. Denial

Keep a record for the next month or so of episodes in which you believe an individual has used one of the forms of coping listed. Among the sources you can use to gather such episodes are movies or television shows, short stories or novels, interactions with friends, conversations you might overhear, experiences someone tells you about, or observations of your own behavior.

Summarize each episode in a few paragraphs, and identify the form of coping that was used by assigning a letter from the above list. After you have collected 20 episodes, consider the following questions:

1. Did any of the forms of coping listed occur much more frequently than others?

2. Do you think the individuals you described were aware of the coping techniques they were using?

3. Was it easier to spot the coping techniques used by others or your own?

CHAPTER 10

Abnormal Behavior

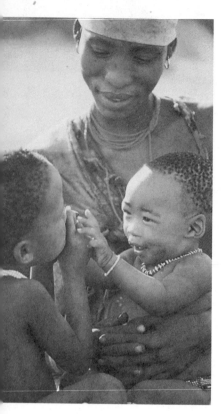

In some hunter-gatherer societies, people spend as little as ten hours per week earning a livelihood. In your society, would such behavior seem normal?

When we imagine someone with a psychological disorder, we may picture a disheveled old man mumbling to himself while pushing a shopping cart full of old belongings, or a withdrawn, dazed woman wandering the halls of a mental institution. Although both images do describe people suffering from mental disorders, they are examples from the extreme end of the spectrum. In contrast, someone with serious depression may appear to be functioning normally in society but may nevertheless be suffering and in need of treatment. People with deep-seated personality disorders may appear charming and engaging at first glance, although time and familiarity will reveal hurtful, destructive, and even dangerous aspects of their personality.

Many of the symptoms described in this chapter will be familiar to you—who among us hasn't experienced an occasional blue mood, intense anxiety, a nagging compulsion? Yet, while all of us may have had some of the same experiences and symptoms as persons clearly identified as abnormal, most of us go through life without ever suffering an actual breakdown in psychological functioning. The task of identifying that breaking point—where the human personality goes significantly awry—is among the most challenging in the field of psychology.

Abnormal Characteristics: Their Nature and Scope

When do people cross the line between what is clearly normal and what is not? Psychologists wouldn't hesitate to label a belligerent man standing on a street corner screaming obscenities at passing strangers as abnormal. Nor would a psychologist hesitate to describe as distinctly normal people who are functioning at the peak of their powers and feeling good about themselves and others. It is virtually impossible, therefore, to arrive at an absolute definition of abnormal behavior. Nevertheless, a good working definition needs to be established. It would be hopeless to study abnormal psychology without setting at least some standards for abnormal behavior—and for differentiating it from normal behavior.

Qualities that Define the Abnormal Personality

Is it abnormal to believe in witches? It was not considered so by the American colonists. Is it abnormal to turn angry and suspicious every time you encounter disappointment and frustration? Among a group of New Guinea natives called the Kaluli, such responses are the accepted norm (Schieffelin, 1985). Is suicide abnormal? To most Americans, it may seem the ultimate in abnormality. Yet in East Asia a Buddhist priest who commits suicide as a form of political protest is regarded as exhibiting strength of character rather than abnormality. All of these examples highlight one of the major themes in psychology emphasized in this textbook—the importance of context in understanding all varieties of human behavior.

From a statistical viewpoint, behavior can be called abnormal if it is uncommon and unusual—as popular terminology recognizes by referring to it as "odd." But this is not the whole story, for even unusual forms of behavior are not generally called abnormal unless they are regarded as undesirable by the particular society in which they occur. In our own society, the habit of working 18 hours a day is probably rarer than heroin addiction. Yet an 18-hour workday is generally considered admirable or at least acceptable and is therefore called normal. Heroin addiction is considered undesirable and therefore called abnormal.

Since personal happiness is highly valued in the United States, people who are happy are generally regarded as being free of any abnormality. Though this criterion is widely accepted, there are some notable exceptions. Many people who commit vicious acts that could hardly be considered normal—such as wartime atrocities and mass murders in peacetime—seem to be perfectly happy.

In general, a useful working definition of abnormal behavior embraces the three features that have been mentioned. An abnormal personality trait or form of behavior is (1) statistically unusual, (2) considered undesirable by most people, and (3) a source of unhappiness to the person who possesses it. It must be admitted that the definition is not satisfactory from a theoretical point of view and would not be accepted enthusiastically by some psychologists—chiefly on the grounds that it sets up rigid standards that enable our society to label as abnormal anybody whose behavior is disliked or considered disruptive.

Many psychologists view as abnormal those behaviors that are **maladaptive**—that is, behaviors that interfere with the individual's functioning. For example, when a person becomes so anxious or depressed that going to work, attending school, or seeing friends becomes impossible, that person's behavior would not be considered normal. Most mental disorders are now characterized by the pattern, severity, and duration of clusters of behavioral symptoms and by the levels of impairment and disruption they produce in people's lives. But, as described later in this chapter, efforts are underway also to develop additional criteria—such as tests of brain structure and activity—that can aid in determining when someone is mentally ill (Kales, Stefanis, & Talbott, 1990).

Maladaptive behavior
A behavior that interferes with an individual's functioning.

The Prevalence and Impact of Psychological Disorders

Psychological disorders affect people of all ages, races, and walks of life, and contrary to a commonly held notion, they are as common in developing countries of the world as in industrialized societies (Léon, 1989). Although statistics on actual prevalence are hard to come by, one U.S. survey attempted an estimate by sampling many households in selected locations around the country and by using carefully constructed interviews that permitted rough diagnoses to be made. The results showed that about 20 percent of the U.S. population suffers from a diagnosable psychological disorder during a six-month period (Myers et al., 1984). The prevalence rates of many of the major disorders that will be discussed in this chapter are shown in Figure 10.1.

Tragically, the highest incidence of most psychological disorders occurs in the prime of life—between 25 and 44 years of age (Freedman, 1984). No age group is spared, however. For example, in the United States, at least 12 percent of the 63 million children under age 18 suffer from one or more psychologically abnormal conditions (Institute of Medicine, 1989).

Among the nation's victims of psychological disorders are those whose conditions are truly severe—individuals who experience long-term, persis-

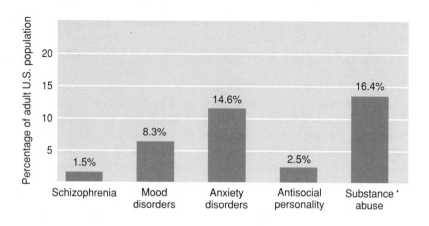

FIGURE 10.1 How widespread are psychological disorders in the United States? From interviews with over 18,000 individuals age 18 or over, it was possible to estimate the percentage of Americans who have experienced one or another major mental disorder in the course of their lifetime (after Regier et al., 1988).

tent, and disabling disorders that have a profound impact on their everyday existence and on that of their families and communities. It is estimated that at one time or another in their lives, at least 15 million Americans have met this painful criterion—and that about 1.7 million Americans now have serious psychological disorders. Of these, 900,000 are residents in institutions, and 800,000 are living—many of them homeless—in the community (National Institute of Mental Health, 1991).

No statistical data, however, can portray the full impact of psychological disorders in human terms. Anyone who has actually experienced periods of intense anxiety or depression knows how disabling they can be and how much agony they can cause. Patients in the throes of terminal-cancer pain who also had a history of severe depression were asked to compare the two. Most reported that the physical pain was more bearable—and far preferable to the psychological pain of their mental disorder (Jamison, 1982).

The Varieties and Origins of Abnormal Behavior

Although the causes of abnormal behavior vary to some degree from one type of disorder to another, in general, people seem to have a "breaking point" at which they lose their psychological balance. That fragile point seems to depend on the kinds and amounts of environmental stressors people face and their abilities to handle them. These abilities, in turn, depend on their biological makeup, their personalities, the kinds of support they get from other people, and their learned styles of coping.

Some people are so biologically susceptible that they seem to develop mental disorders without any pressure from external stressors. Others, as described in the previous chapter, seem practically invulnerable, able to endure and triumph over conditions that would break the minds and spirits of most people. Still others, for reasons not yet clear, seem to develop personalities that are enduringly abnormal. Studies of the sources of psychological disorders strongly underscore the first of the three major themes introduced at the opening of this textbook: Human behavior, whether normal or abnormal, is determined by a complex blend of biological and psychological forces.

Biology's Influence

Just as people vary greatly in their outward physical makeup, they vary greatly in their inner wiring: Wide individual differences exist in glandular activity and sensitivity of the autonomic nervous system—as well as in the activity of the brain centers concerned with emotion. These differences may incline one person to be more easily aroused and more intensely emotional than another. Thus some people, because of their inherited biological makeup, probably experience a great deal more emotional and physical wear and tear than others.

Certainly there is considerable evidence that heredity can contribute to tendencies toward the most severe forms of abnormal behavior. For example, schizophrenia (see page 478) is more common among the close relatives of schizophrenics than among people whose family background shows no other cases. Studies also indicate that hereditary factors may produce tendencies toward disabling forms of depression and perhaps toward other less extreme forms of abnormal behavior as well (Neubauer & Neubauer, 1990). Nevertheless, it is unlikely that a specific gene will be identified as an isolated cause of most mental disorders (Dunn & Plomin, 1990).

Psychology's Influence

Our acquired psychological traits also play a key role in determining how much anxiety and stress we are likely to experience, and how much we can tolerate without succumbing to mental disorder. For example, people who have—but cannot fulfill—high needs for power, achievement, or approval may become extremely vulnerable to tense moods. Our inner standards wield great influence over our psychological well-being. An event—such as receiving a barely passing grade on a final exam—may produce little or no anxiety in a person with relatively low standards of mastery, but it may produce almost unbearable anxiety in a person with higher standards. Clinical psychologists often see people who are crippled by anxiety over violations of norms for sexual behavior, honesty, hostility, or dependency that would seem minor to others.

The Environment's Influence

Environmental stressors are at least partially responsible for many psychological disorders. The role of stressors in precipitating abnormal behavior has been studied since the early part of this century. It is possible to make dogs restless, hostile, destructive, or apathetic by having them perform increasingly difficult—and ultimately impossible—discriminations among shapes.

Research suggests that unfair, harsh, and inconsistent parental discipline is related to adult psychiatric disorders. Such victimizing experiences probably help elicit a disorder to which the child is already predisposed (Holmes & Robins, 1987). The importance of environmental factors is underscored by the consistent evidence that mental disorders disproportionately affect people living in poverty (National Institute of Mental Health, 1991). Perhaps an even clearer example is the breakdown suffered by soldiers enduring the stress and trauma of combat, most recently in Vietnam (Centers for Disease Control, 1988).

A traumatic combat environment can leave emotional scars.

Although stressful events in a person's current social environment can affect vulnerability to mental disorder, the stage may be set by the character of earlier environments. Children who grow up in broken families, or are physically or sexually abused, or who live with a severely mentally ill parent may be vulnerable to mental disorder in later life (Rutter, 1986). Growing up in poverty may also contribute to later vulnerability—perhaps because of the psychologically stressful existence of deprivation, or perhaps because deprived conditions often contribute to poorer physical health before and after birth, and to impaired biological capacity to cope with anxiety and stress.

Abnormality in Its Many Forms

Some deviations from the normal are so slight that they are popularly termed quirks—like eccentricities in dress or speech. People who have picked up such habits may seem a bit odd at times, but they are not seriously discomforted or prevented from functioning effectively. At the other extreme are the serious forms of mental disturbance that render their victims out of touch with reality and incapable of conducting the ordinary affairs of life. These drastic forms of abnormal behavior are relatively rare. In a sort of twilight zone between normal behavior and extreme abnormality are long-lasting emotional disturbances characterized by high levels of anxiety and depression. Their victims usually function day to day but well below par and without feelings of contentment. They are the people who are most likely to seek relief through psychotherapy.

The roster of behavior patterns our society regards as evidence of psychological disorder has evolved over time—based on a combination of social attitudes and values, experiences of people who treat patients, and research on the underlying causes and patterns of abnormal behavior. The classification scheme now used by most psychologists and other mental health professionals is contained in the current, or fourth, edition of the *Diagnostic and Statistical Manual of Mental Disorders,* published in 1994 by the American Psychiatric

TEST YOURSELF

b) Both Tracy and Annette, who work for a large software company, are laid off due to downsizing. During the next six months as the two search for new jobs, Tracy becomes severely depressed, while Annette does not. What factors could account for their differing reactions to this life crisis?

Association. Known as **DSM-IV**, the manual presents detailed descriptions of patterns of abnormal behavior, ranging from those popularly known as "neurotic" to more devastating ones often referred to as "psychotic."

The newest classification scheme may change in time, of course. As our knowledge of abnormal behavior changes, disorders are included, excluded, regrouped, and relabeled. The sections that follow deal with today's major groupings of seriously abnormal personality and behavior patterns.

Schizophrenia: Puzzling and Profound

The symptoms began to appear when Ralph was 19 years old. He became suspicious of his classmates, insisting that they were developing a special language so that they could carry out their secret plans to destroy him. His dress became slovenly, and sometimes, even in the heat of summer, he would wear three sweaters to protect him from "the poisonous rays that will appear at noon." His few friends would often find him in a corner of the library, mumbling to himself. Once Ralph refused to eat for an entire week. He was convinced that the food was poisoned to punish him for his grandmother's death. He imagined that she had died as a result of a magic word he had secretly thought of in his own mind.

As time passed, Ralph's behavior became even more bizarre. He would stand at the window for hours on end, staring at passersby and mumbling nonsensical phrases like "gloop-in-the-soup" or "brangle my strangle." He complained that the neighbors were spying on him, and he would scream obscenities at them. He believed he had enormous powers and wrote letters to the president to offer solutions for all the world's problems. He was chosen, he said, to act as peacemaker not only between nations but also between the United States government and the creatures who were about to arrive from outer space.

Schizophrenia is one of the most serious and debilitating of the mental illnesses.

By the time he was hospitalized, nothing Ralph said or did made any sense. Once he tried to climb into the toilet and have a nurse flush him away. He ordered his doctors to leave the room because, as he explained it, "I am attending a conference with God, George Washington, and IBM."

Ralph is one of the estimated two million people in the United States suffering from **schizophrenia,** a devastating psychological disorder that is often chronic. About 40 percent of the beds in American mental hospitals are now occupied by patients with schizophrenia. The disorder is particularly common among young adults in their twenties and occurs more often among men than among women. Overall, the chances that a person will develop the disease are roughly 1 in 100 (Myers et al., 1984).

Symptoms of Schizophrenia

Individuals are generally considered to be suffering from schizophrenia when they display the following disturbed behavior (Rosenhan & Seligman, 1984):

1. *Perceptual difficulties*—for example, the inability to understand others' speech, to identify people, to gauge the passage of time, or to know what is real and what is not. Often there are **hallucinations,** or false sensory experiences—seeing things, hearing things—that have a compelling sense of reality.
2. *Thought disorders*—including incoherent speech, quick shifts of ideas from one topic to a totally unrelated one. Often there are **delusions,** or false and inane beliefs such as the conviction that other people can hear their thoughts, that they no longer exist, or that their heads and arms are missing. Compared to the delusions of other psychiatric patients, schizophrenic patients' delusions are much more bizarre—often involving the belief they are being controlled by outside forces (Junginger, 1992).
3. *Emotional disturbances*—including the absence of any feeling, remoteness, and inappropriate reactions such as laughing in the face of a sad episode.

In schizophrenia, many of the normal processes described in this book—from the ability to perceive the world to the capacity to relate to other people—unravel completely. People with the disorder lose touch with the real world. They hear voices that are not there, speak a language that does not exist, laugh for no reason, or sit motionless for hours on end (American Psychiatric Association, 1987). What could possibly cause the human personality to become so completely disorganized?

Clues to Schizophrenia's Causes

Most investigators have concluded that schizophrenia is not a single disturbance but is instead made up of several types that have been grouped together because they exhibit certain resemblances. Moreover, these different disturbances probably have different causes, manifestations, and responses to treatment.

There is mounting evidence that heredity may play a large role in who is at risk for the varieties of schizophrenia. One of the possible early markers of the disease in some people is serious retardation in motor development dur-

Schizophrenia

A devastating psychological disorder in which the victim loses touch with reality, and has hallucinations, delusions, or inappropriate emotion.

Hallucination

An imaginary sensation, such as seeing nonexistent things or feeling nonexistent objects under the skin.

Delusion

A false belief, such as the conviction that someone alive is dead.

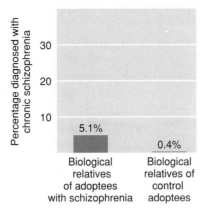

Percentage diagnosed with chronic schizophrenia

5.1%

0.4%

Biological relatives of adoptees with schizophrenia

Biological relatives of control adoptees

FIGURE 10.2 **Heredity and schizophrenia** Biological relatives of adoptees with schizophrenia were about 10 times as likely to be suffering from the disorder as were relatives of adoptees making up a control group (Kety & Ingraham, 1992).

ing the first year of life; these infants are more likely to have parents with schizophrenia (Fish, 1992). Further evidence of a familial factor is shown in Figure 10.2.

Schizophrenia is associated in some, but not all, patients with increased levels of the neurotransmitter dopamine in the brain. Virtually all drugs that are effective in treating schizophrenic symptoms interfere with the action of dopamine. Techniques for observing the brain in action, such as *positron emission tomography (PET)* and new forms of *magnetic resonance imaging (MRI),* offer further indications that some schizophrenics differ from normal people in brain metabolism. Furthermore, in some schizophrenics, the brain ventricles—the fluid-filled cavities of the brain—are enlarged (Meltzer, 1987).

It has also been found that those with the disorder show abnormal patterns of eye movements when they try to track a moving object. Many of their close relatives, though not themselves victims of schizophrenia, display the same unusual tracking pattern, as if there were a family tendency to do so (Holzman, 1992). The unusual patterns might indicate some defect in parts of the nervous system responsible for perception—possibly explaining why schizophrenics seem out of touch with reality as perceived by normal people.

Moreover, individuals with schizophrenia appear to be deficient in their capacity to focus attention—especially when beset by competing stimuli (Grillon et al., 1990). Although they appear to be able to focus attention for a while, they apparently are functioning with a defect in the brain's capacity to pay sustained attention over a period of time—especially when there are distracting inputs (Everett, Laplante, and Thomas, 1989). Recent research has shown that the brains of some schizophrenics are smaller in volume, especially in areas vital to perception, concentration, memory, and thinking (Suddath et al., 1990).

Even if some inherited defect is the basis for the disorder, however, other factors may influence whether the inborn tendency will affect behavior. Environmental stresses may play a role, as might prenatal experiences or injuries during birth. Studies indicate that the disease is more likely to appear in children of families with a high level of communication disorders (Mishler, 1991). The likelihood of developing schizophrenia is also greater among those who are unemployed and unmarried. A job and a spouse seem to offer some buffer against the disease, especially for men (Tien & Eaton, 1992).

TEST YOURSELF

c) What physical evidence is there that the metabolic activity of the brains of schizophrenics are abnormal?

Mood Disorders

Mood (affective) disorders
A form of psychological disorders characterized by abnormalities of emotion, including severe depression and swings of mood from one extreme to another.

All of us know from personal experience that a variety of events—both major and minor—can affect our mood, or what psychologists call our *affect*. There are times when life is marred by grief—when a friend dies, a treasured relationship breaks up, or the job you worked so hard to get is given instead to someone else. These events can sometimes lead to **mood (affective) disorders.**

Depression: Common and Often Curable

Depression
A feeling of severe and prolonged sadness that occurs as a reaction to stress and chemical imbalances in the brain.

All of us are blue or down from time to time, and sometimes we become depressed after a significant setback. Yet, however painful the stress or loss, we expect after a reasonable period to bounce back and feel like our "old self" again. Many people, however, experience a clinical, or major, **depression**—a feeling of severe and prolonged sadness that occurs as a reaction to stress and chemical imbalances in the brain. A bout with depression is very common. The U.S. Agency for Health Care Policy and Research reports that one in eight people will experience a major depression over their lifetime. The incidence of depression appears to be on the rise. In some countries—including the United States—the likelihood that people born after 1955 will suffer major depression is at least three times greater than for their grandparents' generation (Weissman, 1992).

Unipolar disorder
A type of mood disorder that occurs without the swings in mood experienced in bipolar depression.

Bipolar disorder
A type of mood disorder in which a person's lows alternate with exaggerated highs; formerly called manic-depression.

Severely depressed people are quite different from those who are best described as "unhappy" (Gotlib, 1984). They experience not only unrelenting sadness but intense helplessness and hopelessness as well. They lose all semblance of self-esteem and are filled instead with grinding self-recriminations and guilt. They have no zest for either work or play. They may find that even routine acts of thinking and speaking are slowed and take enormous effort. In the most severe cases they may suffer delusions and hallucinations. Depression causes physical problems as well. Sleep is disturbed—especially by early morning awakenings—and the appetite for food and sex tends to diminish or disappear. Depressed people may also complain of poor digestion, heart palpitations, headache, visual disturbances, or dizziness. Other indicators of depression are identified in Figure 10.3.

Depression is accompanied by feelings of futility, hopelessness, and apathy.

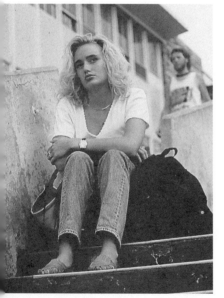

Those in the grip of a depressive episode feel hopeless about virtually everything. Writer William Styron's depression led him to view all the things around him as "potential devices" for his own destruction: "the attic rafter (and an outside maple or two) a means to hang myself, the garage a place to inhale carbon monoxide, the bathtub a vessel to receive the flow of my opened arteries" (Styron, 1990). With an outlook so dark, about 15 percent of depressed people eventually choose suicide as a way out of their misery.

The Turbulent Ups and Downs of Bipolar Disorder

When people have recurrent episodes of depression like the one just described, the disorder is called **unipolar disorder.** But there is another severe affective disorder—known as **bipolar disorder,** and referred to in the past as manic-depression—in which the lows typically alternate with exaggerated highs. Most of us, of course, know that our mood can shift—sometimes for no apparent reason—from bright and joyful to dark and sad. For those suffering from this disorder, the emotional pendulum swings wildly from intense excitement to deep melancholy, at first with long time intervals in

	None or a Little of the Time	Some of the Time	Good Part of the Time	Most or All of the Time
1. I feel downhearted, blue, and sad.				✔
2. Morning is when I feel the best.	✔			
3. I have crying spells or feel like it.				✔
4. I have trouble sleeping through the night.				✔
5. I eat as much as I used to.	✔			
6. I enjoy looking at, talking to, and being with attractive women/men.	✔			
7. I notice that I am losing weight.				✔
8. I have trouble with constipation.				✔
9. My heart beats faster than normal.				✔
10. I get tired for no reason.				✔
11. My mind is as clear as it used to be.	✔			
12. I find it easy to do the things I used to.	✔			
13. I am restless and can't keep still.			✔	
14. I feel hopeful about the future.	✔			
15. I am more irritable than usual.				✔
16. I find it easy to make decisions.	✔			
17. I feel that I am useful and needed.	✔			
18. My life is pretty full.	✔			
19. I feel that others would be better off if I were dead.				✔
20. I still enjoy the things I used to do.	✔			

FIGURE 10.3 A brief test for depression The items are from a test called the Self Rating Depression Scale. The checks in the boxes would be made by a person who is depressed in the most extreme way. Note that such a person would feel that all the positive emotions and experiences mentioned in the test apply "none or a little of the time," while all the negative ones apply "most or all of the time." (Copyright William W. K. Zung, 1965. All rights reserved. Reproduced with author's permission.)

between, but later with frequent and abrupt shifts from high to low (Goodwin & Jamison, 1990).

A recent study of people with bipolar disorder estimates that more than three million Americans have the disorder (National Depressive and Manic-Depressive Association, 1993). Like unipolar depression, it appears to be on the rise—as shown in Figure 10.4. Bipolar disorder affects men and women

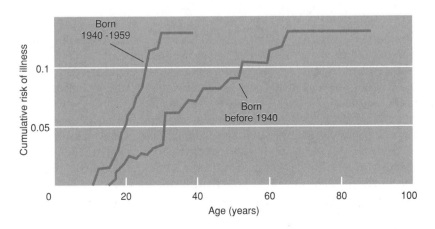

FIGURE 10.4 Generational increase of bipolar disorder The graphs compare two groups related to individuals having bipolar disorder. One group was born before 1940, the other after. Those born after 1940 reveal a greater risk for developing the disorder or a related condition. (Copyright © 1992 by Scientific American. All rights reserved.)

equally, and sometimes appears during childhood. Unfortunately, childhood or adolescent onset predicts more treatment difficulties and increased social disability. The disorder can often be managed fairly well with drug therapy, but people often delay seeking treatment when early symptoms appear, and the problem is often misdiagnosed.

Bipolar disorder magnifies common human experiences to larger-than-life proportions. Among its symptoms are exaggerations of normal sadness and fatigue, joy and exuberance, sensuality and sexuality, irritability and rage, energy and creativity. To those afflicted, it can be so painful that suicide seems the only means of escape; about one of every four untreated for the condition actually does commit suicide.

In the manic phase, people with this disorder tend to be talkative, restless, aggressive, boastful, and destructive. They develop a feeling of intense well-being and even ecstasy. Sexual and moral inhibitions disappear and life is one uninterrupted "high." The manic person needs little sleep and is filled with abundant energy and grandiose notions. Soon, however, most manic individuals plummet back to the depressed phase, becoming so gloomy and hopeless that they are immobilized.

As far back as the ancient Greeks, society has believed that the artistic temperament is often touched by divine madness. In recent years evidence has accumulated linking mood disorders to creativity (Jamison, 1993). From the melancholy Lord Byron to the suicidal Sylvia Plath, biographies of celebrated poets, musicians, and artists have attested to extreme moods in creative people. Here is how writer Virginia Woolf described her divine inspiration:

> As an experience, madness is terrific I can assure you, and not to be sniffed at; and in its lava I still find most of the things I write about. It shoots out of one everything shaped, final, not in mere driblets, as sanity does (Woolf, 1978).

Despite the links between creativity and bipolar disorder, it is important not to glamorize or trivialize the disorder. In fact, most sufferers are not great creative geniuses, and most talented artists are mentally stable. Modern medicine can today offer relief to those who endure the ravages of mood. In the past, artists who were in the clutches of this devastating disorder had nowhere but their art to seek solace. A further discussion of the subject appears in the Psychology and the Media box entitled "Making Art of Madness."

Seasonal Mood Swings

Many people experience a shift in mood, however slight, depending on the brightness of the day. A sunny day helps raise the spirits; a cloudy day helps dampen them. Indeed, a typical pattern is an increase in depressed mood as the day wears on, reaching its peak as darkness falls and night descends (Robbins & Tanck, 1987).

Early in the 1980s, researchers reported a form of mood disorder that exaggerates this pattern of response to light and dark. Called **seasonal affective disorder** (**SAD**), it causes some people to become depressed in the winter, and energetic—and even manic—in the summer. Individuals with SAD turn depressed, unproductive, and lethargic in the winter; they show little interest in sex, their sleep deteriorates, and they tend to overeat. In contrast,

Seasonal affective disorder (SAD)
A form of mood disorder that causes some people to become depressed during the winter months when sunlight is of shorter duration.

Making Art of Madness

On Nov. 15, 1934, Virginia Woolf began her rewrite of a novel eventually titled "The Years." "Lord! Lord!" she noted in her diary, "10 pages a day for 90 days: three months. . . . now, damnably disagreeable, as I see it will be—compacting the vast mass—I am using my faculties again. & all the flies and fleas are forgotten."

Seven years later the flies and fleas and larger plagues drove Woolf, who had fought mental illness throughout her life, to suicide. An increasing number of psychiatrists, neurologists and geneticists, says an article in this week's Science Times, believe there's a link between the genius and madness of artists such as her. Maybe so. But as anyone who's ever read Woolf's letters and diaries can attest, it's the link between imagination and self-discipline that got her a place in literature's pantheon. Her mind may have had a

grasshopper's fleetness, but her industry was the ant's.

"People who have experienced emotional extremes, who have been forced to confront a huge range of feelings and who have successfully coped with those adversities, could end up with a richer organization in memory, a richer palette to work with," said Dr. Ruth Richards, a psychiatrist at McLean Hospital in Belmont, Mass., which often served as a haven for Robert Lowell, the fine American poet.

At least three fine English poets—Byron, Shelley and Coleridge—also suffered from manic depression or severe depression; and so did the composer Robert Schumann, who starved himself to death when he was 46. Dr. Robert M. Post, chief of the biological psychiatry branch at the National Institutes of Health, sees the link between bipolar disorder and creativity as "fortunate," because it is in so many other ways "a devastating illness."

To be mad is not necessarily to be creative, or there'd be a Shelley on every street corner. And to be creative is not necessarily to be mad, or Shakespeare would not have been a monument to shrewdness and adaptability. But to be creative is almost invariably to be diligent—and, manic-depressive or no, to swing high, swing low.

Source: Editorial published in the *New York Times,* October 15, 1993.

Issues to Consider

1. Is abnormal behavior more acceptable in some people than in others?
2. If you could be certain of producing great music or poetry, would you be willing to accept the burden of bipolar disorder?
3. Do you think a person suffering from bipolar disorder could be as creative while depressed as while "high"?

---

they are virtually manic in their summer activity level, showing heightened creativity, interest in sex, and euphoric mood (Wehr, Sack, & Rosenthal, 1984).

A demonstration of this phenomenon emerged from a study that focused on over 1,600 individuals living at varying geographic latitudes along three East Coast areas of the United States, including Florida, Maryland, New York, and New Hampshire. The results showed an increase of SAD in the more northern latitudes, supporting the hypothesis that light deprivation produces the decline in mood (Rosenthal, 1989).

When treated by exposure to light that mimics natural sunlight, individuals suffering from seasonal affective disorder seem to emerge from their dark-induced winter depression. Within a few days, many patients experience dramatic improvements in mood. Some patients find that even an hour or two of bright light exposure a day is sufficient to eliminate their winter symptoms (Rosenthal, 1989).

Less disabling than SAD, but still an impediment to normal living is the "winter blues," experienced by many people during the dark, short days of the year. A surprising number of individuals find that their creativity, energy, and sense of well-being are depleted until the brightness of spring appears (Rosenthal, 1989).

Some people who become depressed in the winter time often feel better if they go south to experience the increased light.

Untangling the Biological and Environmental Components

As with schizophrenia, there is some evidence to suggest that mood disorders have a genetic basis. The risk of developing bipolar disorder is less than 1 percent in the population at large. However, it rises to around 15 percent among the close relatives—parents, siblings, and children—of manic-depressives. One study of depression among female twins found genetics played a substantial, although not overwhelming, role (Kendler, 1992a).

There is evidence also that mood disorders are related to disturbances in the chemistry of the brain—to such an extent that the symptoms sometimes appear without any provocation. The levels of a number of neurotransmitters appear to be disturbed in depression, and various drugs used to treat the disorder—to be described in the next chapter—work by altering the balance of these neurotransmitters. Among depressed individuals, there also appears to be a disturbance in the functioning of hormones regulated by the pituitary and adrenal glands. For instance, many people suffering from severe depression have an excess amount of **cortisol,** a hormone secreted by the adrenal gland during stress or emotional upset (Carroll et al., 1981). Additional evidence of the biological basis of depression comes from observations of the abnormal brain waves of victims of the disorder while they are asleep (Kupfer et al., 1985).

It is not yet clear whether mood disorders are caused by these various biochemical factors or whether the disorder causes the biochemical changes. The most widely held theory is that some people are genetically vulnerable to biochemical imbalances, which are likely to occur in response to intolerably stressful experiences. One such experience, for example, would appear to be the trauma of abuse. Researchers have found an atypically high rate of both physical and sexual abuse in a sample of women hospitalized for depression and other abnormal symptoms (Bryer et al., 1987). The trauma and stress of illnesses ranging from strokes to cancer may also alter the brain's chemistry, leaving one more vulnerable to depression. Even asthma has been found to be associated with depression.

Cortisol

A hormone secreted by the adrenal gland during stress.

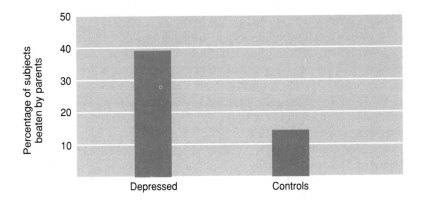

FIGURE 10.5 Childhood abuse and adult depression A history of having been beaten as children is three times as likely among depressed individuals as among those free of depression (after Holmes & Robins, 1987).

Various problems within the family put people at greater risk for depression. As illustrated in Figure 10.5, unfair, harsh, and inconsistent discipline in childhood has been found to be strongly associated with adult depression (Holmes & Robins, 1987). The disruption of divorce may leave children more vulnerable to depression. One study found that children separated from a parent as a result of divorce faced an increased risk of major depression as well as anxiety; this link was not found among children separated from a parent by death (Kendler, 1992b). For more details on depression among children, see the Life Span Perspective box entitled "Depression in the Early Years."

LIFE SPAN PERSPECTIVE

Depression in the Early Years

It seems logical, as studies have found, that the risk of serious depression increases in the later years of life. Less well recognized is the prevalence of depression in early development. Until the early 1960s, the term **childhood depression** did not appear in American textbooks on child psychiatry (Cytryn, McKnew, and Bunney, 1980). Now, however, it has become clear that children as well as adults can suffer from depression. A study of over 5,500 high school students revealed that nearly one in ten suffered from depression, ranging from mild to severe (Whitaker, 1990). Yet the ailment still goes unrecognized—and untreated—in too many cases. Two types of problems often hide an underlying decay of mood in children:

1. Physical complaints, such as headaches, stomachaches, and bed-wetting.
2. School problems, including school phobia, truancy, and poor scholastic performance.

Most parents and pediatricians are likely to overlook the possibility that such conditions may be masking a mood of depression. But careful observa-

Childhood depression
A form of depression in children often characterized by physical complaints.

tion of children by informed child psychiatrists and psychologists can often strip away the mask (Petti, 1981).

Even when the signs of depression are more obvious, the disorder is still easy to overlook in children. Because children are unaware of the meaning of depression, they do not complain of it openly in the same way that adults do. Moreover, many children can still be active and show some interest in their environment even while quite depressed. Closer attention, however, shows that depression produces symptoms in them comparable to those found among severely depressed adults.

Depressed children look sad and feel even sadder, are moody, cry easily, and sleep and eat poorly. They are burdened with a sense of worthlessness, hopelessness, and guilt. Finding no pleasure in life, some entertain thoughts of suicide, and a small but increasing number actually commit the act (Frederick, 1978).

Childhood depression is likely to occur as a result of both genetic vulnerability and a stressful environment. Some long-standing cases arise when children are subjected to continuous stress—repeated separations from loved ones, abuse, family strife and violence, or the daily trauma of being reared by an emotionally disturbed parent. The incidence of depression in children of seriously depressed parents is atypically high (Beardslee et al., 1983). Other cases are much briefer, usually triggered by an identifiable, immediate cause. It could be the sudden death of a parent, an unexpected and uprooting move to a new city, or the arrival of a new sibling. Extremely stressful events, such as divorce or death in the family are strong predictors of later depression (Hoeksema, 1992).

Youth is no shield against the ravages of depression, long regarded to be a painful consequence only of adult stress. More pediatricians, teachers, and parents need to learn to recognize the condition, bringing children and adolescents the appropriate medical treatment they need—and restoring to them their lost well-being and productivity. ■

Introjective depression

A type of depression characterized by feelings of guilt, inferiority, self-criticism, and a sense of having failed to meet expectations.

There also appears to be a link between familial substance abuse and the presence of depression. Children of alcoholic fathers are more prone to **introjective depression**—a type of depression characterized by feelings of guilt, inferiority, self-criticism, and a sense of having failed to meet expectations (Jarmas & Kazak, 1992).

Differences in Depression Among Men and Women

Mood disorders are diagnosed twice as often among women than men, and twice as many women as men take antidepressant drugs (Nolen-Hoeksema, 1990). The reason is not entirely clear. One possibility is that women are more vulnerable because of their biological make-up. Hormonal factors may be partially responsible—for instance, premenstrual and postpartum depression are common and well recognized. Another possibility is social roles. Some theorize that women are encouraged by society to devote themselves to nurturing others, in the process denying their own goals and needs (Jack, 1991). At least one study bears this out. It found that men and women are

Disorders of eating are becoming more common in the United States.

equally capable of adjusting to negative events occurring to them personally. But women were more deeply affected than men by the stressful events occurring to close family and friends—particularly their spouses (Turner & Avison, 1989). As women have emerged from their traditionally passive social roles, their rates of depression have, in fact, declined (F. Goodwin, 1993).

Increasingly unrealistic cultural standards of beauty and thinness may be another reason for higher rates of depression among women. Women from societies that promote extreme thinness have been found to be twice as likely as men to suffer from depression. In contrast, in societies with more realistic ideals of feminine physique, depression for men and women was almost equal (M. McCarthy, 1990). Unrealistic ideals of female body size can also lead to **eating disorders.** The same study also found that eating disorders were almost nonexistent in cultures where the feminine ideal is closer to women's actual body sizes. For more information on eating disorders see the Psychology in Action box, "Eating Disorders: When Food Becomes the Enemy."

Another reason for higher rates of depression among women may be due to errors in diagnosis. According to one study, clinicians overdiagnosed depression among women and underdiagnosed it among men (Potts & Burnam, 1992). Men may tend to deny depression and may be less likely to

Eating disorders

A category of disorders found more often in females who have unrealistic ideals concerning body size.

Eating Disorders: When Food Becomes the Enemy

Katherine is a 5'4" sixteen-year-old who weighs 80 pounds. As her body began going through the changes of puberty, Katherine put on a little bit of weight, which prompted her to begin a demanding regimen of dieting and exercise. Within a month, Katherine had lost the excess weight. But she still saw herself as "fat" and intensified her demanding exercise and diet program. Her daily routine now involves consuming no more than a piece of dry toast, one serving of raw vegetables, a piece of fruit and four glasses of water, and performing at least an hour of aerobic exercise.

Although Katherine doesn't believe she has a problem, clinicians would diagnose her with **anorexia nervosa,** a disorder in which an already thin person continues on a starvation diet to keep weight down. People with this disorder continue to be terrified about gaining weight even when they have already lost as much as 40 percent of their normal body weight. Once the individual has experienced sufficient weight loss, the physiological effects of the malnutrition (such as slower emptying of the stomach) and the psycho-

logical effects (such as increasing social isolation) help perpetuate the disorder (Bloom and Lazerson, 1988).

Even more common is **bulimia nervosa,** a disorder in which a person engages in eating binges and then induces vomiting, takes laxatives or exercises excessively in order to avoid gaining weight. Feelings of depression and shame typically run high during and after binges. As in anorexia, there is a constant preoccupation with food and a morbid fear of being viewed as overweight (Hinz & Williamson, 1987). Eating disorders are particularly common among young women in their teens and early twenties. A variety of causes have been proposed, ranging from chemical and hormonal imbalances, to societal and family pressures. Eating disorders seem to run in families (National Institute of Mental Health, 1987), although it is difficult to tease out the biological from the environmental causes. Often, vulnerable girls come from families that show little cohesion or mutual support (Attie & Brooks-Gunn, 1989). It has also been shown that the families of those with anorexia are often very protective and demanding (Yates, 1990). Yet, the familial link also reveals a genetic component. Among twins, if one has the

disorder, the other is more likely to suffer when the twins are identical rather than fraternal (Fichter & Noegel, 1990).

There is accumulating evidence for an underlying biological component. Researchers have found that women with bulimia tend to binge when levels of the brain chemical serotonin are low (Weltzin, 1993). Low levels of serotonin may encourage binging either by a direct effect on appetite or through its effect on mood. Another study has shown that those with bulimia nervosa have unusually high levels of **vasopressin,** a brain hormone that affects learning and memory and may be released during times of stress (Demitrack, 1992). Bulimics may release higher levels of vasopressin when they are anxious, which may then in turn reinforce the repetitive cycle of dieting, gorging, and vomiting.

Societal standards of thinness share some of the blame for the prevalence of eating disorders among young women. An extremely disturbed body image often underlies eating disorders (Steinberg, 1985). The feminine "ideal" as shown in fashion magazines may be setting an impossible standard by which women evaluate themselves.

Anorexia nervosa

An eating disorder in which an already thin person continues on a starvation diet in order to keep weight down.

express their feelings openly and to seek help. Doctors, on the other hand, may be less likely to ask men about their feelings and may attribute their problems to physical causes. On top of that, men are much less likely to visit a doctor than women are. Some research suggests that men express their dark moods through alcoholism (Bucher et al., 1981). Other methods men may use to mask depression include taking mood-altering drugs, being cranky, irritable or falsely cheerful, abusing their wives or children, becoming workaholics or exercise addicts, and lastly, and most tragically, taking their own lives with little or no warning.

As people become more aware of the hidden symptoms of depression, the gap between men and women may narrow as more men are diagnosed and treated. In fact, the disparity in depression rates between women and men is already closing in among younger generations, with the risk among young men rising toward the levels found among young women (Weisman, 1989).

Anxiety Disorders

Perfectly normal people have many anxious moments because they anticipate an undesirable event—rejection or harm. Anxiety also gnaws at many with mental disorders of all sorts. But in some people, anxiety is the preeminent symptom; it dominates their lives. These are people who suffer from one or another form of **anxiety disorder.** They outnumber virtually all other groups of mentally ill individuals—more than 24 million Americans during the course of their lifetimes (J. Ross, 1990).

Anxiety disorders can take a number of forms. In some cases, conscious worry is clearly the most prominent symptom. In other cases, individuals develop disabling patterns of behavior—such as staying home to avoid crowds or washing their hands every half hour—as a way of keeping their underlying anxiety under control.

Many victims of anxiety disorders function well enough so that even their close friends may not be aware of their symptoms. Moreover, unlike schizophrenics and manic-depressives, they stay in touch with reality and can admit that their feelings and behavior are illogical. However, certain anxiety disorders can be crippling and prevent people from functioning in their social relationships or at work. And cost to society is high. A report from the National Institute of Mental Health found that anxiety disorders account for 32 percent of all mental health costs (NIMH, 1993, Rice & Miller, 1993). There are four common forms of anxiety disorders: (1) generalized anxiety, (2) panic, (3) phobia, and (4) obsessive-compulsive disorder. Discussions of each follow.

Generalized Anxiety Disorder

As the name implies, victims of **generalized anxiety disorder** feel anxious, but their emotion has no specific focus. Freud described the condition as "free-floating anxiety." Each day is filled with a general feeling of tension, uneasiness, and vague fear. People displaying this symptom often feel irritable and jumpy, and they are uncomfortable with other people. They are constantly "on edge," unable to concentrate and filled with doubts about their ability to work or study. Their level of anxiety is likely to shoot up as a result of minor events that would not affect a normal person (Hamilton, 1982).

Many anxious people are constantly concerned about their health—often needlessly, although they may actually develop physical symptoms. Their autonomic nervous system is overactive, producing heart palpitations, shortness of breath, hot flashes, cold sweats, nausea, diarrhea, and frequent urination. Because they find it difficult to "turn off" at night, they wake up feeling as tired as when they went to bed. Sufferers cannot seem to control the apprehension that hovers menacingly over them and clouds virtually every

TEST YOURSELF

d) What are some common symptoms of depression?

e) There is evidence that mood disorders are linked to chemical imbalances in the brain. Some severely depressed people have an excess of which hormone?

f) Jeffrey, a third-grader, complains every morning of a headache or stomachache and says he doesn't want to go to school. What disorder might he be suffering from?

Bulimia nervosa

An eating disorder in which a person engages in eating binges and then induces vomiting, takes laxatives, and exercises excessively in order to avoid weight gain.

Vasopressin

A brain hormone that affects learning and memory and may be released during stress; high levels of vasopressin may be associated with bulimia nervosa.

Anxiety disorder

A psychological disorder in which anxiety is the dominant symptom.

Generalized anxiety disorder

A type of anxiety disorder marked by unfocused feelings of tension, uneasiness, and vague fear.

Typical Statements	Percentage of Cases
I just can't relax	97
I have no powers of concentration	86
I'm tense all over	86
I feel scared all the time	79
I am likely to go out of control	76
I'm afraid of being rejected	72
I just can't control my thinking	72
I feel confused	69
My mind feels like a blur	66
I feel unsteady	62
I get weak all over	59
I can't recall a thing	55
I'm often terrified	52
My hands sweat	52

FIGURE 10.6 What anxiety-ridden people typically say Listed here are statements made by half or more of individuals suffering from generalized anxiety disorder (after Beck & Emery, 1985).

aspect of their lives. Examples of typical complaints of such individuals are contained in Figure 10.6.

As with mood disorders, some people are genetically more susceptible than others. Research has found that when anxiety runs in families, it is more likely to be due to genetic rather than environmental causes (Kendler, 1992c).

Panic Disorder

Panic disorder

A type of anxiety disorder characterized by a sudden and overwhelming sense of disaster or impending death accompanied by physical symptoms like a pounding heart, breathing difficulties, hot flashes, nausea, and dizziness.

Some people unexpectedly experience a flood of terror with no apparent cause. They are said to be suffering from a **panic disorder.** For no clear reason, they are suddenly overwhelmed with a sense of disaster and imminent death, which is usually accompanied by physical symptoms: a pounding heart, breathing difficulties, hot flashes, nausea, and dizziness. They also may have feelings of unreality, or believe that they are about to lose control and "go crazy."

The consequences of untreated panic disorder are similar to those of depression: feelings of poor physical and emotional health, alcohol and drug abuse, increased risk of suicide, and impaired social functioning (Markowitz, 1989). Although panic disorder is usually diagnosed in adulthood, research shows that panic attacks often occur first among children as young as 11 or 12, and the onset is closely linked to the beginning of puberty (Taylor, 1992). Some panic patients become so afraid of having an attack on the street or while driving they are reluctant to leave the safety of their home. When this happens, they are called agoraphobic—meaning fear of the marketplace or fear of being in the world outside of their home.

Phobic Disorder

Phobic disorder

A type of anxiety disorder in which the person has an intense, irrational, and unreasonable fear of a specific object, situation, or activity.

Sometimes anxiety becomes attached to a specific object, situation, or activity. The victim is then regarded as suffering from a **phobic disorder**—in other words, displaying an unreasonable fear. (*Phobia* is the Greek word for fear.) According to the National Institute of Mental Health, phobias are the most common mental health disorder in the United States.

Many of us refer to ourselves casually as having one sort of phobia or another. "I have a phobia about spiders," you might hear some people say as they scrupulously survey the back yard before a picnic. Others will tell you that they become frightened by thunderstorms, and they carefully check and recheck the weather forecast before starting out on a trip. Most of us manage to function quite well despite such fears. Victims of a phobic disorder, in contrast, find that their morbid fears recur so frequently and are so intense that they interfere with day-to-day activities and even become the controlling factors in their lives.

Phobias can be acquired through simple conditioning in childhood, as the child Albert acquired his fear of furry animals (see p. 158). But they can also develop in more complex ways—for instance, as a means of displacing basic anxieties about sex or social interactions onto something more tangible.

The most crippling of all phobias is **agoraphobia,** or fear of public places, which can include streets, stores, buses, trains, or virtually anywhere outside a person's house. In fact, victims often become imprisoned in their own homes, which they perceive as the only safe place to be. As stated earlier, agoraphobia typically takes hold after a number of severe panic attacks. About one third of panic disorder patients develop it (NIH Consensus Paper, 1991). The person then begins to avoid situations in which the attacks happened, but soon this avoidance response spreads to other situations. Eventually it becomes impossible to go anywhere at all—certainly not alone.

Social phobia is an intense fear of being scrutinized by others. Sufferers are preoccupied with the notion that they will be humiliated in some type of social encounter. (Anxiety about public speaking is a mild form of social phobia.) In its most serious form, people with social phobia retreat from social involvement and are handicapped in their work. They often try to calm their fears through alcohol use, which can lead to excessive drinking (Kushner et al., 1990).

Phobias are more likely to be found among adolescents and young adults than older people. Like panic attacks, they are—at least in their milder forms—also more common among females than males (Costello, 1982). One possible explanation of this sex difference is that fearfulness has long been more acceptable among women than men, although genetic causes are likely.

Fear of leaving one's home often follows a series of panic attacks while the person is away from home.

Agoraphobia
(ag-o-rah-FO-be-ah) An abnormal fear of being in public places.

Social phobia
An intense fear of social situations in which one might be scrutinized by others.

Obsessive-Compulsive Disorder

Obsessions are thoughts that keep cropping up in a persistent and disturbing fashion. Some anxiety-ridden people are obsessed with the idea that they have heart trouble or that they are going to die by a certain age. A common and mild form of obsession is the feeling when starting out on a trip that a door has been left unlocked or that the stove is turned on.

Compulsions are irresistible urges to perform some act over and over again, such as washing one's hands dozens of times a day. The hostess who cannot bear to see a knife or fork out of line at the table and keeps emptying her guests' ashtrays is exhibiting mild forms of compulsion. So is the student who cannot get any work done unless his papers are arranged in neat piles on his desk and he has a half-dozen freshly sharpened pencils waiting all in a line.

Obsession
A repetitive thought that occurs in a persistent and disturbing fashion.

Compulsion
A repetitive and irresistible urge to act in a particular way.

Obsessive-compulsive disorder (OCD)

A type of disorder marked by repetitive thoughts (obsessions) and repetitive urges to act (compulsions).

Together, these reactions, when practiced to the extreme, make up **obsessive-compulsive disorder** (OCD), which leads an individual to experience excruciating uncertainties and to practice repeated routines hundreds of times each day. Here are two typical cases, described in a government report on the disorder (Alcohol, Drug Abuse, and Mental Health Administration, 1989):

> Several times a day, a young mother is seized by the fearful thought that she is going to harm her child. However hard she tries, she cannot get rid of this painful and worrisome idea. She even refuses to touch the kitchen knives and other sharp objects because she is afraid that she may use them as weapons.

> Troubled by repeated thoughts that she may have contaminated herself by touching doorknobs and other "dirty" objects, a teenage girl spends hours everyday washing her hands. Her hands are red and raw, and she has little time for social activities, but the washing continues.

The disorder is not at all as rare as was once thought, affecting as many as five million Americans—including a large number of young people. A listing of obsessions and compulsions commonly found among those with this disorder is provided in Figure 10.7.

There is considerable evidence that the disorder has a biological basis—specifically, a disruption of the pathways that link the frontal lobes of the cerebral cortex to areas of the cerebellum and brainstem that govern certain cognitive and motor functions. Moreover, about a fifth of those with obsessive-compulsive disorders have tics such as eye blinks and grimaces. And since the disorder seems to run in families, it may be transmitted genetically (Rapoport, 1989).

TEST YOURSELF

g) A friend is suddenly overwhelmed with a sense of disaster and imminent death. He complains of a pounding heart, difficulty breathing, hot flashes, nausea, and dizziness. What disorder might this be?

h) What age group suffers the most from panic disorder and phobias?

Personality Disorders—Flaws in Character and Temperament

Personality disorders

A category of disorders characterized by ingrained and inflexible habits that are an integral part of the whole personality.

People suffering from schizophrenia, depression, or vared forms of anxiety may have isolated or recurrent episodes of abnormal behavior, but return to their "normal selves" the rest of the time. In contrast, some forms of abnormal behavior are integral parts of the entire personality. These forms of behavior, known as **personality disorders,** may arise out of some underlying and deep-seated conflict, but the person may not feel any discomfort such as depression or panic. But they behave in ways that are often painful to others. They seem to lack a desire—or perhaps ability—to act in ways that are socially acceptable, and they rarely try to change their behavior by getting help. Their patterns of behavior often surface at an early age and become so deeply ingrained that even friends or family members may find it difficult to distinguish the disorder from the person.

Although personality disorders are not easy to classify, it is possible to differentiate over a dozen different types (American Psychiatric Association, 1987). Discussions of three of them follow, and a half dozen others are described in Figure 10.8. In each case, there is no mistaking the central theme, or core, of the personality.

Symptoms of Obsessions	Percentage
Concern with dirt, germs, or environmental toxins	40
Something terrible happening (fire, death or illness of self or loved one)	24
Symmetry, order or exactness	17
Scrupulosity (religious obsessions)	13
Concern or disgust with bodily wastes or secretions (urine, stool, saliva)	8
Lucky or unlucky numbers	8
Forbidden, aggressive, or perverse sexual thoughts, images, or impulses	4
Fear might harm others or oneself	4
Concern with household items	3
Intrusive nonsense sounds, words, or music	1

Symptoms of Compulsions	Percentage
Excessive or ritualized handwashing, showering, bathing, toothbrushing, or grooming	85
Repeating rituals (going in or out of a door, up or down from a chair)	51
Checking (doors, locks, stove, appliances, emergency brake on car, paper route, homework)	46
Rituals to remove contact with contaminants	23
Touching	20
Measures to prevent harm to self or others	16
Ordering or arranging	17
Counting	18
Hoarding or collecting rituals	11
Rituals of cleaning household or inanimate objects	6
Miscellaneous rituals (such as writing, moving, speaking)	26

FIGURE 10.7 When anxiety breeds chronic obsessions and compulsions Indicated here are the most frequent symptoms found in a study of 70 children and adolescents diagnosed as having obsessive-compulsive disorder (Rapoport, 1989).

Antisocial Personality: Recipe for a Criminal

An extreme form of personality disorder is **antisocial personality**. People with this type of personality seem to lack a normal conscience or sense of social responsibility and to have little empathy for other people. Some of these sociopaths, as they are called, may seem on the surface to be quite charming, candid, and generous—but in truth they are selfish, ruthless, and addicted to lying. They have little affection for anyone but themselves and take advantage of others without a shred of guilt. The apparent absence of anxiety or guilt is one of the outstanding characteristics of the sociopath—and, of course, a factor that makes antisocial personality different from most other disorders.

Sociopaths are likely to be in and out of trouble all their lives; they rarely learn from experience and appear to have no desire to help themselves.

Antisocial personality

A personality disorder characterized by a lack of conscience or lack of a sense of social responsibility; a person with this disorder is often referred to as a sociopath.

Type of Personality Disorder	What the Person Is Like
Histrionic	Highly excitable, often reacting to tiny events with gigantic displays of emotion; shallow and not very genuine; quick to form friendships—but soon becomes demanding and inconsiderate; seductive and tries to dominate the opposite sex; egocentric and needs to control others, sometimes even by threatening or actually attempting suicide
Passive-aggressive	Aggressive and resentful toward others—but only indirectly through such annoying techniques as procrastination, stubbornness, and intentional inefficiency; lacks self-confidence and has a pessimistic attitude
Dependent	Lacks self-confidence and initiative; manages to let other people take responsibility for everything in life—even for major decisions about job or career; cannot stand the idea of being self-reliant; needs to depend on others at all costs—even if the other person is mean and abusive; sees self as dumb and helpless
Compulsive	Perfectionistic and so absorbed in trivial details as to be unable to see "the big picture;" overly serious and stingy and rarely does anything spontaneously; intent on having others conform to "my way of doing things;" indecisive, afraid of making a mistake, and unable to establish priorities; puts even routine work ahead of friends
Schizoid	Unable to build close social relationships or even to feel any warmth toward others; indifferent to almost everything, including the feelings of people; reserved and withdrawn—a true "loner;" humorless, dull, and aloof; vague and indecisive; absentminded and given to daydreaming; sometimes seems removed from the real world—but without the seriously abnormal symptoms of schizophrenia
Borderline	Impulsive, unpredictable, and easily upset; gets uncontrollably angry for little reason; quickly shifts mood—from depression to irritability to anxiety; feels empty and bored inside and is unable to establish a firm sense of identity; lives on the border of reality, slipping beyond it during periods of heavy pressure and stress

FIGURE 10.8 Characteristics of people with personality disorders We all know people who have traits somewhat like the ones listed. But for people with personality disorders, the patterns are so pervasive that it becomes virtually impossible for them to adapt to the demands of the real world. As a result, their social relationships and their work are likely to suffer significantly.

Instead of becoming independent, self-supporting adults, they are impulsive and reckless—unable to keep a job, maintain an enduring marital or sexual relationship, or act as a responsible parent. Lacking respect for the law, they often end up spending periods of their lives in prison. Such a person is sometimes also referred to as a "psychopath," a word used frequently to describe criminals who appear to experience no remorse for even the most cruel deeds—examples of the antisocial personality in its most extreme form.

The causes remain a mystery, but antisocial behavior patterns usually begin in childhood, about age seven or eight and is more common in boys. It is rare for people to be diagnosed as having an antisocial personality unless they displayed similar problems before they reached 18 years of age. They have a history of school truancy, stealing, lying, irresponsibility about money, heavy involvement in sex, staying out late, or running away from home. The more antisocial symptoms children displayed, the more likely they were to grow up as antisocial adults (Robins, 1978).

There is some evidence that sociopaths tend to have autonomic nervous systems that are less reactive and more difficult to arouse. Disruptive and antisocial children and adolescents in one study had lower levels of a metabolic neurotransmitter called *serotonin* and had lower levels of arousal (Kruesi, 1992). This biological characteristic might lead them to seek emotional excitement and at the same time to be oblivious to danger (such as the consequences of committing a serious crime). They also seem to respond less to punishment than other people. But as in most other forms of abnormal behavior, it is unlikely that biological factors alone account for an antisocial personality. The social environment appears to weigh heavily in the development of the disorder. The chances of developing an antisocial personality disorder are high for those raised by a parent who has the disorder. Growing up with antisocial companions and in high-crime neighborhoods are also strong factors—but these carry less weight if the parents themselves are free of antisocial behavior (Robins, 1978). The backgrounds of those sociopaths who end up as criminals reveal the same combination of biological traits and environmental circumstances (Wilson & Herrnstein, 1985).

Aggression and stealing, which are on the rise in American cities, are more common in boys than in girls.

Paranoid Personality: Unreasonable Suspicion

All of us feel suspicious at times—and it is a good thing that we do. You would be ignoring your own best interests if you were not wary when hearing strange sounds in your basement at night, or on discovering that a classmate's essay bears an uncanny resemblance to your own. But the basement prowler may turn out to be a cat, and the apparent case of plagiarism a coincidence. For normal people, once there is evidence that such suspicions are not warranted, they are dispelled. Wariness wanes and trust is established.

In contrast, people with a **paranoid personality** are unable to give up their constant suspicions and mistrust of other people—even when the facts clearly point the other way. Worse yet, they may even become suspicious of anyone who tries to reason with them. They expect at any moment to be tricked, and they are always on guard and worried about the hidden motives of others. Paranoid individuals often seem to be devious and scheming. They also appear hostile and defensive—and so stubborn and rigid that they are unable to compromise.

It is extremely hard to build satisfying relationships with paranoid individuals. At work, such people tend to be intensely concerned with rank, always needing to know who is in control. Moreover, everything is taken personally. For example, if a company established a new regulation that required all employees to sign in and out of work, paranoid individuals would feel that the rule was specifically devised only to get at them. In marriage they can become insanely jealous for no reason (read *Othello*), yet they are incapable of intimacy because they can trust no one.

People with a paranoid personality disorder are often quite bright. In their own distorted way, they display highly prized capacities such as sensitivity, quickness of thought, and great consistency. Yet underneath, paranoid persons feel grossly inferior. Because paranoid persons are always fighting off feelings of inadequacy, they tend to blame everything on others. In extreme

Paranoid personality

A personality characterized by constant suspicions and mistrust of others.

cases, this process results in delusions of persecution. Some paranoid individuals manage to compensate for their feelings of inferiority by developing delusions of power and grandeur. Among them are extremely disturbed paranoid persons who end up actually believing that they are the pope or the president. Their delusions are as pervasive as those found in schizophrenia, for whom trying to use reasoning to deal with delusions "is like trying to bail out the ocean with a bucket" (Torrey, 1983).

Narcissistic Personality: Self-Absorption

Narcissistic personality
A personality dominated by self-love.

In an ancient Greek legend, Narcissus was a beautiful young man who fell in love with his own reflection in a pool—so much so that he remained glued there until he died. His name is the basis for a trait known as narcissism—or self-love—which in extreme form dominates the personality of those with a **narcissistic personality.**

People with this disorder are often quite charming and attractive, but once you get to know them, they are easy to dislike. They seem to have an inflated sense of their own importance, acting as if they were God's gift to humanity. Unlike obsessive-compulsive individuals who constantly seek perfection, narcissistic people claim it (Akhtar & Thomson, 1982). They feel entitled to everything and end up using people for their own purposes, including sex. Often they give the impression that they really like you when

Narcissistic personality is a term that Freud used to describe total involvement with the desires of the self.

all they actually want is to get you to do something for them. They offer little in return, and worse still, can excuse nothing of others.

Narcissistic individuals crave constant attention and admiration because they are trying desperately to compensate for painful feelings of emptiness and worthlessness lurking beneath the surface. That is also why they tend to daydream of incredible successes in their work or their love affairs. They are extremely superficial, totally preoccupied with appearances. They would rather be seen with the "right people" than enjoy the company of close friends. They also fake the feelings they think are appropriate in any situation to impress others. How they look is so important to them that they can easily spend hours grooming themselves. The narcissist of today stands transfixed at the mirror instead of the reflecting pool.

Some might claim that this disorder is becoming more common because there is a greater acceptance in our culture of selfish behavior (Wallach & Wallach, 1983). For instance, books intended to teach us how to look out for ourselves first—or how to get everything we want out of life at any cost— tend to become best-sellers. But there is no evidence from research that narcissistic behavior is any more prevalent today than in the days of Narcissus. Moreover, it is wise to remember that to a degree, the urge for self-enhancement can be a healthy and fulfilling goal. It is when the urge becomes overwhelming and dominates one's existence that problems begin to accumulate.

Risky Business: The Abuse of Alcohol and Drugs

So far, this chapter has dealt with alterations in thought, perception, mood and behavior that occur as a result of disorders in which the immediate, precipitating causes are not always clear. In contrast, the final section of this chapter deals with similar changes that take place as a result of an identifiable behavior: the voluntary, frequent, and heavy use of alcohol and other potent drugs, or **substance abuse.** It would be wrong, however, to assume that the two kinds of disorders—for example, depression and alcohol abuse—are mutually exclusive. Substance abuse and mental disorders often go hand in hand.

The Anatomy of an Addiction

The use of alcohol or drugs cannot itself be viewed as a psychological disorder. Otherwise countless people would be considered abnormal for sipping a cocktail to relax before dinner or taking a sedative to get to sleep when upset. The use of substances that affect the central nervous system is considered abnormal when it becomes so frequent and heavy that users can no longer function normally—whether in the family, at school, or at work. Moreover, such people continue to seek alcohol and drugs despite damage to their health and the threat to life itself.

An indication that alcohol or drug use is departing from normal is the development of **psychological dependence.** When this happens, users no longer view the substance as an incidental feature of life or as a way to pro-

Substance abuse
The voluntary, frequent, and heavy use of alcohol, heroin, or other potent addictive drugs.

Psychological dependence
The feeling that the use of alcohol or other drugs is essential in order to handle day-to-day stress.

Physical dependence (addiction)

The state in which the body develops a tolerance for a substance to the point that the person now requires an increasingly large dose to produce the desired effect.

Tolerance

A sign of addiction to alcohol or drugs that occurs when the user begins to require increasingly large doses to produce anything like the desired effect.

Withdrawal symptoms

Painful physical and psychological reactions experienced by individuals after they stop using the substance to which they are addicted.

Delirium tremens (DTs)

A condition that occurs when an alcoholic suddenly withdraws from drinking; a state of intense panic characterized by agitation, tremors, confusion, horrible nightmares, and even hallucinations.

Cirrhosis

A liver condition caused by the excessive and prolonged use of alcohol, in which the liver becomes scarred.

Alcoholism

The abnormal use of alcohol characterized by a strong dependence on alcohol and loss of control over the act of drinking; usually results in serious physical, psychological, and social problems.

mote pleasure and well-being. Instead they believe it to be essential in order to handle the day-to-day stresses of life. An executive might come to believe that he could not possibly endure the daily grind of corporate life without gulping a few swallows of the gin hidden in the desk drawer for "emergencies." Or a student might be convinced that without marijuana there would be no way to survive the tensions of school.

Many people who are psychologically dependent on alcohol and certain drugs become **physically dependent**—or **addicted**—as well. Their bodies develop a **tolerance** for the substance, meaning that they now require increasingly large doses to produce anything like the desired effect. Furthermore, they will now suffer from **withdrawal symptoms**—painful physical and psychological reactions—when they stop using the substance. Withdrawal from alcohol results in **delirium tremens,** popularly known as the "DTs," which are a state of intense panic that includes agitation, tremors, confusion, horrible nightmares, and even hallucinations. It is not unusual for alcoholics in the throes of the DTs to be convinced that bugs are crawling all over their bodies. Withdrawal from stimulants such as cocaine produces depression, disorientation, and irritability.

The suffering produced by withdrawal is usually so great that addicts will go to any lengths to return to using the substance. Many do so despite a strong wish to "kick the habit" and return to a more normal existence.

Alcoholism's Wake of Destruction

The road from an occasional drink to dependence on alcohol is strewn with heavy physical penalties. Over the long haul, alcoholics run into a variety of serious health problems. Alcohol itself has little food value, and because heavy drinkers also usually eat poorly, they often suffer severe malnutrition. **Cirrhosis** of the liver—meaning that the liver has become scarred and hardened—may result from poor nutrition as well as from the irritating effects of alcohol. Alcoholics also run a greater than normal risk of suffering heart problems, high blood pressure, anemia, impotence, gastrointestinal disorders, and cancers of the tongue, mouth, larynx, esophagus, and liver (Eckardt et al., 1981).

Heavy drinking for long periods leads to cognitive and emotional problems as well. Alcohol destroys brain cells—which is why studies of alcoholics show that their perceptual skills and problem-solving abilities are weakened (Silberstein & Parsons, 1981). Although alcohol at first gives users the idea that their feelings of depression are lighter, it actually deepens them (Aneshensel & Huba, 1983). An unusually large number of people with drinking problems commit suicide, and more than a third of all suicides involve alcohol. A significant number of industrial accidents, drownings, burns, and falls have also been attributed to drinking. So, too, have many cases of assault, rape, child abuse and neglect, and family violence.

Measured in both physical and psychological consequences, the price of heavy drinking is heavy indeed. But apparently the price is heavier for some than for others. Recent research indicates that there appear to be two types of alcoholics who differ in defining characteristics and risk factors (Babor, 1992). According to these results, Type A alcoholism is the more benign. Sufferers have fewer childhood risk factors such as conduct and neurological disorders, and they are less pathological. Type B alcoholism is more serious. Members of this group reveal a number of childhood risk factors. There is a great deal of alcoholism in their families, and they begin drinking early in life, experience greater stress, take other drugs, and show greater pathology in their behavior (Babor, 1992).

What Causes Alcoholism?

People from all walks of life can fall victim to alcoholism, as any meeting of the self-help organization known as Alcoholics Anonymous demonstrates. What is the common denominator? While alcoholism has no single cause, heredity apparently plays some role. As in the case of schizophrenia, the chances that twins will both become alcoholics is much greater for identical twins than for fraternal twins. Studies of adopted children have shown that those who had been fathered by alcoholics were four times more likely to develop the disorder later in life than were similar adoptees born to fathers who were not alcoholics. Factors in the children's upbringing—including being raised by an alcoholic or living in a home broken by death or divorce—did not affect the results (Goodwin et al., 1973).

Researchers have not identified an "alcoholic personality," although there is some evidence that individuals who experience a greater-than-usual reduction in autonomic stress reactions with the help of alcohol are at higher risk for the disorder (Sher & Levenson, 1982). The popular image of the alcoholic as a "skid row drunk" does not hold up in real life. It is estimated that only 5 percent of all alcoholics fit this stereotype. People from all walks of life can fall victim, including hard-driving politicians, high-strung performers, harried waitresses, and anxious college students.

Alcoholism, which runs in families, appears to have a modest genetic contribution for some people.

Gender and Alcoholism

Surveys consistently indicate that males are heavier drinkers than females. Moreover, the problems associated with the use of alcohol are much more prevalent among men. Males are twice as likely as females to show signs of dependence on alcohol and are also twice as likely to suffer adverse consequences from alcohol, such as problems in family and social relationships, encounters with police, and auto accidents (Clark & Midanik, 1982).

Women may be less prone than men to try to fight off their feelings of depression and anxiety by drinking. To handle the same complaints, they are more likely to take prescription drugs (Mellinger & Balter, 1981). It may be that some women are turned off to drinking because for them, alcohol is quicker to cause adverse effects. Recent evidence shows that the stomach lining of women manufactures smaller amounts of the enzyme **alcohol dehydrogenase,** which helps in the digestion of alcohol. As a result, more alcohol enters the bloodstream through the stomach wall and goes on to the brain—causing not only the symptoms of intoxication but a greater threat to the liver (Frezza et al., 1990).

Some researchers believe that the actual number of female alcoholics is greater than the statistics show. Because drinking by women is less acceptable, many cases are kept from the attention of doctors and the staffs of clinics treating alcoholics (Sandmaier, 1980). However, the courage of public

Alcohol dehydrogenase
An enzyme that helps in the metabolism of alcohol.

figures such as former First Lady Betty Ford and would-be First Lady Kitty Dukakis to admit publically to their alcohol problems and treatment may encourage more alcoholic women to seek help.

The Highs and Lows of Drug Use

Altered states of consciousness (ASC)

States of consciousness produced by dreams, sleep, hypnosis, alcohol, or mind-altering drugs that differ from normal waking experiences.

Nicotine

A drug in tobacco that acts like a stimulant and may relieve feelings of anxiety.

Caffeine

A central nervous system stimulant found in coffee, tea, and many cola-based beverages.

Humanity has always been interested in finding substances that relieve anxiety, produce feelings of contentment and happiness, and sometimes result in strange experiences that make the user perceive the world in a distorted fashion. Hallucinations of imaginary sights and sounds may result, and sometimes a mystical or religious sense of oneness with the universe may be attained. Such states are referred to as **altered states of consciousness** (ASC).

Some mind-altering substances are used so routinely that they are seldom even thought of as drugs. Alcohol, of course, is probably the best example. **Nicotine,** inhaled through smoking, can act in several different ways—sometimes as a stimulant, sometimes relieving feelings of anxiety. **Caffeine,** found in coffee, tea, and many cola-based beverages is another stimulant.

Popular drugs include a number of substances whose use is illegal, ranging from marijuana to heroin and cocaine, as well as prescription drugs like sleeping pills and stimulants taken for "kicks" rather than on a physician's orders. The use of drugs increased rapidly in the United States during the 1960s and 1970s. More recently, there is evidence that the overall use of illicit drugs has declined. Nevertheless, nearly 37 million Americans—about one in five people 12 years of age or older—use one or more illicit drugs in the course of a year (National Institute on Drug Abuse, 1986).

All the mind-altering drugs create their effects by temporarily changing the activity of the brain—certainly by assisting or hindering the transmission of messages at the brain's innumerable switching points, perhaps also by changing the circuits over which messages ordinarily flow.

Almost invariably, the effect depends not only on the drug itself and the amount used but also on the user's frame of mind, the circumstances in which the drug is used, and the behavior of companions. Certainly the user's expectations play an important part. It has been found that cocaine users, who expect to get "high" from sniffing the powder, may not know the difference when another substance that produces the same sensation in the nose is substituted for the real thing (Van Dyke & Byck, 1982).

What Makes Some Drug Users Addicted?

More than 90 percent of all Americans will at some time in their lives experiment with or try both legal and illegal drugs, and many of these people will continue to use drugs regularly. Yet only a few will ultimately develop a substance abuse problem (Glantz & Pickens, 1992). Why do some people get "hooked" while others do not?

A critical difference, according to the researchers mentioned above, is the condition that existed before drug use started. Those teenagers who end up being heavy drug users, for instance, tend to be aggressive, have strong drives to seek sensation, and reveal a high tolerance for unconventional or deviant behavior. Other factors include poor relations between parent and child, drug use by other family members and peers, and living in an area where drugs are readily available and widely used (Glanz & Pickens, 1992).

After experimenting with drugs, some people develop a belief that they are unable to cope without them. Continued use sets up a vicious circle. As these users rely more and more on drugs to feel in control, they repeatedly confirm their belief that they are powerless to cope on their own. Each failure to function without drugs strengthens that belief until they become addicted and are in actual fact unable to face life without chemical assistance (Gold, 1980).

In the case of heroin, which poses perhaps the most serious drug abuse problem, one investigator found six characteristics prominent among addicts (Nurco, 1979): (1) inability to cope with intense feelings of anger, usually generated by frustration; (2) need for immediate gratification; (3) inability to establish adequate sexual identity; (4) rejection of society's goals and the means typically used to achieve them; (5) proneness to take risks as a way of proving personal adequacy; and (6) constant need to deal with boredom. In another study, addicts were found to be relatively deficient in the capacity for self-regulation—that is, in the ability to plan ahead and anticipate the consequences of their actions (Wilson et al., 1989).

One view of the road to drug abuse is based on a more general principle called the opponent-process theory of emotion (Solomon, 1980). According to this theory, the human nervous system seeks to balance out any deviation from normal equilibrium in emotional experience. Thus every emotion triggers an opposing emotion that lingers after the first one is "switched off." For instance, after fearful flyers endure a frightening trip, they begin to feel ecstatic. Or, as a sequel to the misery of childbirth labor, many women tend to feel euphoric. In the same way, the discomfort, or "low," that a drug user feels when the effects of the drug wear off leads to the motivation for repeated use of the drug as a means for establishing the opposing "high." Ultimately, the result is the onset of tolerance—and addiction. In effect, the drug user becomes an abuser through the frequently repeated experience of contrasting unpleasant and pleasant emotional states (Solomon, 1986).

An Insidious Link: Substance Abuse and Mental Disorder

Alcohol and drug abuse often coexist with mental health problems. One survey has found that 37 percent of people with an alcohol abuse problem also had some kind of mental disorder (Regier, 1990). The causal nature of the relationship is not always clear. Many people use alcohol and drugs to find temporary relief from their depression and anxiety. A survey of people with bipolar disorder, for example, found that 49 percent abused alcohol or drugs during periods when their condition wasn't being treated (National Depressive and Manic-depressive Association, 1993). On the other hand, those who abuse substances may be more prone to developing mental disorders—for instance, phobias. Those suffering from a major mental disorder such as schizophrenia or mood disorders are also often beset by alcohol and drug abuse (Brown et al., 1989). The overlap has been found in nearly a third of all those suffering from depression (Goodwin, 1989).

There may be a genetic susceptibility that leaves people vulnerable to both mental disorders and substance abuse. One study found that people

TEST YOURSELF

k) What type of dependence is experienced by someone who sees alcohol or drugs as essential to handling the day-to-day stresses of life?

l) When individuals who are physically dependent on drugs or alcohol abruptly stop taking the substance, what will they experience?

biologically related to depressed individuals were about twice as likely as relatives of nondepressed people to develop either a depressive or a substance abuse disorder, usually alcoholism (Ingraham, 1992).

As in the case of all mental disorders, by understanding what substance abuse is and how it develops, we may be less fearful of it and more compassionate toward its victims. One of the great challenges for psychology is to learn how to spare more people the pain of mental disorders, lighten the burdens of those who do succumb, and—as described in the next chapter—help our society respond more appropriately to their needs.

SUMMARY REVIEW

Abnormal Characteristics: Their Nature and Scope

1. Abnormal behavior, though difficult to define, is generally considered to be behavior that is:
   a) statistically unusual
   b) considered undesirable by most people
   c) a source of unhappiness to the person who displays it.
2. It is estimated that at least 20 percent of the U.S. population suffers from a diagnosable psychological disorder during a six-month period. At least 15 million Americans are seriously mentally ill.

The Varieties and Origins of Abnormal Behavior

3. Abnormal behavior hinges on two factors:
   a) the amount of stress and anxiety a person experiences
   b) the person's ability to handle this amount.
4. The ability to handle stress and anxiety appears to be determined by
   a) biological factors (such as glandular activity and sensitivity of the autonomic nervous system)
   b) psychological factors (such as motives and anxiety over failure to fulfill them)
   c) environmental influences.

Schizophrenia: Puzzling and Profound

5. **Schizophrenia** is characterized by extreme disorganization of personality. Schizophrenics typically display:
   a) perceptual difficulties, including **hallucinations**
   b) thought disorders, including **delusions**
   c) emotional disturbances.
6. In many patients, schizophrenia is associated with increased levels of the neurotransmitter dopamine in the brain. It has also been found that schizophrenics appear to have defects in brain metabolism and in parts of the nervous system responsible for perception. Evidence for the genetic origin of the disorder is strong.

Mood Disorders

7. Abnormal **depression** is marked by a severe and prolonged mood of sadness, helplessness, and hopelessness. Depressed individuals suffer from lowered self-esteem and motivation, guilt, sleep difficulties, physical complaints, and disturbances of perception and thought. The risk of suicide is especially high in depression.

8. Episodes of depression that recur without other abnormalities of mood are called **unipolar disorder.** Exaggerated mood fluctuations from intense excitement to deep melancholy are characteristic of **bipolar disorder.**

9. One form of mood disorder, called **seasonal affective disorder (SAD),** causes some people to become depressed in the winter, and energetic—even manic—in the summer.

10. Evidence exists that genetic and biochemical factors are involved in the development of mood disorders.

11. **Mood disorders** occur twice as often among women than men. For both sexes, the chance of experiencing depressive episodes increases with age.

12. The risk of serious depression increases in the later years of life—but the disorder affects a considerable number of children as well.

Anxiety Disorders

13. **Anxiety disorders** arise when situations that produce conflict and frustration remain unresolved. Four common types of anxiety disorders are **generalized anxiety disorder, panic disorder, phobic disorder,** and **obsessive-compulsive disorder.**

Personality Disorders: Flaws in Character and Temperament

14. Some forms of abnormal behavior, difficult to classify, are called **personality disorders.** Unlike other forms, they are not expressed in specific symptoms or clearly related to anxiety and stress. People with these disorders seem to lack the desire or ability to act in socially acceptable ways. Three major types are **antisocial personality, paranoid personality,** and **narcissistic personality.**

Risky Business: The Abuse of Alcohol and Drugs

15. Indications that alcohol or drug use is departing from normal are the development of **psychological dependence** and **physical dependence,** or **addiction.** Addiction victims develop **tolerance** for the substance (meaning that they require increasingly large doses to produce the desired effect), and they suffer **withdrawal symptoms** (painful physical and psychological reactions when they stop using the drug).

16. Persons who suffer from **alcoholism** become strongly dependent on alcohol and lose control over the act of drinking. They continue to drink despite the serious physical and psychological problems alcohol

produces, including brain and liver damage, malnutrition, impaired problem-solving abilities, and disruption of family life. Alcoholism has no single cause, but heredity apparently plays some role.

17. **Altered states of consciousness,** in which perception does not operate in the usual fashion, can be produced by a variety of drugs ranging from **nicotine** (in tobacco) and **caffeine** (in coffee, tea, and many cola-based beverages) to heroin and cocaine.

18. Drug abuse results from the repeated use of drugs for other than medical purposes, leading to severe physical and psychological disturbances. Abusers of multiple drugs are likely to have especially serious medical, personal, and social problems.

19. A modern explanation of drug abuse is the opponent-process theory of emotion. It holds that the human nervous system seeks to balance out any deviation from normal equilibrium in emotional experiences. Thus every emotion triggers an opposing emotion that lingers after the first one is "switched off." Ultimately, for the drug abuser, the result is the onset of tolerance and addiction.

TEST YOURSELF ANSWERS

a) Unusual forms of behavior are not considered abnormal unless they are regarded as undesirable within the culture.

b) Tracy may have a greater biological susceptibility to depression than Annette. She may also have other environmental stressors in her life. In addition, Annette may have more avenues of support and better coping skills than Tracy.

c) Physical evidence for schizophrenia include results from PET and MRI scans and the fact that all drugs that effectively treat schizophrenia interfere with the brain chemical dopamine.

d) Unrelenting sadness, intense helplessness and hopelessness, listlessness in work or play, disturbed sleep, impaired appetite, headache, heart palpitations, and dizziness are some of the common symptoms of depression.

e) Some severely depressed people have an excess of cortisol.

f) Jeffrey may be suffering from depression.

g) This person may have panic disorder.

h) Adolescents and young adults suffer the most from panic disorder and phobias.

i) Those with antisocial personality disorder may have insensitive nervous systems.

j) False. The incidence of narcissism has remained steady.

k) Those who see alcohol or drugs as essential to handling life have a psychological dependence.

l) They will experience withdrawal symptoms.

Study Guide

Chapter 10   Abnormal Behavior

LEARNING OBJECTIVES

After studying this chapter, you should be able to:

1. Be familiar with the three-point definition of abnormal behavior, and how it interferes with functioning and development. Understand how abnormal behavior is influenced by biological, psychological, and environmental factors.

2. Be able to describe the major symptoms of schizophrenia and mood disorders.

3. Understand the difference between unipolar and bipolar disorders.

4. Define the following types of anxiety disorders: generalized anxiety disorder, panic disorder, phobic disorder, and obsessive-compulsive disorder.

5. Differentiate among the three types of personality disorders known as antisocial personality, paranoid personality, and narcissistic personality.

6. Know the major signs of substance abuse (alcohol and drugs) and the difference between psychological and physical dependence.

7. Understand that the difference between normal and abnormal behavior is often difficult to define.

8. Know that everyone is likely to experience changes in mood—but in abnormal depression the sadness and feelings of helplessness and hopelessness are intense and prolonged.

9. Be aware that depression carries a higher risk of suicide than any other mental disorder.

10. Recognize that everyone is bound to experience feelings of anxiety, and an anxiety disorder is likely to develop only when conflicts remain unresolved.

11. Understand that antisocial behavior patterns usually begin in childhood and that family environment often plays an important role in their development.

12. Know that the use of alcohol or drugs is considered a psychological disorder when it becomes so frequent and heavy that the individual can no longer function normally.

For an Understanding of the Science

For Application to Life Situations

PROGRAMMED UNIT
ABNORMAL CHARACTERISTICS: THEIR NATURE AND SCOPE

1. One characteristic of *abnormal behavior* is that it is statistically unusual. Since only a few Americans believe in witches, such a belief may be taken as an indication of _____ behavior.

abnormal

unusual

2. Abnormal behavior, besides being statistically _____, is regarded as undesirable by most people.

3. A man who walks down the street talking loudly to himself is considered abnormal partly because most people regard his behavior as _____.

undesirable

statistically
undesirable

4. A third characteristic of abnormal behavior—besides being _____ unusual and considered _____ by most people—is that it is a source of unhappiness to the person who displays it.

5. A woman who is miserable because she cannot give up drinking heavily every day is considered abnormal partly because her behavior is a source of _____.

unhappiness

a source of unhappiness

6. Many psychologists view as abnormal those behaviors that are _____ —that is, behaviors that interfere with the individual's functioning and development.

7. It is estimated that 20 percent of the U.S. population suffers from a diagnosable psychological disorder during a six-month period. This indicates the widespread extent of _____ behavior.

abnormal

THE VARIETIES AND ORIGINS OF ABNORMAL BEHAVIOR

biological

8. Abnormal behavior, though influenced to a degree by an individual's inherited _____ structure, also depends on acquired psychological characteristics.

9. If we have strong motives for power and achievement that are frustrated, we become vulnerable to abnormal behavior. This shows that regardless of the biological structure we inherit, our acquired _____ characteristics also play a role.

psychological

biological, acquired

10. In addition to _____ structure and _____ psychological characteristics, a third factor influencing the development of abnormal behavior is the environment.

11. There is a high rate of mental disorder among people living in poverty. This shows that abnormal behavior is influenced in part by the _____, which also helps determine the particular kinds of abnormal behavior a person is most likely to display.

environment

12. Individuals develop different kinds of abnormal behavior under stress partly as a result of differences in their _____. Abnormal behavior takes so many forms that it can be studied scientifically only if researchers have a common classification scheme.

environment

13. To study abnormal behavior scientifically, scientists must have a common _____ scheme. To provide this, the American Psychiatric Association developed the *Diagnostic and Statistical Manual of Mental Disorders,* now in its fourth edition and known as DSM-IV.

classification

SCHIZOPHRENIA: PUZZLING AND PROFOUND

14. Forty percent of the beds in American mental hospitals are occupied by patients with *schizophrenia,* one of the major disorders in the American Psychiatric Association's classification scheme known as _____.

DSM-IV

15. Patients with schizophrenia, who occupy _____ percent of the beds in American mental hospitals, typically display perceptual difficulties, thought disorders, and emotional disturbances.

40

16. In addition to displaying perceptual difficulties and emotional disturbances, people suffering from schizophrenia also reveal _____ disorders. A prominent symptom among victims of schizophrenia is a false belief, called a *delusion*.

thought

17. If you found a man insisting that his head was missing, you would conclude that he was suffering from a false belief, or a _____.

delusion

18. Often, those with schizophrenia experience false sensory events—for example, seeing things—known as _____.

hallucinations

19. Emotional disturbances, thought disorders, and _____ difficulties are common in schizophrenia.

perceptual

20. Inherited defects in the nervous system and brain chemistry seem to play an important part in the origin of schizophrenia. But the fact that not all people from the same family become schizophrenic points to the influence of psychological and environmental factors as well as inherited _____ structure.

biological

MOOD DISORDERS

21. Stressful events in life can alter a person's mood, or what psychologists call *affect*. The behavior of individuals with an *affective disorder* is marked by extreme abnormalities of _____.

mood

22. Many people react to stress with abnormal *depression*—a plunge in mood so severe and prolonged that it overwhelms the entire personality. Such a person is suffering from one type of _____ disorder.

affective

23. People who are constantly sad and unable to work, eat, or sleep, and feel so hopeless that they often consider suicide are likely to be suffering from abnormal _____.

depression

24. Depressed people, unable to feel any hope for the future are prone to view _____ as a way to end their suffering.

suicide

25. In *unipolar disorder*, the individual is constantly depressed. Such a person has an abnormality of mood, or _____ disorder.

affective

26. An individual with an affective disorder who is constantly depressed is suffering from _____ disorder. In *bipolar disorder*, the person's mood fluctuates from deep melancholy to intense excitement.

unipolar

27. A person who is depressed to the point of suicide one week and higher than a kite the next would probably be diagnosed as suffering from _____ disorder.

bipolar

28. The risk of developing manic-bipolar disorder is 15 times greater among close relatives of manic-depressives than it is in the population at large—which is some evidence that there is a tendency to inherit this form of mood _____.

disorder

29. There is a tendency to inherit _____ disorder, which like other forms of mood disorders appears to be related to chemical disturbances of the brain.

bipolar

mood

30. A person suffering from bipolar disorder experiences wide swings in _____. Mood swings are experienced also by some people in response to the brightness or darkness of the season—a condition called *seasonal affective disorder (SAD)*.

seasonal
affective

31. A person who is depressed during the dark winter and verges on manic activity in the bright summer is probably suffering from _____ _____ disorder.

SAD

32. The disorder just described is also known as _____.

chemical

33. Bipolar and other mood disorders occur among persons showing evidence of _____ disturbances in the brain.

cortisol

34. For example, many people suffering severe depression have an excess amount of _____, a hormone secreted by the adrenal gland to stress.

introjective

35. A type of depression characterized by feelings of guilt, inferiority, and self-criticism is known as _____ depression.

eating

36. Unrealistic standards of beauty and thinness may be a reason for higher rates of depression in women. These standards may also lead to _____ disorders.

anorexia

bulimia

37. One eating disorder, in which an already emaciated person continues on a starvation diet is known as _____ nervosa. Another such disorder, in which a person engages in eating binges and then induces vomiting or takes laxatives, is called _____ nervosa.

serotonin
vasopressin

38. Evidence for a biological basis for eating disorders comes from studies showing alterations in the brain chemical _____, and the brain hormone _____.

ANXIETY DISORDERS

abnormal

39. Anxiety is characteristic of most forms of psychological disorder. Thus it is one of the most important symptoms of _____ behavior.

anxiety

40. Although most people suffering from a psychological disorder experience some symptoms of _____, the term *anxiety disorder* is reserved for cases in which anxiety is the outstanding symptom.

anxiety disorder

41. When anxiety is the obvious and most striking symptom, the patient is suffering from an _____ _____.

42. One form of anxiety disorder is *generalized anxiety*—a sort of "free-floating" anxiety felt not toward anything in particular but to everything in general. Like other anxiety disorders, it occurs in unresolved situations of

frustration

conflict and _____.

43. Mr. X faces each day beset with an unfocused feeling of tension, uneasiness, and vague fear. He is constantly "on edge," and lives as if the world were

generalized

about to cave in. Mr. X shows signs of _____ anxiety disorder.

44. In another form of anxiety disorder, patients experience episodes in which their anxiety erupts into an attack of terror. They are said to be victims of *panic disorder*. Their anxiety is more overwhelming and sharply focused

generalized anxiety

than in _____ _____.

45. Ms. X has attacks of anxiety that overwhelm her "out of the blue." She might be driving her car or walking down the street when suddenly she

feels that she is about to die. Ms. X appears to be suffering from a
_____ _____.

panic disorder

46. In another type of anxiety disorder, called *phobic disorder,* the victim has a crippling fear of something, like being confined in a small space or venturing out into public places or even streets. In a phobic disorder the anxiety is attached to a particular object or situation—rather than producing the unexplained attacks of terror called _____ _____.

panic disorder

47. A crippling fear of public places is called *agoraphobia,* a form of the anxiety disorder called _____ disorder.

phobic

48. A woman who is virtually confined to her home by anxiety over venturing out in public is a victim of _____.

agoraphobia

49. A man with an intense fear of being scrutinized by others—for example, during public speaking—is suffering from a form of phobic disorder called _____ phobia.

social

50. Another type of anxiety disorder—in addition to the vague and free-floating type called _____ anxiety, the attacks of terror known as _____ disorder, and the crippling fear of some object or situation called _____ disorder—takes the form of persistently recurring thoughts or urges. This fourth type of anxiety disorder is *obsessive-compulsive disorder* (OCD).

generalized
panic
phobic

51. An obsession is a thought that keeps cropping up in a persistent and disturbing fashion. A man who cannot help thinking he has heart trouble is exhibiting one of the two symptoms of an _____-_____ disorder, or OCD.

obsessive-compulsive

52. A woman constantly troubled by the thought that she will be killed in an earthquake before her thirty-fifth birthday is displaying an _____.

obsession

53. Just as a persistent and troubling thought is an _____, a persistent and irresistible urge to perform some act over and over again is a *compulsion.*

obsession

54. A man who is driven to wash his hands dozens of times a day is displaying a _____.

compulsion

55. Obsessive-compulsive disorders, phobic disorders, panic disorders, and generalized anxiety disorders are all forms of _____ disorders.

anxiety

PERSONALITY DISORDERS: FLAWS IN CHARACTER AND TEMPERAMENT

56. Some forms of abnormal behavior, rather than being expressed in specific symptoms, appear to exist as part of the entire personality. They are called *personality disorders*—one of the major classifications listed by the American Psychiatric Association in its _____-IV.

DSM

57. Among the various personality disorders, which seem to originate in childhood, is *antisocial personality*—applied to people who seem to lack any normal conscience, sense of responsibility, or feelings for others. These traits seem to pervade their entire _____.

personality

58. A person who constantly behaves in an impulsive and reckless manner, has no respect for the law, and ignores the feelings of family and friends is displaying an _____ personality.

antisocial

childhood

59. Also listed among the personality disorders, which seem to originate in _____, is *paranoid personality,* applied to people who seem consumed by a groundless distrust of others.

60. A man who is constantly suspicious that his wife is unfaithful, even though he has no real reason, is displaying a _____ personality.

paranoid

personality disorder

61. Just as antisocial personality and paranoid personality are forms of _____ _____, so is *narcissistic personality,* applied to people who crave constant attention and admiration and use others for their own purposes and gratifications.

62. A man who never considers the needs of other people but constantly manipulates and exploits them to gain attention and admiration is displaying a _____ personality.

narcissistic

RISKY BUSINESS: THE ABUSE OF ALCOHOL AND DRUGS

63. The use of alcohol or drugs cannot itself be viewed as a psychological disorder. But *substance abuse,* which occurs when the use of these substances becomes so frequent and heavy that users can no longer function normally, is an important topic in _____ psychology.

abnormal

64. One indication that users of alcohol or drugs can no longer function normally and are victims of _____ abuse is the development of *psychological dependence,* or the belief that they need the alcohol or drugs to operate successfully under pressure.

substance

65. Mr. Y, convinced that he can handle the stresses of life only with the help of whisky, is showing signs of _____ _____.

psychological dependence

66. Mr. Y's psychological dependence is typical of those who are beginning to be victims of _____ _____, which usually also makes them dependent, or *addicted.*

substance abuse

67. People who are physically dependent on alcohol or drugs, and are therefore _____, develop a physical tolerance for whatever substance they are using, meaning that they now require increasingly large doses to produce the desired effect.

addicted

68. Mr. Y needs increasing quantities of whiskey to produce the effect he wants. His body is apparently developing a physical _____ for alcohol.

tolerance

addicted

69. When people become physically dependent on a substance, or _____, stopping use of the substance results in painful physical and psychological reactions called *withdrawal symptoms.*

withdrawal

70. Suddenly stopping the use of alcohol often results in the _____ symptoms of *delirium tremens,* popularly known as DTs, a state of intense panic accompanied by tremors, confusion, nightmares, and even hallucinations of nonexistent sights and sounds.

tolerance
delirium tremens, alcoholism

71. People addicted to alcohol, and drinking large amounts because of an increased _____ for it, may suffer the extreme withdrawal symptoms called _____ _____. Their disorder is called _____.

cirrhosis

72. They may also suffer from _____ of the liver—meaning that the liver has become scarred and hardened.

73. Psychological dependence, physical dependence (or addiction), and with-drawal symptoms are all indications of substance _____. *Drug abuse* occurs with the repeated use of drugs for other than medical purposes in ways that result in physical and psychological disturbances.

abuse

74. Jack uses drugs repeatedly, and is now suffering chronic physical and psychological symptoms. He is likely to be a victim of _____ _____.

drug abuse

75. Throughout history, people have sought mind-altering substances, or sub-stances that produce altered states of _____.

consciousness

76. Alcohol is such a substance, and so are _____, inhaled through smoking cigarettes, and _____ found in coffee, tea, and cola-based beverages.

nicotine caffeine

77. One theory about the origins of drug abuse is based on a general principle called the _____-process theory of emotion.

opponent

REVIEW OF IMPORTANT TERMS

agoraphobia (499)

alcohol dehydrogenase (507)

alcoholism (506)

altered states of consciousness (508)

anorexia nervosa (496)

antisocial personality (501)

anxiety disorder (497)

bipolar disorder (488)

bulimia nervosa (497)

caffeine (508)

childhood depression (493)

cirrhosis (506)

compulsion (499)

cortisol (492)

delirium tremens (506)

delusion (486)

depression (488)

DSM-IV (485)

eating disorders (495)

generalized anxiety disorder (497)

hallucination (486)

introjective depression (494)

maladaptive behavior (481)

mood (affective) disorder (488)

narcissistic personality (504)

nicotine (508)

obsession (499)

obsessive-compulsive disorder (OCD) (500)

panic disorder (498)

paranoid personality (503)

personality disorder (500)

phobic disorder (498)

physical dependence (addiction) (506)

psychological dependence (505)

schizophrenia (486)

seasonal affective disorder (SAD) (490)

social phobia (499)

substance abuse (505)

tolerance (506)

unipolar disorder (488)

vasopressin (497)

withdrawal symptoms (506)

PRACTICE TEST

_____ 1. Abnormal behavior is not defined as
  a. statistically unusual.
  b. considered undesirable by most people.
  c. inherited.
  d. a source of unhappiness.

_____ 2. It is estimated that the percentage of Americans suffering from a mental disorder during a six-month period is
  a. 30.
  b. 20.
  c. 50.
  d. 10.

_____ 3. Behaviors that interfere with functioning and development are called
  a. psychotic.
  b. depressive.
  c. bipolar.
  d. maladaptive.

_____ 4. The scheme for classifying mental disorders now used by most psychologists and other mental health professionals was established in 1981 by the American Psychiatric Association and is now known as
  a. DSM-II.
  b. APA-III(R).
  c. DSM-IV.
  d. APA II.

_____ 5. The most devastating of all mental disorders, marked by a dramatic disorganization of personality, is known as
  a. schizophrenia.
  b. affective disorder.
  c. paranoid personality.
  d. phobic disorder.

_____ 6. People with schizophrenia are not likely to display
  a. delusions.
  b. hallucinations.
  c. phobic reactions.
  d. inappropriate emotions.

_____ 7. Which one of the following is an affective disorder?

    a.   Schizophrenia

    b.   Depression

    c.   Generalized anxiety

    d.   Alcoholism

_____ 8. Which one of the following statements is true about depression?

    a.   A tendency to suffer from it may be inherited.

    b.   It is related to a deficiency of cortisol.

    c.   Men are more susceptible than women.

    d.   It is always followed by a period of manic behavior.

_____ 9. An eating disorder, sometimes related to depression, is called

    a.   nervosa.

    b.   unipolar.

    c.   addiction.

    d.   bulimia nervosa.

_____ 10. Depression that occurs mainly in the winter months is typical of a disorder known as

    a.   bipolar disorder

    b.   seasonal affective disorder.

    c.   schizoaffective disorder.

    d.   unipolar disorder.

_____ 11. Which one of the following is *not* a typical symptom of childhood depression?

    a.   School phobia

    b.   Truancy

    c.   Hallucinations

    d.   Bed-wetting

_____ 12. Individuals who are so anxious about being in a public place that they never leave home are suffering from

    a.   claustrophobia.

    b.   agoraphobia.

    c.   generalized anxiety.

    d.   acrophobia.

_____ 13. A person who spends half the day checking and rechecking the doors and windows and still doubts that they are locked is suffering from

    a.   a phobic disorder.

    b.   generalized anxiety.

    c.   depression.

    d.   an obsessive-compulsive disorder.

_____ 14. A person with an antisocial personality is best described as

    a. suspicious and hostile.

    b. withdrawn.

    c. selfish and addicted to lying.

    d. perfectionistic and indecisive.

_____ 15. A person with a narcissistic personality is best described as

    a. craving constant attention and admiration.

    b. suspicious and sensitive.

    c. hostile and defensive.

    d. reckless and ruthless.

_____ 16. "Psychopath" is a term sometimes used to describe a person with

    a. paranoid personality disorder.

    b. narcissistic personality disorder.

    c. sociopathic personality disorder.

    d. borderline personality disorder.

_____ 17. Cirrhosis of the liver is associated with

    a. drug abuse.

    b. organic mental disorder.

    c. alcoholism.

    d. somatoform disorder.

_____ 18. When individuals require increasingly large doses of alcohol or a drug to produce the desired effect, they have developed

    a. withdrawal symptoms.

    b. psychological dependence.

    c. "DTs."

    d. tolerance.

_____ 19. Delirium tremens, known as the "DTs," can be described as a symptom of

    a. tolerance.

    b. blackout.

    c. multiple drug use.

    d. withdrawal.

_____ 20. Another term for addiction is

    a. psychological dependence.

    b. physical dependence.

    c. substance abuse.

    d. alcoholism.

ANSWERS TO PRACTICE TEST

1. c	6. c	11. c	16. c
2. b	7. b	12. b	17. c
3. d	8. a	13. d	18. d
4. c	9. d	14. c	19. d
5. a	10. b	15. a	20. b

EXERCISES

I. On page 485 of the text you will find a description of Ralph, a young man suffering from schizophrenia, and on page 488 a description of William Styron, a victim of depression. Both are brief case histories of the kind one might find in the file of a clinical psychologist or psychiatrist. Here is still another case history:

> Mary is a middle-aged high-school teacher who has not left her home for the past two years. Although she has suffered from episodes of anxiety throughout her life, in recent years these have become excruciatingly intense and overwhelming. At first she felt fear only when riding in a car, which she avoided by using public transportation. But eventually her terror grew unbearable whenever she was on a bus or subway as well, and as a result she began missing day after day of school. Ultimately she became unable even to go to a movie in the evening or to shop at the corner grocery. Now whenever the thought of leaving home occurs to her, she becomes terrified. Mary is virtually imprisoned by her anxieties—a lonely and frightened recluse.

How would you diagnose Mary's case? She is of course suffering from the phobic disorder called *agoraphobia,* described on page 499. Try writing similar brief histories for fictional cases of the five psychological disorders listed below. When you have finished, read them to some classmates and get their diagnosis of the problems. If there is a difference of opinion, discuss the case and revise it until everyone agrees that the description clearly fits the mental disorder indicated.

Case 1: Joseph, bipolar disorder

Case 2: Nancy, generalized anxiety disorder

Case 3: James, obsessive-compulsive disorder

Case 4: Linda, paranoid personality disorder

Case 5: Russell, alcoholism

II. Figure 10.3 in the text (p. 489) is a brief test for depression, with the answers likely to be given by the most extremely depressed individual. Most of us, of course, would answer the test items in a less extreme way. Moreover, depending on our mood, our answers would undoubtedly vary if we took the test on different days.

Two copies of the test are provided in Figure 10.9 on the following pages. Fill in one of them on a day when you are feeling especially "up"—when things are going just right and you are optimistic and content. Then take the test again when you are feeling "down"—a time when you are troubled and "blue." Your answers may vary considerably. If so, you have demonstrated that all of us experience fluctuations in mood. Our spirits rise and fall in the natural course of events. (Remember that a diagnosis of true depression is impossible from the results of any single test—so don't worry if your results seem to point in that direction.)

	None or a Little of the Time	Some of the Time	Good Part of the Time	Most or All of the Time
1. I feel down-hearted, blue, and sad				
2. Morning is when I feel the best				
3. I have crying spells or feel like it				
4. I have trouble sleeping through the night				
5. I eat as much as I used to				
6. I enjoy looking at, talking to, and being with attractive women/men				
7. I notice that I am losing weight				
8. I have trouble with constipation				
9. My heart beats faster than normal				
10. I get tired for no reason				
11. My mind is as clear as it used to be				
12. I find it easy to do the things I used to				
13. I am restless and can't keep still				
14. I feel hopeful about the future				
15. I am more irritable than usual				
16. I find it easy to make decisions				
17. I feel that I am useful and needed				
18. My life is pretty full				
19. I feel that others would be better off if I were dead				
20. I still enjoy the things I used to do				

FIGURE 10.9(a)

	None or a Little of the Time	Some of the Time	Good Part of the Time	Most or All of the Time
1. I feel down-hearted, blue, and sad				
2. Morning is when I feel the best				
3. I have crying spells or feel like it				
4. I have trouble sleeping through the night				
5. I eat as much as I used to				
6. I enjoy looking at, talking to, and being with attractive women/men				
7. I notice that I am losing weight				
8. I have trouble with constipation				
9. My heart beats faster than normal				
10. I get tired for no reason				
11. My mind is as clear as it used to be				
12. I find it easy to do the things I used to				
13. I am restless and can't keep still				
14. I feel hopeful about the future				
15. I am more irritable than usual				
16. I find it easy to make decisions				
17. I feel that I am useful and needed				
18. My life is pretty full				
19. I feel that others would be better off if I were dead				
20. I still enjoy the things I used to do				

FIGURE 10.9(b)

C H A P T E R   11

Psychotherapy and Other Treatment Approaches

More than 15 million Americans undergo psychotherapy each year, according to the National Institute of Mental Health. Today there are bewildering arrays of treatments available for psychological disorders, ranging from drug therapy to encounter groups. Unlike some areas of medicine, there are no definitive formulas for curing psychological disorders. You can't surgically cut out depression, for instance, and even when one drug has successfully helped one person, it may not help another. In addition, mental health providers are often at a loss to explain the mechanisms through which treatments work.

Despite the lack of definitive answers to some treatment questions, most people with mental problems can be helped in some way. If you must suffer from psychological distress, this is a good time to live. Not more than a few centuries ago, most victims of emotional disturbances were likely to face chains and beatings in rat-infested prisons, and total rejection by society. Indeed, the gap between the "treatment" of yesteryear and our own time defines how far society has come in meeting the needs of the mentally ill (National Institute of Mental Health, 1991).

Punishment and incarceration as treatment for psychological disorders were not invented out of the blue. They were based on local theories of causes of abnormal behaviors and how best to deal with them. For example, one notion was that demons had possessed the victims, and brutal remedies were needed to speed the demons' escape (Valenstein, 1986). As late as the opening decades of this century, patients were put in padded cells and severely punished for their deviant behavior, out of a belief that "bizarre illnesses may require bizarre treatment" (Partridge, 1957).

As in the past, today's approaches to treatment are also based on our views of human personality such as those described in Chapter 8, and on assumptions about why a personality goes awry. For instance, psychologists who believe that abnormal behavior originates in the emotional experiences of early life will focus on helping the individual understand and overcome these childhood events. On the other hand, others are convinced that abnormal behavior results from the use of self-defeating responses to people and situations, and they attempt to teach appropriate behavioral responses, while ignoring the patient's past.

The variety of distinct therapeutic techniques used today numbers in the hundreds (Parloff, 1990). This chapter will describe the major contemporary approaches to treatment, which fall into three broad categories:

Psychotherapy

A treatment that uses the discussion of problems to alleviate the patient's anxiety or depression.

- *Psychotherapy,* popularly referred to as the "talking cure," is the treatment of disorders by psychological rather than physical or biological techniques. As described in Chapter 1, **psychotherapy** entails a detailed discussion of problems between patient and therapist in order to alleviate the patient's anxiety or depression—thus modifying attitudes, emotional responses and behavior. The process has been characterized as "an emotionally charged, confiding interaction between a trained, socially sanctioned healer and a sufferer" (Frank, 1982). Psychotherapy, as will be described later, is practiced in a group setting with several patients, as well as on a one-to-one basis.

- *Biological therapy* consists of physical interventions, especially the use of drugs. This approach is based on the evidence, detailed in the previous chapter, that abnormal personality and behavior arise, in part, from disturbances in brain functioning.

Among the many forms of therapy is play therapy, used to study and deal with the psychological problems of children.

- *Community mental health approaches* include less structured techniques—self-help groups, vocational and social rehabilitation programs, telephone hot lines. Sometimes these are used in conjunction with psychotherapy and biological treatment, and sometimes as the sole source of help to those wrestling with mental health problems.

Who does the average person turn to when he or she needs help? A recent survey of more than 20,000 adults found that 43 percent of those seeking help for a mental problem turned to a doctor other than a psychiatrist. Another 40 percent went to a psychiatrist, clinical psychologist, clinical social worker or other trained mental health counselor (Regier, 1993). Finding the right person can be a daunting task, and some suggestions are contained in the Psychology in Action box titled "How to Select a Psychotherapist."

Dynamic Therapy: Probing the Unconscious

Psychotherapists who rely on **dynamic therapy** believe that effective treatment must discover the underlying cognitive and emotional forces that generated the individual's problems. They believe these forces began to influence the person in early childhood.

While it is true enough that all psychotherapy is intended to alter behavior, therapists with a dynamic orientation probe deeply into the individual's makeup in the hope of changing his or her basic attitudes and responses. As we will see, psychotherapists with a different theory see their mission simply as altering behavior and ridding their patients of painful symptoms—without

Dynamic therapy

Therapy based on the belief that effective treatment must focus on the underlying cognitive and emotional forces that generate a person's problems.

How to Select a Psychotherapist

Given the number and variety of therapists, the selection of one by a prospective client is by no means an easy task. Following are some practical steps that can help in the decision:

1. *Ask for referrals.* General practitioners, as well as many medical specialists, often refer patients to psychotherapists and are likely to know who is available and reputable in the community. Others in the service professions may also be of help: lawyers, teachers, school counselors, often stymied by the personality problems of their clients, end up suggesting therapy, and thereby accumulate a knowledge of the professionals in their area. Another good source is the local Mental Health Association.

2. *Talk to former patients.* It is better to interview those who have already completed therapy than those who are still in it. Psychotherapy patients can be emotionally swayed by what happened in their therapy session yesterday, and it might be difficult to correct for their momentary feeling of enthusiasm or disappointment.

3. *Ask for expert consultation.* An appointment with a prominent psychologist or psychiatrist in the community—for example, the head of a university or hospital department—can be used for a "diagnostic consultation." Such a widely experienced person can help narrow down the number of choices—in part by helping match therapists available with the particular problem at hand.

4. *Interview the prospective therapist.* With a few referrals in hand, the most direct way of learning how a particular therapist works is by spending an hour in a "feeling out" interview. In arranging an appointment, it is wise to make clear that the intent is to explore the possibilities, not to actually begin treatment. A number of psychotherapists believe this "courtship" is so important that they do not charge for preliminary visits from prospective clients, unless therapy is actually begun.

The match between patient and "healer" remains a distinctly personal matter. The therapist's personality and how it meshes with the patient's can be even more important than the therapist's theoretical orientation and specific approach.

Insight
The uncovering of the unconscious motives, emotions, and conflicts operating in the individual's unconscious.

Psychoanalysis
A special form of psychotherapy, developed by Freud, in which the chief tools are free association, the study of dreams and slips of the tongue, and transference in an attempt to give the patient insight into unconscious conflicts.

Free association
A psychoanalytic tool in which patients are encouraged to let their minds wander and then speak out every thought that occurs to them.

worrying about the underlying dynamics. For dynamic therapists, however, the crucial element is patient **insight**—the uncovering of the unconscious motives, emotions, and conflicts operating in the individual's unconscious. The hoped-for result is a major change in the individual's personality.

Freudian Analysis in Its Classic Form

Known as **psychoanalysis,** the method of treatment developed by Freud was designed to bring into awareness the unconscious desires and conflicts that he considered the source of abnormal anxiety and guilt. The chief tool in psychoanalysis is **free association,** which can produce insights into hidden psychological processes. If you were to undertake psychoanalysis, you would be asked to lie on a couch, as relaxed as possible, and speak out every thought that occurred to you—no matter how foolish, obscene, or insulting to the analyst it might seem. In this situation, as when drifting off to sleep, conscious control of mental processes is reduced to a minimum and unconscious forces become more apparent. The analyst pays particular attention to occasions when your thoughts encounter **resistance**—that is, when your train of thought seems to be blocked by anxiety and repressions indicating unconscious conflicts. The analyst would also pay attention to your fantasies and slips of the tongue in a search for clues to unconscious desires and conflicts.

Another psychoanalytic technique used to uncover unconscious motives and conflicts is **dream analysis.** Freud believed that dreams often reveal deeply hidden conflicts, though in disguised ways that require painstaking interpretation. Forbidden sexual desires, in particular, he thought, are likely to crop up—often in hidden form in which the male genital organ is symbolized by a snake, a tower, or an airplane, and the female genital organ by a basket or flower. Freud identified more than over two dozen symbols for the male genitals and more than 20 for the female (Rycroft, 1986). Freud labeled the unconscious sexual and aggressive meaning of dreams its **latent content;** in contrast, he identified the conscious material—that is, the actual images of the dream—as its **manifest content.** During therapy, the analyst interprets the manifest content of a patient's dream to expose its latent content—and thereby helps identify and ultimately resolve conflicts deeply rooted in the patient's unconscious. Freud regarded the dream as "the royal road to the unconscious."

Another clue to the unconscious is what analysts call **transference.** Freud believed that in a sense none of us ever completely grows up. Maladjusted people in particular tend to retain their childhood emotional attitudes and combined feelings of love and hate toward their parents and siblings, and they often display or transfer many such attitudes to the analyst. For example, a man who hated his father would transfer that attitude to the analyst, and might act aloof and hostile. At times patients might try desperately to please the analyst, as they once tried to please their parents; at other times they might resent the analyst, who has done nothing to provoke these feelings. The psychoanalyst deliberately remains passive, a neutral listener most of the time, thus providing a blank screen onto which patients can project their feelings about key people in their lives.

Through transference, free associations, dreams, and reports of everyday behavior, the analyst looks for a pattern of the unconscious problems that represent the patient's real-life difficulties. The analyst then interprets the problems and helps the patient to acquire insights into the unconscious processes and to gain control over them. The goal in analysis is to strengthen the ego and provide what an analyst once described as "freedom from the tyranny of the unconscious" (Kubie, 1950).

Modern Dynamic Therapies

Practitioners of classical psychoanalytic therapy approach their patients guided by Freud's views of the origins of abnormal personality development, as described in Chapter 8. For these traditional Freudians—a dwindling number—unconscious sexual and aggressive drives, and how they are handled, are paramount. Following Freud, however, a number of psychoanalytic therapists—taking their cues from the theories of analysts such as Adler, Horney, and Fromm described in Chapter 8—began to place greater emphasis on the importance of social and cultural forces in their patients' lives. Today, many therapists, while still using a dynamic approach, feel that it is important for patients to gain insight into what is happening currently in their lives—in their work, marriage, friendships—and to focus less on what may have happened in childhood.

A number of therapists believe, for example, that substantial changes in attitudes and behavior are possible only by altering the distorted perceptions and interactions of the individual in the presence of the very people with

Resistance

The blocking of a patient's thoughts by anxiety and repression, which often indicates the presence of unconscious conflicts.

Dream analysis

A psychoanalytic technique in which the patient's dreams are analyzed in order to uncover unconscious motives and conflicts.

Latent content

The unconscious sexual and aggressive meaning of a dream.

Manifest content

The conscious material or actual images of a dream.

Transference

The tendency of a patient to transfer the emotional attitudes felt as a child toward much loved or hated persons like parents, siblings, to the therapist.

A therapist and patient meet in face-to-face interaction.

whom problems arise (Wachtel & Wachtel, 1986). They have demonstrated the importance of working with families and spouses as well as with the individual in dealing with a variety of disorders—including agoraphobia, depression, and alcoholism (Goldfried, Greenberg, & Marmar, 1990).

Moreover, practitioners of modern psychodynamic psychotherapy recognize the impact of social and cultural forces in the therapist-client relationship. They no longer regard the major assumptions of psychoanalytic theory as valid for all, for there are often substantial differences in their applicability, depending on the cultural background of the patient. Natives of India, for example, are highly attuned to their inner lives, and once they have established a trusting relationship with a therapist, allow their free associations about the most personal matters to emerge freely. The Japanese, in contrast, tend to be less intimately in touch with their private thoughts and emotions and do not reveal them as easily in therapy (Roland, 1989).

Brief, Goal-Oriented Treatment

Dynamic therapy today diverges from classical psychoanalysis in matters of technique as well as theory. In its classic form, psychoanalysis is a long process, requiring three to five visits a week for two to five years or more, and is, therefore, very expensive. In recent years, however, many dynamically oriented therapists have attempted to shorten the treatment period (Strupp & Binder, 1984). As indicated in Figure 11.1, they have adopted new and faster techniques for helping people achieve, if not full "freedom from the tyranny of the unconscious," at least enough insight to cope with their more serious problems. Some therapists claim patients can be treated in one session (Bloom, 1991).

There is no intention in brief dynamic therapy to affect character change—although such changes sometimes do take hold. During therapy sessions, the therapist takes a more active, directive role in helping patients

Feature	Role of Therapist
Prompt intervention	Offers timely treatment to wide range of patients
Limited time	Estimates the number of sessions required—usually not more than 25—after assessing patient's problems
Limited goals	Helps patient achieve rapid improvement of symptoms, and provides insight into source of problems and future coping strategies
Maintenance of focus	Selects specific area to work on, such as problematic family relationships
High therapist activity	Talks as much as required to make interpretations and offer support and guidance

FIGURE 11.1   The major features of brief psychotherapy For practical reasons, including financial, brief psychotherapy is currently the treatment of choice for many people seeking help (Koss, Butcher, & Strupp, 1986).

focus on and solve specific problems, such as their ways of relating to others rather than on reliving childhood memories. The traditional psychoanalytic couch is no longer in evidence; in its stead there is face-to-face discussion between patient and therapist. And there is less emphasis on free association and more on a focused analysis of specific conflicts and anxieties.

Evidence of the sort shown in Figure 11.2 suggests that such psychotherapy can be as effective as longer-term treatment programs (K. Howard et al., 1986). Brief dynamic therapy can produce positive effects for a number of conditions, including depression in the elderly (Thompson, Gallagher, & Breckenridge, 1987) and stress-induced disorders (Marmar & Horowitz, 1988). There is some evidence, however, that short-term therapy is less useful when the patient is beset by family conflict or is without a social support system (Moos, 1990). Such findings highlight once again one of the three major psychological issues first raised in the opening chapter: the importance of context in understanding the nature of human personality and behavior.

Improving Personal Strengths Through Humanistic Therapy

Unlike psychoanalysis or traditional dynamic therapy, **humanistic therapy** does not demand a rigid set of procedures. The humanistic therapist partici-

Humanistic therapy
A form of psychotherapy in which the therapist encourages the growth of the patient's self-awareness and self-acceptance.

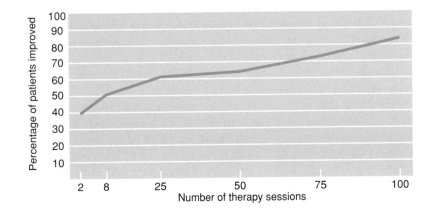

FIGURE 11.2   The impact of brief therapy As shown here, on the basis of patients' own feelings of well-being, over a third feel improved after only a couple of sessions; half after 8 sessions, and two-thirds after about 25 sessions. Subsequent sessions appear to add little of benefit (K. Howard et al., 1986).

pates in the treatment to facilitate self-awareness and self-acceptance. Matters of technique are secondary to the goals of treatment: to explore the client's inner experience from the client's perspective and to encourage personal responsibility, freedom, and will, both with regard to the changes taking place in therapy and the more general ways that individuals choose to conduct their lives (Rosenhan & Seligman, 1989). The traditional assumption in psychoanalysis is that the therapist has a theoretical view of the cause and cure of the patient's symptoms and should attempt to impose that view on the patient. In contrast, in humanistic therapy, the assumption is that the therapist must enter the mind of the patient and try to understand the patient's view of cause and cure.

Person-Centered Therapy

Person-centered (client-centered) therapy

A form of humanistic therapy originally developed by Carl Rogers.

Person-centered therapy, developed by Carl Rogers and originally called by him **client-centered therapy,** is one of the most prominent examples of the humanistic approach. Unlike psychoanalytic therapists who see themselves as the force behind behavior change, client-centered therapists give this responsibility to the client. As Rogers saw it, the task of the therapist is to facilitate—in a nondirective manner—the process of helping individuals understand and control their own lives.

Of central importance to person-centered therapy is the great warmth and acceptance displayed by the therapist toward the client. Unlike the psychoanalytic therapist, who remains aloof, the person-centered therapist creates a nonthreatening situation in which clients explore their thoughts and feelings. In the safety of this accepting relationship, clients are expected to acquire the ability to resolve their conflicts. The process, Rogers taught, requires three steps: (1) clients begin to experience, understand, and accept feelings and desires (such as sexuality and hostility) that they had previously denied to consciousness; (2) they begin to understand the reasons behind their behavior; and (3) they begin to see how they can undertake more positive forms of behavior. In a word, they learn to be themselves. These three goals are also present in psychoanalysis but in person-centered therapy the emphasis is on the third—namely, that the client should begin see how it is possible to undertake more positive forms of behavior.

Unconditional positive regard

The total acceptance of individuals for who and what they are even if one disagrees with their actions.

Rogers identified three important qualities necessary for an effective person-centered therapist: unconditional positive regard, empathy, and genuineness. As described in Chapter 8, **unconditional positive regard** means the acceptance of individuals for who and what they are even if one disagrees with their actions. Such acceptance, free from value judgments and criticism, promotes a trusting relationship between client and therapist. Empathy, according to Rogers, is the ability of the therapist to understand the feelings of the client and to communicate this understanding. Finally, therapists should always be "genuine"—that is, they should frankly describe their own feelings, including disapproval of some of the client's actions.

Humanistic therapists, however, are generally careful to distinguish between criticism of an action and criticism of the person. An important key of humanistic treatment is for the therapist to be viewed as warm and sincere at all times. Thus the match between therapist and client becomes an important factor—as indeed it is in all forms of therapy. Thus the perceived qualities of the therapist are thought to be more important than the actual form of therapy.

Other Humanistic Techniques

The techniques of psychotherapy used by humanistic psychologists are based on the belief that people will grow in constructive ways if they can be helped to explore and use their current hidden potential. **Gestalt therapists** help their patients explore the past, so that they can learn to understand and control the present. Individuals treated by Gestalt therapists are sometimes urged to relive early emotional experiences as vividly as they can. They are even helped to act out feelings—to swear, kick, and scream—but in the interest of teaching them that they now can understand their feelings and be responsible for controlling them (Rosenhan & Seligman, 1989). In confronting their emotions, they are taking a major step in gaining strength to take charge of them.

Practitioners of **existential psychotherapy** also emphasize the ability of people to take control of their lives. In direct contrast to Skinner, they believe in the importance of free will. They maintain that the events in our lives do not control our destinies—what really counts is our attitude toward these events, which we are free to construct for ourselves. Each of us is responsible for our own behavior. We can make our own decisions and thus control our attitudes and thoughts—and thus rise above even the most adverse events in our environment. This was the view of the Judeo-Christian ethic and of the Puritans, and represents a return to the nineteenth-century notion of the power of the individual's will.

Gestalt therapy
A type of therapy that helps patients explore the past so that they can learn to understand and control the present.

TEST YOURSELF

c) What type of therapy gives the responsibility for behavior change to the client? Who developed this therapy?
d) What three important qualities are thought to be necessary for an effective person-centered therapist?

Behavior Therapy: Learning More Effective Responses

Whatever habits have been learned can be unlearned. That is the tenet of **behavior therapy.** Therapists who practice behavior therapy employ techniques based on the principle of learning and conditioning described in Chapter 4. In contrast to dynamic and humanistic therapy, there is no attempt to provide insight or to rely on a person's conscious will and there is no attempt to restructure the individual's underlying personality. Instead, behavioral therapists see the goal as relieving the patient of his troubling symptoms—whether depression, phobias, compulsions, or sexual malfunctions—by modifying the troubling feelings and self-defeating actions directly using the principles of learning. This is done either by rewarding the helpful reactions or punishing the debilitating ones. Behavior therapy uses three techniques: desensitization, reward, and punishment.

Behavior therapists work on behavior and attitudes directly, rather than relying on insight; hence, their approach is useful in ameliorating abnormal, behavioral, and emotional conditions that involve action or behavior—for example, fears and phobias that lead the patient to avoid certain places like elevators, water, or heights. Behavioral therapy is useful also in dealing with problems such as overdrinking, shyness, aggressiveness, or sexual hangups. All of these involve behaviors that can be changed rather than an idea, belief, or attitude.

Behavior therapists try to eliminate whatever conditioned reflex or conditioned response is causing trouble—for example, an unreasonable fear produced by heights or confined spaces, or the habit of responding to certain

Existential psychotherapy
A type of psychotherapy that emphasizes the importance of attitudes in controlling one's destiny.

Behavior therapy
A form of therapy that applies the principles of learning theory and conditioning to help relieve the person of troubled symptoms and problems.

This photo shows a two-day "Achieving Flight" seminar for fearful flyers, in which clinical psychologists demonstrate anxiety-reduction skills. Here, a captain explains safety points.

situations with anxiety or anger. They make a direct attack on such symptoms by trying to break the old stimulus-response connection and substituting a more effective response. Changing the way people think about uncomfortable thoughts and feelings may actually alter brain function. Nine people in one study were taught to recognize obsessions, such as fear of contamination, and to gradually learn to tolerate the fear—for instance, by not being allowed to wash dirt off their hands for an hour each day. After treatment, seven of the nine people treated showed changes in the brain area where habit learning and complex movements are centered (Baxter, 1992).

Systematic Desensitization

Systematic desensitization

A behavioral technique used to eliminate phobias by associating the event that is feared with relaxation rather than the fearful behavior itself.

Deconditioning (counterconditioning)

A form of systematic desensitization.

A behavioral technique often used to eliminate phobias is called **systematic desensitization.** This consists of associating the fear-causing event with relaxation rather than the fearful behavior itself. Because the technique is designed to undo painful associations, it has been referred to also as a **deconditioning (counterconditioning) process.** If you were to seek relief from an unreasonable fear of dogs, for example, the therapist would ask you to relax as much as possible, then to imagine you were looking at a dog in a mildly fear-producing situation. If you could do this you would then be asked to imagine a slightly more threatening sight of a dog and so on until you could remain relaxed while you imagined petting or even holding a dog.

This method can be used to eliminate fears ranging from snakes to flying. One study showed that systematic desensitization can be effective in eliminating chronic nightmares. Patients wrote down their nightmares and later reimagined the nightmare while performing muscular relaxation. They repeated this practice once a week and practiced relaxation before falling asleep (Kellner, 1992).

Relaxation in a feared situation is not absolutely essential. Overwhelming fears—such as the fear of speaking in public—can be desensitized and eliminated simply by visualizing oneself in situations that have caused fear, while in the presence of a therapist who encourages the visualization process and praises improvement in the ability to respond calmly (Barlow & Wolfe, 1981). Apparently, just thinking about the feared stimulus, in an atmosphere that offers support and promises relief, is enough to produce positive results. But in order to build up confidence, it is important to practice the feared public-speaking behavior in a real-life situation (Foa & Kozak, 1986).

Reinforcement: A Positive Approach

Many of us use the technique of **reinforcement** without realizing it, especially with children. A parent or teacher might reward a child with a star whenever he completes his chores, or lavishly praise a toddler every time she successfully uses the toilet. In a clinical setting behavior therapists do much the same thing—offer positive rewards following the display of a more desirable or effective behavior.

The technique, based on reinforcement learning discussed in Chapter 4, has been widely used to improve the emotional and intellectual functioning of autistic children (Lovaas, 1987). Often the rewards that are used to provide positive reinforcement are intended to satisfy basic drives and motives—for instance, the thirst for drink, or for feelings of achievement. It helps, of course, if the rewards offered are personally meaningful to the individual being treated (Koegel & Koegel, 1989).

The technique of reinforcement has also been used in the form of a **token economy** (see Chapter 4), which has produced dramatic improvement in the behavior of mental hospital patients rewarded with tokens exchangeable for movies and other privileges.

Extinction Through Aversive Conditioning

Behavior therapists also use the principle of **extinction** to break a troublesome stimulus response connection. They accomplish this by withholding reward or by introducing a painful, punishing experience.

A nine-month-old boy who had acquired the habit of vomiting shortly after every meal, weighed only 12 pounds and was in danger of starving to death. An electrode was attached to his leg and shocks were administered whenever he began to vomit, continuing until he stopped. After a few experiences, the boy learned to stop vomiting as soon as the shock occurred, soon stopping altogether. After a few weeks he weighed 16 pounds, was released from the hospital, and continued to gain weight at home, showing no signs of going back to the habit (Lang & Melamed, 1969).

The extinction of a response by pairing undesirable stimulus such as electric shock with the response, is called **aversive conditioning.** The person under treatment learns to abandon the undesirable action in order to avoid the unpleasant consequences with which the therapist causes it to be associated. Aversive conditioning is always used with caution—or when nothing else seems possible, as in the case of the starving boy—but has proved effective in a number of situations. For example, behavior therapists have treated alcoholics by giving them a drug that results in extreme nausea when mixed with alcohol, and rapists by administering electric shocks to them while they are experiencing violent sexual fantasies.

Reinforcement
The process of assisting learning by the pairing of desired behaviors with something the organism finds rewarding.

Token economy
A form of behavior modification in which the person earns tokens for appropriate behavior and can later exchange the tokens for privileges or goods.

Extinction
The disappearance of the conditioned response that results from the withdrawal of the reinforcement.

Aversive conditioning
The extinction of a response by the pairing of an undesirable stimulus such as electric shock, with the response.

Although the behavioral therapist and the psychoanalyst would treat a patient afraid of crowds in very different ways, if the therapist is well trained, the success rate is equal for both kinds of therapies. The actual explanation for cure probably lies elsewhere—for instance, in the relation of the patient to the therapist and in the patient's desire to improve and to live up to the standards the therapist has set forth. The key to cure in therapy is one's desire to get better and faith in one's ability to improve.

Cognitive Behavior Therapy

Many behavior therapists have moved away from sole reliance on behavioral techniques such as desensitization, reinforcement, and extinction, and they are using cognitive therapies because they wish to change their clients' thought patterns. In treating depression, for example, therapists who practice **cognitive behavior therapy** try to bring to light the unrealistically negative and self-defeating views that depressed people tend to develop about their own capacities, the world about them, and the future (Beck, 1985). They help their clients by altering these self-defeating thoughts. Some cognitive therapists use **rational-emotive therapy** (**RET**) whose purpose is to expose and to discourage the patient's irrational and illogical ideas (Ellis & Dryden, 1987). It is estimated that as many as 22 variations of cognitive therapy are now in use (Dobson, 1988).

According to many current therapists, the difference between normal and abnormal behavior lies in a person's convictions about the ability or lack of ability to cope with anxiety-producing or stressful situations. Beliefs about **self-efficacy** determine whether individuals will make efforts to cope, how hard they will try, and how long they will persist. The key to therapy success is an enhanced regard for their own self-efficacy. The key to these feelings about themselves, in turn, is successful performance in situations that have previously caused anxiety or stress (Bandura, 1984). For instance, a promising treatment that is used for anxiety related to performing in public has musicians recreate and learn to counter their stage fright during a mock performance with a therapist and other musicians. This cognitive-behavioral method proved superior to a popular antianxiety drug.

TEST YOURSELF

e) An autistic child who has never learned to sit still is rewarded with a treat or attention when he successfully sits for a few minutes. What is this technique called?

f) What type of therapy focuses on changing the unrealistically negative and self-defeating views depressed people have of themselves?

Therapy in Groups

Most of the types of treatment described so far can be practiced with several patients in a group setting, as well as in an individual one. **Group therapy** is the child of necessity, for there are not enough trained therapists to treat all prospective clients individually. But it seems to have genuine advantages with some clients. Joining a group may relieve the individual's anxiety over being different by helping clients see that other people have the same problems. It also creates a social give-and-take that is impossible in a individual session with a therapist. Some psychologists believe many clients show the greatest progress when treated through a combination of group and individual psychotherapy.

Recovering addicts are shown in a group therapy session.

Group Therapy: The Traditional Approach

In the traditional therapy group, the therapist meets with a small number of individuals, usually from six to nine. The therapist typically determines the composition of the group, selecting participants on the basis of what is known of their problems and how each member can be anticipated to engage in the give-and-take of the group situation. Over time, however, each group usually develops its own style, its own way of dealing with explosive subjects such as love and hate, guilt and anger, sex and suspicion. The quality of the leader is important. It takes a well-trained therapist to track the complex interactions among group members and to explain what is happening as the interactions unfold.

For many people, group therapy is an effective vehicle for growth and change (Yalom, 1985). Therapy in a group gives each participant a circle of people who will share feelings with each other and understand and deal with them. In a group setting, interpersonal difficulties can be exposed from behind a facade of "put-ons." Group therapy has been described as a "living laboratory" where therapists can zero in on their patients' usual ways of dealing with people and help them try out new ones.

Healing Through Self-Help

Self-help groups, also referred to as **mutual support groups,** were discussed briefly in Chapter 9. They are based on the belief that when we come together with individuals facing comparable problems, we help ourselves as well as others. Some groups use professional advisers but most do not. They are diverse in size and the structure and frequency of meetings, for the help given does not have the constraints of time, place, or format (Riessman, 1984). Group meetings can take place in a basement, apartment, mental health center, church, school rap room—virtually anywhere in the community.

Self-help (mutual support) groups
A form of community therapy based on the belief that when individuals who are facing comparable problems come together, they can help themselves as well as each other.

Probably no group more clearly reflects the healing effects of mutual support than Alcoholics Anonymous, or A.A. Each chapter is a fellowship of individuals who share their experiences, strengths, and hopes with one another in order to help themselves—and others—recover from the misuse and abuse of alcohol. It is estimated that some 15 million Americans belong to self-help groups, assisting them through a broad spectrum of life crises (Riessman, 1985). Included are groups in which the jobless organize to help one another find work; burned-out professionals sustain one another; parents of young children with cancer see one another through their ordeal; and widows and widowers attempt to pick up the pieces of their lives. There are groups for couples who are infertile, parents whose children use drugs, divorced persons, isolated older people, the handicapped, suicide-prone individuals, and former mental hospital patients. It is estimated that nearly 4 percent of Americans over age 17—more than six million individuals—are currently using such groups as a mental health resource (Jacobs & Goodman, 1989).

Self-help groups are effective for at least three reasons. To begin with, simply to put feelings into words is a healing experience. People find that expressing even their most morbid concerns helps them build a bond with others who are equally troubled. Second, communication helps people recognize that others who face similar problems manage to survive. It helps them discover models with whom they can identify. Third, people learn in self-help groups that reactions to stress are not unnatural. Being unduly anxious, sad, or upset is generally not approved of in our society, and many people struggling with problems are uncomfortable because they see themselves as being more upset than they should be. The company of others gives them the assurance that they are really not so atypical in their emotional reactions to their crises (Segal, 1986).

Assessing the Effectiveness of Encounter Groups

Encounter group
A group of people meeting together, usually led by a trained therapist, who shed emotional masks often worn in public and air their true feelings.

Three decades ago, the **encounter group** emerged as an outgrowth of the humanistic approach stressing openness and honesty in interpersonal relationships. In a traditional encounter group, a number of people would meet with the goal of shedding the masks they usually wear in public and presenting their true feelings. The group was usually led by a trained therapist, though sometimes it would function without a leader. The goal was to throw off the ordinary social restraints and explore what are often called "gut feelings." This is the assumption in humanistic therapy: that people will grow in a positive direction if freed of artificial barriers against perceiving their true selves and interacting with others honestly and openly. The humanistic psychologist Carl Rogers was himself a leader in the encounter group movement.

The effectiveness of encounter groups has always been controversial. At one time, Rogers considered them superior to humanistic therapy as practiced on a one-to-one basis (Rogers, 1969). Abraham Maslow, who devised the humanistic concept of self-actualization, concluded that such groups are useful in encouraging self-awareness and self-expression but can relieve only minor difficulties, not serious psychological problems (Maslow, 1969).

Large group awareness training programs
A form of encounter groups in which the participants are encouraged to interact with open displays of emotions, approval, criticism, affection, and hostility.

In recent years, as the popularity of traditional encounter groups waned, a growing number of individuals have begun to participate in **large group awareness training programs,** which incorporate processes as diverse as education, spiritual enlightenment, encounter, and traditional group psychotherapy (Finkelstein, Wenegrat, & Yalom, 1982). The emphasis is on activities, games, and conversations that encourage members to interact with open displays of emotion, approval, criticism, affection, and hostility. Groups as large as 200 or more are led by a "trainer" through a variety of psychological "exercises," among them aggressive confrontations, relaxation exercises, and situations designed to induce mutual trust. Known under such names as "Lifespring" and "Actualizations," these are self-improvement programs as much as therapy groups. Some, like the program known as "est," are popular for a time and are then replaced by newer ones.

It is estimated that nearly a half million people have participated in these group experiences, and the pace shows little signs of weakening. Although many participants are pleased with the outcome, there is still no evidence that such large group programs have a significant therapeutic effect (Finkelstein, Wenegrat, & Yalom, 1982). The staying power of such groups—and the public's willingness to subscribe to them—underscores an observation made by one leading authority in psychotherapy research: "No form of therapy has ever been initiated without a claim that it had unique therapeutic advantages. And no form of therapy has ever been abandoned because of its failure to live up to these claims" (Parloff, 1979).

Therapy for Specific Problems in Groups

Some therapists address very specific problems in their clients. One example is **assertiveness training** in which the goal is to teach people to stand up for their rights without violating the rights of others in the context of a group. An essential element in the group experience has participants role-play real-life interactions. This allows the leader to provide feedback not only on what clients say and do in situations calling for assertiveness but also on their voice quality and "body language."

The analysis of relationships as played out in life is essential for therapists practicing **family therapy,** an approach based on the belief that the family

Assertiveness training
A technique to teach people to stand up for their rights without violating the rights of others.

Family therapy
A type of therapy based on the assumption that the family plays a key role in producing maladaptive behavior.

Family therapy often pinpoints critical problems in relationships.

plays a key role in producing maladaptive behavior. Underlying this belief is the view that interactions among family members are often the cause of an individual's problems—that the disordered behavior of an individual is merely a symptom of a much larger problem rooted in the family's dynamics. Family therapy sessions typically include mother, father, and children as participants, although extended family members may at times be included as well. Under the therapist's guidance, the family works as a unit, and the goal of the therapist is to resolve any one individual's problems by changing the behavior patterns of the entire family. In this sense, the family as a group—its structure and organization—becomes the therapist's client (Epstein & Vlok, 1981). Thus the therapist may play back video recordings of sessions to allow participants to see how they actually interact, or even visit the home at times to observe the family in its natural setting.

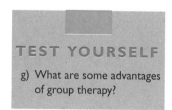

TEST YOURSELF

g) What are some advantages of group therapy?

How Effective Is Psychotherapy?

The National Institute of Mental Health estimates that each year 15.5 million Americans undergo psychotherapy. That number represents millions of dollars spent for various treatments, training of psychotherapists, and research into new and better methods. Are the time and money a good investment? How much does any form of therapy actually help a client?

The Difficulty of Appraising Results

Except in the case of clearly defined problems such as depression, alcoholism, and specific phobias, the results of therapy, unfortunately, are difficult to assess (Strupp, 1986). It is hard to determine for any problem whether a client has improved, much less exactly to what extent. Often different opinions are held by the therapist, the client, and outside observers, such as the client's family and friends (National Institute of Mental Health, 1991). Moreover, many people who experience troublesome psychological symptoms—for instance, mild anxiety or depression—get over them eventually without any treatment at all.

But most psychologists—including those who do not themselves practice therapy—believe that there is value to psychotherapy. Data from 475 controlled studies of about 25,000 clients who had undergone therapy showed that, on the average, they were better off at the end of the treatment than about 80 percent of those with comparable complaints who went without any help (Smith, Glass, & Miller, 1980). It also appears that psychotherapy reduces by about a third, the extent to which clients feel the need to seek care for medical complaints (Mumford et al., 1984).

Do some clients have a better chance for improvement than others? It does not seem to matter whether the client is young or old, male or female. But the nature of the problem does make a considerable difference. The less serious the disturbance, the greater the likelihood of improvement. Thus people with minor maladjustments of recent origin usually do better than people with severe and long-standing problems. Those who are troubled only by anxiety or mild depression are much more likely to benefit than victims of schizophrenia or bipolar depression. Cases of sociopathic personality are extremely resistant to treatment—perhaps because sociopaths do not experience the intense anxiety that most other disturbed people are eager to escape.

A desire to get rid of the psychological problem, a willingness to work at eliminating it, and a firm belief that the treatment will be helpful are the three most important factors in increasing the likelihood of therapeutic success. This is true for all life. Success in a vocation involves the same three factors. Thus, progress in therapy is not a mysterious phenomenon.

Finding the Right Fit Between Patient and Therapist

Clients improve most when they trust, respect, and like their therapist and believe that the therapist understands their predicament, sympathizes with them, and is using a treatment they believe will be effective (Strupp, 1986). The match between patient and "healer" remains a distinctly personal matter. The therapist's personality and beliefs, and how they mesh with the patient's is more important than the therapist's theoretical orientation and specific practices. The analyst, the behavior therapist, and the humanist can all be equally effective if the match between patient and therapist is a good one.

A strong feeling of empathy with the patient by the therapist is necessary if the patient is to feel comfortable sharing troubling thoughts and anxieties. There is some evidence that those who are drawn to become therapists have been wounded themselves and hence can identify with a patient's pain (Pope & Feldman-Sumners, 1992).

Occasionally a therapist's feelings toward a patient can hinder treatment. According to a survey of nearly 300 clinical psychologists, almost one-third reported disliking one or more of their patients, nine out of ten reported being sexually attracted to a patient and 83 percent feared being attacked by at least one patient (Pope & Tabachnick, 1993).

Is One Method Better Than Another?

Granted that psychotherapy is often helpful, a vital question still remains: Is one method of therapy better than another? There is no evidence that the type of treatment makes a difference if the therapist is well-trained. Therapists are about equally helpful regardless of their theoretical background or the techniques they use (Stiles, Shapiro, & Elliot, 1986). Brief dynamic therapy was no better or worse than other forms of nonstandard treatment—for example, mutual support groups, drug counseling, or the administration of a placebo under clinical care (Crits-Christoph, 1992). This may mean that any form of benevolent contact with others is helpful to patients, or that making an effort to do something constructive about one's problems, will make one feel better, at least for awhile. Moreover, for some, the treatment setting may have a powerful impact—as described in the Psychology and the Media box titled "Hospital Healing: A Depressed Patient's View."

One team of investigators compared the results of two different forms of psychotherapy with 250 patients suffering from depression. One form of treatment was interpersonal psychotherapy—a form of dynamic therapy which helps individuals understand their relationships with others and how conflicts in those relationships can result in depression. The second treatment was cognitive behavior therapy which, as described earlier, helps patients correct their distorted, negative thoughts about themselves, their environment,

Hospital Healing: A Depressed Patient's View

Many psychiatrists, who simply do not seem to be able to comprehend the nature and depth of the anguish their patients are undergoing, maintain their stubborn allegiance to pharmaceuticals in the belief that eventually the pills will kick in, the patient will respond, and the somber surroundings of the hospital will be avoided. Dr. Gold was such a type, it seems clear, but in my case he was wrong; I'm convinced I should have been in the hospital weeks before. For, in fact, the hospital was my salvation, and it is something of a paradox that in this austere place with its locked and wired doors and desolate green hall-ways—ambulances screeching night and day ten floors below—I found the repose, the assuagement of the tempest in my brain, that I was unable to find in my quiet farmhouse.

This is partly the result of sequestration, of safety, of being removed to a world in which the urge to pick up a knife and plunge it into one's own breast disappears in the newfound knowledge, quickly apparent even to the depressive's fuzzy brain, that the knife with which he is attempting to cut his dreadful Swiss steak is bendable plastic. But the hospital also offers the mild, oddly gratifying trauma of sudden stabilization—a transfer out of the too familiar surroundings of home, where all is anxiety and discord, into an orderly and benign detention where one's only duty is to try to get well. For me the real healers were seclusion and time.

Source: Excerpted from *Darkness Visible: A Memoir of Madness* by William Styron, New York: Random House, 1990, pp. 68–69.

Issues to Consider

1. Would a hospital setting be the optimum place for recovery for all people suffering from depression?
2. What other nontreatment factors do you think might affect the speed of recovery from a psychological disorder?

Placebo

A sugar pill that has no remedial or medicinal value but may relieve an illness through psychological suggestion.

and their future. A third group was treated with one of a number of drugs, to be described later in this chapter, designed to relieve depression. A fourth group was given only a **placebo**—that is, a sugar pill, with no remedial value at all. The two latter groups, while receiving no formal therapy, also received brief (20 minutes per week) counseling with their pills. As shown in Figure 11.3, all three forms of treatment were about equally effective—and all were superior to the placebo (Elkin et al., 1990).

It is important to keep in mind that the results of this study—and of similar ones—are based on averages across many people that can hide important differences in the effectiveness of particular treatments for a specific individual. For example, in the study just described, the most severely depressed patients

FIGURE 11.3 Comparing treatments for depression Four therapeutic approaches were compared with results as described in the text (Elkin et al., 1990).

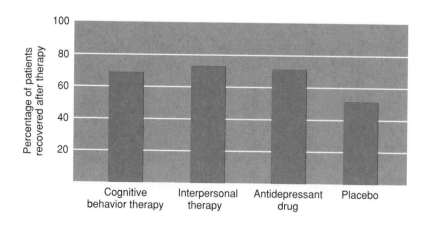

profited most from drug treatment; while those who were only mildly depressed profited, to a surprising degree, from the placebo pill, along with minimal support and encouragement. The effectiveness of a particular type of therapy also depends on the nature of the abnormal condition (Goldfried, Greenber, & Marmar, 1990). As was pointed out, behavioral therapies emphasizing desensitization and extinction have been useful with anxiety disorders such as phobias and compulsions. In contrast, when anxiety and depression are generated by actual life crises such as severe illness or loss of a spouse, group therapy turns out to be the treatment of choice (Yalom, 1985).

To complicate matters further, the cause of the condition is important. Depression can be caused by a recent loss of a loved one, an abusive relationship that has gone on for years, lifelong tendencies for self-blame and a poor self-concept, or a chemical imbalance. The best treatment is likely to be different in each case.

In a surprising number of instances, a physical rather than an emotional disturbance produces the abnormal condition. In such cases, the utility of any form of psychotherapy may be minimal. About 10 percent of patients treated in psychiatric clinics suffer from medical conditions that gave rise to the psychological complaints (Hall, 1980a). With appropriate medical treatment, their symptoms usually clear up rapidly. For instance, people suffering from anemia, a deficiency in red blood cells, often complain of being depressed and unable to concentrate (Schwab, 1980). A diseased thyroid gland can cause rapid swings of mood, uncontrollable restlessness and agitation, disturbed sleep, anxiety to the point of panic and even hallucinations (Hall, 1980b).

Finally, the effectiveness of various therapies must be gauged not only by the reduction of symptoms but by other criteria, including improvement in social and vocational functioning, an increase in the sense of well-being in the patient, and the prevention of harm to the patient and those in the patient's environment (National Institute of Mental Health, 1991).

How Patients Can Help Themselves

"The patient who treats himself has a fool for a doctor." Does this saying apply to psychotherapy as well? Can we solve our own problems and correct any tendencies toward abnormal behavior? How helpful are all the popular, advice-giving articles and books that recommend ways for achieving better mental health and greater self-fulfillment?

There is accumulating evidence that in the case of a handful of well-researched and carefully documented self-help books in which serious therapists explain their theories and methods, reading a book can be as helpful for some as consulting a psychotherapist. But there are many qualifications. For example, the person must be highly motivated and books must be chosen carefully, for there are many useless, and even damaging, self-help books on the market.

A group of elderly men and women, all mildly or moderately depressed, were given two highly regarded books on behavioral and cognitive approaches for dealing with depressed mood. Tests after four weeks showed that two-thirds of the subjects experienced substantial improvement—but only 20 percent of a nonreading control group did. After two years, the gains made by the book-readers were almost fully maintained (Scogin, 1990). In another study, of people with panic disorder, it was found that those who read a book on panic disorder and practiced exercises described there did better after four weeks than those undergoing individual guided imagery therapy (Gould, Clum, & Shapiro, 1991).

Many psychotherapists, prescribe self-help books to their patients. In a survey of 121 psychologists in Boston and San Diego, two-thirds said they consider self-help books helpful and encourage their patients to read them (Starker, 1988). Of course, those who get the most out of self-help products (including audio and video tapes) tend to be highly motivated and well-educated. Reading a book can be especially helpful to older people, who are often reluctant to seek help for mental problems. For more information on how people of different ages respond to treatment, see the Life Span Perspective Box entitled, "Therapeutic Strategies and Developmental Stages."

LIFE SPAN PERSPECTIVE

Therapeutic Strategies and Developmental Stages

Many people find that regular meditation is a therapeutic experience that reduces stress and anxiety.

Therapists do not treat patients of all ages equally. Most of the treatments described in this chapter are designed for adults, before they reach old age. Because of the special physical and developmental needs of the young and the old, traditional therapy techniques for them are often modified or refocused.

Until they are four or five years old, most children's behavioral problems are treated by their pediatricians, unless unusually severe. Symptoms of psychological disturbance among young children often include extreme fears and phobias. Other problems, which are less common, are hyperactivity and extreme disobedience.

Most psychologists and psychiatrists assume that a young child's symptoms are being caused, in part, by the behavior of their parents and the atmosphere in the family. Therefore, therapists usually treat both the child and the family. One therapist may meet with the parents and try to provide insight into the problem and advice as to how they should behave with the child. A second therapist will see the child, often in play sessions with toys, to tempt the child to act out the conflicts that are producing the symptoms. When conflicts, fears, and concerns appear during play sessions, a therapist will encourage the child to discuss them in hopes of alleviating them.

When the patient is an older child or younger adolescent, between 10 to 18 years, the typical behavioral problems are varied, but may include fearfulness, shyness, difficulties in school, antisocial behavior, hyperactivity, distractibility and psychosomatic illnesses like asthma, eczema, or bulimia. The typical treatment will involve psychotherapy or psychotherapy with drugs, or in some cases, drugs alone. Therapy is usually closely matched to the symptom. For example, children with extreme forms of hyperactivity rarely undergo psychotherapy and are simply treated with the drug **ritalin.** Children with problems in school, such as **dyslexia,** a reading impairment, are usually given special tutoring.

During the adult years, 20 to 50, patients are treated with traditional forms of therapy described within this chapter, including psychotherapy, psychotherapy with drugs, drugs alone, group therapy, and encounter groups.

The most common psychological problems among the elderly are depression, complaints about a poor memory, and distractibility. It is less common for older adults to complain of anxiety or psychosomatic ills. Because many of the mental symptoms present among the old are the partial or indirect product of physiological changes in the brain and the body, the therapy often tends to involve drugs rather than individual psychotherapy, but group therapy is often involved, especially to counter the isolation the elderly often feel. ■

Reading books and viewing or listening to tapes are, of course, not the only self-help techniques available. For some people, as reported in Chapter 9, aerobic exercise can prove beneficial in dealing with depression (McCann & Holmes, 1984). Simple exercise such as a brisk ten-minute walk can reduce the urge to smoke or snack, two unhealthy practices (Thayer, 1992). Others find help in dealing with anxiety by practicing breathing exercises or meditation (Weil, 1990). The potential benefits of meditation are illustrated in Figure 11.4.

One difficulty with all attempts at self-therapy, however, is that they lack the support of a warm and encouraging relationship—either with an understanding therapist or with members of a therapeutic group. Without such a relationship, real change and healing are often difficult to accomplish (Strupp, 1989).

TEST YOURSELF

h) What types of mental problems are most amenable to treatment?

i) What type of person is likely to get the most out of a reputable self-help product?

FIGURE 11.4 Meditation as an antidote to emotional distress Patients who took an intensive and highly structured meditation course showed remarkably reduced levels of anxiety and depression after eight weeks, as measured by a widely used rating scale. The reduction was sustained when measured again at 20 weeks (Kabat-Zinn, 1992).

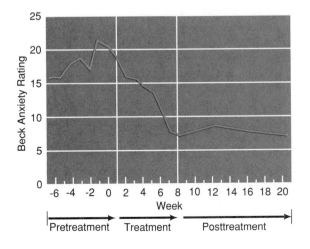

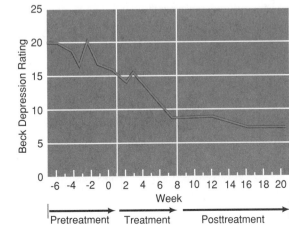

Biological Therapies: Altering Physiological Pathways

Biological therapies

A form of therapy that relies on drugs or other physical treatments to alter brain chemistry.

The therapies described to this point have been based on interpersonal communication between patient and therapist—on that "specialized human relationship designed to facilitate changes in the patient's cognitions, feelings, and actions" (Strupp, 1986). As described in the previous chapter, however, biological factors can play an important role in the development of abnormal behavior. Changes in glandular activity and in brain chemistry are often associated with profound changes in personality and behavior. **Biological therapies** are intended to help the patient by changing these underlying physiological mechanisms. Often, of course, biological approaches are used in conjunction with other therapies described in this chapter.

Drug Therapy

Drug therapy (chemotherapy)

A widely used form of biological treatment in which drugs are prescribed in order to produce specific changes in mood or behavior.

The most widely and successfully used form of biological treatment is **drug therapy**—also called **chemotherapy**—which is the prescription of drugs intended to produce specific changes in mood or behavior. During the early 1950s, the development of drugs that controlled the symptoms of schizophrenia was a major landmark in the treatment of severely disturbed individuals. Patients who were agitated and unmanageable became calm and cooperative. Furthermore, these drugs greatly improved the atmosphere of mental hospitals, making it possible to discharge patients more quickly than ever before. The introduction of drug treatment led to a drastic reduction in the number of patients in institutions for the mentally ill.

Since the early 1950s, a variety of drugs have been shown to be helpful not only in combating the disoriented behavior and hallucinations of schizophrenia, but anxiety states and depression as well. Figure 11.5 identifies the three major classes of drugs used in the treatment of psychological disorders. A more detailed description of them follows.

FIGURE 11.5 Some drugs used in the treatment of psychological disorders
Drugs such as the ones identified here have reduced some of the most grievous symptoms suffered by emotionally disturbed individuals.

Three Major Drug Groups	Trade Names (Examples)	Effects
Drugs for schizophrenia	Thorazine Stelazine Mellaril	Fewer hallucinations and delusions; less disordered thinking, and better emotional expression
Drugs for depression	Nardil Parnate Elavil Trofanil Prozac	Improved mood, sleep, and appetite; fewer negative thoughts
	Eskalith* Lithobid*	Control of mood swings
Drugs for anxiety	Valium Librium	Sedation, muscle relaxation, less anxiety

*Lithium

Drugs for Schizophrenia (Major Tranquilizers)

The **major tranquilizers** (also referred to as **antipsychotic drugs**) have permitted many individuals to be treated in the community rather than in the hospital. Such drugs have proved especially effective in reducing hallucinations, delusions, and the disordered thinking typically displayed by schizophrenic individuals (National Institutes of Health, 1989). They have enabled some patients, though by no means all, to return to a more or less normal life. Moreover, tranquilizing drugs have improved the environment of mental hospitals by calming patients who were previously unmanageable.

The therapeutic effect of some drugs on schizophrenia patients is thought to be related to their impact on the neurotransmitter dopamine. As described in Chapter 10, schizophrenia patients often have unusually high dopamine levels in the brain. By blocking dopamine receptors at the nerve synapses, these drugs reduce the activity of nerve cells that respond to dopamine. The process is illustrated in Figure 11.6.

Although the benefits of antipsychotic drugs are well established, there is growing concern about the risks involved in long-term treatment. After all, **psychopharmacology**—the study of how drugs affect the brain, body, and behavior—is still a young science, limited by lack of knowledge of precisely what goes wrong in the brain in various types of mental illness, and by the current inability to design drugs precise enough to correct only the brain's chemical problems without producing side effects.

For example, some patients who have undergone treatment with tranquilizers for many years develop **tardive dyskinesia,** a serious motor disorder characterized by involuntary movements, primarily of the face, mouth, lips, and tongue. Others may develop tremors or jerking fits, which in turn must be treated with another drug. Although the reduction of dosage may decrease the incidence of such side effects (Kane, 1983), clearly, the continuous use of powerful drugs in the treatment of psychological disorders must be carefully monitored by knowledgeable physicians (Falloon & Liberman, 1983).

Major tranquilizers (antipsychotic drugs)
A group of drugs used to reduce hallucinations, delusions, and the disordered thinking often displayed by schizophrenic individuals.

Psychopharmacology
The study of how drugs affect the brain, body, and behavior.

Tardive dyskinesia
A motor disorder characterized by involuntary movements, primarily of the face, mouth, lips, and tongue; a side effect of some antipsychotic drugs.

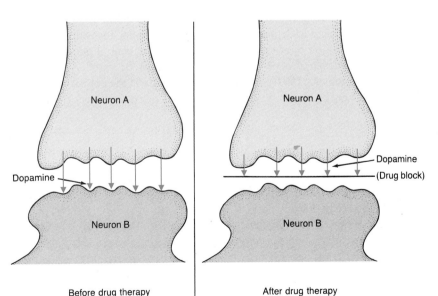

Before drug therapy

After drug therapy

FIGURE 11.6 How drugs may act to help in schizophrenia As described in the text, in many patients with schizophrenia there is an increased level of the neurotransmitter dopamine in the brain. A number of the major tranquilizer drugs—which reduce the most extreme symptoms typical of schizophrenia—prevent dopamine from crossing the synaptic cleft, or gap, between one neuron and the next.

Clozapine

A relatively new antipsychotic drug used in the treatment of schizophrenia.

A promising new antipsychotic drug call **clozapine** seems to hold great promise for treating schizophrenia. Recent studies show it helps about 60 percent of patients, blunting hallucinations and delusions and counteracting passivity and withdrawal. An added bonus is that it does not appear to cause tardive dyskinesia (Meltzer, 1992).

Drugs for Depression

Antidepressant drugs

A group of drugs that act as "psychic energizers" and are often given to depressed patients.

Clomipramine

An antidepressant drug used in the treatment of obsessive-compulsive disorders.

Persons who experience major depression are often treated with **antidepressant drugs.** All act as "psychic energizers." After a period of two to four weeks, individuals treated with these drugs often show significant signs of improvement, including relief from insomnia, a return of appetite for food, and an improvement in mood. The antidepressant drug **clomipramine** has also been used successfully in treating obsessive-compulsive disorders (Rapoport, 1989) and a new study shows it can relieve many of the obsessive-compulsive symptoms associated with autism (Gordon et al., 1993).

Antidepressants are believed to work by increasing the brain's supply of two neurotransmitters—*norepinephrine* and *serotonin*—often found to be deficient in depressed patients. Some studies have shown them to be as effective as various forms of psychotherapy in helping patients overcome depressive symptoms (Elkin et al., 1986). Although used mainly for depression, they can also be effective in blocking repeated panic attacks of agoraphobia patients (Tuma & Maser, 1985).

A new class of antidepressant drugs allows serotonin to act on the brain's neurons for a longer period than it otherwise might, thus helping relieve depressed mood. Prozac is such a drug and has been the center of much attention in recent years, having been both hailed as a wonder cure and reviled as an inducer of violent behavior. Both views are extreme, but Prozac appears to be an effective treatment for many cases of depression, anxiety, and obsessive-compulsive disorder, having fewer side effects than other medications (Kramer, 1993).

Lithium

A drug that is effective in treating the wide mood swings typical of bipolar disorder.

The salts of the metallic element **lithium** are another treatment for depression, especially when it is accompanied by swings toward manic states. This medication, taken regularly, often helps prevent the extreme ups and downs of mood typical of manic-depressive individuals (National Institute of Health, 1984). As in the case of all medications affecting the central nervous system, however, the dosage and possible side effects must be carefully monitored (Goodwin & Jamison, 1990). As shown in Figure 11.7, the course of improvement is not likely be constant, with advances and regressions over time.

Drugs for Anxiety (Minor Tranquilizers)

Minor tranquilizers

A group of drugs like Valium and Librium that are used as antianxiety medications.

Minor tranquilizers, which include such well-known trade names as Valium and Librium, are among the most widely used antianxiety medications. They are often prescribed by doctors to alleviate the symptoms associated with stress and tension. Their effects are believed to arise through an inhibition of activity of parts of the central nervous system. Because of concerns about the chronic use of tranquilizing drugs and subsequent addiction, prescriptions for them have declined notably within the past decade.

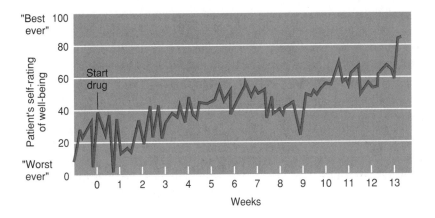

FIGURE 11.7   The course of recovery of a patient with bipolar depression The efficacy of antidepressant medication is clear from this chart, but there is "an uneven, sawtooth nature to the recovery pattern" (after Goodwin & Jamison, 1990).

Combined Therapies

Since the search for powerful medications is still in its infancy, the future will bring many new drugs that work on the biological causes of personality problems. It may even turn out that for some disorders new medications will be a complete cure. However, it is generally believed that abnormal symptoms and behavior typically spring from both psychological and biological causes and, therefore, psychotherapy should accompany treatment with drugs. For this reason, those who treat mentally ill people often use combinations of approaches, giving medications when they are needed but also helping patients understand their problems and cope with the feelings, persons, and situations that they find most troublesome. In the words of one patient being treated for manic-depressive illness:

> At this point in my life, I cannot imagine leading a normal life without both taking lithium and being in psychotherapy. Lithium prevents my seductive but disastrous highs, diminishes my depressions . . . But, ineffably, psychotherapy heals . . . it is where I have believed—or have learned to believe—that I might someday be able to contend with all of this (Goodwin & Jamison, 1990).

Dependence on a pill to dissipate painful anxiety may reduce a person's motivation to get at the underlying cause—and to adopt better ways of coping with stress. For that reason many of the anxiety disorders are best treated with a combination of drug therapy to bring the anxiety under control and ongoing psychotherapy to learn to prevent the spiral of anxiety and panic.

Most patients seeking long-term relief from panic disorder benefit from a combination of drugs—usually antidepressants or tranquilizers—and cognitive-behavioral therapy. Therapists help patients recreate the feelings of an attack, then teach them to deal with those sensations. In one study nearly 90 percent of subjects who participated in 12 sessions over eight to 12 weeks were panic-free afterward and 80 percent were still free of symptoms two years later (Craske & Barlow, 1991).

A combination of drugs and psychotherapy has also been shown to be effective with overcoming the eating disorder *bulimia nervosa*. One study divided patients into groups in which they either received an antidepressant drug, cognitive behavioral therapy, or a combination of the two. The group that improved the most received the drug and the psychotherapy. The group

Bulimia nervosa

An eating disorder in which a person engages in eating binges and then induces vomiting, takes laxatives, and exercises excessively in order to avoid weight gain.

that did the poorest received only the drug (Agras et al., 1992). Another study shows that patients with eating disorders achieve significant improvements when given an antidepressant along with either individual or group therapy that need only be of short term (D. C. Jimerson, 1993).

Electroconvulsive Therapy

Electroconvulsive therapy (ECT)

A biological treatment for severe depression in which electric current is applied to the patient's brain.

Electroconvulsive therapy (**ECT**), known in the past as "electroshock therapy," is the fastest help available for severe or otherwise unresponsive cases of depressive illness. Some patients' moods dramatically lift after only one session. ECT was first used in the 1930s and gained a very negative reputation, especially due to horrific depictions in movies such as *One Flew Over the Cuckoo's Nest*. Current practice is much more humane, administered in millisecond bursts of low voltages while the patient is under general anesthesia and has been given a muscle relaxant. Although ECT's popularity is on the rise and it has lost some of its stigma, it remains controversial (Runck, 1985). Some believe that ECT can cause long-lasting memory impairment and possibly brain damage, and therefore are opposed to its use. The general consensus, however, is that when used with the proper medical safeguards, it can work for patients unresponsive to other approaches and can be a lifesaving technique for those on the brink of suicide.

ECT has been found to be very effective in treating some cases of depression and mania that have not responded to drugs or other treatments (National Institute of Mental Health, 1989). According to one panel of experts assembled to evaluate ECT, "not a single controlled study has shown another form of treatment to be superior to ECT in the short-term management of severe depressions" (National Institutes of Health, 1985).

How does ECT actually work to relieve depression? The answer is not known but it probably increases the brain's supply of norepinephrine and other neurotransmitters. Since the electric current actually shocks the entire brain, identifying the one effective ingredient of ECT is very difficult (Rosenhan and Seligman, 1989).

TEST YOURSELF

j) What is the name for the study of how medically prescribed drugs affect the brain, body, and behavior?

k) What drug can help prevent the extreme mood swings typical of bipolar disorder?

l) For a patient who is extremely depressed and potentially suicidal, what treatment would offer the quickest and possibly most effective relief?

Mental Health in the Community and in Society

Less than a century ago most believed that people who developed a pattern of abnormal behavior were outcasts and should be locked away in "asylums." The belief today is different. We try to incorporate the mentally ill into their communities. This movement began in the early 1960s at the initiative of President John F. Kennedy, who called for a "bold new approach" to mental illness. A law passed by Congress in 1963 mandated the construction and staffing of hundreds of community mental health centers across the country.

Community psychology

A branch of applied psychology that deals with the social environment and how it can better serve human needs.

Rehabilitation

A form of mental health services through which individuals are assisted to perform the physical, intellectual, and emotional tasks necessary to function in their environment.

The field of **community psychology** is oriented not only to meet the needs of individuals who present themselves for treatment but to provide "outreach" services to those in the community in need of mental health services. One such need is for **rehabilitation,** through which individuals are assisted to perform the physical, intellectual, and emotional tasks necessary to function in their environment (Olfson, 1990).

Because community psychology is based in part on the premise that conditions in society can either cause or worsen mental health problems, the field is devoted also to building needed changes into places where people spend so much of their lives, including schools and the workplace. An important goal is to strengthen the mental health of individuals as much by preventing problems as by providing help after the problems have begun taking their toll (Kessler & Goldston, 1986).

Community Mental Health Programs

Community mental health centers were designed to treat mentally disturbed individuals in their communities rather than sending them to hospitals where they are cut off from family and society. The centers provide not only inpatient care, but also partial hospitalization through which individuals receive therapy during the day but return home in the evening. Or patients can work during the day—a therapeutic force in itself—and stay overnight at the center.

Many centers operate so-called "storefront clinics" where staff are available day and night to respond to emergencies such as episodes of abuse in the family, suicide threats, or panic attacks. An important role for psychologists is to offer consultation and education to individuals in the community who are often on the front lines of providing psychological help without actually being trained to do so. For the most part, people do not bring their personal problems and crises to mental health professionals but prefer to talk instead to members of the clergy, lawyers, teachers, physicians, police, or welfare workers (Cowan, 1982). These "natural caregivers," not specifically trained in therapy, profit from the advice and consultation of psychologists who offer them knowledge about the basic concepts and techniques of therapy.

Community programs such as this one can be precious to individuals in psychological pain.

Crisis Intervention

Crisis intervention
A community-based program designed to deal with stress-filled situations that demand immediate attention.

Case management approach
A total program to aid the mentally ill.

Some psychologists and other mental health professionals work in **crisis intervention** programs designed to deal with stress-filled situations that demand immediate attention. The crisis may be an accident, a fire, a runaway child, the loss of a job, a rape—any episode where direct and immediate emotional support is likely to be therapeutic.

The goal in crisis intervention is to use any therapeutic intervention that might be helpful. It can entail home visits to the family, repeated and prolonged telephone contacts, or seeing to it that an abused wife is given shelter. The point is to focus on the immediate circumstances and reduce the troublesome effects of traumatic events. Such intervention is now viewed as an important element in the **case management approach** to serving the mentally ill in the community; other elements of this approach include, for example, helping patients to maintain medication schedules and to address everyday problems of living (National Institute of Mental Health, 1991).

For many people, the nearest source of help in a crisis is the telephone. Thus the "hotline" has emerged as an important therapeutic resource for people in crisis. While the telephone lacks the intimacy and power of face-to-face contact, the delivery of advice, sympathy, and comfort via telephone can be critical in seeing a stressed person through a traumatic episode and preventing breakdown. The hotline also allows callers to be referred to appropriate individuals and agencies for help.

Supporting Patients and Their Families

A "hotline" counselor responds to a distraught caller.

It has been shown repeatedly that those attempting to overcome disabling psychological disorders can benefit from the support of their families and close friends. For instance, people in underdeveloped countries who suffer from serious mental disorders recover more quickly and suffer fewer recurrences than do those in industrially advanced countries (World Health Organization, 1979). With few mental health professionals available, family members in underdeveloped countries are more likely to take responsibility for caring for victims. They are prone to stay close to those relatives who become psychologically disabled and offer them the kind of support and encouragement they need to increase their chances of recovery.

Family support appears to be especially important for victims of serious disorders, such as schizophrenia and severe depression. The risk of suicide is considerably less for deeply depressed persons who have close ties with relatives than those alone (Slater & Depue, 1981). Other studies reveal that recovered schizophrenics are less likely to suffer a relapse if family members minimize their anxiety and instead exert a calming influence (Hooley, 1985).

Family members of the mentally ill, however, often require psychological support, for they face "some of the sternest challenges life provides" (Backer & Richardson, 1989). A recent survey of mental illness among the general population found that 4 percent of the population turns to family for support and solace during a period of mental distress, rather than to a mental health provider (Regier, 1993).

In addition, 65 percent of discharged psychiatric inpatients, approximately 1.5 million per year, return to live with family members. Largely as a result of cost, many of these patients return earlier than they otherwise might, still severely disabled by abnormal symptoms. As a result, the stress and disorganization of family life becomes overwhelming—with a heavy overlay of financial and emotional burdens. Indeed, probably no form of illness so completely destroys the well-being of the family (National Institute of Mental Health, 1991).

Psychologists can play a critical role in the amelioration of the family's burdens—not only by providing appropriate counseling and therapeutic services but by encouraging family members to use appropriate support groups. One organization, the National Alliance for the Mentally Ill (NAMI), has more than 850 local affiliates throughout the United States, representing more than 70,000 families. An essential element of NAMI is its network of support groups, through which burdened family members find needed emotional strength (Backer & Richardson, 1989).

Psychological Disorders Among the Homeless

The importance of a social support system in the recovery of individuals suffering from psychological disorders highlights the special problems of America's homeless—who are "disenfranchised from their families, service providers, and communities" (Levine & Rog, 1990). Although being homeless is not of itself a psychological disorder, a startling number of street-people have histories of psychological disorder. There are more than twice as many people with schizophrenia and bipolar psychosis living in public shelters and on the streets—at least 150,000—than there are in public mental hospitals (Torrey et al., 1990). Yet they do not receive the kinds of treatment and care designed for severe psychological disorders (Levine & Haggard, 1989).

The problem is, in part, an outgrowth of the success of drug treatment in controlling the symptoms of severe psychological disorders and reducing the number of patients cared for in institutions. This trend is graphically shown in Figure 11.8. But the cause-and-effect relationship may run in the opposite direction as well. That is, psychological disorders can be generated—or at least exacerbated—by the conditions of homelessness (Redburn & Buss, 1985). For example, homeless individuals who appear paranoid, depressed, or agitated may be reacting realistically to the abysmal conditions of their lives. It is noteworthy that the newly homeless have atypically high rates of major depression, in part as a response to their plight (National Institute of Mental Health, 1991).

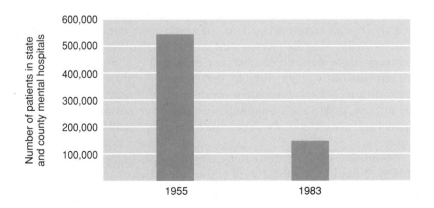

FIGURE 11.8 The drop in mental hospital population In 1955, there were over a half million people in U.S. state and county mental hospitals. By 1983, the total was reduced to one-fourth that number. The sharp decline is due primarily to the development of medicines that eliminate the most disabling symptoms of mental disorder (U.S. Department of Health and Human Services, 1986).

The problem is heightened by the fact that, in many cities, the nation's community mental health centers programs begun in the 1960s have not kept pace with the need to care for the homeless. Not since the early part of the nineteenth century have so many people with serious mental health problems gone untreated (Torrey et al., 1990). The heart of the problem is the public's attitudes toward psychological disorders—specifically, the tendency to reject those whose behavior departs from the community's norm.

Removing the Stigma Surrounding Psychological Disorders

Although more than one in four people in the United States suffer from a psychological or addictive illness at any one time, there is no treatment undertaken in seven out of ten cases (Regier, 1993). Part of the reason may be due to societal stigma about admitting one has a psychological disorder. In the first half of 1993, two prominent Washington, D.C., figures—John Wilson, chairman of the Council of the District of Columbia, and Vincent Foster, a high-ranking attorney at the White House—committed suicide as a result of depression. In both instances colleagues and friends expressed great shock at the suicides, saying they had no idea either man was depressed enough to take his life. In the days and weeks that followed each suicide, many speculated that the men didn't seek the psychological help that could have saved them because of fears of how their depression would be perceived by the public if it were revealed. Possibly Wilson and Foster were haunted by the experience of Senator Thomas Eagleton, who lost a vice-presidential nomination in 1972 when his earlier treatment for depression was revealed. Although more than 20 years have passed since then, society can still be very judgmental about the fitness for public service of those whose lives have been touched by psychological disorders.

How people receiving treatment are viewed by others can be critical. It can help determine whether they will continue to be overwhelmed by their symptoms and even get worse, or become well and function productively in society (National Institute of Mental Health, 1980). Individuals identified as having had a psychological problem are often caught in a vicious cycle. At work they may be unfairly perceived as incompetent and their performance rated as poor for no tangible reason. Feeling alienated and unappreciated, their anxieties may begin to rise and their performance may actually deteriorate (Farina, 1982). Even those who have fully recovered may face discrimination in the workplace.

One of the bitter ironies of life for the psychologically disordered is that when those who have managed to overcome their condition attempt to return to society, they are greeted with distrust and outright prejudice. Their illness suggests to many people that they are "crazy" or "psycho," and, therefore, untrustworthy, unemployable, or perhaps even dangerous. As long as those with psychological disorders are shunned and feared, they cannot be truly integrated into the community. Just when recovering patients need a helping hand and a boost, they experience rejection. Small wonder that some relapse.

A positive response by the community to people who require psychological help can assist even those with serious disturbances to regain full functioning. Therapists work hard with their patients to help them overcome their symptoms, realize their potential, and take their rightful place in society—but full recovery requires society's willingness to accept them as fully capable members of the community. Although it has no name, this itself is a powerful therapy.

SUMMARY REVIEW

Dynamic Therapy: Probing the Unconscious

1. **Dynamic therapy** is based on the assumption that an individual's problems are generated by underlying mental and emotional forces.
2. The most prominent example of dynamic therapy is Sigmund Freud's classical **psychoanalysis.** Freud's method is designed to dredge up into awareness the unconscious desires and conflicts that he considered the source of anxiety and guilt. It uses the techniques of **free association** and examines **transference,** dreams, and slips of the tongue to provide insights and thus achieve "freedom from the tyranny of the unconscious."
3. Modern dynamic therapies diverge from classical psychoanalysis by placing less emphasis on unconscious sexual and aggressive drives and placing greater emphasis on the importance of social and cultural factors.

Improving Personal Strengths Through Humanistic Therapy

4. **Humanistic therapy**—with its emphasis on self-actualization and the perfecting of personal strength—attempts to
   a) explore the client's inner experience solely from the client's own perspective
   b) encourage personal responsibility, freedom, and will.
5. Carl Rogers's humanistic approach—known as **person-centered** or **client-centered therapy**—provides an atmosphere of **unconditional positive regard** in which clients are free to explore all their thoughts and feelings, including those they have been unable to perceive clearly for fear of condemnation by others or by their own consciences. Other humanistic approaches include **Gestalt therapy,** and **existential psychotherapy.**

Behavior Therapy: Learning More Effective Responses

6. **Behavior therapy** regards personality disturbances as learned responses that can be changed through relearning. Its techniques include **systematic desensitization, reinforcement** of more desirable behavior, and extinction of undesired behavior (sometimes through **aversive conditioning**).
7. Many of today's behavior therapists practice **cognitive behavior therapy,** which seeks to change unrealistically negative and self-defeating thought patterns. One such approach is **rational-emotive therapy;** its purpose is to expose and discourage irrational and illogical ideas about life.

TEST YOURSELF

m) A group of people all suffering from cancer get together once a week to discuss their common problems and concerns. What type of program is this?

n) What types of problems are best addressed in these groups?

Therapy in Groups

8. **Group therapy** is the treatment of several patients at the same time. Among the group approaches are
   a) traditional group therapy, which allows the participants to share their feelings with each other
   b) **encounter groups,** which encourage members to interact with open displays of emotion
   c) **large group awareness training,** which comprise elements as diverse as education, spiritual enlightenment, encounter, and traditional group therapy.
9. Other group approaches include **assertiveness training** and **family therapy.**

How Effective Is Therapy?

10. Except in the case of clearly defined problems such as specific phobias, the results of therapy are difficult to assess. The best available evidence, however, indicates that **psychotherapy** benefits many people.
11. The effectiveness of therapy depends on many factors—among them the degree of motivation to change, the nature of the problem, and the qualities of the therapist.

Biological Therapies: Altering Physiological Pathways

12. **Biological therapies** hold that psychological conditions can be influenced by nonpsychological methods—by chemical, hormonal, or physical interventions that affect the brain either directly or indirectly—and thus produce or inhibit certain behaviors that alter mood.
13. The most widely and successfully used form of biological treatment is **drug therapy** (**chemotherapy**), the prescription of drugs intended to produce specific changes in mood or behavior.
14. The three major classes of drugs are
    a) drugs for schizophrenia (major tranquilizers)
    b) drugs for depression,
    c) drugs for anxiety (minor tranquilizers).
15. **Electroconvulsive therapy (ECT),** a highly controversial biological treatment, has been found to be very effective in treating cases of depression that have not responded to other treatments. Persons who are treated in this manner are first sedated and then receive a brief electrical current through electrodes attached to the skull. The result is a convulsion lasting about a minute.

Mental Health in the Community and in Society

16. **Community psychology** is based in part on the premise that the conditions in society can either cause or worsen mental health problems, and thus the field is devoted to providing "outreach" services to society. One such service is rehabilitation, through which individuals are assisted to perform the physical, intellectual, and emotional tasks necessary to function in their environment.

17. Community mental health centers are designed to
    a) treat mentally disturbed individuals in their home communities rather than in a hospital setting
    b) provide outpatient care in clinics through which individuals are treated on an intermittent basis.
18. **Crisis intervention** programs are designed to deal with immediate, stress-filled situations that beg for quick attention. The **case management approach** is one example.
19. **Self-help groups** are effective for three primary reasons:
    a) it is a healing experience to simply put feelings into words
    b) communication allows individuals to recognize that others who face similar problems manage to survive
    c) individuals learn that reactions to stress are not unnatural.
20. Attitudes toward people with psychological disorders can be critical in determining whether or not such individuals will recover sufficiently to function in society. Family support is particularly important.
21. A positive response by the community to people who require psychological help can assist even those with serious disturbances to regain full functioning.

TEST YOURSELF ANSWERS

a) The two types of dream content Freud labeled are manifest content—the actual images of dreams—and latent content—the unconscious sexual and aggressive material symbolized by something else.
b) A therapist takes a more active role in brief, dynamic therapy.
c) Person-centered therapy, developed by Carl Rogers, gives responsibility for change to the client.
d) Unconditional positive regard, empathy, and genuineness are the three qualities Rogers said a therapist must have.
e) This technique is called reinforcement.
f) Cognitive behavior therapy aims to change self-defeating and unrealistic views.
g) Some advantages of group therapy are that it is more cost-effective; it may relieve anxiety by showing that other people have the same problem; and it gives the opportunity of social give-and-take in therapeutic setting.
h) Minor maladjustments of recent origin are the mental problems most amenable to treatment.
i) People who are highly motivated and well-educated are most likely to get something out of a self-help product.
j) Psychopharmacology is the study of how drugs affect the brain, body, and behavior.
k) Lithium can help prevent the mood swings of bipolar disorder.
l) Electroconvulsive therapy (ECT) offers the quickest relief for suicidal depression.
m) People with similar problems can discuss common concerns in self-help or mutual-support group.
n) A broad spectrum of life crises can be addressed in self-help groups.

Study Guide

Chapter 11 Psychotherapy and Other Treatment Approaches

LEARNING OBJECTIVES

After studying this chapter, you should be able to:

For an Understanding of the Science

1. Describe the techniques used in Freudian psychoanalysis, and how dynamic therapies today differ from the classical psychoanalytic approach.

2. Understand the approaches of humanistic therapy and how they differ from those used in psychoanalysis.

3. Know how the techniques of behavior therapy operate, including desensitization, extinction, reinforcement, and cognitive behavior therapy.

4. Recognize the various forms of group therapy, and describe the composition of the groups and their purposes.

5. Understand the importance of evaluating the effectiveness of psychotherapy, and the challenges involved in doing so.

6. Know the range of biological therapies—including drug therapy and electroconvulsive therapy—and what they are intended to accomplish.

7. Understand the origins of the community mental health movement and how its programs are designed to deal both with mental health problems and related social problems.

For Application to Life Situations

8. Recognize that there are many forms of psychotherapy through which a person may seek help for personality disturbances. Though it is difficult to assess their effectiveness, be aware that all of them seem to produce improvement in most clients—especially when therapists themselves are well-adjusted, experienced, and able to establish a warm and close relationship with the client.

9. Know how important it is to choose a therapist carefully, and be aware of the criteria to use in doing so.

10. Understand that the people most likely to profit from therapy are those who are highly motivated to improve, are willing to work hard at eliminating the difficulties, and believe that the treatment will help.

11. Be aware that while attempts at self-therapy such as reading self-help books can sometimes be helpful, they are handicapped by the lack of support from a warm, close, and encouraging relationship with an understanding and sympathetic therapist.

PROGRAMMED UNIT
DYNAMIC THERAPY: PROBING THE UNCONSCIOUS

1. Psychotherapists who employ a *dynamic* approach to therapy believe that effective treatment must focus on the underlying mental and emotional

forces that generated the individual's problems. This would be true, for example, in treating an individual with a phobia—which, as described in the previous chapters, is an _____ disorder.

anxiety

2. Psychotherapists who believe that effective treatment must focus on the underlying mental and emotional forces that generated the individual's problems employ a _____ approach. For such therapists, the crucial element is *insight*—an uncovering and awareness of the forces operating in the individual's unconscious.

dynamic

3. An uncovering and awareness of the forces operating in the individual's unconscious is known as _____. This plays an important part in the method of treatment developed by Freud known as *psychoanalysis*.

insight

4. Freud's method of treatment, known as _____, has as its goal to give individuals insight into their unconscious desires and conflicts that he considered the source of abnormal anxiety and guilt.

psychoanalysis

5. In Freudian psychoanalysis, therapists attempt to bring into awareness the _____ desires and conflicts viewed as the source of extreme anxiety and guilt.

unconscious

6. According to psychoanalysis, people can overcome severe anxiety and guilt by gaining _____ into their unconscious desires and conflicts.

insight

7. In helping an individual acquire insight into unconscious desires and _____, those who practice psychoanalysis use the tool of *free association*—or the speaking out of every thought that occurs to the individual.

conflicts

8. Mary, who is being treated by means of psychoanalysis, lies on a couch and reveals every thought that occurs to her—no matter how foolish or obscene. Mary is using the tool known as free _____. Another technique used by psychoanalysts is *dream analysis*—based on Freud's belief that dreams often reveal deeply hidden conflicts, though in disguised ways that require painstaking interpretation.

association

9. In psychoanalysis, the therapist pays particular attention to occasions when your thoughts encounter _____—that is, when your train of thought seems to be blocked by anxiety and repression.

resistance

10. Based on Freud's belief that dreams often reveal deeply hidden conflicts, psychoanalysts use the technique known as dream _____. In dynamic therapy today, psychotherapists attempt to help individuals gain insight with techniques that shorten the lengthy treatment period required by psychoanalysis.

analysis

11. Freud labeled the unconscious sexual and aggressive material found in dreams as its _____ content. In contrast, he identified the conscious material—that is, the actual images of the dream—as its _____ content.

latent
manifest

12. Freud believed that people tend to display toward the analyst those emotional attitudes they learned to display toward parents and other family members in real life—a process he called _____.

transference

13. Helping individuals gain insight with techniques that shorten the treatment period is typical of today's forms of _____ therapy.

dynamic

IMPROVING PERSONAL STRENGTHS THROUGH HUMANISTIC THERAPY

Freud

14. In contrast to psychoanalysis, which is based on the teachings of Sigmund _____, *humanistic therapy* is based on humanistic theories of personality—with their emphasis on self-actualization and the perfecting of personal strengths.

humanistic

15. Therapy that emphasizes self-actualization and the perfecting of personal strengths is known as _____ therapy. A prime example is the *person-centered therapy* developed by Carl Rogers, who believed that the task of the therapist is to facilitate the process of helping individuals understand and control their own lives.

person

16. An example of humanistic therapy is _____-centered therapy, developed by Carl Rogers.

Rogers
humanistic

17. Person-centered therapy was developed by psychologist Carl _____. It is an example of _____ therapy, and it places emphasis on three qualities of the therapist: *unconditional positive regard,* empathy, and genuineness.

unconditional

18. Clients who received therapy from Carl Rogers would undoubtedly have been viewed with _____ positive regard.

empathy

19. Rogers believed that important qualities for a therapist include unconditional positive regard of the client, _____, and genuineness. His person-centered therapy is one form of humanistic therapy. Another humanistic approach is *Gestalt* therapy, in which therapists try to help individuals confront and understand their feelings, and grow responsible for controlling them.

Gestalt

20. A humanistic form of therapy which attempts to help individuals confront, understand and control their feelings is known as _____ therapy.

existential

21. Practitioners of _____ psychotherapy also emphasize the ability of people to take control of their own lives, and they believe in the capacity of free will.

BEHAVIOR THERAPY: LEARNING MORE EFFECTIVE RESPONSES

humanistic

22. In contrast to practitioners of person-centered and Gestalt therapy, which are two forms of _____ therapy, practitioners of *behavior therapy* use techniques of conditioning and learning.

behavior

23. Therapists who use techniques of conditioning and learning practice _____ therapy, which is an attempt to change behavior rather than to achieve insight. Among the techniques utilized is *desensitization,* which consists of attempts to associate anxiety-provoking stimuli with relaxation rather than with panic.

behavior

24. Behavior therapy is intended not to help individuals achieve insight, but rather to change their _____.

desensitization

25. Attempts to associate anxiety-provoking stimuli with relaxation rather than panic comprise a technique known as systematic _____.

deconditioning

26. Systematic desensitization is also known as a process of _____.

counterconditioning

27. Another term for deconditioning is _____.

28. Mary's therapist urges her to remain calm and relaxed while thinking of the exams that habitually cause her anxiety. Her therapist is using a _____ therapy technique known as desensitization. In the method of *extinction,* the therapist uses a direct attempt to break a troublesome stimulus-response connection.

behavior

29. Behavior therapists who apply direct attempts to break troublesome stimulus-response connections are using the method of _____. The extinction of a response by pairing undesirable behavior with a disagreeable stimulus such as a shock is called *aversive conditioning.*

extinction

30. John, who is suffering from alcoholism, is undergoing a treatment program in which he is given an electrical shock every time he lifts a glass of whiskey. John's therapist is using the technique known as _____ conditioning. Behavior therapists also use a technique that is quite the opposite. Called *reinforcement,* it entails the provision of a reward for more effective and more desirable behavior.

aversive

31. When a therapist provides rewards for more effective and more desirable behavior, the technique being used is _____.

reinforcement

32. A delinquent boy who is given praise for altruistic behavior is being treated with _____. One example of this technique is the reward of mental hospital patients with tokens good for movies and other privileges, referred to as *token economy.*

reinforcement

33. The technique of reinforcement has been used in mental hospitals by offering tokens to patients—a behavior therapy approach referred to as token _____.

economy

34. Therapists who help their clients by altering their self-defeating thoughts are practicing _____ behavior therapy.

cognitive

35. Some cognitive therapists practice rational-_____ therapy, which aims to expose and discourage a client's irrational and illogical ideas.

emotive

36. Convictions about one's ability or lack of ability to cope with anxiety-producing or stressful situations add up to one's convictions about self-_____.

efficacy

THERAPY IN GROUPS

37. The therapist's efforts at desensitization, extinction, or reinforcement—all forms of _____ therapy—typically are directed toward a single individual. But therapists of a number of different orientations have adapted their approaches for use in *group therapy,* or in the treatment of several patients at the same time.

behavior

38. The treatment of several patients at the same time is known as _____ therapy—which has been described as a "living laboratory" where participants can learn new ways of dealing with the world. Of extreme importance is the quality of the leader.

group

39. In group therapy, the quality of the group _____ is of extreme importance. This is true, for example, in an *encounter group,* an outgrowth of the humanistic approach, which stresses openness and honesty in interpersonal relationships.

leader

self-help

support

encounter

awareness

assertiveness

family

40. Groups made up of individuals who share common problems are called _____ groups.

41. Such groups are also called mutual _____ groups.

42. A form of group therapy that emerged as an outgrowth of the humanistic approach is known as the _____ group.

43. More popular today are groups that incorporate processes as diverse as education, spiritual enlightenment, encounter, and traditional group psychotherapy—an approach known as large group _____ training programs.

44. A form of group therapy intended to teach submissive people to stand up for their rights is _____ training. In *family therapy*, participants typically include mother, father, and children, and the goal of the therapist is to help resolve any one individual's problems by changing the behavior patterns of the entire family.

45. John, failing in junior high and increasingly dependent on drugs, is in a therapy group with his mother, father, and two older brothers. He is participating in what is known as _____ therapy.

HOW EFFECTIVE IS PSYCHOTHERAPY?

group

outcome

condition

self

placebo

dyslexia
ritalin

46. Whether individual therapy or _____ therapy, which is used with several patients at the same time, the outcome of psychotherapy is difficult to assess.

47. It is difficult to assess the _____ of various forms of psychotherapy, each of which may depend on the kind of condition being treated.

48. The outcome of various forms of psychotherapy may depend on the kind of _____ being treated. Even self-therapy—that is, serving as your own psychotherapist by reading self-help books—can prove useful sometimes.

49. When you try to serve as your own psychotherapist, you are practicing _____-therapy.

50. A sugar pill with no remedial value at all is called a _____.

51. Children with hyperactivity, or _____, are sometimes treated with the drug _____.

BIOLOGICAL THERAPIES: ALTERING PHYSIOLOGICAL PATHWAYS

biological

biological

52. The previous chapter described how mental disorders can arise not only from psychological and environmental factors but from _____ factors such as changes in brain chemistry and glandular activity. That is why approaches to treatment include *biological therapies*, intended to help the patient by changing these underlying physiological mechanisms.

53. Treatments designed to alter behavior by modifying brain chemistry and glandular activity are referred to as _____ therapies. The most widely and successfully used of these is *drug therapy*—also called *chemotherapy*—which is the prescription of drugs intended to produce specific changes in mood or behavior.

54. The prescription of drugs intended to produce specific changes in mood or behavior is known as _____ therapy. **drug**

55. Their use is based on the study of how drugs affect the brain, body, and behavior—which is the field of _____. **psychopharmacology**

56. Another term for drug therapy is _____. Drugs used to control the most disruptive symptoms of schizophrenia are called *major tranquilizers,* or *antipsychotic drugs*. **chemotherapy**

57. Drugs used to control the most serious symptoms of schizophrenia are called major _____. **tranquilizers**

58. Drugs that treat schizophrenia are also referred to as _____ drugs. **antipsychotic**

59. Some patients who have undergone drug therapy for a long period develop a serious motor disorder characterized by involuntary movements, which is called _____ dyskinesia. **tardive**

60. A promising new antipsychotic drug that appears to avoid such side effects is the drug called _____. Persons who experience major depression are often treated with *antidepressant drugs*. **clozapine**

61. People suffering from depression are often treated with drugs known as _____ drugs. These drugs probably work by increasing the brain's supply of two neurotransmitters, *norepinephrine* and *serotonin*. **antidepressant**

62. Antidepressant drugs work by increasing the brain's supply of the two neurotransmitters known as _____ and _____. **norepinephrine, serotonin**

63. Mary, who is deeply depressed, is being treated with chemotherapy. She is likely to be taking an _____ drug. One such drug, *clomipramine*. has been used to treat obsessive-compulsive disorder. **antidepressant**

64. An antidepressant drug used to treat people with obsessions and compulsions is _____. The drug *lithium,* while sometimes used in depression, is used especially to smooth out the mood swings typical of bipolar disorder. **clomipramine**

65. Sarah has been diagnosed as suffering from bipolar disorder. The drug she is most likely to be given is _____. In treating anxiety, drugs known as *minor tranquilizers* are used. **lithium**

66. To treat cases of anxiety, it is likely that drugs known as minor _____ would be prescribed. One such drug, for example, is Valium. **tranquilizers**

67. Valium is an example of drugs known as _____ tranquilizers. **minor**

68. Paul is suffering from schizophrenia. The drug he is being treated with is likely to be a _____ tranquilizer. Robert, suffering from panic attacks, is more likely to be undergoing treatment with a minor _____. With the advent of drugs for depression, patients are much less likely to be treated with *electroconvulsive therapy (ECT)*, in which a brief electric current or shock is applied through electrodes attached to the skull. **major tranquilizer**

69. In cases of serious and suicidal depression which does not respond to drugs, some patients are treated with a brief electric current applied to the skull—a treatment known as _____ therapy, or ECT. The result is a convulsion lasting about a minute, after which the patient loses consciousness for a short time. **electroconvulsive**

70. In electroconvulsive therapy, or _____, the patient experiences a _____ lasting about a minute and then is unconscious for a short time. **ECT** **convulsion**

biological

71. In contrast to drug therapy or electroconvulsive therapy, both of them belonging to the category of _____ therapies, are approaches that fall under the category of community mental health, and which gave rise to the field of *community psychology.*

community

72. Community mental health approaches gave rise to the field of _____ psychology, oriented not only to meeting the needs of individuals who present themselves for treatment, but to meeting other community needs. One example is *rehabilitation,* through which individuals are assisted to perform the physical, intellectual, and emotional tasks necessary to function in their communities.

rehabilitation

73. One example of community psychology efforts is _____, through which individuals are assisted to perform the physical, intellectual, and emotional tasks necessary to function in their communities. Some psychologists and other mental health professionals provide an important service in *crisis intervention* programs designed to deal with immediate, stress-filled situations that beg for quick attention.

crisis

74. A community mental health program designed to provide help for victims under acute stress such as rape victims is called a _____ intervention program. The *case management approach* includes crisis intervention, and also addresses everyday problems of living.

75. John, recovering from schizophrenia, is being helped by a mental health team which ensures that he takes his medication and gets to work. This is an example of the case _____ approach.

management

REVIEW OF IMPORTANT TERMS

antidepressant drugs (550)

assertiveness training (541)

aversive conditioning (537)

behavior therapy (535)

biological therapies (548)

bulimia nervosa (551)

case management approach (554)

clomipramine (550)

clozapine (550)

cognitive behavior therapy (538)

community psychology (552)

crisis intervention (554)

deconditioning (counterconditioning) (536)

dream analysis (531)

drug therapy (chemotherapy) (548)

dynamic therapy (529)

dyslexia (547)

electroconvulsive therapy (ECT) (552)

encounter group (540)

existential psychotherapy (535)

extinction (537)

family therapy (541)

free association (530)

Gestalt therapy (535)

group therapy (538)

humanistic therapy (533)

insight (530)

large group awareness training **(540)**

latent content **(531)**

lithium **(550)**

major tranquilizers (antipsychotic drugs) **(549)**

manifest content **(531)**

minor tranquilizers **(550)**

person-centered (client-centered) therapy **(534)**

placebo **(544)**

psychoanalysis **(530)**

psychopharmacology **(549)**

psychotherapy **(528)**

rational-emotive therapy (RET) **(538)**

rehabilitation **(552)**

reinforcement **(537)**

resistance **(531)**

ritalin **(547)**

self-efficacy **(538)**

self-help (mutual support) group **(539)**

systematic desensitization **(536)**

tardive dyskinesia **(549)**

token economy **(537)**

transference **(531)**

unconditional positive regard **(534)**

PRACTICE TEST

_____ 1. Psychoanalysis is an outgrowth of the theories of
   a.   Freud.
   b.   Adler.
   c.   Rogers.
   d.   none of the above.

_____ 2. Free association and dream analysis are elements of the form of therapy known as
   a.   behavior therapy.
   b.   humanistic therapy.
   c.   est.
   d.   psychoanalysis.

_____ 3. The name associated with person-centered therapy is
   a.   Freud.
   b.   Adler.
   c.   Rogers.
   d.   Frankl.

_____ 4. Person-centered therapy most emphasizes
   a.   warmth and acceptance by the therapist.
   b.   reinforcing desirable behavior.
   c.   gaining insight into the causes of one's disturbances.
   d.   a cognitive, problem-solving approach.

_____ 5. Existential therapy fits best under the category of
   a. psychoanalysis.
   b. humanistic therapy.
   c. dream analysis.
   d. mutual support therapy.

_____ 6. Which of the following is *not* a technique commonly used by behavior therapists?
   a. Free association
   b. Reinforcement
   c. Observation learning
   d. Desensitization

_____ 7. Behavior therapy is an outgrowth of
   a. psychoanalytic theory.
   b. Gestalt theory.
   c. neopsychoanalysis.
   d. none of the above.

_____ 8. Systematic desensitization is a technique that
   a. helps reduce feelings of inferiority.
   b. grew out of the study of aggressive animals.
   c. attempts to eliminate phobias by new associations.
   d. attempts to discover unconscious conflicts that cause anxiety.

_____ 9. Aversive conditioning is a form of
   a. extinction.
   b. desensitization.
   c. dissonance.
   d. learning by observation.

_____ 10. Henry is afraid of flying. His therapist asks him to imagine being in an airplane and having a good time. The therapist is using the technique called
   a. extinction.
   b. aversive conditioning.
   c. reinforcement.
   d. desensitization.

_____ 11. Another term for drug therapy is
   a. chemotherapy.
   b. logotherapy.
   c. Gestalt therapy.
   d. tranquilizers.

_____ 12. Antipsychotic drugs, or major tranquilizers, are used primarily in the treatment of

    a.   anxiety disorders.

    b.   schizophrenia.

    c.   depression.

    d.   manic-depression.

_____ 13. The therapeutic effect of drugs to treat schizophrenia is thought to be related to their impact on the neurotransmitter

    a.   noradrenalin.

    b.   serotonin.

    c.   tardive dyskinesia.

    d.   dopamine.

_____ 14. Drugs used to combat depression are known as

    a.   minor tranquilizers.

    b.   major tranquilizers.

    c.   neurotransmitters.

    d.   none of the above.

_____ 15. A person who is suffering from bipolar disorder is likely to be treated with

    a.   Valium.

    b.   a major tranquilizer.

    c.   lithium.

    d.   noradrenaline.

_____ 16. Valium is a type of

    a.   antidepressant drug.

    b.   minor tranquilizer.

    c.   major tranquilizer.

    d.   none of the above.

_____ 17. Electroconvulsive therapy is most likely to be used with people who are suffering from

    a.   schizophrenia.

    b.   personality disorders.

    c.   depression.

    d.   manic-depression.

_____ 18. In choosing a psychotherapist, it is wise to

    a.   ask one's doctor for a referral.

    b.   talk to former patients.

    c.   interview the prospective therapist.

    d.   all of the above

_____19. Among the typical psychological problems for which the elderly seek help is

    a. depression.

    b. panic attacks.

    c. schizophrenia.

    d. obsessive-compulsive disorder

_____20. A community psychologist is helping survivors of a hotel fire deal with their trauma on the scene. She is practicing a form of

    a. humanistic therapy.

    b. desensitization.

    c. crisis intervention.

    d. self-help

ANSWERS TO PRACTICE TEST

1. a	6. a	11. a	16. b
2. d	7. d	12. b	17. c
3. c	8. c	13. d	18. d
4. a	9. a	14. d	19. a
5. b	10. d	15. c	20. c

EXERCISES

I.   As explained in this chapter, the chief tool of psychoanalysis is free association, which often produces insights into hidden psychological processes. If you were undergoing psychoanalysis and engaged in free association, you would be urged by the analyst to speak out every thought that occurred to you—no matter how foolish, irrelevant, hostile, or obscene it might seem. But even without the experience of psychoanalysis, it is possible to get at least some idea of what the process is like.

Find a private place—an office, your own room, an empty classroom—where you will have privacy and are not likely to be interrupted. Bring along either a close friend or a tape recorder to record your free associations. To get started think of something specific—a person you know, an incident that occurred to you recently, a wish you have, or a dream that you happen to remember. Now start with the chain of free associations by saying anything and everything that comes to your mind. Doing so may be difficult, but don't hold back any thought that occurs to you even if it seems totally unrelated to the first thought with which you started the chain. And do not be concerned if your associations seem bizarre or abnormal. The process is intended to allow "irrational" thoughts and feelings buried in the unconscious to come to the surface without any inhibition. There may be times when absolutely nothing occurs to you—when you feel "blocked." That, too, is natural. Wait until another thought surfaces in your conscious mind, and you can once again go on with your chain of associations.

After about 10 or 15 minutes, stop the process and review your associations, considering these questions:

1. Did you find the process difficult—and if so, why?

2. Are you able to identify some of the links in the chain of your associations—the threads that tied one thought to another?

3. Is there a major theme or idea that seems to "wrap up" all the thoughts that came to your mind?

4. Do you think it is easier or harder to free associate in the presence of another person?

5. How valuable do you think the technique of free association would be in the process of psychoanalysis?

CHAPTER 12

Infancy and Childhood

Look into a hospital nursery filled with newborn babies and it may be difficult to distinguish one from another. All they seem to do is eat and sleep. But within a few weeks, many differences among these young infants will begin to emerge: One may be cranky and hard to soothe, another will be calm and easy-going. One prefers lots of excitement and stimulation, while another requires quiet and tranquility. With each passing month, more and more clues to each child's personality will begin to emerge. The forces shaping these young individuals are both biological and environmental.

Biological forces guarantee, for example, that all children will normally begin to speak before they are two years old, feel guilt by their fourth birthday, and be able to reason logically by adolescence. These forces also contribute to marked personality differences among children—for example, whether the child will be shy or gregarious, high-strung or placid. Environmental influences arise from both within and outside the family. In the early years, family experiences predominate. Daily interactions with parents and siblings help determine the child's motives, values, sources of anxiety, and ways of coping with conflict. Environmental experiences outside the family—with peers, teachers, even television and movies—gradually begin to exert their powerful influence once children venture out of the confines of the home.

As the child grows, biological and environmental forces become so closely intertwined that it is virtually impossible to distinguish their separate effects. Indeed, one of the three central themes in psychology first raised in the opening chapter—the relationship between biological and psychological forces—is nowhere better illustrated than in the development of the child. The unfolding of that child is the theme of this chapter.

Life's Beginnings: From Conception to Birth

The overture to human development, played out in the mother's womb, is brief but awesome. In only nine months, two microscopic cells become transformed into a fully formed human infant. Developmental psychologists recognize that the future of each of us is shaped to a degree during this period.

To begin with, the impact of heredity is inextricably exerted at the moment of union between the mother's egg cell and the father's sperm cell. Then, from the instant of conception, the impact of the environment begins to leave its mark. When babies give up their home in the womb, they have already undergone experiences that can influence how the characteristics they inherit will actually unfold in the outside world.

The Mechanics of Heredity

A new life begins when the egg cell produced by the mother is penetrated and fertilized by the sperm cell of the father, as shown in Figure 12.1. This fertilized egg contains the key of life. Something inside it directs the entire development from single cell to baby at birth to a fully matured adult. Something in this cell determines the inherited characteristics of the individual to be born—the color of the eyes and hair, the facial features, the potential size,

FIGURE 12.1 The moment of conception The large round object is a human egg cell. In this photo, it is being fertilized by a male sperm cell that has worked its way deep inside and can no longer be seen. Other sperm cells, with small heads and long tails, are also attempting to pierce the egg but have arrived too late.

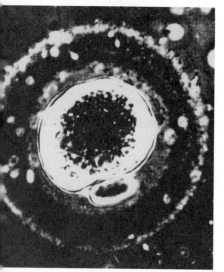

and psychological characteristics such as potential intelligence and patterns of behavior.

This "something" is the **chromosomes**—the tiny structures shown in Figure 12.2 as seen under a powerful microscope. The original fertilized cell contains 46 chromosomes, 23 from each parent. When the cell splits, the chromosomes also divide. Thus each cell of the human body contains exactly the same 46 chromosomes that were present in the fertilized egg with which life began. In the living cell, the 46 chromosomes are arranged in 23 pairs. To form the cells of reproduction—the female egg and the male sperm—the chromosome pairs split apart. One set goes into one egg or sperm cell, and the other half into another reproductive cell. Fertilization of an egg by a sperm, as shown in Figure 12.1, rejoins the chromosomes into the 23 pairs needed for normal growth.

One of the pairs in the fertilized egg cell determines whether the fertilized egg will be a girl or boy. If you look back at Figure 12.2, you will note that two chromosomes are pointed out by arrows. One of them is called an **X chromosome,** the other a **Y chromosome.** The chromosomes in Figure 12.2 are from a cell taken from a male. The X-Y pairing always produces a male; an X-X pair always produces a female.

This is how sex is determined. When the mother's X-X pair of chromosomes splits to form two egg cells, the result is always a cell containing an X chromosome. When the father's X-Y pair splits to form two sperm cells, however, the X chromosome goes to one of the cells, the Y chromosome to the other. If the sperm cell with the X chromosome fertilizes the egg, the result is an X-X pairing and a girl. If the sperm cell with the Y chromosome fertilizes the egg, the result is an X-Y pairing and a boy. The sex of the baby depends on which sperm, an X or a Y, meets the egg.

Each chromosome, though tiny in itself, is composed of hundreds of even smaller structures called **genes,** each of which is a molecule of a complex chemical called DNA (deoxyribonucleic acid). It is believed that there are at least 20,000 genes in each human cell and perhaps as many as 125,000. Each gene is believed to be responsible—sometimes by itself but more often in combination with other genes—for some phase of development. Every human being—except for identical twins—has a unique combination of genes. Never before did the same combination exist; never again is it likely to be repeated.

The World Inside the Womb

The environment, like heredity, begins to exert its influence at the very start of life's journey, when the speck of matter that will one day become a child is just beginning to unfurl in the womb. Over the approximately 280 days of prenatal development, the initial squirming bit of flesh undergoes a remarkable series of changes. During the first eight weeks—between the instant of fertilization and the moment that a recognizable embryonic human being is formed—the infant-to-be increases nearly 2 million percent in size. Alterations in the size, shape, and type of body cells take place with remarkable speed. The number of body cells increases from 1 to 26 billion during the first nine months of life as body structures increase in size and complexity.

All the while, the central nervous system—the machine that will ultimately form the foundation for the child's mental and physical capacities—is

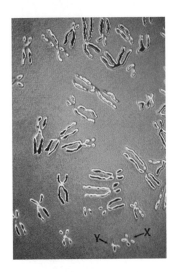

FIGURE 12.2 The human chromosomes When enlarged 750 times, human chromosomes look like this. These are from a man's skin cell, broken down and spread out into a single layer under the microscope. The labels point out the X and Y chromosomes, which determine sex.

Chromosomes

The 23 pairs of tiny structures found in all human cells that make-up the mechanisms of heredity.

X chromosome

One of the two chromosomes that determine the sex of an offspring; an X-X pairing produces a female.

Y chromosome

One of the two chromosomes that determine the sex of an offspring; an X-Y pairing produces a male.

Genes

The smaller structures of a chromosome, composed of molecules of DNA, which are responsible for inherited individual differences.

taking root. During each minute in the womb, the brain of the infant-to-be gains tens of thousands of new cells. As early as seven weeks after conception, some sections of the developing brain can already be discerned, and the nerves that feed electrical impulses from the brain to various parts of the body are in place and beginning to work. The budding arms of the fetus will now move in response to tapping on the sac that protects it. By the time the fetus is 20 weeks old, the nervous system is mature enough to make the developing baby sensitive to touch, pain, and changes in temperature. Surprisingly, the brain waves of a 30-week-old fetus look just the same prior to being born as they do in the real world. The brain is clearly "turned on" long before normal delivery.

The findings from studies of prenatal life show that, starting at the very instant of conception, the development of a child can be affected dramatically by the quality of the environment in the womb. The implications of these findings are discussed in the Psychology in Action entitled "At Risk in the Womb."

PSYCHOLOGY IN ACTION

At Risk in the Womb

There are many factors that can affect the future well-being of children while they are still taking shape in their mother's womb.

If the mother's diet during pregnancy lacks proper nutritional values and vitamins, the baby may have difficulty attaining the IQ level that its genes might otherwise have made possible. Mothers who eat contaminated foods may give birth to children who are less responsive and more easily upset (Jacobson, 1984). Mothers who experience prolonged anxiety or anger during pregnancy may have babies who are of less than average size, overactive, or inclined to digestive problems—as if they, too, had been subjected to damaging stress.

Mothers who smoke constantly may pollute the unborn baby's blood supply with carbon monoxide and thus deprive the baby of oxygen and nutrients essential for healthy development. In one study, maternal cigarette use

during pregnancy was associated with poorer attention in four-year-old preschool children (Streissguth et al., 1984). Smoking marijuana during pregnancy can damage the developing infant's brain. Studies have revealed that the cry of a newborn exposed to marijuana during pregnancy is different from that of a normal baby (Lester & Dreher, 1989).

Infants born to alcoholic or alcohol-abusing mothers are likely to have Fetal Alcohol Syndrome, which causes serious mental and physical handicaps. Even limited alcohol consumption by pregnant women may damage their babies' central nervous system. A group of 4-year-olds whose mothers drank moderately during pregnancy revealed impaired abilities on tests of motor skills such as grasping and manipulating objects or pouring water into a glass (Barr, 1990). The newest drug scourge, crack cocaine, is also harmful to the developing fetus. Children whose mothers smoked crack during pregnancy may have difficulty

concentrating, interacting with others, and playing by themselves. The most common effects are an increased risk of premature birth, decreased birth weight and smaller head circumference (Hawley & Disney, 1992).

Despite these grim facts, the great majority of babies are born healthy, even those of mothers who have smoked some, eaten a less-than-perfect diet, received medication, or experienced some emotional upsets during pregnancy. Moreover, newborns have a surprising capacity to recover from all but the most severe prenatal stress. The effects of many, but not all, early complications can eventually be reversed if the baby's later experiences are good ones (Werner & Smith, 1982). But caring parents-to-be cannot ignore the many factors known to pose a threat to a child's healthy development in the womb. Expectant mothers and fathers need to take every reasonable precaution they can to make sure that their babies get off to the best possible start.

The Birth Process

The vast majority of babies wriggle and squirm into the world as healthy and normal human beings. Nevertheless, events surrounding the birth process can affect the child's later development.

The ease or difficulty with which a baby is born and how quickly the baby begins to breathe can affect the baby's well-being. From the time the first contractions of labor begin and the new baby's head starts to squeeze its way into the world, the tiny brain is vulnerable. If there is very strong pressure on the head of the fetus, the blood vessels in the brain may rupture, leading to **anoxia,** or a loss of oxygen supply to the nerve cells. If the baby fails to begin to breathe soon after being separated from the mother's source of oxygen, the resulting anoxia may affect the brain's metabolism and result in motor paralysis, which is often called cerebral palsy (Rosen, 1985).

Even when complications in the birth process occur, however, most babies eventually show no damage. A lot can depend on what happens later. A group of Hawaiian children who suffered stresses at birth were studied over a period of 18 years. Their early impairments were linked to later problems in physical and psychological development only when combined with persistently poor environmental circumstances such as chronic poverty, family instability, or maternal health problems. Those children who were raised in more affluent homes, with an intact family and a well-educated mother, showed few, if any, negative effects of the stresses endured at birth—unless, of course, there was severe damage to the central nervous system (Werner & Smith, 1982).

Prematurity may also affect the course of the baby's development. The more premature and underweight the newborn is, the greater the likelihood of physical and mental impairment. Premature babies weighing less than 3.3 pounds have significantly more health problems at school age than their normal weight peers (McCormick, 1992). But once again, the eventual outcome

Anoxia
The loss of the oxygen supply to nerve cells, which may negatively affect the brain's metabolism and lead to motor paralysis.

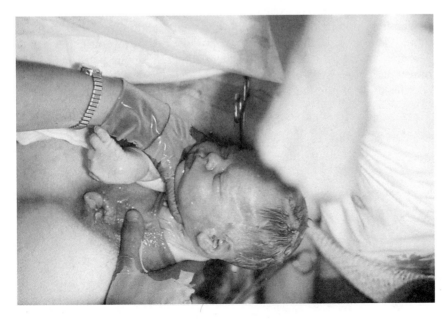

Significant complications at birth can affect later development.

TEST YOURSELF

a) How many chromosomes are present in a fertilized cell?

b) Infants born to mothers who have abused alcohol during pregnancy may suffer from what disorder?

is likely to be influenced by later environment. Early intervention programs have shown great promise in helping premature babies overcome potential handicaps. The simple power of touch in the first weeks after birth can dramatically help premature infants. Those who are gently massaged three times a day show significant weight gain, more rapidly maturing nervous systems, higher activity, and better responsiveness than those left untouched in incubators (Field, 1989).

Newborn Infants: Similarities and Differences

Newborns are miraculous creations. If born healthy, they are remarkably competent—most of their senses are working well and their reflexes will help them adjust to the world. From the moment the first breath is drawn, all normal babies are sensitive to stimuli in their environment. Babies only a few hours old can follow a moving object with their eyes. After only a week, newborns can differentiate between the smell of their own mother's milk and the smell of milk from another mother (Werner & Lipsitt, 1981), and by two weeks they can make a similar discrimination between underarm odors (Crenoch & Porter, 1985).

A newborn inherits a marked preference for the human face and voice. One of the reasons babies gaze so intently into their mother's or father's eyes is that all babies focus on dark contour lines, such as the dark pupils of a parent's eyes (Haith, 1980). When 3-day-old infants were compared to 3-day-old chimpanzees, the chimps and humans showed the same reaction to a variety of stimuli, with the exception of the human face and voice, which human babies greeted with increased attention (Hallock, Worobey & Self, 1989).

Babies respond to stimuli with a wide range of inborn, reflex behaviors that allow them to escape pain, avoid harsh stimuli, and seek food. For example, if the sole of the foot is gently pricked with a pin, infants quickly draw the foot away—a reflex that enables them to escape pain. If a bright light is flashed, they protect themselves by closing their eyelids. And if the side of the mouth is touched, they display the so-called **rooting reflex,** which is explained in Figure 12.3. Some of the infant's reflexes are permanent while others disappear within a few months. The major reflexes of the newborn—and the kinds of stimuli that release them—are listed in Figure 12.4.

Rooting reflex

An inborn reflex in which a newborn turns toward the stimulus when touched near the mouth.

FIGURE 12.3 a–c   The newborn's rooting response When the side of an infant's mouth is touched (A), the reflex response is to turn the head toward the stimulus (B) and then try to suck the finger (C), as if it were a source of food.

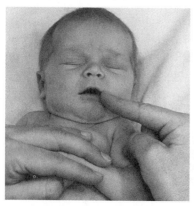
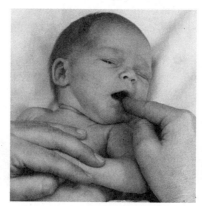
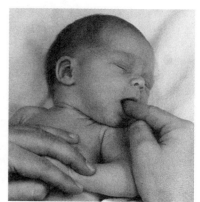

Stimulus	Reflex
Tap upper lips	Lips protrude
Tap bridge of nose	Eyes close tightly
Shine bright light	Eyelids close
Clap hands	Eyelids close
Put fingers in hand	Hand closes
Press the ball of foot	Toes flex
Scratch sole from toe to heel	Big toe bends up, small toes spread
Prick sole with pin	Knee flexes
Touch side of mouth	Turns head, opens mouth, and sucks
Hold baby up, stomach down	Head lifts, legs extend

FIGURE 12.4   The reflexes of healthy newborns At birth, the baby's reflexes are so universal that they are used as a standard test to establish that the new arrival has a healthy nervous system.

Differences in Temperament

Although all normal babies are aware of their environment and can react to the stimuli it presents, they differ in their degree of sensitivity and style of response. They differ also in level of activity, mood, adaptability and other ways that parents are quick to recognize and describe as their babies' "nature." These characteristic styles of behavior, called **temperament,** are displayed so early that they almost surely represent hereditary differences in the physiology of the brain.

Studies have shown wide individual differences in sensory threshold. With some babies, even the most gentle stroking of the skin produces a muscular reflex. Other babies do not respond unless the stroking is fairly firm. There are also differences in how rapidly babies adapt to sensations. Some babies appear to become bored with a stimulus more quickly than others. If a series of pictures of the human face is projected on a screen above the crib, some infants pay close attention for a long time. Others soon stop looking, as if they had rapidly tired of the repetitive stimulus. Similarly, some babies are more attentive and alert than others.

Such early differences in perceptual discrimination, when combined with a stimulating environment, may portend well-developed intellectual capacities later on. In one study, researchers found that babies who react to novelty with increased attention at 3, 4, and 5 months of age tend to have higher IQs when they are 4, 5, and 6 years old (Fagan & Singer, 1983).

Two fundamental temperamental qualities on which infants differ are the ease with which they become aroused by stimulation and the ways in which they regulate, or try to cope with, their arousal. The signs of arousal are motor activity, babbling and crying. Methods of regulation include turning away from the stimulus, retreating, becoming extremely distressed, or approaching the exciting stimulus.

One important difference among infants is their degree of irritability. Some babies begin to fret, whine, or cry at the slightest provocation. Other babies do not fret unless their discomfort and pain is intense or lasts a long time. Even then, they may fret only for a half minute or so and then stop, as if possessing some mechanism that inhibits the buildup of extreme upset.

A major contrast among infants between 3 and 5 months of age is the degree of both motor arousal and irritability they display when exposed to a

Temperament

The characteristic styles of behavior displayed by young babies that probably represent hereditary differences in the physiology of the brain.

stimulus such as a moving mobile. Some babies remain very relaxed, showing little movement in their arms and legs. About 20 percent become very aroused: Their tongues protrude from their mouths, their arms and legs pump vigorously and they often begin to cry. Infants who become highly aroused and irritable are more likely to be fearful and emotionally restrained when they are 2 years old, while infants who remain calm—about 40 percent—often smiling at the same stimulus, tend to become outgoing and sociable children with little fear of unfamiliar events (Kagan, 1994).

The tendency toward irritability seems to be a fairly stable trait. It has been found that children who were irritable as infants were rated as more upset, less attentive, and less responsive to adults when they were 2 years old than were nonirritable newborns (Reite, 1987).

Easy, Slow-to-warm-up, and Difficult Babies

One group of investigators, after studying more than a hundred children from birth through elementary school, came to the conclusion that most American newborns fall into three distinct temperamental groups:

1. *Easy children,* who make up about 40 percent of healthy babies, are generally cheerful. Their reactions to stimuli show a low to moderate intensity. They establish regular habits of eating and sleeping and are quick to adapt to new schedules, foods, and people.
2. *Slow-to-warm-up children,* who make up about 15 percent, are less cheerful; indeed their mood seems slightly sad and tense. Their responses are low in intensity. Their eating and sleeping habits vary and they tend to withdraw initially to new experiences, like unfamiliar people or unfamiliar toys. They take time to adjust to change.
3. *Difficult children,* who make up about 10 percent of infants, become very irritable and cry at unfamiliar events—for instance, when given a bath. Because of this, they are difficult to soothe and their mothers find them hard to please. They show little regularity in eating and sleeping and are easily upset by new experiences.

The remaining 35 percent of children are mixed and not easily typed in temperamental quality (Thomas, Chess, & Birch, 1970).

A striking example of the difference between an easy and a difficult baby is shown in Figure 12.5. The photographs, which were taken several years apart, are of an older sister and a younger brother—an indication that early differences in temperament do not necessarily reflect the parents' personalities or child-rearing methods.

The three types require different treatment during infancy and in the early years of school. Easy children thrive under most family treatments in early childhood. Slow-to-warm-up children require considerable patience. They do their best when encouraged to try new experiences but allowed to adapt at their own pace. Too much pressure heightens their natural inclination to withdraw.

Difficult children present a special problem. Because of their irregular habits, their resistance to adjustment, and their negative attitude, they are hard to live with—a trial to their parents and later to their teachers. There is even evidence that mothers of difficult and irritable 1-year-old boys tend to

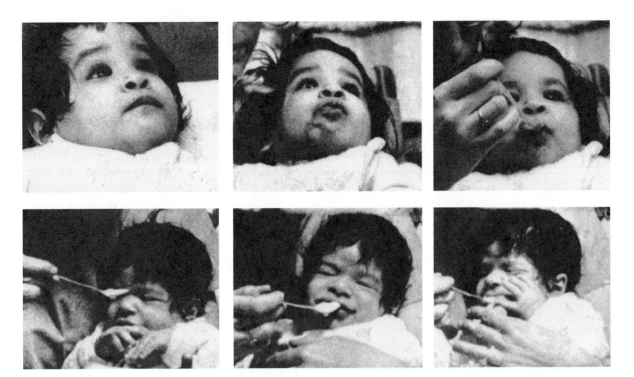

FIGURE 12.5 a–f A contrast in infant temperament Both these babies are three months old and are being offered a new kind of cereal for the first time. The girl at the top, an easy baby, eagerly accepts the new experience. The boy at the bottom, a difficult baby, fights it.

back off from their natural attempts to teach and train (Maccoby, Snow, & Jacklin, 1984). Attempts to force such babies to behave like other children may only make them more difficult. Their parents must exercise exceptional understanding and tolerance to bring them around—slowly and gradually—to getting along with other individuals.

The inborn differences in temperament, together with other new knowledge about variations in sensitivity, activity, and irritability, are of potential value to parents, the staffs of day-care centers, and teachers, especially in the early grades. The findings disprove the popular assumption that all young children are more or less alike and should behave as if cut from the same pattern. Infants require individual treatment if they are to develop to their maximum capability.

The Durability of Early Traits

Two relatively enduring temperamental traits are the excessively cautious and timid child compared with the sociable, outgoing child. The former, a group comprising about 20 percent of healthy infants, is easily aroused as a young infant and usually becomes irritable when stimulated as a 3- or 4-month-old infant. Two-thirds of these "highly reactive" infants become timid, shy, inhibited children in their second, third and fourth years. On the other hand, about 40 percent of 4-month-old infants are very relaxed when stimulated and rarely cry. Almost three-quarters of these children are sociable, outgoing, easy children when they are preschoolers.

These traits appear to be a result of inherited physiological tendencies involving the neurochemistry and physiology of the brain. One research team that followed these two types of children through 13 years of age found that about one-third of the very shy, fearful, inhibited 2-year-olds were still dour, serious and moderately tense when they were adolescents, while one-half of the formerly outgoing, sociable, uninhibited 2-year-olds were still exuberant, minimally fearful, and unusually extroverted in their relationships with others (Kagan, 1994).

The evidence of changes should offer comfort to parents who are worried or pessimistic if a child is difficult, shy, irritable, overactive, or seemingly unable to pay attention. The findings of developmental psychology suggest not pessimism but optimism about children and their potentialities. Difficult babies—boisterous, stubborn, and headstrong—often quiet down as they get older. Babies who seem restless and inattentive in the cradle often learn to concentrate and become star pupils in school. Even babies who seem anxious may turn out to be perfectly normal. If parents can remember that babies show a wide range of individual differences, need individual treatment, and thrive on warmth and love—and if they can tolerate behavior that at the moment may hardly be ideal—their patience will usually be rewarded.

The environment always plays an important role in determining whether an inherited temperamental tendency develops into a permanent personality trait. If highly reactive infants are raised with parents who do not overprotect their child and impose reasonable demands for obedience and socialization, then the 2- and 3-year-old child will be less fearful than a highly reactive infant who is raised with an overprotective, anxious parent who is reluctant to impose any stress on the child.

TEST YOURSELF

c) What do we call characteristic styles of behavior, such as level of activity, mood, and adaptability?

d) In terms of temperamental type, how would you classify an infant who is slightly sad and tense, and who tends to withdraw from new experiences?

The Early Development of Body and Mind

Most new parents are quick to recognize the outward physical growth of the infant. The baby's birth weight doubles in the first three months and triples in one year. By the end of the first year, the baby's height typically increases by almost 50 percent. But there are internal changes as well. The fibers of the nervous system grow and form additional connections to other fibers, and they become faster and more efficient messengers of information to and from the brain. The brain itself grows in size and weight. Its growth spurt during the first three months is more rapid than any other. Neuroscientists suspect that before the first year of life is over, the number of synapses—those critical connections between nerve cells in the brain—reaches a peak never again matched in our lifetime.

The results of all this are some of nature's most spectacular events: the growth of the newborn baby into an eager toddler (sometime after the first birthday), experimenting with language (starting near the end of the second year), and eventually a 6-year-old school child, about to solve the mysteries of reading and writing. How many and varied are the accomplishments of those early years. How many new worlds are faced and conquered.

Part of this rapid early development is the result of **maturation**—the physical changes taking place after birth that continue the biological growth of the organism from fertilized egg cell to adult. Almost day by day, simply as a result of getting older, babies become capable of new feats of physical, perceptual, and mental skill.

Maturation
The physical changes, taking place after birth that continue the biological growth of the organism.

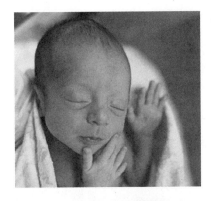

FIGURE 12.6 a–f How the muscles of movement mature The process of maturation accounts for the increasing ability of babies to move around. Shown here is the progress from birth to walking alone and the average age at which each stage of development occurs.

Physical Maturation

Even before birth, babies begin to use their muscles. Their movements can usually be felt in the womb in about the twentieth week of pregnancy. Newborn babies have all the muscle fibers they will ever possess, but the fibers still have a lot of growing to do. Eventually, at full maturity, the muscles will weigh about 40 times as much as they weighed at birth. The muscles of posture, creeping, and standing must mature, as shown in Figure 12.6, before the baby can walk alone, at around the age of 15 months. The muscles of the hands and arms, as they mature, produce increased skill at reaching and grasping. The skeleton at birth is largely composed of cartilage, which is softer and more pliable than bone but gradually hardens. The fibers of the nervous system grow and form additional synaptic connections to other fibers, and some of them develop protective sheaths that make them faster and more efficient conductors of nervous impulses. The brain, in particular, grows in size and weight—very rapidly during the first two years, then more slowly until growth is complete.

Much of the baby's remarkable progress in the early months of life reflects maturation of the body and the nervous system. Thus children all over the world, regardless of child-rearing practices, tend to display various skills at about the same age. They begin to smile at the sight of a human face at about 4 months, show vocal excitement to a new voice at 6 to 7

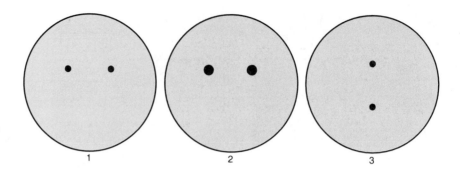

FIGURE 12.7   The visual skills of newborns Infants as young as 5 months are capable of detecting the differences between the pattern shown in circle 1, and variations of that pattern such as those shown in circles 2 and 3 (adapted from Linn et al., 1982).

months, and search for a hidden object that they saw being covered by a piece of cloth at 8 to 12 months. They begin to utter some of the basic sounds of language in the first few days of life—but they cannot really use speech until around 18 months. Evidence suggests that their brains may be mature enough earlier, but their vocal systems are not yet ready (Bonvillian, Orlansky, & Novack, 1983).

The Unfolding of Intellectual Abilities

During the opening years of life, children reveal a dazzling succession of intellectual capacities, each more advanced than the one that preceded it. As early as only a few hours old, babies can distinguish between two designs as subtly different as those shown in Figure 12.7. Although we take such skills for granted in adults, they are remarkable in infants who have only just begun to function in the world. Equally remarkable is the rapid and steady pace at which a given skill develops. The ability to recognize a familiar stimulus, for example, gets better with the passage of time. One-month-old infants who have learned to recognize a frequently repeated word lose the ability if a day passes without their hearing that word spoken. Only three months later, however, they can recognize a familiar word after interruptions of as long as a week or two. The ability of babies to recall past events also becomes more solidly entrenched over the space of only a few months, as shown in Figure 12.8. Such changes appear to be correlated with the maturation of the frontal lobe of the brain, as indicated in Figure 12.9.

As early as three to four months of age, young infants will learn quickly to anticipate an event that will happen in the future. In one study a baby was observed while it lay on its back looking at pictures, which were alternatively placed on the right and left sides. In a short time, the infant learned to look to the alternative side before the picture had appeared, in anticipation of seeing a new scene (Kagan, 1994).

Do these early cognitive skills predict later intelligence? A review of the literature on early intelligence indicates that the encoding, storage, retrieval, discrimination and recognition skills measured by tests described earlier may be related to the vocabulary, abstract reasoning and memory skills measured on childhood intelligence tests (McCall & Carriger, 1993).

Many factors contribute to intellectual development. One is improvement in the process of perception. As children grow older, they begin to know what to search for in the environment and how to go about it. They develop strategies for seeking important information and ignoring irrelevant

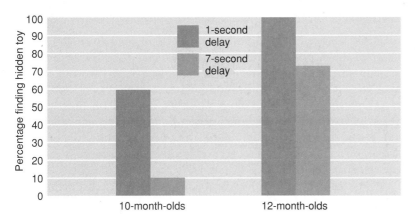

FIGURE 12.8   The baby's progress in short-term memory The bars show the percentages of 10- and 12-month-old babies who could recall where a toy was hidden after brief delays. The babies watched a toy being placed under one of two cloths, and a screen was then lowered to block their view for 1 second or 7 seconds. The task of finding the toy gets harder, of course, as the delay gets longer. But more important, no matter how long the delay, note how sharply the ability to find the toy improves with the passage of only two months (Kagan, Kearsley, & Zelazo, 1978).

information. Their attention becomes more selective and they are able to maintain it over a longer time span. Their scanning of the environment becomes more systematic and orderly. Progress in perceptual efficiency has been charted by recording children's eye movements (Salapatek, 1975). When 1-month-olds are shown a design, they are likely to scan whatever feature their eyes first encounter—usually part of the external border. Only 1 month later, they scan the essential elements of the design. As children get older, they become increasingly efficient in searching for information. They also become more adept at perceiving details (Gibson, 1969) and organizing them into meaningful patterns and entities.

Another important factor in intellectual development is the baby's growing skill in understanding and using language. There is some evidence that parents can help advance this skill by talking to their babies, especially one-to-one (Olson, Bates, & Bayles, 1984). In turn, adeptness with language facilitates the formation of concepts—which helps organize information into categories and facilitates the mental processing that creates long-lasting memories.

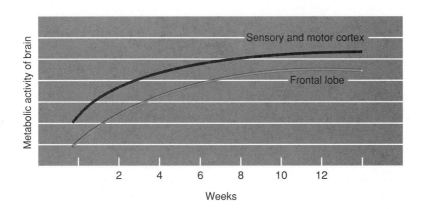

FIGURE 12.9   Changes in brain function in the first year In the opening months of life, the sensory and motor areas of the brain's cortex are more active than the frontal lobe, which does not become significantly active until the babies reach about the eighth month (adapted from Chugani & Phelps, 1986).

Cognitive Development: The Theories of Piaget

During this century, one man's theories have dominated psychology's view of intellectual development in children: Jean Piaget. This Swiss psychologist spent a lifetime studying the mental development of his own and other children as they grew from infancy through adolescence. Piaget's observations have greatly influenced psychology's current position on how we reason, solve problems, and use our intelligence to understand and adapt to our world. He has been a major figure in the rise of the cognitive school, and no introduction to modern psychology would be complete without a discussion of the essential elements of his theory.

Piaget concluded that our mental growth—which he defined as an increased ability to adapt to new situations—takes place because of two key processes that he calls **assimilation** and **accommodation.** Assimilation is the process of incorporating a new event into one's existing cognitive view of the world. Accommodation is the process of changing one's cognitive view and behavior when new information requires such a change.

As a simple example, consider a young boy who has a number of toys. To these familiar old toys we add a new one, a magnet. The boy's initial impulse will be to assimilate the new toy into his existing knowledge of other toys; he may try to bang it like a hammer, throw it like a ball, or blow it like a horn. But once he learns that the magnet has a new and unprecedented quality—the power to attract iron—he accommodates his view of toys to include this previously unfamiliar fact. He now behaves on the revised assumption that some toys are not designed to bang, throw, or make noise with but to attract metal.

There is always tension, Piaget concluded, between assimilation (which in essence represents the use of old ideas to meet new situations) and accommodation (which in essence is a change of old ideas to meet new situations). The resolution of this tension results in intellectual growth. Thus we can develop our cognitive skills only through active interaction with the objects and other people in our world. We need an environment that exposes us to new situations and new problems and thus challenges us to exercise and increase our mental skills.

Another key word in the Piaget theory is **operations.** The term is difficult to define. Roughly, an operation is a sort of dynamic mental rule for manipulating objects or ideas into new forms and back to the original, like the rule that four pieces of candy (or the mere figure 4) can be divided into two parts of two each, then put back again into the original four. The full meaning will become clearer as our discussion proceeds.

Piaget's Four Stages

Piaget found that mental growth, beginning at birth, takes place in a series of four stages, in each of which the child thinks and behaves in quite different fashion than earlier. He maintains that the child grows intellectually not like a leaf, which simply gets larger every day, but like a caterpillar that is eventually transformed into a butterfly (Piaget, 1952).

1. The Sensorimotor Stage In the first or **sensorimotor stage,** during about the first 18 months of life, children have not yet learned to use language and symbols to represent the objects and events in the environment.

Assimilation

The process of incorporating a new event into one's existing cognitive view of the world.

Accommodation

The process of changing one's cognitive view and behavior when new information requires such a change.

Operations

A dynamic mental rule for manipulating ideas or objects into new forms and back to the original.

Sensorimotor stage

According to Piaget, the stage of intellectual development in the first 18 months of life when the child knows the world only in terms of sensory and motor activities.

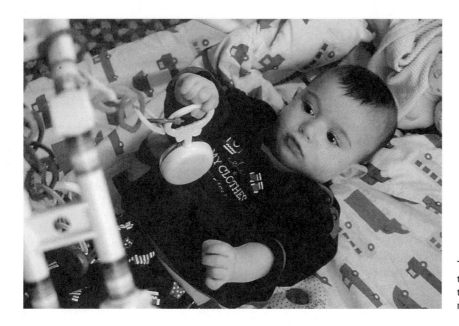

This boy, in Piaget's sensorimotor stage, delights in discovering the results of his own muscular movements.

Infants begin to know the world in terms of their own sensory impressions of its sights, sounds, tastes, and smells. But soon they begin to discover the relationship between their actions toward the objects they perceive and the consequences that follow. By the age of 4 to 6 months, babies are aware that they can produce results through physical activity. They will repeatedly kick at toys hanging over their cribs, apparently to make them swing and thus produce a change of stimulus that they find interesting. By the age of 12 months they act as if they know that objects are permanent and do not mysteriously disappear. If a toy is shown to them and then is hidden behind two pillows side by side in the crib, they know how to find it. They look first behind one of the pillows. If the toy is not there, they look behind the other. If they cannot find a toy at all, they are surprised, indicating that they expect an object that they saw earlier to be somewhere.

2. The Preoperational Stage   From about 18 months to around the seventh birthday, children are in what Piaget calls the **preoperational stage.** They have acquired language and can manipulate symbols. They may behave toward a doll as if it were a child and toward a stick as if it were a gun. They often put objects together in appropriate groups—for example, all their red blocks into one pile and the blue blocks into another. But their actions are still dictated largely by the evidence of their senses. They have not yet developed the kinds of concepts that would enable them to form meaningful categories. They are not yet capable of thinking in terms of the dynamic rules of operations. However, they begin to display autobiographical memories.

Although children as young as two remember incidents from months before, true autobiographical memories that last into adulthood usually don't begin until about age 3½ to 4 (Nelson, 1993). Autobiographical memories seem to form lasting impressions only after children begin to converse with others about what has happened to them. By shaping events into a story, it becomes easier to retrieve the memory many years later. Young children are also easily influenced by suggestions from adults in forming memories, a fact

Preoperational stage
According to Piaget, the stage of intellectual development from ages 2 to 7 years when the child's ability to use language and manipulate symbols dominates intellectual development.

Children's Memories Are Very Susceptible to Revision

Can a child's memory be influenced by an adult's questions? According to researchers led by Stephen Ceci, Ph.D., of Cornell University, persistent questioning may lead young children to develop and believe a description of an event that never happened.

Parents of children between the ages of 4 and 6 helped researchers compile a list of two events that had really happened, and eight that had not. Each week a researcher went through the list with each child, asking him or her after each event, "Did this ever happen?" For example, one of the children was asked whether he had been to the hospital because he had gotten his finger caught in a mousetrap. The first time the child was asked the question, he answered that he had never even *been* to a hospital. The second time he was asked the question, he "remembered" crying when his finger got caught. By the eleventh week, he had developed an elaborate account of how his brother had pushed his finger into the mousetrap. By that same week, 56 percent of the children reported at least one false event as being true, and some reported all of the false events as true.

The children not only believed these stories but also described them in such detail that when researchers showed the videotaped accounts to colleagues, the other professionals were convinced that these events had really happened. The researchers also found that persistent questioning led children to make up new "facts" about false events that the researchers had never introduced.

A question that concerns judges today is whether children elaborate this way when they are being interviewed about possible abuse. But those who defend leading questions have pointed out that children need to be coaxed or else they will never report upsetting events.

Source: Clyman, R., Friedman, M., & Weiss, E. As they grow—0 to 13 years: bulletin on research. *Parents,* November 1993, 68:192–193.

Issues to Consider

1. What safeguards do you think might be introduced in questioning children regarding alleged abuse?
2. Do you think the findings of this research might apply to adults as well?

---

that has bearing when children are called upon to testify in court trials (Bruck and Ceci, 1993). This finding is described in the Psychology and the Media box entitled "Children's Memories Are Very Susceptible to Revision."

(Stage of) Concrete operations

According to Piaget, the stage of intellectual development beginning at 6 to 8 years when children can reason logically about objects they see but cannot yet deal with rules in the abstract.

Conservation

The principle suggesting that qualities such as mass, weight, and volume remain constant regardless of changes in appearance.

3. The Stage of Concrete Operations   Some time between the ages of six and eight, American children enter the stage of **concrete operations**—the period at which, as the name implies, they first begin to reason about concrete events in the world. They now can relate a particular object or event to a larger context. Thus, in the **conservation** experiment illustrated in Figure 12.10, the child is able to relate what he or she sees in Figure C to what he or she saw originally.

Children are now able to learn a variety of operational rules. They know, for example, that if object 1 is heavier than object 2, and object 2 is heavier than 3, then object 1 must be heavier than 3. They have also acquired considerable sophistication in the use of concepts and categories. They realize, for example, that "all the pets that are dogs" plus "all the pets that are not dogs" go to make up a category called "all pets." They also realize that objects or attributes can belong to more than one concept. They know that animals can be tame or wild, furry or feathered. Thus children in the stage of concrete operations show an ability to reason logically and apply operational rules. But as Piaget's name for the stage implies, they reason more effectively about objects that they can see or feel than about verbal statements. Suppose, for example, that children of this age are asked: "A is the same size as B, but B is smaller than C; which is bigger, A or C?" They may not be able to answer—for the question requires thinking about an abstract idea rather than about concrete objects.

4. The Stage of Formal Operations The fourth and final period of mental growth—the stage of **formal operations**—begins at around the age of 11 or 12. In a giant leap toward intellectual skill, children in their adolescent years acquire the ability to reason logically not just about actual objects but about abstract ideas and possibilities. They acquire full mastery of the important rules that Piaget calls operations and can apply them to all kinds of situations, real or imagined. They can assume hypothetical conditions and make correct inferences, thus manipulating their own thoughts as readily as they once manipulated colored blocks. It is probably not a coincidence that the emergence of this stage is associated with maturation of those portions of the brain's frontal cortex that play an important role in thought processes (Stuss & Benson, 1986).

One prominent characteristic of the stage of formal operations is preoccupation with one's own thought processes. Adolescents think about their own thoughts and are curious to learn how these thoughts are organized and where they will lead. This inquiring attitude often causes conflict with the standards of the adult world. Adolescents become keenly aware that people do not always practice what they preach, and they begin to question such ideals as democracy, honesty, self-sacrifice, and turning the other cheek. They may decide that many of the beliefs and values they have been taught are "phony"—and that they want to search instead for a different set of moral principles and a new philosophy of life.

(Stage of) Formal operations

According to Piaget, the stage of intellectual development beginning at about age 11 or 12 when a child becomes capable of thinking in the abstract.

TEST YOURSELF

e) What word do we use to describe the physical changes that take place after birth?

f) Piaget described two key processes that define children's mental growth. What are they?

g) True autobiographical memories that last into adulthood don't usually begin until about what age?

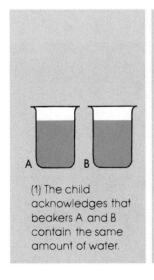
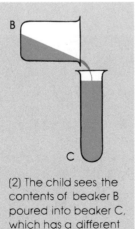
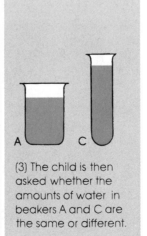

(1) The child acknowledges that beakers A and B contain the same amount of water.

(2) The child sees the contents of beaker B poured into beaker C, which has a different shape.

(3) The child is then asked whether the amounts of water in beakers A and C are the same or different.

FIGURE 12.10 Figuring out the conservation rule A child of 5 still in the preoperational stage, will say that the taller beaker has more water. In contrast, a child of 7 who has entered the concrete operations stage, will say that the glasses still have the same amount of water. The ability to reverse events mentally—for example, to see that it is possible to pour the water from beaker C back to B—is a key advance in concrete operations.

Personality Development: Birth to 18 Months

As with intellectual progress, the development of the personality also seems to proceed in an orderly way, through a series of gradually merging stages. All aspects of personality—emotions, motives, and ways of coping with conflicts—appear first and undergo change. During each stage, there are important qualities developing in all children and the variation in that quality (which is what is meant by personality) is a function of what is happening in the environment.

During the first stage of personality development, which lasts from birth to about the age of 18 months, one of the child's most important tasks is **attachment** to his or her caretakers. Attachment protects a child from too much fear or anxiety. But there is variation in the degree or security of attachment that the infant has to his or her caretakers. This variation depends on the predictability, availability, and sensitivity of the caretaker. When caretakers have these three qualities, children will develop a strong and secure attachment to them. Without these qualities, children become anxious and insecure in their attachment.

Attachment
The tendency of infants to form an emotional bond to their caretakers.

The Process of Attachment

Surrogate mother
A mother substitute.

Much psychological thinking about the very earliest development of attachment stems from a famous series of experiments by Harry F. Harlow, who took baby monkeys from their own mothers and placed them with doll-like objects that he called **surrogate mothers**. As is shown in Figure 12.11, Harlow gave his baby monkeys two such surrogate mothers. One was made of wire, with a bottle and nipple from which the monkey received milk. The other was made of sponge rubber and terry cloth; it was an object to which the baby monkey could cling.

As the photographs show, the baby monkeys strongly preferred the terry-cloth doll to the wire doll. They clung to the terry-cloth mother even when feeding from the other. When a new object was placed in the cage, they clung to the terry-cloth mother while making their first hesitant and tentative

FIGURE 12.11 a–c Baby monkey and surrogate mothers The baby monkey has been taken from its own mother and placed with two surrogate mothers. Note how it clings to the terry-cloth mother, even when feeding from the wire mother and especially when exploring a new and unfamiliar object that has been placed in the cage.

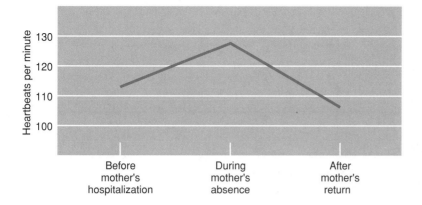

FIGURE 12.12 Baby's response to mother's absence During play sessions, the average heart rate for babies rose sharply while mother was hospitalized and then dropped back when she was home once again.

attempts to discover what this strange and at first frightening object might be (Harlow, 1961). Obviously something about the terry-cloth surrogate provided the baby monkey with what humans could call comfort, protection, and a secure base from which it could explore new aspects of the environment.

In human infants during the first two years of life, attachment takes the form of a strong tendency to approach particular people, to be receptive to care and consolation from them, and to be secure and unafraid in their presence. Human babies, like monkeys, seem to be born with an innate tendency to become attached to the adults who care for them. They show a strong preference for those who have served as continuous caretakers—especially when they are bored, frightened, or distressed by the unfamiliar or unexpected.

One study has shown that young children, separated from their mothers during the birth of another child, became more agitated, depressed, and withdrawn; they also cried more and experienced increased heart rate and awakenings from sleep. As illustrated in Figure 12.12, when mother returned, the symptoms abated (Field & Reite, 1984).

The Effects of Day Care

Such findings have raised many questions in the minds of parents about the advisability of day-care programs. In recent years, especially with both parents frequently working outside the home, day-care programs for young children have grown in popularity. What are the effects on the children? Some authorities have warned that the consequences are likely to be dangerous for the child's emotional development (Dreskin & Dreskin, 1983). But the evidence points to a more qualified conclusion: The consequences depend on the quality of the day-care program itself—on what goes on inside the program. Day-care programs are not universally good or bad. In one study, illustrated in Figure 12.13, children who experienced either high- or low-quality day care in their first year of life were studied later on, during preschool or kindergarten. The results showed that those children who entered high-quality programs were more compliant, capable of self-regulation, task-oriented, and considerate. Those who entered low-quality programs had greater difficulties with their peers and were more distractible and hostile (Howes, 1990).

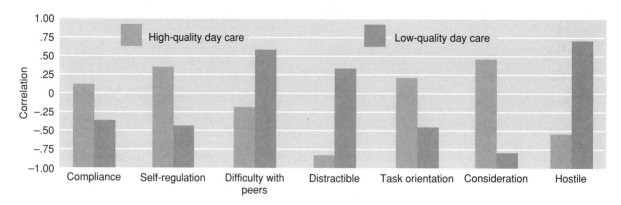

FIGURE 12.13 The results of day-care: it all depends
There are differences in outcome for children who experienced high- and low-quality day-care as infants—as explained in the text (after Howes, 1990).

In well-run, adequate centers, one caretaker is not responsible for more than three to four infants or five to six toddlers. Choice of playthings and learning materials for the children is also important. Infants, for example, should be exposed to a variety of stimulation and have opportunities to practice new abilities as they mature. One study focused on nine day-care centers that differed in the degree of stimulation they offered for language development. Children from those centers where the caregivers talked a lot performed best on tests of language development (McCartney, 1984).

If day care is good, it may even help children in their later adjustment to school (Howes, 1988). Children from disadvantaged homes seem to especially benefit from high quality day care. A study of disadvantaged 4-year-olds found that those who attended high-quality day care had IQs more than 15 points higher than children who had minimal day-care intervention (Burchinal, Lee, & Ramey, 1989). However, if day-care conditions are poor—if the program is understaffed, provides little variety and few pleasures, and restricts the child's explorations—then the child's development can indeed be affected adversely.

Courage for Exploration

Though attachment and exploration seem to be conflicting tendencies, they actually work hand in hand. Note in Figure 12.11 how the baby monkey engages in both activities at once—cautiously exploring a new object while clinging to its terry-cloth surrogate mother. Human babies also seem to gather courage for exploration from their attachment to their mothers. In one experiment, babies just under a year old were placed in a strange room that contained a chair piled high with and surrounded by toys. When baby and mother were in the room together, the baby actively looked at the toys, approached them, and touched them. All this exploratory behavior dropped off, however, if a stranger was present or if the mother left the room (Ainsworth & Bell, 1970).

The First Appearance of Anxiety

Along with the development of attachment during the first 18 months of life comes a related phase—the first appearance of signs of anxiety. In the experiment described above when the babies were left alone in the room, many of them very quickly began to cry, made what appeared to be a rather frantic search for the mother, or did both. They were exhibiting **separation anxiety,** which usually appears among American babies around the age of 8 months.

Separation anxiety seems to emerge as an outgrowth of some of the child's newly developed intellectual skills. At 8 months, most babies are able for the first time not only to recall past events but also to compare them with the here and now. When mother departs, they can now recall her former presence—and at the same time realize that she is no longer there. Not being able to understand the inconsistency, they become anxious and cry. Later, when babies can also anticipate that mother will return, the inconsistency is more easily resolved, and separation anxiety begins to fade.

Separation anxiety appears to be a universal experience regardless of child-rearing practices, as is shown in Figure 12.14. However, the temperamental qualities of the infant do influence how intense the child's separation anxiety is and how long it lasts. Infants who have a temperamental disposition to become highly fearful will show more intense separation anxiety than those who are relaxed and temperamentally are less vulnerable to anxiety (Kagan, 1989a).

A little before separation anxiety becomes apparent, babies show what is called **stranger anxiety.** It first appears at about the age of 7 months, increases to around the first birthday, then declines. Infants will usually smile if the mother shows her face above the crib. But if a stranger appears, they often show anxiety by turning away and perhaps breaking into tears. Again, the explanation is that the appearance of the strange face creates uncertainty. The baby has acquired a mental representation or perceptual expectation of familiar faces. This representation is violated by the unfamiliar face and, as a result, the child becomes fearful. Behavior that seems to indicate stranger anxiety can sometimes be produced by showing the baby a distorted mask of the human face. Although all infants show fear of strangers they will differ in

Separation anxiety
A form of anxiety that appears at about 8 months in which the infant cries when separated from a caretaker.

Stranger anxiety
An early form of anxiety in which a child of about 7 months cries to unfamiliar people.

FIGURE 12.14   The emergence of separation anxiety: A universal pattern In widely different cultures, babies younger than 7 months rarely cry when their mothers leave them. Between 12 and 15 months, however, the experience is almost sure to bring distress and tears—and then the impact begins to weaken. The pattern shown here applies equally everywhere children have been studied, including isolated villages in the Guatemalan highlands and remote areas of the African Kalahari Desert (Kagan, Kearsley, & Zelazo, 1978).

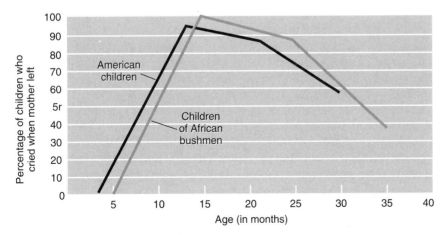

TEST YOURSELF

h) One of a child's most important tasks during the first 18 months is to form a strong bond with his or her caretaker. What is this process called?

i) At what age does separation anxiety usually appear among all babies?

the intensity of their fear, how long it will last, and the ease with which they can be soothed.

The fear that babies show in the presence of strangers reflects a more general principle in psychological development: Anxiety generated by an event is less likely if the event can be anticipated. For example, 1-year-old infants are less frightened by mechanical toys that produce noises on a predictable rather than an unpredictable schedule (Gunnar, Leighton, & Peleaux, 1984).

Thus, at 18 months infants around the world differ in their ease of arousal to unfamiliar events, their tendency to approach or withdraw to the unfamiliar, and their tendency to show positive emotion through smiling and laughter. These differences are a function both of the infant's temperament as well as its experiences in the first 18 months of life.

Learning Society's Rules: 18 Months Through 3 Years

The second important period in personality development, roughly from 18 months through the third year, involves the child's first appreciation of right and wrong; the notion that some behaviors will be met with punishment and disapproval, while others will be met with praise and approval. All children acquire an initial moral sense by the second birthday. The role of the environment is to determine what actions or behaviors the child regards as good and proper and which he or she regards as bad.

Cultures differ on these values. In villages in developing countries, for example, where there are no toilets or bathrooms, it is not wrong for a child to urinate outside the hut. Obviously, in most developed countries that behavior is punished. Thus the environment determines what it is that the child regards as moral. The variation among children will be a function primarily of what standards their families promote. In American society, typically, parents are concerned with teaching the child to control elimination and defecation, to inhibit aggression and destruction, to be clean, and not to cry at every minor frustration.

Initial Moral Sense

Teaching children to adhere to society's rules is helped along considerably by a dramatic change within the child. Around the age of 2, children first develop a sense of right and wrong—inner standards and the desire to live up to them, one of the most powerful motives. In one study, 2-year-olds watched someone play in a complicated manner—such as pretending to use toy kitchenware to cook a meal for a family—and then were told that it was their turn to play with the toys. Just a few months earlier, the process passed without incident. Now, however, many of them broke into tears or ran to their mother. Apparently they felt obligated to play with the toys in an equally sophisticated manner, yet they were unsure of their ability.

This newly developed uncertainty over living up to a self-imposed standard creates anxiety and distress (Kagan, 1981). Even subtle violations of standards appear to be disturbing. Children will now point to a cracked toy, dirty hands, torn clothing, or a missing button and show their concern. They can discern—even from changes in the sound of father's voice or the shape of mother's eyes—that their own behavior elicits judgmental responses from others.

Children in the second year, along with developing inner standards, also are gaining a clearer definition of themselves as individuals. In the company of peers, the 2-year-old begins making sharp distinctions between "I" and "mine" versus "you" and "yours." One investigator, studying peer interactions at this age, has shown how this emerging sense of self leads children to seize toys—not as evidence of selfishness but as a kind of proclamation of self-awareness (Levine, 1983).

Parental Practices and the Development of Morality

In learning to meet social demands, rewards and punishments also play a part. Children are usually rewarded with praise and fondling when they are successful at toilet training or refrain from playing with a lamp after being told "no." And they may be punished, with disapproval if not physically, when they soil themselves, break something, or get into forbidden places. But the desire to live up to standards of proper conduct appears as early as children learn to be anxious over possible punishment—and to have as strong an influence on behavior.

During their first year, babies act without any strong focus on the consequences of their actions and show little emotional reaction when they achieve a specific outcome. But at about 20 months of age, they become more interested in the results of their actions, reflecting the desire to meet inner standards. By the age of 3, the outcome of their efforts has become important. They are proud of success and frustrated with failure (Bullock & Lutkenhaus, 1988).

In addition to the strong influence of parental approval and disapproval in developing a moral sense is the child's own temperament. One researcher has proposed that temperament contributes to two aspects of conscience: guilt and degree of discomfort for doing something wrong, and being able to restrain one's behavior to accord to the rules of society (Kochanska, 1993).

The Role of Punishment

Punishment can actually upset the delicate balance between a child's natural, constructive urge to explore the environment and the requirement of social discipline. This early period of life holds exciting possibilities for children and their self-image as active, competent, and increasingly self-sufficient human beings. By moving about in the world for the first time, they acquire all kinds of fascinating information about the environment. By handling objects—and sometimes, unfortunately, destroying them—they learn that they have some power over their environment. They discover that they can roam about the world and perhaps rearrange it to their liking. They learn that they can satisfy many of their own desires. By reaching into the cookie jar, they can relieve hunger. By crawling under the coat a visitor has thrown on the sofa, they can find warmth. One of the responsibilities of parents is to aid children in their

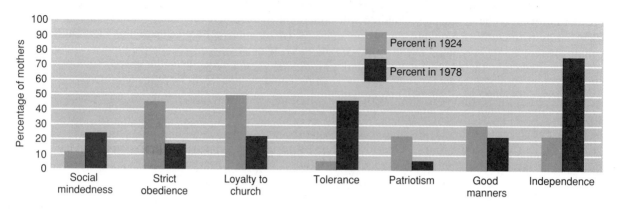

FIGURE 12.15 From obedience to independence In 1924, a group of mothers from Muncie, Indiana, chose three traits they wanted their children to develop. Their choices revealed a strong leaning toward conformity. The preferences of mothers 54 years later, in contrast, emphasized autonomy (Alwin, 1990).

explorations and discoveries while at the same time setting appropriate limits on their behavior.

When and how to punish a child varies by culture. Japanese parents, for instance, rarely punish their young children because they are afraid of making the child angry or anxious. The Japanese believe that it is important to maintain harmonious relations with their infants. Americans, on the other hand, believe that punishment is necessary. Although, as shown in Figure 12.15, American attitudes on obedience have relaxed over the decades, a considerable number still favor the use of corporal punishment as a disciplinary technique.

When Punishment Becomes Abusive

Parents who use corporal punishment are usually convinced that their tactic makes good sense. But the notion that physical pain is an effective teaching device has never been supported by evidence from psychological research. Indeed, study after study reveals that the opposite is true. An unsparing use of the "rod" creates children who in the long run, are less prone to obey, and who are instead more angry and aggressive than other kids. Research shows that corporal punishment can create pent-up feelings of resentment—and the dangerous conviction that, once you're big enough, power and physical force are the only means to get your way in the world (Leach, 1989). The psychological effects of physical punishment can range from apathy to obsessiveness, paranoia, and extreme disassociation (Greven, 1991). Parents tempted to hit their children should consider that as they grow, children will tend to follow the guidance of those who arouse affection and admiration, not loathing and fear.

When does corporal punishment cross the line and become child abuse? All physical punishment of a child by an adult has the potential to become abusive, and carries with it the possibility of lasting harm. Children growing up on a diet of whippings are vulnerable later in life to a variety of mental health problems, including depression and alcoholism (Holmes & Robins, 1987). Investigators studying family violence have also reached this conclu-

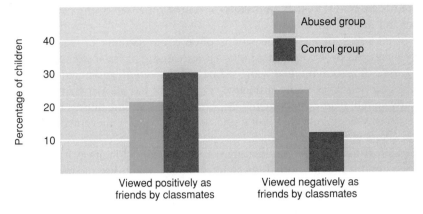

FIGURE 12.16 **The effects of abuse on peer relationships** Researchers compared the social popularity of a large group of abused children between the ages of 8 and 12 with that of an otherwise comparable group of nonabused children. Note that the abused youngsters were considerably less likely to be accepted—and more likely to be spurned—by their peers. They were seen as more aggressive and less cooperative (Salzinger et al., 1993).

sion: "The more children are hit by their parents, the more likely they are to hit others" (Straus, Gelles, & Steinmetz, 1981). Small wonder that, as shown in Figure 12.16, abused children find it relatively difficult to maintain good social relationships (Salzinger et al., 1993).

Venturing into the World: Ages 4 and 5

By the time children are 4, they venture outside the home to play with other children, and they may go to nursery school or kindergarten. This increasing social experience appears to be essential to normal development. As children move into broader social circles, they learn, among other things, that the world is made up of males and females, for whom society decrees different kinds of behavior. Boys begin to take on the characteristics that society considers appropriate to males, and girls to take on the characteristics considered appropriate to females. This is the period in which children begin to identify with their parents.

Emulating a Parent

Children of 4 and 5 have entered a stage of their development where they are mature enough to detect similarities between their parents and themselves, and they begin to feel vicarious emotions—that is, emotions that are appropriate to their parents. For example, when a 5-year-old perceives that her mother is competent, popular, and loved by the father, the child feels a positive emotion of pride because she identifies with her mother.

Children detect many bases of similarity between themselves and their parents. They have the same last name, they are told they look like one or both of their parents, and they begin to imitate their parents, which leads to an increase in perceived similarity. As this perception increases, the child begins to share vicariously in the emotions that come from recognizing the

TEST YOURSELF

j) All children acquire an initial moral sense by about what age?

k) Although corporal punishment may be effective in the short term, what are some of its long-term effects?

parent's strengths, virtues, and skills, or on the other hand, the parent's failures and undesirable traits.

Children with intelligent parents often come to think of themselves as intelligent. A boy whose father holds a job requiring physical strength usually begins to think of himself as being strong, and a girl with an attractive mother thinks of herself as being attractive. One study has shown that mother's clearly stated attitudes about the importance of learning during the child's preschool years is reflected in a higher level of school achievement six years later (Hess et al., 1984).

Unfortunately, children identify with their parents' faults as well as their virtues, and it is not unusual for children to become aware of their parents' defects. They may see that their father is unable to hold a job and is short-tempered or that mother drinks too much and is unwelcome in the neighbor's house. They may hear relatives criticize their parents. Or they may hear warring parents criticize each other. Under such circumstances many children begin to believe that they too are unworthy, unlovable, hateful, stupid, lazy, or mean.

The identification with undesirable qualities can be a burden to children from economically disadvantaged homes or from minority groups beset by prejudice. Children may identify with what they come to believe are undesirable qualities of their social class or ethnic group, and as a result they will experience the anxiety that is the result of such a belief. For tens of thousands of children, numbered among America's homeless, any sense of healthy identification is at a premium—as reflected in the drawings of Figure 12.17.

Same-Sex Identification

Girls and boys identify with the parent of their sex. Even 3-year-old boys and girls reveal their understanding of the differences between mom and dad—the young boy who lathers his face with shaving creams and pretends he is

FIGURE 12.17 The yearning for identification These drawings were made by children in the Homeless Children's Tutorial Project of Washington, D.C., and were presented to the U.S. Senate Subcommittee on Children, Families, Drugs, and Alcoholism in October 1989.

shaving, or the little girl who stuffs a pillow beneath her shirt and announces she has a baby inside.

To start with, differences in behavior between the two sexes may depend in part on the effects of the different hormones produced by the sex glands. The male sex glands produce large amounts of the hormone called **androgen,** the female glands large amounts of the hormone called **estrogen.** Many scientists believe that the two hormones may affect the developing brain. Androgen may program the circuits of the brain to operate in ways distinctively masculine, estrogen in ways typically feminine. One study, for example, shows striking anatomical differences between male and female monkeys in an area of the hypothalamus that influences sexual behavior. In this area the male's neurons contain more numerous and more varied synapses than the female's—probably because of the "masculinizing influence" of the male hormone before birth (Ayoub, Greenough, & Juraska, 1983).

But despite inborn tendencies, experiences in the environment remain crucial. Children learn to act masculine or feminine through a process called **sex typing.** Even parents who say they believe in treating the two sexes in the same way make distinctions. Some convincing evidence comes from an experiment with young and presumably liberated mothers. All these women claimed that boys and girls were alike and should be treated alike. Almost all of them said that they encouraged their girls to be rough-and-tumble and their boys to play with dolls. But their conduct with the child showed otherwise (Will, Self, & Datan, 1974). From infancy onward, fathers exhibit sex-typing behavior as well. They typically offer more attention to sons, and encourage achievement in them while stimulating dependency in their daughters (Sheperd-Look, 1982).

The knowledge of gender differences is present among children as young as 2 years old. When a group of 2-year-old boys and girls were shown sequences that portrayed stereotyped males and females, the boys remembered more of the male, rather than the female stereotypes. The girls remembered the male and female sequences equally well (Bauer, 1993).

Pressures for sex typing can emerge from television, books, and school. The message sinks in very early. When offered a choice, girls as young as 3 or 4 display their femininity in the kinds of toys they select—the customary dolls, toy stoves, and dish sets. Boys shun such toys and prefer guns, trucks, and cowboy suits (Maccoby & Jacklin, 1974). When the opportunities arise, boys are more likely than girls to take risks (Ginsburg & Miller, 1982). But even if books, television, and schools were to abandon sexual stereotyping, children would probably still show sex-type differences. Boys and girls differ in major traits around the world, even in those cultures where there are no schools, no television, no books, and no toys.

Sex differences become prominent when children are among peers. If a fight happens to break out among children, odds are good that it will be the boys rather than the girls who are in the thick of things. Aggression remains more stable in boys than it does in girls, primarily because of sex-typing. Our society has traditionally defined males as being aggressive, independent, and dominant, females as being unaggressive, dependent, and submissive. Hence, girls are more likely than boys to be punished for showing aggression; as they approach kindergarten, aggressive behavior among girls diminishes (Cummings, Iannoti, & Zahn-Waxler, 1989).

Androgen
The hormone produced by the male sex glands.

Estrogen
A hormone produced by the female sex glands.

Sex typing
The process through which society molds its members into its traditional patterns of femininity and masculinity.

But girls are not immune to aggression toward others, usually displaying it through verbal aggression and ostracizing other children (Cairns, 1989). Those who physically develop early tend to have more positive peer relationships. Developing breasts, in particular, makes them feel more mature and hence more secure in their social interactions (Warren, 1988).

The Influence of Television

Long before children begin socializing with classmates and peers, another outside influence enters their lives: television. By the time they are a year old, children are watching and paying attention to the TV. Many parents prop their infants in front of the television to quiet or entertain them, and babies as young as 6 months become upset when the TV picture becomes fuzzy or the sound is distorted. American children spend more time watching television than they do in any other activity excluding sleep.

What are the effects of this powerful medium on children? The answer is mixed. On the one hand, its influence can be deadening, even destructive. On the other hand, TV has the potential to be an educational tool (Huston et al., 1987).

Much of what children watch on television does not have a positive effect. According to one estimate, the child who watches an average two to four hours of television daily will have witnessed 8,000 murders and 100,000 other acts of TV violence by the time he or she graduates from elementary school (Huston et al., 1992). There is evidence that portrayals of violence on TV tend to stimulate aggressive behavior (Liebert & Sprafkin, 1988). Indeed, one study showed a positive correlation between the amount of time children spend viewing television and the seriousness of later criminal behavior (Eron, 1987). Watching television can also reinforce sexual stereotypes. On TV, women cook, clean, care for children, and try to look beautiful. Men on television are aggressive, adventurous, and successful (Calvert & Huston, 1987)

When parents watch television along with their children, they can harness its power in their children's behalf. With very young children, programs like *Sesame Street* can be treated as talking picture books that parents and children discuss (Lemish & Rice, 1986). In addition to its avowed goal of teaching children numbers, the alphabet, and concepts such as *near* and *far*, *Sesame Street* may improve children's vocabulary (Rice et al, 1990). For parents of older children, television offers an opportunity to discuss values as well as news and noteworthy facts.

The effects of television are not likely to be the same for every child. They depend on the child's temperament—for example, level of anxiety or aggressive tendencies—and on what else may be going on in the environment. Clearly, however, all children can use help in learning to relate wisely to that electronic force which, for better or worse, is here to stay.

Divorce and Loss of a Parent

Since children identify so strongly with their parents during the early years, the death of a parent is a keen loss. While it is not clear what the most vulnerable age may be (Garmezy, 1983), it would appear that the loss is often especially painful when it occurs during the preschool years. Of the many ways in which the removal of a parent can hamper a child's development, one is interference with the normal workings of the identification process. But what happens subsequently matters. One study showed that the effects of early loss of mother may be ameliorated if the quality of the child's relationship with the stepmother is a good one, and if a new marriage brings stability to the life of the child (Birtchnell, 1980).

The fate of children of divorce is also not uniform. True enough, many children treated for psychological problems have experienced the distress of parental discord and divorce (Hetherington & Camara, 1984), and the impact on school achievement and emotional well-being may reverberate even in late adolescence and the early adult years (Wallerstein & Blakeslee, 1989). One study, however, reports that the impact of divorce can be slight. Although many children showed some loss of well-being after their parents split up, the differences were too small to be considered very significant (Allison & Furstenberg, 1989).

A study looking at a group of 7- to 11-year-old boys whose parents had divorced found that, although the boys showed more behavioral problems than those from intact homes, most of the problems existed before the actual divorce occurred (Cherlin, 1991). In other words, a significant portion of what is usually considered the ill effects of divorce on children may be due to living in a family in which the parents' marriage was troubled for a long time.

As in the case of bereavement, the results depend on what happens after the breakup. One study found that among girls who were in preschool when their parents separated, school achievement depended on a continuing strong identification with a competent mother and a solid relationship between mother and child. For boys, the key factor was the father's continuing interest or the presence of an involved and committed stepfather (Wallerstein & Kelly, 1980).

TEST YOURSELF

l) What are the names of the hormones produced by the male and female sex glands?

Expanding Social Influences: Ages 6 to 10

As children approach the sixth and seventh birthday and have entered the stage of concrete operations, they can now compare an event with its broader context. At a personal level, this means the child will compare him or herself with others on traits that the child values, such as intelligence, bravery, physical attractiveness, and ability to deal with stress. The child arrives at a conception of self: smart or dumb, pretty or plain, brave or frightened. In our culture, two of the important environmental determinants of these conclusions the child comes to are achievement in school and acceptance by peers. Children who do well in school and are popular with their peers will develop a self-concept that is not anxiety arousing. On the other hand, those who fail in school and have few friends will develop a conceptualization of the self that is anxiety arousing and will influence personality in a major way.

The New World of School

Teachers usually play a dual role in the development of their pupils. First, they teach the intellectual skills appropriate to our society. Second, and perhaps even more important to a child's personality development, they try to encourage a motive for intellectual mastery. It is in the early years of school that children crystallize their inner standards of intellectual mastery and begin to feel anxiety if they do not live up to the standards. By the age of 10, some children have developed an expectancy of success that is likely to bolster their self-confidence throughout life. Others have developed expectations and fears of failure—even the signs of learned helplessness.

Many children who are actually very competent academically develop disparaging self-perceptions and illusions of incompetence (Phillips, 1984). Such outcomes depend largely on the school experience, including the expectations of teachers. Much has been made, for example, of sex differences in intellectual abilities, especially in reading and math. These differences may have more to do with expectations than with innate ability. A team of researchers recently studied the intellectual performance of kindergartners and first- and fifth-graders in the United States, Taiwan, and Japan. They found little evidence that boys and girls differed in their abilities in either reading or math (Lummis & Stevenson, 1990).

As a group however, a large number of American children lag behind their counterparts in Japan and China in level of achievement in mathematics, and the decline becomes more apparent as children progress in school (Stevenson et al., 1993). Part of the reason for this disparity may be the contrasting expectations of children among cultures. Asian parents had much higher expectations than American parents for what their children should achieve, as shown in Figure 12.18. Asian parents were also more likely to attribute their children's academic success to hard work, while American parents attributed it to innate ability.

An extensive study of schools in London attempted to isolate the school factors that make a difference in the child's development. The results showed that physical factors—the size of the school, the age of the buildings, or the space available—do not seem to matter very much. What does matter is the way pupils are dealt with in the school. Children accomplish more and display fewer behavior problems when they are given positions of responsibility and opportunities to help run the school, when they are rewarded and praised for their work, and when staff members are available for consultation and help. They also do better when teachers emphasize their successes and good potential rather than focus on their shortcomings (Rutter, 1983a).

FIGURE 12.18 Differing cultural expectations for achievement Despite their children's lower scores in mathematics, American parents said they were very satisfied with their performances. In contrast, Japanese and Chinese parents, whose children had scored higher, reported lower satisfaction (Stevenson et al., 1993).

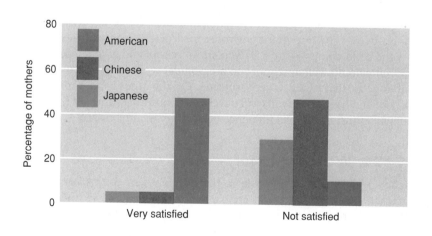

The Power and Pressure of Peers

Besides adjusting to teachers and schoolwork, children must also learn to live with their schoolmates. During the years from 6 to 10 these peers have a particularly strong influence. For one thing, children in school can now evaluate themselves in relation to their classmates (Marsh & Parker, 1984). They can determine their rank on such attributes as intelligence, strength, and skills of various kinds. For another thing, they can freely express among their peers the rebelliousness and hostility they so commonly feel toward the adult world.

Unfortunately for some children, aggression during the school years is often directed at a small minority. One child out of ten is abused by aggressive peers, and girls are as much at risk as boys are. These victims are made up of two kinds of youngsters: those who are bullies themselves and those who are generally passive and frightened (Perry, 1988).

Happily, most children benefit from their relations with each other. Peers can provide models for learning such traits as generosity, empathy, and helpfulness. They can teach other academic skills with surprising effectiveness, and sometimes do a better job than parents of relieving the anxieties and agitation encountered in growing up (Furman, Rahe, & Hartup, 1981).

Early friendships can leave a lasting impression. When presented with pictures of their nursery school playmates, 9-year-old children said they did not recognize them. But measurement of their sweat gland response, subtle changes in electrical activity of their skin, showed that on some unconscious level they did recognize them (Newcombe, Fox, & Prime, In Press). Although early memories fade, some events and people are not completely forgotten.

Becoming Dominant or Submissive

One personality trait that is partially set by the end of the early school years is the tendency to be dominant or submissive in relations with other people. Children of 10 who actively make suggestions to the group, try to influence and persuade others, and resist pressure from others often tend to remain dominant in their social relations. Children who are quiet and like to follow the lead of others often remain passive and submissive.

The tendency to be dominant or submissive is, in part, a function of group acceptance. Children who believe that they are admired by the group are likely to develop enhanced self-confidence and dominance over others. Children who do not consider themselves admired by the group are likely to develop feelings of inferiority and to be submissive. Physical attributes play an important part. The large, strong boy and the attractive girl are more likely to be dominant. The small, frail boy and the unattractive girl are likely to be submissive. Other factors are identification with a dominant or submissive parent and the kind of control exercised by the parents. Permissive parents tend to produce children who are more dominant, while parents who restrict their children's activities tend to produce more submissive youngsters.

The Doorway to Adolescence

By age 10, children have made remarkable progress from their helpless days in the crib. Their bodies and nervous systems have grown to near maturity. They are capable of many physical skills. Intellectually, they are well along in

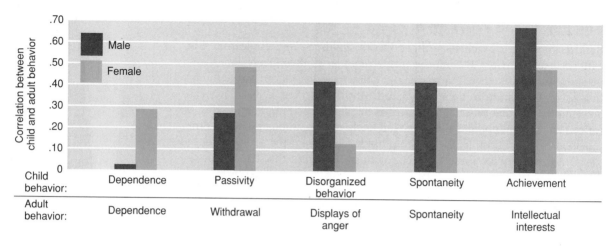

FIGURE 12.19 Some relationships between childhood traits and adult personality The correlations were obtained by rating the behavior of children aged 6 to 14, then making ratings of the same subjects after they had become young adults. For males, note that dependence in childhood shows almost no correlation with dependence as an adult—but striving for achievement shows a high correlation. For females, disorganized behavior in childhood shows little correlation with displays of anger in adulthood—but striving for achievement shows a fairly high correlation (Kagan & Moss, 1962).

Piaget's stage of concrete operations and about to embark on the final stage of formal operations. Their personality has changed and blossomed. They now display many individual differences in personality.

As children approach adolescence, the emotional road ahead will be rockier. A recent study of children ranging in age from 9 to 15 found that as children get older they report fewer occasions of feeling on top of the world and more instances of feeling mildly negative (Larson & Lampman-Petriatis, 1989). Cultural beliefs, values and traditions, and associated child-rearing and socialization practices shape the kinds of problems youngsters show when distressed. One comparison of 11 to 15 year olds from Kenya, Thailand, and the United States (both white and African-American) found strong differences among the behavioral and emotional problems of children from one cultural context to another (Weisz, 1993). White American adolescents displayed more problems like disobedience and cruelty—problems often due to insufficient parental control; Kenyan adolescents, in comparison, displayed more fear and guilt, problems often due to too much control by parents.

In some ways, the 10-year-old child offers a reasonably accurate preview of the future adult. The trend of physical development and the pattern of mental processes have been established. Personality traits have emerged and may persist through adolescence and into adulthood, as indicated by the correlations shown in Figure 12.19. But note that the correlations are by no means perfect. Some are indeed very low. The child's personality is still subject to change—for development, though it proceeds rapidly and dramatically through the first 10 years, does not end at that point. Adolescence and adulthood, as will now be seen, may move development into entirely new channels.

TEST YOURSELF

m) How would you describe a child who actively makes suggestions to a group, tries to influence and persuade others, and resists pressures from peers?

SUMMARY REVIEW

Life's Beginnings: From Conception to Birth

1. Developmental psychology studies the ways in which children gradually acquire their patterns of thinking, emotions, motives, and other aspects of personality—and the ways in which these patterns may change in later life.

2. The mechanisms of human heredity are the 23 pairs of **chromosomes,** 46 in all, found in the fertilized egg cell and repeated through the process of division in every cell of the body that grows from the egg.

3. Being female or male is determined by the **X chromosome** and the **Y chromosome.** An XX pairing in the fertilized egg cell creates a female. An X-Y pairing creates a male.

4. Each chromosome is made up of a large number of **genes,** which are composed of a chemical called DNA. The genes direct the growth of cells into parts of the body and also account for the individual differences we inherit.

5. The development of a child can be affected dramatically by the quality of the environment in the womb.

6. Over approximately 280 days of prenatal development, the developing baby undergoes a remarkable series of changes. During the first eight weeks, an infant increases nearly 2 million percent in size; as early as seven weeks, the nervous system, brain, and parts of the body can be discerned; by 20 weeks, the child is sensitive to touch, pain, and changes in temperature.

7. The ease and difficulty with which a baby is born, how quickly the baby begins to breathe, and the term of pregnancy can affect the baby's wellbeing. Loss of oxygen supply to the nerve cells, which is called **anoxia,** may result in motor paralysis.

Newborn Infants: Similarities and Differences

8. All babies respond to stimuli with a wide range of inborn reflex behavior that allows them to escape pain, avoid harsh stimuli, and seek food. For example, if the side of the mouth is touched, they display the **rooting reflex.**

9. Studies have shown wide individual differences among infants in
   a) the response of sensory threshold
   b) how rapidly babies display sensory adaptation and quit responding
   c) the child's degree of irritability
   d) the child's vulnerability to stress.

10. Babies at birth differ in
   a) sensory thresholds and adaptation
   b) activity and irritability
   c) **temperament.**
   Most newborns fall into three categories: easy children, slow-to-warm-up children, and difficult children.

11. Traits displayed in infancy endure for varying periods of time. Most early traits are altered by childhood environment, although one trait that appears to be relatively persistent is timidity.

12. Human infants are extremely impressionable. An unfavorable environment may produce drastic and sometimes long-lasting abnormalities. But infants are also resilient and malleable—capable of changing when circumstances change.

The Early Development of Body and Mind

13. Physical development, including the acquisition of such skills as walking and talking, depends largely on the process of **maturation**—the physical changes, taking place after birth, that continue biological growth from fertilized egg cell to adult.
14. Factors contributing to intellectual development include improvement in the process of perception and growing skill at understanding and using language.
15. Piaget concluded that intellectual growth is basically an increased ability to adapt to new situations. The key processes in development, he found, are **assimilation** (incorporating a new event into one's existing cognitive view of the world) and **accommodation** (changing one's cognitive view and behavior when new information dictates such a change).
16. A key word in Piaget's theory is **operations**—a dynamic mental rule for manipulating objects or ideas into new forms and back to the original—like the rule that four pieces of candy (or the figure 4) can be divided into two parts of two each, and then restored to the original four.
17. Piaget charted children's intellectual development through four stages:
    a) the **sensorimotor stage,** birth to 18 months, in which children know the world only through their sensory impressions and the results of their motor (or muscular) movements
    b) the **preoperational stage,** 18 months to about 7 years, in which they have acquired language and can manipulate symbols but do not yet grasp the dynamic rules of operation
    c) the **stage of concrete operations,** six to eight years, when they can manipulate ideas mentally and translate them into concrete terms
    d) the **stage of formal operations,** beginning at about age 12, when they can apply operational rules and logical reasoning to abstract ideas and possibilities.

Personality Development: Birth to 18 Months

18. Personality development from birth to 18 months is characterized by **attachment** to the mother or other caretakers. This period is marked by the appearance of **separation anxiety** and **stranger anxiety.**

Learning's Society's Rules: 18 Months Through 3 Years

19. The second important period in personality development, roughly from 18 months through the third year, is dominated by a child's first important experiences with the demands of society.

20. Children in the second year
    a) develop inner standards and desire to live up to them
    b) begin making sharp distinctions between "I" and "mine" and "you" and "yours." In learning to meet social demands, rewards and punishment play a part in influencing behavior.

Venturing into the World: Ages 4 and 5

21. The preschool years, ages 4 and 5, are characterized by
    a) identification with the parents
    b) the first notions of **sex typing** and conduct appropriate to males and females
    c) the first feelings of guilt and conscience.

Expanding Social Influences: Ages 6 to 10

22. From ages 6 to 10, children come under the strong influence of their peers—that is, other children. Peers provide
    a) evaluation
    b) a social role
    c) an opportunity for rebellion against the adult world.
    During this period, children acquire a tendency to be dominant or submissive and strong inner standards calling for
    a) being valued by parents, teachers, and peers
    b) mastering physical and mental skills
    c) achieving harmony between thoughts and behavior.
23. By age 10, a child offers a reasonably accurate preview of the future adult.

TEST YOURSELF ANSWERS

a) There are 46 chromosomes in a fertilized cell.
b) They may suffer from fetal alcohol syndrome.
c) The term is temperament.
d) The description is of a slow-to-warm-up infant.
e) The term is maturation.
f) The two key processes of Piaget are assimilation and accommodation.
g) Autobiographical memories usually don't begin until about age 3½ to 4.
h) This process is called attachment.
i) Separation anxiety usually appears at about 7 months.
j) A moral sense develops by about the age of 2 years.
k) Corporal punishment can lead to disobedience, aggression, resentment, apathy, depression, obsessiveness, and paranoia.
l) Males produce the hormone called androgen and females produce estrogen.
m) This child is dominant in social relations.

Study Guide

Chapter 12   Infancy and Childhood

LEARNING OBJECTIVES

For an Understanding
of the Science

After studying this chapter, you should be able to:

1. Understand that developmental psychology is the study of the ways in which growing children gradually acquire their adult patterns of behavior, thinking, and personality and how the developmental process continues from cradle to grave.

2. Identify the potential influences of diet, alcohol, drugs, and stress during pregnancy on the infant and child.

3. Describe the role of maturation in physical, perceptual, and intellectual development, and be able to characterize the nature of Piaget's four stages of mental development.

4. Identify the events of the first 18 months that are of special importance to personality development, including attachment, stranger anxiety, and separation anxiety.

5. Discuss the important events that occur during the period of first social demands, from 18 months through 3 years.

6. Understand the process of identification with parents in the preschool years (ages 4 and 5).

7. Characterize the influences exerted by the child's teachers and peers during the ages of 6 to 10.

For Application
to Life Sciences

8. Recognize that babies display many individual differences—that some are active and others quiet, some quick to be frightened or to show signs of pain, and some more irritable than others. These differences in temperament mean that babies must be treated differently.

9. Assure parents of difficult and irritable babies that early traits may change during childhood.

10. Understand that it is only natural for young babies to display stranger anxiety (when they see an unfamiliar face) and separation anxiety (when they are left alone by the caretaker).

11. Describe the importance of the period when children meet their first social demands in the form of toilet training and other forms of discipline connected with their increasing exploration of the environment. Parents need to tread a middle course between restrictiveness and encouraging independence.

12. Recognize the importance of providing good models during the preschool period when children identify with their parents and try to imitate their behavior, both their virtues and their faults.

13. Identify the characteristics of early childhood teachers and environments that influence infants and young children, and describe the ideal care environment.

PROGRAMMED UNIT
LIFE'S BEGINNINGS: FROM CONCEPTION TO BIRTH

1. Life beings at *conception,* the instant at which a sperm and egg unite to form a new individual. The child's *heredity* is granted at the moment of _____.   **conception**

2. The characteristics of the parents passed on to the child in its _____ are carried in 46 *chromosomes* arranged in 23 pairs, which are composed of hundreds of smaller *genes.*   **heredity**

3. Each body cell contains 46 _____, 23 from each parent.   **chromosomes**

4. Each chromosome in turn contains from 20,000 to 125,000 _____, which alone, or more likely in combination with each other, influence a particular phase of development and specific physical and behavioral characteristics.   **genes**

5. The sex of the new individual is determined by one particular pair of _____. The sex chromosomes are either in the form of an *X* or a *Y.*   **chromosomes**

6. If the pair of sex chromosomes is *XX,* then the child will be a _____. If the sex chromosomes are *XY,* then the child will be a _____.   **female**
male

7. The mother, being a female, has only *X* _____ to give to her child. The father, being a male, has either an _____ or a _____ chromosome to give to his child.   **chromosomes**
X, Y

8. Therefore, the sex of the child will depend on whether the child receives an *X* or a *Y* chromosome from the _____.   **father**

9. A child's heredity is determined at _____, and the influence of *environmental* factors also starts at this time.   **conception**

10. Whether the mother eats properly, smokes, drinks coffee or alcohol, uses drugs, or is stressed during pregnancy contribute to the prenatal _____ of the fetus, which can influence the child's physical and behavioral characteristics. Similarly, at birth a shortage of oxygen to the brain, a condition called *anoxia,* may lead to later problems.   **environment**

11. Some types of physical paralysis, such as that associated with cerebral palsy, may be caused by _____, insufficient oxygen to certain parts of the brain at birth.   **anoxia**

12. Whether prenatal factors such as substance use or anoxia produce long-term effects in the child may depend on whether the child grows up in a stimulating, supportive _____ after birth.   **environment**

NEWBORN INFANTS: SIMILARITIES AND DIFFERENCES

13. Newborn infants display many *inborn* abilities and behaviors. The ability to follow a moving object with the eyes and pay more attention than chimpanzees to the human face and voice are _____ tendencies.   **inborn**

14. Newborns also have *reflexes* that are _____. For example, the tendency of a newborn to turn toward and suck on a finger that strokes the corner of the mouth is called the *rooting* _____.   **inborn**

    reflex

rooting, reflex

15. While babies learn to improve the efficiency of their sucking with practice, the _____ _____ helps get them started.

temperament

16. Newborn infants differ a great deal in behavior. For example, they differ with respect to *temperament,* or their general pattern of responding to people and events. A baby's general activity, mood, adaptability, and irritability define its _____.

temperament

17. Two fundamental qualities of _____ are how easily the infant will become *aroused* by stimulation and, once aroused, how the infant *copes* with the arousal.

arousal

coping

18. Motor activity, babbling, and crying are signs of _____, and turning away from the arousing stimulus, becoming extremely distressed, and approaching an exciting stimulus are methods of regulating or _____ with arousal.

copes, arousal

irritability

19. How an infant _____ with _____ contributes to the temperamental characteristic of *irritability*. Some infants whine or cry at the slightest provocation while others rarely do so, illustrating differences in _____.

temperament

20. Investigators have found that infants can be grouped into three general types of _____. One type consists of *easy* infants, who are cheerful, react to stimuli with low-to-moderate intensity, have regular habits of eating and sleeping, and are quick to adapt to new schedules, foods, and people. Approximately 40 percent of babies are like this, and parents find these children _____ to deal with.

easy

easy

21. Less cheerful than _____ infants are the *slow-to-warm-up* babies, a category that applies to approximately 15 percent of infants. Their responses are low in intensity, they seem slightly sad and tense, they may withdraw from their first exposure to a new stimulus, and their eating and sleeping habits vary. They seem cautious or _____-_____-_____-_____.

slow-to-warm-up

slow-to-warm-up

22. In addition to the easy infants and those who are _____-_____-_____-_____, other infants, about 10 percent, are termed *difficult.* They seem hard to please, they become very irritable and cry at unfamiliar events, they are difficult to soothe, and they have little regularity in eating and sleeping. For their parents, they are _____.

difficult

temperamental, easy, slow-to-warm-up, difficult

23. While 35 percent of babies have mixed characteristics and are difficult to classify, the remaining fall into three _____ groups: _____, _____-_____-_____-_____, and _____.

24. For some infants, these temperamental characteristics persist into adolescence, while for others they *change*. For example, about one-third of very shy, fearful, inhibited 2-year-olds become dour, serious, and moderately intense adolescents, and approximately half of the outgoing, sociable, uninhibited 2-year-olds become extroverted adolescents; the remainder _____ in _____.

change, temperament

irritable, change

25. Therefore it should come as some comfort to parents who must cope with difficult or _____ infants that most will grow out of it or _____ in temperament by childhood.

26. *Maturation* refers to the physical changes that continue the biological growth of the organism from fertilized cell to adult. As infants and children get older, they become capable of new feats of physical, perceptual, and mental skill that are associated with _____.

maturation

27. These biological processes cannot be speeded up to any great extent, and children from all over the world, regardless of child-rearing practices, tend to display various skills at about the same ages because of biological _____.

maturation

28. Intellectual, as well as physical, development is influenced by _____. Many factors contribute to intellectual development, including improvements in the process of *perception* and skill in understanding and using *language*.

maturation

29. As children grow older, their attention becomes more selective, they can maintain it longer, they scan the environment more systematically, and they become increasingly efficient in searching the environment for information—all because of improvements in the process of _____.

perception

30. In addition, the increasing use of words and concepts helps to organize information into categories and facilitate information processing that creates long-lasting memories—processes reflecting the emerging use of _____.

language

31. The intellectual development of infants and young children has been dominated by the theories of the Swiss psychologist *Jean Piaget*. According to _____, mental growth is the result of an increased ability to adapt to new situations.

Piaget

32. The theories of _____ emphasized the processes of *assimilation* and *accommodation*.

Piaget

33. The process of incorporating a new event into one's existing cognitive view of the world is called _____.

assimilation

34. The process of changing one's cognitive view and behavior when new information dictates such a change is called _____.

accommodation

35. If a young boy is given a new toy—for example, a magnet—he may try to throw it like a ball or bang it like a hammer. These are behaviors he has practiced with other toys, and he is trying to _____ the new toy into existing behavior patterns.

assimilate

36. On the other hand, he may discover the power of the magnet to attract iron and use the magnet to pull other toys toward him, thus _____ his own behavior to fit the unique characteristics of the new object.

accommodating

37. There is always a tension, _____ believed, between _____ and _____, and the resolution of this tension produces intellectual growth. As growth proceeds, the child learns *operations*.

Piaget, assimilation accommodation

38. A mental rule for manipulating objects or ideas into new forms and back to the original is an _____.

operation

39. As children grow older, the sophistication of the _____ of which they are capable increases. According to Piaget, this mental growth occurs in four *stages*. The first, covering approximately the first 18 months of life, is called the *sensorimotor* _____.

operations

stage

sensorimotor stage	40. The period during which infants come to know the environment primarily by their own sensory impressions and the discovery of the relation between their actions with the physical objects in their environment and the consequences of those actions is called the _____ _____.
sensorimotor	41. Following the _____ stage, from approximately 18 months to 7 years, children are in what Piaget calls the *preoperational stage*.
preoperational stage	42. While their actions are still dictated largely by the evidence of their senses, children have acquired language and can manipulate symbols, but they are not capable of forming meaningful categories or thinking according to rules during the _____ _____.
preoperational	43. After the _____ stage, beginning at approximately 6 to 8 years of age, children enter the stage of *concrete operations*.
concrete operations	44. Children become capable of mentally manipulating ideas about events, but only about actual events in the world, during the stage of _____ _____.
concrete operations	45. During the stage of _____ _____, children acquire *conservation* of volume, mass, number, and weight. That is, they understand that these attributes of objects do not change when other attributes are altered. Therefore a child who recognizes that the volume of liquid is the same when the liquid is poured from a short, wide beaker into a tall, narrow beaker has achieved _____ of volume, a skill that is acquired during the stage of _____ _____.
conservation concrete operations	
operational rule	46. During this stage, children also learn a variety of *operational rules*. For example, if they know that object 1 is heavier than object 2, and object 2 is heavier than object 3, then they can conclude that object 1 is heavier than object 3 because they have learned an _____ _____.
concrete operations	47. Following the stage of _____ _____, beginning around the age of 12, children enter the stage of *formal operations*. The ability to reason logically, not just about actual objects but about abstract ideas and possibilities, are the hallmarks of the stage of _____ _____.
formal operations	
formal operations	48. Children who can assume hypothetical conditions and make correct inferences, thus manipulating their own thoughts as readily as they once manipulated colored blocks, are achieving the stage of _____ _____.
Piaget sensorimotor preoperational, concrete formal operations	49. According to the Swiss psychologist _____, the child's mental development goes through four stages, beginning with the _____ stage. This is followed by the _____ stage, and then the _____ and _____ _____ stages.

PERSONALITY DEVELOPMENT: BIRTH TO 18 MONTHS

attachment	50. Personality, like mental development, also seems to grow in stages. A major feature of the first period of personality development is the growing *attachment* between the infant and the person who constitutes the main source of interaction, comfort, and care. The development of a loving relationship between infant and parent (typically) is what psychologists call _____.
attachment	51. In the first two years of life, the infant's strong tendency to approach particular people, to be receptive to care and consolation from them, and to be least afraid when in their presence are signs of _____.

52. Attachment in the infant is promoted by a caretaker who is *predictable, available,* and *sensitive* to the infant's signals and needs. A caretaker who remains in that role over the child's life and who behaves in a similar manner from day to day is _____; one who spends a good deal of time with the infant and responds when needed is _____; and one who adjusts responses to fit the infant's changing needs and abilities is _____.

predictable
available
sensitive

53. The characteristics of _____, _____, and _____ are more important for attachment than satisfying other basic needs, such as food. This was demonstrated in an experiment with baby monkeys who were given two *surrogate* mothers, doll-like objects one of which was made of wire and had a bottle and nipple to feed the infant monkey and one of which was made of sponge rubber and terry cloth to which the infant could cling. The infants preferred the cloth over the feeding _____, especially when frightened, presumably because it provided more comfort, protection, and a secure base.

predictability, availability, sensitivity

surrogate

54. In view of the factors that contribute to attachment, many have wondered whether *day care* is damaging to infants and toddlers. The answer seems to depend upon the quality of care—the extent to which the circumstances and the caretakers are similar to good homes and parents. So, research seems to indicate that good _____ _____ is not damaging and may be good for some infants and toddlers; poor quality care is not good.

day care

55. The desire of most infants to want to be near their parents is a sign of _____. Thus if a parent leaves the infant alone, *separation anxiety* may occur.

attachment

56. At around 8 months of age, infants may become upset and cry as soon as a parent leaves them. That is, they display _____ _____.

separation anxiety

57. In addition to _____ anxiety, infants of approximately the same age show *stranger anxiety.*

separation

58. If an unfamiliar person suddenly appears, especially one who approaches the infant rapidly, the baby may become upset and cry because of _____ _____.

stranger anxiety

59. One of the first events in personality and social development is the formation of _____ between infant and principal caretaker. Later, at approximately 8 months of age, the infant may become upset and cry if the parent leaves, as in _____ _____, and if a new person approaches, as in _____ _____.

attachment

separation anxiety
stranger anxiety

LEARNING SOCIETY'S RULES: 18 MONTHS THROUGH 3 YEARS

60. In the second phase of personality development, from 18 months through 3 years, children meet the first *social demands,* in the form of toilet training and rules against destroying property or getting into danger. They learn to be disciplined members of society by encountering _____ _____.

social demands

61. One aid to parents in imposing this discipline is the fact that by 2 years of age most children have developed some of their own *standards* of behavior. Children who have learned what they are allowed and not allowed to do in particular situations have acquired their own _____ of behavior.

standards

standards

62. In part, these _____ of behavior are created by *rewards* and *punishments*.

rewards, punishments
standards

63. Parents praise, hug, and kiss children for desirable behaviors and scold them for undesirable behaviors, and these _____ and _____ contribute to the establishment of the children's own behavioral _____.

64. The task for the parent during this period is to construct a delicate balance between encouraging exploration, independence, and learning about the child's own effect on the environment on the one hand, and learning and obeying the rules of family and society on the other. Creating this delicate balance between _____ and _____ is the parent's task in the period when children meet their first _____ _____.

rewards, punishments
social demands

VENTURING INTO THE WORLD: AGES 4 AND 5

65. Children during this period begin the process of *identification* with their parents. That is, they see themselves as similar to their parents in many different respects. The result is that they behave like and believe themselves to be similar to their parents, which constitutes part of the _____ process.

identification

66. One aspect of the process of _____ is that children begin to learn about *sex typing*. They come to understand that society considers somewhat different behavior appropriate for males and females, and children of each sex learn the appropriate kind of behavior. This training is called _____ _____.

identification

sex typing

67. Experience with their mothers and fathers as well as the demands of society are not the only contributors to _____ _____. The male hormone *androgen* and the female hormone *estrogen* also play roles.

sex typing

68. Presence of the male hormone _____ tends to "masculinize" the brain and make the developing male more physically aggressive.

androgen

69. The influence of hormones is a matter of degree, because both males and females possess some amount of both sex hormones, _____ and _____.

androgen
estrogen

70. Undoubtedly, however, both hormones and experience in the form of parent behavior, social demands, television, books, and schools combine to foster _____ _____.

sex typing

71. Sex typing and other behaviors are influenced by *television*. Indeed, except for sleeping, American children spend more time watching _____ than any other single activity.

television

72. For example, the average child who watches two to four hours of television per day will witness 8,000 murders and 100,000 other acts of violence before leaving elementary school. On the other hand, if they watch educational programs, such as *Sesame Street* and *Mister Rogers,* they will be exposed to educational information and positive social behavior. Depending upon what children watch, how much they watch, their temperament and personality, and whether their parents watch with them and encourage positive behaviors, the effects of _____ on children can be negative and destructive or positive and beneficial.

television

73. Another factor influencing a child's _____ with parents is *divorce*. The effects of parental separation are not uniform for all ages, sexes, and individual children, and negative effects seem to be associated with amount of parental conflict before and after _____.

identification

divorce

EXPANDING SOCIAL INFLUENCES: AGES 6 TO 10

74. In the next period, when children start school, they must learn to live with some important new people—their *teachers* and their classmates or *peers*. A great deal of their development from ages 6 to 10 is influenced by the fact that they must conform to the discipline and seek the acceptance of new adults in their lives, their _____.

teachers

75. A notable dual role is performed in a pupil's development by the _____ who promotes *intellectual skills* and encourages a motive for *intellectual mastery*. Partly as a result of the practices of teachers, children may develop an expectancy for success or for failure, a situation which may have substantial consequences. A child's intellectual future may be influenced by a teacher's emphasis on, expectancy for, and encouragement of _____ _____ and _____ _____.

teacher

intellectual skills
intellectual mastery

76. Besides developing intellectual _____ and _____, and an expectancy for success or failure, children must also learn to live with their classmates or _____. For one thing, peers provide a standard of *evaluation*. Children decide whether they are competent or incompetent, good or bad, excellent or poor on the basis of how they _____ themselves relative to their _____.

skills, mastery

peers

evaluate
peers

77. By providing a standard of _____, peers advance the development of each other. Children who remain isolated from peers often have problems in social relations, because _____ provide models and encouragement for learning, social skills, and academic abilities that may be necessary for development.

evaluation

peers

78. During this period, children also acquire the personality trait of being *dominant* or *submissive* in relations with other people. Some children have self-confidence and become accustomed to influencing other children while others do not. These patterns of being _____ or _____ develop during this period.

dominant, submissive

79. During the early school years from six to ten, an important influence on child development is the teacher, who serves to promote intellectual _____ and encourage or discourage the motive for intellectual _____. At the same time, peers provide children with a standard of _____, and, as a result of interacting with peers, children acquire the traits of being socially _____ or _____.

skills
mastery
evaluation
dominant, submissive

REVIEW OF IMPORTANT TERMS

accommodation **(586)**

androgen **(599)**

anoxia **(577)**

assimilation **(586)**

attachment **(590)**

chromosomes **(575)**

(stage of) concrete operations **(588)**

conservation **(588)**

estrogen **(599)**

(stage of) formal operations **(589)**

genes **(575)**

maturation **(582)**

operations **(586)**

preoperational stage **(587)**

rooting reflex **(578)**

sensorimotor stage **(586)**

separation anxiety **(593)**

sex typing **(599)**

stranger anxiety **(593)**

surrogate mother **(590)**

temperament **(579)**

X chromosome **(575)**

Y chromosome **(575)**

PRACTICE TEST

_____ 1. The sex of a baby is determined by

    a.   the mother.

    b.   the father.

    c.   both mother and father.

    d.   a single gene X.

_____ 2. Which of the following feats can a 1- or 2-week-old baby _not_ accomplish?

    a.   Follow a moving object with their eyes

    b.   Differentiate between the smell of their own mother's milk and the smell of milk from another mother.

    c.   Display a marked preference for the human face and voice

    d.   Remember where an attractive object is hidden for a few seconds

_____ 3. The rooting reflex occurs when

    a.   the corner of a newborn human's mouth is lightly touched.

    b.   baby pigs dig for roots and mushrooms.

    c.   the heel of a baby is pricked with a pin.

    d.   a bright light is suddenly directed in a baby's eyes.

_____ 4. Differences in temperament between babies in their first months of life

    a.   are similar to the personalities of their parents.

      b.   are permanent dispositions that last in one form or another for most of the child's life.

      c.   reflect differences in child rearing and infant care practices.

      d.   tend to change as the infant gets older.

_____ 5. Infants having a slightly sad and tense mood and low intensity responses, especially to new experiences, are said to be temperamentally

      a.   easy

      b.   slow-to-warm-up.

      c.   difficult.

      d.   none of the above.

_____ 6. Psychology's "optimistic message to parents" is that

      a.   everything will turn out fine.

      b.   it is difficult to predict from the way infants behave how they will behave as children and adolescents.

      c.   almost all harmful experiences will be overcome in time.

      d.   most characteristics are established early so mistakes parents make later do not matter much.

_____ 7. The most persistent early personality trait seems to be

      a.   timidity.

      b.   irritability.

      c.   activity level.

      d.   readiness to smile.

_____ 8. For parents, the most important implication of differences in the temperaments of babies is

      a.   that a single style of child rearing may not be the most appropriate for all babies.

      b.   genetics plays a large part in personality development.

      c.   babies come with different personalities and little can be done to change them.

      d.   babies with extreme irritability are likely to be a problem for many years.

_____ 9. Extremely poor early experiences can

      a.   lead to maladjustment later in life.

      b.   be counteracted by positive environments later.

      c.   both *a* and *b*.

      d.   neither *a* and *b*, the result depends on other factors.

_____ 10. The physical changes that continue the biological growth of the organism throughout life are called

    a.   growth trajectories.

    b.   maturation.

    c.   socialization.

    d.   identification.

_____ 11. Which is *not* true of early physical growth?

    a.   Newborn babies have all the muscle fibers they will ever possess.

    b.   The skeleton at birth is largely composed of cartilage that is softer and more pliable than bone.

    c.   Some of the fibers of the nervous system develop protective sheaths that make them faster and more efficient conductors of nervous impulses.

    d.   The process of maturation can be speeded up to a great extent by exercise and stimulation.

_____ 12. Jason is a quiet and somewhat unresponsive child who tries to avoid new experiences. His parents can probably help him most if they

    a.   gently encourage him to try new experiences at his own pace.

    b.   treat him like any other child.

    c.   create many new experiences for him.

    d.   punish him for being so timid.

_____ 13. Harlow's experiment with surrogate mothers showed that

    a.   attachment in monkeys was not simply a matter of who fed the infant monkey.

    b.   infant monkeys would cling to a soft surrogate when hungry.

    c.   infant monkeys would cling to either surrogate when scared.

    d.   attachment in monkeys is different than in humans.

_____ 14. Placing young children in out-of-home day care typically produces

    a.   different outcomes in the children, depending on the nature of the program of care.

    b.   little effects on the children.

    c.   better social skills.

    d.   improved language performance.

_____ 15. Separation anxiety commonly occurs

    a.   in understaffed nurseries and institutions.

    b.   in infants who have insecure attachment relationships with their mothers.

c. when a stranger rapidly approaches a baby.

d. at approximately 8 months of age in most infants from many different cultures.

_____16. A magazine warns that children will be permanently retarded unless they receive proper stimulation during their first year. Findings on early experience indicate that this advice is incorrect because

a. babies under one year do not know language.

b. the critical period for learning comes at about 4 or 5 years.

c. mental maturation starts at 18 months.

d. development requires continuing encouragement and support and changes can occur at most ages under appropriate circumstances.

_____17. The similarity in attitude and behavior between a child and his or her same-sex parent is most closely associated with the process of

a. socialization.

b. identification.

c. stranger anxiety.

d. maturation.

_____18. Peers

a. often teach a child academic skills

b. can relieve anxieties and agitation in children better than parents.

c. abuse about 1 in 10 classmates.

d. all the above.

_____19. A child 2½ years old who becomes upset because a button is missing or a toy is cracked may be exhibiting

a. excessive anxiety.

b. inner standards.

c. separation anxiety.

d. a reaction to stimulus discrepancy.

_____20. Loss of a parent through death or divorce

a. is more serious for the child if it occurs during midchildhood than at other ages.

b. is made worse on the child if the remaining parent remarries.

c. typically leads to poorer school performance and delinquency in the children.

d. may or may not lead to problems in the children, depending on the quality of the relationship between the child and the remaining parent.

ANSWERS TO PRACTICE TEST

1. b	6. b	11. d	16. d
2. d	7. a	12. a	17. b
3. a	8. a	13. a	18. d
4. d	9. c	14. a	19. b
5. b	10. b	15. d	20. d

EXERCISES

I. Boys and girls are reared differently, even by parents who profess sexual equality. For example, we teach boys to be physically and socially aggressive, to achieve, to get ahead, to be independent. We teach girls, however, to get along with people, to value friendship, and to be a good person.

Ask several students of both sexes to participate. Tell them all they need to do is to write a short story—one paragraph—using the following topic sentence:

"Miguel/Latisha" has just been named first in his/her medical school class at a convocation and reception for the class."*

Use Miguel for male subjects and Latisha for female subjects. (If you have time, also ask some male subjects to respond to Latisha and some female subjects to respond to Miguel.) Examine the stories for male and female respondents separately. Consider these questions:

1. How many positive and how many negative or concerned responses did you get? Were these rates different for males and females?

2. What kinds of reasons for positive and negative feelings were mentioned by males and females? Were there any differences?

3. Was there any hint that one sex was more concerned about losing friendships or disturbing social relations as a result of being first in their class whereas the other sex tended to see the advantage to career and future in this situation?

4. If you have males and females respond to both Miguel and Latisha, did they differ in how they viewed a successful male versus female?

5. Speculate on how the male-female differences you observed might have developed. You might ask some of your subjects why they answered as they did and what experiences led them to believe as they do.

II. Based on what you have learned in this chapter, write a brief paragraph describing how you suspect several of your own prominent personality characteristics developed. Start by identifying three or four traits, both good and bad. Then speculate on how they were created by considering such possible factors as heredity; parental practices and attitudes; the roles of siblings, peers, and teachers; particular experiences; and so forth. In view of this exercise and the material in this chapter, what advice would you give to new parents about rearing their children? What should they do and not do? Write a brief statement as if you were giving advice to parents in a newspaper or magazine.

C H A P T E R   1 3

Adolescence, Adulthood, and Old Age

At 30 a man should know himself like the palm of his hand, know the exact number of his defects and qualities, know how far he can go, foretell his failures—be what he is. And above all accept these things.

—Albert Camus, *Carnets*

Do most 30-year-olds fit this description written by Camus? Adult development, unlike child development, has few clear biological markers. Once adolescents have passed through the physical changes of puberty, most of the influences on a person are the result of experience, not of biology. Psychologist Bernice Neugarten, a pioneer in the field of human development, has pointed out that as we enter adulthood, chronological age is an increasingly unreliable indicator of what people will be like at various ages. Newborns or 6-year-olds show less psychological variation than 35- or 60-year-olds in a particular culture.

Although our society uses the words "adolescent" and "adult," it is difficult to define them. In many simple, nonindustrial cultures there is a clear transition from childhood to full membership in the community, which is often marked by a prescribed ceremony. From this point forward, individuals are treated as adults; they marry, begin a family and get down to the business of planning their role in their community. In our society, the situation is more complex. Most young people remain in school until they are at least 16 to 18 years old. Almost half continue on to college until they are 21 or 22, and only then do they begin to make decisions about specialized schooling or a job and a career. Many postpone marriage and children into their thirties and a few forgo these milestones altogether.

Studies of adulthood have not always been of interest to developmental psychologists. But today we recognize that development does not end when we leave adolescence behind. At 18, we have lived less than a quarter of today's average lifetime. We will face new crises, sometimes solving them and sometimes not, and we may still change remarkably in many respects. As adults, we take on new roles, address new tasks and challenges, enter and leave new relationships. As we do so, we react, learn, and change—sometimes in surprising ways—channeling development into entirely new patterns even in the later years of life. For psychologists interested in **life-span development,** it is essential to study the various physical, psychological, and social changes that accompany not only the early years, but the adult years—the longest period of human life.

Life-span development
The study of the physical, psychological, and social changes that occur throughout life.

Adolescence is characterized by new reasoning abilities and increased freedom, but also a new set of conflicts.

Adolescence: A Time of Struggle and Change

Some parents approach their child's adolescence with anxiety; they fear that adolescence is a synonym for rebellion and conflict. As identified in Figure 13.1, a number of dramatic changes do mark the adolescent's passage from childhood to adulthood.

Although the popular view is that adolescence is a difficult period, psychologists recognize wide individual differences. Three decades ago, for example, substantial numbers of people, looking back on their lives when

Area of Development	When Adolescence Begins	When Adolescence Ends
Biological	Beginning of growth spurt	End of growth spurt
Emotional	Beginning of detachment from parents	Reaching separate sense of identity
Interpersonal	Shifting interest from parents to peers	Development of intimacy with peers
Cognitive	Start of more advanced reasoning abilities	Full development of advanced reasoning
Educational	Entry into junior high school	Completion of schooling
Moral	Becoming tuned in to the expectations of others	Beginning to behave by the dictates of personal conscience

FIGURE 13.1   The adolescent years Psychologists use various markers to distinguish adolescence from childhood on the one hand and from adulthood on the other (Steinberg, 1985). Keep in mind, however, that there is no strict, one-for-all definition. Moreover, although adolescence is regarded as spanning roughly the period between ages 10 and 20, there are wide variations.

they had reached the age of 30, felt that their adolescent years were the time when they were most confused and their morale was at its lowest ebb. They mentioned such difficulties as striving for acceptance from peers of their own and the opposite sex, being under anxiety-producing pressures from their parents for scholastic achievement, and trying to establish their independence while remaining financially dependent on their parents (Macfarlane, 1964).

Today, psychologists are reaching different conclusions. A number of studies have shown that many families with adolescents do not experience as serious a conflict as the earlier generation (Hill, 1987). If this difference is real, it may reflect the fact that today's parents give their adolescents considerably more freedom and the society is more accepting of very different lifestyles. As a result, there may be less conflict over failing to meet family and community standards for what is proper behavior.

The Physical Onset of Adolescence

Puberty is marked by the start of menstruation in the female and the production of sperm in the male. This typically occurs sometime between the ages of 11 and 18, usually a year or two earlier in girls than in boys. The start of puberty is almost invariably accompanied by a spurt in physical growth. A girl may suddenly grow 3 to 5 inches in height in a single year, a boy 4 to 6 inches. Along with growth comes a change in physical proportions and strength. As illustrated in Figure 13.2, the girl begins to look like a woman, the boy like a man. The **primary sex characteristics,** or reproductive organs, develop significantly, and the **secondary sex characteristics** appear—that is, such characteristics as the growth of breasts and enlarged hips in girls, and a deeper voice and facial hair in boys. All these changes are set into motion by increased activity of the pituitary gland, which stimulates the sex glands (ovaries in girls and testes in boys) to produce large quantities of the hormones estrogen in the female and androgen in the male.

The first menstrual period, known as **menarche,** is the benchmark of physical maturity in girls—although fertility often arrives only after the first few cycles. Today, the average age of menarche in the United States is 12½ (Hamburg & Takanishi, 1989). In the past, many American girls entered adolescence with ambivalent feelings—a mixture of excitement and fear.

Primary sex characteristics
The developed reproductive organs like the ovaries in females and the testes in males.

Secondary sex characteristics
Such characteristics as growth of breasts and enlarged hips in females and deepening voice and facial hair in males.

Menarche
The first menstrual period.

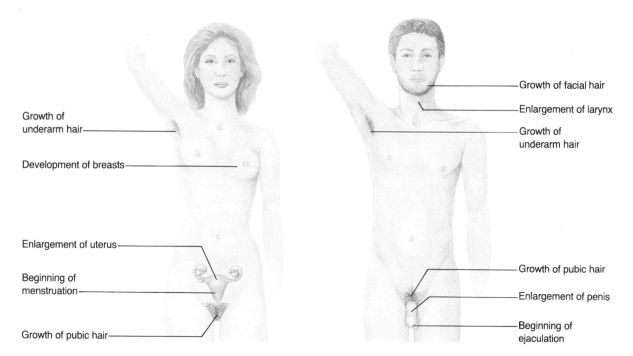

Growth of
underarm hair

Development of breasts

Enlargement of uterus

Beginning of
menstruation

Growth of pubic hair

Growth of facial hair

Enlargement of larynx

Growth of
underarm hair

Growth of pubic hair

Enlargement of penis

Beginning of
ejaculation

FIGURE 13.2 The onset of puberty With the beginning of puberty, both sexes undergo transformations as described in the text.

Recent studies, however, suggest that the attitudes of adolescent girls toward menarche are less negative now than was the case a couple of decades ago. The change is probably due to a more open and less defensive presentation of information about menstruation in homes, schools, and the media (Grief & Ulman, 1982). It is noteworthy that girls with negative feelings about their first menstruation are more likely to be growing up in a family characterized by a lack of openness in discussing physical and sexual issues (Brooks-Gunn, 1987).

The timing of puberty appears to be important psychologically. For boys, reaching puberty early seems to be advantageous in both social and emotional terms. Although later maturation provides added time for both sexes to prepare emotionally for changes in social status, it also means a continued childlike appearance and short stature. This tends to be a particular problem for boys. If they are slow to show the growth spurt, they continue to be treated as "little boys," while their bigger, stronger, and more mature classmates are gaining new respect.

However, along with early sexual maturation comes early sexual activity. Boys who reveal secondary sex characteristics, such as facial hair, deeper voice, and enlarged genitals, earlier than their peers are more likely to become sexually active earlier. Contrary to expectations, increased levels of the male hormone testosterone are not responsible for the greater sexual activity. Instead the boys' feelings of being sexually mature based on their physical development is the main basis for the initiation of sexual behavior (Halpern, 1993). In the view of some, the media can help shape the quality of the adolescent's emerging sexual experiences, as discussed in the Psychology and the Media box entitled "Guide to Responsible Sexual Content in Television, Films, and Music."

Guide to Responsible Sexual Content in Television, Films, and Music

Television and other media can improve dramatically and become important *positive* influences on adolescent cognitive development, says Victor C. Strasburger, M.D., by employing the following guidelines:

- Recognize sex as a healthy and natural part of life.
- Parent and child conversations about sex are important and healthy and should be encouraged.
- Demonstrate that not only the young, unmarried, and beautiful have sexual relationships.

- Show that not all affection and touching must culminate in sex.
- Portray couples having sexual relationships with feelings of affection, love, and respect for one another.
- Consequences of unprotected sex should be discussed or shown.
- Miscarriage should not be used as a dramatic consequence for resolving an unwanted pregnancy.
- Use of contraceptives should be indicated as a normal part of a sexual relationship.
- Avoid associating violence with sex or love.
- Rape should be depicted as a crime of violence, not of passion.
- The ability to say "no" should be recognized and respected.

Source: The Center for Population Options.

Source: From *The Brown University Child and Adolescent Behavior Letter,* March 1992, p. 5.

Issues to Consider

1. Besides the media, what other environmental forces do you think might influence the sexual behavior of adolescents?
2. Do you think the AIDS epidemic has altered the sexual behavior of adolescents?

For girls, early puberty tends to have either little effect or to be a disadvantage, for it reduces the time 12- and 13-year-olds need to prepare for their new status and responsibilities (Brooks-Gunn, 1987). For example, the growth of breasts can make an 11-year-old girl appear sexually provocative at a time when she may be unable, psychologically, to cope with such reactions (Clausen, 1975). For girls, reaching puberty at the same time as peers and classmates would appear to permit the smoothest transition (Powers, 1989).

A number of factors can affect the timing of menarche and its meaning. For example, athletic girls as a group tend to mature late and are thus likely to view themselves as being on schedule rather than behind their peers (Brooks-Gunn, 1987). There is evidence, too, that aspiring dancers are often more successful in that field if they mature late (Petersen, 1987). Differences in age at puberty exist as well among girls from various countries and among subgroups within a country. For example, girls in Czechoslovakia mature later than American girls. Among Americans, black girls tend to reach menarche earlier than white girls (Powers, 1989). This could have implications in some special situations—for example, in the case of an American girl living abroad or a black girl attending school with predominantly white students.

Distorted Body Images: The Path to Eating Disorders

Because adolescence brings dramatic changes in physical appearance, it is a time when self-image is very much dependent on body image. Adolescents who see themselves as deviating from the "ideal" physique can lose their self-

Anorexia nervosa

An eating disorder in which an already emaciated person continues on a starvation diet in order to keep weight down.

Bulimia nervosa

An eating disorder in which a person engages in eating binges and then induces vomiting, takes laxatives, and exercises excessively in order to avoid weight gain.

esteem. Being overweight, for example, can be particularly devastating to teenagers concerned about how they appear to others (Steinberg, 1985).

The concern with weight can lead to the development of a variety of eating problems, including compulsions about food. It is also regarded as one of the factors that lead some adolescents—particularly girls—to embark on abnormal and, ultimately, life-threatening steps to remain thin (Attie & Brooks-Gunn, 1989). The result in some cases is a disorder known as **anorexia nervosa,** in which the already emaciated individual continues on a starvation diet in an effort to keep weight down. Even more common is **bulimia nervosa,** a disorder in which a person engages in eating binges, and then induces vomiting or takes laxatives in order to avoid gaining weight. Both anorexia and bulimia—which in many cases occur together—undoubtedly have complex causes. For example, the disorders may arise out of a biological predisposition such as a hormone imbalance, as well as from chronic anxiety and depression. (See "Eating Disorders, When Food Becomes the Enemy," Chapter 10, pages 495–496.)

An adolescent girl whose self-image is fragile, can be especially sensitive to comments about her body. Girls with eating disorders were much more likely than girls of normal weight to have mothers who urged them to lose weight (Pike & Rodin, 1991). These mothers were also more likely to have eating disorders themselves.

All adolescents can be emotionally hurt when teased or criticized about their appearance by parents, older siblings, teachers, coaches, or other significant people in their lives. Those who were teased between the ages of 8 and 16 are most likely to be dissatisfied with their bodies when they grow up—revealing low self-esteem, depression and a distorted body image—all factors linked to the development of eating disorders (Thompson, 1990).

The Adjustment to Junior High School

The physical changes that accompany the departure from childhood are not the only ones that affect the self-concept of adolescents. So, too, do changes in the social environment—notably the junior high school experience, which imposes a host of challenges that can affect self-esteem. For one thing, students must learn to deal with a more bureaucratic educational institution. They must adapt to a changing cadre of teachers rather than to a single one who was often perceived as a substitute parent. Furthermore, they must respond to heavier academic demands, which if not met change the view that family and peers have of the student's potential (Eccles, 1993). During this transition to junior high school, adolescents are especially vulnerable to troubles at home. Junior high school students whose parents lose their jobs or have their employment status threatened tend to become more disruptive at school (Flanagan, 1993).

Small wonder that motivation wavers and that a sizable number of children who do quite well in elementary school begin to founder in junior high. Many problems, from school failure and dropout to substance abuse, now begin. The Carnegie Council on Adolescent Development formed a Task Force on Education of Young Adolescents to call attention to the needs of 10- to 15-year-olds. This task force has recommended a major restructuring of the nation's middle schools. It has proposed smaller, less competitive

Observer Judgments of Personality at Age 14	Correlation with Increase in Self-Esteem
Females	
Is moralistic	.47
Responds to and appreciates humor.............................	.46
Is protective of those close to him/her	.42
Is turned to or sought out for advice and reassurance	.38
Is cheerful, happy...	.37
Has a clear-cut personality; is relatively easy to understand..	.36
Behaves in a sympathetic and considerate manner	.36
Initiates humor; makes spontaneous funny remarks........	.34
Is giving, generous toward others	.34
Males	
Socially at ease; has social poise and presence	.36
Feels satisfied with self; is unaware of self-concern	.34
Regards self as physically attractive...............................	.33
Is calm, relaxed in manner...	.30
Behaves in masculine style	.27

FIGURE 13.3 Self-esteem among boys and girls Once they reach junior high school, boys tend to have higher self-esteem than girls do, and those qualities associated with high self-esteem differ for males and females (Block & Robins, 1993).

schools that provide more individual attention as well as more effective instruction (Carnegie Council on Adolescent Development, 1989).

The transition to junior high seems to take an especially high toll on the conscious self-esteem of adolescent girls. As they grow, boys' feelings of high self-esteem rise, while girls' drops (Block & Robins, 1993). And the characteristics that lead to conscious high self-esteem differ for adolescent boys and adolescent girls. As Figure 13.3 shows, the girls who increased in self-esteem as they approached adulthood were, at age 14, most likely to have the following qualities: being regarded as moral, appreciating humor, being nur-

The school environment affects the child's view of her intelligence, academic skill, and acceptability.

turant and cheerful. For boys, on the other hand, the important predictors of later high self-esteem were social poise, self-satisfaction, belief in one's attractiveness, and behaving in a masculine way.

Self-esteem problems among junior high school girls may affect their performance in school. Girls show the same aptitudes for math as boys until about the seventh grade, when more girls develop math phobia. About the same time, boys begin to catch up with girls on verbal skills.

Developing a Set of Morals

Moral standards dictating personal behavior usually undergo important and often lasting change during adolescence. Specifically, these ethical standards become a more permanent part of the philosophy of the adolescent. This occurs because of the onset of formal operations. This cognitive advance motivates the adolescent to want to have a set of philosophical premises that are consistent.

The development of moral judgments was studied extensively by Lawrence Kohlberg, who presented boys from seven to adolescence with a number of hypothetical situations involving moral questions such as the following: If a man's wife is dying for lack of an expensive drug that he cannot afford, should he steal the drug? If a patient who is fatally ill and in great pain begs for a mercy killing, should the physician agree? By analyzing the children's answers and particularly the reasoning they used to reach their answers, Kohlberg determined that moral judgments develop through a series of six stages, as shown in Figure 13.4. Children in the two stages of what he calls the "preconventional level" base their ideas of right and wrong largely on self-interest. They are concerned chiefly with avoiding punishment and gaining rewards. Later, in the two stages of what he calls the "conventional level," they become concerned with the approval of other people. Finally, in the two stages of the "postconventional level," they become concerned with abstract moral values and the dictates of their own consciences. Thus the reasons children gave for good behavior progressed from sheer self-interest, to a desire for the approval of others, to a concern for the approval of their own consciences.

Kohlberg conclusions were based primarily on the responses of boys. It has been found recently that many girls respond differently to Kohlberg's moral dilemmas by giving different reasons for a moral behavior. The girls exhibit a greater concern with kind, considerate, human relations than do the boys—who are more concerned with the abstract principles of justice and fairness. For example, when posed with the dilemma of the man who needed a drug for his dying wife, adolescent girls are more likely to reason that helping a loved one at risk takes precedence over the principle that stealing is wrong—which is the view that boys are more likely to offer (Gilligan, 1982).

It should be pointed out, however, that Kohlberg and Gilligan studied the verbal reasons that children and adolescents give for moral and immoral actions. They did not study actual moral behavior. As children grow, they offer more abstract reasons why people should not be cruel or dishonest, but they display more cruelty and dishonesty than six-year-old children.

Preconventional Level

Seven-year-old children are oriented to the consequences of their behavior	**Stage 1.** Defer to the power of adults and obey rules to avoid trouble and punishment.
	Stage 2. Seek to satisfy their own needs by behaving in a manner that will gain rewards and the return of favors.

Conventional Level

At around 10, children begin to become oriented to the expectations of others and to behave in a conventional fashion.	**Stage 3.** Want to be "good" in order to please and help others and thus receive approval.
	Stage 4. Want to "do their duty" by respecting authority (parents, teachers, God) and maintaining the social order for its own sake.

Postconventional Level

Adolescents become oriented to more abstract moral values and their own consciences.	**Stage 5.** Think in terms of the rights of others, the general welfare of the community, and a duty to conform to the laws and standards established by the will of the majority. Behave in ways they believe would be respected by an impartial observer.
	Stage 6. Consider not only the actual laws and rules of society but also their own self-chosen standards of justice and respect for human dignity. Behave in a way that will avoid condemnation by their own consciences.

FIGURE 13.4 Kohlberg's stage theory of moral development Summarized in the table are the six stages in moral development identified by Kohlberg. Among 7-year-olds, almost all moral judgments are made at the preconventional level. By age 16, only a few are made at this level, and judgments made at the postconventional level become important (Kohlberg, 1963, 1967).

Defining Identity

American adolescents crave independence and seek to establish a secure and steady sense of self, called an **identity.** In isolated villages in Latin America and Africa, the main concern of adolescents is more often focused on interpersonal relationships and how choices affect rapport with family members. In our own culture, however, adolescents think of themselves as possessing a distinct and unique personality, of being people in their own right—different from their parents and siblings. The quest for a vague sense of self is surrounded by troublesome questions that often yield contradictory answers: *Who am I? What am I? What do I want to do with my life?*

Having reached a new stage of cognitive development, adolescents are able to think in abstract terms about their identity. They can now form theories about the meaning of life, and contemplate what society might be, rather than what it seems to be. Their new cognitive abilities often make them critical of the values held by society and by their parents.

The task of establishing an identity in contemporary societies inevitably involves a choice of career. It is complicated by the fact that today's world

Identity
A secure sense of self.

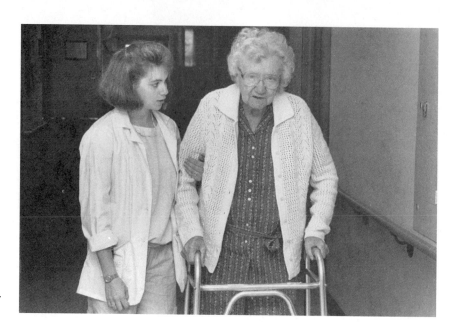

A job can often bolster the adolescent's self-esteem.

seems to offer a large number of possibilities, and adolescents must decide which job best matches their abilities. Proportionately more American teenagers are now employed in part-time jobs than at any other time in recent decades—nearly a third of 16- to 19-year-olds (U.S. Department of Labor, 1989). But this part-time work may have more costs than benefits.

One study of more than 70,000 high school seniors found a positive association between the number of hours worked and a set of undesirable behaviors, including poor school performance, drug use, aggression, fighting with parents, and failing to engage in healthy behaviors, such as eating a good breakfast and getting enough exercise and a good night's sleep (Bachman & Schulenberg, 1993).

An earlier study of high school students that assessed the benefits and costs of part-time employment found that working did encourage a sense of personal responsibility—punctuality, dependability, and self-reliance. But at the same time working reduced commitment to family and friends; led to cynical attitudes toward work, the acceptance of unethical work practices, and paved the way to increased use of cigarettes and marijuana (Steinberg et al., 1982).

During their struggle for identity, adolescents tend to emphasize not only personal concerns such as those dealing with privacy, self-expression, and self-fulfillment, but also moral values like friendship, love, and tolerance. Among girls there is a shift from earlier feelings of certainty and self-confidence to feelings of confusion and self-doubt about what they believe is right and what is wrong.

The Troubles of Adolescence

Some adolescents feel alienated from their society—a fact that may help explain the increase in drinking, delinquency, sexual promiscuity, drug abuse, and even suicide in the last few decades (Education Commission of the States, 1985). More adolescents are experimenting with drugs at a younger age, especially before age 15, and pregnancy rates for 10- to 14-year-olds have increased 23 percent since 1973 (Takanishi, 1993).

A recent survey by the Department of Health and Human Services found that about eight million American junior and senior high school students are weekly users of alcohol, including 454,000 "binge" drinkers—defined as those who drink five or more drinks in a row (Department of Health and Human Services, 1991). Of those students who drink, 31 percent reported drinking alone and 41 percent said they drink when they were upset and 25 percent said they drink to "get high."

In addition, more adolescents seem to be at risk for depression, sometimes leading to suicide. Suicide accounts for 11.3 deaths per 100,000 people among those ages 15 to 19, and is the third leading cause of death in this age group (Garland & Zigler, 1993). More issues involving teenage suicide are discussed in the Psychology in Action box entitled "Teenage Suicides: A Growing Tragedy." When adolescents view parental support as weak or as conditional on their pleasing their parents and meeting their expectations, self-esteem suffers, and feelings of hopelessness and thoughts of suicide may surface (Harter & Marold, 1989).

A recent study calls into question the popular belief that adolescents engage in risky behaviors because they believe that they are protected from catastrophe (Quadrel, Fischhoff, & Davis, 1993). The responses of adolescents were compared to those of adults regarding how probable it was that they would experience eight adverse events ranging from being in an auto accident to getting sick from radiation poisoning. The perception of invulnerability was similar for adolescents and adults.

The frequency of serious problems among the nation's adolescents has grown, in part, because of the deteriorating environment in which young people are raised (National Research Council, 1993). Traditional institutions for helping youth—from the family, and child welfare and neighborhood organizations, to health care groups, schools, and job-training programs—have come under siege and are no longer offering adolescents the support they need. Of the many factors that shape the lives of teenagers, family income is most powerful, according to these findings. Nearly a quarter of families headed by an adult between the ages of 25 and 34 live in poverty. And at all income levels, adolescents living in either single-parent families or in stepfamilies are far more likely to engage in risky behavior, including running away from home, dropping out of school, smoking, and truancy.

Conflicts Within the Family

An adolescent may often find life going less smoothly than it had been just a few years earlier not only at school but also at home. Although family conflict does not dramatically escalate in every home in which a child is reaching adolescence, there is some evidence that arguments and angry confrontations are more prevalent at this time than at other periods of development. Family arguments often occur because adolescents want to apply their newly expanded freedom to many areas of life. They feel that they should be the ones to decide which friends to spend time with, how neat to keep their

Teenage Suicide:
A Growing Tragedy

Suicide rates among teenagers and young adults have almost tripled in the past three decades. Indeed, suicide is the third leading cause of death among young people after accidents and homicide (National Center for Health Statistics, 1992). One study found that 14 percent of all youth reported having made at least one suicide attempt in their life (Wagner, 1993).

Why?

There is no single answer, but various studies offer different reasons for the rise in suicides:

- Society may be changing in ways that have made adolescence a more difficult time—with increased demands and decreased sources of support. Adolescent stresses include the pressure to assume adult roles faster, an increasing rate of family breakup, high rates of mobility, and uncertain career opportunities (Steinberg, 1985).
- Easy availability of firearms may increase suicide. A gun is used in 59 percent of all teen suicide cases and in three-fourths of those committed by adolescent males (Berman & Jobes, 1991).
- Often there is an immediate precipitating cause, such as feeling rejected and running away from

home; being the victim of abuse; experiencing a humiliation before parents and friends; and the breakup of a romantic relationship (Frazier, 1985). Significant predictors of suicide include suicide idealization; stresses involving parents, peers, and sexuality; problems with the police; parental physical abuse; running away from home; living with neither biological parent; and knowing someone who committed suicide (Wagner, 1993).

- Evidence suggests that adolescents predisposed to suicide may be moved to actually commit the act as a result of watching portrayals of teenage suicides in movies or television (Gould & Shaffer, 1986), or in television news stories (Phillips & Carstensen, 1986).
- There may be complex predisposing factors at work early in life. For example, children whose mothers were chronically ill during pregnancy and who experienced significant respiratory problems at birth appear more vulnerable to suicide years later. Such children, because they are at greater-than-usual risk for developmental problems, may be more likely to experience chronically poor relationships with their parents during childhood (Salk et al., 1985).
- Most adolescents who attempt suicide are seriously depressed.

Like depressed adults, they are likely to conclude that there is just never going to be a solution to a serious life problem—and they thus view suicide as their only way out. There are many more unsuccessful attempts at suicide by adolescents than actual suicides. Girls are two or three times more likely to attempt suicide while males more likely to complete suicide (Petti & Larsen, 1987).

In spite of the statistics, keep in mind that most adolescents, however unhappy they may be for a time, never even consider suicide. Although the rate among adolescents has risen, it is lower than among individuals in their twenties and far lower than that among the elderly.

The most effective prevention for suicidal adolescents is to get them help early. Studies show that most suicidal youngsters provide their families or friends with obvious clues to their intent (Berman & Jobes, 1991). A variety of mental health services available in the community can readily be identified by calling the state or county mental health department. Many communities also have a 24-hour suicide prevention hot line listed in the telephone directory. Threats of suicide do not, of course, always result in the act—but they always deserve to be taken seriously by concerned family and friends.

room, or where to go on a free evening. Yet their parents may continue to try to exert control in these areas. Adolescents of both sexes experience more friction in relating to their mothers than to their fathers, presumably because mothers spend more time managing the details of everyday life (Smetana, 1988). In the case of both parents, however, the approach taken can make a difference in the amount and kind of conflict that a family undergoes.

Authoritarian parents often have serious problems with their adolescents. They stress constant obedience and living up to fixed standards, and they do not willingly share power with their adolescent. Punitive parents generate anger when they use harsh discipline to curb what they view as adolescent willfulness. The behaviors of both types of parents can diminish the adolescent's feeling of self-worth.

In contrast, authoritative parents who combine limit-setting with negotiation encounter less turmoil. They do not regard either their standards or themselves as infallible; they are supportive, loving, and committed (Powers, Hauser, & Kilner, 1989). It has also been shown that adolescents with authoritative parents do better in high school than those with authoritarian or very permissive parents (Steinberg, 1992).

It appears that the best antidote to adolescent aches and pains is having the opportunity to identify with parents who are neither too strict nor too permissive. Such parents are warm but firm, and while they are eager for their children to develop autonomy and self-direction, they still leave no doubt that they are responsible for their children's behavior (Biller, 1981; Hill, 1980). Such parents—reasonable, fair, respectful, and eager for their children's advance to maturity—are most likely to lead the child toward adult responsibility and happiness.

In general, despite the problems and the casualties, research indicates that "the great majority of teenagers share a common core of values with their parents, retain harmonious family relationships, and respect the need for discipline" (Graham & Rutter, 1985). Most are reasonably well adjusted, confident about the future, and resilient enough to work through any stresses they encounter in the transition to adulthood.

Teenage pregnancy often leads to early termination of high school and, as a result, a poorer prospect for future vocations.

Adulthood: The Prime Time

As described in the previous chapter, during the opening years of life, maturation of the brain and body sets the path of human development. But with the passage of time, personal life events begin to make it harder to anticipate the course of development. Marriage and parenthood, divorce and remarriage, career choices and changes are among the many critical experiences that help shape the dynamic flow of the adult years.

As a result, the personality and behavior of young adults sometimes seem to bear little relation to those of the earlier years. Although the threads of childhood temperament and adolescent behavior are often still visible, some traits become transfigured in many respects—raising once again the major theme of continuity and change over the life span introduced in the first chapter of this book.

The beginning and end of any one stage of adult life is very difficult to detect. Individuals move at a different pace—and sometimes imperceptibly—from one period to another as they choose careers, marry and build a family, and engage in the world of work. The adult years bring on gradual physical alterations as well. We may continue to look the same to ourselves, but not to our acquaintances. (Indeed, people who attend a fortieth college reunion often have difficulty recognizing old classmates.) At the same time, we change on the inside and personality patterns may become as unrecognizable as faces.

From youth to late adulthood, people exhibit a portrait of change.

New Beginnings

As a child, he was placed in one foster home after another by his widowed father, who was going through difficult times. When he was 16 and his father could finally reassemble his family, he started his first year of high school. But after having been on his own for so many years, he could stand neither the mothering of his three sisters nor the school environment, and so he dropped out and ran away from home to join the Marines. Following three years of service, including World War II combat, he enrolled as a freshman in the University of Southern California, where the admissions personnel failed to notice that he hadn't completed high school. When they discovered their mistake, they were going to expel him, but then relented to let him remain as a special student. He stayed on for three years and became editor of the college humor magazine—but to this day he has earned neither a high school diploma nor a college degree.

His name? Art Buchwald.

The case of this famous humorist and writer is not as unusual as it may seem. Some of the most startling about-faces have been observed among people who were troubled, sometimes seriously, as adolescents. It has been found that even the most maladjusted adolescent—a failure in school, unsuccessful in social contacts, unpopular and despondent—may turn into a successful, happy, well-liked, and highly respected adult. In one study, 166 boys and girls were observed from shortly after birth until they were 18 years old, then observed again at the age of 30. About half the subjects were living richer and more productive lives as adults than could have been predicted from the nature of their adolescent personalities (Macfarlane, 1963).

What causes such marked changes between adolescence and the age of 30? One possibility is that some people are just naturally "late bloomers." It takes them a long time; often a change of environment that gets them away from their parents and to a new community permits them to find themselves. Although there is evidence that, especially for young men, the benefits of staying home with mom and dad well into one's twenties are proving attractive, as shown in Figure 13.5.

Taking on a meaningful job may help young people find purpose and direction in their lives. So may marriage, with all its responsibilities and its opportunities for forming an abiding, supportive relationship. In one study, researchers reconstructed the lives of a group of young women who had been born into abusive and broken families, placed in foster care, and encountered mostly trouble as adolescents. As young adults, however, a sizable number of them were found to be contented, productive, and free of the grinding problems of their earlier years. In many cases, it turned out, they were lucky enough to find supportive and caring husbands, and as a result, they were now enjoying stable family lives far removed from the misery of their younger years (Quinton & Rutter, 1983).

Sometimes a troubled adolescence proves a blessing in disguise as the years go by. If adolescents go through a period of painful experiences but manage to survive them, they may in the long run gain greater insight and stability (Macfarlane, 1964). In effect, stress-filled events can have a "steeling" effect for some that increases their resilience and adaptability as an adult (Rutter, 1983).

FIGURE 13.5 **The not-so-empty nest** Increasing numbers of adults ages 25 to 34, especially young men, are returning home to live with their parents (U.S. Bureau of the Census, 1993).

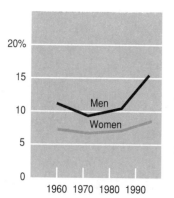

Facing and Meeting Crises: Erikson's Theory

The idea that personality growth depends on dealing with crises is the basis of an influential theory proposed by Erik Erikson, a psychoanalyst who based his conclusions on observations of people he treated at all ages, some in childhood and others at various stages of adulthood. Erikson was concerned with **psychosocial development.** That is, he viewed development as a twofold process in which the psychological development of individuals (their personalities and view of themselves) proceeds hand in hand with the social relations they establish as they go through life. He suggested that this development can be divided into eight stages, in each of which individuals face new social situations and encounter new problems (or "psychosocial crises"). They may emerge from the new experiences with greater maturity and richer personalities—or they may fail to cope successfully with the problems and their development may be warped or arrested. Erikson's eight stages are shown in Figure 13.6.

Psychosocial development

The twofold process, proposed by Erikson, in which the psychological development of individuals proceeds hand in hand with the social relations they establish as they go through life.

Choosing and Succeeding at a Career

Early adulthood demands many new adjustments. One entails job and career and the often intense preoccupation with efforts to start up the vocational ladder. Many young people believe that, while they are still in their early twenties, they must pick an occupation and begin a well-defined path of work. In reality, however, the process is more complicated. The course of a career is usually based on the ebb and flow of decisions made over time.

At least six factors can influence a person's choice of occupation (Kimmel, 1980). These include (1) background factors, such as socioeconomic level, intelligence, sex, prior education—which set boundaries on the range of occupational choice; (2) role models, such as an older sibling with whom individuals identify and wish to emulate; (3) unique life experiences—for example, deciding to become a doctor because of the early death of a parent from cancer; (4) interests and personality traits that can be realized and expressed in a particular occupation; (5) rational assessments of the job market and areas of opportunity; and (6) personality difficulties, which can limit career choice and hamper success in the world of work. A recent study of children who were studied through adulthood for over 40 years found that those who exhibited explosive temper tantrums as children became adults who were significantly less successful in both their jobs and marriages (Caspi, 1987).

Work can affect a person's sense of well-being. Success on the job can have a potent impact on self-esteem, marital satisfaction, and physical health. There is evidence that job satisfaction increases over the years—especially for the middle class (Staines & Quinn, 1979)—and that it is dependent on such factors as the willingness to accept challenges and exercise independence (Gruenberg, 1980).

Until recently, psychologists focused their studies on the role of work in the lives of men, but now there is increased attention to the role of work in the lives of women. The role of women in society combined with an increase in life expectancy and length of marriages, a lower birth rate, and a decline in

Stage	Crisis	Favorable Outcome	Unfavorable Outcome
CHILDHOOD			
First year of life	Trust versus mistrust	Faith in the environment and future events	Suspicion, fear of future events
Second year	Autonomy versus doubt	A sense of self-control and adequacy	Feelings of shame and self-doubt
Third through fifth years	Initiative versus guilt	Ability to be a "self-starter," to initiate one's own activities	A sense of guilt and inadequacy to be on one's own
Sixth year to puberty	Industry versus inferiority	Ability to learn how things work, to understand and organize	A sense of inferiority at understanding and organizing
TRANSITION YEARS			
Adolescence	Identity versus confusion	Seeing oneself as a unique and integrated person	Confusion over who and what one really is
ADULTHOOD			
Early adulthood	Intimacy versus isolation	Ability to make commitments to others, to love	Inability to form affectionate relationships
Middle age	Generativity versus self-absorption	Concern for family and society in general	Concern only for self—one's own well-being and prosperity
Aging years	Integrity versus despair	A sense of integrity and fulfillment; willingness to face death	Dissatisfaction with life; despair over prospect of death

FIGURE 13.6   Erikson's stage theory of "psychosocial crises"   Erikson viewed the life cycle of development, from cradle to grave, as passing through eight stages. Each stage brings new social experiences and new crises—which, if surmounted successfully, lead to constant growth and a steadily enriched personality (Erikson, 1963).

value of the family's income has brought about a remarkable increase in the number of married women—currently over 54 percent—who are paid employees in jobs outside the home (U.S. Department of Labor, 1989).

A majority of married women hold jobs because they need or want the money. Wives' earnings jumped 23.3 percent between 1981 and 1987 while husbands' earnings rose 11.8 percent, but men remained the major breadwinners in most families (U.S. Bureau of the Census, 1989a). But a public opinion poll has also found that a fair number of married women—nearly 15 percent say they work in order to have something interesting to do (Roper Organization, 1980). An in-depth study of about three hundred 35- to 55-year-old women in the Boston area revealed a strong relationship between working for salary and a sense of pride and mastery (Baruch, Barnett, & Rivers, 1983). But because of the persistence of sex-role stereotypes, the path for women in the world of work is not always smooth.

Workplace Inequities: Struggles for Women

Women have never shared equally in society's esteem, praise, privileges, and rewards. In one way or another, they were treated as the inferior sex in ancient Egypt, Greece, and Rome—and, on our own continent, by the Indians. In fact sexual discrimination may have been the first form of social inequality, practiced before people ever thought of discriminating against one another on the basis of race or social class. The division of labor between the sexes has varied from society to society—but no matter how tasks were split up, the jobs assigned to men have always been considered more important (Goode, 1965).

Even today, despite affirmative action programs, relatively few women pursue careers in scientific and technical fields (U.S. Department of Labor, 1989). Although girls do as well as boys in mathematics in the early grades, fewer females take advanced math courses in high school and college and become physicists, engineers, or computer scientists (Meece et al., 1982).

Overall, women have lower rates of employment, more intermittent employment, and lower earning power than men. While 41 percent of male civilian workers earn more than $25,000 per year, only 15 percent of women workers do so (U.S. Bureau of the Census, 1989b). Women are also still at a disadvantage with regard to both private pension plans and social security benefits. Through the year 2055, these benefits are expected to be only two-thirds those for men (U.S. Public Health Service, 1985).

Psychological studies suggest why such differences continue to exist. **Sex-role stereotypes** have changed only a little in the past two decades. Both sexes continue to view men as more forceful, independent, stubborn, and reckless than women, and to view women as more well mannered, kind, emotional, and submissive than men (Werner & LaRussa, 1985). In their day-to-day behavior, many men seem to reinforce the stereotype. They display a greater concern with power than women (Gaeddert, 1985). They also continue to associate sex with power (Hendrick et al., 1985) and, perhaps because of their higher status, take prerogatives at work that women do not. For example, men are much more likely to behave in a dominating fashion toward their female coworkers and to use intimate gestures and sexual innuendos on the job (Radecki & Jennings, 1980). A survey of women lawyers revealed that half find opportunities at their firms better for men, and that nearly two-thirds are the targets of unwanted sexual teasing, jokes, remarks, or questions (Couric, 1989).

The changes in gender role values in certain societies are helping women to fill a greater variety of jobs, many of which were held by men.

Sex-role stereotyping
(sex typing) The process through which society molds its members into its traditional patterns of femininity and masculinity.

Sex Roles in Adulthood: Confusion and Conflicts

Perhaps the greatest problem is that women feel compelled to give full expression to their motives for affiliation, dependency, and nurture, but they are under some pressure to suppress their motive for achievement in the world of work. In the past it was common for women, even the most capable ones, to conceal their intelligence, abandon interest in such "masculine" subjects as mathematics and science, and either shun a career or settle for such traditionally feminine jobs as nursing. One study has shown that at the college level, the proportion of males and females who take bachelor's degrees in mathematics are exactly the same. Yet Ph.D.'s in mathematics are higher for men than for women (Lubinski & Benbow, 1992). The researchers found that it is not that women cannot do mathematics but rather that they decided to do something else.

One common stereotype is that women are inherently more verbal and men are naturally better at math. In the past, studies suggested that, on the average, females outperform males on tests of verbal ability such as vocabulary, spelling, and verbal comprehension. Now, however, indications are that both sexes do equally well (Wilder & Powell, 1989; Hyde & Linn, 1988). On the Scholastic Aptitude Test (SAT), for example, males and females achieve similar scores (ACT, 1987).

As for mathematics, there is evidence that males do better—but the gap is narrowing. And in one area of math—that is, computation—females do as well as males or slightly better (Wilder & Powell, 1989; Hyde, Fennema, & Lamon, 1990). Some researchers believe that the differences that exist stem from the fact that parents and teachers expect boys to be better at math and, therefore, to treat them differently at home and in school. Others have suggested that math ability may be linked to brain functions affected by the male hormone testosterone (Geschwind & Behan, 1984).

Such issues are not of merely academic interest. Many people still do not consider it feminine to be too successful and competent at tasks that have been regarded as for men only. Nor is it feminine to be too competitive and aggressive on the job, especially when these behaviors conflict with a desire to help and support others (Gilligan, 1982).

Men also have problems with their assigned sex roles. The typical male conflicts are the opposite of the usual female conflicts. Boys and men are encouraged to express their motives for power, achievement, and hostility. They are expected to welcome every opportunity to leap into competition and assert their status and position so that they do not appear weak. But they are expected to muffle their motives for affiliation and dependency and to suppress their emotions of sympathy, tenderness, and vulnerability. They have to keep a stiff upper lip—avoiding any show of fear or grief—even in the face of serious disappointment and tragedy.

The struggle to play the masculine role can be fraught with anxiety. The motives for affiliation and dependency, discussed in Chapter 7, are universal. So are the emotions that accompany them. One study showed that men, although they are quite ready to have close social interactions with other men when the situation warrants, actually enjoy fewer close interactions with other men than women do with women (Reis, Senchak, & Solomon, 1985). Society's demands to suppress the motives for affiliation and dependency are a demand to transcend human nature, and such efforts can never completely succeed (B. Stevens, 1974).

The Quest for Love, Intimacy, and Commitment

Erikson believed that the critical event of early adulthood centers on moving into a relationship marked by love, intimacy, and commitment. For most of us, this means marriage. About 95 percent of Americans get married sooner or later—increasingly later in recent decades. As shown in Figure 13.7, between 1960 and 1988, the typical age at first marriage has increased from 20 to 23 for women, and from 23 to 26 for men (U.S. Bureau of the Census, 1989c).

Most of us have wondered what leads to the development of a loving interaction culminating in marriage. Aristotle was among the first to point

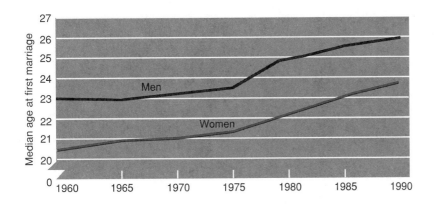

FIGURE 13.7 Marriage and age Americans are waiting longer to get married—as discussed in the text.

out that "we like those who resemble us and are engaged in the same pursuits." Indeed we are more likely to fall in love with and choose as mates someone who shares our beliefs and attitudes. Moreover, most of us do pick a spouse who is of the same religion and race and is similar to us in intelligence, age, educational level, and economic status—although, as interreligious and interracial marriages increase, we see many more exceptions to the pattern (Murstein, 1986).

It is not universally true, of course, that love is a prerequisite for marriage. In a number of non-Western cultures, marriage is based on a contract or on a financial arrangement outside the boundaries of romantic love. In our society, however, the connection between love and marriage is strong. A survey has shown, for example, that only 15 percent of men and women would agree to someone they did not love (Simpson, Campbell, & Berscheid, 1986).

Whatever the motive, marriage seems to help and protect our physical and mental health. People who are either married or living together are ill less often and have fewer chronic conditions that limit their activity than single persons (Schoenborn & Wilson, 1988). Married people feel less lonely, less depressed and less emotionally disturbed than those who remain single (Cargan & Melko, 1982). And for women, being married and having children can buffer them from job stress (Barnett et al, 1992).

Divorced individuals are especially vulnerable to anxiety and unfortunately, the number of unsuccessful marriages continues to be high. Among all adolescent and adult Americans, 14 million are divorced (U.S. Bureau of the Census, 1988). As shown in Figure 13.8, in 1960, there were 35 divorced Americans for every 1,000 married people living with a spouse. By 1988, that number had climbed to 135 (U.S. Bureau of the Census, 1989c). Recent data show that approximately two-thirds of couples who married in the 1980s will probably divorce (Castro-Martin & Bumpass, 1989).

For most people, "unlucky in love" means the tendency to select the wrong partner. Yet one team of researchers suggests that the divorce rate is high not because people make foolish choices, but because they are drawn together for reasons that change as time goes on. What brings a couple together at the start appears to become less important as the years go by, and those qualities that matter most later on are rarely the ones that figure heavily in the early romantic stages of the relationship. Passion is quick to develop, but fades more quickly than other feelings. Feelings of intimacy develop

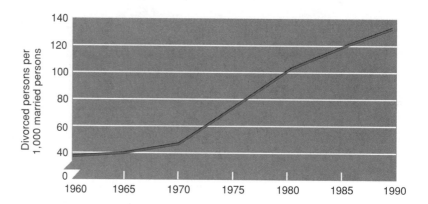

FIGURE 13.8 **Family breakups on the rise** In three decades, the divorce rate among Americans has nearly tripled, as discussed in the text.

Cohabitation

Living together and having a sexual relationship without being married.

more slowly and a sense of commitment grows even more gradually. No relationship is stable over time—but the basic, underlying ingredient of a loving and enduring marriage appears to be the ability to communicate and to satisfy the needs of the partner (Sternberg & Grajek, 1984; Sternberg, 1986).

Cohabitation—living together and having a sexual relationship without being married—has become more prevalent over the past two decades. There were about 2.6 million cohabiting heterosexual couples in 1984—well over five times the number there were in 1970 (U.S. Bureau of the Census, 1988).

Two researchers analyzed data on cohabition, marriage, and divorce gathered from more than 13,000 people. They found that few people who are now in their fifties ever cohabited, but that almost half of those in their thirties have done so. One-fourth of the couples living together married within a year, and another quarter married within three years (Bumpass & Sweet, 1989). There is no good evidence, however, that living together first leads to more satisfying marriages (De Maris & Leslie, 1984). Indeed, it would seem that couples are more likely to get divorced if they have lived together before marriage—perhaps because those who cohabit are likely to be less religious and less subject to family pressure to begin with than those

Raising a child is usually easier with two parents than one.

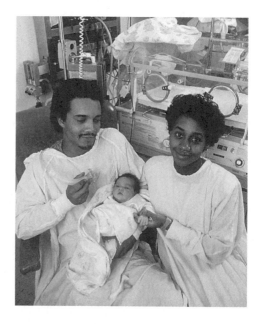

who do not do so. Given the same level of unhappiness, couples who have cohabited before marriage may be more willing to see divorce as a solution (Bumpass & Sweet, 1989).

Rearing Children: Stressful But Rewarding

Couples today have more freedom of choice in deciding whether to become parents than ever before in history. Although there are still many couples who decide not to have children, most choose to do so. One estimate is that 75 to 80 percent of today's young women will eventually have at least one child (Bloom & Trussell, 1983).

The birth of a first child often alters family life more than anticipated. For about half the couples participating in two recent studies, the birth of a first child was followed by more arguments and less satisfaction with the marriage (Belsky & Pensky, 1988; Cowan & Cowan, 1988). The arrival of a baby, however, did not turn a good marriage into a bad one. Those relationships that were most harmonious before the birth of a baby continued to be so afterward (Belsky & Pensky, 1988). Although arguments may be inevitable after a baby appears, the availability of emotional and social support seems to help couples weather the stress. Couples who participated in a small weekly support group during the last three months of pregnancy until the baby was three months old reported more satisfaction with their marriage than comparable couples who did not participate in such a group, and they were far more likely to remain married as late as three years after the group had stopped meeting (Cowan & Cowan, 1988).

Having a child creates complex and sweeping changes in the roles wife and husband play in the marriage and in their lifestyles. Parenthood is hard work; it requires a sense of responsibility; it is often stressful; and once you have begun, you cannot quit when you feel like it (LeMasters & DeFrain, 1983). Most of all, parenting requires skills of various kinds: sensitivity to children's cues and their needs at various stages of development; being able to help them cope with stresses and adversity; knowing how to talk and play with them and to use appropriate disciplinary techniques (Rutter, Quinton, & Liddell, 1983).

Such requirements are easier to satisfy, of course, when parents collaborate. Although we tend to think of parenting as a joint venture undertaken with a spouse, more and more families are headed by just one parent. Single-parent families rose from 13 percent of all families with children in 1970 to 27 percent in 1988. Among blacks, the figure is nearly 60 percent, and for portions of the black community, single-parenthood is becoming the norm. Most of the single parents are mothers, and many of them have never been married (U.S. Bureau of the Census, 1989c).

Three decades ago, most American women who found themselves unmarried and pregnant headed for the altar. But today, the overwhelming majority of unmarried women who become pregnant do not marry before the baby is born, but may later. This trend does not apply only to low-income, minority, or less-educated women. Among white women and women who attended college, the percentage who became mothers without marrying has almost doubled in the past decade (Bachu, 1992). Since research indicates that children in single-parent families tend to have more problems than those raised by two parents, this trend raises questions about the future welfare of children raised by mothers alone.

Even among two-parent families, the quality of the parenthood experience is understandably affected by a number of salient factors. It matters whether one child or several are in the household (Schaffer & Liddell, 1984), whether the parents get along (Hauser, 1985), and whether or not, as noted earlier, there are social supports available to the family (Belsky, 1984). One study found that those couples who coped best with the demands of parenthood were able to communicate their feelings to each other, showed adaptability to the baby's needs, viewed parenthood as a responsibility to be shared, continued to pursue their own adult interests, found some time to spend away from baby, and depended on friends and relatives for information, advice, and help in caring for the child (Miller & Sollie, 1980). All of this is easier, of course, for the affluent than for the poor.

Most young adults who embark on the adventure of parenthood find it a significant and rewarding experience, offering incomparable satisfactions (Veroff, Douvan, & Kulka, 1981). Contentment in marriage does not deteriorate if the children are planned for and if the parents are psychologically prepared for their responsibilities (Feldman, Biringen, & Nash, 1981). Indeed for many adults, according to Erikson, raising children represents their most important achievement.

For some couples, however, the opportunity to raise children is thwarted by biology. Studies indicate that as many as one in six couples will experience difficulty in conceiving a child (Griel, 1991). And research has shown that infertility is a major life crisis for those who experience it. When those who desire children find their efforts unsuccessful, they commonly experience frustration, despair, and helplessness (Jones & Toner, 1993).

Midlife: Radical Changes and Quiet Revelations

When the topic of middle age is brought up, many people think of "midlife crisis," fraught with images of the 45-year-old husband and father of four running off to Aruba with his 20-year old secretary. Many of the popular images of middle age depict it as an unhappy period when people regret the loss of their youth and all the dreams that might have been. But recent research debunks these myths, showing that for many, middle age is the best of times. According to sociologist Ronald Kessler of the University of Michigan's Institute for Social Research:

> When looking at the total U.S. population, the best year is 50. You don't have to deal with the aches and pains of old age or the anxieties of youth . . . Rates of general distress are low—the incidences of depression and anxiety fall at about 35 and don't climb again until the late sixties. You're healthy. You're productive. You have enough money to do some of the things you like to do. You've come to terms with your relationships, and the chance of divorce is very low. Midlife is the "it" you've been working toward. You can turn your attention toward being rather than becoming (Gallagher, 1993).

It is true that people sometimes make radical changes in their lifestyles during middle age. Men may switch careers—moving from a job they have held because of accident or habit, or for financial reasons—into something they have always wanted to do. Women who have spent their early years working as homemakers and mothers may take an outside job for the first time, thus encountering new problems but also finding new satisfactions.

Surveys have shown that 10 to 12 percent of respondents report that they have had a midlife crisis (Gallagher, 1993).

Ideally, according to the theories of Erikson, the crisis of middle age produces a wider outlook on the meaning of life—a sense of kinship with one's fellow human beings, with the ebb and flow of history, with nature itself. Old goals, especially selfish ones, may be abandoned. New satisfactions of the spirit may be found. Recent data tend to bear out Erikson's views. One researcher, for example, analyzed the responses of passersby in a shopping mall to a request by a pregnant woman for donations to help fight birth defects. Generosity increased with age—especially in the middle and later years (Midlarsky, 1989).

One dramatic shift in middle life is often the inclination to begin expressing elements of personality that remained suppressed earlier (Cytrynbaum et al., 1980). With most career goals met and mastered, marital adjustments made, and children reared and grown, many men and women begin to move out of the stereotyped sex roles they maintained during the earlier decades. Men tend in mid-life to become less aggressive and competitive and to take on some of the characteristics of the feminine role. Women become less dependent and submissive and become more independent, assertive, and competitive (Zube, 1982).

The changes are gradual. In one study, students at a women's college were asked to answer a personality questionnaire when they were seniors and then twice in later life—at about age 27 and age 43. At age 27 the women had become more self-controlled and tolerant, and stronger in characteristics traditionally labeled feminine: sympathy and altruism, combined with feelings of vulnerability and inadequacy. By age 43 the women had become more dominant, independent, and psychologically minded, and less flexible and less "feminine." The changes were common in women who were involved in either raising a family or succeeding in a high-level career. Those who were engaged in neither showed few of the changes of their agemates. It may be that the tasks of adulthood—which demand control of impulses, interpersonal skills, independence, perseverance, and goal orientation—propel women to change in adaptive ways (Helson & Moane, 1987).

Women and Menopause

Another negatively depicted aspect of midlife is **menopause**—the time when women stop menstruating and lose the ability to reproduce. Stereotypical images of unhappy middle-aged women going through the change of life, with hormones run amok are not universally true. Although some women do have a difficult time either physically or psychologically, most women pass through menopause without much incident or regret (Budoff, 1994). According to the Massachusetts Women's Health Study, which looked at more than 2500 menopausal women, 42 percent reported relief about ending their menstrual periods, 36 percent reported neutral feelings, 20 percent said they had mixed feelings and only 3 percent conveyed regret.

The worst symptom for most women is experiencing hot flashes, caused by a decline in estrogen that causes the part of the brain that regulates body temperature to behave as if the body is overheated. Studies show that from 50 to 85 percent of menopausal women experience hot flashes to some degree (Budoff, 1994).

Menopause
The time when women stop menstruating and lose the ability to reproduce.

TEST YOURSELF

e) If we describe a typical man as forceful, independent, stubborn and reckless we are describing what type of belief?

f) "Opposites attract," as the old saying goes. But do they usually marry each other?

g) If a couple's marriage is in trouble, would you recommend having a baby to solidify and unite them?

h) Men and women often move away from stereotyped sex roles in mid-life. Is this statement true or false?

Working Toward Successful Transitions

Although personality shifts can create conflicts and stress, in middle age they often reflect increased mellowing and self-assurance. Many adults at middle age are able often by virtue of their experience to cope more successfully than are younger people (Pruett, 1980). When the crisis of middle age is met successfully—and a quieter and deeper attitude toward the rhythm of life is established—people are prepared to grow old with grace and contentment. The process of development, from its seeds in the newborn baby, has come to full flower.

Growing Old: Maintaining Active, Productive Lives

Our society is getting older, but the old are getting younger. The activities and attitudes of a 70-year-old today are equivalent to those of a 50-year-old a few decades ago. During the past few decades, several changes have affected the lives of those over 65. First of all, the financial, physical, and mental health of older people has improved. Because of better medical care, improved diet, and increasing interest in physical fitness, more people are reaching the ages of 65, 75, and older in excellent health. A better understanding of aging has allowed researchers to sort out the inevitable results of biological aging from the effects of illness or social and environmental problems.

The potential for productive and satisfying later years takes on added importance since more and more of us are living increasingly long lives. In 1900, only 1 in 25 Americans was 65 years old or over; by 1986, 1 in 8 was at least 65 (U.S. Senate Special Committee on Aging, 1988). Put another way, as shown in Figure 13.9, the percentage of people who have passed what is generally considered to be the retirement age of 65 will have more than tripled by the turn of the century (U.S. Bureau of the Census, 1989).

Thanks to modern knowledge and technology, the average life expectancy for Americans born today is 75 years (National Center for Health Statistics, 1988), and further strides in curing disease are soon expected to increase it further. Moreover, the 85-plus population is growing especially

FIGURE 13.9 The increasing U.S. population over 65 In 1900, the number of Americans over 65 made up only 4 percent of the population. In the next 80 years their number increased to 12 percent of the population, and this percentage is rising steadily as we approach the end of the century (Brotman, 1981; U.S. Bureau of the Census, 1989b.)

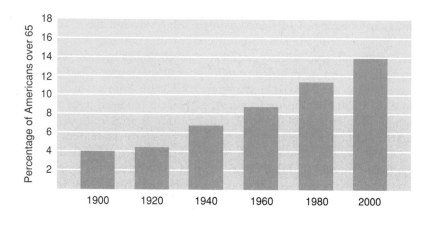

Remaining active in the older years is associated with better health and a longer life.

rapidly. It is expected to rise from 2.2 million in 1980 to 16 million by the year 2050, a sevenfold increase (U.S. Senate Special Committee on Aging, 1988). Small wonder that the nature of the retirement years have become very much a part of psychological investigation.

The retirement years have long been viewed by many in an unfavorable light—so much so that the term **ageism** has come to be used to describe the negative stereotypes and discrimination that take hold solely on the basis of age. Elderly persons have been viewed not only as physically deteriorated, but intellectually and emotionally spent, and there has actually been a decline in the willingness of senior management personnel to use older workers. As this section will make clear, the light of psychological research reveals such pessimistic perceptions to be surprisingly far from reality. Old age is a time of problems for many, to be sure, but of grand pleasures as well.

Ageism
The negative stereotypes and discrimination based solely on age.

The Aging Process

The later years, like earlier periods of life, bring physical alterations. **Senescence,** or the weakening and decline of the body, actually begins almost as soon as we stop growing during young adulthood. Although the changes are not visible, the body reaches its greatest strength in late adolescence, and

Senescence
The gradual weakening and decline in the body that begins in late young adulthood.

then grows weaker throughout our adult years. But the declines—in the output of the heart, in reaction time, in frequency of sexual intercourse—are so gradual that they are of little significance in our day-to-day living.

Although there is no specific age at which these changes become obvious, many of them become apparent as we approach the seventh decade of life. Changes in the spinal column may result in a stooped posture. Acuity in vision and hearing deteriorates. Sensitivity to odor and taste diminishes. Blood arteries and vessels harden. The body's capacity to fight disease weakens, and changes in the central nervous system lead to a slowdown in behavior. There are a number of theories to explain the aging process. Some suggest that aging is caused by the damage that occurs in various body systems throughout life—damage caused by normal "wear and tear," or harmful substances that we breathe or eat. Another theory says that aging results from a slow buildup of damage to the chemical DNA that directs the machinery of every body cell. Others ascribe aging to changes in body hormones, and still others to the breakdown of the immune system, the body's weapon for fighting disease. There are no simple answers to the mystery of aging, and most scientists believe that it is a complex process involving many body systems, with the crucial factor being a growing inability of all the body's cells to function properly (National Institute on Aging, 1984).

The facts of aging have led to a stereotype of the older person as "over the hill"—a portrait that is essentially inaccurate. True enough, in some cases, especially in extreme old age, damage to the brain's cells causes **senile dementia,** or **senility,** with symptoms such as disorientation, poor attention, loss of memory, and inability to store new information. But senility, contrary to popular assumption, is not an inevitable result of aging. Rather, it is a disease that afflicts a small proportion—from 5 to 8 percent—of old people (Kay & Bergmann, 1980).

One neurological illness, **Alzheimer's disease,** is an especially cruel, progressive form of dementia that is now recognized as the most common cause of severe intellectual and emotional impairment in older people (National Institute of Mental Health, 1984). A recent study found that Alzheimer's disease is much more prevalent than was previously thought. It is now estimated that four million older Americans suffer from Alzheimer's disease, and as Figure 13.10 shows, the rate increases dramatically beyond age 65 (Evans et al, 1989). A million and a half older Americans are incapacitated by

Senile dementia

A condition, of serious mental impairment, common in old age, caused by damage to brain cells; sometimes referred to as **senility** with symptoms like disorientation, poor attention, loss of memory, and inability to store new information.

Alzheimer's disease

A progressive form of dementia that causes severe intellectual and emotional impairment, especially in older people.

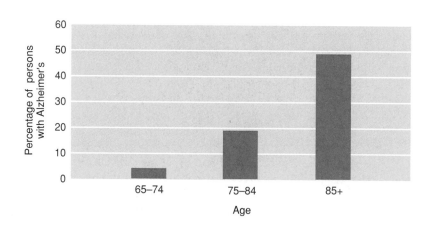

FIGURE 13.10 Alzheimer's disease and age The prevalence of Alzheimer's disease increases by 15 times during the decades from age 65 to age 85 (Evans et al., 1989).

Alzheimer's to the point of needing others to care for them continually (Light & Lebowitz, 1989), and the disease usually leads to death in seven to ten years (Heston & White, 1983). The causes and treatments for Alzheimer's disease are still unknown, but studies of aged primates suggest the possibility of a drug—clonidine—that may one day help improve the memory capacities of elderly people afflicted with this disorder (Arnsten & Goldman-Rakic, 1985). And researchers are getting closer to finding the gene responsible for causing Alzheimer's, which will offer clues to what causes the disease (Marx, 1992).

Despite the realities of the aging body, getting old does not necessarily mean getting weak and sick. Contrary to stereotype, the vast majority of older people view their health positively. Although most older people have at least one chronic condition, seven out of ten older adults who are not living in institutions describe their health as good or excellent compared with others their age (U.S. Senate Special Committee on Aging, 1988). This fact is reflected in the often surprisingly high level of intellectual and emotional functioning of the aged.

Intellectual Capabilities: Slower but Wiser

It is commonly believed that intellectual capacities decline as people grow older—and indeed many studies in the past have pointed in this direction (Willis & Baltes, 1980). One of the problems with such studies, however, is that they are based on the average scores made on tests by many individuals of a given age (Schaie & Hertzog, 1983). In any cross section of older people, researchers are bound to include a number suffering from undiagnosed physical ailments, and the atypically low test scores of these people are likely to pull down the overall average.

More revealing, therefore, are studies that follow a sample of the same people over many years. Such studies tend to present a more optimistic view of the intellectual capacities of older people. In one study, for example, researchers tracked the mental abilities of individuals from age 22 to 67. They found evidence of only slight decline in intellectual functioning before age 60. While more significant changes showed up later, even then there was a wide range of individual differences (Schaie & Hertzog, 1983).

Another problem with past studies of the intellectual capacities of older people is that they gave too much weight to speed of response. True enough, after age 50 we do experience a decrease in the efficiency and speed with which we manipulate information (Cerella, 1985; Salthouse, 1988). But speed itself may indicate very little about the nature and quality of thought in late adulthood. While grandfathers are no match for their grandsons at playing video games, that hardly means that they are deteriorating intellectually.

More than two decades ago, psychologist Raymond Cattell, proposed that intelligence can be divided into two major kinds of abilities. The first is **fluid intelligence,** the capacity to deal with new problems that require such skills as perception (for example, solving a picture puzzle) and memory span (for example, remembering shopping lists and telephone numbers). The second is **crystallized intelligence,** the capacity to use an accumulated body of information to make judgments and solve problems (Cattell, 1971; Horn,

Fluid intelligence

The capacity to deal with new problems that require such skills as perception and memory span; tends to decrease with age.

Crystallized intelligence

The capacity to use an accumulated body of information to make judgments and solve problems; tends to increase with age.

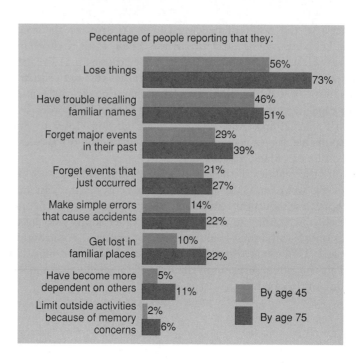

Pecentage of people reporting that they:

	By age 45	By age 75
Lose things	56%	73%
Have trouble recalling familiar names	46%	51%
Forget major events in their past	29%	39%
Forget events that just occurred	21%	27%
Make simple errors that cause accidents	14%	22%
Get lost in familiar places	10%	22%
Have become more dependent on others	5%	11%
Limit outside activities because of memory concerns	2%	6%

FIGURE 13.11 Memory and aging Telephone interviews with more than 600 people showed that certain memory lapses increase with age (World Book Health and Medical Annual, 1994).

1982). Today it is generally agreed that, as we grow older, we experience a decline in the first, but not in the second.

Recent research confirms, for example, that the ability to retain routine information does decline with age. As Figure 13.11 shows, people are more likely to lose things, have trouble recalling names and become forgetful about recent events as they age. In one experiment, both young and older adults kept a diary of occasions in which they could not readily come up with a familiar word that was "on the tip of the tongue." The older adults reported many more such episodes (Burke & Harrold, 1988).

But despite these setbacks, the old outshine the young in other ways. For example, researchers asked young, middle-aged, and older adults to think aloud about how they would solve several difficult life problems faced by fictitious individuals of varying ages. The researchers were trying to measure "wisdom," which they defined as uncommon insight into human development and exceptional judgment about difficult life problems. There was little difference between the age groups, with older adults contributing an equal share of wise responses (Smith & Baltes, 1990).

Even certain deficits in fluid intelligence—for example, in such skills as inductive reasoning and spatial perception—can be reversed with surprising ease with the use of simple exercises (Schaie & Wills, 1986; Baltes, Sowarka, & Kliegl, 1989). It may be that despite a decline in these skills, many older people have a substantial reserve capacity that they can call into play (Baltes, Sowarka, & Kliegl, 1989).

Moreover, not all aspects of memory appear to be equally affected with the passing years. One psychologist tested younger and older adults on tasks involving two types of memory discussed in Chapter 5: **semantic memory** (the retrieval of facts) and **episodic memory** (the retrieval of actual experi-

Semantic memory
The memory or retrieval of facts or bits of information that are without any context.

Episodic memory
The memory or retrieval of personal experiences or events in the context in which they occurred.

ences). He found that the older adults, ages 63 to 80, performed as well as those aged 19 to 32 in the first—for example, in remembering the names of objects shown in pictures—even exhibiting a richer vocabulary while doing so. But they did not do as well in the second—specifically in tasks requiring them to recall the details of recent experiences (Mitchell, 1989).

Aging and Mental Health

Do many people feel contentment and well-being in their aging years—or do they usually encounter a time of agitation and despair? Psychology's findings are, by and large, contrary to what is generally assumed.

In our culture, old age is often thought of as a period of decrepitude and dissatisfaction. Younger people—with their emphasis on growth, progress, and strength—assume that life will become considerably less and less zestful with the passage of time. Therefore they give the aging years the lowest rating of all for happiness and quality of life, and they view any signs of "going downhill" with fear and prejudice (Butler & Lewis, 1977). In fact, however, the vast majority of elderly persons in the community are free of emotional problems and have the psychological resources necessary to manage an effective and independent life (Romaniuk, McAuley, & Arling, 1983).

To be sure, there are problems. Some people, after retiring, are plagued by financial difficulties. Some suffer from chronic illness. Among people 65 and over are about 1.6 million widowers and 8.1 million widows (U.S. Bureau of the Census, 1988), and the stresses they encounter in adjusting to their loneliness are reflected in their own mortality rates. Men especially seem to have a difficult time. One study showed that the mortality rate was 61 percent higher for widowers between the ages of 55 and 64 than for those in the same age range who were married. Among both men and women who lost their mates, the death rate was higher for those who lived alone than for those who shared a household with someone else (Helsing, Szklo, & Comstock, 1981).

Like people of any age, some older adults do, of course, suffer from mental health problems. Sometimes, these may be associated with physical illness or with the stress of caring for a loved one. Depression, for example, is common in stroke and Parkinson's disease (Lebowitz & Cohen, 1991, citing Robinson et al., 1986). And at least 30 percent of those caring for spouses with Alzheimer's disease have been diagnosed as having major depression (Light & Lebowitz, 1989). Suicide rates increase with age among white males, with those over age 85 having the highest recorded suicide rate (Lebowitz & Cohen, 1992). At the same time, however, many psychiatric problems are less common among older people (U.S. Senate Special Committee on Aging, 1988).

The overall picture suggests that, even in late adulthood, patterns of psychological and social adjustment are as varied as in earlier periods of life (Bornstein & Smircina, 1982). Indeed some psychologists who study aging believe that diversity increases with age and that, in the later years, patterns of personality and behavior are more pronounced than at any earlier age (Schaie, 1981). Some examples of extraordinary productivity in the later years are given in Figure 13.12.

Finishing life at home with caring family.

Pablo Picasso

Jessica Tandy

Nelson Mandela

Margaret Chase Smith

Frank Lloyd Wright

FIGURE 13.12 Some great achievers in the "sunset years"

Retirement: Freedom or Boredom?

Retirement has now become an expected and significant period of a person's life. In 1900 the average male spent only 3 percent of his lifetime in retirement; in 1980 the percentage had increased to nearly 20 percent, or 13.8 years.

For many people, retirement is threatening because it is seen as formally ushering in the period of old age (Glick, 1980). But most studies show that when retirees maintain their health and have an adequate income, they find this a rewarding stage of life (Barfield & Morgan, 1978). The concept of retirement often no longer means the end of employment, but rather the initiation of self-chosen and self-directed activity (Atchley, 1982). Most people seem to find that the retirement years are not nearly so bad as they were led to expect—surprisingly full of pleasures that may differ in kind and intensity but are nevertheless as fulfilling as the joys of youth. A key factor appears to be the presence of a network of friends, at least some of whom are viewed as intimates (Heller & Mansbach, 1984).

Even among those who are 85 and older, researchers find diversity not only in physical well-being but in emotional, behavioral, and social characteristics as well. While many people at this stage in life are infirm and dependent, many others are still active and work (Suzman & Riley, 1985).

To Erikson, the aging years represent a fork in the road that can lead either to a heartwarming sense of integrity or to feelings of despair. Putting together a successful life picture with reminiscences from the past can be part of this process. One study has shown that in reviewing their lives, those who age successfully, retrieve memories that enhance their feelings of competence and continuity, rather than dwell with guilt over the past, or in the other extreme, glorify the past and deprecate the present (Wong & Watt, 1991).

People who succeed in negotiating Erikson's final crisis live out the last years of their lives with a sense of self-fulfillment and wisdom. They face the inevitability of death without fear or regret. Those who fail—often because they have not surmounted life's earlier crises—wind up embittered. They are dissatisfied with the way they have lived their lives. They regret what might have been. The prospect of dying fills them with despair.

Coming to Terms with Life's End

The chief reason for today's increased life expectancy is that science has conquered diseases such as pneumonia that formerly killed people in the prime of life. Most deaths today result from chronic, long-lasting conditions—for example, cancer and ailments of the heart and circulatory system (Manton & Soldo, 1985). Thus people are more likely to be aware that they are approaching the end of life—and must somehow reconcile themselves.

Attitudes Toward Death

Death is a reality virtually throughout our lives. When children are between 5 and 7 years old, they already understand the concept that death is universal—and that it is irreversible (Speece & Sandor, 1984). But the challenge of facing death emerges more insistently with the passing years, when the reality of leaving this world is more closely upon us.

Contrary to popular assumption, fear of death is not pervasive among the elderly. Indeed a number of studies show that, with increasing age, earlier anxieties about death become muted. The nature of beliefs about dying appear to be less important in reducing anxiety than the certainty with which these beliefs are held (Smith, Nehemkis, & Charter, 1983–1984), and earlier experience with death—of a close friend or family member—tends to reduce anxiety about death (Cole, 1978–1979).

Death becomes more acceptable if, as older people review their lives, they experience a sense of what Erikson described as integrity and fulfillment—a feeling that they have lived a whole and satisfying life. The capacity to face death with equanimity is diminished among those who have a distinct and pervasive sense of having lived a life that was not fully realized, with tasks or goals that yet remain to be completed, as well as among those who feel that their control over what remains of life has slipped away (Silverberg, 1985). Old people tend to fear a slow and lonely death more than they do death itself (Rogers, 1980). Those who accept death with equanimity view it as part of the continuity of life—"as a point in a journey down an endless road full of travelers who have gone before and will follow. During the journey all leave their own unique mark along the way, enriching those they have encountered and accompanied" (Wyatt, 1985).

Bereavement

Among Americans 65 and over, about 14 million are married and living with their spouses (U.S. Bureau of the Census, 1985). In general these are the most fortunate of the elderly. Studies have shown that older people typically consider their marriage to be just as happy as when they were younger or even more so (Foster, 1982).

Unfortunately, the marriage that prospers into old age, surmounting the problems of retirement and achieving greater happiness than ever before, must inevitably end in sadness when one of the partners dies. Since women, on the average, live about seven years longer than men, usually it is the wife who survives and faces the new crisis of widowhood. There are about 11 million widows in our nation, most of them elderly. Indeed almost half of all women over 65 are widows (U.S. Bureau of the Census, 1988). There are, of course, widowers as well, but not nearly so many—not quite 2 million. And since there are about six times as many widows as widowers of 65 and over, the widowers have a far better chance of remarrying, and many of them do.

Many people believe that normal or "healthy" mourning follows a set pattern: an initial period of great grief or even depression followed by an eventual recovery within some specified period. Psychologists now find that responses are considerably more variable. Recent studies show, for example, that grieving, even soon after a loss, can be a relatively mild experience for some, while for others its debilitating emotional and physical effects can persist for years (Osterweis, Solomon, & Green, 1984). Moreover, some deaths, such as the sudden loss of a child, are particularly hard to recover from (Wortman & Silver, 1989).

Evidence from a number of studies suggests that men suffer more than women when a spouse dies. The death rate for widows is only slightly higher than for other women, but the rate for widowers is over 60 percent greater than for married men (Helsing, Szklo, & Comstock, 1981). The reason probably lies in a combination of factors, including the fact that, without their mates, men are likely to find fewer sources of social support, and that men are, by and large, biologically more vulnerable to stress (Stroebe & Stroebe, 1983). The impact of the death of a spouse, however, is often less traumatic for older people than for younger people because the event is more "on time" (Rodin, 1987).

The Final Stage: Facing Death

Based on intensive work with several hundred patients facing death, Elisabeth Kübler-Ross concluded that most people experience predictable stages in the process (Kübler-Ross, 1969). First comes denial—"I don't believe this is happening to me"; next comes anger—"Why does this have to happen to me?"; then bargaining—"If you let me survive just a few more years, dear God, I'll never get angry again"; then depression—"I'll never see my grandchildren grow up"; and finally acceptance—"I guess my number is up, and that's the way it has to be."

At least some of these stages are probably experienced by most people facing death, but they are hardly predictable for everyone. Moreover, many people, living in the knowledge that the end is near, manage to find new and transforming meanings in what remains of their lives. One investigator, who has worked with terminally ill cancer patients, is struck by "how many of them use their crisis and their danger as an opportunity for change." Many of them rearranged their priorities and began to live fully in the present. They were able to communicate more deeply with loved ones than before they were stricken. And they enjoyed a vivid appreciation of nature and of their relationships with family and friends (Yalom, 1980).

Some people prefer to face death in a hospital setting so that everything possible can be done to postpone the ultimate moment. But the advent of modern medicine has brought with it the capacity to sustain life in ways that many people view as a curse rather than a blessing. Contrary to popular myth, however, most elderly do not die in hospitals hooked up to machines after weeks or months in an intensive care unit, but spend their last days in their own homes, surrounded by family and friends (Brock et al., 1991).

One alternative that encourages a dignified death free of machinery is the **hospice,** a European term meaning a sheltered place for weary travelers, but which now refers to a facility where terminally ill patients are helped to die with a minimum of pain and a maximum of dignity. There are now approximately 1,700 hospice programs in the United States designed to help dying patients maintain a decent quality of life and overcome the emotional trauma of the death experience (National Hospice Organization, 1989). Hospices provide physician-directed medical services—but also psychological, social, and religious assistance as well as sufficient pain-killing drugs to diminish suffering (Wyatt, 1985). Family members are invited to participate as much as they can and at any time. Many hospices have programs of out-patient as well as in-patient care, so that if the patient wishes to die in the familiar surroundings of home, in the midst of family, the required medical and psychological support is available.

Some critics find fault with the hospice concept. For example, they fear that it may cause patients to give in to death too readily, and that, if the concept is widely accepted, there may not be enough medical and psychological specialists available to staff high-quality programs (Aiken & Marx, 1982). But for now, the hospice programs appear to provide an alternative arrangement of care that reduces the anguish of death, and fills the needs of dying patients and their families.

Psychologists have only recently begun to study the cognitive and emotional processes that occur with the knowledge that death is imminent. The findings are sparse and inconclusive. But the search goes on for information that may help ease this final episode and surround dying with a grace and dignity befitting the human spirit and the remarkable flow of events from the cradle to the grave.

Hospice
A facility where terminally ill patients are helped to die with a minimum of pain and a maximum of dignity.

TEST YOURSELF

l) What two processes, described by Erikson, help people accept death?

m) A terminally ill patient who does not want to die in a hospital hooked up to machines might choose what setting to die with a minimum of pain and medical intervention?

SUMMARY REVIEW

Adolescence: A Time of Struggle and Change

1. A number of criteria are used to determine the boundaries of adolescence. Although the period is seen roughly to lie between ages 10 and 20, adolescence has a variety of beginnings and endings for each individual.

2. Psychologically, adolescence may be a period of "storm and stress"—with much confusion over establishing independence, striving for recognition, and being under anxiety-producing scholastic and social pressure. However, some studies have shown that adolescents are well adjusted.

3. In physical terms, adolescence is usually defined as beginning with the onset of puberty—marked by menstruation in females and production of sperm in males. The onset of puberty is almost invariably accompanied by rapid physical growth, and significant development of the **primary sex characteristics** and **secondary sex characteristics.**

4. Concern about body image and being overweight can lead to eating disorders such as *anorexia nervosa* and *bulimia.*

5. The self-concept of adolescents can be affected by the social environment—notably the junior high school experience, which is the occasion for the emergence of many academic and psychological problems.

6. Moral standards usually undergo rapid change during adolescence. From his studies of boys, Kohlberg has suggested that *moral development* occurs in six stages, in which children's reasons for good behavior progress from sheer self-interest to a desire for the approval of others and finally to a concern for their own values and approval of their own consciences. Studies of girls show that they exhibit a greater concern with kind, considerate relationships than do boys—who are more concerned with abstract principles of justice and fairness.

7. Adolescents seek to establish a sense of **identity**—that is, to think of themselves as possessing a distinct and unique character, of being people in their own right.

8. Parental attitudes and approaches to discipline can affect the feelings of self-worth and the degree of turmoil experienced by adolescents.

Adulthood: The Prime Time

9. Continuing development in the years after adolescence often produces striking changes. Some of the most troubled and despondent adolescents turn out to lead happy and fulfilling lives as adults, while some untroubled and self-confident adolescents do not live up to their early promise.

10. One of the prominent proponents of the idea that development is a lifelong process is Erikson, who held that **psychosocial development** (psychological changes occurring with changes in the social environment) proceeds in eight stages extending from infancy to old age.

11. Work often deeply affects an individual's well-being. Success on the job can have a potent impact on self-esteem, marital satisfaction, and physical health.

12. Conflicts for women in our society can be created by **sex role stereo-typing,** often in the workplace, where women are encouraged and often expected to act in traditional feminine roles. In different ways, the stereotyping of sex roles can affect men as well.

13. According to Erikson, the critical event in early adulthood is moving into a relationship (usually marriage) marked by intimacy, commitment, and love. The experience of love differs widely among individuals.

14. The quality of a marriage greatly affects the individual's psychological and physical well-being. **Cohabitation**—living together and having a sexual relationship without being married—has been advocated before marriage to allow participants to learn more about their partners and themselves and thus strengthen a future marriage. However, there is really no evidence that living together first draws a couple closer together.

15. Having a child creates complex and sweeping changes in the roles husband and wife play in their marriage. If the children are planned for and the parents are psychologically prepared for their responsibilities, contentment in marriage does not deteriorate.

16. Middle adulthood is marked by a transition period where people attempt to make the shift to the later stages in life. While such shifts can create conflicts and stress, they often reflect the increased mellowing and self-assurance that middle age brings.

Growing Old: Maintaining Active, Productive Lives

17. With the dramatic increase in the number of people age 65 and over, the problems and pleasures of the retirement years have become very much a part of psychological investigation.

18. Negative stereotypes of the later years have given rise to **ageism,** but psychological research reveals that generalized pessimistic perceptions of the elderly are far from reality.

19. The later years, like the earlier periods of life, bring physical changes. **Senescence,** the weakening and decline of the body, often becomes obvious during the seventh decade of life.

20. **Senile dementia** or **senility,** with symptoms such as disorientation, poor attention, loss of memory, and inability to store new information, is a disease that significantly afflicts a small proportion of old people. A neurological illness, called **Alzheimer's disease,** is a form of dementia that is now recognized as the most common cause of intellectual impairment in older people.

21. Intelligence can be divided into two major kinds of abilities:
    a) **fluid intelligence**
    b) **crystallized intelligence.**
    Fluid abilities are dependent on neurological development and are relatively independent of the impact of education and cultural influences. Crystallized intelligence, in contrast, requires the capacity to use an accumulated body of general information in order to make judgments and solve problems. Today it is generally agreed that, as we grow older, we experience a decline in fluid, but not in crystallized intelligence.

22. Older adults perform well in tasks requiring **semantic memory** (the retrieval of facts), but more poorly in tasks requiring **episodic memory** (the retrieval of actual experiences).

23. Most people seem to cope with the problems of the retirement years and find them fulfilling. A key factor appears to be the presence of a network of friends, at least some of whom are viewed as intimates.

Coming to Terms with Life's End

24. Fear of death is not pervasive among the elderly. Death becomes more acceptable if older people experience a sense of what Erikson described as integrity and fulfillment—a feeling that they have lived a whole and satisfying life.

25. The stages many people experience in the process of facing death are
    a) denial
    b) anger
    c) bargaining
    d) depression
    e) acceptance.

    However, the experiences of grief and mourning vary from one individual to another.

26. The **hospice** is a facility designed to help dying patients maintain a decent quality of life and deal with the emotional trauma of the death experience.

TEST YOURSELF ANSWERS

a) This period of physical maturation is called puberty.
b) Primary sex characteristics refer to direct changes involving the sexual organs. Secondary sex characteristics represent changes in appearance—that is, enlarged hips and breasts in girls, growth of facial hair and deepening voices for boys.
c) Suicide is the third leading cause of death among adolescents.
d) Authoritative parents whose approach is to combine limit-setting with negotiation usually have the least conflict with their teenagers.
e) We are describing a sex-role stereotype.
f) No. People tend to marry those with similar religious beliefs, racial and ethnic backgrounds, education, intelligence, age, and economic status.
g) No. The arrival of a baby, stressful in the best of marriages, will not turn a bad marriage into a good one.
h) True. Men and women often move away from stereotyped sex roles in adulthood.
i) The name is ageism.
j) Alzheimer's disease.
k) We call it crystallized intelligence.
l) The two processes are integrity and fulfillment.
m) The place described is a hospice.

Study Guide

Chapter 13 Adolescence, Adult Life, and Old Age

LEARNING OBJECTIVES

After studying this chapter, you should be able to:

For an Understanding of the Science

1. Understand the impact of the physical development of adolescents on their behavior.

2. Summarize Kohlberg's six-stage theory of moral development and Erikson's eight stages of lifelong development.

3. Know the range of influences that are at play in the choice of a vocation and a mate.

4. Realize the physical changes associated with the aging process, and the nature of memory and personality problems among some older people.

5. Know the difference between fluid and crystallized intelligence, and how confusion between the two often causes people to underestimate the intellectual capacities of older persons.

6. Describe factors associated with successful aging and adaptation to the closing years of life.

7. Discuss the range of attitudes toward death found among aged individuals and the factors that can influence these attitudes.

For Application to Life Situations

8. Understand that some adolescents have special problems in their attempts at independence and need support and encouragement as well as rules and guidance.

9. Understand the significance of Erikson's theory that development is a life-long process, with each new stage from cradle to old age requiring us to face new social situations and encounter new problems that, when surmounted, can lead us to more mature, richer personalities.

10. Know the various factors that are at play in the choice of a career and a marriage partner.

11. Understand how the traditional stereotyping of women's sex roles can create conflicts in their careers and social relationships.

12. Realize how the traditional sex typing of men calls for them to suppress their affiliation and dependency motives and to prove their superiority.

13. Know in what ways parenthood can be both a demanding and rewarding experience.

14. Be aware of the inaccurate stereotypes that are often imposed on older persons.

PROGRAMMED UNIT
ADOLESCENCE: A TIME OF STRUGGLE AND CHANGE

adolescence

puberty

1. The period of *adolescence* is typically one of dynamic and often dramatic change. It is usually defined as beginning with the onset of *puberty*. Thus, the teenage years usually constitute the period called _____.

2. Adolescence is usually defined as beginning with the onset of _____. The period is typically accompanied by rapid physical growth.

adolescence

puberty

3. A girl may grow three to five inches and a boy four to six inches in height in a single year when they enter the period known as _____.

4. The period known as _____ is marked by the onset of menstruation in the female and the production of sperm in the male.

primary

5. The appearance of puberty marks the rapid development of reproductive organs, or _____ sex characteristics.

secondary

6. Also occurring are the growth of breasts and enlarged hips in girls, and a deeper voice and facial hair in boys. These are known as _____ sex characteristics.

menarche

7. The first menstrual period is known as _____.

8. During adolescence, self-image is very much dependent on body image, and a concern with weight can lead some adolescents, especially girls, to develop a disorder known as *anorexia nervosa*. It is marked by the pursuit of a starvation diet by an already emaciated individual.

anorexia nervosa

9. An adolescent girl's concern with body image can lead to an eating disorder known as _____ _____, marked by the pursuit of a starvation diet by someone who is already emaciated. Even more common is *bulimia nervosa,* a disorder in which a person engages in eating binges and then induces vomiting or takes laxatives in order to avoid gaining weight.

bulimia nervosa

10. Nancy regularly gorges herself on food, and then sticks her finger down her throat to induce vomiting. She is suffering from a disorder known as _____ _____. In addition to a concern with body image the period of adolescence is marked by rapid and often lasting change in *moral standards,* an area extensively studied by Lawrence Kohlberg.

Kohlberg

moral

11. The stages of moral development are a subject that was extensively studied by Lawrence _____.

12. Progressive stages of _____ development were studied by Kohlberg. Adolescence brings a dramatic change in moral standards.

moral

13. In adolescence, there is often a dramatic shift in concern from the approval of others to the approval of one's own conscience. This typifies the change taking place in _____ standards. The period is marked as well by the need to establish a sense of *identity*.

identity

14. Teenagers think of themselves as possessing a distinct and unique character and of being people in their own right. In other words, they need to establish a sense of _____. Often this comes down to the matter of choosing a line of work.

standards

15. New principles of behavior emerge during adolescence, marking a change in moral _____.

16. In choosing a line of work, adolescents are demonstrating their need to establish themselves as persons in their own right—that is, with a sense of _____.

identity

ADULTHOOD: THE PRIME TIME

17. Erik Erikson proposed that the psychological development of individuals proceeds hand in hand with the social relations they establish as they go through life—thus the term _____ development.

psychosocial

18. An influential theory of psychosocial development was proposed by psychoanalyst Erik _____. He believed that the really critical event of adulthood centers on moving into a relationship marked by love, intimacy, and commitment.

Erikson

19. For most people, marriage marks the period of _____—the establishment of a relationship marked by love, intimacy, and commitment. Among the adjustments demanded in early adulthood is also one that entails a choice of career.

adulthood

20. Living together in a sexual relationship without marriage is known as _____.

cohabitation

21. In addition to marriage, entry into adulthood entails a choice of _____. In today's society this applies equally to women and to men, but because of the persistence of *sex-role stereotypes,* the path of women in the world of work is not always a smooth one.

career

22. Women often find it difficult to succeed in their choice of careers because of the persistence of _____-_____ stereotypes. As a result, they are under pressure to suppress their motive for achievement.

sex-role

23. Women often find themselves impelled to give full expression to their motives for affiliation and dependency but to suppress their motive for _____. Men, in contrast, are often in conflict because society pressures them to suppress their motives for affiliation and dependency.

achievement

24. For men, achievement and power are the expected norms rather than the motives for _____ and dependency.

affiliation

25. For both men and women, adulthood means facing sex-role _____.

stereotypes

26. According to Erikson, raising children represents the most important achievement of adulthood. This is an element of his theory of psychosocial _____, according to which the crisis of middle age lies in whether we have achieved *generativity,* or "the concern in establishing and guiding the next generation."

development

27. Parents who are concerned about the security and well-being of their children are illustrating the achievement of _____. The crisis of middle age, according to Erikson, produces a wider outlook on the meaning of life.

generativity

28. A negatively depicted aspect of midlife is _____, or the time when women stop menstruating and lose the ability to reproduce.

menopause

GROWING OLD: MAINTAINING ACTIVE, PRODUCTIVE LIVES

29. The retirement years have often been viewed in a negative light—so much so that _____—the negative stereotypes and discrimination associated with aging—is a factor affecting the lives of many of the elderly.

ageism

expectancy	30. The later years, like earlier periods of life, bring physical changes, including a heightening of *senescence,* or the weakening and decline of the body. Still, the average life _____ in the United States continues to increase.
senescence	31. In old age, the weakening or decline of the body—referred to as _____—becomes more apparent. There are no simple answers to the mystery of aging, but most scientists believe that the crucial factor is the growing inability of the body's cells to function adequately.
cells	32. The aging process usually involves the growing inability of the body's _____ to function adequately. The facts of aging—including the onset of *senile dementia,* or senility, among some older persons—had led to an inaccurate stereotype of older persons.
senility	33. The symptoms of senile dementia, or _____, include disorientation, poor attention, loss of memory, and inability to store new information. It is, however, a disease that significantly affects only a small proportion of the aged population.
dementia	34. Senility, or senile _____, affects only a small proportion of the aged population.
memory, information	35. Among the symptoms of senility are disorientation, poor attention, loss of _____, and inability to store new _____. One especially cruel form of senile dementia is known as *Alzheimer's disease.*
disease	36. One especially cruel form of senile dementia, known as Alzheimer's _____, is the most common cause of severe emotional and intellectual impairment in older people.
Alzheimer's disease	37. The most common cause of severe emotional and intellectual impairment in older people is _____ _____.
intellectual	38. Getting old does not necessarily mean getting weak and sick. Most older people do not suffer the severe _____ and emotional impairment caused by senile dementia. Psychologist Raymond Cattell proposed that intelligence is divided into two types of abilities—*fluid intelligence* and *crystallized intelligence*—and that older people experience a decline in the first, but not the second.
intelligence	39. Fluid intelligence is dependent on neurological development and is relatively independent of the impact of education and cultural influences. Thus remembering a series of digits would be a demonstration of fluid _____.
fluid	40. Crystallized intelligence, in contrast, requires the capacity to use an accumulated body of general information in order to make judgments and solve problems. Thus analyzing the reasons for a child's unhappiness would be a demonstration of crystallized rather than _____ intelligence.
crystallized	41. Older people experience a decline in fluid intelligence, but not in _____ intelligence.
fluid	42. Grouping letters or numbers is an example of a task requiring _____ rather than crystallized intelligence.
crystallized, fluid	43. Explaining the motives of political candidates is an example of a task requiring _____ rather than _____ intelligence.
psychosocial	44. To Erikson, the aging years represent a fork in the road that can lead either to a heartwarming sense of integrity or feelings of despair. This is an element in Erikson's theory of _____ development.

45. Two types of intelligence important to distinguish among older people are _____ and _____ intelligence.

fluid, crystallized

COMING TO TERMS WITH LIFE'S END

46. Death becomes more acceptable for older people if they experience what psychoanalyst Erik _____ described in his theory of psychosocial development as a sense of integrity and fulfillment—a feeling that they had lived a whole and satisfying life.

Erikson

47. An aging grandmother who feels that she has fully achieved her life's goals is more likely to accept the prospect of _____ than one who has not. A common crisis among older people is the death of a mate—an experience more common for women than men.

death

48. Comparing men and women, it is more likely that your mate will die before you do if you are a _____. There are about six times as many widows as widowers aged 65 and over in the United States, but the evidence suggests that men who are bereaved suffer more physical and psychological effects.

woman

49. There are many more _____ than widowers over 65 in the United States.

widows

50. Comparing men and women, the experience of bereavement appears to be more difficult for _____. Most persons, according to Elisabeth Kübler-Ross, experience predictable stages in facing their own death.

men

51. Elisabeth Kübler-Ross developed a description of the _____ most people go through in facing death.

stages

52. In facing death, most people go through a number of predictable stages, according to Elisabeth _____-_____. Many people are helped to die with a minimum of pain and a maximum of dignity through a *hospice* program designed to meet the physical and psychological needs of the terminally ill.

Kübler-Ross

53. The needs of the terminally ill can often be met through a _____ program.

hospice

54. Hospice programs can help meet the needs of the _____ ill.

terminally

REVIEW OF IMPORTANT TERMS

ageism **(647)**

Alzheimer's disease **(648)**

anorexia nervosa **(628)**

bulimia nervosa **(628)**

cohabitation **(642)**

crystallized intelligence **(649)**

episodic memory **(650)**

fluid intelligence **(649)**

hospice **(655)**

identity **(631)**

life-span development **(624)**

menarche **(625)**

menopause **(645)**

primary sex characteristics **(625)**

psychosocial development **(637)**

secondary sex characteristics **(625)**

semantic memory **(650)**

senescence **(647)**

senile dementia **(648)**

senility **(648)**

sex-role stereotyping **(639)**

PRACTICE TEST

_____ 1. Adolescence is marked by the onset of
   a. puberty.
   b. conflict.
   c. withdrawal.
   d. frustration.

_____ 2. The name most frequently associated with the study of moral development is
   a. Erikson.
   b. Kohlberg.
   c. Spock.
   d. Skinner.

_____ 3. Erikson's theory emphasizes
   a. identification.
   b. maturation.
   c. psychosocial development.
   d. attachment.

_____ 4. Teenage suicide can be explained by
   a. adolescent stresses.
   b. availability of firearms.
   c. depression.
   d. all of the above.

_____ 5. Kohlberg traced the stages of
   a. puberty.
   b. moral development.
   c. sexuality.
   d. hostility.

_____ 6. Lack of advancement in work by women is often due to the persistence of
   a. prejudice.
   b. sex-role stereotyping.
   c. insufficient physical strength.
   d. emotional instability.

_____ 7. Women are often urged to give up their motive for
   a. affiliation.
   b. dependency.
   c. achievement.
   d. sex.

_____ 8. Men are often pressured to give up their motive for

a.   dependency.

b.   aggression.

c.   achievement.

d.   power.

_____ 9. People who are married

a.   live longer than single people.

b.   die earlier than single people.

c.   are poorer than single people.

d.   take greater risks than single people.

_____ 10. The middle years often bring out long-hidden aspects of

a.   intelligence.

b.   personality.

c.   identity.

d.   conflict.

_____ 11. In Erikson's theory, in middle age there is a decrease in

a.   selfish goals.

b.   generativity.

c.   self-absorption.

d.   psychosocial identification.

_____ 12. The average life expectancy for Americans is now

a.   65 years.

b.   70 years.

c.   75 years.

d.   63 years.

_____ 13. One of the symptoms of senile dementia is

a.   poor attention.

b.   shortness of breath.

c.   stooped appearance.

d.   Alzheimer's disease.

_____ 14. During the later years, the ability that does not decrease is

a.   fluid intelligence.

b.   crystallized intelligence.

c.   memory for digits.

d.   visual acuity.

_____ 15. Aging usually involves the inadequate function of the body's

a.   synapses.

b.   cells.

c.   liver.

d.   hormones.

_____ 16. The most common cause of severe intellectual and emotional impairment in older individuals is

    a. poor attention.

    b. Alzheimer's disease.

    c. loss of memory.

    d. senescence.

_____ 17. Erikson believed that a sense of integrity in old age was most dependent on

    a. financial security.

    b. early childhood experiences.

    c. successfully coping with previous life stages.

    d. physical health.

_____ 18. The weakening and decline of the body is referred to as

    a. wear and tear.

    b. aging.

    c. cell deterioration.

    d. senescence.

_____ 19. A man, told he is dying, responds with "You must be wrong!" In the view of Elisabeth Kübler-Ross, he is expressing

    a. bargaining.

    b. acceptance.

    c. denial.

    d. anger.

_____ 20. A facility where terminally ill patients are helped to die with a minimum of pain and a maximum of dignity is a

    a. hospice.

    b. halfway house.

    c. Heaven's Gate program.

    d. nursing home.

ANSWERS TO PRACTICE TEST

1. a	6. b	11. a	16. b
2. b	7. c	12. c	17. c
3. c	8. a	13. a	18. d
4. d	9. a	14. b	19. c
5. b	10. b	15. b	20. a

EXERCISES

I.   Kohlberg has suggested that moral behavior is based in part on how we intellectually evaluate a situation, and that such evaluations vary in intellectual level. For example, Figure 13.4 in this chapter presents the six stages or levels of moral reasoning proposed by Kohlberg.

Read the paragraph below, entitled "Moral Dilemma," to different students and have them respond, especially to explain their reasoning. Have them write their answers.

After you have accumulated answers from several students, analyze them by taking each statement or reason and attempting to determine its level according to Figure 13.4. You may want to do this together with other students in your class. Count up the number of statements at each level for each subject you assess and also across all the subjects you interview. Then consider these questions:

1. What is the average level of moral reasoning in the group of subjects you tested?

2. Are there statements corresponding to more than one level within the answer from a single person?

3. Do you think that the level of answer might depend on the specific moral dilemma posed to a subject?

4. What are the issues raised by the people in your sample?

5. Speculate on whether your subjects would actually act in the same way as they reasoned on this exercise.

Moral Dilemma

In Europe, a woman was near death from cancer. One drug that might save her was exclusively in the hands of a druggist in the same town. The druggist was charging $2,000, ten times what the drug cost him. The sick woman's husband, Heinz, went to everyone he knew to borrow the money, but he could only get together about half of what it cost. He told the druggist that his wife was dying and asked him to sell it cheaper or let him pay later. But the druggist said, "No." The husband got desperate and broke into the man's store to steal the drug for his wife. Should the husband have done that? Why?*

II.   Review the last four stages of psychosocial development identified by Erikson as described in Figure 13.6 (page 638): adolescence, early adulthood, middle age, and the aging years. From among your friends, relatives, teachers, or school associates, select four people you know well who are at each of these stages. (If you cannot match all four, select as many as you can.)

Using Erikson's criteria as identified in Figure 13.6, do you believe the individuals you selected are negotiating the crises of their periods of development in ways that result in a favorable outcome? Or is the outcome unfavorable? Try to apply Erikson's theory in a similar way to other individuals you know who are at one or another of Erikson's stages of psychosocial development.

*From Kohlberg, L. "Stage and sequence: The cognitive-developmental approach to socialization." In D. A. Goslin (ed.), *Handbook of Socialization Theory and Research,* Chicago: Rand McNally, 1969, p. 379.

CHAPTER 14

Social Psychology: How We Relate to Each Other

American society has a greater variety of people with different values than ever before in its history.

Social psychology
The study of how an individual's thoughts, feelings, and actions are affected by others.

Of all the environmental influences on our behavior, none is so powerful as the people around us. Our dependence on others is evident in childhood, when, as shown in Chapter 12, our psychological development is molded in part by complex relationships with other people. That dependence extends throughout our entire lifetime. As this chapter will show, our identity as adults has been found to be shaped to a significant extent by other people. Thus the importance of **social psychology**—the study of how an individual's thoughts, feelings, and actions are affected by others (Feldman, 1985).

Note that this definition covers cognitive processes and emotions as well as behavior. These processes are, of course, often interrelated—but for the sake of clarity, we will examine them in turn.

How Attitudes Are Shaped

Attitudes
Organized and enduring sets of beliefs and feelings that predispose us to behave in a certain way.

One of the important psychological characteristics we acquire largely through interactions with others is a set of very strong opinions and associated feelings. These are called **attitudes,** and they guide our conduct. Most of us have favorable or unfavorable attitudes toward members of various ethnic groups, foreigners, rich people, poor people, males, females, homosexuals, children, teenagers, and old people. Political parties, national defense, taxation, welfare, crime, and unions are just a few of the issues and institutions that evoke a broad array of attitudes.

Attitudes are not just off-the-cuff judgments that we make casually and change easily. Instead they are deeply ingrained—as if constituting a basic part of our personality. An attitude is defined as an organized and enduring set of beliefs and feelings, predisposing us to behave in a certain way. Although psychology has much yet to learn about the nature and power of attitudes, some broad patterns have been established (Eagly, 1992).

Illogical Attitudes: Prejudices and Stereotypes

It is evident that all attitudes are not based on sound evidence. Some simply represent what we have learned in growing up and interacting with others. We adopt attitudes from the people around us—without looking at the evidence at all.

Nor are they necessarily logical or consistent. Indeed, some psychologists have concluded that the most remarkable thing about our attitudes is the amount of inconsistency we manage to tolerate (Bem, 1970). A study of white college students' ambivalent attitudes toward blacks illustrates this point. When questioned, white students were found to harbor feelings of both friendliness and rejection toward blacks as a group (Katz & Hass, 1988). Moreover, we are surprisingly adept at reconciling dissimilar attributes in a given individual (Asch & Zukier, 1984). That explains why, for example, citizens have voted for—and, in some cases, even elected—officials they liked but who had been found guilty of dishonesty and wrongdoing.

Two kinds of attitudes that often contradict fact are so common that social psychologists have given them special names: prejudice and stereotype.

1. A **prejudice** is an attitude that an individual maintains so stubbornly as to be virtually immune to any information or experience that would disprove it. In our society, one of the most common prejudices is held by some whites against blacks and by some blacks against whites.

2. A **stereotype** is an attitude, shared by a large number of people that disregards individual differences and holds that all members of a certain group behave in the same manner. People are making judgments on the basis of stereotypes when they claim that all women are flighty or that all men are male chauvinists.

We tend to cling to our prejudices and stereotypes—so much so that when we find a member of a group who runs counter to our preconceptions of the group as a whole, we are likely to dismiss the case as atypical, or a "fluke" (Lord, Lepper, & Mackie, 1984). In our personal relationships, we may judge new acquaintances on the basis of stereotypes and thereby become suspicious of certain kinds of people who might actually prove highly congenial if we were only to give them a chance.

Members of various ethnic groups are usually the recipients of society's strongest prejudices and stereotypes. A study of Princeton students shows how irrational such stereotypes can be. The students characterized Turks as cruel, treacherous, sensual, ignorant, and dirty—despite the fact that hardly a single student had ever met a real-life Turk (Brown, 1986).

Prejudice

An attitude that an individual maintains so stubbornly as to be virtually immune to any information or experience that would disprove it.

Stereotype

An attitude, shared by a large number of people, that disregards individual differences and holds that all members of a certain group behave in the same manner.

Developing New Attitudes Throughout Life

We tend to cling to many of our attitudes like a child to a security blanket—and perhaps for some of the same reasons. Yet all attitudes are not permanent. Sometimes the dyed-in-the-wool Republican switches to the Democratic party. Or a confirmed atheist joins a church—and a devout churchgoer drops out. Public opinion polls taken at intervals over recent decades have shown sharp changes in prevailing attitudes toward many institutions and issues.

Socialization

The way that children are integrated into the society through exposure to the actions and opinions of others.

One reason attitudes change is that the process of **socialization**—that is, the way children are integrated into the society through exposure to the actions and opinions of other members—continues throughout life. In our early years, our parents are the chief instruments of socialization and we tend to adopt their attitudes as our own. But as we grow older and are exposed to friends and other socializing influences, the early influence of our parents begins to weaken. Although about 80 percent of elementary school children prefer the same political party as their parents, one study found that the number drops to about 55 percent among college students (Goldsen et al., 1960). The freshman year in college is particularly likely to produce attitude changes (Freedman, Carlsmith, & Sears, 1970).

Individuals are particularly receptive to changes in attitude during adolescence and late adulthood (Krosnick & Alwin, 1989). Part of the reason for this is that we experience more major life shifts between the ages of 18 and 25 than at any other point in our lives. These changes often include graduation from high school, going to college, graduating from college, starting a first job, getting married, becoming a parent, and moving from one place to another—all of which can lead to changes in attitudes.

When we take a job, we undergo a new kind of socialization. Each time we change jobs or get a promotion, each time we move to a new neighborhood or a new community, we come under new influences. We can also be swayed by what we read and by what we see on television. The world changes and we change with it. Our attitudes can be compared to a house that undergoes frequent remodeling, expansion, and repainting over the years. In some ways the house never changes, yet it is never really the same.

The Theory of Cognitive Dissonance

Cognitive dissonance

A feeling generated by the lack of consistency between beliefs and behavior.

What kinds of new experiences and new information are most likely to produce attitude changes? One answer comes from proponents of what is called the theory of **cognitive dissonance.** This theory maintains that we have a strong urge to be consistent and rational in our thinking and to preserve agreement and harmony between our beliefs and behavior—and therefore our many attitudes. There is evidence, for example, that we are more likely to remember information that is consistent with our attitudes than information that runs counter to them (Eagly, 1992). When consistency is broken, we experience cognitive dissonance, making us feel uncomfortable. We may manage to tolerate the inconsistency, but because of our discomfort, we are strongly motivated to restore harmony by making some kind of adjustment in our attitudes.

In some cases, new factual information is enough to create cognitive dissonance and bring about a change in attitude. For example, many people who were once strongly opposed to birth control have been influenced by the information that has appeared in recent years about the population explosion and the dangers of worldwide overcrowding. They once held the belief that a growing population was a good thing. This belief has now changed— and the attitude toward birth control with it.

Events that have a strong emotional impact may also create an inconsistency that calls for change. For example, imagine what would happen if a man who had always regarded women as second-class citizens found himself in love with a woman who was an ardent feminist. Or consider an actual laboratory experiment in which college women underwent a deeply emotional experience related to cigarette smoking. The women, all heavy smokers, were asked to act out a scene in which the experimenter pretended to be a physician and they were his patients. Each subject, visiting the "doctor," got bad news about a persistent cough from which she had been suffering; her X ray had shown lung cancer; immediate surgery was required; before the operation she and the doctor would have to discuss the difficulty, pain, and risk. The experimenter tried to keep the scene as realistic as possible and to involve each subject emotionally to the greatest possible degree. As a result, almost all the women quit or drastically cut down on smoking. A follow-up 18 months later found that they continued to show a significant change in their smoking habits (Mann & Janis, 1968).

How Changes in Behavior Can Change Our Attitudes

It seems logical that a change in an attitude, caused by new beliefs or new emotional responses, should cause a change in behavior. Yet, strangely enough, the sequence of events is often exactly the opposite. In many cases, the change in behavior comes first, and this new behavior creates a change in attitude.

Many studies have shown that experimental manipulation of behavior can produce remarkable results. One such experiment concerned the highly controversial action of President Gerald Ford in extending a blanket pardon to his predecessor, Richard Nixon, for any crimes committed during the Watergate incident. College students who strongly opposed the pardon were asked to write essays taking the opposite view and justifying Ford's action. This simple act of writing an essay created a more favorable attitude toward the pardon (Cooper, Zanna, & Taves, 1978). A similar experiment was conducted with students who favored the legalization of marijuana. After they were asked to write an essay opposing legalization, their attitudes showed considerable change (Fazio, Zanna, & Cooper, 1977).

In our everyday lives, new social situations often push us in the direction of new patterns of behavior, and these in turn often lead to shifts in attitudes. This has been especially noticeable in recent years in the attitudes of whites toward blacks and of blacks toward whites. In general, people who have attended school or worked with members of the other race hold more favorable attitudes, while those who have had no interracial contacts tend to feel less favorably (Pettigrew, 1969). To combat racial animosity at an early age, researchers have been attempting to bring members of different races together early, before prejudices have had a chance to harden. One successful method involves dividing students into interracial learning teams, in the hope that a common purpose can lead to friendship. Such cooperative groups

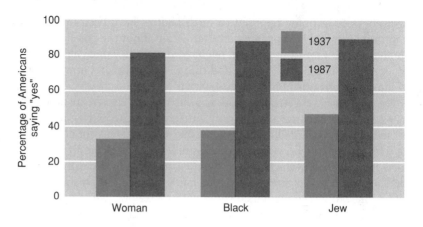

FIGURE 14.1 Would you vote for such a person to be president? As indicated here, Americans have developed more accepting attitudes toward certain social groups in the past half century—for reasons discussed in the text (after Yankelovich, 1988).

reduce prejudice by undercutting the categories that lead to stereotyped thinking (Gaertner, 1989).

Despite highly publicized incidents of racial violence, Americans appear to be more accepting of different groups than ever before (Yankelovich, 1988). Five decades ago, a Gallup poll asked people if they would vote for a well-qualified person for president who was a woman, a black, or a Jew. As shown in Figure 14.1, endorsement of each was low. But by the 1980s, people were much more receptive. More than 80 percent now said they would vote "yes."

Dealing cooperatively with members of another racial or ethnic group—studying or working with them, and treating them as companions—have undoubtedly produced attitude changes. The theory of cognitive dissonance maintains that the friendly behavior produced an imbalance that was remedied by abandoning the disapproving attitude.

Being Persuaded to Change Our Attitudes

Persuasive communications

All attempts to change attitudes by transmitting information and making emotional appeals.

All of us are under constant pressure to adopt new attitudes. Politicians bombard us with speeches and press releases intended to foster favorable attitudes toward them and their party. Advertisers spend millions of dollars every year to try to create favorable attitudes toward their products. Many organizations work hard to win support for such causes as conservation, kindness to animals, and pollution control. To social psychologists, all such attempts to change attitudes by transmitting information and making emotional appeals are known as **persuasive communications.** Because persuasive communications potentially have a great effect on society, they have been studied in considerable depth.

Selective exposure

The idea that people will agree with and pay attention to communications with which they already agree.

Attempts to influence the attitudes of large numbers of people face many handicaps. For one thing, persuasive communications do not ordinarily reach many people. A politician may make the most impassioned and convincing plea for support—yet his speech will be heard in person by only a few thousand people at most. Even if part of the speech is shown on television, it will reach only a small proportion of Americans. Newspaper accounts of a political speech reach and impress an even smaller audience, and editorials have a smaller readership still. It has also been found that the audience likely to watch or read any appeal for attitude change—and to pay attention to it—is determined largely by a factor called **selective exposure.** This means that, by and large, persuasive communications reach people who are already persuaded. Since we tend to associate with people we like and to read or listen to communications we find interesting, we are exposed mostly to people and communications we already agree with.

But let us assume that a persuasive communication does succeed in reaching us, despite the handicaps, and that it argues for a viewpoint to which we are opposed. To adopt it, we will have to change an attitude. Several factors help determine whether we will be persuaded to do so.

1. The Credibility of the Source Some sources are likely to have considerable influence. Others are less likely to convince us and may in fact only make us more opposed to what they are proposing. If the communication comes from someone whose knowledge or motives are suspect—in other words, from a source of low credibility—we tend to disregard it. If it comes from people who clearly know what they are talking about—in other words, from a source of high credibility—we are much more likely to accept it. The effectiveness is enhanced if the source seems to be fair, objective, and not particularly interested in wielding influence. And, of course, it helps if the ideas being communicated match, at least to some degree, the prior beliefs of the audience (Newstead, 1992). Indeed, there is evidence that people often give evidence of what has been termed **belief perseverance**—the tendency to maintain one's beliefs even when faced with evidence to the contrary (Sherman & Kunda, 1989).

Belief perseverance
The tendency to maintain one's beliefs even when faced with evidence to the contrary.

2. The Nature of the Communication What kind of arguments does the source present, and how and when are they presented? In general, appeals to the emotions tend to be especially effective—particularly appeals to fear (Sears, Freedman, & Peplau, 1985). As illustrated in Figure 14.2, such

FIGURE 14.2 Getting scared into taking a tetanus shot The graph illustrates the results of a study in which college students were urged to get inoculations for tetanus. The disease was described in detail—how serious it was and that it was easy to contract—but to different degrees for each of three groups. For one group, the descriptions were extremely vivid, and the disease was made to seem as highly fearsome as possible: for a second group, a moderate amount of fear was aroused; and for a third, only very little. The greater the fear aroused, the more students not only said they intended to take shots, but actually reported to the university health service to be inoculated (Dabbs & Leventhal, 1966). In this case, although the communication aroused strong fear, the person could easily act and do something effective.

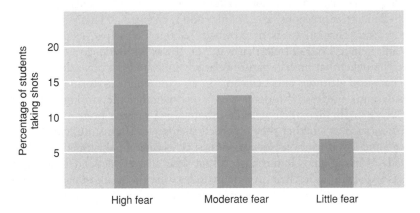

appeals can change not only attitudes but behavior as well. But the arousal of excessive fear will backfire if the person cannot do anything to deal with the danger. Presumably the listener becomes upset and tries to forget the whole matter (Janis, 1967). The effectiveness of a communication appears to be increased if it seems to present a fair rather than a one-sided argument, especially if it is addressed to an intelligent, well-educated audience (Hovland, Lumsdaine, & Sheffield, 1949). With a less intelligent audience, a one-sided argument is likely to be more effective, perhaps because the listeners would be confused by hearing both sides (Aronson, 1984).

3. The Audience Who is listening may be just as important as what is said and the source of the communication. For example, some people are more easily persuaded than others. The crucial factor seems to be one's own opinion of oneself. People who are low in self-esteem tend to be much more easily persuaded than people who are high in self-esteem (Cohen, 1959). Similarly, people who are anxious about social acceptance are more easily persuaded than those who have little anxiety (Sears, 1967). In an odd way, the possibility that listeners will change their arguments is also affected by their beliefs about the relative influence of nature and nurture. This fact is so significant—especially as an influence that can discourage turns for the better—that its implications are discussed in a Life Span Perspective box entitled "How Much Can People Change?"

LIFE SPAN PERSPECTIVE

How Much Can People Change?

One of the great barriers to progress—for both individuals and society as a whole—is the fact that many people take a pessimistic view of the nature-nurture argument. Although there is strong evidence that most human behavior is influenced just as much by environment and learning as by heredity—and often more so—many people still cling to the belief that human nature is determined at birth and resists any attempt to alter or improve it. This belief is evident in such familiar expressions as "People don't change," "That's just human nature," or "That kid was born to be bad." About themselves, people often say, "I can't help it; I'm just built that way," or "I was born unlucky."

The belief that human nature is largely inherited is a powerful deterrent to change in attitudes and behavior. In an experiment performed over four decades ago, university students were asked whether they thought the next five years might alter their attitudes about some of their personality characteristics (such as whether they regarded themselves as trusting, curious, and so on) and toward various social issues (such as capital punishment and legalization of marijuana). It turned out that their answers depended largely on whether they thought their present attitudes were the result of nature or nurture (Festinger, 1954). If they considered an attitude to be largely a matter of learning (as a majority did for being trusted or for favoring legalization of marijuana), they were significantly more likely to foresee possible change than if they regarded the attitude as something innate (as a majority did for the trait of curiosity). The results of that experiment would undoubtedly still hold true today.

Unfortunately our society has a way of implying that personality traits—especially any undesirable ones—are inborn and lasting. Many people become convinced that they are just naturally "dumb," or "awkward," or "bad." Accepting these labels as representing their inherited nature makes it unlikely that they will even consider change possible, much less try to achieve it. Suppose, for example, that an adolescent boy who is in constant trouble feels he was "born" to be a delinquent. He is likely to be totally unresponsive to any options for changing his attitudes and behavior. If he could be convinced that his problems are, at least in part, the result of environmental influences, he would be much more receptive to the possibility of change.

Perhaps the greatest potential contribution of the social psychologists to human happiness and progress is the evidence they have accumulated about the influence of nurture in the form of the social environment. No longer is it possible to assume that our innate biological makeup irrevocably determines our destiny. The findings indicate that personality, attitudes, and behavior are more elastic than is generally realized and that change for the better—in both human happiness and the way society functions—is always possible. ∎

Understanding the Causes of Behavior: Attribution Theories

On December 3, 1979, a crowd of 8,000 people waited for hours in the bitter cold outside the Riverfront Coliseum in Cincinnati to get in to see the rock band The Who perform. Finally, a few doors were opened and the crowd began to surge forward, pushing, shoving, knocking people to the ground, and crushing them. Eleven people were killed. Many were seriously injured. In the wake of this tragedy, the citizens of Cincinnati searched for explanations for the concertgoers' behavior. Were they heartless, cruel people who would literally trample over someone else to get what they wanted? Or were they otherwise considerate people caught in a horrible accident?

To find the answers to these sorts of questions psychologists turn to **attribution theories,** which attempt to infer the causes of behavior. The various theories all assume that we want to know why people act as they do because we want our social interactions to have the most favorable possible outcome (Heider, 1944)—that is, we hope to avoid embarrassing and possibly costly mistakes and maximize the satisfactions and rewards. If we can attribute behavior to some underlying motive or other cause, we have a valuable clue to where we stand, what is likely to happen next, and how we can best deal with the situation. Thus we all perform a good deal of amateur psychoanalysis, seeking in various ways and as best we can to interpret the meanings and future implications of behavior.

Attribution theories

A set of theories stating that a person attributes social behavior to a person's motive or to the context of action.

Person or Situation: The Attribution Error

Dispositional factors

Behavior-producing factors that are deep-seated and consistent personality traits.

Situational factors

Behavior-producing factors that depend on the situations or circumstances of the moment.

Attribution error

The tendency to favor dispositional factors rather than situational factors.

For almost any action, there are a number of possible explanations. Note these simple examples: One morning a waitress smiles at us and says she hopes we enjoy our meal. That same morning the man at the filling station scowls as he takes our money. One possibility is that the waitress is a basically warm and friendly person and that the man at the filling station is hostile and bad tempered. In that event their behavior was due to what are called **dispositional factors,** deep-seated and consistent personality traits. There is also the possibility, however, that the waitress acted as she did only because her boss had just warned her against being her natural surly self around customers—and the man at the filling station, though ordinarily good-humored, had a bad headache. In either case their behavior would have been caused by **situational factors,** or circumstances that forced them in that direction.

We usually attribute other people's actions to dispositional factors, thus ignoring evidence that people are not nearly so consistent as generally assumed, and that their behavior often depends on the circumstances. This tendency to favor dispositional factors—rather than aspects of the situation that may provide a better explanation—is so powerful and widespread that it has been called the **attribution error** (Ross, 1977).

When we try to interpret our own actions, we typically take account of the shifting situations we find ourselves in. For example, we say, "I get angry when someone tries to take advantage of me," or "I feel shy when I am introduced to someone new." But when we try to interpret the actions of other people, we typically commit the fundamental attribution error by pinning these actions on their overall personality traits. For example, we say, "She is hostile," or "he is withdrawn" (McGuire & McGuire, 1986). The tendency to attribute an individual's behavior to enduring personality traits is not nearly so great in certain cultures—for example, among Hindus—as it is among Americans (J. G. Miller, 1984).

Every culture has a set of rules that govern how one person greets another.

Various groups can easily be stigmatized by errors in attribution. For instance, those with illnesses are often blamed for their afflictions. Certain illness are more likely to be seen as within a person's control than others (Weiner, Perry, & Magnusson, 1988). People with physically based illnesses such as cancer and Alzheimer's disease are not considered responsible for their conditions and are thus seen as being deserving of pity and help. On the other hand, those with behavioral or mental illnesses, such as drug abuse or obesity, evoke little compassion and often even hostility.

Mistaken Impressions

The attribution error sometimes gets compounded because we reach our mistaken conclusions on the basis of mistaken impressions. An example occurred in an experiment in which psychologists made a videotape, without a sound track, of a college woman being interviewed. They then showed the videotape to two groups of male subjects. One group was told that the topic of the interview was sex, the other that it was politics. Afterward the subjects were asked to rate the woman on a scale of how nervous and anxious she seemed to be. Their ratings turned out to depend on what they had been told about the interview. If they thought the topic was sex, they thought that the woman showed considerable anxiety. They assumed that the woman would be made anxious by a discussion of sexual behavior. If they thought the topic was politics, they felt that she showed less anxiety. Thus exactly the same behavior—the same videotape of the same woman—created two very different impressions.

The same two groups of subjects were then asked to rate the woman's general tendency to be calm or flustered—in other words, her basic disposition. The results followed the same pattern. Subjects who believed that the interview was about sex, and that it had flustered her, decided she was just naturally inclined to be apprehensive, nervous, and anxious. Those who believed that it was about politics did not make the same judgments (Snyder & Frankel, 1976). The subjects jumped to the erroneous conclusion that acting flustered during a sex interview—a situation that might produce a certain amount of anxiety in almost everyone—indicated a disposition to be easily flustered in general.

All of us are probably guilty at times of this compounded error. We watch person A being treated by person B in what we consider an abusive manner. Such treatment would make us angry—so we assume that A is angry. Then, on the basis of this assumption, we further assume that A tends to be hot-tempered in general. We watch person C making a fuss over person D. Such attention from C, whom we like very much, would greatly please us—so we assume that D is pleased. Then, on the basis of this assumption, we further assume that D is friendly and easily pleased in general. We could be dead wrong in thinking that A is angry or that D is pleased—and how they happen to feel in this particular situation does not necessarily reflect their basic disposition anyway.

Expectations and Social Relationships

It is important to recognize that we ourselves, by the way we act, may produce the very actions that we incorrectly interpret as indicating another person's deep-seated personality traits. This tendency can lead to a **self-fulfilling prophecy**—a prediction that comes true not because it was right but simply because it was made in the first place.

Self-fulfilling prophecies based on false attributions and mistaken impressions are commonplace, with considerable implications for the way we relate to one another. To illustrate the point, a team of psychologists conducted an experiment that was simple in design but that had some surprising and significant results. The subjects were college men. Each of them was merely asked to become acquainted, over the telephone, in a 10-minute conversation, with a college woman he had never met. Before the call was made, the subject saw what he was told was a photograph of the woman. Actually the photograph was of someone else. Half the subjects saw the picture of a woman who had been judged particularly attractive by an independent panel. The other subjects saw the picture of a woman who had been judged physically unattractive.

The phone calls were made and recorded on tape. In analyzing the tapes, the experimenters found something that seems utterly baffling. There seemed to be two completely different types of women on the phone. One type—those believed by the male students to be the person in the attractive photo—sounded warm, charming, and humorous. The other type—those believed by the men to be the person in the unattractive photo—sounded cold, clumsy, and humorless. How could this be? The answer is simple. There also seemed to be two very different types of men on the tapes. If the male subjects thought their telephone partner was attractive, they expected her to be warm and charming—and they themselves were friendly, eager, and easy to respond to. If they thought she was unattractive, they expected her to be cold and humorless—and they themselves cast a pall over the phone call, inviting a chilly and stilted response. By thus setting the tone of the conversation, they pushed their partner into the very kind of behavior they expected (Snyder, Tanke, & Berscheid, 1977).

The gloomy prophecy made by half the male subjects was that their telephone partner would be unsociable—and since they acted accordingly, their prophecy was fulfilled. The other half of the men did exactly the opposite—and made their optimistic predictions come true.

This experiment makes a point worth remembering in social relationships: In everyday dealings with other people, it pays to be an optimist. When you have high hopes that the other person will be likable, your own friendly and accepting actions go a long way toward guaranteeing that the person will indeed behave in a likable manner. But if you expect to dislike someone, your own pessimistic and sour actions almost guarantee a cold and unsympathetic response. It is probably equally true that expecting other people to like us also tends to be a self-fulfilling prophecy. If we expect to be liked, we behave in a likable fashion. If we fear rejection, we tend to act tense, guarded, and not likable at all—and thus bring about the very thing we dreaded. By and large, people treat us not only as we treat them but also as we expect to be treated.

The Potent Effects of Self-Fulfilling Prophecies

One place where the self-fulfilling prophecy flourishes is the classroom. Sometimes the effects are positive. Teachers frequently decide very early in the school year that some students can be expected to do well, and while their judgments are often right, as measured by achievement test scores, the outcome can also be due to the influence of the teacher's expectations. It has been shown that the more favorably teachers viewed students in the beginning of the year, the more these students increased their grade and test scores above the levels that would have been predicted by their prior performance (Jussim & Eccles, 1992).

Unfortunately, sometimes the self-fulfilling prophecy effects are negative. Teachers may decide that some students are not worth much attention. In the elementary schoolroom, for example, they may make this decision on the basis of personal appearance and social class (Rist, 1970). Or they may have taught a pupil's older brother or sister and expect the younger child to be cut from the same cloth (Seaver, 1973). Once teachers have made their prophecy, for whatever reason, they tend to ignore their "dull" pupils and provide much more attention and help to the "bright" ones (H. Cooper, 1979). This behavior has a considerable effect on the pupils' actual progress in the classroom (Crano & Mellon, 1978). The ones tagged as "dull," possibly through no fault of their own, have little opportunity or encouragement to change that reputation.

Compounding the problem is the fact that a prophecy about another person's behavior may seem to come true, in the eyes of the prophecy maker, regardless of how the other person actually does behave. Once we have decided that people are likely to be "bright" or "dull" (or friendly, hostile, charming, humorless, or anything else) we are likely to interpret whatever they do as evidence of that trait. Many actions do not in themselves tell very much about the person who performs them—and an observer who starts with a bias is free to assign whatever meaning the bias dictates (Darley & Fazio, 1980). Teachers may find the very same action to be a sign of stupidity in a "dull" pupil but of intelligence in a "bright" pupil.

Our expectations can be created by a stereotype claiming that certain types of behavior are characteristic of members of racial or ethnic groups, or of social classes or the two sexes. Or the expectation can represent a hasty first impression—or even what we have heard, true or not, of the other person's reputation. Unfortunately, such an expectation can have far-reaching and drastic results, especially when it is held by a person with the power of a teacher, employer, police officer, or psychiatrist. As one study has concluded, an expectation about another person can "significantly affect the life" of that person "perhaps for the better, but as many who do this research fear, often for the worse" (Darley & Fazio, 1980). Some lessons on this subject are contained in the Psychology in Action box entitled "Guidance from Attribution Theories."

Analyzing Our Own Actions

Besides seeking the reasons for other people's behavior, we also make frequent attempts analyze our own actions—especially on occasions when we find ourselves doing something we cannot quite understand. We try to gain some perception of what it was about ourselves or the situation that made us act as we did (Bem, 1972). The way we make the search is the basis of a form of attribution called **self-perception theory.**

Self-perception theory
The theory that says we try to find reasons for our own behavior either in our characteristics or the attitudes and actions of others toward us.

Guidance from Attribution Theorists

Attribution theorists suggest some lessons to guide us in our day-to-day social relationships. They tell us that we had best be cautious and tentative when we act as amateur analysts looking for the reasons behind other people's actions. Yet the attempt at analysis, it must be added, is often useful and not necessarily doomed to failure. Despite the difficulties, we can manage to make a careful enough study to judge people more or less correctly:

- Take into account, when you can, situational factors. If, for example, a person seems withdrawn or confused, try to determine whether that is his or her usual frame of mind or simply the result of anxiety about next Monday's test.

- Search for any information that would indicate whether an act is typical or just an uncharacteristic incident. For example, do not decide that a person is hot-tempered because of a single display of anger.

- When possible, seek and consider the opinions of other observers. These can help you determine whether your attributions are on the mark or way off.

- Other people are so important to us that we simply must try to understand them. We have to make attributions of some kind—and we do the best we can. It is safe to assume that most of the time, a person's behavior is based on a combination of both internal disposition and the particular situation at hand.

Some examples you may have experienced are these: You are playing a friendly game of tennis, lose your temper, and throw your racket into the net—even though the outcome of the game means very little to you. Watching a charity telethon, you impulsively call the number shown on the screen and pledge a contribution much larger than you can really afford. You are puzzled. You are likely to ask yourself, "Why did I do that?"

Again, as in the case of other people's behavior, we can decide that we were pushed into our behavior by situational factors: We lost our temper because our tennis opponent or the spectators did something that was bound to provoke us. We pledged too much to the charity because the people on the telethon were so attractive and persuasive. Or we can decide on dispositional factors: We lost our temper because we hate to lose and are sometimes easily angered. We were overgenerous to the charity because we are generous at heart and do not always stop to think before we act.

When we look for the causes of our own behavior, we often tend to look for situational rather than dispositional factors—just the opposite of what we do when analyzing other people. If we do badly in school, for example, our faculty adviser is likely to attribute our failure to laziness or lack of ability. We ourselves are likely to attribute it to too heavy a course load, emotional strain over personal problems, or some other situational factor (Jones & Nisbett, 1972). In short, we tend to attribute causality to whatever forces we perceive to be paramount (R. Brown, 1986).

Attribution theorists believe that our self-perceptions have an important bearing on changes in attitude. When we manage to find situational factors, as we usually try to do, we have no reason to question or change our attitudes. When we are forced to decide that dispositional factors caused our behavior, however, we may be forced to reexamine and revise our attitudes (Nisbett & Valins, 1972). For example, if we have to admit that our poor grades were indeed caused by our lackadaisical attitude toward study, rather than by circumstances that were beyond our control, we may very well find ourselves jolted into making a change.

Obeying and Conforming to Society's Rules

From the first interactions we have with others, usually our parents and family, followed by teachers and schoolmates, we learn the ways of our own society: How to use a knife and fork, when to cross the street and when to wait for the traffic to pass. Gradually, through socialization, we learn the customs and laws that dictate a whole host of activities, from finding a mate to conducting a business deal.

In many ways, we become creatures of our society, molded by the customs and rules that make up its **culture,** or established way of life. But, to one degree or another, we grow to establish our individual modes of social behavior. The forces that shape both our devotion to society's rules—and our divergence from them—are the subject of this section.

Culture
The customs and rules of an established way of life.

The Urge to Conform and Obey

Life requires that we coordinate or subordinate our actions to fit the larger demands of society. From a very early age, children are taught to obey their parents and follow the rules of the household. As children move out into society, these rules increase and become more formalized: Schools, organizations and businesses all require us to follow agreed upon rules and customs. So it is hardly surprising that most of us will go along with the requests, demands, or in some cases coercions of others.

There are always rebels, of course, who resist the influence of socialization and break the rules or even fail to conform to them most of the time. Despite the exceptions, however, most people follow the customs and rules they have learned and behave as they believe they are expected to behave. Social psychologists have found that most humans everywhere display strong tendencies toward (1) **obedience,** submission to authority, and (2) **conformity,** the yielding by individuals to pressures from the group in which they find themselves. The group applying the pressure may be the society as a whole or any part of it—from family, friends, and classmates, to business associates. It may even be made up of total strangers, such as the people sitting around us on a bus or in a theater. Of course, on many occasions, we tend to believe that there is group pressure on us to conform when, in reality, there is none.

Obedience
The submission to authority.

Conformity
The yielding by individuals to pressures from the group in which they find themselves.

Everyday Gestures of Conformity

The tendencies toward obedience and conformity—and the difference between them—were demonstrated decades ago in a small and simple experiment built around a campus doorway that was in frequent use. On the doorway an urgent sign suddenly appeared:

ABSOLUTELY NO ADMITTANCE
USE ANOTHER ENTRANCE

FIGURE 14.3 Styles change over the years—but people remain look-alikes These street scenes photographed over a span of three-quarters of a century show how the appearance of Americans has shifted since 1910. Yet, no matter when the camera records them, they all look more or less like their contemporaries.

The sign was put up by a psychologist, who then sat by to see what happened. One person after another, even those who had been walking through the doorway every day, turned back—thus exhibiting obedience to society's rules. But then the experimenter arranged for confederates to appear, ignore the sign, and march right in. Given this example, others walked in too (Freed et al., 1955). They were now exhibiting conformity to the behavior of the confederates.

If you make a point of looking for similar examples, you will see them all around you. If a traffic light sticks, showing red to motorists approaching from all four directions, the drivers all come to a halt and wait patiently for a change. But when at last one or two venture across the intersection, others follow. When a pedestrian on a crowded city sidewalk stops to stare at the upper floor of a tall building, others are likely to stop and stare too, even if they find nothing worth watching. People even manage to resemble one another in appearance. As the street scenes in Figure 14.3 show, styles change over the years—but at any given moment in history, everybody looks pretty much like everybody else.

It is amusing but not very significant that all of us tend to gawk at a building when others are doing it—or that we follow the dictates of fashion in

clothing and hairstyles. Often, however, conformity can affect more important aspects of our lives. In a recent study of Princeton University undergrad-
uates, for example, it was found that while most male students felt personally
uncomfortable with the drinking habits of their peers, they believed that their
fellow-students were not similarly uncomfortable—and over time, they shifted
their attitudes toward drinking so that their behavior was more in accord with
what they assumed their peers' attitudes to be. Female students didn't react in
a similar fashion, but the investigators believe that if the behavior being studied were more typical of females, they, too, would have reacted in a similarly
conforming manner (Prentice & Miller, 1993).

The Asch Experiment: Conforming to the Majority

One of the classic experiments on conformity was performed in the 1950s at
Swarthmore College by Solomon Asch. In this experiment, one real subject,
who thought he was taking part in a study of perceptual discrimination, sat at
a table with a group of confederates of the experimenter. The experimenter
showed pairs of white cards with black lines of varying length, such as the
lines shown in their relative sizes in Figures 14.4 and 14.5. The experimenters then asked the group which of the lines in Figure 14.5 matched the
test line. The real subject was always seated where he would hear the judgments of several confederates before making his own.

Sometimes the confederates gave the right answer, but on some trials
they deliberately called out the wrong answer. On these trials, 37 percent of
the answers given by the real subjects who took part in the experiment were
also incorrect. In other words, the subjects conformed with the group's
wrong judgment much of the time.

Only one subject out of four remained completely independent and did
not conform at any time. Even the subjects who showed independence, however, experienced various kinds of conflict and anxiety—as is evident from
Figure 14.6. Some of their comments later were: "At times I had the feeling,
to heck with it, I'll go along with the rest." "I felt disturbed, puzzled, separated, like an outcast from the rest." Thus the urge to conform—to go along
with the group—was strong even among the most independent subjects
(Asch, 1956).

"Just Following Orders": The Milgram Experiment

Another experiment that produced even more dramatic results—and in this
case frightening ones—was performed by Stanley Milgram in a laboratory at
Yale. Milgram selected 80 men of various ages and occupational backgrounds
and asked them to take part in what he said was an important experiment in
learning. Each subject was assigned to a group of four people—the other
three of whom, unknown to the subject, were Milgram's assistants. One of
the assistants was the "learner" in the make-believe experiment. The other
two assistants and the subject were the "teachers," and their job was to
instruct the "learner" by punishing him with an electric shock when he made
an error. The subject was put at the controls that regulated the amount of
shock (see Figure 14.7). Actually, no electricity was hooked up to the controls and no learning took place. The "learner" deliberately made errors and
only pretended to feel pain when punished.

**FIGURE 14.4 A test line in
the Asch experiment** This is
a scaled-down version of one of
the lines Asch showed to the
group. Which of the lines in Figure 14.5, he asked, matches it?

**FIGURE 14.5 Which line
matches?** The group was
asked to judge which of these
lines was the same as the line in
Figure 14.4. The correct answer
is 2. But the experimenter's six
confederates at the table
insisted unanimously that it was
line 1—which is in fact the least
like the test line.

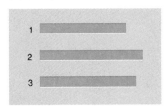

FIGURE 14.6 An "independent" subject—shaken but unyielding These three scenes are from the Asch experiment. In the top photo, student 6 is making his first independent judgment, disagreeing with the group's otherwise unanimous but incorrect verdict. In the other photos, his puzzlement and concern seem to increase until, preserving his independence despite the pressure from the group, he announces (bottom), "I have to call them as I see them."

Of the 80 subjects, half were placed in a control group. These subjects were not subjected to any pressure to raise the shock levels and did not raise them very high. Thirty-four of these 40 control subjects stopped at shock levels listed as "slight" or "moderate." Only six went above 120 volts. But it was a far different story with the other 40 subjects. These 40 were strongly urged by their fellow "teachers" to raise the amount of electricity higher and higher—and they did. Only six of them refused to go above 120 volts. The other 34 went right on, even though the "learner" at first shouted that the shocks were becoming painful and later began to groan and finally scream in pain. Seven of the subjects went up to what they thought was the maximum they could deliver—a "highly dangerous" shock of 450 volts. Many of the experimental subjects showed signs of doubt and distress about engaging in such a cruel act, yet they went along with the group anyway (Milgram, 1964).

Is Blind Conformity the Rule?

Various observers have used Milgram's results to explain how so many "ordinary" people in Nazi Germany could have gone along with the terrible atrocities involved in the systematic murder of millions of innocent people. Although Adolph Hitler may have been a psychopathic monster, most of

A

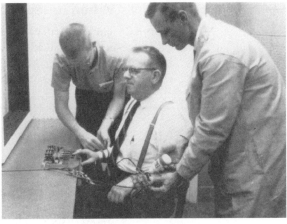

B

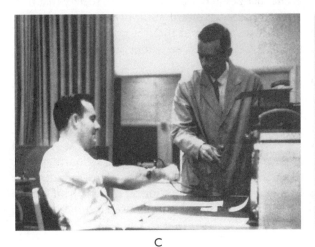

C

D

FIGURE 14.7 Following orders—a high price to pay
In these scenes from a film of the Milgram experiment, A shows the panel, which subjects believed to control the level of shock. In B, electrodes are attached to the wrists of a "learner." In C, a subject who will be at the control panel receives a sample shock of the kind he believes he will administer. In D, a subject breaks off the experiment after reaching as high a shock level as he is willing to administer.

those enlisted with the daily operations of the death camps were not. Social philosopher Hannah Arendt, who followed the trial of Adolph Eichmann, a Nazi war criminal ultimately executed for his crimes, claimed that Eichmann was a rather unremarkable man who simply saw himself as a cog in the bureaucratic wheel (Arendt, 1963).

Most of the actions people unquestioningly perform when following orders are not as horrifying as the examples above. Yet, they can still be dangerous and threatening. In a study showing the potential harm from following orders in more ordinary circumstances, researchers investigated whether a nurse would follow an order that violated hospital rules and professional practice (Horfling et al., 1966). A hospital nurse received a phone call from a doctor she knew of, but had never met, asking her to give a patient a dose of medication. The doctor promised to appear and sign the order within 10 minutes, but instructed the nurse to give the medicine right away. The dose was four times as high as what was written on its container as the usual dosage. The doctor's instructions broke several rules: the dosage was clearly excessive, orders are not to be given over the phone, and the doctor giving the order was unfamiliar. Nonetheless, 95 percent of the nurses were prepared to carry out the order before they were intercepted.

When Independence Replaces Obedience

The obedience displayed in the examples mentioned above does not mean, of course, that adults will inevitably behave in a similar fashion. Nearly two decades after Milgram, a group of scientists conducted a somewhat similar experiment, but with different results. The subjects, living in a working-class town in the Midwest, were persuaded to be videotaped as they discussed the merits of a legal case concerning a service station manager whose license had been revoked because of allegedly immoral behavior. After the coordinator of the experiment had asked a few members of the group to argue as if they were offended by the service station manager's behavior, he requested that all of the subjects sign an affidavit giving the service station the right to introduce the tapes of the group discussion as evidence in court. The result was anger and rebellion on the part of a number of participants (Gamson, Fireman, & Rytina, 1982). The contrast with Milgram's earlier results are probably due to at least two factors: recent changes in our post-Watergate society that have encouraged a more distrustful attitude toward authority than was the case when the Milgram experiment was run, and the fact that there was ample opportunity in this case for group discussion about whether or not the request being made was fair.

It is important to note that people do not always blindly obey authority, despite strong pressures to do so. There are various factors affecting our tendency to obey: First, we are less likely to obey if we are directly causing and witnessing the suffering of others. Second, if we feel personally responsible for our actions, we are less likely to obey something that we oppose. Third, if we see others disobey, we are more likely to disobey ourselves. Fourth, we are less likely to follow orders if we have been encouraged to question the motives, expertise, or judgment of those in authority. And lastly, if we are aware of the power and impact of those in authority, we are more likely to question them (Sears et al., 1988).

The Reasons We Conform

The question, nevertheless, remains: Why do we have a tendency to conform? Why is this tendency so powerful that it can sometimes make us behave in unexpected ways?

1. Our Dependence on Approval   One reason seems to be that it is pleasant to win approval as an accepted, well-liked member of the group. It is highly unpleasant to be rejected by the group and perhaps even subjected to ridicule (Aronson, 1984). Thus it is generally easier and more rewarding to conform—especially when we are members of a group in which there is unanimous agreement.

It can be very difficult to stand alone as a single dissenter in virtually any culture. In Japan, for example, the tendency to conform is even stronger than in the United States. It is more painful for a Japanese adult to rebel against peer values and to experience the rejection of the group than it is for an American (Azuma, 1982).

2. Our Respect for Authority and Its Symbols   Another reason for conformity and obedience is the tendency we have as members of a group to accede to the requests or demands of those who appear to be in legitimate control. In the Milgram study, the experimenter was not a brutish looking man, and he spoke calmly and softly. But he was constantly present and in charge of the situation; he was wearing the scientist's white coat and doing "scientific research." It is noteworthy that when the experimenters left the room and delivered his directions by telephone, the degree of conformity was reduced (Milgram, 1974). The tendency to respect authority begins early in life. Children, for example, have been found to offer specific answers to obviously irrational questions such as "Is a cup sadder than an orange?" Instead of questioning the questioner, they respond because the social situation is one in which it seems natural to comply (Pratt, 1990).

3. Our Need for Guidance   Still another reason for conformity is that we need the help of other people in developing an accurate view of our physical and social environment. We cannot get through life successfully, and we may not even survive, if we do not understand ourselves and our world—and often other people are the only guide we have.

The need for guidance to successful behavior is the basis of an important psychological concept called the **social comparison theory**—the belief that we usually have no objective and scientific way to evaluate our abilities, opinions, or the propriety of our actions (Festinger, 1954). Therefore we can only judge ourselves by comparing ourselves with other people—usually our friends or other people we believe to be similar to ourselves, but sometimes strangers who happen to be around. The more uncertain we are of where we stand and how we should act, the more likely we are to make and rely on the comparisons (Radloff, 1959). For example, if you go to a party where you are the only stranger, how can you fit in without seeing how the others act? On a new campus, how are you expected to dress, behave in the classroom, and get along with your fellow students?

The result of the Milgram experiment can be readily explained by the theory of social comparison. The subjects were in a highly uncertain situation. They had no way of knowing what to think or how to behave—so they looked to others for information. They compared their own opinions with the opinions of the others in the group. When the others proved to be so positive about raising the shock levels, who were they to argue otherwise?

Social comparison theory
A theory suggesting that often we can only evaluate our own abilities, opinions, and behaviors by comparing ourselves with other people.

Comparing Ourselves with Others

The theory of social comparison also holds that our search for guidance strongly influences our self-esteem—indeed our entire self-image. We judge our abilities and our worth, the theory maintains, mostly by comparing ourselves with other people. Otherwise we cannot know if we are good students, good teachers, or good athletes, unless we compare our ability with another person's. Even children feel impelled to try to determine how they rank in comparison with their peers (Marsh & Parker, 1984). We must also ask ourselves, "What do other people think of me?"

The opinions of other people play an important role in self-esteem. For dramatic evidence, note this experiment and its surprising results: The subjects were women attending high school or college. They were asked to try their hand at a problem-solving task containing 25 items. After they had finished, the experimenters pretended to grade their attempts and then told

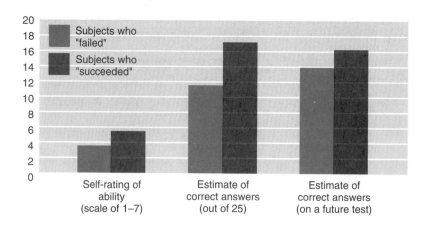

FIGURE 14.8 It is not true—but I believe it! The graph illustrates the results of the experiment with high school and college women discussed in the text. Subjects who were told they failed at a problem-solving task had a significantly lower opinion of their ability than subjects who were told they succeeded—even though they knew that the information about their performance had no relation to the facts (Ross, Lepper, and Hubbard, 1975).

them how they had scored. Actually, no grading was ever done. The experimenters simply decided arbitrarily to tell half the subjects that they had done badly, the other half that they had done very well.

This false information about performance was allowed to "sink in" for a time. Then the experimenters flatly admitted their deception. The women were told that their scores had never actually been compiled and that there was no truth at all in the information that they had done badly or well. Once the truth was out, the women were asked to rate their own ability at that kind of problem solving, estimate how many problems they had in fact solved correctly, and also predict how many they would solve correctly on a future trial. As is shown in Figure 14.8, the results were startling. Apparently the women who had been told they did badly were never quite able to get over the loss of self-esteem they suffered—even though they knew that the unfavorable rating bore no relation to facts and meant absolutely nothing. The women who had been told they did well, on the other hand, were much more confident—even though they too knew that the information was meaningless. There could hardly be a more convincing demonstration of the way other people's opinions shape our own views—even of ourselves.

Interpersonal Behavior: Aggression, Kindness, and Love

- In November 1990, a Brooklyn mother and member of an Orthodox Jewish community that abhors violence, was arrested for the murder of her 8-year-old son. He had died on Yom Kippur day of assorted head injuries and broken bones inflicted at her hands after months, perhaps years, of suffering.
- In January 1982, just after an Air Florida jet crashed into the 14th Street Bridge in Washington, D.C., Arland Williams Jr. jumped into the icy Potomac River and stayed afloat until he caught a rope cast from a hovering helicopter and delivered it to at least three other survivors. Williams died before he himself could be rescued.

These two episodes highlight one of the many questions about social behavior that continue to puzzle scientists. It has to do with the basic quality of human nature. Are humans naturally aggressive and cruel, as crime statistics, episodes of terrorism, and warfare might indicate? Or are they basically kind and helpful, as countless stories of self-sacrifice might seem to say? Are people essentially selfish and mean, as newspapers and television stories so often suggest? Or are they basically nurturing and loving, as the humanistic psychologists have maintained?

Such questions have been answered in the past through philosophical speculation rather than scientific evidence. But science is learning more all the time about how people sometimes treat each other with great kindness and generosity, and sometimes with thoughtless disregard for another person's well-being and even survival. They are also learning how we develop special connections of attraction and love with various individuals who cross our lives.

The Faces of Aggression

Psychologists usually define **aggression** as any action that is intended to hurt others. The clearest example is the kind of aggressive behavior that overtly inflicts physical harm—murder, rape, child abuse—and that our society is primarily concerned about. Even more common, however, are acts that are intended to hurt another person, yet on the surface do not appear to do so. A husband or wife, for example, may initiate an affair which, on the surface, does not seem to constitute an aggressive act—but the intention of which is largely to hurt an indifferent or rejecting spouse. The hurt is psychological rather than physical—but painful nevertheless.

Aggression
Any action that is intended to hurt others.

In contrast, some behaviors are clearly harmful to others—although the intention is absent. Thus a football lineman viciously tackles the opposing team's quarterback, snapping his leg like one might a toothpick. Or, in a competitive office atmosphere, an achievement-oriented staff member works hard to impress the boss—and ends up replacing a colleague in the company hierarchy.

Many behaviors that end up hurting another person fall into a gray area between those that are clearly intentional and those that clearly are not. Indeed often we can only know the true nature of an act by knowing its full context. The surgeon who cuts open the patient's chest and the assailant who stabs his victim in the heart are both behaving in ways that look aggressive from the outside—but the context of one is prosocial and the other antisocial. Moreover, some aggressive acts are fully sanctioned by society—for example, shooting a hostage-holding terrorist, or escorting a murderer to the gas chamber. Examples of the remarkable variety of aggressive behaviors are displayed in Figure 14.9.

The Origins of Aggression: Innate or Learned?

Some scientists, especially biologists, have concluded that aggression is part of our inheritance. They point out that humans are just another form of animal life, and the "law of the jungle" dictates that animals must often kill to survive.

But many psychologists—perhaps a majority—believe otherwise. They have concluded that human aggression, though it may have some basis in biological inheritance, is largely the result of learning and can be controlled.

- A soldier shoots an enemy at the front line.
- The warden of a prison executes a convicted criminal.
- A juvenile gang attacks members of another gang.
- Two men fight for a piece of bread.
- A man viciously kicks a cat.
- A man, while cleaning a window, knocks over a flower pot, which, in falling, injures a pedestrian.
- A girl kicks a wastebasket.
- Mr. X, a notorious gossip, speaks disparagingly of many people of his acquaintance.
- A man mentally rehearses a murder he is about to commit.
- An angry son purposely fails to write to his mother, who is expecting a letter and will be hurt if none arrives.
- A woman daydreams of harming her antagonist but has no hope of doing so.
- A senator does not protest the escalation of bombing to which she is morally opposed.
- A farmer beheads a chicken and prepares it for supper.
- A hunter kills an animal and mounts it as a trophy.
- A physician gives a flu shot to a screaming child.
- A boxer gives his opponent a bloody nose.
- A girl scout tries to assist an elderly woman but trips her by accident.
- A bank robber is shot in the back while trying to escape.
- A tennis player smashes her racket after missing a volley.
- A person commits suicide.

FIGURE 14.9 Which of these constitute aggression? To a creature from space, without knowledge of our society, it would be difficult to tell which examples are aggression. An important criterion is intent—as described in the text (after Benjamin, 1985).

Some children tend to imitate the aggressive behavior they observe—even on television (Turner, Hesse, & Peterson-Lewis, 1986). Similarly, it has been shown that people are more likely to accept and even practice aggression directed toward women after viewing pornography containing violent acts committed toward women (Donnerstein, Linz, & Penrod, 1987). Even a physically uncomfortable environment—overcrowding, loud noise, heat—can apparently help elicit aggressive behavior (Geen, 1976; Anderson, 1989). An example of this can be seen in Figure 14.10.

FIGURE 14.10 Violence and the weather In Houston, between 1980 and 1982, there were more rapes and murders committed on those days when the temperature reached or exceeded 91 degrees Fahrenheit (Anderson & Anderson, 1984).

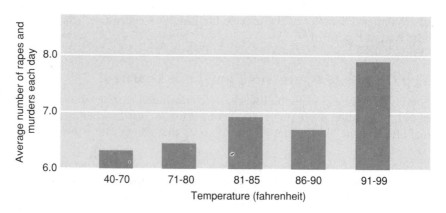

There is evidence, too, that many aggressive people come from aggressive families and were punished severely for childhood misconduct. They may be imitating the behavior of their parents, even though it was once painful to them. Others seem somehow to have decided, from experience, that aggression serves in some way to bring social rewards. Having used it successfully on one occasion, they may adopt it as a way of life.

There seems to be no way, at this stage of psychology's development, to say for sure whether violent behavior is primarily learned or primarily programmed by heredity. Both play a role. Whatever its origins, many scientists agree that it once had clear value in helping the human race survive—but has become obsolete and counterproductive in our present civilization.

The Nature of Caring: Studies of Altruism

Social scientists use the word **altruism** to describe behavior that is kind, generous, and helpful to others. You are not very often likely to read about cases of altruism in the newspapers, but they take place with great frequency. People go to considerable trouble to help a sick neighbor, take in a family left homeless by a fire, and serve as volunteer firemen and hospital attendants. The amount of money donated each year to charities is staggering.

As in the case of aggression, some scientists see in the behavior of animals indications of a hereditary basis for altruism. Chimpanzees, for example, have been observed to share their food with another hungry chimpanzee in an adjoining cage—though they do so somewhat grudgingly (Nissen & Crawford, 1936). Many other animal studies have also produced evidence of an altruistic concern for others (Hebb & Thompson, 1968).

Some scientists maintain that altruism is an innate trait that has been passed along through the process of evolution. They point out that humans have always had a better chance of survival when living with other people than when trying to make it alone. So it seems likely that those who were willing to cooperate with others had a better chance of surviving and passing along their characteristics to future generations (Campbell, 1965). The belief that altruism is an innate trait is somewhat strengthened by recent studies indicating that many children show strong tendencies to perform altruistic acts as early as in the second year of life. Researchers have observed even 18-month-olds giving up food when someone around them is hungry; trying to come to the rescue of victims; consoling adults in distress; and expressing genuine anguish over another child's sorrow (Zahn-Waxler, Radke-Yarrow, & King, 1983).

Other psychologists believe the explanation lies not in heredity but in learning. They point out that there are wide individual differences in tendencies toward altruism. Studies have long shown that the people most likely to be altruistic are those who have learned to experience **empathy**—the ability to feel the mental and emotional states of another person as if they were one's own. The capacity to interpret the psychological states of others and to experience them emotionally appears to emerge as early as the second year of life (Zahn-Waxler & Radke-Yarrow, 1990). Having altruistic parents or other models to imitate and identify with also plays a part (Barnett et al., 1980). Whether altruism is or is not a basic and innate human trait, there seems to

Altruism
Any behavior that is kind, generous, and helpful to others.

Empathy
The ability to feel the mental and emotional states of another person as if they were one's own.

be little doubt that it can at least be encouraged or discouraged by learning and by social influences (Radke-Yarrow, 1989). This topic is discussed in the box on Psychology and the Media entitled "Compassionate Kids."

When No One Cares: Bystander Apathy

In March 1991, a New York man raped his three-year-old niece about 25 feet from the highway during rush hour. According to reports, dozens of people watched the attack without intervening.

Closely related to altruism and aggression is a question stimulated by such episodes. Why do people sometimes help others who are in trouble but sometimes completely ignore them, thus showing a remarkable degree of what social psychologists term **bystander apathy?**

Bystander apathy
The tendency of people, especially under crowded conditions, to ignore others who need help or situations that call for action.

PSYCHOLOGY AND THE MEDIA

Compassionate Kids

Contrary to past popular and professional wisdom, children begin life not as totally selfish creatures, but with a readiness to extend themselves to others in need. What can we do to encourage this positive side of a child's nature? Studies by psychologists suggest five approaches.

- First, it is important to let children know how deeply we feel about their behavior toward others. Theoretical discussions about kindness are not as likely to encourage altruism as is evidence of its importance to the parent. The effective approach, researchers conclude, is not calmly dispensed reasoning, as much as emotional and forceful displays of how much stock we put in being kind to others.
- Second, fostering altruism requires also that parents convey the reasons for the importance they place on helping rather than hurting others. Passion must be accompanied by persuasion. This means taking the time to

explain—with intensity and clarity—the potent consequences our behavior can have in the lives of those around us.

- Third, children need to be exposed to models of altruistic behavior. Where there is a gap between the sermons of parents and their actions, children will model themselves from the living examples they observe rather than the words they hear. Observation learning works where altruistic behavior is concerned. Indeed there is evidence that youngsters tend to emulate models of caring, sharing, and comforting behavior even when they only observe them on TV rather than in the flesh.
- Fourth, it is essential to reinforce caring behavior. Parents ought to be on the lookout, therefore, for signs of children's altruism—and when they find them, to recognize and reward them. Even a generally self-involved child will on occasion act with a surprising degree of consideration for others. The adult's task is to spot the child in the performance of an altruistic

deed and then to reinforce it.
- Fifth, it is important to build a bridge of caring between parent and child. A child's zeal to practice altruism may well depend on the existence of a solid and nurturing bond with mother or father. The nurturance offered by parents to their children is itself a solid model. When children are the beneficiaries of our own acts of caring—self-sacrifice in the face of their needs, compassion when they are in pain, forbearance in the face of their mistakes—they are likely to behave in the same way toward others.

Source: Adapted from "Compassionate Kids," by Julius Segal and Zelda Segal, *Parents Magazine*, September 1988.

Issues to Consider

1. Which of the approaches discussed in this article do you believe to be the most important?
2. What are some other ways that might be used to encourage youngsters to develop compassion as they grow older?

A person is much more likely to help someone in need if no one else does so.

Experiments show a close relationship between the number of people who witness an incident—such as a murder, a theft, or a fire—and the likelihood that anyone will offer assistance. The 3-year-old girl may have been a victim of the fact that, contrary to popular belief, there is not always safety in numbers. Repeated experiments show that a person who needs assistance is more likely to receive it if there is only one person around than if there are many (Latane & Nida, 1981). Several reasons have been suggested. First, the presence of others may relieve any single member of the group from feelings of personal responsibility. Second, apparent indifference on the part of other spectators may cause the individual bystander to downgrade the seriousness of the situation. In some cases, bystander apathy may even represent a type of conformity. If a group of people seems to be ignoring the plight of a person in need, individual members may feel strong pressure to behave as the group is behaving.

Studies also show that people who need help are more likely to receive it in a small town than in a big city (Amato, 1981). As Figure 14.11 portrays, the likelihood of getting such help appears to be twice as good in a small town than it is in a large metropolis. In a large city, people can walk for blocks without meeting anyone they know. They are mere faces in the crowd. They do not have the intimate contact with friends and neighbors that might lead to offers of help.

Any increase in the degree of intimacy serves to reduce bystander apathy. Indeed the size of the group makes little difference when its members know each other and have a sense of group cohesiveness (Rutkowski, Gruder, & Romer, 1983). We are also more prone to empathize with strangers who, we believe, are similar to ourselves (Rushton, Russell, & Wells, 1984).

Bystander apathy is also reduced even when the group members simply anticipate having to interact with each other in the future (Gottlieb & Carver, 1980). This anticipation of face-to-face interaction with other bystanders may increase the possibility of being blamed in the future for inac-

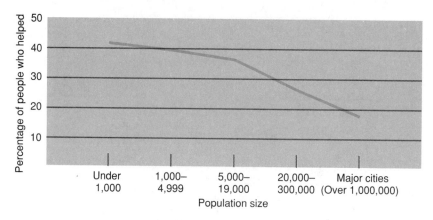

FIGURE 14.11 Helping behavior in communities of different size This graph shows the percentage of passersby who offered to help the investigator after he collapsed in the street, pretending to be in pain. His leg was bandaged and smeared with realistic-looking "blood." Note that the percentage of helpers drops sharply as the community size increases beyond 20,000. The same pattern emerges when the investigator asked for other kinds of help—for example, a charitable donation, or finding directions when "lost" (Amato, 1983).

tion. Or, perhaps the expectation of future interaction induces some degree of group cohesiveness in the group members, thus enhancing their compliance with social norms.

Attraction: What Draws Us Together

Granted that other people influence our behavior, the question now arises: What determines the kinds of people who influence us most? In particular, in this diverse society, why do we become members of one group and not another? And what is the basis of the special connections we build with specific individuals?

It is, of course, the people around us—those with whom we have our closest and most frequent social relationships—who have the greatest impact on our attitudes and our behavior. Therefore social psychology has studied the forces that attract us to others and make us like them and associate with them (Kelley et al., 1983). The key finding has been aptly summarized in a single sentence: "We like those who reward us, and the more they reward us the better we like them" (Berscheid & Walster, 1974). But fully understanding that sentence requires an examination of what it is that we find rewarding about other people—and why. The following are some of the factors that appear to be important:

Proximity

A characteristic of attraction related to nearness.

- *Proximity.* Some social psychologists have concluded that **proximity**—or nearness—is the most powerful factor of all determining who our associates will be. For example, studies conducted in college dormitories revealed that, following a year of school, roommates were twice as apt as floormates to be friends. Moreover, floormates were twice as prone as residents elsewhere in the dorm to be friends (Priest & Sawyer, 1967).

Familiarity

A characteristic of attraction related to the knowledge concerning a person or situation.

- *Familiarity.* The power of proximity in fostering social relationships is, of course, due partly to sheer accessibility. One experiment on the effect of such **familiarity** brought together pairs of subjects who did not know each other. They did not speak but merely sat across from each other in the laboratory. Some pairs saw each other on only a few occasions, others as many as a dozen times. Afterward they were asked how much they liked each other. The more often they had been together—even in this casual fashion—the greater was the mutual attraction (Freedman, Carlsmith, & Sears, 1970). Indeed the process applies to things as well as people. Researchers have shown, for example, that individuals repeatedly exposed to unfamiliar items—for example, nonsense syllables, novel music or geometric patterns, human faces—experience an increased liking for them (Zajonc, 1968; Moreland & Zajonc, 1982). The phenomenon has been aptly named the **mere exposure effect.**

- *Similarity.* One important factor in this picking and choosing is **similarity.** Given the opportunity, and all other things being equal, we tend to be attracted to people who are like us—or at least whom we perceive to be similar. Spouses who enjoy similar interests and activities encounter less conflict and remain closer to one another than spouses who are dissimilar in such respects (Caspi & Herbener, 1989). Moreover, we tend to seek out as friends those who we perceive to be comparable to ourselves in physical attractiveness. In a study of a video dating service, it was found that men and women alike were prone to hook up with a person who resembled them in physical attractiveness (Foulkes, 1982).

- *Reciprocity.* When we believe someone is fond of us, we react with greater warmth—which, in turn, causes them to react even more positively (Curtis & Miller, 1986). This process of **reciprocity** appears to be circular—almost in the manner of a self-fulfilling prophecy.

- *Physical attractiveness.* In actual fact, however, *physical attractiveness* is more influential than most people care to admit. We tend to be "turned off" by people whose appearance—especially the face—we find unattractive (Mueser et al., 1984). Even children judge one another on the basis of appearance. As early as the nursery school years, the attractive boys are the most popular, the unattractive boys the least popular (Dion & Berscheid, 1972). And later, as university students, attractive young men continue to enjoy more social interactions (Reis et al., 1982).

The Staying Power of First Impressions

Why is physical attractiveness so influential? One reason seems to be that it is immediately and obviously apparent. When we meet someone for the first time, we can only guess whether this person is similar to us in attitudes, interests, and tastes. We have no clear clues about competence. We can see at a glance, however, how well the person meets our own standards of attractiveness—and thus move toward acceptance or rejection.

First impressions, it has been found, have a strong and lasting influence. If we like people from the start, even merely because of their physical appearance, we tend to keep on liking them—no matter if some of their subsequent behavior is objectionable. If we dislike them at the start, we are likely to continue to dislike them—even if their subsequent behavior is above reproach.

In one study, subjects were 48 pairs of roommates at a university, all of whom were previously unacquainted. At the end of the year, some of the students decided not to live together any more, while others remained roommates. Whatever the decision, however, it turned out to have been made early in the relationship (Berg, 1984). Evidently the effect of bad first impressions outweighed familiarity.

Why are first impressions of people so strong and long lasting? Social psychologists say the reason is that we carry around a sort of working theory about people and their personalities. We have concluded that certain personality traits generally go together. If something convinces us at the start that a new acquaintance is "cold," for example, we automatically assume that this person is also likely to be irritable, humorless, unsociable, and self-centered. But if we perceive the new acquaintance as "warm," we expect this warmth to be accompanied by a good disposition, a sense of humor, friendliness, and generosity. This belief that personality traits come in clusters is called an **implicit personality theory.** All of us seem to hold such a theory, without being aware of it (Schneider, 1973).

Most of us believe, as part of our implicit personality theory, that physically attractive people also have many other attractive qualities. In one study in which subjects were asked to judge the personality characteristics of people shown in photographs, the subjects read all kinds of virtues into photos of attractive people. They judged the attractive people, as compared with the unattractive ones, to be considerably more interesting, strong, sensitive, sociable, poised, modest, outgoing, and sexually responsible. This was true of both male and female judges (Dion, Berscheid, & Walster, 1972).

Not all physically attractive people, of course, are admirable in every other respect—and the theory that desirable traits always come in clusters can lead us into error in other ways as well. For one thing, it inclines us to think of people as more consistent than they really are. But our theory has been developed through experience and is probably right a good deal more often than it is wrong. Right or wrong, it is one of the tools we use in conducting the social relationships that—as everything in this chapter has emphasized—are such an important part of our lives.

The Elusive Nature of Love

For many years, social psychologists who study interpersonal attraction avoided focusing specifically on the subject of love, believing that the phenomenon is too difficult to define and analyze scientifically. But in recent years, they have attempted to deal with this complex topic, usually reserved for poets and philosophers.

As we know from our own lives, not everyone experiences love in the same way, and thus much of psychology's effort has been devoted to attempts to describe various facets of a loving relationship. One meaningful distinction that emerged is between passionate love and companionate love.

Passionate love has been portrayed as "a wildly emotional state," in which "tender and sexual feelings, elation and pain, anxiety and relief, altruism and jealousy coexist in a confusion of feelings" (Berscheid & Walster, 1974). In such a state of love, emotions run high—fueled by physiological arousal that originates, for example, in sexual longing, fear of rejection, or the anger of a quarrel (Sears et al., 1988). In the view of some, the origins of passionate love lie in our biological nature—ensuring that we unite and reproduce, and stay attached to one another (Buss, 1988). Others argue that such an orientation to love is hardly the rule in all societies—especially those characterized by communal living (Dion & Dion, 1988).

Love Style	Characteristic
Passionate	Early attraction and intense emotion: "I feel that my lover and I were meant for each other."
Game-playing	A sport to be played out with different partners: "I have sometimes had to keep two of my lovers from finding out about each other."
Friendship	A blurring of the borders between platonic and emotional relationships: "I did not realize that I was in love until I actually had been for some time."
Pragmatic	Calculation in a rational, shopping-list fashion of the desired attributes of a partner: "One consideration in choosing a partner is how he/she will reflect on my career."
Possessive	Based on a feeling of uncertainty about oneself and one's lover: "When things aren't right with my lover and me, my stomach gets upset."
All-giving	A view of love as yielding and nondemanding: "I would rather suffer myself than let my lover suffer."

FIGURE 14.12 **Varieties of love** Six styles of love are differentiated here, accompanied by typical test items (answered "yes" or "no") used by researchers to define and measure them. Women scored higher on friendship love and possessive love while men scored higher on game-playing love (Hendrick & Hendrick, 1986).

Companionate love, in contrast, is emotionally more tranquil, not necessarily accompanied by strong sexual feelings, and more typically produces a sense of stability (Brehm, 1985). Among its characteristics are feelings of affection rather than passion, of trust rather than turmoil (Hatfield, 1988). In contrast to passionate love, companionate love is viewed as the basis for enduring relationships. It is less likely to sizzle and fade.

Most psychologists would contend that the two-way distinction just described hardly exhausts the varieties of love we experience. They have attempted, therefore, to make even finer differentiations. Basing their study on 1300 college students, one team of investigators identified six styles of love, described in Figure 14.12. Perhaps human expressions of love are so varied simply because they mirror the remarkable range of personality differences found among us. Moreover, it seems clear that an individual's style of love may vary over the life span. Like other aspects of our social interactions, our expressions of love are marked by diversity and change.

Passionate love

An intense emotional state in which tender and sexual feelings, elation, altruism, and jealousy coexist.

Companionate love

An emotionally tranquil state that produces a sense of stability.

SUMMARY REVIEW

How Attitudes Are Shaped

1. **Attitudes** are strong, deeply ingrained opinions and feelings that we think of as principles that shape our conduct. We are very much "for" things toward which we have a positive attitude, and very much "against" things toward which we have a negative attitude.

2. Attitudes, though powerful, are not necessarily consistent or based on evidence. Two kinds of attitudes that often contradict fact are (a) **prejudices** (for example, against ethnic groups or religions) and (b) **stereotypes,** which assume that all members of a certain group behave in the same manner.

3. Though attitudes tend to persist, they sometimes change because the **socialization** process—that is, the way children are integrated into the society through exposure to others—continues throughout life.

4. One explanation for attitude change is the theory of **cognitive dissonance,** which maintains that we have a strong desire to preserve agreement and harmony among our beliefs, feelings, and behavior. When there is a conflict—caused by factual information, the arousal of emotions, or the fact that circumstances push us into different behavior—we experience cognitive dissonance and may relieve it by changing our attitude.

5. Attempts by other people to change our attitudes—by transmitting information or making emotional appeals—are called **persuasive communications.**

6. The effectiveness of persuasive communications is affected by **selective exposure**—the fact that most such communications reach only people who are already persuaded. It also depends on
   a) the credibility of the source
   b) the nature of the communication
   c) the audience or listener. Listeners who are low in self-esteem or anxious about social acceptance are more easily persuaded.

Understanding the Causes of Behavior: Attribution Theories

7. All of us spend considerable time seeking the reasons other people acted as they did. Why and how we make the search is the subject of various **attribution theories.**

8. Attribution theories all assume that we want to know the reasons behind other people's behavior because we want our social interactions to have the most favorable possible outcome; therefore we seek clues to where we stand, what is likely to happen next, and how best to handle the situation.

9. We have a strong tendency to attribute other people's behavior to **dispositional factors** rather than to **situational factors** that may provide a far better explanation. Because this tendency is so common—and ignores social psychology's finding that people's behavior is not necessarily consistent and often depends on circumstances—it is called **attribution error.**

10. One situational factor we often ignore is the influence of our own behavior on the behavior of others. So strong is this influence that often, because we expect another person to act in a certain way (for example, to be friendly or unfriendly), we push the person into exactly the kind of behavior we expected—thus turning our expectations into a **self-fulfilling prophecy.**

11. In seeking the reasons for our own behavior—the subject of **self-perception theory**—we tend to look for situational rather than dispositional factors. When we are forced to accept a dispositional cause, we may change our attitudes accordingly.

Obeying and Conforming to Society's Rules

12. Humans have been able to survive by establishing some kind of *society*—that is, a group of people who occupy a given geographical area and cooperate in a pattern of living that is accepted by its members.

13. In many ways, we become creatures of our society, molded by the customs and rules that make up its **culture,** or established way of life.

14. Most people follow the customs they have learned and behave as they believe they are expected to behave. They display strong tendencies toward
    a) **obedience,** or submission to authority
    b) **conformity,** or the yielding by individuals to pressures from the group in which they find themselves.

15. One reason for conformity is that we depend on the people around us for many of our psychological satisfactions. It is pleasant to win approval as an accepted member of the group—and highly unpleasant to be rejected.

16. Another reason for conformity is the tendency we have as members of a group to accede to the requests or demands of those we regard as being in control.

17. Still another reason for conformity is that we need guidance from other people in developing an accurate view of our physical and social environment.

18. The need for guidance is the basis for the **social comparison theory,** which holds that to live successfully we must evaluate our own conduct, abilities, and opinions—and often can do so only by comparing ourselves with other people.

Interpersonal Behavior: Aggression, Kindness, and Love

19. The question of whether **aggression** is primarily the result of inborn tendencies or of learning is one of the unresolved issues in psychology.

20. The people most likely to display **altruism** (a tendency to be kind, generous, and helpful to others) are those who feel a personal responsibility for others and have learned to **empathize** (to feel the joys and pains of others as if these emotions were their own).

21. **Bystander apathy** is a failure to assist another person who appears in need of help. Bystander apathy tends to be greatest when there are large numbers of other people around. It is encouraged by the anonymity, lack of intimacy, and the rush of big city life.

22. The forces that attract us to other people—and make us like them and associate with them—are important in social psychology because it is our closest associates who have the greatest effect on our attitudes and behavior. It is a general principle that "we like those who reward us, and the more they reward us the better we like them."

23. The most powerful factor may be **proximity,** or nearness, which occurs by chance because of the family into which we are born, as well as our neighborhood, school companions, and coworkers.

24. Proximity is influential because of the effect of **familiarity**—for, in general, the better we know people the better we like them.

25. We are also attracted to people because of
    a) **similarity,** especially in attitudes;
    b) **reciprocity,** an indication that they like us;
    c) **physical attractiveness.**

26. **First impressions** of other people have a strong and lasting effect. The reason is that we seem to hold an **implicit personality theory** that per-

sonality traits come in clusters—for example, that physically attractive people are also likely to be warm, sociable, poised, and interesting.

27. Psychologists distinguish between two types of love:
    a) **passionate love,** which is marked by strong emotions and sexual feelings
    b) **companionate love,** which is marked by feelings of affection, trust, and stability.

TEST YOURSELF ANSWERS

a) The person would be trying to convey that you have a strong urge to be consistent in your attitudes—in other words, that you would find it hard to tolerate the "dissonance," or disharmony, of inconsistent attitudes.

b) It is called selective exposure.

c) It is an optimistic view of the human ability to change attitudes and behavior over the life span.

d) They call them dispositional factors and situational factors.

e) You would be cautioned against attributing other people's actions to dispositional rather than situational factors.

f) It is called the self-fulfilling prophecy.

g) You are demonstrating conformity.

h) I am likely to display obedience.

i) The theory of social comparison holds that we tend to evaluate our own conduct, abilities, and opinions by comparing ourselves with other people. This theory may thus help explain why Milgram found that some people, seeing others obey a request to act cruelly, ended up doing so themselves.

j) We lack information about the intent of the behavior.

k) The term they use is bystander apathy.

l) Such a belief—that is, that personality traits come in clusters—is called an implicit personality theory.

m) Your friend is contrasting passionate love and companionate love.

Study Guide

Chapter 14   Social Psychology: How We Relate to Each Other

LEARNING OBJECTIVES

After studying this chapter, you should be able to:

For an Understanding of the Science

1. Know that the core of social psychology is the marked extent to which people influence and are influenced by other people.

2. Be aware of how attitudes—including prejudices and stereotypes—influence human behavior. Understand how attitude changes are explained by the theory of cognitive dissonance.

3. Know how attribution theories explain our search for the reasons people act as they do. Know that the fundamental attribution error is the tendency to attribute behavior to dispositional rather than situational causes.

4. Be familiar with the special kind of attribution theory called self-perception theory.

5. Be able to list the factors that attract us to other people and make us like them—including proximity, familiarity, similarity, reciprocity, and physical attractiveness.

6. Understand the relation of implicit personality theory to the importance of first impressions.

7. Understand how the effectiveness of persuasive communications is affected by selective exposure, the credibility of the source, the nature of the communication, and the characteristics of the listener.

8. Understand how strong our tendencies are toward obedience and conformity—and how conformity is further explained by the theory of social comparison and our need for approval and guidance from other people.

9. Explain how conformity stems from our dependence on approval, our respect for authority and its symbols, and our need for guidance.

10. Understand how socialization has affected your own attitudes and behavior.

11. Recognize how new experiences have changed and will continue to change your attitudes throughout life.

12. Be aware of the pitfalls you face in trying to explain other people's behavior, especially the danger of making the fundamental attribution error.

13. Understand how your expectations about other people's behavior can lead them to act that way—thus becoming a self-fulfilling prophecy.

14. Apply the theory of social comparison to an analysis of your own behavior—and the light the theory sheds on your need to judge yourself against other people and the fact that this need is greatest when you are uncertain where you stand or how you should act.

15. Use your knowledge of persuasive communications in an analysis of political campaigns, advertising, and similar efforts to sway public attitudes.

16. Be aware of the argument over whether aggression and altruism are inherited characteristics or the result of learning.

17. Remember how studies of bystander apathy disprove the old adage that there is "safety in numbers."

PROGRAMMED UNIT
HOW ATTITUDES ARE SHAPED

1. *Social psychology* is the study of how an individual's thoughts, feelings, and actions are affected by others. Thus the way people influence and are influenced by others is the core of _____ psychology.   **social**

2. The influence of other people begins in childhood with the process of *socialization,* or integration into society through exposure to the ways the

social

socialization

socialization

attitudes

attitude

prejudice

stereotype

change

socialization

change

cognitive
dissonance

cognitive dissonance

harmony

people in that society think and act. Since socialization helps determine how we behave in the company of others, it is an important topic in _____ psychology.

3. As children grow up, they learn from others how they are expected to behave in society. This process is known as _____.

4. Our behavior is strongly influenced by our *attitudes*, which are deeply ingrained beliefs and feelings predisposing us to behave in a certain way. Since attitudes are acquired in large part from our parents and the other people around us, starting early in life, they are learned as part of the _____ process.

5. The deeply ingrained beliefs we acquire as part of the socialization process—about matters that we are strongly "for" or "against"—are _____ that help shape our behavior.

6. A casual, off-the-cuff belief that pandas are more interesting than polar bears, since we are neither "for" nor "against" pandas or bears, is merely an opinion, not an _____.

7. One kind of attitude that often contradicts fact is a _____, or an attitude that an individual maintains so stubbornly as to be immune to any information or experiences that would disprove it.

8. A _____ is an attitude, shared by large numbers of people, that disregards individual differences and holds that all members of a certain group behave in the same manner.

9. One reason our attitudes are often inconsistent is that we have taken them over from our parents and other people around us—through socialization—without examining the evidence. Yet despite the inconsistencies our attitudes are long-lasting and resistent to _____.

10. We may change an attitude, however, because of new experiences we have and new associates we acquire—reflecting the fact that the _____ process continues throughout life.

11. One explanation of how attitudes change is the *theory of cognitive dissonance*, which maintains that we have a strong urge to preserve agreement and harmony among our beliefs, feelings, and behavior. Lack of harmony produces cognitive dissonance, which is so uncomfortable that we are strongly motivated to relieve it. To do so, we may be forced to _____ an attitude.

12. The suggestion that attitudes may change as a result of lack of harmony among beliefs, feelings, and behavior is the theory of _____ _____.

13. New factual information may shake our beliefs and thus produce _____ _____.

14. Cognitive dissonance may also be produced by new emotional experiences or the fact that we find ourselves acting in ways that create lack of _____ among beliefs, feelings, and behavior.

15. Though it seems only logical that an attitude change should cause a change in behavior, it appears that often the change in behavior, as the result of new experiences, comes first. Many blacks and whites, as a result of studying or working together and treating each other as friendly companions, have abandoned their disapproving attitude toward the other race. The reason

is that the changed behavior produced _____ _____—and harmony could be restored only by changing the attitude.

cognitive dissonance

16. *Persuasive communications* are attempts by other people to win our favor, usually by transmitting information or making emotional appeals. Since they want us to be "for" them, they are seeking to change our _____.

attitudes

17. Attempts by other people to change our attitudes—through political speeches, advertising campaigns, and newspaper editorials—are called _____ _____.

persuasive communications

18. The attempt to influence attitudes is handicapped by *selective exposure,* or the fact that many appeals reach only people who are already convinced. For example, a political rally for Candidate X usually attracts only people who already favor X—and do not need to be convinced by a _____ _____ that makes a factual or emotional appeal in the candidate's behalf.

persuasive communication

19. Since we all tend to seek out people and information with which we already agree, persuasive communications are greatly handicapped by _____ _____.

selective exposure

20. The effectiveness of an appeal depends in large part on the credibility of the source of the communication. The opinion of a good mechanic is more likely than the word of a salesman to persuade us into a favorable _____ toward an automobile.

attitude

21. The effectiveness of an attempt to influence our attitudes depends to a considerable extent on the _____ of the communication.

source

22. Credibility of the source is important. We are likely to be influenced more by a statement about medicine if a noted physician, rather than an electronics engineer, is the _____ of the communication.

source

23. A persuasive communication is more likely to convince us if it comes from an expert source with high _____ and it is presented fairly and logically.

credibility

24. Some people are more easily persuaded than others to change their attitudes. Thus the audience, as well as the credibility of the source, helps determine the effectiveness of a _____ _____.

persuasive communication

25. The effectiveness of an attempt to change attitudes depends not only on the source of the communication but also on the _____ that receives it.

audience

26. The notion that persuasive communications reach people who are already persuaded is referred to as _____ exposure.

selective

27. The tendency to maintain one's beliefs even when faced with evidence to the contrary is termed belief _____.

perseverance

UNDERSTANDING THE CAUSES OF BEHAVIOR: ATTRIBUTION THEORIES

28. To make our interactions with other people have the best possible outcome, it helps to know what their behavior can tell us about where we stand, what is likely to happen, and how we can best deal with the situation. Therefore we constantly try to analyze and search for the causes of people's _____.

behavior

interactions

29. Our search for the causes of behavior is the basis of *attribution theories,* which attempt to explain why and how we make the search. The theories assume that if we can attribute behavior to an underlying motive or some other cause, we can make our _____ with other people have the best possible outcome.

attribution theories

30. Attempts to explain why and how we search for the causes of behavior are called _____ _____.

causes

31. Attribution theories help explain why and how we search for the _____ of people's behavior.

attribution

32. Behavior may spring from *dispositional factors* (deep-seated and consistent personality traits), or *situational factors* (circumstances that cause the actions). Thus both dispositional and situational factors are important considerations in _____ theories.

dispositional

33. If a waitress smiles and speaks cheerfully to us, we may decide that she has a consistently friendly personality, thus attributing her behavior to a _____ factor.

situational

34. We may happen to know, however, that the waitress's boss has just warned her against being her usual surly self around customers—in which case we would attribute her warm smile to a _____ factor.

dispositional

35. We usually attribute other people's behavior to deep-seated and consistent personality traits—in other words, to _____ factors.

situational

36. The tendency to favor dispositional factors is so widespread that it is called the *attribution error.* The error lies in thinking of people as more consistent than they really are and therefore attributing their behavior to deep-seated personality traits—ignoring what may be a better explanation, the particular circumstances, or _____ factors.

attribution error

37. The tendency to attribute behavior to dispositional factors, which often are not the real explanation, is called the _____ _____.

expectation

38. Our actions toward other people are often determined by our expectations of how they will behave. Thus expecting people to like us often becomes a *self-fulfilling prophecy,* because our expectations lead us to behave in a likable fashion—and the other person is likely to respond accordingly. On the other hand, we may invite rejections by being tense and guarded because of an _____ that the other person will not like us.

**self-
fulfilling**

39. Thus fearing that someone will dislike us may make us behave in such a cold and unlikable way that our expectation becomes a _____-_____ prophecy.

attribution

40. Just as we try to attribute other people's behavior to some motive or other cause, we also search for the reasons for our own behavior. Why and how we do this is the basis of *self-perception theory,* which is a special form of _____ theory.

**self-
perception**

41. Especially when we do something we cannot quite understand, we often ask ourselves, "Why did I do that?"—thus seeking the causes of our behavior. Why and how we make the search is the basis of _____-_____ theory.

cause

42. Self-perception theory is concerned with how we try to attribute our behavior to an underlying motive or some other _____, which may be a dispositional or a situational factor.

43. In analyzing the behavior of others, as has been said, we tend to look for dispositional factors. We usually do the opposite in analyzing ourselves, and tend to _____ our behavior to situational factors.

attribute

OBEYING AND CONFORMING TO SOCIETY'S RULES

44. Humans have been able to survive by establishing some kind of *society*—the term applied to any group of people who occupy a given geographical area and cooperate in a pattern of living that is accepted by its members. Thus the Navajo Indians can be described as a _____, with its members molded by the customs and rules that make up its *culture,* or established way of life.

society

45. The customs and rules of a society make up its _____, or established way of life. All of us grow up with strong tendencies to *obedience,* or submission to authority, and *conformity,* or yielding to pressures from the group around us. These tendencies to follow the customs and behave as we think we are expected to behave are acquired through the process of _____.

culture

socialization

46. We depend on the *approval* of the people around us, and it is generally easier and more rewarding to follow their lead. This is one explanation for _____ to the group.

conformity

47. Conformity also develops out of respect for *authority* and its *symbols.* Thus conformity stems from this sense of respect as well as the need for _____.

approval

48. A third factor leading to conformity is the need we feel for *guidance* from other people to understand the world and to learn how to cope with it successfully. This factor is in addition to the _____ for approval and the respect we feel for _____ and its symbols.

need
authority

49. The *social comparison theory* holds that we can usually judge our abilities, opinions, and actions only by comparing ourselves with other people. Thus the theory is based on the idea that conformity often stems from the need for _____.

guidance

50. Our need for guidance, which is especially strong when we are uncertain where we stand or how we should act, is the basis of the _____ _____ theory.

social
comparison

51. We are most likely to seek guidance when we are _____ of how we should act—as on a new campus or when we are the only stranger at a party.

uncertain

52. Our need for approval and guidance from the people around us, and the theory of social comparison, all help explain our strong tendency toward _____ to the group.

conformity

INTERPERSONAL BEHAVIOR: AGGRESSION, KINDNESS, AND LOVE

53. Throughout history, people have speculated whether human behavior is marked by *aggression* or by *altruism.* Because this issue relates to the scientific study of how people feel and behave toward one another, it is in the province of social _____. A major question is whether aggressive and altruistic behavior are part of our biological inheritance or are learned.

psychology

biological
aggression

54. Some psychologists believe that human beings, like animals, live by the "law of the jungle," and because this aggressive approach is bred into our genes, it is part of our _____ inheritance. Others, perhaps most, believe that this tendency toward _____ is learned. They believe the same is true of altruistic behavior, or behavior that is kind, generous, and helpful.

altruism

55. When a person comes to the help of a stranger in distress, we see evidence of _____. Sometimes, however, people ignore others in trouble, a kind of behavior social psychologists call *bystander apathy*.

bystander

56. If your neighbors ignore your cries for help during a robbery, they are showing evidence of _____ apathy.

57. There is evidence that people in small towns are more helpful to others than are people in big cities. Thus you are more likely to find bystander _____ in New York City than in a small town in New England.

apathy

empathy

58. The capacity to feel the mental and emotional states of another person as if they were one's own is called _____.

59. Much of the chapter has stressed how other people influence our behavior—sometimes through persuasive communications, more often because of socialization and our tendency to conform to the group. It is of course the people with whom we have our closest social relationships who influence us the most. Therefore the forces that attract us to others and make us like them and associate with them are important topics in _____ psychology.

social

attract

60. Social psychology has devoted considerable study to the forces that _____ us to other people and make us like them.

61. It has been found that *first impressions* have a strong and lasting influence on how we feel about others. If our first impression of a man who moves in next door is unfavorable, we often continue to dislike him even if his future behavior is charming. If we have a favorable first impression, he probably will continue to _____ us even if some of his future actions are objectionable.

attract

62. Paul is more likely to form a close friendship with students in the adjoining dorm room than with those in the next building. That is an example of the influence of _____.

proximity

familiarity

63. The influence of proximity is related to the factor of _____, or the fact that we are attracted to those we see a lot. The phenomenon has been aptly named mere _____ effect.

exposure

similarity

64. We are also influenced by the factor of _____, or the fact that we tend to be attracted to people who are like us.

65. When we believe someone is fond of us, we react with greater warmth—which, in turn, causes them to react even more positively. This is called _____.

reciprocity

66. Whether people attract us or repel us is strongly influenced by our _____ _____ at our initial meeting.

first impression

67. Physical attractiveness plays a large part in our feelings about other people because it is immediately and obviously apparent. Before we know anything else about new acquaintances, we can see at a glance whether or not we find them physically attractive—and thus we immediately receive a favorable or unfavorable _____ _____.

first impression

68. The belief that personality traits come in clusters is called an *implicit personality theory,* which all of us seem to hold without even being aware of it. One of our beliefs, which is that good-looking people are also warm, good-humored, and sociable, is the reason first impressions are so strongly influenced by _____ _____ .

physical attractiveness

69. All of us seem to hold a sort of working theory about the way good and bad traits come in clusters, known as an _____ _____ theory.

implicit, personality

70. When we meet a person for the first time, the individual's physical attractiveness helps determine the nature of our _____ impression. In studying love, social psychologists distinguish between *passionate love,* a highly emotional and sexually charged state, and *companionate love,* which is accompanied by feelings of affection and trust.

first

71. A person who feels aroused and emotional about another individual is experiencing _____ rather than _____ love.

passionate, companionate

REVIEW OF IMPORTANT TERMS

aggression **(691)**

altruism **(693)**

attitudes **(670)**

attribution error **(678)**

attribution theories **(677)**

belief perseverance **(675)**

bystander apathy **(694)**

cognitive dissonance **(672)**

companionate love **(699)**

conformity **(683)**

culture **(683)**

dispositional factors **(678)**

empathy **(693)**

familiarity **(696)**

first impressions **(697)**

implicit personality theory **(698)**

mere exposure effect **(697)**

obedience **(683)**

passionate love **(699)**

persuasive communications **(674)**

prejudice **(671)**

proximity **(696)**

reciprocity **(697)**

selective exposure **(674)**

self-fulfilling prophecy **(680)**

self-perception theory **(681)**

similarity **(697)**

situational factors **(678)**

social comparison theory **(689)**

social psychology **(670)**

socialization **(672)**

stereotype **(671)**

PRACTICE TEST

_____ 1. Social psychology is best described as the study of

    a. the ways of society.

    b. the effects of socialization.

    c. how other people influence us and we influence them.

    d. how social customs arise and change.

_____ 2. In different parts of the world, people have different ways of expressing emotions, practicing or refraining from aggression, and behaving toward one another. A social psychologist would attribute this to differences in

    a. inherited characteristics.

    b. socialization.

    c. their physical environment.

    d. the social structure they have established.

_____ 3. Attitudes are characterized by their

    a. deeply ingrained quality.

    b. consistency.

    c. susceptibility to change.

    d. backing by evidence.

_____ 4. The theory of cognitive dissonance holds that we have a strong urge to preserve agreement among our

    a. thoughts, words, and actions.

    b. beliefs, attitudes, and actions.

    c. beliefs, feelings, and behavior.

    d. beliefs, feelings, and group pressures.

_____ 5. Cognitive dissonance may be caused by

    a. factual information.

    b. emotional experiences.

    c. social behavior.

    d. all the above.

_____ 6. A woman who has just bought a new car is likely to

    a. read ads for that car.

    b. read ads for other cars.

    c. ask her friends what they think of that make and model.

    d. wish she had taken more time to decide.

_____ 7. Of the following, the best example of a persuasive communication is a

    a. classroom lecture.

    b. news story on passage of a tax law.

    c. coach's pep talk to the team.

    d. friend's invitation to a movie.

_____ 8. The effectiveness of persuasive communication is hampered by all but which one of the following:

    a. the difficulty of reaching a large audience.

    b. selective exposure.

    c. people's reluctance to change attitudes.

    d. the ineffectiveness of appeals to emotion.

_____ 9. Our attempts to explain other people's behavior are the basis of the theory of
   a. cognitive dissonance.
   b. attribution.
   c. social comparisons.
   d. self-perception.

_____ 10. In trying to explain other people's behavior, we are likely to pay special attention to
   a. situational factors.
   b. their facial expressions.
   c. their apparent sincerity.
   d. dispositional factors.

_____ 11. Which one of the following beliefs is most closely related to the attribution error?
   a. People's actions are generally consistent.
   b. People are often forced by circumstances to act as they do.
   c. It is hard to guess a person's motives.
   d. Physically attractive people are usually interesting, poised, and outgoing.

_____ 12. Which one of the following is most central to self-perception theory?
   a. Self-fulfilling prophecies
   b. Situational factors
   c. Dispositional factors
   d. The influence of our own behavior on other people

_____ 13. A college woman is introduced to a male student. Which of the following is least likely to make him seem attractive?
   a. She has seen him on the campus many times.
   b. She has been assigned to work with him on a series of psychology experiments.
   c. He seems similar to her in many ways.
   d. He does not seem attracted to her.

_____ 14. Physical attractiveness plays a big part in attracting people to one another because
   a. everybody agrees on who is and who is not attractive.
   b. of the importance of first impressions.
   c. of the importance of propinquity.
   d. of the importance of similarity.

_____ 15. The belief that personality traits come in clusters is
   a. an implicit personality theory.
   b. part of attribution theory.
   c. false.
   d. all the above.

_____ 16. The belief that altruism is an innate trait is strengthened by evidence that
   a. aggressive behavior is rare in young children.
   b. helpful behavior declines with age.
   c. babies show compassion.
   d. none of the above.

_____ 17. Intimacy among individuals is likely to reduce
   a. cognitive dissonance.
   b. changes of attitude.
   c. bystander apathy.
   d. social comparison.

_____ 18. The tendency to conform is
   a. closely related to the need for approval and guidance.
   b. equally strong in all people.
   c. an inherited trait.
   d. found in some cultures but not others.

_____ 19. To encourage children to behave altruistically, it is important to
   a. say little about it.
   b. avoid criticism.
   c. praise such behavior.
   d. let nature take its course.

_____ 20. An important component of altruism is the capacity to feel
   a. empathy.
   b. intimate.
   c. attracted.
   d. enraged.

ANSWERS TO PRACTICE TEST

1. c	6. a	11. a	16. c
2. b	7. c	12. b	17. c
3. a	8. d	13. d	18. a
4. c	9. b	14. b	19. c
5. d	10. d	15. a	20. a

EXERCISES

I. It is easy to conduct an informal experiment on the effect of your own behavior on the behavior of other people. For a day, or at least part of a day, devote yourself to being as pleasant as you can toward everyone with whom you come in contact—other students, salespeople, waiters, family, neighbors, friends, everybody. Go out of your way to be as cheerful, warm, and friendly as you possibly can, even to the most sour and forbidding of the people you meet. Try to find something nice to say about everyone—a little compliment they may enjoy.

Make mental notes of people's reactions—or jot down reminders—and at the end of your experiment tally the results. How many people showed no response at all? How many seemed to back off from your friendly approach? How many seemed unusually warm and friendly in return? With any luck at all, you should find that most of the reactions fell into the last of the three categories. Your own reactions may also be interesting to analyze. Did you enjoy spreading good cheer? Did the experiment tell you something important about social relationships?

It must be emphasized that this is just an informal experiment with no real claim to being scientific. You have no objective measure of how friendly your behavior actually seemed to others, or how much if at all it differed from your customary behavior. You are also forced to rely on your own subjective judgment of how people responded to you, and you have no way of determining whether there was any change in their customary behavior. Nonetheless the experiment is well worth trying.

II. Along similar lines, you can try an informal attempt to show how one's expectations about another person affect the way one acts—and the way these actions, in turn, influence the other person. Pick out someone you know—a Mr. or Ms. X—who is generally regarded as somewhat cranky, critical, and sharp-tongued. Then arrange to have X meet, for the first time, another of your acquaintances. Before the meeting—preferably at a meal, a sports event, or a long drive that will keep the two together for some time—warn your friend about X's notorious cantankerousness. Note how well, if at all, the two get along. Now arrange a similar meeting between X and Friend No. 2. Tell No. 2 in advance that X, though occasionally a bit outspoken, is a warm and generous person with a delightful sense of humor. See what happens. Is there a difference in the way Friends No. 1 and 2 act toward X? How does X act toward each of them in turn?

A P P E N D I X

Statistical Methods

The use of statistics as a tool in psychology began with Sir Francis Galton, an Englishman who did his most important work in the 1880s. Sir Francis was interested in individual differences—how people vary in height, weight, and such characteristics as color vision, sense of smell, hearing, and ability to judge weights. He was also interested in the workings of heredity. One of the questions that fascinated him was whether taller-than-average people tend to have taller-than-average children. Another was whether successful people tend to have successful children.

Since Galton's time, many investigators have pursued similar questions, such as: Do parents of above-average intelligence tend to have children of above-average intelligence? Do strict parents tend to produce children who are more or less aggressive than the children of lenient parents? Do people of high intelligence tend to be more or less neurotic than people of low intelligence?

To answer these questions, as Galton discovered, one must first make some accurate measurements. Galton himself devised a number of tests for such abilities as vision and hearing. Newer generations of psychologists have tried to perfect tests for intelligence and personality traits. But the results of the tests are meaningless unless they can be analyzed and compared in accordance with sound statistical practices.

Psychological statistics is the application of mathematical principles to the interpretation of the results obtained in psychological studies. It has been aptly called a "way of thinking" (Hebb, 1958)—a problem-solving tool that enables us to summarize our knowledge of psychological events and make legitimate inferences from what we discover.

Probability and Normal Distribution

As an example of how we can profit from thinking in terms of statistical methods, suppose someone shows you two possible bridge hands. One is the bridge player's dream—13 spades. The other is a run-of-the-mill hand containing one ace, a few face cards, and many cards of no special value. The person who has put the hands together asks: "If you play bridge tonight, which of these hands are you less likely to pick up?"

Your first impulse would surely be to say, "The 13 spades." When a bridge player gets such a hand, the newspapers report it as a great rarity. The player is likely to talk about it forever afterward. And, in all truth, a hand of 13 spades is extremely rare. It occurs, as a statistician can quickly calculate, on an average of only once in about 159 billion deals.

But the other hand, whatever it is, is equally rare. The rules of statistical probability say that the chance of getting any particular combination of 13 cards is only one in about 159 billion deals. The reason a hand of 13 spades seems rarer than any other is that bridge players pay attention to it, while lumping all their mediocre hands together as if they were one and the same.

Think about the hand of 13 spades in another way. Since it occurs only once in 159 billion deals, is it not a miracle that it should ever occur at all? No, it is not. It has been estimated that there are about 25 million bridge players in the United States. If each of them deals 20 times a week, that makes 26 billion deals a year. The statistical method tells us that we should expect a hand of 13 spades to be dealt on the average of about once every six years.

Dreams and Prophecies: Why They Often Come True

The fact that we can expect a hand of 13 spades to occur with some regularity explains some events in life that seem baffling to people who do not understand statistics. For example, every once in a while the newspapers report that someone shooting dice in Las Vegas has made 28 passes (or winning throws) in a row. This seems almost impossible, and in fact the mathematical odds are more than 268,000,000 to 1 that it will not happen to anyone who picks up the dice. These are very high odds indeed. Yet, considering the large number of people who step up to all the dice tables in Las Vegas, it is very likely that sooner or later someone will throw the 28 passes.

The laws of probability also explain many of the coincidences that seem—to people unfamiliar with the laws—to represent the working of supernatural powers. A woman in Illinois dreams that her brother in California has died and the next morning gets a telephone call that he was killed in an accident. This may sound like an incredible case of mental telepathy, but the laws of probability offer a much simpler explanation. Most people dream frequently. Dreams of death are by no means rare. In the course of a year millions of people dream of the death of someone in the family. Sooner or later, one of the dreams is almost sure to coincide with an actual death.

Astrologers and other seers also profit from the rules of probability. If an astrologer keeps predicting that a catastrophe will occur, the forecast is bound to be right sooner or later, because the world is almost sure to have some kind of tragedy, from airplane accident to tornado, in any given period. And a prophet who makes a reputation by predicting the death of a world leader knows that there are many world leaders and that many of them are so advanced in age that their death would not be unusual.

In a world as big as ours, all kinds of coincidences are likely to occur. The rules of statistics say that we should expect and not be surprised by them. Statistical analysis lets us view these coincidences for what they are and helps us recognize that they have no real significance.

What Happens When You Toss Coins: A Normal Curve of Distribution

One of the principles of probability, as Galton was the first to notice, has to do with the manner in which many things, including psychological traits, are distributed in the normal course of natural events. The principle can best be demonstrated by a simple experiment. Drop 10 coins into a cup, shake them, throw them on a table, and count the number of heads. Do this a number of times, say 100. Your tally will almost surely turn out to be very much like the one shown in Figure A.1.

What you have come up with is a simple illustration of normal distribution. When you toss 10 coins 100 times—a total of 1,000 tosses—you can expect 500 heads to come up, an average of five heads per toss. As the tally shows, this number came up most frequently. The two numbers on either side, four and six, were close seconds. The numbers farther away from five were increasingly infrequent. Ten came up only once, and zero did not come up at all. (Over a long period, both 10 and zero would be expected to come up on an average of once in every 1,024 tosses.)

The tally shown in Figure A.1 can be converted into the bar graph shown in Figure A.2, which provides a more easily interpreted picture of what hap-

Number of heads						
0						
1	I					
2	HHH	I				
3	HHH	HHH				
4	HHH	HHH	HHH	III		
5	HHH	HHH	HHH	HHH	HHH	II
6	HHH	HHH	HHH	HHH	I	
7	HHH	HHH	I			
8	III					
9	I					
10	I					

FIGURE A.1 A tally of coin tosses Ten coins were shaken in a cup and tossed on a table 100 times. This is a tally of the number of heads that appeared on each toss.

pened in the coin tossing. Note its shape—highest in the middle, then tapering off toward the extreme left and the extreme right. If a curve is drawn to connect the tops of the bars, we have a good example of the *normal curve of distribution*—which, as was explained in Chapter 1, is typical of the results generally found in all tests and measurements, of both physical and psychological traits. The curve for distribution of IQs, which was presented in Chapter 1, is repeated in Figure A.3. Note again that most people fall around the average of 100 and that only a few are found at the far extremes below 40 or above 160. The message of the curve is that in IQ (or height or weight or almost anything else) the people who are about average are in the majority—while some are as rare as those 28 passes in a dice game.

Descriptive Statistics

As a quick and convenient method of summarizing the characteristics of any group under study—as well as the distribution of these characteristics—psychologists use a technique called *descriptive statistics*. For example, suppose

FIGURE A.2 The tally in bar form Here the tally of the coin-tossing experiment has been converted into a bar graph. Note the peak at the center and the rapid falling off toward each extreme.

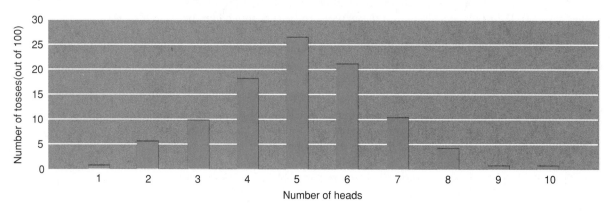

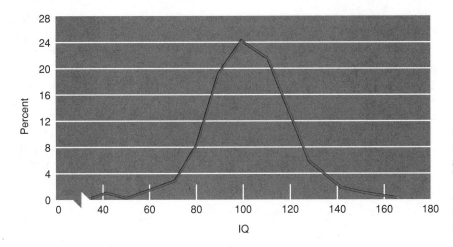

FIGURE A.3 The normal curve of IQ distribution The graph was constructed from IQs found in large-scale testing (Terman and Merrill, 1937). Note that it looks very much like a line connecting the peaks of the bars in Figure A.2.

we draw up a new intelligence test and administer it to 10,000 college students. We wind up with 10,000 raw scores. To pass along what we have learned about the test, however, we need not quote every one of the 10,000 scores. Through the use of descriptive statistics we can summarize and condense. With just a few well-chosen numbers, we can tell other people what they need to know in order to understand our results. Among the most commonly used forms of descriptive statistics are the following.

Number in Group

Number in group is simply the total number of subjects we have studied. It is important because the chances of obtaining accurate results are greater if we study a large group than if we study only a small group. If we test only three people on our new intelligence test, we may happen to select three geniuses or three morons. A large sample is likely to be more representative of the population as a whole.

The Statistical Average (or Mean)

Another useful piece of information is what in everyday language is called the *average*. For example, six students take an examination containing 100 true-false questions and get test scores of 70, 74, 74, 76, 80, and 82. The average score—or in technical language, the *mean*—is the sum of the scores divided by the number of subjects who took the test. In other words, it is 456 divided by 6—or 76. Knowing that the mean is 76 tells us a great deal about the curve of distribution that could be drawn up from the scores. We know that the curve would center on a figure of about 76—and that the majority of scores would be somewhere in this neighborhood.

Another measure of central tendency, or the point around which the scores tend to cluster, is the *median*. This is the halfway point that separates the lower 50 percent of scores from the higher 50 percent. In the example just given, the median would be 75, because half the scores fall below 75 and the other half fall above. The median is an especially useful figure when the data include a small number of exceptionally low or exceptionally high measurements. Let us say, for example, that the six scores on the true-false examination were 70, 74, 74, 76, 80, and 100. The one student who scores 100 brings up the mean score quite sharply to 79. But note that 79 is hardly an "average" score, because only two of the six students scored that high. The median score, which remains at 75, is a better description of the data.

A third measure of central tendency is the *mode*—the measurement or score that applies to the greatest number of subjects. In the case of the true-false examination it would be 74, the only score made by as many as two of the students. The mode tells us where the highest point of the curve of distribution will be found. In a perfectly symmetrical normal curve the mode, the median, and the mean are the same. If the distribution is not symmetrical, but on the contrary tails off more sharply on the below-average side than on the above-average side, or vice versa (as often happens), it is useful to know all three of these figures.

Variability and Standard Deviation

Even when the normal curve is perfectly symmetrical, it may take different forms. Sometimes it is high and narrow. At other times it is shorter and wider. This depends on the *variability* of the measurements, which means the extent to which they differ from one another.

A crude way to describe the variability of scores made on a psychological test is simply to give the *range* of the scores—the highest minus the lowest. A much more sensitive description is provided by what is called the *standard deviation*, often abbreviated to *SD*. The standard deviation, which is computed from the data by a formula that will be explained later, is an especially useful tool because it indicates the proportion of scores or measurements that will be found under any part of the curve. As Figure A.4 shows, the rule is that 34.13 percent of all the scores lie between the mean and a point 1 *SD* above the mean; 13.59 percent lie between 1 *SD* and 2 *SDs* above the mean; and 2.14 percent lie between 2 *SDs* and 3 *SDs* above the mean. Thus the *SD* gives a clear description of the variability of the measurements.

With intelligence quotients, for example, the mean is 100 and the *SD* is approximately 15. That is to say, an IQ one *SD* above the mean is 115. Armed with this knowledge alone, plus the general statistical rule illustrated in Figure A.4, we know that human intelligence tends to be distributed according to the figures in the following table:

IQ	Percentage of People
over 144	0.14
130–144	2.14
115–129	13.59
100–114	34.13
85–99	34.13
70–84	13.59
55–69	2.14
under 55	0.14

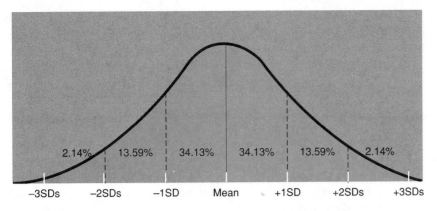

FIGURE A.4 **Using the *SD* to analyze data** In a normal curve of distribution, the standard deviation indicates how many measurements of scores will be found at various distances from the mean. As shown here, 34.13 percent of all measurements lie between the mean and 1 *SD* above the mean. Measurements that are between 1 *SD* and 2 *SDs* above the mean make up 13.59 percent of the total. Measurements between 2 *SDs* and 3 *SDs* above the mean make up 2.14 percent. The same percentages are found below the mean. Note that the figures do not quite add up to 100 percent. This is because 0.14 percent of measurements are found more than 3 *SDs* above the mean and another 0.14 percent are found more than 3 *SDs* below the mean. These various percentages hold for any normal distribution, although the size of the *SD* differs from one curve to another.

The *SD* is also used to compute what are called *standard scores,* or *z-scores,* which are often more meaningful than the raw scores made on a test. The z-score tells how many *SDs* a score is above or below the mean. It is obtained very simply by noting how many points a score is above or below the mean and then dividing by the *SD*. A z-score of 1 is one *SD* above the mean. A z-score of −1.5 is one-and-a-half *SDs* below the mean.

Percentiles

The meaning of *percentile* can best be explained by an example. A college man, a senior who wants to go on to graduate school, is asked to take the Graduate Record Examinations, which are nationally administered aptitude tests often used to screen applicants. He makes a score of 460 on the verbal test and 540 in mathematics. By themselves, these scores do not mean much either to him or to the faculty of the school he wants to attend. But records of other people's results on the test provide a means of comparing his scores with those of other college seniors. A score of 460 on the verbal test, the records show, lies on the 40th percentile for men. This means that 40 percent of all senior men who take the test make a lower score and 60 percent make a higher score. The 540 score in math lies on the 66th percentile for men. In other words, 66 percent of senior men make a lower score, and only 34 percent make higher scores. These percentile figures show the student and the school he hopes to attend how his ability compares with that of other prospective graduate students: He is well above average in mathematics ability (only a third of male college seniors make better scores) but below average in verbal aptitude.

Percentile ratings can be made for any kind of measurement, whether or not it falls into a normal pattern of distribution. A percentile rating of 99—or, to be more exact, 99.99—means that no one had a higher score. A percentile rating of 1—or, to be more exact, 0.01—is the lowest in the group.

Inferential Statistics: The Science of Making Generalizations

Descriptive statistics permits psychologists to summarize the findings of their studies and determine how one individual compares with the others. But psychologists need another tool to help them interpret and make generalizations from their studies. When psychologists study the behavior of a rat in a Skinner box, for example, they are not especially interested in how rapidly that particular animal demonstrates learning. Rather, their primary concern is to discover a general principle of behavior that says something about the learning processes of all rats—and, by implication, perhaps about the learning process in general. Psychologists studying the performance of a group of human subjects who memorize nonsense syllables—or who take part in an experiment on physical attractiveness—are not especially interested in those particular people. Their ultimate goal is to learn something about the behavior of people in general.

The mathematical tool they use is called *inferential statistics*—a set of techniques that enable them to make valid generalizations from their measurements of behavior.

Population and Sample

Inferential statistics is important because science is interested in what is called the *population,* or sometimes the *universe*—that is to say, all people or all events in a particular category. But we cannot study or measure the entire population. We cannot give an intelligence test, for example, to every human being on the face of the earth. Even if we could, we still would not have reached the entire population, because many people would have died and many new people would have been born while we were conducting our test. We must settle for a *sample,* a group of convenient size taken from the population as a whole.

The rules of inferential statistics hold that we can make valid generalizations only if the sample we use is *representative* of the population we want to study. If we are seeking some general conclusions about the intelligence of the American population, we cannot use a sample made up entirely of college students or a sample made up of high-school dropouts. If we want to learn about political attitudes, we cannot poll only Republicans or people who live in big cities or people who belong to one church or one social class. Our sample must be representative of all kinds of Americans.

One way to ensure a representative sample is to choose it entirely at *random*. If each member of the total population has an absolutely equal chance of being studied—and if our sample is large enough—then it is very likely that the sample will represent all segments of the population. For example, the experimenter who wants to study the emotional behavior of rats in a laboratory cannot just reach into a cage and pull out the first dozen animals that are closest at hand. The very fact that they are close at hand may mean that they are tamer than the others and have a different emotional temperament. To achieve a more valid sampling, the experimenter might take the first rat, reject the second, take the third, reject the fourth, and so on. An investigator interested in student attitudes toward marijuana on a particular campus might draw up an alphabetical list of all students, then interview every tenth person on the list.

In the Gallup election polls, the random sampling starts with a list of the approximately 200,000 election districts and precincts in the nation. From this master list, about 300 districts are chosen at random. Then a map of each of the 300 districts is drawn up. On the map, one house is chosen as a starting point—again at random. Beginning at that point and proceeding along a path drawn through the district, the pollsters collect interviews at each third residence or sometimes each fifth or twelfth residence, depending on the size of the sample they want (Gallup, 1972).

Choosing Valid Control Groups

The random technique of obtaining a representative sample is also standard procedure in selecting experimental and control groups. Ideally, every individual in the control group should be identical with a member of the experimental group. But this is of course impossible, because not even identical twins (who are too scarce anyway) are alike in every respect. To ensure as much similarity as possible between the experimental and control groups, subjects are usually assigned to one group or the other at random. Each individual who arrives at the laboratory has a 50–50 chance of being assigned to the experimental group and a 50–50 chance of being assigned to the control group.

Comparing Two Groups

For an example of how inferential statistics is used to compare two groups, such as an experimental group and a control group, let us imagine an experiment in which we try to determine whether physical health affects the learning ability of high school students. We select an experimental group of 16 representative, randomly chosen students who agree to take part in a rigorous health program. We arrange a supervised diet and exercise schedule, give them regular physical examinations, and promptly treat any illnesses or defects such as impaired vision or hearing. We also select a control group of 16 similar students who do not receive any special treatment. At the end of a year, we find that the experimental group has a grade-point mean of 89, with a standard deviation of 3. The control group has a grade-point mean of 85, with a standard deviation of 4. Question: Is this difference of four points between the mean of the experimental group and the mean of the control group just a statistical accident? Or does it really mean that good health produces better grades?

Although four points may sound like a lot, the question is not easy to answer. The reason is that *any* two samples of 16 people each, taken from the high-school population or any other population, are likely to have somewhat different means. Suppose we write the names of all the students in the high school (or in the city) on slips of paper and draw the slips from a hat. The grade-point mean for the first 16 names we draw may be 85, for the next 16 names 88, for the next 16 names 87. If we pull 20 different samples of 16 students each from the hat, we will find that the means vary from sample to sample, perhaps by as much as several points. So the question now becomes: Is the difference between the mean score of 89 for the experimental group and the mean score of 85 for the control group just an accidental result such as we might get by pulling samples from a hat? Or is it *statistically significant*—that is, does it indicate a real difference between our two groups?

Standard Error of the Mean

Helping answer the question is the fact that the means of randomly chosen samples, like raw measurements or scores themselves, tend to fall into a pattern of normal distribution. From our control group of 16 with a grade-point mean of 85 and a standard deviation of 4, we can figure out the distribution of all the means we would be likely to get if we continued to pick samples of 16 students at random, and we find that the curve looks like the one shown on the left in Figure A.5. We get the curve by using the formula (shown later) for the *standard error of the mean*. For the control group, the standard error of the mean turns out to be 1.0. For the experimental group, we get the curve shown at the right in Figure A.5. For this group the standard error of the mean turns out to be .75.

Having found the two curves, we can put them together as in Figure A.6, which shows a very high probability that there is a true difference

FIGURE A.5 How means are distributed These graphs show how the standard error of the mean of a sample is used to infer the true mean that would be found if the entire population could be measured. In the control group of high school students, at left, the mean is 85 and the standard error of the mean is 1.0. Thus we know that the chances are 68.26 percent that the true mean for the population lies between 84 and 86 (1 standard error above or below the mean of our sample), 95.44 percent that the true mean lies between 83 and 87 (2 standard errors above or below), and 99.72 percent that the true mean lies between 82 and 83 (3 standard errors above or below). In the experimental group, at right, the mean is 89 and the standard error of the mean is 0.75. Therefore the chances are 68.26 percent that the true mean of the experimental population would fall between 88.25 and 89.75; the chances are 95.44 percent that the mean would fall between 87.50 and 90.50; and they are 99.72 percent that the mean would fall between 86.75 and 91.25.

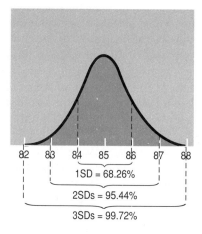

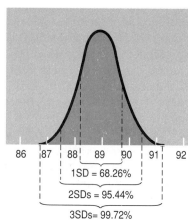

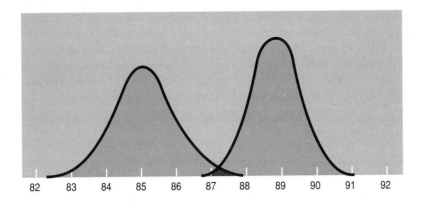

FIGURE A.6 Is the difference between the means significant? When we superimpose the curves shown in Figure A.5, we find that they have only the small dark area in common. This area represents the probability that the difference between the two means was due solely to chance. The probability that the difference is a real one is represented by the blue areas.

between the grades of students who receive special medical care and the grades of students who do not. The possibility that the difference we found is merely a matter of chance is represented by the small area that lies beneath the extreme right-hand end of the control curve and the extreme left-hand of the curve for the experimental group.

Probability and Significance

In actual statistical calculation the curves shown in Figures A.5 and A.6 need not be constructed. We can use the two means and the standard error of each mean to work out what is called *the standard error of the difference between two means*. We can then use this figure to work out the probability that the difference we found was due merely to chance. In the case of the hypothetical experiment we have been describing, the probability comes to less than .01

It is an arbitrary rule of thumb in experimental work that a difference is considered *statistically significant* only when the probability that it might have been obtained by chance is .05 (5 chances in 100, or 1 chance in 20) or less than .05.

In reports on experiments that can be analyzed with this kind of inferential statistics, the probability figure is always given. You will frequently find the note

$$p \le .05$$

This means that the difference would be found by chance only 5 times or less out of 100 and is therefore statistically significant. In virtually all the experiments cited in this book, p was .05 or less.

The Technique and Significance of Correlation

As was said in Chapter 1, *correlation* is a statistical tool used to examine two different measurements (such as the IQs of parents and the IQs of their children)—and to determine, from what would otherwise seem hopelessly jumbled numbers, what relationship if any exists between the two measurements.

Some correlations are *positive*. This means that the higher a person measures on scale X (for example, IQ) the higher that person is likely to measure on scale Y (for example, grades). Other correlations are *negative*. This means that a high score on scale X is likely to be accompanied by a low score on scale Y. For example, the frequency of premature births has been found to be less prematurity among upper-income families than lower-income families. Negative correlations also exist between aggressive behavior in children and social class and between test anxiety and grades made in schools.

Scatter Plots

A rough idea of the degree of correlation between two traits can be obtained by plotting each subject's score on scale X against the subject's score on scale Y. For each person, a dot is entered at a point corresponding to the scores on both scales, as shown in Figure A.7. The result is what is called a *scatter plot*. If the dots are scattered completely at random, we can see that the correlation is 0. If we should happen on one of those extremely rare cases where the dots form a perfectly straight line, running diagonally up or diagonally down, we know that we are dealing with a perfect correlation, either positive or negative. Most scatter diagrams fall somewhere in between. If a fairly narrow diagonal oval would enclose most of the dots, the correlation is rather high. If the oval must be fatter, the correlation is lower.

Correlation Coefficients

A more precise measure of the relationship between scores on the X-scale and scores on the Y-scale can be obtained—without the need for constructing a scatter plot—by using various statistical formulas for calculating a *correlation coefficient*. (The formulas are presented later.) A correlation coefficient can range from 0 (no correlation at all) to +1 (a perfect positive correlation) or −1 (a perfect negative correlation). But correlations of +1 or −1 are very rare. Even such physical traits as height and weight, which would seem to go together in almost perfect proportion, do not reach a correlation of +1. Some typical correlations that have been found in various studies are the following:

- Between IQ and college grades .50
- Between parents' IQ and child's IQ .49
- Between IQ and ability at pitch discrimination .00

FIGURE A.7   Scatter plots of correlations For each subject, a dot has been placed at the point indicating both score on scale X and score on scale Y (Ferguson, G. A. *Statistical analysis in psychology and education*. New York: McGraw-Hill, 1959. Copyright © 1959 by McGraw-Hill Book Co.)

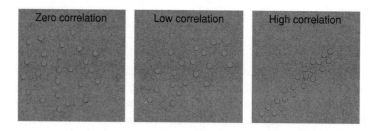

- Between boys' height at age 2 and height at age 18 .60
- Between boys' height at age 10 and height at age 18 .88

Correlation and Prediction

The correlation coefficients in the above table show that there is a considerable relationship between boys' height at age 2 and at age 18—and an even greater relationship between height at age 10 and at age 18. Knowing that these relationships exist, we can make some predictions. We can say that a boy who is taller than average at 2—or especially at 10—has a pretty good chance of also being taller than average at 18. Because of the .50 correlation coefficient between IQ and college grades, we can suggest that high-school seniors who make high scores on intelligence tests have a good chance of getting high grades in college, and that students with very low scores run the risk of failure.

It must always be kept in mind, however, that a coefficient of correlation is less accurate in making predictions than it sounds. Only when the correlation is very close to 1, as in the scatter plot that is shown in Figure A.7, does every subject tend to show a close relationship between score on scale X and score on scale Y. Even in a correlation of .75, which sounds high, there is a considerable amount of scatter, representing subjects who scored relatively low on scale X but relatively high on scale Y, or vice versa. Since most correlations found in psychological studies are lower than .75, we must be quite tentative in making predictions.

Correlation, Cause, and Effect

Just knowing the degree of relationship implied by a correlation coefficient is often of value to psychologists. For example, it has been found that there is a positive correlation between strict discipline on the part of parents and the amount of aggressive behavior displayed by children.

Again, however, it is important not to exaggerate the degree of relationship expressed by a correlation coefficient. We cannot say that strict discipline always—or even usually—is accompanied by aggressive behavior. Moreover we must avoid jumping to conclusions about cause and effect. Did the children become aggressive because the parents were strict, or were the parents strict because the children were aggressive? Is it possible that some third factor caused both the parents' strictness and the children's aggression? (For example, it may be that parents who are generally cold and rejecting of their children tend to be strict and that it is the coldness and rejection, rather than the strictness, that make the children aggressive.)

To avoid the danger of jumping to false conclusions on the basis of correlations, keep in mind that there is a very high correlation between the number of permanent teeth that have erupted through the school-child's gums and the child's raw scores for questions answered correctly on any kind of intelligence or aptitude test. But it would be foolish to conclude that more teeth make the child smarter or that better scores make more teeth appear. Increased maturity produces both the teeth and the higher scores.

The Mathematical Computations

The use of correlations and other descriptive and inferential statistics is not nearly so difficult as might be assumed. The mathematical knowledge required for these kinds of analysis is really not complicated at all. One need only be able to manipulate mathematical symbols, the most frequently used of which are explained in Figure A.8, and to apply the few basic formulas presented in Figure A.9.

The symbols and formulas are given at the start of this section on computations so that they can be found all in one place for future reference. They may seem rather difficult when shown all together in this fashion, but their application should be apparent from the examples that will be presented as we go along.

The kind of measurement that an investigator often wants to analyze is illustrated in Figure A.10. Here 17 students have taken a psychological test and have made scores ranging from 60 to 97. The raw scores are a jumble of figures, from which we now want to determine the mean, the standard deviation, and the standard error of the mean.

FIGURE A.8 Some useful mathematical symbols
These are the symbols used in the statistical formulas discussed in this appendix.

N	Number of subjects from whom a measurement or score has been obtained
X	The numerical value of an individual score
Y	If each subject is measured on two scales, the numerical value of an individual score on the second scale
Σ	The Greek capital letter sigma, standing for "sum of"
ΣX	The sum of all the individual scores on scale X
M	The mean, which is the sum of the scores divided by the number of subjects
x	A deviation score; that is, the difference between an individual score and the mean for the group of which the individual is a member
y	A deviation score on the second scale, or Y-scale
SD	The standard deviation of the scores
SE_M	The standard error of the mean; also called the standard deviation of the mean
D_M	The difference between two means; for example, the difference between the mean (M) of scale X and the mean of scale Y
SE_{DM}	The standard error of the difference between two means, used as a measure of whether the difference is significant
p	Probability, expressed in decimals ranging from .00 (no chance) through .50 (50-50 chance) to 1.00 (100 percent chance). A result is considered statistically significant when $p \leq .05$, meaning that there are only 5 chances in 100 (or fewer) that it was obtained by chance
r	Correlation coefficient obtained by the product-moment method
ρ	Correlation coefficient obtained by the rank-difference method
z	A standard score, expressed in numbers of SDs above or below the mean
C	Coefficient of contingency; type of correlation used to find relationships between events on a nominal scale

1. For determining the mean:

$$M = \frac{\Sigma X}{N}$$

2. For determining a deviation score:

$$x = X - M$$

3. For determining the standard deviation:

$$SD = \sqrt{\frac{\Sigma x^2}{N-1}}$$

4. For determining a z-score:

$$z = \frac{x}{SD}$$

5. For determining the standard error of the mean:

$$SE_M = \frac{SD}{\sqrt{N}}$$

6. For determining the difference between two means:

$$D_M = M_1 - M_2$$

7. For determining the standard error of the difference between two means:

$$SE_{DM} = \sqrt{(SE_{M1})^2 + (SE_{M2})^2}$$

8. For determining the critical ratio:

$$\text{Critical ratio} = \frac{D_M}{SE_{DM}}$$

9. For determining the coefficient of correlation by the product-moment method:

$$r = \frac{\Sigma xy}{(N-1)SD_x SD_y}$$

10. For determining the coefficient of correlation by the rank-difference method:

$$\rho = 1 - \frac{6(\Sigma D)^2}{N(N^2 - 1)}$$

FIGURE A.9   Some statistical formulas These are some of the formulas most frequently used in psychological statistics. Their use is explained in the text and in the following figures.

The Mean

The formula for computing the mean, as shown in Figure A.9, is

$$M = \frac{\Sigma X}{N}$$

These symbols denote, as Figure A.8 shows, that the mean equals the sum of the individual scores divided by the number of subjects.

FIGURE A.10   The raw material of statistical analysis: Test scores of 17 students These raw scores, obtained by students on a psychological test, are analyzed in the text.

1. 78	4. 74	7. 92	10. 74	13. 70	16. 82
2. 97	5. 80	8. 72	11. 85	14. 84	17. 78
3. 60	6. 77	9. 79	12. 68	15. 76	

Test scores (X)	Deviation scores (x)	Deviation scores squared (x^2)
78	0	0
97	+19	361
60	−18	324
74	− 4	16
80	+ 2	4
77	− 1	1
92	+14	196
72	− 6	36
79	+ 1	1
74	− 4	16
85	+ 7	49
68	−10	100
70	− 8	64
84	+ 6	36
76	− 2	4
82	+ 4	16
78	0	0
$\Sigma X = 1{,}326$		$\Sigma x^2 = 1{,}224$

$$M = \frac{\Sigma X}{N} = \frac{1{,}326}{17} = 78$$

$$SD = \sqrt{\frac{\Sigma X^2}{N-1}} = \sqrt{\frac{1{,}224}{16}} = \sqrt{76.5} = 8.75$$

FIGURE A.11   Computing the mean and SD of the 17 scores Using the formulas in Figure A.9, we first compute the mean score (M) for the 17 students, which comes out to 78. Once we have the mean, we can work out the standard deviation (SD). We start by obtaining the deviation scores ($x = \chi - M$), then squaring these deviation scores to get x^2.

The way the formula is applied is illustrated in Figure A.11. The sum of the individual scores, which are shown in column one, is 1,326. The number of subjects is 17. Thus the mean is 1,326 divided by 17, or 78.

The Standard Deviation

The method of finding the standard deviation is also illustrated in Figure A.11. The formula for the standard deviation is

$$SD = \sqrt{\frac{\Sigma x^2}{N-1}}$$

This means that we square each of the deviation scores, add up the total, and divide the total by the number of subjects minus 1. The square root of the figure thus obtained is the standard deviation.

The deviation scores shown in column two have been obtained by the formula $x = X - M$—that is, by subtracting the mean, which is 78, from each individual score. These figures in column two have then been squared to give the figures in column three. The sum of the x^2 figures is 1,224, and this figure divided by 16 (our $N = 1$) comes to 76.5. The standard deviation is the square root of 76.5 or 8.75.

The Standard Error of the Mean

Finding the standard error of the mean for our group is extremely simple. The formula is

$$SE_M = \frac{SD}{\sqrt{N}}$$

We have found that the SD of our sample is 8.75 and our $N = 17$. The formula yields

$$SE_M = \frac{8.75}{\sqrt{17}} = \frac{8.75}{4.12} = 2.12$$

Differences between Groups

For an example of how to apply the formulas for analyzing differences between groups, let us return to the hypothetical experiment mentioned earlier. We had the school grades, you will recall, of an experimental group of 16 students who took part in a health program; the mean was 89 and the standard deviation was 3. We also had the grades of a control group of 16 students; the mean for this group was 85 and the standard deviation was 4.

The difference between the two means is easily computed from the formula

$$D_M = M_1 - M_2$$

which means that the difference between the means is the mean of the first group minus the mean of the second group—in this case, 89 minus 85, or 4. To know whether this difference is statistically significant, however, we must calculate the standard error of the difference between the two means. To do so, as Figure A.9 shows, we must use the fairly complex formula

$$SE_{DM} = \sqrt{(SE_M)^2 + (SE_{M2})^2}$$

Our first step is to compute SE_{M1}, the standard error of the mean of our first or experimental group. We do so as shown earlier, this time with 3 as our standard deviation and 16 as our number of subjects.

$$SE_{M1} = \frac{SD}{\sqrt{N}} = \frac{3}{\sqrt{16}} = \frac{3}{4} = 0.75$$

We also compute SE_{M2}, the standard error of the mean of our second or control group, where the standard deviation is 4 and the number of subjects is 16.

$$SE_{M2} = \frac{SD}{\sqrt{N}} = \frac{4}{\sqrt{16}} = \frac{4}{4} = 1.00$$

The SE_{M1} is 0.75 and SE_{M2} is 1.00, and the standard error of the difference between the two means is computed as follows:

$$
\begin{aligned}
SE_{DM} &= \sqrt{(SE_{M1})^2 + (SE_{M2})^2} \\
&= \sqrt{(0.75)^2 + (1)^2} \\
&= \sqrt{.5625 + 1} \\
&= \sqrt{1.5625} \\
&= 1.25
\end{aligned}
$$

To complete our analysis of the difference between the two groups, we need one more statistical tool—the *critical ratio*. This is given by the formula

$$\text{Critical ratio} = \frac{D_M}{SE_{DM}}$$

In the case of our hypothetical experiment we have found that D_M is 4 and the SE_{DM} is 1.25. Thus,

$$\text{Critical ratio} = \frac{4}{1.25} = 3.2$$

This critical ratio gives us a measure of the probability that our difference was due merely to chance. For reasons that mathematically minded students may be able to work out for themselves but that need not concern the rest of us, the magic numbers for the critical ratio are 1.96 and 2.57. If the critical ratio is as high as 1.96, then $p \leq .05$, and the difference is considered statistically significant. If the critical ratio is as high as 2.57, then $p \leq .01$, and the difference is considered highly significant. The critical ratio we found for our two groups, 3.2, is well over 2.57; thus we can have some confidence that the difference was not the result of chance.

Correlation Coefficients

There are a number of ways of computing correlation coefficients, depending on the type of data that are being studied. The most frequently used is the *product-moment method,* which obtains a coefficient of correlation designated by the letter r for the relationship between two different measurements. The formula is

$$r = \frac{\Sigma xy}{(N-1)SD_x SD_y}$$

To use the formula we have to determine the amount by which each subject's score on scale X differs from the mean for all scores on scale X—in other words the value for x, the deviation score, which may be plus or minus. We must also determine the amount by which the subject's score on the second test, or scale Y, differs from the mean for all scores on scale Y—in other words, the value for y, which also may be plus or minus. We then multiply x by y for each subject and add the xy products for all the subjects in the sample. This gives us the top line, or numerator, of the formula. The bottom line, or denominator, is found by multiplying the number of subjects minus 1 ($N-1$) by the standard deviation of the scores on the X-scale (SD_x) and then multiplying the product by the standard deviation of the scores on the Y-scale (SD_y). An example is shown in Figure A.12.

In some cases it is convenient to use the *rank-difference method,* which produces a different coefficient of correlation called ρ (the Greek letter *rho*), which is similar to but not exactly the same as r. The formula is

$$\rho = 1 - \frac{6(\Sigma D^2)}{N(N^2 - 1)}$$

The method of applying the formula is demonstrated in Figure A.13. Note that the D in the formula refers to the difference between a subject's rank on scale X—that is, whether first, second, third, or so on among all the subjects—and the subject's rank on scale Y. ΣD^2 is found by squaring each subject's difference in rank and adding to get the total for all subjects.

| Subject | Test scores | | Deviation scores | | Product of deviation scores |
	X	Y	x	y	(xy)
1	60	81	−12	+ 1	− 12
2	80	92	+ 8	+12	+ 96
3	70	76	− 2	− 4	+ 8
4	65	69	− 7	−11	+ 77
5	75	88	+ 3	+ 8	+ 24
6	85	96	+13	+16	+208
7	60	64	−12	−16	+192
8	75	75	+ 3	− 5	− 15
9	70	77	− 2	− 3	+ 6
10	80	82	+ 8	+ 2	+ 16
					$\Sigma xy + 600$

$N = 10$

For scale X, $M = 72$, and $SD_x = 8.56$

For scale Y, $M = 80$, and $SD_y = 9.98$

Thus

$$r = \frac{\Sigma xy}{(N-1)SD_x SD_y} = \frac{600}{(10-1) \times 8.56 \times 9.98}$$

$$= \frac{600}{768.9} = .78$$

FIGURE A.12 A product-moment correlation Shown here are the calculations required to determine the product-moment correlation between the scores made by 10 subjects on two different tests, X and Y. First we compute the mean and SD for scales X and Y as was described in Figure A.11. Then we calculate each subject's deviation scores (x and y) for each scale and multiply them together to produce the product of the deviation scores (xy). Note that four subjects who scored above the mean on scale X also scored above the mean on scale Y (subjects 2, 5, 6, and 10). Four students who scored below the mean on scale X also scored below the mean on scale Y (subjects 3, 4, 7, and 9). Only two subjects (1 and 8) scored above the mean on one test and below the mean on the other. Thus multiplying the x deviations times the y deviations gives us eight positive products and two negative products. Σxy, the total of the positive products minus the negative products, comes to 600. The correlation coefficient works out to .78.

Contingency

One other frequently used type of correlation is known as the *coefficient of contingency*, symbolized by the letter C. This is used to find relationships between events that can be measured only on what is called a *nominal scale*— where all we can say about them is that they belong to certain groups. For example, we can set up a nominal scale on which all college students taking a humanities course are grouped in class 1, all taking engineering are grouped in class 2, and all taking a preparatory course for one of the professional schools such as law or medicine are grouped in class 3. We might set up another nominal scale on which we designate the students as males or females. If we then want to determine whether there is any relationship between a student's sex and the kind of college course the student is likely to take, we use the coefficient of contingency. Its meaning is roughly the same as that of any other coefficient of correlation.

Subject	Test scores		Rank		Difference in rank	Difference squared
	X	Y	X	Y	(D)	(D²)
1	60	81	9.5	5	−4.5	20.25
2	80	92	2.5	2	−0.5	0.25
3	70	76	6.5	7	+0.5	0.25
4	65	69	8.0	9	+1.0	1.00
5	75	88	4.5	3	−1.5	2.25
6	85	96	1.0	1	0.0	0.00
7	60	64	9.5	10	−0.5	0.25
8	75	75	4.5	8	−3.5	12.25
9	70	77	6.5	6	−0.5	0.25
10	80	82	2.5	4	+1.5	2.25

$$\Sigma D^2 = 39.0$$

FIGURE A.13 Computing a rank-difference correlation Here the same scores that were shown in Figure A.12 have been used to find the rank-difference correlation, which comes to .76—very close to the .78 found in Figure A.12 for the product-moment correlation. Note that here we disregard the individual scores on scale X and scale Y and use merely the rank of each score as compared with the others on the X scale. Subjects 2 and 10 are tied for second place on the scale. Their rank is therefore considered to be 2.5, halfway between second and third place.

$N = 10$

Thus

$$\rho = 1 - \frac{6(\Sigma D^2)}{N(N^2 - 1)} = 1 - \frac{6(39)}{10(10^2 - 1)}$$

$$= 1 - \frac{234}{990} = 1 - .24 = .76$$

SUMMARY REVIEW

Probability and Normal Distribution

1. *Psychological statistics* is the application of mathematical principles to the interpretation of results obtained in psychological studies.
2. The statistical method is of special importance as a *way of thinking*—reminding us that many events take place in accordance with the laws of probability and that remarkable coincidences can often be explained as occurring by mere chance.
3. Many events in nature, including many human traits, fall into the pattern of the *normal curve of distribution*. In this curve, most such events or traits cluster around the average measurement, and the number then gets smaller toward the lower and upper extremes.

Descriptive Statistics

4. *Descriptive statistics* provides a convenient method of summarizing scores and other psychological measurements. Important types of descriptive statistics are
   a) The *number of subjects,* or *N.*
   b) Measures of central tendency, including the arithmetic average, or *mean* (total of all scores divided by *N*), *median* (point separating the lower half of scores from the upper half), and *mode* (most frequent score in the group).
   c) Index of *variability,* including *range* (obtained by subtracting the lowest score from the highest) and *standard deviation,* symbolized by *SD.* In a normal distribution, 34.13 percent of the scores lie

between the mean and 1 *SD* above the mean, 13.59 percent between 1 *SD* and 2 *SD*s above the mean, and 2.14 percent between 2 *SD*s and 3 *SD*s above the mean, while 0.14 percent lie more than 3 *SD*s above the mean. The same pattern of distribution exists below the mean.

5. *Percentiles* are used to describe the position of an individual score in the total group. A measurement on the 75th percentile is larger than 75 percent of the measurements, or, to put it another way, 25 percent of measurements lie on or above the 75th percentile.

Inferential Statistics: The Science of Making Generalizations

6. *Inferential statistics* is made up of procedures that allow us to make generalizations from measurements. It enables us to infer conclusions about a *population* or *universe,* which is the total of all possible cases in a particular category, by measuring a relatively small *sample.* To permit valid generalization, however, the sample must be *representative.* One way to ensure that the sample is representative is to choose it entirely at *random,* with each member of the population having an equal chance of being selected.

7. A set of findings is considered *statistically significant* when the probability that the findings might have been obtained by chance is only 5 in 100 or less. The figure is expressed mathematically as $p \leq .05$.

The Technique and Significance of Correlation

8. *Correlations* between two measurements—such as scores on two different tests—range from 0 (no relationship) to +1 (perfect positive relationship) or −1 (perfect negative relationship).

The Mathematical Computations

9. The symbols and formulas for the statistical analyses are shown in Figures A.8 and A.9.

REFERENCES AND CREDITS

AACRAO (American Association of Collegiate Registrars and Admissions Officers) and the College Board. *Undergraduate admissions, 1980.* New York: College Entrance Examination Board, 1980.

Abramson, L. Y., Seligman, M. E. P., and Teasdale, J. D. Learned helplessness in humans. *Journal of abnormal psychology,* 1978, *87,* 49–74.

ACT. Are standardized admission tests biased against women? *ACT activity,* July 1987.

Adams, C. G., and Turner, B. F. Reported change in sexuality from young adulthood to old age. *Journal of sex research,* 1985, *21,* 126–41.

Adams, D., and Adams, G. R. Mount Saint Helen's ashfall: Evidence for a disaster stress reaction. *American psychologist,* 1984, *39,* 252–60.

Ader, J., Cohen, N., and Bovbjerg, P. Conditioned suppression of humoral immunity in the rat. *Journal of comparative and physiological psychology,* 1982, *96,* 517–21.

Adler, A. Characteristics of the first, second, and third child. *Children,* 1928, *3,* 14–52.

Agras, W. S., et al. Pharmacologic and cognitive behavioral treatment for bulimia nervosa. *American journal of psychiatry,* 1992, *149,* 82–87.

Ahles, T. A., Cassens, H. C., and Stalling, R. B. Private body consciousness, anxiety, and the perception of pain. *Journal of behavior therapy and experimental psychiatry,* 1987, *18,* 215–22.

Aiken, L. H., and Marx, M. M. Hospices: Perspectives on the public policy debate. *American psychologist,* 1982, *37,* 1271–79.

Ainsworth, M. D. S., and Bell, S. M. Attachment, exploration, and separation. *Child development,* 1970, *41,* 49–68.

Akerstedt, T., Torsvall, L., and Gillberg, M. Sleepiness and shift work: Field studies. *Sleep,* 1982, *5,* 95–106.

Akhtar, S., and Thomson, J. A., Jr. Overview: Narcissistic personality disorder. *American journal of psychiatry,* 1982, *139,* 12–20.

Alcohol, Drug Abuse, and Mental Health Administration. *Obsessive-compulsive disorder.* DHHS Publication No. (ADM) 89–1579, 1989.

Allison, P. D., and Furstenberg, F. F. How marital dissolution affects children: Variations by age and sex. *Developmental psychology,* 1989, *25,* 540–49.

Allport, G. W. *Pattern and growth in personality.* New York: Holt, 1961.

Alwin, D. F. Historical changes in parental orientation to children. In N. Mandell and S. Cahill, eds. *Sociological studies of child development,* vol. 3. Greenwich, CT: JAI Press, 1990, 65–86.

Amabile, T. M. *The social psychology of creativity.* New York: Springer-Verlag, 1983.

Amabile, T. M. Within you, without you: The social psychology of creativity, and beyond. Paper presented at Creativity Conference, Pitzer College, Claremont, CA, November 11–13, 1988.

Amabile, T. M. *Growing up creative.* New York: Crown, 1989.

Amato, P. R. Urban-rural differences in helping: Behavior in Australia and the United States. *Journal of social psychology,* 1981, *114,* 289–90.

Amato, P. R. Helping behavior in urban and rural environments: Field studies based on a taxonomic organization of helping episodes. *Journal of personality and social psychology,* 1983, *45,* 571–86.

Ambady, N., and Rosenthal, R. Half a minute: Predicting teacher evaluations from thin slices of nonverbal behavior and physical attractiveness. *Journal of personality and social psychology,* 1993, *64,* 431–41.

American Psychiatric Association. *Diagnostic and statistical manual of mental disorders,* 3rd ed. Washington, DC, 1980.

American Psychiatric Association. *Diagonstic and statistical manual of mental disorders,* 3rd ed. (revised). Washington, DC, 1987.

American Psychological Association. Ethical principles of psychologists. *American psychologist,* 1990, *45,* 390–95.

Anastasi, A. Coaching, test sophistication, and developed abilities. *American psychologist,* 1981, *36,* 1086–93.

Anastasi, A. *Psychological testing,* 5th ed. New York: Macmillan, 1982.

Anastasi, A. *Psychological testing,* 6th ed. New York: Macmillan, 1988.

Anderson, C. A. Temperature and aggression: Ubiquitous effects of heat on occurrence of human violence. *Psychological bulletin,* 1989, *106,* 74–96.

Anderson, C. A., and Anderson, D. C. Ambient temperature and violent crime: Tests of the linear and curvilinear hypotheses. *Journal of personality and social psychology,* 1984, *46,* 91–97.

Anderson, J. R., and Bower, G. H. *Human associative memory.* Washington, DC: Winston, 1973.

Andrew, R. J. The origins of facial expressions. *Scientific American,* 1965, *213,* 88–94.

Aneshensel, C. S., and Huba, G. J. Depression, alcohol use, and smoking over one year: A four-wave longitudinal case model. *Journal of abnormal psychology,* 1983, *92,* 134–50.

Antoni, M. H. Temporal relationship between life events and two illness measures: A cross-lagged panel analysis. *Journal of human stress,* 1985, *11,* 21–26.

Anthony, E. J., and Cohler, B. J., eds. *The invulnerable child,* New York: Guilford Press, 1988.

Archer, D., et al. Face-ism: Five studies of sex differences in facial prominence. *Journal of personality and social psychology,* 1983, *45,* 725–35.

Arendt, H. *Eichmann in Jerusalem: A report on the banality of evil.* New York: Viking, 1963.

Armstead, C. A., et al. Relationship of racial stressors to blood pressure responses and anger expression in black college students. *Health psychology,* 1989, *8,* 541–56.

Arnold, M. B. Emotion and personality, Vol. 1. New York: Columbia University Press, 1960.

Arnsten, A. F. T., and Goldman-Rakic, P. S. Alpha 2-adrenergic mechanisms in prefrontal cortex associated with cognitive decline in aged nonhuman primates. *Science*, 1985, *230*, 1273–76.

Aronson, E. *The social animal*, 4th ed. San Francisco: Freeman, 1984.

Aronson, E., and Linder, D. Gain and loss of esteem as determinants of interpersonal attractiveness. *Journal of experimental social psychology*, 1965, *1*, 156–71.

Asch, S. E. Studies of independence and submission to group pressure. I: A minority of one against a unanimous majority. *Psychological monographs*, 1956, *70*(No. 416), Fig. 2, p. 7.

Asch, S. E., and Zukier, H. Thinking about persons. *Journal of personality and social psychology*. 1984, *46*, 1230–40.

Astin, A. W. *Minorities in American higher education*. San Francisco: Jossey-Bass, 1982.

Atchley, R. C. Retirement as a social institution. *Annual review of sociology*, 1982, *8*, 263–87.

Atkinson, J. W. The mainsprings of achievement-oriented activity. In J. W. Atkinson and J. O. Raynor, eds. *Personality, motivation, and achievement*. Washington, DC: Winston, 1974.

Atkinson, J. W. Resistance and over-motivation in achievement-oriented activity. In G. Serban, ed. *Psychopathology of human adaptation. Proceedings of the Third International Symposium of the Kittay Scientific Foundation*. New York: Plenum, 1976.

Atkinson, J. W., and Raynor, J. O. *Personality, motivation, and achievement*. New York: Wiley, 1978.

Atkinson, K., MacWhinney, B., and Stoel, C. An experiment on recognition of babbling. In *Papers and reports on child language development*. Stanford, CA: Stanford University Press, 1970.

Attie, I., and Brooks-Gunn, J. Development of eating problems in adolescent girls: A longitudinal study. *Developmental psychology*, 1989, *25*, 70–79.

Averill, J. B. Stress as fact and artifact: An inquiry into the social origins and functions of some stress reactions. In C. D. Spielberger, I. G. Sarason, and J. Strelau, eds. *Stress and anxiety*. New York: Hemisphere, 1989.

Ayllon, T., and Azrin, N. H. *The token economy: A motivational system for therapy and rehabilitation*. New York: Appleton-Century-Crofts, 1965. © 1968. Adapted by permission of Prentice-Hall, Inc. Englewood Cliffs, N.J.

Ayoub, D. M., Greenough, W. T., and Juraska, J. M. Sex differences in dendritic structure in the preoptic area of the juvenile macaque monkey brain. *Science*, 1983, *219*, 197–98.

Azuma, H. Current trends in the study of behavioral development in Japan. *International journal of human development*, 1982, *5*, 163–69.

Babor, T. F., Types of alcoholics, I. *Archives of general psychiatry*, 1992, *49*, 599–608.

Bachman, J. G., and Schulenberg, J. E. How part-time work intensity relates to drug use, problem behavior, time use, and satisfaction among high school seniors: Are these consequences or merely correlates? *Developmental psychology*, 1993, *29*, 220–35.

Bachu, A. *Fertility of women: June, 1992*. U.S. Bureau of the Census. Current Population Reports, Series C-20, No. 470, 1993.

Backer, T. E., and Richardson, D. Building bridges: Psychologists and families of the mentally ill. *American psychologist*, 1989, *44*, 546–50.

Baddeley, A. *Working memory*. London: Oxford University Press, 1986.

Bailey, J. M., and Pillard, R. C. A genetic study of male sexual orientation. *Archives of general psychiatry*, 1991, *48*, 1089–96.

Bailey, J. M., Pillard, R. C., Neale, M. C., and Agyei, Y. Heritable factors influence sexual orientation in women. *Archives of General Psychiatry*, 1993, *50*, 217–23.

Ball, G. G. Vagotomy. *Science*, 1974, *184*, 484–85.

Baltes, P. B., Sowarka, D., and Kliegl, R. Cognitive training research on fluid intelligence in old age: What can older adults achieve by themselves? *Psychology and aging*, 1989, *4*, 217–21.

Bandura, A. *Aggression*. Englewood Cliffs, NJ: Prentice-Hall, 1973.

Bandura, A. Behavior theory and the models of man. *American psychologist*, 1974, *29*, 859–69.

Bandura, A. *Social learning theory*. Englewood Cliffs, NJ: Prentice-Hall, 1977.

Barber, J. D. *The presidential character*. Englewood Cliffs, NJ: Prentice-Hall, 1972.

Bard, M., and Sangrey, D. *The crime victim's book*, 2nd ed. New York: Basic Books, 1986.

Barfield, R. E., and Morgan, J. N. Trends in satisfaction with retirement. *The gerontologist*, 1978, *18*, 19–23.

Barlow, D. H., and Wolfe, B. E. Behavioral approaches to anxiety disorders: A report on the NIMH-SUNY Albany Research Conference. *Journal of consulting and clinical psychology*, 1981, *49*, 448–54.

Barnes, D. M. Silver Spring monkeys yield unexpected data on brain reorganization. *Journal of NIH research*, Spring 1990, *2*, 19–20.

Barnett, M. A., et al. Antecedents of empathy: Retrospective accounts of early socialization. *Personality and social psychology bulletin*, 1980, *6*, 361–65.

Barnett, R. C., et al., Job experiences over time, multiple roles and women's mental health: A longitudinal study. *Journal of personality and social psychology*, 1992, *62*, 634–44.

Baron, R. A., and Lawton, S. F. Environmental influences on aggression. *Psychonomic science*. 1972, *26*, 80–82.

Baron-Cohen, S., and Bolton, P. *Autism: The facts*. New York: Oxford University Press, 1993.

Barr, H. M., et al. Prenatal exposure to alcohol, caffeine, tobacco, and aspirin. *Developmental psychology*, 1990, *26*, 339–48.

Barron, F. *Creativity and personal freedom*. New York: Van Nostrand Reinhold, 1968.

Barron, F., and Harrington, C. L. Creativity, intelligence, and personality. *Annual review of psychology*, 1981, *32*, 439–76.

Barsalou, L. W. Ideals, central tendency, and frequency of instantiation as determinants of graded structure in categories. *Journal of experimental psychology: Learning, memory, and cognition*, 1985, *11*, 629–54.

Baruch, G., Barnett, R., and Rivers, C. *Lifeprints*. New York: McGraw-Hill, 1983.

Baskett, L. M. Ordinal position differences in children's family interactions. *Developmental psychology*, 1984, *20*, 1026–31.

Bauer, P. J. Memory of gender-consistent and gender-inconsistent event sequences by twenty-five-month old children. *Child development*, 1993, *64*, 285–97.

Baumeister, R. F. Choking under pressure: Self-consciousness and paradoxical effects of incentives on skillful performance. *Journal of personality and social psychology*, 1984, *46*, 610–20.

Baumrind, D. Research using intentional deception. *American psychologist*, 1985, *40*, 165–74.

Baumrind, D. The average expectable environment is not good enough: A response to Scarr. *Child development*, 1993, *64*, 1299–317.

Baxter, L. Caudate glucose metabolic rate changes with both drug and behavior therapy for obsessive-compulsive disorder. *Archives of General Psychiatry*, 1992, *49*, 681–89.

Bayley, N. Comparisons of mental and motor test scores for ages 1–15 months by sex, birth order, race, geographic location, and education of parents. *Child development,* 1965, *36,* 379–411.

Bayley, N. Development of mental abilities. In P. Mussen, ed. *Carmichael's manual of child development.* New York: Wiley, 1970.

Beardslee, W. R., et al. Children of parents with major affective disorder: A review. *American journal of psychiatry,* 1983, *140,* 825–44.

Beck, A. T. *Depression: Clinical, experimental, and theoretical aspects.* New York: Harper, 1982.

Beck, A. T., and **Emery, G.** *Anxiety disorders and phobias: A cognitive perspective.* New York: Basic Books, 1985.

Bell, A. P., and **Weinberg, M. S.** *Homosexualities.* New York: Simon and Schuster, 1978.

Bell, A. P., Weinberg, M. S., and **Hammersmith, S. E.** *Sexual preference.* Bloomington, IN: Indiana University Press, 1981.

Belsky, J. The determinants of parenting: A process model. *Child development,* 1984, *55,* 83–96.

Belsky, J., and **Pensky, E.** "Marital change across the transition to parenthood." *Marriage and family review,* 1988, *12,* 133–56.

Bem, D. J. *Beliefs, attitudes, and human affairs.* Belmont, CA: Brooks/Cole, 1970.

Bem, D. J. Self-perception theory. In L. Berkowitz, ed. *Advances in experimental social psychology,* Vol. 6. New York: Academic Press, 1972.

Benjamin, L. T., Jr. Defining aggression: An exercise for classroom discussion. *Teaching of psychology,* 1985, *12,* 40–42.

Berg, I. *Education and jobs.* New York: Praeger, 1970.

Berg, J. H. Development of friendship between roommates. *Journal of personality and social psychology.* 1984, *46,* 346–56.

Berger, K. S. *The developing person through the life span.* New York: Worth, 1983.

Berman, A. L., and **Jobes, D. A.** *Adolescent suicide: Assessment and intervention,* Washington, DC, American Psychological Association, March 1991.

Berry, D. S., and **McArthur, L. Z.** Perceiving character in faces: The impact of age-related craniofacial changes on social perception. *Psychological bulletin.* 1986, *100,* 3–18.

Berscheid, E., and **Walster, E.** Physical attractiveness. In L. Berkowitz, ed. *Advances in experimental social psychology,* vol. 7. New York: Academic Press, 1974.

Bertonici, J., et al. An investigation of young infants' perceptual representations of speech sounds. *Journal of experimental psychology: General.* 1988, *117,* 21–23.

Bettelheim, B. *Freud's Vienna and other essays.* New York: Random House, 1990.

Bhatt, R. S., et al. Conceptual behavior in pigeons: Categorization of both familiar and novel examples from four classes of natural and artificial stimuli. *Journal of experimental psychology: Animal behavior processes,* 1988, *14,* 219–34.

Biller, H. Father absence, divorce, and personality development. In M. Lamb, ed. *The role of the father in child development,* 2nd ed. New York: Wiley, 1981.

Birtchnell, J. Women whose mothers died in childhood: An outcome study. *Psychological medicine,* 1980, *136,* 317–25.

Bjork, R. A. Theoretical implications of directed forgetting. In A. W. Melton and E. Martin, eds. *Coding processes in human memory.* Washington, DC: Winston, 1972.

Bjorkland, A., and **Steveni, A.** Intracerebral neural implants: Neuronal replacement and reconstruction of damaged circuits. *Annual review of neuroscience,* 1984, *7,* 279–308.

Björntorp, P. Disturbances in the regulation of food intake. *Advances in psychosomatic medicine,* 1972, *7,* 116–47.

Black, J. B., and **Bern, H.** Causal coherence and memory for events in narratives. *Journal of verbal learning and verbal behavior,* 1981, *20,* 267–75.

Black, J. B., Turner, T. J., and **Bower, G. H.** Point of view in narrative comprehension, memory, and production. *Journal of verbal learning and verbal behavior,* 1979, *18,* 187–98.

Blass, E. M., and **Hall, W. G.** Drinking termination. *Psychological review,* 1976, *83,* 856–74.

Block, J. *Lives through time.* Berkeley, CA: Bancroft Books, 1971.

Block, J. Some enduring and consequential structures of personality. In A. I. Rabin, ed. *Further explorations in personality.* New York: Wiley, 1981.

Block, J., and **Robins, R. W.** A longitudinal study of consistency and change in self-esteem from early adolescence to early adulthood. *Child development,* 1993, *64,* 909–23.

Block, N. J., and **Dworkin, G.,** eds. *The IQ controversy.* New York: Pantheon, 1976.

Bloom, B. *Planned short-term psychotherapy,* Needham Heights, MA, Allyn and Bacon, 1991.

Bloom, D. E., and **Trussell, J.** *What are the determinants of delayed child-bearing on voluntary childlessness in the United States?* National Bureau of Economic Research, working paper no. 1140, 1983.

Bloom, F. E., and **Lazerson, A.** *Brain, mind, and behavior,* 2nd ed. New York: Freeman, 1988.

Bloom, L. M., Lazerson, A., and **Hofstadter, L.** *Brain, mind, and behavior.* New York: Freeman, 1985.

Bloom, W., and **Fawcett, D. W.** *A textbook of histology,* 9th ed. Philadelphia: Saunders, 1968.

Blumstein, P., and **Schwartz, P.** *American couples.* New York: William Morrow, 1983.

Bogen, J. Drawings by a patient. *Bulletin of the Los Angeles Neurological Society,* 1969, *34,* 73–105.

Boice, R. Increasing the writing activity of "blocked" academicians. *Behavioral research and therapy,* 1982, *20,* 197–207.

Bolles, R. C. Reinforcement, expectancy, and learning. *Psychological review,* 1972, *79,* 394–409.

Bond, E. A. *Tenth-grade abilities and achievements.* New York: Columbia University Teachers College, 1940.

Bonvillian, J. D., Orlansky, M. D., and **Novack, L. L.** Early sign language acquisition and its relation to cognitive and motor development. In J. G. Kyle and B. Woll. *Language in sign: An international perspective on sign language.* London: Croom Helm, 1983.

Boring, E. G. Size constancy in a picture. *American journal of psychology,* 1964, *77,* 494–98.

Bornstein, M. H. Colour-name versus shape-name learning in young children. *Journal of child language,* 1985, *12,* 387–93.

Bornstein, R., and **Smircina, M. T.** The status of the empirical support for the hypothesis of increased variability in aging populations. *The gerontologist,* 1982, *22,* 24–243.

Bower, G. H. Organizational factors in memory. *Cognitive psychology,* 1970, *1,* 18–46.

Bower, G. H. Mental imagery and associative learning. In L. Gregg, ed. *Cognition in learning and memory.* New York: Wiley, 1972.

Bower, G. H. Improving memory. *Human nature,* 1978, *1,* 64–72.

Bower, G. H., and **Clark, M. C.** Narrative stories as mediators for serial learning. *Psychonomic science,* 1969, *14,* 181–82.

Bower, G. H., et al. Hierarchical retrieval schemes in recall of categorized word lists. *Journal of verbal learning and verbal behavior,* 1969, *8,* 323–43.

Bowerman, M. Learning the structure of causative verbs. *Papers and reports on child language development,* Stanford University, 1974, *8,* 142–78.

Boyd, J. H. The increasing rate of suicide by firearms. *New England journal of medicine,* 1983, *308,* 872–74.

Bradley, R. H., et al. Home environment and cognitive development in the first three years of life. *Developmental psychology,* 1989, *25,* 217–35.

Brehm, S. *Intimate relationships.* New York: Random House, 1985.

Breznitz, S. *The denial of stress.* Independence, MO: International University Press, 1983.

Briggs, S. R. Assessing the five-factor model of personality description. *Journal of personality,* 1992, *60,* 253–93.

Brock, D., et al. Methodological issues in a survey of the last days of life. In R. B. Wallace and R. F. Woolson, eds. *The epidemiologic study of the elderly.* New York: Oxford University Press, 1991.

Broen, P. The verbal environment of the language-learning child. *Monographs of the American Speech and Hearing Association,* 1972, p. 17.

Brooks-Gunn, J. Pubertal processes. In V. P. Van Hesselt and M. Hersen, eds. *Handbook of adolescent psychology.* Elmsford, NY: Pergamon, 1987.

Bross, I. D. J. Language in cancer research. In G. P. Murphy, D. Pressman, and E. S. Mirand, eds. *Perspectives in cancer research and treatment.* New York: Liss, 1973.

Brotman, H. B. Supplement to chartbook on aging in America. White House Conference on Aging, 1981.

Brown, Jonathon D. Staying fit and staying well. *Journal of personality and social psychology,* 1991, *60,* 555–561.

Brown, P. L., and **Jenkins, H. M.** Auto-shaping of the pigeon's key peck. *Journal of the experimental analysis of behavior,* 1968, *11,* 1–8.

Brown, R. *A first language.* Cambridge: Harvard University Press, 1973.

Brown, R. *Social psychology,* 2d ed. New York: Free Press, 1986.

Brown, R., and **Kulik, J.** Flashbulb memories. *Cognition,* 1977, *5,* 73–99.

Brown, R., and **Kulik, J.** Flashbulb memories. In U. Neisser, ed. *Memory observed.* San Francisco: Freeman, 1982.

Brown, S. A., et al. Severity of psychosocial stress and outcome of alcoholism treatment. *Journal of abnormal psychology,* 1990, *99,* 344–48.

Brown, V. B., et al. The dual crisis: Mental illness and substance abuse. *American psychologist,* 1989, *44,* 565–69.

Bruck, M., and **Ceci, S. J.** Suggestibility of the child witness: A historical review and synthesis. *Psychological bulletin.* 1993, *113,* 403–39.

Bruner, J. S., Goodnow, J. J., and **Austin, G. A.** *A study of thinking.* New York: Wiley, 1956.

Bryer, J. B., et al. Childhood sexual and physical abuse as factors in adult psychiatric illness. *American journal of psychiatry,* 1987, *144,* 1426–30.

Bucher, K. D., et al. The transmission of manic depressive illness. II: Segregation analysis of the three sets of family data. *Journal of psychiatric research,* 1981, *16,* 65–78.

Budoff, P. W. Straight talk about menopause. *World Book health and medical annual.* Chicago: World Book, 1994.

Bugelski, B. R., and **Alampay, D. A.** The role of frequency in developing perceptual sets. *Canadian journal of psychology,* 1961, *15,* 205–11.

Bullock, M., and **Lutkenhaus, P.** The development of volitional behavior in the toddler years. *Child development,* 1988, *59,* 664–74.

Bumpass, L. Recent trends in marital disruption. *Demography,* February 1989, *26,* 37–52.

Bumpass, L. L., and **Sweet, J. A.** National estimates of cohabitation. *Journal of demography,* 1989, *26,* 615–26.

Burchinal, M., Lee, M., and **Ramey, C.** Type of day care and preschool intellectual development in disadvantaged children. *Child development,* 1989, *60,* 128–37.

Burke, D. M., and **Harrold, R. M.** Aging and semantic processes. In L. L. Light and D. M. Burke, eds., *Language, memory and aging.* New York: Cambridge University Press, 1988.

Buss, A. H., and **Plomin, R.** *Temperament: Early developing personality traits.* Hillsdale, NJ: Erlbaum, 1984.

Buss, D. M. Love acts: The evolutionary biology of love. In R. J. Sternberg and M. L. Barnes, eds. *The psychology of love.* New Haven, CT: Yale University Press, 1988.

Buss, D. M., Larsen, R. J., Westen, D., Semmelroth, J. Sex differences in jealousy: Evolution, physiology, and psychology. *Psychological science,* 1992, *3,* 251–55.

Butler, J. M., and **Haigh, G. V.** Changes in the relation between self-concepts and ideal concepts consequent upon client-centered counseling. In C. R. Rogers and R. F. Dymond, eds. *Psychotherapy and personality change.* Chicago: University of Chicago Press, 1954.

Butler, R. N., and **Lewis, M. I.** *Aging and mental health.* St. Louis: Mosby, 1977.

Butterfield, F. University exams exalt or banish 3 million in China. *New York Times,* July 19, 1980, p. 3.

Cacioppo, J. T., et al. Specific forms of facial EMG response index emotions during an interview: From Darwin to the continuous flow hypothesis of affect-laden information processing. *Journal of personality and social psychology,* 1988, *54,* 592–604.

Cairns, R. B., et al. Growth and aggression. *Developmental psychology,* 1989, *25,* 320–30.

Calderone, M. S. Fetal erection and its message to us. *SIECUS Report,* May–July 1983, 9–10.

Calne, D. B. *The brain.* Publication no. 81-1813, National Institutes of Health, Rockville, MD, 1981.

Calvert, S. L., and **Huston, A. C.** Television and children's gender schemata. In L. Liben and M. Signorella, eds. *New directions in child development: Vol. 38. Children's gender schemata: Origins and implications.* San Francisco: Jossey-Bass, 1987.

Campbell, B. A., and **Church, R. M.,** eds. *Punishment and aversive behavior.* New York: Appleton-Century-Crofts, 1969.

Campbell, D. Ethnocentrism and other altruistic motives. In D. Levine, ed. *Nebraska symposium on motivation, 1965.* Lincoln: University of Nebraska Press, 1965.

Campos, J. J., et al. Socio-emotional Development. In M. M. Haith and J. J. Campos, eds., *Infant Development,* Vol. 2. In P. H. Mussen, ed., *Handbook of Child Psychology,* 4th ed. New York: Wiley, 1983, pp. 783–915.

Carew, T. J., Hawkins, R. D., and **Kandel, E. R.** Differential classical conditioning of a defensive withdrawal reflex in *Aplysia californica. Science,* January 28, 1983, *219,* 397–400.

Cargan, L., and **Melko, M.** *Singles: Myths and realities.* Beverly Hills, CA: Sage, 1982.

Carnegie Council on Adolescent Development. *Turning points,* Washington, DC, 1989.

Carroll, J. B., and **Horn, J. L.** On the scientific basis of ability testing. *American psychologist,* 1981, *36,* 1112–19.

Carroll, J. B., et al. A specific laboratory test for the diagnosis of melancholia. Standardization, validation, and clinical utility. *Archives of general psychiatry,* 1981, *38,* 15–22.

Case, R. B., et al. Type A behavior and survival after acute myocardial infarction. *New England journal of medicine,* 1985, *312,* 737–41.

Caspi, A. Personality in the life course. *Journal of personality and social psychology,* 1987, *53,* 1203–13.

Caspi, A., and **Herbener, E. S.** Continuity and change: Assortive marriage and the consistency of personality in adulthood. 1989, unpublished manuscript, Harvard University.

Castro-Martin, T., and **Bumpass, L. L.** Recent trends in marital disruption. *Journal of demography,* 1989, *26,* 37–52.

Cattell, R. B. *The scientific study of personality.* Baltimore: Penguin, 1965.

Cattell, R. B. *Abilities: Their structure, growth, and action.* Boston: Houghton Mifflin, 1971.

Cattell, R. B. Personality pinned down. *Psychology today,* July 1973, 40–46.

Ceci, S. J. How much does schooling influence general intelligence and its cognitive components? A reassessment of the evidence. *Developmental psychology,* 1991, *27,* 703–22.

Centers for Disease Control. Health status of Vietnam veterans. *Journal of the American Medical Association,* 1988, *259,* 2701–09.

Cerella, J. Information processing rates in the elderly. *Psychological bulletin,* 1985, *98,* 67–83.

Cheng, P. W. Pragmatic reasoning schemas. *Cognitive psychology,* 1985, *17,* 391–416.

Cherlin, A. J., et al. Longitudinal studies of effects of divorce on children in Great Britain and the United States. *Science,* 1991, *252,* 1386–89.

Chipman, S. F., Krantz, D. H., and **Silver, R.** Mathematics anxiety and science careers among able college women. *Psychological science,* 1992, *3,* 292–95.

Chomsky, N. *Aspects of the theory of syntax.* Cambridge: MIT Press, 1965.

Christiaansen, R. E. Prose memory: Forgetting rates for memory codes. *Journal of experimental psychology: Human learning and memory,* 1980, *6,* 611–19.

Christie, K. A., Burke, J. D., Regier, D. A., Rae, D. S., Boyd, J. H., and **Locke, B. Z.** Epidemiologic evidence for early onset of mental disorders and higher risk of drug abuse in young adults. *American journal of psychiatry,* 1988, *145,* 971–75.

Chugani, H. T., and **Phelps, M. E.** Maturational changes in cerebral function in infants determined by [18]FDG positron emission tomography. *Science,* February 21, 1986, *231,* 840–42.

Clark, D. B., and **Agras, W. S.** The assessment and treatment of performance anxiety in musicians. *American journal of psychiatry,* 1991, *148,* 598–605.

Clark, D. C., and **Zeldow, P. B.** Vicissitudes of depressed mood during four years of medical school. *Journal of the American Medical Association,* November 1988, *260,* 2521–28.

Clark, H. H., and **Clark, E. V.** *Psychology and language.* New York: Harcourt, 1977.

Clark, L. A., and **Watson, D.** Mood and the mundane: Relations between daily life events and self-reported mood. *Journal of personality and social psychology,* 1988, *54,* 296–308.

Clark, W. B., and **Midanik, L.** *Report of the 1979 national survey.* National Technical Information Service, Port Royal, VA, PB No. 82-156514, 1982.

Clausen, J. A. The social meaning of differential physical and sexual maturation. In S. E. Dragastin and G. H. Elder, Jr., eds. *Life cycle.* New York: Wiley, 1975.

Clifford, R. E., and **Kolodny, R.** Sex therapy for couples. In B. B. Wolman and G. Stricker, eds. *Handbook of family and marital therapy.* New York: Plenum, 1983.

Clyman, R., Friedman, M., and **Weiss, E.** As they grow—0 to 13 years: Bulletin on research. *Parents,* November 1993, *68,* 192–93.

Coe, C. L. Psychosocial factors in immunity in nonhuman primates: A review. *Psychosomatic medicine,* 1993, *55,* 298–308.

Cohen, A. R. Some implications of self-esteem for social influence. In C. I. Hovland and I. L. Janis, eds. *Personality and persuasibility.* New Haven: Yale University Press, 1959.

Coile, D. C., and **Miller, N. E.** How radical animal activists try to mislead humane people. *American psychologist,* 1984, *39,* 700–01.

Cole, M. A. Sex and marital status differences in death anxiety. *Omega,* 1978–1979, *9,* 139–47.

Collins, A. M., and **Quillian, M. R.** How to make a language user. In E. Tulving and W. Donaldson, eds. *Organization of memory.* New York: Academic Press, 1972.

Conley, J. J. Longitudinal consistency of adult personality: Self-reported psychological characteristics across 45 years. *Journal of personality and social psychology,* 1984, *47,* 1325–33.

Conway, M. A., Cohen, G., and **Stanhope, N.** On the very long-term retention of knowledge acquired through formal education: Twelve years of cognitive psychology. *Journal of experimental psychology: General.* 1991, *120,* 395–409.

Cooper, H. Pygmalion grows up: A model for teacher expectation communication and performance influence. *Review of educational research,* 1979, *49,* 389–410.

Cooper, J. Deception and role-playing. *American psychologist,* 1976, *31,* 605–10.

Cooper, M., Zanna, M. P., and **Taves, P. A.** Arousal as a necessary condition for attitude change following induced compliance. *Journal of personality and social psychology,* 1978, *36,* 1101–06.

Coren, S., Porac, C., and **Ward, L. M.** *Sensation and perception,* 2nd ed. New York: Academic Press, 1984.

Costello, C. G. Fears and phobias in women: A community study. *Journal of abnormal psychology,* 1982, *91,* 280–86.

Couric, E. Women in the law: Awaiting their turn. *The national law journal,* December 11, 1989, S-2.

Cousins, N. *Head first: The biology of hope.* New York: Dutton, 1989.

Cowan, C. P., and **Cowan, P.** Who does what when partners become parents: Implications for men, women, and marriage. *Marriage and family review,* 1988, *12,* 3–4.

Cowan, E. Help is where you find it. *American psychologist,* 1982, *37,* 385–95.

Cowan, N. On short and long auditory stores. *Psychological bulletin,* 1984, *96,* 341–70.

Coyle, J. T., Price, D. L., and **DeLong, M. H.** Alzheimer's disease: A disorder of central cholinergic innervation. *Science,* 1983, *219,* 1184–89.

Coyle, S. L., and **Thurgood, D. H.** *Summary report 1989: Doctorate recipients from U.S. universities.* Washington, DC: National Academy Press, 1989.

Craig, K. D., and **Patrick, C. J.** Facial expression during induced pain. *Journal of personality and social psychology,* 1985, *48,* 1080–91.

Craik, F. I. M., and **Tulving, E.** Depth of processing and the retention of words in episodic memory. *Journal of experimental psychology: General,* 1975, *104,* 268–94.

Crandall, J. E. Adler's concept of social-interest: Theory, measurement, and implications for adjustment. *Journal of personality and social psychology,* 1980, *39,* 481–98.

Crano, W. D., and **Mellon, P. M.** Causal influence of teachers' expectations on children's academic performance. *Journal of educational psychology,* 1978, *70,* 39–49.

Craske, M., Brown, T. A., and **Barlow, D. H.** Behavioral treatment of panic disorder: A two-year follow-up. *Behavior therapy,* 1991, *22,* 289–304.

Crenoch, J. M., and Porter, R. H. Recognition of maternal maxillary odor by infants. *Child development,* 1985, *56,* 1593–98.

Crits-Christoph, A. The efficacy of brief dynamic psychotherapy. *American journal of psychiatry,* 1992, *149,* 151–58.

Crockenburg, S. B. Creativity tests: A boon or boodoogle for education? *Review of educational research,* 1972, *42,* 27–45.

Cronbach, L. J. *Essentials of psychological testing.* New York: Harper, 1949.

Crook, T. H., and West, R. L. Name recall performance across the adult life-span. *British journal of psychology,* 1990, *81,* 335–40.

Crooks, R., and Baur, K. *Our sexuality,* 4th ed. Redwood City, CA: Benjamin/Cummings, 1990.

Crosby, E., Humphrey, T., and Lauer, E. W. *Comparative anatomy of the nervous system.* New York: Macmillan, 1962. Based on the data in Figs. 337 and 339.

Cross-National Collaborative Group. The changing rate of major depression. *Journal of the American Medical Association,* 1992, *268,* 3098–105.

Csikszentmihalyi, M. Toward a psychology of optimal experience. In L. Wheeler, ed. *Review of personality and social psychology,* Vol. 3. Beverly Hills, CA: Sage, 1982.

Csikszentmihalyi, M. *The domain of creativity.* Paper presented at Creativity Conference, Pitzer College, Claremont, CA, November 11–13, 1988.

Csikszentmihalyi, M. *Flow: The psychology of optimal experience.* New York: Harper, 1990.

Cummings, E. M., Iannotti, R. J., and Zahn-Waxler, C. Aggression between peers in early childhood. *Child development,* 1989, *60,* 887–95.

Curtis, R. C., and Miller, K. Believing another likes or dislikes you: Behaviors making the beliefs come true. *Journal of personality and social psychology,* 1986, *51,* 284–90.

Cytryn, L., McKnew, D. H., and Bunney, W. E. Diagnosis of depression in children: A reassessment. *American journal of psychiatry,* 1980, *137,* 22–25.

Cytrynbaum, S., et al. Midlife development: A personality and social systems perspective. In L. Poon, ed. *Aging in the 1980s: Psychological issues.* Washington, DC: American Psychological Association, 1980.

Dabbs, J. M., Jr., and Leventhal, H. Effects of varying the recommendations in a fear-arousing communication. *Journal of personality and social psychology,* 1966, *4,* 525–31.

Damasio, A. R. Category-related recognition deficits as a clue to the neural substrates of knowledge. *Trends in neuroscience,* 1990, 1395–98.

Damasio, A. R., and Damasio, H. Brain and language. *Scientific American,* September 1992, 89–95.

Damasio, A. R., Tranel, D., and Damasio, H. C. Individuals with sociopathic behavior caused by frontal damage fail to respond automatically to social stimuli. *Behavioral brain research*(?), 1990, *14,* 81–94.

Darley, J. M., and Fazio, R. H. Expectancy confirmation processes arising in the social interaction sequence. *American psychologist,* 1980, *35,* 867–81.

Davidson, J., et al. *Patterns of sexual desire.* New York: Guilford Press, 1988.

Davidson, R. J., and Fox, N. A. Frontal brain asymmetry predicts infants' response to maternal separation. *Journal of abnormal psychology,* 1989, *98,* 127–31.

Davidson, R. J., and Tomarken, A. J. Laterality and emotion: An electrophysiological approach. In F. Boller and J. Graffman, eds. *Handbook of neuropsychology.* New York: Elsevier Science, 1989.

Davis, et al. Biological psychology's relationships to psychology and neuroscience. *American psychologist,* 1988, *5,* 359–71.

deCharms, R., and Muir, M. S. Motivation. *Annual review of psychology,* 1978, *29,* 91–113.

deCharms, R., et al. Behavioral correlates of directly measured achievement motivation. In D. C. McClelland, ed. *Studies in motivation.* New York: Appleton-Century-Crofts, 1955.

DeFries, J. C., Plomin, R., and LaBuda, M. C. Genetic stability of cognitive development from childhood to adulthood. *Developmental psychology,* 1987, *23,* 4–12.

Dekker, E., Pelser, H. E., and Groen, J. Conditioning as a cause of asthmatic attacks. *Journal of psychiatric research,* 1957, *2,* 97–108.

DeLacoste-Utamsing, C., and Holloway, R. Sexual dimorphism in the human corpus callosum. *Science,* 1982, *216,* 1431–32.

DeLongis, A., Folkman, S., and Lazarus, R. The impact of daily stress on health and mood: Psychological and social resources as mediators. *Journal of personality and social psychology,* 1988, *54,* 486–95.

DeMaris, A., and Leslie, G. R. Cohabitation with the future spouse: Its influence upon marital satisfaction and communication. *Journal of marriage and the family,* 1984, *46,* 77–84.

Demitrack, M. A. Plasma and cerebrospinal fluid measures of arginine vasopressin secretion in patients with bulimia nervosa and in healthy subjects. *Journal of clinical endocrinology and metabolism,* 1992, *74,* 1277–83.

Department of Health and Human Services, *National survey results on drug use from monitoring the future study, 1975–1992.* NIH Publication No. 93-3497, 1993.

Deutsch, J. A., Puerto, A., and Wang, M. L. The stomach signals satiety. *Science,* 1978, *201,* 165–67.

De Valois, R. L., and Jacobs, G. H. Primate color vision. *Science,* 1968, *162,* 533–40.

de Villiers, J. G., and de Villiers, P. A. *Language acquisition.* Cambridge, MA: Harvard University Press, 1978.

Diamond, A. Frontal lobe involvement in cognitive changes during the first year of life. In K. Gibson and A. Petersen, eds. *Brain maturation and cognitive development.* Hawthorne, NY: Aldine de Greuter, 1991.

Diaz, R. M. Bilingual cognitive development: Addressing three gaps in current research. *Child development,* 1985, *56,* 1376–88.

Diener, E., Sandvik, E., and Pavot, W. Happiness is the frequency not the intensity of positive versus negative affect. In F. Strack, M. Argyle, and N. Schwarz, eds. *The social psychology of subjective well being.* New York: Pergamon, 1990.

Digman, J. M., and Inouye, J. Further specification of the five robust factors of personality. *Journal of personality and social psychology,* 1986, *50,* 116–23.

Dion, K. K., and Berscheid, E. *Physical attractiveness and social perception of peers in preschool children.* Unpublished research report, 1972.

Dion, K. K., Berscheid, E., and Walster E. What is beautiful is good. *Journal of personality and social psychology,* 1972, *24,* 285–90.

Dion, K. L., and Dion, K. K. Romantic love: Individual and cultural perspectives. In R. J. Sternberg and M. L. Barnes, eds. *The psychology of love.* New Haven: Yale University Press, 1988.

Dobson, K. S., ed. *Handbook of cognitive-behavioral therapies.* New York: Guilford, 1988.

Dohrenwend, B., et al. Report on stress and life events. In G. R. Elliott and C. Eisdoefer, eds. *Stress and human health: Analysis and implications of research.* New York: Springer, 1982.

Dohrenwend, B., et al. Life stress and psychopathology: Progress on research begun with Barbara Snell Dohrenwend. *American journal of community psychology,* 1987, *15,* 677–715.

Dollard, J., and **Miller, N. E.** *Personality and psychotherapy.* New York: McGraw-Hill, 1950.

Domjan, M., and **Burkhard, B.** *The principles of learning and behavior,* 2nd ed. Monterey, CA: Brooks/Cole, 1986.

Donnelly, C. M., and **McDaniel, M. A.** Use of analogy in learning scientific concepts. *Journal of experimental psychology: Learning, memory, and cognition.* 1993, *19*, 975–87.

Donnerstein, E., Linz, D., and **Penrod, S.** *The question of pornography: Research findings and implications.* New York: Free Press, 1987.

Doyle, K. O. Theory and practice of ability testing in ancient Greece. *Journal of the history of the behavioral sciences,* 1974, *10*, 202–12.

Dreskin, W., and **Dreskin, W.** *The day care decision: What's best for you and your child.* New York: M. Evans, 1983.

Dreyer, P. Sexuality during adolescence. In B. Wolman, ed. *Handbook of developmental psychology.* Englewood Cliffs, NJ: Prentice-Hall, 1982.

Dubow, E. F., and **Tisak, J.** The relation between stressful life events and adjustment in elementary school children: The role of social support and social problem-solving skills. *Child development,* 1989, *60*, 1412–23.

Dubreuil, D. L., Endler, N. S., and **Spanos, N. P.** Distortion and redefinition in the reduction of low and high intensity experimentally induced pain. *Imagination, cognition, and personality,* 1987–88, *7*, 155–64.

Duncan, O. D., Featherman, D. L., and **Duncan, B.** *Socioeconomic background and achievement.* New York: Seminar Press, 1972.

Duncker, K. On problem solving. *Psychological monographs,* 1945, *58*, 1–113.

Dunn, J., and **Plomin, R.** *Separate lives: Why siblings are so different.* New York: Basic Books, 1990.

Dutton, D. G., and **Strachan, C. E.** Marital needs for power and spouse specific assertiveness in assaultive and nonassaultive men. *Violence and victims,* 1987, *2*, 145–56.

Duyme, M. School success and social class: An adoption study. *Developmental psychology,* 1988, *24*, 203–09.

Eagly, A. H. Uneven progress: Social psychology and the study of attitudes. *Journal of personality and social psychology,* 1992, *63*, 693–710.

Ebbinghaus, H. *Memory.* New York: Columbia University Teachers College, 1913.

Eccles, J. S., et al. Impact of stage-environment fit on young adolescents experiences in schools and in families. *American psychologist,* 1993, *48*, 90–101.

Eckhardt, M. J., et al. Health hazards associated with alcohol consumption. *Journal of the American Medical Association,* 1981, *246*, 648–66.

Edelstein, E. L. Reactivation of concentration camp experiences as a result of hospitalization. In C. D. Spielberger, I. G. Sarason, and N. A. Milgram, eds. *Stress and anxiety,* Vol. 8. Washington, DC: Hemisphere, 1982.

Education Commission of the States. *Reconnecting youth: The next stage of reform.* Denver: October 1985.

Ehrenreich, B., Hess, E., and **Jacobs, G.** *Re-making love.* Garden City, NY: Anchor Press/Doubleday, 1986.

Eich, E., and **Metcalfe, J.** Mood dependent memory for internal versus external events. *Journal of experimental psychology: Learning, memory, and cognition,* 1989, *15*, 443–55.

Eisenberg, L. The epidemiology of suicide in adolescents. *Pediatric annals,* 1984, *13*, 47–54.

Eisenberg, N., et al. Prosocial development in early childhood. *Developmental psychology,* 1987, *23*, 712–18.

Ekman, P. Universals and cultural differences in facial expressions of emotion. In J. K. Cole, ed. *Nebraska symposium on motivation,* Vol. 19. Lincoln: University of Nebraska Press, 1971.

Ekman, P., and **Davidson, R. J.** Voluntary smiling changes regional brain activity. *Psychological science,* 1993, *4*, 342–45.

Ekman, P., and **Friesen, W. V.** A new pan-cultural facial expression of emotion. *Motivation and emotion,* 1986, *10*, 159–67.

Elder, G. H., and **Clipp, E. C.** Combat experience, comradeship, and psychological health. In J. P. Wilson, Z. Harel, and B. Kahana, eds. *Human adaptation to extreme stress.* New York: Plenum, 1988.

Elkin, I., et al. NIMH *treatment of depression collaborative research program: Initial outcome findings.* Paper read at the American Association for the Advancement of Science, May 1986.

Elkin, I., et al. National Institute of Mental Health treatments of depression collaborative research program. *Archives of general psychiatry,* 1990, *46*, 971–83.

Elliot, G. R., and **Eisdorfer, C.** *Stress and human health.* New York: Springer, 1982.

Elliot, R. Tests, abilities, race, and conflict. *Intelligence,* 1988, *12*, 333–50.

Ellis, A., and **Dryden, W.** *The practice of rational emotive therapy.* New York: Springer, 1987.

Ellis, E. M., Atkeson, B. M., and **Calhoun, K. S.** An assessment of long-term reaction to rape. *Journal of abnormal psychology,* 1981, *90*, 263–66.

Ellis, H. C., et al. Emotional mood states and retrieval in episodic memory. *Journal of experimental psychology: Learning, memory, and cognition,* 1985, *11*, 363–70.

Ellis, L., and **Ames, M. A.** Neurohormonal functions and sexual orientation: A theory of homosexuality-heterosexuality. *Psychological bulletin,* 1987, *101*, 233–58.

Elton, C. F., and **Shevel, L. R.** *Who is talented? An analysis of achievement.* Iowa City: American College Testing Program, 1969.

Embertson, S. Intelligence and its measurement: Extending contemporary theory to existing tests. In R. J. Sternberg, ed. *Advances in the psychology of human intelligence.* Hillsdale, NJ: Erlbaum, 1986.

England, P. Women and occupational prestige: A case of vacuous sex equality. *Journal of women in culture and society,* 1979, *5*, 252–65.

Epstein, A. N., Fitzsimons, J. T., and **Simons, B.** Drinking caused by the intercranial injection of angiotensin into the rat. *Journal of physiology* (London), 1969, *200*, 98–100.

Epstein, A. N., Kissileff, H. R., and **Stellar, E.,** eds. *The neuropsychology of thirst.* Washington, DC: Winston, 1973.

Epstein, N. B., and **Vlok, L. A.** Research on the results of psychotherapy: A summary of evidence. *American journal of psychiatry,* 1981, *138*, 1027–35.

Epstein, S. The stability of behavior across time and situations. In R. Zucker, J. Aronoff, and A. I. Rabin, eds. *Personality and the prediction of behavior.* San Diego: Academic Press, 1983.

Erdelyi, M. H. *Psychoanalysis: Freud's cognitive psychology.* San Francisco: Freeman, 1985.

Erikson, E. H. *Childhood and society,* 2nd ed. New York: Norton, 1963.

Erlenmeyer-Kimling, L., and **Jarvik, L. F.** Genetics and intelligence. *Science,* 1963, *142*, 1477–79.

Eron, L. D. The development of aggressive behavior from the perspective of a developing behaviorism. *American psychologist,* 1987, *42*, 435–42.

Evans, D. A., et al. Prevalence of Alzheimer's disease in a community population of older persons. *Journal of the American Medical Association,* 1989, *262*, 2551–56.

Evarts, E. V. Brain mechanisms of movement. In Scientific American's *The brain.* San Francisco: Freeman, 1979.

Everett, J., Laplante, L., and **Thomas, J.** The selective attention deficit in schizophrenia: Limited resources or cognitive fatigue? *The journal of nervous and mental disease,* 1989, *177,* 735–38.

Eysenck, H. J. (with **Kamin, L.**) *The intelligence controversy.* New York: Wiley, 1981.

Facklam, M., and **Facklam, H.** *The brain: Magnificent mind machine.* New York: Harcourt, 1982.

Fagan, J. F., and **Singer, L. T.** Infant recognition memory as a measure of intelligence. In L. P. Lipsitt, ed. *Advances in infancy research,* Vol. 2. Norwood, NJ: Ablex, 1983.

Falbo, T. Relationships between birth category, achievement, and interpersonal orientation. *Journal of personality and social psychology,* 1981, *41,* 121–31.

Falloon, I., and **Liberman, R. P.** Interactions between drug and psychosocial therapy in schizophrenia. *Schizophrenia bulletin,* 1983, *9,* 543–54.

Farina, A. The stigma of mental disorders. In A. G. Miller. *In the eye of the beholder: Contemporary issues in stereotyping.* New York: Praeger, 1982.

Fazio, R. H., Zanna, M. P., and **Cooper, J.** Dissonance and self-perception. *Journal of experimental social psychology,* 1977, *13,* 464–79.

Fehm-Wolsdorf, G., et al. Classically conditioned changes of blood glucose level in humans. *Physiology and behavior,* 1993, *54,* 155–60.

Feldman, D. H., and **Goldsmith, L. T.** *Nature's gambit: Child prodigies and the development of human potential.* New York: Basic Books, 1986.

Feldman, R. S. *Social psychology: Theories, research, and applications.* New York: McGraw-Hill, 1985.

Feldman, S. S., Biringen, Z. C., and **Nash, S. C.** Fluctuations of sex-related self-attributions as a function of stage of family life cycle. *Developmental psychology,* 1981, *17,* 24–35.

Fernald, A. The perceptual and affective salience of mother's speech to infants. In L. Feagans, ed. *The origins and growth of communication.* New Brunswick, NJ: Ablex, 1983, pp. 5–29.

Fernald, A., and **Simon, T.** Expanded intonation contours in mother's speech to newborns. *Developmental psychology,* 1984, *20,* 104–13.

Feshbach, N. D. Learning to care: A positive approach to child training and discipline. *Journal of clinical child psychology,* 1983, *12,* 266–71.

Feshbach, S., and **Weiner, B.** *Personality,* 2nd ed. Lexington, MA: Heath, 1986.

Festinger, L. A. A theory of social comparison processes. *Human relations,* 1954, *7,* 117–40.

Fichter, M. M., and **Noegel, R.** Concordance for bulimia nervosa in twins. *International journal of eating disorders,* 1990, *9,* 255–63.

Field, T. Stressors during pregnancy and the postnatal period. *New directions in child development,* 1989, *45,* 19–31.

Field, T., and **Reite, M.** Children's responses to separation from mother during the birth of another child. *Child development,* 1984, *55,* 1308–16.

Fillion, T. J., and **Blass, E. M.** Infantile experiences with suckling odors determines adult sexual behavior in rats. *Science,* February 1986, *231,* 729–31.

Fine, M. A., Moreland, J. R., and **Schwebel, A. I.** Long-term effects of divorce on parent-child relationships. *Developmental psychology,* 1983, *19,* 703–13.

Finkelstein, P., Wenegrat, B., and **Yalom, I.** Large group awareness training. *Annual review of psychology,* 1982, *33,* 515–39.

Fischbach, G. D. Mind and brain. *Scientific American,* September 1992, 48–59.

Fish, B. Infants at risk for schizophrenia: Sequelae of a genetic neurointegrative defect. *Archives of general psychiatry,* 1992, *49,* 221–35.

Flanagan, C. *Economic hardship, parents' regrets, and adolescents' achievement motivation.* Paper presented at Society for Research in Child Development, Kansas City, MO, 1989.

Flanagan, C. A. Changes in parent's work status and adolescents adjustment at school. *Child development,* 1993, *64,* 246–57.

Foa, E. B., and **Kozak, M. J.** Emotional processing of fear: Exposure to corrective information. *Psychological bulletin,* 1986, *99,* 20–35.

Fodor, E. M., and **Smith, T.** The power motive as an influence on group decision making. *Journal of personality and social psychology,* 1982, *42,* 178–85.

Folkes, V. S. Forming relationships and the matching hypothesis. *Personality and social psychology bulletin,* 1982.

Follingstad, D. R., and **Kimbill, C. D.** Sex fantasies revisited. *Archives of sexual behavior,* 1986, *15,* 475–86.

Forster, C., et al. Measurement of the analgesic effects of aspirin on the new analgesmetric procedure. *Pain,* 1988, *32,* 215–22.

Forward, J., Canter, R., and **Kirsch, N.** Role-enactment and deception methodologies. *American psychologist,* 1976, *31,* 595–604.

Foster, B. G. Self-disclosure and intimacy in long-term marriages. In N. Stinnett et al., eds. *Family strengths 4: Positive support systems.* Lincoln: University of Nebraska Press, 1982.

Frank, J. D. Therapeutic components shared by all psychotherapies. In J. H. Harvey and M. M. Parks, eds. *The master lecture series: Vol. 1: Psychotherapy research and behavior change.* Washington, DC: American Psychological Association, 1982.

Frazier, K., ed. *Science confronts the paranormal.* Buffalo: Prometheus Books, 1986.

Frazier, S. H. *Preventing youth suicide: A collaborative effort.* Paper presented at the National Conference on Youth Suicide, Washington, DC, June 19, 1985.

Frederick, C. Current trends in suicidal behavior in the United States. *American journal of psychotherapy,* 1978, *32,* 172–200.

Freed, A., et al. Stimulus and background factors in sign violation. *Journal of personality,* 1955, *23,* 499.

Freed, W. J., deMedinaceli, L., and **Wyatt, R. J.** Promoting functional plasticity in the nervous system. *Science,* 1985, *227,* 1544–52.

Freedman, D. X. Psychiatric epidemiology counts. *Archives of general psychiatry,* 1984, *41,* 931–33.

Freedman, J. L., Carlsmith, J. M., and **Sears, D. O.** *Social psychology.* Englewood Cliffs, NJ: Prentice-Hall, 1970.

French, E. G. Development of a measure of complex motivation. In J. W. Atkinson, ed. *Motives in fantasy, action and society.* Princeton, NJ: Van Nostrand, 1959.

Frezza, M., et al. High blood alcohol levels in women: The role of decreased gastric alcohol dehydrogenase activity and first-pass metabolism. *New England journal of medicine,* January 11, 1990, *322,* 95–99.

Friedman, M., and **Ulmer, D.** *Type A behavior—your heart.* New York: Fawcett, 1985.

Fromm, E. *The sane society.* New York: Holt, 1955.

Furman, W., Rahe, D. F., and **Hartup, W. W.** Rehabilitation of socially-withdrawn preschool children through mixed-age and same-age socialization. In E. M. Hetherington and R. D. Parke, eds. *Contemporary readings in child psychology,* 2nd ed. New York: McGraw-Hill, 1981.

Furstenberg, F. F., Jr., Brooks-Gunn, J., and **Morgan, S. P.** *Adolescent mothers in later life.* New York: Cambridge University Press, 1987.

Furumoto, L., and **Scarborough, E.** Placing women in the history of psychology: The first American women psychologists. *American psychologist,* 1986, *41,* 35–42.

Gaeddert, W. P. Sex and sex-role effects on achievement strivings: Dimensions of similarity and difference. *Journal of personality,* 1985, *53,* 286–305.

Gaeddert, W. P. The relationship of gender, gender-related traits, and achievement orientation to achievement attributions: A study of subject-selected accomplishments. *Journal of personality,* 1987, *55,* 687–710.

Gaertner, S. Researching intergroup bias: The benefits of intercategorization. *Journal of personality and social psychology,* 1989, *57,* 239–49.

Galaburda, A. M. Anatomical asymmetries. In N. Geschwind and A. M. Galaburda, eds. *Cerebral dominance: The biological foundations.* Cambridge: Harvard University Press, 1984.

Gallagher, W. Midlife myths. *The Atlantic,* 1993, *271*(5), 51–68.

Gallup, G. *The sophisticated poll watcher's guide.* Princeton, NJ: Princeton Opinion Press, 1972.

Gamson, W. A., Fireman, B., and **Rytina, S.** *Encounters with unjust authority.* Homewood, IL: Dorsey, 1982.

Garb, J. J., and **Stunkard, A. J.** Taste aversion in man. *American journal of psychiatry,* 1974, *131,* 1204–07.

Garber, J., and **Hollon, S.** *Depression and the expectancy of success for self and for others.* Unpublished manuscript, University of Minnesota, 1977.

Gardner, H. *Frames of mind: The theory of multiple intelligence.* New York: Basic Books, 1983.

Gardner, H. Creativity: An interdisciplinary perspective. *Creativity research journal,* 1988, *1,* 8–26.

Gardner, R. A., and **Gardner, B. T.** Communication with a young chimpanzee. In R. Chauvin, ed. *Edition du centre national de la recherche scientific.* Paris: 1972.

Garland, A., and **Zigler, E.** Adolescent suicide prevention: Current research and social policy. *American psychologist,* 1993, *48,* 169–82.

Garmezy, N. Stressors of childhood. In N. Garmezy and M. Rutter, eds. *Stress, coping, and child development.* New York: McGraw-Hill, 1983, pp. 43–84.

Garmezy, N., and **Rutter, M.** Acute reactions to stress. In M. Rutter, and L. Hersov. *Child and adolescent psychiatry: Modern approaches,* 2nd ed. Oxford: Blackwell, 1985, pp. 152–76.

Gates, A. L. Recitation as a factor in memorizing. *Archives of psychology, No. 40.* New York: Columbia University, 1917.

Gati, I., and **Tversky, A.** Weighing common and distinctive features in perceptual and conceptual judgments. *Cognitive psychology,* 1984, *16,* 341–70.

Geen, R. G. *Personality.* St. Louis: Mosby, 1976.

Geen, R. G., and **O'Neil, E. C.** Activation of cue-elicited aggression by general arousal. *Journal of personality and social psychology,* 1969, *ii,* 289–92.

Geer, J. H., and **Fuhr, R.** Cognitive factors in sexual arousal: The role of distraction. *Journal of consulting and clinical psychology,* 1976, *44,* 238–43.

Geracioti, T. D., Jr., and **Liddle, R. A.** Impaired cholecystokinin secretion in bulimia nervosa. *The New England journal of medicine,* September 15, 1988, *319,* 683–88.

Gerstein, D. R., et al. *The behavioral and social sciences: Achievements and opportunities.* Washington, DC: National Academy Press, 1988.

Geschwind, N., and **Behan, P. O.** Laterality, hormones, and immunity. In N. Geschwind and A. M. Galaburda, eds. *Cerebral dominance: The biological foundations.* Cambridge: Harvard University Press, 1984.

Getzels, J. W., and **Jackson, P. W.** *Creativity and intelligence.* New York: Wiley, 1962.

Gibson, E. J. *Principles of perceptual learning and development.* New York: Appleton-Century-Crofts, 1969.

Gibson, E. J., and **Walk, R. D.** The "visual cliff." *Scientific American,* 1960, *202,* 64–71.

Gigerenzer, G., and **Hug, K.** Domain specific reasoning: social contracts, cheating and perspective change. *Cognition,* 1992, *43,* 127–71.

Gilbert, A. N., and **Wysocki, C. J.** The smell survey: Results. *National geographic,* 1987, *172,* 514–25.

Gilligan, C. *In a different voice.* Cambridge: Harvard University Press, 1982.

Gillian, C. Making connections: The relational worlds of adolescent girls at Emma Willard School. Cambridge: Harvard University Press, 1988.

Gilovich, T., Vallone, R., and **Tversky, A.** The hot hand in basketball: On the misperception of random sequences. *Cognitive psychology,* 1985, *17,* 295–314.

Ginsburg, H. J., and **Miller, S. M.** Sex differences in children's risk-taking behavior. *Child development,* 1982, *53,* 426–28.

Gladue, B. A., Green, R., and **Hellman, R. E.** Neuroendocrine response to estrogen and sexual orientation. *Science,* 1984, *225,* 1496–99.

Glantz, M., and **Pickens, R.** *Vulnerability to drug abuse,* Washington, DC: American Psychological Association, 1992.

Glaser, R., and **Bond, L.** Introduction to a special issue on testing: Concepts, policy, practice, and research. *American psychologist,* 1981, *36,* 997–1000.

Glaser, R., et al. Stress-induced modulation of the immune response to recombinant hepatitis B vaccine. *Psychosomatic medicine,* 1992, *54,* 22–29.

Gleitman, L. R., Newport, E. L., and **Gleitman, H.** The current status of the motherese hypothesis. *Journal of child language,* 1984, *11,* 43–79.

Glick, R. Promoting competence and coping through retirement planning. In L. A. Bond and J. C. Rosen, eds. *Competence and coping during adulthood.* Hanover, NH: University Press of New England, 1980.

Gold, S. R. The CAP control theory of drug abuse. In D. J. Lettieri, M. Sayers, and H. W. Pearson, eds. *Theories on drug abuse: Selected contemporary perspectives.* National Institute on Drug Abuse, DHHS Publication No. (ADM) 80-967, 1980, pp. 8–11.

Goldberg, I. R. Language and individual differences: The search for universal in personality lexicons. In L. Wheeler, ed. *Review of personality and social psychology,* Vol. 2. Beverly Hills, CA: Sage, 1981.

Goldfarb, W. Effects of early institutional care on adolescent personality. *American journal of orthopsychiatry,* 1944, *14,* 441–47.

Goldfield, B. A. Pointing, naming, and talk about objects: Referential behavior in children and mothers. *First language,* 1990, *10,* 231–42.

Goldfried, M. R., Greenberg, L. S., and **Marmar, C.** Individual psychotherapy: Process and outcome. *Annual review of psychology,* 1990, *41,* 659–88.

Goldman, P. An alternative to developmental plasticity: Heterology of CNS structures in infants and adults. In D. G. Stein, J. J. Rosen, and N. Butters, eds. *Plasticity and recovery of function in the central nervous system.* New York: Academic Press, 1974.

Goldman-Rakic, P. S. Working memory and the mind. *Scientific American,* September 1992, 110–17.

Goldsen, R., et al. *What college students think.* Princeton, NJ: Van Nostrand, 1960.

Goldstein, J. H., and **Arms, R. L.** Effects of observing athletic contests on hostility. *Sociometry,* 1971, *234,* 83–90.

Goleman, D. Hypnosis comes of age. *Psychology today,* July 1977, *11,* 54–56+.

Goodall, J. *The chimpanzees of Gombe.* Cambridge: Harvard University Press, 1986.

Goode, W. J. *The family.* Englewood Cliffs, NJ: Prentice-Hall, 1965.

Goodwin, D. W., et al. Alcohol problems in adoptees raised apart from biological parents. *Archives of general psychiatry,* 1973, *28,* 238–43.

Goodwin, F. Personal communication, 1993.

Goodwin, F. J., and Jamison, K. R. *Manic-depressive illness.* New York: Oxford University Press, 1990.

Goodwin, F. K. From the Alcohol, Drug Abuse, and Mental Health Administration. *Journal of the American Medical Association,* June 23/30, 1989, *261,* 3517.

Gopnik, A. The acquisition of *gone* and the development of the object concept. *Journal of child language,* 1984, *11,* 273–92.

Gopnik, A., and Meltzoff, A. N. Semantic and cognitive development in 15- to 21-month-old children. *Journal of child language,* 1984, *11,* 495–513.

Gordon, A. M. Adequacy of responses given by low-income and middle-income kindergarten children in structured adult-child conversations. *Developmental psychology,* 1984, *20,* 881–92.

Gordon, D., State, R., Nelson, J., Hamburger, S. and Rapoport, J. A double blind comparison of clomipramine, desipramine and placebo in the treatment of autistic disorder., 1993 *50:* 441–447. *Archives of general psychiatry,* June 1993.

Gormezano, I., Kehoe, E. J., and Marshall, B. S. Twenty years of classical conditioning research with the rabbit. In J. M. Sprague and A. N. Epstein, eds. *Progress in psychobiological and physiological research,* Vol. 10. New York: Academic Press, 1983.

Gortmaker, S. L., Must, A., Perrin, J. M., Sobol, A. M., Dietz, W. H. Social and economic consequences of overweight in adolescence and young adulthood. *New England journal of medicine,* 1993, *329,* 1008–12.

Gotlib, I. H. Depression and general psychopathology in university students. *Journal of abnormal psychology,* 1984, *93,* 19–30.

Gottesman, I. I. Biogenetics of race and class. In M. Deutsch, I. Katz, and A. B. Jensen, eds. *Social class, race, and psychological development.* New York: Holt, 1963.

Gottesman, I. I., and Shields, J. *Schizophrenia: The epigenetic puzzle.* New York: Cambridge University Press, 1982.

Gottlieb, J., and Carver, C. S. Anticipation of future interaction and the bystander effect. *Journal of experimental social psychology,* 1980, *16,* 253–60.

Gottschalk, E. C. Student shock. Stress is more severe for collegians today; counselors keep busy. *Wall Street journal,* June 1, 1983.

Gould, M. S., and Shaffer, D. The impact of suicide in television movies: Evidence of imitation. *New England journal of medicine,* Sept. 11, 1986, *315,* 690–94.

Gouras, P. Color vision. In E. R. Kandel and J. H. Schwartz, eds. *Principles of neural science.* New York: Elsevier, 1985.

Graf, P., and Schacter, D. L. Selective effects of interference on implicit and explicit memory for new associations. *Journal of experimental psychology: Learning, memory, and cognition,* 1987, *13,* 45–53.

Graf, P., Squire, L. R., and Mandler, G. The information that amnesic patients do not forget. *Journal of experimental psychology: Learning, memory, and cognition,* 1984, *10,* 164–78.

Graf, R. C. Speed reading. *Psychology today,* December 1973, 112–13.

Graham, P., and Rutter, M. Adolescent disorders. In M. Rutter and L. Hersov, eds. *Child and adolescent psychiatry: Modern approaches.* London: Blackwell, 1985.

Graziano, W. G., Feldesman, A. B., and Rahe, D. F. Extraversion, social cognition, and the salience of aversiveness in social encounters. *Journal of personality and social psychology.* 1985, *49,* 971–80.

Greenblatt, M., Becerra, R. M., and Serafetinides, E. A. Social networks in mental health: An overview. *The American journal of psychiatry,* 139, August 1982, 977–84.

Greene, W. A., Goldstein, S., and Moss, A. J. Psychosocial aspects of sudden death. *Archives of internal medicine,* 1972, *129,* 725–31.

Gregersen, E. *Sexual practices.* New York: Franklin Watts, 1983.

Greven, P. *Spare the child.* New York: Knopf, 1991.

Grief, E., and Ulman, K. The psychological impact of menarche on early adolescent females: A review of the literature. *Child development,* 1982, *53,* 1413–30.

Griel, A. *Not yet pregnant,* New Brunswick, NJ: Rutgers University Press, 1991.

Grillon, C., et al. Increased distractibility in schizophrenic patients. *Archives of general psychiatry,* 1990, *47,* 171–79.

Grinker, J. A. Physiological and behavioral basis of human obesity. In D. W. Pfaff, ed. *The physiological mechanisms of motivation.* New York: Springer-Verlag, 1982.

Gross, A. E. and Fleming, I. Twenty years of deception in social psychology. *Personality and social psychology,* 1982, *8,* 402–08.

Gruenberg, B. The happy worker: An analysis of educational and occupational differences in determinants of job satisfaction. *American journal of sociology,* 1980, *86,* 247–71.

Guerin, B. Mere presence effects in humans: A review. *Journal of personality and social psychology,* 1986, *22,* 38–77.

Guilford, J. P. A factor analytic study across the domains of reasoning, creativity, and evaluation. *Reports from the psychology laboratory,* University of Southern California, 1954.

Guilford, J. P. *The nature of human intelligence.* New York: McGraw-Hill, 1967.

Gunnar, M. R., Leighton, K., and Peleaux, R. Effects of temporal predictability on the reactions of 1-year-olds to potentially frightening toys. *Developmental psychology,* 1984, *20,* 449–58.

Gunter, B., Berry, C., and Clifford, B. R. Proactive interference effects with television news items: Further evidence. *Journal of experimental psychology: Human learning and memory,* 1981, *7,* 480–87.

Haig, N. D. The effect of feature displacement on face recognition. *Perception,* 1984, *13,* 505–12.

Haith, M. *Rules babies look by.* Hillsdale, NJ: Erlbaum, 1980.

Hall, C. S., and Lindzey, G. *Theories of personality,* 3rd ed. New York: Wiley, 1978.

Hall, R. C. W. Anxiety. In R. C. W. Hall, ed. *Psychiatric presentations of medical illness: Somatopsychic disorders.* New York: Spectrum, 1980a.

Hall, R. C. W. Medically induced psychiatric disease—an overview. In R. C. W. Hall, ed. *Psychiatric presentations of medical illness: Somatopsychic disorders.* New York: Spectrum, 1980b.

Hall, R. C. W., Stickney, S. K., and Gardner, E. R. Behavioral toxicity of nonpsychiatric drugs. In R. C. W. Hall. *Psychiatric presentations in medical illness: Somatopsychic disorders.* New York: Spectrum, 1980.

Hall, W. S. *Science and public policy seminars: Some recent developments in the study of children's language,* Washington, DC: Federation of Behavioral, Psychological and Cognitive Sciences, 1986.

Hallock, M. B., Worobey, J., and Self, P. A. Behavioral development in chimpanzee and human newborns across the first month of life. *International journal of behavioral development,* 1989, *12,* 526–40.

Halpern, A. R. Organization and memory for familiar songs. *Journal of experimental psychology: Learning, memory, and cognition,* 1984, *10,* 496–512.

Halpern, C. T. et al. Testosterone and pubertal development as predictors of sexual activity: A panel analysis of adolescent males. *Psychosomatic medicine,* 1993, *55,* 436–47.

Hamburg, D. A., and Takanishi, R. Preparing for life: The critical transition of adolescence. *American psychologist,* 1989, *44,* 825–27.

Hamer, D., Hu, S., Magnuson, V. L., Hu, N., and Pattatucci, A. M. L. A linkage between DNA markers on the X chromosome and male sexual orientation. *Science,* 1993, *261,* 321–27.

Hamilton, M. Diagnosis of anxiety states. In R. J. Mathew, ed. *The biology of anxiety.* New York: Bruner/Mazel, 1982.

Hammen, C., et al. Psychiatric history and stress: Predictors of severity of unipolar depression. *Journal of abnormal psychology,* 1992, *101,* 45–52.

Hansel, C. E. M. *ESP.* New York: Scribners, 1966.

Hargadon, F. Tests and college admissions. *American psychologist,* 1981, *36,* 1112–19.

Harlow, H. F. The formation of learning sets. *Psychological review,* 1949, *56,* 51–65.

Harlow, H. F. The development of affectional patterns in infant monkeys. In B. M. Foss, ed. *Determinants of infant behaviour.* London: Methuen, 1961.

Harlow, H. F., and Harlow, M. K. Learning to love. *American scientist,* 1966, *54,* 244–72.

Harrell, T. W., and Harrell, M. S. Army general classification test scores for civilian occupations. *Educational and psychological measurement,* 1945, *5,* 229–39.

Harris, B. Whatever happened to little Albert? *American psychologist,* 1979, *34,* 151–60.

Harris, F. R., et al. Effects of positive social reinforcement on regressed crawling of a nursery school child. In L. Ullmann and L. Krasner, eds. *Case studies in behavior modification.* New York: Holt, 1965.

Hart, J., and Gordon, B. Neural subsystems for direct knowledge. *Nature,* 1992, *359,* 60–64.

Harter, S., and Marold, D. A model of risk factors in adolescent suicide: The mediational role of self-worth. Presented at the Society for Research in Child Development, Kansas City, MO, April 1989.

Hartmann, E. *The nightmare.* New York: Basic Books, 1984.

Hartmann, H. Ego psychology and the problem of adaptation. In D. Rapaport, ed. *Organization and pathology of thought.* New York: Columbia University Press, 1951.

Harvard Medical School. *Mental health letter,* December 1989, *6,* 1–3.

Harvard Medical School. *Mental health letter,* February 1991, *7,* 1–4.

Harvey, S. M. Female sexual behavior: Fluctuations during the menstrual cycle. *Journal of psychosomatic research,* 1987, *31,* 101–10.

Hatfield, E. Passionate and companionate love. In R. J. Sternberg and M. L. Barnes, eds. *The psychology of love.* New Haven: Yale University Press, 1988.

Hathaway, S. R., et al. *Minnesota Multiphasic Personality Inventory-II: Manual for administration and scoring.* Minneapolis: University of Minnesota Press, 1989.

Hauri, P. J. *The sleep disorders.* Kalamazoo, MI: Upjohn, 1982.

Hauser, B. B. Custody in dispute: Legal and psychological profiles of contesting families. *Journal of the academy of child psychiatry,* 1985, *24,* 575–82.

Hawley, T. L. and Disney, E. R. Crack's children: The consequences of maternal cocaine abuse. *Social policy report,* 1992, *VI,* 4.

Hayward, C., et al. Pubertal stage and panic attack history in sixth- and seventh-grade girls. *American journal of psychiatry,* 1992, *149,* 1239–43.

Hebb, D. O., and Thompson, W. The social significance of animal studies. In G. Lindzey and E. Aronson, eds. *The handbook of social psychology,* 2nd ed., Vol. 2 (research methods). Reading, MA: Addison-Wesley, 1968.

Heider, F. Social perception and phenomenal causality. *Psychological review,* 1944, *51,* 358–74.

Heller, K., and Mansbach, W. E. The multifaceted nature of social support in a community sample of older women. *Journal of social issues,* 1984, *40,* 99–112.

Helsing, K. L., Szklo, M., and Comstock, G. W. Factors associated with mortality after widowhood. *American journal of public health,* 1981, *71,* 802–09.

Helson, R., and Moane, G. Personality change in women from college to midlife. *Journal of personality and social psychology,* 1987, *53,* 176–86.

Helzer, J. E., Robins, L. N., and McEvoy, L. Post-traumatic stress disorder in the general population: Findings of the epidemiologic catchment area survey. *New England journal of medicine,* 1987, *317,* 1630–34.

Hendrick, C., and Hendrick, S. A theory and method of love. *Journal of personality and social psychology,* 1986, *50,* 392–402.

Hendrick, S., et al. Gender differences in sexual attitudes. *Journal of personality and social psychology,* 1985, *48,* 1630–42.

Henke, P. G. Electrophysiological activity in the central nucleus of the amygdala: Emotionality and stress ulcers in rats. *Behavioral neuroscience,* 1988, *102,* 77–83.

Herrmann, T. F., Hurwitz, H. M. B., and Levine, S. Behavioral control, aversive stimulus frequency, and pituitary-adrenal response. *Behavioral neuroscience,* 1984, *98,* 1094–99.

Herrnstein, R. J., and de Villiers, P. A. Fish as a natural category for people and pigeons. In G. H. Bower, ed. *Psychology of learning and motivation,* Vol. 14. New York: Academic Press, 1980.

Herzog, E., and Lewis, H. Children in poor families. *American journal of orthopsychiatry,* 1970, *40,* 375–87.

Hess, R. D., et al. Maternal variables as predictors of children's school readiness and later achievement in vocabulary and mathematics in the sixth grade. *Child development,* 1984, *55,* 1902–12.

Heston, L. H., and White, J. A. *Dementia: A practical guide to Alzheimer's disease and related illness.* San Francisco: Freeman, 1983.

Hetherington, E. M., and Camara, K. A. Families in transition: The process of dissolution and reconstitution. In R. D. Parke, ed. *Review of child development research: The family,* Vol. 7. Chicago: University of Chicago Press, 1984.

Hilgard, E. R., and Hilgard, J. R. *Hypnosis in the relief of pain.* Los Altos, CA: William Kaufmann, 1975.

Hill, J. The family. In M. Johnson, ed. *Toward adolescence: The middle school years.* Chicago: University of Chicago Press, 1980.

Hill, J. P. Research on adolescents and their families: Past and prospect. In C. E. Irwin, ed. *Adolescent social behavior and health.* San Francisco: Jossey-Bass, 1987.

Hilton, I. Differences in the behavior of mothers toward first- and later-born children. *Journal of personality and social psychology,* 1967, *7,* 282–90.

Hinz, L. D., and Williamson, D. A. Bulimia and depression: A review of the affective variant hypothesis. *Psychological Bulletin,* 1987, *102,* 150–58.

Hiroto, D. S. Locus of control and learned helplessness. *Journal of experimental psychology,* 1974, *102,* 187–93.

Hitchcock, J. M., and **Davis, M.** Efferent pathway of the amygdala involved in conditioned fear as measured with the fear-potentiated startle paradigm. *Behavioral neuroscience,* 1991, *105,* 826–42.

Hobson, J. A. *Sleep.* New York: Scientific American Library, 1989.

Hochberg, J. *Perception.* 2nd ed. Englewood Cliffs, NJ: Prentice-Hall, 1978.

Hoeksema, S. N. Predictors and consequences of childhood depressive symptoms: A 5-year longitudinal study. *Journal of abnormal psychology,* 1992, *101,* 405–22.

Hogan, J. Personality correlates of physical fitness. *Journal of personality and social psychology,* 1989, *56,* 284–88.

Holahan, C. J., and **Moos, R. H.** Personality, coping, and family resources in stress resistance: A longitudinal analysis. *Journal of personality and social psychology,* 1986, *51,* 389–95.

Holahan, C. J., and **Moos, R. H.** Life stressors, personal and social resources, and depression: A 4-year structural model. *Journal of abnormal psychology,* 1991, *100,* 31–38.

Holder, M. D., Bermudez-Rattoni, F., and **Garcia, J.** Taste-potentiated noise-illness associations. *Behavioral neuroscience,* 1988, *102,* 363–70.

Holmes, S. J., and **Robins, L. N.** The influence of childhood disciplinary experience on the development of alcoholism and depression. *Journal of child psychology and psychiatry,* 1987, *28,* 399–415.

Holmes, T. H., and **Rahe, R. H.** The social readjustment rating scale. *Journal of psychosomatic research,* 1967, *11,* 213–18.

Holyrod, K. A., et al. Performance, cognition, and physiological responding in test anxiety. *Journal of abnormal psychology,* 1978, *87,* 442–51.

Holzman, P. H. Behavioral markers of schizophrenia useful for genetic studies. *Journal of psychiatric research,* 1992, *26,* 427–45.

Honzik, M. P., Macfarlane, J. W., and **Allen, L.** The stability of mental test performance between two and eighteen years. *Journal of experimental education,* 1948, *17,* 454–55.

Hooley, J. M. Expressed emotion: A review of the critical literature. *Clinical psychology review,* 1985, *5,* 119–39.

Horfling, C. K., et al. An experimental study in nurse-physician relationships. *Journal of nervous and mental disease,* 1966, *143,* 171–80.

Horn, J. L. The aging of human abilities. In J. Woolman, ed. *Handbook of developmental psychology.* Englewood Cliffs, NJ: Prentice-Hall, 1982.

Horne, J. *Why we sleep: The functions of sleep in humans and other mammals.* Oxford, England: Oxford University Press, 1988.

Horney, K. *Our inner conflicts.* New York: Norton, 1945.

Horowitz, F. D., and **O'Brien, M.** Gifted and talented children: State of knowledge and directions for research. *American psychologist,* 1986, *41,* 1147–52.

Horowitz, J. H., and **Stefanko, M.** Toxic waste: Behavioral effects of an environmental stressor. *Behavioral medicine,* 1989, *15,* 23–28.

Horowitz, M. J. *Introduction to psychodynamics.* New York: Basic Books, 1988.

House, J. S., Landis, K. R., and **Umberson, D.** Social relationships and health. *Science,* 1988, *241,* 540–45.

Hovland, C. I., Lumsdaine, A. A., and **Sheffield, F. C.** *Experiments on mass communication,* Princeton, NJ: Princeton University Press, 1949.

Howard, A., et al. The changing face of American psychology: A report from the committee on employment and human resources. *American psychologist,* 1986, *41,* 1311–27.

Howard, K., et al. The dose-effect relationship in psychotherapy. *American psychologist,* 1986, *41,* 159–64.

Howes, C. The relation between early child care and schooling. *Developmental psychology,* 1988, *24,* 53–57.

Howes, C. Can the age of entry into child care and the quality of child care predict adjustment in kindergarten? *Developmental psychology,* 1990, *26,* 292–303.

Hoyenga, K. B., and **Hoyenga, K. T.** *Psychobiology: The neuron and behavior.* Pacific Grove, CA: Brooks/Cole, 1988.

Hubel, D. H. The visual cortex of the brain. *Scientific American,* 1963, *209,* 54–62.

Hubel, D. H. Vision and the brain. *Bulletin of the American Academy of Arts and Sciences,* 1978, *31,* 17–28.

Hubel, D. H. The brain. In Scientific American's *The brain.* San Francisco: Freeman, 1979.

Hubel, D. H. *Eye, brain, and vision.* New York: Scientific American Library, 1988.

Hubel, D. H., and **Wiesel, T. N.** Receptive fields and functional architecture in two non-striate visual areas (18 and 19) of the cat. *Journal of neurophysiology,* 1965, *28,* 229–89.

Hubel, D. H., and **Wiesel, T. N.** Brain mechanisms of vision. In Scientific American's *The brain.* San Francisco: Freeman, 1979.

Hudspeth, A. J. The cellular basis of hearing: The biophysics of hair cells. *Science,* November 15, 1985, *230,* 745–52.

Hunt, E. Verbal ability. In R. J. Sternberg, ed. *Human abilities: An information-processing approach.* New York: Freeman, 1985.

Huston, A., et al. *Big world, small screen: The role of television in American society.* Lincoln: University of Nebraska Press, 1992.

Huston, A. C., et al. The development of television viewing patterns in early childhood: A longitudinal investigation. Paper presented at the meeting of the Society for Research in Child Development, Baltimore, April 1987.

Hyde, J. S., Fennema, E., and **Lamon, S. J.** Gender differences in mathematics performance: A meta-analysis. *Psychological bulletin,* 1990, *107,* 139–55.

Hyde, J. S., and **Linn, M. C.** Gender differences in verbal ability: A meta-analysis. *Psychological bulletin,* 1988, *104,* 53–69.

Ilfeld, F. W. Coping styles of Chicago adults: Description. *Journal of human stress,* 1980, *6,* 2–10.

Ingraham, L. J. Risk for affective disorder and alcohol and other drug abuse in the relatives of affectively ill adoptees. *Journal of affective disorders,* 1992, *26,* 45–57.

Institute of Medicine. *Research on children and adolescents with mental, behavioral and developmental disorders.* Washington, DC: National Academy Press, 1989.

Institute for Mental Health Initiatives. *Channeling children's anger.* Washington, DC, 1988.

Iversen, L. L. The chemistry of the brain. *Scientific American,* 1979, *241,* 14+, 134–35+.

Iversen, L. L. Neurotransmitters and CNS disease: Introduction, *Lancet,* 1982, II, *8304,* 914–16.

Izard, C. E. *Human emotions.* New York: Plenum, 1977.

Jack, D. C. *Silencing the self,* Cambridge: Harvard University Press, 1991.

Jackson, J. F. Human behavioral genetics, Scarr's theory, and her views on interventions: A critical review and commentary on their implications for African-American children. *Child development,* 1993, *64,* 1318–32.

Jacobowitz, D. M. Personal communication, 1989.

Jacobs, M. K., and **Goodman, G.** Psychology and self-help groups. *American psychologist,* 1989, *44,* 536–45.

Jacobson, J. L., et al. Prenatal exposure to an environmental toxin: A test of the multiple effects model. *Developmental psychology,* 1984, *20,* 523–32.

Jacquart, D., and **Thomassat, C.** *Sexuality and medicine in the Middle Ages,* Princeton, NJ: Princeton University Press, 1988.

James, W. *Principles of psychology.* New York: Holt, 1890.

Jamison, K. R. Personal communication, 1982.

Jamison, K. R. *Touched with fire.* New York: Free Press, 1993.

Janis, I. L. Effects of fear arousal on attitude change: recent developments in theory and experimental research. In L. Berkowitz, ed. *Advances in experimental social psychology,* Vol. 3. New York: Academic Press, 1967.

Janke, L. L., and **Havighurst, R. J.** Relation between ability and social-status in a midwestern community. II: Sixteen-year-old boys and girls. *Journal of educational psychology,* 1945, *36,* 499–509.

Jankelovich, D. *Coming to public judgment.* Syracuse, NY: Syracuse University Press, 1988.

Janos, P. M., **Fung, H. C.,** and **Robinson, N. M.** Self-concept, self-esteem, and peer relations among gifted children who feel different. *The gifted child quarterly,* 1985, *29,* 78–82.

Jarmas, A. L., and **Kazak, A. E.** Young adult children of alcoholic fathers: Depressive experiences, coping styles, and family systems. *Journal of consulting and clinical psychology.* 1992. *60,* 244–51.

Jencks, C., et al. *Inequality.* New York: Basic Books, 1972.

Jensen, A. R. How much can we boost IQ and school achievement? *Harvard educational review,* 1969, *39,* 1–123.

Jensen, A. R. The heritability of intelligence. *Saturday evening post,* 1972, *244,* 9.

Jensen, A. R. *Bias in mental testing.* New York: Free Press, 1980.

Jensen, M. R. Psychobiological factors predicting the course of breast cancer. *Journal of personality,* 1987, *55,* 317–42.

Jimerson, D. C., **Herzog, D. B.,** and **Brotman, A. W.** Pharmacologic approaches in the treatment of eating disorders. *Harvard review of psychiatry,* 1993, *1,* 82–93.

Johansson, G. Visual motion perception. In R. Held and W. Richards, eds. *Recent progress in perception: Readings from Scientific American.* San Francisco: Freeman, 1976, pp. 67–75.

John, E. R., et al. Observation learning in cats. *Science,* 1968, *159,* 1489–91.

Jones, E. E., and **Nisbett, R. E.** The actor and the observer. In E. E. Jones, et al., eds. *Attribution.* Morristown, NJ: General Learning Press, 1972.

Jones, H. W. and **Toner, J. P.** The infertile couple. *New England journal of medicine,* 1993, *329,* 1710–15.

Julien, E., and **Over, R.** Male sexual arousal across five modes of erotic stimulation. *Archives of sexual behavior,* 1988, *17,* 131–47.

Junginger, J. Mood theme and bizarreness of delusions of schizophrenia and mood psychosis. *Journal of abnormal psychology,* 1992, *101,* 287–92.

Jussim, L., and **Eccles, J. S.** Teacher expectations II: Construction and reflection of student achievement. *Journal of personality and social psychology,* 1992, *63,* 947–61.

Kabat-Zinn, J. Effectiveness of a meditation based stress reduction program. *American journal of psychiatry,* 1992, *149,* 936–43.

Kagan, J. *Galen's prophecy,* New York: Basic Books, 1994.

Kagan, J. *The second year: The emergence of self-awareness.* Cambridge: Harvard University Press, 1981.

Kagan, J. *The nature of the child.* New York: Basic Books, 1984.

Kagan, J. Temperamental contributions to social behavior. *American psychologist,* 1989a, *44,* 668–74.

Kagan, J. *Unstable ideas: Temperament, cognition, and self.* Cambridge: Harvard Univ. Press, 1989b.

Kagan, J., **Kearsley, R. B.,** and **Zelazo, P. R.** *Infancy: Its place in human development.* Cambridge: Harvard University Press, 1978.

Kagan, J., and **Klein, R. E.** Cross-cultural perspectives on early development. *American psychologist,* 1973, *28,* 947–61.

Kagan, J., and **Moss, H. A.** *Birth to maturity.* New York: Wiley, 1962.

Kagan, J., **Reznick, J. S.,** and **Snidman, N.** Biological bases of childhood shyness. *Science,* 1988, *240,* 167–71.

Kagan, J., and **Snidman, N.** Infant predictors of inhibited and uninhibited profiles. *Psychological science,* in press.

Kagan, J., et al. Childhood derivatives of inhibition and lack of inhibition to the unfamiliar. *Child development,* 1988, *59,* 1580–89.

Kail, R., and **Pellegrino, J. W.** *Human intelligence.* New York: Freeman, 1985.

Kales, A., **Stefanis, C. N.,** and **Talbott, J.** *Recent advances in schizophrenia.* New York: Springer-Verlag, 1990.

Kalil, R. E. Synapse formation in the developing brain. *Scientific American,* December 1989, 76–85.

Kamin, L. (with Eysenck, H. J.) *The intelligence controversy.* New York: Wiley, 1981.

Kandel, E. R., and **Schwartz, J. H.** Molecular-biology of learning-modulation of transmitter release. *Science,* 1982, *218,* 433–43.

Kandel, E. R., and **Schwartz, J. H.** *Principles of neural science,* 2nd ed. New York: Elsevier, 1985.

Kane, J. M. Low dose medication strategies in the maintenance treatment of schizophrenia. *Schizophrenia bulletin,* 1983, *9,* 528–32.

Kang, D. H., et al. Frontal brain asymmetry and immune function. *Behavioral neuroscience,* 1991, *105,* 860–69.

Karasek, R. A., et al. Job characteristics in relation to the prevalence of myocardial infarction in the U.S. Health Examination Survey (**HES**) and the Health and Nutrition Examination Survey (**HANES**). *The American journal of public health,* 1988, *78,* 810–18.

Katchadourian, H. A., and **Lunde, D. T.** *Fundamentals of human sexuality,* 3rd ed. New York: Holt, 1980.

Katz, I., and **Hass, R. G.** Racial ambivalence and American value conflict: Correlational and priming studies of dual cognitive structures. *Journal of personality and social psychology,* 1988, *55,* 893–905.

Kay, D., and **Bergmann, K.** Epidemiology of mental disorders among the aged in the community. In J. Birren and R. Sloan, eds. *Handbook of mental health and aging.* Englewood Cliffs, NJ: Prentice-Hall, 1980.

Kay, P. Synchronic variability and diachronic changes in basic color terms. *Language in society,* 1975, *4,* 257–70.

Kehoe, P., and **Blass, E. M.** Conditioned opioid release in ten-day-old rats. *Behavioral neuroscience,* 1989, *103,* 423–28.

Keith-Spiegel, P., and **Koocher, G. P.** *Ethics in psychology.* San Francisco: Random House-Knopf, 1985.

Kelley, H., et al. *Close relationships.* San Francisco: Freeman, 1983.

Kelley, K., and **Musialowski, D.** Repeated exposure to sexually explicit stimuli. *Archives of sexual behavior,* 1986, *15,* 487–98.

Kellner, R. Changes in chronic nightmares, *American journal of psychiatry,* 1992, *149,* 659–63.

Kendler, K. S. Childhood parental loss and adult psychopathology in women. *Archives of general psychiatry,* 1992a, *49,* 109–16.

Kendler, K. S. A population-based twin study of major depression in women. *Archives of general psychiatry,* 1992b, *49,* 257–66.

Kendler, K. S., Neale, M. C., Kessler, R. C., Heath, A. C., and Eaves, L. J. A population-based twin study of major depression in women: The impact of varying definitions of illness. *Archives of general psychiatry,* 1992a, *49,* 257–66.

Kendler, K. S., Neale, M. C., Kessler, R. C., Heath, A. C., and Eaves, L. J. Childhood parental loss and adult psychopathology in women: A twin study perspective. *Archives of general psychiatry,* 1992b, *49,* 109–16.

Kendler, K. S., Neale, M. C., Kessler, R. C., Heath, A. C., and Eaves, L. J. Major depression and generalized anxiety disorder: Same genes, (partly) different environments? *Archives of general psychiatry,* 1992c, *49,* 716–22.

Kenrick, D. T., and Stringfield, D. O. Personality traits and the eye of the beholder: Crossing some traditional philosophical boundaries in the search for consistency in all of the people. *Psychological review,* 1980, *87,* 88–104.

Kermis, M. D. *The psychology of human aging.* Boston: Allyn and Bacon, 1984.

Kessler, M., and Goldston, S. E., eds. *A decade of progress in primary prevention.* Hanover, NH: University Press of New England, 1986.

Kessler, R. C., et al. Lifetime and 12-month prevalence of DSM-III (R) Psychiatric Disorders in the United States. *Archives of general psychiatry,* 1994, *51,* 8–19.

Kety, S. S. The impact of neurobiology in the concept of the mind. Paper presented at European Neuroscience Congress, Malaga, Spain, September 1982.

Kety, S. S., and Ingraham, L. J. Genetic transmission and improved diagnosis of schizophrenia from pedigrees of adoptees. *Journal of psychiatric research,* 1992, *26,* 247–55.

Kiecolt-Glaser, J. K., et al. Psychosocial modifiers of immunocompetence in medical students. *Psychosomatic medicine,* 1984, *46,* 7–14.

Kiecolt-Glaser, J. K., and Glaser, R. Stress and immune function in humans. In R. Ader, D. Felten, and N. Cohen, eds. *Psychoneuroimmunology II.* San Diego: Academic Press, 1991.

Kielcolt-Glaser, J. K., et al. Chronic stress and immunity in family caregivers of Alzheimer's disease victims. *Psychosomatic medicine,* 1987, *49,* 523–35.

Kiester, E., Jr. Spare parts for damaged brains. *Science,* 1986, *7,* 33–41.

Kimmel, D. C. *Adulthood and aging: An interdisciplinary developmental view,* 2nd ed. New York: Wiley, 1980.

Kimura, D. Male brain, female brain: The hidden difference. *Psychology today,* November 1985, 50–58.

Kimura, D., and Hampson, E. Neural and hormonal mechanisms mediating sex differences in cognition. London, Canada: Department of Psychology, University of Western Ontario, 1990.

Kindred, D. Yancey: Fall into darkness. *Washington post,* March 24, 1978.

Kinsey, A. C., Pomeroy, W. B., and Martin, C. E. *Sexual behavior in the human male.* Philadelphia: Saunders, 1948.

Kinsey, A. C., et al. *Sexual behavior in the human female.* Philadelphia: Saunders, 1953.

Kintsch, W. *Memory and cognition,* 2nd ed. New York: Wiley, 1977.

Kirk-Smith, M. D., and Booth, D. A. Effects of androstenone on choice of location in each other's presence. In H. van der Starre, ed. *Olfaction and taste VII.* London: IRL Press, 1980, 397–400.

Kirk-Smith, M. D., et al. Human social attitudes affected by androstenol. *Research communications in psychology, psychiatry and behavior,* 1978, *3,* 379–84.

Klatzky, R. L. *Human memory: Structures and processes,* 2nd ed. San Francisco: Freeman, 1980.

Kleinmuntz, B., and Szucko, J. J. A field study of the fallibility of polygraph lie detection. *Nature,* 1984, *308,* 449–50.

Klerman, G. L., and Weisman, M. M. Increasing rates of depression. *Journal of the American Medical Association,* 1989, *261,* 2229–35.

Kliegl, R., Smith, J., and Baltes, P. B. Testing-the-limits and the study of adult age differences in cognitive plasticity of a mnemonic skill. *Developmental psychology,* 1989, *25,* 247–56.

Klopfer, B., and Davidson, H. H. *The Rorschach technique.* New York: Harcourt, 1962.

Knapp, R. R. Relationship of a measure of self-actualization to neuroticism and extraversion. *Journal of consulting psychology,* 1965, *29,* 168–72.

Kobari, M., Meyer, J. S., and Ichijo, M. Leuko-araiosis, cerebral atrophy, and cerebral perfusion in normal aging. *Archives of neurology,* 1990, *47,* 161–65.

Kochanska, G. Toward a synthesis of parental socialization and child temperament in early development of conscience. *Child development,* 1993, *64,* 325–47.

Koegel, R. L. Personal communication, 1991.

Koegel, R. L., and Koegel, L. K. Motivating language use. Paper presented at Proceedings of the 1989 Autism Society of America, National Conference. Seattle, 1989.

Kohlberg, L. The development of children's orientations toward a moral order. I: Sequence in the development of moral thought. *Vita humana,* 1963, *6,* 11–33.

Kohlberg, L. Moral and religious education and the public schools. In T. Sizer, ed. *Religion and public education.* Boston: Houghton Mifflin, 1967.

Köhler, W. *The mentality of apes.* New York: Harcourt, 1925.

Kolata, G. Why do people get fat? *Science,* March 15, 1985, *227,* 1327–28.

Kolata, G. Early signs of school age IQ. *Science,* 1987, *236,* 774–75.

Koss, M. P., Butcher, J. N., and Strupp, H. H. Brief psychotherapy methods in clinical research. *Journal of consulting and clinical psychology,* 1986, *54,* 60–67.

Kramer, P. *Listening to Prozac.* New York: Viking, 1993.

Krantz, D., et al. *Behavior and health.* Paper commissioned by NRC/ABASS Committee on Basic Research in Behavioral and Social Sciences and Social Science Research Council, 1981.

Kretschmer, E. *Physique and character.* New York: Harcourt, 1925.

Krippner, S. *Experimentally induced effects in dreams and other altered conscious states.* 20th International Congress of Psychology, Tokyo, Aug. 1972.

Krosnick, J. A., and Alwin, D. F. Aging and susceptibility to attitude change. *Journal of personality and social psychology,* 1989, *57,* 416–25.

Kubie, L. S. *Practical and theoretical aspects of psychoanalysis.* New York: International University Press, 1950.

Kübler-Ross, E. *On death and dying.* New York: Macmillan, 1969.

Kruesi, M. J. P. A 2-year prospective follow-up study of children and adolescents with disruptive behavior disorders. *Archives of general psychiatry,* 1992, *49,* 429–53.

Kupfer, D. J., et al. Electroencephalographic sleep of younger depressives: Comparison with normals. *Archives of general psychiatry,* 1985, *42,* 806–10.

Kushner, M. G., Sher, K. J., Beltman, B. D. The relation between alcohol problems and the anxiety disorders. *American journal of psychiatry,* 1990, *147,* 685–95.

Labows, J. N., Jr. What the nose knows: Investigating the significance of human odors. *The sciences,* November 1980, 10–13.

Lacey, J. I., and Lacey, B. C. Verification and extension of the principle of autonomic response-stereotype. *American journal of psychology,* 1958, *71,* 50–73.

Lamb, S. Internal state words: Their relation to moral development and to maternal communications about moral development in the second year of life. *First language,* 1991, *11,* 391–406.

Lang, P. J. and Melamed, B. G. Avoidance conditioning therapy of an infant with chronic ruminative vomiting. *Journal of abnormal psychology,* 1969, *74,* 1–8.

Langley, P., et al. *Scientific discovery.* Cambridge: MIT Press, 1987.

Larsen, R. J., Diener, E., and Emmons, R. A. Affect intensity and reactions to daily life events. *Journal of personality and social psychology,* 1986, *51,* 803–14.

Larsen, R. J., and Lampman-Petraitis, C. Daily emotional states as reported by children and adolescents. *Child development,* 1989, *60,* 1250–60.

Latane, B., and Nida, S. Ten years of research on group size and helping. *Psychological bulletin,* 1981, *89,* 308–24.

Laudenslager, M. L., and Ryan, S. M. Coping and immunosuppression: Inescapable but not escapable shock suppresses lymphocyte proliferation. *Science,* 1983, *221,* 568–70.

Lazarus, R. S. *The stress and coping paradigm.* Paper delivered at the University of Washington conference on the critical evaluation of behavioral paradigms for psychiatric science, 1978.

Lazarus, R. S., and Averill, J. R. Emotion and cognition. In C. D. Spielberger, ed. *Anxiety.* New York: Academic Press, 1972.

Lazarus, R. S., and Folkman, S. *Stress, appraisal, and coping.* New York: Springer, 1984.

Leach, P. *Your growing child: From babyhood through adolescence.* New York: Knopf, 1989.

Leahey, T. H., and Harris, R. J. *Human learning,* 2nd ed. Englewood Cliffs, NJ: Prentice-Hall, 1989.

Lebowitz, B. D., and Cohen, G. D. Psychotropic drugs and geriatric patients. In C. Sulzman, ed., *Geriatric psychopharmacology.* Baltimore: Williams and Wilkins, 1991.

Lebowitz, B. D., and Cohen, G. C. The elderly and their illness. In C. Salzman, ed. *Clinical geriatric psychopharmacology,* 2nd ed. Baltimore: Williams and Wilkins, 1992.

Leedy, M. G., and Wilson, M. S. Testosterone and cortisol levels in crewmen of U.S. Air Force fighter and cargo planes. *Psychosomatic medicine,* 1985, *47,* 333–38.

Lefcourt, H. M., et al. Locus of control as a modifier of the relationship between stressors and moods. *Journal of personality and social psychology,* 1981, *41,* 357–69.

LeGoff, D. B., and Spigelman, M. N. Salivary response to olfactory food stimuli as a function of dietary restraint and body weight. *Appetite,* 1987, *8,* 29–35.

Le Magnen, J. Is regulation of body weight elucidated? *Neuroscience and biobehavior reviews,* 1984, *8,* 515–22.

LeMasters, E. E., and DeFrain, J. *Parents in contemporary America.* Homewood, IL: Dorsey, 1983.

Lemish, D., and Rice, M. L. Television as a talking picture book: A prop for language acquisition. *Journal of child language,* 1986, *13,* 251–74.

Lenneberg, E. H. *Biological foundations of language.* New York: Wiley, 1967.

Léon, C. A. Clinical course and outcome of schizophrenia in Cali, Colombia. *Journal of nervous and mental disease,* 1989, *177,* 593–606.

Leon, M. R., and Revelle, W. Effects of anxiety on analogical reasoning: A test of three theoretical models. *Journal of personality and social psychology,* 1985, *49,* 1302–15.

Lester, B., and Dreher, M. Effects of marijuana use during pregnancy on the newborn cry. *Child development,* 1989, *60,* 765–71.

LeVay, S. A difference in hypothalamic structure between heterosexual and homosexual men. *Science,* 1991, *253,* 1034–37.

Levenson, R. W. and Ruef, A. M. Empathy: A physiological substrate. *Journal of personality and social psychology,* 1992, *63,* 234–46.

Levine, I. S., and Haggard, L. K. Homelessness as a public mental health problem. In D. A. Rochefort, ed. *Handbook on mental health policy in the United States.* Boston: Greenwood Press, 1989.

Levine, I. S., and Rog, D. J. Mental health services for homeless mentally ill persons. *American psychologist,* 1990, *45,* 963–68.

Levine, L. E. Mine: Self-definition in 2-year-old boys. *Developmental psychology,* 1983, *19,* 544–49.

Levine, M. W., and Shefner, J. M. *Fundamentals of sensation and perception.* Reading, MA: Addison-Wesley, 1981.

Levinson, B., and Reese, H. W. Patterns of discrimination learning set in preschool children, fifth-graders, college freshmen, and the aged. *Monographs of the society for research in child development,* 1967, 32(No. 7), 1–92.

Levinson, D. J. *The seasons of a man's life.* New York: Knopf, 1978.

Levy, J. Right brain, left brain: Fact and fiction. *Psychology today,* May 1985, 38–44.

Levy, R. I. The emotions in comparative perspective. In K. R. Scherer and P. Ekman, eds. *Approaches to emotion: A book of readings.* Hillsdale, NJ: Erlbaum, 1984.

Lewis, E. R., Zeevi, Y. Y., and Everhart, T. E. Studying neural organization in *Aplysia* with scanning electron microscope. *Science,* 1969, *165,* 1140–42.

Lewontin, R. C. Race and intelligence. In N. J. Block and G. Dworkin, eds. *The IQ controversy.* New York: Pantheon, 1976.

Libet, B. Unconscious cerebral initiative and the role of conscious will in voluntary action. *The behavioral and brain sciences,* 1985, *8,* 529–39.

Liebert, R. M., and Sprafkin, J. *The early window: Effects of television on children and youth,* 3rd ed. New York: Pergamon, 1988.

Liebeskind, J. C., and Paul, L. A. Psychological and physiological mechanisms of pain. *Annual review of psychology,* 1977, *28,* 41–60.

Light, E., and Lebowitz, B. Alzheimer's disease treatment and family stress: Directions for research. Rockville, MD: National Institute of Mental Health, 1989. DHHS Publication No. (ADM) 89-1569, 1989.

Linn, S., et al. Salience of visual patterns in the human infant. *Developmental psychology,* 1982, *18,* 651–57.

Lipsitt, L. P. Personal communication, 1990.

Lloyd, R. L., and Kling, A. S. Delta activity from squirrel monkeys (Saimiri sciureus): Influence of social and environmental context. *Behavioral neuroscience,* 1991, *105,* 223–29.

Loehlin, J. C., Lindzey, G., and Spuhler, J. N. *Race differences in intelligence.* San Francisco: Freeman, 1975.

Loevinger, J., and Knoll, E. Personality: Stages, traits, and the self. *Annual review of psychology,* 1983, *34,* 195–222.

Loftus, E. F. When a lie becomes memory's truth: Memory distortion after exposure to misinformation. *Psychological science,* 1992, *1,* 121–23.

Loftus, E. F. The reality of repressed memories. *American psychologist,* 1993, *48,* 518–37.

Loftus, E. F., Miller, D. G., and **Burns, H. J.** Semantic integration of verbal information into a visual memory. *Journal of experimental psychology,* 1978, *4,* 19–31.

Logue, A. W., Ophir, I., and **Strauss, K. E.** The acquisition of taste aversion in humans. *Behavior research and therapy,* 1981, *19,* 319–33.

Lord, C. G., Lepper, M. R., and **Mackie, D.** Attitude prototypes as determinants of attitude-behavior consistency. *Journal of personality and social psychology,* 1984, *46,* 1254–66.

Lovaas, O. I. Behavioral treatment and normal educational and intellectual functioning in young autistic children. *Journal of consulting and clinical psychology,* 1987, *55,* 3–9.

Lubinski, D., and **Benbow, D. P.** Gender differences in abilities and preferences among the gifted: Implications for the math-science pipeline. *Current directions in psychological science,* 1992, *2,* 61–66.

Lummis, M., and **Stevenson, H. W.** Gender differences in beliefs and achievement: A cross-cultural study. *Developmental psychology,* 1990, *26,* 254–63.

Lykken, D. T. *A tremor in the blood: Uses and abuses of the lie detector.* New York: McGraw-Hill, 1981.

Lynn, S. J., and **Rhue, J. W.** Hypnosis, developmental antecedents, and psychopathology. *American psychologist,* 1988, *43,* 35–44.

Lyon, D. R. Individual differences in immediate serial recall: A matter of mnemonics. *Cognitive psychology,* 1977, *9,* 403–11.

Maccoby, E. E., and **Jacklin, C. N.** *The psychology of sex differences.* Stanford, CA: Stanford University Press, 1974.

Maccoby, E. E., Snow, M. E., and **Jacklin, C. N.** Children's dispositions and mother-child interaction at 12 and 18 months: A short-term longitudinal study. *Developmental psychology,* 1984, *20,* 459–72.

Macfarlane, J. W. From infancy to adulthood. *Child education,* 1963, *39,* 336–42.

Macfarlane, J. W. Perspectives on personality consistency and change from the guidance study. *Vita humana,* 1964, *7,* 115–26.

Mackenzie, B. Explaining race differences in IQ: The logic, the methodology, and the evidence. *American psychologist,* 1984, *39,* 1214–33.

MacKinnon, D. W. The nature and nurture of creative talent. *American psychologist,* 1962, *17,* 484–95.

MacKinnon, D. W. *The personality of correlates of creativity.* In G. S. Neilson, ed. *Proceedings of the XIV international congress of applied psychology,* Copenhagen, 1961. Copenhagen: Munksgaard, 1962.

MacKinnon, D. W. Stress interview. In D. N. Jackson and S. Messick, eds. *Problems in human assessment.* New York: McGraw-Hill, 1967.

Maddi, S. R. *Personality theories,* rev. ed. Homewood, IL: Dorsey, 1972.

Maddi, S. R., Barone, P. T., and **Puccetti, M. C.** Stressful events are indeed a factor in physical illness: Reply to Schroeder and Costa (1984). *Journal of personality and social psychology,* 1987, *52,* 833–43.

Maddi, S. R., and **Kobasa, S. C.** *The hardy executive: Health under stress.* Homewood, IL: Dow Jones–Irwin, 1984.

Maier, S. F., Seligman, M. E. P., and **Solomon, R. L.** Pavlovian fear conditioning and learned helplessness. In B. A. Campbell and R. M. Church, eds. *Punishment and aversive behavior.* New York: Appleton-Century-Crofts, 1969.

Mann, L., and **Janis, I. L.** A followup study on the long-term effects of emotional role playing. *Journal of personality and social psychology,* 1968, *8,* 338–42.

Manton, K. G., and **Soldo, B. J.** Dynamics of health changes in the oldest old: New perspectives and evidence. *Milbank memorial fund quarterly,* 1985, *63,* 206–85.

Manuck, S. B., et al. Individual differences in cellular immune responses to stress. *Psychological science,* March 1991, *2,* 111–15.

Markovitz, J. H., et al. Psychological predictors of hypertension in the Framingham study: Is there tension in hypertension? *Journal of the American Medical Association,* November 24, 1993, *270,* 2439–43.

Markowitz, J. S. Long-term psychological distress among chemically exposed firefighters. *Behavioral medicine,* 1989, *15,* 75–83.

Markowitz, J. S., Weissman, M. M., Ouelette, R., Lish, J. D., and **Klevman, G. L.** Quality of life in panic disorder. *Archives of general psychiatry,* 1989, *46,* 984–92.

Marks, D. F. Investigating the paranormal. *Nature,* 1986, *320,* 119–24.

Marks, I. M. Aversion therapy. *British journal of medical psychology,* 1968, *41,* 47–52.

Marmar, C. R., and **Horowitz, M. J.** Diagnosis and phase-oriented treatment of post-traumatic stress disorder. In J. P. Wilson, Z. Harel, and B. Kahana, eds. *Human adaptation to extreme stress.* 1988, 81–103.

Marsh, H. W., and **Parker, J. W.** Determinants of student self-concept: Is it better to be a relatively large fish in a small pond even if you don't learn to swim as well? *Journal of personality and social psychology,* 1984, *47,* 213–31.

Martin, J. L. The effects of social support on psychological distress among Vietnam veterans and their peers. Paper presented to the annual meetings of the American Psychological Association, Washington, DC, August 1982.

Marx, J. Familial Alzheimers linked to chromosome 14 gene. *Science,* 1992, *258,* 550.

Marx, J. L. The immune system "belongs in the body." *Science,* 1985, *227,* 1190–92.

Maslow, A. H. Personal communication, 1969.

Maslow, A. H. *Motivation and personality,* 2nd ed. New York: Harper, 1970.

Mason, J. W., et al. The use of psychoendocrine strategies in post-traumatic stress disorder. *Journal of applied social psychology,* 1990, *21,* 1822–46.

Masserman, J. H. *Principles of dynamic psychiatry,* 2nd ed. Philadelphia: Saunders, 1961.

Masters, W. H., and **Johnson, V. E.** *Human sexual response.* Boston: Little, Brown, 1966.

Matson, F. W. Humanistic theory: The third revolution in psychology. *The humanist,* March/April 1971, 7–11.

Maugh, T. M., II. Sleep-promoting factor isolated. *Science,* 1982, *216,* 1400.

Mayer, R. E. *Thinking, problem solving, and cognition.* San Francisco: Freeman, 1983.

Mayes, A. R. *Human organic memory disorders.* London: Cambridge University Press, 1988.

Mayr, E. *Growth of biological thought: Diversity, evolution, and inheritance.* Cambridge: Harvard University Press, 1985.

McAdams, D. P. *The person: Introduction to personality psychology.* San Diego: Harcourt, 1990.

McAdams, D. P. The five-factor model in personality: A critical appraisal. *Journal of personality,* 1992, *60,* 329–61.

McCall, R. B., Applebaum, M. I., and **Hogarty, P. S.** Developmental changes in mental performance. *Monographs of the society for research in child development,* 1973, *38,* Serial No. 150.

McCall, R. B. and **Carriger, M. S.** A meta-analysis of infant habituation and recognition memory performance as predictors of later IQ. *Child development,* 1993, *64,* 57–79.

McCann, I. L., and **Holmes, D. S.** Influence of aerobic exercise on depression. *Journal of personality and social psychology,* 1984, *46,* 1142–47.

McCarthy, G. Echo-planar magnetic resonance imaging studies of frontal cortex activation during word generation in humans. *Proceedings of the National Academy of Sciences,* 1993, *90,* 4952–56.

McCarthy, M. The thin ideal: Depression and eating disorders in women. *Behavior research and therapy,* 1990, *28,* 205–15.

McCartney, K. Effect of quality of day care environment on children's language development. *Developmental psychology,* 1984, *20,* 244–60.

McCaul, K. D. Sensory information, fear level, and reactions to pain. *Journal of personality,* 1980, *48,* 494–504.

McCaul, K. D., Holmes, D. S., and Solomon, S. Voluntary expressive changes in emotion. *Journal of personality and social psychology,* 1982, *42,* 145–52.

McClelland, D. C. Inhibited power motive and high blood pressure in men. *Journal of abnormal psychology,* 1979, *88,* 182–90.

McClelland, D. C. How motives, skills, and values determine what people do. *American psychologist,* 1985, *40,* 812–25.

McClelland, D. C. Motivational factors in health and disease. *American psychologist,* 1989, *44,* 675–82.

McClelland, D. C., and Atkinson, J. W. The projective expression of needs. I: The effect of different intensities of the hunger drive on perception. *Journal of psychology,* 1948, *25,* 205–22.

McClelland, D. C., Clark, R. A., and Lowell, E. L. *The achievement motive.* New York: Appleton-Century-Crofts, 1953.

McClelland, D. C., et al. *The drinking man.* New York: Free Press, 1972.

McClelland, J. L. *The role of the behavioral sciences in mental health (framing piece).* Washington, DC: National Institute of Mental Health, 1988.

McClenon, J. A survey of elite scientists: Their attitudes toward ESP and parapsychology. *Journal of parapsychology,* 1982, *46,* 127–52.

McClintock, M. K. Menstrual synchrony and suppression. *Nature,* 1971, *229,* 224–45.

McClintock, M. K. Estrous synchrony: Modulation of ovarian cycle length by female pheromones. *Physiology and behavior,* 1984, *32,* 701–05.

McCormick, M. C., et al. The health and developmental status of very low-birth-weight children at school age. *Journal of the American Medical Association,* 1992, *267,* 2204–08.

McCullough, C. Color adaptation of edge-detectors in the human visual system. *Science,* 1965, *149,* 1115–16.

McDonald, R. J., and White, N. M. A triple dissociation of memory systems: Hippocampus, amygdala, and dorsal striatum. *Behavioral neuroscience,* 1993, *107,* 3–22.

McGaugh, J. L. Preserving the presence of the past: Hormonal influences on memory storage. *American psychologist,* 1983, *38,* 161–74.

McGeoch, J. A. The influence of associative value upon the difficulty of nonsense-syllable lists. *Journal of genetic psychology,* 1930, *37,* 421–26.

McGlynn, S. M. Behavioral approaches to neuropsychological rehabilitation. *Psychological bulletin.* 1990, *108,* 420–41.

McGuire, W. J., and McGuire, C. V. Differences in conceptualizing self versus conceptualizing other people as manifested by contrasting verbs used in natural speech. *Journal of personality and social psychology,* 1986, *51,* 1135–43.

McKeachie, W., et al. Student affiliation, motives, teacher warmth and academic achievement. *Journal of personality and social psychology,* 1966, *4,* 457–61.

McNally, R. J., et al. Selective processing of threat cues in post-traumatic stress disorder. *Journal of abnormal psychology,* 1990, *99,* 398–402.

McNemar, Q. *The revision of the Stanford-Binet scale.* Boston: Houghton Mifflin, 1942.

McRae, R., and Costa, P. T., Jr. Clinical assessment can benefit from recent advances in personality psychology. *American psychologist,* 1986, *41,* 1001–03.

Meece, J. L., Parsons, J. E., Kaczaia, C. M., and Goff, S. B. Sex differences in math achievement: Toward models of academic choice. *Psychological bulletin,* 1982, *91,* 324–48.

Mellinger, G. D., and Balter, M. B. Prevalence and patterns of use of psychotherapeutic drugs: Results from a 1979 national survey of American adults. In G. Tognoni, C. Bellantuono, and M. Lader, eds. *Epidemiological impact of psychotropic drugs.* Amsterdam: Elsevier/North Holland Biomedical Press, 1981.

Meltzer, H. Y. Biological studies in schizophrenia. *Schizophrenia bulletin,* National Institute of Mental Health, 1987, *13,* 77–111.

Meltzer, H. Y. Dimensions of outcome with clozapine. *British journal of psychiatry,* 1992, *160,* 46–53.

Melzack, R. *The puzzle of pain.* New York: Basic Books, 1973.

Mendelson, W. B., et al. The experience of insomnia and daytime and nighttime functioning. *Psychiatry research,* 1984, *12,* 235–50.

Metcalfe, J. Premonitions of insight predict impending error. *Journal of experimental psychology: Learning, memory, and cognition,* 1986, *12,* 623–34.

Meyer, C. B., and Taylor, S. E. Adjustment to rape. *Journal of personality and social psychology,* 1986, *50,* 1226–34.

Midlarsky, E., and Hannah, M. E. The generous elderly: Naturalistic studies of donations along the life span. *Psychology and aging,* 1989, *4,* 346–51.

Milgram, S. Group pressure and action against a person. *Journal of abnormal and social psychology,* 1964, *69,* 137–43.

Milgram, S. *Obedience to authority.* New York: Harper, 1974.

Miller, B. C., and Sollie, D. L. Normal stress during the transition to parenthood. *Family relations,* 1980, *29,* 459–65.

Miller, B. D., and Strunk, R. C. Circumstances surrounding the deaths of children due to asthma: A case-control study. *American journal of diseases of children.* 1989, *143,* 1294–99.

Miller, G. A. *Language and communication.* New York: McGraw-Hill, 1951.

Miller, G. A. The magical number seven, plus or minus two: Some limits on our capacity for processing information. *Psychological review,* 1956, *63,* 81–97.

Miller, G. A. Language and psychology. In E. H. Lenneberg, ed. *New directions in the study of language.* Cambridge: MIT Press, 1964.

Miller, G. A. *Language and speech.* San Francisco: Freeman, 1981.

Miller, J. G. Culture and the development of everyday social explanation. *Journal of personality and social psychology,* 1984, *46,* 961–78.

Miller, N. E. How the brain affects the health of the body. In K. D. Craig and S. M. Weiss, eds. *Health enhancement, disease prevention, and early intervention.* New York: Springer, 1990.

Miller, N. E. *Behavioral sciences report for the overview cluster of the President's biomedical research panel,* 1975.

Miller, N. E. Behavioral medicine: Symbiosis between laboratory and clinic. *Annual review of psychology,* 1983, *34,* 1–31.

Miller, N. E. The value of behavioral research on animals. *American psychologist,* 1985a, *40,* 423–40.

Miller, N. E. Rx: Biofeedback. *Psychology today.* February 1985b, 54–59.

Miller, N. E., and Dollard, J. *Social learning and imitation.* New Haven: Yale University Press, 1941.

Milner, B. Memory and the medial temporal regions of the brain. In K. K. Pribram and D. E. Broadbent, eds. *Biology of memory*. New York: Academic Press, 1970, 29–50.

Mischel, W. *Personality and assessment*. New York: Wiley, 1968.

Mischel, W. Convergences and challenges in the search for consistency. *American psychologist*, 1984, *39*, 351–64.

Mishkin, M. Personal communication, 1986.

Mishkin, M., and **Appenzeller, T.** The anatomy of memory. *Scientific american*, June 1987, 80–89.

Mishler, E. Families and schizoprenia. *Harvard mental health letter*, 1991, *7*, 3–6.

Mitchell, D. B. How many memory systems? Evidence from aging. *Journal of experimental psychology: Learning, memory, and cognition*, 1989, *15*, 31–49.

Moberg, G. P. Influence of stress on reproduction: Measure of well-being. In G. P. Moberg, ed. *Animal stress*. Bethesda, MD: American Physiological Society, 1987, 161–267.

Money, J. Sin, sickness, or status? Homosexuality, gender identity, and psychoneuroendicronology. *American psychologist*, 1987, *42*, 384–99.

Montie, J. E., and **Fagan, J. F.** Racial differences in IQ: Item analysis of the Stanford-Binet at 3 years. *Intelligence*, 1988, *12*, 315–32.

Moos, R. H. Depressed outpatients' life contexts, amount of treatment, and treatment outcome. *Journal of nervous and mental disease*, 1990, *178*, 105–12.

Moreland, R. L., and **Zajonc, R. B.** Exposure effects in person perception: Familiarity, similarity, and attraction. *Journal of experimental social psychology*, 1982, *18*, 395–415.

Moss, H. A., and **Susman, E. J.** Longitudinal study of personality development. *Constancy and change in human development*. Cambridge: Harvard University Press, 1980.

Moyer, J. A., **Herrenkohl, L. R.**, and **Jacobowitz, D. M.** Stress during pregnancy: Effect on catecholamines in discrete brain regions of offspring as adults. *Brain research*, 1978, *144*, 173–78.

Mozel, M. M., et al. Nasal chemoreception in flavor identification. *Archives of otolaryngology, 90*, 367–73.

Mueser, K. T., et al. You're only as pretty as you feel: Facial expression as a determinant of physical attractiveness. *Journal of personality and social psychology*, 1984, *46*, 469–78.

Mumford, J., et al. A new look at evidence about reduced cost of medical utilization following mental health treatment. *American journal of psychiatry*, 1984, *141*, 1145–58.

Munn, N. L., **Fernald, L. D., Jr.**, and **Fernald, P. S.** *Introduction to psychology*, 2nd ed. Boston: Houghton Mifflin, 1969.

Murphy, C., and **Cain, W. S.** Taste and olfaction: Independence vs. interaction. *Physiology and behavior*, 1980, *24*, 601–05.

Murphy, G. L., and **Medin, D. L.** The role of theories in conceptual coherence. *Psychological review*, 1985, *92*, 289–316.

Murray, E. A., and **Mishkin, M.** Amygdalectomy impairs crossmodal association in monkeys. *Science*, 1985, *228*, May 3, 1985, 604–06.

Murstein, B. L. *Paths to marriage*. Newbury Park, CA: Sage, 1986.

Mussen, P. H., et al. *Child development and personality*, 7th ed. New York: Harper, 1990.

Myers, J. K., et al. Six-month prevalence of psychiatric disorders in three communities. *Archives of general psychiatry*, 1984, *41*, 959–67.

National Center for Health Statistics. *Vital statistics of the United States: Annual volume on mortality, 1986*, Washington, DC: 1988.

National Center for Health Statistics. Advanced report of final mortality statistics, 1991. *Monthly Vital Statistics Report*, 1993 (*supplement*), *42*, 2.

National Depressive and Manic-Depressive Association, *Bipolar disorder: Self-portrait of an illness*. Chicago, 1993.

National Hospice Organization. *Guide to the nation's hospice*. Arlington, VA: 1989.

National Institute of Mental Health. *Attitudes toward the mentally ill: Research perspectives*. **DHHS** Publication No. (ADM) 80-1031, 1980.

National Institute of Mental Health. *Alzheimer's disease*. **DHHS** Publication No. (ADM) 84-1323, September 1984.

National Institute of Mental Health. Useful information on anorexia nervosa and bulimia. **DHHS** Publication No. (ADM) 87-1514, 1987.

National Institute of Mental Health. *Approaching the 21st century: Opportunities for NIMH neuroscience research*. **DHHS** Pub. No. (ADM) 88-1580, 1988.

National Institute of Mental Health. *A national plan for schizophrenia research*. **DHHS** Pub. No. (ADM) 88-1570, 1989a.

National Institute of Mental Health. *Animal research: The search for life-saving answers*. **DHHS** Pub. No. (ADM) 92-1771, 1991.

National Institute of Mental Health, *Consensus paper on panic disorder*, 1991.

National Institute of Mental Health. *Animals in medical science*. **DHHS** Pub. No. (ADM) 92-1961, 1992.

National Institute on Aging. *Age page: Can life be extended?* **DHHS,** National Institutes of Health, June 1984.

National Institute on Drug Abuse. *Overview of the 1985 National Household Survey on Drug Abuse*, 1986.

National Institute on Drug Abuse. *Overview of the national household survey on drug use*, 1988.

National Institutes of Health. Coronary-prone behavior and coronary heart disease. A critical review. *Circulation*, 1981, *63*, 1199–1215.

National Institutes of Health. Mood disorders: Pharmacologic prevention of recurrences. *Consensus development conference*, vol. 4 no. 5, 1984.

National Institutes of Health. *Electroconvulsive therapy: Consensus development* (Consensus statement). Bethesda, MD: June 1985, (5).

National Institutes of Health. *Decade of the brain*. **NIH** Pub. No. 88-2957, 1989.

National Institutes of Health. Treatment of Panic Disorder. **NIH** Consens Dev Conf Consens Statement, Sept 25–27, 1991, 9(2).

National Research Council. *Ability testing: Uses, consequences and controversies*. Washington, DC: National Academy Press, 1982.

National Research Council. *Losing generations: Adolescents in high-risk settings*. Washington, DC: National Academy Press, 1993.

Neisser, U., and **Becklen, R.** Selective looking. *Cognitive psychology*, 1975, *7*, 480–94.

Nelson, K. The psychological and social origins of autobiographical memory. *Psychological science*, 1993, *4*, 7–14.

Neubauer, P. B., and **Neubauer, A.** *Nature's thumbprint*. Reading, MA: Addison-Wesley, 1990.

Newcombe, N., **Fox, F.**, and **Prime, A.** Preschool memories: Through a glass darkly. In press.

Newport, E. L. Motherese. *Technical report no. 52. Center for Human Information Processing*. San Diego: University of California, 1975.

Newstead, S. E., et al. The source of belief bias effects in syllogistic reasoning. *Cognition*, 1992, *45*, 257–84.

Nielsen, S. L., and Sarason, I. G. Emotion, personality, and selective attention. *Journal of personality and social psychology*, 1981, *41*, 945–60.

Nieuwenhuise, B., Offenberg, L., and Frijda, N. H. Subjective emotion and reported body experience. *Motivation and emotion*, 1987, *11*, 169–82.

Nisbett, R. E. Taste, deprivation, and weight determinants of eating behavior. *Journal of personality and social psychology*, 1968, *10*, 107–16.

Nisbett, R. E. Hunger, obesity, and the ventromedial hypothalamus. *Psychological review*, 1972, *79*, 433–53.

Nisbett, R. E., and Valins, S. Perceiving the causes of one's own behavior. In E. E. Jones et al., eds. *Attribution*. Morristown, NJ: General Learning Press, 1972.

Nissen, H., and Crawford, M. A. A preliminary study of food-sharing behavior in young chimpanzees. *Journal of comparative psychology*, 1936, *22*, 283–419.

Nolen-Hoeksema, S. *Sex differences in depression*. Palo Alto, CA: Stanford University Press, 1990.

Novak, M. A., and Suomi, S. J. Psychological well-being of primates in captivity. *American psychologist*, 1988, *43*, 765–73.

Nurco, D. N. Etiological aspects of drug abuse. In R. I. Dupont, A. Goldstein, and J. O'Donnell, eds. *Handbook on drug abuse*. Washington, DC: GPO, January 1979, 315–34.

O'Connor, M. J., Cohen, S., and Parmelee, A. H. Infant auditory discrimination in preterm and full-term infant as a predictor of 5-year intelligence. *Developmental psychology*, 1984, *20*, 159–65.

Offir, C. W. *Human sexuality*. San Diego: Harcourt, 1982.

Oggins, J., and Veroff, J. The interaction of communication behaviors and attitudes in predicting marital well-being. Paper presented at the Midwest Psychological Association, Chicago, May 1989.

O'Leary, K. D., and Drabman, R. Token reinforcement programs in the classroom. *Psychological bulletin*, 1971, *75*, 379–98.

Olfson, M. Assertive community treatment: An evaluation of the experimental evidence. *Hospital and community psychiatry*, 1990, *4*, 634–41.

Olson, S. L., Bates, J. E., and Bayles, K. Mother-infant interaction and the development of individual differences in children's cognitive competence. *Developmental psychology*, 1984, *20*, 166–79.

Olweus, D. Continuity in aggressive and withdrawn, inhibited behavior patterns. *Psychiatry and social sciences*, 1981, *1*, 141–59.

O'Neil, H. F., Jr., Spielberger, C. D., and Hansen, D. N. Effects of state anxiety and task difficulty on computer-assisted learning. *Journal of educational psychology*, 1969, *60*, 343–50.

Orne, M. Lecture to American Association for the Advancement of Science. Washington, DC, 1982.

Ornstein, R. The split and the whole brain. *Human nature*, 1978, *1*, 76–83.

Ornstein, R., and Thompson, R. F. *The amazing brain*. Boston: Houghton Mifflin, 1984.

Osterweis, M., Solomon, F., and Green, M. *Bereavement: Reactions, consequences, and care*. Washington, DC: National Academy of Sciences, 1984.

Oyama, S. *A sensitive period for the acquisition of a second language*. Unpublished doctoral dissertation, Harvard University, 1973.

Pachura, C. M., and Martin, J. B. *Mapping the brain and its functions*. Washington, DC: National Academy Press, 1991.

Paddock, J., O'Neill, C. W., and Haver, W. *Faces of anti-violence*. International Society for Research on Aggression, Washington, DC, September 1978.

Parloff, M. B. Can psychotherapy research guide the policymaker? A little knowledge may be a dangerous thing. *American psychologist*, 1979, *34*, 296–306.

Parloff, M. B. Personal communication, 1990.

Partridge, M. *Prefrontal leucotomy: A survey of 300 cases followed over 1½ to 3 years*. Springfield, IL: Charles C. Thomas, 1957.

Passingham, R. E. Memory of monkeys (Macaca mulatta) with lesions in prefrontal cortex. *Behavioral neurosciences*, 1985, *99*, 3–21.

Patterson, G. R., Hops, H., and Weiss, R. L. Interpersonal skills training for couples in early stages of conflict. *Journal of marriage and the family*, 1975, *37*, 295–303.

Pavlov, I. P. *Conditioned reflexes*. London: Oxford University Press, 1927 (reprinted by Dover, New York, 1960).

Pearson, C. Intelligence of Honolulu preschool children in relation to parents' education. *Child development*, 1969, *40*, 647–50.

Peele, S. Reductionism in the psychology of the eighties: Can biochemistry eliminate addiction, mental illness, and pain? *American psychologist*, 1981, *36*, 807–18.

Penick, S., and Solomon, P. R. Hippocampus, context, and conditioning. *Behavioral neuroscience*, 1991 *105*, 611–17.

Pennebaker, J. W. Confession, inhibition, and disease. *Advances in experimental social psychology*, 1989, *22*, 211–44.

Pennebaker, J. W., Kiecolt-Glaser, J. K., and Glaser, R. Disclosure of traumas and immune function: Health implications for psychotherapy. *Journal of consulting and clinical psychology*, 1988, *56*, 239–45.

Perin, C. T. A quantitative investigation of the delay of reinforcement gradient. *Journal of experimental psychology*, 1943, *32*, 37–51.

Perkins, D. Creativity and the quest for mechanism. In R. J. Sternberg and E. E. Smith, eds. *The psychology of human thought*. Cambridge, England: Cambridge University Press, 1988.

Perry, D. G., et al. Victims of pure aggression. *Developmental psychology*, 1988, *24*, 807–14.

Petersen, A. C. Those gangly years. *Psychology today*, September 1987, 28–34.

Peterson, C., and Seligman, M. E. P. Causal explanations as a risk factor in depression. *Psychological review*, 1984, *91*, 347–74.

Petti, T. A. Depression in children: A significant disorder. *Psychosomatics*, 1981, *22*, 444–47.

Petti, T. A., and Larson, C. N. Depression and suicide. In V. P. Van Hesselt and M. Hersen, eds. *Handbook of adolescent psychology*. New York: Pergamon, 1987.

Pettigrew, T. F. Racially separate or together? *Journal of social issues*, 1969, *25*, 43–69.

Pettingale, K. W., et al. Mental attitudes to cancer: An additional prognostic factor. *Lancet*, March 30, 1985.

Pevsner, J., et al. Molecular cloning of odorant binding protein: Member of a ligand carrier family. *Science*, 1988, *241*, 336–39.

Pezdek, K., et al. Memory for real-world scenes: The role of consistency with schema expectations. *Journal of experimental psychology: Learning, memory, and cognition*, 1989, *15*, 587–95.

Phares, E. J., and Lamiell, J. T. Internal-external control, interpersonal judgments of others in need, and attribution of responsibility. *Journal of personality*, 1975, *43*, 23–38.

Phillips, D. The illusion of incompetence among academically competent children. *Child development*, 1984, *55*, 2000–16.

Phillips, D. P., and Carstensen, L. L. Clustering of teenage suicides after television news stories about suicide. *New England journal of medicine*, September 11, 1986, *315*, 685–89.

Piaget, J. *The origins of intelligence in children*. New York: International University Press, 1952.

Pick, H. L. Information and the effects of early perceptual experience. In N. Eisenberg, ed. *Contemporary topics in developmental psychology*. New York: Wiley, 1987, 59–76.

Piet, S. What motivates stunt men? *Motivation and emotion*, 1987, *11*, 195–213.

Pietropinto, A. Misconceptions about male sexuality. *Medical aspects of human sexuality*, 1986, *20*, 80–85.

Pike, K., and Rodin, J. Mothers, daughters, and disordered eating. *Journal of abnormal psychology*, 1991, *100*, 198–204.

Pillemer, D. H. Flashbulb memories of the assassination attempt of President Reagan. *Cognition*, 1984, *16*, 63–80.

Pine, C. J. Anxiety and eating behavior in obese and nonobese American Indians and white Americans. *Journal of personality and social psychology*, 1985, *49*, 774–80.

Pion, G. Psychologists wanted: Employment trends over the last decade. In R. Kilburg, ed. *Managing your psychological career*. Washington, DC: American Psychological Association, 1990.

Plomin, R. Environment and genes. *American psychologist*, 1989, *44*, 105–11.

Plomin, R. Behavioral genetics: Nature and nurture. *Harvard Medical School mental health letter*, May 1990, 4–6.

Plomin, R., and McClearn, G. E., eds. *Nature-nurture and psychology*. Washington, DC: American Psychological Association, 1993.

Polivy, J. On the induction of emotion in the laboratory: Discrete moods or multiple affect states? *Journal of personality and social psychology*, 1981, *41*, 803–17.

Pollack, I., and Pickett, J. M. Intelligibility of excerpts from fluent speech. *Journal of verbal learning and verbal behavior*, 1964, *3*, 79–84.

Pollitt, E., et al. *Iron deficiency and school achievement in Thailand*. Paper presented at meeting of the Society for Research in Child Development. Kansas City, MO, 1989.

Pomerantz, J. R. The grass is always greener: An ecological analysis of an old aphorism. *Perception*, 1983, *12*, 501–02.

Pope, K., and Feldman-Summers, S. National survey of psychologists' sexual and physical abuse history and their evaluation of training and competence in these areas. *Professional psychology: Research and practice*, 1992, *23*, 353–61.

Pope, K. S., and Tabachnick, B. G. Therapists' anger, hate, fear and sexual feelings: National survey of therapist responses, client characteristics, critical events, formal complaints, and training. *Professional psychology: Research and practice*, 1993, *24*, 142–52.

Postman, L., Bruner, B., and McGinnies, E. Personal values as selective factors in perception. *Journal of abnormal and social psychology*, 1948, *43*, 142–54.

Potts, M. K., Burnam, M. A., and Wells, K. B. Gender differences in depression detection: A comparison of clinical diagnosis and standardized assessment. *Psychological assessment*, 1991, *3*, 609–15.

Powers, S. I., Hauser, S. T., and Kilner, L. A. Adolescent mental health. *American psychologist*, 1989, *44*, 200–208.

Pratt, C. On asking children—and adults—bizarre questions. *First language*, 1990, *10*, 167–75.

Premack, D. *Intelligence in ape and man*. Hillsdale, NJ: Erlbaum, 1976.

Premack, D. "Gavagai!" or the future history of the animal language controversy. *Cognition*, 1985, *19*, 207–96.

Prentice, D. A., and Miller, D. T. Pluralistic ignorance and alcohol use on campus: Some consequences of misperceiving the social norm. *Journal of personality and social psychology*, 1993, *64*, 243–56.

Priest, R. F., and Sawyer, J. Proximity and peership: Bases of balance in interpersonal attraction. *American journal of sociology*, 1967, *72*, 633–649.

Pritchard, R. M. Stabilized images on the retina. *Scientific American*, 1961, *204*, 72–78.

Pruett, H. L. Stressors in middle adulthood. *Family and community health*, 1980, *2*, 53–60.

Quadrel, M. J., Fischhoff, B. and Davis, W. Adolescent (in)vulnerability. *American psychologist*, 1993, *48*, 102–16.

Quinn, S. *A mind of her own: The life of Karen Horney*. New York: Basic Books, 1987.

Quinton, D., and Rutter, M. Parenting behavior of mothers raised "in care." In A. R. Nicol, ed. *Practical lessons from longitudinal studies*. Chichester, England: Wiley, 1983.

Rabkin, J. G., and Struening, E. L. Life events, stress, and illness. *Science*, 1976, *194*, 1013–20.

Radecki, C., and Jennings, J. Sex as a status variable in work settings: Female and male reports of dominance behavior. *Journal of applied social psychology*, 1980, *10*, 71–85.

Radke-Yarrow, M. Personal communication, 1989.

Radke-Yarrow, M., Zahn Waxler, C., and Chapman, M. Children's prosocial dispositions and behavior. In P. H. Mussen, ed. *Handbook of child psychology*, 4th ed, Vol 4. New York: Wiley, 1983.

Radloff, R. *Opinion and affiliation*. Unpublished doctoral dissertation, University of Minnesota, 1959.

Rahe, R. H., et al. Psychological and physiological assessments on American hostages freed from captivity in Iran. *Psychosomatic medicine*, 1990, 1–16.

Rajram, S., and Roediger, H. L. Direct comparison of four implicit memory tests. *Journal of experimental psychology: Learning, memory, and cognition*. 1993, *19*, 765–76.

Rakic, P. et al. Concurrent overproduction of synapses in diverse regions of the primate cortex. *Science*, 1986, *232*, 232–35.

Rapoport, J. L. The biology of obsessions and compulsions. *Scientific American*, March 1989, 83–89.

Reason, J. The psychopathology of everyday slips. *The sciences*, September/October 1984, 45–49.

Redburn, F. S., and Buss, T. F. *Responding to America's homeless*. New York: Praeger, 1985.

Reece, R. D., and Siegal, H. A. *Studying people: A primer in the ethics of social research*. Macon, GA: Mercer University Press, 1986.

Reeve, J., Cole, S. G., and Olson, B. C. Zeigarnik effect and instrinsic motivation. *Motivation and emotion*, 1986, *10*, 233–45.

Regier, D. A. Comorbidity of mental disorders with alcohol and other drug abuse. *Journal of the American Medical Association*. 1990, *264*, 2511–18.

Regier, D. A. The de facto U.S. mental and addictive disorders service system. *Archives of general psychiatry*, 1993, *50*, 85–94.

Regier, D. A., et al. One-month prevalence of mental disorders in the United States. *Archives of general psychiatry*, 1988, *45*, 977–86.

Reis, H. T., Senchak, M., and Solomon, B. Sex differences in the intimacy of social interaction: Further examination of potential explanations. *Journal of personality and social psychology*, 1985, *48*, 1204–17.

Reis, H. T., et al. Physical attractiveness in social interaction: II: Why does appearance affect social experience? *Journal of personality and social psychology*, 1982, *43*, 979–96.

Reite, M. L. Temperament stability between prenatal period and 24 months. *Developmental psychology*, 1987, *23*, 216–22.

Reno, R. M., and Halaris, A. E. The relationship between life stress and depression in an endogenous sample. *Comprehensive psychiatry*, 1990, *31*, 25–33.

Rescorla, R. A., and Holland, P. C. Behavioral studies of associative learning in animals. In M. R. Rosenzweig and L. W. Porter, eds. *Annual review of psychology*, 1982, *33*, 265–308.

Reynolds, B. A., and Weiss, S. Generation of neurons and astrocytes from isolated cells of the adult mammalian central nervous system. *Science*, March 1992, *255*, 1707–10.

Reynolds, C. R., and Gutkin, T. B. A multivariate comparison of the intellectual performance of blacks and whites matched on four demographic variables. *Personality and individual differences*, 1981, *2*, 175–80.

Reznick, J. S. Visual preference as a test of infant word comprehension. *Applied psycholinguistics*, 1990, *11*, 145–66.

Rhine, J. B., and Pratt, J. G. *Parapsychology*. Springfield, IL: Thomas, 1957.

Rice, D. P., and Miller, L. S. The economic burden of mental disorders. Paper presented at the American Psychiatric Association, 1993 Annual Meeting, May 26, 1993.

Rice, M. L., et al. Words from "Sesame Street": Learning vocabulary while viewing. *Developmental psychology*, 1990, *26, 3*, 421–28.

Richlin, M., et al. Five-year medical followup of Vietnam POWs: Preliminary results: *U.S. Navy medicine*, August 1980, *71*, 19–28.

Riessman, F. *Support groups as preventive intervention*. Paper presented to Vermont Conference on Primary Prevention of Psychology. June 29, 1984, Burlington, VT.

Riessman, F. Personal communication, 1985.

Rist, R. C. Student social class and teacher expectations: The self-fulfilling prophecy in ghetto education. *Harvard educational review*, 1970, *40*, 411–51.

Rizley, R. Depression and distortion in the attribution of causality. *Journal of abnormal psychology*, 1978, *87*, 32–48.

Robbins, D. Partial reinforcement. *Psychological bulletin*, 1971, *76*, 415–31.

Robbins, P. R., and Tanck, R. H. A study of diurnal patterns of depressed mood. *Motivation and emotion*, 1987, *11*, 37–49.

Roberts, L. Vietnam's psychological toll. *Science*, 1988, *241*, 159–61.

Robins, L. N. Sturdy childhood predictors of adult outcomes: Replications from longitudinal studies. *Psychological medicine*, 1978, *8*, 611–22.

Robinson, R. G., et al. Two-year longitudinal study of post-stroke mood disorders: Comparison of acute-onset with delayed-onset depression. *American journal of psychiatry*, 1986, *143*, 1238–44.

Rock, I. *Perception*, Washington, DC: Scientific American Library, 1984.

Rodin, J. Managing the stress of aging: The role of control and coping. In S. Levine and H. Ursin, eds. *Coping and health*. New York: Plenum, 1980.

Rodin, J. Insulin levels, hunger, and food intake: An example of feedback loops in body weight regulation. *Health psychology*, 1985, *4*, 1–18.

Rodin, J. The determinants of successful aging. Washington, DC: Federation of Behavioral, Psychological and Cognitive Sciences, 1987.

Roediger, H. L. Implicit memory: Retention without remembering. *American psychologist*, 1990, *45*, 1043–56.

Rogel, M. J. A critical evaluation of the possibility of higher primate reproductive and sexual pheromones. *Psychological bulletin*, 1978, *85*, 810–30.

Rogers, C. Personal communication, 1969.

Rogers, C. R. *A way of being*. Boston: Houghton Mifflin, 1980.

Roland, A. *In search of self in India and Japan*. Princeton, NJ: Princeton University Press, 1989.

Rolls, B. J., and Rolls, E. T. *Thirst*. New York: Cambridge University Press, 1982.

Romaniuk, M., McAuley, W. J., and Arling, G. An examination of the prevalance of mental disorders among the elderly in the community. *Journal of abnormal psychology*, 1983, *92*, 458–67.

Rook, K. S. Social support versus companionship: Effects on life stress, loneliness, and evaluations by others. *Journal of personality and social psychology*, 1987, *52*, 1132–47.

Roper Organization. *Virginia Slims American women's opinion poll*. New York, 1980.

Roper Organization. *Virginia Slims American women's opinion poll*. New York, 1990.

Rorer, L. G., and Widiger, J. A. Personality structure and assessment. *Annual review of psychology*, 1983, *34*, 431–63.

Rosch, E. H. Natural categories. *Cognitive psychology*, 1973, *4*, 328–50.

Rosch, E. H. Human categorization. In E. Warren, ed. *Advances in cross-cultural psychology*, Vol. 1. London: Academic Press, 1977.

Rosch, E. H., and Mervis, C. B. Family resemblances: studies in the internal structure of categories. *Cognitive psychology*, 1975, *7*, 573–605.

Rose, R. M. Endocrine responses to stressful psychological events. *Psychiatric clinics of North America*, 1980, *3*, 251–76.

Rose, R. M., Jenkins, C. D., and Hurst, M. W. *Air traffic controller health change study*. Boston: Boston University School of Medicine, 1978.

Rose, S. A., and Wallace, I. F. Visual recognition memory: A predictor of later cognitive functioning in preterms. *Child development*, 1985, *56*, 843–52.

Rosekrans, M., and Hartup, W. W. Imitative influences of consistent and inconsistent response consequences to a model of aggressive behavior in children. *Journal of personality and social psychology*, 1967, *7*, 429–34.

Rosen, M. G. Factors during labor and delivery that influence brain disorders. In J. M. Freeman, ed. *Prenatal and perinatal factors associated with brain disorders*. National Institute of Child Health and Human Development, NIH Publication No. 85-1149, April 1985.

Rosenhan, D., and Seligman, M. E. P. *Abnormal psychology*, 2nd ed. New York: Norton, 1989.

Rosenhan, D. L., and Seligman, M. E. P. *Abnormal psychology*. New York: Norton, 1984.

Rosenthal, N. E. *Seasons of the mind: Why you get the winter blues and what you can do about it*. New York: Bantam, 1989.

Rosenthal, N. E., Sack, D. A., Gillin, J. C., Lewy, A. J., Goodwin, F. K., Davenport, Y., Mueller, P. S., Newsome, D. A., and Wehr, T. A. Seasonal affective disorder: A description of the syndrome and preliminary findings with light therapy *Archives of general psychiatry*, 1984, *41*, 72–80.

Rosenthal, N. E., Sack, D., and Wehr, T. A. Seasonal variation in affective disorders. In T. A. Wehr and F. K. Goodwin, eds. *Circadian rhythms in psychiatry*. Pacific Grove, CA: Boxwood, 1983.

Rosenzweig, M. R., and Lieman, A. L. *Physiological psychology*. Lexington, MA: Heath, 1982.

Ross, G. Concept categorization in one- to two-year-olds. *Developmental psychology*, 1980, *16*, 391–96.

Ross, J. Welcome and orientation. Paper presented to the Anxiety Disorders Association of America, Bethesda, MD, March 15, 1990.

Ross, L. The intuitive psychologist and his shortcomings. In L. Berkowitz, ed. *Advances in experimental social psychology*, Vol. 10. New York: Academic Press, 1977.

Ross, L., Lepper, M. R., and Hubbard, M. Perseverance in self-perception and social perception. Stanford, CA: Stanford University *Journal of personality and social psychology,* 1975, *32,* 880–92.

Roth, D. L., and Holmes, D. S. Influence of physical fitness in determining the impact of stressful life events on physical and psychological health. *Psychosomatic medicine,* 1985, *47,* 164–73.

Roth, F. P. Accelerating language learning in young children. *Journal of child language,* 1984, *11,* 89–107.

Rozanski, A., et al. Mental stress and the induction of silent myocardial ischemia in patients with coronary artery disease. *New England journal of medicine.* 1988, *318,* 1005–12.

Rubin, D. C. Very long-term memory for prose and verse. *Journal of verbal learning and verbal behavior,* 1977, *16,* 611–21.

Rubin, D. C., ed. *Autobiographical memory.* New York: Cambridge University Press, 1986.

Rubin, D. C., and Kozin, M. Vivid memories. *Cognition,* 1984, *16,* 81–95.

Runck, B. Consensus panel backs cautious use of ECT for severe disorders. *Hospital and community psychiatry,* 1985, *36,* 943–46.

Rushton, J. P., Russell, R. J. H., and Wells, P. A. Genetic similarity theory: Beyond kin selection. *Behavior genetics,* 1984, *14,* 179–93.

Rutkowski, G. K., Gruder, C. L., and Romer, D. Group cohesiveness, social norms, and bystander intervention. *Journal of personality and social psychology,* 1983, *44,* 545–52.

Rutter, M. School effects on pupil progress: Research findings and policy implications. *Child development,* 1983a, *54,* 1–29.

Rutter, M. Stress, coping, and development: Some issues and some questions. In N. Garmezy and M. Rutter, eds. *Stress, coping, and development in children.* New York: McGraw-Hill, 1983b.

Rutter, M. Infantile autism and other pervasive developmental disorders. In M. Rutter and L. Hersov, eds. *Child and adolescent psychiatry: Modern approaches,* 2nd ed. London: Blackwell, 1985.

Rutter, M. Meyerian psychobiology, personality development and the role of life experiences. *American journal of psychiatry,* 1986, *143,* 1077–87.

Rutter, M., Quinton, D., and Liddell, C. Parenting in two generations: Looking backwards and looking forwards. In N. Madge, ed. *Families at risk.* London: Heinemann Educational, 1983, 60–98.

Rutter, M., and Rutter, M. *Developing minds: Challenge and continuity across the life span.* New York: Basic Books, 1993.

Rycroft, C. *Psychoanalysis and beyond.* Chicago: University of Chicago Press, 1986.

Salapatek, P. Pattern perception in early infancy. In L. Cohen and P. Salapatek, eds. *Infant perception: From sensation to cognition: Vol. 1: Basic visual processes.* New York: Academic Press, 1975.

Salapatek, P., and Kessen, W. Visual scanning of triangles of the human newborn. *Journal of experimental child psychology,* 1966, *3,* 155–67.

Salk, L., et al. Relationship of maternal and perinatal conditions to eventual adolescent suicide. *Lancet,* March 16, 1985, vol. I, *8429,* 624–27.

Salthouse, T. A. Effects of aging on verbal abilities. In L. L. Light and D. M. Burke, eds., *Language, memory and aging.* New York: Cambridge University Press, 1988.

Salzinger, S., Feldman, R., Hammer, M., and Rosario, M. The effects of physical abuse on children's social relationships. *Child development,* 1993, *64,* 169–87.

Sandmaier, M. *The invisible alcoholics: Women and alcohol abuse in America.* New York: McGraw-Hill, 1980.

Sands, S. F., and Wright, A. A. Monkey and human pictorial memory scanning. *Science,* 1982, *216,* 1333–34.

Sarason, I. G., and Sarason, B. R., eds. *Social support: Theory, research, and applications.* Hingham, MA: Klumer, 1985.

Sarrel, P. M. Sexuality and menopause. *Obstetrics and gynecology,* April 1990, *75*(Supplement 4), 26S–30S.

Sattler, J. M. *Assessment of children.* San Diego: Jerome M. Sattler, 1988.

Savage-Rumbaugh, E. S., et al. The capacity of animals to acquire language: Do species differences have anything to say to us? *Philosophical Transactions—Royal Society of London,* 1985, *B308,* 177–85.

Sawrey, W. L., Conger, J. J., and Turrell, E. S. An experimental investigation of the role of psychological factors in the production of gastric ulcers of rats: *Journal of comparative and physiological psychology,* 1956, *49,* 457–61.

Scarborough, E., and Furumoto, L. *Untold lives: The first generation of American women psychologists.* New York: Columbia University Press, 1987.

Scarr, S. Testing for children. *American psychologist,* 1981, *36,* 1159–66.

Scarr, S., and Grajek, S. Similarities and differences among siblings. In M. E. Lamb and B. Sutton Smith, eds. *Sibling relationships: Their nature and significance across the lifespan.* Hillsdale, NJ: Erlbaum, 1982.

Scarr, S., and Weinberg, R. A. IQ test performance of black children adopted by white families. *American psychologist,* 1976, *31,* 726–39.

Scarr-Salapatek, S. Race, social class, and IQ. *Science,* 1971a, *174,* 1286–95.

Scarr-Salapatek, S. Unknowns in the IQ equation. *Science,* 1971b, *174,* 1223–28.

Schachter, S. *Psychology of affiliation.* Stanford, CA: Stanford University Press, 1959.

Schachter, S. Some extraordinary facts about obese humans and rats. *American psychologist,* 1971, *26,* 129–44.

Schachter, S., and Singer, J. E. Cognitive, social and physiological determinants of emotional state. *Psychological review,* 1962, *69,* 379–99.

Schacter, D. L. Implicit memory: History and current status. *Journal of experimental psychology: Learning, memory, and cognition,* 1987, *3,* 501–18.

Schaefer, C., Coyne, J. C., and Lazarus, R. S. The health-related functions of social support. *Journal of behavioral medicine,* 1981, *4,* 381–406.

Schaefer, E. S., and Burnett, C. K. Stability and predictability of quality of women's marital relationships and demoralization. *Journal of personality and social psychology,* 1987, *53,* 1129–36.

Schaeffer, M. A., and Baum, A. Adrenal cortical response to stress at Three Mile Island. *Psychosomatic medicine,* 1984, *46,* 227–37.

Schaffer, H. R., and Liddell, C. Adult-child interaction under dyadic and polyadic conditions. *British journal of developmental psychology,* 1984, *2,* 33–42.

Schaie, K. W. Psychological changes from midlife to early old age: Implications for the maintenance of mental health. *American journal of orthopsychiatry,* 1981, *51,* 199–218.

Schaie, K. W., and Hertzog, C. Fourteen-year cohort-sequential analyses of adult intellectual development. *Developmental psychology,* 1983, *19,* 531–43.

Schaie, K. W., and Willis, S. L. Can decline in adult intellectual functioning be reversed? *Developmental psychology,* 1986, *22,* 223–232.

Scheils, D. A cross-cultural study of beliefs in out-of-the-body experiences, waking and sleeping. *Journal of the society for psychical research,* 1978, *49,* 697–741.

Scherer, K. R. Vocal affect expression: A review and a model for future research. *Psychological bulletin,* 1986, *99,* 143–65.

Scherer, K. R., and **Tannenbaum, P. H.** Emotional experience in everyday life. *Motivation and emotion,* 1986, *10,* 295–314.

Schieffelin, E. L. The cultural analysis of depressive affect: An example from New Guinea. In A. Kleinman and B. Good, *Culture and depression.* Berkeley: University of California Press, 1985.

Schiff, M., and **Leowontin, R.** *Education and class.* Oxford: Clarendon Press, 1986.

Schiff, M., et al. How much could we boost scholastic achievement and IQ scores: A direct answer from a French adoption study. *Cognition,* 1982, *12,* 165–96.

Schiffman, S. S. Food recognition by the elder. *Journal of gerontology,* 1977, *32,* 586–92.

Schmolling, P. Human reactions to the Nazi concentration camps: A summing up. *Journal of human stress,* 1984, *10,* 108–20.

Schnall, P. L., et al. The relationship between "job strain," workplace diastolic blood pressure, and left ventricular mass index: Results of a case-control study. *Journal of the American medical association,* 1990, *236,* 1929–35.

Schneider, D. J. Implicit personality theory: A review. *Psychological bulletin,* 1973, *79,* 294–309.

Schoenborn, C. A., and **Wilson, B. F.** Are married people healthier? Health characteristics of married and unmarried U.S. men and women. Paper presented to the American Public Health Association, Boston, 1988.

Schwab, J. J. Psychiatric manifestations of infectious diseases. In R. C. W. Hall, ed. *Psychiatric presentations of medical illness: Somatopsychic disorders.* New York: Spectrum, 1980.

Schwartz, G. E. Psychophysiological patterning and emotion revisited: A system perspective. In C. E. Izard, ed. *Measuring emotions in infants and children.* Cambridge, England: Cambridge University Press, 1982, 67–93.

Scogin, F., Jamison, D., and **Davis, N.** A two-year follow-up of the effects of bibliotherapy for depressed older adults. *Journal of clinical and consulting psychology,* 1990, *58,* 665–67.

Sears, D. O. Social anxiety, opinion structure, and opinion change. *Journal of personality and social psychology,* 1967, *7,* 142–51.

Sears, D. O., Freedman, J. L., and **Peplau, L. A.** *Social Psychology,* 5th ed. Englewood Cliffs, NJ: Prentice-Hall, 1985.

Sears, D. O., et al. *Social psychology,* 6th ed. Englewood Cliffs, NJ: Prentice-Hall, 1988.

Seaver, W. B. Effects of naturally induced teacher expectancies. *Journal of personality and social psychology,* 1973, *28,* 333–42.

Segal, J. *Winning life's toughest battles: Roots of human resilience.* New York: McGraw-Hill, 1986.

Segal, J., and **Segal, Z.** *Growing up smart and happy.* New York: McGraw-Hill, 1985.

Segal, N. L. Monozygotic and dizygotic twins: A comparative analysis of mental ability profiles. *Child development,* 1985, *56,* 1051–58.

Segerberg, O. *Living to be 100: 1,200 who did and how they did it.* New York: Scribners, 1982.

Segraves, R. T., and **Schoenberg, H. W.** *Diagnosis and treatment of erectile disturbances: A guide for clinicians.* New York: Plenum, 1985.

Sekuler, R., and **Levinson, E.** The perception of moving targets. *Scientific American,* 1977, *236,* 60–73.

Seligman, M. E. P. Explanatory style: Depression, Lyndon Baines Johnson, and the Baseball Hall of Fame. Paper presented at meeting of the American Psychological Association, Washington, DC, 1986.

Seligman, M. E. P. *Predicting depression, poor health and presidential elections.* Federation of Behavioral, Psychological and Cognitive sciences, Washington, DC, 1988.

Seligman, M. E. P. *Learned optimism.* New York: Knopf, 1991.

Selkoe, D. J. Aging brain, aging mind. *Scientific American,* September 1992, 135–42.

Selye, H. *The stress of life.* New York: McGraw-Hill, 1956.

Sethi, S., and **Seligman, M. E. P.** Optimism and fundamentalism. *Psychological science,* 1993, *4,* 256–59.

Shapiro, S., et al. Utilization of health and mental health services. *Archives of general psychiatry,* 1984, *41,* 971–78.

Shapley, R. Personal communication, 1986.

Shatz, C. J. The developing brain. *Scientific American,* September 1992, *267,* 61–67.

Sheperd-Look, D. L. Sex differentiation and the development of sex roles. In B. B. Wolman, ed. *Handbook of developmental psychology.* Englewood Cliffs, NJ: Prentice-Hall, 1982.

Shephard, R. N. Recognition memory for words, sentences, and pictures. *Journal of verbal learning and verbal behavior,* 1967, *6,* 156–63.

Sher, K. J., and **Levenson, R. W.** Risk for alcoholism and individual differences in the stress-response dampening effect of alcohol. *Journal of abnormal psychology,* 1982, *91,* 350–67.

Sherman, B. R., and **Kunda, Z.** Motivated evaluation of scientific evidence. Paper presented at meetings of American Psychological Society, Arlington, VA, 1989.

Sherman, S. J. Internal-external control and its relationship to attitude change under different social influence techniques. *Journal of personality and social psychology,* 1973, *26,* 23–29.

Shields, S. A. Distinguishing between emotion and nonemotion: Judgments about experience. *Motivation and emotion,* 1984, *8,* 355–69.

Shiffrin, R. M., and **Atkinson, R. C.** Storage and retrieval processes in long-term memory. *Psychological review,* 1969, *76,* 179–93.

Shimamura, A. P., and **Squire, L. R.** A neuropsychological study of fact memory and source amnesia. *Journal of experimental psychology: Learning, memory, and cognition,* 1987, *13,* 464–73.

Shore, C., O'Connell, B., and **Bates, E.** First sentences in language and symbolic play. *Developmental psychology,* 1984, *20,* 872–80.

Siegel, S. Classical conditioning, drug tolerance, and drug dependence. In R. G. Smart et al., eds. *Research advances in alcohol and drug problems,* Vol. 7. New York: Plenum, 1983.

Silberstein, J. A., and **Parsons, O. A.** Neuropsychological impairment in female alcoholics: Replication and extension. *Journal of abnormal psychology,* 1981, *90,* 179–82.

Silver, L. B. *Adolescent suicide.* Unpublished paper, National Institute of Mental Health, April 19, 1984.

Silver, L. B., and **Segal, J.** Psychology and mental health: An enduring partnership. *American psychologist,* 1984, *39,* 804–09.

Silverberg, R. A. Men confronting death: Management versus self-determination. *Clinical social work journal,* 1985, *13,* 157–69.

Simenauer, J., and **Carroll, D.** *Singles: The new Americans.* New York: Simon and Schuster, 1982.

Simon, H. A. Unity of the arts and sciences: The psychology of thought and discovery. *Bulletin of the American academy of arts and sciences,* March 1982, *35,* 26–53.

Simpson, J. A., Campbell, B., and Berscheid, E. The association between romantic love and marriage: Kephart 1967 twice revisited. *Personality and social psychology bulletin,* 1986, *12,* 363–72.

Skinner, B. F. *The behavior of organisms.* New York: Appleton-Century-Crofts, 1938.

Skinner, B. F. *Science and human behavior.* New York: Macmillan, 1953.

Skinner, B. F. *Verbal behavior.* Englewood Cliffs, NJ: Prentice-Hall, 1957.

Skinner, B. F. Can psychology be a science of mind? *American psychologist,* 1990, *45,* 1206–10.

Slater, J., and Depue, R. A. The contribution of environmental events and social support to serious suicide attempts in primary depressive disorder. *Journal of abnormal psychology,* 1981, *90,* 275–85.

Slobin, D. I. *Psycholinguistics.* Glenview, IL: Scott, Foresman, 1971.

Slobin, D. I. Cognitive prerequisites for the acquisition of grammar. In C. A. Ferguson and D. I. Slobin, eds. *Studies of child language development.* New York: Holt, 1973.

Slobin, D. I. *Cross-cultural study of language acquisition.* Hillsdale, NJ: Erlbaum, 1985.

Smetana, J. G. Concepts of self and social convention: Adolescents' and parents' reasoning about hypothetical and actual family conflicts. In M. R. Gunnar and W. A. Collins, eds. *The Minnesota Symposia,* Vol. 21. Hillsdale, NJ: Erlbaum, 1988.

Smith, C. A., and Ellsworth, P. C. Patterns of cognitive appraisal in emotion. *Journal of personality and social psychology,* 1987, *52,* 475–88.

Smith, C. B., Adamson, L. B., and Bakeman, R. B. Interactional predictors of early language. *First language,* 1988, *8,* 143–56.

Smith, D. K., Nehemkis, A. M., and Charter, R. A. Fear of death, death attitudes, and religious conviction in the terminally ill. *International journal of psychiatry and medicine,* 1983–1984, *13,* 221–32.

Smith, E. E., and Medin, D. L. *Categories and concepts.* Cambridge: Harvard University Press, 1981.

Smith, J., and Baltes, P. B. Wisdom-related knowledge: Age/cohort differences in response to life-planning problems. *Developmental psychology,* 1990, *26,* 494–505.

Smith, M. E. An investigation of the development of the sentence and the extent of vocabulary in young children. *University of Iowa studies in child welfare,* 1926, *3*(5).

Smith, M. L., Glass, G. V., and Miller, T. I. *The benefits of psychotherapy.* Baltimore: Johns Hopkins University Press, 1980.

Smith, S. M. Remembering in and out of context. *Journal of experimental psychology,* 1979, *5,* 460–71.

Snow, C. Mother's speech to children learning language. *Child development,* 1972, *43,* 549–65.

Snow, C. E., et al. Mothers' speech in three social classes. *Journal of psycholinguistic research,* 1976, *5,* 1–20.

Snow, C. E., and Dickinson, D. K. Social sources of narrative skills at home and at school. *First language,* 1990, *10,* 87–103.

Snyder, M., Tanke, E. D., and Berscheid, E. Social perception and interpersonal behavior. *Journal of personality and social psychology,* 1977, *35,* 656–66.

Snyder, M. L., and Frankel, A. Observer bias. *Journal of personality and social psychology,* 1976, *34,* 857–64.

Snyder, S. H. Neurotransmitters and CNS disease: Schizophrenia. *Lancet,* 1982, II, 8305, 970–73.

Snyder, S. H. Neurosciences: An integrative discipline. *Science,* December 21, 1984, *225,* 1255–57.

Snyderman, M., and Rothman, S. Survey of expert opinion on intelligence and aptitude testing. *American psychologist,* 1987, *42,* 137–44.

Solomon, R. L. Punishment. *American psychologist,* 1964, *19,* 239–53.

Solomon, R. L. The opponent-process theory of acquired motivation: The costs of pleasure and the benefits of pain. *American psychologist,* 1980, *35,* 691–712.

Solomon, R. L. The costs of pleasure and the benefits of pain. Paper presented at the meetings of the American Association for the Advancement of Science, Philadelphia, 1986.

Solomon, R. L., and Turner, C. H. Discriminative classical conditioning in dogs paralyzed by curare can later control discriminative avoidance response in the normal state. *Psychological review,* 1962, *69,* 202–19.

Sontag, L. W., Baker, C. T., and Nelson, V. L. Mental growth and personality development. *Monographs of the society for research in child development,* 1958, *23,* (No. 2).

Spanos, N. P., et al. Suffering for science: The effects of implicit social demands on response to experimentally induced pain. *Journal of personality and social psychology,* 1984, *46,* 1162–72.

Spearman, C. *The abilities of man.* London: Macmillan, 1927.

Speece, M. W., and Sandor, B. B. Children's understanding of death: A review of three components of a death concept. *Child development,* Oct. 1984, *55,* 1671–86.

Sperling, G. The information available in brief visual presentations. *Psychological monographs,* 1960, *74.* Copyright 1960 by the American Psychological Association.

Sperling, G. Successive approximations to a model for short-term memory. *Acta psychologica,* 1967, *27,* 285–92.

Sperry, R. Some effects of disconnecting the cerebral hemispheres. *Science,* 1982, *217,* 1223–26.

Sperry, R. W. Psychology's mentalist paradigm and the religion/science tension. *American psychologist,* 1988, *43,* 607–13.

Spitz, R. A. Hospitalism. In R. S. Eissler, et al., eds. *Psychoanalytic study of the child,* Vol. 2. New York: International University Press, 1946.

Springer, S. P. Educating the two sides of the brain: Separating fact from fiction. *American educator,* Spring 1989, *13,* 32–52.

Squire, L. Memory and the hippocampus: A synthesis from findings with rats, monkeys, and humans. *Psychological review,* 1992, *99,* 195–231.

Squire, L. R. *Memory and brain.* New York: Oxford University Press, 1987.

Squire, L. R. On the course of forgetting in very long-term memory. *Journal of experimental psychology: Learning, memory, and cognition.* 1989, *15,* 241–45.

Squire, L. R., and Davis, H. P. The pharmacology of memory: A neurobiological perspective. *Annual review of pharmacology and toxicology,* 1981, *21,* 323–56.

Squire, L. R., Zola-Morgan, S., and Chen, K. S. Human amnesia and animal models of amnesia: Performance of amnesic patients on tests designed for the monkey. *Behavioral neuroscience,* 1988, *102,* 210–21.

Staddon, J. E. R., and Ettinger, R. H. *Learning: An introduction to the principles of adaptive behavior.* San Diego: Harcourt, 1989.

Staines, G. L., and Quinn, R. P. American workers evaluate the quality of their jobs. *Monthly labor review,* January 1979, *13,* 3–12.

Stapp, J., Tucker, A. M., and VandenBos, G. R. Census of psychological personnel: 1983. *American psychologist,* 1985, *40,* 1317–51.

Starker, S. Do-it-yourself therapy: The prescription of self-help books by psychologists. *Psychotherapy,* 1988, *25,* 142–46.

Steinberg, L. *Adolescence*. New York: Knopf, 1985.

Steinberg, L., Dornbusch, S. M., Brown, R. B. Ethnic differences in adolescent achievement: An ecological perspective. *American psychologist*, 1992, *47*, 723–29.

Steinberg, L., et al. Effects of working on adolescent development. *Developmental psychology*, 1982, *18*, 3, 385–95.

Steinberg, L., et al. Impact of parenting practices on adolescent achievement: Authoritative parenting, school involvement, and encouragement to succeed. *Child development*, 1992, *63*, 1266–81.

Stellar, E., McHugh, P. R., and Moran, T. H. The stomach: A conception of its dynamic role in satiety. *Progress in psychobiology and physiological psychology*, Vol. 11. New York: Academic Press, 1985, 197–232.

Stephens, T. Physical activity and mental health in the United States and Canada: Evidence from four population surveys. *Preventive medicine*, 1988, *17*, 35–47.

Stepper, S., and Strack, F. Proprioceptive determinants of emotional and nonemotional feelings. *Journal of personality and social psychology*, 1993, *64*, 211–20.

Stern, W. Wirklichkeitsversuche. *Beitrage zur psychologie der aussage*, 1904, *2*, 1–31.

Sternberg, R. J. Testing intelligence without IQ tests. *Phi Delta Kappan*, 1984, *65*, 694–98.

Sternberg, R. J. Implicit theories of intelligence, creativity, and wisdom. In R. J. Sternberg, ed. *Journal of personality and social psychology*, 1985, *49*, 607–27.

Sternberg, R. J. *Beyond IQ: A Triarchic theory of human intelligence*. New York: Cambridge University Press, 1985.

Sternberg, R. J. *Intelligence applied: Understanding and increasing your intellectual skills*. San Diego: Harcourt, 1986.

Sternberg, R. J. A triangular theory of love. *Psychological review*, 1986, *93*, 119–35.

Sternberg, R. J., and Grajek, S. The nature of love. *Journal of personality and social psychology*, 1984, *47*, 312–29.

Sternberg, R. J., et al. People's conceptions of intelligence. *Journal of personality and social psychology*, 1981, *41*, 37–55.

Stevens, B. The sexually oppressed male. *Psychotherapy*, 1974, *11*, 16–21.

Stevens, C. F. *The neuron*. In Scientific American's *The brain*. San Francisco: Freeman, 1979.

Stevenson, H. W., and Lee, S. Contexts of achievement. *Monographs of the Society for Research in Child Development*, 1990, *55*.

Stevenson, H. W., Lee, S., and Stingler, J. W. Mathematics achievement of Chinese, Japanese, and American children. *Science*, Feb. 14, 1986, *231*, 693–99.

Stevenson, H. W., et al. Cognitive performance and academic achievement of Japanese, Chinese, and American children. *Child development*, 1985, *56*, 718–34.

Stevenson, H. W., et al. Mathematics achievement of Chinese, Japanese, and American children: Ten years later. *Science*, 1993, *259*, 53–58.

Stewart, A. J. *Longitudinal prediction from personality to life outcomes among college-educated women*. Unpublished doctoral dissertation, Harvard University 1975.

Stewart, A. J., and Rubin, Z. Power motivation in the dating couple. *Journal of personality and social psychology*, 1976, *34*, 305–09.

Stiles, W. B., Shapiro, D. A., and Elliot, R. Are all psychotherapies equivalent? *American psychologist*, 1986, *41*, 165–80.

Stock, M. B., and Smythe, P. M. Does undernutrition during infancy inhibit brain growth and subsequent intellectual development? *Archives of disorders in children*, 1963, *38*, 546–52.

Stolz, S. B., Wienckowski, L. A., and Brown, B. S. Behavior modification. *American psychologist*, 1975, *30*, 1027–48.

Straus, M. A., Gelles, R. J., and Steinmetz, S. K. *Behind closed doors: Violence in the American family*. Garden City, NY: Doubleday/Anchor Books, 1981.

Streissguth, A. P., et al. Intrauterine alcohol and nicotine exposure: Attention and reaction time in 4-year-old children. *Developmental psychology*, 1984, *20*, 533–41.

Strickland, B. R. Internal-external control of reinforcement. In T. Blass, ed. *Personality variables in social behavior*. Hillsdale, NJ: Erlbaum, 1977.

Strickland, B. R. Internal-external control expectancies. *American psychologist*, 1989, *44*, 1–12.

Stroebe, M. S., and Stroebe, W. Who suffers more? Sex differences in health risks of the widowed. *Psychological bulletin*, 1983, *93*, 279–301.

Stroop, J. R. Studies of interface in serial verbal reactions. *Journal of experimental psychology*, 1935, *18*, 643–62.

Strupp, H. H. Psychotherapy: Research, practice, and public policy (how to avoid dead ends). *American psychologist*, 1986, *41*, 120–30.

Strupp, H. H. Can the practitioner learn from the researcher? *American psychologist*, 1989, *44*, 717–24.

Strupp, H. H., and Binder, J. L. *A guide to time-limited dynamic psychotherapy*. New York: Basic Books, 1984.

Stunkard, A. J. Behavioral management of obesity. *Medical journal of Australia*, 1985, *142*, (7 supplement), 513–20.

Stunkard, A. J., Foch, T. T., and Hrubec, H. A twin study of human obesity. *Journal of the American Medical Association*, 1986, *256*, 51–54.

Stuss, D. T., and Benson, D. F. *The frontal lobes*. New York: Raven Press, 1986.

Styron, W. *Darkness visible: A memoir of madness*. New York: Random House, 1990.

Suarez, E. C., and Williams, R. B., Jr. Situational determinants of cardiovascular and emotional reactivity in high- and low-hostile men. *Psychosomatic medicine*, 1989, *51*, 404–18.

Suddath, R. E., et al. Anatomical abnormalities in the brains of monozygotic twins discordant for schizophrenia. *New England journal of medicine*, 1990, *322*, 789–94.

Suedfeld, P. Sensory deprivation stress. *Journal of personality and social psychology*, 1969, *11*, 70–74.

Sulloway, F. Personal communication, 1990.

Sumi, S. Upside-down presentation of the Johansson moving light-spot pattern. *Perception*, 1984, *13*, 283–86.

Suomi, S. J., and Harlow, H. F. Social rehabilitation of isolate-reared monkeys. *Developmental psychology*, 1972, *6*, 487–96.

Sutton-Smith, B. Birth order and sibling status effects. *Sibling relationships: Their nature and significance across the lifespan*. Hillsdale, NJ: Erlbaum, 1982.

Suzman, R., and Riley, M. W. Introducing the "oldest old." *Milbank memorial fund quarterly*, 1985, *63*, 177–205.

Swaab, D. F., and Hofman, M. A. An enlarged suprachiasmatic nucleus in homosexual men. *Brain research*, 1990, *537*, 141–48.

Takanishi, R. The opportunities of adolescence: Research initiatives and policies. *American psychologist*, 1993, *48*, 85–87.

Tanner, J. M. *Foetus into man*. Cambridge: Harvard University Press, 1978.

Tarler-Benlolo, L. The role of relaxation in biofeedback training. *Psychological bulletin*, 1978, *85*, 727–55.

Tarpy, R. M., and Mayer, R. E. *Foundations of learning and memory*. Glenview, IL: Scott, Foresman, 1978.

Tavris, C., and Wade, C. *The longest war*. San Diego: Harcourt, 1984.

Taylor, C., Smith, W. R., and Ghiselin, B. The creative and other contributions of one sample of research scientists. In C. Taylor and F. Barron, eds. *Scientific creativity.* New York: Wiley, 1963.

Taylor, S. E. *Health Psychology.* New York: Random House, 1986.

Taylor, S. E. Health psychology: The science and the field. *American psychologist,* 1990, *45,* 40–50.

Teasdale, J. D. Effects of real and recalled success on learned helplessness and depression. *Journal of abnormal psychology,* 1978, *87,* 155–64.

Tellegen, A., et al. Personality similarity in twins reared apart and together. *Journal of personality and social psychology,* 1988, *54,* 1031–39.

Tennes, K. H., and Mason, J. W. Developmental psychoendocrinology: An approach to the study of emotions. In C. E. Izard, ed. *Measuring emotions in infants and children.* Cambridge, England: Cambridge University Press, 1982.

Terman, L. M., and Merrill, M. A. *Stanford-Binet intelligence scale: Manual for the third revision, form L-M,* 1937.

Thayer, R. *Moderate exercise and mood.* Paper presented at the American Psychological Association Convention, 1992.

Theorell, T., et al. "Person under train" incidents: Medical consequences for subway drivers. *Psychosomatic medicine,* 1992, *54,* 480–88.

Thomas, A., Chess, S., and Birch, H. G. The origin of personality. *Scientific American,* 1970, *223,* 106–07.

Thompson, C. Personal communication, 1989.

Thompson, J. K., Penner, L. A., and Altabe, M. N. Procedures, problems and progress in the assessment of body images. In T. Cash and T. Pruzinsky, eds. *Body images.* New York: Guilford Press, 1990.

Thompson, L. W., Gallagher, D., and Breckenridge, J. S. Comparative effectiveness of psychotherapies for depressed elders. *Journal of consulting and clinical psychology,* 1987, *55,* 385–90.

Thorndike, E. L., et al. Intelligence and its measurement: A symposium. *Journal of educational psychology,* 1921, *12,* 123–47.

Tien, A. Y., and Eaton, W. W. Psychopathologic precursors and sociodemographic risk factors for the schizophrenia syndrome. *Archives of general psychiatry,* 1992, *49,* 37–46.

Tolman, E. C. Cognitive maps in rats and men. *Psychological review,* 1948, *55,* 189–208.

Tolman, E. C., and Honzik, C. H. Introduction and removal of reward and maze performance in rats. *University of California publications in psychology,* 1930, *4,* 257–75.

Tomarken, A. J., Davidson, R. J., and Henriques, J. B. Resting frontal brain asymmetry predicts affective responses to films. *Journal of personality and social psychology,* 1990, *59,* 791–801.

Tomarken, A. J., et al. Individual differences in anterior brain asymmetry and fundamental dimensions of emotion. *Journal of personality and social psychology,* 1992, *62,* 676–87.

Tomkins, S. S. *Affect, imagery, consciousness, vol. 1. The positive affects.* New York: Springer, 1962.

Torrance, E. P. *Torrance tests of creative thinking.* Princeton, NJ: Personnel Press, 1966.

Torrey, E. F. *Surviving schizophrenia.* New York: Harper, 1983.

Torrey, E. F., et al. *Care of the seriously mentally ill: A rating of state programs,* 3rd ed. Washington, DC: Public Citizen Health Research Group and National Alliance for the Mentally Ill, 1990.

Tranel, D., and Damasio, A. O. Knowledge without awareness. *Science,* 1985, *228,* 1453–54.

Triplett, N. The dynamogenic factors in pace making and competition. *American journal of psychology,* 1898, *9,* 507–33.

Trusheim, D., and Crouse, J. The DTS admissions formula: Does the SAT add useful information? *Phi Delta Kappan,* Sept. 1982, 59–61.

Tucker, L. A. Muscular strength and mental health. *Journal of personality and social psychology,* 1983, *45,* 1355–60.

Tulving, E. Remembering and knowing the past. *American scientist,* 1989, *77,* 361–67.

Tuma, A. H., and Maser, J. D., eds. *Anxiety and the anxiety disorders.* Hillsdale, NJ: Erlbaum, 1985.

Turnbull, C. M. Some observations regarding the experiences and behavior of the Ma Mbuti pygmies. *American journal of psychology,* 1961, *74,* 304–08.

Turner, C. W., Hesse, B. W., and Peterson-Lewis, S. Naturalistic studies of the long-term effects of television violence. *Journal of social issues,* 1986, *42,* 7–28.

Turner, R. J., and Avison, W. R. Gender and depression: Assessing exposure and vulnerability to life events in a chronically strained population. *Journal of nervous and mental diseases,* 1989, *177,* 443–55.

Tversky, A., and Kahneman, D. Availability: A heuristic for judging frequency and probability. *Cognitive psychology,* 1973, *5,* 207–32.

Tyler, L. E. The intelligence we test—An evolving concept. In L. B. Resnick, ed. *The nature of intelligence.* New York: Erlbaum, 1976.

Underwood, B. J. Interference and forgetting. *Psychological review,* 1957, *64,* Fig. 1, p. 61.

U.S. Bureau of the Census. *Marital status and living arrangements.* Current Population Reports, Series P-20, No. 410, 1985.

U.S. Bureau of the Census. *Marital status and living arrangements.* Current Population Reports. Series P-20, No. 533, 1988.

U.S. Bureau of the Census. *Earnings of married couple families.* Current Population Reports, Series P-60, No. 165, 1989a.

U.S. Bureau of the Census. *Money Income and poverty status in the United States: 1988.* Consumer Income Reports, Series P-60, No. 166, 1989b.

U.S. Bureau of the Census. *Studies in marriage and the family.* Current Population Reports, Series P-23, No. 162, 1989c.

U.S. Bureau of the Census. *Marital status and living arrangements.* Current Population Reports, Series P-20, No. 478, 1993.

U.S. Department of Health and Human Services. *Myths and facts about sleep.* DHHS Publication No. (ADM) 81-1108, 1981.

U.S. Department of Health and Human Services. *Use of mental health services.* ADMAHA update, No. 6, July 1986.

U.S. Department of Labor. *Handbook of labor statistics,* 236, August 1989.

U.S. House Select Committee on Children, Youth, and Families. *U.S. children and their families: Current conditions and recent trends, 1989.* Washington, DC: US House of Representatives, October 2, 1989.

U.S. Office of Strategic Services, Assessment Staff. *Assessment of men.* New York: Holt, 1948.

U.S. Public Health Service. *Women's health: Report of the Public Health Service Task Force on women's health issues. Public health reports,* January–February 1985, *100,* 73–106.

U.S. Senate Special Committee on Aging. *Aging in America: Trends and projections, 1987–88 edition.* Washington, DC: U.S. Department of Health and Human Services, 1988.

Vaillant, G. E. Alcoholism and drug dependence. In A. M. Nicholi, Jr., ed. *The Harvard guide to modern psychiatry.* Cambridge: Harvard University Press, 1978.

Valdes-Dapena, M. A. Sudden infant death syndrome: A review of the medical literature, 1974–1979. *Pediatrics,* 1980, *66,* 597–614.

Valenstein, E. S. *Great and desperate cures.* New York: Basic Books, 1986.

Valenta, J. G., and **Rigby, M. K.** Discrimination of the odor of distressed rats. *Science,* 1968, *161,* 599–601.

Van Dyke, C., and **Byck, R.** Cocaine. *Scientific American,* 1982, *246,* 3, 128–41.

Vennemann, T. An explanation of drift. In C. N. Li, ed. *Word order and word order change.* Austin: University of Texas Press, 1975.

Verhave, T. The pigeon as a quality-control inspector. *American psychologist,* 1966, *21,* 109–15.

Vernon, P. A., ed. *Speed of information-processing and intelligence.* Norwood, NJ: Ablex, 1987.

Veroff, J., Douvan, E., and **Kulka, R.** *The inner American.* New York: Basic Books, 1981.

Vescey, G. Moral of the U.S. Open: You just never know. *The New York times,* September 11, 1989, C-3.

Vierling, J. S., and **Rock, J.** Variations of olfactory sensitivity to exaltolide during the menstrual cycle. *Journal of applied physiology,* 1967, *22,* 311–15.

Vihman, M. M. Language differentiation by a bilingual infant. *Journal of child language,* 1985, *12,* 297–324.

Wachtel, E. F., and **Wachtel, P. L.** *Family dynamics in individual psychotherapy.* New York: Guilford, 1986.

Wadden, T. A., and **Anderson, C. H.** The clinical use of hypnosis. *Psychological bulletin, 91,* 215–43.

Wagner, B. M., et al. Prediction of suicide attempts among junior and senior high school youth. Paper presented at the Meeting of the Society for Research in Child Development, New Orleans, March 1993.

Wagner, H. L. The spontaneous facial expression of differential positive and negative emotions. *Motivation and emotion,* 1990, *14,* 27–43.

Wagner, K. R. How much do children say in a day? *Journal of child language,* 1985, *12,* 475–87.

Wagner, M. W., and **Monnett, M.** Attitudes of college professors toward extrasensory perception. *Zetetic scholar,* 1979, *5,* 7–16.

Wakefield, J. C. The semantics of success: Do masturbation exercises lead to partner orgasm? *Journal of sex and marital therapy,* 1987, *13,* 3–14.

Wald, G. The photochemical basis of rod vision. *Journal of the Optical Society of America,* 1951, *41,* 949–56.

Walker, E., and **Emory, E.** Commentary: Interpretive bias and behavioral genetic research. *Child development,* 1985, *56,* 775–78.

Walker, J. I. The psychological problems of Vietnam veterans. *Journal of the American Medical Association,* 1981, *246,* 781–82.

Walker, P. A. The role of antiandrogens in the treatment of sex offenders. In C. B. Qualls, J. P. Wincze, and D. H. Barlow, eds. *The prevention of sexual disorders,* New York: Plenum, 1978, 117–36.

Wallach, M. A. *The intelligence-creativity distinction.* Morristown, NJ: General Learning Corporation, 1971.

Wallach, M. A. Tests tell us little about talent. *American scientist,* 1976, *64,* 57–63.

Wallach, M. A. Creativity testing and giftedness. In F. Horowitz and O'Brien, eds. *The gifted and talented.* Washington, DC: American Psychological Association, 1985.

Wallach, M. A., and **Kogan, N.** Modes of thinking in young children: A study of the creativity-intelligence distinction. New York: Holt, 1965.

Wallach, M. A., and **Wallach, L.** *Psychology's sanction of selfishness.* New York: Freeman, 1983.

Wallerstein, J., and **Blakeslee, S.** *Second chances: Men, women and children a decade after divorce.* New York: Ticknor and Fields, 1989.

Wallerstein, J., and **Kelley, J.** *Surviving the breakup: How children and parents cope with divorce.* New York: Basic Books, 1980.

Warren, M. P. The psychological significance of secondary sexual characteristics in 9 to 11 year old girls. *Child development,* 1988, *59,* 1061–69.

Wason, P. C. Problem solving and reasoning. *Cognitive psychology,* British Medical Bulletin, 1971, *27.*

Watson, J. B., and **Rayner, R.** Conditioned emotional reactions. *Journal of experimental psychology,* 1920, *3,* 1–14.

Webb, W. B., and **Cartwright, R. D.** Sleep and dreams. *Annual review of psychology,* 1978, *29,* 223–52.

Wechsler, D. Intelligence defined and undefined. *American psychologist,* 1975, *30,* 135–59.

Weil, A. *Natural health, natural medicine.* Boston: Houghton Mifflin, 1990.

Weinberg, R. A. Intelligence and IQ: Landmark issues and great debates. *American psychologist,* 1989, *44,* 98–104.

Weinberger, D. R., and **Kleinman, J. E.** Observations in the brain in schizophrenia. *Psychiatric update,* chap. 3. Washington, DC: American Psychiatric Association, 1986.

Weinberger, M., Hiner, S. L., and **Tierney, W. M.** In support of hassles as a measure of stress in predicting health outcomes. *Journal of behavioral medicine,* 1987, *10,* 19–31.

Weiner, B. *Achievement motivation and attribution theory.* Morristown, NJ: General Learning Press, 1974.

Weiner, B., Perry, P. P., and **Magnusson, J.** An attributional analysis of reactions to stigmas. *Journal of personality and social psychology,* 1988, *55,* 738–48.

Weiner, H. Psychobiology of essential hypertension. In R. J. Mathew, ed. *The biology of anxiety.* New York: Brunner/Mazel, 1982.

Weiskrantz, L. Experimental studies of amnesia. In C. W. M. Whitty and O. L. Zangwill, eds. *Amnesia.* London: Butterworths, 1966.

Weiss, J. M. Somatic effects of predictable and unpredictable shock. *Psychosomatic medicine,* 1970, *32,* 397–409.

Weissman, M. M., et al. Affective disorders. In L. Robins and D. A. Regier, eds. *Psychiatric disorders in America.* New York: Free Press, 1992.

Weisz, J. R., et al. Parent reports of behavioral and emotional problems among children in Kenya, Thailand, and the United States. *Child development,* 1993, *64,* 98–109.

Wells, G. L., and **Loftus, E. F.,** eds. *Eyewitness testimony: Psychological perspectives.* Cambridge, England: Cambridge University Press, 1984.

Weltzin, T. E., Fernstrom, J. D., McConaha, C., and **Kaye, W. H.** Acute tryptophan depletion in bulimia: Effects on large neutral amino acids. *Biological psychiatry,* 1994, *35,* 388–97.

Werker, J. F. Becoming a native listener. *American scientist,* 1989, *77,* 54–59.

Werker, J. F., et al. Developmental aspects of cross-language speech perception. *Child development,* 1981, *52,* 349–53.

Werner, E. E., and **Smith, R. S.** *Vulnerable but invincible.* New York: McGraw-Hill, 1982.

Werner, P. D., and **LaRussa, G. W.** Persistence and change in sex-role stereotypes. *Sex Roles,* 1985, *12,* 1089–100.

Wessels, M. G. *Cognitive psychology.* New York: Harper, 1982.

Whalen, R. W. *Bitter wounds: German victims of the Great War, 1914–1939.* Ithaca, NY: Cornell University Press, 1984.

Whitaker, A., et al. Uncommon troubles in young people: Prevalence estimates of selected psychiatric disorders in a nonreferred adolescent population. *Archives of general psychiatry,* 1990, *47,* 487–96.

Whitfield, I. C., and **Evans, E. F.** Responses of auditory cortical neurons to stimuli of changing frequency. *Journal of neurophysiology*, 1965, *28*, 655–72.

Whorf, B. L. Science and linguistics. In J. B. Carroll, ed. *Language, thought, and reality*. Cambridge: MIT Press, 1956.

Wickelgren, W. A. *Learning and memory*. Englewood Cliffs, NJ: Prentice-Hall, 1977.

Wickelgren, W. A. Human learning and memory. *Annual review of psychology*, 1981, *32*, 21–52.

Wickens, C. D. *Engineering psychology and human performance*. Columbus, OH: Charles Merrill, 1984.

Wiesel, T. N., and **Hubel, D. H.** Ordered arrangement of orientation columns in monkeys lacking visual experience. *Journal of comparative neurology*, 1974, *158*, 307–18.

Wilder, G. Z., and **Powell, K.** *Sex differences in test performance: A survey of the literature*. New York: College Entrance Examination Board, 1989.

Will, J., Self, P., and **Datan, N.** Paper presented to the American Psychological Association, 1974.

Williams, R. B., Jr. *The trusting heart: Great news about type A behavior*. New York: Random House, 1989.

Willis, S. L., and **Baltes, P. B.** Intelligence in adulthood and aging: Contemporary issues. In L. W. Poon, ed. *Aging in the 80's: Psychological issues*. Washington, DC: American Psychological Association, 1980.

Wilson, A., et al. A hierarchical model of opiate addiction: Failures of self-regulation as a central aspect of substance abuse. *The journal of nervous and mental disease*, 1989, *177*, 390–99.

Wilson, J. Q., and **Herrnstein, R. J.** *Crime and human nature*. New York: Simon and Schuster, 1985.

Wine, J. *Investigations of attentional interpretation of test anxiety*. Unpublished doctoral dissertation, University of Waterloo, Ontario, 1971.

Wing, C. W., Jr., and **Wallach, M. A.** *College admissions and the psychology of talent*. New York: Holt, 1971.

Winter, D. G. *The power motive*. New York: Free Press, 1973.

Winter, D. G., and **Stewart, A. J.** The power motive. In H. London and J. E. Exner, eds. *Dimensions of personality*. New York: Wiley, 1978.

Winterbottom, M. R. *The relation of childhood training in independence to achievement motivation*. Unpublished doctoral dissertation, University of Michigan, 1953. Summarized in D. C. McClelland, et al. *The achievement motive*. New York: Irvington, 1953.

Witelson, S. Hand and sex differences in the isthmus and the genu of the human corpus collosum. *Brain*, 1989, *112*, 799–835.

Wolf, D. Novelty, creativity, and child development. *Newsletter of the society for research in child development*. University of Chicago Press, spring 1989.

Wolf, R. M. *The identification and measurement of environmental process variables related to intelligence*. Unpublished doctoral dissertation, University of Chicago, 1963.

Wong, P. T. P., and **Watt, L. M.** What types of reminiscence are associated with successful aging? *Psychology and aging*, 1991, *6*, 272–79.

Wood, J. M., et al. Effects of the 1989 San Francisco earthquake on frequency and content of nightmares. *Journal of abnormal psychology*, 1992, *101*, 219–24.

Woodrow, K. M., and **Eltherington, L. G.** Feeling no pain. *Pain*, 1988, *32*, 159–63.

Woolf, V. *The Letters of Virginia Woolf*. Nicholson, N., and Trautman, J., eds. New York: Harcourt, 1975–1980.

World Health Organization. *Schizophrenia: An international follow-up study*. New York: Wiley, 1979.

Wortman, C., and **Silver, R. C.** The myths of coping with loss. *Journal of consulting and clinical psychology*, 1989, *57*, 349–57.

Wright, L. The type A behavior pattern and coronary artery disease: Quest for the active ingredients and the elusive mechanism. *American psychologist*, 1988, *43*, 12–14.

Wyatt, G., Peters, S., and **Guthrie, D.** Kinsey revisited, part I: Comparisons of the sexual socialization and sexual behavior of white women over 33 years. *Archives of sexual behavior*, 1988, *17*, 201–39.

Wyatt, R. J. *After middle age*. New York: McGraw-Hill, 1985.

Wyatt, R. J., and **Freed, W. J.** Progress in neurografting as a treatment for degenerative brain disease: The Parkinson's model. In W. Regelson, ed. *Intervention in the aging process*. New York: Alan R. Liff, 1983.

Yalom, I. *Existential psychotherapy*. New York: Basic Books, 1980.

Yalom, I. D. *The theory and practice of group psychotherapy*, 3rd ed. New York: Basic Books, 1985.

Yankelovich, D. The work ethic is underemployed. *Psychology today*, May 1988, *16*, 5–8.

Yarbus, A. L. *Eye movements and vision*. Translated by L. A. Riggs. New York: Plenum, 1967.

Yates, A. Curin press perspectives on the eating disorders: II. Treatment, outcome, and research directions. *Journal of the American Academy of Child and Adolescent Psychiatry*, 1990, *29*, 1–9.

Yerkes, R. M., and **Morgulis, S.** The methods of Pavlov in animal psychology. *Psychological bulletin*, 1909, *6*, 257–73.

Young, P. T. *Motivation and emotion*. New York: Wiley, 1961.

Yule, W. *Behavioral approaches*. In M. Rutter and L. Hersov, eds. *Child and adolescent psychiatry: Modern approaches*, 2nd ed. London: Blackwell, 1985.

Zahn-Waxler, C., and **Radke-Yarrow, M.** The origins of empathic concern. *Motivation and emotion*, 1990, *14*, 107–30.

Zahn-Waxler, C., Radke-Yarrow, M., and **King, R. A.** Child rearing and children's prosocial initiations toward victims in distress. *Child development*, 1979, *50*, 319–30.

Zahn-Waxler, C., Radke-Yarrow, M., and **King, R.** Early altruism and guilt. *Academic psychology bulletin*, 1983, *5*, 247–59.

Zajonc, R. B. The decline and rise of scholastic aptitude scores: A prediction derived from the confluence model. *American psychologist*, August 1986, *41*, 862–67.

Zajonc, R. B. The face as a primary instrument of social process. In R. B. Zajonc and S. Moscovici, eds. *Social psychology and the emotions*. Cambridge: Cambridge University Press, 1989.

Zeldow, P. B., Daugherty, S. R., Leksas, L. A four-year longitudinal study of personality changes in medical students. *Journal of medical education*, 1987, *62*, 992–95.

Zika, S., and **Chamberlain, K.** Relation of hassles and personality to subjective well-being. *Journal of personality and social psychology*, 1987, *53*, 155–62.

Zillman, D., and **Bryant, J.** Effects of massive exposure to pornography. In N. Malamuth and E. Donnerstein, eds. *Pornography and aggression*. Orlando, FL: Academic Press, 1988.

Zillman, D., Katcher, A. H., and **Milavsky, B.** Excitation transfer from physical exercise to subsequent aggressive behavior. *Journal of experimental social psychology*, 1972, *8*, 247–59.

Zipf, G. K. *Human behavior and the principle of least effort*. Reading, MA: Addison-Wesley, 1949.

Zube, M. Changing behavior and outlook of aging men and women. *Family relations*, 1982, *31*, 147–56.

Zuckerman, M., ed. *Biological bases of sensation seeking, impulsivity, and anxiety*. Hillsdale, NJ: Erlbaum, 1983.

Zuckerman, M. Sensation seeking: The balance between risk and reward. In L. P. Lipsitt and L. L. Mitmick, eds. *Self-regulatory behavior and risk taking: Causes and consequences*. Norwood, NJ Ablex, 1991.

Zung, W. W. K. A self-rating depression scale. *Archives of general psychiatry*, 1965, *12*, 63–70.

PHOTO/TEXT CREDITS

Page 2: ©Stock Boston. Page 5: ©Tony Freeman/PhotoEdit. Page 8: UPI/Bettmann. Page 9: (left) ©Van Bucher/Photo Researchers, Inc., (right) ©Richard Pasley/Stock Boston. Page 11: Edmund Engelman, NY. Page 12: ©Stock Boston. Page 18: (left, right) ©Garrison/Hewitt Photography. Page 21: Culver Pictures, Inc. Page 29: ©PhotoEdit. Page 48: ©Allsport. Page 50: ©A. Glauberman, Science Source/Photo Researchers, Inc. Page 54: Courtesy of the American Association for the Advancement of Science. Page 55: ©1991 Custom Medical Stock Photo. All rights reserved. Page 59: ©Photo Researchers, Inc. Page 60: ©Allsport. Page 63: ©Stock Boston. Page 66: Erik Arneson. Page 69: (top, left, right) Arthur Leipzig, (bottom) ©Stock Boston. Pages 70–71: "Zone of Brain Linked to Men's Sexual Orientation" by Natalie Angier. Copyright © 1994 by The New York Times Company. Reprinted by permission. Page 76: Courtesy of Dr. Marcus E. Raichle, Washington University, St. Louis. Page 96: ©Robert McElroy/Woodfin Camp & Associates. Page 98: ©T.J. Florian/Rainbow. Page 104: ©Photo Researchers, Inc. Page 116: ©Rich Freidman/Black Star. Page 118: ©Robert McElroy/Woodfin Camp & Associates. Page 123: ©Robert Brenner/PhotoEdit. Page 125: (left, right) A.L. Yarbus. Page 128: (top) David Moskowitz, (bottom) ©Garrison/Hewitt Photography. Page 129: (left, right) William Vandivert. Page 154: ©Jerry Berndt/Stock Boston. Page 157: Culver Pictures, Inc. Page 165: ©Louis Goldman/Photo Researchers, Inc. Page 168: Nina Lean, Life Magazine ©Time Warner, Inc. Page 169: M.S. Terrace, Columbia University. Page 170: Yerkes Regional Primate Research Center of Emory University. Page 179: ©Allsport. Page 184: ©Jerry Berndt/Stock Boston. Page 204: ©Charles Gupton/Stock Boston. Page 206: ©Charles Gupton/Stock Boston. Page 212: ©Richard Hutchings/PhotoEdit. Page 213: Courtesy of Dr. Endel Tulving, University of Toronto. Page 217: ©CoCo McCoy/Rainbow. Page 218: "Drug is Found to Improve Memory in Tests on Rats" by Philip J. Hilts. Copyright © 1991 by The New York Times Company. Reprinted by permission. Page 223: ©Melanie Kaestner. Page 224: ©Black Star. Page 227: ©Jeff Greenberg/PhotoEdit. Page 229: Harlow Primate Lab. Page 252: ©Michael Newman/PhotoEdit. Page 254: ©Michael Newman/PhotoEdit. Page 261: ©Elizabeth Crews. Page 263: ©Elizabeth Crews. Page 267: B.T. Gardner. Page 268: ©Elizabeth Crews. Page 270: (top) ©Garrison/Hewitt Photography. Page 271: ©Robert Brenner/PhotoEdit. Page 275: ©Hank Morgan/Rainbow. Page 282: (top, bottom) ©Garrison/Hewitt Photography. Page 283: ©Stock Boston. Page 298: Reuters/Bettmann. Page 300: Reuters/Bettmann. Page 303: ©Walter Chandoha. Page 306: (bottom, left & right) ©Neil Robinson. Page 314: ©Bill Gallery/Stock Boston. Page 318: ©Dan McCoy/Rainbow. Pages 322–323: "The Great American Sleep Debt" by Sandy Rovner. Copyright © 1994 The Washington Post. Reprinted with permission. Page 324: ©Galen Rowell/FPG International. Page 332: ©Liane Enkelis/Stock Boston. Page 358: ©David Young-Wolff/PhotoEdit. Page 361: ©Anthro-Photo. Page 364: Bettmann Archive. Page 366: ©Lew Merrim/Monkmeyer Press. Page 371: ©David Young-Wolff/PhotoEdit. Page 377: ©Jeffrey Myers/Stock Boston. Page 384: Harcourt Brace Collection. Page 385: (top left) ©Moss/Outline; (top right) ©Sygma; (middle left) ©J.P. Laffont/Sygma; (middle right) Bettmann Newsphotos; (bottom left) ©Lange/Outline; (bottom right) ©Frank Trapper/Sygma. Page 386: ©Little/Outline. Pages 392–393: "Spit Tasting May be Hard to Swallow in the Workplace." Reprinted by permission of The Wall Street Journal, © 1993 Dow Jones & Company, Inc. All Rights Reserved Worldwide. Page 426: ©Sygma. Page 429: ©Richard Hutchings/PhotoEdit. Page 432: ©Les Stone/Sygma. Page 433: ©Owen Franken/Stock Boston. Page 439: ©Stock Boston. Page 444: ©Stock Boston. Page 447: ©Black Star. Page 448: ©Sygma. Page 453: ©Stock Boston. Page 459: ©Stock Boston. Page 461: ©Stock Boston. Page 462: Julius H. Masserman, M.D., Co-Chairman of Psychology, Northwestern, IL. Page 478: AP/Wide World Photos. Page 480: ©Anthro-Photo. Page 484: UPI/Bettmann. Page 485: ©Dan McCoy/Rainbow. Page 488: ©Black Star. Page 489 from "Major Disorders of Mind and Brain" by Elliot S. Gershon and Ronald O. Rieder. Copyright © 1992 by Scientific American, Inc. All rights reserved. Page 491 "Making Art of Madness" (Editorial). Copyright © 1993 by The New York Times Company. Reprinted by permission. Page 492: ©Stock Boston. Page 495: ©Tony Freeman/PhotoEdit. Page 499: ©William McCoy/Rainbow. Page 503: AP/Wide World Photos. Page 504: ©Sygma. Page 507: ©Tony Stone Worldwide. Page 526: ©Stock Boston. Page 529: Copyright 1989 by SIU/Photo Researchers, Inc. Page 532: ©Stock Boston. Page 536: ©Stock Boston. Page 539: ©Stock Boston. Page 541: ©Stock Boston. Page 546: ©Felicia Martinez/PhotoEdit. Page 553: ©Stock Boston. Page 554: ©Stock Boston. Page 572: ©Elizabeth Crews. Page 574: Dr. Landrum B. Shettles. Page 575: ©Howard Sochurek/MediChrome-The Stock Shop, Inc. Page 577: ©Peter Byron. Page 578: Heinz Prechtl. Page 581: Edwin and Lillian Robbins. Page 583: (top left) ©Elizabeth Crews; (top middle) ©Elizabeth Crews; (top right) ©Raith/G & J/Black Star; (bottom left) ©Peter Vandermark/Stock Boston; (bottom middle) ©Stock Boston; (bottom right) ©Elizabeth Crews. Page 587: ©Peter Southwick/Stock Boston. Page 590: Fred Sponholz. Page 598: Courtesy Broderick Johnson, Homeless Children's Tutorial Project, Washington D.C. Page 622: ©Bill Aron/PhotoEdit. Page 624: ©Stock Boston. Page 629: ©Stock Boston. Page 632: ©Stock Boston. Page 635: ©1988 Myrleen Ferguson/PhotoEdit. Page 636: ©Bill Aron/PhotoEdit. Page 639: ©Stock Boston. Page 642: ©Dan McCoy/Rainbow. Page 647: ©Stock Boston. Page 651: ©1985 Lynn Johnson/Black Star. Page 652: (top left)

NAME INDEX

Brehm, S., 699
Breznitz, S., 463
Briggs, S. R., 393
Brock, D., 655
Bronzaft, Arlene, 109
Brooks-Gunn, J., 328, 496, 626, 627, 628
Bross, I. D. J., 272
Brotman, H. B., *646*
Brown, B. S., 173
Brown, Jonathon D., 457
Brown, P. L., 170
Brown, R., 225, 265, 671, 682
Brown, R. B., 336
Brown, S. A., 431
Brown, T. A., 551
Brown, V. B., 509
Bruck, M., 588
Bruner, B., 123
Bruner, J. S., 271
Bryer, J. B., 492
Bucher, K. D., 496
Buchwald, Art, 636
Budoff, P. W., 645
Bugelski, B. R., *132*
Bukowski, Charles, 433
Bullock, M., 595
Bumpass, L. L., 641, 642, 643
Bunney, W. E., 493
Burchinal, M., 592
Burke, D. M., 213, 650
Burkhard, B., *159*
Burnam, M. A., 495
Buss, D. M., 330, 698
Buss, T. F., 555
Butcher, J. N., *533*
Butler, R. N., 651
Byck, R., 508
Byron, Lord, 490, 491

C

Cacioppo, J. T., 306
Cain, W. S., 113
Cairns, R. B., 600
Calderone, M. S., 327
Calhoun, K. S., 448
Calkins, Mary, 8
Calvert, S. L., 600
Camara, K. A., 601
Campbell, B., 641
Campbell, B. A., 177
Campbell, D., 693
Campos, J. J., 303
Camus, Albert, 624
Carew, T. J., 158
Cargan, L., 641
Carnegie Council on Adolescent Development, 629
Carriger, M. S., 584
Carroll, J. B., 372, 492
Carskadon, Mary, 323
Carlsmith, J. M., 672, 697
Carstensen, L. L., 634
Cartwright, R. D., 320
Carver, C. S., 695
Case, R. B., 444

Caspi, A., 637, 697
Cassens, H. C., 323
Castro-Martin, T., 641
Cattell, Raymond B., 649
Ceci, Stephen J., 368, 588
Centers for Disease Control, 483
Cerella, J., 649
Chamberlain, K., 434
Charter, R. A., 653
Chase-Lansdale, L., 328
Chen, K. S., 63
Cheng, P. W., 277
Cherlin, A. J., 601
Chess, S., 580
Chipman, S. F., 335, 340
Chomsky, Noam, 257, 266
Christiaansen, R. E., 221
Chugani, H. T., *585*
Church, R. M., 177
Clark, E. V., 224, 257, 259, 260, 272, 275, 276
Clark, H. H., 224, 257, 259, 260, 272, 275, 276
Clark, L. A., 433
Clark, M. C., *234*
Clark, W. B., 507
Clifford, B. R., *220*
Clifford, R. E., 328
Clinton, Hillary Rodham, *385*
Clum, G., 546
Clyman, R., 588
Coe, C. L., 442, 454
Cohen, A. R., 676
Cohen, G., 211, *211*
Cohen, G. D., 651
Cohen, N., 160
Coile, D. C., 30
Cole, M. A., 653
Cole, S. G., 334
Coleridge, Samuel Taylor, 491
Collins, A. M., 271
Columbus, Christopher, 278
Comstock, G. W., 651, 654
Conger, J. J., 160
Conway, M. A., 211, *211*
Cooper, H., 681
Cooper, J., 673
Cooper, M., 673
Copernicus, 386
Coren, S., 115, 116, 120, *122*, 131
Costa, P. T., Jr., *394*
Costello, C. G., 499
Couric, E., 639
Cousins, N., 456
Cowan, *64*
Cowan, C. P., 643
Cowan, E., 553
Cowan, N., 209
Cowan, P., 643
Coyle, S. L., 7
Coyne, J. C., 454
Craig, K. D., 307
Craik, F. I. M., 224, 227
Crandall, J. E., 384
Crano, W. D., 681
Craske, M., 551
Crawford, M., 693
Crenoch, J. M., 578

Crick, G., 321
Crick, Francis, 337
Crits-Christoph, A., 543
Crockenburg, S. B., 371
Cronbach, L. J., 364
Crook, T. H., 213, *213*
Crooks, R., 328, 330
Crosby, E., *73*
Crouse, J., 366
Crutchfield, R. S., *130*
Cummings, E. M., 599
Curtis, R. C., 697
Cytryn, L., 493
Cytrynbaum, S., 645

D

Dabbs, James M., Jr., 392, 393, *675*
Damasio, A. O., 15
Damasio, A. R., 58, 62, *270*
Damasio, H., *270*
Damasio, H. C., 62
Darley, J. M., 681
Darwin, Charles, 386
Datan, N., 599
Davidson, H. H., *398*
Davidson, J., 326
Davidson, R. J., 74, 309
Davis et al., 75
Davis, M., 68, 164, 633
de Medinaceli, L., 57
De Valois, R. L., 106
de Villiers, J. G., 266
de Villiers, P. A., 266, 269
DeFrain, J., 643
DeFries, J. C., 372
DeLongis, A., 434
DeMaris, A., 642
Dement, William, 322
Demitrack, M. A., 496
Depue, R. A., 554
Deutsch, J. A., 313
Diamond, A., 62
Diaz, R. M., 261
Dickinson, D. K., 265
Diener, E., 311
Digman, J. M., 392
Dion, K. K., 697, 698
Dion, K. L., 698
Disney, E. R., 576
Dobson, K. S., 538
Dohrenwend, B., 431, 450
Dollard, John, 181, 390
Domjan, M., *159*
Donnelly, C. M., 227
Donnerstein, E., 692
Dornbusch, S. M., 336
Dougherty, L. M., 306, 309
Douvan, E., 644
Drabman, R., 173
Dreher, M., 576
Dreskin, W., 591
Dreyer, P., 331
Dryden, W., 538
Dubow, E. F., 454
Dubreuil, D. L., 325
Dukakis, Kitty, 508

Grief, E., 626
Griel, A., 644
Grillon, C., 487
Grinker, J. A., 314
Gruder, C. L., 695
Gruenberg, B., 637
Guilford, J. P., 362–63, *363*, 364
Gunnar, M. R., 594
Gunter, B., *220*
Guthrie, D., 328
Gutkin, T. B., 375

H

Haggard, L. K., 555
Haig, N. D., 121
Haith, M., 578
Halaris, R. M., 450
Hall, R. C. W., 545
Hall, W. G., 316
Hall, W. S., 261, 262, 263
Hallock, M. B., 578
Halpern, A. R., 221
Halpern, C. T., 626
Hamburg, D. A., 625
Hamer, D., 332
Hamilton, M., 497
Hammen, C., 450
Hammersmith, S. E., 331
Hannah, M. E., 645
Hansen, D. N., 447
Harlow, Harry F., *229*, 590–91
Harrell, M. S., 368
Harrell, T. W., 368
Harrington, C. L., 370
Harris, F. R., 173
Harris, R. J., 165, 172
Harrold, R. M., 213, 650
Hart, J., 62
Harter, S., 633
Hartmann, E., 321
Hartmann, Heinz, 387
Hartup, W. W., 186, 603
Harvey, S. M., 326
Hass, R. G., 671
Hatfield, E., 699
Hathaway, S. R., 396
Hauser, B. B., 644
Hauser, S. T., 635
Hawkins, R. D., 158
Hawley, T. L., 576
Hebb, 716
Hebb, D. O., 693
Hebb, Donald O., 25
Heider, F., 677
Heller, K., 653
Hellman, R. E., 331
Helsing, K. L., 651, 654
Helson, R., 645
Helzer, J. E., 449
Hendrick, C., *699*
Hendrick, S., 639, *699*
Henriques, J. B, 74
Herbener, E. S., 697
Herrenkohl, L. R., 331
Herrmann, T. F., 68

Herrnstein, R. J., 269, 503
Hertzog, C., 649
Hess, E., 328
Hess, R. D., 598
Hesse, B. W., 692
Heston, L. H., 649
Hetherington, E. M., 601
Hill, J., 635
Hill, J. P., 625
Hilton, I., 384
Hilts, Philip J., 218
Hinz, L. D., 496
Hiroto, D. S., 179
Hitchcock, J. M., 68, 164
Hitler, Adolph, 686
Hobson, J. A., 65, 319, 321
Hochberg, J., 128, 129
Hoeksema, S. N., 494
Hofman, M. A., 332
Hofstadter, L., 78
Hogan, J., 458
Holahan, C. J., 442, 454
Holder, M. D., 167
Holland, P. C., 164, 183
Hollon, S., 179
Holmes, D. S., 309, 442, *458*, 547
Holmes, S. J., 483, 493, *493*, 596
Holmes, T. H., *441*
Holyrod, K. A., 447
Holzman, P. H., 487
Honzik, C. H., 181, *182*
Hooley, J. M., 554
Hops, H., 176
Horfling, C. K., 687
Horn, J. L., 372, 649–50
Horne, J., 320
Horney, Karen, *384*, 387, 388, 531
Horowitz, M. J., 461, 533
House, J. S., 453, 454
Hovland, C. I., 676
Howard, A., 8
Howard, K., 533, *533*
Howes, C., 591, 592, *592*
Hoyenga, K. B., 52
Hoyenga, K. T., 52
Hrubec, H., 316, *316*
Huba, G. J., 506
Hubbard, M., *690*
Hubel, David H., 56, 120, 121
Hug, K., 278
Humphrey, T., 73
Hurst, M. W., 440
Hurwitz, H. M. B., 68
Huston, A. C., 600
Hyde, J. S., 640

I

Iannotti, R. J., 599
Ilfeld, F. W., 452
Ingraham, L. J., *487*, 510
Inouye, J., 392
Insel, Thomas R., 70
Institute for Mental Health Initiatives, 445
Institute of Medicine, 481
Isen, Alice M., 456

Iversen, L. L., 78, 117
Izard, C. E., *302*, 305, 306, 309

J

Jack, D. C., 494
Jacklin, C. N., 581
Jackson, Jacquelyn F., 374
Jacobowitz, D. M., 331
Jacobs, G., 328
Jacobs, G. H., 106
Jacobs, M. K., 540
Jacobson, J. L., 576
James, William, 21, 22, 25, 26–27, 228–29, 271, 307–08
Jamison, K. R., 322, 449, 482, 489, 490, 550, 551, *551*
Janis, I. L., 673, 676
Jarmas, A. L., 494
Jarvik, L. F., *373*
Jeffery, R. W., 180
Jencks, C., 370, *373*
Jenkins, C. D., 440
Jenkins, H. M., 170
Jennings, J., 639
Jensen, A. R., 375
Jensen, M. R., 440
Jimerson, D. C., 552
Jobes, D. A., 634
John, E. R., 185
Johnson, V. E., 13
Jones, E. E., 682
Jones, H. W., 644
Jung, Carl, 383, 392, 394
Junginger, J., 486
Juraska, J. M., 599
Jussim, L., 681

K

Kabat-Zinn, J., *547*
Kagan, J., 311, 397, 580, 582, 584, 585, 593, *593*, 594, *604*
Kahneman, D., 282, 283
Kail, R., 362
Kales, A., 481
Kamin, Leon, 372, 376
Kandel, E. R., 77, 158
Kane, J. M., 549
Kang, D. H., 75
Karasek, R. A., 453
Katchadourian, H. A., 331
Katz, I., 671
Kay, D., 648
Kay, P., 275
Kazak, A. E., 494
Kearsley, R. B., *585*, 593
Kehoe, E. J., 158
Kelley, H., 696
Kelley, J., 601
Kelley, K., 329
Kellner, R., 536
Kendler, K. S., 492, 493, 498
Kennedy, John F., 225, 552
Kessen, W., 122
Kessler, M., 553

Weiss, S., 57
Weissman, M. M., 488
Weisz, J. R., 604
Wells, P. A., 695
Weltzin, 496
Wenegrat, B., 541
Werker, J. F., 261, 263, *263*
Werner & Lipsitt, 578
Werner, E. E., 576, 577
Werner, P. D., 639
Wertheimer, Max, 25
Wessels, M. G., 279
West, R. L., 213, *213*
Whitaker, A., 493
White, J. A., 649
White, N. M., 63
Whitehurst, G. J., 17, *19*
Whitfield, I. C., 120
Whorf, Benjamin L., 274
Wickelgren, W. A., 171, 212, 217, 227, 272
Wickens, C. D., 124
Wienckowski, L. A., 173
Wiesel, Torsten N., 56, 61, 106, 120, *120*, 121
Wilder, G. Z., 640
Will, J., 599
Williams, Arland, Jr., 690

Williams, R. B., Jr., 444
Williamson, D A., 496
Willis, S. L., 649, 650
Wilson, A., 509
Wilson, B. F., 641
Wilson, J. Q., 503
Wilson, John, 556
Wilson, M. S., 452
Wing, C. W., Jr., 368
Winter, D. G, 336
Winterbottom, M. R., 335
Wolf, R. M., 374
Wolfe, B. E., 537
Wong, P. T. P., 653
Wood, J. M., 432
Woodrow, K. M., 322
Woolf, Virginia, 490, 491
World Health Organization, 554
Worobey, J., 578
Wortman, C., 654
Wright, A. A., 234
Wright, Frank Lloyd, *652*
Wright, L., 443, 444
Wundt, William, 20, 21, 25
Wyatt, G., 328
Wyatt, R. J., 57, 65, 654, 655
Wysocki, C. J., 114

Y

Yalom, I. D., 539, 541, 545, 655
Yankelovich, D., 674, *674*
Yarbus, A. L., *125*
Yates, A., 496
Yerkes, R. M., *158*
Young, P. T., *303*
Yule, W., 173

Z

Zahn-Waxler, C., 599, 693
Zajonc, R. B., 308–9, 386, 697
Zanna, M. P., 673
Zeevi, Y. Y., *54*
Zelazo, P. R., *585*, *593*
Zeldow, P. B., 450
Zigler, E., 633
Zika, S., 434
Zipf, G. K., 276
Zola-Morgan, S., 63
Zube, M., 645
Zuckerman, M., 311
Zukier, H., 671
Zung, William W. K., *489*

SUBJECT INDEX

first impressions and, 697–98
inconsistent, 671
toward the mentally ill, 556–57
pressure to change, 674–77
stress and, 454–56, *457*
See also Prejudice; Stereotypes
Attraction, 696–97
Attribution error, 678–79
Attribution theories, 677–83
Auditory canal, *108*
Auditory nerve, *108*, 109
Authority, respect for, 688–89. *See also*
Conformity; Obedience
Autonomic nervous system (ANS),
69–74, *73*
defined, 69–70
emotion and, 303–4, 311
endocrine glands in, 70–71, *72*
parasympathetic division of, 72–73, *73*
sympathetic division of, 73–74
Autoshaping, 170
Average, statistical, 719–20
Aversive conditioning, 537–38
Avoidance, operant, 175
Avoidance-avoidance conflict, 434
Axon, 52, *52*, 54

B

"**Babbling**," 262–63
Backward pairing, 162, *163*
Balance, cerebellum and, 61
Basic anxiety, 387
Basic science, 7
Basilar membrane, 109, *110*
Behavior
abnormal. *See* Abnormal psychology
attitude changes and, 673–74
attribution theories of, 677–83
brain and, 51–56, 65
built-in patterns of, 156
changes in, 27, 676–77
continuity in, 27
control of, 6
coping and, 451–52
drives and, 312–16
hereditary and environmental influences on, 26–27
interpersonal, 690–99
motives and, 339–40
operant, 168
personality as learned, 390–91
psychobiology and, 26
punishment and, 176–77
shaping and operant conditioning, 169, *169*
See also specific topics
Behavior genetics, 27
Behavior modification, 173, *174*
Behavior therapy (behavior therapists), 535–38
cognitive, 538
defined, 391, 535
extinction, 537–38
reinforcement, 537
systemic desensitization, 536–37
Behavioral sciences, 6

Behavioral theories, 390–91
Behaviorism, 21–22
Belief perseverance, 675
Bereavement
old age and, 654
immune response to, 443
Bias, 367
Bilingualism and education, 260–62
Binocular vision, 129
Biofeedback, 174
Biological therapies, 528, 548–52
Bipolar disorder, 488–90, *489*, *551*
Birth process, 577–78
Bisexual, 330–31
Bladder, 73
Blind spot, 103, *103*
Blood pressure, 445–46
Bodily movement, 60–61, 118–19
Body image, 627–28
Borderline personality, *502*
Brain, 50–80, *50*, *55*, *59*, *64*, *76*
alcohol and, 507
anxiety and, 500
cerebellum and, 61
cerebral cortex, 55–56, *56*, *58*
cerebrum, 56
chemical activity of, 77–78
of child, 582, *585*
communication system in, 51–56
depression and, 492
drug use and, 506
electroconvulsive therapy and, 552
emotions and, 66–75
hemispheres of, *55*, 56, *64*, 65,
74–75
hippocampus, 622–63, *67*, 68
hunger and, 312
hypothalamus, *59*, *67*, 68, 69
of infant, 576
intellectual development and, 63–64
limbic system, 67–68, *67*
maturational changes in, 65
memory and, 61–63
movement and, 60–61
neurotransmitters of, 77–78
Parkinson's disease and, 65
peptides of, 77–78
repair of, 57
in schizophrenia, 65, 487
sensory information and, 57–60
in senile dementia, 648
thought and, 61–62
Brain imaging, 75–77
Brain stem, *59*
Brief psychotherapy, 532–33, *533*
Brightness, 100, *101*
Brightness constancy, 128, 129
Bulimia nervosa, *496*, 551–52, 628
Bystander apathy, 694–96, *696*

C

Caffeine, 508
**California Personality Inventory
(CPI)**, 396, *397*
Cannon-Bard theory, 309–10, *309*,
310

Careers
choosing, 637–38
IQ and, 368–69
See also Employment
Case history, 13
Case management approach, 554
CAT (computerized axial tomography) scan, 76
Catastrophes as stressors, 431–33, *432*
Categories, 230–31, *230*, *231*
Cause and effect
correlation and, 17
relationship, 232–33, *232*
Cell body, 52, *52*
Central nervous system, 55
Cerebellum, 61
Cerebral cortex
association, 61
hearing and, *58*
language and, *58*
memory and, 61, 62–63
movement and, *58*, 60–61
size of, 56
somatosensory, 57–58
vision and, *58*
Cerebrum, 56, 57, *59*
Change
of attitudes, 673–74
of behavior, 27
perception of, 121
Chemotherapy, 548. *See also* Drug
therapy
Childhood depression, 493
Children, 643–44
abuse of, *597*
achievement motivation in, 334–36,
335
aggression in, 692
altruism in, 693
anxiety in, 592–94, *593*
bilingualism and, 260–62
compassion in, 694
depression and, 493–94
hyperactivity in, 546–47
intellectual growth of, 63–64
language development in, 17, 18, 19,
265–66
learned helplessness in, 179
memory revision in, 588
motive for certainty in, 338
Oedipus complex and, 381
personality development and,
384–87
punishment used with, 177
school and, 601–3
social development of, 594–604
socialization of, 672
stress and, 429–30
temperament in, 579–82, *581*
therapeutic strategies and, 546–47
Chromosomes, 575
Chunking, 222, *223*
Ciliary muscles, *102*, 103
Cirrhosis, 506
Classical conditioning, 156–67
basic steps in, *163*
built-in predispositions in learning
and, 167

sex typing and, 599
See also Alcoholism; Substance abuse
Dependency motive, 338
Dependent personality, *502*
Dependent variable, 17
Depression, 488–90, *489, 491, 544*
  abuse and, *493*
  in adolescence, 633
  bipolar, 488–90, *489, 551*
  childhood, 493–94
  defined, 449, 488
  drug therapy for, *548,* 550, *551*
  endogenous causes of, 450
  exercise and, *458*
  in the homeless, 555
  introjective, 494
  learned helplessness and, 179–80
  old age and, 651
  stress and, 449–50
  substance abuse and, 494
  test for, *489*
  unipolar, 488
Depth, perception of, 128–29
Descriptive statistics, 718–22
Development, 378
Developmental psychologists, 9, 574
Diagnostic and Statistical Manual of Mental Disorders: Fourth Edition (DSM-IV), 485
Difference threshold, 100
Difficult children, 580–81
Displacement, 461–62
Distance, perception of, 128–29
Divorce, 600–1, 642–43, *642*
Dominance, 603
Dopamine, 77, 487
Double approach-avoidance conflict, 434–35
Double-blind technique, 20
Draw-a-person test, 398
Dream analysis, 531
Drive(s), 301, 312–33
  behavior and, 312–16
  defined, 301, 390
  hunger and, 312–16
  pain, 321, 322–25
  sex, 326
  sleep, 317–21, *320, 322–23*
  temperature, 325
  thirst, 316
Drive state, 312
Drugs
  abuse of. *See* Substance abuse
  addiction to, 505–6, 508–9
  classes of, *548*
  heroin, 509
  mind-altering, 508
  side effects of, 549, 550
  See also specific drugs
Drug therapy, 548–53, *548, 555*
  for anxiety, *548,* 550
  defined, 548
  for depression, *548,* 550, *551*
  psychotherapy and, 551–52
  for schizophrenia, *548,* 549–50
DSM-IV *(Diagnostic and Statistical Manual of Mental Disorders: Fourth Edition),* 485

Ductless glands, 70–71, *72*
Dynamic therapy, 529–33
Dyslexia, 547

E

Ear
  equilibrium and, 118–19, *119*
  structures of, 108–9, *108*
  See also Hearing; Sound
Eardrum, 108, *108*
Easy children, 580
Eating disorders, 495–97, *496,* 627–28
Education, bilingualism and, 260–62
Educational psychologists, 10
EEG (electroencephalogram), 76
Efferent neurons, 55
Ego, 381
Ego ideal, 339
Electroconvulsive therapy (ECT), 552
Electroencephalogram (EEG), 76
Emotion, 300–11, 326–33
  bodily changes in, 301–6
  brain and, 66–75
  Cannon-Bard theory of, 309–10, *309,* 310
  cognitive theory of, 310
  defined, 301
  facial expressions and, 304–7, *306*
  individual differences in, 311
  infants and, *306*
  James-Lange theory of, 307–9, *308,* 310
  meditation and, 546, *547*
  opponent–process theory of, 509
  range of, *302*
  regulation of, 74–75
  schizophrenia and, 486
  sex as, 326–27
  speech patterns and, *304*
Emotional stress, 314–15
Empathy, 693
Employment
  in adolescence, 632
  IQ and, 368–69
  sex roles and, 639–40
  of women, 637–39
  See also Careers
Encoding
  defined, 210
  categories as an aid to, 230–31, *230, 231*
  in memory, 226–29
Encounter groups, 540
End branches, 52, *52*
Endocrine glands, 70–71, *72*
Endogenous causes, 450
Endorphins, 78, 323
Environment
  behavior influenced by, 26–27
  behaviorism and, 21–22
  bystander apathy and, 694–96, *696*
  coping with, 451
  noise and, 109
  IQ and, 372–75
  perception of, 57–58

  sociopaths and, 503
  stress and, 428–29, 451
Environmental psychologists, 10
Epinephrine, 78
Episodic memory, 212, 213, 650–51
Equilibrium, 118–19, *119*
Erikson's theory of psychosocial development, 637, *638*
Escape and avoidance in operant conditioning, 174–76
Estrogen, 326, 599, 645
Ethics, 28–30
Ethnicity and IQ tests, 375–76
Eustachian tube, *108*
Exercise
  depression and, *458*
  stress and, 456–58
Exhaustion stage, 439, *439*
Existential psychotherapy, 535
Expectancies
  in cognitive learning, 184
  defined, 165
Expectations, perceptual, 132, *133*
Experiment
  defined, 17
  experimental and control groups in, 18–19
  single-blind and double-blind, 19–20
  variables in, 17–18
Experimental group, 18–19
Experimental psychologists, 8
Exploration
  attachment and, 592
  and perception, 124
Extinction
  defined, 165, 537
  and operant conditioning, 169
  resistance to, 217
Extrinsic motivation, 371
Extrovert, 383
Eye, *73*
  blink reflex of, *159*
  movement in sleep, 65, 319, 321
  structures of, 102–3, *102*
  See also Vision

F

Facial expressions, 304–7, *306*
Failure
  intelligence and, *370*
  learned helplessness and, 179–80
Familiarity, 696–97
Family
  adolescence and, 633–35
  divorce and, 600–1, 642–3, *642*
  IQ similarities in, 372–73, *373*
  single parent, 633
Family therapy, 541
"Fast" fibers, 117
Fat cells, 313
Fear
  in anxiety disorders, 497
  of death, 654–55
  as learned response, 158–59
Feature detectors, 120, *120*
Feelings. *See* Emotions

physical growth in, 583–84, *584*
reflexes in, 578–79, *579*
stress in, 429–30
temperament in, 579–82, *581*
Inference, 271–72
Inferential statistics, 722–25
Information, retention of, 209–10, *209*
Information processing, 23
Innate mechanism, 266
Inner ear, 109
Inputs, attention to simultaneous, 124
Insight, 181, *182*, 530
Instincts, 156
Insulin, 314
Intellectual development
  brain and, 63–64
  in children, 586–89
  in infants, 584–85
Intelligence, 360–63
  crystallized, 649
  defined, 360
  failure and, *370*
  fluid, 649
  g factor of, 361
  Gardner's theory of, 363
  Guilford's theory of, 362–63, *363*
  s factor of, 361
  Sternberg's theory of, 363
  Thurstone's theory of, 362
  Wechsler's view of, 360
  See also Creativity; Intelligence quotient; Intelligence tests
Intelligence quotient (IQ), 16, 17
  creativity and, 370–71
  defined, 364
  environment and, 372–75
  family resemblances in, 372–73, *373*
  job success and, 368–69
  normal curve and, *16*
  race and, 375–76
  ranges of, 365
  school success and, 367–68
  success in life and, 369–70
  See also Intelligence tests
Intelligence tests, 364–67
  aptitude, 366–67
  defined, 364
  group, 366
  history of, 364
  individual, 366
  social implications of, 371–72
  Stanford-Binet Intelligence Scale, 364, 365, *365*, 366
  Wechsler, 365, 366
Intensity, 100, 101
Interaction
  language skills and, 263–64
  reciprocal, 391
Interference
  and forgetting, 219–21, *220*
  proactive, 219–20, *220*, 229
  retroactive, 221, 229
Interpersonal behavior, 690–99
Interposition, 129, *130*
Interpretation, 131–33
Interval schedules, 172, *172*
Interviews, 13

Intrinsic motivation, 371
Introjective depression, 494
Introspection, 21
Introvert, 383
IQ. *See* Intelligence quotient
Iris, 102, *102*

J

James-Lange theory, 307–9, *308*, 310
Jealousy, sexual differences in, *331*
Jobs. *See* Careers; Employment
Just noticeable difference (j.n.d.), 100

K

Knowledge, 184
Kohlberg's stage theory of moral development, 630, *631*

L

Language, 585
  in apes, 266–67
  bilingualism and, 260–62
  as communication, 254–55, 258–61
  concepts in, 268–76
  development of, 17, 18, 19
  function of, 254–55
  interaction affecting, 263–64
  learning and, 262–68
  structure of, 255–58
  thinking and, 275–76
  world view and, 274–75
Large group awareness training programs, 540
Latent content, 531
Law of overlearning, 228
Learned helplessness
  children and, 179
  defined, 167
  failure and, 179–80
  operant conditioning and, 177–80, *178*
Learning, 229–35
  and age, 184–85
  aggression and, 691–93
  through biofeedback, 174
  categories as an aid to, 230–31, *230, 231*
  classical conditioning and, 156–67
  cognitive, 180–86
  concepts and memory in, 272–73
  defined, 156
  language and, 262–68
  memory and, 225–33
  observational, 185–86, 391
  operant conditioning and, 167–80
  without reinforcement, 181–83
  without response, 183
  role of built-in predispositions in, 167
  by rote, 227–28
  by rules, 227–28
  social theories of, 391

SQ3R system of, 227
  See also Behavior modification; Classical conditioning; Operant conditioning
Learning set, 230
Learning through observation, 185–86, *186*
Left hemisphere, 55, 56, 57
Lens, 102, *102*
Libido, 379
Lie detectors, *305*
Life Stress Scale, *441*
Life transitions as stressors, 431
Life-span development, 624
Light waves, 101–2
Limbic system, 67–68, *67*
Linear perspective, 129
Listening skills, 259–60
Lithium, 550
Liver, *73*
Long-term memory, 210–11
  categories to aid encoding for, 230–31, *230, 231*
  clustering techniques for, 231–33, *232, 233*
Love, 698–99, *699*
Lungs, *73*

M

Magnetic resonance imaging (MRI) scan, 76, 487
Major tranquilizers, 549
Maladaptive behavior, 481
Manifest content, 531
Marriage, 640–43, *641*
  power motive and, 336
  punishment in, 176
  social and cultural influences on, 330
Mathematical computations, 728–34
Maturation, 582–84
  of brain, 65
Mean, 719–20, *721*, 729–30, *730*
  standard error of, 724–25, *724*, 730–31
Meaning, as a role in memory, 226–27
Measurement, 14
Median, 719–20
Meditation, *546, 547*
Medulla, *59, 69*
Memory, 206–35
  aging and, 650–51, *650*
  associative, 223–24, 362
  and brain, 61–63
  concepts and learning in, 272–73
  content of, 212–14
  encoding of, 210, 222–25, 226–29
  episodic, 212, 650–51
  flashbulb, 225
  imagery in, 232
  learning and, 225–33
  long-term, 210–11, *211*, 231–33, *233*
  mnemonic devices in, 232, 233
  primary effect, 210
  procedural, 63, 215

recency effect, 210
rehearsal system, 210
retrieval process of, 62–63, 212, 224
role of meaning and organization in, 226–27
rule use to aid in, 227–28
scanning, 210
schema, 210
semantic, 63, 212, 215, 650
sensory, 207–9, *208*
short–term, 209–10, *209*, 222, *223*, *585*
stages of, 207–12, *208*
storage of, 62–63
transfer process of, 210, 222–25
visual information and, 234
See also Forgetting
Memory trace, 216–18
Men
alcoholism and, 507–8
depression and, 494–97
midlife changes in, 644–45
motivation and, 444–45
power motive in, 336
sex roles of, 639–40
See also Gender differences
Menarche, 625
Menopause, 326, 645
Mental abilities. *See* Intelligence; Intelligence quotient; Intelligence tests; Thinking
Mental health
community. *See* Community mental health
old age and, 651
stress and, 446–50
See also Coping
Mental hospital population, *555*
Mental illness. *See* Abnormal psychology
Mental models of reality, 23
Mere exposure effect, 697
Middle ear, 108, *108*
Minnesota Multiphasic Personality Inventory (MMPI), 396
Minor tranquilizers, 550
Mnemonic device, 232, 233, 234, 235
Mode, 720
Modeling, learning through, 185–86, *186*
Mood, perception and, 123. *See also* Emotion
Mood (affective) disorders, 488–97
anxiety, 497–500
biological causes of, 492–93
in children, 493–94
defined, 488
depression. *See* Depression
gender and, 494–97
seasonal affective disorder, 490–91
Moral development, 594–95
in adolescence, 630, *631*
Morpheme, 255–56
Mothers
separation anxiety and, 592–93, *593*
surrogate, 590
teenage, 635
working, 637–39

Motivated forgetting, 221–22
Motivation (motives), 301, 333–40
achievement, 334–36, *335*, 339, 400, 443–44
affiliation, 338
behavior and, 339–40
for certainty, 338–39
creativity and, 371
defined, 301
dependency, 338
extrinsic, 371
hierarchy of, 340
hostility, 337
intrinsic, 371
power, 336–37, 444
sexual, 326–28
standards met by, 339
Motive for certainty, 338
Motive to live up to our standards, 339
Motor cortex, 60
Movement
brain and, 60–61
defined, 121
perception of, 121–22
MRI (magnetic resonance imaging) scan, 76, 487
Mutual support groups, 539–40
Myelin sheath, 52, *52*
Myoclonic jerk, 318

N

Narcissistic personality, 504–5
Naturalistic observation, 12
Nature-nurture controversy, 27, 676–77
IQ and, 372–73
race and, 375
Needs, basic human, 387–88, *388*
Negative reinforcement, 175, *175*
Neopsychoanalysts, 387
Nerve cells. *See* Neurons
Nervous system
perception and, 120
peripheral, 55
reflex responses and, 157
type A personality and, 443–44
See also Autonomic nervous system; Brain; Central nervous system; Neurons
Neurons (nerve cells), 549
afferent, 55
all or none principle of, 53
brain, 51–54, *52*
color sensing, 105
connecting, 55
defined, 51
efferent, 55
hearing, 109
transmission of messages by, 53–55
Neuroscience, 75–79
Neurotransmitters, 53, 54
acetylcholine, 77
defined, 53
and depression, 492

dopamine, 77, *549*
epinephrine, 78
norepinephrine, 77
Newborns. *See* Infancy
Nicotine, 508
Nodes, 52–53, *52*
Noise and aggression, 109
Norepinephrine, 77
Normal curve of distribution, 15–16, *16*, 717–18, *721*
Nose, 112–13, *113*
Nucleus, 52, *52*
Number
in group, 719
as primary mental ability, 362
Nutrition, 374

O

Obedience
blind, 686–87
defined, 683
Milgram's experiments in, 685–87, *686*, *687*
rebellion and, 688
Objective tests, 396
Objectivity, 399
Observation, 12–13
Observational learning, 185–86, *186*, 391
Obsessions, 499
Obsessive-compulsive disorder (OCD), 499–500, *501*
Occupation. *See* Careers; Employment
OCD (obsessive-compulsive disorder), 499–500, *501*
Oedipus complex, 381
Old age, 646–55
attitudes toward death and, 653–54
bereavement and, 654
intellectual changes in, 649–51
life expectancy in, 646–47, *646*
memory and, 213–14
mental health and, 651
physical changes in, 647–49
retirement and, 652–53
sexuality in, 328
stress in, 430
therapeutic strategies and, 546–47
Olfactory epithelium, 112, *113*
120-factory theory of intelligence, *363*
Operant avoidance, 175
Operant behavior, 168
Operant conditioning, 167–80
behavior shaping and, 169, *169*
biofeedback and, 174
defined, 168
escape and avoidance in, 174–76
learned helplessness and, 177–80, *178*
punishment in, 175, 176–77
reinforcement in, 170–172
Skinner box and, 168–69
superstitions and, 170
token economies and, 173
Operant escape, 175
Operations, 586

Sexual orientation, 330–33, *333*
Shape constancy, 127
Shaping, 169
Short-term memory, 209–10, *209*, *585*
  chunking techniques used in, 222, *223*
  defined, 209
Sibling order, personality development
    and, 384–87
Sight. *See* Eye; Vision
Significance, 725
Similarity, 126–27, *127*, 697
Simultaneous brightness contrast, 122
Simultaneous inputs, attention to, 124
Simultaneous pairing, 162, 163
Single-blind technique, 19–20
Situational factors, 678
Situational test, 397
Size
  perception of, 129–30
  relative, 129
Size constancy, 127–28, *128*
Skin senses, 116–18
Skinner box, 168
Sleep
  delta, 319
  depression and, 488
  deprivation, *322–23*
  need for, 320–21
  paradoxical, 319
  REM, 319, 321
  stages of, 317–19, *320*
Sleep drive, 317–21, *320*, *322–23*
Sleep stages (I, II, III, IV), 318–19
"Slow" fibers, 117
Slow-to-warm-up children, 580
Smell senses, 112–13
Social comparison theory, 689
Social context. *See* Context, social
Social development, 594–604
  in adolescence, 628–30
  identification in, 597–600
  influence of television on, 600
  peer influences on, 603
  in school, 601–3
Social learning theory, 391
Social phobia, 499
Social psychology (social psycholo-
    gists), 9
  aggression and altruism in, 690–94
  attitudes in, 670–77
  attribution theories of, 677–83
  defined, 670
  interpersonal behavior and, 690–99
  obedience and conformity in,
    683–90
Social relationships. *See* Relationships,
    social
Social sciences, 6–7
Social support network, 453–54
Social implications of IQ testing,
    371–72
Socialization, 672
Somatosensory cortex, 57–58
Sound (sound waves), 106–11, *107*, *110*
  language and, 255–56, *256*
  See also Ear; Hearing
Space, as primary mental ability, 362
Speech

feature detectors of, 120
patterns of, *304*
See also Communication; Language
Spinal cord, 55, 73
  gate-control mechanism in, 117
Spleen, 73
Spontaneous recovery, 166
  and operant conditioning, 169
SQ3R system of learning, 227
Standard deviation, 720–21, *721*, 730,
    730
Standard error of mean, 724–25, *724*,
    730–31
Standardization, 400
Stanford-Binet Intelligence Scale,
    364
Stapes, *108*, 109
Statistical methods, 716–34
  descriptive, 718–22
  inferential, 722–25
  mathematical computations used in,
    728–34
Statistics, 15
Stereotype
  racial, 671
  sex-role, 639
  See also Attitudes; Prejudice
Stimulus, 21, 98–9, 162
Stimulus discrimination, 166
  and operant conditioning, 169
Stimulus generalization, 166
Stomach, *73*
Stranger anxiety, 593
Strength, 217
Stress (stressors)
  age and, 429–30
  anxiety and, 446–47
  appraisal of, 436–37, *436*
  catastrophes as, 431–33, *432*
  conflict as, 434–35
  coping with, 450–63
  daily hassles as, 433–34
  defined, 428
  depression and, 449–50
  general adaptation syndrome and,
    437–39, *438*
  health and, 437–46
  humor and, *456–57*
  immune systems and, 442–43, *443*
  life crisis as, 430–31, 440–42, *441*
  life transitions as, 431
  personality and, 443–46, *445*
  post-traumatic stress disorder and,
    447–49, *449*, 454
  psychosomatic illness and, 439–40
  sources of, 428–29
  uncertainty and doubt as, 435–36, *436*
Sublimation, 459–60
Submissiveness, 603
Substance abuse
  in adolescence, 632–33
  defined, 505
  depression and, 494
  drugs and, 505–6, 508–9
  mental disorders and, 509–10
  opponent-process theory of emotion
    and, 509
  See also Alcoholism

Success
  achievement motivation in, 334–36,
    335
  gauging odds of, 340
  IQ and, 368–70
Suicide
  adolescence and, 633, 634
  old age and, 651
  Vietnam War veterans and, 449
Superego, 381
Superstitions, 170
Support network, social, 453–54
Surrogate mothers, 590
Surveys, public opinion, 13–14
Symbolic concepts, 268–69, 363
Sympathetic division, 73–74
Synapse, 53, *54*
Synaptic cleft, 53, *54*
Synaptic knobs, 53, *54*
Synaptic vesicles, 53, *54*
Syntax, 257
Systematic desensitization, 536–37

T

Tardive dyskinesia, 549
Taste buds, 111
Taste senses, 111–12, *112*
  smell connection in, 113–15, *115*
Television, social development and, 600
Temperament
  defined, 383, 579
  in infancy, 579–82, *581*
Temperature drive, 325
Testosterone, 78, *392–93*
Tests (testing), 14
  achievement, 367
  aptitude, 366–67
  bias in, 367
  depression, *489*
  intelligence. *See* Intelligence tests
  normal curve of distribution of,
    15–16, *16*, 717–18, *721*
  objectivity of, 399
  personality. *See* Personality tests
  reliability of, 399
  standardization of, 400
  statistical measurements and, 728–34
  validity of, 399
Thalamus, 59, *59*, *103*
Thematic Apperception Test (TAT),
    397
Theory of self-actualization, 389
Therapy
  behavior, 535–38
  biological, 528, 548–52
  community mental health, 539–40
  drug, 544, 548–53, *548*
  effectiveness of, 542–46
  electroconvulsive, 552
  group, 538–42
  self-help, 547
  See also types of therapy; Psychotherapy
Thinking
  defined, 276
  language and, 275–76
  logical versus illogical, 277–78

premises of, 277
problem-solving techniques and, 278–83
rules of, 276–77
Thirst, 312
Thirst drive, 316
Thought and brain, 61–62
Thought disorders in schizophrenia, 486
Timbre, 107, *108*
Timing and classical conditioning, 162–64, *164*
Token economy, 173, 537
Tolerance, 506
Touch, 116–18
perceptual illusions and, 130–31
Traits
in children, *596*, 603, *604*
in newborns, 581–82
Tranquilizers, 549, 550
Transfer process, 210
Transference, 531
Type A personality, 337, 443, 444
Type B personality, 443–44

U

Unconditional positive regard, 389, 534
Unconditioned response, 162
Unconditioned stimulus, 162

Unconscious mind, 379
Unconscious motives, 379
Unconscious processes, 25
Unipolar disorder, 488

V

Validity, 399
Variability, 720
Variable schedules, 172, *172*
Variables, experimental, 17–18
Vasopressin, *496*
Verbal comprehension, 362
Verbal skills, 259
Vestibular sacs, 119, *119*
Violence, 690–93, *692*
influence of TV and, 600
Vision, 101–6
binocular, 129
color, 105–6
feature detectors of, 120, *120*
newborns and, *584*
pathway for, *103*
perceptual illusions and, 129–31
perceptual organization of, 125–33
scanning process of, *125*
See also Eye
Visual cliff, 129, *129*
Visual cortex, 103
Visual information and memory, 234
Vocabulary, 257

W

Wavelength, 100, 101
Weber's law, 100
Weight, 316, *316*
Withdrawal symptoms, 506
Women
alcoholism and, 507–8
dependency motive in, 338
depression and, 494–97
employment of, 8, 637–39
Horney's view of, 387
menopause and, 645
midlife changes in, 644–45
post–traumatic stress disorder and, 448–49
self-esteem and, 689–90
sex roles of, 639–40
See also Gender differences
Word association test, 398
Word fluency, 362

X

X chromosome, 575

Y

Y chromosome, 575